INSIGHT INTO ETHICS

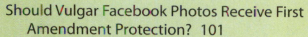

LINKING BUSINESS LAW to . . .

8th EDITION

THE LEGAL ENVIRONMENT TODAY

(photastic/Brocreative/Shutterstock.com)

Roger LeRoy Miller

Institute for University Studies, Arlington, Texas

Frank B. Cross

Herbert D. Kelleher
Centennial Professor in Business Law
University of Texas at Austin

CENGAGE
Learning™

Australia • Brazil • Japan • Korea • Mexico • Singapore • Spain • United Kingdom • United States

The Legal Environment Today

Eighth Edition

Roger LeRoy Miller

Frank B. Cross

Vice President and General Manager, Social Sciences & Qualitative Business:
Erin Joyner

Product Director:
Michael Worls

Senior Product Manager:
Vicky True-Baker

Managing Developer:
Rebecca von Gillern

Product Assistant:
Ryan McAndrews

Marketing Director:
Kristen Hurd

Senior Marketing Manager:
Katie Jergens

Marketing Coordinator:
Chris Walz

Senior Art Director:
Michelle Kunkler

Senior Content Project Manager:
Ann Borman

Manufacturing Planner:
Kevin Kluck

Compositor:
Parkwood Composition Service, Inc.

Cover and Internal Designer:
Stratton Design

Cover Image:
blue globe: photastic/Shutterstock.com
courthouse: Brocreative/Shutterstock.com

Interior Design Logo Credits:
touch pad: Peshkova/Shutterstock.com; themis in spotlight: Dariush M/Shutterstock.com; spiral staircase: iStockPhoto.com/Johnny Greig; spotlight: iStockPhoto.com/julioechandia.

For product information and technology assistance, contact us at
Cengage Learning Customer & Sales Support
1-800-354-9706

For permission to use material from this text or product,
submit all requests online at
www.cengage.com/permissions.

Further permissions questions can be e-mailed to
permissionrequest@cengage.com.

Library of Congress Control Number: 2014944118

Student Edition ISBN-13: 978-1-305-07545-0

Cengage Learning
200 First Stamford Place, 4th Floor
Stamford, CT 06902
USA

Cengage Learning is a leading provider of customized learning solutions with office locations around the globe, including Singapore, the United Kingdom, Australia, Mexico, Brazil, and Japan. Locate your local office at: **www.cengage.com/global.**

Cengage Learning products are represented in Canada by Nelson Education, Ltd.

To learn more about Cengage Learning, visit **www.cengage.com.**

Purchase any of our products at your local college store or at our preferred online store **www.cengagebrain.com.**

Printed in the United States of America
Print Number: 01   Print Year: 2014

Contents in Brief

Detailed Contents

UNIT 3

Business and Employment 393

CHAPTER 14 Small Business Organizations 395

CHAPTER 15 Corporations 426

CHAPTER 16 Agency Relationships 462

CHAPTER 17 Employment, Immigration, and Labor Law 487

Preface

The study of the legal environment of business has universal applicability. A student entering any field of business must have at least a passing understanding of business law in order to function in the real world.

Additionally, students preparing for a career in accounting, government and political science, economics, and even medicine can use much of the information that they learn in a legal environment of business course. In fact, every individual throughout his or her lifetime can benefit from a knowledge of contracts, employment relationships, real property law, land-use control, and other legal topics. Consequently, we have fashioned this text as a useful "tool for living" for all of your students (including those taking the CPA exam).

For the Eighth Edition, we have spent a great deal of effort making this book more contemporary, exciting, and visually appealing than ever before. We have also added many new features and special pedagogical devices that focus on legal, ethical, global, and corporate issues, while addressing core curriculum requirements.

Unique New Digital Learning Systems

Before we discuss the many new aspects of this text, however, we wish to point out the exciting new digital products offered in conjunction with the text.

MindTap Legal Environment for The Legal Environment Today, *Eighth Edition*

MindTap™ Legal Environment is a fully online, highly personalized learning experience built upon authoritative Cengage Learning content. By combining readings, multimedia, activities, and assessments into a singular Learning Path, *MindTap* guides students through their course with ease and engagement. Instructors personalize the Learning Path by customizing Cengage Learning resources and adding their own content via apps that integrate into the *MindTap* framework seamlessly with Learning Management Systems.

Legal environment instructors have told us that it is important to help students **Prepare** for class, **Engage** with the course concepts to reinforce learning, **Apply** these concepts in real-world scenarios, and use legal reasoning and critical thinking to **Analyze** business law and legal environment content.

Accordingly, the *MindTap Legal Environment* product provides a four-step Learning Path designed to meet these critical needs while also allowing instructors to measure skills and outcomes with ease.

1. **Prepare**—Interactive worksheets are guided readings designed to prepare students for classroom discussion by ensuring reading and comprehension.
2. **Engage**—Real-world videos with related questions help engage students by displaying the relevance of business law in everyday life.
3. **Apply**—Brief hypotheticals help students practice spotting issues and applying the law in the context of short factual scenarios.
4. **Analyze**—Case-problem blueprints promote deeper critical thinking and legal reasoning by building on acquired knowledge to truly assess students' understanding of legal principles.

Each and every item in the Learning Path is assignable and gradable. This gives instructors the knowledge of class standings and concepts that may be difficult. Additionally, students gain knowledge about where they stand—both individually and compared to the highest performers in class.

To view a demo video and learn more about *MindTap Legal Environment*, please visit **www.cengage.com/mindtap**.

CourseMate

CourseMate for *The Legal Environment Today* brings business law concepts to life with interactive learning, study, and exam preparation tools that support the printed textbook. Built-in engagement tracking tools allow you to assess the study activities of your students.

Additionally, *The Legal Environment Today* CourseMate includes an interactive online textbook, which contains the complete content of the print textbook enhanced by the many advantages of a digital environment.

Cengage Learning Testing Powered by Cognero

Cengage Learning Testing Powered by Cognero is a flexible, online system that allows you to do the following:

- Author, edit, and manage *Test Bank* content from multiple Cengage Learning solutions.
- Create multiple test versions in an instant.
- Deliver tests from your Learning Management System (LMS), your classroom, or wherever you want.

Start Right Away! *Cengage Learning Testing Powered by Cognero* works on any operating system or browser.

- No special installs or downloads are needed.
- Create tests from school, home, the coffee shop—anywhere with Internet access.

What Will You Find

- *Simplicity at every step.* A desktop-inspired interface features drop-down menus and familiar intuitive tools that take you through content creation and management with ease.
- *Full-featured test generator.* Create ideal assessments with your choice of fifteen question types—including true/false, multiple choice, opinion scale/Likert, and essay. Multi-language support, an equation editor, and unlimited metadata help ensure your tests are complete and compliant.
- *Cross-compatible capability.* Import and export content into other systems.

What Is New in the Eighth Edition

Instructors have come to rely on the coverage, accuracy, and applicability of *The Legal Environment Today*. To make sure that our text engages your students, solidifies their understanding of legal concepts, and provides the best teaching tools available, we now offer the following items in the text.

New Chapter on Internet Law, Social Media, and Privacy

For the Eighth Edition, we have included an entirely new chapter (Chapter 9) entitled **Internet Law, Social Media, and Privacy**. Social media have entered the mainstream and become a part of everyday life for many businesspersons. Throughout the text, we recognize this trend by incorporating the Internet and social media as they relate to the topics under discussion.

We also give the legal issues and laws surrounding the Internet, social media, and privacy special emphasis in this new chapter. In addition, the chapter discusses recent legal developments concerning the protection of social media passwords and the use of social media by employers and law enforcement.

New *Managerial Strategy* Features

For the Eighth Edition, we have created a new feature entitled *Managerial Strategy* that focuses on the management aspects of business law. Special emphasis is given to sustainability, ethical trends, and changing managerial responsibilities.

Each feature includes a short section entitled *Managerial Implications* that provides concrete information for managers and connects the topic under discussion to operating a business. Each feature also concludes with two *Business Questions* that prompt students to further examine the issues discussed. **Suggested answers to all the *Business Questions* are included in the *Solutions Manual* for this text.**

Topics examined in these features include:

- Budget Cuts for State Courts Can Affect Businesses (Chapter 3).
- Marriage Equality and the Constitution (Chapter 4).
- Many Companies Have to Revise Their Social Media Policies (Chapter 17).

New *Spotlight Cases* and *Spotlight Case Problems*

For the Eighth Edition of *The Legal Environment Today,* certain cases and case problems have been carefully chosen as exceptionally good teaching cases. *Spotlight Cases* and *Spotlight Case Problems* are labeled either by the name of one of the parties or by the subject involved. Some examples include *Spotlight on Apple, Spotlight on Beer Labels, Spotlight on Gucci, Spotlight on Macy's, Spotlight on Nike,* and *Spotlight on the Seattle Mariners.*

Instructors will find these *Spotlight Cases* useful to illustrate the legal concepts under discussion. Students will enjoy studying these cases because the parties are often familiar and the cases involve interesting and memorable facts. **Suggested answers to all case-ending questions and case problems are included in the *Solutions Manual* for this text.**

New *Legal Reasoning Group Activities*

For instructors who want their students to engage in group projects, each unit of the Eighth Edition concludes with a **special new *Legal Reasoning Group Activity*.** Each activity begins by describing a business scenario and then requires each group of students to answer a specific question pertaining to the scenario based on the information that they learned in the chapter. These projects may be used in class to spur discussion or as homework assignments. **Suggested answers to the *Legal Reasoning Group Activities* are included in the *Solutions Manual* for this text.**

New *Insight into Ethics* Features

For the Eighth Edition, we have created many **new *Insight into Ethics* features** that appear in selected chapters. These features provide valuable insights into how the courts and the law are dealing with specific issues. Each of these features ends with a **For Critical Analysis** question that explores some cultural, environmental, or technological aspect of the issue. The following are some of the topics explored in these features:

- The Emergence of Patent Trolls (Chapter 8)
- Boasting on Facebook Can Have Consequences (Chapter 9)

- Warning Labels for Video Games (Chapter 12)
- Appearance-Based Discrimination (Chapter 18)

Suggested answers to the *For Critical Analysis* questions are included in the *Solutions Manual* for this text.

New *Debate This* Feature

To encourage student participation and motivate students to think critically about the rationale underlying the law on a particular topic, a new feature has been created for the Eighth Edition. Entitled *Debate This,* it consists of a brief statement or question concerning the chapter material that can be used to spur lively classroom or small group discussions. It can also be used as a written assignment. This feature follows the *Reviewing . . .* feature at the end of each chapter.

Suggested pro and con responses to the *Debate This* features can be found in the *Solutions Manual* for this text.

New Cases and Case Problems

The Eighth Edition of *The Legal Environment Today* is filled with new cases and case problems. Every chapter features new cases and case problems from 2013 and 2014, and some chapters include three new cases. That means more than 85 percent of the cases are new to this edition.

The new cases have been carefully selected based on three criteria:

1. They illustrate important points of law.
2. They are of high interest to students and instructors.
3. They are simple enough factually for legal environment students to understand.

We have made it a point to find recent cases that enhance learning. We have also eliminated cases that are too difficult procedurally or factually.

Improved Ethics Coverage

For the Eighth Edition of *The Legal Environment Today,* we have significantly revised and updated the chapter on ethics and business decision making (Chapter 2). The chapter now presents a more practical, realistic, case-study approach to business ethics and the dilemmas facing businesspersons today. It also provides step-by-step guidance for making ethical business decisions.

The emphasis on ethics is reiterated in materials throughout the text, particularly the *Insight into Ethics* features and the pedagogy that accompanies selected cases and features. We also discuss **corporate governance issues** in Chapter 24. Finally, each chapter in the text includes *A Question of Ethics* case problem that provides a modern-day example of the kinds of ethical issues faced by businesspersons and explores the ways that courts can resolve them.

Additional Features of This Text

The Legal Environment Today, Eighth Edition, includes a number of pedagogical devices and special features, including those discussed here.

Linking Business Law to . . . Feature

The Eighth Edition also includes a **special feature entitled** *Linking Business Law to . . .* [one of the six functional fields of business]. As will be discussed in Chapter 1, the six functional fields of business are *corporate management, production and transportation, marketing, research and development, accounting and finance,* and *human resources management.*

This feature appears in selected chapters to underscore how the law relates to other fields of business. Some of the new *Linking Business Law to . . .* features include:

- *Linking Business Law to Marketing*—Is Pretexting Illegal? (Chapter 4)
- *Linking Business Law to Accounting and Finance*—Protecting Your Company against Hacking of Its Bank Accounts (Chapter 6)
- *Linking Business Law to Marketing*—Trademarks and Service Marks (Chapter 8)
- *Linking Business Law to Corporate Management*—What Can You Do to Prepare for a Chapter 11 Reorganization? (Chapter 13)

Preventing Legal Disputes

The Eighth Edition of *The Legal Environment Today* continues the emphasis on providing practical information in most chapters through a special feature entitled **Preventing Legal Disputes**. These brief, integrated sections offer sensible guidance on steps that businesspersons can take in their daily transactions to avoid legal disputes and litigation in a particular area.

Online Developments

The Eighth Edition contains many new **Online Developments** features, which examine cutting-edge cyberlaw issues coming before today's courts. Here are some examples of these features:

- Corporate Reputations under Attack (Chapter 2)
- Facebook Uses Privacy Concerns to Smear Google (Chapter 5)
- Even Smartphones Are Vulnerable to Cyber Attacks (Chapter 6)
- The New Era of Crowdfunding (Chapter 15)
- Social Media in the Workplace Come of Age (Chapter 17)
- The Justice Department Goes after E-Book Pricing (Chapter 23)

Each feature concludes with a *Critical Thinking* question that asks the student to analyze some facet of the issues discussed in the feature. **Suggested answers to these questions are included in the** *Solutions Manual* **for this text.**

Emphasis on Business and on Critical Thinking

For the Eighth Edition, we have focused on making the text more business related. To that end, we have carefully chosen cases, features, and problems that are relevant to operating a business.

In addition, we recognize that today's business leaders must often think "outside the box" when making business decisions. For this reason, we have included numerous critical thinking and legal reasoning elements in this text. Almost all of the features and cases presented in the text conclude with some type of critical thinking question.

Cases may include one or more of the following critical thinking questions:

- *What If the Facts Were Different?*
- *The Ethical Dimension*
- *The E-Commerce Dimension*
- *The Global Dimension*
- *The Legal Environment Dimension*

Suggested answers to all questions following cases can be found in the *Solutions Manual* **for this text.**

Managerial Implications in Selected Cases

In addition to the critical thinking questions, we have included special case pedagogy at the end of selected cases that have particular importance for business managers. This section, called *Managerial Implications,* points out the significance of the court's ruling in the case for business owners and managers.

Highlighted and Numbered
Examples and *Case Examples*

Many instructors use cases and examples to illustrate how the law applies to business. For this edition, we have expanded both our in-text examples and our discussion of case law by adding highlighted numbered *Examples* and *Case Examples* in every chapter.

These two features are uniquely designed and consecutively numbered throughout each chapter for easy reference. *Examples* illustrate how the law applies in a specific situation. *Case Examples* present the facts and issues of an actual case, and then describe the court's decision and rationale. The numbered *Examples* and *Case Examples* features are integrated throughout the text to help students better understand how courts apply the principles in the real world.

Two *Issue Spotters*

At the conclusion of each chapter, we include **two *Issue Spotters* related to the chapter's topics** that facilitate student learning and review of the materials. **Suggested answers to the *Issue Spotters* in every chapter are provided in Appendix D at the end of the text.**

Reviewing Features in Every Chapter

In the Eighth Edition of *The Legal Environment Today,* we continue to offer a *Reviewing* feature at the end of every chapter to help solidify students' understanding of the chapter materials. Each *Reviewing* feature presents a hypothetical scenario and then asks a series of questions that require students to identify the issues and apply the legal concepts discussed in the chapter.

These features are designed to help students review the chapter topics in a simple and interesting way and see how the legal principles discussed in the chapter affect the world in which they live. An instructor can use these features as the basis for in-class discussion or encourage students to use them for self-study prior to completing homework assignments. **Suggested answers to the questions posed in the *Reviewing* features can be found in the *Solutions Manual* for this text.**

Exhibits

When appropriate, we also illustrate important aspects of the law in graphic form in exhibits. In all, nearly fifty exhibits are featured in *The Legal Environment Today,* Eighth Edition. Several of these exhibits are new, and we have modified existing exhibits to achieve better clarity.

Case Problems

Every chapter includes a 2013 and 2014 case problem in the *Business Scenarios and Case Problems* that appear at the end of the chapter. These problems are designed to clarify how modern courts deal with the business issues discussed in the chapter.

At the request of instructors, we have given every business scenario and case problem a label that identifies the chapter topic to which the question relates. These labels make it easier for instructors who wish to assign only certain questions to their students. In addition, for this edition, we have added references to the section in the text where the problem's answer can be found.

We have also included two special problems—the *Spotlight Case Problems* (in selected chapters, as mentioned earlier), which are based on good teaching cases with interesting facts, and the *Business Case Problem with Sample Answer* (discussed next).

Suggested answers to all *Business Scenarios and Case Problems* are included in the *Solutions Manual* for this text.

Business Case Problem with Sample Answer in Each Chapter

In response to those instructors who would like students to have sample answers available for some of the questions and case problems, we include a *Business Case Problem with Sample Answer* in each chapter. The *Business Case Problem with Sample Answer* is based on an actual case, and students can access a sample answer in Appendix E at the end of the text.

A Complete Supplements Package

This edition of *The Legal Environment Today* is accompanied by many teaching and learning supplements, which are available on the password-protected portion of the Instructor's Companion Web Site.

The complete teaching/learning package includes the supplements listed next. For further information on *The Legal Environment Today* teaching/learning package, contact your local sales representative or visit *The Legal Environment Today* Web site.

Instructor's Companion Web Site

The Instructor's Companion Web Site contains the following supplements:

- *Instructor's Manual.* Includes sections entitled "Additional Cases Addressing This Issue" at the end of selected case synopses.
- *Solutions Manual.* Provides answers to all questions presented in the text, including the questions in each case, feature, and unit-ending feature.
- *Test Bank.* A comprehensive test bank that contains multiple choice, true/false, and short essay questions.
- *Case-Problem Cases.*
- *Case Printouts.*
- *PowerPoint slides.*
- *Lecture Outlines.*
- *Business Law Digital Video Library.* Provides access to ninety videos, including the *Drama of the Law* videos and video clips from actual Hollywood movies. Access to our Digital Library is available in an optional package with each new text at no additional cost. You can access the Business Law Digital Video Library, along with corresponding *Video Questions* that are related to specific chapters in the text, at **www.cengagebrain.com**.

For Users of the Seventh Edition

First of all, we want to thank you for helping make *The Legal Environment Today* the best-selling legal environment text in America today. Second, we want to make you aware of the numerous additions and changes that we have made in this edition—many in response to comments from reviewers.

New Chapter and Special Pedagogy

For this edition, we have added more material on Internet law and social media throughout the text. We have also created an entire chapter (Chapter 9) on Internet law, social media, and privacy.

We have also added the following entirely new elements for the Eighth Edition:

- *Learning Objectives* in the margin.
- New *Managerial Strategy* features.
- New *Spotlight Cases* and *Spotlight Case Problems.*
- New *Debate This* features at the end of every chapter.
- New *Legal Reasoning Group Activities* for every unit.

Significantly Revised Chapters

Every chapter of the Eighth Edition has been revised as necessary to incorporate new developments in the law or to streamline the presentations. Other major changes and additions for this edition include the following:

- **Chapter 2 (Business Ethics)**—This chapter has been thoroughly revised with all new cases, business scenarios, and many new case problems. It includes a new section on business ethics and social media, as well as an in-depth discussion of stakeholders and corporate social responsibility. The chapter also provides step-by-step guidance on making ethical business decisions and includes materials on global business ethics. An *Online Developments* feature examines Corporate Reputations under Attack.

- **Chapter 4 (Business and the Constitution)**—The chapter has been revised and updated to be more business oriented. It has numerous new *Examples* and *Case Examples,* many of which are based on United States Supreme Court decisions. The chapter includes an updated discussion of privacy rights and the equal protection clause. We have added two new cases and four new features, which discuss computers and free speech, Facebook photos and the First Amendment, same-sex marriages, and pretexting.

- **Chapter 5 (Torts and Strict Liability)**—This chapter has been thoroughly revised and updated. It includes a new defamation case example involving soccer player David Beckham. All of the cases presented in the chapter are new to this edition, including a *Spotlight on the Seattle Mariners.* An *Online Developments* feature involves Facebook and privacy concerns.

- **Chapter 6 (Criminal Law and Cyber Crime)**—The chapter includes many new examples and case examples. There is a new subsection and 2014 case on the reasonable expectation of privacy, and a new *Linking Business Law to Accounting and Finance* addresses Protecting Your Company against Hacking of Its Bank Accounts.

- **Chapter 7 (International Law in a Global Economy)**—The chapter now discusses international dispute resolution and includes a feature on border searches of electronic devices. There are three new cases, including a new *Spotlight on International Torts* that involves Mercedes-Benz Argentina, and several new examples, such as one concerning the 2014 Russian takeover of Crimea.

- **Chapter 8 (Intellectual Property Rights)**—The materials on intellectual property rights have been thoroughly revised and updated to reflect the most current laws and trends. Two of the cases are new, and a United States Supreme Court decision is presented as a *Spotlight Case.* There is a discussion of the dispute between Apple, Inc., and Samsung Electronics Company over smartphones, and many new examples, including one on Sherlock Holmes to illustrate how works fall into the public domain. There are numerous new features. An *Insight into Ethics* discusses The Emergence of Patent Trolls. A *Beyond Our Borders* discusses a 2013 United States Supreme Court decision on the resale on eBay of textbooks purchased abroad. The case problems include a *Spotlight on Macy's.*

- **Chapter 9 (Internet Law, Social Media, and Privacy)**—This chapter is all new and was created for the Eighth Edition to explore timely topics. It discusses legal issues that are unique to the Internet, such as spam, domain name disputes, cybersquatting, digital copyright laws, and file-sharing. It also discusses social media, company-wide social media networks, state legislation on social media, the Electronic Communications Privacy Act, and password protection. The chapter also covers online defamation, data collection and cookies, and online privacy, and includes several features.

- **Chapters 10 and 11 (the contracts materials)**—The materials on contracts have been substantially revised and updated to include numerous new examples and case examples. Five of the six cases are new, and they include a new *Spotlight on Nike*. Both of the chapters have new *Online Developments* features—one concerns the validity of e-signatures in contracts with online schools and another discusses catfishing and online friends. There are also new *Insight into Ethics* features in both chapters, a *Spotlight on Taco Bell* case problem in Chapter 10, and a new *Preventing Legal Disputes* in Chapter 11.

- **Chapter 12 (Sales, Leases, and Product Liability)**—This chapter includes two new cases, and a *Spotlight on Baseball Cards*. Three new features have been added, one on how local governments are attempting to levy taxes on online travel companies, another on warning labels for video games, and another on imposing product liability in China. A *Spotlight on Apple* case problem is included.

- **Chapter 13 (Creditor-Debtor Relations and Bankruptcy)**—This chapter has been revised to be more up to date and comprehensible. We have streamlined the materials to focus on those concepts that students need to know and included updated dollar amounts of various provisions of the Bankruptcy Code. There are three new cases, several new features, and a new section and *Spotlight Case* on Mortgages.

- **Chapter 14 (Small Business Organizations)**—This chapter now provides more practical information and recent examples. There are two new cases and a *Classic Case*, new *Managerial Strategy* and *Insight into Ethics* features, and a *Spotlight on Liberty Tax* case problem.

- **Chapter 15 (Corporations)**—The chapter has been streamlined and revised to be more up to date. It includes a new subsection and discussion of benefit corporations, two new features, including one on crowdfunding, and a new *Spotlight on Smart Inventions* case problem.

- **Chapter 16 (Agency Relationships)**—Many new case examples have been added to this chapter, as well as three new cases, including a *Spotlight Case*. The chapter also includes two new features and several new case problems.

- **Chapter 17 (Employment, Immigration, and Labor Law)**—This chapter discusses many legal issues facing employers today, and includes updated minimum wage figures and Social Security and Medicare percentages. We have also included a discussion of the Affordable Care Act (Obamacare) and a new *Preventing Legal Disputes*. The materials on immigration law have been streamlined and updated, and include a discussion of state immigration legislation and its constitutionality. A *Managerial Strategy* feature covers how many companies are changing their social media policies, and an *Online Developments* feature discusses social media in the workplace. A *Spotlight on Coca-Cola* case problem is included.

- **Chapter 18 (Employment Discrimination)**—We have added *Examples* and *Case Examples* throughout this chapter, as well as new numbered lists of elements, and two new cases. A new *Insight into Ethics* feature examines appearance-based discrimination. We discuss relevant United States Supreme Court decisions affecting employment issues throughout this chapter, including a 2014 decision on affirmative action.

- **Chapter 20 (Consumer Protection)**—This chapter has been streamlined and updated. The chapter also includes a *Spotlight on Honda* case and a *Spotlight on McDonald's* case problem.

- **Chapter 22 (Real Property and Land-Use Control)**—Parts of this chapter have been significantly revised. Several new terms and new *Case Examples* were added. The discussion of eminent domain for economic development was updated. A *Spotlight Case* covers whether the buyer of an allegedly haunted house can seek rescission of the sale. The discussion of zoning laws has been reworked, and several numbered lists explain permissible uses of land and requirements for variances.

- **Chapter 23 (Antitrust Law and Promoting Competition)**—We have added a new exhibit, several new *Examples* and *Case Examples,* and expanded coverage of leading cases. An *Online Developments* feature discusses price fixing and e-books. Updated thresholds for interlocking directorates have been incorporated.
- **Chapter 24 (Investor Protection and Corporate Governance)**—This chapter has been substantially revised, updated, and simplified. It includes new numbered lists of elements, two new cases, and a *Classic Case.* A new *Insight into Ethics* feature covers shareholder "say-on-pay" provisions.

Acknowledgments for Previous Editions

Since we began this project many years ago, a sizable number of legal environment of business professors and others have helped us in various phases of the undertaking. The following reviewers offered numerous constructive criticisms, comments, and suggestions during the preparation of the previous editions.

Muhammad Abdullah
Pfeiffer University

Jane Bennett
Orange Coast College

Robert C. Bird
University of Connecticut

Dean Bredeson
University of Texas at Austin

Martin D. Carrigan
The University of Findlay

Thomas D. Cavenagh
*North Central College
Naperville, Illinois*

Wade M. Chumney
Georgia Tech

Corey Ciocchetti
University of Denver

Brent D. Clark
Davenport University

Richard L. Coffinberger
George Mason University

Teri Elkins
University of Houston

Joan Gabel
Florida State University

Teresa Gillespie
Seattle Pacific University

Jeanne M. Gohl-Noice
Parkland College

Gary Greene
Manatee Community College

Ruth Ann Hall
University of Alabama

Eloise Hassell
*University of North Carolina,
Greensboro*

Penelope L. Herickhoff
Mankato State University

Arlene M. Hibschweiler
University at Buffalo

Whitney Johnson
Saint Cloud State University

James F. Kelley
Santa Clara University

Susan Key
University of Alabama at Birmingham

Karrin Klotz
University of Washington

Y. S. Lee
Oakland University

William J. McDevitt
Saint Joseph's University

Tom Moore
Georgia College and State University

Michael J. O'Hara
University of Nebraska at Omaha

Mark Phelps
University of Oregon

Lemoine D. Pierce
Georgia State University

G. Keith Roberts
University of Redlands

Jeanette Rogers
Jefferson State Community College

Gary Sambol
Rutgers, the State University of New Jersey, Camden Campus

Linda Samuels
George Mason University

Martha Wright Sartoris
North Hennepin Community College

Gwen Seaquist
Ithaca College

Craig Stilwell
Michigan State University

Joyce Stoneking
Orange Coast College

Dawn R. Swink
University of St. Thomas

Daphyne Thomas
James Madison University

Carrie Vaia
North Hennepin Community College

Wayne Wells
St. Cloud State University

Eric D. Yordy
Northern Arizona University

We also wish to extend special thanks to Diane May, Winona State University, for her contributions to the Eighth Edition, specifically for preparing the Blueprint Cases that are included in *MindTap* for this edition.

As in all past editions, we owe a debt of extreme gratitude to the numerous individuals who worked directly with us or at Cengage Learning. In particular, we wish to thank Vicky True-Baker and Michael Worls for their helpful advice and guidance during all of the stages of this new edition. We extend our thanks to Rebecca von Gillern, our content developer, for her many useful suggestions and for her efforts in coordinating and ensuring the timely and accurate publication of all supplemental materials. We are also indebted to Katie Jergens for her excellent marketing advice.

Our content project manager, Ann Borman, and our art director, Michelle Kunkler, made sure that we came out with an error-free, visually attractive Eighth Edition. We appreciate their efforts. We are also indebted to the staff at Parkwood Composition, our compositor. Their ability to generate the pages for this text quickly and accurately made it possible for us to meet our ambitious printing schedule.

We especially wish to thank Katherine Marie Silsbee for her management of the entire project, as well as for the application of her superb research and editorial skills. We also wish to thank William Eric Hollowell, who co-authored the *Solutions Manual* and the *Test Bank* for his excellent research efforts. We were fortunate enough to have the copyediting services of Beverly Peavler and the proofreading services of Jeanne Yost. We are grateful for the efforts of Vickie Reierson and Roxanna Lee for their proofreading and other assistance, which helped to ensure an error-free text. Finally, we thank Suzanne Jasin of K & M Consulting for her many special efforts on this project.

In addition, we would like to give special thanks to all of the individuals who were instrumental in developing and implementing the new *MindTap Legal Environment* for *The Legal Environment Today*. These include Michael Worls, Vicky True-Baker, Rebecca von Gillern, Kristen Meere, Katie Jergens, and Javan Kline at Cengage, and Katherine Marie Silsbee, Roger Meiners, Lavina Leed Miller, William Eric Hollowell, Kimberly Wallan, Kristi Wiswell, and Joseph Zavaleta who helped develop the content for this unique Web-based product.

Through the years, we have enjoyed an ongoing correspondence with many of you who have found points on which you wish to comment. We continue to welcome all comments and promise to respond promptly. By incorporating your ideas, we can continue to write a business law text that is best for you and best for your students.

F.B.C.
R.L.M.

Dedication

To my parents and sisters.

F.B.C.

To Sophie and Philippe,

Writing is life.
Let's continue forever.

R.L.M.

(BackyardProduction/iStockphoto.com)

The Foundations

CHAPTER 1

Business and Its Legal Environment

(JustASC/Shutterstock.com)

CONTENTS

- Business Activities and the Legal Environment
- Sources of American Law
- The Common Law Tradition
- Classifications of Law

LEARNING OBJECTIVES

The five learning objectives below are designed to help improve your understanding of the chapter. After reading this chapter, you should be able to answer the following questions:

1. What are four primary sources of law in the United States?
2. What is the common law tradition?
3. What is a precedent? When might a court depart from precedent?
4. What is the difference between remedies at law and remedies in equity?
5. What are some important differences between civil law and criminal law?

---

*"Laws should be like clothes.
They should be made to fit the people they are meant to serve."*
—Clarence Darrow, 1857–1938 (American lawyer)

In the chapter-opening quotation, Clarence Darrow asserts that law should be created to serve the public. As you are part of that public, the law is important to you. Those entering the world of business will find themselves subject to numerous laws and government regulations. A basic knowledge of these laws and regulations is beneficial—if not essential—to anyone contemplating a successful career in today's business environment.

Although the law has various definitions, they all are based on the general observation that **law** consists of *enforceable rules governing relationships among individuals and between individuals and their society*. In some societies, these enforceable rules consist of unwritten principles of behavior, while in other societies they are set forth in ancient or contemporary law codes. In the United States, our rules consist of written laws and court decisions created by modern legislative and judicial bodies. Regardless of how such rules are created, they all have one feature in common: they establish *rights, duties, and privileges that are consistent with the values and beliefs of a society or its ruling group.*

Law A body of enforceable rules governing relationships among individuals and between individuals and their society.

In this introductory chapter, we look first at an important question for any student reading this text: How do business law and the legal environment affect business decision making? Next, we describe the basic sources of American law, the common law tradition, and some schools of legal thought. We conclude the chapter with a discussion of some general classifications of law.

Business Activities and the Legal Environment

As those entering the business world will learn, laws and government regulations affect all business activities—hiring and firing decisions, workplace safety, the manufacturing and marketing of products, and business financing, to name just a few. To make good business decisions, a basic understanding of the laws and regulations governing these activities is essential. Moreover, in today's setting, simply being aware of what conduct can lead to legal **liability** is not enough. Businesspersons must develop critical thinking and legal reasoning skills so that they can evaluate how various laws might apply to a given situation and determine the potential result of their course of action. Businesspersons are also under increasing pressure to make ethical decisions and to consider the consequences of their decisions for stockholders and employees (as will be discussed in Chapter 2).

Liability The state of being legally responsible (liable) for something, such as a debt or obligation.

Many Different Laws May Affect a Single Business Transaction

As you will note, each chapter in this text covers a specific area of the law and shows how the legal rules in that area affect business activities. Although compartmentalizing the law in this fashion facilitates learning, it does not indicate the extent to which many different laws may apply to just one transaction. This is where the critical thinking skills that you will learn throughout this book become important. You need to be able to identify the various legal issues, apply the laws that you learn about, and arrive at a conclusion on the best course of action.

EXAMPLE 1.1 Suppose that you are the president of NetSys, Inc., a company that creates and maintains computer network systems for other business firms. NetSys also markets software for internal computer networks. One day, Janet Hernandez, an operations officer for Southwest Distribution Corporation (SDC), contacts you by e-mail about a possible contract involving SDC's computer network. In deciding whether to enter into a contract with SDC, you need to consider, among other things, the legal requirements for an enforceable contract. Are the requirements different for a contract for services and a contract for products? What are your options if SDC **breaches** (breaks, or fails to perform) the contract? The answers to these questions are part of contract law and sales law.

Breach The failure to perform a legal obligation.

Other questions might concern payment under the contract. How can you guarantee that NetSys will be paid? For example, if SDC pays with a check that is returned for insufficient funds, what are your options? Answers to these questions can be found in the laws that relate to negotiable instruments (such as checks) and creditors' rights. Also, a dispute may arise over the rights to NetSys's software, or there may be a question of liability if the software is defective. There may even be an issue as to whether you and Hernandez had the authority to make the deal in the first place. Resolutions of these questions may be found in the laws that relate to intellectual property, e-commerce, torts, product liability, agency, business organizations, or professional liability. ●

Finally, if any dispute cannot be resolved amicably, then the laws and the rules concerning courts and court procedures spell out the steps of a lawsuit. Exhibit 1–1 that follows illustrates the various areas of the law that may influence business decision making.

To avoid potential legal disputes, be aware of the many different laws that may apply to a single business transaction. Become familiar with the laws that affect your business operations, but always consult an expert. Attorneys must keep up with the myriad rules and regulations that govern the conduct of business in the United States. When you need to choose an attorney, obtain recommendations from friends, relatives, or business associates who have had long-standing relationships with their attorneys. If that fails, contact your local or state bar association, or check FindLaw's online directory (at lawyers.findlaw.com).

Linking Business Law to the Six Functional Fields of Business

In all likelihood, you are taking a business law or legal environment course because you intend to enter the business world, though some of you may also plan to become full-time practicing attorneys. Many of you are taking other business school courses and may therefore be familiar with the functional fields of business listed below:

1. Corporate management.
2. Production and transportation.
3. Marketing.
4. Research and development.
5. Accounting and finance.
6. Human resource management.

Exhibit 1–1 Areas of the Law That May Affect Business Decision Making

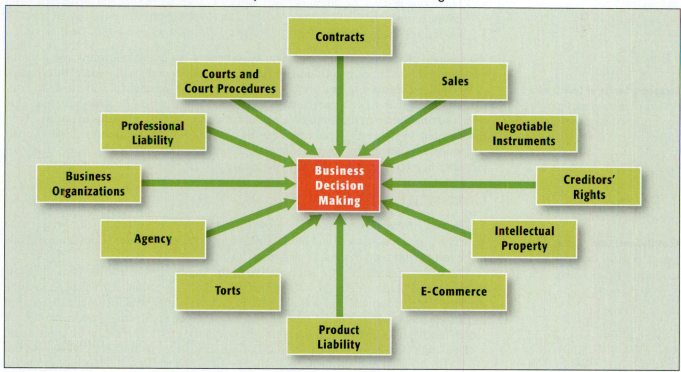

Every small-business person will at some time need to look up laws relating to his or her commercial activities.

One of our goals in this text is to show how legal concepts can be useful for managers and businesspersons, whether their activities focus on management, marketing, accounting, or some other field. To that end, several chapters conclude with a special feature called "*Linking Business Law to* [one of the six functional fields of business]."

The Role of the Law in a Small Business

Some of you may end up working in a small business or even owning and running one yourselves. The small business owner/operator is the most general of managers. When you seek additional financing, you become a finance manager. When you "go over the books" with your bookkeeper, you become an accountant. When you decide on a new advertising campaign, you are suddenly the marketing manager. When you hire employees and determine their salaries and benefits, you become a human resources manager.

Just as the functional fields of business are linked to the law, so too are all of these different managerial roles that a small-business owner must perform. See Exhibit 1–2, which shows some of the legal issues that may arise as part of the management of a small business. Large businesses face most of these issues, too.

Sources of American Law

Learning Objective 1
What are four primary sources of law in the United States?

Primary Source of Law A document that establishes the law on a particular issue, such as a constitution, a statute, an administrative rule, or a court decision.

There are numerous sources of American law. **Primary sources of law,** or sources that establish the law, include the following:

- The U.S. Constitution and the constitutions of the various states.
- Statutes, or laws, passed by Congress and by state legislatures.
- Regulations created by administrative agencies, such as the federal Food and Drug Administration.
- Case law (court decisions).

We describe each of these important primary sources of law in the following pages and discuss how to find statutes, regulations, and case law in the appendix at the end of this chapter.

Secondary Source of Law A publication that summarizes or interprets the law, such as a legal encyclopedia, a legal treatise, or an article in a law review.

Secondary sources of law are books and articles that summarize and clarify the primary sources of law. Legal encyclopedias, compilations (such as *Restatements of the Law,* which summarize court decisions on a particular topic), official comments to statutes, treatises, articles in law reviews published by law schools, and articles in other legal journals are examples of secondary sources of law. Courts often refer to secondary sources of law for guidance in interpreting and applying the primary sources of law discussed here.

Constitutional Law

Constitutional Law The body of law derived from the U.S. Constitution and the constitutions of the various states.

The federal government and the states have separate written constitutions that set forth the general organization, powers, and limits of their respective governments. **Constitutional law** is the law as expressed in these constitutions.

The U.S. Constitution is the supreme law of the land. As such, it is the basis of all law in the United States. A law in violation of the U.S. Constitution, if challenged, will be declared unconstitutional and will not be enforced, no matter what its source. Because of its paramount importance in the American legal system, we discuss the U.S. Constitution at length in Chapter 4 and present the complete text of the U.S. Constitution in Appendix B.

The Tenth Amendment to the U.S. Constitution reserves to the states all powers not granted to the federal government. Each state in the union has its own constitution. Unless

Exhibit 1–2 Linking Business Law to the Management of a Small Business

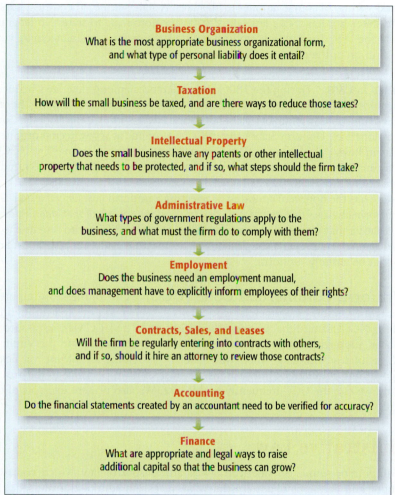

Business Organization
What is the most appropriate business organizational form, and what type of personal liability does it entail?

Taxation
How will the small business be taxed, and are there ways to reduce those taxes?

Intellectual Property
Does the small business have any patents or other intellectual property that needs to be protected, and if so, what steps should the firm take?

Administrative Law
What types of government regulations apply to the business, and what must the firm do to comply with them?

Employment
Does the business need an employment manual, and does management have to explicitly inform employees of their rights?

Contracts, Sales, and Leases
Will the firm be regularly entering into contracts with others, and if so, should it hire an attorney to review those contracts?

Accounting
Do the financial statements created by an accountant need to be verified for accuracy?

Finance
What are appropriate and legal ways to raise additional capital so that the business can grow?

it conflicts with the U.S. Constitution or a federal law, a state constitution is supreme within that state's borders.

Statutory Law

Laws enacted by legislative bodies at any level of government, such as the statutes passed by Congress or by state legislatures, make up the body of law generally referred to as **statutory law.** When a legislature passes a statute, that statute ultimately is included in the federal code of laws or the relevant state code of laws. Whenever a particular statute is mentioned in this text, we usually provide a footnote showing its **citation** (a reference to a publication in which a legal authority—such as a statute or a court decision—or other source can be found). In the appendix following this chapter, we explain how you can use these citations to find statutory law.

Statutory law also includes local **ordinances**—statutes (laws, rules, or orders) passed by municipal or county governing units to administer matters not covered by federal or state

Statutory Law The body of law enacted by legislative bodies (as opposed to constitutional law, administrative law, or case law).

Citation A reference to a publication in which a legal authority—such as a statute or a court decision—or other source can be found.

Ordinance A regulation enacted by a city or county legislative body that becomes part of that state's statutory law.

Many cities have passed local ordinances banning texting while driving.

Uniform Law A model law developed by the National Conference of Commissioners on Uniform State Laws for the states to consider enacting into statute.

law. Ordinances commonly have to do with city or county land use (zoning ordinances), building and safety codes, and other matters affecting only the local governing unit.

A federal statute, of course, applies to all states. A state statute, in contrast, applies only within the state's borders. State laws thus may vary from state to state. No federal statute may violate the U.S. Constitution, and no state statute or local ordinance may violate the U.S. Constitution or the relevant state constitution.

Uniform Laws   During the 1800s, the differences among state laws frequently created difficulties for businesspersons conducting trade and commerce among the states. To counter these problems, a group of legal scholars and lawyers formed the National Conference of Commissioners on Uniform State Laws (NCCUSL, online at **www.nccusl.org**) in 1892 to draft **uniform laws** ("model statutes") for the states to consider adopting. The NCCUSL still exists today and continues to issue uniform laws: it has issued more than two hundred uniform acts since its inception.

Each state has the option of adopting or rejecting a uniform law. *Only if a state legislature adopts a uniform law does that law become part of the statutory law of that state.* Furthermore, a state legislature may choose to adopt only part of a uniform law or to rewrite the sections that are adopted. Hence, even though many states may have adopted a uniform law, those laws may not be entirely "uniform."

The Uniform Commercial Code (UCC)   One of the most important uniform acts is the Uniform Commercial Code (UCC), which was created through the joint efforts of the NCCUSL and the American Law Institute.[1] The UCC was first issued in 1952 and has been adopted in all fifty states,[2] the District of Columbia, and the Virgin Islands. The UCC facilitates commerce among the states by providing a uniform, yet flexible, set of rules governing commercial transactions. Because of its importance in the area of commercial law, we cite the UCC frequently in this text. We also present excerpts of the UCC in Appendix C.

Administrative Law

Another important source of American law is administrative law, which consists of the rules, orders, and decisions of administrative agencies. An administrative agency is a federal, state, or local government agency established to perform a specific function. Rules issued by various administrative agencies now affect almost every aspect of a business's operations, including the firm's capital structure and financing, its hiring and firing procedures, its relations with employees and unions, and the way it manufactures and markets its products. Because of its significance and influence on businesses, we discuss administrative law in detail in Chapter 19.

Case Law and Common Law Doctrines

Case Law The rules of law announced in court decisions. Case law interprets statutes, regulations, constitutional provisions, and other case law.

The rules of law announced in court decisions constitute another basic source of American law. These rules of law include interpretations of constitutional provisions, of statutes enacted by legislatures, and of regulations created by administrative agencies. Today, this body of judge-made law is referred to as **case law.** Case law—the doctrines and principles announced in cases—governs all areas not covered by statutory law or administrative law

---

1. This institute was formed in the 1920s and consists of practicing attorneys, legal scholars, and judges.
2. Louisiana has adopted only Articles 1, 3, 4, 5, 7, 8, and 9.

and is part of our common law tradition. We look at the origins and characteristics of the common law tradition in some detail in the pages that follow.

The Common Law Tradition

Because of our colonial heritage, much of American law is based on the English legal system. A knowledge of this tradition is crucial to understanding our legal system today because judges in the United States still apply common law principles when deciding cases.

Early English Courts

After the Normans conquered England in 1066, William the Conqueror and his successors began the process of unifying the country under their rule. One of the means they used to do this was the establishment of the king's courts, or *curiae regis*. Before the Norman Conquest, disputes had been settled according to the local legal customs and traditions in various regions of the country. The king's courts sought to establish a uniform set of rules for the country as a whole. What evolved in these courts was the beginning of the **common law**—a body of general rules that applied throughout the entire English realm. Eventually, the common law tradition became part of the heritage of all nations that were once British colonies, including the United States.

Courts developed the common law rules from the principles underlying judges' decisions in actual legal controversies. Judges attempted to be consistent, and whenever possible, they based their decisions on the principles suggested by earlier cases. They sought to decide similar cases in a similar way and considered new cases with care because they knew that their decisions would make new law. Each interpretation became part of the law on the subject and served as a legal **precedent**—that is, a court decision that furnished an example or authority for deciding subsequent cases involving identical or similar legal principles or facts.

In the early years of the common law, there was no single place or publication where court opinions, or written decisions, could be found. Beginning in the late thirteenth and early fourteenth centuries, however, portions of significant decisions from each year were gathered together and recorded in *Year Books*. The *Year Books* were useful references for lawyers and judges. In the sixteenth century, the *Year Books* were discontinued, and other reports of cases became available. (See the appendix to this chapter for a discussion of how cases are reported, or published, in the United States today.)

Common Law The body of law developed from custom or judicial decisions in English and U.S. courts, not attributable to a legislature.

Learning Objective 3
What is a precedent? When might a court depart from precedent?

Precedent A court decision that furnishes an example or authority for deciding subsequent cases involving identical or similar legal principles or facts.

Stare Decisis

The practice of deciding new cases with reference to former decisions, or precedents, eventually became a cornerstone of the English and U.S. judicial systems. The practice forms a doctrine called **stare decisis**[3] ("to stand on decided cases").

Stare Decisis A common law doctrine under which judges are obligated to follow the precedents established in prior decisions.

The Importance of Precedents in Judicial Decision Making
Under the doctrine of *stare decisis,* once a court has set forth a principle of law as being applicable to a certain set of facts, that court and courts of lower rank must adhere to that principle and apply it in future cases involving similar fact patterns. *Stare decisis* has two aspects: (1) decisions made by a higher court are binding on lower courts, and (2) a court should not overturn its own precedents unless there is a strong reason to do so.

Controlling precedents in a *jurisdiction* (an area in which a court or courts have the power to apply the law) are referred to as binding authorities. A **binding authority** is any source of law that a court *must* follow when deciding a case. Binding authorities include

Binding Authority Any source of law that a court *must* follow when deciding a case.

---

3. Pronounced *stah-ree dih-si-sis.*

constitutions, statutes, and regulations that govern the issue being decided, as well as court decisions that are controlling precedents within the jurisdiction. United States Supreme Court case decisions, no matter how old, remain controlling until they are overruled by a subsequent decision of the Supreme Court, by a constitutional amendment, or by congressional legislation.

***Stare Decisis* and Legal Stability**   The doctrine of *stare decisis* helps the courts to be more efficient because if other courts have carefully reasoned through a similar case, their legal reasoning and opinions can serve as guides. *Stare decisis* also makes the law more stable and predictable. If the law on a given subject is well settled, someone bringing a case to court can usually rely on the court to make a decision based on what the law has been.

Departures from Precedent   Although courts are obligated to follow precedents, sometimes a court will depart from the rule of precedent. If a court decides that a precedent is simply incorrect or that technological or social changes have rendered the precedent inapplicable, the court may rule contrary to the precedent. Cases that overturn precedent often receive a great deal of publicity.

CASE EXAMPLE 1.2   In *Brown v. Board of Education of Topeka*,[4] the United States Supreme Court expressly overturned precedent when it concluded that separate educational facilities for whites and blacks, which had been upheld as constitutional in numerous previous cases,[5] were inherently unequal. The Supreme Court's departure from precedent in the *Brown* decision received a tremendous amount of publicity as people began to realize the ramifications of this change in the law. ●

(Library of Congress)

School integration occurred after *Brown v. Board of Education of Topeka*.

When There Is No Precedent   At times, a case may raise issues that have not been raised before in that jurisdiction, so the court has no precedents on which to base its decision. When deciding such cases, called "cases of first impression," courts often look at precedents established in other jurisdictions for guidance. Precedents from other jurisdictions, because they are not binding on the court, are referred to as **persuasive authorities.**

A court may also consider other factors, including legal principles and policies underlying previous court decisions or existing statutes, fairness, social values and customs, public policy, and data and concepts drawn from the social sciences.

Can a court consider unpublished decisions as persuasive precedent? See this chapter's *Online Developments* feature that follows for a discussion of this issue.

Persuasive Authority Any legal authority or source of law that a court may look to for guidance but need not follow when making its decision.

Equitable Remedies and Courts of Equity

A **remedy** is the means given to a party to enforce a right or to compensate for the violation of a right.   **EXAMPLE 1.3**   Elena is injured because of Rowan's wrongdoing. If Elena files a lawsuit and is successful, a court can order Rowan to compensate Elena for the harm by paying her a certain amount. The compensation is Elena's remedy. ●

The kinds of remedies available in the early king's courts of England were severely restricted. If one person wronged another, the king's courts could award as compensation either money or property, including land. These courts became known as *courts of law,* and the remedies were called *remedies at law.* Even though this system introduced uniformity in the settling of disputes, when a person wanted a remedy other than economic compensation, the courts of law could do nothing, so "no remedy, no right."

Remedy The relief given to an innocent party to enforce a right or compensate for the violation of a right.

Learning Objective 4
What is the difference between remedies at law and remedies in equity?

---

4. 347 U.S. 483, 74 S.Ct. 686, 98 L.Ed. 873 (1954).
5. See *Plessy v. Ferguson*, 163 U.S. 537, 16 S.Ct. 1138, 41 L.Ed. 256 (1896).

ONLINE DEVELOPMENTS

How the Internet Has Expanded Precedent

The notion that courts should rely on precedents to decide the outcome of similar cases has long been a cornerstone of U.S. law. Nevertheless, the availability of "unpublished opinions" over the Internet has changed what the law considers to be precedent.

An *unpublished opinion* is a decision issued by an appellate (reviewing) court that is not intended for publication in a reporter (the bound books that contain court opinions).**ᵃ** Courts traditionally did not consider unpublished opinions to be "precedents," binding or persuasive, and often did not allow attorneys to refer to (cite) these decisions in their arguments.

Increased Online Availability of Unpublished Decisions

The number of court decisions not published in printed books has risen dramatically in recent years. Nearly 80 percent of the decisions of the federal appellate courts are unpublished, and the number is equally high in some state court systems.

Even though certain decisions are not intended for publication, they are posted ("published") almost immediately in online legal databases, such as Westlaw and Lexis. With the proliferation of free legal databases and court Web sites, the general public also has almost instant access to the unpublished decisions of most courts. This situation has caused many to question why these opinions have no precedential effect.

Before the Internet, not considering unpublished decisions as precedent might have been justified on the grounds of fairness. How could lawyers know about decisions if they were not printed in the case reporters? Now that opinions are so readily available on the Web, however, this justification is no

longer valid. Moreover, it now seems unfair not to consider these decisions as precedent because they are so publicly accessible. Some claim that unpublished decisions could make bad precedents because these decisions frequently are written by staff attorneys and law clerks, rather than by judges, so the reasoning may be inferior. If the decision is considered merely as persuasive precedent, however, judges who disagree with the reasoning are free to reject the conclusion.

The Federal Rules Now Allow Judges to Consider Unpublished Opinions

The United States Supreme Court made history in 2006 when it announced that it would allow lawyers to cite unpublished decisions in all federal courts. Rule 32.1 of the Federal Rules of Appellate Procedure states that federal courts may not prohibit or restrict the citation of federal judicial opinions that have been designated as "not for publication," "nonprecedential," or "not precedent." The rule applies only to federal courts and only to unpublished opinions issued after January 1, 2007. It does not specify what weight a court must give to its own unpublished opinions or to those from another court.

Basically, Rule 32.1 establishes a uniform rule for all of the federal courts that allows attorneys to cite—and judges to consider as persuasive precedent—unpublished decisions.

Critical Thinking

Only a few states, such as Massachusetts, have followed the federal courts in allowing unpublished decisions to be used as persuasive precedent. The other states claim that doing so would increase the already heavy workload of their courts. Under the current system, a judge who designates an opinion as unpublished does not have to take the time to provide a complete set of facts, references, and views. Does this argument justify the different treatment for unpublished opinions in the state and federal courts? Explain.

---

a. Recently decided cases that are not yet published are also sometimes called *unpublished opinions*, but because these decisions will eventually be printed in reporters, we do not include them here.

Remedies in Equity   *Equity* is a branch of law, founded on what might be described as notions of justice and fair dealing, that seeks to supply a remedy when no adequate remedy at law is available. When individuals could not obtain an adequate remedy in a court of law, they petitioned the king for relief. Most of these petitions were referred to the *chancellor*, an adviser to the king who had the power to grant new and unique remedies. Eventually, formal chancery courts, or *courts of equity*, were established. Thus, two distinct court systems were created, each having its own set of judges and its own set of remedies. The remedies granted by the chancery courts were called *remedies in equity*.

Plaintiff One who initiates a lawsuit.

Defendant One against whom a lawsuit is brought, or the accused person in a criminal proceeding.

Plaintiffs (those bringing lawsuits) had to specify whether they were bringing an "action at law" or an "action in equity," and they chose their courts accordingly. **EXAMPLE 1.4** A plaintiff might ask a court of equity to order the **defendant** (the person against whom a lawsuit is brought) to perform within the terms of a contract. A court of law could not issue such an order because its remedies were limited to the payment of money or property as compensation for damages. A court of equity, however, could issue a decree for *specific performance*—an order to perform what was promised. A court of equity could also issue an *injunction,* directing a party to do or refrain from doing a particular act. In certain cases, a court of equity could allow for the *rescission* (cancellation) of the contract, thereby returning the parties to the positions that they held prior to the contract's formation. ● Equitable remedies will be discussed in Chapter 11.

The Merging of Law and Equity

Today, in most states, the courts of law and equity have merged, and thus the distinction between the two courts has largely disappeared. A plaintiff may now request both legal and equitable remedies in the same action, and the trial court judge may grant either form—or both forms—of relief.

The distinction between legal and equitable remedies remains significant, however, because a court normally will grant an equitable remedy only when the remedy at law (monetary damages) is inadequate. To request the proper remedy, a businessperson (or her or his attorney) must know what remedies are available for the specific kinds of harms suffered. Exhibit 1–3 summarizes the procedural differences (applicable in most states) between an action at law and an action in equity.

Equitable Principles and Maxims General propositions or principles of law that have to do with fairness (equity).

Equitable Principles and Maxims

Over time, the courts have developed a number of **equitable principles and maxims** that provide guidance in deciding whether plaintiffs should be granted equitable relief. Because of their importance, both historically and in our judicial system today, we present these principles and maxims in this chapter's *Landmark in the Legal Environment* feature.

Schools of Legal Thought

How judges apply the law to specific cases, including disputes relating to the business world, depends on their philosophical approaches to law, among other things. The study of law, often referred to as **jurisprudence**, includes learning about different schools of legal thought and discovering how each school's approach to law can affect judicial decision making.

Jurisprudence The science or philosophy of law.

Natural Law The oldest school of legal thought, based on the belief that the legal system should reflect universal ("higher") moral and ethical principles that are inherent in human nature.

The Natural Law School

Those who adhere to the **natural law** theory believe that a higher, or universal, law exists that applies to all human beings and that written

Exhibit 1–3 Procedural Differences between an Action at Law and an Action in Equity

PROCEDURE	ACTION AT LAW	ACTION IN EQUITY
Initiation of lawsuit	By filing a complaint.	By filing a petition.
Decision	By jury or judge.	By judge (no jury).
Result	Judgment.	Decree.
Remedy	Monetary damages.	Injunction, specific performance, or rescission.

laws should imitate these inherent principles. If a written law is unjust, then it is not a true (natural) law and need not be obeyed.

The natural law tradition is one of the oldest and most significant schools of jurisprudence. It dates back to the days of the Greek philosopher Aristotle (384–322 B.C.E.), who distinguished between natural law and the laws governing a particular nation. According to Aristotle, natural law applies universally to all humankind.

The notion that people have "natural rights" stems from the natural law tradition. Those who claim that certain nations, such as China and North Korea, are depriving many of their citizens of their human rights are implicitly appealing to a higher law that has universal applicability. The question of the universality of basic human rights also comes into play in the context of international business operations. For example, U.S. companies that have operations abroad often hire foreign workers as employees. Should the same laws that protect U.S. employees apply to these foreign employees? This question is rooted implicitly in a concept of universal rights that has its origins in the natural law tradition.

Legal Positivism In contrast, *positive*, or national, law (the written law of a given society at a particular point in time) applies only to the citizens of that nation or society. Those who adhere to **legal positivism** believe that there can be no higher law than a

> **Legal Positivism** A school of legal thought centered on the assumption that there is no law higher than the laws created by a national government. Laws must be obeyed, even if they are unjust, to prevent anarchy.

LANDMARK IN THE LEGAL ENVIRONMENT
Equitable Principles and Maxims

In medieval England, courts of equity were expected to use discretion in supplementing the common law. Even today, when the same court can award both legal and equitable remedies, it must exercise discretion. Students of business law should know that courts often invoke equitable principles and maxims when making their decisions.

Here are some of the most significant equitable principles and maxims:

1. *Whoever seeks equity must do equity.* (Anyone who wishes to be treated fairly must treat others fairly.)
2. *Where there is equal equity, the law must prevail.* (The law will determine the outcome of a controversy in which the merits of both sides are equal.)
3. *One seeking the aid of an equity court must come to the court with clean hands.* (Plaintiffs must have acted fairly and honestly.)
4. *Equity will not suffer a wrong to be without a remedy.* (Equitable relief will be awarded when there is a right to relief and there is no adequate remedy at law.)
5. *Equity regards substance rather than form.* (Equity is more concerned with fairness and justice than with legal technicalities.)
6. *Equity aids the vigilant, not those who rest on their rights.* (Equity will not help those who neglect their rights for an unreasonable period of time.)

The last maxim has come to be known as the *equitable doctrine of laches*. The doctrine arose to encourage people to bring lawsuits while the evidence was fresh. If they failed to do so, they would not be allowed to bring a lawsuit. What constitutes a reasonable time, of course, varies according to the circumstances of the case.

Time periods for different types of cases are now usually fixed by *statutes of limitations*—that is, statutes that set the maximum time period during which a certain action can be brought. After the time allowed under a statute of limitations has expired, no action can be brought, no matter how strong the case was originally.

Application to Today's Legal Environment *The equitable maxims listed underlie many of the legal rules and principles that are commonly applied by the courts today—and that you will read about in this book.*

For instance, in Chapter 11 you will read about the doctrine of substantial performance. Under this doctrine of contract law, a party who in good faith substantially performs as required under a contract may be entitled to compensation even if the performance was defective in some way. A key requirement is good faith, meaning that the defect in the party's performance was unintentional or accidental. The requirement of good faith reflects the first and third maxims on the list, that whoever seeks to recover and be treated fairly by a court must have acted fairly and honestly in the situation.

nation's positive law. According to the positivist school, there is no such thing as "natural rights." Rather, human rights exist solely because of laws. If the laws are not enforced, anarchy will result. Thus, whether a law is morally "bad" or "good" is irrelevant. The law is the law and must be obeyed until it is changed—in an orderly manner through a legitimate lawmaking process.

A judge with positivist leanings probably would be more inclined to defer to an existing law than would a judge who adheres to the natural law tradition.

The Historical School

Historical School A school of legal thought that looks to the past to determine what the principles of contemporary law should be.

The Historical School   The **historical school** of legal thought emphasizes the evolutionary process of law by concentrating on the origin and history of the legal system. This school looks to the past to discover what the principles of contemporary law should be. The legal doctrines that have withstood the passage of time—those that have worked in the past—are deemed best suited for shaping present laws. Hence, law derives its legitimacy and authority from adhering to the standards that historical development has shown to be workable.

Followers of the historical school are more likely than those of other schools to adhere strictly to decisions made in past cases.

Legal Realism A school of legal thought that holds that the law is only one factor to be considered when deciding cases and that social and economic circumstances should also be taken into account.

Legal Realism   In the 1920s and 1930s, a number of jurists and scholars, known as *legal realists,* rebelled against the historical approach to law. **Legal realism** is based on the idea that law is just one of many institutions in society and that it is shaped by social forces and needs. This school holds that because the law is a human enterprise, judges should look beyond the law and take social and economic realities into account when deciding cases. Legal realists also believe that the law can never be applied with total uniformity. Given that judges are human beings with unique experiences, personalities, value systems, and intellects, different judges will obviously bring different reasoning processes to the same case. Female judges, for instance, might be more inclined than male judges to consider whether a decision might have a negative impact on the employment of women or minorities.

Classifications of Law

The law may be broken down according to several classification systems. For instance, one classification system divides law into **substantive law** (all laws that define, describe, regulate, and create legal rights and obligations) and **procedural law** (all laws that establish the methods of enforcing the rights established by substantive law).

Substantive Law Law that defines, describes, regulates, and creates legal rights and obligations.

Procedural Law Law that establishes the methods of enforcing the rights established by substantive law.

EXAMPLE 1.5   A state law that provides employees with the right to workers' compensation benefits for any on-the-job injuries they sustain is a substantive law because it creates legal rights (workers' compensation laws will be discussed in Chapter 17). Procedural laws, in contrast, establish the method by which an employee must notify the employer about an on-the-job injury, prove the injury, and periodically submit additional proof to continue receiving workers' compensation benefits. Note that a law concerning workers' compensation may contain both substantive and procedural provisions. ●

Other classification systems divide law into (1) federal law and state law, or (2) private law (dealing with relationships between persons) and public law (addressing the relationship between persons and their governments). Frequently, people use the term **cyberlaw** to refer to the emerging body of law that governs transactions conducted via the Internet.

Cyberlaw An informal term used to refer to all laws governing transactions conducted via the Internet.

Cyberlaw is not really a classification of law, nor is it a new *type* of law. Rather, it is an informal term used to describe traditional legal principles that have been modified and adapted to fit situations that are unique to the online world. Of course, in some areas new statutes have been enacted, at both the federal and state levels, to cover specific types of problems stemming from online communications. Throughout this book, you will read about how the law is evolving to govern specific legal issues that arise in the online context.

Civil Law and Criminal Law

Civil law spells out the rights and duties that exist between persons and between persons and their governments, and the relief available when a person's rights are violated. Typically, in a civil case, a private party sues another private party (although the government can also sue a party for a civil law violation) to make sure that the other party complies with a duty or pays for the damage caused by the failure to comply with a duty.

EXAMPLE 1.6 If a seller fails to perform a contract with a buyer, the buyer may bring a lawsuit against the seller. The purpose of the lawsuit will be either to compel the seller to perform as promised or, more commonly, to obtain monetary damages for the seller's failure to perform. ●

Much of the law that we discuss in this text is civil law. Contract law, for example, which we will discuss in Chapters 10 and 11, is civil law. The whole body of tort law (see Chapter 5) is civil law. Note that *civil law* is not the same as a *civil law system*. As you will read shortly, a **civil law system** is a legal system based on a written code of laws.

Criminal law has to do with wrongs committed against society for which society demands redress. Criminal acts are proscribed by local, state, or federal government statutes (see Chapter 6 and many of the laws discussed in Chapters 21 and 24). Thus, criminal defendants are prosecuted by public officials, such as a district attorney (D.A.), on behalf of the state, not by their victims or other private parties. Whereas in a civil case the object is to obtain a remedy (such as monetary damages) to compensate the injured party, in a criminal case the object is to punish the wrongdoer in an attempt to deter others from similar actions. Penalties for violations of criminal statutes consist of fines and/or imprisonment—and, in some cases, death. We will discuss the differences between civil and criminal law in greater detail in Chapter 6.

Civil Law The branch of law dealing with the definition and enforcement of all private or public rights, as opposed to criminal matters.

Learning Objective 5
What are some important differences between civil law and criminal law?

Civil Law System A system of law derived from Roman law that is based on codified laws (rather than on case precedents).

Criminal Law The branch of law that defines and punishes wrongful actions committed against the public.

National and International Law

Although the focus of this book is U.S. business law, increasingly businesspersons in this country engage in transactions that extend beyond our national borders. In these situations, the laws of other nations or the laws governing relationships among nations may come into play. For this reason, those who pursue a career in business today should have an understanding of the global legal environment (discussed further in Chapter 7).

National Law Law that pertains to a particular nation (as opposed to international law).

International Law The law that governs relations among nations.

National Law The law of a particular nation, such as the United States or Sweden, is **national law.** National law, of course, varies from country to country because each country's law reflects the interests, customs, activities, and values that are unique to that nation's culture. Even though the laws and legal systems of various countries differ substantially, broad similarities do exist, as discussed in the following *Beyond Our Borders* feature.

International Law In contrast to national law, international law applies to more than one nation. **International law** can be defined as a body of written and unwritten laws observed by independent nations and governing the acts of individuals as well as governments. It is a mixture of rules and constraints derived from a variety of sources, including the laws of individual nations, customs developed among nations, and international treaties and organizations. Each nation is motivated not only by the need to be the final authority over its own

A witness points out someone in the courtroom to the judge.

(Junial Enterprises/Shutterstock.com)

affairs, but also by the desire to benefit economically from trade and harmonious relations with other nations. In essence, international law is the result of centuries-old attempts to strike a balance between these competing needs.

The key difference between national law and international law is that government authorities can enforce national law. If a nation violates an international law, however, enforcement is up to other countries or international organizations, which may or may not choose to act. If persuasive tactics fail, the only option is to take coercive actions against the violating nation. Coercive actions range from the severance of diplomatic relations and boycotts to, as a last resort, war. We will examine the laws governing international business transactions in Chapter 7.

BEYOND OUR BORDERS   National Law Systems

Despite their varying cultures and customs, almost all countries have laws governing torts, contracts, employment, and other areas. Two types of legal systems predominate around the globe today. One is the common law system of England and the United States, which we have discussed elsewhere. The other system is based on Roman civil law, or "code law," which relies on the legal principles enacted into law by a legislature or governing body.

Civil Law Systems

Although national law systems share many commonalities, they also have distinct differences. In a *civil law system,* the primary source of law is a statutory code, and case precedents are not judicially binding, as they normally are in a common law system. Although judges in a civil law system commonly refer to previous decisions as sources of legal guidance, those decisions are not binding precedents (*stare decisis* does not apply).

Exhibit 1–4 lists some countries that today follow either the common law system or the civil law system. Generally, those countries that were once colonies of Great Britain have retained their English common law heritage. The civil law system, which is used in most continental European nations, has been retained in the countries that were once colonies of those nations. In the United States, the state of Louisiana, because of its historical ties to France, has in part a civil law system, as do Haiti, Québec, and Scotland.

Islamic Legal Systems

A third, less prevalent legal system is common in Islamic countries, where the law is often influenced by *sharia,* the religious law of Islam. Islam is both a religion and a way of life. *Sharia* is a comprehensive code of principles that governs the public and private lives of Islamic persons and directs many aspects of their day-to-day life, including politics, economics, banking, business law, contract law, and social issues.

Although *sharia* affects the legal codes of many Muslim countries, the extent of its impact and its interpretation vary widely. In some Middle Eastern nations, aspects of *sharia* have been codified in modern legal codes and are enforced by national judicial systems.

Critical Thinking

Does the civil law system offer any advantages over the common law system, or vice versa? Explain.

Exhibit 1–4   The Legal Systems of Selected Nations

CIVIL LAW		COMMON LAW	
Argentina	Indonesia	Australia	Nigeria
Austria	Iran	Bangladesh	Singapore
Brazil	Italy	Canada	United Kingdom
Chile	Japan	Ghana	United States
China	Mexico	India	Zambia
Egypt	Poland	Israel	
Finland	South Korea	Jamaica	
France	Sweden	Kenya	
Germany	Tunisia	Malaysia	
Greece	Venezuela	New Zealand	

Reviewing . . . Business and Its Legal Environment

Suppose that the California legislature passes a law that severely restricts carbon dioxide emissions from automobiles in that state. A group of automobile manufacturers files a suit against the state of California to prevent the enforcement of the law. The automakers claim that a federal law already sets fuel economy standards nationwide and that these standards are essentially the same as carbon dioxide emission standards. According to the automobile manufacturers, it is unfair to allow California to impose more stringent regulations than those set by the federal law. Using the information presented in the chapter, answer the following questions.

1. Who are the parties (the plaintiffs and the defendant) in this lawsuit?
2. Are the plaintiffs seeking a legal remedy or an equitable remedy? Why?
3. What is the primary source of the law that is at issue here?
4. Read through the appendix that follows this chapter, and then answer the following question: Where would you look to find the relevant California and federal laws?

Debate This Under the doctrine of *stare decisis,* courts are obligated to follow the precedents established in their jurisdiction unless there is a compelling reason not to do so. Should U.S. courts continue to adhere to this common law principle, given that our government now regulates so many areas by statute?

Key Terms

binding authority 9	cyberlaw 14	liability 4	primary source of law 6
breach 4	defendant 12	majority opinion 27	procedural law 14
case law 8	dissenting opinion 27	national law 15	remedy 10
citation 7	equitable principles and maxims 12	natural law 12	secondary source of law 6
civil law 15	historical school 14	ordinance 7	*stare decisis* 9
civil law system 15	international law 15	*per curiam* opinion 28	statutory law 7
common law 9	jurisprudence 12	persuasive authority 10	substantive law 14
concurring opinion 27	law 3	plaintiff 12	uniform law 8
constitutional law 6	legal positivism 13	plurality opinion 28	
criminal law 15	legal realism 14	precedent 9	

Chapter Summary: Business and Its Legal Environment

Sources of American Law	1. *Constitutional law*—The law as expressed in the U.S. Constitution and the various state constitutions. The U.S. Constitution is the supreme law of the land. State constitutions are supreme within state borders to the extent that they do not violate the U.S. Constitution or a federal law.
	2. *Statutory law*—Laws or ordinances created by federal, state, and local legislatures and governing bodies. None of these laws can violate the U.S. Constitution or the relevant state constitutions. Uniform laws, when adopted by a state legislature, become statutory law in that state.
	3. *Administrative law*—The rules, orders, and decisions of federal or state government administrative agencies.
	4. *Case law and common law doctrines*—Judge-made law, including interpretations of constitutional provisions, of statutes enacted by legislatures, and of regulations created by administrative agencies. The common law—the doctrines and principles embodied in case law—governs all areas not covered by statutory law or administrative law.

Continued

Chapter Summary: Business and Its Legal Environment—Continued

| The Common Law Tradition | 1. **Common law**—Law that originated in medieval England with the creation of the king's courts, or *curiae regis*, and the development of a body of rules that were common to (or applied in) all regions of the country.
2. **Stare decisis**—A doctrine under which judges "stand on decided cases"—or follow the rule of precedent—in deciding cases. *Stare decisis* is the cornerstone of the common law tradition.
3. **Remedies**—A remedy is the means by which a court enforces a right or compensates for a violation of a right. Courts typically grant legal remedies (monetary damages) but may also grant equitable remedies (specific performance, injunction, or rescission) when the legal remedy is inadequate or unavailable.
4. **Schools of legal thought**—Judges' decision making is influenced by their philosophy of law. The following are four important schools of legal thought, or legal philosophies:
    a. Natural law tradition—One of the oldest and most significant schools of legal thought. Those who believe in natural law hold that there is a universal law applicable to all human beings and that this law is of a higher order than positive, or conventional, law.
    b. Legal positivism—A school of legal thought centered on the assumption that there is no law higher than the laws created by the government. Laws must be obeyed, even if they are unjust, to prevent anarchy.
    c. Historical school—A school of legal thought that stresses the evolutionary nature of law and looks to doctrines that have withstood the passage of time for guidance in shaping present laws.
    d. Legal realism—A school of legal thought that generally advocates a less abstract and more realistic approach to the law that takes into account customary practices and the circumstances in which transactions take place. |
| Classifications of Law | The law may be broken down according to several classification systems, such as substantive or procedural law, federal or state law, and private or public law. Two broad classifications are civil and criminal law, and national and international law. Cyberlaw is not really a classification of law but a term that is used for the growing body of case and statutory law that applies to Internet transactions. |

Issue Spotters

1. The First Amendment to the U.S. Constitution provides protection for the free exercise of religion. A state legislature enacts a law that outlaws all religions that do not derive from the Judeo-Christian tradition. Is this law valid within that state? Why or why not? (See *Sources of American Law*.)
2. Under what circumstances might a judge rely on case law to determine the intent and purpose of a statute? (See *The Common Law Tradition*.)

—**Check your answers to the Issue Spotters against the answers provided in Appendix D at the end of this text.**

For Review

1. What are four primary sources of law in the United States?
2. What is the common law tradition?
3. What is a precedent? When might a court depart from precedent?
4. What is the difference between remedies at law and remedies in equity?
5. What are some important differences between civil law and criminal law?

Business Scenarios and Case Problems

1–1. Binding versus Persuasive Authority. A county court in Illinois is deciding a case involving an issue that has never been addressed before in that state's courts. The Iowa Supreme Court, however, recently decided a case involving a very similar fact pattern. Is the Illinois court obligated to follow the Iowa Supreme Court's decision on the issue? If the United States Supreme Court had decided a similar case, would that decision be binding on the Illinois court? Explain. (See *The Common Law Tradition*.)

1–2. Remedies. Arthur Rabe is suing Xavier Sanchez for breaching a contract in which Sanchez promised to sell Rabe a Van Gogh painting for $150,000. (See *The Common Law Tradition*.)

1. In this lawsuit, who is the plaintiff, and who is the defendant?
2. If Rabe wants Sanchez to perform the contract as promised, what remedy should Rabe seek?
3. Suppose that Rabe wants to cancel the contract because Sanchez fraudulently misrepresented the painting as an original Van Gogh when in fact it is a copy. In this situation, what remedy should Rabe seek?
4. Will the remedy Rabe seeks in either situation be a remedy at law or a remedy in equity?
5. Suppose that the court finds in Rabe's favor and grants one of these remedies. Sanchez then appeals the decision to a higher court. Read through the subsection entitled "Parties to Lawsuits" in the appendix following this chapter. On appeal, which party in the Rabe-Sanchez case will be the appellant (or petitioner), and which party will be the appellee (or respondent)? (See *Reading and Understanding Case Law.*)

1–3. Philosophy of Law. After World War II ended in 1945, an international tribunal of judges convened at Nuremberg, Germany. The judges convicted several Nazi war criminals of "crimes against humanity." Assuming that the Nazis who were convicted had not disobeyed any law of their country and had merely been following their government's (Hitler's) orders, what law had they violated? Explain. (See *Schools of Legal Thought.*)

1–4. Spotlight on AOL—Common Law. AOL, LLC, mistakenly made public the personal information of 650,000 of its members. The members filed a suit, alleging violations of California law. AOL asked the court to dismiss the suit on the basis of a "forum-selection" clause in its member agreement that designates Virginia courts as the place where member disputes will be tried. Under a decision of the United States Supreme Court, a forum-selection clause is unenforceable "if enforcement would contravene a strong public policy of the forum in which suit is brought." California has declared in other cases that the AOL clause contravenes a strong public policy. If the court applies the doctrine of *stare decisis,* will it dismiss the suit? Explain. [*Doe 1 v. AOL, LLC,* 552 F.3d 1077 (9th Cir. 2009)] (See *The Common Law Tradition.*)

1–5. Sources of Law. Under a Massachusetts state statute, large wineries could sell their products through wholesalers or to consumers directly, but not both. Small wineries could use both methods. Family Winemakers of California filed a suit against the state, arguing that this restriction gave small wineries a competitive advantage in violation of the U.S. Constitution. The court agreed that the statute was in conflict with the Constitution. Which source of law takes priority, and why? [*Family Winemakers of California v. Jenkins,* 592 F.3d 1 (1st Cir. 2010)] (See *Sources of American Law.*)

1–6. Business Case Problem with Sample Answer— Law Around the World. Karen Goldberg's husband was killed in a terrorist bombing in Israel. She filed a suit in a U.S. federal court against UBS AG, a Switzerland-based global financial services company. She claimed that UBS aided her husband's killing because it provided services to the terrorists. UBS argued that the case should be transferred to another country. Like many nations, the United States has a common law system. Other nations have civil law systems. What are the key differences between these systems? [*Goldberg v. UBS AG,* 690 F.Supp.2d 92 (E.D.N.Y. 2010)] (See *Classifications of Law.*)

—**For a sample answer to Problem 1–6, go to Appendix E at the end of this text.**

1–7. Reading Citations. Assume that you want to read the court's entire opinion in the case of *People v. Tuttle,* 304 Mich.App. 72, 850 N.W.2d 484 (2014). Read the section entitled "Finding Case Law" in the appendix that follows this chapter, and then explain specifically where you would find the court's opinion. (See *Finding Case Law.*)

1–8. A Question of Ethics—*Stare Decisis.* On July 5, 1884, Dudley, Stephens, and Brooks—"all able-bodied English seamen"—and a teenage English boy were cast adrift in a lifeboat following a storm at sea. They had no water with them in the boat, and all they had for sustenance were two one-pound tins of turnips. On July 24, Dudley proposed that one of the four in the lifeboat be sacrificed to save the others. Stephens agreed with Dudley, but Brooks refused to consent—and the boy was never asked for his opinion. On July 25, Dudley killed the boy, and the three men then fed on the boy's body and blood. Four days later, the men were rescued by a passing vessel. They were taken to England and tried for the murder of the boy. If the men had not fed on the boy's body, they would probably have died of starvation within the four-day period. The boy, who was in a much weaker condition, would likely have died before the rest. [*Regina v. Dudley and Stephens,* 14 Q.B.D. (Queen's Bench Division, England) 273 (1884)] (See *The Common Law Tradition.*)

1. The basic question in this case is whether the survivors should be subject to penalties under English criminal law, given the men's unusual circumstances. You be the judge and decide the issue. Give the reasons for your decision.
2. Should judges ever have the power to look beyond the written "letter of the law" in making their decisions? Why or why not?

Appendix to Chapter 1:

Finding and Analyzing the Law

This text includes numerous references, or *citations,* to primary sources of law—federal and state statutes, the U.S. Constitution and state constitutions, regulations issued by administrative agencies, and court cases.

As mentioned in Chapter 1, a citation identifies the publication in which a legal authority—such as a statute or a court decision or other source—can be found. In this appendix, we explain how you can use citations to find primary sources of law. Note that in addition to being published in sets of books, as described next, most federal and state laws and case decisions are available online.

Finding Statutory and Administrative Law

When Congress passes laws, they are collected in a publication titled *United States Statutes at Large.* When state legislatures pass laws, they are collected in similar state publications. Most frequently, however, laws are referred to in their codified form—that is, the form in which they appear in the federal and state codes. In these codes, laws are compiled by subject.

United States Code

The *United States Code* (U.S.C.) arranges all existing federal laws of a public and permanent nature by subject. Each of the fifty subjects into which the U.S.C. arranges the laws is given a title and a title number. For example, laws relating to commerce and trade are collected in "Title 15, Commerce and Trade." Titles are subdivided by sections.

A citation to the U.S.C. includes title and section numbers. Thus, a reference to "15 U.S.C. Section 1" means that the statute can be found in Section 1 of Title 15. ("Section" may be designated by the symbol §, and "Sections" by §§.) In addition to the print publication, the federal government also provides a searchable online database of the *United States Code* at **www.gpo.gov** (click on "Libraries" and then "Core Documents of Our Democracy" to find the *United States Code*).

Commercial publications of these laws are available and are widely used. For example, Thomson Reuters publishes the *United States Code Annotated* (U.S.C.A.). The U.S.C.A. contains the complete text of laws included in the U.S.C., notes of court decisions that interpret and apply specific sections of the statutes, and the text of presidential proclamations and executive orders. The U.S.C.A. also includes research aids, such as cross-references to related statutes, historical notes, and other references. A citation to the U.S.C.A. is similar to a citation to the U.S.C.: "15 U.S.C.A. Section 1."

State Codes

State codes follow the U.S.C. pattern of arranging laws by subject. The state codes may be called codes, revisions, compilations, consolidations, general statutes, or statutes, depending on the state.

In some codes, subjects are designated by number. In others, they are designated by name. For example, "13 Pennsylvania Consolidated Statutes Section 1101" means that the statute can be found in Title 13, Section 1101, of the Pennsylvania code. "California Commercial Code Section 1101" means the statute can be found in Section 1101 under the subject heading

"Commercial Code" of the California code. Abbreviations are commonly used. For instance, "13 Pennsylvania Consolidated Statutes Section 1101" may be abbreviated "13 Pa. C.S. § 1101," and "California Commercial Code Section 1101" may be abbreviated "Cal. Com. Code § 1101."

Administrative Rules

Rules and regulations adopted by federal administrative agencies are initially published in the *Federal Register,* a daily publication of the U.S. government. Later, they are incorporated into the *Code of Federal Regulations* (C.F.R.).

Like the U.S.C., the C.F.R. is divided into fifty titles. Rules within each title are assigned section numbers. A full citation to the C.F.R. includes title and section numbers. For example, a reference to "17 C.F.R. Section 230.504" means that the rule can be found in Section 230.504 of Title 17.

Finding Case Law

Before discussing the case reporting system, we need to look briefly at the court system (which will be discussed in detail in Chapter 3). There are two types of courts in the United States: federal courts and state courts.

Both the federal and state court systems consist of several levels, or tiers, of courts. *Trial courts,* in which evidence is presented and testimony is given, are on the bottom tier (which also includes lower courts handling specialized issues). Decisions from a trial court can be appealed to a higher court, which commonly would be an intermediate *court of appeals,* or an *appellate court.* Decisions from these intermediate courts of appeals may be appealed to an even higher court, such as a state supreme court or the United States Supreme Court.

State Court Decisions

Most state trial court decisions are not published in books (except in New York and a few other states, which publish selected trial court opinions). Decisions from state trial courts are typically filed in the office of the clerk of the court, where the decisions are available for public inspection. (Increasingly, they can be found online as well.)

Written decisions of the appellate, or reviewing, courts, however, are published and distributed (in print and online). As you will note, most of the state court cases presented in this textbook are from state appellate courts. The reported appellate decisions are published in volumes called *reports* or *reporters,* which are numbered consecutively. State appellate court decisions are found in the state reporters of that particular state. Official reports are published by the state, whereas unofficial reports are published by nongovernment entities.

Regional Reporters State court opinions appear in regional units of the West's National Reporter System, published by Thomson Reuters. Most lawyers and libraries have these reporters because they publish cases more quickly and are distributed more widely than the state-published reporters. In fact, many states have eliminated their own reporters in favor of the West's National Reporter System.

The West's National Reporter System divides the states into the following geographic areas: *Atlantic* (A., A.2d, or A.3d), *North Eastern* (N.E. or N.E.2d), *North Western* (N.W. or N.W.2d), *Pacific* (P., P.2d, or P.3d), *South Eastern* (S.E. or S.E.2d), *South Western* (S.W., S.W.2d, or S.W.3d), and *Southern* (So., So.2d, or So.3d). (The *2d* and *3d* in the preceding abbreviations refer to *Second Series* and *Third Series,* respectively.) The states included in each of these regional divisions are indicated in Exhibit 1A–1 that follows, which illustrates the West's National Reporter System.

Exhibit 1A–1 West's National Reporter System—Regional/Federal

Regional Reporters	Coverage Beginning	Coverage
Atlantic Reporter (A., A.2d, or A.3d)	1885	Connecticut, Delaware, District of Columbia, Maine, Maryland, New Hampshire, New Jersey, Pennsylvania, Rhode Island, and Vermont.
North Eastern Reporter (N.E. or N.E.2d)	1885	Illinois, Indiana, Massachusetts, New York, and Ohio.
North Western Reporter (N.W. or N.W.2d)	1879	Iowa, Michigan, Minnesota, Nebraska, North Dakota, South Dakota, and Wisconsin.
Pacific Reporter (P., P.2d, or P.3d)	1883	Alaska, Arizona, California, Colorado, Hawaii, Idaho, Kansas, Montana, Nevada, New Mexico, Oklahoma, Oregon, Utah, Washington, and Wyoming.
South Eastern Reporter (S.E. or S.E.2d)	1887	Georgia, North Carolina, South Carolina, Virginia, and West Virginia.
South Western Reporter (S.W., S.W.2d, or S.W.3d)	1886	Arkansas, Kentucky, Missouri, Tennessee, and Texas.
Southern Reporter (So., So.2d, or So.3d)	1887	Alabama, Florida, Louisiana, and Mississippi.

Federal Reporters		
Federal Reporter (F., F.2d, or F.3d)	1880	U.S. Circuit Courts from 1880 to 1912; U.S. Commerce Court from 1911 to 1913; U.S. District Courts from 1880 to 1932; U.S. Court of Claims (now called U.S. Court of Federal Claims) from 1929 to 1932 and since 1960; U.S. Courts of Appeals since 1891; U.S. Court of Customs and Patent Appeals since 1929; U.S. Emergency Court of Appeals since 1943.
Federal Supplement (F.Supp. or F.Supp.2d)	1932	U.S. Court of Claims from 1932 to 1960; U.S. District Courts since 1932; U.S. Customs Court since 1956.
Federal Rules Decisions (F.R.D.)	1939	U.S. District Courts involving the Federal Rules of Civil Procedure since 1939 and Federal Rules of Criminal Procedure since 1946.
Supreme Court Reporter (S.Ct.)	1882	United States Supreme Court since the October term of 1882.
Bankruptcy Reporter (Bankr.)	1980	Bankruptcy decisions of U.S. Bankruptcy Courts, U.S. District Courts, U.S. Courts of Appeals, and the United States Supreme Court.
Military Justice Reporter (M.J.)	1978	U.S. Court of Military Appeals and Courts of Military Review for the Army, Navy, Air Force, and Coast Guard.

NATIONAL REPORTER SYSTEM MAP

- Pacific
- North Western
- South Western
- North Eastern
- Atlantic
- South Eastern
- Southern

Case Citations   After appellate decisions have been published, they are normally referred to (cited) by the name of the case; the volume, name, and page number of the state's official reporter (if different from the National Reporter System); the volume, name, and page number of the West's National Reporter; and the volume, name, and page number of any other selected reporter. (Citing a reporter by volume number, name, and page number, in that order, is common to all citations. The year that the decision was issued is often included at the end in parentheses.) When more than one reporter is cited for the same case, each reference is called a *parallel citation*.

Note that some states have adopted a "public domain citation system" that uses a somewhat different format for the citation. For example, in Ohio, a Ohio court decision might be designated "2014-Ohio-1838," meaning that the case was decided in the year 2014 by an Ohio state court and was the 1838th decision issued by that court during that year. Parallel citations to the *Ohio Appellate Reporter* and the *North Eastern Reporter* are still included after the public domain citation.

Consider the following case citation: *Wells Fargo Bank, N.A. v. Strong,* 149 Conn.App. 384, 89 A.3d. 392 (2014). We see that the opinion in this case can be found in Volume 149 of the official *Connecticut Appellate Court Reports,* on page 384. The parallel citation is to Volume 89 of the *Atlantic Reporter, Third Series,* page 392.

When we present opinions in this text (starting in Chapter 2), in addition to the reporter, we give the name of the court hearing the case and the year of the court's decision. Sample citations to state court decisions are explained in Exhibit 1A–2 that follows.

Federal Court Decisions

Federal district (trial) court decisions are published unofficially in the *Federal Supplement* (F. Supp. or F.Supp.2d), and opinions from the circuit courts of appeals (federal reviewing courts) are reported unofficially in the *Federal Reporter* (F., F.2d, or F.3d). Cases concerning federal bankruptcy law are published unofficially in West's *Bankruptcy Reporter* (Bankr. or B.R.).

The official edition of United States Supreme Court decisions is the *United States Reports* (U.S.), which is published by the federal government. Unofficial editions of Supreme Court cases include West's *Supreme Court Reporter* (S.Ct.) and the *Lawyers' Edition of the Supreme Court Reports* (L.Ed. or L.Ed.2d). Sample citations for federal court decisions are also listed and explained in Exhibit 1A–2.

Unpublished Opinions

Many court opinions that are not yet published or that are not intended for publication can be accessed through Westlaw® (abbreviated in citations as "WL"), an online legal database. When no citation to a published reporter is available for cases cited in this text, we give the WL citation (such as 2014 WL 238128, which means it was case number 238128 decided in the year 2014). Sometimes, both in this text and in other legal sources, you will see blanks left in a citation. This occurs when the decision will be published, but the particular volume number or page number is not yet available.

Old Case Law

On a few occasions, this text cites opinions from old, classic cases dating to the nineteenth century or earlier. Some of these cases are from the English courts. The citations to these cases may not conform to the descriptions given above because they were published in reporters that are no longer used today.

Exhibit 1A–2 How to Read Citations

STATE COURTS

287 Neb. 261, N.W.2d (2014)[a]

> *N.W.* is the abbreviation for the publication of state court decisions rendered in the *North Western Reporter* of West's National Reporter System. *2d* indicates that this case was included in the *Second Series* of that reporter. The number 825 refers to the volume number of the reporter; the number 429 refers to the page in that volume on which this case begins.

> *Neb.* is an abbreviation for *Nebraska Reports,* Nebraska's official reports of the decisions of its highest court, the Nebraska Supreme Court.

58 Cal.App.4th 500, 167 Cal.Rptr.3d 87 (2014)

> *Cal.Rptr.* is the abbreviation for the unofficial reports—titled *California Reporter*—of the decisions of California courts.

115 A.D.3d 177, 981 N.Y.S.2d 5 (2014)

> *N.Y.S.* is the abbreviation for the unofficial reports—titled *New York Supplement*—of the decisions of New York courts.

> *A.D.* is the abbreviation for *Appellate Division*, which hears appeals from the New York Supreme Court—the state's general trial court. The New York Court of Appeals is the state's highest court, analogous to other states' supreme courts.

325 Ga.App. 579, 754 S.E.2d 157 (2014)

> *Ga.App.* is the abbreviation for *Georgia Appeals Reports,* Georgia's official reports of the decisions of its court of appeals.

FEDERAL COURTS

___ U.S. ___, 134 S.Ct. 870, 187 L.Ed.2d 729 (2014)

> *L.Ed.* is an abbreviation for *Lawyers' Edition of the Supreme Court Reports*, an unofficial edition of decisions of the United States Supreme Court.

> *S.Ct.* is the abbreviation for West's unofficial reports—titled *Supreme Court Reporter*—of decisions of the United States Supreme Court.

> *U.S.* is the abbreviation for *United States Reports*, the official edition of the decisions of the United States Supreme Court. The blank lines in this citation (or any other citation) indicate that the appropriate volume of the case reporter has not yet been published and no page number is available.

a. The case names have been deleted from these citations to emphasize the publications. It should be kept in mind, however, that the name of a case is as important as the specific page numbers in the volumes in which it is found. If a citation is incorrect, the correct citation may be found in a publication's index of case names. In addition to providing a check on errors in citations, the date of a case is important because the value of a recent case as an authority is likely to be greater than that of older cases from the same court.

Exhibit 1A–2 How to Read Citations, Continued

FEDERAL COURTS (Continued)

742 F.3d 330 (8th Cir. 2014)

> *8th Cir.* is an abbreviation denoting that this case was decided in the U.S. Court of Appeals for the Eighth Circuit.

994 F.Supp.2d 558 (D.D.C. 2014)

> *D.D.C.* is an abbreviation indicating that the U.S. District Court for the Southern District of Florida decided this case.

ENGLISH COURTS

9 Exch. 341, 156 Eng.Rep. 145 (1854)

> *Eng.Rep.* is an abbreviation for *English Reports, Full Reprint,* a series of reports containing selected decisions made in English courts between 1378 and 1865.

> *Exch.* is an abbreviation for *English Exchequer Reports,* which includes the original reports of cases decided in England's Court of Exchequer.

STATUTORY AND OTHER CITATIONS

18 U.S.C. Section 1961(1)(A)

> *U.S.C.* denotes *United States Code,* the codification of *United States Statutes at Large.* The number 18 refers to the statute's U.S.C. title number and 1961 to its section number within that title. The number 1 in parentheses refers to a subsection within the section, and the letter A in parentheses to a subsection within the subsection.

UCC 2–206(1)(b)

> *UCC* is an abbreviation for *Uniform Commercial Code.* The first number 2 is a reference to an article of the UCC, and 206 to a section within that article. The number 1 in parentheses refers to a subsection within the section, and the letter b in parentheses to a subsection within the subsection.

Restatement (Third) of Torts, **Section 6**

> *Restatement (Third) of Torts* refers to the third edition of the American Law Institute's *Restatement of the Law of Torts.* The number 6 refers to a specific section.

17 C.F.R. Section 230.505

> *C.F.R.* is an abbreviation for *Code of Federal Regulations,* a compilation of federal administrative regulations. The number 17 designates the regulation's title number, and 230.505 designates a specific section within that title.

Continued

Exhibit 1A–2 How to Read Citations, Continued

WESTLAW® CITATIONS[b]

2014 WL 340977

WL is an abbreviation for Westlaw. The number 2014 is the year of the document that can be found with this citation in the Westlaw database. The number 340977 is a number assigned to a specific document. A higher number indicates that a document was added to the Westlaw database later in the year.

UNIFORM RESOURCE LOCATORS (URLs)

http://www.westlaw.com[c]

The suffix *com* is the top level domain (TLD) for this Web site. The TLD *com* is an abbreviation for "commercial," which usually means that a for-profit entity hosts (maintains or supports) this Web site.

westlaw is the host name—the part of the domain name selected by the organization that registered the name. In this case, West registered the name. This Internet site is the Westlaw database on the Web.

www is an abbreviation for "World Wide Web." The Web is a system of Internet servers that support documents formatted in *HTML* (hypertext markup language) and other formats as well.

http://www.uscourts.gov

This is "The Federal Judiciary Home Page." The host is the Administrative Office of the U.S. Courts. The TLD *gov* is an abbreviation for "government." This Web site includes information and links from, and about, the federal courts.

http://www.law.cornell.edu/index.html

This part of a URL points to a Web page or file at a specific location within the host's domain. This page is a menu with links to documents within the domain and to other Internet resources.

This is the host name for a Web site that contains the Internet publications of the Legal Information Institute (LII), which is a part of Cornell Law School. The LII site includes a variety of legal materials and links to other legal resources on the Internet. The TLD *edu* is an abbreviation for "educational institution" (a school or a university).

http://www.ipl2.org/div/news

This part of the URL points to a static *news* page at this Web site, which provides links to online newspapers from around the world.

div is an abbreviation for "division," which is the way that ipl2 tags the content on its Web site as relating to a specific topic.

The site *ipl2* was formed from the merger of the Internet Public Library and the Librarians' Internet Index. It is an online service that provides reference resources and links to other information services on the Web. The site is supported chiefly by the *iSchool* at Drexel College of Information Science and Technology. The TLD *org* is an abbreviation for "organization" (normally nonprofit).

b. Many court decisions that are not yet published or that are not intended for publication can be accessed through Westlaw, an online legal database.

c. The basic form for a URL is "service://hostname/path." The Internet service for all of the URLs in this text is *http* (hypertext transfer protocol). Because most Web browsers add this prefix automatically when a user enters a host name or a hostname/path, we have generally omitted the *http://* from the URLs listed in this text.

Reading and Understanding Case Law

The cases in this text have been condensed from the full text of the courts' opinions and paraphrased by the authors. For those wishing to review court cases for future research projects or to gain additional legal information, the following sections will provide useful insights into how to read and understand case law.

Case Titles and Terminology

The title of a case, such as *Adams v. Jones,* indicates the names of the parties to the lawsuit. The *v.* in the case title stands for *versus,* which means "against." In the trial court, Adams was the plaintiff—the person who filed the suit. Jones was the defendant. If the case is appealed, however, the appellate court will sometimes place the name of the party appealing the decision first, so the case may be called *Jones v. Adams.* Because some reviewing courts retain the trial court order of names, it is often impossible to distinguish the plaintiff from the defendant in the title of a reported appellate court decision. You must carefully read the facts of each case to identify the parties.

The following terms and phrases are frequently encountered in court opinions and legal publications. Because it is important to understand what these terms and phrases mean, we define and discuss them here.

Parties to Lawsuits   As mentioned in Chapter 1, the party initiating a lawsuit is referred to as the *plaintiff* or *petitioner,* depending on the nature of the action, and the party against whom a lawsuit is brought is the *defendant* or *respondent.* Lawsuits frequently involve more than one plaintiff and/or defendant. When a case is appealed from the original court or jurisdiction to another court or jurisdiction, the party appealing the case is called the *appellant.* The *appellee* is the party against whom the appeal is taken. (In some appellate courts, the party appealing a case is referred to as the *petitioner,* and the party against whom the suit is brought or appealed is called the *respondent.*)

Judges and Justices   The terms *judge* and *justice* are usually synonymous and are used to refer to the judges in various courts. All members of the United States Supreme Court, for example, are referred to as justices. And justice is the formal title usually given to judges of appellate courts, although this is not always the case. In New York, a justice is a judge of the trial court (which is called the Supreme Court), and a member of the Court of Appeals (the state's highest court) is called a judge. The term *justice* is commonly abbreviated to J., and *justices* to JJ. A Supreme Court case might refer to Justice Sotomayor as Sotomayor, J., or to Chief Justice Roberts as Roberts, C.J.

Decisions and Opinions   Most decisions reached by reviewing, or appellate, courts are explained in written *opinions.* The opinion contains the court's reasons for its decision, the rules of law that apply, and the judgment. You may encounter several types of opinions as you read appellate cases, including the following:

- When all the judges (or justices) agree, a *unanimous opinion* is written for the entire court.
- When there is not unanimous agreement, a **majority opinion** is generally written. It outlines the views of the majority of the judges deciding the case.
- A judge who agrees (concurs) with the majority opinion as to the result but not as to the legal reasoning often writes a **concurring opinion.** In it, the judge sets out the reasoning that he or she considers correct.
- A **dissenting opinion** presents the views of one or more judges who disagree with the majority view.

Majority Opinion A court opinion that represents the views of the majority (more than half) of the judges or justices deciding the case.

Concurring Opinion A court opinion by one or more judges or justices who agree with the majority but want to make or emphasize a point that was not made or emphasized in the majority's opinion.

Dissenting Opinion A court opinion that presents the views of one or more judges or justices who disagree with the majority's decision.

Plurality Opinion A court opinion that is joined by the largest number of the judges or justices hearing the case, but less than half of the total number.

Per Curiam Opinion A court opinion that does not indicate which judge or justice authored the opinion.

- Sometimes, no single position is fully supported by a majority of the judges deciding a case. In this situation, we may have a **plurality opinion.** This is the opinion that has the support of the largest number of judges, but the group in agreement is less than a majority.
- Finally, a court occasionally issues a ***per curiam* opinion** (*per curiam* is Latin for "of the court"), which does not indicate which judge wrote the opinion.

A Sample Court Case

Knowing how to read and analyze a court opinion is an essential step in undertaking accurate legal research. A further step involves "briefing" the case. Legal researchers routinely brief cases by summarizing and reducing the texts of the opinions to their essential elements. Briefing cases facilitates the development of critical thinking skills that are crucial for businesspersons when evaluating relevant business law. (For instructions on how to brief a case, go to Appendix A at the end of this text.)

The cases contained within the chapters of this text have already been analyzed and partially briefed by the authors, and the essential aspects of each case are presented in a convenient format consisting of three basic sections: *Background and Facts, In the Words of the Court* (excerpts from the court's opinion), and *Decision and Remedy,* as shown in Exhibit 1A–3 on the pages that follow, which has also been annotated to illustrate the kind of information that is contained in each section.

Throughout this text, in addition to this basic format, we sometimes include a *Company Profile* to provide background on one of the parties to the lawsuit. Each case is followed by two critical-thinking questions regarding some issue raised by the case. A section entitled *Impact of This Case on Today's Law* concludes the *Classic Cases* that appear throughout the text to indicate the significance of the case for today's legal landscape.

To illustrate the elements in a court opinion, we present an annotated opinion in Exhibit 1A–3. The opinion is from an actual case that the United States Court of Appeals for the Ninth Circuit, decided in 2014. You will note that triple asterisks (* * *) and quadruple asterisks (* * * *) frequently appear in the opinion. The triple asterisks indicate that we have deleted a few words or sentences from the opinion for the sake of readability or brevity. Quadruple asterisks mean that an entire paragraph (or more) has been omitted.

Additionally, when the opinion cites another case or legal source, the citation to the case or other source has been omitted to save space and to improve the flow of the text. These editorial practices are continued in the other court opinions presented in this book. In addition, whenever we present a court opinion that includes a term or phrase that may not be readily understandable, a bracketed definition or paraphrase has been added.

THE SAMPLE COURT CASE FOLLOWS.

Exhibit 1A–3   A Sample Court Case

This section contains the citation—the name of the case, the name of the court that heard the case, the year of the decision, and reporter in which the court's opinion can be found.

This line provides the name of the judge (or justice) who authored the court's opinion.

L.L.C. is an abbreviation for limited liability company, a hybrid form of business enterprise that offers the limited liability of the corporation and the tax advantages of a partnership.

The court divides the opinion into three sections, each headed by an explanatory heading. The first section summarizes the factual background of the case.

In the context of this case, a *license* is an agreement permitting the license holder to use a trademark for certain limited purposes

A *domain name* is the last part of an Internet address (such as hendrixlicensing.com).

EXPERIENCE HENDRIX L.L.C. v. HENDRIXLICENSING.COM LTD.

United States Court of Appeals, Ninth Circuit,

742 F.3d 377 (2014).

DAVID M. EBEL, Circuit Judge.

The sole heir of deceased rock legend Jimi Hendrix formed two companies, * * * Experience Hendrix, **L.L.C.**, and its wholly owned subsidiary, Authentic Hendrix, L.L.C. (collectively "Experience Hendrix").

* * * *

BACKGROUND

Experience Hendrix holds a number of trademarks associated with Jimi Hendrix, including the names "Hendrix" and "Jimi Hendrix" and Jimi Hendrix's signature, as well as logos incorporating a "headshot" of Hendrix. Experience Hendrix uses these trademarks to market, sell and **license** Hendrix-related merchandise, including apparel, posters, and artwork sold to the public through Internet websites and brick-and-mortar retail stores throughout the United States.

[Andrew Pitsicalis and his company, Hendrixlicensing.com, L.L.C. (collectively "Pitsicalis")] has also used Jimi Hendrix's celebrity status commercially. Pitsicalis owns, or has licenses to use, photographs and original pieces of art depicting Hendrix, as well as visual artwork created by Hendrix himself. In 2008, Pitsicalis began licensing the right to use these images to produce and sell Hendrix-related merchandise, including apparel, posters and household items. Like Experience Hendrix, Pitsicalis's licensees sold this merchandise over the Internet and in brick-and-mortar stores. Pitsicalis placed marks on his licensed products that used the names "Hendrix" and "Jimi Hendrix," as well as Jimi Hendrix's signature and a logo of Hendrix's headshot with a guitar. In conducting his business, Pitsicalis also used two websites with the **domain names** hendrixlicensing.com and hendrixartwork.com.

Continued

Exhibit 1A–3 A Sample Court Case, Continued

To *allege* is to assert to be true as described.	In March 2009, Experience Hendrix sued Pitsicalis [in a federal district court]. * * * Experience Hendrix **alleged** that Pitsicalis was infringing Experience Hendrix's trademarks in violation of the federal **Lanham Act.** * * * The district court granted Experience Hendrix
The *Lanham Act* is a federal statute enacted in 1946 that protects the owner of a trademark against the use of a similar mark if any consumer confusion might result.	* * * **summary judgment** on the federal Lanham Act claim, concluding that Pitsicalis had infringed Experience Hendrix's trademarks. The court permanently **enjoined** Pitsicalis's infringing activity. * * * Although the jury awarded Experience Hendrix **damages** * * *
A *summary judgment* is a judgment that a court enters without beginning or continuing a trial. This judgment can be entered only if no facts are in dispute and the only question is how the law applies to the facts.	totaling [$366,650], the district court reduced the jury's award to $60,000. These cross-appeals followed.
To *enjoin* is to issue an injunction—a court decree ordering a person to do or refrain from doing a certain activity.	**DISCUSSION**

* * * *

On appeal, Pitsicalis challenges * * * the district court's conclusion that he is liable for infringing Experience Hendrix's trademarks: Pitsicalis argues that his domain names hendrixlicensing.com and hendrixartwork.com did not violate the federal Lanham Act by infringing Experience Hendrix's trademark "Hendrix."

Damages is money sought as a remedy for a wrongful act.

The second major section of the opinion responds to the parties' appeals.

* * * On appeal. Experience Hendrix seeks reinstatement of the jury's entire damages award.

* * * *

Nominative fair use refers to the reasonable and limited use of a name without the owner's permission. Fair use is a defense to an infringement claim, depending on such factors as, in this case, the purpose and character of the use.

Pitsicalis defended his use of the trademark "Hendrix" in his domain names only as **nominative fair use.** Nominative fair use applies where a defendant has used the plaintiff's mark to describe the plaintiff's product. The district court rejected Pitsicalis's nominative fair use defense, concluding that Pitsicalis used "Hendrix" in his domain names to refer, not to Experience Hendrix's products (as is required for a nominative fair use defense), but only to Pitsicalis's own product or service, licensing and marketing Hendrix-related goods (which is not protected under the nominative fair use defense). On appeal, Pitsicalis does not argue that his domain names refer to Experience Hendrix's products. Nor does he contend

Exhibit 1A–3 A Sample Court Case, Continued

To *affirm* is to validate or give legal force to.	that Jimi Hendrix is Experience Hendrix's product. We, therefore, **affirm** the district court's decision to enter * * * summary judgment for Experience Hendrix.

* * * *

Based on Pitsicalis's infringing Experience Hendrix's trademarks in violation of the Lanham Act, the jury awarded Experience Hendrix 1) $60,000, representing the profits Pitsicalis made from licensing his infringing goods; and 2) $306,650 to compensate Experience Hendrix for the profits Experience Hendrix lost because of Pitsicalis's infringing conduct.

* * * * |

In this context, to *strike* is to remove or expunge.

* * * After the jury's verdict, the district court * * * **struck,** as unsupported by the evidence, all of the damages awarded except the $60,000 award.

* * * *

* * * In striking the jury's award for Experience Hendrix's lost profits, the district court held that, while Experience Hendrix had presented evidence of its lost revenue, it had failed to offer any evidence as to its expenses, which the jury was required to deduct from the lost revenue in order to calculate Experience Hendrix's lost profits.

Sufficient evidence is evidence that is sufficient to satisfy an unprejudiced mind seeking the truth.

[But] there was **sufficient evidence** before the jurors from which they could calculate the profits Experience Hendrix lost due to Pitsicalis's infringing conduct. That evidence included the following: There was undisputed evidence that, at the same time that Pitsicalis was licensing his infringing goods, Experience Hendrix suffered a significant decline in its own licensing revenue earned from products similar to Pitsicalis's infringing merchandise.

A *licensee* is one who receives a license to use another's property.

There was also testimony describing the nature of licensing revenue generally as a **licensee's** payment to the **licensor** of a percentage of the licensee's revenue in return for the use of

A *licensor* is one who grants the right to use his or her property to another.

the licensor's **intellectual property.** In addition, the jury had before it financial documents

Intellectual property is property resulting from intellectual, creative processes, such as a trademark.

* * * which summarized and compared Experience Hendrix's licensing revenue from 2006 through 2009. * * * So we conclude that the district court erred in * * * **vacating** the

To *vacate* is to cancel, invalidate, or void.

damages of $306,650 in Experience Hendrix's lost profits.

Continued

Exhibit 1A–3 A Sample Court Case, Continued

* * * *

In the third major section of the opinion, the court states its decision.

CONCLUSION

For the foregoing reasons, we * * * AFFIRM the district court's decision granting Experience Hendrix * * * summary judgment on its claim that Pitsicalis's use of "Hendrix" in its domain names infringed Experience Hendrix's mark "Hendrix." * * * We **REVERSE**

Here, to *reverse* is to reject or overrule the court's judgment.

* * * the district court's * * * decision to strike most of the jury's award of damages. * * *

In this context, to *remand* is to send back to the lower court.

We * * * **REMAND** for a new trial on such damages.

AFFIRMED IN PART, REVERSED IN PART, * * * AND REMANDED.

CHAPTER 2

Business Ethics

(pixeldeluxe/iStockphoto.com)

CONTENTS

- Business Ethics
- Business Ethics and Social Media
- Approaches to Ethical Reasoning
- Making Ethical Business Decisions
- Global Business Ethics

LEARNING OBJECTIVES

The five learning objectives below are designed to help improve your understanding of the chapter. After reading this chapter, you should be able to answer the following questions:

1. What is business ethics, and why is it important?
2. How do duty-based ethical standards differ from outcome-based ethical standards?
3. What are five steps that a businessperson can take to evaluate whether his or her actions are ethical?
4. How can business leaders encourage their employees to act ethically?
5. What types of ethical issues might arise in the context of international business transactions?

"New occasions teach new duties."
—James Russell Lowell, 1819–1891 (American editor, poet, and diplomat)

One of the most complex issues businesspersons and corporations face is ethics. As noted in the chapter-opening quotation, "New occasions teach new duties." Ethics is not as well defined as the law, and yet it can have tremendous impacts on a firm's finances and reputation. Consider, for instance, the experience of the Chick-fil-A restaurant chain in 2012 when its chief operating officer made several statements about the company's commitment to supporting traditional marriage.

After those comments were made, it became public knowledge that Chick-fil-A had made donations to Christian organizations perceived to be opposed to same-sex marriage. Opponents of same-sex marriage held support rallies and Chick-fil-A appreciation days. Supporters of same-sex marriage held "kiss-ins" at local Chick-fil-A restaurants. Some politicians denounced Chick-fil-A's position and said that they would block expansion of the company in their cities. Eventually, Chick-fil-A issued a statement saying that it had ceased donations to any organization that promotes discrimination in any way. Chick-fil-A no longer sponsors charities that discriminate against same-sex couples or those who identify themselves as gay, lesbian, bisexual, or transgendered.

(Lucas JACKSON/Reuters /Landov)

Bernard Madoff (right) perpetuated the largest fraudulent investment scheme in modern history.

Ethics Moral principles and values applied to social behavior.

Business Ethics What constitutes right or wrong behavior and the application of moral principles in a business context.

Learning Objective 1
What is business ethics, and why is it important?

Triple Bottom Line Focuses on a corporation's profits, its impact on people, and its impact on the planet.

Chick-fil-A was not accused of violating any laws, but its actions raised questions about the role of corporations and the effect of corporate ethics on profit. This chapter addresses some of those same questions. First, we look at business ethics—its definitions, its importance, and its relationship to the law. Next, we examine the philosophical bases for making ethical decisions. Finally, we discuss the application of business ethics to global situations.

Business Ethics

As you might imagine, business ethics is derived from the concept of ethics. **Ethics** can be defined as the study of what constitutes right or wrong behavior. It is the branch of philosophy that focuses on morality and the way in which moral principles are derived and applied to one's conduct in daily life. Ethics has to do with questions relating to the fairness, justness, rightness, or wrongness of an action.

Business ethics focuses on what constitutes right or wrong behavior in the business world and on how businesspersons apply moral and ethical principles to situations that arise in the workplace. Because business decision makers often address more complex ethical dilemmas than they face in their personal lives, business ethics is more complicated than personal ethics.

Why Is Studying Business Ethics Important?

Over the last two hundred years, the public perception of the corporation has changed from an entity that primarily generates revenues for its owners to an entity that participates in society as a corporate citizen. Originally, the only goal or duty of a corporation was to maximize profits. Although many people today may view this idea as greedy or inhumane, the rationale for the profit-maximization theory is still valid.

Profit Maximization   In theory, if all firms strictly adhere to the goal of profit maximization, resources flow to where they are most highly valued by society. Corporations can focus on their strengths, and other entities that are better suited to deal with social problems and perform charitable acts can specialize in those activities. The government, through taxes and other financial allocations, can shift resources to those other entities to perform public services. Thus, in an ideal world, profit maximization leads to the most efficient allocation of scarce resources.

The Rise of Corporate Citizenship   Over the years, as resources were not sufficiently reallocated to cover the costs of social needs, many people became dissatisfied with the profit-maximization theory. Investors and others began to look beyond profits and dividends and to consider the **triple bottom line**—a corporation's profits, its impact on people, and its impact on the planet. Magazines and Web sites began to rank companies based on their environmental impacts and their ethical decisions. The corporation came to be viewed as a "citizen" that was expected to participate in bettering communities and society.

Even so, many still believe that corporations are fundamentally profit-making entities that should have no responsibility other than profit maximization.

The Importance of Ethics in Making Business Decisions

Whether one believes in the profit-maximization theory or corporate citizenship, ethics is important in making business decisions. Corporations should strive to be "good citizens." When making decisions, a business should evaluate:

1. The legal implications of each decision.
2. The public relations impact.
3. The safety risks for consumers and employees.
4. The financial implications.

This analysis will assist the firm in making decisions that not only maximize profits but also reflect good corporate citizenship.

Long-Run Profit Maximization   In attempting to maximize profits, however, corporate executives and employees have to distinguish between *short-run* and *long-run* profit maximization. In the short run, a company may increase its profits by continuing to sell a product, even though it knows that the product is defective. In the long run, though, because of lawsuits, large settlements, and bad publicity, such unethical conduct will cause profits to suffer. Thus, business ethics is consistent only with long-run profit maximization. An overemphasis on short-term profit maximization is the most common reason that ethical problems occur in business.

CASE EXAMPLE 2.1   When the powerful narcotic painkiller OxyContin was first marketed, its manufacturer, Purdue Pharma, claimed that it was unlikely to lead to drug addiction or abuse. Internal company documents later showed that the company's executives knew that OxyContin could be addictive, but kept this risk a secret to boost sales and maximize short-term profits.

Subsequently, Purdue Pharma and three former executives pleaded guilty to criminal charges that they misled regulators, patients, and physicians about OxyContin's risks of addiction. Purdue Pharma agreed to pay $600 million in fines and other payments. The three former executives agreed to pay $34.5 million in fines and were barred from federal health programs for a period of fifteen years. Thus, the company's focus on maximizing profits in the short run led to unethical conduct that hurt profits in the long run.[1] •

The Internet Can Ruin Reputations   In the past, negative information or opinions about a company might remain hidden. Now, however, cyberspace provides a forum where disgruntled employees, unhappy consumers, or special interest groups can post derogatory remarks. Thus, the Internet has increased the potential for a major corporation (or other business) to suffer damage to its reputation or loss of profits through negative publicity.

Wal-Mart and Nike in particular have been frequent targets for advocacy groups that believe that those corporations exploit their workers. Although some of these assertions may be unfounded or exaggerated, the courts generally have refused to consider them *defamatory* (the tort of defamation will be discussed in Chapter 5). Most courts regard online attacks as simply the expression of opinion and therefore a form of speech protected by the First Amendment. Even so, corporations often incur considerable expense in running marketing campaigns to thwart bad publicity and may even face legal costs (if the complaint leads to litigation).

Image Is Everything   The study of business ethics is concerned with the purposes of a business and how that business achieves those purposes. Thus, business ethics is concerned with the image of the business and the impacts that the business has on the environment, customers, suppliers, employees, and the global economy.

Unethical corporate decision making can negatively affect suppliers, consumers, the community, and society as a whole. It can also have a negative impact on the reputation of the company and the individuals who run that company. Hence, an in-depth understanding of business ethics is important to the long-run viability of any corporation today.

1. *United States v. Purdue Frederick Co.*, 495 F.Supp.2d 569 (W.D.Va. 2007).

"It's easy to make a buck. It's a lot tougher to make a difference."

Tom Brokaw, 1940–present
(American television journalist)

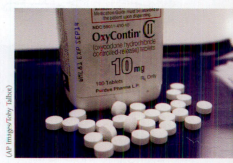

(AP Images/Toby Talbot)

What were the long-run consequences of aggressively marketing OxyContin?

"Have you noticed ethics creeping into some of these deals lately?"

Moral Minimum The minimum degree of ethical behavior expected of a business firm, which is usually defined as compliance with the law.

The Relationship of Law and Ethics

Because the law does not codify all ethical requirements of all persons, compliance with the law is not always sufficient to determine "right" behavior. Laws have to be general enough to apply in a variety of circumstances. Laws are broad in their purpose and their scope. They prohibit or require certain actions to avoid significant harm to society.

When two competing companies secretly agree to set prices on products, for instance, society suffers harm—typically, the companies will charge higher prices than they could if they continued to compete. This harm inflicted on consumers has negative consequences for the economy, and so colluding to set prices is an illegal activity. Similarly, when a company is preparing to issue stock, the law requires certain disclosures to potential investors. This requirement is meant to avoid harms that come with uninformed investing, such as occurred in the 1920s and contributed to the stock market crash and the Great Depression.

Moral Minimum   Compliance with the law is sometimes called the **moral minimum.** If people and entities merely comply with the law, they are acting at the lowest ethical level society will tolerate. The study of ethics goes beyond those legal requirements to evaluate what is right for society.

Businesspersons must remember that just because an action is legal does not mean it is ethical. For instance, no law specifies the salaries that publicly held corporations (companies that sell their shares to the public) can pay their officers (executive employees). Nevertheless, if a corporation pays its officers an excessive amount relative to other employees, or relative to what officers at other corporations are paid, the executives' compensation might be viewed as unethical.

The following case illustrates some consequences of failure to meet the minimum acceptable standard for behavior—the moral minimum.

Case 2.1

Scott v. Carpanzano
United States Court of Appeals, Fifth Circuit, 2014 WL 274493 (2014).

BACKGROUND AND FACTS Rick Scott deposited $2 million into an escrow account maintained by a company owned by Salvatore Carpanzano. Immediately after the deposit was made, in violation of the escrow agreement, the funds were withdrawn. When Scott was unable to recover his money, he filed a suit against Salvatore Carpanzano and others, including Salvatore's daughter Carmela Carpanzano. In the complaint, Scott made no allegations of acts or knowledge on Carmela's part. Salvatore failed to cooperate with discovery and did not respond to attempts to contact him by certified mail, regular mail, or e-mail. Salvatore also refused to make an appearance in the court, and did not finalize a settlement negotiated between the parties' attorneys. Carmela denied that she was involved in her father's business or the Scott transaction. The court found that the defendants had intentionally failed to respond to the litigation and issued a judgment for more than $6 million in Scott's favor. The defendants appealed to the U.S. Court of Appeals for the Fifth Circuit.

When is certified mail used?

IN THE WORDS OF THE COURT . . .
PER CURIAM.
    * * * *

A willful default is an *intentional failure to respond to litigation.* The district court found that [the] Defendants willfully defaulted based on evidence that the Defendants were aware of the proceedings against them and that [their] attorneys were specifically instructed not to enter an appearance [participate] in this case. [Emphasis added.]

Case 2.1—Continued

The evidence substantially supports the district court's finding as to Mr. Carpanzano. First, Mr. Carpanzano's first attorney withdrew [from the case] because Mr. Carpanzano failed to cooperate with the discovery process and refused to appear as requested and ordered. Second, * * * Mr. Carpanzano instructed his second set of attorneys to negotiate settlement of this matter but not to enter an appearance in the district court. Significantly, Mr. Carpanzano never denies this allegation. Third, * * * Mr. Carpanzano and his attorneys were well aware that the case was proceeding toward default and that they were in communication with each other during this time. Fourth, * * * once final execution of settlement papers was at hand, Mr. Carpanzano also ceased communication with his second set of attorneys and did not finalize the settlement. Finally, other than ambiguously suggesting that a health condition (unsupported by any evidence of what the condition was) and absence from the country (unsupported by any evidence that electronic communication was not possible from that country) prevented him from defending this action, Mr. Carpanzano offers no real reason why he did not answer the * * * complaint.

* * * *

By contrast, the record does not support the district court's finding that * * * Ms. Carpanzano also willfully defaulted.

* * * Ms. Carpanzano repeatedly indicated that [she was] relying on Mr. Carpanzano * * * to make sure [her] interests were protected. Nothing in the record contradicts this assertion. While [her] reliance on Mr. Carpanzano acting with the attorneys he retained may have been negligent, it does not amount to an intentional failure to respond to litigation.

* * * *

* * * [Furthermore] the * * * complaint * * * contains no factual allegations of acts or omissions on the part of Ms. Carpanzano. It does not allege that she ever was in contact with Scott, that she was in control of the * * * escrow account, or that she wrongfully transferred any funds out of the account. Nor does it allege any intent or knowledge on the part of Ms. Carpanzano * * *. Indeed, an examination of the complaint reveals that there is not a sufficient basis in the pleadings for the judgment * * * entered against Ms. Carpanzano.

The defenses presented by Ms. Carpanzano to the district court assert that she had no knowledge of the details of her father's business transactions, she did not personally enter into any contracts with Scott or seek to defraud him, and * * * she had limited involvement in the facts of this case.

* * * *

* * * Even if Scott were able to prove the entirety of the * * * complaint, we fail to see how it would justify a judgment * * * against Ms. Carpanzano.

DECISION AND REMEDY The U.S. Court of Appeals for the Fifth Circuit affirmed the judgment against Salvatore, but reversed the decision against Carmela. Scott had made no allegations of acts on Carmela's part.

THE LEGAL ENVIRONMENT DIMENSION *Did Carmela Carpanzano meet the minimum acceptable standard for ethical business behavior? Explain.*

THE ETHICAL DIMENSION *Are the defendants' actions likely to affect their ability to profit from their business in the long run? Discuss.*

Ethics and Company Codes of Ethics

Most companies attempt to link ethics and law through the creation of internal codes of ethics. (We present the code of ethics of Costco Wholesale Corporation as an example in the appendix following this chapter.) Company codes are not law. Instead, they are rules that the company sets forth that it can also enforce (by terminating an employee who does not follow them, for instance). Codes of conduct typically outline the company's policies on particular issues and indicate how employees are expected to act.

EXAMPLE 2.2 Google's code of conduct starts with the motto "Don't be evil." The code then makes general statements about how Google promotes integrity, mutual respect, and the highest standard of ethical business conduct. Google's code also provides specific rules on a number of issues, such as privacy, drugs and alcohol, conflicts of interest, co-worker relationships, and confidentiality—it even has a dog policy. The company takes a stand against employment discrimination that goes further than the law requires. It prohibits discrimination based on sexual orientation, gender identity or expression, and veteran status. ●

Numerous industries have also developed their own codes of ethics. The American Institute of Certified Public Accountants (AICPA) has a comprehensive Code of Professional Conduct for the ethical practicing of accounting. The American Bar Association has model rules of professional conduct for attorneys, and the American Nurses Association has a code of ethics that applies to nurses. These codes can give guidance to decision makers facing ethical questions. Violation of a code may result in discipline of an employee or sanctions against a company from the industry organization. Remember, though, that these internal codes are not laws, so their effectiveness is determined by the commitment of the industry or company leadership to enforcing the codes.

"Never let your sense of morals prevent you from doing what is right."

Isaac Asimov, 1920–1992
(Russian-born writer and scientist)

Ethical Uncertainty and "Gray Areas"   Ethics can be a difficult subject for corporate officers to fully understand. Because it is often highly subjective and subject to change over time without any sort of formal process, ethics is less certain than law.

The law can also be uncertain, however, and contains numerous "gray areas" that make it difficult to predict with certainty how a court will apply a given law to a particular action. Uncertainty can make decision making difficult, especially when a law requires a court to determine what is "foreseeable" or "reasonable" in a particular situation. Because a business has no way of predicting how a specific court will decide these issues, decision makers need to proceed with caution and evaluate an action and its consequences from an ethical perspective.

Ethics is based more on judgment than research. A company that can show it acted ethically, responsibly, and in good faith (honestly) has a better chance of succeeding in a dispute than one that cannot make such a showing.

In the following case, the court considered whether an employer's response to complaints about harassment against one of its employees warranted a large penalty against the employer.

Case 2.2

May v. Chrysler Group, LLC
United States Court of Appeals, Seventh Circuit, 716 F.3d 963 (2013).

What other ways can employees be harassed?

COMPANY PROFILE   *Chrysler Corporation, founded in 1925 by Walter Chrysler, emerged from bankruptcy in 2009 as Chrysler Group, LLC. Today, Chrysler is a wholly owned subsidiary of the Italian automaker Fiat S.p.A. Chrysler makes and markets vehicles under the Chrysler, Dodge, Jeep, Ram, and Fiat USA brands. Headquartered in Auburn Hills, Michigan, the company employs more than 65,000 people at twenty-six manufacturing facilities in five countries, including an assembly plant in Belvedere, Illinois.*

BACKGROUND AND FACTS   Between 2002 and 2005, Otto May, Jr., a pipefitter at Chrysler's Belvedere Assembly Plant (Illinois), was the target of over fifty racist, homophobic, and anti-Semitic messages and graffiti. He received death threats, his bike and car tires were punctured, and someone poured sugar into the gas tanks of his two cars. A dead bird wrapped in toilet paper to look like a member of the Ku Klux Klan was placed at his workstation. May complained to Chrysler.

The employer documented the complaints and began an investigation. Records were checked to determine who was in the building when the incidents occurred, and the graffiti handwriting was analyzed. The company held meetings and reminded its workers that harassment was not acceptable. The harassers were never caught, but the incidents became fewer and eventually stopped. May filed a suit against Chrysler in a federal district court for hostile work environment harassment. A jury awarded May $709,000 in compensatory damages and $3.5 million in punitive damages. When the judge overturned the punitive damages award, May appealed.

IN THE WORDS OF THE COURT . . .
PER CURIAM [By the Whole Court]
* * * *

May can recover punitive damages only if he presented sufficient evidence for the jury to conclude that Chrysler acted with malice or with reckless indifference to [his] federally protected rights. [Emphasis added.]

* * * Chrysler employed several strategies to stop and prevent the harassment of May. When May's cars were vandalized

Case 2.2—Continued

in early 2002, Chrysler allowed him to park in the salaried lot, which is monitored * * * by cameras. Chrysler had all supervisors meet with their employees to review Chrysler's anti-harassment policy. And in September 2002, [Chrysler] held a pair of meetings with [its employees] about Chrysler's harassment policy. * * * In 2003, Chrysler implemented a protocol for handling incidents against May, which included prompt clean-up of graffiti, documentation of the incidents, taking photographs if possible, notification to * * * security, and discussions with the person or persons who discovered the graffiti or note and any other persons in the area when the graffiti or note was found.

Chrysler worked with its security team to increase their presence in area walk-throughs and heightened the supervisors' and managers' awareness and attentiveness to the harassment. Management increased its presence with walk-throughs as well.

When the harassment did not stop, Chrysler continued and even increased, to some extent, its efforts to protect May. * * * Beginning in May 2003, Chrysler conducted diversity training to raise awareness among all employees. Also in May 2003, Chrysler retained a handwriting analyst and continued to utilize his expertise in 2004 and 2005. Then in early August 2003, * * * Steve Hughes took over as paint shop manager * * * . Hughes held town hall meetings with his employees in all three shifts in which he * * * addressed May's situation, stating that the harassment needed to stop

* * *. While far from perfect, Chrysler's actions did have a positive effect on the harassment: the harassment's frequency gradually decreased from one year to the next, and eventually ceased in December 2005.

* * * The district court was correct to conclude that the evidence is simply insufficient to support a finding that Chrysler acted with malice or reckless indifference to May's federally protected rights.

DECISION AND REMEDY The U.S. Court of Appeals for the Seventh Circuit affirmed the lower court's judgment. Chrysler could have done more to prevent the harassment against May, but the company did not act with malice or reckless indifference to his federally protected rights, as required for an award of punitive damages.

THE ETHICAL DIMENSION *Does an organization have an ethical obligation to secure a safe and harassment-free workplace for its employees? Why or why not? Discuss.*

MANAGERIAL IMPLICATIONS *It is clear from this opinion that employers have a significant duty to take complaints of harassment seriously. Even if an employer believes that an employee may be staging harassment against himself or herself (possibly to obtain compensation from the company), the employer has an obligation to set up clear policies and procedures and follow those procedures when a complaint is made.*

Business Ethics and Social Media

Although most young people think of social media—Facebook, Twitter, Pinterest, Google+, MySpace, LinkedIn, and the like—as simply ways to communicate rapidly, businesses face ethical issues with respect to these same social media platforms.

Hiring Procedures

In the past, to learn about a prospective employee, the employer would ask the candidate's former employers for references. Today, employers are likely to also conduct Internet searches to discover what job candidates have posted on their Facebook pages, blogs, and tweets. Nevertheless, many people believe that judging a job candidate based on what she or he does outside the work environment is unethical.

Sometimes, too, the opposite situation occurs, and job candidates are rejected because they *do not* participate in any social media. Given that the vast majority of younger people do use social media, some employers have decided that the failure to do so raises a red flag. Some consider this employer behavior to be unethical as well.

(iStockphoto.com/Erik Khalitov)

What restrictions can there be on employees' use of social media to discuss work-related issues?

The Use of Social Media to Discuss Work-Related Issues

Because so many Americans use social media many times a day, they often discuss work-related issues there. Numerous companies have provided strict guidelines about what is appropriate and inappropriate when making posts on one's own or others' social media accounts. A number of companies have fired employees for such activities as criticizing other employees or managers through social media outlets. Until recently, such disciplinary measures were considered ethical and legal.

Today, in contrast, a ruling by the National Labor Relations Board (NLRB—the federal agency that investigates unfair labor practices) has changed the legality of such actions. **EXAMPLE 2.3**   Costco's social media policy specified that its employees should not make statements that would damage the company, harm another person's reputation, or violate the company's policies. Employees who violated these rules were subject to discipline and could be fired.

In 2012, the NLRB ruled that Costco's social media policy violated federal labor law, which protects employees' right to engage in "concerted activities." Employees can freely associate with each other and have conversations about common workplace issues without employer interference. This right extends to social media posts. Therefore, Costco cannot broadly prohibit its employees from criticizing the company or co-workers, supervisors, or managers via social media. ●

Ethics in Reverse

While most of the discussion in this chapter involves business ethics, employee ethics is also an important issue. For instance, is it ethical for employees to make negative posts in social media about other employees or, more commonly, about managers? After all, negative comments about managers reflect badly on those managers, who often are reluctant to respond via social media to such criticism. Disgruntled employees may exaggerate the negative qualities of managers whom they do not like.

Some may consider the latest decision by the National Labor Relations Board outlined in *Example 2.3* to be too lenient toward employees and too stringent toward management. There is likely to be an ongoing debate about how to balance employees' right to free expression against employers' right to prevent inaccurate negative statements being spread across the Internet.

Learning Objective 2
How do duty-based ethical standards differ from outcome-based ethical standards?

Ethical Reasoning A reasoning process in which an individual links his or her moral convictions or ethical standards to the particular situation at hand.

Duty-based Ethics An ethical philosophy rooted in the idea that every person has certain duties to others, including both humans and the planet. Those duties may be derived from religious principles or from other philosophical reasoning.

Approaches to Ethical Reasoning

As Dean Krehmeyer, executive director of the Business Roundtable's Institute for Corporate Ethics, once said, "Evidence strongly suggests being ethical—doing the right thing—pays." Instilling ethical business decision making into the fabric of a business organization is no small task, even if ethics "pays." How do business decision makers decide whether a given action is the "right" one for their firms? What ethical standards should be applied?

Broadly speaking, **ethical reasoning**—the application of morals and ethics to a situation—applies to businesses just as it does to individuals. As businesses make decisions, they must analyze the alternatives in a variety of ways, one of which is the ethical implications.

Generally, the study of ethics is divided into two major categories—duty-based ethics and outcome-based ethics. **Duty-based ethics** is rooted in the idea that every person has certain duties to others, including both humans and the planet. Those duties may be derived from religious principles or from other philosophical reasoning. **Outcome-based ethics** focuses on the impacts of a decision on society or on key *stakeholders*.

Duty-Based Ethics

Duty-based ethics focuses on the obligations of the corporation. It deals with standards for behavior that traditionally were derived from revealed truths, religious authorities, or philosophical reasoning. These standards involve concepts of right and wrong, duties owed, and rights to be protected.

Corporations today often describe these values or duties in their mission statements or strategic plans. Some companies base their statements on a nonreligious rationale, but others still derive their values from religious doctrine (such as the statements of Chick-fil-A, discussed in the introduction to this chapter).

Religious Ethical Principles   Nearly every religion has principles or beliefs about how one should treat others. In the Judeo-Christian tradition, which is the dominant religious tradition in the United States, the Ten Commandments of the Old Testament establish these fundamental rules for moral action. The principles of the Muslim faith are set out in the Qur'an, and Hindus find their principles in the four Vedas.

Religious rules generally are absolute with respect to the behavior of their adherents. **EXAMPLE 2.4**   The commandment "Thou shalt not steal" is an absolute mandate for a person who believes that the Ten Commandments reflect revealed truth. Even a benevolent motive for stealing (such as Robin Hood's) cannot justify the act because the act itself is inherently immoral and thus wrong. ●

For businesses, religious principles can be a unifying force for employees or a rallying point to increase employee motivation. They can also be problematic, however, because different owners, suppliers, employees, and customers may all have different religious backgrounds. As the introduction to this chapter illustrated, taking an action based on religious principles, especially when those principles address socially or politically controversial topics, can lead to negative publicity and even to protests or boycotts.

The Principle of Rights   Another view of duty-based ethics focuses on basic rights. The principle that human beings have certain fundamental rights (to life, freedom, and the pursuit of happiness, for example) is deeply embedded in Western culture. As discussed in Chapter 1, the natural law tradition embraces the concept that certain actions (such as killing another person) are morally wrong because they are contrary to nature (the natural desire to continue living).

Those who adhere to this **principle of rights,** or "rights theory," believe that a key factor in determining whether a business decision is ethical is how that decision affects the rights of others. These others include the firm's owners, its employees, the consumers of its products or services, its suppliers, the community in which it does business, and society as a whole.

Conflicting Rights   A potential dilemma for those who support rights theory, however, is that they may disagree on which rights are most important. When considering all those affected by a business decision to downsize a firm, for example, how much weight should be given to employees relative to shareholders? Which employees should be laid off first—those with the highest salaries or those who have worked there for less time (and have less seniority)? How should the firm weigh the rights of customers relative to the community, or those of employees relative to society as a whole?

Outcome-based Ethics An ethical philosophy that focuses on the impacts of a decision on society or on key stakeholders.

"When I do good, I feel good. When I do bad, I feel bad. And that's my religion."

Abraham Lincoln, 1809–1865 (Sixteenth president of the United States, 1861–1865)

Principle of Rights The belief that human beings have certain fundamental rights. Whether an action or decision is ethical depends on how it affects the rights of various groups, such as owners, employees, consumers, suppliers, the community, and society.

Resolving Conflicts   In general, rights theorists believe that whichever right is stronger in a particular circumstance takes precedence. **EXAMPLE 2.5**   Murray Chemical Corporation has to decide whether to keep a chemical plant in Utah open, thereby saving the jobs of a hundred and fifty workers, or shut it down. Closing the plant will avoid contaminating a river with pollutants that would endanger the health of tens of thousands of people. In this situation, a rights theorist can easily choose which group to favor because the value of the right to health and well-being is obviously stronger than the basic right to work. (Not all choices are so clear-cut, however.) ●

Kantian Ethical Principles

Duty-based ethical standards may also be derived solely from philosophical reasoning. The German philosopher Immanuel Kant (1724–1804) identified some general guiding principles for moral behavior based on what he thought to be the fundamental nature of human beings. Kant believed that human beings are qualitatively different from other physical objects and are endowed with moral integrity and the capacity to reason and conduct their affairs rationally.

People Are Not a Means to an End   Based on this view of human beings, Kant said that when people are treated merely as a means to an end, they are being treated as the equivalent of objects and are being denied their basic humanity. For instance, a manager who treats subordinates as mere profit-making tools is less likely to retain motivated and loyal employees than a manager who respects his or her employees. Management research has shown that employees who feel empowered to share their thoughts, opinions, and solutions to problems are happier and more productive.

Categorical Imperative   When a business makes unethical decisions, it often rationalizes its action by saying that the company is "just one small part" of the problem or that its decision would have "only a small impact." A central theme in Kantian ethics is that individuals should evaluate their actions in light of the consequences that would follow if everyone in society acted in the same way. This **categorical imperative** can be applied to any action.

Categorical Imperative An ethical guideline developed by Immanuel Kant under which an action is evaluated in terms of what would happen if everybody else in the same situation, or category, acted the same way.

EXAMPLE 2.6   CHS Fertilizer is deciding whether to invest in expensive equipment that will decrease profits but will also reduce pollution from its factories. If CHS has adopted Kant's categorical imperative, the decision makers will consider the consequences if every company invested in the equipment (or if no company did so). If the result would make the world a better place (less polluted), CHS's decision would be clear. ●

Outcome-Based Ethics: Utilitarianism

In contrast to duty-based ethics, outcome-based ethics focuses on the consequences of an action, not on the nature of the action itself or on any set of preestablished moral values or religious beliefs. Outcome-based ethics looks at the impacts of a decision in an attempt to maximize benefits and minimize harms. The premier philosophical theory for outcome-based decision making is **utilitarianism**, a philosophical theory developed by Jeremy Bentham (1748–1832) and modified by John Stuart Mill (1806–1873)—both British philosophers.

"The greatest good for the greatest number" is a paraphrase of the major premise of the utilitarian approach to ethics.

Utilitarianism An approach to ethical reasoning in which an action is evaluated in terms of its consequences for those whom it will affect. A "good" action is one that results in the greatest good for the greatest number of people.

Cost-Benefit Analysis

Under a utilitarian model of ethics, an action is morally correct, or "right," when, among the people it affects, it produces the greatest amount of good for the greatest number or creates the least amount of harm for the fewest people.

When an action affects the majority adversely, it is morally wrong. Applying the utilitarian theory thus requires the following steps:

1. A determination of which individuals will be affected by the action in question.
2. A **cost-benefit analysis,** which involves an assessment of the negative and positive effects of alternative actions on these individuals.
3. A choice among alternative actions that will produce maximum societal utility (the greatest positive net benefits for the greatest number of individuals).

Thus, if expanding a factory would provide hundreds of jobs but generate pollution that could endanger the lives of thousands of people, a utilitarian analysis would find that saving the lives of thousands creates greater good than providing jobs for hundreds.

Problems with the Utilitarian Approach   There are problems with a strict utilitarian analysis. In some situations, an action that produces the greatest good for the most people may not seem to be the most ethical. **EXAMPLE 2.7**   Phazim Company is producing a drug that will cure a disease in 85 percent of patients, but the other 15 percent will experience agonizing side effects and a horrible, painful death. A quick utilitarian analysis would suggest that the drug should be produced and marketed because the majority of patients will benefit. Many people, however, have significant concerns about manufacturing a drug that will cause such harm to anyone. ●

Corporate Social Responsibility

In pairing duty-based concepts with outcome-based concepts, strategists and theorists developed the idea of the corporate citizen. **Corporate social responsibility (CSR)** combines a commitment to good citizenship with a commitment to making ethical decisions, improving society, and minimizing environmental impact.

CSR is a relatively new concept in the history of business, but a concept that becomes more important every year. Although CSR is not imposed on corporations by law, it does involve a commitment to self-regulation in a way that attends to the text and intent of the law, ethical norms, and global standards. A survey of U.S. executives undertaken by the Boston College Center for Corporate Citizenship found that more than 70 percent of those polled agreed that corporate citizenship must be treated as a priority. More than 60 percent said that good corporate citizenship added to their companies' profits.

CSR can be an incredibly successful strategy for companies, but corporate decision makers must not lose track of the two descriptors in the title: *corporate* and *social*. The company must link the responsibility of citizenship with the strategy and key principles of the business. Incorporating both the social and the corporate components of CSR and making ethical decisions can help companies grow and prosper.

The Social Aspects of CSR   First, the social aspect requires that corporations demonstrate that they are promoting goals that society deems worthwhile and are moving toward solutions to social problems. Because business controls so much of the wealth and power of this country, business, in turn, has a responsibility to society to use that wealth and power in socially beneficial ways.

Companies may be judged on how much they donate to social causes, as well as how they conduct their operations with respect to employment discrimination, human rights, environmental concerns, and similar issues. Some corporations publish annual social responsibility reports, which may also be called corporate sustainability (referring to the capacity to endure) or citizenship reports. (See the *Linking Business Law to Accounting and Finance* feature at the end of this chapter for several examples.)

Cost-Benefit Analysis A decision-making technique that involves weighing the costs of a given action against the benefits of that action.

"Next to doing the right thing, the most important thing is to let people know you are doing the right thing."

John D. Rockefeller, 1839–1897 (American industrialist and philanthropist)

Corporate Social Responsibility (CSR) The idea that corporations can and should act ethically and be accountable to society for their actions.

Stakeholders Groups, other than the company's shareholders, that are affected by corporate decisions. Stakeholders include employees, customers, creditors, suppliers, and the community in which the corporation operates.

The Corporate Aspects of CSR   Arguably, any socially responsible activity will benefit a corporation. The corporation may see an increase in goodwill from the local community for creating a park. Corporations may see increases in sales if they are viewed as good citizens.

At times, the benefit may not be immediate. Constructing a new plant that meets the high Leadership in Energy and Environmental Design (LEED) standards may cost more initially. Nevertheless, over the life of the building, the savings in maintenance and utilities may more than make up for the extra cost of construction.

Surveys of college students about to enter the job market confirm that young people are looking for socially responsible employers. Socially responsible activities may cost a corporation now but may lead to more impressive, and more committed, employees. Corporations that engage in meaningful social activities retain workers longer, particularly younger ones.

Corporate responsibility is most successful when a company undertakes activities that are significant and related to its business operations. **EXAMPLE 2.8**   The Walt Disney Company announced in 2012 that in an effort to curb childhood obesity, it was issuing strict nutritional standards for all products advertised through its media outlets. In addition to focusing on a major social issue, the initiative was intended to clarify Disney's mission and values, as well as enhance its reputation as a trustworthy, family-friendly company. The initiative has been praised by commentators and politicians, and is expected to increase Disney's revenue in the long term. ●

Stakeholders   One view of CSR stresses that corporations have a duty not just to shareholders, but also to other groups affected by corporate decisions—called **stakeholders.** The rationale for this "stakeholder view" is that, in some circumstances, one or more of these other groups may have a greater stake in company decisions than the shareholders do.

Under this approach, a corporation considers the impact of its decisions on its employees, customers, creditors, suppliers, and the community in which it operates. Stakeholders could also include advocacy groups such as environmental groups and animal rights groups. To avoid making a decision that may be perceived as unethical and result in negative publicity or protests, a corporation should consider the impact of its decision on the stakeholders. The most difficult aspect of the stakeholder analysis is determining which group's interests should receive greater weight if the interests conflict.

For instance, during the last ten years, layoffs numbered in the millions. Nonetheless, some corporations succeeded in reducing labor costs without layoffs. To avoid slashing their workforces, these employers turned to alternatives such as (1) four-day workweeks, (2) unpaid vacations and voluntary furloughs, (3) wage freezes, (4) pension cuts, and (5) flexible work schedules. Some companies asked their workers to accept wage cuts to prevent layoffs, and the workers agreed. Companies finding alternatives to layoffs included Dell (extended unpaid holidays), Cisco Systems (four-day end-of-year shutdowns), Motorola (salary cuts), and Honda (voluntary unpaid vacation time).

Making Ethical Business Decisions

Even if officers, directors, and others in a company want to make ethical decisions, it is not always clear what is ethical in a given situation. Thinking beyond things that are easily measured, such as profits, can be challenging. Although profit projections are not always accurate, they are more objective than considering the personal impacts of decisions on employees, shareholders, customers, and even the community. But this subjective component to decision making potentially has a great influence on a company's profits.

Companies once considered leaders in their industry, such as Enron and the worldwide accounting firm Arthur Andersen, were brought down by the unethical behavior of a few.

A two-hundred-year-old British investment banking firm, Barings Bank, was destroyed by the actions of one employee and a few of his friends. Clearly, ensuring that all employees get on the ethical business decision-making "bandwagon" is crucial in today's fast-paced world.

Individuals entering the global corporate community, even in entry-level positions, must be prepared to make hard decisions. Sometimes, there is no "good" answer to the questions that arise. Therefore, it is important to have tools to help in the decision-making process and a framework for organizing those tools. Business decisions can be complex and may involve legal concerns, financial questions, possibly health and safety concerns, and ethical components.

A Systematic Approach

Organizing the ethical concerns and issues and approaching them systematically can help a businessperson eliminate various alternatives and identify the strengths and weaknesses of the remaining alternatives. Ethics consultant Leonard H. Bucklin of Corporate-Ethics.US™ has devised a procedure that he calls Business Process Pragmatism™. It involves five steps:

Step 1: Inquiry. First, the decision maker must understand the problem. To do this, one must identify the parties involved (the stakeholders) and collect the relevant facts. Once the ethical problem or problems are clarified, the decision maker lists any relevant legal and ethical principles that will guide the decision.

Step 2: Discussion. In this step, the decision maker lists possible actions. The ultimate goals for the decision are determined, and each option is evaluated using the laws and ethical principles listed in Step 1.

Step 3: Decision. In this step, those participating in the decision making work together to craft a consensus decision or consensus plan of action for the corporation.

Step 4: Justification. In this step, the decision maker articulates the reasons for the proposed action or series of actions. Generally these reasons should come from the analysis done in Step 3. This step essentially results in documentation to be shared with stakeholders explaining why the proposal is an ethical solution to the problem.

Step 5: Evaluation. This final step occurs once the decision has been made and implemented. The solution should be analyzed to determine if it was effective. The results of this evaluation may be used in making future decisions.

The Importance of Ethical Leadership

Talking about ethical business decision making is meaningless if management does not set standards. Furthermore, managers must apply the same standards to themselves as they do to the company's employees.

Attitude of Top Management One of the most important ways to create and maintain an ethical workplace is for top management to demonstrate its commitment to ethical decision making. A manager who is not totally committed to an ethical workplace rarely succeeds in creating one. Management's behavior, more than anything else, sets the ethical tone of a firm. Employees take their cues from management. **EXAMPLE 2.9** Devon, a BioTek

Learning Objective 3
What are five steps that a businessperson can take to evaluate whether his or her actions are ethical?

Microsoft founder Bill Gates and his wife, Melinda, are shown below with financier Warren Buffett (right) after Buffett gave $40 billion to the Bill and Melinda Gates Foundation.

(Keith Meyers/The New York Times/Redux)

> "What you do speaks so loudly that I cannot hear what you say."
>
> Ralph Waldo Emerson, 1803–1882
> (American essayist and poet)

Learning Objective 4
How can business leaders encourage their employees to act ethically?

employee, observes his manager cheating on her expense account. Later, when Devon is promoted to a managerial position, he "pads" his expense account as well, knowing that he is unlikely to face sanctions for doing so. •

Managers who set unrealistic production or sales goals increase the probability that employees will act unethically. If a sales quota can be met only through high-pressure, unethical sales tactics, employees will try to act "in the best interest of the company" and will continue to behave unethically.

A manager who looks the other way when she or he knows about an employee's unethical behavior also sets an example—one indicating that ethical transgressions will be accepted. Managers have found that discharging even one employee for ethical reasons has a tremendous impact as a deterrent to unethical behavior in the workplace. This is true even if the company has a written code of ethics. If management does not enforce the company code, the code is essentially nonexistent.

Behavior of Owners and Managers
Business owners and managers sometimes take more active roles in fostering unethical and illegal conduct. This may indicate to their co-owners, co-managers, employees, and others that unethical business behavior will be tolerated. Business owners' misbehavior can have negative consequences for themselves and their business. Not only can a court sanction the owners and managers, but it can also issue an injunction that prevents them from engaging in similar patterns of conduct in the future.

In the following case, the court had to determine if a repair shop was entitled to receive full payment of an invoice or a lesser amount given its conduct in the matter.

Case 2.3

Johnson Construction Co. v. Shaffer
Court of Appeal of Louisiana, Second Circuit, 87 So.3d 203 (2012).

BACKGROUND AND FACTS A truck owned by Johnson Construction Company needed repairs. John Robert Johnson, Jr., the company's president, took the truck with its attached fifteen-ton trailer to Bubba Shaffer, doing business as Shaffer's Auto and Diesel Repair. The truck was supposedly fixed, and Johnson paid the bill. The truck continued to leak oil and water. Johnson returned the truck to Shaffer, who again claimed to have fixed the problem. Johnson paid the second bill. The problems with the truck continued, however, so Johnson returned the truck and trailer a third time. Shaffer gave a verbal estimate of $1,000 for the repairs, but he ultimately sent an invoice for $5,863.49. Johnson offered to settle for $2,480, the amount of the initial estimate ($1,000), plus the costs of parts and shipping. Shaffer refused the offer and would not return Johnson's truck or trailer until full payment was made. Shaffer also charged Johnson a storage fee of $50 a day and 18 percent interest on the $5,863.49.

Johnson Construction filed a suit against Shaffer alleging unfair trade practices. The trial court determined that Shaffer had acted deceptively and wrongfully in maintaining possession of the trailer, on which no work had been performed. The trial court awarded Johnson $3,500 in general damages, plus $750 in attorneys' fees. Shaffer was awarded the

initial estimate of $1,000 and appealed.

IN THE WORDS OF THE COURT . . .
LOLLEY, J. [Judge]
* * * *

* * * At the outset, we point out that Mr. Johnson maintained he had a verbal agreement with Bubba Shaffer, the owner of Shaffer's Auto Diesel and Repair, that the repairs to the truck would cost $1,000. Mr. Johnson also testified that he was not informed otherwise.

The existence or nonexistence of a contract is a question of fact, and the finder of fact's determination may not be set aside unless it is clearly wrong.
* * * *

* * * At the trial of the matter, the trial court was presented with testimony from Mr. Johnson, Mr. Shaffer, and Michael Louton, a mechanic employed by Shaffer. * * * The trial court did not believe Mr. Johnson was informed of the cost for the additional work.

* * * We cannot say that the trial court was clearly wrong in its determination. * * * The trial court viewed Mr. Shaffer's

Can an auto repair shop hold a truck "hostage" during a payment dispute with its owner?

Case 2.3—Continued

testimony on the issue as "disingenuous" and we cannot see where that was an error.

As for the amount that Shaffer contends is due for storage, had it invoiced Mr. Johnson the amount of the original estimate in the first place, there would have been no need to store the truck or trailer. * * * We cannot see how Shaffer would be entitled to any payment for storage when it failed to return the truck and trailer where an offer of payment for the agreed upon price had been conveyed.

* * * *

* * * So considering, we see no error in the trial court's characterization of Shaffer's actions with the trailer as holding "hostage in an effort to force payment for unauthorized repairs." * * * Shaffer had no legal right to retain possession of the trailer * * * . Thus, the trial court did not err in its determination that Shaffer's

retention of Johnson Construction's trailer [for four years!] was a deceptive conversion of the trailer. [Emphasis added.]

DECISION AND REMEDY The state appellate court affirmed the judgment of the trial court in favor of Johnson Construction Company. It affirmed the award of $3,500, plus $750 in attorneys' fees, as well as Shaffer's original award of $1,000.

WHAT IF THE FACTS WERE DIFFERENT? Suppose that Shaffer had invoiced Johnson for only $1,500. Would the outcome have been different?

THE ETHICAL DIMENSION Would it have been ethical for Shaffer's mechanic to lie to support his employer's case? Discuss.

To avoid disputes over ethical violations, you should first create a written ethical code that is expressed in clear and understandable language. The code should establish specific procedures that employees can follow if they have questions or complaints. It should assure employees that their jobs will be secure and that they will not face reprisals if they do file a complaint. A well-written code might also include examples to clarify what the company considers to be acceptable and unacceptable conduct. You should also hold periodic training meetings so that you can explain to employees face to face why ethics is important to the company. If your company does business internationally, you might also communicate the code to firms in your supply chain and make sure they follow your ethics policies.

PREVENTING LEGAL DISPUTES

The Sarbanes-Oxley Act The Sarbanes-Oxley Act[2] requires companies to set up confidential systems so that employees and others can "raise red flags" about suspected illegal or unethical auditing and accounting practices.

Some companies have implemented online reporting systems to accomplish this goal. In one such system, employees can click on an icon on their computers that anonymously links them with NAVEX Global, an organization based in Oregon. Through NAVEX, employees can report suspicious accounting practices, sexual harassment, and other possibly unethical behavior. NAVEX, in turn, alerts management personnel or the audit committee at the designated company to the possible problem. Those who have used the system say that it is less inhibiting than calling a company's toll-free number.

Global Business Ethics

Given the various cultures and religions throughout the world, it is not surprising that conflicts in ethics frequently arise between foreign and U.S. businesspersons. For instance, in certain countries, the consumption of alcohol and specific foods is forbidden for religious reasons. Under such circumstances, it would be considered unethical for a U.S.

---

2. 15 U.S.C. Sections 7201 *et seq.*

businessperson to start a business that produces alcohol and employs local workers in an area where alcohol is forbidden.

We look here at how laws governing workers in other countries, particularly developing countries, have created some especially difficult ethical problems for U.S. sellers of goods manufactured in foreign countries. We also examine some of the ethical ramifications of laws prohibiting U.S. businesspersons from bribing foreign officials to obtain favorable business contracts.

Learning Objective 5
What types of ethical issues might arise in the context of international business transactions?

Employment Practices of Foreign Suppliers

Many U.S. businesses now contract with companies in developing nations to produce goods, such as shoes and clothing, because the wage rates in those nations are significantly lower than wages in the United States. Yet what if a foreign company exploits its workers—by hiring women and children at below-minimum-wage rates, for example, or by requiring its employees to work long hours in a workplace full of health hazards? What if the company's supervisors routinely engage in workplace conduct that is offensive to women? What if plants that are operated abroad routinely violate labor and environmental standards?

EXAMPLE 2.10   Like other high-tech companies, Apple, Inc., relies heavily on foreign suppliers for components and assembly of many of its products. Following a number of high-profile labor problems with its foreign suppliers and manufacturers, Apple started to evaluate practices at companies in its supply chain and to communicate its ethics policies to them. After its audits revealed numerous violations, in 2012 Apple released a list of its suppliers for the first time. Apple's five-hundred-page "Supplier Responsibility Report" showed that sixty-seven facilities had docked worker pay as a disciplinary measure. Some had falsified pay records and forced workers to use machines without safeguards. Others had engaged in unsafe environmental practices, such as dumping wastewater on neighboring farms. Apple terminated its relationship with one supplier and turned over its findings to the Fair Labor Association for further inquiry. •

Given today's global communications network, few companies can assume that their actions in other nations will go unnoticed by "corporate watch" groups that discover and publicize unethical corporate behavior. As a result, U.S. businesses today usually take steps to avoid such adverse publicity—either by refusing to deal with certain suppliers or by arranging to monitor their suppliers' workplaces to make sure that the employees are not being mistreated.

For a discussion of how the Internet has increased the ability of critics to publicize a corporation's misdeeds, see this chapter's *Online Developments* feature.

> "Never doubt that a small group of committed citizens can change the world; indeed, it is the only thing that ever has."
>
> Margaret Mead, 1901–1978
> (American anthropologist)

The Foreign Corrupt Practices Act

Another ethical problem in international business dealings has to do with the legitimacy of certain "side" payments to government officials. In the United States, most contracts are formed within the private sector. In many countries, however, government regulation and control over trade and industry are much more extensive than in the United States, so government officials make the decisions on most major construction and manufacturing contracts. Side payments to government officials in exchange for favorable business contracts are not unusual in such countries, where they are not considered to be unethical. In the past, U.S. corporations doing business in these countries largely followed the dictum "When in Rome, do as the Romans do."

In the 1970s, however, large side payments by U.S. corporations to foreign representatives for the purpose of securing advantageous international trade contracts led to a

ONLINE DEVELOPMENTS

Corporate Reputations under Attack

In the pre-Internet days, disgruntled employees and customers wrote letters of complaint to corporate management or to the editors of local newspapers. Occasionally, an investigative reporter would write an exposé of alleged corporate misdeeds. Today, those unhappy employees and customers have gone online. To locate them, just type in the name of any major corporation. You will find electronic links to blogs, wikis, message boards, and online communities—many of which post harsh criticisms of corporate giants. Some disgruntled employees and consumers have even created rogue Web sites that mimic the look of the target corporation's official Web site—except that the rogue sites feature chat rooms and postings of "horror stories" about the corporation.

Damage to Corporate Reputations

Clearly, by providing a forum for complaints, the Internet has increased the potential for damage to the reputation of any major (or minor) corporation. Now a relatively small number of unhappy employees, for example, may make the entire world aware of a single incident that is not at all representative of how the corporation ordinarily operates.

Special Interest Groups Go on the Attack

Special interest groups are also using the Internet to attack corporations they do not like. Rather than writing letters or giving speeches to a limited audience, a special interest group can now go online and mercilessly "expose" what it considers to be a corporation's "bad practices." Wal-Mart and Nike in particular have been frequent targets for advocacy groups that believe that those corporations exploit their workers.

Online Attacks: Often Inaccurate, but Probably Legal

Corporations often point out that many of the complaints and charges leveled against them are unfounded or exaggerated. Sometimes, management has tried to argue that the online attacks are libelous. The courts, however, disagree. To date, most courts have regarded online attacks as simply the expression of opinion and therefore a form of speech protected by the First Amendment.

In contrast, if employees breach company rules against the disclosure of internal financial information or trade secrets, the courts have been willing to side with the employers. Note, also, that companies that succeed in lawsuits against inappropriate employee online disclosures always have a clear set of written guidelines about what employees can do when they blog or generate other online content.

Critical Thinking

How might online attacks actually help corporations in the long run? (Hint: Some online criticisms might be accurate.)

---

number of scandals. In response, in 1977 Congress passed the Foreign Corrupt Practices Act[3] (FCPA), which prohibits U.S. businesspersons from bribing foreign officials to secure advantageous contracts.

Prohibition against the Bribery of Foreign Officials   The first part of the FCPA applies to all U.S. companies and their directors, officers, shareholders, employees, and agents. This part prohibits the bribery of officials of foreign governments if the purpose of the payment is to induce the officials to act in their official capacity to provide business opportunities.

The FCPA does not prohibit payment of substantial sums to minor officials whose duties are ministerial. These payments are often referred to as "grease," or facilitating payments. They are meant to accelerate the performance of administrative services that might otherwise be carried out at a slow pace. Thus, for example, if a firm makes a payment to a minor official to speed up an import licensing process, the firm has not violated the FCPA. Generally, the

---

3. 15 U.S.C. Sections 78 dd-1 *et seq.*

act, as amended, permits payments to foreign officials if such payments are lawful within the foreign country. The act also does not prohibit payments to private foreign companies or other third parties unless the U.S. firm knows that the payments will be passed on to a foreign government in violation of the FCPA.

Business firms that violate the FCPA may be fined up to $2 million. Individual officers or directors who violate the act may be fined up to $100,000 (the fine cannot be paid by the company) and may be imprisoned for up to five years.

Accounting Requirements   In the past, bribes were often concealed in corporate financial records. Thus, the second part of the FCPA is directed toward accountants. All companies must keep detailed records that "accurately and fairly" reflect the company's financial activities. In addition, all companies must have an accounting system that provides "reasonable assurance" that all transactions entered into by the company are accounted for and legal. These requirements assist in detecting illegal bribes. The FCPA further prohibits any person from making false statements to accountants or false entries in any record or account.

Reviewing . . . Business Ethics

Isabel Arnett was promoted to be chief executive officer of Tamik, Inc., a pharmaceutical company that manufactures a vaccine called Kafluk, which supposedly provides some defense against bird flu. The company began marketing Kafluk throughout Asia. After numerous media reports that bird flu might soon become a worldwide epidemic, the demand for Kafluk increased, sales soared, and Tamik earned record profits. Arnett then began receiving disturbing reports from Southeast Asia that in some patients, Kafluk had caused psychiatric disturbances, including severe hallucinations, and heart and lung problems. She was also informed that six children in Japan had committed suicide by jumping out of windows after receiving the vaccine. To cover up the story and prevent negative publicity, Arnett instructed Tamik's partners in Asia to offer cash to the Japanese families whose children had died in exchange for their silence. Arnett also refused to authorize additional research within the company to study the potential side effects of Kafluk. Using the information presented in the chapter, answer the following questions.

1. This scenario illustrates one of the main reasons why ethical problems occur in business. What is that reason?
2. Would a person who adheres to the principle of rights consider it ethical for Arnett not to disclose potential safety concerns and to refuse to perform additional research on Kafluk? Why or why not?
3. If Kafluk prevented fifty Asian people who were exposed to bird flu from dying, would Arnett's conduct in this situation be ethical under a utilitarian cost-benefit analysis? Why or why not?
4. Did Tamik or Arnett violate the Foreign Corrupt Practices Act in this scenario? Why or why not?

Debate This   Executives in large corporations are ultimately rewarded if their companies do well, particularly as evidenced by rising stock prices. Consequently, shouldn't we just let those who run corporations decide what level of negative side effects of their goods or services is "acceptable"?

LINKING BUSINESS LAW to Accounting and Finance

Managing a Company's Reputation

While in business school, all of you must take basic accounting courses. Accounting generally is associated with developing balance sheets and profit-and-loss statements, but it can also be used as a support system to provide information that can help managers do their jobs correctly. Enter managerial accounting, which involves the provision of accounting information for a company's internal use. Managerial accounting is used within a company for planning, controlling, and decision making.

Increasingly, managerial accounting is also being used to *manage corporate reputations*. To this end, more than 2,500 multinationals now release to the public large quantities of managerial accounting information.

Internal Reports Designed for External Scrutiny

Some large companies refer to the managerial accounting information that they release to the public as their corporate sustainability reports. Dow Chemical Company, for example, issues its Global Reporting Initiative Sustainability Report annually. So does Waste Management, Inc., which calls its report "The Color of Our World."

Other corporations call their published documents social responsibility reports. The software company Symantec Corporation issues corporate responsibility reports to demonstrate its focus on critical environmental, social, and governance issues. In its 2012 report, Symantec pointed out that 88 percent of facilities it owns or leases on a long-term basis are certified as environmentally friendly by the LEED program. LEED stands for Leadership in Energy and Environmental Design. Certification requires the achievement of high standards for energy efficiency, material usage in construction, and other environmental qualities.

A smaller number of multinationals provide what they call citizenship reports. For example, in 2011 General Electric (GE)

released its Seventh Annual Citizenship Report, which it calls "Sustainable Growth." GE's emphasis is on energy and climate change, demographics, growth markets, and financial markets. It even has a Web site that provides detailed performance metrics (www.ge.com/citizenship).

The Hitachi Group releases an Annual Corporate Social Responsibility Report, which outlines its environmental strategy, including its attempts to reduce carbon dioxide emissions (so-called greenhouse gases). It typically discusses its human rights policies and its commitment to diversity and human rights awareness.

Why Use Managerial Accounting to Manage Reputations?

We live in an age of information. Any news, whether positive or negative, about a corporation will be known throughout the world almost immediately given the 24/7 cable and online news networks, social media, Internet bloggers, and smartphones. Consequently, corporations want to manage their reputations by preparing and releasing the news that the public, their shareholders, and government officials will receive.

In a world in which corporations are often blamed for anything bad that happens, corporations are finding that managerial accounting information can provide a useful counterweight. To this end, some corporations have combined their social responsibility reports with their traditional financial accounting information. When a corporation's reputation is on the line, the future is at stake.

Critical Thinking

Valuable company resources are used to create and publish corporate social responsibility reports. Under what circumstances can a corporation justify such expenditures?

Key Terms

Chapter Summary: Business Ethics

Business Ethics	1. *Ethics*—Business ethics focuses on how moral and ethical principles are applied in the business context. 2. *The moral minimum*—Lawful behavior is the moral minimum. The law has its limits, though, and some actions may be legal but not ethical. 3. *Short-term profit maximization*—One of the most pervasive reasons why ethical breaches occur is the focus on short-term profit maximization. Executives should distinguish between short-run and long-run profit goals and focus on maximizing profits over the long run because only long-run profit maximization is consistent with business ethics. 4. *Legal uncertainties*—It may be difficult to predict with certainty whether particular actions are legal, given the numerous and frequent changes in the laws regulating business and the "gray areas" in the law. 5. *The importance of ethical leadership*—Management's commitment and behavior are essential in creating an ethical workplace. Management's behavior, more than anything else, sets the ethical tone of a firm and influences the behavior of employees. 6. *Ethical codes*—Most large firms have ethical codes or policies and training programs to help employees determine whether specific actions are ethical. In addition, the Sarbanes-Oxley Act requires firms to set up confidential systems so that employees and others can report suspected illegal or unethical auditing or accounting practices.
Business Ethics and Social Media	Employers today may conduct Internet searches to see what job candidates have posted on social media. Employers may also look at, but not interfere with, the social media posts of their employees. Many companies have explicit policies regarding the use of social media by workers, but employers must be careful when considering disciplinary action for violations of these policies.
Approaches to Ethical Reasoning	1. *Duty-based ethics*—Ethics based on religious beliefs; philosophical reasoning, such as that of Immanuel Kant; and the basic rights of human beings (the principle of rights). A potential problem for those who support this approach is deciding which rights are more important in a given situation. Management constantly faces ethical conflicts and trade-offs when considering all those affected by a business decision. 2. *Outcome-based ethics (utilitarianism)*—Ethics based on philosophical reasoning, such as that of Jeremy Bentham and John Stuart Mill. Applying this theory requires a cost-benefit analysis, weighing the negative effects against the positive and deciding which course of action produces the better outcome. 3. *Corporate social responsibility*—A number of theories based on the idea that corporations can and should act ethically and be accountable to society for their actions. These include the stakeholder approach and corporate citizenship.
Making Ethical Business Decisions	Making ethical business decisions is crucial in today's legal environment. Doing the right thing pays off in the long run, both by increasing profits and by avoiding negative publicity and the potential for bankruptcy. Corporate ethics officers and ethics committees require a practical method to investigate and solve specific ethics problems. We provide a five-step pragmatic procedure to solve ethical problems.
Global Business Ethics	Businesses must take account of the many cultural, religious, and legal differences among nations. Notable differences relate to the role of employment laws governing workplace conditions and the practice of giving side payments to foreign officials to secure favorable contracts.

Issue Spotters

1. Acme Corporation decides to respond to what it sees as a moral obligation to correct for past discrimination by adjusting pay differences among its employees. Does this raise an ethical conflict between Acme and its employees? Between Acme and its shareholders? Explain your answers. (See *Approaches to Ethical Reasoning.*)
2. Delta Tools, Inc., markets a product that under some circumstances is capable of seriously injuring consumers. Does Delta have an ethical duty to remove this product from the market, even if the injuries result only from misuse? Why or why not? (See *Making Ethical Business Decisions.*)

—**Check your answers to the Issue Spotters against the answers provided in Appendix D at the end of this text.**

For Review

1. What is business ethics, and why is it important?
2. How do duty-based ethical standards differ from outcome-based ethical standards?
3. What are five steps that a businessperson can take to evaluate whether his or her actions are ethical?

4. How can business leaders encourage their employees to act ethically?

5. What types of ethical issues might arise in the context of international business transactions?

Business Scenarios and Case Problems

2–1. Business Ethics. Jason Trevor owns a commercial bakery in Blakely, Georgia, that produces a variety of goods sold in grocery stores. Trevor is required by law to perform internal tests on food produced at his plant to check for contamination. Three times in 2011, the tests of food products that contained peanut butter were positive for salmonella contamination. Trevor was not required to report the results to U.S. Food and Drug Administration officials, however, so he did not. Instead, Trevor instructed his employees to simply repeat the tests until the outcome was negative. Therefore, the products that had originally tested positive for salmonella were eventually shipped out to retailers.

Five people who ate Trevor's baked goods in 2011 became seriously ill, and one person died from salmonella. Even though Trevor's conduct was legal, was it unethical for him to sell goods that had once tested positive for salmonella? If Trevor had followed the five-step systematic approach for making ethical business decisions, would he still have sold the contaminated goods? Why or why not? (See *Making Ethical Business Decisions*.)

2–2. Ethical Conduct. Internet giant Zoidle, a U.S. company, generated sales of £2.5 billion in the United Kingdom in 2013 (approximately $4 billion in U.S. dollars). Its net profits before taxes on these sales were £200 million, and it paid £6 million in corporate tax, resulting in a tax rate of 3 percent. The corporate tax rate in the United Kingdom is between 20 percent and 24 percent.

The CEO of Zoidle held a press conference stating that he was proud of his company for taking advantage of tax loopholes and for sheltering profits in other nations to avoid paying taxes. He called this practice "capitalism at its finest." He further stated that it would be unethical for Zoidle not to take advantage of loopholes and that it would be borderline illegal to tell shareholders that the company paid more taxes than it had to pay because it felt that it should. Zoidle receives significant benefits for doing business in the United Kingdom, including tremendous sales tax exemptions and some property tax breaks. The United Kingdom relies on the corporate income tax to provide services to the poor and to help run the agency that regulates corporations. Is it ethical for Zoidle to avoid paying taxes? Why or why not? (See *Business Ethics*.)

2–3. ▨ **Spotlight on Pfizer—Corporate Social Responsibility.** Methamphetamine (meth) is an addictive drug made chiefly in small toxic labs (STLs) in homes, tents, barns, or hotel rooms. The manufacturing process is dangerous, often resulting in explosions, burns, and toxic fumes. Government entities spend time and resources to find and destroy STLs, imprison meth dealers and users, treat addicts, and provide services for affected families. Meth cannot be made without ingredients that are also used in cold and allergy medications. Arkansas has one of the highest numbers of STLs in the United States. To recoup the costs of fighting the meth epidemic, twenty counties in Arkansas filed a suit against Pfizer, Inc., which makes cold and allergy medications. What is Pfizer's ethical responsibility here, and to whom is it owed? Why? [*Ashley County, Arkansas v. Pfizer, Inc.,* 552 F.3d 659 (8th Cir. 2009)] (See *Approaches to Ethical Reasoning*.)

2–4. Ethical Leadership. David Krasner, who worked for HSH Nordbank AG, complained that his supervisor, Roland Kiser, fostered an atmosphere of sexism that was demeaning to women. Among other things, Krasner claimed that career advancement was based on "sexual favoritism." He objected to Kiser's relationship with a female employee, Melissa Campfield, who was promoted before more qualified employees, including Krasner. How do a manager's attitudes and actions affect the workplace? [*Krasner v. HSH Nordbank AG,* 680 F.Supp.2d 502 (S.D.N.Y. 2010)] (See *Making Ethical Business Decisions*.)

2–5. Business Ethics on a Global Scale. After the fall of the Soviet Union, the new government of Azerbaijan began converting certain state-controlled industries to private ownership. Ownership in these companies could be purchased through a voucher program. Frederic Bourke, Jr., and Viktor Kozeny wanted to purchase the Azerbaijani oil company, SOCAR, but it was unclear whether the Azerbaijani president would allow SOCAR to be put up for sale. Kozeny met with one of the vice presidents of SOCAR (who was also the son of the president of Azerbaijan) and other Azerbaijani leaders to discuss the sale of SOCAR. To obtain their cooperation, Kozeny set up a series of parent and subsidiary companies through which the Azerbaijani leaders would eventually receive two-thirds of the SOCAR profits without ever investing any of their own funds. In return, the Azerbaijani leaders would attempt to use their influence to convince the president to put SOCAR up for sale. Assume that Bourke and Kozeny are operating out of a U.S. company. Discuss the ethics of this scheme, both in terms of the Foreign Corrupt Practices Act (FCPA) and as a general ethical issue. What duties did Kozeny have under the FCPA? [*United States v. Kozeny,* 667 F.3d 122 (2d Cir. 2011)] (See *Global Business Ethics*.)

2–6. ⚖ **Business Case Problem with Sample Answer— Online Privacy.** Facebook, Inc., launched a program called "Beacon" that automatically updated the profiles of users on Facebook's social networking site when those users had any activity on Beacon "partner" sites. For example, one partner site was Blockbuster.com. When a user rented or purchased a movie through Blockbuster.com, the user's Facebook profile would be updated to share the purchase. The Beacon program was set up as a default setting, so users never consented to the program, but they could opt out. What are the ethical implications of an opt-in program versus an opt-out program in social media? [*Lane v. Facebook, Inc.,* 696 F.3d 811 (9th Cir. 2012)] (See *Business Ethics and Social Media.*)

—For a sample answer to Problem 2–6, go to Appendix E at the end of this text.

2–7. Business Ethics. Mark Ramun worked as a manager for Allied Erecting and Dismantling Co. where he had a tense relationship with his father, John Ramun, who was also Allied's president. After more than ten years, Mark left Allied, taking 15,000 pages of Allied's documents on DVDs and CDs (trade secrets). Later, he joined Allied's competitor, Genesis Equipment & Manufacturing, Inc. Genesis soon developed a piece of equipment that incorporated elements of Allied equipment. How might business ethics have been violated in these circumstances? Discuss. [*Allied Erecting and Dismantling Co. v. Genesis Equipment & Manufacturing, Inc.,* 2013 WL 85907 (6th Cir. 2013)] (See *Making Ethical Business Decisions.*)

2–8. Business Ethics. Stephen Glass became infamous as a dishonest journalist after fabricating the content of more than forty articles for *The New Republic* magazine and other publications. He also manufactured supporting materials to delude *The New Republic's* fact checkers and avoid detection. At the time, he was a law student at Georgetown University. Later, Glass applied for admission to the California bar. The California Supreme Court denied his application, citing "numerous instances of dishonesty and disingenuousness" during his "rehabilitation" following the exposure of his misdeeds. How do these circumstances underscore the importance of ethics? Discuss. [*In re Glass,* 58 Cal.4th 500, 316 P.3d 1199 (2014)] (See *Business Ethics.*)

2–9. ⬄ **A Question of Ethics—Consumer Rights.** Best Buy, a national electronics retailer, offered a credit card that allowed users to earn "reward points" that could be redeemed for discounts on Best Buy goods. After reading a newspaper advertisement for the card, Gary Davis applied for, and was given, a credit card. As part of the application process, he visited a Web page containing Frequently Asked Questions as well as terms and conditions for the card. He clicked on a button affirming that he understood the terms and conditions. When Davis received his card, it came with seven brochures about the card and the reward point program. As he read the brochures, he discovered that a $59 annual fee would be charged for the card. Davis went back to the Web pages he had visited and found a statement that the card "may" have an annual fee. Davis sued, claiming that the company did not adequately disclose the fee. [*Davis v. HSBC Bank Nevada, N.A.,* 691 F.3d 1152 (9th Cir. 2012)] (See *Business Ethics.*)

1. Online applications frequently have click-on buttons or check boxes for consumers to acknowledge that they have read and understand the terms and conditions of applications or purchases. Often, the terms and conditions are so long that they cannot all be seen on one screen and users must scroll to view the entire document. Is it unethical for companies to put terms and conditions, especially terms that may cost the consumer, in an electronic document that is too long to read on one screen? Why or why not? Does this differ from having a consumer sign a hard-copy document with terms and conditions printed on it? Why or why not?

2. The Truth-in-Lending Act requires that credit terms be clearly and conspicuously disclosed in application materials. Assuming that the Best Buy credit-card materials had sufficient legal disclosures, discuss the ethical aspects of businesses strictly following the language of the law as compared to following the intent of the law.

Appendix to Chapter 2: Costco Code of Ethics

COSTCO

CODE OF ETHICS

By Jim Sinegal

OBEY THE LAW

The law is irrefutable! Absent a moral imperative to challenge a law, we must conduct our business in total compliance with the laws of every community where we do business.

- Comply with all statutes.
- Cooperate with authorities.
- Respect all public officials and their positions.
- Avoid all conflict of interest issues with public officials.
- Comply with all disclosure and reporting requirements.
- Comply with safety and security standards for all products sold.
- Exceed ecological standards required in every community where we do business.
- Comply with all applicable wage and hour laws.
- Comply with all applicable anti-trust laws.
- Protect "inside information" that has not been released to the general public.

TAKE CARE OF OUR MEMBERS

The member is our key to success. If we don't keep our members happy, little else that we do will make a difference.

- Provide top-quality products at the best prices in the market.
- Provide a safe shopping environment in our warehouses.
- Provide only products that meet applicable safety and health standards.
- Sell only products from manufacturers who comply with "truth in advertising/packaging" standards.
- Provide our members with a 100% satisfaction guaranteed warranty on every product and service we sell, including their membership fee.
- Assure our members that every product we sell is authentic in make and in representation of performance.
- Make our shopping environment a pleasant experience by making our members feel welcome as our guests.
- Provide products to our members that will be ecologically sensitive.

Our member is our reason for being. If they fail to show up, we cannot survive. Our members have extended a "trust" to Costco by virtue of paying a fee to shop with us. We can't let them down or they will simply go away. We must always operate in the following manner when dealing with our members:
Rule #1 – The member is always right.
Rule #2 – In the event the member is ever wrong, refer to rule #1.

There are plenty of shopping alternatives for our members. We will succeed only if we do not violate the trust they have extended to us. We must be committed at every level of our company, with every ounce of energy and grain of creativity we have, to constantly strive to "bring goods to market at a lower price."

If we do these four things throughout our organization, we will realize our ultimate goal, which is to REWARD OUR SHAREHOLDERS.

TAKE CARE OF OUR EMPLOYEES

To claim "people are our most important asset" is true and an understatement. Each employee has been hired for a very important job. Jobs such as stocking the shelves, ringing members' orders, buying products, and paying our bills are jobs we would all choose to perform because of their importance. The employees hired to perform these jobs are performing as management's "alter egos." Every employee, whether they are in a Costco warehouse, or whether they work in the regional or corporate offices, is a Costco ambassador trained to give our members professional, courteous treatment.

Today we have warehouse managers who were once stockers and callers, and vice presidents who were once in clerical positions for Costco. We believe that Costco's future executive officers are currently working in our warehouses, depots, buying offices, and accounting departments, as well as in our home offices.

To that end, we are committed to these principles:

- Provide a safe work environment.
- Pay a fair wage.
- Make every job challenging, but make it fun!
- Consider the loss of any employee as a failure on the part of the company and a loss to the organization.
- Teach our people how to do their jobs and how to improve personally and professionally.
- Promote from within the company to achieve the goal of a minimum of 80% of management positions being filled by current employees.
- Create an "open door" attitude at all levels of the company that is dedicated to "fairness and listening."

RESPECT OUR VENDORS

Our vendors are our partners in business and for us to prosper as a company, they must prosper with us. It is important that our vendors understand that we will be tough negotiators, but fair in our treatment of them.

- Treat all vendors and their representatives as you would expect to be treated if visiting their places of business.
- Pay all bills within the allocated time frame.
- Honor all commitments.
- Protect all vendor property assigned to Costco as though it were our own.
- Always be thoughtful and candid in negotiations.
- Provide a careful review process with at least two levels of authorization before terminating business with an existing vendor of more than two years.
- Do not accept gratuities of any kind from a vendor.

These guidelines are exactly that - guidelines, some common sense rules for the conduct of our business. Intended to simplify our jobs, not complicate our lives, these guidelines will not answer every question or solve every problem. At the core of our philosophy as a company must be the implicit understanding that not one of us is required to lie or cheat on behalf of PriceCostco. In fact, dishonest conduct will be tolerated. To do any less would be unfair to the overwhelming majority of our employees who support and respect Costco's commitment to ethical business conduct.

If you are ever in doubt as to what course of action to take on a business matter that is open to varying ethical interpretations, take the high road and do what is right.

If you want our help, we are always available for advice and counsel. That's our job and we welcome your questions or comments.

Our continued success depends on you. We thank each of you for your contribution to our past success and for the high standards you have insisted upon in our company.

"Truth in advertising/packaging" legal standards are part of the statutes and regulations that are discussed in Chapter 20, which deals with consumer law.

If the company did not provide products that comply with safety and health standards, it could be held liable in civil suits on legal grounds that are classified as torts (see Chapter 5).

Disclosure of "inside information" that constitutes trade secrets could subject an employee to civil liability or criminal prosecution (see Chapters 6 and 8).

Antitrust laws apply to illegal restraints of trade–arrangement between competitors to set prices, for example, or an attempt by one company to control an entire market. Antitrust laws will be discussed in Chapter 23.

Failure to comply with "ecological" standards could be a violation of environmental laws (see Chapter 21).

Accepting "gratuities" from a vendor might be interpreted as accepting a bribe. This can be a crime (see Chapter 6). In an international context, a bribe can be a violation of the Foreign Corrupt Practices Act as discussed in this chapter.

If the company fails to honor one of its commitments, it may be sued for breach of contract (see Chapter 11).

Failing to pay bills when they become due could subject the company to the creditors' remedies discussed in Chapter 13. The company might even be forced into involuntary bankruptcy.

Promotions and other benefits of employment cannot be granted or withheld on the basis of discrimination. This is against the law. Employment discrimination is the subject of Chapter 18.

Safety standards for the work environment are governed by the Occupational Safety and Health Act and other statutes. Laws regulating safety in the workplace will be discussed in Chapter 17.

Costco Background

Costco Wholesale Corporation operates a chain of cash-and-carry membership warehouses that sell high-quality, nationally branded, and selected private-label merchandise at low prices. Its target markets include both businesses that buy goods for commercial use or resale and individuals who are employees or members of specific organizations and associations. The company tries to reach high sales volume and fast inventory turnover by offering a limited choice of merchandise in many product groups at competitive prices.

The company takes a strong position on behaving ethically in all transactions and relationships. It expects employees to behave ethically. For example, no one can accept gratuities from vendors. The company also expects employees to behave ethically, according to domestic ethical standards, in any country in which it operates.

Courts and Alternative Dispute Resolution

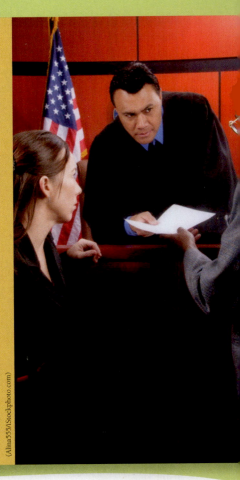

(Alina555/iStockphoto.com)

LEARNING OBJECTIVES

The five learning objectives below are designed to help improve your understanding of the chapter. After reading this chapter, you should be able to answer the following questions:

1. What is judicial review? How and when was the power of judicial review established?

2. Before a court can hear a case, it must have jurisdiction. Over what must it have jurisdiction? How are the courts applying traditional jurisdictional concepts to cases involving Internet transactions?

3. What is the difference between a trial court and an appellate court?

4. What is discovery, and how does electronic discovery differ from traditional discovery?

5. What are three alternative methods of resolving disputes?

"An eye for an eye will make the whole world blind."
—Mahatma Gandhi, 1869–1948 (Indian political and spiritual leader)

Every society needs to have an established method for resolving disputes. Without one, as Mahatma Gandhi implied in the chapter-opening quotation, the biblical "eye for an eye" would lead to anarchy. This is particularly true in the business world—almost every businessperson will face a lawsuit at some time in his or her career. For this reason, anyone involved in business needs to have an understanding of court systems in the United States, as well as the various methods of dispute resolution that can be pursued outside the courts.

In this chapter, after examining the judiciary's overall role in the American governmental scheme, we discuss some basic requirements that must be met before a party may bring a lawsuit before a particular court. We then look at the court systems of the United States in some detail and, to clarify judicial procedures, follow a hypothetical case through a state court system. Because Islamic legal systems are prevalent in many parts of the world, some judges in this country have been asked to accept some Islamic law. You will read later in this chapter about this controversy.

Throughout this chapter, we indicate how court doctrines and procedures are being adapted to the needs of a cyber age. The chapter concludes with an overview of some alternative methods of settling disputes, including online dispute resolution.

The Judiciary's Role

As you learned in Chapter 1, the body of American law includes the federal and state constitutions, statutes passed by legislative bodies, administrative law, and the case decisions and legal principles that form the common law. These laws would be meaningless, however, without the courts to interpret and apply them. This is the essential role of the judiciary—the courts—in the American governmental system: to interpret and apply the law.

Judicial Review

As the branch of government entrusted with interpreting the laws, the judiciary can decide, among other things, whether the laws or actions of the other two branches are constitutional. The process for making such a determination is known as **judicial review**. The power of judicial review enables the judicial branch to act as a check on the other two branches of government, in line with the checks-and-balances system established by the U.S. Constitution. (Today, nearly all nations with constitutional democracies, including Canada, France, and Germany, have some form of judicial review.)

The Origins of Judicial Review in the United States

The power of judicial review is not mentioned in the U.S. Constitution (although many constitutional scholars believe that the founders intended the judiciary to have this power). The United States Supreme Court explicitly established this power in 1803 in the case *Marbury v. Madison*.[1] In that decision, the Court stated, "It is emphatically the province [authority] and duty of the Judicial Department to say what the law is. . . . If two laws conflict with each other, the courts must decide on the operation of each. . . . [I]f both [a] law and the Constitution apply to a particular case, . . . the Court must determine which of these conflicting rules governs the case. This is of the very essence of judicial duty." Since the *Marbury v. Madison* decision, the power of judicial review has remained unchallenged. Today, this power is exercised by both federal and state courts.

Basic Judicial Requirements

Before a court can hear a lawsuit, certain requirements must first be met. These requirements relate to jurisdiction, venue, and standing to sue. We examine each of these important concepts here.

Jurisdiction

In Latin, *juris* means "law," and *diction* means "to speak." Thus, "the power to speak the law" is the literal meaning of the term **jurisdiction.** Before any court can hear a case, it must have jurisdiction over the person (or company) against whom the suit is brought (the defendant) or over the property involved in the suit. The court must also have jurisdiction over the subject matter of the dispute.

Learning Objective 1
What is judicial review? How and when was the power of judicial review established?

Judicial Review The process by which a court decides on the constitutionality of legislative enactments and actions of the executive branch.

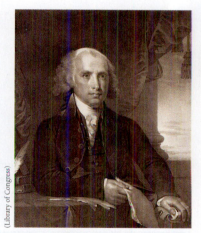
(Library of Congress)

James Madison (1751–1836) wrote in favor of the states' adopting the new Constitution. What did he think of judicial review?

Jurisdiction The authority of a court to hear and decide a specific case.

---

1. 5 U.S. (1 Cranch) 137, 2 L.Ed. 60 (1803).

Jurisdiction over Persons or Property
Generally, a court can exercise personal jurisdiction (*in personam* jurisdiction) over any person or business that resides in a certain geographic area. A state trial court, for example, normally has jurisdictional authority over residents (including businesses) in a particular area of the state, such as a county or district. A state's highest court (often called the state supreme court, as will be discussed shortly) has jurisdiction over all residents of that state.

A court can also exercise jurisdiction over property that is located within its boundaries. This kind of jurisdiction is known as *in rem* jurisdiction, or "jurisdiction over the thing." **EXAMPLE 3.1** A dispute arises over the ownership of a boat in dry dock in Fort Lauderdale, Florida. The boat is owned by an Ohio resident, over whom a Florida court normally cannot exercise personal jurisdiction. The other party to the dispute is a resident of Nebraska. In this situation, a lawsuit concerning the boat could be brought in a Florida state court on the basis of the court's *in rem* jurisdiction. ●

Long Arm Statute A state statute that permits a state to exercise jurisdiction over nonresident defendants.

Long Arm Statutes Under the authority of a state **long arm statute,** a court can exercise personal jurisdiction over certain out-of-state defendants based on activities that took place within the state. Before exercising long arm jurisdiction over a nonresident, however, the court must be convinced that the defendant had sufficient contacts, or *minimum contacts,* with the state to justify the jurisdiction.[2] Generally, this means that the defendant must have enough of a connection to the state for the judge to conclude that it is fair for the state to exercise power over the defendant. If an out-of-state defendant caused an automobile accident or sold defective goods within the state, for instance, a court will usually find that minimum contacts exist to exercise jurisdiction over that defendant.

CASE EXAMPLE 3.2 After an Xbox game system caught fire in Bonnie Broquet's home in Texas and caused substantial personal injuries, Broquet filed a lawsuit in a Texas court against Ji-Haw Industrial Company, a nonresident company that made the Xbox components. Broquet alleged that Ji-Haw's components were defective and had caused the fire. Ji-Haw argued that the Texas court lacked jurisdiction over it, but in 2008, a state appellate court held that the Texas long arm statute authorized the exercise of jurisdiction over the out-of-state defendant.[3] ●

Similarly, a state may exercise personal jurisdiction over a nonresident defendant who is sued for breaching a contract that was formed within the state, even when that contract was negotiated over the phone or through correspondence. **EXAMPLE 3.3** Sharon Mills, a California resident, forms a corporation to distribute a documentary film on global climate change. Brad Cole, an environmentalist who lives in Ohio, loans the corporation funds that he borrows from an Ohio bank. A year later, the film is still not completed. Mills agrees to repay Cole's loan in a contract arranged through phone calls and correspondence between California and Ohio. When Mills does not repay the loan, Cole files a lawsuit in an Ohio court. In this situation, the Ohio court can likely exercise jurisdiction over Mills because her phone calls and letters have established sufficient contacts with the state of Ohio. ●

Suppose that a young gamer is injured because Microsoft's Xbox, shown below, released an electrical shock. Who can the parents sue?

(Bloomberg/Getty Images)

Corporate Contacts Because corporations are considered legal persons, courts use the same principles to determine whether it is fair to exercise jurisdiction over a corporation.[4] A corporation normally is subject to personal

---

2. The minimum-contacts standard was established in *International Shoe Co. v. State of Washington,* 326 U.S. 310, 66 S.Ct. 154, 90 L.Ed. 95 (1945).
3. *Ji-Haw Industrial Co. v. Broquet,* 2008 WL 441822 (Tex.App.—San Antonio 2008).
4. In the eyes of the law, corporations are "legal persons"—entities that can sue and be sued. See Chapter 15.

jurisdiction in the state in which it is incorporated, has its principal office, and/or is doing business. Courts apply the minimum-contacts test to determine if they can exercise jurisdiction over out-of-state corporations.

The minimum-contacts requirement is usually met if the corporation advertises or sells its products within the state, or places its goods into the "stream of commerce" with the intent that the goods be sold in the state. **EXAMPLE 3.4** A business is incorporated under the laws of Maine but has a branch office and manufacturing plant in Georgia. The corporation also advertises and sells its products in Georgia. These activities would likely constitute sufficient contacts with the state of Georgia to allow a Georgia court to exercise jurisdiction over the corporation. •

Some corporations do not sell or advertise products or place any goods in the stream of commerce. Determining what constitutes minimum contacts in these situations can be more difficult. **CASE EXAMPLE 3.5** Independence Plating Corporation is a New Jersey corporation that provides metal-coating services. Its only office and all of its personnel are located in New Jersey, and it does not advertise out of state. Independence had a long-standing business relationship with Southern Prestige Industries, Inc., a North Carolina company. Eventually, Southern Prestige filed suit in North Carolina against Independence for defective workmanship. Independence argued that North Carolina did not have jurisdiction over it, but the court held that Independence had sufficient minimum contacts with the state to justify jurisdiction. The two parties had exchanged thirty-two separate purchase orders in a period of less than twelve months.[5] •

Jurisdiction over Subject Matter

Jurisdiction over subject matter is a limitation on the types of cases a court can hear. In both the federal and state court systems, there are courts of *general* (unlimited) *jurisdiction* and courts of *limited jurisdiction*. An example of a court of general jurisdiction is a state trial court or a federal district court. An example of a state court of limited jurisdiction is a probate court. **Probate courts** are state courts that handle only matters relating to the transfer of a person's assets and obligations after that person's death, including matters relating to the custody and guardianship of children. An example of a federal court of limited subject-matter jurisdiction is a bankruptcy court. **Bankruptcy courts** handle only bankruptcy proceedings, which are governed by federal bankruptcy law (discussed in Chapter 13).

A court's jurisdiction over subject matter is usually defined in the statute or constitution creating the court. In both the federal and state court systems, a court's subject-matter jurisdiction can be limited not only by the subject of the lawsuit but also by the amount in controversy, by whether a case is a felony (a more serious type of crime) or a misdemeanor (a less serious type of crime), or by whether the proceeding is a trial or an appeal.

Original and Appellate Jurisdiction

The distinction between courts of original jurisdiction and courts of appellate jurisdiction normally lies in whether the case is being heard for the first time. Courts having original jurisdiction are courts of the first instance, or trial courts—that is, courts in which lawsuits begin, trials take place, and evidence is presented. In the federal court system, the *district courts* are trial courts. In the various state court systems, the trial courts are known by various names, as will be discussed shortly.

The key point here is that any court having original jurisdiction is normally known as a trial court. Courts having appellate jurisdiction act as reviewing courts, or appellate courts. In general, cases can be brought before appellate courts only on appeal from an order or a judgment of a trial court or other lower court.

Probate Court A state court of limited jurisdiction that conducts proceedings relating to the settlement of a deceased person's estate.

Bankruptcy Court A federal court of limited jurisdiction that handles only bankruptcy proceedings, which are governed by federal bankruptcy law.

---

5. *Southern Prestige Industries, Inc. v. Independence Plating Corp.*, 690 S.E.2d 768 (N.C. 2010).

(iStockphoto.com/Alina Solovyova-Vincent/Alina555)

Can a judge hear any case?

Federal Question A question that pertains to the U.S. Constitution, an act of Congress, or a treaty and provides a basis for federal jurisdiction in a case.

Diversity of Citizenship A basis for federal court jurisdiction over a lawsuit between citizens of different states and countries.

Jurisdiction of the Federal Courts   Because the federal government is a government of limited powers, the jurisdiction of the federal courts is limited. Federal courts have subject-matter jurisdiction in two situations.

Federal Questions   Article III of the U.S. Constitution establishes the boundaries of federal judicial power. Section 2 of Article III states that "[t]he judicial Power shall extend to all Cases, in Law and Equity, arising under this Constitution, the Laws of the United States, and Treaties made, or which shall be made, under their Authority." This clause means that whenever a plaintiff's cause of action is based, at least in part, on the U.S. Constitution, a treaty, or a federal law, then a **federal question** arises, and the federal courts have jurisdiction. Any lawsuit involving a federal question, such as a person's rights under the U.S. Constitution, can originate in a federal court. Note that in a case based on a federal question, a federal court will apply federal law.

Diversity of Citizenship   Federal district courts can also exercise original jurisdiction over cases involving **diversity of citizenship.** The most common type of diversity jurisdiction has two requirements:[6]

1. The plaintiff and defendant must be residents of different states.
2. The dollar amount in controversy must exceed $75,000.

For purposes of diversity jurisdiction, a corporation is a citizen of both the state in which it is incorporated and the state in which its principal place of business is located. A case involving diversity of citizenship can be filed in the appropriate federal district court. If the case starts in a state court, it can sometimes be transferred, or "removed," to a federal court. A large percentage of the cases filed in federal courts each year are based on diversity of citizenship.

As noted, a federal court will apply federal law in cases involving federal questions. In a case based on diversity of citizenship, in contrast, a federal court will apply the relevant state law (which is often the law of the state in which the court sits).

Concurrent Jurisdiction Jurisdiction that exists when two different courts have the power to hear a case.

Exclusive Jurisdiction Jurisdiction that exists when a case can be heard only in a particular court or type of court.

Exclusive versus Concurrent Jurisdiction   When both federal and state courts have the power to hear a case, as is true in lawsuits involving diversity of citizenship, **concurrent jurisdiction** exists. When cases can be tried only in federal courts or only in state courts, **exclusive jurisdiction** exists. Federal courts have exclusive jurisdiction in cases involving federal crimes, bankruptcy, most patent and copyright claims, suits against the United States, and in some areas of admiralty law (law governing transportation on the seas and ocean waters). State courts also have exclusive jurisdiction over certain subject matter—for instance, divorce and adoption.

When concurrent jurisdiction exists, a party may bring a suit in either a federal court or a state court. Many factors can affect a party's decision to litigate in a federal versus a state court. Examples include the availability of different remedies, the distance to the respective courthouses, or the experience or reputation of a particular judge. For instance, if the dispute involves a trade secret, a party might conclude that a federal court—which has exclusive jurisdiction over copyrights, patents, and trademarks—would have more expertise in the matter.

A resident of another state might also choose a federal court over a state court if he or she is concerned that a state court might be biased against an out-of-state plaintiff. In

---

6. Diversity jurisdiction also exists in cases between (1) a foreign country and citizens of a state or of different states and (2) citizens of a state and citizens or subjects of a foreign country. These bases for diversity jurisdiction are less commonly used.

contrast, a plaintiff might choose to litigate in a state court if it has a reputation for award-ing substantial amounts of damages or if the judge is perceived as being pro-plaintiff. The concepts of exclusive and concurrent jurisdiction are illustrated in Exhibit 3–1.

Jurisdiction in Cyberspace

The Internet's capacity to bypass political and geographic boundaries undercuts the traditional basis on which courts assert personal jurisdiction. As already discussed, for a court to compel a defendant to come before it, there must be at least minimum contacts—the presence of a sales-person within the state, for example. Are there sufficient minimum contacts if the defendant's only connection to a jurisdiction is an ad on a Web site originating from a remote location?

The "Sliding-Scale" Standard   The courts have developed a "sliding-scale" standard to determine when they can exercise personal jurisdiction over an out-of-state defendant based on the defendant's Web activities. The sliding-scale standard identifies three types of Internet business contacts and outlines the following rules for jurisdiction:

1. When the defendant conducts substantial business over the Internet (such as contracts and sales even using a smartphone), jurisdiction is proper.
2. When there is some interactivity through a Web site, jurisdiction may be proper, depending on the circumstances. Even a single contact can satisfy the minimum-contacts requirement in certain situations.
3. When a defendant merely engages in passive advertising on the Web, jurisdiction is never proper. An Internet communication is typically considered passive if people have to voluntarily access it to read the message and active if it is sent to specific individuals.

In certain situations, even a single contact can satisfy the minimum-contacts requirement.
CASE EXAMPLE 3.6   A Louisiana resident, Daniel Crummey, purchased a used recreational vehicle (RV) from sellers in Texas after viewing photos of it on eBay. The sellers' statements on eBay claimed that "everything works great on this RV and will provide comfort and dependability for years to come. This RV will go to Alaska and back without problems!"

Learning Objective 2
Before a court can hear a case, it must have jurisdiction. Over what must it have jurisdiction? How are the courts applying traditional jurisdictional concepts to cases involving Internet transactions?

(Alex Segre/Alamy)

Which court would have jurisdiction over a dispute between an online customer and Amazon.com?

Exhibit 3–1 Exclusive and Concurrent Jurisdiction

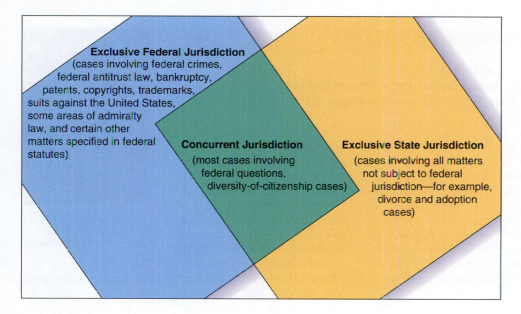

Exclusive Federal Jurisdiction
(cases involving federal crimes, federal antitrust law, bankruptcy, patents, copyrights, trademarks, suits against the United States, some areas of admiralty law, and certain other matters specified in federal statutes)

Concurrent Jurisdiction
(most cases involving federal questions, diversity-of-citizenship cases)

Exclusive State Jurisdiction
(cases involving all matters not subject to federal jurisdiction—for example, divorce and adoption cases)

Crummey picked up the RV in Texas, but on the drive home, the RV quit working. He filed a suit in Louisiana against the sellers alleging that the vehicle was defective, but the sellers claimed that the Louisiana court lacked jurisdiction. Because the sellers had used eBay to market and sell the RV to a Louisiana buyer—and had regularly used eBay to sell vehicles to remote parties in the past—the court found that jurisdiction was proper.[7] •

PREVENTING LEGAL DISPUTES

Those of you with an entrepreneurial spirit may be eager to establish Web sites to promote products and solicit orders. Be aware, however, that you can be sued in states in which you have *never* been physically present if you have had sufficient contacts with residents of those states over the Internet. Before you create a Web site that is the least bit interactive, you need to consult an attorney to find out whether you will be subjecting yourself to jurisdiction in every state. Becoming informed about the extent of your potential exposure to lawsuits in various locations is an important part of preventing litigation.

International Jurisdictional Issues   Because the Internet is global in scope, it obviously raises international jurisdictional issues. The world's courts seem to be developing a standard that echoes the minimum-contacts requirement applied by U.S. courts.

Most courts are indicating that minimum contacts—doing business within the jurisdiction, for example—are enough to compel a defendant to appear and that a physical presence is not necessary. The effect of this standard is that a business firm has to comply with the laws in any jurisdiction in which it targets customers for its products. This situation is complicated by the fact that many countries' laws on particular issues—free speech, for example—are very different from U.S. laws

The following *Spotlight Case* illustrates how federal courts apply a sliding-scale standard to determine if they can exercise jurisdiction over a foreign defendant whose only contact with the United States is through a Web site.

---

7. *Crummey v. Morgan,* 965 So.2d 497 (La.App.1 Cir. 2007). But note that a single sale on eBay does not necessarily confer jurisdiction. Jurisdiction depends on whether the seller regularly uses eBay as a means for doing business with remote buyers. See *Boschetto v. Hansing,* 539 F.3d 1011 (9th Cir. 2008).

Spotlight on Gucci

Case 3.1
Gucci America, Inc. v. Wang Huoqing
United States District Court, Northern District of California, 2011 WL 30972 (2011).

COMPANY PROFILE *Gucci America, Inc., a New York corporation headquartered in New York City, is part of Gucci Group, a global fashion firm with offices in Italy, France, Great Britain, China, and Japan. Gucci makes and sells high-quality luxury goods, including footwear, belts, sunglasses, handbags, wallets, jewelry, fragrances, and children's clothing, which are sold worldwide. In connection with its products, Gucci uses more than twenty federally registered trademarks (trademark law will be discussed in Chapter 8). Gucci also operates a number of boutiques, some of which are located in California.*

BACKGROUND AND FACTS Wang Huoqing, a resident of the People's Republic of China, operates numerous Web sites. When Gucci discovered that Wang Huoqing's Web sites offered for sale counterfeit goods—products that bear Gucci's trademarks but are not genuine Gucci articles— it hired a private investigator in San Jose, California, to buy goods from the Web sites. The investigator purchased a wallet that

(Alessia Pierdomenico/ Bloomberg/GettyImages)

Gucci luxury leather products are often counterfeited. Can Gucci sue an Asian company in the United States, nonetheless?

Spotlight Case 3.1—Continued

was labeled Gucci but was counterfeit. Gucci filed a trademark infringement lawsuit against Wang Huoqing in a federal district court in California seeking damages and an injunction to prevent further infringement. Wang Huoqing was notified of the lawsuit via e-mail but did not appear in court. Gucci asked the court to enter a default judgment—that is, a judgment entered when the defendant fails to appear—but the court first had to determine whether it had personal jurisdiction over Wang Huoqing based on the Internet sales.

IN THE WORDS OF THE COURT . . .
Joseph C. *SPERO*, United States Magistrate Judge.

* * * *

* * * Under California's long-arm statute, federal courts in California may exercise jurisdiction to the extent permitted by the Due Process Clause of the Constitution. The Due Process Clause allows federal courts to exercise jurisdiction where * * * the defendant has had sufficient minimum contacts with the forum to subject him or her to the specific jurisdiction of the court. The courts apply a three-part test to determine whether specific jurisdiction exists:

> (1) The nonresident defendant must do some act or consummate some transaction with the forum or perform some act by which he purposefully avails himself of the privilege of conducting activities in the forum, thereby invoking the benefits and protections of its laws; (2) the claim must be one which arises out of or results from the defendant's forum-related activities; and (3) exercise of jurisdiction must be reasonable.

* * * *

In order to satisfy the first prong of the test for specific jurisdiction, a defendant must have either purposefully availed itself of [taken advantage of] the privilege of conducting business activities within the forum or purposefully directed activities toward the forum. *Purposeful availment typically consists of action taking place in the forum that invokes the benefits and protections of the laws of the forum, such as executing or performing a contract within the forum.* To show purposeful availment, a plaintiff must show that the defendant "engage[d] in some form of affirmative conduct allowing or promoting the transaction of business within the forum state." [Emphasis added.]

"In the Internet context, the Ninth Circuit utilizes a sliding scale analysis under which 'passive' websites do not create sufficient contacts to establish purposeful availment, whereas interactive websites may create sufficient contacts, depending on how interactive the website is." * * * *Personal jurisdiction is appropriate where an entity is conducting business over the Internet and has offered for sale and sold its products to forum [California] residents.* [Emphasis added.]

Here, the allegations and evidence presented by Plaintiffs in support of the Motion are sufficient to show purposeful availment on the part of Defendant Wang Huoqing. Plaintiffs have alleged that Defendant operates "fully interactive Internet websites operating under the Subject Domain Names" and have presented evidence in the form of copies of web pages showing that the websites are, in fact, interactive. * * * Additionally, Plaintiffs allege Defendant is conducting counterfeiting and infringing activities within this Judicial District and has advertised and sold his counterfeit goods in the State of California. * * * Plaintiffs have also presented evidence of one actual sale within this district, made by investigator Robert Holmes from the website bag2do.cn. * * * Finally, Plaintiffs have presented evidence that Defendant Wang Huoqing owns or controls the twenty-eight websites listed in the Motion for Default Judgment. * * * Such commercial activity in the forum amounts to purposeful availment of the privilege of conducting activities within the forum, thus invoking the benefits and protections of its laws. Accordingly, the Court concludes that Defendant's contacts with California are sufficient to show purposeful availment.

DECISION AND REMEDY   The U.S. District Court for the Northern District of California held that it had personal jurisdiction over the foreign defendant, Wang Huoqing. The court entered a default judgment against Wang Huoqing and granted Gucci an injunction.

WHAT IF THE FACTS WERE DIFFERENT?   *Suppose that Gucci had not presented evidence that Wang Huoqing had made one actual sale through his Web site to a resident (the private investigator) of the court's district. Would the court still have found that it had personal jurisdiction over Wang Huoqing? Why or why not?*

THE LEGAL ENVIRONMENT DIMENSION   *Is it relevant to the analysis of jurisdiction that Gucci America's principal place of business is in New York rather than California? Explain.*

Venue

Jurisdiction has to do with whether a court has authority to hear a case involving specific persons, property, or subject matter. **Venue**[8] is concerned with the most appropriate physical location for a trial. Two state courts (or two federal courts) may have the authority to

Venue The geographic district in which a legal action is tried and from which the jury is selected.

---

8. Pronounced *ven-yoo.*

exercise jurisdiction over a case, but it may be more appropriate or convenient to hear the case in one court than in the other.

Basically, the concept of venue reflects the policy that a court trying a suit should be in the geographic neighborhood (usually the county) where the incident leading to the lawsuit occurred or where the parties involved in the lawsuit reside. Venue in a civil case typically is where the defendant resides, whereas venue in a criminal case normally is where the crime occurred.

Pretrial publicity or other factors, though, may require a change of venue to another community, especially in criminal cases when the defendant's right to a fair and impartial jury has been impaired. **EXAMPLE 3.7** Police raid a compound of religious polygamists in Texas and remove many children from the ranch. Authorities suspect that some of the girls were being sexually and physically abused. The raid receives a great deal of media attention, and the people living in the nearby towns are likely influenced by this publicity. In this situation, if the government files criminal charges against a member of the religious sect, that individual may request—and will probably receive—a change of venue to another location. •

Note, though, that venue has lost some significance in today's world because of the Internet and 24/7 news reporting. Courts now rarely grant requests for a change of venue. Because everyone has instant access to all information about a purported crime, courts reason that no community is more or less informed or prejudiced for or against a defendant.

Standing to Sue

Standing to Sue The legal requirement that an individual must have a sufficient stake in a controversy before he or she can bring a lawsuit.

Before a person can bring a lawsuit before a court, the party must have **standing to sue**, or a sufficient "stake" in the matter to justify seeking relief through the court system. In other words, to have standing, a party must have a legally protected and tangible interest at stake in the litigation.

The party bringing the lawsuit must have suffered a harm, or have been threatened by a harm, as a result of the action about which she or he has complained. At times, a person can have standing to sue on behalf of another person, such as a minor (child) or mentally incompetent person. Standing to sue also requires that the controversy at issue be a **justiciable**[9] **controversy**—a controversy that is real and substantial, as opposed to hypothetical or academic.

Justiciable Controversy A controversy that is not hypothetical or academic but real and substantial; a requirement that must be satisfied before a court will hear a case.

CASE EXAMPLE 3.8 Harold Wagner obtained a loan through M.S.T. Mortgage Group to buy a house in Texas. After the sale, M.S.T. transferred its interest in the loan to another lender, which assigned it to another lender, as is common in the mortgage industry. Eventually, when Wagner failed to make the loan payments, CitiMortgage, Inc., notified him that it was going to foreclose on the property and sell the house. Wagner filed a lawsuit claiming that the lenders had improperly assigned the mortgage loan. In 2014, a federal district court ruled that Wagner lacked standing to assert defects in the assignment. Under Texas law, only the parties directly involved in an assignment can challenge its validity. In this case, the assignment was between two lenders and did not directly involve Wagner.[10] •

The State and Federal Court Systems

As mentioned earlier in this chapter, each state has its own court system. Additionally, there is a system of federal courts. Even though there are fifty-two court systems—one for each of the fifty states, one for the District of Columbia, plus a federal system—similarities abound.

---

9. Pronounced *jus-tish-uh-bul*.
10. *Wagner v. CitiMortgage, Inc.*, 2014 WL 462655 (N.D. Tex. 2014).

Exhibit 3–2 illustrates the basic organizational structure characteristic of the court systems in many states. The exhibit also shows how the federal court system is structured. Keep in mind that the federal courts are not superior to the state courts. They are simply an independent system of courts, which derives its authority from Article III, Sections 1 and 2, of the U.S. Constitution. We turn now to an examination of these court systems, beginning with the state courts.

The State Court Systems

Typically, a state court system will include several levels, or tiers, of courts. As indicated in Exhibit 3–2, state courts may include (1) trial courts of limited jurisdiction, (2) trial courts of general jurisdiction, (3) appellate courts, and (4) the state's highest court (often called the state supreme court).

Generally, any person who is a party to a lawsuit has the opportunity to plead the case before a trial court and then, if he or she loses, before at least one level of appellate court. If the case involves a federal statute or a federal constitutional issue, the decision of a state supreme court on that issue may be further appealed to the United States Supreme Court. (See this chapter's *Managerial Strategy* feature that follows for a discussion of how state budget cuts are making it more difficult to bring cases in some state courts.)

Trial Courts   Trial courts are exactly what their name implies—courts in which trials are held and testimony taken. State trial courts have either general or limited jurisdiction. Trial courts that have general jurisdiction as to subject matter may be called county, district, superior, or circuit courts.[11] The jurisdiction of these courts is often determined by the size of the county in which the court sits. State trial courts of general jurisdiction have jurisdiction over a wide variety of subjects, including both civil disputes and criminal prosecutions. (In some states, trial courts of general jurisdiction may hear appeals from courts of limited jurisdiction.)

---

11. The name in Ohio is court of common pleas, and the name in New York is supreme court.

Exhibit 3–2 The State and Federal Court Systems

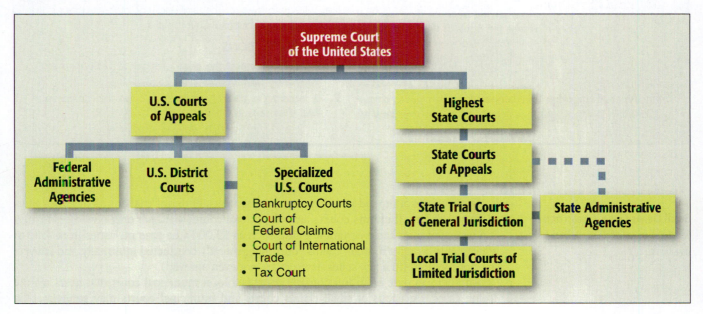

MANAGERIAL STRATEGY

Budget Cuts for State Courts Can Affect Businesses

In the United States, businesses use the courts far more than anyone else. Most civil court cases involve a business suing another business for breach of contract or fraud, for instance. Additionally, when one company fails to pay another company for products or services, the unpaid company will often turn to the court system. If that firm does not have ready access to the courts, its financial stability can be put at risk.

Court Budgets Have Been Reduced According to the National Center for State Courts, since 2008 forty-two state legislatures have reduced funding for their state courts. California's courts have experienced the steepest cuts—$844 million from their annual budget since 2011. Recently, the Alabama legislature cut its court funding by almost 9 percent. As a result, the state's chief justice ordered courthouses to close on Fridays. The number of weeks that jury trials are available to civil litigants in Alabama has been reduced by 50 percent.

Intellectual Property Cases Take Longer to Resolve Today, the value of a company's intellectual property, such as its copyrights and patents, often exceeds the value of its physical property. Not surprisingly, disputes over intellectual property have grown in number and importance. As a result of the court budget cuts, these disputes also take longer to resolve. In California, for example, a typical patent lawsuit used to last twelve months. Today, that same lawsuit might take three to five years.

Investors are reluctant to invest in a company that is the object of a patent or copyright lawsuit because they fear that if the company loses, it may lose the rights to its most valuable product. Consequently, when litigation drags on for years, some companies may suffer because investors abandon them even though the companies are otherwise healthy.

Other Types of Litigation Take Longer, Too Other types of lawsuits are also taking longer to conclude. Now attorneys must tell

businesses to consider not only the cost of bringing a lawsuit, but also the length of time involved. The longer the litigation lasts, the larger the legal bills and the greater the drain on company employees' time. Roy Weinstein, managing director of Micronomics in California, argues that the economic impact of court delays on businesses is substantial. During the years that a lawsuit can take, some businesses find that they cannot expand or hire new employees, and they are reluctant to spend on additional marketing and advertising.

In fact, it is not unusual for a company to win its case but end up going out of business. As a result of putting its business on hold for years, the company becomes insolvent.

Some Meritorious Cases Are Never Filed Facing long delays in litigation with potential negative effects on their companies, business managers are becoming reluctant to bring lawsuits, even when their cases clearly have merit. In Alabama, for instance, the number of civil cases filed has dropped by more than a third in the last few years. Judge J. Scott Vowell of Jefferson County attributes this decline to delays and higher court costs.

MANAGERIAL IMPLICATIONS

Before bringing a lawsuit, a manager must now take into account the possibility of long delays before the case is resolved. A cost-benefit analysis for undertaking litigation must include the delays in the calculations. Managers can no longer just stand on principle because they know that they are right and that they will win a lawsuit. They have to look at the bigger picture, which includes substantial court delays.

BUSINESS QUESTIONS

1. What are some of the costs of increased litigation delays caused by court budget cuts?
2. In response to budget cuts, many states have increased their filing fees. Is this fair? Why or why not?

Small Claims Court A special court in which parties can litigate small claims without an attorney.

Some courts of limited jurisdiction are called special inferior trial courts or minor judiciary courts. **Small claims courts** are inferior trial courts that hear only civil cases involving claims of less than a certain amount, such as $5,000 (the amount varies from state to state). Suits brought in small claims courts are generally conducted informally, and lawyers are not required (in a few states, lawyers are not even allowed).

Another example of an inferior trial court is a local municipal court that hears mainly traffic cases. Decisions of small claims courts and municipal courts may sometimes be appealed to a state trial court of general jurisdiction. Other courts of limited jurisdiction as to subject matter include domestic relations or family courts, which handle primarily divorce actions and child-custody disputes, and probate courts, as mentioned earlier. A few states have even established Islamic law courts, which are courts of limited jurisdiction that serve the American Muslim community. (See this chapter's *Beyond Our Borders* feature for a discussion of the rise of Islamic law courts.)

Appellate, or Reviewing, Courts

Every state has at least one court of appeals (appellate court, or reviewing court), which may be an intermediate appellate court or the state's highest court. About three-fourths of the states have intermediate appellate courts. Generally, courts of appeals do not conduct new trials, in which evidence is submitted to the court and witnesses are examined. Rather, an appellate court panel of three

BEYOND OUR BORDERS   Islamic Law Courts Abroad and at Home

As mentioned in Chapter 1, Islamic law is one of the world's three most common legal systems, along with civil law and common law systems. In most Islamic countries, the law is based on *sharia*, a system of law derived from the Qur'an and the sayings and doings of Muhammad and his companions. Today, many non-Islamic countries are establishing Islamic courts for their Muslim citizens.

Islamic Law in Britain, Canada, and Belgium

For several years, Great Britain has had councils that arbitrate disputes between British Muslims involving child custody, property, employment, and housing. These councils do not deal with criminal law or with any civil issues that would put *sharia* in direct conflict with British statutory law. Most Islamic law cases involve marriage or divorce. Starting in 2008, Britain officially sanctioned the authority of *sharia* judges to rule on divorce and financial disputes of Muslim couples. Britain now has eighty-five officially recognized *sharia* courts that have the full power of their equivalent courts within the traditional British judicial system.

In Ontario, Canada, a group of Canadian Muslims established a judicial tribunal using *sharia*. To date, this tribunal has resolved only marital disagreements and some other civil disputes. Under Ontario law, the regular judicial system must uphold such agreements as long as they are voluntary and negotiated through an arbitrator. Any agreements that violate Canada's Charter of Rights and Freedoms will not be upheld.

In 2011, Belgium established its first *sharia* court. This court also handles primarily family law disputes for Muslim immigrants in Belgium.

Islamic Law Courts in the United States

The use of Islamic courts in the United States has been somewhat controversial. The legality of arbitration clauses that require disputes to be settled in Islamic courts has been upheld by regular state courts in some states, including Minnesota and Texas.

In the Texas case, an American Muslim couple was married and was issued an Islamic marriage certificate. Years later, a dispute arose over marital property and the nonpayment of a "dowry for the bride." The parties involved had signed an arbitration agreement stating that all claims and disputes were to be submitted to arbitration in front of the Texas Islamic Court. A Texas appeals court ruled that the arbitration agreement was valid and enforceable.[a]

In some other states, however, there has been a public backlash against the use of Islamic courts. For instance, in Detroit, Michigan, which has a large American Muslim population, a controversy erupted over the community's attempt to establish Islamic courts. A legislator in Michigan then introduced legislation that would prohibit judges from enforcing foreign laws. More than twenty other states have also attempted to pass laws to restrict judges from consulting *sharia* law. Voters in Oklahoma enacted a referendum banning courts from considering *sharia* law, but the ban was later held to be unconstitutional.[b]

Critical Thinking

One of the arguments against allowing sharia courts in the United States is that we would no longer have a common legal framework within our society. Do you agree or disagree? Why?

---

a. *Jabri v. Qaddura,* 108 S.W.3d 404 (Tex.App.— Fort Worth 2003).

b. *Awad v. Zirax,* 670 F.3d 1111 (10th Cir. 2012). A lower court later issued a permanent injunction to prevent enforcement of the ban, *Awad v. Zirax,* 966 F.Supp.2d 1198 (W.D. Okla. 2013).

or more judges reviews the record of the case on appeal, which includes a transcript of the trial proceedings, and determines whether the trial court committed an error.

Focus on Questions of Law   Appellate courts generally focus on questions of law, not questions of fact. A **question of fact** deals with what really happened in regard to the dispute being tried—such as whether a party actually burned a flag. A **question of law** concerns the application or interpretation of the law—such as whether flag-burning is a form of speech protected by the First Amendment to the U.S. Constitution. Only a judge, not a jury, can rule on questions of law.

Question of Fact In a lawsuit, an issue that involves only disputed facts, and not what the law is on a given point.

Question of Law In a lawsuit, an issue involving the application or interpretation of a law.

Defer to the Trial Court's Findings of Fact   Appellate courts normally defer (or give weight) to a trial court's findings on questions of fact because the trial court judge and jury were in a better position to evaluate testimony by directly observing witnesses' gestures, demeanor, and nonverbal behavior during the trial. At the appellate level, the judges review the written transcript of the trial, which does not include these nonverbal elements.

An appellate court will challenge a trial court's finding of fact only when the finding is clearly erroneous (that is, when it is contrary to the evidence presented at trial) or when there is no evidence to support the finding. **EXAMPLE 3.9**   A jury concludes that a manufacturer's product harmed the plaintiff, but no evidence was submitted to the court to support that conclusion. In this situation, the appellate court will hold that the trial court's decision was erroneous. ● The options exercised by appellate courts will be discussed further later in this chapter.

Learning Objective 3
What is the difference between a trial court and an appellate court?

Highest State Courts   The highest appellate court in a state is usually called the supreme court but may be called by some other name. For example, in both New York and Maryland, the highest state court is called the court of appeals. The decisions of each state's highest court are final on all questions of state law. Only when issues of federal law are involved can a decision made by a state's highest court be overruled by the United States Supreme Court.

The Federal Court System

The federal court system is basically a three-tiered model consisting of (1) U.S. district courts (trial courts of general jurisdiction) and various courts of limited jurisdiction, (2) U.S. courts of appeals (intermediate courts of appeals), and (3) the United States Supreme Court.

Unlike state court judges, who are usually elected, federal court judges—including the justices of the Supreme Court—are appointed by the president of the United States and confirmed by the U.S. Senate. All federal judges receive lifetime appointments because under Article III they "hold their offices during Good Behavior."

U.S. District Courts   At the federal level, the equivalent of a state trial court of general jurisdiction is the district court. There is at least one federal district court in every state. The number of judicial districts can vary over time, primarily owing to population changes and corresponding caseloads. Today, there are ninety-four federal judicial districts. U.S. district courts have original jurisdiction in federal matters. Federal cases typically originate in district courts. Federal courts with original, but special (or limited), jurisdiction include the bankruptcy courts and others shown in Exhibit 3–2 presented earlier.

U.S. Courts of Appeals   In the federal court system, there are thirteen U.S. courts of appeals—also referred to as U.S. circuit courts of appeals. The federal courts of appeals for twelve of the circuits, including the U.S. Court of Appeals for the District of Columbia Circuit, hear appeals from the federal district courts located within their

respective judicial circuits. The Court of Appeals for the Thirteenth Circuit, called the Federal Circuit, has national appellate jurisdiction over certain types of cases, such as cases involving patent law and cases in which the U.S. government is a defendant.

The decisions of the circuit courts of appeals are final in most cases, but appeal to the United States Supreme Court is possible. Exhibit 3–3 shows the geographic boundaries of the U.S. circuit courts of appeals and the boundaries of the U.S. district courts within each circuit.

The United States Supreme Court The highest level of the three-tiered model of the federal court system is the United States Supreme Court. According to the language of Article III of the U.S. Constitution, there is only one national Supreme Court. All other courts in the federal system are considered "inferior." Congress is empowered to create other inferior courts as it deems necessary. The inferior courts that Congress has created include the second tier in our model—the U.S. courts of appeals—as well as the district courts and any other courts of limited, or specialized, jurisdiction.

The United States Supreme Court consists of nine justices. Although the Supreme Court has original, or trial, jurisdiction in rare instances (set forth in Article III, Section 2), most of its work is as an appeals court. The Supreme Court can review any case decided by any of the federal courts of appeals, and it also has appellate authority over some cases decided in the state courts.

Exhibit 3–3 Boundaries of the U.S. Courts of Appeals and U.S. District Courts

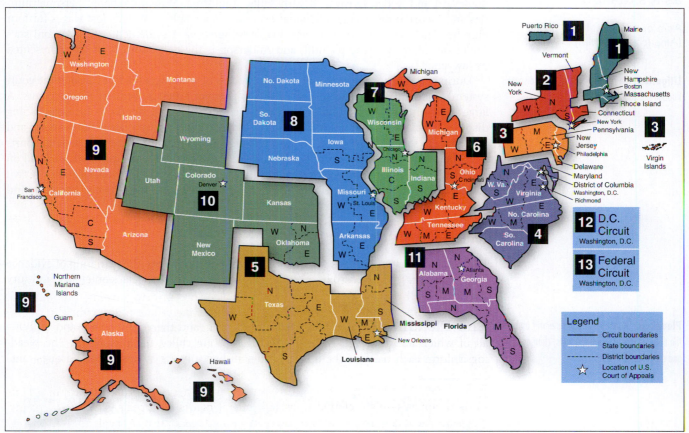

Source: Administrative Office of the United States Courts.

Writ of *Certiorari* A writ from a higher court asking a lower court for the record of a case.

Rule of Four A rule of the United States Supreme Court under which the Court will not issue a writ of *certiorari* unless at least four justices approve of the decision to issue the writ.

Appeals to the Supreme Court To bring a case before the Supreme Court, a party requests that the Court issue a writ of *certiorari*. A **writ of *certiorari***[12] is an order issued by the Supreme Court to a lower court requiring that court to send the record of the case for review. Under the **rule of four,** the Court will not issue a writ unless at least four of the nine justices approve.

Whether the Court will issue a writ of *certiorari* is entirely within its discretion. The Court is not required to issue one, and most petitions for writs are denied. (Although thousands of cases are filed with the Supreme Court each year, it hears, on average, fewer than one hundred of these cases.)[13] A denial is not a decision on the merits of a case, nor does it indicate agreement with the lower court's opinion. Furthermore, a denial of the writ has no value as a precedent.

Petitions Granted by the Court Typically, the Court grants petitions when cases raise important constitutional questions or when the lower courts are issuing conflicting decisions on a significant issue. The justices, however, never explain their reasons for hearing certain cases and not others, so it is difficult to predict which type of case the Court might select.

Following a State Court Case

"Lawsuit: A machine which you go into as a pig and come out of as a sausage."

Ambrose Bierce, 1842–1914 (American journalist)

Litigation The process of resolving a dispute through the court system.

To illustrate the procedures that would be followed in a civil lawsuit brought in a state court, we present a hypothetical case and follow it through a state court system. The case involves an automobile accident in which Kevin Anderson, driving a Lexus, struck Lisa Marconi, driving a Hyundai Genesis. The accident occurred at the intersection of Wilshire Boulevard and Rodeo Drive in Beverly Hills, California. Marconi suffered personal injuries and incurred medical and hospital expenses as a result, as well as lost wages for four months. Anderson and Marconi are unable to agree on a settlement, and Marconi sues Anderson. Marconi is the plaintiff, and Anderson is the defendant. Both are represented by lawyers.

During each phase of the **litigation** (the process of working a lawsuit through the court system), Marconi and Anderson will have to observe strict procedural requirements. A large body of law—procedural law—establishes the rules and standards for determining disputes in courts. Procedural rules are very complex, and they vary from court to court and from state to state. In addition to the various sets of rules for state courts, the federal courts have their own rules of procedure. Additionally, the applicable procedures will depend on whether the case is a civil or criminal proceeding. Generally, the Marconi-Anderson civil lawsuit will involve the procedures discussed in the following subsections. Keep in mind that attempts to settle the case may be ongoing throughout the trial.

Pretrial Procedures

The pretrial litigation process involves the filing of the *pleadings*, the gathering of evidence (called *discovery*), and possibly other procedures, such as a pretrial conference and jury selection.

Pleadings Statements by the plaintiff and the defendant that detail the facts, charges, and defenses of a case.

The Pleadings
The complaint and answer (and the counterclaim and reply)—all of which are discussed next—taken together are called the **pleadings.** The pleadings inform each party of the other's claims and specify the issues (disputed questions)

---

12. Pronounced sur-shee-uh-*rah*-ree.
13. From the mid-1950s through the early 1990s, the United States Supreme Court reviewed more cases per year than it has in the last few years. In the Court's 1982–1983 term, for example, the Court issued opinions in 151 cases. In contrast, in its 2013–2014 term, the Court issued opinions in only 75 cases.

involved in the case. The style and form of the pleadings may be quite different in different states.

The Plaintiff's Complaint Marconi's suit against Anderson commences when her lawyer files a **complaint** with the appropriate court. The complaint contains a statement alleging (1) the facts necessary for the court to take jurisdiction, (2) a brief summary of the facts necessary to show that the plaintiff is entitled to relief (a remedy), and (3) a statement of the remedy the plaintiff is seeking. Complaints may be lengthy or brief, depending on the complexity of the case and the rules of the jurisdiction.

> **Complaint** The pleading made by a plaintiff alleging wrongdoing on the part of the defendant. When filed with a court, the complaint initiates a lawsuit.

Service of Process Before the court can exercise personal jurisdiction over the defendant (Anderson)—in effect, before the lawsuit can begin—the court must have proof that the defendant was notified of the lawsuit. Formally notifying the defendant of a lawsuit is called **service of process.**

The plaintiff must deliver, or serve, a copy of the complaint and a **summons** (a notice requiring the defendant to appear in court and answer the complaint) to the defendant. The summons notifies Anderson that he must file an answer to the complaint within a specified time period (typically twenty to thirty days) or suffer a default judgment against him. A **default judgment** in Marconi's favor would mean that she would be awarded the damages alleged in her complaint because Anderson failed to respond to the allegations.

How service of process occurs depends on the rules of the court or jurisdiction in which the lawsuit is brought. Usually, the server hands the summons and complaint to the defendant personally or leaves it at the defendant's residence or place of business. In some states, process can be served by mail if the defendant consents (accepts service). When the defendant cannot be reached, special rules provide for alternative means of service, such as publishing a notice in the local newspaper or serving process via e-mail.

> **Service of Process** The delivery of the complaint and summons to the defendant.
>
> **Summons** A document informing a defendant that a legal action has been commenced against her or him and that the defendant must appear in court on a certain date to answer the plaintiff's complaint.
>
> **Default Judgment** A judgment entered by a court against a defendant who has failed to appear in court to answer or defend against the plaintiff's claim.

The Defendant's Answer The defendant's **answer** either admits the statements or allegations set forth in the complaint or denies them and outlines any defenses that the defendant may have. If Anderson admits to all of Marconi's allegations in his answer, the court will enter a judgment for Marconi. If Anderson denies any of Marconi's allegations, the litigation will go forward.

Anderson can deny Marconi's allegations and set forth his own claim that Marconi was negligent and therefore owes him compensation for the damage to his Lexus. This is appropriately called a **counterclaim.** If Anderson files a counterclaim, Marconi will have to answer it with a pleading, normally called a **reply,** which has the same characteristics as an answer.

Anderson can also admit the truth of Marconi's complaint but raise new facts that may result in dismissal of the action. This is called raising an *affirmative defense.* For example, Anderson could assert the expiration of the time period under the relevant *statute of limitations* (a state or federal statute that sets the maximum time period during which a certain action can be brought or rights enforced) as an affirmative defense.

> **Answer** Procedurally, a defendant's response to the plaintiff's complaint.
>
> **Counterclaim** A claim made by a defendant in a civil lawsuit against the plaintiff. In effect, the defendant is suing the plaintiff.
>
> **Reply** Procedurally, a plaintiff's response to a defendant's answer.

Motion to Dismiss A **motion to dismiss** requests the court to dismiss the case for stated reasons. Grounds for dismissal of a case include improper delivery of the complaint and summons, improper venue, and the plaintiff's failure to state a claim for which a court could grant relief. For instance, if Marconi had suffered no injuries or losses as a result of Anderson's negligence, Anderson could move to have the case dismissed because Marconi would not have stated a claim for which relief could be granted.

If the judge grants the motion to dismiss, the plaintiff generally is given time to file an amended complaint. If the judge denies the motion, the suit will go forward, and the

> **Motion to Dismiss** A pleading in which a defendant admits the facts as alleged by the plaintiff but asserts that the plaintiff's claim to state a cause of action has no basis in law.

(Bajinda/Shutterstock.com)

When does a coffee company have to abide by a forum-selection clause in its contract?

Motion for Judgment on the Pleadings
A motion by either party to a lawsuit at the close of the pleadings requesting the court to decide the issue solely on the pleadings without proceeding to trial. The motion will be granted only if no facts are in dispute.

Motion for Summary Judgment A motion requesting the court to enter a judgment without proceeding to trial. The motion can be based on evidence outside the pleadings and will be granted only if no facts are in dispute.

Discovery A method by which the opposing parties obtain information from each other to prepare for trial.

Learning Objective 4
What is discovery, and how does electronic discovery differ from traditional discovery?

defendant must then file an answer. Note that if Marconi wishes to discontinue the suit because, for instance, an out-of-court settlement has been reached, she can likewise move for dismissal. The court can also dismiss the case on its own motion.

CASE EXAMPLE 3.10   Espresso Disposition Corporation 1 entered into a contract with Santana Sales & Marketing Group, Inc. The agreement included a mandatory *forum-selection clause*—that is, a provision designating that any disputes arising under the contract will be decided by a court in Illinois. When Santana Sales filed a lawsuit against Espresso in a Florida state court, Espresso filed a motion to dismiss based on the agreement's forum-selection clause. Santana claimed that the forum-selection clause had been a mistake. The court denied Espresso's motion to dismiss. Espresso appealed. A state intermediate appellate court reversed the trial court's denial of Espresso's motion to dismiss and remanded the case to the lower court for the entry of an order of dismissal.[14] ●

Pretrial Motions   Either party may attempt to get the case dismissed before trial through the use of various pretrial motions. We have already mentioned the motion to dismiss. Two other important pretrial motions are the motion for judgment on the pleadings and the motion for summary judgment.

At the close of the pleadings, either party may make a **motion for judgment on the pleadings,** or on the merits of the case. The judge will grant the motion only when there is no dispute over the facts of the case and the sole issue to be resolved is a question of law. In deciding on the motion, the judge may consider only the evidence contained in the pleadings.

In contrast, in a **motion for summary judgment,** the court may consider evidence outside the pleadings, such as sworn statements (affidavits) by parties or witnesses, or other documents relating to the case. Either party can make a motion for summary judgment. Like the motion for judgment on the pleadings, a motion for summary judgment will be granted only if there are no genuine questions of fact and the sole question is a question of law.

Discovery   Before a trial begins, each party can use a number of procedural devices to obtain information and gather evidence about the case from the other party or from third parties. The process of obtaining such information is known as **discovery.** Discovery includes gaining access to witnesses, documents, records, and other types of evidence.

The Federal Rules of Civil Procedure and similar rules in the states set forth the guidelines for discovery. Generally, discovery is allowed regarding any matter that is not privileged and is relevant to the claim or defense of any party. Discovery rules also attempt to protect witnesses and parties from undue harassment and to safeguard privileged or confidential material from being disclosed.

If a discovery request involves privileged or confidential business information, a court can deny the request and can limit the scope of discovery in a number of ways. For instance, a court can require the party to submit the materials to the judge in a sealed envelope so that the judge can decide if they should be disclosed to the opposing party.

Discovery prevents surprises at trial by giving parties access to evidence that might otherwise be hidden. This allows both parties to learn what to expect during a trial before they reach the courtroom. Discovery also serves to narrow the issues so that trial time is spent on the main questions in the case. The following case shows how vital discovery can be to the outcome of litigation.

---

14. *Espresso Disposition Corp. 1 v. Santana Sales & Marketing Group, Inc.,* 105 So.3d 592 (Fla.App. 3 Dist. 2013).

Case 3.2

Brothers v. Winstead

Supreme Court of Mississippi, 129 So.3d 906 (2014).

BACKGROUND AND FACTS Phillips Brothers, LP (limited partnership), Harry Simmons, and Ray Winstead were the three owners of Kilby Brake Fisheries, LLC, a catfish farm in Mississippi. Winstead operated a hatchery for the firm for about eight years. During this time, the hatchery had only two profitable years. Consequently, Winstead was fired. He filed a suit in a Mississippi state court against Kilby Brake and its other owners, alleging a "freeze-out." (A freeze-out occurs when a majority of the owners of a firm exclude other owners from certain benefits of participating in the firm.) The defendants filed a counterclaim of theft. To support this claim, the defendants asked the court to allow them to obtain documents from Winstead regarding his finances, particularly income from his Winstead Cattle Company. The court refused this request. A jury awarded Winstead more than $1.7 million, and the defendants appealed.

IN THE WORDS OF THE COURT . . .
WALLER, Chief Justice for the Court.
   * * * *

During discovery, Winstead produced his tax returns from 2006 to 2009, which showed substantial income as coming from the Winstead Cattle Company. The only other income listed on Winstead's tax returns was from Kilby Brake * * * . Winstead had also produced [other documents showing income] from a fish farmer named Scott Kiker, which did not appear on his tax returns. [The documents supposedly involved income from sales of cattle.] Kilby Brake's theory was the entries for "cattle" represented income from sales of Kilby Brake fish Winstead was brokering and thus, it sought to compel [discovery] of all of the Winstead Cattle Company's financial records. Winstead [testified] in his deposition and again at trial that the Winstead Cattle Company did no actual business, and it was simply his hunting camp. The trial court denied Kilby Brake's motion to compel discovery into Winstead's finances.

Why was Winstead fired from his catfish hatchery position?

* * * [Winstead was questioned about the forms he] had produced in discovery showing income from Kiker. Winstead testified that he would often act as a middle man if he knew of a farmer who was in need of fish and another who had fish for sale; taking a commission for brokering the deal.
   * * * *

* * * Kiker testified that he had received a load of fish from Kilby Brake [but that] there was no paperwork on the transaction [and] that he sold this load of fish, gave Winstead a commission and did not pay Kilby Brake for the sales.

*From the evidence noted above, we find the trial court's refusal to allow both discovery into the finances of Winstead and questions concerning Winstead Cattle Company on his tax return prevented Kilby Brake and the jury from finding out whether Winstead was selling fish from Kilby Brake and disguising it on his income tax returns * * * .* Importantly, the decisions by the trial court denied Kilby Brake the ability to present its case as to what happened to the fish. The record shows there were years in which Winstead received substantial income from brokering fish sales, almost $20,000 in one year. He [testified] that Winstead Cattle Company did no business and was simply his hunting camp, yet it made significant amounts of money. [Emphasis added.]

DECISION AND REMEDY The Mississippi Supreme Court reversed the lower court's decision to deny discovery of information concerning Winstead's outside finances, especially regarding income from Winstead Cattle Company. The state supreme court remanded the case for a new trial.

THE LEGAL ENVIRONMENT DIMENSION *Do the reasons for discovery support the defendants' request for information regarding Winstead's outside income? Explain.*

THE ETHICAL DIMENSION *Does Winstead have an ethical duty to comply with the defendants' discovery request? Discuss.*

Depositions and Interrogatories Discovery can involve the use of depositions or interrogatories, or both. A **deposition** is sworn testimony by a party to the lawsuit or any witness. The person being deposed gives testimony and answers questions asked by the attorneys from both sides. The questions and answers are recorded, sworn to, and signed.

Deposition The testimony of a party to a lawsuit or a witness taken under oath before a trial.

(Occasionally, written depositions are taken when witnesses are unable to appear in person.) These answers, of course, will help the attorneys prepare for the trial. They can also be used in court to impeach (challenge the credibility of) a party or a witness who changes her or his testimony at the trial. In addition, a witness's deposition can be used as testimony if he or she is not available for the trial.

Interrogatories A series of written questions for which written answers are prepared by a party to a lawsuit, usually with the assistance of the party's attorney, and then signed under oath.

Interrogatories are written questions for which written answers are prepared and then signed under oath. The main difference between interrogatories and written depositions is that interrogatories are directed to a party to the lawsuit (the plaintiff or the defendant), not to a witness, and the party can prepare answers with the aid of an attorney. The scope of interrogatories is broader because parties are obligated to answer the questions, even if that means disclosing information from their records and files.

Note that, as with discovery requests, a court can impose sanctions on a party who fails to answer interrogatories. **CASE EXAMPLE 3.11** Computer Task Group, Inc. (CTG), sued a former employee, William Brotby, for violating the terms of his employment agreement. During discovery, Brotby refused to respond fully to CTG's interrogatories. He gave contradictory answers, made frivolous objections, filed baseless motions, and never disclosed all the information that CTG sought. The court ordered Brotby to comply with discovery requests five times. Nevertheless, Brotby continued to make excuses and changed his story repeatedly, making it impossible for CTG to establish basic facts with any certainty. Eventually, CTG requested and the court granted a default judgment against Brotby based on his failure to cooperate.[15] ●

Requests for Other Information   A party can serve a written request on the other party for an admission of the truth on matters relating to the trial. Any matter admitted under such a request is conclusively established for the trial. For example, Marconi can ask Anderson to admit that his driver's license was suspended at the time of the accident. A request for admission saves time at trial because the parties will not have to spend time proving facts on which they already agree.

A party can also gain access to documents and other items not in her or his possession in order to inspect and examine them. Likewise, a party can gain "entry upon land" to inspect the premises. Anderson's attorney, for instance, normally can gain permission to inspect and make copies of Marconi's car repair bills.

When the physical or mental condition of one party is in question, the opposing party can ask the court to order a physical or mental examination. The court will do so only if the need for the information outweighs the right to privacy of the person to be examined.

Electronic Discovery

Any relevant material, including information stored electronically, can be the object of a discovery request. The federal rules and most state rules now specifically allow all parties to obtain electronic "data compilations." Electronic evidence, or **e-evidence**, includes all types of computer-generated or electronically recorded information, such as e-mail, voice mail, tweets, blogs, social media posts, and spreadsheets, as well as documents and other data stored on computers.

E-Evidence A type of evidence that consists of all computer-generated or electronically recorded information.

Metadata Data that are automatically recorded by electronic devices and provide information about who created a file and when, and who accessed, modified, or transmitted it on their hard drives. Can be described as data about data.

E-evidence can reveal significant facts that are not discoverable by other means. Computers, smartphones, cameras, and other devices automatically record certain information about files—such as who created the file and when, and who accessed, modified, or transmitted it—on their hard drives. This information is called **metadata**, which can be thought of as "data about data." Metadata can be obtained only from the file in its electronic format—not from printed-out versions.

---

15. *Computer Task Group, Inc. v. Brotby,* 364 F.3d 1112 (9th Cir. 2004).

EXAMPLE 3.12   In 2012, John McAfee, the programmer responsible for creating McAfee antivirus software, was wanted for questioning in the murder of his neighbor in Belize. McAfee left Belize and was on the run from police, but he allowed a journalist to come with him and photograph him. When the journalist posted photos of McAfee online, some metadata were attached to a photo. The police used the metadata to pinpoint the latitude and longitude of the image and subsequently arrested McAfee in Guatemala. ●

E-Discovery Procedures   The Federal Rules of Civil Procedure deal specifically with the preservation, retrieval, and production of electronic data. Although traditional means, such as interrogatories and depositions, are still used to find out about the e-evidence, a party must usually hire an expert to retrieve evidence in its electronic format. The expert uses software to reconstruct e-mail, text, and other exchanges to establish who knew what and when they knew it. The expert can even recover files that the user thought had been deleted from a computer.

Advantages and Disadvantages   E-discovery has significant advantages over paper discovery. Back-up copies of documents and e-mail can provide useful—and often quite damaging—information about how a particular matter progressed over several weeks or months. E-discovery can uncover the proverbial smoking gun that will win the lawsuit, but it is also time consuming and expensive, especially when lawsuits involve large firms with multiple offices. Also, many firms are finding it difficult to fulfill their duty to preserve electronic evidence from a vast number of sources. For a discussion of some of the problems associated with preserving e-evidence for discovery, see this chapter's *Online Developments* feature that follows.

Pretrial Conference
Either party or the court can request a pretrial conference, or hearing. Usually, the hearing consists of an informal discussion between the judge and the opposing attorneys after discovery has taken place. The purpose of the hearing is to explore the possibility of a settlement without trial and, if this is not possible, to identify the matters that are in dispute and to plan the course of the trial.

Jury Selection
A trial can be held with or without a jury. The Seventh Amendment to the U.S. Constitution guarantees the right to a jury trial for cases in *federal* courts when the amount in controversy exceeds $20, but this guarantee does not apply to state courts. Most states have similar guarantees in their own constitutions (although the threshold dollar amount is higher than $20). The right to a trial by jury does not have to be exercised, and many cases are tried without a jury. In most states and in federal courts, one of the parties must request a jury in a civil case, or the judge presumes that the parties waive the right.

Before a jury trial commences, a jury must be selected. The jury selection process is known as **voir dire**.[16] During *voir dire* in most jurisdictions, attorneys for the plaintiff and the defendant ask prospective jurors oral questions to determine whether a potential jury member is biased or has any connection with a party to the action or with a prospective witness. In some jurisdictions, the judge may do all or part of the questioning based on written questions submitted by counsel for the parties.

During *voir dire,* a party may challenge a prospective juror *peremptorily*—that is, ask that an individual not be sworn in as a juror without providing any reason. Alternatively, a party may challenge a prospective juror *for cause*—that is, provide a reason why an individual should not be sworn in as a juror. If the judge grants the challenge, the individual is asked to step down. A prospective juror may not be excluded from the jury by the use of discriminatory challenges, however, such as those based on racial criteria or gender.

---

16. Pronounced vwahr *deehr.*

> "The judicial system is the most expensive machine ever invented for finding out what happened and what to do about it."
>
> Irving R. Kaufman, 1910–1992 (American jurist)

Voir Dire An important part of the jury selection process in which the attorneys question prospective jurors about their backgrounds, attitudes, and biases to ascertain whether they can be impartial jurors.

Can a lawyer choosing a jury exclude potential jurors for any reason whatsoever?

(moodboard/Veta/Getty Images)

ONLINE DEVELOPMENTS

The Duty to Preserve E-Evidence for Discovery

Today, less than 0.5 percent of new information is created on paper. Instead of sending letters and memos, people send e-mails and text messages, creating a massive amount of electronically stored information (ESI). The law requires parties to preserve ESI whenever there is a "reasonable anticipation of litigation."

Why Companies Fail to Preserve E-Evidence

Preserving e-evidence can be a challenge, though, particularly for large corporations that have electronic data scattered across multiple networks, servers, desktops, laptops, iPhones, iPads, and other smartphones and tablets. Although many companies have policies regarding back-up of office e-mail and computer systems, these may cover only a fraction of the e-evidence requested in a lawsuit.

Technological advances further complicate the situation. Users of BlackBerrys, for example, can configure them so that messages are transmitted with limited or no archiving rather than going through a company's servers and being recorded. How can a company preserve e-evidence that is never on its servers? In one case, the court held that a company had a duty to preserve transitory "server log data," which exist only temporarily on a computer's memory.[a]

Potential Sanctions and Malpractice Claims

A court may impose sanctions (such as fines) on a party that fails to preserve electronic evidence or to comply with e-evidence requests. A firm may be sanctioned if it provides e-mails without the attachments, does not produce all of the e-discovery requested, overwrites the contents of files, or fails to suspend its automatic e-mail deletion procedures.[b] Sanctions for e-discovery violations have become increasingly common in recent years.[c] Attorneys who fail to properly advise their clients concerning the duty to preserve e-evidence or who fail to supervise vendors, contract attorneys, or subordinates who work for the clients also often face sanctions and malpractice claims.[d]

Lessons from Intel

A party that fails to preserve e-evidence may even find itself at such a disadvantage that it will settle a dispute rather than continue litigation. For instance, Advanced Micro Devices, Inc. (AMD), sued Intel Corporation, one of the world's largest microprocessor suppliers, for violating antitrust laws. Immediately after the lawsuit was filed, Intel began collecting and preserving the ESI on its servers. Although the company instructed its employees to retain documents and e-mails related to competition with AMD, many employees saved only copies of the e-mails that they had received and not e-mails that they had sent.

In addition, Intel did not stop its automatic e-mail deletion system, causing other information to be lost. In the end, although Intel produced data that were equivalent to "somewhere in the neighborhood of a pile 137 miles high" in paper, its failure to preserve e-discovery led it to settle the dispute.[e]

Critical Thinking

How might a large company protect itself from allegations that it intentionally failed to preserve electronic data?

---

a. See *Columbia Pictures v. Brunnell*, 2007 WL 2080419 (C.D.Cal. 2007).
b. See, for example, *Io Group, Inc. v. GLBT, Ltd.*, 2011 WL 4974337 (N.D.Cal. 2011); *E. I. Du Pont de Nemours & Co. v. Kolon Industries, Inc.*, 803 F.Supp.2d 469 (E.D.Va. 2011); *Genger v. TR Investors, LLC*, 26 A.3d 180 (Del.Supr. 2011); *PIC Group, Inc. v. LandCoast Insulation, Inc.*, 2011 WL 2669144 (S.D.Miss. 2011).
c. Elizabeth E. McGinn and Karen M. Morgan, "New Ethical Issues and Challenges in E-Discovery," *New York Law Journal*, October 5, 2011.
d. See, for example, *Surowiec v. Capital Title Agency, Inc.*, 790 F.Supp.2d 997 (D.Ariz. 2011).
e. See *In re Intel Corp. Microprocessor Antitrust Litigation*, 2008 WL 2310288 (D.Del. 2008). See also *Net2Phone, Inc. v. eBay, Inc.*, 2008 WL 8183817 (D.N.J. 2008).

At the Trial

At the beginning of the trial, the attorneys present their opening arguments, setting forth the facts that they expect to prove during the trial. Then the plaintiff's case is presented. In our hypothetical case, Marconi's lawyer would introduce evidence (relevant documents, exhibits, and the testimony of witnesses) to support Marconi's position. The defendant has the opportunity to challenge any evidence introduced and to cross-examine any of the plaintiff's witnesses.

Directed Verdicts   At the end of the plaintiff's case, the defendant's attorney has the opportunity to ask the judge to direct a verdict for the defendant on the ground that the plaintiff has presented no evidence that would justify the granting of the plaintiff's remedy. This is called a **motion for a directed verdict** (known in federal courts as a *motion for judgment as a matter of law*). If the motion is not granted (it seldom is granted), the defendant's attorney then presents the evidence and witnesses for the defendant's case. At the conclusion of the defendant's case, the defendant's attorney has another opportunity to make a motion for a directed verdict. The plaintiff's attorney can challenge any evidence introduced and cross-examine the defendant's witnesses.

Closing Arguments and Awards   After the defense concludes its presentation, the attorneys present their closing arguments, each urging a verdict in favor of her or his client. The judge instructs the jury in the law that applies to the case (these instructions are often called *charges*), and the jury retires to the jury room to deliberate a verdict. In the Marconi-Anderson case, the jury will not only decide for the plaintiff or for the defendant but, if it finds for the plaintiff, will also decide on the amount of the **award** (the compensation to be paid to her).

Posttrial Motions

After the jury has rendered its verdict, either party may make a posttrial motion. If Marconi wins and Anderson's attorney has previously moved for a directed verdict, Anderson's attorney may make a **motion for judgment *n.o.v.*** (from the Latin *non obstante veredicto,* which means "notwithstanding the verdict"—called a *motion for judgment as a matter of law* in the federal courts). Such a motion will be granted only if the jury's verdict was unreasonable and erroneous. If the judge grants the motion, the jury's verdict will be set aside, and a judgment will be entered in favor of the opposite party (Anderson).

Alternatively, Anderson could make a **motion for a new trial,** asking the judge to set aside the adverse verdict and to hold a new trial. The motion will be granted if, after looking at all the evidence, the judge is convinced that the jury was in error but does not feel that it is appropriate to grant judgment for the other side. A judge can also grant a new trial on the basis of newly discovered evidence, misconduct by the participants or the jury during the trial, or error by the judge.

The Appeal

Assume here that any posttrial motion is denied and that Anderson appeals the case. (If Marconi wins but receives a smaller monetary award than she sought, she can appeal also.) Keep in mind, though, that a party cannot appeal a trial court's decision simply because he or she is dissatisfied with the outcome of the trial. A party must have legitimate grounds to file an appeal. In other words, he or she must be able to claim that the lower court committed an error. If Anderson has grounds to appeal the case, a notice of appeal must be filed with the clerk of the trial court within a prescribed time. Anderson now becomes the appellant, or petitioner, and Marconi becomes the appellee, or respondent.

Filing the Appeal   Anderson's attorney files the record on appeal with the appellate court. The record includes the pleadings, the trial transcript, the judge's rulings on motions made by the parties, and other trial-related documents. Anderson's attorney will also provide the reviewing court with a condensation of the record, known as an *abstract,* and a brief. The **brief** is a formal legal document outlining the facts and issues of the case, the judge's rulings or jury's findings that should be reversed or modified, the applicable law, and arguments on Anderson's behalf (citing applicable statutes and relevant cases as precedents).

Motion for a Directed Verdict A motion for the judge to take the decision out of the hands of the jury and to direct a verdict for the party making the motion on the ground that the other party has not produced sufficient evidence to support her or his claim.

Award The monetary compensation given to a party at the end of a trial or other proceeding.

Motion for Judgment *N.O.V.* A motion requesting the court to grant judgment in favor of the party making the motion on the ground that the jury's verdict against him or her was unreasonable and erroneous.

Motion for a New Trial A motion asserting that the trial was so fundamentally flawed (because of error, newly discovered evidence, prejudice, or another reason) that a new trial is necessary to prevent a miscarriage of justice.

Brief A written summary or statement prepared by one side in a lawsuit to explain its case to the judge.

Marconi's attorney will file an answering brief. Anderson's attorney can file a reply to Marconi's brief, although it is not required. The reviewing court then considers the case.

Appellate Review   As explained earlier, a court of appeals does not hear evidence. Instead, the court reviews the record for errors of law. Its decision concerning a case is based on the record on appeal, the abstracts, and the attorneys' briefs. The attorneys can present oral arguments, after which the case is taken under advisement.

After reviewing a case, an appellate court has the following options:

1. The court can *affirm* the trial court's decision.
2. The court can *reverse* the trial court's judgment if it concludes that the trial court erred or that the jury did not receive proper instructions.
3. The appellate court can *remand* (send back) the case to the trial court for further proceedings consistent with its opinion on the matter.
4. The court might also affirm or reverse a decision *in part.* For example, the court might affirm the jury's finding that Anderson was negligent but remand the case for further proceedings on another issue (such as the extent of Marconi's damages).
5. An appellate court can also *modify* a lower court's decision. If the appellate court decides that the jury awarded an excessive amount in damages, for example, the court might reduce the award to a more appropriate, or fairer, amount.

The members of the California Supreme Court, that state's highest court, ready themselves for a hearing. Do all parties to legal disputes have a right to be heard by an appellate court?

(AP Photo/Paul Sakuma)

Appeal to a Higher Appellate Court   If the reviewing court is an intermediate appellate court, the losing party may decide to appeal to the state supreme court (the highest state court). Such a petition corresponds to a petition for a writ of *certiorari* from the United States Supreme Court. Although the losing party has a right to ask (petition) a higher court to review the case, the party does not have a right to have the case heard by the higher appellate court.

Appellate courts normally have discretionary power and can accept or reject an appeal. Like the United States Supreme Court, state supreme courts generally deny most appeals. If the appeal is granted, new briefs must be filed before the state supreme court, and the attorneys may be allowed or requested to present oral arguments. Like the intermediate appellate court, the supreme court may reverse or affirm the appellate court's decision or remand the case. At this point, the case typically has reached its end (unless a federal question is at issue and one of the parties has legitimate grounds to seek review by a federal appellate court).

Enforcing the Judgment

The uncertainties of the litigation process are compounded by the lack of guarantees that any judgment will be enforceable. Even if a plaintiff wins an award of damages in court, the defendant may not have sufficient assets or insurance to cover that amount. Usually, one of the factors considered before a lawsuit is initiated is whether the defendant has sufficient assets to pay the damages sought, should the plaintiff win the case.

The Courts Adapt to the Online World

We have already mentioned that the courts have attempted to adapt traditional jurisdictional concepts to the online world. Not surprisingly, the Internet has also brought about changes in court procedures and practices, including new methods for filing pleadings and other documents and issuing decisions and opinions. Some jurisdictions are exploring the possibility of cyber courts, in which legal proceedings could be conducted totally online.

Electronic Filing

The federal court system has now implemented its electronic filing system, Case Management/Electronic Case Files (CM/ECF), in nearly all of the federal courts. The system is available in federal district, appellate, and bankruptcy courts, as well as the U.S. Court of International Trade and the U.S. Court of Federal Claims. More than 33 million cases are on the CM/ECF system. Users can create a document using conventional document-creation software, save it as a PDF (portable digital file), then log on to a court's Web site and submit the PDF to the court via the Internet. Access to the electronic documents filed on CM/ECF is available through a system called PACER (Public Access to Court Electronic Records), which is a service of the U.S. Courts.

A majority of the states have some form of electronic filing, although often it is not yet available in state appellate courts. Some states, including Arizona, California, Colorado, Delaware, Mississippi, New Jersey, New York, and Nevada, offer statewide e-filing systems. Generally, when electronic filing is made available, it is optional. Nonetheless, some state courts have now made e-filing mandatory in certain types of disputes, such as complex civil litigation.

Courts Online

Most courts today have sites on the Web. Of course, each court decides what to make available at its site. Some courts display only the names of court personnel and office phone numbers. Others add court rules and forms. Many appellate court sites include judicial decisions, although the decisions may remain online for only a limited time. In addition, in some states, including California and Florida, court clerks offer **docket** (the court's schedule of cases to be heard) information and other searchable databases online.

Docket The list of cases entered on a court's calendar and thus scheduled to be heard by the court.

Appellate court decisions are often posted online immediately after they are rendered. Recent decisions of the U.S. courts of appeals, for example, are available online at their Web sites. The United States Supreme Court also has an official Web site and publishes its opinions there immediately after they are announced to the public. In fact, even decisions that are designated as "unpublished" opinions by the appellate courts are usually published online (as discussed in the *Online Developments* feature in Chapter 1).

Cyber Courts and Proceedings

Someday, litigants may be able to use cyber courts, in which judicial proceedings take place only on the Internet. The parties to a case could meet online to make their arguments and present their evidence. This might be done with e-mail submissions, through video cameras, in designated chat rooms, at closed sites, or through the use of other Internet and social media facilities. These courtrooms could be efficient and economical. We might also see the use of virtual lawyers, judges, and juries—and possibly the replacement of court personnel with computer software.

Already the state of Michigan has passed legislation creating cyber courts that will hear cases involving technology issues and high-tech businesses. The state of Wisconsin has also enacted a rule authorizing the use of videoconferencing in both civil and criminal trials, at the discretion of the trial court.[17] In some situations, a Wisconsin judge can allow videoconferencing even if the parties object, provided that certain operational criteria are met.

When is video conferencing acceptable during a trial?

(David R. Frazier Photolibrary, Inc./Alamy Limited)

---

17. Wisconsin Statute Section 751.12.

Learning Objective 5
What are three alternative methods of resolving disputes?

The courts may also use the Internet in other ways. For instance, some bankruptcy courts in Arizona, New Mexico, and Nevada recently began offering online chatting at their Web sites, which you will read about in Chapter 13. The model for these online chats came from retailers in the private sector, and chatting may eventually be offered on all federal bankruptcy court Web sites. Other courts are ordering parties to use the Internet as part of their judgments. A Florida county court granted "virtual" visitation rights in a couple's divorce proceedings so that the child could visit with each parent online (through a videoconferencing system or Skype, for instance) during stays at the other parent's residence.

Alternative Dispute Resolution

Alternative Dispute Resolution (ADR)
The resolution of disputes in ways other than those involved in the traditional judicial process, such as negotiation, mediation, and arbitration.

Litigation is expensive. It is also time consuming. Because of the backlog of cases pending in many courts, several years may pass before a case is actually tried. For these and other reasons, more and more businesspersons are turning to **alternative dispute resolution (ADR)** as a means of settling their disputes.

The great advantage of ADR is its flexibility. Methods of ADR range from the parties sitting down together and attempting to work out their differences to multinational corporations agreeing to resolve a dispute through a formal hearing before a panel of experts. Normally, the parties themselves can control how they will attempt to settle their dispute, what procedures will be used, whether a neutral third party will be present or make a decision, and whether that decision will be legally binding or nonbinding.

Today, more than 90 percent of cases are settled before trial through some form of ADR. Indeed, most states either require or encourage parties to undertake ADR prior to trial. Many federal courts have instituted ADR programs as well. In the following subsections, we examine the basic forms of ADR. Keep in mind, though, that new methods of ADR—and new combinations of existing methods—are constantly being devised and employed.

Negotiation

Negotiation A process in which parties attempt to settle their dispute informally, with or without attorneys to represent them.

The simplest form of ADR is **negotiation,** in which the parties attempt to settle their dispute informally, with or without attorneys to represent them. Attorneys frequently advise their clients to negotiate a settlement voluntarily before they proceed to trial. Parties may even try to negotiate a settlement during a trial or after the trial but before an appeal. Negotiation traditionally involves just the parties themselves and (typically) their attorneys. The attorneys, though, are advocates—they are obligated to put their clients' interests first.

Mediation

Mediation A method of settling disputes outside the courts by using the services of a neutral third party, who acts as a communicating agent between the parties and assists them in negotiating a settlement.

In **mediation,** a neutral third party acts as a mediator and works with both sides in the dispute to facilitate a resolution. The mediator talks with the parties separately as well as jointly and emphasizes their points of agreement in an attempt to help the parties evaluate their options. Although the mediator may propose a solution (called a *mediator's proposal*), he or she does not make a decision resolving the matter. States that require parties to undergo ADR before trial often offer mediation as one of the ADR options or (as in Florida) the only option.

One of the biggest advantages of mediation is that it is not as adversarial as litigation. In a trial, the parties "do battle" with each other in the courtroom, trying to prove each other wrong, while the judge is usually a passive observer. In mediation, the mediator takes an active role and attempts to bring the parties together so that they can come to a mutually satisfactory resolution. The mediation process tends to reduce the hostility between the disputants, allowing them to resume their former relationship without bad feelings. For this reason, mediation is often the preferred form of ADR for disputes involving business partners, employers and employees, or other parties involved in long-term relationships.

EXAMPLE 3.13 Two business partners, Mark Shalen and Charles Rowe, have a dispute over how the profits of their firm should be distributed. If the dispute is litigated, Shalen and Rowe will be adversaries, and their respective attorneys will emphasize how the parties' positions differ, not what they have in common. In contrast, when the dispute is mediated, the mediator emphasizes the common ground shared by Shalen and Rowe and helps them work toward agreement. The two men can work out the distribution of profits without damaging their continuing relationship as partners. •

Arbitration

In **arbitration,** a more formal method of ADR, an arbitrator (a neutral third party or a panel of experts) hears a dispute and imposes a resolution on the parties. Arbitration differs from other forms of ADR in that the third party hearing the dispute makes a decision for the parties. Exhibit 3–4 outlines the basic differences among the three traditional forms of ADR. Usually, the parties in arbitration agree that the third party's decision will be *legally binding,* although the parties can also agree to *nonbinding* arbitration. (Arbitration that is mandated by the courts often is nonbinding.) In nonbinding arbitration, the parties can go forward with a lawsuit if they do not agree with the arbitrator's decision.

    In some respects, formal arbitration resembles a trial, although usually the procedural rules are much less restrictive than those governing litigation. In the typical arbitration, the parties present opening arguments and ask for specific remedies. Both sides present evidence and may call and examine witnesses. The arbitrator then renders a decision.

Arbitration The settling of a dispute by submitting it to a disinterested third party (other than a court), who renders a decision.

The Arbitrator's Decision   The arbitrator's decision is called an *award.* It is usually the final word on the matter. Although the parties may appeal an arbitrator's decision, a court's review of the decision will be much more restricted in scope than an appellate court's review of a trial court's decision. The general view is that because the parties were free to frame the issues and set the powers of the arbitrator at the outset, they cannot complain about the results. A court will set aside an award only in the event of one of the following:

1. The arbitrator's conduct or "bad faith" substantially prejudiced the rights of one of the parties.
2. The award violates an established public policy.
3. The arbitrator exceeded her or his powers—that is, arbitrated issues that the parties did not agree to submit to arbitration.

Exhibit 3–4 Basic Differences in the Traditional Forms of Alternative Dispute Resolution

TYPE OF ADR	DESCRIPTION	NEUTRAL THIRD PARTY PRESENT	WHO DECIDES THE RESOLUTION
Negotiation	The parties meet informally with or without their attorneys and attempt to agree on a resolution.	No	The parties themselves reach a resolution.
Mediation	A neutral third party meets with the parties and emphasizes points of agreement to help them resolve their dispute.	Yes	The parties decide the resolution, but the mediator may suggest or propose a resolution.
Arbitration	The parties present their arguments and evidence before an arbitrator at a hearing, and the arbitrator renders a decision resolving the parties' dispute.	Yes	The arbitrator imposes a resolution on the parties that may be either binding or nonbinding.

Arbitration Clause A clause in a contract that provides that, in the event of a dispute, the parties will submit the dispute to arbitration rather than litigate the dispute in court.

Arbitration Clauses

Just about any commercial matter can be submitted to arbitration. Frequently, parties include an **arbitration clause** in a contract. The clause provides that any dispute that arises under the contract will be resolved through arbitration rather than through the court system. Parties can also agree to arbitrate a dispute after a dispute arises.

Arbitration Statutes

Most states have statutes (often based in part on the Uniform Arbitration Act) under which arbitration clauses will be enforced, and some state statutes compel arbitration of certain types of disputes, such as those involving public employees. At the federal level, the Federal Arbitration Act (FAA), enacted in 1925, enforces arbitration clauses in contracts involving maritime activity and interstate commerce (though its applicability to employment contracts has been controversial, as discussed in a later subsection). Because of the breadth of the commerce clause (see Chapter 4), arbitration agreements involving transactions only slightly connected to the flow of interstate commerce may fall under the FAA.

CASE EXAMPLE 3.14 Buckeye Check Cashing, Inc., cashes personal checks for consumers in Florida. Buckeye would agree to delay submitting a consumer's check for payment if the consumer paid a "finance charge." For each transaction, the consumer signed an agreement that included an arbitration clause. A group of consumers filed a lawsuit claiming that Buckeye was charging an illegally high rate of interest in violation of state law. Buckeye filed a motion to compel arbitration, which the trial court denied, and the case was appealed. The plaintiffs argued that the entire contract—including the arbitration clause—was illegal and therefore arbitration was not required. The United States Supreme Court found that the arbitration provision was *severable,* or capable of being separated, from the rest of the contract. The Court held that when the challenge is to the validity of a contract as a whole, and not specifically to an arbitration clause within the contract, an arbitrator must resolve the dispute. Even if the contract itself later proves to be unenforceable, arbitration will still be required because the FAA established a national policy favoring arbitration and that policy extends to both federal and state courts.[18] ●

In the following case, the parties had agreed to arbitrate disputes involving their contract, but a state law allowed one party to void a contractual provision that required arbitration outside the state. The court had to decide if the FAA preempted the state law.

---

18. *Buckeye Check Cashing, Inc. v. Cardegna,* 546 U.S. 440, 126 S.Ct. 1204, 163 L.Ed.2d 1038 (2006).

Case 3.3

Cleveland Construction, Inc. v. Levco Construction, Inc.

Court of Appeals of Texas, First District, 359 S.W.3d 843 (2012).

An excavation machine.

BACKGROUND AND FACTS Cleveland Construction, Inc. (CCI), was the general contractor on a project to build a grocery store in Houston, Texas. CCI hired Levco Construction, Inc., as a subcontractor to perform excavation and grading. The contract included an arbitration provision stating that any disputes would be resolved by arbitration in Ohio. When a dispute arose between the parties, Levco filed a suit against CCI in a Texas state court. CCI sought to compel arbitration in Ohio under the Federal Arbitration Act (FAA), but a Texas statute allows a party to void a contractual provision that requires arbitration outside Texas. The Texas court granted an emergency motion preventing arbitration. CCI appealed.

IN THE WORDS OF THE COURT . . .
Evelyn N. *KEYES*, Justice.
* * * *

[Texas] Business and Commerce Code section 272.001 provides:

Case 3.3—Continued

If a contract contains a provision making * * * any conflict arising under the contract subject to * * * arbitration in another
state, that provision is voidable by the party obligated by the
contract to perform the construction * * * .

Levco argues * * * that it "exercised its option to void the
requirement in the Contract to arbitrate in Lake County, Ohio."

*The FAA preempts all otherwise applicable inconsistent state
laws * * * under the Supremacy Clause of the United States
Constitution. The FAA declares written provisions for arbitration
"valid, irrevocable, and enforceable, save upon such grounds
as exist at law or in equity for the revocation of any contract."*
[Emphasis added.]

* * * Applying section 272.001 as Levco asks us to do
here would prevent us from enforcing a term of the parties'
arbitration agreement—the venue—on a ground that is not recognized by the FAA or by general state-law contract principles.
We hold that the FAA preempts application of this provision
under the facts of this case.

* * * By allowing a party to * * * declare void a previously
bargained-for provision, application of section 272.001 would
undermine the declared federal policy of rigorous enforcement
of arbitration agreements.

DECISION AND REMEDY   The Texas appellate court reversed
the trial court, holding that the FAA preempts the Texas statute.
CCI could compel arbitration in Ohio.

THE LEGAL ENVIRONMENT DIMENSION   *How would business
be affected if each state could pass a statute, like the one in
Texas, allowing parties to void out-of-state arbitrations?*

THE SOCIAL DIMENSION   *Considering the relative bargaining power of the parties, was it fair to enforce the arbitration
clause in this contract? Why or why not?*

The Issue of Arbitrability   Notice that in the preceding *Case Example 3.14,*
the issue before the United States Supreme Court was *not* the basic controversy (whether
the interest rate charged was illegally high) but rather the issue of arbitrability—that is,
whether the matter had to be resolved by arbitration under the arbitration clause. Actions
over arbitrability often occur when a dispute arises over an agreement that contains an arbitration clause: one party files a motion to compel arbitration, while the other party wants
to have the dispute settled by a court, not by arbitration. If the court finds that the dispute
is covered by the arbitration clause, it may compel the other party to submit to arbitration,
even though his or her claim involves the violation of a statute, such as an employment
statute. Usually, if the court finds that the legislature, in enacting the statute, did not intend
to prohibit arbitration, the court will allow the claim to be arbitrated.

No party will be ordered to submit a particular dispute to arbitration, however, unless
the court is convinced that the party consented to do so. Additionally, the courts will not
compel arbitration if it is clear that the prescribed arbitration rules and procedures are
inherently unfair to one of the parties.

The terms of an arbitration agreement can limit the types of disputes that the parties
agree to arbitrate. When the parties do not specify limits, however, disputes can arise as
to whether a particular matter is covered by the arbitration agreement. Then it is up to the
court to resolve the issue of arbitrability.

Mandatory Arbitration in the Employment Context   A significant
question in the last several years has concerned mandatory arbitration clauses in employment contracts. Many claim that employees' rights are not sufficiently protected when
workers are forced, as a condition of being hired, to agree to arbitrate all disputes and thus
waive their rights under statutes specifically designed to protect employees. The United
States Supreme Court, however, has generally held that mandatory arbitration clauses in
employment contracts are enforceable.

CASE EXAMPLE 3.15   In a landmark decision, *Gilmer v. Interstate Johnson Lane Corp.*,[19] the Supreme Court held that a claim brought under a federal statute prohibiting age discrimination (see Chapter 18) could be subject to arbitration. The Court concluded that the employee had waived his right to sue when he agreed, as part of a required registration application to be a securities representative with the New York Stock Exchange, to arbitrate "any dispute, claim, or controversy" relating to his employment. ●

Since the *Gilmer* decision, some courts have refused to enforce one-sided arbitration clauses on the ground that they are *unconscionable* (see Chapter 10). Thus, businesspersons considering using arbitration clauses in employment contracts should be careful that they are not too one sided—especially provisions on how the parties will split the costs of the arbitration procedure.

Private Arbitration Proceedings

In 2011, the Delaware Chancery Court established a new confidential arbitration process, which allows parties to arbitrate their disputes in private. Because many companies are headquartered in Delaware, the court's caseload is heavy, and its influence on the business environment is significant. Delaware's decision to authorize secret arbitration proceedings has been controversial.

EXAMPLE 3.16   Two smartphone makers were the first to use Delaware's confidential arbitration procedures to reach a settlement of their dispute. Skyworks Solutions, Inc., makes technology that transmits signals from smartphones, and Advanced Analogic Technologies, Inc. (AATI), makes power management devices for smartphones. Skyworks had agreed to a merger deal with AATI for $262.5 million, but then backed out, claiming that AATI had not properly accounted for revenue. Both parties filed lawsuits and ended up arbitrating using Delaware's new process. The two reached a settlement to complete the merger for $256 million, without disclosing the details of their agreement. ●

Providers of ADR Services

ADR services are provided by both government agencies and private organizations. A major provider of ADR services is the American Arbitration Association (AAA), which handles more than 200,000 claims a year in its numerous offices worldwide. Most of the largest U.S. law firms are members of this nonprofit association. Cases brought before the AAA are heard by an expert or a panel of experts in the area relating to the dispute and are usually settled quickly. The AAA has a special team devoted to resolving large, complex disputes across a wide range of industries.

Hundreds of for-profit firms around the country also provide various forms of dispute-resolution services. Typically, these firms hire retired judges to conduct arbitration hearings or otherwise assist parties in settling their disputes. The judges follow procedures similar to those of the federal courts and use similar rules. Usually, each party to the dispute pays a filing fee and a designated fee for a hearing session or conference.

Online Dispute Resolution

Online Dispute Resolution (ODR) The resolution of disputes with the assistance of organizations that offer dispute-resolution services via the Internet.

An increasing number of companies and organizations offer dispute-resolution services using the Internet. The settlement of disputes in these online forums is known as **online dispute resolution (ODR).** The disputes have most commonly involved disagreements over the rights to domain names or over the quality of goods sold via the Internet, including goods sold through Internet auction sites.

ODR may be best suited for resolving small- to medium-sized business liability claims, which may not be worth the expense of litigation or traditional ADR. Rules being developed

---

19. 500 U.S. 20, 111 S.Ct. 1647, 114 L.Ed.2d 26 (1991).

in online forums may ultimately become a code of conduct for everyone who does business in cyberspace. Most online forums do not automatically apply the law of any specific jurisdiction. Instead, results are often based on general, universal legal principles. As with most offline methods of dispute resolution, any party may appeal to a court at any time.

Interestingly, some local governments are using ODR to resolve claims. **EXAMPLE 3.17** New York City has used Cybersettle.com to resolve auto accident, sidewalk, and other personal-injury claims made against the city. Parties with complaints submit their demands, and the city submits its offers confidentially online. If an offer exceeds a demand, the claimant keeps half the difference as a bonus. ●

Reviewing . . . Courts and Alternative Dispute Resolution

Stan Garner resides in Illinois and promotes boxing matches for SuperSports, Inc., an Illinois corporation. Garner created the promotional concept of the "Ages" fights—a series of three boxing matches pitting an older fighter (George Foreman) against a younger fighter, such as John Ruiz or Riddick Bowe. The concept included titles for each of the three fights ("Challenge of the Ages," "Battle of the Ages," and "Fight of the Ages"), as well as promotional epithets to characterize the two fighters ("the Foreman Factor"). Garner contacted George Foreman and his manager, who both reside in Texas, to sell the idea, and they arranged a meeting at Caesar's Palace in Las Vegas, Nevada. At some point in the negotiations, Foreman's manager signed a nondisclosure agreement prohibiting him from disclosing Garner's promotional concepts unless they signed a contract. Nevertheless, after negotiations between Garner and Foreman fell through, Foreman used Garner's "Battle of the Ages" concept to promote a subsequent fight. Garner filed a lawsuit against Foreman and his manager in a federal district court in Illinois, alleging breach of contract. Using the information presented in the chapter, answer the following questions.

1. On what basis might the federal district court in Illinois exercise jurisdiction in this case?
2. Does the federal district court have original or appellate jurisdiction?
3. Suppose that Garner had filed his action in an Illinois state court. Could an Illinois state court exercise personal jurisdiction over Foreman or his manager? Why or why not?
4. Assume that Garner had filed his action in a Nevada state court. Would that court have personal jurisdiction over Foreman or his manager? Explain.

Debate This   In this age of the Internet, when people communicate via e-mail, tweets, FaceBook, and Skype, is the concept of jurisdiction losing its meaning?

Key Terms

Chapter Summary: Courts and Alternative Dispute Resolution

The Judiciary's Role	The role of the judiciary—the courts—in the American governmental system is to interpret and apply the law. Through the process of judicial review—determining the constitutionality of laws—the judicial branch acts as a check on the executive and legislative branches of government.

Basic Judicial Requirements	1. *Jurisdiction*—Before a court can hear a case, it must have jurisdiction over the person against whom the suit is brought or the property involved in the suit, as well as jurisdiction over the subject matter.
	  a. Limited versus general jurisdiction—Limited jurisdiction exists when a court is limited to a specific subject matter, such as probate or divorce. General jurisdiction exists when a court can hear any kind of case.
	  b. Original versus appellate jurisdiction—Original jurisdiction exists when courts have authority to hear a case for the first time (trial courts). Appellate jurisdiction is exercised by courts of appeals, or reviewing courts, which generally do not have original jurisdiction.
	  c. Federal jurisdiction—Arises (1) when a federal question is involved (when the plaintiff's cause of action is based, at least in part, on the U.S. Constitution, a treaty, or a federal law) or (2) when a case involves diversity of citizenship (citizens of different states, for example) and the amount in controversy exceeds $75,000.
	  d. Concurrent versus exclusive jurisdiction—Concurrent jurisdiction exists when two different courts have authority to hear the same case. Exclusive jurisdiction exists when only state courts or only federal courts have authority to hear a case.
	2. *Jurisdiction in cyberspace*—Because the Internet does not have physical boundaries, traditional jurisdictional concepts have been difficult to apply in cases involving activities conducted via the Web. Gradually, the courts are developing standards to use in determining when jurisdiction over a Web site owner or operator located in another state is proper.
	3. *Venue*—Venue has to do with the most appropriate location for a trial, which is usually the geographic area where the event leading to the dispute took place or where the parties reside.
	4. *Standing to sue*—A requirement that a party must have a legally protected and tangible interest at stake sufficient to justify seeking relief through the court system. The controversy at issue must also be a justiciable controversy—one that is real and substantial, as opposed to hypothetical or academic.

The State and Federal Court Systems	1. *Trial courts*—Courts of original jurisdiction, in which legal actions are initiated.
	  a. State—Courts of general jurisdiction can hear any case. Courts of limited jurisdiction include domestic relations courts, probate courts, traffic courts, and small claims courts.
	  b. Federal—The federal district court is the equivalent of the state trial court. Federal courts of limited jurisdiction include the U.S. Tax Court, the U.S. Bankruptcy Court, and the U.S. Court of Federal Claims.
	2. *Intermediate appellate courts*—Courts of appeals, or reviewing courts, which generally do not have original jurisdiction. Many states have an intermediate appellate court. In the federal court system, the U.S. circuit courts of appeals are the intermediate appellate courts.
	3. *Supreme (highest) courts*—Each state has a supreme court, although it may be called by some other name. Appeal from the state supreme court to the United States Supreme Court is possible only if the case involves a federal question. The United States Supreme Court is the highest court in the federal court system and the final arbiter of the U.S. Constitution and federal law.

Following a State Court Case	Rules of procedure prescribe the way in which disputes are handled in the courts. Rules differ from court to court, and separate sets of rules exist for federal and state courts, as well as for criminal and civil cases. A civil court case in a state court would involve the following procedures:
	1. *The pleadings*—
	  a. Complaint—Filed by the plaintiff with the court to initiate the lawsuit. The complaint is served with a summons on the defendant.
	  b. Answer—A response to the complaint in which the defendant admits or denies the allegations made by the plaintiff. The answer may assert a counterclaim or an affirmative defense.
	  c. Motion to dismiss—A request to the court to dismiss the case for stated reasons, such as the plaintiff's failure to state a claim for which relief can be granted.
	2. *Pretrial motions* (in addition to the motion to dismiss)—
	  a. Motion for judgment on the pleadings—May be made by either party. It will be granted if the parties agree on the facts and the only question is how the law applies to the facts. The judge bases the decision solely on the pleadings.

Chapter Summary: Courts and Alternative Dispute Resolution— Continued

Following a State Court Case— Continued	b. Motion for summary judgment—May be made by either party. It will be granted if the parties agree on the facts and the sole question is a question of law. The judge can consider evidence outside the pleadings when evaluating the motion.
	3. *Discovery*—The process of gathering evidence concerning the case. Discovery involves depositions (sworn testimony by a party to the lawsuit or any witness), interrogatories (written questions and answers to these questions made by parties to the action with the aid of their attorneys), and various requests (for admissions, documents, and medical examinations, for example). Discovery may also involve electronically recorded information, such as e-mail, voice mail, word-processing documents, and other data compilations. Although electronic discovery has significant advantages over paper discovery, it is also more time consuming and expensive and often requires the parties to hire experts.
	4. *Pretrial conference*—Either party or the court can request a pretrial conference to identify the matters in dispute after discovery has taken place and to plan the course of the trial.
	5. *Trial*—Following jury selection *(voir dire)*, the trial begins with opening statements from both parties' attorneys. The following events then occur:
	  a. The plaintiff's introduction of evidence (including the testimony of witnesses) supporting the plaintiff's position. The defendant's attorney can challenge evidence and cross-examine witnesses.
	  b. The defendant's introduction of evidence (including the testimony of witnesses) supporting the defendant's position. The plaintiff's attorney can challenge evidence and cross-examine witnesses.
	  c. Closing arguments by the attorneys in favor of their respective clients, the judge's instructions to the jury, and the jury's verdict.
	6. *Posttrial motions*—
	  a. Motion for judgment *n.o.v.* ("notwithstanding the verdict")—Will be granted if the judge is convinced that the jury was in error.
	  b. Motion for a new trial—Will be granted if the judge is convinced that the jury was in error. The motion can also be granted on the grounds of newly discovered evidence, misconduct by the participants during the trial, or error by the judge.
	7. *Appeal*—Either party can appeal the trial court's judgment to an appropriate court of appeals. After reviewing the record on appeal, the abstracts, and the attorneys' briefs, the appellate court holds a hearing and renders its opinion.

The Courts Adapt to the Online World	A number of state and federal courts now allow parties to file litigation-related documents with the courts via the Internet or other electronic means. Nearly all of the federal appellate courts and bankruptcy courts and a majority of the federal district courts have implemented electronic filing systems. Almost every court now has a Web page offering information about the court and its procedures, and increasingly courts are publishing their opinions online. In the future, we may see cyber courts, in which all trial proceedings are conducted online.
Alternative Dispute Resolution	1. *Negotiation*—The parties come together, with or without attorneys to represent them, and try to reach a settlement without the involvement of a third party. 2. *Mediation*—The parties themselves reach an agreement with the help of a neutral third party, called a mediator. The mediator may propose a solution but does not make a decision resolving the matter. 3. *Arbitration*—A more formal method of ADR in which the parties submit their dispute to a neutral third party, the arbitrator, who renders a decision. The decision may or may not be legally binding, depending on the circumstances. 4. *Other types of ADR*—These include assisted negotiation, early neutral case evaluation, mini-trials, and summary jury trials (SJTs). 5. *Providers of ADR services*—The leading nonprofit provider of ADR services is the American Arbitration Association. Hundreds of for-profit firms also provide ADR services. 6. *Online dispute resolution*—A number of organizations and firms are now offering negotiation, mediation, and arbitration services through online forums. These forums have been a practical alternative for the resolution of domain name disputes and e-commerce disputes in which the amount in controversy is relatively small.

Issue Spotters

1. At the trial, after Sue calls her witnesses, offers her evidence, and otherwise presents her side of the case, Tom has at least two choices between courses of action. Tom can call his first witness. What else might he do? (See *Following a State Court Case.*)

2. Sue contracts with Tom to deliver a quantity of computers to Sue's Computer Store. They disagree over the amount, the delivery date, the price, and the quality. Sue files a suit against Tom in a state court. Their state requires that their dispute

be submitted to mediation or nonbinding arbitration. If the dispute is not resolved, or if either party disagrees with the decision of the mediator or arbitrator, will a court hear the case? Explain. (See *Alternative Dispute Resolution.*)

—**Check your answers to the Issue Spotters against the answers provided in Appendix D at the end of this text.**

For Review

1. What is judicial review? How and when was the power of judicial review established?
2. Before a court can hear a case, it must have jurisdiction. Over what must it have jurisdiction? How are the courts applying traditional jurisdictional concepts to cases involving Internet transactions?
3. What is the difference between a trial court and an appellate court?
4. What is discovery, and how does electronic discovery differ from traditional discovery?
5. What are three alternative methods of resolving disputes?

Business Scenarios and Case Problems

3–1. Standing to Sue. Jack and Maggie Turton bought a house in Jefferson County, Idaho, located directly across the street from a gravel pit. A few years later, the county converted the pit to a landfill. The landfill accepted many kinds of trash that cause harm to the environment, including major appliances, animal carcasses, containers with hazardous content warnings, leaking car batteries, and waste oil. The Turtons complained to the county, but the county did nothing. The Turtons then filed a lawsuit against the county alleging violations of federal environmental laws pertaining to groundwater contamination and other pollution. Do the Turtons have standing to sue? Why or why not? (See *Basic Judicial Requirements.*)

3–2. Jurisdiction. Marya Callais, a citizen of Florida, was walking along a busy street in Tallahassee when a large crate flew off a passing truck and hit her. Callais sustained numerous injuries. She incurred a great deal of pain and suffering plus significant medical expenses, and she could not work for six months. She wishes to sue the trucking firm for $300,000 in damages. The firm's headquarters are in Georgia, although the company does business in Florida. In what court may Callais bring suit—a Florida state court, a Georgia state court, or a federal court? What factors might influence her decision? (See *Basic Judicial Requirements.*)

3–3. Discovery. Advance Technology Consultants, Inc. (ATC), contracted with RoadTrac, LLC, to provide software and client software systems for the products of global positioning satellite (GPS) technology being developed by RoadTrac. RoadTrac agreed to provide ATC with hardware with which ATC's software would interface. Problems soon arose, however, and RoadTrac filed a lawsuit against ATC alleging breach of contract. During discovery, RoadTrac requested ATC's customer lists and marketing procedures. ATC objected to providing this information because RoadTrac and ATC had

become competitors in the GPS industry. Should a party to a lawsuit have to hand over its confidential business secrets as part of a discovery request? Why or why not? What limitations might a court consider imposing before requiring ATC to produce this material? (See *Following a State Court Case.*)

3–4. Venue. Brandy Austin used powdered infant formula to feed her infant daughter shortly after her birth. Austin claimed that a can of Nestlé Good Start Supreme Powder Infant Formula was contaminated with *Enterobacter sakazakii* bacteria, which can cause infections of the bloodstream and central nervous system, in particular, meningitis (inflammation of the tissue surrounding the brain or spinal cord). Austin filed an action against Nestlé in Hennepin County District Court in Minnesota. Nestlé argued for a change of venue because the alleged tortious action on the part of Nestlé occurred in South Carolina. Austin is a South Carolina resident and gave birth to her daughter in that state. Should the case be transferred to a South Carolina venue? Why or why not? [*Austin v. Nestle USA, Inc.*, 677 F.Supp.2d 1134 (D.Minn. 2009)] (See *Basic Judicial Requirements.*)

3–5. Spotlight on National Football—Arbitration. Bruce Matthews played football for the Tennessee Titans. As part of his contract, he agreed to submit any dispute to arbitration. He also agreed that Tennessee law would determine all matters related to workers' compensation. After Matthews retired, he filed a workers' compensation claim in California. The arbitrator ruled that Matthews could pursue his claim in California but only under Tennessee law. Should this award be set aside? Explain. [*National Football League Players Association v. National Football League Management Council*, 2011 WL 1137334 (S.D.Cal. 2011)] (See *Alternative Dispute Resolution.*)

3–6. Minimum Contacts. Seal Polymer Industries sold two freight containers of latex gloves to Med-Express, Inc., a company based in North Carolina. When Med-Express failed to pay the $104,000 owed for the gloves, Seal Polymer sued in an Illinois court and obtained a judgment against Med-Express. Med-Express argued that it did not have minimum contacts with Illinois and therefore the Illinois judgment based on personal jurisdiction was invalid. Med-Express stated that it was incorporated under North Carolina law, had its principal place of business in North Carolina, and therefore had no minimum contacts with Illinois. Was this statement alone sufficient to prevent the Illinois judgment from being collected against Med-Express in North Carolina? Why or why not? [*Seal Polymer Industries v. Med-Express, Inc.*, 725 S.E.2d 5 (N.C.App. 2012)] (See *Basic Judicial Requirements.*)

3–7. Arbitration. Horton Automatics and the Industrial Division of the Communications Workers of America—the union that represented Horton's workers—negotiated a collective bargaining agreement. If an employee's discharge for a workplace-rule violation was submitted to arbitration, the agreement limited the arbitrator to determining whether the rule was reasonable and whether the employee had violated it. When Horton discharged its employee, Ruben de la Garza, the union appealed to arbitration. The arbitrator found that de la Garza had violated a reasonable safety rule, but "was not totally convinced" that Horton should have treated the violation more seriously than other rule violations. The arbitrator ordered de la Garza reinstated to his job. Can a court set aside this order from the arbitrator? Explain. [*Horton Automatics v. The Industrial Division of the Communications Workers of America, AFL-CIO,* 2013 WL 59204 (5th Cir. 2013)] (See *Alternative Dispute Resolution.*)

3–8. Business Case Problem with Sample Answer— Discovery. Jessica Lester died from injuries suffered in an auto accident caused by the driver of a truck owned by Allied Concrete Co. Jessica's widower, Isaiah, filed a suit against Allied for damages. The defendant requested copies of all of Isaiah's Facebook photos and other postings. Before responding, Isaiah "cleaned up" his Facebook page. Allied suspected that some of the items had been deleted, including a photo of Isaiah holding a beer can while wearing a T-shirt that declared "I [heart] hotmoms." Can this material

be recovered? If so, how? What effect might Isaiah's "misconduct" have on the result in this case? Discuss. [*Allied Concrete Co. v. Lester,* 736 S.E.2d 699 (Va. 2013)] (See *Following a State Court Case.*)

—**For a sample answer to Problem 3–8, go to Appendix E at the end of this text.**

3–9. Electronic Filing. Betsy Faden worked for the U.S. Department of Veterans Affairs. Faden was removed from her position in April 2012 and was given until May 29 to appeal the removal decision. She submitted an appeal through the Merit Systems Protection Board's e-filing system seven days after the deadline. Ordered to show good cause for the delay, Faden testified that she had attempted to e-file the appeal while the board's system was down. The board acknowledged that its system had not been functioning on May 27, 28, and 29. Was Faden sufficiently diligent in ensuring a timely filing? Discuss. [*Faden v. Merit Systems Protection Board,* 2014 WL 163394 (Fed.Cir. 2014)] (See *The Courts Adapt to the Online World.*)

3–10. ⬌ A Question of Ethics—Agreement to Arbitrate. Nellie Lumpkin, who suffered from dementia, was admitted to the Picayune Convalescent Center, a nursing home. Because of her mental condition, her daughter, Beverly McDaniel, signed the admissions agreement. It included a clause requiring the parties to submit any dispute to arbitration. After Lumpkin left the center two years later, she filed a suit against Picayune to recover damages for mistreatment and malpractice. [*Covenant Health & Rehabilitation of Picayune, LP v. Lumpkin,* 23 So.2d 1092 (Miss. App. 2009)] (See *Alternative Dispute Resolution.*)

1. Is it ethical for this dispute—involving negligent medical care, not a breach of a commercial contract—to be forced into arbitration? Why or why not? Discuss whether medical facilities should be able to impose arbitration when there is generally no bargaining over such terms.

2. Should a person with limited mental capacity be held to the arbitration clause agreed to by her next of kin who signed on her behalf? Why or why not?

4 CHAPTER

Business and the Constitution

(JustASC/Shutterstock.com)

LEARNING OBJECTIVES

The five learning objectives below are designed to help improve your understanding of the chapter. After reading this chapter, you should be able to answer the following questions:

1. What is the basic structure of the U.S. government?

2. What constitutional clause gives the federal government the power to regulate commercial activities among the various states?

3. What constitutional clause allows laws enacted by the federal government to take priority over conflicting state laws?

4. What is the Bill of Rights? What freedoms does the First Amendment guarantee?

5. Where in the Constitution can the due process clause be found?

"The United States Constitution has proved itself the most marvelously elastic compilation of rules of government ever written."
—Franklin D. Roosevelt, 1882–1945 (Thirty-second president of the United States, 1933–1945)

The U.S. Constitution is brief. (See Appendix B for the full text of the U.S. Constitution.) It contains only about seven thousand words—less than one-third of the number of words in the average state constitution. Perhaps its brevity explains, in part, why the Constitution has proved to be so "marvelously elastic," as Franklin Roosevelt pointed out in the chapter-opening quotation, and why it has survived for more than two hundred years—longer than any other written constitution in the world.

Laws that govern business have their origin in the lawmaking authority granted by the Constitution, which is the supreme law in this country. As mentioned in Chapter 1, neither Congress nor any state can enact a law that is in conflict with the Constitution. Constitutional disputes frequently come before the courts. For example, numerous states have challenged the Obama administration's Affordable Care Act on constitutional grounds.[1]

---

1. *National Federation of Independent Business v. Sebelius,* ___ U.S. ___, 132 S.Ct. 2566, 183 L.Ed.2d 450 (2012).

The United States Supreme Court had to decide if the provisions of this law that required most Americans to have health insurance by 2014 exceeded the constitutional authority of the federal government. In 2012, the Court upheld the constitutionality of this provision— a decision that significantly impacts business because many individuals obtain insurance through their employers.

In this chapter, we first look at some basic constitutional concepts and clauses and their significance for business. Then, we examine how certain fundamental freedoms guaranteed by the Constitution affect businesspersons and the workplace. We also examine the constitutional protection of privacy rights. In recent years, many users of online social networks have become concerned at the amount of their personal information that exists in cyberspace and the possibility that it might be misused. Such concerns recently led the Federal Trade Commission to charge Facebook, Twitter, and Google with misleading users about the way their personal data were being used. All three companies agreed to revise their privacy policies as a result.

Does the Constitution limit the powers of the national government?

The Constitutional Powers of Government

Following the Revolutionary War, the states created a *confederal* form of government in which the states had the authority to govern themselves and the national government could exercise only limited powers. When problems arose because the nation was facing an economic crisis and state laws interfered with the free flow of commerce, a national convention was called, and the delegates drafted the U.S. Constitution. This document, after its ratification by the states in 1789, became the basis for an entirely new form of government.

A Federal Form of Government

The new government created by the Constitution reflected a series of compromises made by the convention delegates on various issues. Some delegates wanted sovereign power to remain with the states, whereas others wanted the national government alone to exercise sovereign power. The end result was a compromise—a **federal form of government** in which the national government and the states *share* sovereign power.

The Constitution sets forth specific powers that can be exercised by the national government and provides that the national government has the implied power to undertake actions necessary to carry out its expressly designated powers. All other powers are "reserved" to the states. The broad language of the Constitution, though, has left much room for debate over the specific nature and scope of these powers. Generally, it has been the task of the courts to determine where the boundary line between state and national powers should lie—and that line changes over time. In the past, for instance, the national government met little resistance from the courts when extending its regulatory authority over broad areas of social and economic life. Today, the courts are sometimes willing to curb the national government's regulatory powers.

Federal Form of Government A system of government in which the states form a union and the sovereign power is divided between the central government and the member states.

The Separation of Powers

To make it difficult for the national government to use its power arbitrarily, the Constitution divided the national government's powers among the three branches of government. The legislative branch makes the laws, the executive branch enforces the laws, and the judicial branch interprets the laws. Each branch performs a separate function, and no branch may exercise the authority of another branch.

Learning Objective 1
What is the basic structure of the U.S. government?

Checks and Balances The principle under which the powers of the national government are divided among three separate branches — the executive, legislative, and judicial branches — each of which exercises a check on the actions of the others.

Additionally, a system of **checks and balances** allows each branch to limit the actions of the other two branches, thus preventing any one branch from exercising too much power. The following are examples of these checks and balances:

1. The legislative branch (Congress) can enact a law, but the executive branch (the president) has the constitutional authority to veto that law.
2. The executive branch is responsible for foreign affairs, but treaties with foreign governments require the advice and consent of the Senate.
3. Congress determines the jurisdiction of the federal courts, and the president appoints federal judges, with the advice and consent of the Senate, but the judicial branch has the power to hold actions of the other two branches unconstitutional.[2]

Learning Objective 2
What constitutional clause gives the federal government the power to regulate commercial activities among the various states?

Commerce Clause The provision in Article I, Section 8, of the U.S. Constitution that gives Congress the power to regulate interstate commerce.

The Commerce Clause

To prevent states from establishing laws and regulations that would interfere with trade and commerce among the states, the Constitution expressly delegated to the national government the power to regulate interstate commerce. Article I, Section 8, of the U.S. Constitution expressly permits Congress "[t]o regulate Commerce with foreign Nations, and among the several States, and with the Indian Tribes." This clause, referred to as the **commerce clause,** has had a greater impact on business than any other provision in the Constitution.

Initially, the commerce power was interpreted as being limited to *interstate* commerce (commerce among the states) and not applicable to *intrastate* commerce (commerce within a state). In 1824, however, in the case of *Gibbons v. Ogden* (see the chapter's *Landmark in the Legal Environment* feature), the United States Supreme Court held that commerce within a state could also be regulated by the national government as long as the commerce *substantially affected* commerce involving more than one state.

The Expansion of National Powers under the Commerce Clause
In *Gibbons v. Ogden*, the commerce clause was expanded to regulate activities that "substantially affect interstate commerce." As the nation grew and faced new kinds of problems, the commerce clause became a vehicle for the additional expansion of the national government's regulatory powers. Even activities that seemed purely local came under the regulatory reach of the national government if those activities were deemed to substantially affect interstate commerce. **CASE EXAMPLE 4.1** In 1942, in *Wickard v. Filburn*,[3] the Supreme Court held that wheat production by an individual farmer intended wholly for consumption on his own farm was subject to federal regulation. The Court reasoned that the home consumption of wheat reduced the market demand for wheat and thus could have a substantial effect on interstate commerce. •

The Commerce Clause Today
Today, at least theoretically, the power over commerce authorizes the national government to regulate almost every commercial enterprise in the United States. The breadth of the commerce clause permits the national government to legislate in areas in which Congress has not explicitly been granted power.

In the last twenty years, the Supreme Court has on occasion curbed the national government's regulatory authority under the commerce clause. In 1995, the Court held—for the first time in sixty years—that Congress had exceeded its regulatory authority under the commerce clause. The Court struck down an act that banned the possession of guns

---

2. See the *Landmark in the Legal Environment* feature in Chapter 3 on the case of *Marbury v. Madison* (1803), in which the doctrine of judicial review was clearly enunciated by Chief Justice John Marshall.
3. 317 U.S. 111, 63 S.Ct. 82, 87 L.Ed. 122 (1942).

LANDMARK IN THE LEGAL ENVIRONMENT
Gibbons v. Ogden (1824)

The commerce clause of the U.S. Constitution gives Congress the power "[t]o regulate Commerce with foreign Nations, and among the several States, and with the Indian Tribes." Prior to the commerce clause, states tended to restrict commerce within and beyond their borders, which made trade more costly and inefficient. The goal of the clause was to unify the states' commerce policies and improve the efficiency of exchanges.

The problem was that although the commerce clause gave Congress some authority to regulate trade among the states, the extent of that power was unclear. What exactly does "to regulate commerce" mean? What does "commerce" entail? These questions came before the United States Supreme Court in 1824 in the case of *Gibbons v. Ogden.*[a]

Background In 1803, Robert Fulton, the inventor of the steamboat, and Robert Livingston, who was the ambassador to France, secured a monopoly from the New York legislature on steam navigation on the waters in the state of New York. Their monopoly extended to interstate waters—waterways between New York and another state. Fulton and Livingston licensed Aaron Ogden, a former governor of New Jersey and a U.S. senator, to operate steam-powered ferryboats between New York and New Jersey.

Thomas Gibbons already operated a ferry service between New Jersey and New York, which had been licensed by Congress under a 1793 act regulating the coastal trade. Although the federal government had licensed Gibbons to operate boats in interstate waters, he did not have the state of New York's permission to compete with Ogden in that area. Ogden sued Gibbons. The New York state courts granted Ogden's request for an injunction—an order prohibiting Gibbons from operating in New York waters. Gibbons appealed the decision to the United States Supreme Court.

Marshall's Decision The issue before the Court was whether the law regulated commerce that was "among the several states." The chief justice on the Supreme Court was John Marshall, an advocate of a strong national government. Marshall defined the word *commerce* as used in the commerce clause to mean all commercial intercourse—that is, all business dealings that affect more than one state. This broader definition included navigation.

In addition to expanding the definition of commerce, Marshall also validated and increased the power of the national legislature to regulate commerce. Said Marshall, "What is this power? It is the power . . . to prescribe the rule by which commerce is to be governed." Marshall held that the power to regulate interstate commerce is an exclusive power of the national government and that this power includes the power to regulate any intrastate commerce that substantially affects interstate commerce. Accordingly, the Court held in favor of Gibbons.

Application to Today's Legal Environment *Marshall's broad definition of the commerce power established the foundation for the expansion of national powers in the years to come. Today, the national government continues to rely on the commerce clause for its constitutional authority to regulate business activities.*

Marshall's conclusion that the power to regulate interstate commerce was an exclusive power of the national government has also had significant consequences. By implication, this means that a state cannot regulate activities that extend beyond its borders, such as out-of-state online gambling operations that affect the welfare of in-state citizens. It also means that state regulations over in-state activities normally will be invalidated if the regulations substantially burden interstate commerce.

a. 22 U.S. (9 Wheat.) 1, 6 L.Ed. 23 (1824).

---

within one thousand feet of any school because the act attempted to regulate an area that had "nothing to do with commerce."[4] Subsequently, the Court invalidated key portions of two other federal acts on the ground that they exceeded Congress's commerce clause authority.[5]

4. The Court held the Gun-Free School Zones Act of 1990 to be unconstitutional in *United States v. Lopez,* 514 U.S. 549, 115 S.Ct. 1624, 131 L.Ed.2d 626 (1995).
5. See *Printz v. United States,* 521 U.S. 898, 117 S.Ct. 2365, 138 L.Ed.2d 914 (1997), involving the Brady Handgun Violence Prevention Act of 1993; and *United States v. Morrison,* 529 U.S. 598, 120 S.Ct. 1740, 146 L.Ed.2d 658 (2000), concerning the federal Violence Against Women Act of 1994.

Because the Constitution reserves to the states all powers not delegated to the national government, the states can and do regulate many types of commercial activities within their borders. So, too, do municipalities. One of these powers is the imposition of building codes. What is the general term that applies to such powers?

Police Powers Powers possessed by the states as part of their inherent sovereignty. These powers may be exercised to protect or promote the public order, health, safety, morals, and general welfare.

In one notable case, however, the Supreme Court did allow the federal government to regulate noncommercial activities taking place wholly within a state's borders. **CASE EXAMPLE 4.2**   A growing number of states, including California, have adopted laws that legalize marijuana for medical purposes (and recreational use of marijuana is legal in a few states). Marijuana possession, however, is illegal under the federal Controlled Substances Act (CSA).[6] After the federal government seized the marijuana that two seriously ill California women were using on the advice of their physicians, the women filed a lawsuit. They argued that it was unconstitutional for the federal statute to prohibit them from using marijuana for medical purposes that were legal within the state. The Supreme Court, though, held that Congress has the authority to prohibit the *intra*state possession and noncommercial cultivation of marijuana as part of a larger regulatory scheme (the CSA).[7] In other words, the federal government may prosecute individuals for possession of marijuana regardless of whether they reside in a state that allows the medical or recreational use of marijuana. ●

The Regulatory Powers of the States   As part of their inherent sovereignty, state governments have the authority to regulate affairs within their borders. This authority stems in part from the Tenth Amendment to the Constitution, which reserves to the states all powers not delegated to the national government. State regulatory powers are often referred to as **police powers**. The term encompasses not only the enforcement of criminal law but also the right of state governments to regulate private activities in order to protect or promote the public order, health, safety, morals, and general welfare. Fire and building codes, antidiscrimination laws, parking regulations, zoning restrictions, licensing requirements, and thousands of other state statutes have been enacted pursuant to a state's police powers. Local governments, including cities, also exercise police powers.[8] Although a state may not directly regulate interstate commerce, it may indirectly affect interstate commerce through the reasonable exercise of its police powers. Generally, state laws enacted pursuant to a state's police powers carry a strong presumption of validity.

The "Dormant" Commerce Clause   The United States Supreme Court has interpreted the commerce clause to mean that the national government has the *exclusive* authority to regulate commerce that substantially affects trade and commerce among the states. This express grant of authority to the national government, which is often referred to as the "positive" aspect of the commerce clause, implies a negative aspect—that the states do *not* have the authority to regulate interstate commerce. This negative aspect of the commerce clause is often referred to as the "dormant" (implied) commerce clause.

The dormant commerce clause comes into play when state regulations affect interstate commerce. In this situation, the courts normally weigh the state's interest in regulating a certain matter against the burden that the state's regulation places on interstate commerce. Because courts balance the interests involved, predicting the outcome in a particular case can be extremely difficult.

CASE EXAMPLE 4.3   Tri-M Group, LLC, a Pennsylvania electrical contractor, was hired to work on a veteran's home in Delaware that was partially state funded. Delaware's regulations allowed contractors on state-funded projects to pay a lower wage rate to apprentices if the

---

6. 21 U.S.C. Sections 801 *et seq.*
7. *Gonzales v. Raich*, 545 U.S. 1, 125 S.Ct. 2195, 162 L.Ed.2d 1 (2005).
8. Local governments derive their authority to regulate their communities from the state because they are creatures of the state. In other words, they cannot come into existence unless authorized by the state to do so.

contractors had registered their apprenticeship programs in the state. Out-of-state contractors, however, were not eligible to pay the lower rate unless they maintained a permanent office in Delaware. Tri-M filed a suit in federal court claiming that Delaware's regulations discriminated against out-of-state contractors in violation of the dormant commerce clause. The state argued that the regulations were justified because it had a legitimate interest in safeguarding the welfare of all apprentices by requiring a permanent place of business in Delaware. But the court held that the state had not overcome the presumption of invalidity that applies to discriminatory regulations and that nondiscriminatory alternatives existed for ensuring the welfare of apprentices. Therefore, the regulations violated the dormant commerce clause.[9] ●

The Supremacy Clause

Article VI of the Constitution provides that the Constitution, laws, and treaties of the United States are "the supreme Law of the Land." This article, commonly referred to as the **supremacy clause**, is important in the ordering of state and federal relationships. When there is a direct conflict between a federal law and a state law, the state law is rendered invalid. Because some powers are *concurrent* (shared by the federal government and the states), however, it is necessary to determine which law governs in a particular circumstance.

Preemption occurs when Congress chooses to act exclusively in a concurrent area. In this circumstance, a valid federal statute or regulation will take precedence over a conflicting state or local law or regulation on the same general subject. Often, it is not clear whether Congress, in passing a law, intended to preempt an entire subject area against state regulation. In these situations, the courts determine whether Congress intended to exercise exclusive power over a given area. No single factor is decisive as to whether a court will find preemption. Generally, congressional intent to preempt will be found if a federal law regulating an activity is so pervasive, comprehensive, or detailed that the states have little or no room to regulate in that area. Also, when a federal statute creates an agency—such as the National Labor Relations Board—to enforce the law, matters that may come within the agency's jurisdiction will likely preempt state laws.

CASE EXAMPLE 4.4 The United States Supreme Court ruled on a case involving a man who alleged that he had been injured by a faulty medical device (a balloon catheter that had been inserted into his artery following a heart attack). The Court noted that the Medical Device Amendments of 1976 had included a preemption provision. The medical device had passed the U.S. Food and Drug Administration's rigorous premarket approval process. Therefore, the Court ruled that the federal regulation of medical devices preempted the man's state law claims for negligence, strict liability, and implied warranty (see Chapter 5).[10] ●

Business and the Bill of Rights

The importance of having a written declaration of the rights of individuals eventually caused the first Congress of the United States to enact twelve amendments to the Constitution and submit them to the states for approval. The first ten of these amendments, commonly known as the **Bill of Rights**, were adopted in 1791 and embody a series of protections for the individual against various types of interference by the federal government.[11]

Some constitutional protections apply to business entities as well. For example, corporations exist as separate legal entities, or legal persons, and enjoy many of the same rights and

Can state and city governments regulate the ingredients in fast food?

Supremacy Clause The requirement in Article VI of the U.S. Constitution that provides that the Constitution, laws, and treaties of the United States are "the supreme Law of the Land."

Preemption A doctrine under which certain federal laws preempt, or take precedence over, conflicting state or local laws.

Learning Objective 3
What constitutional clause allows laws enacted by the federal government to take priority over conflicting state laws?

Bill of Rights The first ten amendments to the U.S. Constitution.

---

9. *Tri-M Group, LLC v. Sharp*, 638 F.3d 406 (3d Cir. 2011). Sharp was the name of the secretary of the Delaware Department of Labor.
10. *Riegel v. Medtronic, Inc.*, 552 U.S. 312, 128 S.Ct. 999, 169 L.Ed.2d 892 (2008).
11. One of the proposed amendments was ratified more than two hundred years later (in 1992) and became the Twenty-seventh Amendment to the Constitution. See Appendix B.

Learning Objective 4
What is the Bill of Rights? What freedoms does the First Amendment guarantee?

privileges as natural persons do. Summarized here are the protections guaranteed by these ten amendments (see the Constitution in Appendix B for the complete text of each amendment):

1. The First Amendment guarantees the freedoms of religion, speech, and the press and the rights to assemble peaceably and to petition the government.
2. The Second Amendment guarantees the right to keep and bear arms.
3. The Third Amendment prohibits, in peacetime, the lodging of soldiers in any house without the owner's consent.
4. The Fourth Amendment prohibits unreasonable searches and seizures of persons or property.
5. The Fifth Amendment guarantees the rights to *indictment* (formal accusation) by a grand jury, to *due process of law*, and to fair payment when private property is taken for public use. The Fifth Amendment also prohibits compulsory self-incrimination and double jeopardy (trial for the same crime twice).
6. The Sixth Amendment guarantees the accused in a criminal case the right to a speedy and public trial by an impartial jury and with counsel. The accused has the right to cross-examine witnesses against him or her and to solicit testimony from witnesses in his or her favor.
7. The Seventh Amendment guarantees the right to a trial by jury in a civil (noncriminal) case involving at least twenty dollars.[12]
8. The Eighth Amendment prohibits excessive bail and fines, as well as cruel and unusual punishment.
9. The Ninth Amendment establishes that the people have rights in addition to those specified in the Constitution.
10. The Tenth Amendment establishes that those powers neither delegated to the federal government nor denied to the states are reserved for the states.

We will look closely at several of these amendments in Chapter 6, in the context of criminal law and procedures. In this chapter, we examine two important guarantees of the First Amendment—freedom of speech and freedom of religion—after we look at how the Bill of Rights puts certain limits on government.

Limits on Federal and State Governmental Actions

As originally intended, the Bill of Rights limited only the powers of the national government. Over time, however, the United States Supreme Court "incorporated" most of these rights into the protections against state actions afforded by the Fourteenth Amendment to the Constitution. That amendment, passed in 1868 after the Civil War, provides, in part, that "[n]o State shall . . . deprive any person of life, liberty, or property, without due process of law." Starting in 1925, the Supreme Court began to define various rights and liberties guaranteed in the national Constitution as constituting "due process of law," which was required of state governments under the Fourteenth Amendment. Today, most of the rights and liberties set forth in the Bill of Rights apply to state governments as well as to the national government.

The rights secured by the Bill of Rights are not absolute. Many of the rights guaranteed by the first ten amendments are described in very general terms. For example, the Second

---

12. Twenty dollars was forty days' pay for the average person when the Bill of Rights was written.

Amendment states that people have a right to keep and bear arms, but it does not explain the extent of this right. As the Supreme Court noted in 2008, this does not mean that people can "keep and carry any weapon whatsoever in any manner whatsoever and for whatever purpose."[13] Legislatures can prohibit the carrying of concealed weapons or certain types of weapons, such as machine guns.

Ultimately, it is the Supreme Court, as the final interpreter of the Constitution, that gives meaning to these rights and determines their boundaries. (For a discussion of how the Supreme Court may consider other nations' laws when determining the appropriate balance of individual rights, see this chapter's *Beyond Our Borders* feature.)

The First Amendment— Freedom of Speech

A democratic form of government cannot survive unless people can freely voice their political opinions and criticize government actions or policies. Freedom of speech, particularly political speech, is thus a prized right, and traditionally the courts have protected this right to the fullest extent possible.

Symbolic speech—gestures, movements, articles of clothing, and other forms of expressive conduct—is also given substantial protection by the courts. The Supreme Court held that the burning of the American flag to protest government policies is a constitutionally

The European Court of Human Rights meets in the French city of Strasbourg on a regular basis. Most lawsuits heard by these seven judges involve appeals concerning actions by European governments. Should judges and justices in the United States give deference to decisions made by this foreign court?

(Johanna Leguerre/AFP/Getty Images)

Symbolic Speech Nonverbal expressions of beliefs. Symbolic speech, which includes gestures, movements, and articles of clothing, is given substantial protection by the courts.

---

13. *District of Columbia v. Heller*, 554 U.S. 570, 128 S.Ct. 2783, 171 L.Ed.2d 637 (2008).

BEYOND OUR BORDERS

The Impact of Foreign Law on the United States Supreme Court

The United States Supreme Court interprets the rights provided in the U.S. Constitution. Changing public views on controversial topics, such as privacy in an era of terrorist threats or the rights of gay men and lesbians, may affect the way the Supreme Court decides a case. But should the Court also consider other nations' laws and world opinion when balancing individual rights in the United States?

Justices on the Supreme Court have increasingly considered foreign law when deciding issues of national importance. This trend started in 2003 when, for the first time ever, foreign law was cited in a majority opinion of the Supreme Court. The case was a controversial one in which the Court struck down laws that prohibited oral and anal sex between consenting adults

of the same gender. In the majority opinion (an opinion that the majority of justices have signed), Justice Anthony Kennedy mentioned that the European Court of Human Rights and other foreign courts have consistently acknowledged that homosexuals have a right "to engage in intimate, consensual conduct."[a] The Supreme Court again looked at foreign law when deciding whether the death penalty was an appropriate punishment for persons who were juveniles when they committed their crimes.[b]

The practice of looking at foreign law has many critics, including Justice Antonin

---

a. *Lawrence v. Texas*, 539 U.S. 558, 123 S.Ct. 2472, 156 L.Ed.2d 508 (2003).
b. *Roper v. Simmons*, 543 U.S. 551, 125 S.Ct. 1183, 161 L.Ed.2d 1 (2005).

Scalia and other more conservative members of the Supreme Court, who believe that foreign views are irrelevant to rulings on U.S. law. Other Supreme Court justices, however, including Justice Stephen Breyer and Justice Ruth Bader Ginsburg, have publicly stated that in our increasingly global community we should not ignore the opinions of courts in the rest of the world.

Critical Thinking

Should U.S. courts, and particularly the United States Supreme Court, look to other nations' laws for guidance when deciding important issues—including those involving rights granted by the Constitution? If so, what impact might this have on their decisions? Explain.

> "If the freedom
> of speech is taken
> away, then dumb
> and silent we may be
> led like sheep to the
> slaughter."
>
> George Washington, 1732–1799
> (First president of
> the United States, 1789–1797)

protected form of expression.[14] Similarly, wearing a T-shirt with a photo of a presidential candidate would be a constitutionally protected form of expression. The test is whether a reasonable person would interpret the conduct as conveying some sort of message. **EXAMPLE 4.5** As a form of expression, Nam has gang signs tattooed on his torso, arms, neck, and legs. If a reasonable person would interpret this conduct as conveying a message, then it might be a protected form of symbolic speech. •

An interesting topic in today's legal environment is whether computers should have free speech rights. For a discussion of this issue, see the *Online Developments* feature later in this chapter.

Reasonable Restrictions Expression—oral, written, or symbolized by conduct—is subject to reasonable restrictions. A balance must be struck between a government's obligation to protect its citizens and those citizens' exercise of their rights. Reasonableness is analyzed on a case-by-case basis.

Content-Neutral Laws Laws that regulate the time, manner, and place, but not the content, of speech receive less scrutiny by the courts than do laws that restrict the content of expression. If a restriction imposed by the government is content neutral, then a court may allow it. To be content neutral, the restriction must be aimed at combating some secondary societal problem, such as crime, and not be aimed at suppressing the expressive conduct or its message.

Courts have often protected nude dancing as a form of symbolic expression. Nevertheless, the courts typically allow content-neutral laws that ban *all* public nudity. **CASE EXAMPLE 4.6** Ria Ora was charged with dancing nude at an annual "anti-Christmas" protest in Harvard Square in Cambridge, Massachusetts. Ora argued that the statute was overbroad and unconstitutional, and a trial court agreed. On appeal, a state appellate court reversed. The court found that the statute was constitutional because it banned public displays of open and gross lewdness in situations in which there was an unsuspecting or unwilling audience.[15] •

At issue in the following case was an Indiana state law that barred most sex offenders from using social networking sites (such as Facebook), instant messaging services (such as Twitter), and chat programs that the offenders knew were accessible to minors. The question before the court was whether this law was unconstitutional under the First Amendment.

---

14. See *Texas v. Johnson*, 491 U.S. 397, 109 S.Ct. 2533, 105 L.Ed.2d 342 (1989).
15. *Commonwealth v. Ora*, 451 Mass. 125, 883 N.E.2d 1217 (2008).

Case 4.1

Doe v. Prosecutor, Marion County, Indiana
United States Court of Appeals, Seventh Circuit, 705 F.3d 694 (2013).

BACKGROUND AND FACTS John Doe was arrested in Marion County, Indiana, and convicted of child exploitation. Although he was released from prison and was not on any form of supervised release, he was required to register as a sex offender with the state of Indiana. Under an Indiana statute that covered child exploitation and other sex offenses, Doe could not use certain Web sites and programs. Doe filed a lawsuit in a federal district court against the Marion County prosecutor, alleging that the statute violated his right to freedom of speech under the First Amendment. Doe asked the court to issue an injunction to block the enforcement of the law. The court held that "the regulation is narrowly tailored to serve a significant state interest" and entered a judgment for the defendant. Doe appealed to the U.S. Court of Appeals for the Seventh Circuit.

IN THE WORDS OF THE COURT . . .
FLAUM, Circuit Judge.
* * * *

Indiana Code Section 35-42-4-12 prohibits certain sex offenders from "knowingly or intentionally using: a social

Case 4.1—Continued

networking web site" or "an instant messaging or chat room program" that "the offender knows allows a person who is less than eighteen (18) years of age to access or use the web site or program." The law applies broadly to all individuals required to register as sex offenders.

* * * *

This case presents a single legal question * * * . The statute clearly implicates Doe's First Amendment rights * * * . It not only precludes expression through the medium of social media, it also limits his right to receive information and ideas. The Indiana law, however, is content neutral because it restricts speech without reference to the expression's content. As such, it may impose reasonable time, place, or manner restrictions. To do so, the law * * * must be narrowly tailored to serve a significant governmental interest.

The state initially asserts an interest in "protecting public safety, and specifically in protecting minors from harmful online communications." Indiana is certainly justified in shielding its children from improper sexual communication.

* * * *

* * * The state agrees there is nothing dangerous about Doe's use of social media as long as he does not improperly communicate with minors. Further, there is no disagreement that illicit communication comprises a minuscule subset of the universe of social network activity. As such, *the Indiana law targets substantially more activity than the evil it seeks to redress.* * * * *Indiana has other methods to combat unwanted and inappropriate communication between minors and sex offenders.* For instance, [under Indiana Code Section 35-42-4-6] it is a felony in Indiana for persons over twenty-one to "solicit" children under sixteen "to engage in: (1) sexual intercourse; (2) deviate sexual conduct; or

(3) any fondling intended to arouse or satisfy the sexual desires of either the child or the older person." A separate statute goes further. [Indiana Code Section 35-42-4-13] punishes mere "inappropriate communication with a child" and communication "with the intent to gratify the sexual desires of the person or the individual." Significantly, both statutes have enhanced penalties for using a computer network and better advance Indiana's interest in preventing harmful interaction with children (by going beyond social networks). They also accomplish that end more narrowly (by refusing to burden benign Internet activity). That is, they are neither over nor under-inclusive like the statute at issue here. [Emphasis added.]

* * * *

For the foregoing reasons, we REVERSE the district court's decision, and REMAND with instructions to enter judgment in favor of Doe and issue the injunction.

DECISION AND REMEDY   The U.S Court of Appeals for the Seventh Circuit reversed the lower court's judgment in the defendant's favor and remanded the case for the entry of a judgment for Doe. A law that concerns rights under the First Amendment must be narrowly tailored to accomplish its objective. The blanket ban on social media in this case did not pass this test.

THE LEGAL ENVIRONMENT DIMENSION   *What is an injunction? What did the plaintiff in this case hope to gain by seeking an injunction?*

THE ETHICAL DIMENSION   *Could a state effectively enforce a law that banned all communication between minors and sex offenders through social media sites? Why or why not?*

Laws That Restrict the Content of Speech   If a law regulates the content of the expression, it must serve a compelling state interest and must be narrowly written to achieve that interest. Under the **compelling government interest** test, the government's interest is balanced against the individual's constitutional right to be free of law. For the statute to be valid, there must be a compelling governmental interest that can be furthered only by the law in question.

The United States Supreme Court has held that schools may restrict students' speech at school events.   **CASE EXAMPLE 4.7**   Some high school students held up a banner saying "Bong Hits 4 Jesus" at an off-campus but school-sanctioned event. The majority of the Court ruled that school officials did not violate the students' free speech rights when they confiscated the banner and suspended the students for ten days. Because the banner could reasonably be interpreted as promoting drugs, the Court concluded that the school's actions were justified. Several justices disagreed, however, noting that the majority's holding creates a special exception that will allow schools to censor any student speech that mentions drugs.[16] ●

Compelling Government Interest A test of constitutionality that requires the government to have convincing reasons for passing any law that restricts fundamental rights, such as free speech, or distinguishes among people based on a suspect trait.

---

16. *Morse v. Frederick,* 551 U.S. 393, 127 S.Ct. 2618, 168 L.Ed.2d 290 (2007).

ONLINE DEVELOPMENTS

Do Computers Have Free Speech Rights?

When you do a Web search using Bing, Google, or any other search engine, the program inherent in the engine gives you a list of results. When you use a document-creation program, such as Microsoft Word, it often guesses what you intend and corrects your misspellings automatically. Do computers that make such choices engage in "speech," and if so, do they enjoy First Amendment protection? This question is not as absurd as it may seem at first.

Are Google's Search Results "Speech"?

More than a decade ago, a company dissatisfied with its rankings in Google's search results sued. Google argued that its search results were constitutionally protected speech. The plaintiff, Search King, Inc., sought an injunction against Google, but a federal district court decided in Google's favor. The court ruled that the ranking of results when a search is undertaken "constitutes opinions protected by the First Amendment. . . . *Page Ranks* are opinions—opinions are the significance of particular Web sites as they correspond to a search query." Therefore, the First Amendment applied to the search results.[a]

Google versus the Federal Trade Commission

For the last few years, Google has been the dominant search engine. Yet in the 1990s, the federal government was worried that Microsoft's search engine was too dominant and was crushing the search engines of Yahoo!, AltaVista, and Lycos. Today, of course, AltaVista and Lycos no longer exist, and Microsoft's new search engine, Bing, is a relatively minor player in the field.

Fast-forward to 2011. The Federal Trade Commission (FTC) contemplated bringing charges against Google for favoring its own offerings, such as restaurant reviews, in its search results. Now it was Microsoft that was encouraging the FTC to proceed. After a nineteen-month investigation, in early 2013 the FTC announced that it would *not* prosecute Google. The FTC's decision was a blow to search engines that compete with Google, including Microsoft's Bing.

The First Amendment Protection Argument

Google commissioned Eugene Volokh and Donald Falk, two legal experts in this field, to research the issue of whether search engine results are protected by the First Amendment.[b] The researchers concluded that search engine results are the same as the editorial judgments that a newspaper makes in deciding which wire service stories to run and which op-ed and business columnists to feature. The authors further claim that free speech applies to editorial choices no matter what their format. Search engines are protected even when they are "unfair" in ranking search results. Whether the search engine uses a computerized algorithm to compile its rankings is irrelevant.

Columbia Law professor Tim Wu disagrees. He argues that the First Amendment was intended to protect humans against the evils of state censorship and that protecting a computer's speech is not related to that purpose. At best, he says, search engine results are *commercial speech*, which has always received limited protection under the First Amendment. After all, computers make trillions of invisible decisions each day. Is each of those decisions protected speech?

Critical Thinking

Facebook has numerous computers, all programmed by humans, of course. If Facebook's computers make decisions that allow your private information to be shared without your knowledge, should the First Amendment protect Facebook? Why or why not?

---

a. *Search King, Inc. v. Google Technology, Inc.*, 2003 WL 21464568 (W.D.Okla. 2003). See also *Langdon v. Google, Inc.*, 474 F.Supp.2d 622 (D.Del. 2007).

b. Eugene Volokh and Donald Falk, "First Amendment Protection for Search Engine Search Results: White Paper Commissioned by Google" (UCLA School of Law Research Paper No. 12-22, April 20, 2012).

Can a high school suspend teenagers from extracurricular activities because they posted suggestive photos of themselves online at social networking sites? For a discussion of this issue, see this chapter's *Insight into Ethics* feature.

Corporate Political Speech   Political speech by corporations also falls within the protection of the First Amendment. Many years ago, the United States Supreme Court reviewed a Massachusetts statute that prohibited corporations from making political contributions or expenditures that individuals were permitted to make. The Court ruled that the Massachusetts law was unconstitutional because it violated the right of corporations to freedom of speech.[17] The Court has also held that a law prohibiting a corporation from including inserts with its bills to express its views on controversial issues violates the First Amendment.[18]

Corporate political speech continues to be given significant protection under the First Amendment. **CASE EXAMPLE 4.8** In *Citizens United v. Federal Election Commission,*[19] the Supreme Court issued a landmark decision that overturned a twenty-year-old precedent

17. *First National Bank of Boston v. Bellotti,* 435 U.S. 765, 98 S.Ct. 1407, 55 L.Ed.2d 707 (1978).

18. *Consolidated Edison Co. v. Public Service Commission,* 447 U.S. 530, 100 S.Ct. 2326, 65 L.Ed.2d 319 (1980).

19. 558 U.S. 310, 130 S.Ct. 876, 175 L.Ed.2d 753 (2010).

INSIGHT INTO ETHICS

SHOULD VULGAR FACEBOOK PHOTOS RECEIVE FIRST AMENDMENT PROTECTION?

A federal judge in Indiana ruled that a high school did not have the right to punish students for posting raunchy photos of themselves on the Internet. According to the court, "the case poses timely questions about the limits school officials can place on out-of-school speech by students in the information age where Twitter, Facebook, MySpace, texts, and the like rule the day."[a]

High School Suspended the Teens from Extracurricular Activities

T.V. and M.K. were both entering the tenth grade at a public high school. During summer sleepovers, the girls took photos of each other pretending to suck penis-shaped rainbow-colored lollipops and holding them in various suggestive positions. They later posted the photos on Facebook, MySpace, and Photo Bucket to be seen by persons granted "friend" status or given a password. The images did not identify the school that the girls attended.

When a parent complained to the school about the provocative online display, school officials suspended both girls from extracurricular activities for a portion of the upcoming school year. Both T.V. and M.K. were members of the high school's volleyball team, and M.K. was also a member of the cheerleading squad and the show choir. Through their parents, the girls filed a lawsuit claiming that the school had violated their First Amendment rights.

Can Online Photos Qualify as Symbolic Speech?

Expressive conduct is entitled to First Amendment protection if it meets a two-part intent-plus-perception test. Conduct is symbolic speech if the "intent to convey a particularized message was present" and if "the likelihood was great that the message would

be understood by those who viewed it."[b] Here, both girls testified that they were just trying to be funny when they took the photos and posted them online for their friends to see. Although the photos were suggestive, the girls were fully clothed, and the images were not pornographic or obscene. The court reasoned that the conduct depicted in the photos was intended to be humorous and would be understood as such by their teenage audience. Therefore, the photos were entitled to First Amendment protection as symbolic speech, even if they were "juvenile and silly."

Did the Off-Campus Speech Substantially Disrupt School Activities?

Although schools can restrict students' speech at times, this was not one of those times, according to the court. The conduct took place off campus and did not substantially disrupt the work and discipline of the high school. Schools generally can punish students only for off-campus speech that becomes an in-school problem, such as bullying, but here, the photos had only a minimal effect on the volleyball team. (Some of the other players and two parents had complained that the photos were inappropriate.) The court also struck down the provision in the student handbook banning out-of-school conduct that brings discredit or dishonor on the school, finding that it was impermissibly broad and vague.

For Critical Analysis
Insight into the Social Environment

How might the outcome of this case have been different if the girls had posted the photos on the high school's public Web site for all to see?

a. *T.V. ex rel. E.V. v. Smith-Green Community School Corp.,* 807 F.Supp.2d 767 (N.D.Ind. 2011).

b. See *Texas v. Johnson,* 491 U.S. 397, 109 S.Ct. 2533, 105 L.Ed.2d 342 (1989).

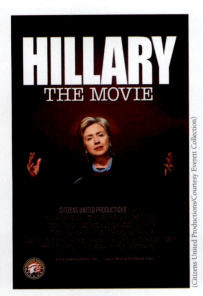

Can independent political expenditures by corporations be used to broadcast a movie that portrays a candidate in an unfavorable light?

on campaign financing. The case involved Citizens United, a nonprofit corporation that has a *political action committee* (an organization that registers with the government and campaigns for or against political candidates).

Citizens United had produced a film called *Hillary: The Movie* that was critical of Hillary Clinton, who was seeking the Democratic nomination for presidential candidate. Campaign-finance law restricted Citizens United from broadcasting the movie, however. The Court ruled that the restrictions were unconstitutional and that the First Amendment prevents limits from being placed on independent political expenditures by corporations. ●

Commercial Speech   The courts also give substantial protection to *commercial speech,* which consists of communications—primarily advertising and marketing—made by business firms that involve only their commercial interests. The protection given to commercial speech under the First Amendment is not as extensive as that afforded to non-commercial speech, however. A state may restrict certain kinds of advertising, for instance, in the interest of protecting consumers from being misled. States also have a legitimate interest in the beautification of roadsides, and this interest allows states to place restraints on billboard advertising. **CASE EXAMPLE 4.9**   Café Erotica, a nude dancing establishment, sued the state after being denied a permit to erect a billboard along an interstate highway in Florida. The state appellate court decided that because the law directly advanced a substantial government interest in highway beautification and safety, it was not an unconstitutional restraint on commercial speech.[20] ●

Generally, a restriction on commercial speech will be considered valid as long as it (1) seeks to implement a substantial government interest, (2) directly advances that interest, and (3) goes no further than necessary to accomplish its objective. A substantial government interest is a significant or important connection or concern of the government with respect to a particular matter. Examples of such interests are given in *Case Example 4.9* in the previous paragraph. This substantial-interest requirement limits the power of the government to regulate commercial speech.

At issue in the following *Spotlight Case* was whether a government agency had unconstitutionally restricted commercial speech when it prohibited the inclusion of a certain illustration on beer labels.

20. *Café Erotica v. Florida Department of Transportation,* 830 So.2d 181 (Fla.App. 1 Dist. 2002); review denied, *Café Erotica/We Dare to Bare v. Florida Department of Transportation,* 845 So.2d 888 (Fla. 2003).

Spotlight on Beer Labels

Case 4.2
Bad Frog Brewery, Inc. v. New York State Liquor Authority
United States Court of Appeals, Second Circuit, 134 F.3d 87 (1998).

BACKGROUND AND FACTS   Bad Frog Brewery, Inc., makes and sells alcoholic beverages. Some of the beverages feature labels with a drawing of a frog making the gesture generally known as "giving the finger." Bad Frog's authorized New York distributor, Renaissance Beer Company, applied to the New York State Liquor Authority (NYSLA) for brand label approval, as required by state law before the beer could be sold in New York. The

NYSLA denied the application, in part, because "the label could appear in grocery and convenience stores, with obvious exposure on the shelf to children of tender age." Bad Frog filed a suit in a federal district court against the NYSLA, asking for, among other things, an injunction against the denial of the application. The court granted summary judgment in favor of the NYSLA. Bad Frog appealed to the U.S. Court of Appeals for the Second Circuit.

Spotlight Case 4.2—Continued

IN THE WORDS OF THE COURT . . .
Jon O. *NEWMAN*, Circuit Judge.

* * * *

* * * To support its asserted power to ban Bad Frog's labels [NYSLA advances] * * * the State's interest in "protecting children from vulgar and profane advertising" * * * .

[This interest is] substantial * * * . *States have a compelling interest in protecting the physical and psychological well-being of minors* * * * . [Emphasis added.]

* * * *

* * * NYSLA endeavors to advance the state interest in preventing exposure of children to vulgar displays by taking only the limited step of barring such displays from the labels of alcoholic beverages. *In view of the wide currency of vulgar displays throughout contemporary society, including comic books targeted directly at children, barring such displays from labels for alcoholic beverages cannot realistically be expected to reduce children's exposure to such displays to any significant degree.* [Emphasis added.]

* * * If New York decides to make a substantial effort to insulate children from vulgar displays in some significant sphere of activity, at least with respect to materials likely to be seen by children, NYSLA's label prohibition might well be found to make a justifiable contribution to the material advancement of such an effort, but its currently isolated response to the perceived problem, applicable only to labels on a product that children cannot purchase, does not suffice. * * * A state must demonstrate that its commercial speech limitation is part of a substantial effort to advance a valid state interest, not merely the removal of a few grains of offensive sand from a beach of vulgarity.

* * * *

* * * Even if we were to assume that the state materially advances its asserted interest by shielding children from viewing the Bad Frog labels, it is plainly excessive to prohibit the labels from all use, including placement on bottles displayed in bars and taverns where parental supervision of children is to be expected. Moreover, to whatever extent NYSLA is concerned that children will be harmfully exposed to the Bad Frog labels when wandering without parental supervision around grocery and convenience stores where beer is sold, that concern could be less intrusively dealt with by placing restrictions on the permissible locations where the appellant's products may be displayed within such stores.

DECISION AND REMEDY The U.S. Court of Appeals for the Second Circuit reversed the judgment of the district court and remanded the case for the entry of a judgment in favor of Bad Frog. The NYSLA's ban on the use of the labels lacked a "reasonable fit" with the state's interest in shielding minors from vulgarity, and the NYSLA did not adequately consider alternatives to the ban.

WHAT IF THE FACTS WERE DIFFERENT? *If Bad Frog had sought to use the label to market toys instead of beer, would the court's ruling likely have been the same? Explain your answer.*

THE LEGAL ENVIRONMENT DIMENSION *Whose interests are advanced by the banning of certain types of advertising?*

Unprotected Speech
The United States Supreme Court has made it clear that certain types of speech will not be given any protection under the First Amendment. Speech that harms the good reputation of another, or defamatory speech (see Chapter 5), will not be protected. Speech that violates criminal laws (such as threatening speech) is not constitutionally protected. Other unprotected speech includes "fighting words," or words that are likely to incite others to respond violently.

The First Amendment, as interpreted by the Supreme Court, also does not protect obscene speech. Establishing an objective definition of obscene speech has proved difficult, however.[21] Numerous state and federal statutes make it a crime to disseminate and possess obscene materials, including child pornography. But, obviously, it is even more difficult to prohibit the dissemination of obscenity and pornography online.

Most of Congress's attempts to pass legislation protecting minors from pornographic materials on the Internet have been struck down on First Amendment grounds when

---

21. For a leading case on this issue, see *Miller v. California*, 413 U.S. 15, 93 S.Ct. 2607, 37 L.Ed.2d 419 (1973).

(AP Photo/Rick Bowmer)

These policemen look on at the Occupy Portland encampment set up in a public place. When the mayor of Portland, Oregon, ordered the demonstrators to "pull up stakes," was he violating their right to free speech?

challenged in court. One exception was a law that passed in 2000, which requires schools public schools and libraries to install **filtering software** on computers to keep children from accessing adult content.[22] Such software is designed to prevent persons from viewing certain Web sites based on a site's Internet address or its **meta tags,** or key words. The Supreme Court held that the act does not unconstitutionally burden free speech because it is flexible and libraries can disable the filters for any patrons who ask.[23]

Another statute that passed in 2003 makes it a crime to intentionally distribute *virtual child pornography*—which uses computer-generated images, not actual people—without indicating that it is computer-generated.[24] In a case challenging its constitutionality, the Supreme Court held that the statute was valid because it does not prohibit a substantial amount of protected speech.[25] Nevertheless, because of the difficulties of policing the Internet, as well as the constitutional complexities of prohibiting online obscenity through legislation, it remains a problem worldwide.

Filtering Software A computer program that is designed to block access to certain Web sites, based on their content.

Meta Tag A key word in a document that can serve as an index reference to the document. Online search engines return results based, in part, on the tags in Web documents.

Establishment Clause The provision in the First Amendment that prohibits the government from establishing any state-sponsored religion or enacting any law that promotes religion or favors one religion over another.

The First Amendment—Freedom of Religion

The First Amendment states that the government may neither establish any religion nor prohibit the free exercise of religious practices. The first part of this constitutional provision is referred to as the *establishment clause,* and the second part is known as the *free exercise clause.* Government action, both federal and state, must be consistent with this constitutional mandate.

The Establishment Clause   The **establishment clause** prohibits the government from establishing a state-sponsored religion, as well as from passing laws that promote (aid or endorse) religion or show a preference for one religion over another. Although the establishment clause involves the separation of church and state, it does not require a complete separation.

Applicable Standard   Establishment clause cases often involve such issues as the legality of allowing or requiring school prayers, using state-issued vouchers to pay tuition at religious schools, and teaching creation theories versus evolution. Federal or state laws that do not promote or place a significant burden on religion are constitutional even if they have some impact on religion. For a government law or policy to be constitutional, it must not have the primary effect of promoting or inhibiting religion.

Religious Displays   Religious displays on public property have often been challenged as violating the establishment clause, and the United States Supreme Court has ruled on a number of such cases. Generally, the Court has focused on the proximity of the religious display to nonreligious symbols, such as reindeer and candy canes, or to symbols from different religions, such as a menorah (a nine-branched candelabrum used in celebrating

---

22. Children's Internet Protection Act (CIPA), 17 U.S.C. Sections 1701–1741.
23. *United States v. American Library Association,* 539 U.S. 194, 123 S.Ct. 2297, 156 L.Ed.2d 221 (2003).
24. The Prosecutorial Remedies and Other Tools to End the Exploitation of Children Today Act (Protect Act), 18 U.S.C. Section 2252A(a)(5)(B).
25. *United States v. Williams,* 553 U.S. 285, 128 S.Ct. 1830, 170 L.Ed.2d 650 (2008).

Hanukkah). The Supreme Court eventually took a slightly different approach when it held that public displays having historical, as well as religious, significance do not necessarily violate the establishment clause.[26]

CASE EXAMPLE 4.10 Mount Soledad is a prominent hill near San Diego. There has been a forty-foot cross on top of Mount Soledad since 1913. In the 1990s, a war memorial was constructed next to the cross that included six walls listing the names of veterans. The site was privately owned until 2006, when Congress authorized the property's transfer to the federal government "to preserve a historically significant war memorial."

Steve Trunk and the Jewish War Veterans filed lawsuits claiming that the cross display violated the establishment clause because it endorsed the Christian religion. A federal appellate court agreed, finding that the primary effect of the memorial as a whole sent a strong message of endorsement and exclusion (of non-Christian veterans). The court noted that although not all cross displays at war memorials violate the establishment clause, the cross in this case physically dominated the site, was originally dedicated to religious purposes, had a long history of religious use, and was the only portion visible to drivers on the freeway below.[27] •

(AP Photo/Denis Poroy)

This large cross on Mount Soledad in San Diego sits on land that became public property. Should it be removed as a violation of the establishment clause?

The Free Exercise Clause

The **free exercise clause** guarantees that a person can hold any religious belief that she or he wants, or a person can have no religious belief. The constitutional guarantee of personal religious freedom restricts only the actions of the government, however, and not those of individuals or private businesses.

Free Exercise Clause The provision in the First Amendment that prohibits the government from interfering with people's religious practices or forms of worship.

Restrictions Must Be Necessary The government must have a compelling state interest for restricting the free exercise of religion, and the restriction must be the only way to further that interest. **CASE EXAMPLE 4.11** Members of a particular Mennonite church must use horses and buggies for transportation, but they can use tractors to take their agricultural products to market. Their religion requires the tractors to have steel cleats on the tires, and they drove tractors with cleats on county roads for many years. Then the county passed an ordinance that prohibited the use of steel cleats because the cleats tend to damage newly surfaced roads.

When a member of the church received a citation for driving a tractor with cleats, he claimed that the ordinance violated the church's right to freely exercise its religion. Ultimately, the court ruled in his favor. The county had not met its burden of showing that the ordinance served a compelling state interest and was the least restrictive means of attaining that interest. There was no evidence of how much the cleats harmed the roads, other events also harmed the roads, and the county had allowed the cleats to be used for many years. Therefore, the ordinance was not carefully tailored to achieve the stated objective of road preservation.[28] •

Public Welfare Exception When religious *practices* work against public policy and the public welfare, though, the government can act. For instance, the government can require that a child receive certain types of vaccinations or medical treatment if his or her life is in danger—regardless of the child's or parent's religious beliefs. When public safety is an issue, an individual's religious beliefs often have to give way to the government's interest in protecting the public.

26. See *Van Orden v. Perry*, 545 U.S. 677, 125 S.Ct. 2854, 162 L.Ed.2d 607 (2005). The Court held that a six-foot-tall monument of the Ten Commandments on the Texas state capitol grounds did not violate the establishment clause because the Ten Commandments had historical significance

27. *Trunk v. City of San Diego*, 629 F.3d 1099 (9th Cir. 2011).

28. *Mitchell County v. Zimmerman*, 810 N.W.2d 1 (Iowa Sup.Ct. 2012).

EXAMPLE 4.12 In the Muslim faith, it is a religious violation for a woman to appear in public without a scarf over her head. Due to public safety concerns, many courts today do not allow any headgear to be worn in courtrooms. A courthouse in Georgia prevented a Muslim woman from entering because she refused to remove her scarf. As she left, she uttered an expletive at the court official and was arrested and brought before the judge, who ordered her to serve ten days in jail. •

Due Process and Equal Protection

Learning Objective 5
Where in the Constitution can the due process clause be found?

Two other constitutional guarantees of great significance to Americans are mandated by the due process clauses of the Fifth and Fourteenth Amendments and the equal protection clause of the Fourteenth Amendment.

Due Process

Due Process Clause The provisions in the Fifth and Fourteenth Amendments that guarantee that no person shall be deprived of life, liberty, or property without due process of law. State constitutions often include similar clauses.

Both the Fifth and the Fourteenth Amendments provide that no person shall be deprived "of life, liberty, or property, without due process of law." The **due process clause** of each of these constitutional amendments has two aspects—procedural and substantive. Note that the due process clause applies to "legal persons," such as corporations, as well as to individuals.

Procedural Due Process *Procedural* due process requires that any government decision to take life, liberty, or property must be made fairly. This means that the government must give a person proper notice and an opportunity to be heard, and that it must use fair procedures in determining whether a person will be subjected to punishment or have some burden imposed on him or her.

Fair procedure has been interpreted as requiring that the person have at least an opportunity to object to a proposed action before a fair, neutral decision maker (who need not be a judge). **EXAMPLE 4.13** Doyle Burns, a nursing student in Kansas, poses for a photograph standing next to a placenta used as a lab specimen. Although she quickly deletes the photo from her library, it ends up on Facebook. When the director of nursing sees the photo, Burns is expelled. She sues for reinstatement and wins. The school violated Burns's due process rights by expelling her from the nursing program for taking a photo without giving her an opportunity to present her side to school authorities. •

PREVENTING LEGAL DISPUTES

Many of the constitutional protections discussed in this chapter have become part of our culture in the United States. Due process, especially procedural due process, has become synonymous with what Americans consider "fair." For this reason, if you wish to avoid legal disputes, consider giving due process to anyone who might object to some of your business decisions or actions, whether that person is an employee, a partner, an affiliate, or a customer. For instance, provide ample notice of new policies to all affected persons, and give them at least an opportunity to express their opinions on the matter. Providing an opportunity to be heard is often the ideal way to make people feel that they are being treated fairly. People are less likely to sue a businessperson or firm that they believe is fair and listens to both sides of an issue.

Substantive Due Process *Substantive* due process focuses on the content of legislation rather than the fairness of procedures. Substantive due process limits what the government may do in its legislative and executive capacities. Legislation must be fair and reasonable in content and must further a legitimate governmental objective. Only when state conduct is arbitrary or shocks the conscience, however, will it rise to the level of violating substantive due process.

If a law or other governmental action limits a fundamental right, the courts will hold that it violates substantive due process unless it promotes a compelling or overriding state interest. Fundamental rights include interstate travel, privacy, voting, marriage and family, and all First Amendment rights. Thus, a state must have a substantial reason for taking any action that infringes on a person's free speech rights.

In situations not involving fundamental rights, a law or action does not violate substantive due process if it rationally relates to any legitimate governmental end. It is almost impossible for a law or action to fail the "rationality" test. Under this test, almost any government regulation of business will be upheld as reasonable.

> "Our Constitution protects aliens [extraterrestrials], drunks, and U.S. senators."
>
> Will Rogers, 1879–1935
> (American humorist)

Equal Protection

Under the Fourteenth Amendment, a state may not "deny to any person within its jurisdiction the equal protection of the laws." The United States Supreme Court has used the due process clause of the Fifth Amendment to make the **equal protection clause** applicable to the federal government as well. Equal protection means that the government cannot enact laws that treat similarly situated individuals differently.

Equal protection, like substantive due process, relates to the substance of the law or other governmental action. When a law or action limits the liberty of all persons to do something, it may violate substantive due process. When a law or action limits the liberty of some persons but not others, it may violate the equal protection clause. **EXAMPLE 4.14** If a law prohibits all persons from buying contraceptive devices, it raises a substantive due process question. If it prohibits only unmarried persons from buying the same devices, it raises an equal protection issue. ●

In an equal protection inquiry, when a law or action distinguishes between or among individuals, the basis for the distinction—that is, the classification—is examined. Depending on the classification, the courts apply different levels of scrutiny, or "tests," to determine whether the law or action violates the equal protection clause. The courts use one of three standards: strict scrutiny, intermediate scrutiny, or the "rational basis" test.

Equal Protection Clause The provision in the Fourteenth Amendment that requires state governments to treat similarly situated individuals in a similar manner.

Strict Scrutiny If a law or action prohibits or inhibits some persons from exercising a fundamental right, the law or action will be subject to "strict scrutiny" by the courts. A classification based on a *suspect trait*—such as race, national origin, or citizenship status—will also be subject to strict scrutiny. Under this standard, the classification must be necessary to promote a *compelling government interest.*

Compelling state interests include remedying past unconstitutional or illegal discrimination, but do not include correcting the general effects of "society's discrimination." **EXAMPLE 4.15** For a city to give preference to minority applicants in awarding construction contracts, it normally must identify past unconstitutional or illegal discrimination against minority construction firms. Because the policy is based on suspect traits (race and national origin), it will violate the equal protection clause *unless* it is necessary to promote a compelling state interest. ● Generally, few laws or actions survive strict-scrutiny analysis by the courts.

Does the equal protection clause protect the homeless? If so, how?

Intermediate Scrutiny Another standard, that of "intermediate scrutiny," is applied in cases involving discrimination based on gender or legitimacy. Laws using these classifications must be *substantially related to important government objectives.* **EXAMPLE 4.16** An important government objective is preventing illegitimate teenage pregnancies. Because males and females are not similarly situated in this regard—only females can become pregnant—a law that punishes men but not women for statutory rape will be upheld even though it treats men and women unequally. ●

The state also has an important objective in establishing time limits (called *statutes of limitation*) for how long after an event a particular type of action can be brought. Nevertheless, the limitation period must be substantially related to the important objective of preventing fraudulent or outdated claims. **EXAMPLE 4.17** A state law requires illegitimate children to bring paternity suits within six years of their births in order to seek support from their fathers. A court will strike down this law if legitimate children are allowed to seek support from their parents at any time because distinguishing between support claims on the basis of legitimacy is not related to the important government objective of preventing fraudulent or outdated claims. ●

The "Rational Basis" Test

In matters of economic and social welfare, a classification will be considered valid if there is any conceivable "rational basis" on which the classification might relate to a *legitimate government interest*. It is almost impossible for a law or action to fail the rational basis test. **EXAMPLE 4.18** A city ordinance that in effect prohibits all pushcart vendors, except a specific few, from operating in a particular area of the city will be upheld if the city offers a rational basis—such as reducing traffic in that area—for the ordinance. In contrast, a law that provides for unemployment benefits to be paid only to people over six feet tall would clearly fail the rational basis test because it could not further any legitimate government interest. ●

In the following case, the court applied the rational basis test to a statute that prohibits certain businesses from applying for a license to sell wine and liquor.

Case 4.3

Maxwell's Pic-Pac, Inc. v. Dehner
United States Court of Appeals, Sixth Circuit, 739 F.3d 936 (2014).

(Jeff Greenberg/Alamy)

Who can prevent a grocery store from selling wine and liquor?

BACKGROUND AND FACTS A Kentucky statute prohibits businesses that sell substantial amounts of staple groceries or gasoline from applying for a license to sell wine and liquor. The provision applies to retailers that sell those items at a rate of at least 10 percent of gross monthly sales. Maxwell's Pic-Pac (a grocer) and Food with Wine Coalition (a group of grocers) filed a suit in a federal district court against Tony Dehner, the commissioner of the Kentucky Department of Alcoholic Beverage Control, and Danny Reed, the distilled spirits administrator of the Kentucky Department of Alcoholic Beverage Control. The plaintiffs alleged that the statute and the regulation were unconstitutional under the equal protection clause. The court ruled in the plaintiffs' favor, and the defendants appealed. The defendants contended that a rational basis—reducing access to products with high alcohol content—supported distinguishing grocery stores and gas stations from other retailers.

IN THE WORDS OF THE COURT . . .
COOK, Circuit Judge.
* * * *

* * * *The general rule is that legislation is presumed to be valid and will be sustained if the classification drawn by the statute is rationally related to a legitimate state interest. We must uphold an economic regulation if there is any reasonably conceivable state of facts that could provide a rational basis for the classification. [Emphasis added.]

The state indisputably maintains a legitimate interest in reducing access to products with high alcohol content. * * * Products with high alcohol content exacerbate [worsen] the problems caused by alcohol, including drunken driving. The state's interest applies not only to the general public; minors, inexperienced and impressionable, require particular vigilance. And the state's interest applies to abstinent citizens [nondrinkers] who, morally or practically objecting to alcohol exposure, wish to avoid retailers that sell such drinks.

We conclude that reasonably conceivable facts support the contention that grocery stores and gas stations pose a greater risk of exposing citizens to alcohol than do other retailers. A

Case 4.3—Continued

legislature could rationally believe that average citizens spend more time in grocery stores and gas stations than in other establishments; people typically need to buy staple groceries (for sustenance) and gas (for transportation) more often than items from retailers that specialize in other, less-frequently-used products. * * * Kentucky could believe that its citizenry visits grocery stores and gas stations more often than pharmacies—people can survive without ever visiting a pharmacy given that many grocery stores fill prescriptions. On the other hand, most people who object to confronting wine and liquor conceivably cannot avoid grocery stores and gas stations. Though some modern pharmacies sell staple groceries, grocery stores may remain the go-to place for life's essentials. And though Kentucky otherwise reduces access to wine and liquor by capping the *number* of places that supply it, the state can also reduce access by limiting the *types* of places that supply it—just as a parent can reduce a child's access to liquor by keeping smaller amounts in the house *and* by locking it in the liquor cabinet.

Our conclusion also rings true regarding minors. According to a plausible set of facts, more minors work at grocery stores and gas stations than other retailers; after all, grocery stores

and gas stations conceivably provide more low-skilled and low-experience jobs, including clerks, baggers, and stockers. Kentucky could also believe that grocery stores typically outweigh other retailers in size and traffic, allowing minors to more easily steal wine or liquor. Regarding gas stations, their convenience and prevalence near highways suggest an even greater danger in allowing alcohol sales.

DECISION AND REMEDY The U.S. Court of Appeals for the Sixth Circuit reversed the judgment of the lower court. The appellate court held that the statute and the regulation were rationally related to a legitimate state interest in reducing access to products with high alcohol content.

WHAT IF THE FACTS WERE DIFFERENT? *Suppose that the state restricted packaged beer sales by bars but not breweries. Would this pass the rational basis test under the equal protection clause? Why or why not?*

THE GLOBAL DIMENSION *Could the licensing measure imposed by the state in this case work in every other state and country? Explain.*

Privacy Rights

The U.S. Constitution does not explicitly mention a general right to privacy. In a 1928 Supreme Court case, *Olmstead v. United States*,[29] Justice Louis Brandeis stated in his dissent that the right to privacy is "the most comprehensive of rights and the right most valued by civilized men." The majority of the justices at that time, however, did not agree with Brandeis.

It was not until the 1960s that a majority on the Supreme Court endorsed the view that the Constitution protects individual privacy rights. In a landmark 1965 case, *Griswold v. Connecticut*,[30] the Supreme Court invalidated a Connecticut law that effectively prohibited the use of contraceptives on the ground that it violated the right to privacy. The Supreme Court held that a constitutional right to privacy was implied by the First, Third, Fourth, Fifth, and Ninth Amendments.

Today, privacy rights receive protection under various federal statutes as well the U.S. Constitution. State constitutions and statutes also secure individuals' privacy rights, often to a significant degree. Privacy rights are also protected to an extent under tort law (see Chapter 5), consumer law (see Chapter 20), Internet law (see Chapter 9), and employment law (see Chapter 17). In this section, after a brief look at some of the most important federal statutes protecting the privacy of individuals, we examine some current topics related to privacy rights. One such topic, the debate over marriage equality laws, is discussed next in this chapter's *Managerial Strategy* feature.

"There was, of course, no way of knowing whether you were being watched at any given moment."

George Orwell, 1903–1950
(English author,
from his famous novel *1984*)

---

29. 277 U.S. 438, 48 S.Ct. 564, 72 L.Ed. 944 (1928).
30. 381 U.S. 479, 85 S.Ct. 1678, 14 L.Ed.2d 510 (1965).

MANAGERIAL STRATEGY

Marriage Equality and the Constitution

The debate over whether to allow same-sex marriage has been raging across the country for years. The legal issues raised by marriage equality involve both the privacy rights protected by state and federal constitutions and the full faith and credit clause of the U.S. Constitution, which requires states to enforce judicial decisions (and marriage decrees) issued in other states.

Although marriage equality may not appear at first glance to be business related, it is a pertinent legal issue for managers. For example, Target Corporation once contributed $150,000 to a group backing a Republican candidate in Minnesota who had taken a stand against same-sex marriage. Boycotts of Target stores sprang up across the country.

In 2013, Guido Barilla, the head of the world's largest pasta manufacturer, stated in an interview that he would never use homosexuals in Barilla Pasta advertising. His statements sparked anger and resulted in a boycott of the company's products, despite his prompt apology on Twitter and Facebook. Other businesses, such as Chick-fil-A and Exxon Mobil, have also lost business for supporting anti-gay organizations and legislation.

Federal Law Before 1996, federal law did not define marriage, and the U.S. government recognized any marriage that was recognized by a state. Then Congress passed the Defense of Marriage Act (DOMA), which explicitly defined marriage as a union of one man and one woman.

DOMA was later challenged in the federal court system. Eight federal courts found it to be unconstitutional in a variety of contexts, including bankruptcy, public employee benefits, estate taxes, and immigration. In 2013, in a review of several of these cases, the United States Supreme Court struck down part of the DOMA as unconstitutional.[a] In 2014, the federal government went one step further and clarified that same-sex couples had equal rights in federal legal matters such as bankruptcies, prison visits, and survivor benefits. These federal benefits are available to same-sex couples even in states that do not recognize same-sex marriages. Today, once again, no federal law defines marriage, and marriage law is determined at the state level.

State Laws Twenty-seven states prohibit same-sex marriages in their constitutions. Another four states forbid such marriages through state statutes that define marriage as a union between a man and a woman.

Marriage laws that do not permit or recognize same-sex marriage have increasingly led to court challenges. For ex-

ample, in California, same-sex couples could obtain marriage certificates before 2008. That year, voters enacted Proposition 8 to restrict marriage to one man and one woman. In 2012, a federal appellate court struck down Proposition 8 as a violation of the equal protection clause, reasoning that it was not rationally related to a legitimate state interest. The court noted that the U.S. Constitution "requires that there be at least a legitimate reason for the passage of a law that treats different classes of people differently." In the court's view, Proposition 8 served no legitimate purpose other than to "lessen the status and human dignity of gay men and lesbians in California."[b]

Federal courts have become increasingly likely to invalidate state bans on same-sex marriage. In 2013, a federal district court held that Utah's same-sex marriage ban was unconstitutional.[c] In 2014, a federal district court in Oklahoma struck down that state's constitutional prohibition against same-sex marriage.[d] Moreover, public sentiment on the issue has shifted, and more states are recognizing the rights of same-sex couples. As of 2014, seventeen states, as well as the District of Columbia, had legalized same-sex marriage.

MANAGERIAL IMPLICATIONS

In this era of social networking, a company's policies can become public almost instantly—the boycotts of Target and Barilla were largely organized via Facebook. Consequently, businesspersons must carefully consider their policies toward employees and others who have different sexual orientations, taking into account such factors as their firms' size, location, composition, and client base. At a minimum, company policies should clearly specify how same-sex partners will be treated in terms of family and medical leave, health insurance coverage, pensions, and other benefits.

BUSINESS QUESTIONS

1. Should a business manager's religious beliefs factor into the business's treatment of same-sex partners with regard to family and medical leave and health insurance? Why or why not?

2. Why might business owners who live in states that currently ban same-sex marriage want to provide the same benefits to employees in a same-sex union as they do to married employees?

a. *United States v. Windsor*, ___ U.S. ___, 133 S.Ct. 2675, 186 L.Ed.2d 808 (2013).

b. *Perry v. Brown*, 671 F.3d 1052 (9th Cir. 2012).
c. *Kitchen v. Herbert*, 961 F.Supp.2d 1181 (D.Utah 2013).
d. *Bishop v. U.S. ex rel. Holder*, 962 F.Supp.2d 1252 (N.D.Okla. 2013).

Federal Privacy Legislation

In the last several decades, Congress has enacted a number of statutes that protect the privacy of individuals in various areas of concern. Most of these statutes deal with personal information collected by governments or private businesses. In the 1960s, Americans were sufficiently alarmed by the accumulation of personal information in government files that they pressured Congress to pass laws permitting individuals to access their files. Congress responded in 1966 with the Freedom of Information Act, which allows any person to request copies of any information on her or him contained in federal government files. In 1974, Congress passed the Privacy Act, which also gives persons the right to access such information.

These and other major federal laws protecting privacy rights are listed and described in Exhibit 4–1. (See the *Linking Business Law to Marketing* feature at the end of this chapter for a discussion of some laws pertaining to the collection of personal information by businesses.)

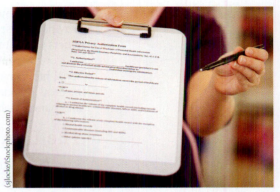

(sjlocke/iStockphoto.com)

Hospital patients are always informed about privacy rights under HIPAA.

Medical Information

Responding to the growing need to protect the privacy of individuals' health records—particularly computerized records—Congress passed the Health Insurance Portability and Accountability Act (HIPAA).[31] This act defines and limits the circumstances in which an individual's "protected health information" may be used or disclosed.

HIPAA requires health-care providers and health-care plans, including certain employers who sponsor health plans, to inform patients of their privacy rights and of how their personal

---

31. HIPAA was enacted as Pub. L. No. 104-191 (1996) and is codified in 29 U.S.C.A. Sections 1181 *et seq.*

Exhibit 4–1 Federal Legislation Relating to Privacy

TITLE OF ACT	PROVISIONS CONCERNING PRIVACY
Freedom of Information Act (1966)	Provides that individuals have a right to obtain access to information about them collected in government files.
Family and Educational Rights and Privacy Act (1974)	Limits access to computer-stored records of education-related evaluations and grades in private and public colleges and universities.
Privacy Act (1974)	Protects the privacy of individuals about whom the federal government has information. Under this act, agencies that use or disclose personal information must make sure that the information is reliable and guard against its misuse. Individuals must be able to find out what data concerning them the agency is compiling and how the data will be used. In addition, the agency must give individuals a means to correct inaccurate data and must obtain their consent before using the data for any other purpose.
Tax Reform Act (1976)	Preserves the privacy of personal financial information.
Right to Financial Privacy Act (1978)	Prohibits financial institutions from providing the federal government with access to a customer's records unless the customer authorizes the disclosure.
Electronic Communications Privacy Act (1986)	Prohibits the interception of information communicated by electronic means.
Driver's Privacy Protection Act (1994)	Prevents states from disclosing or selling a driver's personal information without the driver's consent.
Health Insurance Portability and Accountability Act (1996)	Prohibits the use of a consumer's medical information for any purpose other than that for which such information was provided, unless the consumer expressly consents to the use.
Financial Services Modernization Act (Gramm-Leach-Bliley Act) (1999)	Prohibits the disclosure of nonpublic personal information about a consumer to an unaffiliated third party unless strict disclosure and opt-out requirements are met.

medical information may be used. The act also generally states that a person's medical records may not be used for purposes unrelated to health care—such as marketing—or disclosed to others without the individual's permission.

Congress later expanded HIPAA's provisions to apply to *vendors* (those who maintain personal health records for health-care providers) and to electronic records shared by multiple medical providers. Congress also authorized the Federal Trade Commission to enforce HIPAA and pursue violators.[32]

The USA Patriot Act

The USA Patriot Act was passed by Congress in the wake of the terrorist attacks of September 11, 2001, and then reauthorized twice.[33] The Patriot Act has given government officials increased authority to monitor Internet activities (such as e-mail and Web site visits) and to gain access to personal financial information and student information. Law enforcement officials may now track the telephone and e-mail communications of one party to find out the identity of the other party or parties.

To gain access to these communications, the government must certify that the information likely to be obtained by such monitoring is relevant to an ongoing criminal investigation. The government need not provide proof of any wrongdoing.

EXAMPLE 4.19   In 2012, General David Petraeus, who ran the wars in Iraq and Afghanistan, resigned as director of the Central Intelligence Agency after his extramarital affair with Paula Broadwell, his biographer, became public. Apparently, after Petraeus broke off the affair with Broadwell, she sent harassing e-mails to another woman who reported the harassment. The FBI investigated, accessed Petraeus's e-mail accounts, and discovered that he had communicated with Broadwell via messages left in a draft folder on his e-mail account. Although there was no evidence that Petraeus did anything illegal, he was urged to resign and did so. •

> "The things most people want to know about are usually none of their business."
>
> George Bernard Shaw, 1856–1950 (Irish dramatist and socialist)

---

32. These provisions were part of the American Recovery and Reinvestment Act (ARRA) of 2009, popularly known as the stimulus law. See 45 C.F.R. Sections 164.510 and 164.512(f)(2).

33. The Uniting and Strengthening America by Providing Appropriate Tools Required to Intercept and Obstruct Terrorism Act of 2001, also known as the USA Patriot Act, was enacted as Pub. L. No. 107-56 (2001). While the bulk of the Patriot Act is permanent law, the most controversial surveillance provisions must be reauthorized every four years and were reauthorized by Pub. L. No. 109-173 (2006) and Pub. L. No. 112-114 (2011).

Reviewing . . . Business and the Constitution

A state legislature enacted a statute that required any motorcycle operator or passenger on the state's highways to wear a protective helmet. Jim Alderman, a licensed motorcycle operator, sued the state to block enforcement of the law. Alderman asserted that the statute violated the equal protection clause because it placed requirements on motorcyclists that were not imposed on other motorists. Using the information presented in the chapter, answer the following questions.

1. Why does this statute raise equal protection issues instead of substantive due process concerns?
2. What are the three levels of scrutiny that the courts use in determining whether a law violates the equal protection clause?
3. Which level of scrutiny or test would apply to this situation? Why?
4. Applying this standard or test, is the helmet statute constitutional? Why or why not?

Debate This Legislation aimed at protecting people from themselves concerns the individual as well as the public in general. Protective helmet laws are just one example of such legislation. Should individuals be allowed to engage in unsafe activities if they choose to do so?

LINKING BUSINESS LAW to Marketing

Is "Pretexting" Illegal?

Most businesses, institutions, and organizations gather information from and about their customers, constituents, or members. Many businesses also want information about potential customers and may obtain names from a mailing list of some other business or organization. Unless the owner of the list has a privacy policy that prohibits the sharing of certain information without the person's consent, a business may purchase the list and proceed to offer its product or service to all the people on it. Locating potential customers in this manner may be completely legal, depending on how the information was obtained in the first place. Pretexting is a method of collecting personal information that skirts the boundary between legal and illegal.

What Is "Pretexting"?

A *pretext* is a false motive put forth to hide the real motive, and *pretexting* is the process of obtaining information by false means. The term *pretexting* was first used in the 1990s when scammers obtained Social Security numbers by claiming that they were from the Social Security Administration and that their computer had broken down.

Pretexters may try to obtain personal data by claiming that they are taking a survey for a research firm, a political party, or even a charity. Then they proceed to ask for information such as the person's insurance or telephone company, where he or she banks, and perhaps the name of his or her broker. Once they obtain the information, the pretexters sell it to a data broker, who in turn sells it to someone else, who may be a legitimate businessperson, a private investigator, or an individual intent on identity theft.

Pretexting Legislation

In 1999, Congress passed the Gramm-Leach-Bliley Act, which made pretexting to obtain financial information illegal. Initially, it was not clear whether that law prohibited lying to obtain *nonfinancial* information for purposes other than identity theft.

Fueling the debate over pretexting was a scandal involving Hewlett-Packard's board of directors. To find out who had leaked confidential company information to the press, Hewlett-Packard chair, Patricia C. Dunn, hired private investigators who used false pretenses to gain access to individuals' personal cell phone records. Dunn claimed that she was not aware of the investigators' methods and had assumed that they had obtained the information from public records. Although criminal charges that were brought against her were later dropped, several civil lawsuits followed. The company eventually paid $14.5 million in fines to settle a lawsuit filed by the California attorney general. In 2008, Hewlett-Packard reached a settlement with the New York Times Company and three *BusinessWeek* magazine journalists in connection with the scandal.

To clarify the law on pretexting to gain access to phone records, Congress enacted the Telephone Records and Privacy Protection Act. This act makes it a federal crime to pretend to be someone else or to make false representations for the purpose of obtaining another person's confidential phone records. The act also prohibits the buying, selling, transferring, or receiving of such phone records without the phone owner's permission. The Federal Trade Commission investigates and prosecutes violators, who can be fined and sentenced to up to ten years in prison.

Critical Thinking

How might a business obtain a list of potential customers for marketing purposes without violating the laws pertaining to pretexting?

Key Terms

Chapter Summary: Business and the Constitution

The Constitutional Powers of Government	The U.S. Constitution established a federal form of government, in which government powers are shared by the national government and the state governments. At the national level, government powers are divided among the legislative, executive, and judicial branches.
The Commerce Clause	1. *The expansion of national powers*—The commerce clause expressly permits Congress to regulate commerce. Over time, courts expansively interpreted this clause, thereby enabling the national government to wield extensive powers over the economic life of the nation. 2. *The commerce power today*—Today, the commerce power authorizes the national government, at least theoretically, to regulate almost every commercial enterprise in the United States. In recent years, the Supreme Court has reined in somewhat the national government's regulatory powers under the commerce clause. 3. *The regulatory powers of the states*—The Tenth Amendment reserves to the states all powers not expressly delegated to the national government. Under their police powers, state governments may regulate private activities in order to protect or promote the public order, health, safety, morals, and general welfare. 4. *The "dormant" commerce clause*—If state regulations substantially interfere with interstate commerce, they will be held to violate the "dormant" commerce clause of the U.S. Constitution. The positive aspect of the commerce clause, which gives the national government the exclusive authority to regulate interstate commerce, implies a "dormant" aspect—that the states do *not* have this power.
The Supremacy Clause	The U.S. Constitution provides that the Constitution, laws, and treaties of the United States are "the supreme Law of the Land." Whenever a state law directly conflicts with a federal law, the state law is rendered invalid.
Business and the Bill of Rights	The Bill of Rights, which consists of the first ten amendments to the U.S. Constitution, was adopted in 1791 and embodies a series of protections for individuals—and, in some instances, business entities—against various types of interference by the federal government. Today, most of the protections apply against state governments as well. Freedoms guaranteed by the First Amendment that affect businesses include the following: 1. *Freedom of speech*—Speech, including symbolic speech, is given the fullest possible protection by the courts. Corporate political speech and commercial speech also receive substantial protection under the First Amendment. Certain types of speech, such as defamatory speech and lewd or obscene speech, are not protected under the First Amendment. Government attempts to regulate unprotected forms of speech in the online environment have, to date, met with numerous challenges. 2. *Freedom of religion*—Under the First Amendment, the government may neither establish any religion (the establishment clause) nor prohibit the free exercise of religion (the free exercise clause).
Due Process and Equal Protection	1. *Due process*—Both the Fifth and the Fourteenth Amendments provide that no person shall be deprived of "life, liberty, or property, without due process of law." Procedural due process requires that any government decision to take life, liberty, or property must be made fairly, using fair procedures. Substantive due process focuses on the content of legislation. Generally, a law that limits a fundamental right violates substantive due process unless the law promotes a compelling state interest, such as public safety. 2. *Equal protection*—Under the Fourteenth Amendment, a law or action that limits the liberty of some persons but not others may violate the equal protection clause. Such a law may be upheld, however, if there is a rational basis for the discriminatory treatment of a given group or if the law substantially relates to an important government objective.
Privacy Rights	Americans are increasingly becoming concerned about privacy issues raised by Internet-related technology. The Constitution does not contain a specific guarantee of a right to privacy, but such a right has been derived from guarantees found in several constitutional amendments. A number of federal statutes protect privacy rights. Privacy rights are also protected by many state constitutions and statutes, as well as under tort law.

Issue Spotters

1. Can a state, in the interest of energy conservation, ban all advertising by power utilities if conservation could be accomplished by less restrictive means? Why or why not? (See *Business and the Bill of Rights*.)
2. Suppose that a state imposes a higher tax on out-of-state companies doing business in the state than it imposes on in-state companies. Is this a violation of equal protection if the only reason for the tax is to protect the local firms from out-of-state competition? Explain. (See *Due Process and Equal Protection*.)

—**Check your answers to the Issue Spotters against the answers provided in Appendix D at the end of this text.**

For Review

1. What is the basic structure of the U.S. government?
2. What constitutional clause gives the federal government the power to regulate commercial activities among the various states?
3. What constitutional clause allows laws enacted by the federal government to take priority over conflicting state laws?
4. What is the Bill of Rights? What freedoms does the First Amendment guarantee?
5. Where in the Constitution can the due process clause be found?

Business Scenarios and Case Problems

4–1. Freedom of Speech. A mayoral election is about to be held in Bay City. One of the candidates is Donita Estrella, and her supporters wish to post campaign signs on streetlights and utility posts. A Bay City ordinance prohibits the posting of signs on public property. The purpose of the ordinance is to improve the appearance of the city. Estrella's supporters contend that the ordinance violates their rights to free speech. What factors might a court consider in determining the constitutionality of this ordinance? (See *Business and the Bill of Rights.*)

4–2. Freedom of Religion. Thomas worked in the nonmilitary operations of a large firm that produced both military and non-military goods. When the company discontinued the production of nonmilitary goods, Thomas was transferred to the plant producing military equipment. Thomas left his job, claiming that it violated his religious principles to participate in the manufacture of goods to be used in destroying life. In effect, he argued, the transfer to the military equipment plant forced him to quit his job. He was denied unemployment compensation by the state because he had not been effectively "discharged" by the employer but had voluntarily terminated his employment. Did the state's denial of unemployment benefits to Thomas violate the free exercise clause of the First Amendment? Explain. (See *Business and the Bill of Rights.*)

4–3. The Equal Protection Clause. With the objectives of preventing crime, maintaining property values, and preserving the quality of urban life, New York City enacted an ordinance to regulate the locations of commercial establishments that featured adult entertainment. The ordinance expressly applied to female, but not male, topless entertainment. Adele Buzzetti owned the Cozy Cabin, a New York City cabaret that featured female topless dancers. Buzzetti and an anonymous dancer filed a suit in a federal district court against the city, asking the court to block the enforcement of the ordinance. The plaintiffs argued, in part, that the ordinance violated the equal protection clause. Under the equal protection clause, what standard should the court apply in considering this ordinance? Under this test, how should the court rule? Why? (See *Due Process and Equal Protection.*)

4–4. **Spotlight on Plagiarism—Due Process.** The Russ College of Engineering and Technology of Ohio University announced in a press conference that it had found "rampant and flagrant plagiarism" in the theses of mechanical

engineering graduate students. Faculty singled out for "ignoring their ethical responsibilities" included Jay Gunasekera, chair of the department. Gunasekera was prohibited from advising students. He filed a suit against Dennis Irwin, the dean of Russ College, for violating his due process rights. What does due process require in these circumstances? Why? [*Gunasekera v. Irwin*, 551 F.3d 461 (6th Cir. 2009)] (See *Due Process and Equal Protection.*)

4–5. The Commerce Clause. Under the federal Sex Offender Registration and Notification Act (SORNA), sex offenders must register and update their registration as sex offenders when they travel from one state to another. David Hall, a convicted sex offender in New York, moved to Virginia, where he did not update his registration. He was charged with violating SORNA. He claimed that the statute is unconstitutional, arguing that Congress cannot criminalize interstate travel if no commerce is involved. Is that reasonable? Why or why not? [*United States v. Guzman*, 591 F.3d 83 (2d Cir. 2010)] (See *The Constitutional Powers of Government.*)

4–6. **Business Case Problem with Sample Answer— Establishment Clause.** Judge James DeWeese hung a poster in his courtroom showing the Ten Commandments. The American Civil Liberties Union (ACLU) filed a suit, alleging that the poster violated the establishment clause. DeWeese responded that his purpose was not to promote religion but to express his view about "warring" legal philosophies—moral relativism and moral absolutism. "Our legal system is based on moral absolutes from divine law handed down by God through the Ten Commandments." Does this poster violate the establishment clause? Why or why not? [*American Civil Liberties Union of Ohio Foundation, Inc. v. DeWeese*, 633 F.3d 424 (6th Cir. 2011)] (See *Business and the Bill of Rights.*)

—For a sample answer to Problem 4–6, go to Appendix E at the end of this text.

4–7. The Dormant Commerce Clause. In 2001, Puerto Rico enacted a law that requires specific labels on cement sold in Puerto Rico and imposes fines for any violations of these requirements. The law prohibits the sale or distribution of cement manufactured outside Puerto Rico that does not carry a required label warning that the cement may not be used in government-financed construction projects. Antilles Cement Corp., a Puerto Rican firm that imports foreign cement, filed a complaint in federal court, claiming that this law violated the dormant commerce clause. (The dormant commerce clause doctrine applies not only to commerce among the states and U.S. territories, but also to international commerce.) Did the 2001 Puerto Rican law violate the dormant commerce clause? Why or why not? [*Antilles Cement Corp. v. Fortuno,* 670 F.3d 310 (1st Cir. 2012)] (See *The Constitutional Powers of Government.*)

4–8. Freedom of Speech. Mark Wooden sent e-mail to an alderwoman for the city of St. Louis. Attached was a nineteen-minute audio that compared her to the biblical character, Jezebel—she was a "bitch in the Sixth Ward," spending too much time with the rich and powerful and too little time with the poor. In a menacing, maniacal tone, Wooden said that he was "dusting off a sawed-off shotgun," called himself a "domestic terrorist," and referred to the assassination of President John F. Kennedy, the murder of a federal judge, and the shooting of Congresswoman Gabrielle Giffords. Feeling threatened, the alderwoman called the police. Wooden was convicted of harassment under a state criminal statute. Was this conviction unconstitutional under the First Amendment? Discuss. [*State v. Wooden,* 388 S.W.3d 522 (Mo. 2013)] (See *Business and the Bill of Rights.*)

4–9. Equal Protection. Abbott Laboratories licensed SmithKline Beecham Corp. to market a human immunodeficiency virus (HIV) drug manufactured by Abbot in conjunction with one of SmithKline's drugs. Abbott then increased the price of its drug fourfold, forcing SmithKline to increase its prices and thereby driving business to Abbott's own combination drug. SmithKline filed a suit in a federal district court against Abbott, alleging violations of the implied covenant of good faith and fair dealing. During jury selection, Abbott struck the only self-identified gay person among the potential jurors. (The pricing of HIV drugs is of considerable concern in the gay community.) Could the equal protection clause be applied to prohibit discrimination based on sexual orientation in jury selection? Discuss. [*SmithKline Beecham Corp. v. Abbott Laboratories,* 740 F.3d 471 (9th Cir. 2014)] (See *Due Process and Equal Protection.*)

4–10. A Question of Ethics—Freedom of Speech. Aric Toll owns and manages the Balboa Island Village Inn, a restaurant and bar in Newport Beach, California. Anne Lemen lives across from the Inn. Lemen complained to the authorities about the Inn's customers, whom she called "drunks" and "whores." Lemen told the Inn's bartender Ewa Cook that Cook "worked for Satan." She repeated her statements to potential customers, and the Inn's sales dropped more than 20 percent. The Inn filed a suit against Lemen. [*Balboa Island Village Inn, Inc. v. Lemen,* 40 Cal.4th 1141, 156 P.3d 339 (2007)] (See *Business and the Bill of Rights.*)

1. Are Lemen's statements about the Inn's owners and customers protected by the U.S. Constitution? In whose favor should the court rule? Why?
2. Did Lemen behave unethically in the circumstances of this case? Explain.

CHAPTER 5

(Creativeye99/iStockphoto.com)

Torts and Strict Liability

LEARNING OBJECTIVES

The five learning objectives below are designed to help improve your understanding of the chapter. After reading this chapter, you should be able to answer the following questions:

1. What is the purpose of tort law? What types of damages are available in tort lawsuits?
2. What are two basic categories of torts?
3. What is defamation? Name two types of defamation.
4. Identify the four elements of negligence.
5. What is meant by strict liability? In what circumstances is strict liability applied?

> "Two wrongs do not make a right."
> —English Proverb

Torts are wrongful actions (the word *tort* is French for "wrong"). Most of us agree with the chapter-opening quotation—two wrongs do not make a right. Part of doing business today—and, indeed, part of everyday life—is the risk of being involved in a lawsuit. The list of circumstances in which businesspersons can be sued is long and varied. A customer who is injured by a security guard at a business establishment, for instance, may sue the business owner, claiming that the security guard's conduct was intentionally wrongful. A man who slips and falls on a wet floor at a Walgreens store may sue the company for *negligence* (an unintentional tort explained later in this chapter). Any time that one party's allegedly wrongful conduct causes injury to another, an action may arise under the law of *torts*.

Through tort law, society compensates those who have suffered injuries as a result of the wrongful conduct of others. Even conduct that is not wrongful but is abnormally dangerous can lead to liability under the doctrine of strict liability, which is *liability without fault*. Many of the lawsuits brought by or against business firms are based on the tort theories discussed in this chapter, which covers intentional torts, negligence, and strict liability. In

Tort A wrongful act (other than a breach of contract) that results in harm or injury to another and leads to civil liability.

addition, Chapter 9 discusses how tort law applies to wrongful actions in the online environment and Chapter 12 discusses product liability.

The Basis of Tort Law

Two notions serve as the basis of all torts: wrongs and compensation. Tort law is designed to compensate those who have suffered a loss or injury due to another person's wrongful act. In a tort action, one person or group brings a personal suit against another person or group to obtain compensation (monetary **damages**) or other relief for the harm suffered.

The Purpose of Tort Law

Generally, the purpose of tort law is to provide remedies for the violation of various *protected interests*. Society recognizes an interest in personal physical safety. Thus, tort law provides remedies for acts that cause physical injury or that interfere with physical security and freedom of movement.

Society recognizes an interest in protecting property, and tort law provides remedies for acts that cause destruction of or damage to property. Note that in legal usage, the singular *damage* is used to refer to harm or injury to persons or property, and the plural *damages* is used to refer to monetary compensation for such harm or injury.

Damages Available in Tort Actions

Because the purpose of tort law is to compensate the injured party for the damage suffered, it is important to have a basic understanding of the types of damages that plaintiffs seek in tort actions.

Compensatory Damages
Compensatory damages are intended to compensate or reimburse plaintiffs for actual losses—to make the plaintiffs whole and put them in the same position that they would have been in had the tort not occurred. Compensatory damages awards are often broken down into *special damages* and *general damages*.

Special damages compensate the plaintiff for quantifiable monetary losses, such as medical expenses, lost wages and benefits (now and in the future), extra costs, the loss of irreplaceable items, and the costs of repairing or replacing damaged property.

CASE EXAMPLE 5.1   Seaway Marine Transport operates the *Enterprise,* a large cargo ship with twenty-two hatches for storing coal. When the *Enterprise* moved into position to receive a load of coal on the shores of Lake Erie in Ohio, it struck a land-based coal-loading machine operated by Bessemer & Lake Erie Railroad Company. A federal court found Seaway liable for negligence and awarded $522,000 in special damages to compensate Bessemer for the cost of repairing the damage to the loading machine.[1] ●

General damages compensate individuals (not companies) for the nonmonetary aspects of the harm suffered, such as pain and suffering. A court might award general damages for physical or emotional pain and suffering, loss of companionship, loss of consortium (losing the emotional and physical benefits of a spousal relationship), disfigurement, loss of reputation, or loss or impairment of mental or physical capacity.

Punitive Damages
Occasionally, **punitive damages** may also be awarded in tort cases to punish the wrongdoer and deter others from similar wrongdoing. Punitive damages are appropriate only when the defendant's conduct was particularly egregious (bad) or reprehensible (unacceptable).

---

1. *Bessemer & Lake Erie Railroad Co. v. Seaway Marine Transport,* 596 F.3d 357 (6th Cir. 2010).

Damages A monetary award sought as a remedy for a breach of contract or a tortious action.

Learning Objective 1
What is the purpose of tort law? What types of damages are available in tort lawsuits?

Compensatory Damages A monetary award equivalent to the actual value of injuries or damage sustained by the aggrieved party.

Punitive Damages Monetary damages that may be awarded to a plaintiff to punish the defendant and deter similar conduct in the future.

This photo shows a South Korean ferry that sank, killing hundreds of passengers. Would relatives of the deceased be able to sue for damages?

(Ed Jones/AFP/Getty Images)

Usually, this means that punitive damages are available mainly in intentional tort actions and only rarely in negligence lawsuits (*intentional torts* and *negligence* will be explained later in the chapter). They may be awarded, however, in suits involving *gross negligence,* which can be defined as an intentional failure to perform a manifest duty in reckless disregard of the consequences of such a failure for the life or property of another.

Courts exercise great restraint in granting punitive damages to plaintiffs in tort actions because punitive damages are subject to the limitations imposed by the due process clause of the U.S. Constitution (discussed in Chapter 4). The United States Supreme Court has held that a punitive damages award that is grossly excessive furthers no legitimate purpose and violates due process requirements.[2] Consequently, an appellate court will sometimes reduce the amount of punitive damages awarded to a plaintiff because the amount was excessive and thereby violates the due process clause.

Tort Reform

Tort law performs a valuable function by enabling injured parties to obtain compensation. Nevertheless, critics contend that certain aspects of today's tort law encourage too many trivial and unfounded lawsuits, which clog the courts and add unnecessary costs. They say that damages awards are often excessive and bear little relationship to the actual damage suffered, which inspires more plaintiffs to file lawsuits. The result, in the critics' view, is a system that disproportionately rewards a few plaintiffs while imposing a "tort tax" on business and society as a whole. For instance, to avoid medical malpractice (negligence) lawsuits, physicians and hospitals order more tests than necessary.

Measures to reduce the number of tort cases include (1) limiting the amount of both punitive damages and general damages that can be awarded, (2) capping the amount that attorneys can collect in *contingency fees* (attorneys' fees that are based on a percentage of the damages awarded to the client), and (3) requiring the losing party to pay both the plaintiff's and the defendant's expenses.

The Class Action Fairness Act (CAFA) of 2005[3] shifted jurisdiction over large interstate tort and product liability class-action lawsuits (lawsuits filed by a large number of plaintiffs) from the state courts to the federal courts. The intent was to prevent plaintiffs' attorneys from *forum shopping*—looking for a state court known to be sympathetic to their clients' cause and predisposed to award large damages. At the state level, half of the states have placed caps on general damages, such as for pain and suffering, and more than thirty states have limited punitive damages, with some imposing outright bans.

Classifications of Torts

There are two broad classifications of torts: *intentional torts* and *unintentional torts* (torts involving negligence). The classification of a particular tort depends largely on how the tort occurs (intentionally or negligently) and the surrounding circumstances. Intentional torts result from the intentional violation of person or property (fault plus intent). Negligence results from the breach of a duty to act reasonably (fault without intent). In addition, as you will read later in this chapter, in certain circumstances, strict liability may be imposed (liability without fault).

Learning Objective 2
What are two basic categories of torts?

Defenses

Even if a plaintiff proves all the elements of a tort, the defendant can raise a number of legally recognized **defenses** (reasons why the plaintiff should not obtain damages). The defenses available may vary depending on the specific tort involved. A common defense

Defense A reason offered and alleged by a defendant in an action or lawsuit as to why the plaintiff should not recover or establish what she or he seeks.

---

2. *State Farm Mutual Automobile Insurance Co. v. Campbell,* 538 U.S. 408, 123 S.Ct. 1513, 155 L.Ed.2d 585 (2003).
3. 28 U.S.C. Sections 1453, 1711–1715.

to intentional torts against persons, for instance, is *consent.* When a person consents to the act that damages her or him, there is generally no liability. The most widely used defense in negligence actions is *comparative negligence* (discussed later in this chapter). A successful defense releases the defendant from partial or full liability for the tortious act.

Intentional Torts against Persons

Intentional Tort A wrongful act knowingly committed.

Tortfeasor One who commits a tort.

An **intentional tort,** as the term implies, requires *intent.* The **tortfeasor** (the one committing the tort) must intend to commit an act, the consequences of which interfere with the personal or business interests of another in a way not permitted by law. An evil or harmful motive is not required—in fact, the person committing the action (the actor) may even have a beneficial motive for committing what turns out to be a tortious act.

In tort law, intent means only that the actor intended the consequences of his or her act or knew with substantial certainty that certain consequences would result from the act. The law generally assumes that individuals intend the *normal* consequences of their actions. Thus, forcefully pushing another—even if done in jest and without any evil motive—is an intentional tort if injury results, because the object of a strong push can ordinarily be expected to fall down.

Transferred intent A legal principle under which a person who intends to harm one individual, but unintentionally harms a second person, can be liable to the second victim for an intentional tort.

In addition, intent can be transferred when a defendant intends to harm one individual, but unintentionally harms a second person. This is called **transferred intent.** **EXAMPLE 5.2** Alex swings a bat intending to hit Blake but misses and hits Carson instead. Carson can sue Alex for the tort of battery (discussed shortly) because Alex's intent to harm Blake can be transferred to Carson. ●

Assault

Assault Any word or action intended to make another person fearful of immediate physical harm—a reasonably believable threat.

An **assault** is any intentional and unexcused threat of immediate harmful or offensive contact—words or acts that create a reasonably believable threat. An assault can occur even if there is no actual contact with the plaintiff, provided that the defendant's conduct creates a reasonable apprehension of imminent harm in the plaintiff. Tort law aims to protect individuals from having to expect harmful or offensive contact.

Battery

Battery Unexcused, harmful or offensive, physical contact with another that is intentionally performed.

If the act that created the apprehension is *completed* and results in harm to the plaintiff, it is a **battery**—an unexcused and harmful or offensive physical contact *intentionally* performed. **EXAMPLE 5.3** Ivan threatens Jean with a gun and then shoots her. The pointing of the gun at Jean is an assault. The firing of the gun (if the bullet hits Jean) is a battery. ●

The contact can be harmful, or it can be merely offensive (such as an unwelcome kiss). Physical injury need not occur. The contact can involve any part of the body or anything attached to it—for instance, a hat, a purse, or a jacket. The contact can be made by the defendant or by some force set in motion by the defendant, such as by throwing a rock. Whether the contact is offensive is determined by the *reasonable person standard.*[4]

If the plaintiff shows that there was contact, and the jury (or judge, if there is no jury) agrees that the contact was offensive, then the plaintiff has a right to compensation. A plaintiff may be compensated for the emotional harm or loss of reputation resulting from a battery, as well as for physical harm. A defendant may assert self-defense or defense of others in an attempt to justify his or her conduct.

---

4. The reasonable person standard is an "objective" test of how a reasonable person would have acted under the same circumstances. See "The Duty of Care and Its Breach" later in this chapter.

False Imprisonment

False imprisonment is the intentional confinement or restraint of another person's activities without justification. False imprisonment interferes with the freedom to move without restraint. The confinement can be accomplished through the use of physical barriers, physical restraint, or threats of physical force. Moral pressure or threats of future harm do not constitute false imprisonment. It is essential that the person under restraint does not wish to be restrained.

Businesspersons are often confronted with suits for false imprisonment after they have attempted to confine a suspected shoplifter for questioning. Under the "privilege to detain" granted to merchants in most states, a merchant can use *reasonable force* to detain or delay a person suspected of shoplifting the merchant's property. Although the details of the privilege vary from state to state, generally laws require that any detention be conducted in a *reasonable* manner and for only a *reasonable* length of time. Undue force or unreasonable detention can lead to liability for the business.

Cities and counties may also face lawsuits for false imprisonment if they detain individuals without reason. **EXAMPLE 5.4** Police arrested Adetokunbo Shoyoye for an unpaid subway ticket and for a theft that had been committed by someone who had stolen his identity. A court ordered him to be released, but a county employee mistakenly confused Shoyoye's paperwork with that of another person—who was scheduled to be sent to state prison. As a result, instead of being released, Shoyoye was held in county jail for more than two weeks. Shoyoye later sued the county for false imprisonment and won.[5] ●

Intentional Infliction of Emotional Distress

The tort of *intentional infliction of emotional distress* can be defined as an extreme and outrageous act, intentionally committed, that results in severe emotional distress to another. To be **actionable** (capable of serving as the ground for a lawsuit), the conduct must be so extreme and outrageous that it exceeds the bounds of decency accepted by society.

Actionable Capable of serving as the basis of a lawsuit. An actionable claim can be pursued in a lawsuit or other court action.

Outrageous Conduct
Courts in most jurisdictions are wary of emotional distress claims and confine them to truly outrageous behavior. Generally, repeated annoyances (such as those experienced by a person who is being stalked), coupled with threats, are sufficient to support a claim. Acts that cause indignity or annoyance alone usually are not enough. **EXAMPLE 5.5** A father attacks a man who has had consensual sexual relations with the father's nineteen-year-old daughter. The father handcuffs the man to a steel pole and threatens to kill him unless he leaves town immediately. The father's conduct may be sufficiently extreme and outrageous to be actionable as an intentional infliction of emotional distress. ●

Limited by the First Amendment
Note that when the outrageous conduct consists of speech about a public figure, the First Amendment's guarantee of freedom of speech also limits emotional distress claims. **CASE EXAMPLE 5.6** *Hustler* magazine once printed a fake advertisement that showed a picture of the Reverend Jerry Falwell and described him as having lost his virginity to his mother in an outhouse while he was drunk. Falwell sued the magazine for intentional infliction of emotional distress and won, but the United States Supreme Court overturned the decision. The Court held that creators of parodies of public figures are protected under the First Amendment from claims of intentional infliction of emotional distress. (The Court applied the same standards that apply to public figures in defamation lawsuits, discussed next.)[6] ●

---

5. *Shoyoye v. County of Los Angeles*, 203 Cal.App.4th 947, 137 Cal.Rptr.3d 839 (2012).
6. *Hustler Magazine, Inc. v. Falwell*, 485 U.S. 46, 108 S.Ct. 876, 99 L.Ed.2d 41 (1988). For another example of how the courts protect parody, see *Busch v. Viacom International, Inc.*, 477 F.Supp.2d 764 (N.D.Tex. 2007), involving a fake endorsement of televangelist Pat Robertson's diet shake.

Defamation

Learning Objective 3
What is defamation? Name two
types of defamation.

Defamation Anything published or publicly spoken that causes injury to another's good name, reputation, or character.

Libel Defamation in writing or another form having the quality of permanence (such as a digital recording).

Slander Defamation in oral form.

As discussed in Chapter 4, the freedom of speech guaranteed by the First Amendment to the U.S. Constitution is not absolute. In interpreting the First Amendment, the courts must balance free speech rights against other strong social interests, including society's interest in preventing and redressing attacks on reputation. (Nations with fewer free speech protections have seen an increase in defamation lawsuits targeting U.S. citizens and journalists as defendants. See this chapter's *Beyond Our Borders* feature for a discussion of this trend.)

Defamation of character involves wrongfully hurting a person's good reputation. The law has imposed a general duty on all persons to refrain from making *false*, defamatory *statements of fact* about others. Breaching this duty in writing or in another permanent form (such as a digital recording) constitutes the tort of **libel.** Breaching this duty orally is the tort of **slander.** As you will read later in this chapter, the tort of defamation can also arise when a false statement of fact is made about a person's product, business, or legal ownership rights to property.

To establish defamation, a plaintiff normally must prove the following:

1. The defendant made a false statement of fact.
2. The statement was understood as being about the plaintiff and tended to harm the plaintiff's reputation.
3. The statement was published to at least one person other than the plaintiff.
4. If the plaintiff is a public figure, she or he must prove *actual malice* (discussed shortly).

Statement of Fact Requirement

Often at issue in defamation lawsuits (including online defamation, discussed in Chapter 9) is whether the defendant made a statement of fact or a *statement of opinion*.[7] Statements of opinion normally are not actionable because they are protected under the First Amendment.

In other words, making a negative statement about another person is not defamation unless the statement is false and represents something as a fact rather than a personal opinion. **EXAMPLE 5.7**   The statement "Lane cheats on his taxes," if false, can lead to liability for defamation. The statement "Lane is a jerk," however, cannot constitute defamation because it is an opinion. •

The Publication Requirement

The basis of the tort of defamation is the publication of a statement or statements that hold an individual up to contempt, ridicule, or hatred. *Publication* here means that the defamatory statements are communicated to persons other than the defamed party. **EXAMPLE 5.8**   If Rodriques writes Andrews a private letter falsely accusing him of embezzling funds, the action does not constitute libel. If Peters falsely states that Gordon is dishonest and incompetent when no one else is around, the action does not constitute slander. In neither instance was the message communicated to a third party. •

The courts have generally held that even dictating a letter to a secretary constitutes publication, although the publication may be privileged (privileged communications will be discussed shortly). Moreover, if a third party overhears defamatory statements by chance, the courts usually hold that this also constitutes publication. Defamatory statements made via the Internet are also actionable (see Chapter 9). Note further that anyone who republishes or repeats defamatory statements is liable even if that person reveals the source of the statements.

Damages for Libel

Once a defendant's liability for libel is established, general damages are presumed as a matter of law. General damages are designed to compensate

---

7. See, for example, *Lott v. Levitt*, 469 F.Supp.2d 575 (N.D.Ill. 2007).

BEYOND OUR BORDERS   "Libel Tourism"

As mentioned earlier, U.S. plaintiffs sometimes engage in forum shopping by trying to have their complaints heard by a particular state court that is likely to be sympathetic to their claims. *Libel tourism* is essentially forum shopping on an international scale. Rather than filing a defamation lawsuit in the United States where the freedoms of speech and press are strongly protected, a plaintiff files it in a foreign jurisdiction where there is a greater chance of winning.

The Threat of Libel Tourism Libel tourism can have a chilling effect on the speech of U.S. journalists and authors because the fear of liability in other nations may prevent them from freely discussing topics of profound public importance. Libel tourism could even increase the threat to our nation's security if it discourages authors from writing about persons who support or finance terrorism or other dangerous activities.

The threat of libel tourism captured media attention when Khalid bin Mahfouz, a Saudi Arabian businessman, sued U.S.

resident Dr. Rachel Ehrenfeld in London, England. Ehrenfeld had written a book on terrorist financing that claimed Mahfouz financed Islamic terrorist groups. Mahfouz filed the case in England because English law assumes that the offending speech is false (libelous), and the author must prove that the speech is true in order to prevail.

The English court took jurisdiction because twenty-three copies of the book had been sold online to residents of the United Kingdom. Ehrenfeld did not go to England to defend herself, and the court entered a judgment of $225,000 against her. She then countersued Mahfouz in a U.S. court in an attempt to show that she was protected under the First Amendment and had not committed libel, but that case was dismissed for lack of jurisdiction.[a]

The U.S. Response In response to the *Ehrenfeld* case, the New York state legislature enacted the Libel Terrorism

Reform Act in 2008.[b] That act enables New York courts to assert jurisdiction over anyone who obtains a foreign libel judgment against a writer or publisher living in New York State. It also prevents courts from enforcing foreign libel judgments unless the foreign country provides equal or greater free speech protection than is available in the United States and New York. In 2010, the federal government passed similar legislation that makes foreign libel judgments unenforceable in U.S. courts unless they comply with the First Amendment.[c]

Critical Thinking
Why do we need special legislation designed to control foreign libel claims against U.S. citizens? Explain.

---

a. *Ehrenfeld v. Mahfouz*, 518 F.3d 102 (2d Cir. 2008).

b. McKinney's Consolidated Laws of New York, Sections 302 and 5304.

c. Securing the Protection of Our Enduring and Established Constitutional Heritage Act, 28 U.S.C. Sections 4101–4105.

---

the plaintiff for nonspecific harms such as disgrace or dishonor in the eyes of the community, humiliation, injured reputation, and emotional distress—harms that are difficult to measure. In other words, to recover damages in a libel case, the plaintiff need not prove that she or he was actually harmed in any specific way as a result of the libelous statement.

Damages for Slander

In contrast to cases alleging libel, in a case alleging slander, the plaintiff must prove *special damages* to establish the defendant's liability. In other words, the plaintiff must show that the slanderous statement caused the plaintiff to suffer actual economic or monetary losses. Unless this initial hurdle of proving special damages is overcome, a plaintiff alleging slander normally cannot go forward with the suit and recover any damages. This requirement is imposed in cases involving slander because slanderous statements have a temporary quality. In contrast, a libelous (written) statement has the quality of permanence, can be circulated widely, especially through tweets and blogs, and usually results from some degree of deliberation on the part of the author.

Exceptions to the burden of proving special damages in cases alleging slander are made for certain types of slanderous statements. If a false statement constitutes "slander *per se*," no proof of special damages is required for it to be actionable. The following four types of false utterances are considered to be slander *per se*:

> "My initial response was to sue her for defamation of character, but then I realized that I had no character."
>
> Charles Barkley, 1963–present (National Basketball Association player, 1984–2000)

1. A statement that another has a loathsome disease (historically, leprosy and sexually transmitted diseases, but now also including allegations of mental illness).
2. A statement that another has committed improprieties while engaging in a business, profession, or trade.
3. A statement that another has committed or has been imprisoned for a serious crime.
4. A statement that a person (usually only unmarried persons and sometimes only women) is unchaste or has engaged in serious sexual misconduct.

Defenses against Defamation   Truth is normally an absolute defense against a defamation charge. In other words, if the defendant in a defamation suit can prove that his or her allegedly defamatory statements were true, normally no tort has been committed.

Other defenses to defamation may exist if the statement is privileged or concerns a public figure. Note that the majority of defamation actions in the United States are filed in state courts, and the states may differ both in how they define defamation and in the particular defenses they allow, such as privilege (discussed shortly).

At the heart of the following case were allegedly defamatory statements posted online by a medical patient's son, which criticized a doctor for his perceived rude and insensitive behavior.

Case 5.1

(Shutterstock.com)

McKee v. Laurion
Supreme Court of Minnesota, 825 N.W.2d 725 (2013).

BACKGROUND AND FACTS   Kenneth Laurion was admitted to St. Luke's Hospital in Duluth, Minnesota, after suffering a hemorrhagic stroke. Two days later, he was transferred from the intensive care unit (ICU) of St. Luke's to a private room. The attending physician arranged for Dr. David McKee, a neurologist, to examine him. Kenneth's son, Dennis, and other Laurion family members were present during the examination. After Kenneth was discharged from the hospital, Dennis posted the following statements on "rate-your-doctor" Web sites:

> [Dr. McKee] seemed upset that my father had been moved [into a private room]. Never having met my father or his family, Dr. McKee said, "When you weren't in ICU, I had to spend time finding out if you transferred or died." When we gaped at him, he said, "Well, 44 percent of hemorrhagic strokes die within 30 days. I guess this is the better option." * * * When my father said his gown was just hanging from his neck without a back, Dr. McKee said, "That doesn't matter." My wife said, "It matters to us; let us go into the hall."

After learning of the posts, Dr. McKee filed a suit in a Minnesota state court against Dennis, asserting defamation. The court issued a summary judgment in Dennis's favor. A state intermediate appellate court reversed this judgment. Dennis appealed to the Minnesota Supreme Court.

IN THE WORDS OF THE COURT . . .
PAGE, Justice.
* * * *

Truth is a complete defense to a defamation action and true statements, however disparaging, are not actionable. * * * *If the statement is true in substance, minor inaccuracies of expression or detail are immaterial. Minor inaccuracies do not amount to falsity so long as the substance, the gist, the sting, of the libelous charge is justified.* A statement is substantially true if it would have the same effect on the mind of the reader or listener as that which the pleaded truth would have produced. [Emphasis added.]

* * * As to Statement 1 (Dr. McKee said he had to "spend time finding out if you transferred or died."), Dr. McKee described his account of the statement in his deposition testimony:

> I made a jocular comment * * * to the effect of I had looked for Kenneth Laurion up in the intensive care unit and was glad to find that, when he wasn't there, that he had been moved to a regular hospital bed, because you only go one of two ways when you leave the intensive care unit; you either have improved to the point where you're someplace like this or you leave because you've died.

Case 5.1—Continued

In light of the substantial similarity between Statement 1 and Dr. McKee's account, we conclude that any differences between the two versions are nothing more than minor inaccuracies that cannot serve as a basis for satisfying the falsity element of a defamation claim. Here, the gist or sting of Laurion's and Dr. McKee's versions are the same. Both communicate the notion that patients in the intensive care unit who have suffered a hemorrhagic stroke leave the intensive care unit either because they have been transferred to a regular room or they have died.

As to Statement 2 (Dr. McKee said, "Well, 44 percent of hemorrhagic strokes die within 30 days. I guess this is the better option."), Dr. McKee acknowledged in his deposition that during the examination of Kenneth Laurion, he communicated to those present that some ICU patients die. However, he denies referencing a specific percentage. Thus, Dr. McKee posits that Statement 2 is false, or that, at the least, there is a genuine issue of material fact as to the falsity of Statement 2 because he never stated a specific percentage. The problem for Dr. McKee with respect to Statement 2 is that the gist or sting of Statement 2 is the mention of hemorrhagic stroke patients dying and not the percentage referenced. Statement 2 squarely satisfies the test for substantial truth because it would have the same effect on the reader regardless of whether a specific percentage is referenced (or whether the percentage is accurate).

As to Statement [3] (Dr. McKee said, "That doesn't matter" that the patient's gown did not cover his backside), Dr. McKee testified that he told the patient that the gown "looks like it's okay" because it did not appear that the gown was at risk of falling off. We are not persuaded that there is any meaningful difference between the two versions of the statements sufficient to create a genuine issue as to the falsity of Statement [3]. The substance or gist of the two versions is the same.

DECISION AND REMEDY   The Minnesota Supreme Court concluded that the lower court properly granted summary judgment in favor of Dennis and reversed the decision of the intermediate appellate court. Dennis's statements were not actionable as defamatory. There was no genuine question as to the falsity of the statements—they were substantially true.

THE LEGAL ENVIRONMENT DIMENSION   *What are the required elements to establish a claim of defamation? Which party has to plead and prove these elements?*

WHAT IF THE FACTS WERE DIFFERENT?   *Suppose that Laurion had posted online, "When I mentioned Dr. McKee's name to a friend who is a nurse, she said, 'Dr. McKee is a real tool!'" Would this statement have been defamatory? Explain.*

Privileged Communications   In some circumstances, a person will not be liable for defamatory statements because she or he enjoys a **privilege**, or immunity. Privileged communications are of two types: absolute and qualified.[8] Only in judicial proceedings and certain government proceedings is an absolute privilege granted. Thus, statements made in a courtroom by attorneys and judges during a trial are absolutely privileged, as are statements made by government officials during legislative debate.

In other situations, a person will not be liable for defamatory statements because he or she has a *qualified,* or conditional, privilege. An employer's statements in written evaluations of employees are an example of a qualified privilege. Generally, if the statements are made in good faith and the publication is limited to those who have a legitimate interest in the communication, the statements fall within the area of qualified privilege.

EXAMPLE 5.9   Jorge worked at Facebook for five years and was being considered for a management position. His supervisor, Lydia, wrote a memo about Jorge's performance to those evaluating him for the management position. The memo contained certain negative statements, which Lydia honestly believed were true. If Lydia limits her disclosure to company representatives, her statements would likely be protected by a qualified privilege. ●

Privilege A special right, advantage, or immunity granted to a person or a class of persons, such as a judge's absolute privilege to avoid liability for defamation over statements made in the courtroom during a trial.

---

8. Note that the term *privileged communication* in this context is not the same as privileged communication between a professional, such as an attorney, and his or her client.

Public Figures   Politicians, entertainers, professional athletes, and other persons who are in the public eye are considered *public figures*. In general, public figures are considered fair game, and false and defamatory statements about them that appear in the media will not constitute defamation unless the statements are made with **actual malice**.[9] To be made with actual malice, a statement must be made *with either knowledge of its falsity or a reckless disregard of the truth.*

Statements about public figures, especially when made via a public medium, are usually related to matters of general interest. They are made about people who substantially affect all of us. Furthermore, public figures generally have some access to a public medium for answering disparaging (belittling, discrediting) falsehoods about themselves, whereas private individuals do not. For these reasons, public figures have a greater burden of proof in defamation cases (they must prove actual malice) than do private individuals.

CASE EXAMPLE 5.10   *In Touch* magazine published a story about a former high-class call girl who claimed to have slept with legendary soccer player, David Beckham, more than once. Beckham sued *In Touch* magazine for libel seeking $25 million in damages. He said that he had never met the woman, did not cheat on his wife with her, or pay her for sex. After months of litigation, a federal district court dismissed the case because Beckham could not show that the magazine acted with actual malice. Whether or not the statements in the article were accurate, there was no evidence that the defendants acted with willful falsity or reckless disregard for the truth.[10] •

Invasion of Privacy

A person has a right to solitude and freedom from prying public eyes—in other words, to privacy. As discussed in Chapter 4, the Supreme Court has held that a fundamental right to privacy is implied by various amendments to the U.S. Constitution. Some state constitutions explicitly provide for privacy rights, as do a number of federal and state statutes. Tort law also safeguards these rights through the torts of *invasion of privacy,* discussed next.

Intrusion into an Individual's Affairs or Seclusion   Invading someone's home or illegally searching someone's briefcase is an invasion of privacy. The tort has been held to extend to eavesdropping by wiretap, the unauthorized scanning of a bank account, compulsory blood testing, and window peeping. **EXAMPLE 5.11**   A female sports reporter for ESPN was digitally videoed while naked through the peephole in the door of her hotel room. She subsequently won a lawsuit against the man who took the video and posted it on the Internet. •

False Light   Publication of information that places a person in a false light is also an invasion of privacy. For instance, writing a story about a person that attributes ideas and opinions not held by that person is an invasion of privacy. (Publishing such a story could involve the tort of defamation as well.)

EXAMPLE 5.12   An Arkansas newspaper printed an article with the headline "Special Delivery: World's oldest newspaper carrier, 101, quits because she's pregnant!" Next to the article was a picture of a ninety-six-year-old woman who was not the subject of the article (and not pregnant). She sued the paper for false light and won. •

Public Disclosure of Private Facts   This type of invasion of privacy occurs when a person publicly discloses private facts about an individual that an ordinary person would find objectionable or embarrassing. A newspaper account of a private citizen's sex life or financial affairs could be an actionable invasion of privacy, even if the information revealed is true, because it should not be a matter of public concern.

---

9. *New York Times Co. v. Sullivan*, 376 U.S. 254, 84 S.Ct. 710, 11 L.Ed.2d 686 (1964).
10. *Beckham v. Bauer Pub. Co., L.P.*, 2011 WL 977570 (2011).

Appropriation of Identity   Under the common law, using a person's name, picture, or other likeness for commercial purposes without permission is a tortious invasion of privacy. An individual's right to privacy normally includes the right to the exclusive use of her or his identity.   **EXAMPLE 5.13**   An advertising agency asks a singer with a distinctive voice and stage presence to do a marketing campaign for a new automobile. The singer rejects the offer. If the agency then uses someone who imitates the singer's voice and dance moves in the ad, this would be actionable as an appropriation of identity. •

Most states today have codified the common law tort of appropriation of identity in statutes that establish the distinct tort of **appropriation** or right of publicity. States differ as to the degree of likeness that is required to impose liability for appropriation, however.

Some courts have held that even when an animated character in a video or a video game is made to look like an actual person, there are not enough similarities to constitute appropriation.   **CASE EXAMPLE 5.14**   The Naked Cowboy, Robert Burck, is a street entertainer in New York City who performs for tourists wearing only a white cowboy hat, white cowboy boots, and white underwear. He carries a guitar strategically placed to give the illusion of nudity and has become famous. Burck sued Mars, Inc., the maker of M&Ms candy, over a video it showed on billboards in Times Square that depicted a blue M&M dressed exactly like The Naked Cowboy. The court, however, held that the use of Burck's signature costume did not amount to appropriation.[11] •

> **Appropriation**   In tort law, the use by one person of another person's name, likeness, or other identifying characteristic without permission and for the benefit of the user.

Fraudulent Misrepresentation

A misrepresentation leads another to believe in a condition that is different from the condition that actually exists. This is often accomplished through a false or incorrect statement. Although persons sometimes make misrepresentations accidentally because they are unaware of the existing facts, the tort of **fraudulent misrepresentation**, or fraud, involves *intentional* deceit for personal gain. The tort includes several elements:

1. A misrepresentation of material facts or conditions with knowledge that they are false or with reckless disregard for the truth.
2. An intent to induce another party to rely on the misrepresentation.
3. A justifiable reliance on the misrepresentation by the deceived party.
4. Damages suffered as a result of that reliance.
5. A causal connection between the misrepresentation and the injury suffered.

> **Fraudulent Misrepresentation**   Any misrepresentation, either by misstatement or by omission of a material fact, knowingly made with the intention of deceiving another and on which a reasonable person would and does rely to his or her detriment.

For fraud to occur, more than mere **puffery**, or *seller's talk,* must be involved. Fraud exists only when a person represents as a fact something he or she knows is untrue. For instance, it is fraud to claim that the roof of a building does not leak when one knows that it does. Facts are objectively ascertainable, whereas seller's talk (such as "I am the best accountant in town") is not.

Normally, the tort of fraudulent misrepresentation occurs only when there is reliance on a *statement of fact.* Sometimes, however, reliance on a *statement of opinion* may involve the tort of fraudulent misrepresentation if the individual making the statement of opinion has superior knowledge of the subject matter. For instance, when a lawyer makes a statement of opinion about the law in a state in which the lawyer is licensed to practice, a court might treat it as a statement of fact.

> **Puffery**   A salesperson's often exaggerated claims concerning the quality of property offered for sale. Such claims involve opinions rather than facts and are not legally binding promises or warranties.

Abusive or Frivolous Litigation

Tort law recognizes that people have a right not to be sued without a legally just and proper reason. It therefore protects individuals from the misuse of litigation. If the party that initiated a lawsuit did so out of malice and without a legitimate legal reason, and ended up losing that suit, the party can be sued for *malicious prosecution.*

---

11. *Burck v. Mars, Inc.,* 571 F.Supp.2d 446 (S.D.N.Y. 2008).

Abuse of process can apply to any person using a legal process against another in an improper manner or to accomplish a purpose for which the process was not designed. The key difference between the torts of abuse of process and malicious prosecution is the level of proof. Abuse of process is not limited to prior litigation and does not require the plaintiff to prove malice. It can be based on the wrongful use of subpoenas, court orders to attach or seize real property, or other types of formal legal process.

Wrongful Interference

Business Tort Wrongful interference with another's business rights and relationships.

Business torts involving wrongful interference are generally divided into two categories: wrongful interference with a contractual relationship and wrongful interference with a business relationship.

Wrongful Interference with a Contractual Relationship   Three elements are necessary for wrongful interference with a contractual relationship to occur:

1. A valid, enforceable contract must exist between two parties.
2. A third party must know that this contract exists.
3. The third party must *intentionally* induce a party to breach the contract.

> **CASE EXAMPLE 5.15**   A classic case involved an opera singer, Joanna Wagner, who was under contract to sing for a man named Lumley for a specified period of years. A man named Gye, who knew of this contract, nonetheless "enticed" Wagner to refuse to carry out the agreement, and Wagner began to sing for Gye. Gye's action constituted a tort because it wrongfully interfered with the contractual relationship between Wagner and Lumley.[12] (Of course, Wagner's refusal to carry out the agreement also entitled Lumley to sue Wagner for breach of contract.) •

The body of tort law relating to intentional interference with a contractual relationship has expanded greatly in recent years. In principle, any lawful contract can be the basis for an action of this type. The contract could be between a firm and its employees or a firm and its customers. Sometimes, a competitor draws away one of a firm's key employees. To recover damages from the competitor, the original employer must show that the competitor knew of the contract's existence and intentionally induced the breach.

Wrongful Interference with a Business Relationship   Businesspersons devise countless schemes to attract customers, but they are prohibited from unreasonably interfering with another's business in their attempts to gain a share of the market. There is a difference between *competitive methods* and *predatory behavior*—actions undertaken with the intention of unlawfully driving competitors completely out of the market.

Attempting to attract customers in general is a legitimate business practice, whereas specifically targeting the customers of a competitor is more likely to be predatory. **EXAMPLE 5.16**   A shopping mall contains two athletic shoe stores: Joe's and Ultimate Sport. Joe's cannot station an employee at the entrance of Ultimate Sport to divert customers by telling them that Joe's will beat Ultimate Sport's prices. This type of activity constitutes the tort of wrongful interference with a business relationship, which is commonly considered to be an unfair trade practice. If this activity were permitted, Joe's would reap the benefits of Ultimate Sport's advertising. •

Defenses to Wrongful Interference   A person will not be liable for the tort of wrongful interference with a contractual or business relationship if it can be shown that the interference was justified or permissible. Bona fide competitive behavior—through aggressive marketing and advertising strategies, for instance—is a permissible interference even if it results in the breaking of a contract.

---

12. *Lumley v. Gye,* 118 Eng.Rep. 749 (1853).

EXAMPLE 5.17   Taylor Meats advertises so effectively that it induces Sam's Restaurant to break its contract with Burke's Meat Company. In that situation, Burke's will be unable to recover against Taylor Meats on a wrongful interference theory. After all, the public policy that favors free competition in advertising outweighs any possible instability that such competitive activity might cause in contractual relations. ● (For a discussion of Facebook's advertising campaign that alleged sweeping privacy violations by Google's social network, see this chapter's *Online Developments* feature.)

Intentional Torts against Property

Intentional torts against property include trespass to land, trespass to personal property, conversion, and disparagement of property. These torts are wrongful actions that interfere with individuals' legally recognized rights with regard to their land or personal property.

The law distinguishes real property from personal property (see Chapter 22). *Real property* is land and things "permanently" attached to the land. *Personal property* consists of all other items, which are basically movable. Thus, a house and lot are real property, whereas the furniture inside the house is personal property. Cash and stocks and bonds are also personal property.

ONLINE DEVELOPMENTS

Facebook Uses Privacy Concerns to "Smear" Google

With close to one billion users, Facebook is the largest social network in the world. Although Facebook has had various competitors, none has posed as much of a threat as Google. Several years ago, Google added a social-networking feature called Social Circles that eventually became part of Google+. Today, Google+ has more than 100 million users and is growing faster than Facebook.

Privacy Policies Matter

For many users of social networks, privacy is a major concern. Facebook has faced a number of complaints about its privacy policy and has changed its policy several times to satisfy its critics and to ward off potential government investigations. One of Google's main advertising points has been its social network's ability to keep "conversations" private and limited to as few individuals as users desire.

As the rivalry between Google and Facebook intensified, Facebook hired Burson-Marsteller, a public relations firm, to plant anonymous stories raising questions about Google's privacy policy. Although Facebook later claimed that Burson-Marsteller was only supposed to investigate how Social Circles collected and used data, several influential bloggers reported that they were approached by Burson-Marsteller and asked to publish negative stories about privacy concerns on Social Circles. In some instances, Burson-Marsteller even offered to

supply the stories—one would have claimed that Social Circles "enables people to trace their contacts' connections and profile information by crawling and scraping the sites you and your contacts use, such as Twitter, YouTube, and Facebook."

The Campaign Backfires

If Facebook's goal was to discredit Google, the plan failed dramatically. Bloggers across the Web responded with a mixture of derision and amazement. Some pointed out that planting anonymous stories violated Facebook's privacy policy for its own site, while others said that Facebook's effort to attack Google showed that the social-networking giant was running scared. Writing in *Wired* magazine, Steven Levy concluded that "Facebook was running a smear campaign against itself."[a]

Critical Thinking

If you were part of Google's legal team, on what basis might you think that you could sue Facebook and its public relations firm?

---

a. Steven Levy, "Facebook's Stealth Attack on Google Exposes Its Own Privacy Problem," *Wired*, May 12, 2011. See also Sam Gustin, "Burson-Marsteller Deletes Critical Facebook Posts, Spares Google-Smear Flacks," *Wired*, May 13, 2011; David Sarno, "Sibling Rivalry? Facebook vs. Google," *Los Angeles Times*, May 13, 2011; and Barbara Ortutay, "Facebook-Google Rivalry Intensifies with PR Fiasco," *Huffington Post*, May 12, 2011.

Trespass to Land

A **trespass to land** occurs when a person, without permission, does any of the following:

1. Enters onto, above, or below the surface of land that is owned by another.
2. Causes anything to enter onto land owned by another.
3. Remains on land owned by another or permits anything to remain on it.

Actual harm to the land is not an essential element of this tort because the tort is designed to protect the right of an owner to exclusive possession.

Common types of trespass to land include walking or driving on another's land, shooting a gun over another's land, and throwing rocks at a building that belongs to someone else. Another common form of trespass involves constructing a building so that part of it extends onto an adjoining landowner's property.

Establishing Trespass

Before a person can be a trespasser, the real property owner (or other person in actual and exclusive possession of the property) must establish that person as a trespasser. For instance, "posted" trespass signs expressly establish as a trespasser a person who ignores these signs and enters onto the property. A guest in your home is not a trespasser—unless she or he has been asked to leave but refuses. Any person who enters onto your property to commit an illegal act (such as a thief entering a lumberyard at night to steal lumber) is established impliedly as a trespasser, without posted signs.

At common law, a trespasser is liable for any damage caused to the property and generally cannot hold the owner liable for injuries sustained on the premises. This common law rule is being abandoned in many jurisdictions in favor of a *reasonable duty of care* rule that varies depending on the status of the parties. For instance, a landowner may have a duty to post a notice that guard dogs patrol the property. Also, under the *attractive nuisance* doctrine, if young children were attracted to the property by some object, such as a swimming pool, an abandoned building, or a sand pile, the landowner may still be held liable. Trespassers normally can be removed from the premises through the use of reasonable force without the owner being liable for assault, battery, or false imprisonment.

Defenses against Trespass to Land

One defense to a claim of trespass to land is to show that the trespass was warranted—such as when the trespasser entered a building to assist someone in danger. Another defense is for the trespasser to show that he or she had a **license** to come onto the land. A *licensee* is one who is invited (or allowed to enter) onto the property of another for the licensee's benefit. A person who enters another's property to read an electric meter, for example, is a licensee. When you purchase a ticket to attend a movie or sporting event, you are licensed to go onto the property of another to view that movie or event.

Note that licenses to enter are *revocable* by the property owner. If a property owner asks a meter reader to leave and the meter reader refuses to do so, the meter reader at that point becomes a trespasser.

Trespass to Personal Property

Whenever an individual wrongfully takes or harms the personal property of another or otherwise interferes with the lawful owner's possession of personal property, **trespass to personal property** occurs (also called *trespass to chattels* or *trespass to personalty*[13]). In this context, harm means not only destruction of the property, but also anything that diminishes its value, condition, or quality.

Trespass to personal property involves intentional meddling with a possessory interest (the right to possess), including barring an owner's access to personal property.

---

13. Pronounced *per*-sun-ul-tee.

EXAMPLE 5.18 Kelly takes Ryan's business law book as a practical joke and hides it so that Ryan is unable to find it for several days before the final examination. Here, Kelly has engaged in a trespass to personal property. (Kelly has also committed the tort of *conversion*—to be discussed next.) •

If it can be shown that the trespass to personal property was warranted, then a complete defense exists. Most states, for example, allow automobile repair shops to retain a customer's car (under what is called an *artisan's lien*—see Chapter 13) when the customer refuses to pay for repairs already completed.

Conversion

Whenever a person wrongfully possesses or uses the personal property of another without permission, the tort of **conversion** occurs. Any act that deprives an owner of personal property or the use of that property without that owner's permission and without just cause can be conversion. Even the taking of electronic records and data can be a form of conversion.

Often, when conversion occurs, a trespass to personal property also occurs because the original taking of the personal property from the owner was a trespass, and wrongfully retaining it is conversion. Conversion is the civil side of crimes related to theft, but it is not limited to theft. Even if the rightful owner consented to the initial taking of the property, so there was no theft or trespass, a failure to return the personal property may still be conversion.

EXAMPLE 5.19 Chen borrows Mark's iPad Air to use while traveling home from school for the holidays. When Chen returns to school, Mark asks for his iPad back. Chen tells Mark that she gave it to her little brother for Christmas. In this situation, Mark can sue Chen for conversion, and Chen will have to either return the iPad or pay damages equal to its replacement value. •

Even if a person mistakenly believed that she or he was entitled to the goods, the tort of conversion may occur. In other words, good intentions are not a defense against conversion. Someone who buys stolen goods, for instance, may be sued for conversion even if he or she did not know that the goods were stolen. If the true owner brings a tort action against the buyer, the buyer must either return the property to the owner or pay the owner the full value of the property, despite having already paid the purchase price to the thief.

In the following case, the court was asked to decide whether the tort of conversion was an appropriate cause of action for the misappropriation and use of a credit card.

Conversion Wrongfully taking or retaining possession of an individual's personal property and placing it in the service of another.

Case 5.2

Welco Electronics, Inc. v. Mora

Court of Appeal, Second District, Division 5, California, 223 Cal.App.4th 202, ___ P.2d ___, 166 Cal.Rptr.3d 877 (2014).

How can a portable credit card terminal be used for conversion?

BACKGROUND AND FACTS Darrel Derouis, the president of Welco Electronics, Inc., hired Lidia Gimenes, a certified bookkeeper, to help him "find where his money went." In her investigation, Gimenes discovered discrepancies in Welco's credit card statements. Statements she obtained from the credit card company contained charges to "AQM Supplies," a company established by Nicholas Mora. The charges, which totaled $376,142.70, did not appear on Welco's copies of the statements. Mora worked as a quality assurance manager for Welco. At the time of the transactions, AQM leased a portable credit card terminal, and money paid through the terminal was electronically deposited into Mora's bank account. Welco filed a suit in a California state court against Mora, alleging conversion.

Welco sought the value of the money allegedly converted, as well as interest, expenses, punitive damages, and costs. The court ruled in the plaintiff's favor, and the defendant appealed.

IN THE WORDS OF THE COURT . . .
MOSK, J. [Judge]
* * * *

Defendant wrongfully caused a charge to plaintiff's credit card account by having a specific sum of money paid through

Case 5.2—Continues ➡

Case 5.2—Continued

defendant's credit card terminal into defendant's bank account. Plaintiff had a property right in its credit card account because plaintiff's interest was specific, control over its credit card account, and an exclusive claim to the balance. Defendant obtained the money from the credit card company. As a result, plaintiff became indebted to the credit card company. Thus, when defendant * * * misappropriated plaintiff's credit card and used it, part of plaintiff's credit balance with the credit card company was taken by defendant and what resulted was an unauthorized transfer to defendant of plaintiff's property rights—i.e., in money from the available credit line belonging to plaintiff with the credit card company. That the taking was something that affected plaintiff's rights with a third party does not mean that there has not been a conversion of intangible property. * * * *There can be a conversion of intangible rights represented by special instruments such as a check bank book, insurance policy, or stock certificate, all of which involve a taking by the defendant of the plaintiff's property rights exercised through a third party.* [Emphasis added.]

* * * *

Credit card, debit card, or PayPal information may be the subject of a conversion. * * * Historically, the tort of conversion was limited to tangible property and did not apply to intangible property (with an exception for intangible property represented by documents, such as stock certificates). Modern courts, however, have permitted conversion claims against intangible interests such as checks and customer lists. * * * Possession of the debit card or PayPal account information is similar to the intangible property interest in a check.

Defendant * * * had to take plaintiff's credit card or its information in order to obtain the money from the credit card company,

resulting in charges showing up on the statement for which plaintiff was responsible to pay. Taking a credit card or its information in order to obtain money is not materially different in effect than conversion by taking other instruments such as checks, bonds, notes, bills of exchange, warehouse receipts, stock certificates, and information related to those instruments, to obtain someone else's money. Nor is the taking of a credit card or its number to obtain money that could otherwise be used by the owner materially different from the taking of private payment information or other property held to be capable of being converted.

* * * *

Although the parties have not cited any authority that expressly covers the facts here, our application of the tort of conversion in this case is consistent with existing legal principles. As what was found to have occurred here was a theft, the tort of conversion was an appropriate cause of action.

DECISION AND REMEDY   A state intermediate appellate court affirmed the lower court's judgment. "The tort of conversion has been adapted to new property rights and modern means of commercial transactions."

THE LEGAL ENVIRONMENT DIMENSION   *Does the holding in this case mean that any transaction involving a credit card that leads to a dispute is subject to a cause of action for conversion? Why or why not?*

THE E-COMMERCE DIMENSION   *Can the appropriation of an Internet domain name constitute conversion? Explain.*

Disparagement of Property

Disparagement of Property An economically injurious falsehood about another's product or property.

Slander of Quality (Trade Libel) The publication of false information about another's product, alleging that it is not what its seller claims.

Slander of Title The publication of a statement that denies or casts doubt on another's legal ownership of any property, causing financial loss to that property's owner.

Disparagement of property occurs when economically injurious falsehoods are made about another's product or property, not about another's reputation. Disparagement of property is a general term for torts specifically referred to as *slander of quality* or *slander of title*.

Publication of false information about another's product, alleging that it is not what its seller claims, constitutes the tort of **slander of quality,** or **trade libel.** To establish trade libel, the plaintiff must prove that the improper publication caused a third party to refrain from dealing with the plaintiff and that the plaintiff sustained economic damages (such as lost profits) as a result.

An improper publication may be both a slander of quality and defamation of character. For instance, a statement that disparages the quality of a product may also, by implication, disparage the character of the person who would sell such a product.

When a publication denies or casts doubt on another's legal ownership of any property, and the property's owner suffers financial loss as a result, the tort of **slander of title** may exist. Usually, this is an intentional tort that occurs when someone knowingly publishes an untrue statement about property with the intent of discouraging a third party from dealing with the property's owner. For instance, a car dealer would have difficulty attracting customers after competitors published a notice that the dealer's stock consisted of stolen automobiles.

Negligence

The tort of **negligence** occurs when someone suffers injury because of another's failure to live up to a required *duty of care*. In contrast to intentional torts, in torts involving negligence, the tortfeasor neither wishes to bring about the consequences of the act nor believes that they will occur. The actor's conduct merely creates a *risk* of such consequences. If no risk is created, there is no negligence. Moreover, the risk must be foreseeable—that is, it must be such that a reasonable person engaging in the same activity would anticipate the risk and guard against it. In determining what is reasonable conduct, courts consider the nature of the possible harm.

Many of the actions discussed earlier in the chapter in the section on intentional torts constitute negligence if the element of intent is missing. **EXAMPLE 5.20** Juan walks up to Maya and intentionally shoves her. Maya falls and breaks an arm as a result. In this situation, Juan has committed an intentional tort (assault and battery). If Juan carelessly bumps into Maya, however, and she falls and breaks an arm as a result, Juan's action will constitute negligence. In either situation, Juan has committed a tort. •

To succeed in a negligence action, the plaintiff must prove each of the following:

1. *Duty*. The defendant owed a duty of care to the plaintiff.
2. *Breach*. The defendant breached that duty.
3. *Causation*. The defendant's breach caused the plaintiff's injury.
4. *Damages*. The plaintiff suffered a legally recognizable injury.

The Duty of Care and Its Breach

Central to the tort of negligence is the concept of a **duty of care.** The basic principle underlying the duty of care is that people in society are free to act as they please so long as their actions do not infringe on the interests of others.

When someone fails to comply with the duty to exercise reasonable care, a potentially tortious act may have been committed. Failure to live up to a standard of care may be an act (setting fire to a building) or an omission (neglecting to put out a campfire). It may be a careless act or a carefully performed but nevertheless dangerous act that results in injury. Courts consider the nature of the act (whether it is outrageous or commonplace), the manner in which the act was performed (cautiously versus heedlessly), and the nature of the injury (whether it is serious or slight).

The Reasonable Person Standard Tort law measures duty by the **reasonable person standard.** In determining whether a duty of care has been breached, the courts ask how a reasonable person would have acted in the same circumstances. The reasonable person standard is said to be (though in an absolute sense it cannot be) objective. It is not necessarily how a particular person would act. It is society's judgment on how people *should* act. If the so-called reasonable person existed, he or she would be careful, conscientious, even tempered, and honest.

The courts frequently use this hypothetical reasonable person in decisions relating to other areas of law as well. That individuals are required to exercise a reasonable standard of care in their activities is a pervasive concept in business law, and many of the issues discussed in subsequent chapters of this text have to do with this duty.

Negligence The failure to exercise the standard of care that a reasonable person would exercise in similar circumstances.

Learning Objective 4
Identify the four elements of negligence.

Duty of Care The duty of all persons, as established by tort law, to exercise a reasonable amount of care in their dealings with others. Failure to exercise due care, which is normally determined by the reasonable person standard, constitutes the tort of negligence.

Reasonable Person Standard The standard of behavior expected of a hypothetical "reasonable person." It is the standard against which negligence is measured and that must be observed to avoid liability for negligence.

"Do you have any picture books that could help a child understand tort reform?"

"A little neglect may breed great mischief."

Benjamin Franklin, 1706–1790
(American politician
and inventor)

In negligence cases, the degree of care to be exercised varies, depending on the defendant's occupation or profession, her or his relationship with the plaintiff, and other factors. Generally, whether an action constitutes a breach of the duty of care is determined on a case-by-case basis. For instance, pharmacists are generally not held liable for any negative effects resulting from medications that were prescribed by a patient's physician. Nevertheless, if the pharmacist is aware of a customer-specific risk of taking the prescribed medication, such as an allergy, the pharmacist may be liable for failing to warn the customer.[14] The outcome depends on how the judge (or jury, if it is a jury trial) decides a reasonable person in the position of the defendant would act in the particular circumstances of the case.

The Duty of Landowners

Landowners are expected to exercise reasonable care to protect persons coming onto their property from harm. As mentioned earlier, in some jurisdictions, landowners are held to owe a duty to protect even trespassers against certain risks. Landowners who rent or lease premises to tenants (see Chapter 22) are expected to exercise reasonable care to ensure that the tenants and their guests are not harmed in common areas, such as stairways, entryways, and laundry rooms.

Business Invitee A person, such as a customer or a client, who is invited onto business premises by the owner of those premises for business purposes.

Duty to Warn Business Invitees of Risks   Retailers and other firms that explicitly or implicitly invite persons to come onto their premises are usually charged with a duty to exercise reasonable care to protect those persons, who are considered **business invitees.** **EXAMPLE 5.21**   Liz enters a supermarket, slips on a wet floor, and sustains injuries as a result. If there was no sign warning that the floor was wet when Liz slipped, the owner of the supermarket would be liable for damages. A court would hold that the business owner was negligent because the owner failed to exercise a reasonable degree of care in protecting the store's customers against foreseeable risks about which the owner knew or *should have known*. That a patron might slip on the wet floor and be injured was a foreseeable risk, and the owner should have taken care to avoid this risk or to warn the customer of it (by posting a sign or setting out orange cones, for example). ●

The landowner also has a duty to discover and remove any hidden dangers that might injure a customer or other invitee. Store owners have a duty to protect customers from potentially slipping and injuring themselves on merchandise that has fallen off the shelves, for instance.

Does a "Wet Floor" sign relieve a restaurant owner from being held negligent if a customer slips?

(James Leynse/CORBIS/Glow Images)

Obvious Risks Are an Exception   Some risks, of course, are so obvious that the owner need not warn of them. For instance, a business owner does not need to warn customers to open a door before attempting to walk through it. Other risks, however, may seem obvious to a business owner but may not be so to someone else, such as a child. In addition, even if a risk is obvious, that does not necessarily excuse a business owner from the duty to protect its customers from foreseeable harm.

CASE EXAMPLE 5.22   Giorgio's Grill is a restaurant that becomes a nightclub after hours. At those times, traditionally, as the manager of Giorgio's knew, the staff and customers throw paper napkins into the air as the music played. The napkins land on the floor, but no one picks them up. One night, Jane Izquierdo went to Giorgio's. Although she had been to the club on other occasions and knew about the napkin-throwing tradition, she slipped on a napkin and fell, breaking her leg. She sued Giorgio's for negligence but lost at trial because the jury found that the risk of slipping on the napkins was obvious. A state appellate court reversed, however, holding that the obviousness of a risk does not discharge a business owner's duty to its invitees to maintain the premises in a safe condition.[15] ●

---

14. See, for example, *Klasch v. Walgreen Co.*, 264 P.3d 1155 (Nev. 2011).
15. *Izquierdo v. Gyroscope, Inc.*, 946 So.2d 115 (Fla.App. 2007).

It can be difficult to determine whether a risk is obvious. Because you can be held liable if you fail to discover hidden dangers on business premises that could cause injuries to customers, you should post warnings of any conceivable risks on the property. Be vigilant and frequently reassess potential hazards. Train your employees to be on the lookout for possibly dangerous conditions at all times and to notify a superior immediately if they notice something. Remember that a finding of liability in a single lawsuit can leave a small enterprise close to bankruptcy. To prevent potential negligence liability, make sure that your business premises are as safe as possible for all persons who might be there, including children, senior citizens, and individuals with disabilities.

The Duty of Professionals   If an individual has knowledge, skill, or training superior to that of an ordinary person, the individual's conduct must be consistent with that status. Because professionals—such as physicians, dentists, architects, engineers, accountants, and lawyers—are required to have a certain level of knowledge and training, a higher standard of care applies. In determining whether professionals have exercised reasonable care, the law takes their training and expertise into account. Thus, an accountant's conduct is judged not by the reasonable person standard, but by the reasonable accountant standard.

If a professional violates her or his duty of care toward a client, the professional may be sued for **malpractice**, which is essentially professional negligence. For instance, a patient might sue a physician for *medical malpractice*. A client might sue an attorney for *legal malpractice*.

Malpractice Professional misconduct or the lack of the requisite degree of skill as a professional. Negligence — the failure to exercise due care — on the part of a professional, such as a physician, is commonly referred to as malpractice.

Causation

Another necessary element in a negligence action is *causation*. If a person fails in a duty of care and someone suffers an injury, the wrongful act must have caused the harm for the act to be considered a tort.

Courts Ask Two Questions   In deciding whether there is causation, the court must address two questions:

1. *Is there causation in fact?* Did the injury occur because of the defendant's act, or would it have occurred anyway? If an injury would not have occurred without the defendant's act, then there is causation in fact.

   Causation in fact can usually be determined by the use of the but for test: "but for" the wrongful act, the injury would not have occurred. Theoretically, causation in fact is limitless. One could claim, for example, that "but for" the creation of the world, a particular injury would not have occurred. Thus, as a practical matter, the law has to establish limits, and it does so through the concept of proximate cause.

2. *Was the act the proximate cause of the injury?* **Proximate cause,** or legal cause, exists when the connection between an act and an injury is strong enough to justify imposing liability. Courts use proximate cause to limit the scope of the defendant's liability to a subset of the total number of potential plaintiffs that might have been harmed by the defendant's actions.

   EXAMPLE 5.23 Ackerman carelessly leaves a campfire burning. The fire not only burns down the forest but also sets off an explosion in a nearby chemical plant that spills chemicals into a river, killing all the fish for a hundred miles downstream and ruining the economy of a tourist resort. Should Ackerman be liable to the resort owners? To the tourists whose vacations were ruined? These are questions of proximate cause that a court must decide.•

Causation in Fact An act or omission without which an event would not have occurred.

Proximate Cause Legal cause. It exists when the connection between an act and an injury is strong enough to justify imposing liability.

Both of these questions regarding causation in fact and proximate cause must be answered in the affirmative for liability in tort to arise. If a defendant's action constitutes causation in fact but a court decides that the action was not the proximate cause of the plaintiff's injury, the causation requirement has not been met—and the defendant normally will not be liable to the plaintiff.

Foreseeability   Questions of proximate cause are linked to the concept of foreseeability because it would be unfair to impose liability on a defendant unless the defendant's actions created a foreseeable risk of injury.

Probably the most cited case on proximate cause is the *Palsgraf* case, which is discussed in this chapter's *Landmark in the Legal Environment* feature. In determining the issue of proximate cause, the court addressed the following question: Does a defendant's duty of care extend only to those who may be injured as a result of a foreseeable risk, or does it also extend to a person whose injury could not reasonably be foreseen?

The Injury Requirement and Damages

For a tort to have been committed, the plaintiff must have suffered a *legally recognizable* injury. To recover damages (receive compensation), the plaintiff must have suffered some loss, harm, wrong, or invasion of a protected interest. Essentially, the purpose of tort law

LANDMARK IN THE LEGAL ENVIRONMENT
Palsgraf v. Long Island Railroad Co. (1928)

In 1928, the New York Court of Appeals (that state's highest court) issued its decision in *Palsgraf v. Long Island Railroad Co.*,[a] a case that has become a landmark in negligence law and proximate cause.

The Facts of the Case   The plaintiff, Helen Palsgraf, was waiting for a train on a station platform. A man carrying a small package wrapped in newspaper was rushing to catch a train that had begun to move away from the platform. As the man attempted to jump aboard the moving train, he seemed unsteady and about to fall. A railroad guard on the train car reached forward to grab him, and another guard on the platform pushed him from behind to help him board the train. In the process, the man's package fell on the railroad tracks and exploded, because it contained fireworks. The repercussions of the explosion caused scales at the other end of the train platform to fall on Palsgraf, who was injured as a result. She sued the railroad company for damages in a New York state court.

The Question of Proximate Cause   At the trial, the jury found that the railroad guards were negligent in their conduct. On appeal, the question before the New York Court of Appeals was whether the conduct of the railroad guards was the proximate cause of Palsgraf's injuries. In other words, did the guards' duty of care extend to Palsgraf, who was outside the zone of danger and whose injury could not reasonably have been foreseen?

The court stated that the question of whether the guards were negligent *with respect to Palsgraf* depended on whether her injury was *reasonably foreseeable* by the railroad guards. Although the guards may have acted negligently with respect to the man boarding the train, this had no bearing on the question of their negligence with respect to Palsgraf. This was not a situation in which a person committed an act so potentially harmful (for example, firing a gun at a building) that he or she would be held responsible for any harm that resulted.

The court stated that here "there was nothing in the situation to suggest to the most cautious mind that the parcel wrapped in news-paper would spread wreckage through the station." The court thus concluded that the railroad guards were not negligent with respect to Palsgraf because her injury was not reasonably foreseeable.

Application to Today's Legal Environment   *The Palsgraf case established foreseeability as the test for proximate cause. Today, the courts continue to apply this test in determining proximate cause—and thus tort liability for injuries. Generally, if the victim of a harm or the consequences of a harm done are unforeseeable, there is no proximate cause. Note, though, that in the online environment, distinctions based on physical proximity, such as the "zone of danger" cited by the court in this case, are largely inapplicable.*

a. 248 N.Y. 339, 162 N.E. 99 (1928).

is to compensate for legally recognized injuries resulting from wrongful acts.

If no harm or injury results from a given negligent action, there is nothing to compensate—and no tort exists. **EXAMPLE 5.24** If you carelessly bump into a passerby, who stumbles and falls as a result, you may be liable in tort if the passerby is injured in the fall. If the person is unharmed, however, there normally cannot be a suit for damages because no injury was suffered. •

Compensatory damages are the norm in negligence cases. As noted earlier, a court will award punitive damages only if the defendant's conduct was grossly negligent, reflecting an intentional failure to perform a duty with reckless disregard of the consequences to others.

Defenses to Negligence

Defendants often defend against negligence claims by asserting that the plaintiffs failed to prove the existence of one or more of the required elements for negligence. Additionally, there are three basic *affirmative* defenses in negligence cases (defenses that a defendant can use to avoid liability even if the facts are as the plaintiff states): (1) assumption of risk, (2) superseding cause, and (3) contributory and comparative negligence.

(Joyce Marshall/Fort Worth Star-Telegram/MCT via Getty Images)

Injuries from car accidents can cause handicaps that last a lifetime. Do such injuries satisfy the injury requirement for a finding of a negligence tort?

Assumption of Risk
A plaintiff who voluntarily enters into a risky situation, knowing the risk involved, will not be allowed to recover. This is the defense of **assumption of risk,** which requires (1) knowledge of the risk and (2) voluntary assumption of the risk. The assumption of risk defense is frequently asserted when the plaintiff is injured during recreational activities that involve known risk, such as skiing and skydiving. Assumption of risk can apply not only to participants in sporting events, but also to spectators and bystanders who are injured while attending those events.

The risk can be assumed by express agreement, or the assumption of risk can be implied by the plaintiff's knowledge of the risk and subsequent conduct. Courts do not apply the assumption of risk doctrine in emergency situations, though.

In the following case, the issue was whether a spectator at a baseball game voluntarily assumed the risk of being hit by an errant ball thrown while the players were warming up before the game.

Assumption of Risk A defense to negligence. A plaintiff may not recover for injuries or damage suffered from risks he or she knows of and has voluntarily assumed.

Spotlight on the Seattle Mariners

Case 5.3
Taylor v. Baseball Club of Seattle, L.P.
Court of Appeals of Washington, 132 Wash.App. 32, 130 P.3d 835 (2006).

(Otto Greule Jr/Allsport/Getty Images)

Many fans arrive at baseball games early so they can watch the players warm up.

BACKGROUND AND FACTS Delinda Taylor went to a Seattle Mariners baseball game at Safeco Field with her boyfriend and two minor sons. Their seats were four rows up from the field along the rightfield foul line. They arrived more than an hour before the game so they could see the players warm up and get their autographs. When she walked in, Taylor saw that Mariners pitcher, Freddy Garcia, was throwing a ball back and forth with José Mesa right in front of their seats.

As Taylor stood in front of her seat, she looked away from the field, and a ball thrown by Mesa got past Garcia and struck her in the face, causing serious injuries. Taylor sued the Mariners for the allegedly

Spotlight Case 5.3—Continues ➡

Spotlight Case 5.3—Continued

negligent warm-up throw. The Mariners filed a motion for a summary judgment in which they argued that Taylor, a longtime Mariners fan, was familiar with baseball and the inherent risk of balls entering the stands, and therefore, she had assumed the risk of her injury. The trial court granted the motion and dismissed Taylor's case. Taylor appealed.

IN THE WORDS OF THE COURT . . .
DWYER, J. [Judge]
* * * *

* * * For many decades, courts have required baseball stadiums to screen some seats—generally those behind home plate—to provide protection to spectators who choose it.

A sport spectator's assumption of risk and a defendant sports team's duty of care are accordingly discerned under the doctrine of primary assumption of risk. * * * "Implied *primary* assumption of risk arises where a plaintiff has impliedly consented (often in advance of any negligence by defendant) to relieve defendant of a duty to plaintiff regarding specific known and appreciated risks." [Emphasis in original.]
* * * *

Under this implied primary assumption of risk, defendant must show that plaintiff had full subjective understanding of the specific risk, both its nature and presence, and that he or she voluntarily chose to encounter the risk.

* * * It is undisputed that the warm-up is part of the sport, that spectators such as Taylor purposely attend that portion of the event, and that the Mariners permit ticket-holders to view the warm-up.

* * * We find the fact that Taylor was injured during warm-up is not legally significant because that portion of the event is necessarily incident to the game.
* * * *

Here, there is no evidence that the circumstances leading to Taylor's injury constituted an unusual danger. It is undisputed that it is the normal, every-day practice at all levels of baseball for pitchers to warm up in the manner that led to this incident. *The risk of injuries such as Taylor's are within the normal comprehension of a spectator who is familiar with the game.* Indeed, the possibility of an errant ball entering the stands is part of the game's attraction for many spectators. [Emphasis added.]

* * * The record contains substantial evidence regarding Taylor's familiarity with the game. She attended many of her sons' baseball games, she witnessed balls entering the stands, she had watched Mariners' games both at the Kingdome and on television, and she knew that there was no screen protecting her seats, which were close to the field. In fact, as she walked to her seat she saw the players warming up and was excited about being in an unscreened area where her party might get autographs from the players and catch balls.

DECISION AND REMEDY   The state intermediate appellate court affirmed the lower court's judgment. As a spectator who chose to sit in an unprotected area of seats, Taylor voluntarily undertook the risk associated with being hit by an errant baseball thrown during warm-ups before the start of the game.

WHAT IF THE FACTS WERE DIFFERENT?   *Would the result in this case have been different if it had been Taylor's minor son, rather than Taylor herself, who had been struck by the ball? Should courts apply the doctrine of assumption of risk to children? Discuss.*

THE LEGAL ENVIRONMENT DIMENSION   *What is the basis underlying the defense of assumption of risk? How does that support the court's decision in this case?*

Superseding Cause   An unforeseeable intervening event may break the connection between a wrongful act and an injury to another. If so, the event acts as a *superseding cause*—that is, it relieves a defendant of liability for injuries caused by the intervening event.

EXAMPLE 5.25   While riding his bicycle, Derrick negligently hits Julie, who is walking on the sidewalk. As a result of the impact, Julie falls and fractures her hip. While she is waiting for help to arrive, a small plane crashes nearby and explodes, and some of the fiery debris hits her, causing her to sustain severe burns. Derrick will be liable for Julie's fractured hip because the risk of hitting her with his bicycle was foreseeable. Normally, Derrick will not be liable for the burns caused by the plane crash—because the risk of a plane's crashing nearby and injuring Julie was not foreseeable. ●

Contributory and Comparative Negligence   All individuals are expected to exercise a reasonable degree of care in looking out for themselves. In the past, under the common law doctrine of **contributory negligence**, a plaintiff who was also negligent (failed to exercise a reasonable degree of care) could not recover anything from the defendant. Under this rule, no matter how insignificant the plaintiff's negligence was relative to the defendant's negligence, the plaintiff was precluded from recovering any damages. Today, only a few jurisdictions still follow this doctrine.

In most states, the doctrine of contributory negligence has been replaced by a **comparative negligence** standard. Under this standard, both the plaintiff's and the defendant's negligence are computed, and the liability for damages is distributed accordingly. Some jurisdictions have adopted a "pure" form of comparative negligence that allows the plaintiff to recover, even if the extent of his or her fault is greater than that of the defendant. For example, if the plaintiff was 80 percent at fault and the defendant 20 percent at fault, the plaintiff may recover 20 percent of his or her damages. Many states' comparative negligence statutes, however, contain a "50 percent" rule that prevents the plaintiff from recovering any damages if she or he was more than 50 percent at fault. Under this rule, a plaintiff who is 35 percent at fault could recover 65 percent of his or her damages, but a plaintiff who is 65 percent (more than 50 percent) at fault could recover nothing.

> **Contributory Negligence** A rule in tort law, used in only a few states, that completely bars the plaintiff from recovering any damages if the damage suffered is partly the plaintiff's own fault.

> **Comparative Negligence** A rule in tort law, used in the majority of states, that reduces the plaintiff's recovery in proportion to the plaintiff's degree of fault, rather than barring recovery completely.

Special Negligence Doctrines and Statutes

There are a number of special doctrines and statutes relating to negligence. We examine a few of them here.

Res Ipsa Loquitur   Generally, in lawsuits involving negligence, the plaintiff has the burden of proving that the defendant was negligent. In certain situations, however, under the doctrine of *res ipsa loquitur*[16] (meaning "the facts speak for themselves"), the courts may infer that negligence has occurred. Then the burden of proof rests on the defendant—to prove she or he was *not* negligent. This doctrine is applied only when the event creating the damage or injury is one that ordinarily would occur only as a result of negligence.

> **Res Ipsa Loquitur** A doctrine under which negligence may be inferred simply because an event occurred, if it is the type of event that would not occur in the absence of negligence. Literally, the term means "the facts speak for themselves."

CASE EXAMPLE 5.26   A kidney donor, Darnell Backus, sustained injuries to his cervical spine and to the muscles on the left side of his body as a result of the surgery to harvest his kidney. He sued the hospital and physicians involved in the transplant operation for damages. Backus asserted *res ipsa loquitor* because the injury was the kind that ordinarily does not occur in the absence of someone's negligence. The burden of proof shifted to the defendants, and because they failed to show that they had *not* been negligent, Backus won.[17] ●

Negligence *Per Se*   Certain conduct, whether it consists of an action or a failure to act, may be treated as **negligence *per se*** (*per se* means "in or of itself"). Negligence *per se* may occur if an individual violates a statute or ordinance and thereby causes the kind of harm that the statute was intended to prevent. The statute must clearly set out what standard of conduct is expected, when and where it is expected, and of whom it is expected. The standard of conduct required by the statute is the duty that the defendant owes to the plaintiff, and a violation of the statute is the breach of that duty.

> **Negligence *Per Se*** An action or failure to act in violation of a statutory requirement.

CASE EXAMPLE 5.27   A Delaware statute states that anyone "who operates a motor vehicle and who fails to give full time and attention to the operation of the vehicle" is guilty of inattentive driving. Michael Moore was cited for inattentive driving after he collided with Debra Wright's car when he backed a truck out of a parking space. Moore paid the ticket,

---

16. Pronounced *rehz ihp-suh low-kwuh-tuhr.*
17. *Backus v. Kaleida Health,* 91 A.D.3d 1284, 937 N.Y.S.2d 773 (N.Y.A.D. 4 Dept. 2012).

which meant that he pleaded guilty to violating the statute. The day after the accident, Wright began having back pain, which eventually required surgery. She sued Moore for damages, alleging negligence *per se*. The Delaware Supreme Court ruled that the inattentive driving statute set forth a sufficiently specific standard of conduct to warrant application of negligence *per se*.[18] ●

"Danger Invites Rescue" Doctrine

Sometimes, a person who is trying to avoid harm—such as an individual who swerves to avoid a head-on collision with a drunk driver—ends up causing harm to another (such as a cyclist riding in the bike lane) as a result. In those situations, the original wrongdoer (the drunk driver in this scenario) is liable to anyone who is injured, even if the injury actually resulted from another person's attempt to escape harm. The "danger invites rescue" doctrine extends the same protection to a person who is trying to rescue another from harm—the original wrongdoer is liable for injuries to an individual attempting a rescue. The idea is that the rescuer should not be held liable for any damages because he or she did not cause the danger and because danger invites rescue.

EXAMPLE 5.28   Ludley drives down a street but fails to see a stop sign because he is trying to quiet his squabbling children in the car's back seat. Salter, who is standing on the curb, realizes that Ludley is about to hit a pedestrian and runs into the street to push the pedestrian out of the way. If Ludley's vehicle hits Salter instead, Ludley will be liable for Salter's injury, as well as for any injuries the other pedestrian sustained. ● Whether rescuers injure themselves, the person rescued, or even a stranger, the original wrongdoer will still be liable.

Good Samaritan Statutes

Most states have enacted what are called **Good Samaritan statutes**.[19] Under these statutes, someone who is aided voluntarily by another cannot turn around and sue the "Good Samaritan" for negligence. These laws were passed largely to protect physicians and medical personnel who voluntarily render medical services in emergency situations to those in need, such as individuals hurt in car accidents.

Dram Shop Acts

Many states have also passed **dram shop acts**,[20] under which a tavern owner or bartender may be held liable for injuries caused by a person who became intoxicated while drinking at the bar or who was already intoxicated when served by the bartender.

Some states' statutes also impose liability on *social hosts* (persons hosting parties) for injuries caused by guests who became intoxicated at the hosts' homes. Under these statutes, it is unnecessary to prove that the tavern owner, bartender, or social host was negligent. **EXAMPLE 5.29**   Selena hosts a Super Bowl party at which Raul, a minor, sneaks alcoholic drinks. Selena is potentially liable for damages resulting from Raul's drunk driving after the party. ●

Strict Liability

Another category of torts is called **strict liability,** or *liability without fault*. Intentional torts and torts of negligence involve acts that depart from a reasonable standard of care and cause injuries. Under the doctrine of strict liability, liability for injury is imposed for reasons other than fault.

---

18. *Wright v. Moore*, 931 A.2d 405 (Del.Supr. 2007).
19. These laws derive their name from the Good Samaritan story in the Bible. In the story, a traveler who had been robbed and beaten lay along the roadside, ignored by those passing by. Eventually, a man from the country of Samaria (the "Good Samaritan") stopped to render assistance to the injured person.
20. Historically, a *dram* was a small unit of liquid, and spirits were sold in drams. Thus, a dram shop was a place where liquor was sold in drams.

Good Samaritan Statute A state statute stipulating that persons who provide emergency services to, or rescue, someone in peril cannot be sued for negligence unless they act recklessly, thereby causing further harm.

Dram Shop Act A state statute that imposes liability on the owners of bars and taverns, as well as those who serve alcoholic drinks to the public, for injuries resulting from accidents caused by intoxicated persons when the sellers or servers of alcoholic drinks contributed to the intoxication.

Learning Objective 5
What is meant by strict liability? In what circumstances is strict liability applied?

Strict Liability Liability regardless of fault, which is imposed on those engaged in abnormally dangerous activities, on persons who keep dangerous animals, and on manufacturers or sellers that introduce into commerce defective and unreasonably dangerous goods.

Abnormally Dangerous Activities

Strict liability for damages proximately caused by an abnormally dangerous or exceptional activity is one application of this doctrine. Courts apply the doctrine of strict liability in such cases because of the extreme risk of the activity. For instance, even if blasting with dynamite is performed with all reasonable care, there is still a risk of injury. Because of the potential for harm, the person who is engaged in an abnormally dangerous activity—and benefits from it—is responsible for paying for any injuries caused by that activity. Although there is no fault, there is still responsibility because of the dangerous nature of the undertaking.

Other Applications of Strict Liability

The strict liability principle is also applied in other situations. Persons who keep wild animals, for example, are strictly liable for any harm inflicted by the animals. In addition, an owner of domestic animals may be strictly liable for harm caused by those animals if the owner knew, or should have known, that the animals were dangerous or had a propensity to harm others.

A significant application of strict liability is in the area of *product liability*—liability of manufacturers and sellers for harmful or defective products. Liability here is a matter of social policy and is based on two factors:

1. The manufacturer or seller can better bear the cost of injury because it can spread the cost throughout society by increasing prices of goods and services.
2. The manufacturer or seller is making a profit from its activities and therefore should bear the cost of injury as an operating expense.

We will discuss product liability in Chapter 12.

Reviewing . . . Torts and Strict Liability

Elaine Sweeney went to Ragged Mountain Ski Resort in New Hampshire with a friend. Elaine went snow tubing down a snow-tube run designed exclusively for snow tubers. There were no Ragged Mountain employees present in the snow-tube area to instruct Elaine on the proper use of a snow tube. On her fourth run down the trail, Elaine crossed over the center line between snow-tube lanes, collided with another snow tuber, and was injured. Elaine filed a negligence action against Ragged Mountain seeking compensation for the injuries that she sustained. Two years earlier, the New Hampshire state legislature had enacted a statute that prohibited a person who participates in the sport of skiing from suing a ski-area operator for injuries caused by the risks inherent in skiing. Using the information presented in the chapter, answer the following questions.

1. What defense will Ragged Mountain probably assert?
2. The central question in this case is whether the state statute establishing that skiers assume the risks inherent in the sport bars Elaine's suit. What would your decision be on this issue? Why?
3. Suppose that the court concludes that the statute applies only to skiing and not to snow tubing. Will Elaine's lawsuit be successful? Explain.
4. Now suppose that the jury concludes that Elaine was partly at fault for the accident. Under what theory might her damages be reduced in proportion to the degree to which her actions contributed to the accident and her resulting injuries?

Debate This Each time a state legislature enacts a law that applies the assumption of risk doctrine to a particular sport, participants in that sport suffer.

Key Terms

actionable 121

actual malice 126

appropriation 127

assault 120

assumption of risk 137

battery 120

business invitee 134

business tort 128

causation in fact 135

comparative negligence 139

compensatory damages 118

contributory negligence 139

conversion 131

damages 118

defamation 122

defense 119

disparagement of property 132

dram shop act 140

duty of care 133

fraudulent misrepresentation 127

Good Samaritan statute 140

intentional tort 120

libel 122

license 130

malpractice 135

negligence 133

negligence *per se* 139

privilege 125

proximate cause 135

puffery 127

punitive damages 118

reasonable person standard 133

res ipsa loquitur 139

slander 122

slander of quality (trade libel) 132

slander of title 132

strict liability 140

tort 117

tortfeasor 120

transferred intent 120

trespass to land 130

trespass to personal property 130

Chapter Summary: Torts and Strict Liability

Intentional Torts against Persons	1. *Assault and battery*—An assault is an unexcused and intentional act that causes another person to be apprehensive of immediate harm. A battery is an assault that results in physical contact.
	2. *False imprisonment*—The intentional confinement or restraint of another person's movement without justification.
	3. *Intentional infliction of emotional distress*—An extreme and outrageous act, intentionally committed, that results in severe emotional distress to another.
	4. *Defamation (libel or slander)*—A false statement of fact, not made under privilege, that is communicated to a third person and that causes damage to a person's reputation. For public figures, the plaintiff must also prove actual malice.
	5. *Invasion of the right to privacy*—Includes four acts: wrongful intrusion into a person's private activities; publication of information that places a person in a false light; disclosure of private facts that an ordinary person would find objectionable; and appropriation of identity, which involves the use of a person's name, likeness, or other identifying characteristic, without permission and for a commercial purpose. Most states have enacted statutes establishing appropriation of identity as the tort of *appropriation* or right of publicity. Courts differ on the degree of likeness required.
	6. *Misrepresentation (fraud)*—A false representation made by one party, through misstatement of facts or through conduct, with the intention of deceiving another and on which the other reasonably relies to his or her detriment. Negligent misrepresentation occurs when a person supplies information without having a reasonable basis for believing its truthfulness.
	7. *Abusive or frivolous litigation*—When a person initiates a lawsuit out of malice and without probable cause, and loses the suit, he or she can be sued for the tort of *malicious prosecution*. When a person uses a legal process against another improperly or to accomplish a purpose for which it was not designed, she or he can be sued for *abuse of process*.
	8. *Wrongful interference*—The knowing, intentional interference by a third party with an enforceable contractual relationship or an established business relationship between other parties for the purpose of advancing the economic interests of the third party.
Intentional Torts against Property	1. *Trespass to land*—The invasion of another's real property without consent or privilege.
	2. *Trespass to personal property*—Unlawfully damaging or interfering with the owner's right to use, possess, or enjoy her or his personal property.
	3. *Conversion*—Wrongfully taking or using the personal property of another without permission.
	4. *Disparagement of property*—Any economically injurious falsehood that is made about another's product or property. The term includes the torts of *slander of quality* and *slander of title*.
Negligence	1. *Negligence*—The careless performance of a legally required duty or the failure to perform a legally required act. Elements that must be proved are that a legal duty of care existed, that the defendant breached that duty, that the breach caused the plaintiff's injury, and that the plaintiff suffered a legally recognizable injury.
	2. *Defenses to negligence*—The basic affirmative defenses in negligence cases are assumption of risk, superseding cause, and contributory or comparative negligence.
	3. *Special negligence doctrines and statutes*—
	a. *Res ipsa loquitur*—A doctrine under which a plaintiff need not prove negligence on the part of the defendant because "the facts speak for themselves."

Chapter Summary: Torts and Strict Liability—Continued

Negligence—*Continued*	b. Negligence *per se*—A type of negligence that may occur if a person violates a statute or an ordinance and the violation causes another to suffer the kind of injury that the statute or ordinance was intended to prevent.
	c. Special negligence statutes—State statutes that prescribe duties and responsibilities in certain circumstances. Violation of these statutes will impose civil liability. Dram shop acts and Good Samaritan statutes are examples of special negligence statutes.
Strict Liability	Under the doctrine of strict liability, a person may be held liable, regardless of the degree of care exercised, for damages or injuries caused by her or his product or activity. Strict liability includes liability for harms caused by abnormally dangerous activities, by dangerous animals, and by defective products (product liability).

Issue Spotters

1. Jana leaves her truck's motor running while she enters a Kwik-Pik Store. The truck's transmission engages and the vehicle crashes into a gas pump, starting a fire that spreads to a warehouse on the next block. The warehouse collapses, causing its billboard to fall and injure Lou, a bystander. Can Lou recover from Jana? Why or why not? (See *Negligence*.)
2. A water pipe bursts, flooding a Metal Fabrication Company utility room and tripping the circuit breakers on a panel in the room. Metal Fabrication contacts Nouri, a licensed electrician with five years' experience, to check the damage and turn the breakers back on. Without testing for short circuits, which Nouri knows that he should do, he tries to switch on a breaker. He is electrocuted, and his wife sues Metal Fabrication for damages, alleging negligence. What might the firm successfully claim in defense? (See *Negligence*.)

—**Check your answers to the Issue Spotters against the answers provided in Appendix D at the end of this text.**

For Review

1. What is the purpose of tort law? What types of damages are available in tort lawsuits?
2. What are two basic categories of torts?
3. What is defamation? Name two types of defamation.
4. Identify the four elements of negligence.
5. What is meant by strict liability? In what circumstances is strict liability applied?

Business Scenarios and Case Problems

5–1. Defamation. Richard is an employee of the Dun Construction Corp. While delivering materials to a construction site, he carelessly backs Dun's truck into a passenger vehicle driven by Green. This is Richard's second accident in six months. When the company owner, Dun, learns of this latest accident, a heated discussion ensues, and Dun fires Richard. Dun is so angry that he immediately writes a letter to the union of which Richard is a member and to all other construction companies in the community, stating that Richard is the "worst driver in the city" and that "anyone who hires him is asking for legal liability." Richard files a suit against Dun, alleging libel on the basis of the statements made in the letters. Discuss the results. (See *Intentional Torts against Persons*.)

5–2. Liability to Business Invitees. Kim went to Ling's Market to pick up a few items for dinner. It was a stormy day, and the wind had blown water through the market's door each time it opened. As Kim entered through the door, she slipped and fell in the rainwater that had accumulated on the floor. The manager knew of the weather conditions but had not posted any sign to warn customers of the water hazard. Kim injured her back as a result of the fall and sued Ling's for damages. Can Ling's be held liable for negligence? Discuss. (See *Negligence*.)

5–3. **Spotlight on Intentional Torts—Defamation.** Sharon Yeagle was an assistant to the vice president of student affairs at Virginia Polytechnic Institute and State University (Virginia Tech). As part of her duties, Yeagle helped students participate in the Governor's Fellows Program. The *Collegiate Times*, Virginia Tech's student newspaper, published an article about the university's success in placing students in the program. The article's text surrounded a block quotation attributed to Yeagle with the phrase "Director of Butt Licking" under her name. Yeagle sued the *Collegiate Times* for defamation. She argued that the phrase implied the commission of sodomy and was therefore actionable. What is *Collegiate Times's* defense to this claim? [*Yeagle v. Collegiate Times,* 497 S.E.2d 136 (Va. 1998)] (See *Intentional Torts against Persons.*)

5–4. Libel and Invasion of Privacy. The *Northwest Herald,* a newspaper, received regular e-mail reports from police departments about criminal arrests. When it received a report that Caroline Eubanks had been charged with theft, the *Herald* published the information. Later, the police sent an e-mail that retracted the report about Eubanks. The *Herald* published a correction. Eubanks filed a suit against the paper for libel and invasion of privacy. Does Eubanks have a good case for either tort? Why or why not? [*Eubanks v. Northwest Herald Newspapers,* 397 Ill.App.3d 746, 922 N.E.2d 1196 (2010)] (See *Intentional Torts against Persons.*)

5–5. Proximate Cause. Galen Stoller was killed at a railroad crossing when an Amtrak train hit his car. The crossing was marked with a stop sign and a railroad-crossing symbol but there were no flashing lights. Galen's parents filed a suit against National Railroad Passenger Corporation (Amtrak) and Burlington Northern & Santa Fe Railroad Corp alleging negligence in the design and maintenance of the crossing. The defendants argued that Galen had not stopped at the stop sign. Was Amtrak negligent? What was the proximate cause of the accident? [*Henderson v. National Railroad Passenger Corp.,* 2011 WL 14458 (10th Cir. 2011)] (See *Negligence.*)

5–6. Business Torts. Medtronic, Inc., is a medical technology company that competes for customers with St. Jude Medical S.C., Inc. James Hughes worked for Medtronic as a sales manager. His contract prohibited him from working for a competitor for one year after leaving Medtronic. Hughes sought a position as a sales director for St. Jude. St. Jude told Hughes that his contract with Medtronic was unenforceable and offered him a job. Hughes accepted. Medtronic filed a suit, alleging wrongful interference. Which type of interference was most likely the basis for this suit? Did it occur here? Explain. [*Medtronic, Inc. v. Hughes,* 2011 WL 134973 (Minn. App. 2011)] (See *Intentional Torts against Persons.*)

5–7. Intentional Infliction of Emotional Distress. While living in her home country of Tanzania, Sophia Kiwanuka signed an employment contract with Anne Margareth Bakilana, a Tanzanian living in Washington, D.C. Kiwanuka traveled to the United States to work as a babysitter and maid in Bakilana's house. When Kiwanuka arrived, Bakilana confiscated her passport, held her in isolation, and forced her to work long hours under threat of having her deported. Kiwanuka worked seven days a week without breaks and was subjected to regular verbal and psychological abuse by

Bakilana. Kiwanuka filed a complaint against Bakilana for intentional infliction of emotional distress, among other claims. Bakilana argued that Kiwanuka's complaint should be dismissed because the allegations were insufficient to show outrageous intentional conduct that resulted in severe emotional distress. If you were the judge, in whose favor would you rule? Why? [*Kiwanuka v. Bakilana,* 844 F.Supp.2d 107 (D.D.C. 2012)] (See *Intentional Torts against Persons.*)

5–8.   Business Case Problem with Sample Answer— Negligence. At the Weatherford Hotel in Flagstaff, Arizona, in Room 59, a balcony extends across thirty inches of the room's only window, leaving a twelve-inch gap with a three-story drop to the concrete below. A sign prohibits smoking in the room but invites guests to "step out onto the balcony" to smoke. Toni Lucario was a guest in Room 59 when she climbed out of the window and fell to her death. Patrick McMurtry, her estate's personal representative, filed a suit against the Weatherford. Did the hotel breach a duty of care to Locario? What might the Weatherford assert in its defense? Explain. [*McMurtry v. Weatherford Hotel, Inc.,* 293 P.3d 520 (Ariz.App. 2013)] (See *Negligence.*)

—For a sample answer to Problem 5–8, go to Appendix E at the end of this text.

5–9. Negligence. Ronald Rawls and Zabian Bailey were in an auto accident in Bridgeport, Connecticut. Bailey rear-ended Rawls at a stoplight. Evidence showed it was more likely than not that Bailey failed to apply his brakes in time to avoid the collision, failed to turn his vehicle to avoid the collision, failed to keep his vehicle under control, and was inattentive to his surroundings. Rawls filed a suit in a Connecticut state court against his insurance company, Progressive Northern Insurance Co., to obtain benefits under an underinsured motorist clause, alleging that Bailey had been negligent. Could Rawls collect? Discuss. [*Rawls v. Progressive Northern Insurance Co.,* 310 Conn. 768, 83 A.3d 576 (2014)] (See *Negligence.*)

5–10.   ⬌ A Question of Ethics—Wrongful Interference. White Plains Coat & Apron Co. and Cintas Corp. are competitors. White Plains had five-year exclusive contracts with some of its customers. As a result of Cintas's soliciting of business, dozens of White Plains' customers breached their contracts and entered into rental agreements with Cintas. White Plains filed a suit against Cintas, alleging wrongful interference. [*White Plains Coat & Apron Co. v. Cintas Corp.,* 8 N.Y.3d 422, 867 N.E.2d 381 (2007)] (See *Intentional Torts against Persons.*)

1. What are the two policies at odds in wrongful interference cases? When there is an existing contract, which of these interests should be accorded priority? Why?

2. Is a general interest in soliciting business for profit a sufficient defense to a claim of wrongful interference with a contractual relationship? What do you think? Why?

CHAPTER 6

Criminal Law and Cyber Crime

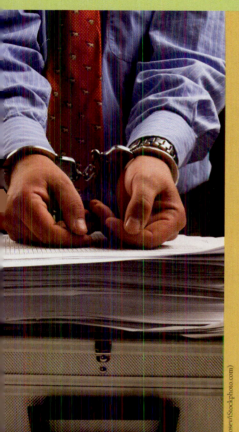

(Alex Kosev/iStockphoto.com)

LEARNING OBJECTIVES

The five learning objectives below are designed to help improve your understanding of the chapter. After reading this chapter, you should be able to answer the following questions:

1. What two elements normally must exist before a person can be held liable for a crime?

2. What are five broad categories of crimes? What is white-collar crime?

3. What defenses can be raised to avoid liability for criminal acts?

4. What constitutional safeguards exist to protect persons accused of crimes?

5. How has the Internet expanded opportunities for identity theft?

> "The crime problem is getting really serious.
> The other day, the Statue of Liberty had both hands up."
> —Jay Leno, 1950–present (American comedian and television host)

Criminal law is an important part of the legal environment of business. Various sanctions are used to bring about a society in which businesses can compete and flourish. These sanctions include damages for various types of tortious conduct (see Chapter 5), damages for breach of contract (see Chapter 11), and various equitable remedies (see Chapter 1). Additional sanctions are imposed under criminal law. Many statutes regulating business provide for criminal as well as civil sanctions.

In this chapter, after a brief summary of the major differences between criminal and civil law, we look at the elements that must be present for criminal liability to exist. We then examine various categories of crimes, the defenses that can be raised to avoid liability for criminal actions, and the rules of criminal procedure. Advances in technology allow authorities to trace phone calls and track vehicle movements with greater ease and precision. One such technique is attaching tracking devices to a suspect's vehicle. Is such an action a violation of the constitutional rights of those suspects who are being tracked? You will discover what the courts have to say on this question later in this chapter.

Civil Law and Criminal Law

Remember from Chapter 1 that *civil law* spells out the duties that exist between persons or between persons and their governments, excluding the duty not to commit crimes. Contract law, for example, is part of civil law. The whole body of tort law, which deals with the infringement by one person on the legally recognized rights of another, is also an area of civil law.

Criminal law, in contrast, has to do with crime. A **crime** can be defined as a wrong against society proclaimed in a statute and, if committed, punishable by society through fines and/or imprisonment—and, in some cases, death. As mentioned in Chapter 1, because crimes are *offenses against society as a whole,* criminals are prosecuted by a public official, such as a district attorney (D.A.), rather than by the crime victims. Victims often report the crime to the police, but ultimately it is the D.A.'s office that decides whether to file criminal charges and to what extent to pursue the prosecution or carry out additional investigation.

Key Differences between Civil Law and Criminal Law

Because the state has extensive resources at its disposal when prosecuting criminal cases, and because the sanctions can be so severe, there are numerous procedural safeguards to protect the rights of defendants. We look here at one of these safeguards—the higher burden of proof that applies in a criminal case—and at the sanctions imposed for criminal acts. Exhibit 6–1 summarizes these and other key differences between civil law and criminal law.

Burden of Proof

In a civil case, the plaintiff usually must prove his or her case by a *preponderance of the evidence.* Under this standard, the plaintiff must convince the court that, based on the evidence presented by both parties, it is more likely than not that the plaintiff's allegation is true.

In a criminal case, in contrast, the state must prove its case **beyond a reasonable doubt.** If the jury views the evidence in the case as reasonably permitting either a guilty or a not guilty verdict, then the jury's verdict must be *not* guilty. In other words, the government (prosecutor) must prove beyond a reasonable doubt that the defendant has committed every essential element of the offense with which she or he is charged.

If the jurors are not convinced of the defendant's guilt beyond a reasonable doubt, they must find the defendant not guilty. Note also that in a criminal case, the jury's verdict normally must be unanimous—agreed to by all members of the jury—to convict the defendant.[1] (In a civil trial by jury, in contrast, typically only three-fourths of the jurors need to agree.)

---

1. Note that a few states allow jury verdicts that are not unanimous. Arizona, for example, allows six of eight jurors to reach a verdict in criminal cases. Louisiana and Oregon have also relaxed the requirement of unanimous jury verdicts.

Crime A wrong against society proclaimed in a statute and, if committed, punishable by society through fines, imprisonment, or death.

Beyond a Reasonable Doubt The standard of proof used in criminal cases.

Exhibit 6–1 Key Differences between Civil Law and Criminal Law

ISSUE	CIVIL LAW	CRIMINAL LAW
Party who brings suit	The person who suffered harm.	The state.
Wrongful act	Causing harm to a person or to a person's property.	Violating a statute that prohibits some type of activity.
Burden of proof	Preponderance of the evidence.	Beyond a reasonable doubt.
Verdict	Three-fourths majority (typically).	Unanimous (almost always).
Remedy	Damages to compensate for the harm or a decree to achieve an equitable result.	Punishment (fine, imprisonment, or death).

Criminal Sanctions   The sanctions imposed on criminal wrongdoers are also harsher than those applied in civil cases. Remember from Chapter 5 that the purpose of tort law is to allow persons harmed by the wrongful acts of others to obtain compensation from the wrongdoer rather than to punish the wrongdoer.

In contrast, criminal sanctions are designed to punish those who commit crimes and to deter others from committing similar acts in the future. Criminal sanctions include fines as well as the much harsher penalty of the loss of one's liberty by incarceration in a jail or prison. The harshest criminal sanction is, of course, the death penalty.

Civil Liability for Criminal Acts

Some torts, such as assault and battery, provide a basis for a criminal prosecution as well as a tort action.   **EXAMPLE 6.1**   Carlos is walking down the street, minding his own business, when suddenly a person attacks him. In the ensuing struggle, the attacker (assailant) stabs Carlos several times, seriously injuring him. A police officer restrains and arrests the wrongdoer. In this situation, the attacker may be subject both to criminal prosecution by the state and to a tort lawsuit brought by Carlos. •

Criminal Liability

Two elements normally must exist simultaneously for a person to be convicted of a crime: (1) the performance of a prohibited act and (2) a specified state of mind or intent on the part of the actor. Note that to establish criminal liability, there must be a *concurrence* between the act and the intent. In other words, these two elements must occur together.

Learning Objective 1
What two elements normally must exist before a person can be held liable for a crime?

The Criminal Act

Every criminal statute prohibits certain behavior. Most crimes require an act of *commission.* That is, a person must *do* something in order to be accused of a crime. In criminal law, a prohibited act is referred to as the ***actus reus,***[2] or guilty act. In some situations, an act of *omission* can be a crime, but only when a person has a legal duty to perform the omitted act, such as failing to file a tax return.

The *guilty act* requirement is based on one of the premises of criminal law—that a person is punished for harm done to society. For a crime to exist, the guilty act must cause some harm to a person or to property. Thinking about killing someone or about stealing a car may be wrong, but the thoughts do no harm until they are translated into action. Of course, a person can be punished for attempting murder or robbery, but normally only if he or she took substantial steps toward the criminal objective.

Actus reus A guilty (prohibited) act. The commission of a prohibited act is one of the two essential elements required for criminal liability, the other element being the intent to commit a crime.

State of Mind

A wrongful mental state (***mens rea***)[3] is generally required to establish criminal liability. What constitutes such a mental state varies according to the wrongful action. For murder, the act is the taking of a life, and the mental state is the intent to take life. For theft, the guilty act is the taking of another person's property, and the mental state involves both the knowledge that the property belongs to another and the intent to deprive the owner of it.

Mens rea The wrongful mental state ("guilty mind"), or intent, that is one of the key requirements to establish criminal liability for an act.

Recklessness and Criminal Negligence   A court can also find that the required mental state is present when a defendant's acts are reckless or criminally negligent.

---

2. Pronounced ak-tuhs ray-uhs.
3. Pronounced *mehns ray-uh.*

A defendant is *criminally reckless* if he or she consciously disregards a substantial and unjustifiable risk. **EXAMPLE 6.2** A fourteen-year-old New Jersey girl posted a Facebook message saying that she was going to launch a terrorist attack on her high school and asking if anyone wanted to help. The police arrested the girl for the crime of making a terrorist threat, which requires the intent to commit an act of violence with "the intent to terrorize" or "in reckless disregard of the risk of causing" terror or inconvenience. Although the girl claimed that she did not intend to cause harm, she was prosecuted under the "reckless disregard" part of the statute. •

Criminal negligence occurs when the defendant takes an unjustified, substantial, and foreseeable risk that results in harm. A defendant can be negligent even if she or he was not actually aware of the risk but *should have been aware* of it.[4] A homicide is classified as *involuntary manslaughter* when it results from an act of criminal negligence and there is no intent to kill. **EXAMPLE 6.3** Dr. Conrad Murray, the personal physician of pop star Michael Jackson, was convicted of involuntary manslaughter in 2011 for prescribing the drug that led to Jackson's sudden death in 2009. Murray had given Jackson propofol, a powerful anesthetic normally used in surgery, as a sleep aid on the night of his death, even though Murray knew that Jackson had already taken other sedatives. •

Strict Liability and Overcriminalization
An increasing number of laws and regulations have imposed criminal sanctions for strict liability crimes—that is, offenses that do not require a wrongful mental state, or malice, to establish criminal liability.

Federal Crimes The federal criminal code now lists more than four thousand criminal offenses, many of which do not require a specific mental state. There are also at least ten thousand federal rules that can be enforced through criminal sanctions, and many of these rules do not require intent. **EXAMPLE 6.4** Eddie Leroy Anderson, a retired logger and former science teacher, and his son went digging for arrowheads near a campground in Idaho. They did not realize that they were on federal land and that it is a crime to take artifacts off federal land without a permit. Although the penalty could be as much as two years in prison, father and son pleaded guilty and were sentenced to probation and a $1,500 fine each. •

Strict liability crimes are particularly common in environmental laws, laws aimed at combating illegal drugs, and other laws related to public health, safety, and welfare. Under federal law, for instance, tenants can be evicted from public housing if one of their relatives or guests used illegal drugs—regardless of whether the tenant knew or should have known about the drug activity.

State Crimes Many states have also enacted laws that punish behavior as criminal without the need to show criminal intent. **EXAMPLE 6.5** In Arizona, a hunter who shoots an elk outside the area specified by his or her permit has committed a crime. The hunter can be convicted of the crime regardless of his or her intent or knowledge of the law. •

Overcriminalization Proponents of laws that establish strict liability crimes argue that they are necessary to protect the public and the environment. Critics say that the laws have led to *overcriminalization,* or the use of criminal law to attempt to solve social problems, such as illegal drug use. They argue that

CEO Mary Barro testifies before Congress about when General Motors knew that some of its cars had faulty ignition switches. Ultimately, from 2003 until recently, 36 persons purportedly died because of this electrical defect. Could GM face criminal liability?

Pete Marovich/Bloomberg/Getty Images

---

4. Model Penal Code Section 2.02(2)(d).

when the requirement of intent is removed from criminal offenses, people are more likely to commit crimes unknowingly—and perhaps even innocently. When an honest mistake can lead to a criminal conviction, the role of criminal law as a deterrent to future wrongful conduct is undermined.

Corporate Criminal Liability

As will be discussed in Chapter 15, a *corporation* is a legal entity created under the laws of a state. At one time, it was thought that a corporation could not incur criminal liability because, although a corporation is a legal person, it can act only through its agents (corporate directors, officers, and employees). Therefore, the corporate entity itself could not "intend" to commit a crime. Over time, this view has changed. Obviously, corporations cannot be imprisoned, but they can be fined or denied certain legal privileges (such as necessary licenses).

Liability of the Corporate Entity   Today, corporations are normally liable for the crimes committed by their agents and employees within the course and scope of their employment.[5] For such criminal liability to be imposed, the prosecutor typically must show that the corporation could have prevented the act or that a supervisor within the corporation authorized or had knowledge of the act. In addition, corporations can be criminally liable for failing to perform specific duties imposed by law (such as duties under environmental laws or securities laws).

   CASE EXAMPLE 6.6   A prostitution ring, the Gold Club, was operating out of motels in West Virginia. A motel manager, who was also an officer in the corporation that owned the motels, gave discounted rates to Gold Club prostitutes, and they paid him in cash. The corporation received a portion of the funds generated by the Gold Club's illegal operations. At trial, the jury found that the corporation was criminally liable because a supervisor within the corporation—the motel manager—had knowledge of the prostitution and the corporation had allowed it to continue.[6] ●

Liability of Corporate Officers and Directors   Corporate directors and officers are personally liable for the crimes they commit, regardless of whether the crimes were committed for their personal benefit or on the corporation's behalf. Additionally, corporate directors and officers may be held liable for the actions of employees under their supervision. Under the *responsible corporate officer doctrine,* a court may impose criminal liability on a corporate officer regardless of whether she or he participated in, directed, or even knew about a given criminal violation.[7]

   CASE EXAMPLE 6.7   The Roscoe family owned the Customer Company, which operated an underground storage tank that leaked gasoline. After the leak occurred, an employee, John Johnson, notified the state environmental agency, and the Roscoes hired an environmental services firm to clean up the spill. The clean-up did not occur immediately, however, and the state sent many notices to John Roscoe, a corporate officer, warning him that the company was violating federal and state environmental laws. Roscoe gave the letters to Johnson, who passed them on to the environmental services firm, but the spill was not cleaned up. The state eventually filed criminal charges against the corporation and the Roscoes individually, and they were convicted. On appeal, the court affirmed the Roscoes' convictions under the responsible corporate officer doctrine. The Roscoes were in positions

Gary Foster, formerly a Citigroup vice president, embezzled $22 million from his employer. Are corporate officers liable for their crimes?

(AP Photo/Seth Wenig)

---

5. See Model Penal Code Section 2.07.
6. As a result of the convictions, the motel manager was sentenced to fifteen months in prison, and the corporation was ordered to forfeit the motel property. *United States v. Singh,* 518 F.3d 236 (4th Cir. 2008).
7. For a landmark case in this area, see *United States v. Park,* 421 U.S. 658, 95 S.Ct. 1903, 44 L.Ed.2d 489 (1975).

of responsibility, they had influence over the corporation's actions, and their failure to act constituted a violation of environmental laws.[8] ●

....
**PREVENTING
LEGAL DISPUTES**

If you become a corporate officer or director at some point in your career, you need to be aware that you can be held liable for the crimes of your subordinates. You should always be familiar with any criminal statutes relevant to the corporation's particular industry or trade. Also, make sure that corporate employees are trained in how to comply with the multitude of applicable laws, particularly environmental laws and health and safety regulations, which frequently involve criminal sanctions.

Types of Crimes

Learning Objective 2
What are five broad categories of crimes? What is white-collar crime?

Federal, state, and local laws provide for the classification and punishment of hundreds of thousands of different criminal acts. Traditionally, though, crimes have been grouped into five broad categories: violent crime (crimes against persons), property crime, public order crime, white-collar crime, and organized crime. Within each of these categories, crimes may also be separated into more than one classification. Note also that many crimes may be committed in cyberspace, as well as the physical world. When they occur in the virtual world, we refer to them as cyber crimes, as will be discussed later in the chapter.

Violent Crime

Robbery The act of forcefully and unlawfully taking personal property of any value from another.

Crimes against persons, because they cause others to suffer harm or death, are referred to as *violent crimes*. Murder is a violent crime. So, too, is sexual assault, or rape. **Robbery**—defined as the taking of cash, personal property, or any other article of value from a person by means of force or fear—is another violent crime. Typically, states have more severe penalties for *aggravated robbery*—robbery with the use of a deadly weapon.

Assault and battery, which were discussed in Chapter 5 in the context of tort law, are also classified as violent crimes. Recall that assault can involve an object or force put into motion by a person. **EXAMPLE 6.8**   Former rap star Flavor Flav (whose real name is William Drayton) was arrested in Las Vegas in 2012 on assault and battery charges. During an argument with his fiancée, Drayton allegedly threw her to the ground and then grabbed two kitchen knives and chased her son. ●

Each violent crime is further classified by degree, depending on the circumstances surrounding the criminal act. These circumstances include the intent of the person committing the crime and whether a weapon was used. For crimes other than murder, the level of pain and suffering experienced by the victim is also a factor.

Property Crime

The most common type of criminal activity is property crime—crimes in which the goal of the offender is some form of economic gain or the damaging of property. Robbery is a form of property crime, as well as a violent crime, because the offender seeks to gain the property of another. We look here at a number of other crimes that fall within the general category of property crime. (Note also that many types of cyber crime are forms of property crime as well.)

---

8. The Roscoes and the corporation were sentenced to pay penalties of $2,493,250. *People v. Roscoe*, 169 Cal.App.4th 829, 87 Cal.Rptr.3d 187 (3 Dist. 2008).

Burglary Traditionally, **burglary** was defined under the common law as breaking and entering the dwelling of another at night with the intent to commit a felony. Originally, the definition was aimed at protecting an individual's home and its occupants. Most state statutes have eliminated some of the requirements found in the common law definition. The time of day at which the breaking and entering occurs, for example, is usually immaterial. State statutes frequently omit the element of breaking, and some states do not require that the building be a dwelling. When a deadly weapon is used in a burglary, the person can be charged with *aggravated burglary* and punished more severely.

Burglary The unlawful entry or breaking into a building with the intent to commit a felony.

Larceny Under the common law, the crime of **larceny** involved the unlawful taking and carrying away of someone else's personal property with the intent to permanently deprive the owner of possession. Put simply, larceny is stealing, or theft.

Whereas robbery involves force or fear, larceny does not. Therefore, picking pockets is larceny, not robbery. Similarly, an employee who takes company products and supplies home for personal use without authorization commits larceny. (Note that a person who commits larceny generally can also be sued under tort law because the act of taking possession of another's property involves a trespass to personal property.)

Most states have expanded the definition of property that is subject to larceny statutes. Stealing computer programs may constitute larceny even though the "property" is not physical (see the discussion of computer crime later in this chapter). So, too, can the theft of natural gas or Internet and television cable service.

Larceny The wrongful taking and carrying away of another person's personal property with the intent to permanently deprive the owner of the property.

Obtaining Goods by False Pretenses

Obtaining goods by means of false pretenses is a form of theft that involves trickery or fraud, such as paying for an iPad with a stolen credit-card number. Statutes dealing with such illegal activities vary widely from state to state. They often apply not only to acquiring property, but also to obtaining services or funds by false pretenses—for example, selling an iPad that you claim is yours when you actually do not own it.

At one time, the common law did not recognize the crime of obtaining goods by false pretenses. The remedy for someone defrauded out of property was a civil suit. The crime of theft by fraud can be traced to an Act of the Parliament of Great Britain in 1757. This law served as a template for most of the false pretense statutes in the United States. The crimes of larceny and embezzlement required that property be taken without the owner's consent. The crime of obtaining goods by false pretenses was designed to protect persons from those who would obtain their property with their consent by misrepresentation. The following case involved the application of a current state theft-by-fraud statute.

Case 6.1

State of Wisconsin v. Steffes

Supreme Court of Wisconsin, 347 Wis.2d 683, 832 N.W.2d 101 (2013).

(Thinkstock Images/Getty Images)

BACKGROUND AND FACTS While Matthew Steffes was incarcerated, he participated in a scheme to make free collect calls from prison. His friends and family members would set up a phone number by giving false information to AT&T, Inc. This information included fictitious business names, such as "Nick's Heating & Cooling" and "Douyette Typing Service," and personal identifying information stolen from a health care clinic. Once the number was set up, Steffes could make unlimited collect calls to it. The bills went unpaid, the phone company would shut down the number, and the process would start again. Over an eighteen-month period, Steffes used sixty fraudulently obtained phone numbers to make 322 calls totaling 6,562 minutes. The loss to AT&T was $28,061.41.

Steffes was charged with and convicted of two counts of conspiracy to commit theft by fraud of property in excess of $10,000. The court sentenced him to two years in prison and

Case 6.1—Continues ➡

Case 6.1—Continued

thirty months of supervision (probation), and ordered him to pay $28,061.41 in restitution to AT&T. A state intermediate appellate court affirmed the conviction. Steffes appealed. He claimed that there had not been any false representations to the phone company that he would pay for the calls and that telephone services did not constitute goods (property).

IN THE WORDS OF THE COURT . . .
Michael J. *GABLEMAN*, J. [Justice]
    * * * *

Two issues are presented in this case. The first is whether submitting fictitious business names and stolen personal identifying information is a "false representation" under Wisconsin Statute Section 943.20(1)(d). Steffes alleges that such conduct is not a false representation because the statute requires that the actor make an express promise to pay. The second issue is whether the applied electricity that AT&T uses to power its network is included within the definition of "property" found in Section 943.20(2)(b). Steffes argues that his conviction cannot be sustained because the evidence at trial showed that he stole telephone *services* and not *property*.

On the first issue we hold that Steffes made "false representations" to AT&T. The theft-by-fraud statute says that *"false representation includes a promise made with intent not to perform if it is part of a false and fraudulent scheme."* Because the word "includes" is not restrictive, the statute clearly anticipates that other conduct aside from an express promise falls under the umbrella of a "false representation." The scope and history of the theft-by-fraud statute make plain that providing fictitious business names and stolen personal identifying information to a phone company as a way of avoiding payment falls within the meaning of "false representation." [Emphasis added.]

As to the second issue, "property" under the theft-by-fraud statute is defined as "all forms of tangible property, whether real or personal, without limitation including electricity, gas and documents which represent or embody * * * intangible rights." Relying on the plain language of the statute in conjunction with commonly used dictionaries, we conclude that Steffes stole electricity from AT&T. AT&T purchases and stores electricity to power its network. *When consumers make phone calls, AT&T must buy more electricity. The conspiracy perpetrated against AT&T therefore deprived the company of its property.* [Emphasis added.]

DECISION AND REMEDY   The Wisconsin Supreme Court affirmed the judgment of the lower court. Steffes made "false representations" to AT&T so that he could make phone calls without paying for them, depriving the company of its "property"—its electricity.

THE LEGAL ENVIRONMENT DIMENSION   *Besides the defendant, who may have committed a crime in this case? Explain.*

THE ETHICAL DIMENSION   *How might the crimes in this case have been avoided? Discuss.*

Receiving Stolen Goods   It is a crime to receive goods that a person knows or should have known were stolen or illegally obtained. To be convicted, the recipient of such goods need not know the true identity of the owner or the thief, and need not have paid for the goods. All that is necessary is that the recipient knows or should have known that the goods were stolen, and intended to deprive the true owner of those goods.

Arson   The willful and malicious burning of a building (and, in some states, vehicles and other items of personal property) is the crime of **arson.** At common law, arson traditionally applied only to burning down another person's house. The law was designed to protect human life. Today, arson statutes have been extended to cover the destruction of any building, regardless of ownership, by fire or explosion.

Arson The intentional burning of a building.

Every state has a special statute that covers the act of burning a building for the purpose of collecting insurance. **EXAMPLE 6.9**   Benton owns an insured apartment building that is falling apart. If he sets fire to it or pays someone else to do so, he is guilty not only of arson but also of defrauding the insurer, which is attempted larceny. ● Of course, the insurer need not pay the claim when insurance fraud is proved.

Forgery

Forgery   The fraudulent making or altering of any writing (including electronic records) in a way that changes the legal rights and liabilities of another is **forgery.** **EXAMPLE 6.10** Without authorization, Severson signs Bennett's name to the back of a check made out to Bennett and attempts to cash it. Severson has committed the crime of forgery. ● Forgery also includes changing trademarks, falsifying public records, counterfeiting, and altering a legal document.

Public Order Crime

Historically, societies have always outlawed activities that are considered to be contrary to public values and morals. Today, the most common public order crimes include public drunkenness, prostitution, gambling, and illegal drug use. These crimes are sometimes referred to as victimless crimes because they normally harm only the offender. From a broader perspective, however, they are deemed detrimental to society as a whole because they may create an environment that gives rise to property and violent crimes.

EXAMPLE 6.11 A flight attendant observed a man and woman engaging in sex acts while on a flight to Las Vegas in 2013. A criminal complaint was filed, and the two defendants pleaded guilty in federal court to misdemeanor disorderly conduct. ●

(Gene Blevins/Reuters/Landov)

This carport fire was one of twelve such fires that were set by an individual during a short time period. What type of crime was that person guilty of committing?

White-Collar Crime

Crimes that typically occur only in the business context are popularly referred to as **white-collar crimes.** Although there is no official definition of white-collar crime, the term is commonly used to mean an illegal act or series of acts committed by an individual or business entity using some nonviolent means. Usually, this kind of crime is committed in the course of a legitimate occupation. Corporate crimes fall into this category. In addition, certain property crimes, such as larceny and forgery, may also be white-collar crimes if they occur within the business context.

Embezzlement

Embezzlement   When a person who is entrusted with another person's funds or property fraudulently appropriates it, **embezzlement** occurs. Typically, embezzlement is carried out by an employee who steals funds. Banks are particularly prone to this problem, but embezzlement can occur in any firm. In a number of businesses, corporate officers or accountants have fraudulently converted funds for their own benefit and then "fixed" the books to cover up their crime. Embezzlement is not larceny, because the wrongdoer does not physically take the property from another's possession, and it is not robbery, because force or fear is not used.

Embezzlement occurs whether the embezzler takes the funds directly from the victim or from a third person. If the financial officer of a corporation pockets checks from third parties that were given to her to deposit into the corporate account, she is embezzling. Frequently, an embezzler takes a relatively small amount at one time but does so repeatedly over a long period. The embezzler might underreport income or deposits and keep the remaining amount, for example, or create fictitious persons or accounts and write checks to them from the corporate account. An employer's failure to remit state withholding taxes that were collected from employee wages can also constitute embezzlement.

The intent to return embezzled property—or its actual return—is not a defense to the crime of embezzlement, as the following *Spotlight Case* illustrates.

Forgery The fraudulent making or altering of any writing in a way that changes the legal rights and liabilities of another.

White-Collar Crime Nonviolent crime committed by individuals or corporations to obtain a personal or business advantage.

Embezzlement The fraudulent appropriation of funds or other property by a person who was entrusted with the funds or property.

Spotlight on White-Collar Crime

Case 6.2
People v. Sisuphan
Court of Appeal of California, First District, 181 Cal.App.4th 800, 104 Cal.Rptr.3d 654 (2010).

A Toyota dealership employee committed embezzlement but returned the funds. Is this a defense?

(Joe Raedle/Getty Images)

BACKGROUND AND FACTS Lou Sisuphan was the director of finance at a Toyota dealership. His responsibilities included managing the financing contracts for vehicle sales and working with lenders to obtain payments. Sisuphan complained repeatedly to management about the performance and attitude of one of the finance managers, Ian McClelland. The general manager, Michael Christian, would not terminate McClelland "because he brought a lot of money into the dealership." One day, McClelland accepted $22,600 in cash and two checks totaling $7,275.51 from a customer in payment for a car. McClelland placed the cash, the checks, and a copy of the receipt in a large envelope. As he tried to drop the envelope into the safe through a mechanism at its top, the envelope became stuck. While McClelland went for assistance, Sisuphan wiggled the envelope free and kept it. On McClelland's return, Sisuphan told him that the envelope had dropped into the safe. When the payment turned up missing, Christian told all the managers he would not bring criminal charges if the payment was returned within twenty-four hours.

After the twenty-four-hour period had lapsed, Sisuphan told Christian that he had taken the envelope, and he returned the cash and checks to Christian. Sisuphan claimed that he had no intention of stealing the payment but had taken it to get McClelland fired. Christian fired Sisuphan the next day, and the district attorney later charged Sisuphan with embezzlement. After a jury trial, Sisuphan was found guilty. Sisuphan appealed, arguing that the trial court had erred by excluding evidence that he had returned the payment. The trial court had concluded that the evidence was not relevant because return of the property is not a defense to embezzlement.

IN THE WORDS OF THE COURT . . .
JENKINS, J. [Judge]
* * * *

Fraudulent intent is an essential element of embezzlement. Although restoration of the property is not a defense, evidence of repayment may be relevant to the extent it shows that a defendant's intent at the time of the taking was not fraudulent. Such evidence is admissible "only when [a] defendant shows a relevant and probative [tending to prove] link in his subsequent actions from which it might be inferred his original intent was innocent." The question before us, therefore, is whether evidence that Sisuphan returned the money reasonably tends to prove he lacked the requisite intent at the time of the taking. [Emphasis added.]

Section 508 [of the California Penal Code], which sets out the offense of which Sisuphan was convicted, provides: "Every clerk, agent, or servant of any person who fraudulently appropriates to his own use, or secretes with a fraudulent intent to appropriate to his own use, any property of another which has come into his control or care by virtue of his employment * * * is guilty of embezzlement." Sisuphan denies he ever intended "to use the [money] to financially better himself, even temporarily" and contends the evidence he sought to introduce showed "he returned the [money] without having appropriated it to his own use in any way." He argues that this evidence negates fraudulent intent because it supports his claim that he took the money to get McClelland fired and acted "to help his company by drawing attention to the inadequacy and incompetency of an employee." We reject these contentions.

In determining whether Sisuphan's intent was fraudulent at the time of the taking, the issue is not whether he intended to spend the money, but whether he intended to use it for a purpose other than that for which the dealership entrusted it to him. The offense of embezzlement contemplates a principal's entrustment of property to an agent for certain purposes and the agent's breach of that trust by acting outside his authority in his use of the property. * * * Sisuphan's undisputed purpose—to get McClelland fired—was beyond the scope of his responsibility and therefore outside the trust afforded him by the dealership. Accordingly, even if the proffered [submitted] evidence shows he took the money for this purpose, it does not tend to prove he lacked fraudulent intent, and the trial court properly excluded this evidence. [Emphasis added.]

DECISION AND REMEDY The California appellate court affirmed the trial court's decision. The fact that Sisuphan had returned the payment was irrelevant. He was guilty of embezzlement.

THE LEGAL ENVIRONMENT DIMENSION Why was Sisuphan convicted of embezzlement instead of larceny? What is the difference between these two crimes?

THE ETHICAL DIMENSION Given that Sisuphan returned the cash, was it fair for the dealership's general manager to terminate Sisuphan's employment? Why or why not?

Mail and Wire Fraud

One of the most potent weapons against white-collar criminals are the federal laws that prohibit mail fraud[9] and wire fraud.[10] These laws make it a federal crime to devise any scheme that uses the U.S. mail, commercial carriers—such as FedEx or UPS—or wire, including telegraph, telephone, television, e-mail, or online social media, with the intent to defraud the public. These laws are often applied when persons send out advertisements or e-mails with the intent to obtain cash or property by false pretenses.

CASE EXAMPLE 6.12 Cisco Systems, Inc., offers a warranty program to authorized resellers of Cisco parts. Iheanyi Frank Chinasa and Robert Kendrick Chambliss formulated a scheme to use this program to defraud Cisco by obtaining replacement parts to which they were not entitled. The two men sent numerous e-mails and Internet service requests to Cisco to convince the company to ship them new parts via commercial carriers. Ultimately, Chinasa and Chambliss were convicted of mail and wire fraud, and conspiracy to commit mail and wire fraud.[11] •

The maximum penalty under these statutes is substantial. Persons convicted may be imprisoned for up to twenty years and/or fined. If the violation affects a financial institution or involves fraud in connection with emergency disaster-relief funds, the violator may be fined up to $1 million, imprisoned for up to thirty years, or both.

Bribery

The crime of bribery involves offering something of value to someone in an attempt to influence that person, who is usually, but not always, a public official, to act in a way that serves a private interest. Three types of bribery are considered crimes: bribery of public officials, commercial bribery, and bribery of foreign officials. As an element of the crime of bribery, intent must be present and proved. The bribe itself can be anything the recipient considers to be valuable. Realize that the *crime of bribery occurs when the bribe is offered*—it is not required that the bribe be accepted. *Accepting a bribe* is a separate crime.

Commercial bribery involves corrupt dealings between private persons or businesses. Typically, people make commercial bribes to obtain proprietary information, cover up an inferior product, or secure new business. Industrial espionage sometimes involves commercial bribes. **EXAMPLE 6.13** Kent Peterson works at the firm of Jacoby & Meyers. He offers to pay Laurel, an employee in a competing firm, if she will give him her firm's trade secrets and pricing schedules. Kent has committed commercial bribery. • So-called kickbacks, or payoffs for special favors or services, are a form of commercial bribery in some situations.

Theft of Trade Secrets

As will be discussed in Chapter 8, trade secrets constitute a form of intellectual property that can be extremely valuable for many businesses. The Economic Espionage Act[12] made the theft of trade secrets a federal crime. The act also made it a federal crime to buy or possess trade secrets of another person, knowing that the trade secrets were stolen or otherwise acquired without the owner's authorization.

Violations of the act can result in steep penalties. An individual who violates the act can be imprisoned for up to ten years and fined up to $500,000. If a corporation or other organization violates the act, it can be fined up to $5 million. Additionally, the law provides that any property acquired as a result of the violation, such as airplanes and automobiles, and any property used in the commission of the violation, such as servers and other electronic devices, are subject to criminal *forfeiture*—meaning that the government can take the property. A theft of trade secrets conducted via the Internet, for example, could result in the forfeiture of every computer or other device used to commit or facilitate the crime.

> "It was beautiful and simple as all truly great swindles are."
>
> O. Henry, 1862–1910
> (American writer)

---

9. The Mail Fraud Act of 1990, 18 U.S.C. Sections 1341–1342.
10. 18 U.S.C. Section 1343.
11. *United States v. Chinasa*, 789 F.Supp.2d 691 (E.D.Va. 2011).
12. 18 U.S.C. Sections 1831–1839.

Insider Trading The purchase or sale of securities on the basis of *inside information* (information that has not been made available to the public).

Insider Trading

An individual who obtains "inside information" about the plans of a publicly listed corporation can often make stock-trading profits by purchasing or selling corporate securities based on the information. **Insider trading** is a violation of securities law and will be considered more fully in Chapter 24. Generally, the rule is that a person who possesses inside information and has a duty not to disclose it to outsiders may not profit from the purchase or sale of securities based on that information until the information is made available to the public.

Organized Crime

As mentioned, white-collar crime takes place within the confines of the legitimate business world. *Organized crime,* in contrast, operates *illegitimately* by, among other things, providing illegal goods and services. For organized crime, the traditional preferred markets are gambling, prostitution, illegal narcotics, and loan sharking (lending at higher than legal interest rates), along with counterfeiting and credit-card scams.

Money Laundering

Organized crime and other illegal activities generate many billions of dollars in profits each year from illegal drug transactions and, to a lesser extent, from racketeering, prostitution, and gambling. Under federal law, banks and other financial institutions are required to report currency transactions involving more than $10,000. Consequently, those who engage in illegal activities face difficulties when they try to deposit their cash profits from illegal transactions.

Money Laundering Engaging in financial transactions to conceal the identity, source, or destination of illegally gained funds.

As an alternative to simply storing cash from illegal transactions in a safe-deposit box, wrongdoers and racketeers launder their "dirty" money to make it "clean" by passing it through a legitimate business. **Money laundering** is engaging in financial transactions to conceal the identity, source, or destination of illegally gained funds.

EXAMPLE 6.14 Leo Harris, a successful drug dealer, becomes a partner with a restaurateur. Little by little, the restaurant shows increasing profits. As a partner in the restaurant, Harris is able to report the "profits" of the restaurant as legitimate income on which he pays federal and state taxes. He can then spend those funds without worrying that his lifestyle may exceed the level possible with his reported income. ●

Vincent Gotti (center) is an alleged mobster—member of organized crime—in New York and Sicily, Italy. What types of crimes are the most commonly committed by such individuals?

(Debbie Egan-Chin/NY Daily News via Getty Images)

The Racketeer Influenced and Corrupt Organizations Act

To curb the entry of organized crime into the legitimate business world, Congress enacted the Racketeer Influenced and Corrupt Organizations Act (RICO).[13] The statute, which was enacted as part of the Organized Crime Control Act, makes it a federal crime to (1) use income obtained from racketeering activity to purchase any interest in an enterprise, (2) acquire or maintain an interest in an enterprise through racketeering activity, (3) conduct or participate in the affairs of an enterprise through racketeering activity, or (4) conspire to do any of the preceding activities.

Broad Application of RICO The broad language of RICO has allowed it to be applied in cases that have little or nothing to do with organized crime. RICO incorporates by reference twenty-six separate types of federal crimes and nine types of state felonies[14] and declares that if a person commits two of these offenses, he or she is guilty of "racketeering activity."

---

13. 18 U.S.C. Sections 1961–1968.
14. See 18 U.S.C. Section 1961(1)(A).

Under the criminal provisions of RICO, any individual found guilty is subject to a fine of up to $25,000 per violation, imprisonment for up to twenty years, or both. Additionally, the statute provides that those who violate RICO may be required to forfeit (give up) any assets, in the form of property or cash, that were acquired as a result of the illegal activity or that were "involved in" or an "instrumentality of" the activity.

Civil Liability   In the event of a RICO violation, the government can seek civil penalties, such as the divestiture of a defendant's interest in a business (called forfeiture) or the dissolution of the business.

Moreover, in some cases, the statute allows private individuals to sue violators and potentially to recover three times their actual losses (treble damages), plus attorneys' fees, for business injuries caused by a violation of the statute. This is perhaps the most controversial aspect of RICO and one that continues to cause debate in the nation's federal courts. The prospect of receiving treble damages in civil RICO lawsuits has given plaintiffs a financial incentive to pursue businesses and employers for violations.

Classification of Crimes

In addition to being grouped into the five categories just discussed, crimes are also classified as felonies or misdemeanors depending on their degree of seriousness. **Felonies** are serious crimes punishable by death or by imprisonment for more than a year. Many states also define different degrees of felony offenses and vary the punishment according to the degree. **Misdemeanors** are less serious crimes, punishable by a fine or by confinement for up to a year. In most jurisdictions, **petty offenses** are considered to be a subset of misdemeanors. Petty offenses are minor violations, such as jaywalking or violations of building codes. Even for petty offenses, however, a guilty party can be put in jail for a few days, fined, or both, depending on state or local law.

Defenses to Criminal Liability

Persons charged with crimes may be relieved of criminal liability if they can show that their criminal actions were justified under the circumstances. In certain circumstances, the law may also allow a person to be excused from criminal liability because she or he lacks the required mental state. We look at several of the defenses to criminal liability here.

Note that procedural violations, such as obtaining evidence without a valid search warrant, may also operate as defenses. As you will read later in this chapter, evidence obtained in violation of a defendant's constitutional rights normally may not be admitted in court. If the evidence is suppressed, then there may be no basis for prosecuting the defendant.

Justifiable Use of Force

Probably the best-known defense to criminal liability is **self-defense.** Other situations, however, also justify the use of force: the defense of one's dwelling, the defense of other property, and the prevention of a crime. In all of these situations, it is important to distinguish between deadly and nondeadly force. *Deadly force* is likely to result in death or serious bodily harm. *Nondeadly force* is force that reasonably appears necessary to prevent the imminent use of criminal force.

Generally speaking, people can use the amount of nondeadly force that seems necessary to protect themselves, their dwellings, or other property or to prevent the commission of a crime. Deadly force can be used in self-defense if the defender *reasonably believes* that imminent death or grievous bodily harm will otherwise result. In addition, normally the

Felony A crime—such as arson, murder, rape, or robbery—that carries the most severe sanctions, ranging from more than one year in a state or federal prison to the death penalty.

Misdemeanor A lesser crime than a felony, punishable by a fine or incarceration in jail for up to one year.

Petty Offense The least serious kind of criminal offense, such as a traffic or building-code violation.

Learning Objective 3
What defenses can be raised to avoid liability for criminal acts?

Self-Defense The legally recognized privilege to do what is reasonably necessary to protect oneself, one's property, or someone else against injury by another.

attacker must be using unlawful force, and the defender must not have initiated or provoked the attack.

Traditionally, deadly force could be used to defend a dwelling only when the unlawful entry was violent and the person believed deadly force was necessary to prevent imminent death or great bodily harm. Today, however, in some jurisdictions, deadly force can also be used if the person believes it is necessary to prevent the commission of a felony in the dwelling. Many states are expanding the situations in which the use of deadly force can be justified. Florida, for example, allows the use of deadly force to prevent the commission of a "forcible felony," including robbery, carjacking, and sexual battery. Similar laws have been passed in at least seventeen other states.

Necessity

Sometimes, criminal defendants can be relieved of liability by showing *necessity*—that a criminal act was necessary to prevent an even greater harm. **EXAMPLE 6.15** Jake Trevor is a convicted felon and, as such, is legally prohibited from possessing a firearm. While he and his wife are in a convenience store, a man draws a gun, points it at the cashier, and demands all the cash. Afraid that the man will start shooting, Trevor grabs the gun and holds on to it until police arrive. In this situation, if Trevor is charged with possession of a firearm, he can assert the defense of necessity. ●

Insanity

A person who suffers from a mental illness may be incapable of the state of mind required to commit a crime. Thus, insanity can be a defense to a criminal charge. Note that an insanity defense does not allow a person to avoid imprisonment. It simply means that if the defendant successfully proves insanity, she or he will be placed in a mental institution. **EXAMPLE 6.16** James Holmes opened fire with an automatic weapon in a crowded Colorado movie theater during the screening of *The Dark Knight Rises*, killing twelve people and injuring more than fifty. Holmes had been a graduate student until he suffered from mental health problems. Before the incident, he had no criminal history. Holmes's attorneys have asserted the defense of insanity to try to avoid a possible death penalty. If the defense is successful, Holmes will be confined to a mental institution, rather than a prison. ●

The courts have had difficulty deciding what the test for legal insanity should be, however, and psychiatrists as well as lawyers are critical of the tests used. Federal courts and some states use the *substantial-capacity test* set forth in the Model Penal Code. Under this test, "A person is not responsible for criminal conduct if at the time of such conduct as a result of mental disease or defect he [or she] lacks substantial capacity either to appreciate the wrongfulness of his [or her] conduct or to conform his [or her] conduct to the requirements of the law."

Some states use the *M'Naghten* test,[15] under which a criminal defendant is not responsible if, at the time of the offense, he or she did not know the nature and quality of the act or did not know that the act was wrong. Other states use the *irresistible-impulse test*. A person operating under an irresistible impulse may know an act is wrong but cannot refrain from doing it. Under any of these tests, proving insanity is extremely difficult. For this reason, the insanity defense is rarely used and usually is not successful.

Mistake

Everyone has heard the saying "Ignorance of the law is no excuse." Ordinarily, ignorance of the law or a mistaken idea about what the law requires is not a valid defense. A *mistake*

Amy Bishop, shown with her attorney, killed three fellow college professors. She pleaded not guilty by reason of insanity. What does she have to prove to prevail at trial?

(AP Photo/The Huntsville Times, Glenn Baeske)

---

15. A rule derived from *M'Naghten's* Case, 8 Eng.Rep. 718 (1843).

of fact, as opposed to a *mistake of law,* can excuse criminal responsibility if it negates the mental state necessary to commit a crime.

EXAMPLE 6.17 If Oliver Wheaton mistakenly walks off with Julie Tyson's briefcase because he thinks it is his, there is no crime. Theft requires knowledge that the property belongs to another. (If Wheaton's act causes Tyson to incur damages, however, she may sue him in a civil action for trespass to personal property or conversion—torts that were discussed in Chapter 5.) ●

Duress

Duress exists when the *wrongful threat* of one person induces another person to perform an act that she or he would not otherwise perform. In such a situation, duress is said to negate the mental state necessary to commit a crime because the defendant was forced or compelled to commit the act.

Duress can be used as a defense to most crimes except murder. The states vary in how duress is defined and what types of crimes it can excuse, however. Generally, to successfully assert duress as a defense, the defendant must reasonably believe in the immediate danger, and the jury (or judge) must conclude that the defendant's belief was reasonable.

Duress Unlawful pressure brought to bear on a person, causing the person to perform an act that she or he would not otherwise perform.

Entrapment

Entrapment is a defense designed to prevent police officers or other government agents from enticing persons to commit crimes so that they can later be prosecuted for criminal acts. In the typical entrapment case, an undercover agent *suggests* that a crime be committed and pressures or induces an individual to commit it. The agent then arrests the individual for the crime.

For entrapment to succeed as a defense, both the suggestion and the inducement must take place. The defense is not intended to prevent law enforcement agents from ever setting a trap for an unwary criminal. Rather, its purpose is to prevent them from pushing the individual into a criminal act. The crucial issue is whether the person who committed a crime was predisposed to commit the illegal act or did so only because the agent induced it.

Entrapment A defense in which a defendant claims that he or she was induced by a public official to commit a crime that he or she would otherwise not have committed.

Statute of Limitations

With some exceptions, such as for the crime of murder, statutes of limitations apply to crimes just as they do to civil wrongs. In other words, the state must initiate criminal prosecution within a certain number of years. If a criminal action is brought after the statutory time period has expired, the accused person can raise the statute of limitations as a defense.

Immunity

Accused persons are understandably reluctant to give information if it will be used to prosecute them, and they cannot be forced to do so. The privilege against **self-incrimination** is granted by the Fifth Amendment to the U.S. Constitution, which reads, in part, "nor shall [any person] be compelled in any criminal case to be a witness against himself." When the state wishes to obtain information from a person accused of a crime, the state can grant *immunity* from prosecution or agree to prosecute for a less serious offense in exchange for the information. Once immunity is given, the person can no longer refuse to testify on Fifth Amendment grounds because he or she now has an absolute privilege against self-incrimination.

Often, a grant of immunity from prosecution for a serious crime is part of the **plea bargaining** between the defendant and the prosecuting attorney. The defendant may be

Self-Incrimination Giving testimony in a trial or other legal proceeding that could expose the person testifying to criminal prosecution.

Plea Bargaining The process by which a criminal defendant and the prosecutor work out an agreement to dispose of the criminal case, subject to court approval.

convicted of a lesser offense, while the state uses the defendant's testimony to prosecute accomplices for serious crimes carrying heavy penalties.

Criminal Procedures

Learning Objective 4
What constitutional safeguards exist to protect persons accused of crimes?

Criminal law brings the force of the state, with all its resources, to bear against the individual. Criminal procedures are designed to protect the constitutional rights of individuals and to prevent the arbitrary use of power by the government.

The U.S. Constitution provides specific safeguards for those accused of crimes. The United States Supreme Court has ruled that most of these safeguards apply not only in federal court but also in state courts by virtue of the due process clause of the Fourteenth Amendment. These protections include the following:

1. The Fourth Amendment protection from unreasonable searches and seizures.
2. The Fourth Amendment requirement that no warrant for a search or an arrest be issued without probable cause.
3. The Fifth Amendment requirement that no one be deprived of "life, liberty, or property without due process of law."
4. The Fifth Amendment prohibition against **double jeopardy** (trying someone twice for the same criminal offense).[16]
5. The Fifth Amendment requirement that no person be required to be a witness against (incriminate) himself or herself.
6. The Sixth Amendment guarantees of a speedy trial, a trial by jury, a public trial, the right to confront witnesses, and the right to a lawyer at various stages in some proceedings.
7. The Eighth Amendment prohibitions against excessive bail and fines and against cruel and unusual punishment.

Double Jeopardy The Fifth Amendment requirement that prohibits a person from being tried twice for the same criminal offense.

Fourth Amendment Protections

The Fourth Amendment protects the "right of the people to be secure in their persons, houses, papers, and effects." Before searching or seizing private property, normally law enforcement officers must obtain a **search warrant**—an order from a judge or other public official authorizing the search or seizure.

Search Warrant An order granted by a public authority, such as a judge, that authorizes law enforcement personnel to search particular premises or property.

Advances in technology allow the authorities to track phone calls and vehicle movements with greater ease and precision. Nevertheless, the use of such technology can still constitute a search within the meaning of the Fourth Amendment. **CASE EXAMPLE 6.18** Antoine Jones owned and operated a nightclub. Police suspected that he was also trafficking in narcotics. As part of their investigation, police obtained a warrant to attach a Global Positioning System (GPS) device to his wife's car. Although the warrant specified that the GPS device had to be attached within ten days, officers did not attach it until eleven days later.

Law enforcement then tracked the vehicle's movement for about a month, eventually arresting Jones for possession and intent to distribute cocaine. Jones was convicted. He appealed, arguing that police did not have a warrant for the GPS tracking. The United States Supreme Court held that the attachment of a GPS tracking device to a suspect's vehicle constitutes a Fourth Amendment search. The Court did not rule on whether the search in this case was unreasonable and required a warrant, however, and allowed Jones's conviction to stand.[17] ●

---

16. Once a criminal defendant is found not guilty of a particular crime, the government may not indict that person again and retry him or her for the same crime. Double jeopardy does *not* preclude the crime victim from bringing a *civil* suit against that same person to recover damages, however. Additionally, a state's prosecution of a crime will not prevent a separate federal prosecution of the same crime, and vice versa.
17. *United States v. Jones,* __ U.S. __, 132 S.Ct. 945, 181 L.Ed.2d 911 (2012).

Probable Cause To obtain a search warrant, law enforcement officers must convince a judge that they have reasonable grounds, or **probable cause**, to believe a search will reveal a specific illegality. Probable cause requires the officers to have trustworthy evidence that would convince a reasonable person that the proposed search or seizure is more likely justified than not.

Furthermore, the Fourth Amendment prohibits general warrants. It requires a particular description of what is to be searched or seized. General searches through a person's belongings are impermissible. The search cannot extend beyond what is described in the warrant. Although search warrants require specificity, if a search warrant is issued for a person's residence, items in that residence may be searched even if they do not belong to that individual.

Because of the strong governmental interest in protecting the public, a warrant normally is not required for seizures of spoiled or contaminated food. Nor are warrants required for searches of businesses in such highly regulated industries as liquor, guns, and strip mining.

Probable Cause Reasonable grounds for believing that a search should be conducted or that a person should be arrested.

Reasonable Expectation of Privacy The Fourth Amendment only protects against searches that violate a person's *reasonable expectation of privacy*. A reasonable expectation of privacy exists if (1) the individual actually expects privacy, and (2) the person's expectation is one that society as a whole would think is legitimate.

The issue before the court in the following case was whether a defendant had a reasonable expectation of privacy in cell phone texts stored in the account of another person.

Case 6.3

State of Oklahoma v. Marcum
Court of Criminal Appeals of Oklahoma, 319 P.3d 681 (2014).

Is there an absolute right to privacy for text messages?

BACKGROUND AND FACTS Angela Marcum, a drug court coordinator associated with the District County Court of Pittsburg County, Oklahoma, was romantically involved with James Miller, an assistant district attorney in Pittsburg County. When Miller learned that state officials were "in town" investigating suspected embezzlement, he quickly sent Marcum text messages from his personal phone. She sent messages back. The state obtained a search warrant and collected the records of the messages from U.S. Cellular, Miller's phone company. Later, the state charged Marcum with obstructing the investigation and offered in evidence the messages obtained pursuant to the warrant. Marcum filed a motion to suppress the records, which the court granted. The state appealed.

IN THE WORDS OF THE COURT . . .
SMITH, Vice Presiding Judge.
* * * *

The initial issue below and on appeal is whether Marcum has a reasonable expectation of privacy in the U.S. Cellular records of Miller's phone account. * * * Fourth Amendment rights are personal, may not be asserted on behalf of another, and will be enforced only where a search and seizure infringes on a defendant's own rights. * * * *Marcum must prove she exhibited an actual, subjective expectation of privacy, which society is*

prepared to recognize as reasonable. [Emphasis added.]

* * * Generally, the issuance of a subpoena to a third party to obtain the records of that party does not violate the rights of a defendant, even if a criminal prosecution is contemplated at the time the subpoena is issued. * * * *There is no reasonable expectation of privacy in call records of phone numbers kept by a telephone company.* Here, the records consist of more than account numbers, and include the contents of the text messages themselves. Also, of course, here Marcum is not the account holder on the U.S. Cellular account named in the warrant. [Emphasis added.]

* * * *

* * * Marcum's strongest claim to an expectation of privacy is in the texts she sent to Miller's phone, which were received by him and recorded on Miller's account records. This is similar to mailing a letter; there is no expectation of privacy once the letter is delivered. It is like leaving a voice mail message, having the recipient receive and play the message, and then claiming the message is private. * * * Once the messages were both transmitted and received, the expectation of privacy was

Case 6.3—Continues ➡

Case 6.3—Continued

lost. * * * It is the individual's decision to transmit a message to an electronic device that could be in anybody's possession * * * that defeats the individual's expectation of privacy in that communication.

Marcum has not demonstrated a reasonable expectation of privacy in the records seized from U.S. Cellular for Miller's phone account. * * * *There is no expectation of privacy in the text messages or account records of another person, where the defendant has no possessory interest in the cell phone in question, and particularly where, as here, the actual warrant is directed to a third party.* The trial court abused its discretion in finding that Marcum had a reasonable expectation of privacy in the records of text messages sent from and received by Miller's phone, and kept by U.S. Cellular. [Emphasis added.]

DECISION AND REMEDY   A state intermediate appellate court reversed the ruling of the lower court, holding that Marcum had no reasonable expectation of privacy in the text messages in Miller's account. "Once the messages were both transmitted and received, the expectation of privacy was lost." The case was reversed and remanded for further proceedings.

WHAT IF THE FACTS WERE DIFFERENT?   *Suppose that the phones Miller and Marcum used to text each other had belonged to their employer. What factors might have shaped the court's decision in that situation?*

THE E-COMMERCE DIMENSION   *If Miller and Marcum had used smartphones and U.S. Cellular had stored its records in the "cloud," would the outcome likely have been different? Explain.*

The Exclusionary Rule

Exclusionary Rule A rule that prevents evidence that is obtained illegally or without a proper search warrant—and any evidence derived from illegally obtained evidence—from being admissible in court.

Under what is known as the **exclusionary rule**, all evidence obtained in violation of the constitutional rights spelled out in the Fourth, Fifth, and Sixth Amendments, as well as all evidence derived from illegally obtained evidence, normally must be excluded from the trial. Evidence derived from illegally obtained evidence is known as the "fruit of the poisonous tree." If a confession is obtained after an illegal arrest, for instance, the arrest is "the poisonous tree," and the confession, if "tainted" by the arrest, is the "fruit." The purpose of the exclusionary rule is to deter police from conducting warrantless searches and engaging in other misconduct.

CASE EXAMPLE 6.19   Lonnie Oliver gained access to people's personal information and then filed for and received unemployment benefits in their names. Oliver and another person were later arrested. Oliver's co-defendant told police that Oliver kept a laptop computer and a box of items at the apartment of his girlfriend, Erica Armstrong. Police searched the box and laptop and found evidence of the crime. Oliver argued that the evidence was "fruit of the poisonous tree," and should be excluded. The court, however, held that the search was legal. Armstrong had looked through the box before the police arrived. When a private individual examines the contents of a closed container, a later search of the container by the police is lawful. In addition, the police had an independent source of information concerning the laptop—Oliver's co-defendant, who had admitted using a laptop to further their scheme. Evidence obtained through a legal, independent source is admissible.[18] ●

The *Miranda* Rule

In *Miranda v. Arizona,* a case decided in 1966, the United States Supreme Court established the rule that individuals who are arrested must be informed of certain constitutional rights, including their Fifth Amendment right to remain silent and their Sixth Amendment right to counsel. If the arresting officers fail to inform a criminal suspect of these constitutional rights, any statements the suspect makes normally will not be admissible in court.

---

18. *United States v. Oliver,* 630 F.3d 397 (5th Cir. 2011).

Although the Supreme Court's *Miranda* ruling was controversial, the decision has survived attempts by Congress to overrule it.[19] Because of its importance in criminal procedure, the *Miranda* case is presented as this chapter's *Landmark in the Legal Environment* feature.

Over time, as part of a continuing attempt to balance the rights of accused persons against the rights of society, the United States Supreme Court has carved out numerous exceptions to the *Miranda* rule. For instance, the "public safety" exception allows certain statements—such as statements concerning the location of a weapon—to be admissible even if the defendant was not given *Miranda* warnings.

Criminal Process

As mentioned, as a result of the effort to safeguard the rights of the individual against the state, a criminal prosecution differs from a civil case in several respects. We now discuss three phases of the criminal process—arrest, indictment or information, and trial—in more detail. Exhibit 6–2 summarizes the major procedural steps in processing a criminal case.

---

19. *Dickerson v. United States*, 530 U.S. 428, 120 S.Ct. 2326, 147 L.Ed.2d 405 (2000).

LANDMARK IN THE LEGAL ENVIRONMENT
Miranda v. Arizona (1966)

The United States Supreme Court's decision in *Miranda v. Arizona*[a] has been cited in more court decisions than any other case in the history of U.S. law. Through television shows and other media, the case has also become familiar to most of the adult population in the United States.

The case arose after Ernesto Miranda was arrested in his home on March 13, 1963, for the kidnapping and rape of an eighteen-year-old woman. Miranda was taken to a police station in Phoenix, Arizona, and questioned by two police officers. Two hours later, the officers emerged from the interrogation room with a written confession signed by Miranda.

Rulings by the Lower Courts The confession was admitted into evidence at the trial, and Miranda was convicted and sentenced to prison for twenty to thirty years. Miranda appealed his conviction, claiming that he had not been informed of his constitutional rights. He did not assert that he was innocent of the crime or that his confession was false or made under duress. He claimed only that he would not have confessed if he had been advised of his right to remain silent and to have an attorney. The Supreme Court of Arizona held that Miranda's constitutional rights had not been violated and affirmed his conviction. In its decision, the court emphasized that Miranda had not specifically requested an attorney.

---

a. 384 U.S. 436, 86 S.Ct. 1602, 16 L.Ed.2d 694 (1966).

The Supreme Court's Decision The *Miranda* case was subsequently consolidated with three other cases involving similar issues and reviewed by the United States Supreme Court. In its decision, the Court stated that whenever an individual is taken into custody, "the following measures are required: He must be warned prior to any questioning that he has the right to remain silent, that anything he says can be used against him in a court of law, that he has the right to the presence of an attorney, and that if he cannot afford an attorney one will be appointed for him prior to any questioning if he so desires." If the accused waives his or her rights to remain silent and to have counsel present, the government must be able to demonstrate that the waiver was made knowingly, intelligently, and voluntarily.

Application to Today's Legal Environment *Today, both on television and in the real world, police officers routinely advise suspects of their "Miranda rights" on arrest. When Ernesto Miranda himself was later murdered, the suspected murderer was "read his Miranda rights." Interestingly, this decision has also had ramifications for criminal procedure in Great Britain. British police officers are required, when making arrests, to inform suspects, "You do not have to say anything. But if you do not mention now something which you later use in your defense, the court may decide that your failure to mention it now strengthens the case against you. A record will be made of everything you say, and it may be given in evidence if you are brought to trial."*

Exhibit 6–2 Major Procedural Steps in a Criminal Case

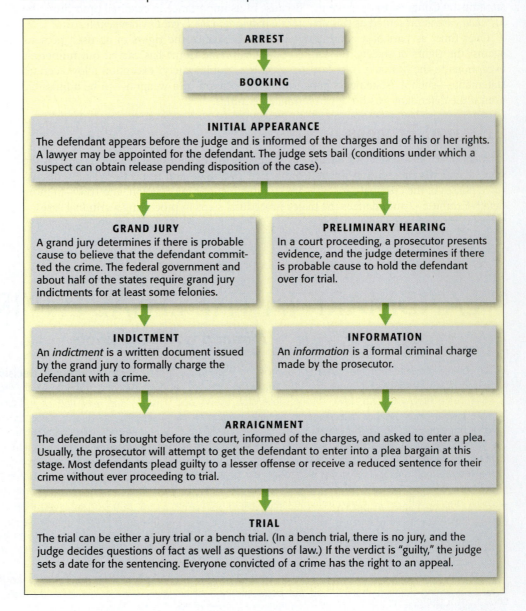

Arrest   Before a warrant for arrest can be issued, there must be probable cause to believe that the individual in question has committed a crime. As discussed earlier, *probable cause* can be defined as a substantial likelihood that the person has committed or is about to commit a crime. Note that probable cause involves a likelihood, not just a possibility. An arrest can be made without a warrant if there is no time to get one, but the action of the arresting officer is still judged by the standard of probable cause.

Indictment or Information   Individuals must be formally charged with having committed specific crimes before they can be brought to trial. If issued by a grand jury, this charge is called an **indictment**.[20] A **grand jury** usually consists of more jurors than the ordinary trial jury. A grand jury does not determine the guilt or innocence of an accused party. Rather, its function is to hear the state's evidence and to determine whether a reasonable basis (probable cause) exists for believing that a crime has been committed and that a trial ought to be held.

Usually, grand juries are used in cases involving serious crimes, such as murder. For lesser crimes, an individual may be formally charged with a crime by what is called an **information**, or criminal complaint. An information will be issued by a government prosecutor if the prosecutor determines that there is sufficient evidence to justify bringing the individual to trial.

Trial At a criminal trial, the accused person does not have to prove anything—the entire burden of proof is on the prosecutor (the state). As mentioned earlier, the prosecution must show that, based on all the evidence presented, the defendant's guilt is established *beyond a reasonable doubt*. If there is a reasonable doubt as to whether a criminal defendant committed the crime with which she or he has been charged, then the verdict must be "not guilty." Note that giving a verdict of "not guilty" is not the same as stating that the defendant is innocent. It merely means that not enough evidence was properly presented to the court to prove guilt beyond a reasonable doubt.

Courts have complex rules about what types of evidence may be presented and how the evidence may be brought out in criminal cases. These rules are designed to ensure that evidence in trials is relevant, reliable, and not prejudicial toward the defendant.

Federal Sentencing Guidelines

The Sentencing Reform Act created the U.S. Sentencing Commission, which performs the task of standardizing sentences for *federal* crimes. The commission's guidelines establish a range of possible penalties for each federal crime. Originally, the guidelines were mandatory, in that the judge was required to select a sentence from within the set range and was not allowed to deviate from it.

Problems with Constitutionality In 2005, the United States Supreme Court held that certain provisions of the federal sentencing guidelines were unconstitutional. **CASE EXAMPLE 6.20** Freddie Booker was arrested with 92.5 grams of crack cocaine in his possession. Booker admitted to police that he had sold an additional 566 grams of crack cocaine, but he was never charged with, or tried for, possession of this additional quantity. Nevertheless, under the federal sentencing guidelines the judge was required to sentence Booker to twenty-two years in prison. The Court ruled that this sentence was unconstitutional because a jury did not find beyond a reasonable doubt that Booker had possessed the additional 566 grams of crack.[21] ●

Essentially, the Court's ruling changed the federal sentencing guidelines from mandatory to advisory. Depending on the circumstances of the case, a federal trial judge may now depart from the guidelines if she or he believes that it is reasonable to do so.

Factors That Increase Criminal Penalties Sentencing guidelines still exist and provide for enhanced punishment for certain types of crimes. Penalties can be enhanced for white-collar crimes, violations of the Sarbanes-Oxley Act (mentioned in Chapter 2), and violations of securities laws (see Chapter 24).[22]

Indictment A formal charge by a grand jury that there is probable cause to believe that a named person has committed a crime.

Grand Jury A group of citizens who decide, after hearing the state's evidence, whether probable cause exists for believing that a crime has been committed and that a trial ought to be held.

Information A formal accusation or complaint (without an indictment) issued in certain types of actions by a government prosecutor.

"In school, every period ends with a bell. Every sentence ends with a period. Every crime ends with a sentence."

Steven Wright, 1955–present (American comedian)

---

20. Pronounced in-dyte-ment.
21. *United States v. Booker*, 543 U.S. 220, 125 S.Ct. 738, 160 L.Ed.2d 621 (2005).
22. The sentencing guidelines were amended in 2003, as required under the Sarbanes-Oxley Act of 2002, to impose stiffer penalties for corporate securities fraud.

The sentencing judge must take into account the various sentencing factors that apply to an individual defendant before concluding that a particular sentence is reasonable. When the defendant is a business firm, these factors include the company's history of past violations, management's cooperation with federal investigators, and the extent to which the firm has undertaken specific programs and procedures to prevent criminal activities by its employees.

Cyber Crime

Computer Crime The unlawful use of a computer or network to take or alter data, or to gain the use of computers or services without authorization.

Cyber Crime A crime that occurs in the online environment rather than in the physical world.

The U.S. Department of Justice broadly defines **computer crime** as any violation of criminal law that involves knowledge of computer technology for its perpetration, investigation, or prosecution. Many computer crimes fall under the broad label of **cyber crime,** which describes any criminal activity occurring via a computer in the virtual community of the Internet.

Most cyber crimes are simply existing crimes, such as fraud and theft of intellectual property, in which the Internet is the instrument of wrongdoing. **EXAMPLE 6.21**   Richard O'Dwyer ran TVShack.net, a Web site with links directing users to copyrighted TV shows and movies. U.S. authorities seized his .net domain name, claiming that the site was nothing more than a search engine for pirated content. O'Dwyer simply moved the site to a .cc domain over which the United States apparently has no authority. ●

Here we look at several types of activities that constitute cyber crimes against persons or property. (Of course, just as computers and the Internet have expanded the scope of crime, they have also provided new ways of detecting and combatting crime. For instance, police are using social media as an investigative tool, as discussed in Chapter 9.)

Cyber Fraud

Cyber Fraud Any misrepresentation knowingly made over the Internet with the intention of deceiving another for the purpose of obtaining property or funds.

As mentioned in Chapter 5, fraud is any misrepresentation knowingly made with the intention of deceiving another and on which a reasonable person would and does rely to her or his detriment. **Cyber fraud** is fraud committed over the Internet.

Online Auction Fraud
Online auction fraud, in its most basic form, is a simple process. A person puts up an expensive item for auction, on either a legitimate or a fake auction site, and then refuses to send the product after receiving payment. Or, as a variation, the wrongdoer may send the purchaser an item that is worth less than the one offered in the auction.

The larger online auction sites, such as eBay, try to protect consumers against such schemes by providing warnings about deceptive sellers or offering various forms of insurance. It is nearly impossible to completely block fraudulent auction activity on the Internet, however. Because users can assume multiple identities, it is very difficult to pinpoint fraudulent sellers—they will simply change their screen names with each auction.

A state government official examines counterfeit jewelry, much of which would have been sold online.

(AP Photo/Paul Sakuma)

Online Retail Fraud
Somewhat similar to online auction fraud is online retail fraud, in which consumers pay directly (without bidding) for items that are never delivered. As with other forms of online fraud, it is difficult to determine the actual extent of online sales fraud, but anecdotal evidence suggests that it is a substantial problem. **CASE EXAMPLE 6.22**   Jeremy Jaynes grossed more than $750,000 per week selling nonexistent or worthless products such as "penny stock pickers" and "Internet history erasers." By the time he was arrested, he had amassed an estimated $24 million from his various fraudulent schemes.[23] ●

---

23. *Jaynes v. Commonwealth of Virginia,* 276 Va.App. 443, 666 S.E.2d 303 (2008).

Cyber Theft

In cyberspace, thieves are not subject to the physical limitations of the "real" world. A thief can steal data stored in a networked computer with Internet access from anywhere on the globe. Only the speed of the connection and the thief's computer equipment limit the quantity of data that can be stolen.

Identity Theft   Not surprisingly, there has been a marked increase in identity theft in recent years. **Identity theft** occurs when the wrongdoer steals a form of identification—such as a name, date of birth, or Social Security number—and uses the information to access the victim's financial resources. This crime existed to a certain extent before the widespread use of the Internet. Thieves would rifle through garbage to find credit-card or bank account numbers and then use those numbers to purchase goods or to withdraw funds from the victims' accounts.

The Internet has provided even easier access to private data, as we will discuss further in Chapter 9. Frequent Web surfers surrender a wealth of information about themselves without knowing it. Most Web sites use "cookies" to collect data on those who visit their sites. The data may include the areas of the site the user visits and the links on which the user clicks.

Furthermore, Web browsers often store information such as the consumer's name and e-mail address. Finally, every time a purchase is made online, the item is linked to the purchaser's name, allowing Web retailers to amass a database of who is buying what. Of course, the database also includes purchasers' credit-card numbers. Cyber criminals who steal people's identities normally do not use the identifying information themselves. Instead, they sell the credit-card numbers and other information on the Internet.

Phishing   A distinct form of identity theft known as **phishing** has added a different wrinkle to the practice. In a phishing attack, the perpetrators "fish" for financial data and passwords from consumers by posing as a legitimate business such as a bank or credit-card company. The "phisher" sends an e-mail asking the recipient to "update" or "confirm" vital information, often with the threat that an account or some other service will be discontinued if the information is not provided. Once the unsuspecting individual enters the information, the phisher can use it to masquerade as that person or to drain his or her bank or credit account.

EXAMPLE 6.23   Customers of Wachovia Bank (now owned by Wells Fargo) received official-looking e-mails telling them to type in personal information on a Web form to complete a mandatory installation of a new Internet security certificate. But the Web site was bogus. When people filled out the forms, their computers were infected and funneled their data to a computer server. The cyber criminals then sold the data. ●

Employment Fraud   Cyber criminals also look for victims at online job-posting sites. Claiming to be an employment officer in a well-known company, the criminal sends bogus e-mail messages to job seekers. The messages ask the unsuspecting job seekers to reveal enough information to allow for identity theft. As the unemployment rate has remained high, cyber criminals have found many opportunities for employment fraud.

EXAMPLE 6.24   The job site Monster.com once asked 4.5 million users to change their passwords. Cyber thieves had broken into its databases and stolen user identities, passwords, and other data in one of Britain's largest cyber theft cases. ●

Credit-Card Numbers   Companies take risks by storing their online customers' credit-card numbers. Although the consumer can make a purchase more quickly without

---

Identity Theft The illegal use of someone else's personal information to access the victim's financial resources.

Learning Objective 5
How has the Internet expanded opportunities for identity theft?

Phishing An e-mail fraud scam in which the messages purport to be from legitimate businesses to induce individuals into revealing their personal financial data, passwords, or other information.

entering a lengthy card number, the electronic warehouses that store the numbers are targets for cyber thieves.

Stolen credit-card numbers are much more likely to hurt merchants and credit-card issuers (such as banks) than consumers. In most situations, the legitimate holders of credit cards are not held responsible for the costs of purchases made with a stolen number.

EXAMPLE 6.25   During the 2013 Christmas shopping season, a security breach at Target Corporation exposed the personal information of 70 million Target customers. Hackers stole credit and debit card numbers and debit-card PINs from the embedded code on the magnetic strips of the cards, as well as customers' names, addresses, and phone numbers. Target's sales plummeted and profits dropped. JPMorgan Chase Bank, the world's largest issuer of credit cards, had to replace 2 million credit and debit cards as a result of the breach. ●

Hacking

A **hacker** is someone who uses one computer to break into another. The danger posed by hackers has increased significantly because of **botnets,** or networks of computers that have been appropriated by hackers without the knowledge of their owners. A hacker may secretly install a program on thousands, if not millions, of personal computer "robots," or "bots," that allows him or her to forward transmissions to an even larger number of systems.

EXAMPLE 6.26   When a hacker broke into Sony Corporation's PlayStation 3 video gaming and entertainment networks, the company had to temporarily shut down its online services. This single hacking incident affected more than 100 million online accounts that provide gaming, chat, and music streaming services. ●

Hacker A person who uses computers to gain unauthorized access to data.

Botnet Short for robot network—a group of computers that run an application that is controlled and manipulated only by the software source. Usually this term is reserved for networks that have been infected by malicious software.

Malware   Botnets are one of the latest forms of malware, a term that refers to any program that is harmful to a computer or, by extension, a computer user. A **worm**, for example, is a software program that is capable of reproducing itself as it spreads from one computer to the next.

EXAMPLE 6.27   Within three weeks, the computer worm called "Conflicker" spread to more than a million personal computers around the world. It was transmitted to some computers through the use of Facebook and Twitter. This worm also infected servers and devices plugged into infected computers, via USB ports, such as iPads, iPhones, and flash drives. ●

A **virus,** another form of malware, is also able to reproduce itself, but must be attached to an "infested" host file to travel from one computer network to another. For instance, hackers are now capable of corrupting banner ads that use Adobe's Flash Player. When an Internet user clicks on the banner ad, a virus is installed. Worms and viruses can be programmed to perform a number of functions, such as prompting host computers to continually "crash" and reboot, or otherwise infect the system. (For a discussion of how malware is now affecting smartphones, see this chapter's *Online Developments* feature that follows.)

Worm A type of malware that is designed to copy itself from one computer to another without human interaction. A worm can copy itself automatically and can replicate in great volume and with great speed. Worms, for example, can send out copies of themselves to every contact in your e-mail address book.

Virus A type of malware that is transmitted between computers and attempts to do deliberate damage to systems and data.

Cyberterrorism   Cyberterrorists, as well as hackers, may target businesses. The goals of a hacking operation might include a wholesale theft of data, such as a merchant's customer files, or the monitoring of a computer to discover a business firm's plans and transactions. A cyberterrorist might also want to insert false codes or data. For instance, the processing control system of a food manufacturer could be changed to alter the levels of ingredients so that consumers of the food would become ill.

A cyberterrorist attack on a major financial institution, such as the New York Stock Exchange or a large bank, could leave securities or money markets in flux and seriously

ONLINE DEVELOPMENTS

Even Smartphones Are Vulnerable to Cyber Attacks

Recent statistics show that the number of bank robberies occurring annually is on the decline. Criminals have learned that it is easier, less risky, and more profitable to steal via the Internet. Advances in the speed and use of the Internet have fostered the growth of a relatively new criminal industry that uses malware to conduct espionage and profit from crime.

Who Are the Creators of Malware?

While any smart teenager can buy prepackaged hacking software on the Internet, the malware that businesses and governments are worried about is much more sophisticated. There is evidence that malware that can be used for international diplomatic espionage as well as industrial espionage is most often developed by so-called cyber mercenaries. According to Steve Sachs of the cyber security firm FireEye, "There are entire little villages dedicated to malware in Russia, villages in China, very sophisticated, very organized, very well-funded."

Flame Malware

The most sophisticated globally created and propagated malware has been labeled Flame. Flame was discovered in 2012, although experts believe that it was lying dormant in thousands of computers worldwide for at least five years.

Flame can record screen shots, keyboard strokes, network traffic, and audio. It can also record Skype conversations. It can even turn infected computers into Bluetooth beacons, which can then attempt to download contact information from nearby Bluetooth-enabled devices.

The Malware Can Infect Smartphones

Many smartphone owners are unaware that their Apple, Nokia, and Microsoft Windows mobile phones can be infected with Flame malware or variants of it without their knowledge. The information that is hacked from smartphones can then be sent on to a series of command-and-control servers and ultimately to members of international criminal gangs.

Once a computer or smartphone is infected with this malware, all information in the device can be transferred. Additionally, files can be deleted, and furthermore, files that have been erased on hard drives can be resurrected. This malware has been responsible for stealing e-mail databases from Microsoft's e-mail program Outlook and has even been able to capture e-mail from remote servers.[a]

Until recently, most attacks involved diplomatic espionage, but cyber technicians at large business enterprises are now worried that industrial espionage may be taking place. In fact, an extensive hacking operation was uncovered in 2013 that was linked to a Chinese military unit (the "Comment Crew"). The wide-ranging cyber attacks involved the theft of hundreds of terabytes of data and intellectual property of more than 140 corporations in twenty different industries. The goal of the attacks was to help Chinese companies better compete against U.S. and foreign firms.[b]

Critical Thinking

What entities might pay "cyber mercenaries" to create some of the malware described in this feature?

---

a. Mark Stevens, "CWI Cryptanalyst Discovers New Cryptographic Attack Variant in Flame Spy Malware," June 7, 2012, www.cwi.nl/news/2012.
b. David E. Sanger, David Barboza, and Nicole Perlroth, "Chinese Army Unit Is Seen as Tied to Hacking Against U.S.," www.nytimes.com/2013.

---

affect the daily lives of millions of citizens. Similarly, any prolonged disruption of computer, cable, satellite, or telecommunications systems due to the actions of expert hackers would have serious repercussions on business operations—and national security—on a global level.

Prosecuting Cyber Crime

Cyber crime has raised new issues in the investigation of crimes and the prosecution of offenders. Determining the "location" of a cyber crime and identifying a criminal in cyberspace are two significant challenges for law enforcement.

"THE PRISONS ARE FILLED WITH CYBER-CRIMINALS, SO I'M SENTENCING YOU TO FOUR YEARS OF WAITING FOR INTERNET ACCESS."

Jurisdiction and Identification Challenges A threshold issue is, of course, jurisdiction. Jurisdiction is normally based on physical geography, as discussed in Chapter 3. Each state and nation has jurisdiction over crimes committed within its boundaries. But geographic boundaries simply do not apply in cyberspace. A person who commits an act against a business in California, where the act is a cyber crime, might never have set foot in California but might instead reside in New York, or even in Canada, where the act may not be a crime.

Identifying the wrongdoer can also be difficult. Cyber criminals do not leave physical traces, such as fingerprints or DNA samples, as evidence of their crimes. Even electronic "footprints" (digital evidence) can be hard to find and follow. For example, e-mail may be sent through a remailer, an online service that guarantees that a message cannot be traced to its source.

For these reasons, laws written to protect physical property are often difficult to apply in cyberspace. Nonetheless, governments at both the state and the federal level have taken significant steps toward controlling cyber crime, both by applying existing criminal statutes and by enacting new laws that specifically address wrongs committed in cyberspace. California, for instance, which has the highest identity theft rate in the nation, established a special eCrime unit in 2011 to investigate and prosecute cyber crimes. Other states, including Florida, Louisiana, and Texas, also have special law enforcement units that focus solely on Internet crimes.

The Computer Fraud and Abuse Act Perhaps the most significant federal statute specifically addressing cyber crime is the Counterfeit Access Device and Computer Fraud and Abuse Act.[24] This act is commonly known as the Computer Fraud and Abuse Act, or CFAA.

Among other things, the CFAA provides that a person who accesses a computer online, without authority, to obtain classified, restricted, or protected data (or attempts to do so) is subject to criminal prosecution. Such data could include financial and credit records, medical records, legal files, military and national security files, and other confidential information in government or private computers. The crime has two elements: accessing a computer without authority and taking the data.

This theft is a felony if it is committed for a commercial purpose or for private financial gain, or if the value of the stolen information exceeds $5,000. Penalties include fines and imprisonment for up to twenty years.

---

24. 18 U.S.C. Section 1030.

Reviewing . . . Criminal Law and Cyber Crime

Edward Hanousek worked for Pacific & Arctic Railway and Navigation Company (P&A) as a roadmaster of the White Pass & Yukon Railroad in Alaska. As an officer of the corporation, Hanousek was responsible "for every detail of the safe and efficient maintenance and construction of track, structures, and marine facilities of the entire railroad," including special projects. One project was a rock quarry, known as "6-mile," above the Skagway River. Next to the quarry, and just beneath the surface, ran a high-pressure oil pipeline owned by Pacific & Arctic Pipeline, Inc., P&A's sister company. When the quarry's backhoe operator punctured the pipeline, an estimated 1,000 to 5,000 gallons of oil were discharged into the river. Hanousek was charged with negligently discharging a harmful quantity of oil into a navigable water of the United States in violation of the criminal provisions of the Clean Water Act (CWA). Using the information presented in the chapter, answer the following questions.

1. Did Hanousek have the required mental state (*mens rea*) to be convicted of a crime? Why or why not?
2. Which theory discussed in the chapter would enable a court to hold Hanousek criminally liable for violating the statute regardless of whether he participated in, directed, or even knew about the specific violation?
3. Could the quarry's backhoe operator who punctured the pipeline also be charged with a crime in this situation? Explain.
4. Suppose that, at trial, Hanousek argued that he could not be convicted because he was not aware of the requirements of the CWA. Would this defense be successful? Why or why not?

Debate This Because of overcriminalization, particularly by the federal government, Americans may be breaking the law regularly without knowing it. Should Congress rescind many of the more than four thousand federal crimes now on the books?

LINKING BUSINESS LAW to Accounting and Finance

Protecting Your Company against the Hacking of Its Bank Accounts

Each year, conventional, old-fashioned crooks rob banks to the tune of about $50 million. In contrast, every year cybercrooks steal billions of dollars from the bank accounts of small and mid-size companies in Europe and the United States. Why? The reason is that small businesses tend to be lax in protecting themselves from hackers. They keep their accounts in community or regional banks, have only rudimentary security measures, and usually fail to hire an on-site cyber security expert.

You May Not Receive Compensation for Your Losses

Many small-business owners believe that if their bank accounts are hacked and disappear, their banks will reimburse them. That is not always the case, however. Just ask Mark Patterson, the owner of Patco Construction in Stanford, Maryland. He lost more than $350,000 to cyberthieves. When People's United Bank would not agree to a settlement, Patterson sued, claiming that the bank

should have monitored his account. So far, federal judges have agreed with the bank—that its protections were "commercially reasonable," which is the only standard that banks have to follow.

Insurance May Not Be the Answer

Similarly, small-business owners often think that their regular insurance policy will cover cyber losses at their local banks. In reality, unless there is a specific "rider" to a business's insurance policy, its bank accounts are not covered. So, just because your business will be reimbursed if thieves break in and steal your machines and network servers, that does not mean you will be covered if cybercrooks break into your bank account.

Critical Thinking

What steps can a businessperson take with the company's bank and its employees to minimize the risk of hacking?

Key Terms

Chapter Summary: Criminal Law and Cyber Crime

Civil Law and Criminal Law	1. *Civil law*—Spells out the duties that exist between persons or between persons and their governments, excluding the duty not to commit crimes. 2. *Criminal law*—Has to do with crimes, which are wrongs against society proclaimed in statutes and, if committed, punishable by society through fines and/or imprisonment—and, in some cases, death. Because crimes are *offenses against society as a whole*, they are prosecuted by a public official, not by the victims. 3. *Key differences*—An important difference between civil and criminal law is that the standard of proof is higher in criminal cases (see Exhibit 6–1 for other differences between civil and criminal law). 4. *Civil liability for criminal acts*—A criminal act may give rise to both criminal liability and tort liability.
Criminal Liability	1. *Guilty act*—In general, some form of harmful act must be committed for a crime to exist. 2. *Intent*—An intent to commit a crime, or a wrongful mental state, is generally required for a crime to exist.

Types of Crimes	1. Crimes fall into five general categories: violent crime, property crime, public order crime, white-collar crime, and organized crime.
	    a. Violent crimes are those that cause others to suffer harm or death, including murder, assault and battery, sexual assault (rape), and robbery.
	    b. Property crimes are the most common form of crime. The offender's goal is to obtain some economic gain or to damage property. This category includes burglary, larceny, obtaining goods by false pretenses, receiving stolen property, arson, and forgery.
	    c. Public order crimes are acts, such as public drunkenness, prostitution, gambling, and illegal drug use, that a statute has established are contrary to public values and morals.
	    d. White-collar crimes are illegal acts committed by a person or business using nonviolent means to obtain a personal or business advantage. Usually, such crimes are committed in the course of a legitimate occupation. Examples include embezzlement, mail and wire fraud, bribery, theft of trade secrets, and insider trading.
	    e. Organized crime is a form of crime conducted by groups operating illegitimately to satisfy the public's demand for illegal goods and services (such as gambling or illegal narcotics). This category of crime also includes money laundering and racketeering (RICO) violations.
	2. Crimes may also be classified according to their degree of seriousness. Felonies are serious crimes punishable by death or by imprisonment for more than one year. Misdemeanors are less serious crimes punishable by fines or by confinement for up to one year.

Defenses to Criminal Liability	Defenses to criminal liability include justifiable use of force, necessity, insanity, mistake, duress, entrapment, and the statute of limitations. Also, in some cases defendants may be relieved of criminal liability, at least in part, if they are given immunity.

Criminal Procedures	1. *Fourth Amendment*—Provides protection against unreasonable searches and seizures, and requires that probable cause exist before a warrant for a search or an arrest can be issued.
	2. *Fifth Amendment*—Requires due process of law, prohibits double jeopardy, and protects against self-incrimination.
	3. *Sixth Amendment*—Guarantees a speedy trial, a trial by jury, a public trial, the right to confront witnesses, and the right to counsel.
	4. *Eighth Amendment*—Prohibits excessive bail and fines, and cruel and unusual punishment.
	5. *Exclusionary rule*—A criminal procedural rule that prohibits the introduction at trial of all evidence obtained in violation of constitutional rights, as well as any evidence derived from the illegally obtained evidence.
	6. *Miranda rule*—A rule set forth by the Supreme Court in *Miranda v. Arizona* holding that individuals who are arrested must be informed of certain constitutional rights, including their right to counsel.
	7. *Criminal Process*—
	    a. *Arrest, indictment, and trial*—Procedures governing arrest, indictment, and trial for a crime are designed to safeguard the rights of the individual against the state. See Exhibit 6–2 for a summary of the procedural steps involved in prosecuting a criminal case.
	    b. *Sentencing guidelines*—The federal government has established sentencing laws or guidelines, which are no longer mandatory but provide a range of penalties for each federal crime.

Cyber Crime	1. *Cyber fraud*—Occurs when misrepresentations are knowingly made over the Internet to deceive another. Two widely reported forms are online auction fraud and online retail fraud. 2. *Cyber theft*—In cyberspace, thieves can steal data from anywhere in the world. Identity theft is made easier by the fact that many e-businesses store information such as the consumer's name, e-mail address, and credit-card numbers. Phishing and employment fraud are variations of identity theft. The financial burden of stolen credit-card numbers falls more on merchants and credit-card issuers than on consumers. 3. *Hacking*—A hacker is a person who uses one computer to break into another.

Chapter Summary: Criminal Law and Cyber Crime—Continued

Cyber Crime—Continued	4. *Cyberterrorism*—Cyberterrrorists aim to cause serious problems for computer systems. A cyberterrorist attack on a major U.S. financial institution or telecommunications system could have serious repercussions, including jeopardizing national security.
	5. *Prosecution of cyber crime*—Prosecuting cyber crime is more difficult than prosecuting traditional crime. Identifying the wrongdoer through electronic footprints left on the Internet is complicated, and jurisdictional issues may arise when the suspect lives in another jurisdiction or nation. A significant federal statute addressing cyber crime is the Computer Fraud and Abuse Act.

Issue Spotters

1. Dana takes her roommate's credit card, intending to charge expenses that she incurs on a vacation. Her first stop is a gas station, where she uses the card to pay for gas. With respect to the gas station, has she committed a crime? If so, what is it? (See *Types of Crimes.*)
2. Without permission, Ben downloads consumer credit files from a computer belonging to Consumer Credit Agency. He then sells the data to Dawn. Has Ben committed a crime? If so, what is it? (See *Types of Crimes.*)

—**Check your answers to the Issue Spotters against the answers provided in Appendix D at the end of this text.**

For Review

1. What two elements normally must exist before a person can be held liable for a crime?
2. What are five broad categories of crimes? What is white-collar crime?
3. What defenses can be raised to avoid liability for criminal acts?
4. What constitutional safeguards exist to protect persons accused of crimes?
5. How has the Internet expanded opportunities for identity theft?

Business Scenarios and Case Problems

6–1. Types of Cyber Crimes. The following situations are similar, but each represents a variation of a particular crime. Identify the crime and point out the differences in the variations. (See *Cyber Crime.*)

1. Chen, posing fraudulently as Diamond Credit Card Co., sends an e-mail to Emily, stating that the company has observed suspicious activity in her account and has frozen the account. The e-mail asks her to reregister her credit-card number and password to reopen the account.
2. Claiming falsely to be Big Buy Retail Finance Co., Conner sends an e-mail to Dino, asking him to confirm or update his personal security information to prevent his Big Buy account from being discontinued.
3. Felicia posts her résumé on GotWork.com, an online job-posting site, seeking a position in business and managerial finance and accounting. Hayden, who misrepresents himself as an employment officer with International Bank & Commerce Corp., sends her an e-mail asking for more personal information.

6–2. Cyber Scam. Kayla, a student at Learnwell University, owes $20,000 in unpaid tuition. If Kayla does not pay the tuition, Learnwell will not allow her to graduate. To obtain the funds to pay the debt, she sends e-mails to people that she does not know asking them for financial help to send her child, who has a disability, to a special school. In reality, Kayla has no children. Is this a crime? If so, which one? (See *Cyber Crime.*)

6–3. Fourth Amendment. Three police officers, including Maria Trevizo, pulled over a car with suspended registration. One of the occupants, Lemon Johnson, wore clothing consistent with membership in the Crips gang. Trevizo searched him "for officer safety" and found a gun. Johnson was charged with illegal possession of a weapon. What standard should apply to an officer's search of a passenger during a traffic stop? Should a warrant be required? Could a search proceed solely on the basis of probable cause? Would a reasonable suspicion short of probable cause be enough? Discuss. [*Arizona v. Johnson*, 555 U.S. 323, 129 S.Ct. 781, 172 L.Ed.2d 694 (2009)] (See *Criminal Procedures.*)

6–4. Searches. Charles Byrd was in a minimum-security county jail awaiting trial. A team of sheriff's deputies wearing T-shirts and jeans took Byrd and several other inmates into a room for a strip search without any apparent justification. Byrd was ordered to remove all his clothing except his boxer shorts. A female deputy searched Byrd while several male deputies watched. One of the male deputies videotaped the search. Byrd filed a suit against the sheriff's department. Did the search violate Byrd's rights? Discuss. [*Byrd v. Maricopa County Sheriff's Department,* 629 F.3d. 1135 (9th Cir. 2011)] (See *Criminal Procedures.*)

6–5. Credit- and Debit-Card Theft. Jacqueline Barden was shopping for school clothes with her children when her purse and automobile were taken. In Barden's purse were her car keys, credit and debit cards for herself and her children, as well as the children's Social Security cards and birth certificates needed for enrollment at school. Immediately after the purse and car were stolen, Rebecca Mary Turner attempted to use Barden's credit card at a local Exxon gas station, but the card was declined. The gas station attendant recognized Turner because she had previously written bad checks and used credit cards that did not belong to her.

Turner was later arrested while attempting to use one of Barden's checks to pay for merchandise at a Wal-Mart—where the clerk also recognized Turner from prior criminal activity. Turner claimed that she had not stolen Barden's purse or car, and that a friend had told her he had some checks and credit cards and asked her to try using them at Wal-Mart. Turner was convicted at trial. She appealed, claiming that there was insufficient evidence that she committed credit- and debit-card theft. Was the evidence sufficient to uphold her conviction? Why or why not? [*Turner v. State of Arkansas,* 2012 Ark.App. 150 (2012)] (See *Cyber Crime.*)

6–6. ⚖ **Business Case Problem with Sample Answer— Criminal Liability.** During the morning rush hour, David Green threw bottles and plates from a twenty-sixth-floor hotel balcony overlooking Seventh Avenue in New York City. A video of the incident also showed him doing cartwheels while holding a beer bottle and sprinting toward the balcony while holding a glass steadily in his hand. When he saw police on the street below and on the roof of the building across the street, he suspended his antics but resumed tossing objects off the balcony after the police left. He later admitted that he could recall what he had done, but claimed to have been intoxicated and said his only purpose was to amuse himself and his friends. Did Green have the mental state required to establish criminal liability? Discuss. [*People v. Green,* 104 A.D.3d 126, 958 N.Y.S.2d 138 (1 Dept. 2013)] (See *Criminal Liability.*)

—For a sample answer to Problem 6–6, go to Appendix E at the end of this text.

6–7. White-Collar Crime. Matthew Simpson and others created and operated a series of corporate entities to defraud telecommunications companies, creditors, credit reporting agencies, and others. Through these entities, Simpson and the others used routing codes and spoofing services to make long-distance calls appear to be local. They stole other firms' network capacity and diverted payments to themselves. They leased goods and services without paying for them. To hide their association with their corporate entities and with each other, they used false identities, addresses, and credit histories, and issued false bills, invoices, financial statements, and credit references,. Did these acts constitute mail and wire fraud? Discuss. [*United States v. Simpson,* 741 F.3d 539 (5th Cir. 2014)] (See *Types of Crimes.*)

6–8. ⬌ **A Question of Ethics—Identity Theft.** Twenty-year-old Davis Omole had good grades in high school, where he played on the football and chess teams, and went on to college. Omole worked at a cell phone store where he stole customers' personal information. He used the stolen identities to create a hundred different accounts on eBay, and held more than three hundred auctions listing for sale items that he did not own (including cell phones, plasma televisions, and stereos). From these auctions, he collected $90,000. To avoid getting caught, he continuously closed and opened the eBay accounts, activated and deactivated cell phone and e-mail accounts, and changed mailing addresses and post office boxes. Omole, who had previously been convicted in a state court for Internet fraud, was convicted in a federal district court of identity theft and wire fraud. [*United States v. Omole,* 523 F.3d 691 (7th Cir. 2008)] (See *Cyber Crime.*)

1. Omole displayed contempt for the court and ridiculed his victims, calling them stupid for having been cheated. What does this behavior suggest about Omole's ethics?

2. Under federal sentencing guidelines, Omole could have been imprisoned for more than eight years. He received only three years, however, two of which comprised the mandatory sentence for identity theft. Was this sentence too lenient? Explain.

CHAPTER 7

(AP Photo/Shuji Kajiyama)

International Law in a Global Economy

CONTENTS

- International Law
- Doing Business Internationally
- Regulation of Specific Business Activities
- International Contracts
- Payment Methods
- U.S. Laws in a Global Context

LEARNING OBJECTIVES

The five learning objectives below are designed to help improve your understanding of the chapter. After reading this chapter, you should be able to answer the following questions:

1. What is the principle of comity, and why do courts deciding disputes involving a foreign law or judicial decree apply this principle?

2. What is the act of state doctrine? In what circumstances is this doctrine applied?

3. Under the Foreign Sovereign Immunities Act, in what situations is a foreign state subject to the jurisdiction of U.S. courts?

4. What are three clauses commonly included in international business contracts?

5. What federal law allows U.S. citizens, as well as citizens of foreign nations, to file civil actions in U.S. courts for torts that were committed overseas?

"The merchant has no country."
—Thomas Jefferson, 1743–1826 (Third president of the United States, 1801–1809)

International business transactions are not unique to the modern world. Indeed, commerce has always crossed national borders, as President Thomas Jefferson noted in the chapter-opening quotation. What is new in our day is the dramatic growth in world trade and the emergence of a global business community. Because exchanges of goods, services, and intellectual property on a global level are now routine, students of business law and the legal environment should be familiar with the laws pertaining to international business transactions.

Laws affecting the international legal environment of business include both international law and national law. As discussed in Chapter 1, *international law* is defined as a body of law—formed as a result of international customs, treaties, and organizations—that governs relations among or between nations.

International law may be public, creating standards for the nations themselves. It may also be private, establishing international standards for private transactions that cross national borders. (Can officials legally search electronic devices, including laptops and smartphones, of persons who cross national borders? See this chapter's *Beyond Our Borders* feature for the answer.) *National law,* as pointed out in Chapter 1, is the law of a particular nation, such as Brazil, Germany, Japan, or the United States. In this chapter, we examine how both international law and national law frame business operations in the global context.

International Law

The major difference between international law and national law is that government authorities can enforce national law. What government, however, can enforce international law? By definition, a *nation* is a sovereign entity—meaning that there is no higher authority to which that nation must submit.

If a nation violates an international law and persuasive tactics fail, other countries or international organizations have no recourse except to take coercive actions. Coercive actions might include economic sanctions, severance of diplomatic relations, boycotts, and, as a last resort, war against the violating nation. **EXAMPLE 7.1**   In 2014, Russia sent troops into the neighboring nation of Ukraine and supported an election that allowed Crimea (part of Ukraine) to secede from Ukraine. Because Russia's actions violated Ukraine's independent sovereignty, the U.S. and the European Union imposed economic sanctions on Russia. ●

BEYOND OUR BORDERS   Border Searches of Your Electronic Devices

Every year, tens of millions of travelers arrive at U.S. borders where they are subject to a search. Of these travelers, about 12 million undergo a secondary screening, and approximately five thousand of these screenings involve an electronic device. About three hundred devices—computers, BlackBerrys, tablets, and smartphones—are sent to the Immigration and Customs Enforcement forensics laboratory in Fairfax, Virginia, for further examination.

The U.S. government has historically had a broad power to search travelers and their property when they enter this country. That power includes the right to inspect papers and other physical documents in the possession of anyone entering the United States, including U.S. citizens.

A Legal Challenge to Extensive Searches of Electronic Devices

Increasingly, however, instead of being carried in physical form, documents are carried on the hard drives of laptop computers, in tablets, or in smartphones. Indeed, a person might have thousands and thousands of photos, e-mails, video clips, and

documents on the hard drive of a laptop. Does the government's power to conduct border searches give it the right to rummage through all of the data on an electronic device? Several recent lawsuits have raised this issue.

When Pascal Abidor, a Ph.D. student who has dual U.S. and French citizenship, traveled by train from Canada to New York, U.S. Customs and Border Control agents pulled him aside and required him to log on to his computer. They then examined much of its contents. Abidor was released after a few hours, but the Department of Homeland Security kept his laptop for eleven days. Abidor challenged the search. His complaint alleged:

> [A government policy that authorizes] the suspicionless search of the contents of Americans' laptops, cell phones, cameras, and other electronic devices at the international border . . . violates the constitutional rights of American citizens to keep the private and expressive details of their lives, as well as sensitive information obtained or created in the course of their work, free from unwarranted government scrutiny.

The lawsuit was dismissed in 2013 when the federal court concluded that Abidor lacked standing (see Chapter 3) to challenge the government's border search policies.[a]

Protecting Attorney-Client Privilege

Border searches present a special problem for attorneys because they have a duty to protect the attorney-client privilege by preventing anyone, including the government, from accessing client communications. To avoid this problem, attorneys should never keep client files on a digital device that they are taking abroad. If the attorneys will need the files during the trip abroad, they can be put on a server in the "cloud."

Critical Thinking

What are some steps that businesspersons can take to avoid any issues at the border with respect to the contents of their electronic devices?

---

a. *Abidor v. Napolitano,* ___ F.Supp.2d ___, 2013 WL 6912654 (E.D.N.Y. 2013).

International law attempts to reconcile the need of each country to be the final authority over its own affairs with the desire of nations to benefit economically from trade and harmonious relations with one another. Sovereign nations can, and do, voluntarily agree to be governed in certain respects by international law for the purpose of facilitating international trade and commerce, as well as civilized discourse. As a result, a body of international law has evolved.

Sources of International Law

Basically, there are three sources of international law: international customs, treaties and international agreements, and international organizations. We look at each of these sources here.

International Customs
One important source of international law consists of the international customs that have evolved among nations in their relations with one another. Article 38(1) of the Statute of the International Court of Justice refers to an international custom as "evidence of a general practice accepted as law." The legal principles and doctrines that you will read about shortly are rooted in international customs and traditions that have evolved over time in the international arena.

Treaties and International Agreements
Treaties and other explicit agreements between or among foreign nations provide another important source of international law. A **treaty** is an agreement or contract between two or more nations that must be authorized and ratified by the supreme power of each nation. Under Article II, Section 2, of the U.S. Constitution, the president has the power "by and with the Advice and Consent of the Senate, to make Treaties, provided two-thirds of the Senators present concur."

A *bilateral* agreement, as the term implies, is an agreement formed by two nations to govern their commercial exchanges or other relations with one another. A *multilateral* agreement is formed by several nations. For instance, regional trade associations such as the Andean Common Market (ANCOM), the Association of Southeast Asian Nations (ASEAN), and the European Union (EU) are the result of multilateral trade agreements.

Treaty A formal international agreement negotiated between two nations or among several nations. In the United States, all treaties must be approved by the Senate.

International Organizations
In international law, the term **international organization** generally refers to an organization that is composed mainly of member nations and usually established by treaty. The United States is a member of more than one hundred bilateral and multilateral organizations, including at least twenty through the United Nations.

International Organization An organization that is composed mainly of member nations and usually established by treaty—for example, the United Nations.

Adopt Resolutions These organizations adopt resolutions, declarations, and other types of standards that often require nations to behave in a particular manner. The General Assembly of the United Nations, for instance, has adopted numerous nonbinding resolutions and declarations that embody principles of international law. Disputes with respect to these resolutions and declarations may be brought before the International Court of Justice. That court, however, normally has authority to settle legal disputes only when nations voluntarily submit to its jurisdiction.

Create Uniform Rules The United Nations Commission on International Trade Law has made considerable progress in establishing uniformity in international law as it relates to trade and commerce. One of the commission's most significant creations to date is the 1980 Convention on Contracts for the International Sale of Goods (CISG).

As you will read in Chapter 12, the CISG is similar to Article 2 of the Uniform Commercial Code in that it is designed to settle disputes between parties to sales contracts. It spells out the duties of international buyers and sellers that will apply if the parties have not agreed otherwise in their contracts. The CISG governs only sales contracts between trading partners in nations that have ratified the CISG, however.

General-Secretary of the United Nations (UN) Ban Ki-moon shakes hands with former U.S. secretary of state Hillary Clinton. Why do governments support the UN?

Comity The principle by which one nation defers to and gives effect to the laws and judicial decrees of another nation. This recognition is based primarily on respect.

Learning Objective 1
What is the principle of comity, and why do courts deciding disputes involving a foreign law or judicial decree apply this principle?

International Principles and Doctrines

Over time, a number of legal principles and doctrines have evolved and have been employed by the courts of various nations to resolve or reduce conflicts that involve a foreign element. The three important legal principles discussed next are based primarily on courtesy and respect, and are applied in the interests of maintaining harmonious relations among nations.

The Principle of Comity   Under the principle of **comity,** one nation will defer to and give effect to the laws and judicial decrees of another country, as long as they are consistent with the law and public policy of the accommodating nation. For instance, a U.S. court ordinarily will recognize and enforce a default judgment (see Chapter 3) from an Australian court because the legal procedures in Australia are compatible with those in the United States. Nearly all nations recognize the validity of marriage decrees (at least those between a man and a woman) issued in another country.

CASE EXAMPLE 7.2   Karen Goldberg's husband was killed in a terrorist bombing in Israel. She filed a lawsuit in a federal court in New York against UBS AG, a Switzerland-based global financial services company with many offices in the United States. Goldberg claimed that UBS was liable under the U.S. Anti-Terrorism Act for aiding and abetting the murder of her husband. She argued that UBS was liable because it provided financial services to the international terrorist organizations responsible for his murder.

UBS requested that the case be transferred to a court in Israel, which would offer a remedy "substantially the same" as the one available in the United States. The court refused, however. Transferring the case would require an Israeli court to take evidence and judge the emotional damage suffered by Goldberg, "raising distinct concerns of comity and enforceability."[1] ●

In the following case, the court was asked to balance interests that were significant and serious to all of the parties. The defendant wanted the court to give particular weight to the principle of comity.

1. *Goldberg v. UBS AG*, 690 F.Supp.2d 92 (E.D.N.Y. 2010).

Case 7.1

Linde v. Arab Bank, PLCᵃ
United States Court of Appeals, Second Circuit, 706 F.3d 92 (2013).

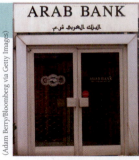

COMPANY PROFILE *Founded in 1930, Arab Bank is one of the largest financial institutions in the Middle East. Headquartered in Jordan, it serves clients in more than 500 branches in thirty countries, including branches in Australia, New York, and Switzerland. The bank is a major economic engine in Jordan and throughout the Middle East/Northern Africa, providing modern banking services and capital, and facilitating development and trade throughout the region.*

BACKGROUND AND FACTS Victims of terrorist attacks that were committed in Israel between 1995 and 2004—during a period commonly referred to as the Second Intifada—filed a

---

a. *PLC stands for public liability company, which is a publicly traded company in England and Ireland. This business form is the equivalent of a publicly traded corporation in the United States.*

Case 7.1—Continued

suit in a federal district court against Arab Bank, PLC, seeking damages under the Anti-Terrorism Act (ATA) and the Alien Tort Claims Act. According to plaintiffs, Arab Bank provided financial services and support to the terrorists. Over several years and despite multiple discovery orders, the bank failed to produce certain documents relevant to the case. As a result, the court issued an order imposing sanctions. Arab Bank appealed to the U.S. Court of Appeals for the Second Circuit, arguing that the order was an abuse of discretion.

IN THE WORDS OF THE COURT . . .
Susan L. *CARNEY,* Circuit Judge:
   * * * *
   * * * The Bank argues that the documents are covered by foreign bank secrecy laws such that their disclosure would subject the Bank to criminal prosecution and other penalties in several foreign jurisdictions. The sanctions order takes the form of a jury instruction that would permit—but not require—the jury to infer from the Bank's failure to produce these documents that the Bank provided financial services to designated foreign terrorist organizations, and did so knowingly.
   * * * *
   The District Court carefully explained its decision to impose this sanction. It noted that many of the documents that plaintiffs had already obtained tended to support the inference that Arab Bank knew that its services benefited terrorists. According to the District Court, these documents included * * * documents from Arab Bank's Lebanon branch that suggested * * * Arab Bank officials approved the transfer of funds into an account at that branch despite the fact that the transfers listed known terrorists as beneficiaries. As a consequence of * * * Arab Bank's non-disclosure, the court reasoned, plaintiffs would be "hard-pressed to show that * * * these transfers were not approved by mistake, but instead are representative of numerous other transfers to terrorists." The permissive inference instruction will, according to the District Court, help to rectify this evidentiary imbalance.
   * * * *
   Arab Bank argues that the District Court's decisions ordering production and imposing sanctions should be vacated because they offend international comity. This argument derives from the notion that the sanctions force foreign authorities either to waive enforcement of their bank secrecy laws or to enforce those laws,

and in so doing create an allegedly devastating financial liability for the leading financial institution in their region. The Bank asserts, further, that international comity principles merit special weight here because the District Court's decisions affect the United States' interests in combating terrorism and pertain to a region of the world pivotal to United States foreign policy.
   * * * The [District] Court expressly noted that it had "considered the interests of the United States *and* the foreign jurisdictions whose foreign bank secrecy laws are at issue."
   Additionally, international comity calls for more than an examination of only some of the interests of some foreign states. Rather, the concept of international comity requires a particularized analysis of the respective interests of the foreign nation and the requesting nation. In other words, the analysis invites a weighing of all *of the relevant interests of* all *of the nations affected by the court's decision.* * * * The District Court recognized the legal conflict faced by Arab Bank and the comity interests implicated by the bank secrecy laws. But [the Court] also observed—and properly so—that Jordan and Lebanon have expressed a strong interest in deterring the financial support of terrorism, and that these interests have often outweighed the enforcement of bank secrecy laws, even in the view of the foreign states. Moreover, * * * the District Court took into account the United States' interests in the effective prosecution of civil claims under the ATA [Anti-Terrorism Act]. This type of holistic, multi-factored analysis does not so obviously offend international comity. [Emphasis added.]

DECISION AND REMEDY   The U.S. Court of Appeals for the Second Circuit affirmed the lower court's decision and order. There is no abuse of discretion in concluding that the interest of other nations in enforcing bank secrecy laws are outweighed by the need to impede terrorism "as embodied in the tort remedies provided by U.S. civil law and the stated commitments of the foreign nations."

THE ETHICAL DIMENSION   *Is it unethical to give the interest of fighting terrorism precedence over an international legal principle? Discuss.*

THE LEGAL ENVIRONMENT DIMENSION   *What interests were at stake in the dispute at the heart of this case?*

The Act of State Doctrine

The **act of state doctrine** provides that the judicial branch of one country will not examine the validity of public acts committed by a recognized foreign government within its own territory.

CASE EXAMPLE 7.3   Spectrum Stores, Inc., a gasoline retailer in the United States, filed a lawsuit in a U.S. court against Citgo Petroleum Corporation, which is owned by the

> **Act of State Doctrine** A doctrine providing that the judicial branch of one country will not examine the validity of public acts committed by a recognized foreign government within its own territory.

Learning Objective 2
What is the act of state doctrine? In what circumstances is this doctrine applied?

government of Venezuela. Spectrum alleged that Citgo had conspired with other oil companies in Venezuela and Saudi Arabia to limit production of crude oil and thereby fix the prices of petroleum products sold in the United States.

Because Citgo is owned by a foreign government, the U.S. court dismissed the case under the act of state doctrine. A government controls the natural resources, such as oil reserves, within its territory. A U.S. court will not rule on the validity of a foreign government's acts within its own territory.[2] ●

When a Foreign Government Takes Private Property   The act of state doctrine can have important consequences for individuals and firms doing business with, and investing in, other countries. This doctrine is frequently employed in situations involving expropriation or confiscation.

Expropriation   A government's seizure of a privately owned business or personal property for a proper public purpose and with just compensation.

Confiscation   A government's taking of a privately owned business or personal property without a proper public purpose or an award of just compensation.

Expropriation occurs when a government seizes a privately owned business or privately owned goods for a proper public purpose and awards just compensation. When a government seizes private property for an illegal purpose or without just compensation, the taking is referred to as a **confiscation.** The line between these two forms of taking is sometimes blurred because of differing interpretations of what is illegal and what constitutes just compensation.

EXAMPLE 7.4   Flaherty, Inc., a U.S. company, owns a mine in Argentina. The government of Argentina seizes the mine for public use and claims that the profits that Flaherty realized from the mine in preceding years constitute just compensation. Flaherty disagrees, but the act of state doctrine may prevent the company's recovery in a U.S. court. ● Note that in a case alleging that a foreign government has wrongfully taken the plaintiff's property, the defendant government has the burden of proving that the taking was an expropriation, not a confiscation.

Doctrine May Immunize a Foreign Government's Actions   When applicable, both the act of state doctrine and the doctrine of *sovereign immunity* (to be discussed next) tend to immunize (protect) foreign governments from the jurisdiction of U.S. courts. This means that firms or individuals who own property overseas often have diminished legal protection against government actions in the countries in which they operate.

The Doctrine of Sovereign Immunity

When certain conditions are satisfied, the doctrine of **sovereign immunity** immunizes foreign nations from the jurisdiction of U.S. courts. In 1976, Congress codified this rule in the Foreign Sovereign Immunities Act (FSIA).[3] The FSIA exclusively governs the circumstances in which an action may be brought in the United States against a foreign nation, including attempts to attach a foreign nation's property. Because the law is jurisdictional in nature, a plaintiff has the burden of showing that a defendant is not entitled to sovereign immunity.

Sovereign Immunity   A doctrine that immunizes foreign nations from the jurisdiction of U.S. courts when certain conditions are satisfied.

Section 1605 of the FSIA sets forth the major exceptions to the jurisdictional immunity of a foreign state. A foreign state is not immune from the jurisdiction of U.S. courts in the following situations:

1. When the foreign state has waived its immunity either explicitly or by implication.
2. When the foreign state has engaged in commercial activity within the United States or in commercial activity outside the United States that has "a direct effect in the United States."[4]
3. When the foreign state has committed a tort in the United States or has violated certain international laws.

Learning Objective 3
Under the Foreign Sovereign Immunities Act, in what situations is a foreign state subject to the jurisdiction of U.S. courts?

---

2. *Spectrum Stores, Inc. v. Citgo Petroleum Corp.,* 632 F.3d 938 (5th Cir. 2011).
3. 28 U.S.C. Sections 1602–1611.
4. See, for example, *Triple A. Intern., Inc. v. Democratic Republic of Congo,* 852 F.Supp.2d 839 (E.D. Mich. 2012).

In applying the FSIA, questions frequently arise as to whether an entity is a "foreign state" and what constitutes a "commercial activity." Under Section 1603 of the FSIA, a *foreign state* includes both a political subdivision of a foreign state and an instrumentality of a foreign state. Section 1603 broadly defines a *commercial activity* as a commercial activity that is carried out by a foreign state within the United States, but it does not describe the particulars of what constitutes a commercial activity. Thus, the courts are left to decide whether a particular activity is governmental or commercial in nature.

Doing Business Internationally

A U.S. domestic firm can engage in international business transactions in a number of ways. The simplest way is for U.S. firms to **export** their goods and services to markets abroad. Alternatively, a U.S. firm can establish foreign production facilities so as to be closer to the foreign market or markets in which its products are sold. The advantages may include lower labor costs, fewer government regulations, and lower taxes and trade barriers. A domestic firm may engage in manufacturing abroad by licensing its technology to an existing foreign company or by establishing overseas subsidiaries or joint ventures.

Export The sale of goods and services by domestic firms to buyers located in other countries.

Exporting

Exporting can take two forms: direct exporting and indirect exporting. In *direct exporting*, a U.S. company signs a sales contract with a foreign purchaser that provides for the conditions of shipment and payment for the goods. (How payments are made in international transactions will be discussed later in this chapter.) If sufficient business develops in a foreign country, a U.S. corporation may set up a specialized marketing organization in that foreign market by appointing a foreign agent or distributor. This is called *indirect exporting*.

When a U.S. firm desires to limit its involvement in an international market, it will typically establish an *agency relationship* with a foreign firm. (*Agency* will be discussed in Chapter 16.) The foreign firm then acts as the U.S. firm's agent and can enter into contracts in the foreign location on behalf of the principal (the U.S. company).

"Commerce is the great civilizer. We exchange ideas when we exchange fabrics."

Robert G. Ingersoll, 1833–1899 (American politician and orator)

Distributorships
When a foreign country represents a substantial market, a U.S. firm may wish to appoint a distributor located in that country. The U.S. firm and the distributor enter into a **distribution agreement.** This is a contract setting out the terms and conditions of the distributorship, such as price, currency of payment, availability of supplies, and method of payment. Disputes concerning distribution agreements may involve jurisdictional or other issues, as well as contract law, which will be discussed later in this chapter.

Distribution Agreement A contract between a seller and a distributor of the seller's products setting out the terms and conditions of the distributorship.

The National Export Initiative
Although the United States is one of the world's major exporters, exports make up a much smaller share of annual output in the United States than they do in our most important trading partners. In the past, the United States has not promoted exports as actively as many other nations have.

In an effort to increase U.S. exports, the Obama administration created the National Export Initiative (NEI) with a goal of doubling U.S. exports by 2015. Some commentators believe that another goal of the NEI is to reduce outsourcing—the practice of having manufacturing or other activities performed in lower-wage countries such as China and India.

Export Promotion An important component of the NEI is the Export Promotion Cabinet, which includes officials from sixteen government agencies and departments. All cabinet members must submit detailed plans to the president, outlining the steps that they will take to increase U.S. exports.

The U.S. Commerce Department plays a leading role in the NEI, and hundreds of its trade experts serve as advocates to help some twenty thousand U.S. companies increase their export sales. In addition, the Commerce Department and other cabinet members work to promote U.S. exports in the high-growth developing markets of Brazil, China, and India. The members also identify market opportunities in fast-growing sectors, such as environmental goods and services, biotechnology, and renewable energy.

Increased Export Financing   Under the NEI, the Export-Import Bank of the United States increased the financing that it makes available to small and medium-sized businesses by 50 percent. In the initial phase, the bank added hundreds of new small-business clients that sell a wide variety of products, from sophisticated polymers to date palm trees and nanotechnology-based cosmetics.

PREVENTING LEGAL DISPUTES   In light of the National Export Initiative, managers in companies that are now outsourcing or thinking of doing so may wish to reconsider. Increasingly, the federal government is taking a stance against outsourcing. As long as unemployment remains high in the United States, the emphasis will be on the creation of jobs at home. These efforts will often be backed by subsidies and access to federally supported borrowing initiatives.

Manufacturing Abroad

An alternative to direct or indirect exporting is the establishment of foreign manufacturing facilities. Typically, U.S. firms establish manufacturing plants abroad if they believe that doing so will reduce their costs—particularly for labor, shipping, and raw materials—and enable them to compete more effectively in foreign markets. Foreign firms have done the same in the United States. Sony, Nissan, and other Japanese manufacturers have established U.S. plants to avoid import duties that the U.S. Congress may impose on Japanese products entering this country.

Licensing   A U.S. firm may license a foreign manufacturing company to use its copyrighted, patented, or trademarked intellectual property or trade secrets. A licensing agreement with a foreign-based firm calls for a payment of royalties on some basis—such as so many cents per unit produced or a certain percentage of profits from units sold in a particular geographic territory.

Chinese workers assemble cars at a Ford plant in Chongqing, China. Why would Ford build a plant outside the United States?

(AP Photo)

EXAMPLE 7.5   The Coca-Cola Bottling Company licenses firms worldwide to use (and keep confidential) its secret formula for the syrup used in its soft drink. In return, the foreign firms licensed to make the syrup pay Coca-Cola a percentage of the income earned from the sale of the soft drink. ● Once a firm's trademark is known worldwide, the firm may experience increased demand for other products it manufactures or sells. As will be discussed in Chapter 14, franchising is a well-known form of licensing.

Subsidiaries   A U.S. firm can also expand into a foreign market by establishing a wholly owned subsidiary firm in a foreign country. When a wholly owned subsidiary is established, the parent company, which remains in the United States, retains complete ownership of all the facilities in the foreign country, as well as total authority and control over all phases of the operation.

A U.S. firm can also expand into international markets through a joint venture. In a joint venture, the U.S. company owns only part of the operation. The rest is owned either by local owners in the foreign country or by another foreign entity. All of the firms involved in a joint venture share responsibilities, as well as profits and liabilities.

Regulation of Specific Business Activities

Doing business abroad can affect the economies, foreign policies, domestic policies, and other national interests of the countries involved. For this reason, nations impose laws to restrict or facilitate international business. Controls may also be imposed by international agreements. Here, we discuss how different types of international activities are regulated.

Investment Protections

Firms that invest in foreign nations face the risk that the foreign government may take possession of the investment property. Expropriation, as already mentioned, occurs when property is taken and the owner is paid just compensation for what is taken. Expropriation does not violate generally observed principles of international law.

Confiscating property without compensation (or without adequate compensation), in contrast, normally violates international law. Few remedies are available for confiscation of property by a foreign government. Claims are often resolved by lump-sum settlements after negotiations between the United States and the taking nation.

Because the possibility of confiscation may deter potential investors, many countries guarantee that foreign investors will be compensated if their property is taken. A guaranty can take the form of statutory laws or provisions in international treaties. As further protection for foreign investments, some countries provide insurance for their citizens' investments abroad.

Export Controls

The U.S. Constitution provides in Article I, Section 9, that "No Tax or Duty shall be laid on Articles exported from any State." Thus, Congress cannot impose any export taxes. Congress can, however, use a variety of other devices to restrict or encourage exports, including the following:

1. *Export quotas.* Congress sets export quotas on various items, such as grain being sold abroad.
2. *Restrictions on technology exports.* Under the Export Administration Act,[5] the flow of technologically advanced products and technical data can be restricted.
3. *Incentives and subsidies.* The United States (and other nations) also uses incentives and subsidies to stimulate other exports and thereby aid domestic businesses. **EXAMPLE 7.6** Under the Export Trading Company Act,[6] U.S. banks are encouraged to invest in export trading companies, which are formed when exporting firms join together to export a line of goods. The Export-Import Bank of the United States provides financial assistance, primarily in the form of credit guaranties given to commercial banks that in turn lend funds to U.S. exporting companies. ●

(Imaginechina via AP Images)

What type of legal agreement do the distributors of Coca-Cola in China have with the Coca-Cola Company?

---

5. 50 U.S.C. Sections 2401–2420.
6. 15 U.S.C. Sections 4001, 4003.

> "The notion dies hard that in some sort of way exports are patriotic but imports are immoral."
>
> Lord Harlech, 1918–1985 (British writer)

Import Controls

All nations have restrictions on imports, and the United States is no exception. Restrictions include strict prohibitions, quotas, and tariffs.

Prohibited Goods
Under the Trading with the Enemy Act,[7] no goods may be imported from nations that have been designated enemies of the United States. Other laws prohibit the importation of illegal drugs, books that urge insurrection against the United States,[8] and agricultural products that pose dangers to domestic crops or animals.

The importation of goods that infringe U.S. patents is also prohibited. The International Trade Commission is the government agency that investigates allegations that imported goods infringe U.S. patents and imposes penalties if necessary. **CASE EXAMPLE 7.7** Fuji Photo Film Company owned numerous patents for disposable cameras, including the plastic shell covering. Jazz Photo Corporation collected used plastic shells in the United States, shipped them abroad to have new film inserted, and imported the refurbished shells back into the United States for sale. The International Trade Commission (ITC) determined that Jazz's resale of shells originally sold outside the United States infringed Fuji's patents. The ITC ordered Jazz to stop the imports. When Jazz imported and sold 27 million more refurbished shells, Fuji complained to the ITC, which fined Jazz more than $13.5 million.[9] ●

Quota A set limit on the amount of goods that can be imported.

Tariff A tax on imported goods.

Quotas and Tariffs
Limits on the amounts of goods that can be imported are known as **quotas**. At one time, the United States had legal quotas on the number of automobiles that could be imported from Japan. Today, Japan "voluntarily" restricts the number of automobiles exported to the United States (but it builds most cars in U.S. factories).

Tariffs are taxes on imports. A tariff usually is a percentage of the value of the import, but it can be a flat rate per unit (for example, per barrel of oil). Tariffs raise the prices of goods, causing some consumers to purchase more domestically manufactured goods and fewer imported goods.

Political Factors
Sometimes, countries impose tariffs on goods from a particular nation in retaliation for political acts. **EXAMPLE 7.8** In 2009, Mexico imposed tariffs of 10 to 20 percent on ninety products exported from the United States in retaliation for the Obama administration's cancellation of a cross-border trucking program. The program had been instituted to comply with a provision in the North American Free Trade Agreement (to be discussed shortly) that called for Mexican trucks to eventually be granted full access to U.S. highways.

U.S truck drivers opposed the program, however, and consumer protection groups claimed that the Mexican trucks posed safety issues. Because the Mexican tariffs were imposed annually on $2.4 billion of U.S. goods, in 2011 President Barack Obama negotiated a deal that allowed Mexican truckers to enter the United States. In exchange, Mexico agreed to suspend half of the tariffs immediately and the remainder when the first Mexican hauler complied with the new U.S. requirements. ●

Dumping The sale of goods in a foreign country at a price below the price charged for the same goods in the domestic market.

Antidumping Duties
The United States has specific laws directed at what it sees as unfair international trade practices. **Dumping**, for instance, is the sale of imported goods at "less than fair value." "Fair value" is usually determined by the price of those goods in the exporting country. Foreign firms that engage in dumping in the United States hope

---

7. 12 U.S.C. Section 95a.
8. Because numerous sites that advocate the overthrow of the U.S. government are available on the Internet, this prohibition against importing books that urge insurrection is rather meaningless.
9. *Fuji Photo Film Co. v. International Trade Commission*, 474 F.3d 1281 (Fed.Cir. 2007).

A commercial truck crosses the border between Mexico and the United States. What treaty made this possible?

(AP Photo/*The Laredo Morning Times*, Ricardo Santos)

to undersell U.S. businesses to obtain a larger share of the U.S. market. To prevent this, an extra tariff—known as an *antidumping duty*—may be assessed on the imports.

Two U.S. government agencies are instrumental in imposing antidumping duties: the International Trade Commission (ITC) and the International Trade Administration (ITA). The ITC assesses the effects of dumping on domestic businesses and then makes recommendations to the president concerning temporary import restrictions. The ITA, which is part of the Department of Commerce, decides whether imports were sold at less than fair value. The ITA's determination establishes the amount of antidumping duties, which are set to equal the difference between the price charged in the United States and the price charged in the exporting country. A duty may be retroactive to cover past dumping.

Minimizing Trade Barriers

Restrictions on imports are also known as *trade barriers*. The elimination of trade barriers is sometimes seen as essential to the world's economic well-being. Most of the world's leading trading nations are members of the World Trade Organization (WTO), which was established in 1995.

To minimize trade barriers among nations, each member country of the WTO is required to grant **normal trade relations (NTR) status** to other member countries. This means each member is obligated to treat other members at least as well as it treats the country that receives its most favorable treatment with regard to imports or exports. Various regional trade agreements and associations also help to minimize trade barriers between nations.

Normal Trade Relations (NTR) Status
A legal trade status granted to member countries of the World Trade Organization.

The European Union (EU)
The European Union (EU) arose out the 1957 Treaty of Rome, which created the Common Market, a free trade zone comprising the nations of Belgium, France, Italy, Luxembourg, the Netherlands, and West Germany. Today, the EU is a single integrated trading unit made up of twenty-eight European nations.

The EU has gone a long way toward creating a new body of law to govern all of the member nations—although some of its efforts to create uniform laws have been confounded by nationalism. The EU's council and commission issue regulations, or directives, that define EU law in various areas, such as environmental law, product liability, anticompetitive practices, and corporations. The directives normally are binding on all member countries.

The North American Free Trade Agreement (NAFTA)
The North American Free Trade Agreement (NAFTA) created a regional trading unit consisting of Canada, Mexico, and the United States. The goal of NAFTA was to eliminate tariffs among

Flags from European countries fly in front of the European Parliament in Strasbourg, France.

these three countries on substantially all goods by reducing the tariffs incrementally over a period of time.

NAFTA gives the three countries a competitive advantage by retaining tariffs on goods imported from countries outside the NAFTA trading unit. Additionally, NAFTA provides for the elimination of barriers that traditionally have prevented the cross-border movement of services, such as financial and transportation services. NAFTA also attempts to eliminate citizenship requirements for the licensing of accountants, attorneys, physicians, and other professionals.

The Central America–Dominican Republic–United States Free Trade Agreement (CAFTA-DR)

The Central America–Dominican Republic–United States Free Trade Agreement (CAFTA-DR) was formed by Costa Rica, the Dominican Republic, El Salvador, Guatemala, Honduras, Nicaragua, and the United States. Its purpose is to reduce tariffs and improve market access among all of the signatory nations, including the United States. Legislatures in all seven countries have approved the CAFTA-DR, despite significant opposition in certain nations.

The Republic of Korea–United States Free Trade Agreement (KORUS FTA)

In 2011, the United States ratified its first free trade agreement with South Korea—the Republic of Korea–United States Free Trade Agreement (KORUS FTA). The treaty's provisions will eliminate 95 percent of each nation's tariffs on industrial and consumer exports within five years.

KORUS is the largest free trade agreement the United States has entered since NAFTA, and may boost U.S. exports by more than $10 billion a year. It will benefit U.S. automakers, farmers, ranchers, and manufacturers by enabling them to compete in new markets.

Other Free Trade Agreements

Also in 2011, Congress ratified free trade agreements with Colombia and Panama. The Colombian trade agreement included a provision requiring an exchange of tax information, and the Panama bill incorporated labor rights assurances. The administration believes that the agreements will provide an impetus for continuing the negotiation of the trans-Pacific trade initiative, aimed at increasing exports to Japan and other Asian nations.

International Contracts

Like all commercial contracts, an international contract should be in writing. For an example of an actual international sales contract from Starbucks Coffee Company, see the appendix at the end of Chapter 12.

Contract Clauses

Learning Objective 4
What are three clauses commonly included in international business contracts?

Language and legal differences among nations can create special problems for parties to international contracts when disputes arise. To avoid these problems, parties should include special provisions in the contract that designate the language of the contract, the jurisdiction where any disputes will be resolved, and the substantive law that will be applied in settling any disputes. Parties to international contracts should also indicate in their contracts what acts or events will excuse the parties from performance under the contract and whether disputes under the contract will be arbitrated or litigated.

Choice-of-Language Clause

A deal struck between a U.S. company and a company in another country normally involves two languages. Typically, many phrases in one language are not readily translatable into another. Consequently, the complex contractual terms involved may not be understood by one party in the other party's language. To make sure that no disputes arise out of this language problem, an international sales contract should have a **choice-of-language clause** designating the official language by which the contract will be interpreted in the event of disagreement.

Note also that some nations have mandatory language requirements. In France, for instance, certain legal documents, such as the prospectuses used in securities offerings (see Chapter 24), must be written in French. In addition, contracts with any departmental or local authority in France, instruction manuals, and warranties for goods and services offered for sale in France must also be written in French.

> **Choice-of-Language Clause** A clause in a contract designating the official language by which the contract will be interpreted in the event of a disagreement over the contract's terms.

Forum-Selection Clause

When a dispute arises, litigation may be pursued in courts of different nations. There are no universally accepted rules as to which court has jurisdiction over a particular subject matter or parties to a dispute. Consequently, parties to an international transaction should always include in the contract a **forum-selection clause** indicating what court, jurisdiction, or tribunal will decide any disputes arising under the contract. It is especially important to indicate the specific court that will have jurisdiction. The forum does not necessarily have to be within the geographic boundaries of the home nation of either party.

> **Forum-Selection Clause** A provision in a contract designating the court, jurisdiction, or tribunal that will decide any disputes arising under the contract.

CASE EXAMPLE 7.9 Intermax Trading Corporation, a New York firm, contracted to act as the North American sales agent for Garware Polyester, Ltd., based in Mumbai, India. The parties executed a series of contracts with provisions stating that the courts of Mumbai, India, would have exclusive jurisdiction over any disputes relating to the agreements.

When Intermax fell behind in its payments to Garware, Garware filed a lawsuit in a U.S. court to collect the balance due, claiming that the forum-selection clause did not apply to sales of warehoused goods. The court, however, sided with Intermax. Because the forum-selection clause was valid and enforceable, Garware had to bring its complaints against Intermax in a court in India.[10] ●

Choice-of-Law Clause

A contractual provision designating the applicable law—such as the law of Germany or the United Kingdom or California—is called a **choice-of-law clause.** Every international contract typically includes a choice-of-law clause. At common law (and in European civil law systems), parties are allowed to choose the law that will govern their contractual relationship, provided that the law chosen is the law of a jurisdiction that has a substantial relationship to the parties and to the international business transaction.

> **Choice-of-Law Clause** A clause in a contract designating the law (such as the law of a particular state or nation) that will govern the contract.

Under Section 1–105 of the Uniform Commercial Code (see Chapter 12), parties may choose the law that will govern the contract as long as the choice is "reasonable." Article 6 of the United Nations Convention on Contracts for the International Sale of Goods, however, imposes no limitation on the parties' choice. Similarly, the 1986 Hague Convention on the Law Applicable to Contracts for the International Sale of Goods—often referred to as the Choice-of-Law Convention—allows unlimited autonomy in the choice of law. The Hague Convention indicates that whenever a contract does not specify a choice of law, the governing law is that of the country in which the *seller's* place of business is located.

Force Majeure Clause

Every contract, particularly those involving international transactions, should have a *force majeure* clause. *Force majeure* is a French term meaning "impossible or irresistible force"—sometimes loosely identified as "an act of God." In international business contracts, *force majeure* clauses commonly stipulate that in addition to acts of God, a number of other eventualities (such as government orders or embargoes, for example) may excuse a party from liability for nonperformance.

> ***Force Majeure* Clause** A provision in a contract stipulating that certain unforeseen events—such as war, political upheavals, or acts of God—will excuse a party from liability for nonperformance of contractual obligations.

---

10. *Garware Polyester, Ltd. v. Intermax Trading Corp.,* 2001 WL 1035134 (S.D.N.Y. 2001). See also *Laasko v. Xerox Corp.,* 566 F.Supp.2d 1018 (C.D.Cal. 2008).

Civil Dispute Resolution

International contracts frequently include arbitration clauses. By means of such clauses, the parties agree in advance to be bound by the decision of a specified third party in the event of a dispute, as discussed in Chapter 3. The United Nations Convention on the Recognition and Enforcement of Foreign Arbitral Awards (often referred to as the *New York Convention*) assists in the enforcement of arbitration clauses, as do provisions in specific treaties among nations.

Basically, the convention requires courts in nations that have signed it to honor private agreements to arbitrate and recognize arbitration awards made in other contracting states. The New York Convention has been implemented in nearly one hundred countries, including the United States.

Under the New York Convention, a court will compel the parties to arbitrate their dispute if all of the following are true:

1. There is a written (or recorded) agreement to arbitrate the matter.
2. The agreement provides for arbitration in a convention signatory nation.
3. The agreement arises out of a commercial legal relationship.
4. One party to the agreement is not a U.S. citizen. In other words, both parties cannot be U.S. citizens.

In the following case, the parties had agreed to arbitrate any disputes in Guernsey, which is a British Crown dependency in the English Channel. The court had to decide whether the agreement was enforceable even though one party was a U.S. company and the other party may have had its principal place of business in the United States.

Case 7.2

S&T Oil Equipment & Machinery, Ltd. v. Juridica Investments, Ltd.

United States Court of Appeals, Fifth Circuit, 2012 WL 28242 (2012).

BACKGROUND AND FACTS Juridica Investments, Ltd. (JIL), entered into a financing contract with S&T Oil Equipment & Machinery, Ltd., a U.S. company. The contract included an arbitration provision stating that any disputes would be arbitrated "in St. Peter Port, Guernsey, Channel Islands." The contract also stated that it was executed in Guernsey and would be fully performed there. When a dispute arose between the parties, JIL initiated arbitration in Guernsey. Nevertheless, S&T filed a suit in federal district court in the United States. When JIL filed a motion to dismiss in favor of arbitration, the court granted the motion and compelled arbitration under the Convention on the Recognition and Enforcement of Foreign Arbitral Awards. S&T appealed.

IN THE WORDS OF THE COURT . . .
PER CURIAM [By the Whole Court]
* * * *

* * * "A court should compel arbitration if (1) there is a written agreement to arbitrate the matter; (2) the agreement provides

for arbitration in a Convention signatory nation; (3) the agreement arises out of a commercial legal relationship; and (4) a party to the agreement is not an American citizen."

The parties dispute whether the fourth * * * factor is satisfied in this case. In considering this fourth factor, courts must ask the following: Is a party to the agreement not an American citizen or does the commercial relationship have some reasonable relation with one or more foreign states? If either question is answered in the affirmative, then the fourth * * * factor is satisfied.

* * * *

Although it is not absolutely clear where JIL has its principal place of business, it is evident that the commercial relationship between S&T and JIL has some reasonable relation with one or more foreign states. Even if JIL's principal place of business is in the United States, the * * * agreement's arbitral clause can still

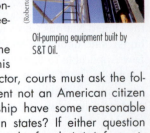

Oil-pumping equipment built by S&T Oil.

Case 7.2—Continued

be enforceable under the Convention if the legal relationship between JIL and S&T involved "property abroad, envisages performance or enforcement abroad, or has some other reasonable relation with one or more foreign states." As we stated in [another case], this reasonable relation with a foreign state must be "independent of the arbitral clause itself." [Emphasis added.]

Here, it is evident that the legal relationship between JIL and S&T envisaged performance abroad. The * * * agreement specifically states that it was executed in Guernsey and would be performed by JIL "exclusively and wholly in and from Guernsey." Indeed, pursuant to the terms of the * * * agreement, JIL performed part of the agreement abroad when it wired funds from Guernsey to cover * * * legal fees and costs * * * .

Given these facts, it is evident that the commercial relationship between S&T and JIL has some reasonable relation with one or more foreign states that is independent of the arbitral clause itself. As such, the fourth * * * factor is satisfied in

this case. The district court therefore did not err in compelling arbitration.

DECISION AND REMEDY The U.S. Court of Appeals for the Fifth Circuit held that arbitration was required under the Convention on the Recognition and Enforcement of Foreign Arbitral Awards. It therefore affirmed the district court's judgment compelling arbitration.

THE GLOBAL DIMENSION *What would happen if Congress did not require a reasonable relationship with a foreign state for arbitration agreements between U.S. citizens doing business abroad? Would there be more or fewer agreements to arbitrate disputes abroad?*

THE TECHNOLOGICAL DIMENSION *How might these parties have avoided the time and expense of settling their dispute in a foreign jurisdiction?*

Payment Methods

Currency differences between nations and the geographic distance between parties to international sales contracts add a degree of complexity to international sales that does not exist in the domestic market. Because international contracts involve greater financial risks, special care should be taken in drafting these contracts to specify both the currency in which payment is to be made and the method of payment.

Monetary Systems

Although our national currency, the U.S. dollar, is one of the primary forms of international currency, any U.S. firm undertaking business transactions abroad must be prepared to deal with one or more other currencies. After all, a Japanese firm may want to be paid in Japanese yen for goods and services sold outside Japan. Both firms therefore must rely on the convertibility of currencies.

Currencies are convertible when they can be freely exchanged one for the other at some specified market rate in a **foreign exchange market.** Foreign exchange markets make up a worldwide system for the buying and selling of foreign currencies. The foreign exchange rate is simply the price of a unit of one country's currency in terms of another country's currency. For instance, if today's exchange rate is eighty Japanese yen for one dollar, that means that anybody with eighty yen can obtain one dollar, and vice versa. Like other prices, the exchange rate is set by the forces of supply and demand.

Frequently, a U.S. company can rely on its domestic bank to take care of all international transfers of funds. Commercial banks often transfer funds internationally through their **correspondent banks** in other countries. **EXAMPLE 7.10** A customer of Citibank wishes to pay a bill in euros to a company in Paris. Citibank can draw a bank check payable in euros on its account in Crédit Agricole, a Paris correspondent bank, and then send the check to the French company to which its customer owes the funds. Alternatively, Citibank's

(Ralf Siemieniec/Shutterstock.com)

How do businesses pay foreign firms?

Foreign Exchange Market A worldwide system in which foreign currencies are bought and sold.

Correspondent Bank A bank in which another bank has an account (and vice versa) for the purpose of facilitating fund transfers.

customer can request a wire transfer of the funds to the French company. Citibank instructs Crédit Agricole by wire to pay the necessary amount in euros. ●

Letters of Credit

Because buyers and sellers engaged in international business transactions are frequently separated by thousands of miles, special precautions are often taken to ensure performance under the contract. Sellers want to avoid delivering goods for which they might not be paid. Buyers desire the assurance that sellers will not be paid until there is evidence that the goods have been shipped. Thus, **letters of credit** are frequently used to facilitate international business transactions.

Letter of Credit A written document in which the issuer (usually a bank) promises to honor drafts or other demands for payment by third persons in accordance with the terms of the instrument.

Parties to a Letter of Credit   In a simple letter-of-credit transaction, the *issuer* (a bank) agrees to issue a letter of credit and to ascertain whether the *beneficiary* (seller) performs certain acts. In return, the *account party* (buyer) promises to reimburse the issuer for the amount paid to the beneficiary. The transaction may also involve an *advising bank* that transmits information and a *paying bank* that expedites payment under the letter of credit. See Exhibit 7–1 for an illustration of a letter-of-credit transaction.

Under a letter of credit, the issuer is bound to pay the beneficiary (seller) when the beneficiary has complied with the terms and conditions of the letter of credit. The beneficiary looks to the issuer, not to the account party (buyer), when it presents the documents required by the letter of credit.

Typically, the letter of credit will require that the beneficiary deliver a *bill of lading* to the issuing bank to prove that shipment has been made. A letter of credit assures the

Exhibit 7–1 A Letter-of-Credit Transaction

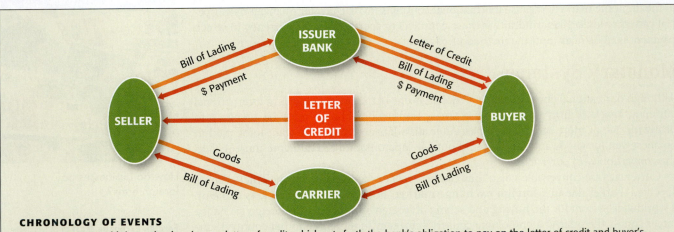

CHRONOLOGY OF EVENTS

1. Buyer contracts with issuer bank to issue a letter of credit, which sets forth the bank's obligation to pay on the letter of credit and buyer's obligation to pay the bank.
2. Letter of credit is sent to seller informing seller that on compliance with the terms of the letter of credit (such as presentment of necessary documents—in this example, a bill of lading), the bank will issue payment for the goods.
3. Seller delivers goods to carrier and receives a bill of lading.
4. Seller delivers the bill of lading to issuer bank and, if the document is proper, receives payment.
5. Issuer bank delivers the bill of lading to buyer.
6. Buyer delivers the bill of lading to carrier.
7. Carrier delivers the goods to the buyer.
8. Buyer settles with issuer bank.

beneficiary (seller) of payment and at the same time assures the account party (buyer) that payment will not be made until the beneficiary has complied with the terms and conditions of the letter of credit.

The Value of a Letter of Credit The basic principle behind letters of credit is that payment is made against the documents presented by the beneficiary and not against the facts that the documents purport to reflect. Thus, in a letter-of-credit transaction, the issuer does not police the underlying contract. A letter of credit is independent of the underlying contract between the buyer and the seller. Eliminating the need for banks (issuers) to inquire into whether actual contractual conditions have been satisfied greatly reduces the costs of letters of credit. Moreover, the use of a letter of credit protects both buyers and sellers.

U.S. Laws in a Global Context

The internationalization of business raises questions about the extraterritorial application of a nation's laws—that is, the effect of the country's laws outside its boundaries. To what extent do U.S. domestic laws apply to other nations' businesses? To what extent do U.S. domestic laws apply to U.S. firms doing business abroad? Here, we discuss the extraterritorial application of certain U.S. laws, including antitrust laws, tort laws, and laws prohibiting employment discrimination.

U.S. Antitrust Laws

U.S. antitrust laws (to be discussed in Chapter 23) have a wide application. They may *subject* firms in foreign nations to their provisions, as well as *protect* foreign consumers and competitors from violations committed by U.S. citizens. Section 1 of the Sherman Act— the most important U.S. antitrust law—provides for the extraterritorial effect of the U.S. antitrust laws.

The United States is a major proponent of free competition in the global economy. Thus, any conspiracy that has a *substantial effect* on U.S. commerce is within the reach of the Sherman Act. The law applies even if the violation occurs outside the United States, and foreign governments as well as businesses can be sued for violations.

EXAMPLE 7.11 An investigation by the U.S. government revealed that a Tokyo-based auto parts supplier, Furukawa Electric Company, and its executives conspired with competitors in an international price-fixing agreement (an agreement to set prices—see Chapter 23). The agreement lasted more than ten years and resulted in automobile manufacturers paying noncompetitive and higher prices for parts in cars sold to U.S. consumers. Because the conspiracy had a substantial effect on U.S. commerce, the United States had jurisdiction to prosecute the case. In 2011, Furukawa agreed to plead guilty and pay a $200 million fine. The Furukawa executives from Japan also agreed to serve up to eighteen months in a U.S. prison and to cooperate fully with the ongoing investigation. ●

International Tort Claims

The international application of tort liability is growing in significance and controversy. An increasing number of U.S. plaintiffs are suing foreign (or U.S.) entities for torts that these entities have allegedly committed overseas. Often, these cases involve human rights violations by foreign governments. The Alien Tort Claims Act (ATCA),[11] allows even foreign citizens to bring civil suits in U.S. courts for injuries caused by violations of international law or a treaty of the United States.

Learning Objective 5
What federal law allows U.S. citizens, as well as citizens of foreign nations, to file civil actions in U.S. courts for torts that were committed overseas?

---

11. 28 U.S.C. Section 1350.

Since 1980, plaintiffs have increasingly used the ATCA to bring actions against companies operating in other countries. ATCA actions have been brought against companies doing business in various nations, including Colombia, Ecuador, Egypt, Guatemala, India, Indonesia, Nigeria, and Saudi Arabia. Some of these cases have involved alleged environmental destruction. In addition, mineral companies in Southeast Asia have been sued for collaborating with oppressive government regimes.

In the following *Spotlight Case,* the United States Supreme Court considers the parameters of the ATCA (which the Court refers to as the Alien Tort Statute, or ATS). The question is whether the statute allows U.S. courts to exercise jurisdiction over a cause of action that occurred outside the United States.

Spotlight on International Torts

Case 7.3
Daimler AG v. Bauman
United States Supreme Court, ___ U.S. ___, 134 S.Ct. 746, 187 L.Ed.2d 624 (2014)

(Juan Mabromata/AFP/Getty Images/Newscom)

Victims of Argentina's "Dirty War."

BACKGROUND AND FACTS   Barbara Bauman and twenty-one other residents of Argentina filed a suit in a federal district court in California against Daimler AG, a German company, alleging that Mercedes-Benz Argentina (MB Argentina), an Argentinean subsidiary of Daimler, had collaborated with state security forces to kidnap, detain, torture, and kill certain MB Argentina workers, including the plaintiffs and relatives of the plaintiffs. These claims were asserted under the Alien Tort Claims Act (ATCA). Personal jurisdiction was based on the California contacts of Mercedes-Benz USA, LLC (MBUSA), a Daimler subsidiary incorporated in Delaware with its principal place of business in New Jersey. MBUSA distributes Daimler-made vehicles to dealerships throughout the United States, including California. The court dismissed the suit for lack of jurisdiction. The U.S. Court of Appeals for the Ninth Circuit reversed this ruling. Daimler appealed.

IN THE WORDS OF THE COURT . . .
Justice *GINSBURG* delivered the opinion of the Court.
    * * * *

Even if we were to assume that MBUSA is at home in California, and further to assume MBUSA's contacts are imputable [attributable] to Daimler, there would still be no basis to subject Daimler to general jurisdiction in California, for Daimler's slim contacts with the State hardly render it at home there.

* * * Only a limited set of affiliations with a forum will render a defendant amenable to all-purpose jurisdiction there. For an individual, the paradigm forum [the typical forum] for the exercise of general jurisdiction is the individual's domicile; for a corporation, it is an equivalent place, one in which the corporation is fairly regarded as at home. *With respect to a corporation, the place of incorporation and principal place of business are paradigm * * * bases for general jurisdiction.*

Those affiliations have the virtue of being unique—that is, each ordinarily indicates only one place—as well as easily ascertainable. These bases afford plaintiffs recourse to at least one clear and certain forum in which a corporate defendant may be sued on any and all claims. [Emphasis added.]

[This does not mean] that a corporation may be subject to general jurisdiction *only* in a forum where it is incorporated or has its principal place of business * * * . [But] plaintiffs would have us look beyond the exemplar bases identified [above] and approve the exercise of general jurisdiction in every State in which a corporation engages in a substantial, continuous, and systematic course of business. That formulation, we hold, is unacceptably grasping.

* * * The inquiry * * * is not whether a foreign corporation's in-forum contacts can be said to be in some sense continuous and systematic; it is whether that corporation's affiliations with the State are so continuous and systematic as to render it essentially at home in the forum State.

Here, neither Daimler nor MBUSA is incorporated in California, nor does either entity have its principal place of business there. If Daimler's California activities sufficed to allow adjudication of this Argentina-rooted case in California, the same global reach would presumably be available in every other State in which MBUSA's sales are sizable. Such exorbitant exercises of all-purpose jurisdiction would scarcely permit out-of-state defendants to structure their primary conduct with some minimum assurance as to where that conduct will and will not render them liable to suit.

It was therefore error for the Ninth Circuit to conclude that Daimler, even with MBUSA's contacts attributed to it, was at home in California, and hence subject to suit there on claims by foreign plaintiffs having nothing to do with anything that occurred or had its principal impact in California.

Spotlight Case 7.3—Continued

DECISION AND REMEDY The United States Supreme Court reversed the decision of the lower court. A federal district court in California could not exercise jurisdiction over Daimler in this case, given the absence of any California connection to the atrocities, perpetrators, or victims described in the complaint.

THE LEGAL ENVIRONMENT DIMENSION *What are the consequences for Daimler of the decision in this case?*

THE GLOBAL DIMENSION *If the Court had adopted the plaintiffs' argument, how might U.S. citizens have been affected?*

Antidiscrimination Laws

Laws in the United States prohibit discrimination on the basis of race, color, national origin, religion, gender, age, and disability, as will be discussed in Chapter 18. These laws, as they affect employment relationships, generally apply extraterritorially. U.S. employees working abroad for U.S. employers are protected under the Age Discrimination in Employment Act. The Americans with Disabilities Act, which requires employers to accommodate the needs of workers with disabilities, also applies to U.S. nationals working abroad for U.S. firms.

In addition, the major law regulating employment discrimination—Title VII of the Civil Rights Act—also applies extraterritorially to all U.S. employees working for U.S. employers abroad. U.S. employers must abide by U.S. discrimination laws unless to do so would violate the laws of the country where their workplaces are located. This "foreign laws exception" prevents employers from being subjected to conflicting laws.

Reviewing . . . International Law in a Global Economy

Robco, Inc., was a Florida arms dealer. The armed forces of Honduras contracted to purchase weapons from Robco over a six-year period. After the government was replaced and a democracy installed, the Honduran government sought to reduce the size of its military, and its relationship with Robco deteriorated. Honduras refused to honor the contract by purchasing the inventory of arms, which Robco could sell only at a much lower price. Robco filed a suit in a federal district court in the United States to recover damages for this breach of contract by the government of Honduras. Using the information provided in the chapter, answer the following questions.

1. Should the Foreign Sovereign Immunities Act preclude this lawsuit? Why or why not?
2. Does the act of state doctrine bar Robco from seeking to enforce the contract? Explain.
3. Suppose that prior to this lawsuit, the new government of Honduras had enacted a law making it illegal to purchase weapons from foreign arms dealers. What doctrine might lead a U.S. court to dismiss Robco's case in that situation?
4. Now suppose that the U.S. court hears the case and awards damages to Robco, but the government of Honduras has no assets in the United States that can be used to satisfy the judgment. Under which doctrine might Robco be able to collect the damages by asking another nation's court to enforce the U.S. judgment?

Debate This The U.S. federal courts are accepting too many lawsuits initiated by foreigners that concern matters not relevant to this country.

Key Terms

act of state doctrine 179

choice-of-language clause 187

choice-of-law clause 187

comity 178

confiscation 180

correspondent bank 189

distribution agreement 181

dumping 185

export 181

expropriation 180

force majeure clause 187

foreign exchange market 189

forum-selection clause 187

international organization 177

letter of credit 190

normal trade relations (NTR) status 185

quota 184

sovereign immunity 180

tariff 184

treaty 177

Chapter Summary: International Law in a Global Economy

International Law	1. *Principle of comity*—Under this principle, nations give effect to the laws and judicial decrees of other nations for reasons of courtesy and international harmony. 2. *Act of state doctrine*—Under this doctrine, U.S. courts avoid passing judgment on the validity of public acts committed by a recognized foreign government within its own territory. 3. *Doctrine of sovereign immunity*—When certain conditions are satisfied, foreign nations are immune from U.S. jurisdiction under the Foreign Sovereign Immunities Act. Exceptions are made when a foreign state (a) has waived its immunity either explicitly or by implication, (b) has engaged in commercial activity within the United States, or (c) has committed a tort within the United States.
Doing Business Internationally	U.S. domestic firms may engage in international business transactions in several ways including (1) exporting, which may involve foreign agents or distributors, and (2) manufacturing abroad through licensing arrangements, franchising operations, wholly owned subsidiaries, or joint ventures.
Regulation of Specific Business Activities	In the interests of their economies, foreign policies, domestic policies, or other national priorities, nations impose laws that restrict or facilitate international business. Such laws regulate foreign investments, exporting, and importing. The World Trade Organization attempts to minimize trade barriers among nations, as do regional trade agreements and associations, including the European Union and the North American Free Trade Agreement.
International Contracts	International business contracts often include choice-of-language, forum-selection, and choice-of-law clauses to reduce the uncertainties associated with interpreting the language of the agreement and dealing with legal differences. Most domestic and international contracts include *force majeure* clauses. They commonly stipulate that acts of God and certain other events may excuse a party from liability for nonperformance of the contract. Arbitration clauses are also frequently found in international contracts.
Payment Methods	1. *Currency conversion*—Because nations have different monetary systems, payment on international contracts requires currency conversion at a rate specified in a foreign exchange market. 2. *Correspondent banking*—Correspondent banks facilitate the transfer of funds from a buyer in one country to a seller in another. 3. *Letters of credit*—Letters of credit facilitate international transactions by ensuring payment to sellers and assuring buyers that payment will not be made until the sellers have complied with the terms of the letters of credit. Typically, compliance occurs when a bill of lading is delivered to the issuing bank.
U.S. Laws in a Global Context	1. *Antitrust laws*—U.S. antitrust laws may be applied beyond the borders of the United States. Any conspiracy that has a substantial effect on commerce within the United States may be subject to the Sherman Act, even if the violation occurs outside the United States. 2. *Tort laws*—U.S. tort laws may be applied to wrongful acts that take place in foreign jurisdictions under the Alien Tort Claims Act. This act allows even foreign citizens to bring civil suits in U.S. Courts for injuries caused by violations of international law or a treaty of the United States. 3. *Antidiscrimination laws*—The major U.S. laws prohibiting employment discrimination, including Title VII of the Civil Rights Act, the Age Discrimination in Employment Act, and the Americans with Disabilities Act, cover U.S. employees working abroad for U.S. firms—*unless* to apply the U.S. laws would violate the laws of the host country.

Issue Spotters

1. Café Rojo, Ltd., an Ecuadoran firm, agrees to sell coffee beans to Dark Roast Coffee Company, a U.S. firm. Dark Roast accepts the beans but refuses to pay. Café Rojo sues Dark Roast in an Ecuadoran court and is awarded damages, but Dark Roast's assets are in the United States. Under what circumstances would a U.S. court enforce the judgment of the Ecuadoran court? (See *International Law.*)

2. Gems International, Ltd., is a foreign firm that has a 12 percent share of the U.S. market for diamonds. To capture a larger share, Gems offers its products at a below-cost discount to U.S. buyers (and inflates the prices in its own country to make up the difference). How can this attempt to undersell U.S. businesses be defeated? (See *Regulation of Specific Business Activities.*)

—Check your answers to the Issue Spotters against the answers provided in Appendix D at the end of this text.

For Review

1. What is the principle of comity, and why do courts deciding disputes involving a foreign law or judicial decree apply this principle?
2. What is the act of state doctrine? In what circumstances is this doctrine applied?
3. Under the Foreign Sovereign Immunities Act, in what situations is a foreign state subject to the jurisdiction of U.S. courts?
4. What are three clauses commonly included in international business contracts?
5. What federal law allows U.S. citizens, as well as citizens of foreign nations, to file civil actions in U.S. courts for torts that were committed overseas?

Business Scenarios and Case Problems

7–1. Letters of Credit. Antex Industries, a Japanese firm, agreed to purchase 92,000 electronic integrated circuits from Electronic Arrays. The Swiss Credit Bank issued a letter of credit to cover the transaction. The letter of credit specified that the chips would be transported to Tokyo by ship. Electronic Arrays shipped the circuits by air. Payment on the letter of credit was dishonored because the shipment by air did not fulfill the precise terms of the letter of credit. Should a court compel payment? Explain. (See *Payment Methods.*)

7–2. Dumping. U.S. pineapple producers alleged that producers of canned pineapple from the Philippines were selling their canned pineapple in the United States for less than its fair market value (dumping). The Philippine producers also exported other products, such as pineapple juice and juice concentrate, which used separate parts of the same fresh pineapple, so they shared raw material costs, according to the producers' own financial records. To determine fair value and antidumping duties, the plaintiffs argued that a court should calculate the Philippine producers' cost of production and allocate a portion of the shared fruit costs to the canned fruit. The result of this allocation showed that more than 90 percent of the canned fruit sales were below the cost of production. Is this a reasonable approach to determining the production costs and fair market value of canned pineapple in the United States? Why or why not? (See *Regulation of Specific Business Activities.*)

7–3. Doing Business Internationally. Macrotech, Inc., develops an innovative computer chip and obtains a patent on it. The firm markets the chip under the trade-marked brand name "Flash." Macrotech wants to sell the chip to Nitron, Ltd., in Pacifica, a foreign country. Macrotech is concerned, however, that after an initial purchase, Nitron will duplicate the chip, pirate it, and sell the pirated version to computer manufacturers in Pacifica. To avoid this possibility, Macrotech could

establish its own manufacturing facility in Pacifica, but it does not want to do this. How can Macrotech, without establishing a manufacturing facility in Pacifica, protect Flash from being pirated by Nitron? (See *Doing Business Internationally.*)

7–4. Dumping. Nuclear power plants use low-enriched uranium (LEU) as a fuel. LEU consists of feed uranium enriched by energy to a certain assay—the percentage of the isotope necessary for a nuclear reaction. The amount of energy required is described by an industry standard as a "separative work unit" (SWU). A nuclear utility may buy LEU from an enricher, or the utility may provide an enricher with feed uranium and pay for the SWUs necessary to produce LEU. Under an SWU contract, the LEU returned to the utility may not be exactly the uranium the utility provided. This is because feed uranium is fungible and trades like a commodity (such as wheat or corn), and profitable enrichment requires the constant processing of undifferentiated stock. Foreign enrichers, including Eurodif, S.A., allegedly exported LEU to the United States and sold it for "less than fair value." Did this constitute dumping? Explain. If so, what could be done to prevent it? [*United States v. Eurodif, S.A.*, 555 U.S. 305, 129 S.Ct. 878, 172 L.Ed.2d 679 (2009)] (See *Regulation of Specific Business Activities.*)

7–5. International Agreements and Jurisdiction. U.S. citizens who were descendants of victims of the Holocaust (the mass murder of 6 million Jews by the Nazis during World War II) in Europe filed a claim for breach of contract in the United States against an Italian insurance company, Assicurazioni Generali, S.P.A. (Generali). Before the Holocaust, the plaintiffs' ancestors had purchased insurance policies from Generali, but Generali refused to pay them benefits under the policies. Due to certain agreements among nations after World War II, such lawsuits could not be filed for many years. In 2000, however, the United States agreed that Germany could establish a foundation—the

International Commission on Holocaust-Era Insurance Claims, or ICHEIC—that would compensate victims who had suffered losses at the hands of the Germans during the war.

Whenever a German company was sued in a U.S. court based on a Holocaust-era claim, the U.S. government would inform the court that the matter should be referred to the ICHEIC as the exclusive forum and remedy for the resolution. There was no such agreement with Italy, however, so the federal district court dismissed the suit. The plaintiffs appealed. Did the plaintiffs have to take their claim to the ICHEIC rather than sue in a U.S. court? Why or why not? [*In re Assicurazioni Generali, S.P.A.*, 592 F.3d 113 (2d Cir. 2010)] (See *International Contracts*.)

7–6. **Business Case Problem with Sample Answer— Sovereign Immunity.** Bell Helicopter Textron, Inc., designs, makes, and sells helicopters with distinctive and famous trade dress that identifies them as Bell aircraft. Bell also owns the helicopters' design patents. Bell's Model 206 Series includes the Jet Ranger. Thirty-six years after Bell developed the Jet Ranger, the Islamic Republic of Iran began to make and sell counterfeit Model 206 Series helicopters and parts. Iran's counterfeit versions—the Shahed 278 and the Shahed 285— used Bell's *trade dress* (see Chapter 8). The Shahed aircraft was promoted at an international air show in Iran to aircraft customers. Bell filed a suit in a U.S. district court against Iran, alleging violations of trademark and patent laws. Is Iran—a foreign nation—exempt in these circumstances from the jurisdiction of U.S. courts? Explain. [*Bell Helicopter Textron, Inc. v. Islamic Republic of Iran*, 892 F.Supp.2d 219 (D.D.C. 2012)] (See *International Law*.)

—For a sample answer to Problem 7–6, go to Appendix E at the end of this text.

7–7. **Commercial Activity Exception.** Technology Incubation and Entrepreneurship Training Society (TIETS) entered into a joint-venture agreement with Mandana Farhang and M.A. Mobile to develop and market certain technology for commercial purposes. Farhang and M.A. Mobile filed a suit in a federal district court in California, where they both were based, alleging claims under the joint-venture agreement and a related nondisclosure agreement. The parties agreed that TIETS was a "foreign state" covered by the Foreign Sovereign Immunities Act because it was a part of the Indian government. Nevertheless, Farhang and M.A. Mobile argued that TIETS did not enjoy sovereign immunity because it had engaged in a commercial activity that had a direct effect in the United States. Could TIETS still be subject to the jurisdiction of U.S. courts under the commercial activity exception even though the joint venture was to take place outside the United States? If so, how? [*Farhang v. Indian Institute of Technology, Kharagpur*, 2012 WL 113739 (N.D.Cal. 2012)] (See *International Law*.)

7–8. **Sovereign Immunity.** In 1954, the government of Bolivia began expropriating land from Francisco Loza. One such public project included an international airport. The government directed the payment of compensation in exchange for at least some of his land for the airport. The government, however, never paid the full amount. Decades later, his heirs, Genoveva and Marcel Loza, who were both U.S. citizens, filed a suit in a U.S. federal district court against the government of Bolivia, seeking damages for the taking. Can the court exercise jurisdiction? Explain. [*Santivanez v. Estado Plurinacional de Bolivia*, 2013 WL 879983 (11th Cir. 2013)] (See *International Law*.)

7–9. **Import Controls.** The Wind Tower Trade Coalition is an association of domestic manufacturers of utility-scale wind towers. The Coalition filed a suit in the U.S. Court of International Trade against the U.S. Department of Commerce, challenging its decision to impose only *prospective* antidumping duties, rather than *retrospective* (retroactive) duties, on imports of utility-scale wind towers from China and Vietnam. The Commerce Department had found that the domestic industry had not suffered any "material injury" or "threat of material injury" from such imports and that it would be protected by a prospective assessment. Can an antidumping duty be assessed retrospectively? If so, should it be assessed here? Discuss. [*Wind Tower Trade Coalition v. United States*, 741 F.3d 89 (Fed. Cir. 2014)] (See *Regulation of Specific Business Activities*.)

7–10. ⬌ **A Question of Ethics—Terrorism.** On December 21, 1988, Pan Am Flight 103 exploded 31,000 feet in the air over Lockerbie, Scotland, killing all 259 passengers and crew on board and 11 people on the ground. Among those killed was Roger Hurst, a U.S. citizen. An investigation determined that a portable radio-cassette player packed in a brown Samsonite suitcase smuggled onto the plane was the source of the explosion. The explosive device was constructed with a digital timer specially made for, and bought by, Libya. Abdel Basset Ali Al-Megrahi, a Libyan government official and an employee of the Libyan Arab Airline (LAA), was convicted by the Scottish High Court of Justiciary on criminal charges that he planned and executed the bombing in association with members of the Jamahiriya Security Organization (JSO)—an agency of the former Libyan government that performed security and intelligence functions—or the Libyan military. Members of the victims' families filed a suit in a U.S. federal district court against the JSO, the LAA, Al-Megrahi, and others. The plaintiffs claimed violations of U.S. federal law, including the Anti-Terrorism Act, and state law, including the intentional infliction of emotional distress. [*Hurst v. Socialist People's Libyan Arab Jamahiriya*, 474 F.Supp.2d 19 (D.D.C. 2007)] (See *International Law*.)

1. Under what doctrine, codified in which federal statute, might the defendants have claimed to be immune from the jurisdiction of a U.S. court? Should this law include an exception for "state-sponsored terrorism"? Why or why not?

2. The defendants agreed to pay $2.7 billion, or $10 million per victim, to settle all claims for "compensatory death damages." The families of eleven victims, including Hurst, were excluded from the settlement because they were "not wrongful death beneficiaries under applicable state law." These plaintiffs continued the suit. The defendants filed a motion to dismiss. Should the motion have been granted on the ground that the settlement barred the plaintiffs' claims? Explain.

UNIT 1   Cumulative Business Hypothetical

CompTac, Inc., which is headquartered in San Francisco, California, is one of the leading software manufacturers in the United States. The company invests millions of dollars in research and development of new software applications and computer games, which are sold worldwide. It also has a large service department and has taken great pains to offer its customers excellent support services.

1. CompTac routinely purchases some of the materials necessary to produce its computer games from a New York firm, Electrotex, Inc. A dispute arises between the two firms, and CompTac wants to sue Electrotex for breach of contract. Can CompTac bring the suit in a California state court? Can CompTac bring the suit in a federal court? Explain.

2. A customer at one of CompTac's retail stores stumbles over a crate in the parking lot and breaks her leg. The crate had just moments before fallen off a CompTac truck that was delivering goods from a CompTac warehouse to the store. The customer sues CompTac, alleging negligence. Will she succeed in her suit? Why or why not?

3. Roban Electronics, a software manufacturer and one of CompTac's major competitors, has been trying to convince one of CompTac's key employees, Jim Baxter, to come to work for Roban. Roban knows that Baxter has a written employment contract with CompTac, which Baxter would breach if he left CompTac before the contract expired. Baxter goes to work for Roban, and the departure of its key employee causes CompTac to suffer substantial losses due to delays in completing new software. Can CompTac sue Roban to recoup some of these losses? If so, on what ground?

4. One of CompTac's employees in its accounting division, Alan Green, has a gambling problem. To repay a gambling debt of $10,000, Green decides to "borrow" some money from CompTac to cover the debt. Using his "hacking" skills and his knowledge of CompTac account numbers, Green electronically transfers CompTac funds into his personal checking account. A week later, he is luckier at gambling and uses the same electronic procedures to transfer funds from his personal checking account to the relevant CompTac account. Has Green committed any crimes? If so, what are they?

5. One of CompTac's best-selling products is a computer game that includes some extremely violent actions. Groups of parents, educators, and consumer activists have bombarded CompTac with letters and e-mail messages calling on the company to stop selling the product. CompTac executives are concerned about the public outcry, but at the same time they realize that the game is a major source of profits. If it ceased marketing the game, the company could go bankrupt. If you were a CompTac decision maker, what would your decision be in this situation? How would you justify your decision from an ethical perspective?

6. CompTac wants to sell one of its best-selling software programs to An Phat Company, a firm located in Ho Chi Minh City, Vietnam. CompTac is concerned, however, that after an initial purchase, An Phat will duplicate the software without permission (and in violation of U.S. copyright laws) and sell the illegal bootleg software to other firms in Vietnam. How can CompTac protect its software from being pirated by An Phat Company?

Legal Reasoning Group Activity

Free Speech and Equal Protection.   For many years, New York City has had to deal with the vandalism and defacement of public property caused by unauthorized graffiti. In an effort to stop the damage, the city banned the sale of aerosol spray-paint cans and broad-tipped indelible markers to persons under twenty-one years of age. The new rules also prohibited people from possessing these items on property other than their own. Within a year, five people under age twenty-one were cited for violations of these regulations, and 871 individuals were arrested for actually making graffiti.

Legal Reasoning Group Activity—Continues ➡

Legal Reasoning Group Activity—Continued

Lindsey Vincenty and other artists wished to create graffiti on legal surfaces, such as canvas, wood, and clothing. Unable to buy her supplies in the city or to carry them in the city if she bought them elsewhere, Vincenty and others filed a lawsuit on behalf of themselves and other young artists against Michael Bloomberg, the city's mayor, and others. The plaintiffs claimed that, among other things, the new rules violated their right to freedom of speech. (See Chapter 4.)

1. One group will argue in favor of the plaintiffs and provide several reasons why the court should hold that the city's new rules violate the plaintiffs' freedom of speech.
2. Another group will develop a counterargument that outlines the reasons why the new rules do not violate free speech rights.
3. A third group will argue that the city's ban violates the equal protection clause because it applies only to persons under age twenty-one.

(Edhar/Shutterstock.com)

The Commercial Environment

UNIT CONTENTS

CHAPTER 8

(Login/Shutterstock.com)

Intellectual Property Rights

CONTENTS

- Trademarks
- Patents
- Copyrights
- Trade Secrets
- International Protections

LEARNING OBJECTIVES

The five learning objectives below are designed to help improve your understanding of the chapter. After reading this chapter, you should be able to answer the following questions:

1. What is intellectual property?
2. Why is the protection of trademarks important?
3. How does the law protect patents?
4. What laws protect authors' rights in the works they create?
5. What are trade secrets, and what laws offer protection for this form of intellectual property?

"My words and my ideas are my property, and I'll keep and protect them as surely as I do my stable of unicorns."
—Jarod Kintz, 1982–present (American author)

Intellectual property is any property resulting from intellectual, creative processes—the products of an individual's mind, as noted in the chapter-opening quotation. Although it is an abstract term for an abstract concept, intellectual property is nonetheless familiar to almost everyone. The information contained in books and computer files is intellectual property. The apps for your iPhone and iPad, the movies you watch, and the music you listen to are all forms of intellectual property. Although the need to protect creative works was first recognized in Article I, Section 8, of the U.S. Constitution (see Appendix B), statutory protection of these rights began in the 1940s and continues to evolve to meet the needs of modern society.

Of significant concern to businesspersons is the need to protect their rights in intellectual property, which may be more valuable than their physical property, such as machines and buildings. Consider, for instance, the importance of intellectual property rights to technology companies, such as Apple, Inc., the maker of the iPhone and iPad. In today's

Intellectual Property Property resulting from intellectual and creative processes.

Learning Objective 1
What is intellectual property?

world, intellectual property rights can be a company's most valuable assets, which is why Apple sued rival Samsung Electronics Company. Apple claimed that Samsung's Galaxy line of mobile phones and tablets (those that run Google's Android software) copy the look, design, and user interface of Apple's iPhone and iPad. Although Apple is one of Samsung's biggest customers and buys many of its components from Samsung, Apple also needs to protect its iPhone and iPad revenues from competing Android products. You will read about the verdict in this case later in this chapter.

In today's global economy, however, protecting intellectual property in one country is no longer sufficient. The United States is participating in various international agreements to secure ownership rights in intellectual property in other countries as you will learn in this chapter.

Trademarks

Trademark A distinctive word, symbol, or design that identifies the manufacturer as the source of particular goods and distinguishes its products from those made or sold by others.

A **trademark** is a distinctive word, symbol, sound, or design that identifies the manufacturer as the source of particular goods and distinguishes its products from those made or sold by others. At common law, the person who used a symbol or mark to identify a business or product was protected in the use of that trademark. Clearly, by using another's trademark, a business could lead consumers to believe that its goods were made by the other business. The law seeks to avoid this kind of confusion. (For information on how companies use trademarks and service marks, see this chapter's *Linking Business Law to Marketing* feature at the end of this chapter.)

Learning Objective 2
Why is the protection of trademarks important?

In the following *Classic Case* concerning Coca-Cola, the defendants argued that the Coca-Cola trademark was not entitled to protection under the law because the term did not accurately represent the product.

✳ Classic Case 8.1

Coca-Cola Co. v. Koke Co. of America
Supreme Court of the United States, 254 U.S. 143, 41 S.Ct. 113, 65 L.Ed. 189 (1920).

(Rob Wilson/Shutterstock.com)

How is Coca-Cola protected?

COMPANY PROFILE *John Pemberton, an Atlanta pharmacist, invented a caramel-colored, carbonated soft drink in 1886. His bookkeeper, Frank Robinson, named the beverage Coca-Cola after two of the ingredients, coca leaves and kola nuts. Asa Candler bought the Coca-Cola Company in 1891 and, within seven years, had made the soft drink available throughout the United States and in parts of Canada and Mexico as well. Candler continued to sell Coke aggressively and to open up new markets, reaching Europe before 1910. In doing so, however, he attracted numerous competitors, some of whom tried to capitalize directly on the Coke name.*

BACKGROUND AND FACTS The Coca-Cola Company brought an action in a federal district court to prevent other beverage companies from using the words *Koke* and *Dope* for their products. The defendants contended that the Coca-Cola trademark was a fraudulent representation and that Coca-Cola was therefore not entitled to any help from the courts. By use of the Coca-Cola name, the defendants alleged, the Coca-Cola Company represented that the beverage contained cocaine (from coca leaves). The district court granted the injunction, but the federal appellate court reversed. The Coca-Cola Company appealed to the United States Supreme Court.

IN THE WORDS OF THE COURT . . .
Mr. Justice *HOLMES* delivered the opinion of the Court.
  * * * *
  * * * Before 1900 the beginning of [Coca-Cola's] good will was more or less helped by the presence of cocaine, a drug that, like alcohol or opium, may be described as a deadly poison or as a valuable item of the pharmacopœa [collection

Classic Case 8.1—Continued

of pharmaceuticals] according to the [purposes of the speaker]. * * * After the Food and Drug Act of June 30, 1906, if not earlier, long before this suit was brought, it was eliminated from the plaintiff's compound.

　* * * Since 1900 the sales have increased at a very great rate corresponding to a like increase in advertising. The name now characterizes a beverage to be had at almost any soda fountain. It means a single thing coming from a single source, and well known to the community. It hardly would be too much to say that the drink characterizes the name as much as the name the drink. In other words Coca-Cola probably means to most persons the plaintiff's familiar product to be had everywhere rather than a compound of particular substances. * * * Before this suit was brought the plaintiff had advertised to the public that it must not expect and would not find cocaine, and had eliminated everything tending to suggest cocaine effects except the name and the picture of the leaves and nuts, which probably conveyed little or nothing to most who saw it. It appears to us that it would be going too far to deny the plaintiff relief against a palpable fraud because possibly here and there an ignorant person might call for the drink with the hope

for incipient cocaine intoxication. The plaintiff's position must be judged by the facts as they were when the suit was begun, not by the facts of a different condition and an earlier time.

DECISION AND REMEDY The United States Supreme Court upheld the district court's injunction. The competing beverage companies were prevented from calling their products *Koke*. The Court did not prevent them from calling their products *Dope*, however.

WHAT IF THE FACTS WERE DIFFERENT? *Suppose that Coca-Cola had been trying to make the public believe that its product contained cocaine. Would the result in the case likely have been different? Explain your answer.*

IMPACT OF THIS CASE ON TODAY'S LEGAL ENVIRONMENT *In this early case, the United States Supreme Court made it clear that trademarks and trade names (and nicknames for those marks and names, such as "Coke" for "Coca-Cola") that are in common use receive protection under the common law. This holding is significant historically because it is the predecessor to the federal statute later passed to protect trademark rights (the Lanham Act of 1946).*

Statutory Protection of Trademarks

Statutory protection of trademarks and related property is provided at the federal level by the Lanham Act of 1946.[1] The Lanham Act was enacted in part to protect manufacturers from losing business to rival companies that used confusingly similar trademarks.

　The Lanham Act incorporates the common law of trademarks and provides remedies for owners of trademarks who wish to enforce their claims in federal court. Many states also have trademark statutes.

Trademark Dilution

In 1995, Congress amended the Lanham Act by passing the Federal Trademark Dilution Act,[2] which allowed trademark owners to bring a suit in federal court for trademark *dilution*. In 2006, Congress further amended the law on trademark dilution by passing the Trademark Dilution Revision Act (TDRA).[3]

　Under the TDRA, to state a claim for trademark dilution, a plaintiff must prove the following:

1. The plaintiff owns a famous mark that is distinctive.
2. The defendant has begun using a mark in commerce that allegedly is diluting the famous mark.
3. The similarity between the defendant's mark and the famous mark gives rise to an *association* between the marks.
4. The association is likely to impair the distinctiveness of the famous mark or harm its reputation.

---

1. 15 U.S.C. Sections 1051–1128.
2. 15 U.S.C. Section 1125.
3. Pub. L. No. 103-312, 120 Stat. 1730 (2006).

When an Oregon woman opened this store, its sign read "Sambuck's." On what ground did Starbuck's sue her so that she had to change the store's name?

Trademark dilution laws protect "distinctive" or "famous" trademarks (such as Rolls Royce, McDonald's, and Apple) from certain unauthorized uses even when the use is on noncompeting goods or is unlikely to confuse. More than half of the states have also enacted trademark dilution laws.

Use of a Similar Mark May Constitute Trademark Dilution   A famous mark may be diluted not only by the use of an *identical* mark but also by the use of a *similar* mark.[4]

CASE EXAMPLE 8.1   Samantha Lundberg opened a coffee shop under the name "Sambuck's Coffee" in Astoria, Oregon, even though she knew that "Starbucks" is the largest coffee chain in the nation. When Starbucks Corporation filed a dilution lawsuit, the federal court ruled that use of the "Sambuck's" mark constituted trademark dilution because it created confusion for consumers. Not only was there a "high degree" of similarity between the marks, but also both companies provided coffee-related services through "stand-alone" retail stores. Therefore, the use of the similar mark (Sambuck's) reduced the value of the famous mark (Starbucks).[5] ●

Trademark Registration

Trademarks may be registered with the state or with the federal government. To register for protection under federal trademark law, a person must file an application with the U.S. Patent and Trademark Office in Washington, D.C. A mark can be registered (1) if it is currently in commerce or (2) if the applicant intends to put the mark into commerce within six months.

In special circumstances, the six-month period can be extended by thirty months, giving the applicant a total of three years from the date of notice of trademark approval to make use of the mark and to file the required use statement. Registration is postponed until the mark is actually used.

During this waiting period, the applicant's trademark is protected against any third party who has neither used the mark previously nor filed an application for it. Registration is renewable between the fifth and sixth years after the initial registration and every ten years thereafter (every twenty years for trademarks registered before 1990).

Trademark Infringement

Registration of a trademark with the U.S. Patent and Trademark Office gives notice on a nationwide basis that the trademark belongs exclusively to the registrant. The registrant is also allowed to use the symbol ® to indicate that the mark has been registered. Whenever someone else uses that trademark in its entirety or copies it to a substantial degree, intentionally or unintentionally, the trademark has been *infringed* (used without authorization).

When a trademark has been infringed, the owner has a cause of action against the infringer. To succeed in a lawsuit for trademark infringement, the owner must show that the defendant's use of the mark created a likelihood of confusion about the origin of the defendant's goods or services. The owner need not prove that the infringer acted intentionally or that the trademark was registered (although registration does provide proof of the date of inception of the trademark's use).

---

4. See *Louis Vuitton Malletier S.A. v. Haute Diggity Dog, LLC,* 507 F.3d 252 (4th Cir. 2007); and *Moseley v. V Secret Catalogue, Inc.,* 537 U.S. 418, 123 S.Ct. 1115, 155 L.Ed.2d 1 (2003).
5. *Starbucks Corp. v. Lundberg,* 2005 WL 3183858 (D.Or. 2005).

See this chapter's *Online Developments* feature that follows for a discussion of how some companies are turning first to Internet forums, before they resort to costly trademark litigation.

The remedy most commonly granted for trademark infringement is an *injunction* to prevent further infringement. Under the Lanham Act, a trademark owner who successfully proves infringement can recover actual damages, plus the profits that the infringer wrongfully received from the unauthorized use of the mark. A court can also order the destruction of any goods bearing the unauthorized trademark. In some situations, the trademark owner may also be able to recover attorneys' fees.

Distinctiveness of the Mark

A central objective of the Lanham Act is to reduce the likelihood that consumers will be confused by similar marks. For that reason, only those trademarks that are deemed sufficiently distinctive from all competing trademarks will be protected. In addition, a trademark may not be derogatory to a person, institution, belief, or national symbol.

ONLINE DEVELOPMENTS

Using Online Shame in Trademark Disputes

Claims of trademark infringement have risen 5 percent each year for the past several years and exceeded four thousand in 2014. Trademark litigation is costly and can drag on for years. Small businesses, particularly start-ups, typically do not have the resources to engage in such lengthy litigation.

Yet claims of infringement, even when they seem dubious, must be addressed. Some entrepreneurs are finding that online publicity and the shame it can bring are an effective alternative to going to federal court to resolve trademark disputes.

Can a Company Trademark the Letter "K"?

When Phil Michaelson created the Web site KeepRecipes.com to provide an Internet cookbook where people could collect and share recipes, he never thought the word "Keep" and the letter "K" could be someone's trademarks.

On his site, users click on "K," which is short for "Keep," when they want to save the instructions for a recipe. Nevertheless, AdKeeper, a New York–based service company, immediately sent Michaelson a cease-and-desist letter. AdKeeper claimed that the use of "K" and "Keep," as well as the Web site name *KeepRecipes.com*, constituted "blatant trademark infringement."

Online Publicity Provides a Solution

Michaelson did not have the resources to engage in a prolonged legal battle with AdKeeper, even though he thought its claims had no merit. Instead, he turned to Chillingeffects.org, a Web site created by several universities to foster lawful online activity. Soon after he described his problem and posted the cease-and-desist letter, several lawyers who deal with Web site issues offered to represent him in his trademark dispute at no charge.

Using Social Media

Other small entrepreneurs facing lawsuits are turning to social media, especially Facebook and Twitter, where large companies' threats to sue small companies for trademark infringement are generally met with displeasure.

When the restaurant company Chick-fil-A, Inc., for example, threatened Vermont T-shirt manufacturer Bo Muller-Moore with a lawsuit, he created a Facebook page. Chick-fil-A claimed that Muller-Moore had infringed its trademarked slogan "Eat Mor Chikin" when he used the slogan "Eat More Kale" on his T-shirts—even though Muller-Moore used correct spelling and kale and chicken would seem to be rather different foods. Several thousand supporters regularly look at Muller-Moore's Facebook page and have donated $10,000 for his defense.

Critical Thinking

As social media becomes ever more pervasive in our lives, what do you expect to occur with respect to trademark disputes?

A controversial issue in trademark law has to do with the use of slang terms for American Indians, such as "redskins" and "braves." Many Native Americans find the use of these names offensive. **EXAMPLE 8.2** In 2014, the United States Patent and Trademark Office (USPTO) rejected an application to trademark "Washington Redskin Potatoes," in part because the name could be seen as derogatory to Native Americans. Numerous football and sports teams (including the Washington Redskins) have had their trademarks challenged for the same reason. It has proved more difficult for the USPTO to cancel an existing trademark than to refuse to register a new mark, however. •

Strong Marks

Fanciful, arbitrary, or suggestive trademarks are generally considered to be the most distinctive (strongest) trademarks. Because they are normally taken from outside the context of the particular product, strong marks provide the best means of distinguishing one product from another. Fanciful trademarks include invented words, such as *Xerox* for one manufacturer's copiers and *Google* for search engines. Arbitrary trademarks use common words that would not ordinarily be associated with the product, such as *Dutch Boy* as a name for paint.

A single letter used in a particular style can be an arbitrary trademark. **CASE EXAMPLE 8.3** Sports entertainment company ESPN, Inc., sued Quiksilver, Inc., a maker of youth-oriented clothing, alleging trademark infringement. ESPN claimed that Quiksilver had used on its clothing the stylized "X" mark that ESPN uses in connection with the "X Games" (competitions in extreme action sports). Quiksilver filed counterclaims for trademark infringement and dilution, arguing that it had a long history of using the stylized X on its products.

ESPN created the X Games in the mid-1990s, and Quiksilver has used the X mark since 1994. ESPN asked the court to dismiss Quiksilver's counterclaims, but the court refused, holding that the X on Quiksilver's clothing was clearly an arbitrary mark. The court found that the two Xs were "similar enough that a consumer might well confuse them."[6] •

Suggestive Trademarks

Suggestive trademarks bring to mind something about a product without describing the product directly. For instance, "Dairy Queen" suggests an association between its products and milk, but it does not directly describe ice cream. "Blu-ray" is a suggestive mark that is associated with the high-quality, high-definition video contained on a particular optical data storage disc. Although blue-violet lasers are used to read blu-ray discs, the term *blu-ray* does not directly describe the disc.

Secondary Meaning

Descriptive terms, geographic terms, and personal names are not inherently distinctive and do not receive protection under the law *until* they acquire a secondary meaning. A secondary meaning arises when customers begin to associate a specific term or phrase, such as "London Fog," with specific trademarked items (coats with "London Fog" labels) made by a particular company.

CASE EXAMPLE 8.4 Frosty Treats, Inc., sells frozen desserts out of ice cream trucks. The video game series *Twisted Metal* depicted an ice cream truck with a clown character on it that was similar to the clowns on Frosty Treats' trucks. In the last game of the series, the truck bears the label "Frosty Treats." Frosty Treats sued for trademark infringement, but the court held that "Frosty Treats" is a descriptive term that is not protected by trademark law unless it has acquired a secondary meaning. To establish secondary meaning, Frosty Treats would have to show that the public recognizes its trademark and associates it with a single source. Because Frosty Treats failed to do so, the court entered a judgment in favor of the video game producer.[7] •

---

6. *ESPN, Inc. v. Quiksilver, Inc.*, 586 F.Supp.2d 219 (S.D.N.Y. 2008).
7. *Frosty Treats, Inc. v. Sony Computer Entertainment America, Inc.*, 426 F.3d 1001 (8th Cir. 2005).

Once a secondary meaning is attached to a term or name, a trademark is considered distinctive and is protected. Even a color can qualify for trademark protection, such as the color schemes used by state university sports teams, including Ohio State University and Louisiana State University.[8]

Generic Terms   Generic terms are terms that refer to an entire class of products, such as *bicycle* and *computer.* Generic terms receive no protection, even if they acquire secondary meanings. A particularly thorny problem for a business arises when its trademark acquires generic use. For instance, *aspirin* and *thermos* were originally trademarked products, but today the words are used generically. Other trademarks that have acquired generic use include *escalator, trampoline, raisin bran, dry ice, lanolin, linoleum, nylon,* and *cornflakes.*

Service, Certification, and Collective Marks

A **service mark** is essentially a trademark that is used to distinguish the *services* (rather than the products) of one person or company from those of another. For instance, each airline has a particular mark or symbol associated with its name. Titles and character names used in radio and television are frequently registered as service marks.

Other marks protected by law include certification marks and collective marks. A **certification mark** is used by one or more persons, other than the owner, to certify the region, materials, mode of manufacture, quality, or other characteristic of specific goods or services. Certification marks include such marks as "Good Housekeeping Seal of Approval" and "UL Tested."

When used by members of a cooperative, association, labor union, or other organization, a certification mark is referred to as a **collective mark.** **EXAMPLE 8.5** Collective marks appear at the end of a movie's credits to indicate the various associations and organizations that participated in making the movie. The labor union marks found on the tags of certain products are also collective marks. ●

Service Mark A trademark that is used to distinguish the services (rather than the products) of one person or company from those of another.

Certification Mark A mark used by one or more persons, other than the owner, to certify the region, materials, mode of manufacture, quality, or other characteristic of specific goods or services.

Collective Mark A mark used by members of a cooperative, association, union, or other organization to certify the region, materials, mode of manufacture, quality, or other characteristic of specific goods or services.

Trade Dress

The term **trade dress** refers to the image and overall appearance of a product. Trade dress is a broad concept that can include all or part of the total image or overall impression created by a product or its packaging. **EXAMPLE 8.6** The distinctive decor, menu, and style of service of a particular restaurant may be regarded as the restaurant's trade dress. Similarly, trade dress can include the layout and appearance of a mail-order catalogue, the use of a lighthouse as part of a golf hole, the fish shape of a cracker, or the G-shaped design of a Gucci watch. ●

Basically, trade dress is subject to the same protection as trademarks. In cases involving trade dress infringement, as in trademark infringement cases, a major consideration is whether consumers are likely to be confused by the allegedly infringing use.

Trade Dress The image and overall appearance ("look and feel") of a product that is protected by trademark law.

Counterfeit Goods

Counterfeit goods copy or otherwise imitate trademarked goods but are not genuine. The importation of goods bearing counterfeit (fake) trademarks poses a growing problem for U.S. businesses, consumers, and law enforcement. In addition to having negative financial effects on legitimate businesses, sales of certain counterfeit goods, such as pharmaceuticals and nutritional supplements, can present serious public health risks.

Although Congress has enacted statutes against counterfeit goods (discussed next), the United States cannot prosecute foreign counterfeiters because our national laws do not

---

8. *Board of Supervisors of LA State University v. Smack Apparel Co.,* 438 F.Supp.2d 653 (2006). See also *Qualitex Co. v. Jacobson Products Co.,* 514 U.S. 159, 115 S.Ct. 1300, 131 L.Ed.2d 248 (1995).

(AP Photo/Nick Ut)

A federal customs officer displays about $4 million of counterfeit goods that were seized in the Los Angeles area. Is it possible to control the foreign sources of such merchandise?

apply to them. Instead, one effective tool that U.S. officials are using to combat online sales of counterfeit goods is to obtain a court order to close down the domain names of Web sites that sell such goods. **EXAMPLE 8.7** In 2013, U.S. agents shut down 297 domain names on the Monday after Thanksgiving ("Cyber Monday," the online version of "Black Friday," the day after Thanksgiving when the holiday shopping season begins). Europol, an international organization, shut down 393 domain names. Although the criminal enterprises may continue selling counterfeit versions of brand-name products under different domain names, shutting down the Web sites, particularly on key shopping days, prevents some counterfeit goods from entering the United States. •

Stop Counterfeiting in Manufactured Goods Act

In 2006, Congress enacted the Stop Counterfeiting in Manufactured Goods Act[9] (SCMGA) to combat counterfeit goods. The act made it a crime to intentionally traffic in, or attempt to traffic in, counterfeit goods or services, or to knowingly use a counterfeit mark on or in connection with goods or services.

Before this act, the law did not prohibit the creation or shipment of counterfeit labels that were not attached to any product. Therefore, counterfeiters would make labels and packaging bearing a fake trademark, ship the labels to another location, and then affix them to inferior products to deceive buyers. The SCMGA closed this loophole by making it a crime to traffic in counterfeit labels, stickers, packaging, and the like, whether or not they are attached to goods.

Penalties for Counterfeiting

Persons found guilty of violating the SCMGA may be fined up to $2 million or imprisoned for up to ten years (or more if they are repeat offenders). If a court finds that the statute was violated, it must order the defendant to forfeit the counterfeit products (which are then destroyed), as well as any property used in the commission of the crime. The defendant must also pay restitution to the trademark holder or victim in an amount equal to the victim's actual loss.

CASE EXAMPLE 8.8 Wajdi Beydoun pleaded guilty to conspiring to import cigarette-rolling papers from Mexico that were falsely marked as "Zig-Zags" and sell them in the United States. The defendant was sentenced to prison and ordered to pay $566,267 in restitution. On appeal, the court affirmed the prison sentence but ordered the trial court to reduce the amount of restitution because it exceeded the actual loss suffered by the legitimate sellers of Zig-Zag rolling papers.[10] •

Trade Names

Trade Name A name that a business uses to identify itself and its brand. A trade name that is the same as the company's trademarked product is protected as a trademark, and unique trade names are protected under the common law.

Trademarks apply to *products*. A **trade name** indicates part or all of a *business's name,* whether the business is a sole proprietorship, a partnership, or a corporation. Generally, a trade name is directly related to a business and its goodwill.

Trade names may be protected as trademarks if the trade name is the same as the company's trademarked product—for example, Coca-Cola. Unless it is also used as a trademark or service mark, a trade name cannot be registered with the federal government.

Trade names are protected under the common law, however. As with trademarks, words must be unusual or fancifully used if they are to be protected as trade names. For instance,

---

9. Pub. L. No. 109-181 (2006), which amended 18 U.S.C. Sections 2318–2320.
10. *United States v. Beydoun,* 469 F.3d 102 (5th Cir. 2006).

the courts held that the word *Safeway* was sufficiently fanciful to obtain protection as a trade name for a grocery chain.

Licensing

One way to avoid litigation and still make use of another's trademark or other form of intellectual property is to obtain a license to do so. A **license** in this context is an agreement permitting the use of a trademark, copyright, patent, or trade secret for certain limited purposes. The party that owns the intellectual property rights and issues the license is the *licensor,* and the party obtaining the license is the *licensee.*

A license grants only the rights expressly described in the license agreement. A licensor might, for example, allow the licensee to use the trademark as part of its company name, or as part of its domain name, but not otherwise use the mark on any products or services. Disputes frequently arise over licensing agreements, particularly when the license involves Internet uses.

Typically, license agreements are very detailed and should be carefully drafted. **CASE EXAMPLE 8.9** George V Restauration S.A. and others owned and operated the Buddha Bar Paris, a restaurant with an Asian theme in Paris, France. In 2005, one of the owners allowed Little Rest Twelve, Inc., to use the Buddha Bar trademark and its associated concept in New York City under the name *Buddha Bar NYC.* Little Rest paid royalties for its use of the Buddha Bar mark and advertised Buddha Bar NYC's affiliation with Buddha Bar Paris, a connection also noted on its Web site and in the media.

When a dispute arose, the owners of Buddha Bar Paris withdrew their permission for Buddha Bar NYC's use of their mark, but Little Rest continued to use it. The owners of the mark filed a suit in a New York state court against Little Rest, and ultimately a state appellate court granted an injunction preventing Little Rest from using the mark.[11] ●

License An agreement by the owner of intellectual property to permit another to use a trademark, copyright, patent, or trade secret for certain limited purposes.

PREVENTING LEGAL DISPUTES

Consult with an attorney before signing any licensing contract to make sure that the wording of the contract is very clear as to what rights are or are not being conveyed. This can help to avoid litigation. Moreover, to prevent misunderstandings over the scope of the rights being acquired, determine whether any other parties hold licenses to use that particular intellectual property and the extent of those rights.

Patents

A **patent** is a grant from the government that gives an inventor the exclusive right to make, use, and sell an invention for a period of twenty years. Patents for designs, as opposed to inventions, are given for a fourteen-year period.

Until recently, patent law in the United States differed from the laws of many other countries because the first person to invent a product or process obtained the patent rights rather than the first person to file for a patent. It was often difficult to prove who invented an item first, however, which prompted Congress to change the system in 2011 by passing the America Invents Act.[12] Now the first person to file an application for a patent on a product or process will receive patent protection. In addition, the new law established a nine-month limit for challenging a patent on any ground.

Patent A property right granted by the federal government that gives an inventor an exclusive right to make, use, sell, or offer to sell an invention in the United States for a limited time.

Learning Objective 3
How does the law protect patents?

---

11. *George V Restauration S.A. v. Little Rest Twelve, Inc.,* 58 A.D.3d 428, 871 N.Y.S.2d 65 (2009).
12. The full title of this law is the Leahy-Smith America Invents Act, Pub. L. No. 112-29 (2011), which amended 35 U.S.C. Sections 1, 41, and 321.

The period of patent protection begins on the date when the patent application is filed, rather than when the patent is issued, which can sometimes be years later. After the patent period ends (either fourteen or twenty years later), the product or process enters the public domain, and anyone can make, sell, or use the invention without paying the patent holder.

Searchable Patent Databases

This is the home page of the U.S. Patent and Trademark Office. Is its database searchable?

A significant development relating to patents is the availability online of the world's patent databases. The Web site of the U.S. Patent and Trademark Office (www.uspto.gov) provides searchable databases covering U.S. patents granted since 1976. The Web site of the European Patent Office (www.epo.org) provides online access to 50 million patent documents in more than seventy nations through a searchable network of databases. Businesses use these searchable databases in many ways. Because patents are valuable assets, businesses may need to perform patent searches to list or inventory their assets. Patent searches may also be conducted to study trends and patterns in a specific technology or to gather information about competitors in the industry.

What Is Patentable?

Under federal law, "[w]hoever invents or discovers any new and useful process, machine, manufacture, or composition of matter, or any new and useful improvement thereof, may obtain a patent therefor, subject to the conditions and requirements of this title."[13] Thus, to be patentable, an invention must be *novel, useful,* and *not obvious* in light of current technology.

Almost anything is patentable, except the laws of nature, natural phenomena, and abstract ideas (including algorithms[14]). Even artistic methods and works of art, certain business processes, and the structures of storylines are patentable, provided that they are novel and not obvious.[15]

Plants that are reproduced asexually (by means other than from seed), such as hybrid or genetically engineered plants, are patentable in the United States, as are genetically engineered (or cloned) microorganisms and animals. **CASE EXAMPLE 8.10** Monsanto, Inc., sells its patented genetically modified (GM) seeds to farmers as a way to achieve higher yields from crops using fewer pesticides. It requires farmers who buy GM seeds to sign licensing agreements promising to plant the seeds for only one crop and to pay a technology fee for each acre planted. To ensure compliance, Monsanto has many full-time employees whose job is to investigate and prosecute farmers who use the GM seeds illegally. Monsanto has filed nearly 150 lawsuits against farmers in the United States and has been awarded more than $15 million in damages (not including out-of-court settlement amounts).[16] •

Patent Infringement

If a firm makes, uses, or sells another's patented design, product, or process without the patent owner's permission, it commits the tort of patent infringement. Patent infringement may occur even though the patent owner has not put the patented product in commerce.

> "To invent, you need a good imagination and a pile of junk."
>
> Thomas Edison, 1847–1931
> (American inventor)

---

13. 35 U.S.C. 101.
14. An *algorithm* is a step-by-step procedure, formula, or set of instructions for accomplishing a specific task—such as the set of rules used by a search engine to rank the listings contained within its index in response to a particular query.
15. For a United States Supreme Court case discussing the obviousness requirement, see *KSR International Co. v. Teleflex, Inc.,* 550 U.S. 398, 127 S.Ct. 1727, 167 L.Ed.2d 705 (2007). For a discussion of business process patents, see *In re Bilski,* 535 F.3d 943 (Fed.Cir. 2008).
16. See, for example, *Monsanto Co. v. Scruggs,* 459 F.3d 1328 (2006); *Monsanto Co. v. McFarling,* 2005 WL 1490051 (E.D.Mo. 2005); and *Sample v. Monsanto Co.,* 283 F.Supp.2d 1088 (2003).

Patent infringement may also occur even though not all features or parts of an invention are copied. (To infringe the patent on a process, however, all steps or their equivalent must be copied.) To read about an important issue in patent infringement today, see this chapter's *Insight into Ethics* feature that follows.

Patent Infringement Suits and High-Tech Companies

Obviously, companies that specialize in developing new technology stand to lose significant profits if someone "makes, uses, or sells" devices that incorporate their patented inventions. Because these firms are the holders of numerous patents, they are frequently involved in patent infringement lawsuits (as well as other types of intellectual property disputes). Many companies that make and sell electronics and computer software and hardware are based in foreign nations (for example, Samsung Electronics Company is a Korean firm). Foreign firms can apply for and obtain U.S. patent protection on items that they sell within the United States, just as U.S. firms can obtain protection in foreign nations where they sell goods.

Nevertheless, as a general rule, no patent infringement occurs under U.S. law when a patented product is made and sold in another country. The United States Supreme Court has narrowly construed patent infringement as it applies to exported software.

CASE EXAMPLE 8.11 AT&T Corporation holds a patent on a device used to digitally encode, compress, and process recorded speech. AT&T brought an infringement case against Microsoft Corporation, which admitted that its Windows operating system incorporated software code that infringed on AT&T's patent. The case reached the United States Supreme Court on the question of whether Microsoft's liability extended to computers made in another country. The Court held that it did not. Microsoft was liable only for infringement in the United States and not for the Windows-based computers produced in foreign locations. The Court reasoned that Microsoft had not "supplied" the software for the computers but had only electronically transmitted a master copy, which the foreign manufacturers then copied and loaded onto the computers.[17] ●

Apple, Inc. v. Samsung Electronics Company

As mentioned in the chapter introduction, Apple sued Samsung in federal court in 2011 alleging that Samsung's Galaxy mobile phones and tablets infringe on Apple's patents. The complaint also included allegations of trade dress violations (that Samsung copied the "look and feel" of iPhones and iPads) and trademark infringement (that the icons used for many of the apps on Samsung's products are nearly identical to Apple's apps).

Apple claimed that its design patents cover the graphical user interface (the display of icons on the home screen), the device's shell, and the screen and button design. It also claimed that its patents cover the way information is displayed on iPhones and other devices, the way windows pop open, and the way information is scaled and rotated, among other things. Apple argued that Samsung's phones and tablets that use Google's HTC Android operating system violate all of these patents.

In 2012, a jury issued a verdict in favor of Apple and awarded more than $1 billion in damages.[18] The jury found that Samsung had willfully infringed five of Apple's patents and had "diluted" Apple's registered iPhone trade dress. The jury's award was one of the largest ever in a patent case. The case also provides an important precedent for Apple in its legal attacks against Android devices made by other companies worldwide. In fact, Apple filed another infringement lawsuit against Samsung over different patents in 2014.

(SeongJoon Cho/Bloomberg via Getty Images)

Galaxy Tab 10.1 tablet computer at the company's Galaxy Zone showroom in Seoul, Korea.

"The patent system . . . added the fuel to the fire of genius."

Abraham Lincoln, 1809–1865 (The sixteenth president of the United States, 1861–1865)

---

17. *Microsoft Corp. v. AT&T Corp.,* 550 U.S. 437, 127 S.Ct. 1746, 167 L.Ed.2d 737 (2007).
18. *Apple, Inc. v. Samsung Electronics Co.,* Case Nos. CV 11-1846 and CV 12-0630 (N.D. Cal. August 24, 2012).

INSIGHT INTO ETHICS

THE EMERGENCE OF PATENT TROLLS

In recent years, a huge number of patent infringement lawsuits have been filed against software and technology firms. Many patent cases involve companies defending real innovations, but some lawsuits are "shakedowns" by patent trolls.

Patent trolls—more formally called nonpracticing entities (NPEs) or patent assertion entities (PAEs)—are firms that do not make or sell products or services but are in the business of patent litigation. These firms buy patents and then assert them against companies that *do* sell products or services, demanding licensing fees and threatening infringement lawsuits. Such business practices, although ethically questionable, are not illegal under current law.

"I'm Going to Sue You Unless You Pay Me to Go Away"

Patent trolls literally bank on the fact that when threatened with infringement suits, most companies would rather pay to settle than engage in costly litigation, even if they believe they could win. Consider an example. Soverain Software, LLC, sued dozens of online retailers, including Amazon, Avon, Home Depot, Macy's, Nordstrom, Kohl's, RadioShack, The Gap, and Victoria's Secret. Soverain claimed that it owned patents that covered nearly any use of online shopping-cart technology and that all these retailers had infringed on its patents. Amazon paid millions to settle with Soverain, as did most of the other defendants.

Interestingly, one online retailer, Newegg, Inc., refused to pay Soverain and ultimately won in court. In 2013, a federal appellate court held that the shopping-cart patent claim was invalid on the ground of obviousness because the technology for it already existed before Soverain obtained its patent.[a]

The Role of Software Patents

The patent troll problem is concentrated in software patents, which often include descriptions of what the software does rather than the computer code involved. Many software patents are vaguely worded and overly broad. In the United States, both the patent system and the courts have had difficulty evaluating and protecting such patents.

As a result, nearly any business that uses basic technology can be a target of patent trolls. In fact, *more than 60 percent of all new patent cases* are filed by patent trolls. The firms most commonly targeted by patent trolls, however, are large technology companies, including AT&T, Google, Apple, Samsung, Amazon, and Verizon.[b] In 2013 alone, "AT&T was sued for patent infringement by so-called patent trolls a startling 54 times—more than once a week."[c]

Reforms on the Horizon

There is widespread agreement that patent trolls are stifling innovation and clogging our courts with patent suits that are sometimes without merit. Patent trolls also make it more difficult for start-up companies to attract investors (because of the potential for infringement claims). As a result, every branch of our government is considering reforms.

President Barack Obama issued five executive orders designed to deal with patent trolls. These orders require officials at the Patent and Trademark Office to stop issuing overly broad patents, and force patent applicants to provide more details about their claims. One order opens up the patent application approval process for public scrutiny.

In his 2014 State of the Union address, President Obama urged Congress to "pass a patent reform bill that allows our businesses to stay focused on innovation, not costly and needless litigation." Congress is debating what provisions to include in patent reform legislation. In addition, the United States Supreme Court is considering a case concerning whether patent trolls should pay legal fees to the other side if they lose in court.[d]

For Critical Analysis

Some argue that the best way to stop patent trolls from taking advantage of the system would be to eliminate software patents completely and pass a law that makes software unpatentable. Would this be fair to software and technology companies? Why or why not?

---

a. *Soverain Software, LLC v. Newegg, Inc.*, 728 F.3d 1332 (Fed.Cir. 2013), cert. denied, ___ U.S. ___, 134 S.Ct. 910, 187 L.Ed.2d 779 (2014).

b. Roger Parloff, "10 Biggest Patent Troll Targets in Business," *Fortune*, February 27, 2014.

c. Roger Parloff, "Taking on the Patent Trolls," *Fortune*, February 27, 2014.

d. *Highmark, Inc. v. Allcare Health Management System, Inc.*, 687 F.3d 1300 (Fed.Cir. 2012), cert. granted, ___ U.S. ___, 134 S.Ct. 48, 186 L.Ed.2d 962 (2013).

Remedies for Patent Infringement

If a patent is infringed, the patent holder may sue for relief in federal court. The patent holder can seek an injunction against the infringer and can also request damages for royalties and lost profits. In some cases, the court may grant the winning party reimbursement for attorneys' fees and costs. If the court determines that the infringement was willful, the court can triple the amount of damages awarded (treble damages).

In the past, permanent injunctions were routinely granted to prevent future infringement. In 2006, however, the United States Supreme Court ruled that patent holders are not automatically entitled to a permanent injunction against future infringing activities. According to the Supreme Court, a patent holder must prove that it has suffered irreparable injury and that the public interest would not be *disserved* by a permanent injunction.[19] This decision gives courts discretion to decide what is equitable in the circumstances and allows them to consider the public interest rather than just the interests of the parties.

CASE EXAMPLE 8.12 In the first case applying this rule, a court found that although Microsoft had infringed on the patent of a small software company, the latter was not entitled to an injunction. According to the court, the small company was not irreparably harmed and could be adequately compensated by monetary damages. Also, the public might suffer negative effects from an injunction because the infringement involved part of Microsoft's widely used Office suite software.[20] •

Copyrights

A **copyright** is an intangible property right granted by federal statute to the author or originator of certain literary or artistic productions. The Copyright Act of 1976,[21] as amended, governs copyrights. Works created after January 1, 1978, are automatically given statutory copyright protection for the life of the author plus 70 years. For copyrights owned by publishing companies, the copyright expires 95 years from the date of publication or 120 years from the date of creation, whichever is first. For works by more than one author, the copyright expires 70 years after the death of the last surviving author.[22]

CASE EXAMPLE 8.13 The popular character Sherlock Holmes originated in stories written by Arthur Conan Doyle. Over the years, elements of the characters and stories created by Doyle have appeared in books, movies, and television series, including the recent *Elementary* on CBS and *Sherlock* on BBC. Prior to 2013, those wanting to use the copyrighted Sherlock story had to pay a licensing fee to Doyle's estate. Then, in 2013, the editors of a book of Holmes-related stories filed a lawsuit in federal court claiming that the basic Sherlock Holmes story elements introduced before 1923 should no longer be protected. The court agreed and ruled that these elements have entered the public domain—that is, the copyright has expired and they can be used without permission.[23] •

Copyrights can be registered with the U.S. Copyright Office (www.copyright.gov) in Washington, D.C. A copyright owner no longer needs to place a © or *Copr.* or *Copyright* on the work, however, to have the work protected against infringement. Chances are that if somebody created it, somebody owns it.

Copyright The exclusive right of an author or originator of a literary or artistic production to publish, print, sell, or otherwise use that production for a statutory period of time.

Learning Objective 4
What laws protect authors' rights in the works they create?

---

19. *eBay, Inc. v. MercExchange, LLC*, 547 U.S. 388, 126 S.Ct. 1837, 164 L.Ed.2d 641 (2006).
20. See *Z4 Technologies, Inc. v. Microsoft Corp.*, 434 F.Supp.2d 437 (2006).
21. 17 U.S.C. Sections 101 *et seq.*
22. These time periods reflect the extensions of the length of copyright protection enacted by Congress in the Copyright Term Extension Act of 1998, 17 U.S.C. Section 302.
23. *Klinger v. Conan Doyle Estate, Ltd.*, ___ F.Supp.2d ___, 2013 WL 6824923 (N.D.Ill. 2013).

Artist Shepard Fairey created a poster portrait of Barack Obama. It was clearly based on an Associated Press file photo taken by Manny Garcia. Did Fairey violate copyright law?

(Jewel Samad/AFP/Getty Images)

Generally, copyright owners are protected against the following:

1. Reproduction of the work.
2. Development of derivative works.
3. Distribution of the work.
4. Public display of the work.

What Is Protected Expression?

Works that are copyrightable include books, records, films, artworks, architectural plans, menus, music videos, product packaging, and computer software. To be protected, a work must be "fixed in a durable medium" from which it can be perceived, reproduced, or communicated. Protection is automatic. Registration is not required.

Section 102 of the Copyright Act explicitly states that it protects original works that fall into one of the following categories:

1. Literary works (including newspaper and magazine articles, computer and training manuals, catalogues, brochures, and print advertisements).
2. Musical works and accompanying words (including advertising jingles).
3. Dramatic works and accompanying music.
4. Pantomimes and choreographic works (including ballets and other forms of dance).
5. Pictorial, graphic, and sculptural works (including cartoons, maps, posters, statues, and even stuffed animals).
6. Motion pictures and other audiovisual works (including multimedia works).
7. Sound recordings.
8. Architectural works.

Section 102 Exclusions
It is not possible to copyright an idea. Section 102 of the Copyright Act specifically excludes copyright protection for any "idea, procedure, process, system, method of operation, concept, principle, or discovery, regardless of the form in which it is described, explained, illustrated, or embodied." Thus, others can freely use the underlying ideas or principles embodied in a work.

What is copyrightable is the particular way in which an idea is *expressed*. Whenever an idea and an expression are inseparable, the expression cannot be copyrighted. Generally, anything that is not an original expression will not qualify for copyright protection. Facts widely known to the public are not copyrightable. Page numbers are not copyrightable because they follow a sequence known to everyone. Mathematical calculations are not copyrightable.

As noted above, an idea and its expression must be separable for the expression to be copyrightable. Similarly, for the design of a useful article to be copyrightable, the sculptural features of the article (the way it looks) must be separate from the article's utilitarian (functional) purpose. In the following case, the court was asked to apply this principle.

Case 8.2

Inhale, Inc. v. Starbuzz Tobacco, Inc.
United States Court of Appeals for the Ninth Circuit, 739 F.3d 446 (2014).

(megastocker/Shutterstock)

BACKGROUND AND FACTS A hookah is a device for smoking tobacco by filtering the smoke through water. The water is held in a container at the base of the hookah. Inhale, Inc., claimed to hold a registered copyright on a hookah that covered the shape of the hookah's water container. Inhale filed a suit in a federal district court against Starbuzz Tobacco, Inc., alleging copyright infringement for the sale of hookahs with identically shaped water containers.

Case 8.2—Continued

The court determined that the shape of the water container on Inhale's hookahs was not copyrightable and issued a summary judgment in Starbuzz's favor. Inhale appealed.

IN THE WORDS OF THE COURT . . .
O'SCANNLAIN, Circuit Judge.

* * * *

Because ownership of a valid copyright is an element of copyright infringement, summary judgment was appropriate if the shape of Inhale's hookah water container is not copyrightable.

* * * *

The parties agree that Inhale's hookah water container is a "useful article." *As the design of a useful article, the shape of the container is copyrightable only if, and only to the extent that, it incorporates* * * * *sculptural features that can be identified separately from, and are capable of existing independently of, the utilitarian aspects of the container.* [Emphasis added.]

This statutory standard is satisfied by either physical or conceptual separability. Inhale, Inc., does not argue that the container's shape satisfies the requirements of physical separability. Thus, we consider only conceptual separability.

* * * *

* * * The district court ruled that the container's shape is not conceptually separable from its utilitarian features. * * * However, Inhale emphasizes the distinctive shape of its hookah water container. Therefore, we must determine whether distinctiveness of shape affects separability.

* * * *

* * * [In an earlier case involving bottle designs,] the Copyright Office has determined that whether an item's shape is distinctive does not affect separability. That determination was based on the principle that analogizing the general shape of a useful article to works of modern sculpture is insufficient for conceptual separability. Although Inhale's water container, like a piece of modern sculpture, has a distinctive shape, the shape of the alleged artistic features and of the useful article are one and the same.

Because the Copyright Office's reasoning is persuasive, we adopt it for this case. The shape of a container is not independent of the container's utilitarian function—to hold the contents within its shape—because the shape accomplishes the function. The district court correctly concluded that the shape of Inhale's hookah water container is not copyrightable.

DECISION AND REMEDY   The U.S. Court of Appeals for the Ninth Circuit affirmed the lower court's judgment. "The shape of a container is not independent of the container's utilitarian function—to hold the contents within its shape—because the shape accomplishes the function."

WHAT IF THE FACTS WERE DIFFERENT?   *Suppose that Inhale had claimed a copyright in the design of a vodka bottle instead of a hookah. Would the result have been different? Why or why not?*

THE LEGAL ENVIRONMENT DIMENSION   *How could Inhale hold a registered copyright on its hookah if the shape of the water container was not copyrightable?*

Compilations of Facts   Unlike ideas, *compilations* of facts are copyrightable. Under Section 103 of the Copyright Act, a compilation is a work formed by the collection and assembling of preexisting materials or of data that are selected, coordinated, or arranged in such a way that the resulting work as a whole constitutes an original work of authorship.

The key requirement for the copyrightability of a compilation is originality. The White Pages of a telephone directory do not qualify for copyright protection because they simply list alphabetically names and telephone numbers. The Yellow Pages of a directory can be copyrightable, provided that the information is selected, coordinated, or arranged in an original way.

Copyright Infringement

Whenever the form or expression of an idea is copied, an infringement of copyright occurs. The reproduction does not have to be exactly the same as the original, nor does it have to reproduce the original in its entirety. If a substantial part of the original is reproduced, copyright infringement has occurred.

Remedies for Copyright Infringement   Those who infringe copyrights may be liable for damages or criminal penalties. These range from actual damages or statutory damages, imposed at the court's discretion, to criminal proceedings for willful violations. Actual damages are based on the harm caused to the copyright holder by the infringement, while statutory damages, not to exceed $150,000, are provided for under the Copyright Act. In addition, criminal proceedings may result in fines and/or imprisonment. In some instances, a court may grant an injunction against a defendant when the court deems it necessary to prevent future copyright infringement.

CASE EXAMPLE 8.14   Rusty Carroll operated an online term paper business, R2C2, Inc., that offered up to 300,000 research papers for sale at nine Web sites. Individuals whose work was posted on these Web sites without their permission filed a lawsuit against Carroll for copyright infringement. Because Carroll had repeatedly failed to comply with court orders regarding discovery, the court found that the copyright infringement was likely to continue unless an injunction was issued. The court therefore issued a permanent injunction prohibiting Carroll and R2C2 from selling any term paper without sworn documentary evidence that the paper's author had given permission.[24] •

The "Fair Use" Exception

An exception to liability for copyright infringement is made under the "fair use" doctrine. In certain circumstances, a person or organization can reproduce copyrighted material without paying royalties (fees paid to the copyright holder for the privilege of reproducing the copyrighted material). Section 107 of the Copyright Act provides as follows:

> [T]he fair use of a copyrighted work, including such use by reproduction in copies or phono-records or by any other means specified by [Section 106 of the Copyright Act], for purposes such as criticism, comment, news reporting, teaching (including multiple copies for classroom use), scholarship, or research, is not an infringement of copyright. In determining whether the use made of a work in any particular case is a fair use the factors to be considered shall include—
>
> (1) the purpose and character of the use, including whether such use is of a commercial nature or is for nonprofit educational purposes;
> (2) the nature of the copyrighted work;
> (3) the amount and substantiality of the portion used in relation to the copyrighted work as a whole; and
> (4) the effect of the use upon the potential market for or value of the copyrighted work.

What Is Fair Use?

Because these guidelines are very broad, the courts determine whether a particular use is fair on a case-by-case basis. Thus, anyone reproducing copyrighted material may be committing a violation. In determining whether a use is fair, courts have often considered the fourth factor to be the most important.

CASE EXAMPLE 8.15   The owner of copyrighted music, BMG Music Publishing, granted a license to Leadsinger, Inc., a manufacturer of karaoke devices. The license gave Leadsinger permission to reproduce the sound recordings, but not to reprint the song lyrics, which appeared at the bottom of a TV screen when the karaoke device was used. BMG demanded that Leadsinger pay a "lyric reprint" fee and a "synchronization" fee. Leadsinger refused to pay, claiming that its use of the lyrics was educational and thus did not constitute copyright infringement under the fair use exception. A federal appellate court disagreed. The court held that Leadsinger's display of the lyrics was not a fair use because it would have a negative effect on the value of the copyrighted work.[25] •

The First Sale Doctrine

Section 109(a) of the Copyright Act—also known as the *first sale doctrine*—provides that "the owner of a particular copy or phonorecord

---

24. *Weidner v. Carroll*, 2010 WL 310310 (S.D.Ill. 2010).
25. *Leadsinger, Inc. v. BMG Music Publishing*, 512 F.3d 522 (9th Cir. 2008).

lawfully made under [the Copyright Act], or any person authorized by such owner, is entitled, without the authority of the copyright owner, to sell or otherwise dispose of the possession of that copy or phonorecord."

In other words, once a copyright owner sells or gives away a particular copy of a work, the copyright owner no longer has the right to control the distribution of that copy. **EXAMPLE 8.16**   Miranda buys a copyrighted book, such as *The Hunger Games* by Suzanne Collins. She can legally sell it to another person. •

In 2012, the United States Supreme Court heard the appeal of a case involving the resale of textbooks on eBay. To read about the Court's decision in this important case, see this chapter's *Beyond Our Borders* feature.

BEYOND OUR BORDERS

The Resale of Textbooks Purchased Abroad

Students and professors alike complain about the high price of college textbooks. Some enterprising students have found that if they purchase textbooks printed abroad, they can sometimes save enough to justify the shipping charges. Textbook prices are lower in other countries because (1) production costs are lower there and (2) average incomes are also lower, so students are unable to pay the higher prices that U.S. students face. (Also, neither students nor professors abroad have the full range of paper and digital supplements that are offered with most textbooks in the United States.)

A Cornell University Student Starts a Side Business Supap Kirtsaeng, a citizen of Thailand, started his studies at Cornell University and then went on to a Ph.D. program at the University of Southern California. He enlisted friends and family in Thailand to buy copies of textbooks there and ship them to him in the United States. To pay for his education, Kirtsaeng resold the textbooks on eBay, where he eventually made about $100,000.

John Wiley & Sons, Inc., which had printed eight of those textbooks in Asia, sued Kirtsaeng in federal district court for copyright infringement under Section 602(a)(1) of the Copyright Act. Wiley claimed that it is

impermissible to import a work "without the authority of the owner." Kirtsaeng's defense was that Section 109(a) of the Copyright Act allows the first purchaser-owner of a book to sell or otherwise dispose of it without the copyright owner's permission. Kirtsaeng did not prevail.[a]

Kirtsaeng appealed to the U.S. Court of Appeals for the Second Circuit, but the court upheld the lower court's judgment.[b] The court reasoned that the first sale doctrine of the Copyright Act refers specifically to works that are manufactured in the United States. Therefore, the doctrine does not apply to textbooks printed and sold abroad, and then resold in the United States. Kirtsaeng appealed to the United States Supreme Court.

The Supreme Court Weighs In The Supreme Court had to decide this question: Can any copy of a book or CD or DVD that was legally produced abroad, acquired abroad, and then imported into the United States be resold in the United States without the copyright owner's permission? The answer to this question has implications for

discount sellers, such as Costco, and online businesses, such as eBay and Google, all of which offer "good" prices on many products that were made abroad.

The Supreme Court ruled in Kirtsaeng's favor, reversing the appellate court's decision.[c] The majority of the Court ruled that the first sale doctrine applies, even when the good was purchased abroad: " [T]he common-law history of the 'first-sale' doctrine . . . favors a non-geographical interpretation. We . . . doubt that Congress would have intended to create the practical copyright-related harms with which a geographical interpretation would threaten ordinary scholarly, artistic, commercial activities."

Much of the Court's decision concerned the potential consequences of what might occur if the Court did not reverse the appellate court's decision. Allowing that decision to stand would have meant that one "could prevent a buyer from domestically selling or even giving away copies of a video game made in Japan, a film made in Germany or a dress (with a design copyright) made in China."

Critical Thinking
What options do textbook publishers face given this Supreme Court decision?

---

a. *John Wiley & Sons, Inc. v. Kirtsaeng*, 93 U.S.P.Q.2d 1432 (S.D.N.Y. 2009).
b. *John Wiley & Sons, Inc. v. Kirtsaeng*, 654 F.3d 210 (2d Cir. 2011).
c. *Kirtsaeng v. John Wiley & Sons, Inc.*, ___ U.S. ___, 133 S.Ct. 1351, 185 L.Ed.2d 392 (2013).

Copyright Protection for Software

In 1980, Congress passed the Computer Software Copyright Act, which amended the Copyright Act to include computer programs in the list of creative works protected by federal copyright law.[26] Generally, copyright protection extends to those parts of a computer program that can be read by humans, such as the "high-level" language of a source code. Protection also extends to the binary-language object code, which is readable only by the computer, and to such elements as the overall structure, sequence, and organization of a program.

Not all aspects of software are protected, however. Courts typically have not extended copyright protection to the "look and feel"—the general appearance, command structure, video images, menus, windows, and other screen displays—of computer programs. **EXAMPLE 8.17** MiTek develops a software program for laying out wood trusses (used in construction). Another company comes out with a different program that includes similar elements, such as the menu and submenu command tree-structures. MiTek cannot successfully sue for copyright infringement because the command structure of software is not protected. • (Note that copying the "look and feel" of another's product may be a violation of trade dress or trademark laws, however.)

As will be explored in Chapter 9, technology has vastly increased the potential for copyright infringement via the Internet.

Trade Secrets

The law of trade secrets protects some business processes and information that are not or cannot be protected under patent, copyright, or trademark law against appropriation by a competitor. A **trade secret** is basically information of commercial value. Trade secrets may include customer lists, plans, research and development, pricing information, marketing techniques, and production methods—anything that makes an individual company unique and that would have value to a competitor.

Unlike copyright and trademark protection, protection of trade secrets extends both to ideas and to their expression. (For this reason, and because there are no registration or filing requirements for trade secrets, trade secret protection may be well suited for software.) Of course, the secret formula, method, or other information must be disclosed to some persons, particularly to key employees. Businesses generally attempt to protect their trade secrets by having all employees who use the process or information agree in their contracts, or in confidentiality agreements, never to divulge it.

State and Federal Law on Trade Secrets

Under Section 757 of the *Restatement of Torts,* those who disclose or use another's trade secret, without authorization, are liable to that other party if:

1. They discovered the secret by improper means, or
2. Their disclosure or use constitutes a breach of a duty owed to the other party.

Stealing of confidential business data by industrial espionage, as when a business taps into a competitor's computer, is a theft of trade secrets without any contractual violation and is actionable in itself.

Although trade secrets have long been protected under the common law, today most states' laws are based on the Uniform Trade Secrets Act, which has been adopted in forty-seven states. Additionally, in 1996 Congress passed the Economic Espionage Act, which

Trade Secret A formula, device, idea, process, or other information used in a business that gives the owner a competitve advantage in the marketplace.

Learning Objective 5
What are trade secrets, and what laws offer protection for this form of intellectual property?

---

26. Pub. L. No. 96-517 (1980), amending 17 U.S.C. Sections 101, 117.

made the theft of trade secrets a federal crime. We examined the provisions and significance of this act in Chapter 6, in the context of crimes related to business.

Trade Secrets in Cyberspace

Today's computer technology undercuts a business firm's ability to protect its confidential information, including trade secrets. For instance, a dishonest employee could e-mail trade secrets in a company's computer to a competitor or a future employer. If e-mail is not an option, the employee might walk out with the information on a flash pen drive.

A former employee's continued use of a Twitter account after leaving the company may be the grounds for a suit alleging misappropriation of trade secrets. **CASE EXAMPLE 8.18**   Noah Kravitz worked for a company called PhoneDog for four years as a product reviewer and video blogger. PhoneDog provided him with the Twitter account "@PhoneDog_Noah." Kravitz's popularity grew, and he had approximately 17,000 followers by the time he quit in 2010. PhoneDog requested that Kravitz stop using the Twitter account. Although Kravitz changed his handle to "@noahkravitz," he continued to use the account. PhoneDog subsequently sued Kravitz for misappropriation of trade secrets, among other things. Kravitz moved for a dismissal, but the court found that the complaint adequately stated a cause of action for misappropriation of trade secrets and allowed the suit to continue.[27] ●

For a summary of trade secrets and other forms of intellectual property, see Exhibit 8.1 that follows.

---

27. *PhoneDog v. Kravitz*, 2011 WL 5415612 (N.D.Cal. 2011).

Exhibit 8–1   Forms of Intellectual Property

	DEFINITION	HOW ACQUIRED	DURATION	REMEDY FOR INFRINGEMENT
Patent	A grant from the government that gives an inventor exclusive rights to an invention.	By filing a patent application with the U.S. Patent and Trademark Office and receiving its approval.	Twenty years from the date of the application; for design patents, fourteen years.	Monetary damages, including royalties and lost profits, *plus* attorneys' fees. Damages may be tripled for intentional infringements.
Copyright	The right of an author or originator of a literary or artistic work, or other production that falls within a specified category, to have the exclusive use of that work for a given period of time.	Automatic (once the work or creation is put in tangible form). Only the *expression* of an idea (and not the idea itself) can be protected by copyright.	For authors: the life of the author, plus 70 years. For publishers: 95 years after the date of publication or 120 years after creation.	Actual damages plus profits received by the party who infringed *or* statutory damages under the Copyright Act, *plus* costs and attorneys' fees in either situation.
Trademark (service mark and trade dress)	Any distinctive word, name, symbol, or device (image or appearance), or combination thereof, that an entity uses to distinguish its goods or services from those of others. The owner has the exclusive right to use that mark or trade dress.	1. At common law, ownership created by use of the mark. 2. Registration with the appropriate federal or state office gives notice and is permitted if the mark is currently in use or will be within the next six months.	Unlimited, as long as it is in use. To continue notice by registration, the owner must renew by filing between the fifth and sixth years, and thereafter, every ten years.	1. Injunction prohibiting the future use of the mark. 2. Actual damages plus profits received by the party who infringed (can be increased under the Lanham Act). 3. Destruction of articles that infringed. 4. *Plus* costs and attorneys' fees.
Trade Secret	Any information that a business possesses and that gives the business an advantage over competitors (including formulas, lists, patterns, plans, processes, and programs).	Through the originality and development of the information and processes that constitute the business secret and are unknown to others.	Unlimited, so long as not revealed to others. Once revealed to others, it is no longer a trade secret.	Monetary damages for misappropriation (the Uniform Trade Secrets Act also permits punitive damages if willful), *plus* costs and attorneys' fees.

International Protections

For many years, the United States has been a party to various international agreements relating to intellectual property rights. For example, the Paris Convention of 1883, to which about 173 countries are signatory, allows parties in one country to file for patent and trademark protection in any of the other member countries. Other international agreements include the Berne Convention, the Trade-Related Aspects of Intellectual Property Rights (known as the TRIPS agreement), the Madrid Protocol, and the Anti-Counterfeiting Trade Agreement.

The Berne Convention

Under the Berne Convention of 1886, an international copyright agreement, if a U.S. citizen writes a book, every country that has signed the convention must recognize her or his copyright in the book. Also, if a citizen of a country that has not signed the convention first publishes a book in one of the 163 countries that have signed, all other countries that have signed the convention must recognize that author's copyright. Copyright notice is not needed to gain protection under the Berne Convention for works published after March 1, 1989.

This convention and other international agreements have given some protection to intellectual property on a worldwide level. None of them, however, has been as significant and far reaching in scope as the TRIPS agreement, discussed in the next subsection.

In 2011, the European Union agreed to extend the period of royalty protection for musicians from fifty years to seventy years. This decision aids major record labels as well as performers and musicians who previously faced losing royalties from sales of their older recordings. The profits of musicians and record companies have been shrinking in recent years because of the sharp decline in sales of compact discs and the rise in digital downloads (both legal and illegal).

In the following case, the United States Supreme Court had to decide if Congress had exceeded its authority under the U.S. Constitution when it enacted a law that restored copyright protection to many foreign works that were already in the public domain.

Spotlight on Congressional Authority and Copyright Law

Case 8.3

Golan v. Holder
Supreme Court of the United States, ____ U.S. ____, 132 S.Ct. 873, 181 L.Ed.2d 835 (2012).

Does a U.S. singer owe royalties to the owner of a foreign-created song?

BACKGROUND AND FACTS The United States joined the Berne Convention in 1989, but it failed to give foreign copyright holders the same protections enjoyed by U.S. authors. Contrary to the Berne Convention, the United States did not protect any foreign work that had already entered the public domain.

In 1994, Congress enacted the Uruguay Round Agreements Act (URAA), which "restored" copyright protection for many foreign works that were already in the public domain. The URAA put foreign and domestic works on the same footing, allowing their copyrights to extend for the same number of years. Lawrence Golan, along with a group of musicians, conductors, and publishers, filed a suit against Eric Holder, in his capacity as the U.S. attorney general. These individuals had enjoyed free access to foreign works in the public domain before the URAA's enactment. They claimed that the URAA violated the copyright clause of the U.S. Constitution and thus that Congress had exceeded its constitutional authority in passing the URAA.

Spotlight Case 8.3—Continued

A federal appellate court held that Congress did not violate the copyright clause by passing the URAA. The petitioners appealed. The United States Supreme Court granted *certiorari* to resolve the matter.

IN THE WORDS OF THE COURT . . .

Justice *GINSBURG* delivered the opinion of the Court.

* * * *

* * * The Constitution states that "Congress shall have Power . . . to promote the Progress of Science . . . by securing for limited Times to Authors . . . the exclusive Right to their . . . Writings." Petitioners [Golan and others] find in this grant of authority an impenetrable [impassable] barrier to the extension of copyright protection to authors whose writings, for whatever reason, are in the public domain. We see no such barrier in the text of the Copyright Clause * * * .

* * * *

The text of the Copyright Clause does not exclude application of copyright protection to works in the public domain. * * * Petitioners' contrary argument relies primarily on the Constitution's confinement of a copyright's lifespan to a "limited Tim[e]." "Removing works from the public domain," they contend, "violates the 'limited times' restriction by turning a fixed and predictable period into one that can be reset or resurrected at any time, even after it expires."

Our decision in [a prior case] is largely dispositive [capable of settling a dispute] of petitioners' limited-time argument.[a] There we addressed the question of whether Congress violated the Copyright Clause when it extended, by 20 years, the terms of existing copyrights. Ruling that Congress acted within constitutional bounds, we

declined to infer from the text of the Copyright Clause "the command that a time prescription, once set, becomes forever 'fixed' or 'inalterable.'" *"The word 'limited,'* we observed, *"does not convey a meaning so constricted." Rather, the term is best understood to mean "confine[d] within certain bounds," "restrain[ed]," or "circumscribed."* The construction petitioners tender closely resembles the definition rejected in *Eldred* [the prior case] and is similarly infirm [weak]. [Emphasis added.]

* * * *

* * * In aligning the United States with other nations bound by the Berne Convention, and thereby according equitable treatment to once disfavored foreign authors, Congress can hardly be charged with a design to move stealthily toward a regime of perpetual copyrights.

DECISION AND REMEDY The United States Supreme Court affirmed the federal appellate court's ruling that the URAA does not violate the U.S. Constitution's copyright clause. Thus, Golan and the others could no longer use, without permission, any of the foreign works that were previously in the public domain. By passing the URAA in the United States, Congress, in effect, took those works out of the public domain and extended copyright protection to them. Henceforth, U.S. copyright and patent laws cover all such foreign intellectual property.

THE GLOBAL DIMENSION *What does the Court's decision in this case mean for copyright holders in the United States who want copyright protection in other countries? Will other nations be more or less inclined to protect U.S. authors? Explain.*

THE ECONOMIC DIMENSION *Why did a group of musicians, conductors, publishers, and others file this suit? What did they hope to gain by a decision in their favor?*

---

a. See *Eldred v. Ashcroft,* 537 U.S. 186, 123 S.Ct. 769, 154 L.Ed.2d 683 (2003).

The TRIPS Agreement

Representatives from more than one hundred nations signed the TRIPS agreement in 1994. The agreement established, for the first time, standards for the international protection of intellectual property rights, including patents, trademarks, and copyrights for movies, computer programs, books, and music. The TRIPS agreement provides that each member country of the World Trade Organization must include in its domestic laws broad intellectual property rights and effective remedies (including civil and criminal penalties) for violations of those rights.

Generally, the TRIPS agreement forbids member nations from discriminating against foreign owners of intellectual property rights (in the administration, regulation, or adjudication of such rights). In other words, a member nation cannot give its own nationals (citizens) favorable treatment without offering the same treatment to nationals of all other member countries. **EXAMPLE 8.19** A U.S. software manufacturer brings a suit for the infringement of intellectual property rights under Germany's national laws. Because Germany is a member of the TRIPS agreement, the U.S. manufacturer is entitled to receive the same treatment as a German manufacturer. ●

Each member nation must also ensure that legal procedures are available for parties who wish to bring actions for infringement of intellectual property rights. Additionally, a related document established a mechanism for settling disputes among member nations.

The Madrid Protocol

In the past, one of the difficulties in protecting U.S. trademarks internationally was the time and expense required to apply for trademark registration in foreign countries. The filing fees and procedures for trademark registration vary significantly among individual countries. The Madrid Protocol, which was signed into law in 2003, may help to resolve these problems.

The Madrid Protocol is an international treaty that has been signed by eighty-six countries. Under its provisions, a U.S. company wishing to register its trademark abroad can submit a single application and designate other member countries in which the company would like to register its mark. The treaty was designed to reduce the costs of international trademark protection by more than 60 percent.

Although the Madrid Protocol may simplify and reduce the cost of trademark registration in foreign countries, it remains to be seen whether it will provide significant benefits to trademark owners. Even with an easier registration process, there are still questions as to whether all member countries will enforce the law and protect the mark.

The Anti-Counterfeiting Trade Agreement

In 2011, Australia, Canada, Japan, Korea, Morocco, New Zealand, Singapore, and the United States signed the Anti-Counterfeiting Trade Agreement (ACTA), an international treaty to combat global counterfeiting and piracy. The members of the European Union, Mexico, Switzerland, and other nations that support ACTA are still developing domestic procedures to comply with its provisions. Once a nation has adopted appropriate procedures, it can ratify the treaty.

Provisions and Goals
The goals of the treaty are to increase international cooperation, facilitate the best law enforcement practices, and provide a legal framework to combat counterfeiting. The treaty will have its own governing body.

ACTA applies not only to counterfeit physical goods, such as medications, but also to pirated copyrighted works being distributed via the Internet. The idea is to create a new standard of enforcement for intellectual property rights that goes beyond the TRIPS agreement and encourages international cooperation and information sharing among signatory countries.

Border Searches
Under ACTA, member nations are required to establish border measures that allow officials, on their own initiative, to search commercial shipments of imports and exports for counterfeit goods. The treaty neither requires nor prohibits random border searches of electronic devices, such as laptops, tablet devices, and smartphones, for infringing content. If border authorities reasonably believe that any goods in transit are counterfeit, the treaty allows them to keep the suspect goods unless the owner proves that the items are authentic and noninfringing.

The treaty allows member nations, in accordance with their own laws, to order online service providers to furnish information about (including the identity of) suspected trademark and copyright infringers.

Reviewing . . . Intellectual Property Rights

Two computer science majors, Trent and Xavier, have an idea for a new video game, which they propose to call "Hallowed." They form a business and begin developing their idea. Several months later, Trent and Xavier run into a problem with their design and consult a friend, Brad, who is an expert in designing computer source codes. After the software is completed but before Hallowed is marketed, a video game called Halo 2 is released for both the Xbox and the Playstation systems. Halo 2 uses source codes similar to those of Hallowed and imitates Hallowed's overall look and feel, although not all the features are alike. Using the information presented in the chapter, answer the following questions.

1. Would the name *Hallowed* receive protection as a trademark or as trade dress? Explain.
2. If Trent and Xavier had obtained a patent on Hallowed, would the release of Halo 2 have infringed on their patent? Why or why not?
3. Based only on the facts described above, could Trent and Xavier sue the makers of Halo 2 for copyright infringement? Why or why not?
4. Suppose that Trent and Xavier discover that Brad took the idea of Hallowed and sold it to the company that produced Halo 2. Which type of intellectual property issue does this raise?

Debate This   Congress has impeded the spread of ideas by amending copyright law several times to give copyright holders protection for many decades.

LINKING BUSINESS LAW to Marketing

Trademarks and Service Marks

In your marketing courses, you have learned or will learn about the importance of trademarks. If you become a marketing manager, you will be involved in creating trademarks or service marks for your firm, protecting the firm's existing marks, and ensuring that you do not infringe on anyone else's marks.

The Broad Range of Trademarks and Service Marks

The courts have held that trademarks and service marks consist of much more than well-known brand names, such as Apple or Amazon. As a marketing manager, you will need to be aware that parts of a brand or other product identification often qualify for trademark protection.

- **Catchy Phrases**—Certain brands have established phrases that are associated with them, such as Nike's "Just Do It!" As a marketing manager for a competing product, you will have to avoid such catchy phrases in your own

marketing program. Note, though, that not all phrases can become part of a trademark or service mark. When a phrase is extremely common, the courts normally will not grant trademark or service mark protection to it.

- **Abbreviations**—The public sometimes abbreviates a well-known trademark. For example Budweiser beer is known as Bud and Coca-Cola as Coke. As a marketing manager, you should avoid using any name for a product or service that closely resembles a well-known abbreviation, such as Koke for a cola drink.

- **Shapes**—The shape of a brand name, a service mark, or a container can take on exclusivity if the shape clearly aids in product or service identification. For example, just about everyone throughout the world recognizes the shape of a Coca-Cola bottle. As a marketing manager, you would do

Continued

Linking Business Law to Marketing—Continued

well to avoid using a similar shape for a new carbonated drink.

- **Ornamental Colors**—Sometimes color combinations can become part of a service mark or trademark. For example, FedEx established its unique identity with the use of bright orange and purple. The courts have protected this color combination. The same holds for the black-and-copper color combination of Duracell batteries.

- **Ornamental Designs**—Symbols and designs associated with a particular mark are normally protected. Marketing managers should not attempt to copy them. Levi's places a small tag on the left side of the rear pocket of its jeans. Cross uses a cutoff black cone on the top of its pens.

- **Sounds**—Sounds can also be protected. For example, the familiar roar of the Metro-Goldwyn-Mayer (MGM) lion is protected.

When to Protect Your Trademarks and Service Marks

Every business should register its logo as a trademark, and perhaps also its business name and Web site address, to provide the company with the highest level of protection. A trademark will discourage counterfeiting and will give your firm the advantage in the event of future infringement.

Once your company has established a trademark or a service mark, as a manager, you will have to decide how aggressively you wish to protect those marks. If you fail to protect them, your company faces the possibility that they will become generic. Remember that *aspirin, cellophane, thermos, dry ice, shredded wheat,* and many other familiar terms were once legally protected trademarks. Protecting exclusive rights to a mark can be expensive, however, so you will have to determine how much it is worth to your company to protect your rights. If you work in a small company, making major expenditures to protect your trademarks and service marks might not be cost-effective.

Critical Thinking

The U.S. Patent and Trademark Office requires that a registered trademark or service mark be put into commercial use within three years after the application has been approved. Why do you think the federal government established this requirement?

Key Terms

Chapter Summary: Intellectual Property Rights

Trademarks and Related Property	1. *A trademark* is a distinctive word, symbol, or design that identifies the manufacturer as the source of the goods and distinguishes its products from those made or sold by others.
	2. The major federal statutes protecting trademarks and related property are the Lanham Act of 1946 and the Federal Trademark Dilution Act of 1995. Generally, to be protected, a trademark must be sufficiently distinctive from all competing trademarks.
	3. *Trademark infringement* occurs when one uses a mark that is the same as, or confusingly similar to, the protected trademark, service mark, trade name, or trade dress of another without permission when marketing goods or services.
Patents	1. *A patent* is a grant from the government that gives an inventor the exclusive right to make, use, and sell an invention for a period of twenty years (fourteen years for a design patent) from the date when the application for a patent is filed. To be patentable, an invention (or a discovery, process, or design) must be genuine, novel, useful, and not obvious in light of current technology. Computer software may be patented.
	2. Almost anything is patentable, except the laws of nature, natural phenomena, and abstract ideas (including algorithms). Even business processes or methods are patentable if they relate to a machine or transformation.
	3. *Patent infringement* occurs when one uses or sells another's patented design, product, or process without the patent owner's permission. The patent holder can sue the infringer in federal court and request an injunction, but must prove irreparable injury to obtain a permanent injunction against the infringer. The patent holder can also request damages and attorneys' fees. If the infringement was willful, the court can grant treble damages.

Chapter Summary: Intellectual Property Rights—Continued

Copyrights	1. *A copyright* is an intangible property right granted by federal statute to the author or originator of certain literary or artistic productions. The Copyright Act of 1976, as amended, governs copyrights. 2. *Copyright infringement* occurs whenever the form or expression of an idea is copied without the permission of the copyright holder. An exception applies if the copying is deemed a "fair use." 3. Computer software may be copyrighted.
Trade Secrets	*Trade secrets* include customer lists, plans, research and development, and pricing information. Trade secrets are protected under the common law and, in some states, under statutory law against misappropriation by competitors. The Economic Espionage Act made the theft of trade secrets a federal crime (see Chapter 6).
International Protections	Various international agreements provide international protection for intellectual property. A landmark agreement is the agreement on Trade-Related Aspects of Intellectual Property Rights (TRIPS), which provides for enforcement procedures in all countries signatory to the agreement.

Issue Spotters

1. Roslyn is a food buyer for Organic Cornucopia Food Company when she decides to go into business for herself as Roslyn's Kitchen. She contacts Organic's suppliers, offering to buy their entire harvest for the next year, and Organic's customers, offering to sell her products for less than her ex-employer. Has Roslyn violated any of the intellectual property rights discussed in this chapter? Explain. (See *Trade Secrets.*)
2. Global Products develops, patents, and markets software. World Copies, Inc., sells Global's software without the maker's permission. Is this patent infringement? If so, how might Global save the cost of suing World for infringement and at the same time profit from World's sales? (See *Patents.*)

—Check your answers to the Issue Spotters against the answers provided in Appendix D at the end of this text.

For Review

1. What is intellectual property?
2. Why is the protection of trademarks important?
3. How does the law protect patents?
4. What laws protect authors' rights in the works they create?
5. What are trade secrets, and what laws offer protection for this form of intellectual property?

Business Scenarios and Case Problems

8–1. Patent Infringement. John and Andrew Doney invented a hard-bearing device for balancing rotors. Although they obtained a patent for their invention from the U.S. Patent and Trademark Office, it was never used as an automobile wheel balancer. Some time later, Exetron Corp. produced an automobile wheel balancer that used a hard-bearing device with a support plate similar to that of the Doneys' device. Given that the Doneys had not used their device for automobile wheel balancing, does Exetron's use of a similar device infringe on the Doneys' patent? (See *Patents.*)

8–2. Fair Use. Professor Wise is teaching a summer seminar in business torts at State University. Several times during the course, he makes copies of relevant sections from business law texts and distributes them to his students. Wise does not realize that the daughter of one of the textbook authors is a member of his seminar. She tells her father about Wise's copying activities, which have taken place without her father's or his publisher's permission. Her father sues Wise for copyright infringement. Wise claims protection under the fair use doctrine. Who will prevail? Explain. (See *Copyrights.*)

8–3. Licensing. Redwin Wilchcombe composed, performed, and recorded a song called *Tha Weedman* at the request of Lil Jon, a member of Lil Jon & the East Side Boyz (LJESB), for LJESB's album *Kings of Crunk*. Wilchcombe was not paid, but was given credit on the album as a producer. After the album had sold two million copies, Wilchcombe filed a suit against LJESB, alleging copyright infringement. The defendants claimed that they had a license to use the song. Do the facts support this claim? Explain. [*Wilchcombe v. TeeVee Toons, Inc.,* 555 F.3d 949 (11th Cir. 2009)] (See *Trademarks.*)

8–4.   **Business Case Problem with Sample Answer— Trade Secrets.** Jesse Edwards, an employee of Carbon Processing and Reclamation, LLC (CPR), put unmarked boxes of company records in his car. Edwards's wife, Channon, who suspected him of hiding financial information from her, gained access to the documents. William Jones, the owner of CPR, filed a suit, contending that Channon's unauthorized access to the files was a theft of trade secrets. Could the information in the documents be trade secrets? Should liability be imposed? Why or why not? [*Jones v. Hamilton,* 59 So.3d 134 (Ala.Civ.App. 2010)] (See *Trade Secrets.*)

—For a sample answer to Problem 8–4, go to Appendix E at the end of this text.

8–5.   **Spotlight on Macy's—Copyright Infringement.** United Fabrics International, Inc., bought a fabric design from an Italian designer and registered a copyright to it with the U.S. Copyright Office. When Macy's, Inc., began selling garments with a similar design, United filed a copyright infringement suit against Macy's. Macy's argued that United did not own a valid copyright to the design and so could not claim infringement. Does United have to prove that the copyright is valid to establish infringement? Explain. [*United Fabrics International, Inc. v. C & J Wear, Inc.,* 630 F.3d 1255 (9th Cir. 2011)] (See *Copyrights.*)

8–6.   **Theft of Trade Secrets.** Hanjuan Jin, a citizen of the People's Republic of China, began working at Motorola in 1998. He worked as a software engineer in a division that created proprietary standards for cellular communications. In 2004 and 2005, in contradiction to Motorola's policies, Jin also began working as a consultant for Lemko Corp. Lemko introduced Jin to Sun Kaisens, a Chinese software company. During 2005, Jin returned to Beijing on several occasions and began working with Sun Kaisens and with the Chinese military. The following year, she started corresponding with Sun Kaisens's management about a possible full-time job in China. During this period, she took several medical leaves of absence from Motorola. In February 2007, after one of these medical leaves, she returned to Motorola.

During the next several days at Motorola, she accessed and downloaded thousands of documents on her personal laptop as well as on pen drives. On the following day, she attempted to board a flight to China but was randomly searched by U.S. Customs and Border Protection officials at Chicago's O'Hare International Airport. Ultimately, U.S. officials discovered the thousands of downloaded Motorola documents. Are there any circumstances under which Jin could avoid being prosecuted for theft of trade secrets? If so, what are these circumstances? Discuss fully. [*United States v. Hanjuan Jin,* 833 F.Supp.2d 977 (N.D.Ill. 2012)] (See *Trade Secrets.*)

8–7.   **Copyright Infringement.** SilverEdge Systems Software hired Catherine Conrad to perform a singing telegram. SilverEdge arranged for James Bendewald to record Conrad's performance of her copyrighted song to post on its Web site. Conrad agreed to wear a microphone to assist in the recording, told Bendewald what to film, and asked for an additional fee only if SilverEdge used the video for a commercial purpose. Later, the company chose to post the video of a different performer's singing telegram instead. Conrad filed a suit in a federal district court against SilverEdge and Bendewald for copyright infringement. Are the defendants liable? Explain. [*Conrad v. Bendewald,* 2013 WL 310194 (7th Cir. 2013)] (See *Copyrights.*)

8–8.   **Patents.** The U.S. Patent and Trademark Office (PTO) denied Raymond Gianelli's application for a patent for a "Rowing Machine"—an exercise machine on which a user *pulls* on handles to perform a rowing motion against a selected resistance. The PTO considered the device obvious in light of a previously patented "Chest Press Apparatus for Exercising Regions of the Upper Body"—an exercise machine on which a user *pushes* on handles to overcome a selected resistance. On what ground might this result be reversed on appeal? Discuss. [*In re Gianelli,* 739 F.3d 1375 (Fed. Cir. 2014)] (See *Patents.*)

8–9.   **A Question of Ethics—Copyright Infringement.** Custom Copies, Inc., prepares and sells coursepacks, which contain compilations of readings for college courses. A teacher selects the readings and delivers a syllabus to the copy shop, which obtains the materials from a library, copies them, and binds the copies. Blackwell Publishing, Inc., which owns the copyright to some of the materials, filed a suit, alleging copyright infringement. [*Blackwell Publishing, Inc. v. Custom Copies, Inc.,* 2006 WL 152950 (N.D.Fla. 2006)] (See *Copyrights.*)

1. Custom Copies argued, in part, that it did not "distribute" the coursepacks. Does a copy shop violate copyright law if it only copies materials for coursepacks? Does the fair use doctrine apply in these circumstances? Discuss.

2. What is the potential impact if copies of a book or journal are created and sold without the permission of, and the payment of royalties or a fee to, the copyright owner? Explain.

CHAPTER 9

(Alamy)

Internet Law, Social Media, and Privacy

CONTENTS

- Internet Law
- Copyrights in Digital Information
- Social Media
- Online Defamation
- Privacy

LEARNING OBJECTIVES

The five learning objectives below are designed to help improve your understanding of the chapter. After reading this chapter, you should be able to answer the following questions:

1. What is cybersquatting, and when is it illegal?
2. What steps have been taken to protect intellectual property rights in the digital age?
3. When does the law protect a person's electronic communications from being intercepted or accessed?
4. What law governs whether Internet service providers are liable for online defamatory statements made by users?
5. How do online retailers track their users' Web browsing activities?

"The Internet is just the world passing around notes in a classroom."
—Jon Stewart, 1962–present (American comedian and host of *The Daily Show*)

The Internet has changed our lives and our laws. Technology has put the world at our fingertips and now allows even the smallest business to reach customers around the globe. Because the Internet allows the world to "pass around notes" so quickly, as Jon Stewart joked in the chapter-opening quotation, it presents a variety of challenges for the law. Courts are often in uncharted waters when deciding disputes that involve the Internet, social media, and online privacy. There may not be any common law precedents for judges to rely on when resolving a case. Long-standing principles of justice may be inapplicable. New rules are evolving, as we discuss in this chapter, but often not as quickly as technology.

Internet Law

A number of laws specifically address issues that arise only on the Internet. Three such issues are unsolicited e-mail, domain names, and cybersquatting, as we discuss here. We also discuss how the law is dealing with problems of trademark infringement and dilution online.

Spam

Spam Bulk, unsolicited (junk) e-mail.

Businesses and individuals alike are targets of **spam.**[1] Spam is the unsolicited "junk e-mail" that floods virtual mailboxes with advertisements, solicitations, and other messages. Considered relatively harmless in the early days of the Internet, by 2015 spam accounted for roughly 75 percent of all e-mails.

(Shutterstock)

Have state and federal laws against spam reduced its use?

State Regulation of Spam

In an attempt to combat spam, thirty-seven states have enacted laws that prohibit or regulate its use. Many state laws that regulate spam require the senders of e-mail ads to instruct the recipients on how they can "opt out" of further e-mail ads from the same sources. For instance, in some states, an unsolicited e-mail must include a toll-free phone number or return e-mail address that the recipient can use to ask the sender to send no more unsolicited e-mails.

The Federal CAN-SPAM Act

In 2003, Congress enacted the Controlling the Assault of Non-Solicited Pornography and Marketing (CAN-SPAM) Act.[2] The legislation applies to any "commercial electronic mail messages" that are sent to promote a commercial product or service. Significantly, the statute preempts state antispam laws except for those provisions in state laws that prohibit false and deceptive e-mailing practices.

Generally, the act permits the sending of unsolicited commercial e-mail but prohibits certain types of spamming activities. Prohibited activities include the use of a false return address and the use of false, misleading, or deceptive information when sending e-mail. The statute also prohibits the use of "dictionary attacks"—sending messages to randomly generated e-mail addresses—and the "harvesting" of e-mail addresses from Web sites through the use of specialized software.

EXAMPLE 9.1 Federal officials arrested Robert Alan Soloway, considered to be one of the world's most prolific spammers. Soloway, known as the "Spam King," had been using *botnets* (automated spamming networks) to send out hundreds of millions of unwanted e-mails. In 2008, Soloway pleaded guilty to mail fraud, spam, and failure to pay taxes. •

Arresting prolific spammers, however, has done little to curb spam, which continues to flow at a rate of 70 billion messages per day.

The U.S. Safe Web Act

After the CAN-SPAM Act prohibited false and deceptive e-mails originating in the United States, spamming from servers located in other nations increased. These cross-border spammers generally were able to escape detection and legal sanctions because the Federal Trade Commission (FTC) lacked the authority to investigate foreign spamming.

Congress sought to rectify the situation by enacting the U.S. Safe Web Act (also known as the Undertaking Spam, Spyware, and Fraud Enforcement with Enforcers Beyond Borders Act).[3] The act allows the FTC to cooperate and share information with foreign agencies in investigating and prosecuting those involved in spamming, spyware, and various Internet frauds and deceptions.

Internet Service Provider (ISP)
A business or organization that offers users access to the Internet and related services.

The Safe Web Act also provides a "safe harbor" for **Internet service providers (ISPs)**—that is, organizations that provide access to the Internet. The safe harbor gives ISPs immunity from liability for supplying information to the FTC concerning possible unfair or deceptive conduct in foreign jurisdictions.

---

1. The term *spam* is said to come from the lyrics of a Monty Python song that repeats the word *spam* over and over.
2. 15 U.S.C. Sections 7701 *et seq.*
3. Pub. L. No. 109-455, 120 Stat. 3372 (2006), codified in various sections of 15 U.S.C. and 12 U.S.C. Section 3412.

Domain Names

As e-commerce expanded worldwide, one issue that emerged involved the rights of a trademark owner to use the mark as part of a domain name. A **domain name** is part of an Internet address, such as "cengage.com."

Structure of Domain Names

Every domain name ends with a top-level domain (TLD), which is the part of the name to the right of the period that often indicates the type of entity that operates the site. For instance, *com* is an abbreviation for *commercial,* and *edu* is short for *education.*

The second-level domain (SLD)—the part of the name to the left of the period—is chosen by the business entity or individual registering the domain name. Competition for SLDs among firms with similar names and products has led to numerous disputes. By using an identical or similar domain name, parties have attempted to profit from a competitor's **goodwill** (the nontangible value of a business). For instance, a party might use a similar domain name to sell pornography, offer for sale another party's domain name, or otherwise infringe on others' trademarks.

Distribution System

The Internet Corporation for Assigned Names and Numbers (ICANN), a nonprofit corporation, oversees the distribution of domain names and operates an online arbitration system. Due to numerous complaints, ICANN completely overhauled the domain name distribution system.

In 2012, ICANN started selling new generic top-level domain names (gTLDs) for an initial price of $185,000 plus an annual fee of $25,000. Whereas TLDs were limited to only a few terms (such as "com," "net," and "org"), gTLDs can take any form. By 2015, many companies and corporations had acquired gTLDs based on their brands, such as .aol, .bmw, .canon, .gap, .target, .toyota, and .walmart. Some companies have numerous gTLDs. Google's gTLDs, for instance, include .android, .chrome, .gmail, .goog, and .YouTube.

Cybersquatting

One of the goals of the new gTLD system is to alleviate the problem of *cybersquatting.* **Cybersquatting** occurs when a person registers a domain name that is the same as, or confusingly similar to, the trademark of another and then offers to sell the domain name back to the trademark owner.

EXAMPLE 9.2 Apple, Inc., has repeatedly sued cybersquatters that registered domain names similar to its products, such as iphone4s.com and ipods.com. In 2012, Apple won a judgment in litigation at the World Intellectual Property Organization (WIPO) against a company that was squatting on the domain name iPhone5.com.[4] •

Anticybersquatting Legislation

Because cybersquatting has led to so much litigation, Congress enacted the Anticybersquatting Consumer Protection Act (ACPA),[5] which amended the Lanham Act—the federal law protecting trademarks, discussed in Chapter 8. The ACPA makes cybersquatting illegal when both of the following are true:

1. The name is identical or confusingly similar to the trademark of another.
2. The one registering, trafficking in, or using the domain name has a "bad faith intent" to profit from that trademark.

Domain Name The series of letters and symbols used to identify site operators on the Internet; Internet "addresses."

Goodwill In the business context, the valuable reputation of a business viewed as an intangible asset.

"Almost overnight, the Internet's gone from a technical wonder to a business must."

Bill Schrader, 1953–present (Internet pioneer and co-founder of the first commercial Internet service provider)

Cybersquatting The act of registering a domain name that is the same as, or confusingly similar to, the trademark of another and then offering to sell that domain name back to the trademark owner.

Learning Objective 1
What is cybersquatting, and when is it illegal?

---

4. WIPO Case No. D2012-0951.
5. 15 U.S.C. Section 1129.

The Ongoing Problem of Cybersquatting Despite the ACPA, cybersquatting continues to present a problem for businesses, largely because more TLDs and gTLDs are now available and many more companies are registering domain names. Indeed, domain name registrars have proliferated. Registrar companies charge a fee to businesses and individuals to register new names and to renew annual registrations (often through automated software). Many of these companies also buy and sell expired domain names.

All domain name registrars are supposed to relay information about these transactions to ICANN and other companies that keep a master list of domain names, but this does not always occur. The speed at which domain names change hands and the difficulty in tracking mass automated registrations have created an environment where cybersquatting can flourish.

CASE EXAMPLE 9.3 OnNet USA, Inc., owns the English-language rights to 9Dragons, a game with a martial arts theme, and operates a Web site for its promotion. When a party known as "Warv0x" began to operate a pirated version of the game at Play9D.com, OnNet filed an action under the ACPA in a federal court. OnNet was unable to obtain contact information for the owner of Play9D.com through its Australian domain name registrar, however, and thus could not complete service of process (see Chapter 3). Therefore, the federal court allowed OnNet to serve the defendant by publishing a notice of the suit in a newspaper in Gold Coast, Australia.[6] ●

Typosquatting Cybersquatters have also developed new tactics, such as **typosquatting,** or registering a name that is a misspelling of a popular brand, such as googl.com or appple.com. Because many Internet users are not perfect typists, Web pages using these misspelled names receive a lot of traffic.

More traffic generally means increased profit (advertisers often pay Web sites based on the number of unique visits, or hits), which in turn provides incentive for more cybersquatters. Also, if the misspelling is significant, the trademark owner may have difficulty proving that the name is identical or confusingly similar to the trademark of another as the ACPA requires.

Cybersquatting is costly for businesses, which must attempt to register all variations of a name to protect their domain name rights from would-be cybersquatters and typosquatters. Large corporations may have to register thousands of domain names across the globe just to protect their basic brands and trademarks.

Applicability and Sanctions of the ACPA The ACPA applies to all domain name registrations of trademarks. Successful plaintiffs in suits brought under the act can collect actual damages and profits, or they can elect to receive statutory damages ranging from $1,000 to $100,000.

Although some companies have been successful suing under the ACPA, there are roadblocks to pursuing such lawsuits. Some domain name registrars offer privacy services that hide the true owners of Web sites, making it difficult for trademark owners to identify cybersquatters. Thus, before bringing a suit, a trademark owner has to ask the court for a subpoena to discover the identity of the owner of the infringing Web site. Because of the high costs of court proceedings, discovery, and even arbitration, many disputes over cybersquatting are settled out of court.

To facilitate dispute resolution, ICANN now offers the Uniform Rapid Suspension (URS) system. URS allows trademark holders with clear-cut infringement claims to obtain rapid relief. **EXAMPLE 9.4** In the first dispute filed involving gTLDs, IBM filed a complaint with URS against an individual who registered the domain names IBM.guru and IBM.ventures in February 2014. A week later, the URS panel decided in IBM's favor and suspended the two domain names. ●

Typosquatting A form of cybersquatting that relies on mistakes, such as typographical errors, made by Internet users when inputting information into a Web browser.

---

6. *OnNet USA, Inc. v. Play9D.com,* 2013 WL 120319 (N.D.Cal. 2013).

Meta Tags

Search engines compile their results by looking through a Web site's key-word field. As noted in Chapter 4, *meta tags* are key words that are inserted into the HTML (hypertext markup language) code to tell Internet browsers specific information about a Web page. Meta tags increase the likelihood that a site will be included in search engine results, even though the site may have nothing to do with the key words. Using this same technique, one site may appropriate the key words of other sites with more frequent hits so that the appropriating site will appear in the same search engine results as the more popular sites.

Using another's trademark in a meta tag without the owner's permission, however, normally constitutes trademark infringement. Some uses of another's trademark as a meta tag may be permissible if the use is reasonably necessary and does not suggest that the owner authorized or sponsored the use.

CASE EXAMPLE 9.5 Farzad and Lisa Tabari are auto brokers—the personal shoppers of the automotive world. They contact authorized dealers, solicit bids, and arrange for customers to buy from the dealer offering the best combination of location, availability, and price. The Tabaris offered this service at the Web sites buy-a-lexus.com and buyorleaselexus.com.

Toyota Motor Sales U.S.A., Inc., the exclusive distributor of Lexus vehicles and the owner of the Lexus mark, objected to the Tabaris' practices. The Tabaris removed Toyota's photographs and logo from their site and added a disclaimer in large type at the top, but they refused to give up their domain names. Toyota sued for infringement. The court forced the Tabaris to stop using any "domain name, service mark, trademark, trade name, meta tag or other commercial indication of origin that includes the mark LEXUS."[7] ●

Trademark Dilution in the Online World

As discussed in Chapter 8, trademark *dilution* occurs when a trademark is used, without authorization, in a way that diminishes the distinctive quality of the mark.

Unlike trademark infringement, a claim of dilution does not require proof that consumers are likely to be confused by a connection between the unauthorized use and the mark. For this reason, the products involved need not be similar, as the following *Spotlight Case* illustrates.

---

7. *Toyota Motor Sales, U.S.A., Inc. v. Tabari*, 610 F.3d 171 (9th Cir. 2011).

Spotlight on Internet Porn

Case 9.1
Hasbro, Inc. v. Internet Entertainment Group, Ltd.
United States District Court, Western District of Washington, 1996 WL 84858 (1996).

Candy Land is a children's board game. Why did its parent company, Hasbro, Inc., sue a Web site?

(Reuters/Hasbro/Ray Stubblebine/Landov)

BACKGROUND AND FACTS In 1949, Hasbro, Inc.—then known as the Milton Bradley Company—published its first version of Candy Land, a children's board game. Hasbro is the owner of the trademark "Candy Land," which has been registered with the U.S. Patent and Trademark Office since 1951. Over the years, Hasbro has produced several versions of the game, including Candy Land puzzles, a travel version, a computer game, and a handheld electronic version. In the mid-1990s, Brian Cartmell and his employer, the Internet Entertainment Group, Ltd., used the term *candyland.com* as a domain name for a sexually explicit Internet site. Anyone who performed an online search using the word *candyland* was directed to this adult Web site. Hasbro filed a trademark dilution claim in a federal court, seeking a permanent injunction to prevent the defendants from using the Candy Land trademark.

Spotlight Case 9.1—Continues ➡

Spotlight Case 9.1—Continued

IN THE WORDS OF THE COURT . . .
DWYER, U.S. District Judge.
* * * *

2. Hasbro has demonstrated a probability of proving that defendants Internet Entertainment Group, Ltd., Brian Cartmell and Internet Entertainment Group, Inc. (collec-tively referred to as "defendants") have been diluting the value of Hasbro's CANDY LAND mark by using the name CANDYLAND to iden-tify a sexually explicit Internet site, and by using the name string "candyland.com" as an Internet domain name which, when typed into an Internet-connected computer, provides Internet users with access to that site.
* * * *

4. Hasbro has shown that defendants' use of the CANDY LAND name and the domain name candyland.com in con-nection with their Internet site is causing irreparable injury to Hasbro.

5. *The probable harm to Hasbro from defendants' conduct outweighs any inconvenience that defendants will experience if they are required to stop using the CANDYLAND name.* [Emphasis added.]

* * * *

THEREFORE, IT IS HEREBY ORDERED that Hasbro's motion for preliminary injunction is granted.

DECISION AND REMEDY The federal district court granted Hasbro an injunction against the defendants, agreeing that the domain name *candyland* was "causing irreparable injury to Hasbro." The judge ordered the defendants to immediately remove all content from the *candyland.com* Web site and to stop using the Candy Land mark.

THE ECONOMIC DIMENSION *How can companies protect themselves from others who create Web sites that have similar domain names, and what limits each company's ability to be fully protected?*

WHAT IF THE FACTS WERE DIFFERENT? *Suppose that the site using* candyland.com *had not been sexually explicit but had sold candy. Would the result have been the same? Explain.*

Licensing

Recall from Chapter 8 that a company may permit another party to use a trademark (or other intellectual property) under a license. A licensor might grant a license allowing its trademark to be used as part of a domain name, for example.

Indeed, licensing is ubiquitous in the online world. When you download an application on your smartphone, tablet, or other mobile device, for instance, you are typically entering into a license agreement. You are obtaining only a *license* to use that app and not ownership rights in it. Apps published on Google Play, for instance, may use its licensing service to prompt users to agree to a license at the time of installation and use.

Licensing agreements frequently include restrictions that prohibit licensees from shar-ing the file and using it to create similar software applications. The license may also limit the use of the application to a specific device or give permission to the user for a certain time period. For further discussion of licensing and e-contracts, see Chapter 10.

Copyrights in Digital Information

Learning Objective 2
What steps have been taken to protect intellectual property rights in the digital age?

Copyright law is probably the most important form of intellectual property protection on the Internet. This is because much of the material on the Internet (including software and database information) is copyrighted, and in order to transfer that material online, it must be "copied." Generally, whenever a party downloads software or music into a com-puter's random access memory, or RAM, without authorization, a copyright is infringed. Technology has vastly increased the potential for copyright infringement.

CASE EXAMPLE 9.6   In one case, a rap song that was included in the sound track of a movie had used only a few seconds from the guitar solo of another's copyrighted sound recording without permission. Nevertheless, a federal court held that digitally sampling a copyrighted sound recording of any length constitutes copyright infringement.[8] ●

Some other federal courts have not found that digital sampling is always illegal. Some courts have allowed the defense of fair use (see Chapter 8), while others have not. **EXAMPLE 9.7**   Hip hop stars Jay-Z and Kanye West were sued for digitally sampling music by soul musician Syl Johnson. Given the uncertain outcome of the litigation, they ended up settling the suit in 2012 for an undisclosed amount. ●

Initially, criminal penalties for copyright violations could be imposed only if unauthorized copies were exchanged for financial gain. Yet much piracy of copyrighted materials online was "altruistic" in nature—unauthorized copies were made simply to be shared with others. Then, Congress amended the law and extended criminal liability for the piracy of copyrighted materials to persons who exchange unauthorized copies of copyrighted works without realizing a profit.

Digital Millennium Copyright Act

In 1998, Congress passed further legislation to protect copyright holders—the Digital Millennium Copyright Act (DMCA).[9] The DMCA gave significant protection to owners of copyrights in digital information. Among other things, the act established civil and criminal penalties for anyone who circumvents (bypasses) encryption software or other technological antipiracy protection. Also prohibited are the manufacture, import, sale, and distribution of devices or services for circumvention.

The DMCA provides for exceptions to fit the needs of libraries, scientists, universities, and others. In general, the law does not restrict the "fair use" of circumvention methods for educational and other noncommercial purposes. For instance, circumvention is allowed to test computer security, to conduct encryption research, to protect personal privacy, and to enable parents to monitor their children's use of the Internet. The exceptions are to be reconsidered every three years.

The DMCA also limits the liability of Internet service providers (ISPs). Under the act, an ISP is not liable for copyright infringement by its customer *unless* the ISP is aware of the subscriber's violation. An ISP may be held liable only if it fails to take action to shut down the subscriber after learning of the violation. A copyright holder must act promptly, however, by pursuing a claim in court, or the subscriber has the right to be restored to online access.

MP3 and File-Sharing Technology

Soon after the Internet became popular, a few enterprising programmers created software to compress large data files, particularly those associated with music. The best-known compression and decompression system is MP3, which enables music fans to download songs or entire CDs onto their computers or onto portable listening devices, such as smartphones. The MP3 system also made it possible for music fans to access other fans' files by engaging in file-sharing via the Internet.

CASE EXAMPLE 9.8   The issue of file-sharing infringement has been the subject of an ongoing debate since the highly publicized cases against two companies (Napster, Inc. and Grokster, Ltd.) that created software used for copyright infringement. In the first case, Napster operated a Web site with free software that enabled users to copy and transfer MP3

> "The Internet is the world's largest library. It's just that all the books are on the floor."
>
> John Allen Paulos, 1945–present (American mathematics professor)

---

8. *Bridgeport Music, Inc. v. Dimension Films*, 410 F.3d 792 (6th Cir. 2005).
9. 17 U.S.C. Sections 512, 1201–1205, 1301–1332; and 28 U.S.C. Section 4001.

files via the Internet. Firms in the recording industry sued Napster. Ultimately, the court held that Napster was liable for contributory and vicarious[10] (indirect) copyright infringement.

As technology evolved, Grokster, Ltd., and several other companies created and distributed new types of file-sharing software. This software did not maintain a central index of content, but allowed P2P network users to share stored music files. The court held that because the companies distributed file-sharing software "with the object of promoting its use to infringe the copyright," they were liable for the resulting acts of infringement by the software's users.[11] •

Peer-to-peer (P2P) Networking The sharing of resources (such as files, hard drives, and processing styles) among multiple computers without the requirement of a central network server.

Distributed Network A network that can be used by persons located (distributed) around the country or the globe to share computer files.

Cloud Computing The delivery to users of on-demand services from third-party servers over a network.

Methods of File-Sharing   File-sharing is accomplished through **peer-to-peer (P2P) networking.** The concept is simple. Rather than going through a central Web server, P2P networking uses numerous personal computers (PCs) that are connected to the Internet. Individuals on the same network can access files stored on one another's PCs through a **distributed network.** Parts of the network may be distributed all over the country or the world, which offers an unlimited number of uses. Persons scattered throughout the country or the world can work together on the same project by using file-sharing programs.

A newer method of sharing files via the Internet is **cloud computing,** which is essentially a subscription-based or pay-per-use service that extends a computer's software or storage capabilities. Cloud computing can deliver a single application through a browser to multiple users. Alternatively, cloud computing might be a utility program to pool resources and provide data storage and virtual servers that can be accessed on demand. Amazon, Facebook, Google, IBM, and Sun Microsystems are using and developing more cloud computing services.

> "We're into a whole new world with the Internet, and whenever we sort of cross another plateau in our development, there are those who seek to take advantage of it. So this is a replay of things that have happened throughout our history."
>
> Bill Clinton, 1946–present (42nd President of the United States)

Sharing Stored Music Files   When file-sharing is used to download others' stored music files, copyright issues arise. Recording artists and their labels stand to lose large amounts of royalties and revenues if relatively few digital downloads or CDs are purchased and then made available on distributed networks. Anyone can get the music for free on these networks, which has prompted recording companies to pursue individuals for file-sharing copyrighted works.

CASE EXAMPLE 9.9   Maverick Recording Company and other recording companies sued Whitney Harper in federal court for copyright infringement. Harper had used a file-sharing program to download a number of copyrighted songs from the Internet and had then shared the audio files with others via a P2P network. The plaintiffs sought $750 per infringed work—the minimum amount of statutory damages available under the Copyright Act.

Harper claimed that she was an "innocent" infringer because she was unaware that her actions constituted copyright infringement. Under the act, innocent infringement can result in a reduced penalty. The court, however, noted that a copyright notice appeared on all the songs that Harper had downloaded. She therefore could not assert the innocent infringer defense, and the court ordered her to pay damages of $750 per infringed work.[12] •

---

10. *Vicarious (indirect) liability* exists when one person is subject to liability for another's actions. A common example occurs in the employment context, when an employer is held vicariously liable by third parties for torts committed by employees in the course of their employment.
11. *A&M Records, Inc. v. Napster, Inc.,* 239 F.3d 1004 (9th Cir. 2001); and *Metro-Goldwyn-Mayer Studios, Inc. v. Grokster, Ltd.,* 545 U.S. 913, 125 S.Ct. 2764, 162 L.Ed.2d 781 (2005). Grokster, Ltd., later settled this dispute out of court and stopped distributing its software.
12. *Maverick Recording Co. v. Harper,* 598 F.3d 193 (5th Cir. 2010).

DVDs and File-Sharing   File-sharing also creates problems for the motion picture industry, which loses significant amounts of revenue annually as a result of pirated DVDs. Numerous Web sites offer software that facilitates the illegal copying of movies, such as BitTorrent, which enables users to download high-quality files from the Internet.

CASE EXAMPLE 9.10   TorrentSpy, a popular BitTorrent indexing Web site, enabled users to locate and exchange files. The Motion Picture Association of America (MPAA) and Columbia Pictures, Inc., brought a lawsuit against the operators of TorrentSpy for facilitating copyright infringement. The MPAA also claimed that the operators had destroyed evidence that would reveal the identity of individual infringers. The operators had ignored a court order to keep server logs of the Internet addresses of people who facilitated the trading of files via the site. Because TorrentSpy's operators had willfully destroyed evidence, a federal court found in favor of the MPAA and ordered the defendants to pay a judgment of $111 million.[13] ●

(Alamy)

Movie piracy is becoming ubiquitous just like illegal music downloading. Why?

Social Media

Social media provide a means by which people can create, share, and exchange ideas and comments via the Internet. Social networking sites, such as Facebook, Google+, MySpace, LinkedIn, Pinterest, and Tumblr, have become ubiquitous. Studies show that Internet users spend more time on social networks than at any other sites. The amount of time people spend accessing social networks on their smartphones and other mobile devices has increased every year (by nearly 37 percent in 2014 alone).

EXAMPLE 9.11   Facebook, which was launched in 2004, had more than a billion active users by 2015. Individuals of all ages use Facebook to maintain social contacts, update friends on events, and distribute images to others. Facebook members often share common interests based on their school, location, or recreational affiliation, such as a sports team. ●

Legal Issues

The emergence of Facebook and other social networking sites has created a number of legal and ethical issues for businesses. For instance, a firm's rights in valuable intellectual property may be infringed if users post trademarked images or copyrighted materials on these sites without permission.

Social media posts now are routinely included in discovery in litigation (see Chapter 3) because they can provide damaging information that establishes a person's intent or what she or he knew at a particular time. Like e-mail, posts on social networks can be the smoking gun that leads to liability.

Tweets and other social media posts can also be used to reduce damages awards. **EXAMPLE 9.12**   Omeisha Daniels sued for injuries she sustained in a car accident. She claimed that her injuries made it impossible for her to continue working as a hairstylist. The jury originally awarded her $237,000, but when the jurors saw Daniels's tweets and photographs of her partying in New Orleans and vacationing on the beach, they reduced the damages to $142,000. ● See this chapter's *Insight into Ethics* that follows for a discussion of one case in which a daughter's social media post invalidated a father's settlement agreement.

Social Media Forms of communication through which users create and share information, ideas, messages, and other content via the Internet.

> "Twitter is just a multiplayer notepad."
>
> Ben Maddox
> (Global technology officer at New York University)

---

13. *Columbia Pictures, Inc., v. Bunnell*, 2007 WL 4877701 (C.D.Cal. 2007).

INSIGHT INTO ETHICS

BOASTING ON FACEBOOK CAN HAVE CONSEQUENCES

Patrick Snay was the headmaster of Gulliver Preparatory School in Miami, Florida. When Gulliver did not renew Snay's employment contract for 2010–2011, Snay sued the school for age discrimination (see Chapter 18). During mediation, Snay agreed to settle the case for $80,000 (plus $60,000 in attorney's fees and $10,000 in back pay).

The settlement agreement included a confidentiality clause that required Snay and his wife to keep the "terms and existence" of the agreement private. Nevertheless, Snay and his wife told their daughter, Dana, that the dispute had been settled and that they were happy with the results. Dana, a college student, had recently graduated from Gulliver and, according to Snay, had suffered retaliation at the school.

The Facebook Post

Four days after the settlement agreement was signed, Dana posted a Facebook comment that said "Mama and Papa Snay won the case against Gulliver. Gulliver is now officially paying for my vacation to Europe this summer. SUCK IT." The comment went out to 1,200 of Dana's Facebook friends, many of whom were either current or past Gulliver students, and school officials soon learned of it. The school immediately notified Snay that, through the Facebook post, he had breached the confidentiality clause in the settlement agreement. Snay filed a motion

to enforce the agreement. The court held that Snay was not in breach, and Gulliver appealed.

Appellate Court Throws Out the Settlement Agreement

The state intermediate appellate court held that Snay had breached the confidentiality clause. The plain language of the clause was clear. It stipulated "that neither Snay nor his wife would 'either directly or *indirectly*' disclose to anyone (other than their lawyers or other professionals) 'any information' regarding the existence or the terms of the parties' agreement." Snay had admitted telling his daughter that the dispute had been settled and that he was happy with the result. Because he had breached the provisions of the confidentiality clause, the court held that the settlement agreement was no longer enforceable.[a]

For Critical Analysis
Insight into the Technological Environment
Is it fair that the father lost his settlement because of his daughter's Facebook post? What might this case mean for a business firm that enters into a settlement agreement with a confidentiality clause?

_____

a. *Gulliver Schools, Inc. v. Snay,* 137 So.3d 1045 (Fla.App. 2014).

Criminal Investigations Law enforcement uses social media to detect and prosecute criminals. **EXAMPLE 9.13** A nineteen-year-old posts a message on Facebook bragging about how drunk he was on New Year's Eve and apologizing to the owner of the parked car that he hit. The next day, police officers arrest him for drunk driving and leaving the scene of an accident. •

Administrative Agencies Federal regulators also use social media posts in their investigations into illegal activities. **EXAMPLE 9.14** Reed Hastings, the top executive of Netflix, stated on Facebook that Netflix subscribers had watched a billion hours of video the previous month. As a result, Netflix's stock price rose, which prompted a federal agency investigation. Because such a statement is considered to be material information to investors, it must be disclosed to all investors under securities law (see Chapter 24). The agency ultimately concluded that it could not hold Hastings responsible for any wrongdoing because the agency's policy on social media use was not clear. The agency then issued new guidelines that allow companies to disclose material information through social media if investors have been notified in advance. •

The decision in a hearing before an administrative law judge can turn on the content of two Facebook posts, as occurred in the case that follows.

(1000 words/Shutterstock.com)

Case 9.2

In re O'Brien

Superior Court of New Jersey, Appellate Division, 2013 WL 132508 (2013).

BACKGROUND AND FACTS   Jennifer O'Brien was a tenured teacher at School No. 21 in Paterson, New Jersey, when she posted the following messages on her Facebook page: "I'm not a teacher—I'm a warden for future criminals!" and "They had a scared straight program in school—why couldn't I bring first graders?" Not surprisingly, outraged parents protested. The deputy superintendent of schools filed a complaint against O'Brien with the commissioner of education, charging her with conduct unbecoming a teacher. After a hearing, an administrative law judge (ALJ) ordered that O'Brien be removed from her teaching position. The commissioner issued a final decision, concluding that removal was the appropriate penalty. O'Brien appealed to a state court.

IN THE WORDS OF THE COURT . . .
PER CURIAM [By the Whole Court].
    * * * *

O'Brien argues that her Facebook postings are protected by the First Amendment to the United States Constitution and, therefore, she could not be disciplined or discharged for having posted those statements. We cannot agree.

To determine whether a public employee's statements are protected by the First Amendment, we balance the employee's interest as a citizen, in commenting upon matters of public concern, and the interest of the State, as an employer, in promoting the efficiency of the public services it performs through its employees. [Emphasis added.]

Here, O'Brien claimed that her statements were addressed to a matter of genuine public concern, specifically student behavior in the classroom. The ALJ and Commissioner found, however, that O'Brien was not endeavoring to comment on a matter of public interest, that is, the behavior of students in school but was making a personal statement, driven by her dissatisfaction with her job and conduct of some of her students. The ALJ and * * * Commissioner further found that, even if O'Brien's comments were on a matter of public concern, her right to express those comments was outweighed by the district's interest in the efficient operation of its schools. There is sufficient credible evidence in the record to support these findings. *Therefore, O'Brien failed to establish that her Facebook postings were protected speech under the * * * balancing test.* [Emphasis added.]

O'Brien additionally argues that there was insufficient evidence to support the ALJ's and the * * * Commissioner's finding that she engaged in conduct unbecoming a tenured teacher. We do not agree. As the ALJ pointed out in her initial decision, *conduct unbecoming* is a term that encompasses any conduct that has a tendency to destroy public respect for government employees and confidence in the operation of public services.

The ALJ found that, by posting her comments on Facebook, O'Brien "showed a disturbing lack of self-restraint, violated any notion of good behavior, and acted in a manner that was inimical [contrary] to her role as a professional educator." The * * * Commissioner said that O'Brien's actions constituted unbecoming conduct, noting that the posting of such derogatory [insulting] and demeaning comments about first-grade students showed a lack of self-control, insensitivity and a lack of professionalism. We are satisfied that there is sufficient credible evidence in the record to support those findings.

O'Brien additionally argues that the penalty of removal is arbitrary, capricious and unreasonable. She argues that, assuming her comments were inappropriate, this was her "sole transgression" in an otherwise unblemished career of more than a decade. She further argues that the ALJ and * * * Commissioner erred by relying in part on the fact that she did not apologize to the community, the students or their parents. O'Brien contends that, if a penalty should be imposed, it should be minimal.

Again, we disagree. We are satisfied that, in determining the appropriate penalty, the ALJ and * * * Commissioner considered all relevant factors and reasonably concluded that the seriousness of O'Brien's conduct warranted her removal from her tenured position in the district.

DECISION AND REMEDY   The state intermediate appellate court affirmed the commissioner's final decision to remove O'Brien from her position. The court was "satisfied" with this outcome for the reasons stated by the ALJ and the commissioner in their decisions.

WHAT IF THE FACTS WERE DIFFERENT?   *Would the outcome have been different if the plaintiff had apologized? Discuss.*

THE LEGAL ENVIRONMENT DIMENSION   *Certain interests of public employees and their employer are balanced to determine whether the First Amendment protects an employee's Facebook posts. What are those interests?*

Employers' Social Media Policies

Employees who use social media in a way that violates their employer's stated policies may be disciplined or fired from their jobs. (Many large corporations have established specific guidelines on creating a social media policy in the workplace.) Courts and administrative agencies usually uphold an employer's right to terminate a person based on his or her violation of a social media policy.

CASE EXAMPLE 9.15   Virginia Rodriquez worked for Wal-Mart Stores, Inc., for almost twenty years and had been promoted to management. Then she was disciplined for violating the company's policies by having a fellow employee use Rodriquez's password to alter the price of an item that she purchased. Under Wal-Mart's rules, another violation within a year would mean termination.

Nine months later, on Facebook, Rodriquez publicly chastised employees under her supervision for calling in sick to go to a party. The posting violated Wal-Mart's "Social Media Policy," which was "to avoid public comment that adversely affects employees." Wal-Mart terminated Rodriquez. She filed a lawsuit, alleging discrimination, but the court issued a summary judgment in Wal-Mart's favor.[14] ● Note, however, that employees' posts on social media may be protected under labor law, as discussed in *Example 2.3* in Chapter 2.

The Electronic Communications Privacy Act

Learning Objective 3
When does the law protect a person's electronic communications from being intercepted or accessed?

The Electronic Communications Privacy Act (ECPA)[15] amended federal wiretapping law to cover electronic forms of communications. Although Congress enacted the ECPA many years before social media networks existed, it nevertheless applies to communications through social media.

The ECPA prohibits the intentional interception of any wire, oral, or electronic communication. It also prohibits the intentional disclosure or use of the information obtained by the interception.

Exclusions

Excluded from the ECPA's coverage are any electronic communications through devices that an employer provides for its employee to use "in the ordinary course of its business." Consequently, if a company provides the electronic device (cell phone, laptop, tablet) to the employee for ordinary business use, the company is not prohibited from intercepting business communications made on it.

This "business-extension exception" to the ECPA permits employers to monitor employees' electronic communications made in the ordinary course of business. It does not, however, permit employers to monitor employees' personal communications. Another exception allows an employer to avoid liability under the act if the employees consent to having their electronic communications monitored by the employer.

Can employers monitor and regulate employees' use of social media such as Instagram?

Stored Communications

Part of the ECPA is known as the Stored Communications Act (SCA).[16] The SCA prohibits intentional and unauthorized access to *stored* electronic communications and sets forth criminal and civil sanctions for violators. A person can violate the SCA by intentionally accessing a stored electronic communication. The SCA also prevents "providers" of communication services (such as cell phone companies and social media networks) from divulging private communications to certain entities and individuals.

CASE EXAMPLE 9.16   Two restaurant employees, Brian Pietrylo and Doreen Marino, were fired after their manager uncovered their password-protected MySpace group. The group's communications, stored on MySpace's Web site, contained sexual remarks about customers

---

14. *Rodriguez v. Wal-Mart Stores, Inc.,* ___ F.Supp.2d ___, 2013 WL 102674 (N.D.Tex. 2013).
15. 18 U.S.C. Sections 2510–2521.
16. 18 U.S.C. Sections 2701–2711.

(Alamy)

and management, and comments about illegal drug use and violent behavior. One employee said the group's purpose was to "vent about any BS we deal with out of work without any outside eyes spying on us."

The restaurant learned about the private MySpace group when a hostess showed it to a manager who requested access. The hostess was not explicitly threatened with termination but feared she would lose her job if she did not comply. The court allowed the employees' SCA claim, and the jury awarded them $17,003 in compensatory and punitive damages.[17] ●

Protection of Social Media Passwords

In recent years, employees and applicants for jobs or colleges have sometimes been asked to divulge their social media passwords. Employers and schools have sometimes looked at an individual's Facebook or other account to see if it included controversial postings such as racially discriminatory remarks or photos of drug parties. Such postings can have a negative effect on a person's prospects even though they were made years earlier or have been taken out of context.

By 2014, eleven states (Arkansas, California, Colorado, Illinois, Maryland, Michigan, Nevada, New Mexico, Oregon, Utah, and Washington) had enacted legislation to protect individuals from having to disclose their social media passwords. Each state's law is slightly different. Some states, such as Michigan, prohibit employers from taking adverse action against an employee or job applicant based on what the person has posted online. Michigan's law also applies to e-mail and cloud storage accounts. The federal government is also considering legislation that would prohibit employers and schools from demanding passwords to social media accounts.

Even if legislation is passed, however, it will not completely prevent employers and others from taking actions against a person based on his or her social network postings. Management and human resources personnel are unlikely to admit that they looked at someone's Facebook page and that it influenced their decision. How would a person who does not get a job be able to prove that she or he was rejected because the employer accessed social media? Also, the employer or school may use private browsing, which enables people to keep their Web browsing activities confidential.

(Alamy)

Suppose that two employees use a private MySpace account to share sometimes offensive remarks about customers. If their employer, without their permission, gains access to that account, can that employer retaliate against the employees for their social media behavior?

Company-wide Social Media Networks

Many companies, including Dell, Inc., and Nikon Instruments, form their own internal social media networks. Software companies offer a variety of systems, including Salesforce.com's Chatter, Microsoft's Yammer, and Cisco Systems' WebEx Social. Posts on these internal networks are quite different from the typical posts on Facebook, LinkedIn, and Twitter. Employees use these intranets to exchange messages about topics related to their work such as deals that are closing, new products, production flaws, how a team is solving a problem, and the details of customer orders. Thus, the tone is businesslike.

Protection of Trade Secrets An important advantage to using an internal system for employee communications is that the company can better protect its trade secrets. The company usually decides which employees can see particular intranet files and which employees will belong to each specific "social" group within the company. Companies providing internal social media networks often keep the resulting data on their own servers in secure "clouds."

> "My favorite thing about the Internet is that you get to go into the private world of real creeps without having to smell them."
>
> Penn Jillette, 1955–present (American illusionist, comedian, author)

---

17. *Pietrylo v. Hillstone Restaurant Group*, 2009 WL 3128420 (D.N.J. 2009).

Other Advantages   Internal social media systems also offer additional benefits such as real-time information about important issues, such as production glitches. Additionally, posts can include tips on how to best sell new products or deal with difficult customers, as well as information about competitors' products and services.

Another major benefit of intranets is a significant reduction in the use of e-mail. Rather than wasting fellow employees' time reading mass e-mailings, workers can post messages or collaborate on presentations via the company's social network.

Online Defamation

Cyber Tort   A tort committed via the Internet.

"In cyberspace, the First Amendment is a local ordinance."

John Perry Barlow, 1947–present (American poet and essayist)

Cyber torts are torts that arise from online conduct. One of the most prevalent cyber torts is online defamation. Recall from Chapter 5 that defamation is wrongfully hurting a person's reputation by communicating false statements about that person to others. Because the Internet enables individuals to communicate with large numbers of people simultaneously (via a blog or tweet, for instance), online defamation has become a problem in today's legal environment.

EXAMPLE 9.17   Courtney Love was sued for defamation based on remarks she posted about fashion designer Dawn Simorangkir on Twitter. Love claimed that her statements were opinion (rather than statements of fact, as required) and therefore were not actionable as defamation. Nevertheless, Love ended up paying $430,000 to settle the case out of court. ●

Identifying the Author of Online Defamation

An initial issue raised by online defamation is simply discovering who is committing it. In the real world, identifying the author of a defamatory remark generally is an easy matter. Suppose, though, that a business firm has discovered that defamatory statements about its policies and products are being posted in an online forum. Such forums allow anyone—customers, employees, or crackpots—to complain about a firm that they dislike while remaining anonymous.

Therefore, a threshold barrier to anyone who seeks to bring an action for online defamation is discovering the identity of the person who posted the defamatory message. An Internet service provider (ISP) can disclose personal information about its customers only when ordered to do so by a court. Consequently, businesses and individuals are increasingly bringing lawsuits against "John Does" (John Doe, Jane Doe, and the like are fictitious names used in lawsuits when the identity of a party is not known or when a party wishes to conceal his or her name for privacy reasons). Then, using the authority of the courts, the plaintiffs can obtain from the ISPs the identity of the persons responsible for the defamatory messages.

Does requiring an ISP to reveal the identities of its anonymous users violate those users' rights under the First Amendment? That was the question before the court in the case that follows.

Case 9.3

Yelp, Inc. v. Hadeed Carpet Cleaning, Inc.
Court of Appeals of Virginia, 62 Va.App. 678, 752 S.E.2d 554 (2014).

BACKGROUND AND FACTS   Yelp, Inc., operates a social networking Web site that allows users to post and read reviews on local businesses. The site, which has more than 100 million visitors per month, features about 40 million local reviews. Yelp records and stores the Internet Protocol address from which

(Alamy)

Case 9.3—Continued

each posting is made. Seven users posted negative reviews of Hadeed Carpet Cleaning, Inc., of Alexandria, Virginia. Hadeed brought an action in a Virginia state court against the anonymous posters, claiming defamation. Hadeed alleged that the reviewers were not actual customers. Their statements that Hadeed had provided them with shoddy service were therefore false and defamatory. When Yelp failed to comply with a subpoena seeking the users' identities, the court held the site in contempt. Yelp appealed, arguing that the subpoena violated the users' First Amendment rights.

IN THE WORDS OF THE COURT . . .
PETTY, Judge.
* * * *

The First Amendment to the United States Constitution provides, in relevant part, that "Congress shall make no law * * * abridging the freedom of speech."
* * * *

An Internet user does not shed his free speech rights at the log-in screen. The right to free speech is assiduously guarded in all mediums of expression, from the analog to the digital.
* * * *

* * * [Thus] it is without dispute that the Doe defendants have a constitutional right to speak anonymously over the Internet. However, that right must be balanced against Hadeed's right to protect its reputation.
* * * *

Generally, a Yelp review is entitled to First Amendment protection because it is a person's opinion about a business that they patronized. But this general protection relies upon an underlying assumption of fact: that the reviewer was a customer of the specific company and he posted his review based on his personal experience with the business. *If this underlying assumption of fact proves false, in that the reviewer was never a customer of the business, then the review is not an opinion; instead, the review is based on a false statement of fact—that the reviewer is writing his review based on personal*

experience. And there is no constitutional value in false statements of fact. [Emphasis added.]

Here, Hadeed attached sufficient evidence to its subpoena * * * indicating that it made a thorough review of its customer database to determine whether all of the Yelp reviews were written by actual customers. After making such a review, Hadeed discovered that it could not match the seven Doe defendants' reviews with actual customers in its database. Thus, the evidence presented by Hadeed was sufficient to show that the reviews are or may be defamatory, if not written by actual customers of Hadeed.
* * * *

* * * Hadeed first contacted Yelp to obtain the identity of the Doe defendants. Yelp refused to comply. Thus, Hadeed was then forced to resort to a subpoena * * * to obtain the identity of the Doe defendants.

* * * Without the identity of the Doe defendants, Hadeed cannot move forward with its defamation lawsuit. There is no other option. The identity of the Doe defendants is not only important, it is necessary.

DECISION AND REMEDY A state intermediate appellate court affirmed the lower court's ruling. Hadeed had showed that the negative reviews might be defamatory, and "without the identity of the Doe defendants, Hadeed cannot move forward with its defamation lawsuit." Thus, "the judgment of the [lower] court does not constitute a forbidden intrusion on the field of free expression."

THE LEGAL ENVIRONMENT DIMENSION *Should a party seeking the identity of an anonymous poster be required to exhaust all other means before an ISP can be ordered to reveal that information? Explain.*

THE ETHICAL DIMENSION *Why would someone post a negative review of a business that he or she had never patronized? Discuss the ethics of this practice.*

It is relatively common for disgruntled employees, unhappy customers, and competitors to post negative comments online about business firms. Obviously, these "cyber slurs" can damage a firm's reputation and profitability. One way for business owners to deal with online defamation without resorting to costly (and sometimes unsuccessful) litigation is to retain an online reputation management service. Some such services use automated software to identify negative comments and attempt to get them removed. Owners can often pay a monthly monitoring fee without entering a long-term contract.

**PREVENTING
LEGAL DISPUTES**

Liability of Internet Service Providers

Learning Objective 4
What law governs whether Internet service providers are liable for online defamatory statements made by users?

Recall from the discussion of defamation in Chapter 5 that normally one who repeats or otherwise republishes a defamatory statement is subject to liability as if he or she had originally published it. Thus, newspapers, magazines, and television and radio stations are subject to liability for defamatory content that they publish or broadcast, even though the content was prepared or created by others.

Applying this rule to cyberspace, however, raises an important issue: Should ISPs be regarded as publishers and therefore be held liable for defamatory messages that are posted by their users in online forums or other arenas?

General Rule   The Communications Decency Act (CDA) states that "[n]o provider or user of an interactive computer service shall be treated as the publisher or speaker of any information provided by another information content provider."[18] Thus, under the CDA, ISPs usually are treated differently from publishers in print and other media and are not liable for publishing defamatory statements that come from a third party.

Exceptions   Although the courts generally have construed the CDA as providing a broad shield to protect ISPs from liability for third party content, some courts have started establishing some limits to this immunity. **EXAMPLE 9.18** Roommate.com, LLC, operates an online roommate-matching Web site that helps individuals find roommates based on their descriptions of themselves and their roommate preferences. Users respond to a series of online questions, choosing from answers in drop-down and select-a-box menus.

Some of the questions asked users to disclose their sex, family status, and sexual orientation—which is not permitted under the federal Fair Housing Act. When a nonprofit housing organization sued Roommate.com, the company claimed it was immune from liability under the CDA. A federal appellate court disagreed and ruled that Roommate.com was not immune from liability. Roommate.com was ordered to pay nearly $500,000 for prompting discriminatory preferences from users and matching users based on these criteria in violation of federal law.[19] ●

Privacy

Facebook, Google, and Yahoo have all been accused of violating users' privacy rights. As discussed in Chapter 4, the courts have held that the right to privacy is guaranteed by the Bill of Rights, and some state constitutions guarantee it as well. To maintain a suit for the invasion of privacy, though, a person must have a reasonable expectation of privacy in the particular situation (see Chapter 4).

Boston Red Sox baseball player David Ortiz takes a selfie with President Obama. Can the maker of the smartphone (Samsung) use that photo in its Twitter ads?

(Getty Images/Win McNamee)

People clearly have a reasonable expectation of privacy when they enter their personal banking or credit-card information online. They also have a reasonable expectation that online companies will follow their own privacy policies. But it is probably not reasonable to expect privacy in statements made on Twitter—or photos posted on Twitter, for that matter. **EXAMPLE 9.19** In 2014, Boston Red Sox player David Ortiz used his cell phone to take a "selfie" showing him standing with President Barack Obama. Ortiz tweeted the photo to his followers, who then resent it tens of thousands of times. Eventually, Samsung used the picture in an ad on Twitter (because Ortiz had taken it with a Samsung phone), which prompted an objection from the White House. ●

---

18. 47 U.S.C. Section 230.
19. *Fair Housing Council of San Fernando Valley v. Roommate.com, LLC,* 666 F.3d 1216 (9th Cir. 2012).

Sometimes, people are confused and mistakenly believe that they are making statements or posting photos in a private forum. **EXAMPLE 9.20**   Randi Zuckerberg, the older sister of Mark Zuckerberg (the founder of Facebook), used a mobile app called "Poke" to post a "private" photo on Facebook of their family gathering during the holidays. Poke allows the sender to decide how long the photo can be seen by others. Facebook allows users to configure their privacy settings to limit access to photos, which Randi thought she had done. Nonetheless, the photo showed up in the Facebook feed of Callie Schweitzer, who then put it on Twitter where it eventually went viral. Schweitzer apologized and removed the photo, but it had already gone public for the world to see. •

Data Collection and Cookies

Whenever a consumer purchases items from an online retailer, such as Amazon.com, or a retailer that sells both offline and online, such as Best Buy, the retailer collects information about the consumer. **Cookies** are invisible files that computers, smartphones, and other mobile devices create to track a user's Web browsing activities. Cookies provide detailed information to marketers about an individual's behavior and preferences, which is then used to personalize online services.

Over time, the retailer can amass considerable data about a person's shopping habits. Does collecting this information violate a consumer's right to privacy? Should retailers be able to pass on the data they have collected to their affiliates? Should they be able to use the information to predict what a consumer might want and then create online "coupons" customized to fit the person's buying history?

EXAMPLE 9.21   Facebook, Inc., recently settled a lawsuit over its use of a targeted advertising technique called "Sponsored Stories." An ad would display a Facebook friend's name, profile picture, and a statement that the friend "likes" the company sponsoring the advertisement, alongside the company's logo. A group of plaintiffs filed suit, claiming that Facebook had used their pictures for advertising without their permission. When a federal court refused to dismiss the case, Facebook agreed to settle. •

Internet Companies' Privacy Policies

The Federal Trade Commission (FTC) investigates consumer complaints of privacy violations. The FTC has forced many companies, including Google, Facebook, Twitter, and MySpace, to enter a consent decree that gives the FTC broad power to review their privacy and data practices. It can then sue companies that violate the terms of the decree.

EXAMPLE 9.22   In 2012, Google settled a suit brought by the FTC alleging that it had misused data from Apple's Safari users. Google allegedly had used cookies to trick the Safari browser on iPhones and iPads so that Google could monitor users who had blocked such tracking. This violated the consent decree with the FTC. Google agreed to pay $22.5 million to settle the suit without admitting liability. •

Facebook has faced a number of complaints about its privacy policy and has changed its policy several times to satisfy its critics and ward off potential government investigations. Other companies, including mobile app developers, have also changed their privacy policies to provide more information to consumers. Consequently, it is frequently the companies, rather than courts or legislatures, that are defining the privacy rights of their online users.

Protecting Consumer Privacy

To protect consumers' personal information, the Obama administration has proposed a consumer privacy bill of rights (see the *Online Developments* feature that follows for details). The goal is to ensure that personal information is safe online.

"Science fiction does not remain fiction for long. And certainly not on the Internet."

—Vinton Cerf, 1943–present (American Internet pioneer, comedian, author)

Cookie A small file sent from a Web site and stored in a user's Web browser to track the user's Web-browsing activities.

Learning Objective 5
How do online retailers track their users' Web browsing activities?

If this proposed privacy bill of rights becomes law, retailers will have to change some of their procedures. Retailers will have to give customers better choices about what data are collected and how the data are used for marketing. They may also have to take into account consumers' expectations about how their information will be used once it is collected.

ONLINE DEVELOPMENTS

A Consumer Privacy Bill of Rights

Whenever consumers purchase items from an online retailer, such as Amazon.com, or a retailer that sells both offline and online, such as Target Brands, Inc., the retailer collects information about the consumer. Over time, the retailer can amass considerable data about a person's shopping habits. Does collecting this information violate a consumer's right to privacy? Should the retailers be able to pass on the data they have collected to their affiliates? Should they be able to use the information to predict what a consumer might want and then create online "coupons" customized to fit the person's buying history?

The President Proposes a Consumer Privacy Bill of Rights

To protect consumers' personal information, the Obama administration drafted a consumer privacy bill of rights that would apply both online and offline. In introducing the bill of rights and asking Congress to enact it into law, President Obama said that "American consumers can't wait any longer for clear rules of the road that ensure their personal information is safe online."

The following is the bill of rights proposed by the president:

1. **Individual Control**—Consumers have a right to exercise control over what personal data organizations collect from them and how they use it.
2. **Transparency**—Consumers have the right to easily understandable information about privacy and security practices.
3. **Respect for Context**—Consumers have a right to expect that organizations will collect, use, and disclose personal data in ways that are consistent with the context in which consumers provide the data.
4. **Security**—Consumers have the right to secure and responsible handling of personal data.

5. **Access and Accuracy**—Consumers have a right to access and correct personal data in usable formats, in a manner that is appropriate to the sensitivity of the data and the risk of adverse consequences to consumers if the data are inaccurate.
6. **Focus Collection**—Consumers have a right to reasonable limits on the personal data that companies collect and retain.
7. **Accountability**—Consumers have a right to have personal data handled by companies with appropriate measures in place to assure that they adhere to the Consumer Privacy Bill of Rights.

The Implications of the Consumer Privacy Bill of Rights

If this proposed privacy bill of rights becomes law, retailers will have to change some of their procedures:

1. Retailers will have to give customers better choices about what data are collected and how the data are used for marketing.
2. Retailers will have to take into account consumers' expectations about how their information will be used once it is collected.
3. Retailers will have to allow consumers to set reasonable limits on the personal information that is collected about them.

Critical Thinking

Some argue that restricting retailers' tracking ability will actually make consumers worse off. How would this be possible?

Reviewing . . . Internet Law, Social Media, and Privacy

While he was in high school, Joel Gibb downloaded numerous songs to his smartphone from an unlicensed file-sharing service. He used portions of the copyrighted songs when he recorded his own band and posted videos on YouTube and Facebook. Gibb also used BitTorrent to download several movies from the Internet. Now he has applied to Boston University. The admissions office has requested access to his Facebook password, and he has complied. Using the information presented in the chapter, answer the following questions.

1. What laws, if any, did Gibb violate by downloading the music and videos from the Internet?
2. Was Gibb's use of portions of copyrighted songs in his own music illegal? Explain.
3. Can individuals legally post copyrighted content on their Facebook pages? Why or why not?
4. Did Boston University violate any laws when it asked Joel to provide his Facebook password? Explain.

Debate This Internet service providers should be subject to the same defamation laws as newspapers, magazines, and television and radio stations.

Key Terms

cloud computing 234
cookie 243
cybersquatting 229

cyber tort 240
distributed network 234
domain name 229

goodwill 229
Internet service provider (ISP) 228
peer-to-peer (P2P) networking 234

social media 235
spam 228
typosquatting 230

Chapter Summary: Internet Law, Social Media, and Privacy

Internet Law	
	1. *Spam*—Unsolicited junk e-mail accounts for about three-quarters of all e-mails. Laws to combat spam have been enacted by thirty-seven states and the federal government, but the flow of spam continues.
	a. The Controlling the Assault of Non-Solicited Pornography and Marketing (CAN-SPAM) Act prohibits false and deceptive e-mails originating in the United States.
	b. The U.S. Safe Web Act allows U.S. authorities to cooperate and share information with foreign agencies in investigating and prosecuting those involved in spamming, spyware, and various Internet frauds and deceptions. The act includes a safe harbor for Internet service providers.
	2. *Domain names*—Trademark owners often use their mark as part of a domain name (Internet address). The Internet Corporation for Assigned Names and Numbers (ICANN) oversees the distribution of domain names. ICANN recently expanded the available domain names to include new generic top-level domain names (gTLDs).
	3. *Cybersquatting*—Disputes arise when a person registers a domain name that is the same as, or confusingly similar to, the trademark of another and then offers to sell the domain name back to the trademark owner. This is known as cybersquatting, and it is illegal if the one registering, trafficking in, or using the domain name has a "bad faith intent" to profit from that mark. Anticybersquatting legislation is aimed at combatting the problem, but it has had only limited success.
	4. *Meta tags*—Search engines compile their results by looking through a Web site's *meta tags,* or key words, inserted into the HTML code. Using another's trademark in a meta tag without the owner's permission normally constitutes trademark infringement.
	5. *Trademark dilution*—When a trademark is used online, without authorization, in a way that diminishes the distinctive quality of the mark, it constitutes trademark dilution. Unlike infringement actions, trademark dilution claims do not require proof that consumers are likely to be confused by a connection between the unauthorized use and the mark.
	6. *Licensing*—Many companies choose to permit others to use their trademarks and other intellectual property online under a license. Licensing agreements frequently include restrictions that prohibit licensees from sharing the file and using it to create similar software applications.

Continued

Chapter Summary: Internet Law, Social Media, and Privacy— Continued

Copyrights in Digital Information	1. *Copyrighted works online*—Much of the material on the Internet (including software and database information) is copyrighted, and in order to transfer that material online, it must be "copied." Generally, whenever a party downloads software or music without authorization, a copyright is infringed. 2. *Digital Millennium Copyright Act*—To protect copyrights in digital information, Congress passed the Digital Millennium Copyright Act (DMCA). The DMCA establishes civil and criminal penalties for anyone who bypasses encryption software or other antipiracy technologies, but provides exceptions for certain educational and nonprofit uses. It also limits the liability of Internet service providers for infringement unless the ISP is aware of the user's infringement and fails to take action. 3. *File-sharing technology*—When file sharing is used to download others' stored music files or illegally copy movies, copyright issues arise. Individuals who download the music or movies in violation of copyright laws are liable for infringement. Companies that distribute file-sharing software or provide such services have been held liable for the copyright infringement of their users if the software or technology involved promoted copyright infringement.

Social Media	1. *Legal issues*—The emergence of Facebook and other social networking sites has created a number of legal and ethical issues. Law enforcement and administrative agencies now routinely use social media to detect illegal activities and conduct investigations, as do many businesses.
	2. *The Electronic Communications Privacy Act (ECPA)*—The ECPA prohibits the intentional interception or disclosure of any wire, oral, or electronic communication.
	    a. The ECPA includes a "business-extension exception" that permits employers to monitor employees' electronic communications made in the ordinary course of business (but not personal communications).
	    b. The Stored Communications Act is part of the ECPA and prohibits intentional unauthorized access to *stored* electronic communications (such as backup data stored by an employer).
	3. *Social media passwords*—Private employers and schools have sometimes looked at an individual's Facebook or other social media account to see if it included controversial postings such as racially discriminatory remarks or photos of drug parties. A number of states have enacted legislation that protects individuals from having to divulge their social media passwords. Such laws may not be completely effective in preventing employers from rejecting applicants or terminating workers based on their social media postings.
	4. *Company-wide social media networks*—Many companies today form their own internal social media networks through which employees can exchange messages about topics related to their work.

Online Defamation	Federal and state statutes apply to certain forms of cyber torts, or torts that occur in cyberspace, such as online defamation. Under the federal Communications Decency Act (CDA), Internet service providers generally are not liable for defamatory messages posted by their subscribers.
Privacy	Numerous Internet companies have been accused of violating users' privacy rights. To sue for invasion of privacy, though, a person must have a reasonable expectation of privacy in the particular situation. It is often difficult to determine how much privacy it is reasonable for a person to expect on the Internet. Whenever a consumer purchases items online from a retailer, the retailer collects information about the consumer through "cookies." Consequently, retailers have gathered large amounts of data about individuals' shopping habits. It is not clear, however, whether collecting such information violates a person's right to privacy. Many companies establish Internet privacy policies, which typically inform users what types of data they are gathering and for what purposes it will be used. People have a reasonable expectation that online companies will follow their own privacy policies.

Issue Spotters

1. Karl self-publishes a cookbook titled *Hole Foods,* in which he sets out recipes for donuts, Bundt cakes, tortellini, and other foods with holes. To publicize the book, Karl designs the Web site **holefoods.com**. Karl appropriates the key words of other cooking and cookbook sites with more frequent hits so that **holefoods.com** will appear in the same search engine results as the more popular sites. Has Karl done anything wrong? Explain. (See *Internet Law.*)
2. Eagle Corporation began marketing software in 2001 under the mark "Eagle." In 2013, Eagle.com, Inc., a different company selling different products, begins to use *eagle* as part of its URL and registers it as a domain name. Can Eagle Corporation stop this use of *eagle?* If so, what must the company show? (See *Internet Law.*)

—Check your answers to the Issue Spotters against the answers provided in Appendix D at the end of this text.

For Review

1. What is cybersquatting, and when is it illegal?
2. What steps have been taken to protect intellectual property rights in the digital age?
3. When does the law protect a person's electronic communications from being intercepted or accessed?
4. What law governs whether Internet service providers are liable for online defamatory statements made by users?
5. How do online retailers track their users' Web browsing activities?

Business Scenarios and Case Problems

9–1. Domain Names. Tony owns Antonio's, a pub in a small town in Iowa. Universal Dining, Inc., opens a chain of pizza parlors in California called "Antonio's." Without Tony's consent, Universal uses "antoniosincalifornia" as part of the domain name for the chain's Web site. Has Universal committed trademark dilution or any other violation of the law? Explain. (See *Internet Law.*)

9–2. Internet Service Providers. CyberConnect, Inc., is an Internet service provider (ISP). Pepper is a CyberConnect subscriber. Market Reach, Inc., is an online advertising company. Using sophisticated software, Market Reach directs its ads to those users most likely to be interested in a particular product. When Pepper receives one of the ads, she objects to the content. Further, she claims that CyberConnect should pay damages for "publishing" the ad. Is the ISP regarded as a publisher and therefore liable for the content of Market Reach's ad? Why or why not? (See *Online Defamation.*)

9–3. Privacy. SeeYou, Inc., is an online social network. SeeYou's members develop personalized profiles to interact and share information—photos, videos, stories, activity updates, and other items—with other members. Members post the information that they want to share and decide with whom they want to share it. SeeYou launched a program to allow members to share with others what they do elsewhere online. For example, if a member rents a movie through Netflix, SeeYou will broadcast that information to everyone in the member's online network. How can SeeYou avoid complaints that this program violates its members' privacy? (See *Privacy.*)

9–4. Copyrights in Digital Information. When she was in college, Jammie Thomas-Rasset wrote a case study on Napster, the online peer-to-peer (P2P) file-sharing network, and knew that it was shut down because it was illegal. Later, Capitol Records, Inc., which owns the copyrights to a large number of music recordings, discovered that "tereastarr"—a user name associated with Thomas-Rasset's Internet protocol address—had made twenty-four songs available for distribution on KaZaA, another P2P network. Capitol notified Thomas-Rasset that she had been identified as engaging in the unauthorized trading of music. She replaced the hard drive on her computer with a new drive that did not contain the songs in dispute. Is Thomas-Rasset liable for copyright infringement? Explain. [*Capitol Records, Inc. v. Thomas-Rasset*, 692 F.3d 899 (8th Cir. 2012)] (See *Copyrights in Digital Information.*)

9–5. Domain Names. Austin Rare Coins, Inc., buys and sells rare coins, bullion, and other precious metals through eight Web sites with different domain names. An unknown individual took control of Austin's servers and transferred the domain names to another registrant without Austin's permission. The new registrant began using the domain names to host malicious content—including hate letters to customers and fraudulent contact information—and to post customers' credit-card numbers and other private information, thereby tarnishing Austin's goodwill. Austin filed a suit in a federal district court against the new registrant under the Anticybersquatting Consumer Protection Act. Is Austin entitled to a transfer of the domain names? Explain. [*Austin Rare Coins, Inc. v. Acoins.com*, __ F.Supp.2d __, 2013 WL 85142 (E.D.Va. 2013)] (See *Internet Law.*)

9–6. Business Case Problem with Sample Answer— Privacy. Using special software, South Dakota law enforcement officers found a person who appeared to possess child pornography at a specific Internet protocol address. The officers subpoenaed Midcontinent Communications, the service that assigned the address, for the personal information of its subscriber. With this information, the officers obtained a search warrant for the residence of John Rolfe, where they found a laptop that contained child pornography. Rolfe argued that the subpoenas violated his "expectation of privacy." Did Rolfe have a privacy interest in the information obtained by the subpoenas issued to Midcontinent? Discuss. [*State of South Dakota v. Rolfe*, 825 N.W.2d 901 (S.Dak. 2013)] (See *Privacy.*)

—For a sample answer to Problem 9–6, go to Appendix E at the end of this text.

9–7. File-Sharing. Dartmouth College professor M. Eric Johnson, in collaboration with Tiversa, Inc., a company that monitors peer-to-peer networks to provide security services, wrote an article titled "Data Hemorrhages in the Health-Care Sector." In preparing the article, Johnson and Tiversa searched the networks for data that could be used to commit medical or financial identity theft. They found a document that contained the Social Security numbers, insurance information, and treatment codes for patients of LabMD, Inc. Tiversa notified LabMD of the find in order to solicit its business. Instead of hiring Tiversa, however, LabMD filed a suit in a federal district court against the company, alleging trespass, conversion, and violations of federal statutes. What do these facts indicate about the security of private information? Explain. How should the court rule? [*LabMD, Inc. v. Tiversa, Inc.*, 2013 WL 425983 (11th Cir. 2013)] (See *Copyrights in Digital Information.*)

9–8. Social Media. Mohammad Omar Aly Hassan and nine others were indicted in a federal district court on charges of conspiring to advance violent jihad (holy war against enemies of Islam) and other offenses related to terrorism. The evidence at Hassan's trial included postings he made on Facebook concerning his adherence to violent jihadist ideology. Convicted, Hassan appealed, contending that the Facebook items had not been properly authenticated (established as his comments). How might the government show the connection between postings on Facebook and those who post them? Discuss. [*United States v. Hassan*, 742 F.3d 104 (4th Cir. 2014)] (See *Social Media.*)

9–9. 💡 **Critical-Thinking Managerial Question.** Sync Computers, Inc., makes computer-related products under the brand name "Sync," which the company registers as a trademark. Without Sync's permission, E-Product Corp. embeds the Sync mark in E-Product's Web site, in black type on a blue background. This tag causes the E-Product site to be returned at the top of the list of results on a search engine query for "Sync." Does E-Product's use of the Sync mark as a meta tag without Sync's permission constitute trademark infringement? Explain. (See *Internet Law.*)

9–10. ↔ **A Question of Ethics—Criminal Investigations.** After the unauthorized release and posting of classified U.S. government documents to WikiLeaks.org, involving Bradley Manning, a U.S. Army private first class, the U.S. government began a criminal investigation. The government obtained a court order to require Twitter, Inc., to turn over subscriber information and communications to and from the e-mail addresses of Birgitta Jonsdottir and others. The court sealed the order and the other documents in the case, reasoning that "there exists no right to public notice of all the types of documents filed in a . . . case." Jonsdottir and the others appealed this decision. [*In re Application of the United States of America for an Order Pursuant to 18 U.S.C. Section 2703(d)*, 707 F.3d 283 (4th Cir. 2013)] (See *Social Media.*)

1. Why would the government want to "seal" the documents of an investigation? Why would the individuals under investigation want those documents to be "unsealed"? What factors should be considered in striking a balance between these competing interests?

2. How does law enforcement use social media to detect and prosecute criminals? Is this use of social media an unethical invasion of individuals' privacy? Discuss.

CHAPTER 10

The Formation of Traditional and E-Contracts

(nuno/iStockphoto.com)

LEARNING OBJECTIVES

The five learning objectives below are designed to help improve your understanding of the chapter. After reading this chapter, you should be able to answer the following questions:

1. What are the four basic elements necessary to the formation of a valid contract?

2. What is the difference between express and implied contracts?

3. What are the elements necessary for an effective acceptance?

4. How do shrink-wrap and click-on agreements differ from other contracts? How have traditional laws been applied to these agreements?

5. Under what circumstances will a covenant not to compete be enforced? When will such covenants not be enforced?

"All sensible people are selfish,
and nature is tugging at every contract to make the terms of it fair."

—Ralph Waldo Emerson, 1803–1882 (American poet)

As Ralph Waldo Emerson observed in the chapter-opening quotation, people tend to act in their own self-interest, and this influences the terms they seek in their contracts. Contract law must therefore provide rules to determine which contract terms will be enforced and which promises must be kept. A **promise** is a declaration by a person (the *promisor*) to do or not to do a certain act. As a result, the person to whom the promise is made (the *promisee*) has a right to expect or demand that something either will or will not happen in the future.

Like other types of law, contract law reflects our social values, interests, and expectations at a given point in time. It shows, for instance, what kinds of promises our society thinks should be legally binding. It distinguishes between promises that create only *moral* obligations (such as a promise to take a friend to lunch) and promises that are legally binding (such as a promise to pay for merchandise purchased).

Contract law also demonstrates which excuses our society accepts for breaking certain types of promises. In addition, it indicates which promises are considered to be contrary to public policy—against the interests of society as a whole—and therefore legally invalid.

Promise A declaration by a person (the promisor) to do or not to do a certain act.

When the person making a promise is a child or is mentally incompetent, for example, a question will arise as to whether the promise should be enforced. Resolving such questions is the essence of contract law.

An Overview of Contract Law

Before we look at the numerous rules that courts use to determine whether a particular promise will be enforced, it is necessary to understand some fundamental concepts of contract law. In this section, we describe the sources and general function of contract law and introduce the objective theory of contracts.

Sources of Contract Law

The common law governs all contracts except when it has been modified or replaced by statutory law, such as the Uniform Commercial Code (UCC),[1] or by administrative agency regulations. Contracts relating to services, real estate, employment, and insurance, for instance, generally are governed by the common law of contracts.

Contracts for the sale and lease of goods, however, are governed by the UCC—to the extent that the UCC has modified general contract law. The relationship between general contract law and the law governing sales and leases of goods will be explored in detail in Chapter 12. In the discussion of general contract law that follows, we indicate in footnotes the areas in which the UCC has significantly altered common law contract principles.

The Definition of a Contract

Contract A set of promises constituting an agreement between parties, giving each a legal duty to the other and also the right to seek a remedy for the breach of the promises or duties.

A **contract** is "a promise or a set of promises for the breach of which the law gives a remedy, or the performance of which the law in some way recognizes as a duty."[2] Put simply, a contract is an agreement that can be enforced in court. It is formed by two or more parties who agree to perform or to refrain from performing some act now or in the future.

Generally, contract disputes arise when there is a promise of future performance. If the contractual promise is not fulfilled, the party who made it is subject to the sanctions of a court (see Chapter 11). That party may be required to pay damages for failing to perform the contractual promise. In a few instances, the party may be required to perform the promised act.

The Objective Theory of Contracts

Objective Theory of Contracts The view that contracting parties shall only be bound by terms that can objectively be inferred from promises made.

In determining whether a contract has been formed, the element of intent is of prime importance. In contract law, intent is determined by what is called the **objective theory of contracts,** not by the personal or subjective intent, or belief, of a party. The theory is that a party's intention to enter into a legally binding agreement, or contract, is judged by outward, objective facts. The facts are as interpreted by a *reasonable* person, rather than by the party's own secret, subjective intentions. Objective facts may include:

1. What the party said when entering into the contract.
2. How the party acted or appeared (intent may be manifested by conduct as well as by oral or written words).
3. The circumstances surrounding the transaction.

A party may have many unexpressed reasons for entering into an agreement—such as obtaining real property, goods, or services—and profiting from the deal. Any of these purposes

---

1. See Chapters 1 and 12 for further discussions of the significance and coverage of the UCC. Excerpts from the UCC are presented in Appendix C at the end of this book.
2. *Restatement (Second) of Contracts,* Section 1. As mentioned in Chapter 1, *Restatements of the Law* are scholarly books that restate the existing common law principles distilled from court opinions as a set of rules on a particular topic. Courts often refer to the *Restatements* for guidance.

may provide a motivation for performing the contract. If one party has a goal of *not* performing, normally that party will be liable to the other. The case that follows illustrates this point.

Case 10.1

Pan Handle Realty, LLC v. Olins

Appellate Court of Connecticut, 140 Conn.App. 556, 59 A.3d 842 (2013).

REAL ESTATE CONTRACT
CANCELED

(Olivier Le Queinec/
Shutterstock.com)

BACKGROUND AND FACTS Pan Handle Realty, LLC, built a luxury home in Westport, Connecticut. Robert Olins proposed to lease the property. Pan Handle forwarded a draft lease to Olins. On January 17, 2009, the parties met and negotiated changes to the terms. After the final draft of the lease was signed, Olins gave Pan Handle a check for the amount of the annual rent—$138,000—and said that he planned to move into the home on January 28. Before that date, according to the lease, Pan Handle removed all of the furnishings. On January 27, Olins's bank informed Pan Handle that payment had been stopped on the rental check. Olins then told Pan Handle that he was "unable to pursue any further interest in the property." Pan Handle made substantial efforts to find a new tenant, but was unable to do so. Consequently, Pan Handle filed a lawsuit in a Connecticut state court against Olins, alleging that he had breached the lease. From a decision in Pan Handle's favor—and an award of damages in the amount of $138,000 in unpaid rent, $8,000 in utility fees, interest, and attorneys' fees—Olins appealed.

IN THE WORDS OF THE COURT . . .
SHELDON, J. [Judge]
* * * *

The defendant's * * * claim on appeal is that the court improperly determined that the parties entered into a valid lease agreement. The defendant contends that because "material terms were still being negotiated and various issues were unresolved," there was no meeting of the minds, which is required to form a contract.
* * * *

In order for an enforceable contract to exist, the court must find that the parties' minds had truly met. * * * *If there has been a misunderstanding between the parties, or a misapprehension by one or both so that their minds have never met, no contract has been entered into by them and the court will not make for them a contract which they themselves did not make.* [Emphasis added.]

There was evidence in the record to support the court's finding that the parties entered into a valid lease agreement because there was a true meeting of the parties' minds as to the essential terms of the agreement. Prior to the January 17 meeting,

the plaintiff [Pan] had provided the defendant [Olins] with a draft lease agreement * * * . The defendant testified that at the January 17 meeting, he and the plaintiff's representative * * * made * * * revisions and signed the lease. It was then that the defendant tendered a check, post-dated to the start of the lease period, on which he noted payment for a one-year lease of the premises.

There is no evidence in the record to support the defendant's contention that he did not intend to be bound by the lease when he signed it or that terms of the lease were still being negotiated at that time. Pursuant to the lease, the plaintiff was obligated to make modifications to the premises * * * . The defendant's apparent unilateral change of heart regarding the lease agreement does not negate the parties' prior meeting of the minds that occurred at the time the lease was executed. There is ample evidence in the record evincing the intent of the parties to be bound by the lease when they signed it and, thus, to support the court's finding that "the lease agreement was a valid and binding contract which the defendant * * * has breached."
* * * *

* * * As in any other contract action the measure of damages is that the award should place the injured party in the same position as he would have been in had the contract been fully performed. * * * As a consequence, the unpaid rent * * * may be used by the court in computing the losses suffered by the plaintiff by reason of the defendant's breach of contract of lease.

DECISION AND REMEDY The state intermediate appellate court affirmed the lower court's judgment. The objective fact, as supported by the evidence, was that the parties intended to be bound by the lease when they signed it. That Olins had a different intent or a later "change of heart" was not in evidence.

THE ETHICAL DIMENSION *Did the measure of damages assessed in this case place Pan Handle in the same position that it would have been in if the lease had been fully performed? Discuss.*

THE LEGAL ENVIRONMENT DIMENSION *How did the objective theory of contracts affect the result in this case? Explain.*

Elements of a Valid Contract

The following list briefly describes the four requirements that must be met before a valid contract exists. If any of these elements is lacking, no contract will have been formed. (Each requirement will be explained more fully later in this chapter.)

1. *Agreement.* An agreement to form a contract includes an *offer* and an *acceptance.* One party must offer to enter into a legal agreement, and another party must accept the terms of the offer.
2. *Consideration.* Any promises made by the parties to the contract must be supported by legally sufficient and bargained-for *consideration* (something of value received or promised, such as money, to convince a person to make a deal).
3. *Contractual capacity.* Both parties entering into the contract must have the contractual *capacity* to do so. The law must recognize them as possessing characteristics that qualify them as competent parties.
4. *Legality.* The contract's purpose must be to accomplish some goal that is legal and not against public policy.

Defenses to the Enforceability of a Contract

Even if all of the requirements listed above are satisfied, a contract may be unenforceable if the following requirements are not met. These requirements typically are raised as *defenses* to the enforceability of an otherwise valid contract.

1. *Voluntary consent.* The consent of both parties must be voluntary. For instance, if a contract was formed as a result of fraud, undue influence, mistake, or duress, the contract may not be enforceable (see Chapter 11).
2. *Form.* The contract must be in whatever form the law requires. Some contracts must be in writing to be enforceable, as discussed later in this chapter.

Types of Contracts

There are many types of contracts. They are categorized based on legal distinctions as to their formation, performance, and enforceability.

Contract Formation

Contracts can be classified according to how and when they are formed. Exhibit 10–1 that follows shows three such classifications, and the following subsections explain them in greater detail.

Bilateral versus Unilateral Contracts
Every contract involves at least two parties. The *offeror* is the party making the offer. The *offeree* is the party to whom the offer is made. Whether the contract is classified as *bilateral* or *unilateral* depends on what the offeree must do to accept the offer and bind the offeror to a contract.

Bilateral Contracts   If the offeree can accept simply by promising to perform, the contract is a **bilateral contract.** Hence, a bilateral contract is a "promise for a promise." No performance, such as payment of funds or delivery of goods, need take place for a bilateral contract to be formed. The contract comes into existence at the moment the promises are exchanged.
   EXAMPLE 10.1 Javier offers to buy Ann's smartphone for $200. Javier tells Ann that he will give her the $200 for the smartphone next Friday, when he gets paid. Ann accepts

Bilateral Contract A type of contract that arises when a promise is given in exchange for a return promise.

Exhibit 10–1 Classifications Based on Contract Formation

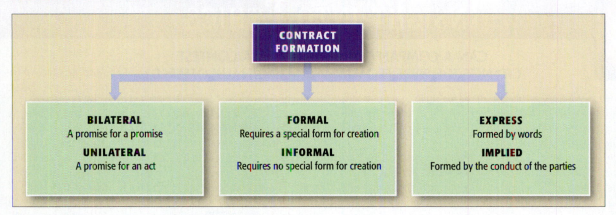

Javier's offer and promises to give him the smartphone when he pays her on Friday. Javier and Ann have formed a bilateral contract. ●

Unilateral Contracts If the offer is phrased so that the offeree can accept the offer only by completing the contract performance, the contract is a **unilateral contract.** Hence, a unilateral contract is a "promise for an act."[3] In other words, a unilateral contract is formed not at the moment when promises are exchanged but at the moment when the contract is *performed.* **EXAMPLE 10.2** Reese says to Celia, "If you drive my car from New York to Los Angeles, I'll give you $1,000." Only on Celia's completion of the act—bringing the car to Los Angeles—does she fully accept Reese's offer to pay $1,000. If she chooses not to accept the offer to drive the car to Los Angeles, there are no legal consequences. ●

Contests, lotteries, and other competitions involving prizes are examples of offers to form unilateral contracts. If a person complies with the rules of the contest—such as by submitting the right lottery number at the right place and time—a unilateral contract is formed. The organization offering the prize is then bound to a contract to perform as promised in the offer. If the person fails to comply with the contest rules, however, no binding contract is formed. (See this chapter's *Insight into Ethics* feature that follows for a discussion of whether a company can change a contest prize from what it originally advertised.)

Revocation of Offers for Unilateral Contracts A problem arises in unilateral contracts when the promisor attempts to *revoke* (cancel) the offer after the promisee has begun performance but before the act has been completed. **EXAMPLE 10.3** Seiko offers to buy Jin's sailboat, moored in San Francisco, on delivery of the boat to Seiko's dock in Newport Beach, three hundred miles south of San Francisco. Jin rigs the boat and sets sail. Shortly before his arrival at Newport Beach, Jin receives a message from Seiko withdrawing her offer. Seiko's offer was for a unilateral contract, and only Jin's delivery of the sailboat at her dock is an acceptance. ●

In contract law, offers are normally *revocable* (capable of being taken back, or canceled) until accepted. Under the traditional view of unilateral contracts, Seiko's revocation would terminate the offer. Because of the harsh effect on the offeree of the revocation of an offer to form a unilateral contract, the modern-day view is different.

Today, once performance has been *substantially* undertaken, the offeror cannot revoke the offer. Thus, in *Example 10.3*, even though Jin has not yet accepted the offer by complete

Unilateral Contract *A contract that results when an offer can be accepted only by the offeree's performance.*

---

3. The phrase *unilateral contract*, if read literally, is a contradiction in terms. A contract cannot be one sided because, by definition, an agreement implies the existence of two or more parties.

INSIGHT INTO ETHICS

CAN A COMPANY THAT SPONSORS A CONTEST CHANGE THE PRIZE FROM WHAT IT ORIGINALLY OFFERED?

Courts have historically treated contests as unilateral contracts, which typically cannot be modified by the offeror after the offeree has begun to perform. But this principle may not always apply to contest terms or advertisements.

John Rogalski entered a poker tournament conducted by Little Poker League, LLC (LPL). The tournament lasted several months as players competed for spots in a winner-take-all final event. During the final event, Rogalski and the other contestants signed a "World Series of Poker (WSOP) Agreement," which stated that LPL would pay the $10,000 WSOP entry fee on the winner's behalf and provide $2,500 for travel-related expenses. The agreement also stated that if the winner did not attend the WSOP, he or she would relinquish the WSOP seat and return the expense money to LPL.

Rogalski won and took the $2,500 for travel expenses, but did not attend the WSOP. He then filed a suit for $10,000 against LPL, arguing that it had advertised that the winner could choose to receive the cash value of the prizes ($12,500) instead

of going to the WSOP. Rogalski claimed that, by participating in the tournament, he had accepted the advertised offer to take the cash in lieu of entering the WSOP. He further claimed that the later agreement was an invalid contract modification. LPL filed a counterclaim to recover the $2,500 in expenses. The court ruled in favor of LPL, finding that the contract was not formed when Rogalski began participating in the contest. Rather, it was formed when he signed the WSOP agreement. Under the contest rules as stated in the WSOP agreement, Rogalski had to return the $2,500 of expenses to LPL.[a]

For Critical Analysis
Insight into the Social Environment
Why would a company that changes its advertised prizes have to worry about its reputation?

a. *Rogalski v. Little Poker League, LLC*, 2011 WL 589636 (Minn.App. 2011).

---

performance, Seiko is normally prohibited from revoking it. Jin can deliver the boat and bind Seiko to the contract.

Formal Contract An agreement that by law requires a specific form for its validity.

Formal versus Informal Contracts
Another classification system divides contracts into formal contracts and informal contracts. **Formal contracts** are contracts that require a special form or method of creation (formation) to be enforceable.[4] One example is *negotiable instruments,* which include checks, drafts, promissory notes, bills of exchange, and certificates of deposit. Negotiable instruments are formal contracts because, under the Uniform Commercial Code (UCC), a special form and language are required to create them.

Letters of credit, which are frequently used in international sales contracts (see Chapter 7), are another type of formal contract. Letters of credit are agreements to pay contingent on the purchaser's receipt of invoices and *bills of lading* (documents evidencing receipt of, and title to, goods shipped).

Informal Contract A contract that does not require a specific form or method of creation to be valid.

Informal contracts (also called *simple contracts*) include all other contracts. No special form is required (except for certain types of contracts that must be in writing), as the contracts are usually based on their substance rather than their form. Typically, businesspersons put their contracts in writing to ensure that there is some proof of a contract's existence should disputes arise.

---

4. See *Restatement (Second) of Contracts,* Section 6, which explains that formal contracts include (1) contracts under seal, (2) recognizances, (3) negotiable instruments, and (4) letters of credit.

Express versus Implied Contracts   Contracts may also be categorized as *express* or *implied*. In an **express contract,** the terms of the agreement are fully and explicitly stated in words, oral or written. A signed lease for an apartment or a house is an express written contract. If one classmate calls another on the phone and agrees to buy her textbooks from last semester for $300, an express oral contract has been made.

A contract that is implied from the conduct of the parties is called an **implied contract** (or sometimes an *implied-in-fact contract*). This type of contract differs from an express contract in that the conduct of the parties, rather than their words, creates and defines the terms of the contract.

Requirements for Implied Contracts   For an implied contract to arise, certain requirements must be met. Normally, if the following conditions exist, a court will hold that an implied contract was formed:

1. The plaintiff furnished some service or property.
2. The plaintiff expected to be paid for that service or property, and the defendant knew or should have known that payment was expected.
3. The defendant had a chance to reject the services or property and did not.

EXAMPLE 10.4   Oleg, a small-business owner, needs an accountant to complete his tax return. He drops by a local accountant's office, explains his situation to the accountant, and learns what fees she charges. The next day, he returns and gives the receptionist all of the necessary documents to complete his return. Then he walks out without saying anything further to the accountant. In this situation, Oleg has entered into an implied contract to pay the accountant the usual fees for her services. The contract is implied because of Oleg's conduct and hers. She expects to be paid for completing the tax return, and by bringing in the records she will need to do the job, Oleg has implied an intent to pay her. ●

Contracts with Express and Implied Terms   Note that a contract may be a mixture of an express contract and an implied contract. In other words, a contract may contain some express terms, while others are implied. During the constructions of a home, for instance, the homeowner often asks the builder to make changes in the original specifications.

CASE EXAMPLE 10.5   Lamar Hopkins hired Uhrhahn Construction & Design, Inc., for several projects during the construction of his home. Each project was based on a cost estimate and specifications, and had a signed contract that required modifications to be in writing. When work was in progress, however, Hopkins made several requests for changes. There was no written record of these changes, but Uhrhahn performed the work and Hopkins paid for it. A dispute arose after Hopkins requested that Uhrhahn use Durisol blocks rather than cinder blocks. Uhrhahn orally agreed to the modification, but then demanded extra payment because the Durisol blocks were more complicated and costly to install. Hopkins refused to pay. Uhrhahn sued and won. The court found that that there was an implied contract for the Durisol blocks. The builder did the work, and the buyer accepted the work. Such oral modification of the original contract creates an enforceable contract, and payment is due for the extra work.[5] ●

Contract Performance

Contracts are also classified according to the degree to which they have been performed. A contract that has been fully performed on both sides is called an **executed contract.** A contract that has not been fully performed by the parties is called an **executory contract.**

---

5. *Uhrhahn Construction & Design, Inc. v. Hopkins,* 179 P.3d 808 (Utah App. 2008).

Express Contract A contract in which the terms of the agreement are stated in words, oral or written.

Implied Contract A contract formed in whole or in part from the conduct of the parties.

Learning Objective 2
What is the difference between express and implied contracts?

Executed Contract A contract that has been fully performed by both parties.

Executory Contract A contract that has not yet been fully performed.

If one party has fully performed but the other has not, the contract is said to be executed on the one side and executory on the other, but the contract is still classified as executory. **EXAMPLE 10.6** Rosanno agreed to buy ten tons of coal from Western Coal Company. Western has delivered the coal to his steel mill, where it is now being burned. At this point, the contract is an executory contract—it is executed on the part of Western and executory on Rosanno's part. After he pays Western for the coal, the contract will be executed on both sides. •

Contract Enforceability

Valid Contract A contract that results when the elements necessary for contract formation are present.

A **valid contract** has the elements necessary to entitle at least one of the parties to enforce it in court. In other words, it meets the four basic requirements listed earlier (agreement, consideration, capacity, and legality). As you can see in Exhibit 10–2 that follows, valid contracts may be enforceable, voidable, or unenforceable. Additionally, a contract may be referred to as a *void contract*. We look next at the meaning of the terms *voidable, unenforceable,* and *void* in relation to contract enforceability.

Voidable Contract A contract that may be legally avoided at the option of one or both of the parties.

Voidable Contracts

A **voidable contract** is a valid contract but one that can be avoided at the option of one or both of the parties. The party having the option can elect either to avoid any duty to perform or to *ratify* (make valid) the contract. If the contract is avoided, both parties are released from it. If it is ratified, both parties must fully perform their respective legal obligations.

As you will read later in this chapter, contracts made by minors generally are voidable at the option of the minor (with certain exceptions). Contracts made by mentally incompetent persons and intoxicated persons sometimes may also be voidable. Additionally, contracts entered into under duress, fraudulent conditions, or undue influence are voidable.

Unenforceable Contract A valid contract rendered unenforceable by some statute or law.

Unenforceable Contracts

An **unenforceable contract** is one that cannot be enforced because of certain legal defenses against it. It is not unenforceable because a party

Exhibit 10–2 Enforceable, Voidable, Unenforceable, and Void Contracts

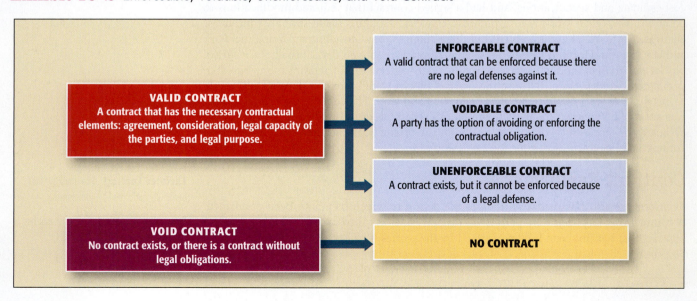

VALID CONTRACT
A contract that has the necessary contractual elements: agreement, consideration, legal capacity of the parties, and legal purpose.

ENFORCEABLE CONTRACT
A valid contract that can be enforced because there are no legal defenses against it.

VOIDABLE CONTRACT
A party has the option of avoiding or enforcing the contractual obligation.

UNENFORCEABLE CONTRACT
A contract exists, but it cannot be enforced because of a legal defense.

VOID CONTRACT
No contract exists, or there is a contract without legal obligations.

NO CONTRACT

failed to satisfy a legal requirement of the contract. Rather, it is a valid contract rendered unenforceable by some statute or law. For instance, certain contracts must be in writing, and if they are not, they will not be enforceable except in certain exceptional circumstances.

Void Contracts   A **void contract** is no contract at all. The terms *void* and *contract* are contradictory. None of the parties have any legal obligations if a contract is void. A contract can be void because the purpose of the contract was illegal (as you will read later in this chapter).

Void Contract A contract having no legal force or binding effect.

Agreement

Whether a contract is formed in the traditional way (on paper) or online, an essential element for contract formation is **agreement**—the parties must agree on the terms of the contract and manifest to each other their *mutual assent* (agreement) to the same bargain. Ordinarily, agreement is evidenced by two events: an *offer* and an *acceptance*. One party offers a certain bargain to another party, who then accepts that bargain.

Agreement A mutual understanding or meeting of the minds between two or more individuals regarding the terms of a contract.

The agreement does not necessarily have to be in writing. Both parties, however, must manifest their assent, or voluntary consent, to the same bargain. Once an agreement is reached, if the other elements of a contract (consideration, capacity, and legality—discussed later in this chapter) are present, a valid contract is formed. Generally, the contract creates enforceable rights and duties between the parties.

Requirements of the Offer

An **offer** is a promise or commitment to do or refrain from doing some specified action in the future. As mentioned, the parties to a contract are the *offeror,* the one who makes an offer or proposal to another party, and the *offeree,* the one to whom the offer or proposal is made. Under the common law, three elements are necessary for an offer to be effective:

Offer A promise or commitment to perform or refrain from performing some specified act in the future.

1. The offeror must have a serious intention to become bound by the offer.
2. The terms of the offer must be reasonably certain, or definite, so that the parties and the court can ascertain the terms of the contract.
3. The offer must be communicated to the offeree.

Once an effective offer has been made, the offeree's acceptance of that offer creates a legally binding contract (providing the other essential elements for a valid and enforceable contract are present).

Intention   The first requirement for an effective offer is a serious intent on the part of the offeror. Serious intent is not determined by the subjective intentions, beliefs, and assumptions of the offeror. Rather, it is determined by what a reasonable person in the offeree's position would conclude that the offeror's words and actions meant. Offers made in obvious anger, jest, or undue excitement do not meet the serious-and-objective-intent test because a reasonable person would realize that a serious offer was not being made. Because these offers are not effective, an offeree's acceptance does not create an agreement.

A classic contracts case from 1954 illustrates the serious-and-objective-intent requirement in the context of an offer made "after a few drinks." **CASE EXAMPLE 10.7**   W. O. Lucy had known A. H. Zehmer more than fifteen years and had offered to buy the Ferguson Farm from him many times. One night, Lucy stopped to visit the Zehmers at the restaurant and gas station they operated and tried to buy the Ferguson Farm once again. Lucy said to Zehmer, "I bet you wouldn't take $50,000 for that place." Zehmer replied, "Yes, I would too; you wouldn't give fifty." Throughout the evening, both men continued to drink whiskey while talking, and the conversation returned to the sale of the Ferguson Farm for $50,000.

Eventually, Lucy enticed Zehmer to write up an agreement to the effect that the Zehmers would sell the Ferguson Farm to Lucy for $50,000 complete. Later, Lucy sued Zehmer to compel him to go through with the sale. Zehmer argued that he had been drunk and that the offer had been made in jest and hence was unenforceable. The trial court agreed with Zehmer, and Lucy appealed. The Virginia Supreme Court looked at the parties' outward expressions of intent and held in favor of Lucy. The parties had discussed the terms of the sale for at least forty minutes and had done two drafts of the contract before both men agreed to sign it. Therefore, the serious-intent requirement had been met, and the contract was binding.[6] ●

Situations When Intent May Be Lacking

The concept of intention can be further clarified through an examination of types of statements that are *not* offers. We look at these expressions and statements in the subsections that follow.

Expressions of Opinion   An expression of opinion is not an offer. It does not indicate an intention to enter into a binding agreement.

CASE EXAMPLE 10.8   George Hawkins took his son to McGee, a physician, and asked McGee to operate on the son's hand. McGee said that the boy would be in the hospital three or four days and that the hand would *probably* heal a few days later. The son's hand did not heal for a month, but the father did not win a suit for breach of contract. The court held that McGee had not made an offer to heal the son's hand in a few days. He had merely expressed an opinion as to when the hand would heal.[7] ●

Statements of Future Intent   A statement of an intention to do something in the future is not an offer.   **EXAMPLE 10.9**   Samir says, "I *plan* to sell my stock in Novation, Inc., for $150 per share." If John "accepts" and tenders the $150 per share for the stock, no contract is created. Samir has merely expressed his intention to enter into a future contract for the sale of the stock. No contract is formed because a reasonable person would conclude that Samir was only *thinking about* selling his stock, not *promising* to sell it. ●

Preliminary Negotiations   A request or invitation to negotiate is not an offer. It only expresses a willingness to discuss the possibility of entering into a contract. Statements such as "Will you sell Blythe Estate?" or "I wouldn't sell my car for less than $5,000" are examples. A reasonable person in the offeree's position would not conclude that these statements indicated an intention to enter into a binding obligation.

Likewise, when the government or private firms require construction work, they invite contractors to submit bids. The *invitation* to submit bids is not an offer, and a contractor does not bind the government or private firm by submitting a bid. (The bids that the contractors submit are offers, however, and the government or private firm can bind the contractor by accepting the bid.)

Advertisements   In general, advertisements (including representations made in catalogues, price lists, circulars, and Web sites) are treated not as offers to contract but as invitations to negotiate.

Price lists are another form of invitation to negotiate or trade. A seller's price list is not an offer to sell at that price. It merely invites the buyer to offer to buy at that price. In fact, the seller usually puts "prices subject to change" on the price list. Only in rare circumstances will a price quotation be construed as an offer.

When a contractor submits a bid proposal, is that proposal binding on the entity to whom the bid was addressed?

(Alexskopje/Shutterstock.com)

---

6. *Lucy v. Zehmer*, 196 Va. 493, 84 S.E.2d 516 (1954).
7. *Hawkins v. McGee*, 84 N.H. 114, 146 A. 641 (1929).

Although most advertisements and price lists are treated as invitations to negotiate, this does not mean that they can never be an offer. On some occasions, courts have construed advertisements to be offers because the ads contained definite terms that invited acceptance (such as an ad offering a reward for the return of a lost dog).

Preliminary Agreements   Increasingly, the courts are holding that a preliminary agreement constitutes a binding contract if the parties have agreed on all essential terms and no disputed issues remain to be resolved. In contrast, if the parties agree on certain major terms but leave other terms open for further negotiation, a preliminary agreement is not binding. The parties are bound only in the sense that they have committed themselves to negotiate the undecided terms in good faith in an effort to reach a final agreement.

CASE EXAMPLE 10.10   Basis Technology Corporation entered into several contracts with Amazon.com, Inc., to create software and provide technical services. When a dispute arose over payment for services rendered, Basis sued. During the trial, the two parties appeared to reach an agreement to settle out of court via a series of e-mail exchanges outlining the settlement, and the trial stopped. Afterward, Amazon rejected the language of the settlement agreement prepared by Basis, so Basis filed suit again to enforce a proposed settlement. Amazon claimed that the proposed terms were not sufficiently complete and definite to form a binding agreement.

The court looked at the parties' statements in the e-mail exchange, and concluded that it was clear that a settlement had been reached. Basis's attorney had written, "This e-mail confirms the essential business terms of the settlement between our respective clients." The e-mail also indicated that the parties "agree that they promptly will take all reasonable steps to memorialize" those terms. Amazon's counsel had responded with an e-mail saying "correct." Therefore, the court held that the settlement agreement was enforceable and that Amazon had intended to be bound by its terms.[8] •

Jeff Bezos, the founder and CEO of Amazon.com, with a Japanese manager.

PREVENTING LEGAL DISPUTES

To avoid potential legal disputes, be cautious when drafting a memorandum that outlines a preliminary agreement or understanding with another party. If all the major terms are included, a court might hold that the agreement is binding even though you intended it to be only a tentative agreement. One way to avoid being bound is to include in the writing the points of disagreement, as well as those points on which you and the other party agree. Alternatively, you could add a disclaimer to the memorandum stating that, although you anticipate entering a contract in the future, neither party intends to be legally bound to the terms that were discussed. That way, the other party cannot claim that you have already reached an agreement on all essential terms.

Definiteness of Terms   The second requirement for an effective offer involves the definiteness of its terms. An offer must have reasonably definite terms so that a court can determine if a breach has occurred and give an appropriate remedy.[9] The specific terms required depend, of course, on the type of contract.

Generally, a contract must include the following terms, either expressed in the contract or capable of being reasonably inferred from it:

1. The identification of the parties.
2. The identification of the object or subject matter of the contract (also the quantity, when appropriate), including the work to be performed, with specific identification of such items as goods, services, and land.

---

8. *Basis Technology Corp. v. Amazon.com, Inc.*, 71 Mass.App.Ct. 29, 878 N.E.2d 952 (2008).
9. *Restatement (Second) of Contracts*, Section 33.

3. The consideration to be paid.
4. The time of payment, delivery, or performance.

An offer may invite an acceptance to be worded in such specific terms that the contract is made definite. **EXAMPLE 10.11**   Nintendo of America, Inc., contacts your Play 2 Win Games store and offers to sell "from one to twenty-five Nintendo 3DS gaming systems for $75 each. State number desired in acceptance." You agree to buy twenty systems. Because the quantity is specified in the acceptance, the terms are definite, and the contract is enforceable. •

When the parties have clearly manifested an intent to form a contract, courts sometimes are willing to supply a missing term in a contract, especially a sales contract (see Chapter 12). But a court will not rewrite a contract if the parties' expression of intent is too vague or uncertain to be given any precise meaning.

Communication

Communication   The third requirement for an effective offer is communication—the offer must be communicated to the offeree. Ordinarily, one cannot agree to a bargain without knowing that it exists. **EXAMPLE 10.12**   Tolson advertises a reward for the return of her lost cat. Dirk, not knowing of the reward, finds the cat and returns it to Tolson. Usually, Dirk cannot recover the reward because an essential element of a reward contract is that the one who claims the reward must have known it was offered. •

Termination of the Offer

The communication of an effective offer to an offeree gives the offeree the power to transform the offer into a binding, legal obligation (a contract) by an acceptance. This power of acceptance does not continue forever, though. It can be terminated either by action of the parties or by operation of law.

Termination by Action of the Parties

Termination by Action of the Parties   An offer can be terminated by action of the parties in any of three ways: by revocation, by rejection, or by counteroffer.

Revocation The withdrawal of a contract offer by the offeror. Unless an offer is irrevocable, it can be revoked at any time prior to acceptance without liability.

Revocation   The offeror's act of withdrawing (revoking) an offer is known as **revocation.** Unless an offer is irrevocable, the offeror usually can revoke the offer, as long as the revocation is communicated to the offeree before the offeree accepts. Revocation may be accomplished by either of the following:

1. Express repudiation of the offer (such as "I withdraw my previous offer of October 17").
2. Performance of acts that are inconsistent with the existence of the offer and are made known to the offeree (for instance, selling the offered property to another person in the presence of the offeree).

In most states, a revocation becomes effective when the offeree or the offeree's *agent* (a person acting on behalf of the offeree) actually receives it. Therefore, a revocation sent via FedEx on April 1 and delivered at the offeree's residence or place of business on April 3 becomes effective on April 3. An offer made to the general public can be revoked in the same manner that the offer was originally communicated, such as by being broadcast over a local television news program.

Irrevocable Offers   Although most offers are revocable, some can be made irrevocable—that is, they cannot be revoked. Increasingly, courts refuse to allow an offeror to revoke an offer when the offeree has changed position because of justifiable reliance on the offer. In some circumstances, "firm offers" made by merchants may also be considered irrevocable—see the discussion of a "merchant's firm offer" in Chapter 12.

Another form of irrevocable offer is an **option contract.** An option contract is created when an offeror promises to hold an offer open for a specified period of time in return for

Option Contract A contract under which the offeror cannot revoke the offer for a stipulated time period (because the offeree has given consideration for the offer to remain open).

a payment (consideration) given by the offeree. An option contract takes away the offeror's power to revoke the offer for the period of time specified in the option.

Option contracts are frequently used in conjunction with the sale or lease of real estate. **EXAMPLE 10.13**   Tyrell agrees to lease a house from Jackson, the property owner. The lease contract includes a clause stating that Tyrell is paying an additional $15,000 for an option to purchase the property within a specified period of time. If Tyrell decides not to purchase the house after the specified period has lapsed, he loses the $15,000, and Jackson is free to sell the property to another buyer. •

Rejection   If the offeree rejects the offer—by words or by conduct—the offer is terminated. Any subsequent attempt by the offeree to accept will be construed as a new offer, giving the original offeror (now the offeree) the power of acceptance. Like a revocation, a rejection of an offer is effective only when it is actually received by the offeror or the offeror's agent.

Merely inquiring about an offer does not constitute rejection. When the offeree merely inquires as to the "firmness" of the offer, there is no reason to presume that he or she intends to reject it. **EXAMPLE 10.14**   Raymond offers to buy Francie's iPhone 5 for $200, and Francie responds, "Is that your best offer?" or "Will you pay me $275 for it?" A reasonable person would conclude that Francie did not reject the offer but merely made an inquiry about it. She can still accept and bind Raymond to the $200 purchase price. •

Counteroffer   A **counteroffer** is a rejection of the original offer and the simultaneous making of a new offer. **EXAMPLE 10.15**   Burke offers to sell his home to Lang for $270,000. Lang responds, "Your price is too high. I'll offer to purchase your house for $250,000." Lang's response is called a counteroffer because it rejects Burke's offer to sell at $270,000 and creates a new offer by Lang to purchase the home at a price of $250,000. •

At common law, the **mirror image rule** requires the offeree's acceptance to match the offeror's offer exactly—to mirror the offer. Any change in, or addition to, the terms of the original offer automatically terminates that offer and substitutes the counteroffer. The counteroffer, of course, need not be accepted, but if the original offeror does accept the terms of the counteroffer, a valid contract is created.[10]

> **Counteroffer**   An offeree's response to an offer in which the offeree rejects the original offer and at the same time makes a new offer.

> **Mirror Image Rule**   A common law rule that requires the terms of the offeree's acceptance to exactly match the terms of the offeror's offer for a valid contract to be formed.

Termination by Operation of Law   The power of the offeree to transform the offer into a binding, legal obligation can be terminated by operation of law through the occurrence of any of the following events:

1. Lapse of time.
2. Destruction of the specific subject matter of the offer (such as a smartphone or a house).
3. Death or incompetence of the offeror or the offeree.
4. Supervening illegality of the proposed contract. (A statute or court decision that makes an offer illegal automatically terminates the offer.)

Lapse of Time   An offer terminates automatically by law when the period of time *specified in the offer* has passed. If the offer states that it will be left open until a particular date, then the offer will terminate at midnight on that day. If the offer states that it will be open for a number of days, this time period normally begins to run when the offeree *receives* the offer (not when it is formed or sent).

If the offer does not specify a time for acceptance, the offer terminates at the end of a *reasonable* period of time. What constitutes a reasonable period of time depends on the

---

10. The mirror image rule has been greatly modified in regard to sales contracts. Section 2–207 of the UCC provides that a contract is formed if the offeree makes a definite expression of acceptance (such as signing the form in the appropriate location), even though the terms of the acceptance modify or add to the terms of the original offer (see Chapter 12).

subject matter of the contract, business and market conditions, and other relevant circumstances. An offer to sell farm produce, for example, will terminate sooner than an offer to sell farm equipment because farm produce is perishable. Produce is also subject to greater fluctuations in market value.

Supervening Illegality of the Proposed Contract   A statute or court decision that makes an offer illegal automatically terminates the offer.[11]   **EXAMPLE 10.16**   Lee offers to lend Kim $10,000 at an annual interest rate of 15 percent. Before Kim can accept the offer, a law is enacted that prohibits interest rates higher than 12 percent. Lee's offer is automatically terminated. (If the statute is enacted after Kim accepts the offer, a valid contract is formed, but the contract may still be unenforceable.) ●

Acceptance

Acceptance is a voluntary act by the offeree that shows assent (agreement) to the terms of an offer. The offeree's act may consist of words or conduct. The acceptance must be unequivocal and must be communicated to the offeror. Generally, only the person to whom the offer is made or that person's agent can accept the offer and create a binding contract.

Unequivocal Acceptance   To exercise the power of acceptance effectively, the offeree must accept unequivocally. This is the *mirror image rule* previously discussed. An acceptance may be unequivocal even though the offeree expresses dissatisfaction with the contract. For instance, "I accept the offer, but can you give me a better price?" is an effective acceptance.

An acceptance cannot impose new conditions or change the terms of the original offer. If it does, the acceptance may be considered a counteroffer, which is a rejection of the original offer. For instance, the statement "I accept the offer but only if I can pay on ninety days' credit" is a counteroffer and not an unequivocal acceptance.

Certain terms, when included in an acceptance, will not change the offer sufficiently to constitute rejection.   **EXAMPLE 10.17**   In response to an art dealer's offer to sell a painting, the offeree, Ashton Gibbs, replies, "I accept. Please send a written contract." Gibbs is requesting a written contract but is not making it a condition for acceptance. Therefore, the acceptance is effective without the written contract. In contrast, if Gibbs replies, "I accept *if* you send a written contract," the acceptance is expressly conditioned on the request for a writing, and the statement is not an acceptance but a counteroffer. (Notice how important each word is!)[12] ●

Silence as Acceptance   Ordinarily, silence cannot constitute acceptance, even if the offeror states, "By your silence and inaction, you will be deemed to have accepted this offer." An offeree should not be obligated to act affirmatively to reject an offer when no consideration (nothing of value) has passed to the offeree to impose such a duty.

In some instances, however, the offeree does have a duty to speak, and her or his silence or inaction will operate as an acceptance. Silence may constitute an acceptance in the following circumstances:

1. When an offeree takes the benefit of offered services even though he or she had an opportunity to reject them and knew that they were offered with the expectation of compensation.

Acceptance The act of voluntarily agreeing, through words or conduct, to the terms of an offer, thereby creating a contract.

Learning Objective 3
What are the elements necessary for an effective acceptance?

---

11. *Restatement (Second) of Contracts*, Section 36.
12. As noted in footnote 10, in regard to sales contracts, the UCC provides that an acceptance may still be valid even if some terms are added. The new terms are simply treated as proposed additions to the contract.

2. When the offeree has had prior dealings with the offeror. For instance, a merchant routinely receives shipments from a certain supplier and always notifies that supplier when defective goods are rejected. The merchant's silence regarding a particular shipment (failure to reject the goods) will constitute acceptance.

Communication of Acceptance

In a bilateral contract, acceptance is in the form of a promise (not performance). Because bilateral contracts are formed when the promise is made (rather than when the act is performed), communication of acceptance is necessary. Communication of acceptance may not be necessary if the offer dispenses with the requirement, however, or if the offer can be accepted by silence.

CASE EXAMPLE 10.18 Powerhouse Custom Homes, Inc., owed $95,260.42 to 84 Lumber Company under a credit agreement. When Powerhouse failed to pay, 84 Lumber filed a suit to collect. During mediation, the parties agreed to a deadline for objections to whatever agreement they might reach. If there were no objections, the agreement would be binding.

Powerhouse then offered to pay less than the amount owed, and 84 Lumber did not respond. Powerhouse argued that 84 Lumber accepted the offer by not objecting to it within the deadline. The court, however, held that for a contract to be formed, an offer must be accepted unequivocally. Although Powerhouse had made an offer of a proposed settlement, 84 Lumber did not communicate its acceptance. Thus, the court reasoned that the parties did not reach an agreement on the proposed settlement.[13] •

Because a unilateral contract calls for the full performance of some act, acceptance is usually evident, and notification is therefore unnecessary. Nevertheless, exceptions do exist, such as when the offeror requests notice of acceptance or has no way of determining whether the requested act has been performed.

Mode and Timeliness of Acceptance

In bilateral contracts, acceptance must be timely. The general rule is that acceptance in a bilateral contract is timely if it is made before the offer is terminated. Problems may arise, though, when the parties involved are not dealing face to face. In such situations, the offeree should use an authorized mode of communication.

The Mailbox Rule Acceptance takes effect, thus completing formation of the contract, at the time the offeree sends or delivers the communication via the mode expressly or impliedly authorized by the offeror. This is the so-called **mailbox rule**, also called the *deposited acceptance rule*, which the majority of courts follow. Under this rule, if the authorized mode of communication is the mail, then an acceptance becomes valid when it is dispatched (placed in the control of the U.S. Postal Service)—*not* when it is received by the offeror. (Note, however, that if the offer stipulates when acceptance will be effective, then the offer will not be effective until the time specified.)

The mailbox rule does not apply to instantaneous forms of communication, such as when the parties are dealing face to face, by telephone, by fax, and usually by e-mail. Under the law of most states (based on the Uniform Electronic Transactions Act), e-mail is considered sent when it either leaves the control of the sender or is received by the recipient. This rule takes the place of the mailbox rule when the parties have agreed to conduct transactions electronically and allows an e-mail acceptance to become effective when sent.

Authorized Means of Acceptance A means of communicating acceptance can be expressly authorized by the offeror or impliedly authorized by the facts and circumstances of the situation. An acceptance sent by means not expressly or impliedly authorized normally is not effective until it is received by the offeror.

Mailbox Rule A common law rule that acceptance takes effect, and thus a contract is formed, at the time the offeree sends or delivers the acceptance using the communication mode expressly or impliedly authorized by the offeror.

---

13. *Powerhouse Custom Homes, Inc. v. 84 Lumber Co.*, 307 Ga.App. 605, 705 S.E.2d 704 (2011).

When an offeror specifies how acceptance should be made (for example, by overnight delivery), *express authorization* is said to exist. The contract is not formed unless the offeree uses that specified mode of acceptance. Moreover, both offeror and offeree are bound in contract the moment this means of acceptance is employed. **EXAMPLE 10.19** Motorola Mobility, Inc., offers to sell 144 Atrix 4G smartphones and 72 Lapdocks to Call Me Plus phone stores. The offer states that Call Me Plus must accept the offer via FedEx overnight delivery. The acceptance is effective (and a binding contract is formed) the moment that Call Me Plus gives the overnight envelope containing the acceptance to the FedEx driver. •

If the offeror does not expressly authorize a certain mode of acceptance, then acceptance can be made by *any reasonable means*.[14] Courts look at the prevailing business usages and the surrounding circumstances to determine whether the mode of acceptance used was reasonable. Usually, the offeror's choice of a particular means in making the offer implies that the offeree can use the *same or a faster means* for acceptance. Thus, if the offer is made via Priority U.S. mail, it would be reasonable to accept the offer via Priority mail or by a faster method, such as signed scanned documents sent as attachments via e-mail or overnight delivery.

Substitute Method of Acceptance   Sometimes, the offeror authorizes a particular method of acceptance, but the offeree accepts by a different means. In that situation, the acceptance may still be effective if the substituted method serves the same purpose as the authorized means.

The acceptance by a substitute method is not effective on dispatch, though, and no contract will be formed until the acceptance is received by the offeror. For instance, an offer specifies acceptance by FedEx overnight delivery, but the offeree instead accepts by overnight delivery from another carrier. The substitute method of acceptance will still be effective, but the contract will not be formed until the offeror receives it.

E-Contracts

E-Contract A contract that is formed electronically.

Numerous contracts are formed online. Electronic contracts, or **e-contracts,** must meet the same basic requirements (agreement, consideration, contractual capacity, and legality) as paper contracts. Disputes concerning e-contracts, however, tend to center on contract terms and whether the parties voluntarily agreed to those terms.

Online contracts may be formed not only for the sale of goods and services but also for *licensing*. As you may recall from Chapter 8, the purchase of software generally involves a license, or a right to use the software, rather than the passage of title (ownership rights) from the seller to the buyer. **EXAMPLE 10.20** Lynn downloads an app on her iPad that enables her to work on spreadsheets. During the transaction, she has to select "I agree" several times to indicate that she understands that she is purchasing only the right to use the software under specific terms. After she agrees to these terms (the licensing agreement), she can use the application. •

"If two men agree on everything, you can be sure one of them is doing the thinking."

Lyndon Baines Johnson, 1908–1973 (Thirty-sixth president of the United States, 1963–1969)

Online Offers

Sellers doing business via the Internet can protect themselves against contract disputes and legal liability by creating offers that clearly spell out the terms that will govern their transactions if the offers are accepted. All important terms should be conspicuous and easy to view.

The seller's Web site should include a hypertext link to a page containing the full contract so that potential buyers are made aware of the terms to which they are assenting. The

---

14. *Restatement (Second) of Contracts*, Section 30. This is also the rule under UCC 2–206(1)(a).

contract generally must be displayed online in a readable format, such as a twelve-point typeface.

Provisions to Include

An important rule to keep in mind is that the offeror (the seller) controls the offer and thus the resulting contract. The seller should therefore anticipate the terms he or she wants to include in a contract and provide for them in the offer. At a minimum, an online offer should include the following provisions:

1. *Acceptance of terms.* A clause that clearly indicates what constitutes the buyer's agreement to the terms of the offer, such as a box containing the words "I accept" that the buyer can click.
2. *Payment.* A provision specifying how payment for the goods (including any applicable taxes) must be made.
3. *Return policy.* A statement of the seller's refund and return policies.
4. *Disclaimer.* Disclaimers of liability for certain uses of the goods. For instance, an online seller of business forms may add a disclaimer that the seller does not accept responsibility for the buyer's reliance on the forms rather than on an attorney's advice.
5. *Limitation on remedies.* A provision specifying the remedies available to the buyer if the goods are found to be defective or if the contract is otherwise breached. Any limitation of remedies should be clearly spelled out.
6. *Privacy policy.* A statement indicating how the seller will use the information gathered about the buyer.
7. *Dispute resolution.* Provisions relating to dispute settlement, such as an arbitration clause or a forum-selection clause (discussed next).

Dispute-Settlement Provisions

Online offers frequently include provisions relating to dispute settlement. For instance, the offer might include an arbitration clause specifying that any dispute arising under the contract will be arbitrated in a designated forum. For a discussion of how some online schools use arbitration agreements, see this chapter's *Online Developments* feature that follows.

Forum-Selection Clause Many online contracts contain a **forum-selection clause** indicating the forum, or location (such as a court or jurisdiction), in which contract disputes will be resolved. As discussed in Chapter 3, significant jurisdictional issues may arise when parties are at a great distance, as they often are when they form contracts via the Internet. A forum-selection clause will help to avert future jurisdictional problems and also help to ensure that the seller will not be required to appear in court in a distant state.

> **Forum-Selection Clause** A provision in a contract designating the court, jurisdiction, or tribunal that will decide any disputes arising under the contract.

CASE EXAMPLE 10.21 Before advertisers can place ads through Google, Inc., they must agree to certain terms that are displayed in an online window. These terms include a forum-selection clause, which provides that any dispute is to be "adjudicated in Santa Clara County, California." Lawrence Feldman, who advertised through Google, complained that he was overcharged and filed a lawsuit against Google in a federal district court in Pennsylvania. The court held that Feldman had agreed to the forum-selection clause in Google's online contract and transferred the case to a court in Santa Clara County.[15] •

Choice-of-Law Clause Some online contracts may also include a *choice-of-law clause* specifying that any contract dispute will be settled according to the law of a particular jurisdiction, such as a state or country. As discussed in Chapter 7, choice-of-law clauses are particularly common in international contracts, but they may also appear in e-contracts to specify which state's laws will govern in the United States.

---

15. *Feldman v. Google, Inc.,* 513 F.Supp.2d 229 (E.D.Pa. 2007).

ONLINE DEVELOPMENTS

The Validity of E-Signatures on Agreements with Online Colleges and Universities

The number of online institutions offering bachelor's, master's, and even doctoral degrees has grown dramatically in recent years. Enrollment for these online colleges and universities is conducted online. Most, if not all, of these schools ask enrolling students to agree that any disputes will be solved by arbitration. How valid are these enrollment agreements when the students simply indicate their assent via electronic signatures, or e-signatures?

Two Students Claimed That E-Signatures Were Invalid

One student, Scott Rosendahl, alleged that online Ashford University's enrollment adviser claimed that Ashford offered one of the cheapest undergraduate degree programs in the country. In fact, it did not. Another student, Veronica Clarke, enrolled in the doctor of psychology program at the online University of the Rockies. She alleged that its enrollment adviser told her that the doctor of psychology program would qualify her to become a clinical psychologist in the U.S. military, but that statement was false.

Rosendahl and Clarke sued their respective universities for violation of unfair competition laws and false advertising laws, fraud, and negligent misrepresentation. These students claimed that their e-signatures were invalid.

The Online Universities Argued for Arbitration

The universities pointed out that each student had electronically assented to the enrollment agreement, which clearly required that all disputes be arbitrated. Each agreement stated, "Such arbitration shall be the sole remedy for the resolution of any dispute or controversies between the parties to this agreement."

One issue was whether the e-signatures on the agreement were valid. Each application form had an "acknowledgment and signature" paragraph that stated, "My signature on this application certifies that I have read, understood, and agreed to my rights and responsibilities as set forth in this application."

Both students had to click on an electronic box acknowledging that they had read the agreement and consented to it. When they clicked on the box, the phrase "Signed by E-Signature" appeared on the signature line.

The Court Ruled in Favor of the Online Universities

The universities submitted copies of Rosendahl's and Clarke's online application forms to the court. Both forms contained the arbitration agreement and were signed with e-signatures. Rosendahl and Clarke provided no proof that they had not consented to the enrollment agreements. Thus, the court held that the online universities had proved the existence of valid arbitration agreements.[a]

Critical Thinking

Would the fact that the arbitration agreements were valid have prevented Rosendahl and Clarke from pursuing their claims for negligent misrepresentation and fraud? Why or why not?

---

a. *Rosendahl v. Bridgepoint Education, Inc.*, 2012 WL 667049 (S.D.Cal. 2012).

Online Acceptances

The *Restatement (Second) of Contracts,* which, as noted earlier, is a compilation of common law contract principles, states that parties may agree to a contract "by written or spoken words or by other action or by failure to act."[16] The Uniform Commercial Code (UCC), which governs sales contracts, has a similar provision. Section 2–204 of the UCC states that any contract for the sale of goods "may be made in any manner sufficient to show agreement, including conduct by both parties which recognizes the existence of such a contract."

Learning Objective 4
How do shrink-wrap and click-on agreements differ from other contracts? How have traditional laws been applied to these agreements?

Click-On Agreements   The courts have used the *Restatement* and UCC provisions to conclude that a binding contract can be created by conduct. This includes the act of clicking on a box indicating "I accept" or "I agree" to accept an online offer. The agreement

---

16. *Restatement (Second) of Contracts,* Section 19.

resulting from such an acceptance is often called a **click-on agreement** (sometimes referred to as a *click-on license* or *click-wrap agreement*). Exhibit 10–3 that follows shows a portion of a typical click-on agreement that accompanies a software package.

Generally, the law does not require that the parties have read all of the terms in a contract for it to be effective. Therefore, clicking on a box that states "I agree" to certain terms can be enough. The terms may be contained on a Web site through which the buyer is obtaining goods or services. They may also appear on a screen when software is loaded from a CD-ROM or DVD or downloaded from the Internet.

CASE EXAMPLE 10.22   The "Terms of Use" that govern Facebook users' accounts include a forum-selection clause that provides for the resolution of all disputes in a court in Santa Clara County, California. To sign up for a Facebook account, a person must click on a box indicating that he or she has agreed to this term.

Mustafa Fteja was an active user of facebook.com when his account was disabled. He sued Facebook in a federal court in New York, claiming that it had disabled his Facebook page without justification and for discriminatory reasons. Facebook filed a motion to transfer the case to California under the forum-selection clause. The court found that the clause in Facebook's online contract was binding and transferred the case. When Fteja clicked on the button to accept the "Terms of Use" and become a Facebook user, he agreed to resolve all disputes with Facebook in Santa Clara County, California.[17] ●

Shrink-Wrap Agreements   With a **shrink-wrap agreement** (or *shrink-wrap license*), the terms are expressed inside the box in which the goods are packaged. (The term *shrink-wrap* refers to the plastic that covers the box.) Usually, the party who opens the box is told that she or he agrees to the terms by keeping whatever is in the box. Similarly, when a purchaser opens a software package, he or she agrees to abide by the terms of the limited license agreement.

EXAMPLE 10.23   Ava orders a new iMac from Big Dog Electronics, which ships it to her. Along with the iMac, the box contains an agreement setting forth the terms of the sale, including what remedies are available. The document also states that Ava's retention of the iMac for longer than thirty days will be construed as an acceptance of the terms. ●

In most instances, a shrink-wrap agreement is not between a retailer and a buyer, but between the manufacturer of the hardware or software and the ultimate buyer-user of the product. The terms generally concern warranties, remedies, and other issues associated with the use of the product.

Shrink-Wrap Agreements and Enforceable Contract Terms

In some cases, the courts have enforced the terms of shrink-wrap agreements in the same way as the terms of other contracts. These courts have reasoned that by including the terms with the product, the seller proposed a contract. The buyer could accept this contract by using the product after having an opportunity to read the terms. Thus, a buyer's failure to object to terms contained within a shrink-wrapped software package may constitute an acceptance of the terms by conduct.

Shrink-Wrap Terms That May Not Be Enforced   Sometimes,

however, the courts have refused to enforce certain terms included in shrink-wrap agreements because the buyer did not expressly consent to them. An important factor is when the parties formed their contract.

Click-On Agreement An agreement that arises when an online buyer clicks on "I agree," or otherwise indicates her or his assent to be bound by the terms of an offer.

Shrink-Wrap Agreement An agreement whose terms are expressed in a document located inside a box in which goods (usually software) are packaged.

Exhibit 10–3   A Sample Click-On Agreement

This exhibit illustrates an online offer to form a contract. To accept the offer, the user simply scrolls down the page and clicks on the "I Accept" button.

17. *Fteja v. Facebook, Inc.,* 841 F.Supp.2d 829 (S.D.N.Y. 2012).

If a buyer orders a product over the telephone, for instance, and is not informed of an arbitration clause or forum-selection clause at that time, the buyer clearly has not expressly agreed to these terms. If the buyer discovers the clauses *after* the parties entered into a contract, a court may conclude that those terms were proposals for additional terms and were not part of the contract.

Browse-Wrap Term A term or condition of use that is presented when an online buyer downloads a product but that does not require the buyer's explicit agreement.

Browse-Wrap Terms   Like the terms of click-on agreements, **browse-wrap terms** can occur in transactions conducted over the Internet. Unlike click-on agreements, however, browse-wrap terms do not require Internet users to assent to the terms before downloading or using certain software. In other words, a person can install the software without clicking "I agree" to the terms of a license. Browse-wrap terms are often unenforceable because they do not satisfy the agreement requirement of contract formation.[18]

E-Signature Technologies

E-Signature An electronic sound, symbol, or process attached to or logically associated with a record and adopted by a person with the intent to sign the record.

Today, numerous technologies allow electronic documents to be signed. An **e-signature** has been defined as "an electronic sound, symbol, or process attached to or logically associated with a record and executed or adopted by a person with the intent to sign the record."[19] Thus, e-signatures include encrypted digital signatures, names (intended as signatures) at the end of e-mail messages, and clicks on a Web page if the click includes some means of identification.

Federal Law on E-Signatures and E-Documents

The Electronic Signatures in Global and National Commerce Act (E-SIGN Act)[20] provides that no contract, record, or signature may be "denied legal effect" solely because it is in electronic form. In other words, under this law, an electronic signature is as valid as a signature on paper, and an e-document can be as enforceable as a paper one.

For an e-signature to be enforceable, the contracting parties must have agreed to use electronic signatures. For an electronic document to be valid, it must be in a form that can be retained and accurately reproduced.

Many e-signatures are legally binding today.

(Terry Davis/Shutterstock.com)

The E-SIGN Act does not apply to all types of documents. Contracts and documents that are exempt include court papers, divorce decrees, evictions, foreclosures, health-insurance terminations, prenuptial agreements, and wills. Also, the only agreements governed by the UCC that fall under this law are those covered by Articles 2 and 2A (sales and lease contracts) and UCC 1–107 and 1–206. Despite these limitations, the E-SIGN Act significantly expanded the possibilities for contracting online.

The Uniform Electronic Transactions Act

Although most states have laws governing e-signatures and other aspects of electronic transactions, these laws vary. In an attempt to create more uniformity among the states, in 1999 the National Conference of Commissioners on Uniform State Laws and the American Law Institute promulgated the Uniform Electronic Transactions Act (UETA). The UETA has been adopted, at least in part, by forty-eight states. Among other things, the UETA declares that a signature may not be denied legal effect or enforceability solely because it is in electronic form.

The primary purpose of the UETA is to remove barriers to e-commerce by giving the same legal effect to electronic records and signatures as is given to paper documents and signatures. As mentioned earlier, the UETA broadly defines an *e-signature* as "an electronic sound, symbol, or process attached to or logically associated with a record and executed or

---

18. See, for example, *Jesmer v. Retail Magic, Inc.*, 863 N.Y.S.2d 737 (2008).
19. This definition is from the Uniform Electronic Transactions Act, which will be discussed shortly.
20. 15 U.S.C. Sections 7001 *et seq.*

adopted by a person with the intent to sign the record."[21] A **record** is "information that is inscribed on a tangible medium or that is stored in an electronic or other medium and is retrievable in perceivable [visual] form."[22]

Record Information that is either inscribed on a tangible medium or stored in an electronic or other medium and is retrievable.

Scope and Applicability

The UETA does not create new rules for electronic contracts but rather establishes that records, signatures, and contracts may not be denied enforceability solely due to their electronic form. The UETA does not apply to all writings and signatures. It covers only electronic records and electronic signatures *relating to a transaction* between two or more people in a business, commercial, or governmental context.

The act specifically does not apply to wills or testamentary trusts or to transactions governed by the UCC (other than those covered by Articles 2 and 2A).[23] In addition, the provisions of the UETA allow the states to exclude its application to other areas of law.

The UETA does not apply to a transaction unless each of the parties has previously agreed to conduct transactions by electronic means. The agreement need not be explicit, however. It can be implied by the conduct of the parties and the surrounding circumstances, such as negotiating a contract via e-mail. The parties can agree to opt out of all or some of the terms of the UETA, but if they do not, then the UETA terms will govern their electronic transactions.

The Federal E-SIGN Act and the UETA

Congress passed the E-SIGN Act in 2000, a year after the UETA was presented to the states for adoption. The E-SIGN Act refers explicitly to the UETA and provides that if a state has enacted the uniform version of the UETA, it is not preempted by the E-SIGN Act.[24]

In other words, if the state has enacted the UETA without modification, state law will govern. The problem is that many states have enacted nonuniform (modified) versions of the UETA, usually to exclude other areas of state law from the UETA's terms. The E-SIGN Act specifies that those exclusions will be preempted to the extent that they are inconsistent with the E-SIGN Act's provisions.

The E-SIGN Act explicitly allows the states to enact alternative requirements for the use of electronic records or electronic signatures. Generally, however, the requirements must be consistent with the provisions of the E-SIGN Act, and the state must not give greater legal status or effect to one specific type of technology. Additionally, if a state enacts alternative requirements after the E-SIGN Act was adopted, the state law must specifically refer to the E-SIGN Act. The relationship between the UETA and the E-SIGN Act is illustrated in Exhibit 10–4 that follows.

Signatures on Electronic Records

Under the UETA, if an electronic record or signature is the act of a particular person, the record or signature may be attributed to that person. If a person types her or his name at the bottom of an e-mail purchase order, for instance, that name would qualify as a "signature." The signature would therefore be attributed to the person whose name appeared.

The UETA does not contain any express provisions about what constitutes fraud or whether an agent is authorized to enter a contract. Other state laws control if any issues relating to agency, authority, forgery, or contract formation arise.

Under the UETA, an electronic record is considered *sent* when it is properly directed to the intended recipient in a form readable by the recipient's computer system. Once the electronic record leaves the control of the sender or comes under the control of the recipient, the UETA deems it to have been sent. An electronic record is considered *received* when it enters the recipient's processing system in a readable form—*even if no individual is aware of its receipt.*

---

21. UETA 102(8).
22. UETA 102(15).
23. UETA 3(b).
24. 15 U.S.C. Section 7002(2)(A)(i).

Exhibit 10–4 The E-SIGN Act and the UETA

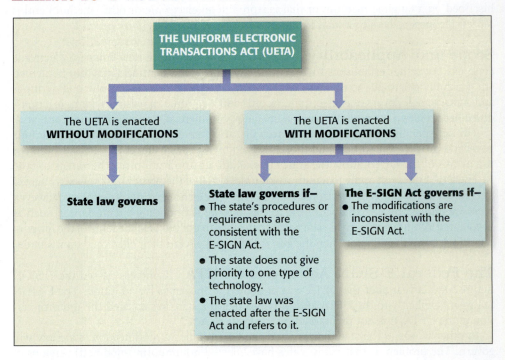

Consideration

The fact that a promise has been made does not mean the promise can or will be enforced. Under the common law, a primary basis for the enforcement of promises is consideration. **Consideration** usually is defined as the value (such as cash) given in return for a promise (in a bilateral contract) or in return for a performance (in a unilateral contract). As long as consideration is present, the courts generally do not interfere with contracts based on the amount of consideration paid.

Elements of Consideration

Often, consideration is broken down into two parts: (1) something of *legally sufficient value* must be given in exchange for the promise, and (2) there must be a *bargained-for* exchange.

Legally Sufficient Value   To be legally sufficient, consideration must be something of value in the eyes of the law. The "something of legally sufficient value" may consist of the following:

1. A promise to do something that one has no prior legal duty to do.
2. The performance of an action that one is otherwise not obligated to undertake.
3. The refraining from an action that one has a legal right to undertake (called a **forbearance**).

Consideration in bilateral contracts normally consists of a promise in return for a promise, as explained earlier. In a contract for the sale of goods, for instance, the seller promises to ship specific goods to the buyer, and the buyer promises to pay for those goods. Each of these promises constitutes consideration for the contract.

Consideration The value given in return for a promise or performance in a contractual agreement.

"No cause of action arises from a bare promise."

Legal Maxim

Forbearance The act of refraining from an action that one has a legal right to undertake.

In contrast, unilateral contracts involve a promise in return for a performance. **EXAMPLE 10.24** Anita says to her neighbor, "When you finish painting the garage, I will pay you $800." Anita's neighbor paints the garage. The act of painting the garage is the consideration that creates Anita's contractual obligation to pay her neighbor $800. •

What if, in return for a promise to pay, a person refrains from pursuing harmful habits (a forbearance), such as the use of tobacco and alcohol? In most situations, such forbearance constitutes legally sufficient consideration.[25]

Bargained-for Exchange The second element of consideration is that it must provide the basis for the bargain struck between the contracting parties. The item of value must be given or promised by the promisor (offeror) in return for the promisee's promise, performance, or promise of performance.

This element of bargained-for exchange distinguishes contracts from gifts. **EXAMPLE 10.25** Sheng-Li says to his son, "In consideration of the fact that you are not as wealthy as your brothers, I will pay you $5,000." The fact that the word *consideration* is used does not, by itself, mean that consideration has been given. Indeed, Sheng-Li's promise is not enforceable because the son does not have to do anything in order to receive the $5,000 promised. Because the son does not need to give Sheng-Li something of legal value in return for his promise, there is no bargained-for exchange. Rather, Sheng-Li has simply stated his motive for giving his son a gift. •

Agreements That Lack Consideration

Sometimes, one of the parties (or both parties) to an agreement may think that consideration has been exchanged when in fact it has not. Here, we look at some situations in which the parties' promises or actions do not qualify as contractual consideration.

Preexisting Duty Under most circumstances, a promise to do what one already has a legal duty to do does not constitute legally sufficient consideration. The preexisting legal duty may be imposed by law or may arise out of a previous contract. A sheriff, for instance, has a duty to investigate crime and to arrest criminals. Hence, a sheriff cannot collect a reward for providing information leading to the capture of a criminal.

Likewise, if a party is already bound by contract to perform a certain duty, that duty cannot serve as consideration for a second contract. **EXAMPLE 10.26** Ajax Contractors begins construction on a seven-story office building and after three months demands an extra $75,000 on its contract. If the extra $75,000 is not paid, the contractor will stop working. The owner of the land, finding no one else to complete the construction, agrees to pay the extra $75,000. The agreement is unenforceable because it is not supported by legally sufficient consideration. Ajax Contractors had a preexisting contractual duty to complete the building. •

Unforeseen Difficulties The rule regarding preexisting duty is meant to prevent extortion and the so-called holdup game. Nonetheless, if, during performance of a contract, extraordinary difficulties arise that were totally unforeseen at the time the contract was formed, a court may allow an exception to the rule. The key is whether the court finds the modification is fair and equitable in view of circumstances not anticipated by the parties when the contract was made.

Suppose that in *Example 10.26,* Ajax Contractors had asked for the extra $75,000 because it encountered a rock formation that no one knew existed. If the

"Understanding does not necessarily mean agreement."

Howard Vernon, 1918–1992 (American author)

Can a contractor who is performing under a contract legally demand a payment that was greater than what was stated in the contract?

(George Muresan/Shutterstock.com)

---

25. For a classic case holding that a person's promise to refrain from using alcohol and tobacco was sufficient consideration, see *Hamer v. Sidway,* 124 N.Y. 538, 27 N.E. 256 (1891).

landowner agrees to pay the extra $75,000 to excavate the rock and the court finds that it is fair to do so, Ajax Contractors can enforce the agreement. If rock formations are common in the area, however, the court may determine that the contractor should have known of the risk. In that situation, the court may choose to apply the preexisting duty rule and prevent Ajax Contractors from obtaining the extra $75,000.

Rescission and New Contract   The law recognizes that two parties can mutually agree to rescind, or cancel, their contract, at least to the extent that it is *executory* (still to be carried out). **Rescission**[26] is the unmaking of a contract so as to return the parties to the positions they occupied before the contract was made.

Sometimes, parties rescind a contract and make a new contract at the same time. When this occurs, it is often difficult to determine whether there was consideration for the new contract, or whether the parties had a preexisting duty under the previous contract. If a court finds there was a preexisting duty, then the new contract will be invalid because there was no consideration.

Past Consideration
Promises made in return for actions or events that have already taken place are unenforceable. These promises lack consideration in that the element of bargained-for exchange is missing. In short, you can bargain for something to take place now or in the future but not for something that has already taken place. Therefore, **past consideration** is no consideration.

CASE EXAMPLE 10.27   Jamil Blackmon became friends with Allen Iverson when Iverson was a high school student who showed tremendous promise as an athlete. One evening, Blackmon suggested that Iverson use "The Answer" as a nickname in the summer league basketball tournaments. Blackmon said that Iverson would be "The Answer" to all of the National Basketball Association's woes. Later that night, Iverson said that he would give Blackmon 25 percent of any proceeds from the merchandising of products that used "The Answer" as a logo or a slogan. Because Iverson's promise was made in return for past consideration, it was unenforceable. In effect, Iverson stated his intention to give Blackmon a gift.[27] ●

In a variety of situations, an employer will often ask an employee to sign a **covenant not to compete,** also called a *noncompete agreement*. Under such an agreement, the employee agrees not to compete with the employer for a certain period of time after the employment relationship ends. When a current employee is required to sign a noncompete agreement, his or her employment is not sufficient consideration for the agreement because the individual is already employed. To be valid, the agreement requires new consideration.

In the next case, the court had to decide if new consideration supported a noncompete agreement between physicians and a medical clinic.

---

26. Pronounced reh-*sih*-zhen.
27. *Blackmon v. Iverson*, 324 F.Supp.2d 602 (E.D.Pa. 2003).

Margin definitions

Rescission A remedy whereby a contract is canceled and the parties are returned to the positions they occupied before the contract was made.

Past Consideration An act that has already taken place at the time a contract is made and that ordinarily, by itself, cannot be consideration for a later promise to pay for the act.

Covenant Not to Compete A contractual promise of one party to refrain from competing with another party for certain period of time and within a certain geographic area.

(Feng Yu/Shutterstock.com)

Case 10.2

Baugh v. Columbia Heart Clinic, P.A.[a]
Court of Appeals of South Carolina, 402 S.C. 1, 738 S.E.2d 480 (2013).

BACKGROUND AND FACTS   Columbia Heart Clinic, P.A., in Columbia, South Carolina, provides comprehensive cardiology services. Its physicians are all cardiologists. When Kevin Baugh, M.D., and Barry Feldman, M.D., became employees and shareholders of Columbia Heart, and again several years later, they signed noncompete agreements. Under these agreements, Baugh and Feldman would forfeit certain payments if they competed with Columbia Heart within a year after their

---

a. *P.A.* means "professional association."

Case 10.2—Continued

employment ended. Specifically, they were not to practice cardiology "within a twenty (20) mile radius of any Columbia Heart office at which [they] routinely provided services." Later, Baugh and Feldman left Columbia Heart and opened a new cardiology practice near one of Columbia Heart's offices. They then filed a suit in a South Carolina state court against Columbia Heart, seeking a ruling that their noncompete agreements were unenforceable. From a judgment in favor of Baugh and Feldman, Columbia Heart appealed.

IN THE WORDS OF THE COURT . . .
THOMAS, J. [Judge]
* * * *
    * * * Article 5 [of the agreements] says the following:
Physician, in the event of termination * * * for any reason, during the twelve (12) month period immediately following the date of termination * * * shall not Compete * * * with Columbia Heart * * * within a twenty (20) mile radius of any Columbia Heart office at which Physician routinely provided services during the year prior to the date of termination.
    No separate monetary consideration was paid to any shareholder-physician to sign the Agreements, nor did the Agreements change the [established] compensation system.
    * * * *
    [Baugh and Feldman] contend * * * that the Agreements are unenforceable because they are not supported by new consideration. We disagree.
    When a covenant not to compete is entered into after the inception of employment, separate consideration, in addition to continued at-will employment, is necessary in order for the covenant to be enforceable. There is no consideration when the contract containing the covenant is exacted after several

years' employment and the employee's duties and position are left unchanged. [Emphasis added.]
    [Baugh and Feldman] executed the Agreements after they became employed by Columbia Heart, and the Agreements did not change the general compensation system agreed to by the parties under their prior employment contracts. However, * * * Article 4 of the Agreements provides the following:

> Physician shall be paid Five Thousand and No/100 Dollars ($5,000.00) per month for each of the twelve (12) months following termination, so long as the Physician is not in violation of Article 5 of this Agreement.

This language established that Columbia Heart promised to pay [Baugh and Feldman] each * * * a total of $60,000 over twelve months after termination so long as they did not violate the non-competition provision in Article 5. * * * Consequently, the Agreements are supported by new consideration.

DECISION AND REMEDY   A state intermediate appellate court reversed the lower court's finding that the noncompete provisions were unenforceable. The agreements were supported by new consideration because they provided for compensation to physicians who left Columbia Heart so long as they did not compete with the clinic's cardiology practice.

THE LEGAL ENVIRONMENT DIMENSION   *Did the court hold that the noncompete agreement at the heart of the dispute was supported by consideration? Why or why not?*

THE ETHICAL DIMENSION   *When a noncompete agreement is entered into after employment has begun, is continued employment sufficient consideration for the agreement? Explain.*

Contractual Capacity

In addition to agreement and consideration, for a contract to be deemed valid, the parties to the contract must have **contractual capacity**—the legal ability to enter into a contractual relationship. Courts generally presume the existence of contractual capacity, but in some situations, as when a person is young or mentally incompetent, capacity may be lacking or questionable.

Contractual Capacity   The legal ability to enter into contracts. The threshold mental capacity required by law for a party who enters into a contract to be bound by that contract.

Minors

Today, in almost all states, the *age of majority* (when a person is no longer a minor) for contractual purposes is eighteen years.[28] In addition, some states provide for the termination of minority on marriage. Minority status may also be terminated by a minor's *emancipation*, which occurs when a child's parent or legal guardian relinquishes the legal right to exercise

---

28. The age of majority may still be twenty-one for other purposes, such as the purchase and consumption of alcohol.

control over the child. Normally, minors who leave home to support themselves are considered emancipated.

The general rule is that a minor can enter into any contract that an adult can, except contracts prohibited by law for minors (for instance, the purchase of tobacco or alcoholic beverages). A contract entered into by a minor, however, is voidable at the option of that minor, subject to certain exceptions.

Disaffirmance The legal avoidance, or setting aside, of a contractual obligation.

The legal avoidance, or setting aside, of a contractual obligation is referred to as **disaffirmance.** To disaffirm, a minor must express his or her intent, through words or conduct, not to be bound to the contract.

CASE EXAMPLE 10.28　　Fifteen-year-old Morgan Kelly was a cadet in her high school's Navy Junior Reserve Officer Training Corps. As part of the program, she visited a U.S. Marine Corps training facility. To enter the camp, she was required to sign a waiver that exempted the Marines from all liability for any injuries arising from her visit. While participating in activities on the camp's confidence-building course, Kelly fell from the "Slide for Life" and suffered serious injuries. She filed a suit to recover her medical costs. The Marines asserted that she had signed their waiver of liability. Kelly claimed that she had disaffirmed the waiver when she filed suit. The court ruled in Kelly's favor. Liability waivers are generally enforceable contracts, but a minor can avoid a contract by disaffirming it.[29] •

Note that an adult who enters into a contract with a minor cannot avoid his or her contractual duties on the ground that the minor can do so. Unless the minor exercises the option to disaffirm the contract, the adult party normally is bound by it.

Intoxication

Intoxication is a condition in which a person's normal capacity to act or think is inhibited by alcohol or some other drug. A contract entered into by an intoxicated person can be either voidable or valid (and thus enforceable).

If the person was sufficiently intoxicated to lack mental capacity, then the agreement may be voidable even if the intoxication was purely voluntary. If a contract is voidable because one party was intoxicated, that person has the option of disaffirming it while intoxicated and for a reasonable time after becoming sober. If, despite intoxication, the person understood the legal consequences of the agreement, the contract will be enforceable.

Courts look at objective indications of the intoxicated person's condition to determine if he or she possessed or lacked the required capacity. It is difficult to prove that a person's judgment was so severely impaired that he or she could not comprehend the legal consequences of entering into a contract. Therefore, courts rarely permit contracts to be avoided due to intoxication.

Mental Incompetence

Contracts made by mentally incompetent persons can be void, voidable, or valid. If a court has previously determined that a person is mentally incompetent, any contract made by that person is *void*—no contract exists. Only a guardian appointed by the court to represent a mentally incompetent person can enter into binding legal obligations on that person's behalf.

If a court has not previously judged a person to be mentally incompetent but the person was incompetent at the time the contract was formed, the contract may be voidable.[30] A contract is *voidable* in the majority of states if the person did not know he or she was entering into the contract or lacked the mental capacity to comprehend its nature, purpose, and consequences.

---

29. *Kelly v. United States*, 809 F.Supp.2d 429 (E.D.N.C. 2011).
30. This is the rule in the majority of states. See, for example, *Hernandez v. Banks*, 65 A.3d 59 (D.C. 2013).

EXAMPLE 10.29   Larry agrees to sell his stock in Google, Inc., to Sergey for substantially less than its market value. At the time of the deal, Larry is confused about the purpose and details of the transaction, but he has not been declared incompetent. Nonetheless, if a court finds that Larry did not understand the nature and consequences of the contract due to a lack of mental capacity, he can avoid the sale. ●

A contract entered into by a mentally incompetent person (whom a court has not previously declared incompetent) may also be *valid* if the person had capacity *at the time the contract was formed*. Some people who are incompetent due to age or illness have *lucid intervals*—temporary periods of sufficient intelligence, judgment, and will. During such intervals, they will be considered to have legal capacity to enter into contracts.

Legality

Legality is the fourth requirement for a valid contract to exist. For a contract to be valid and enforceable, it must be formed for a legal purpose. A contract to do something that is prohibited by federal or state statutory law is illegal and, as such, void from the outset and thus unenforceable. Additionally, a contract to commit a tortious act—such as an agreement to engage in fraudulent misrepresentation (see Chapter 5)—is contrary to public policy and therefore illegal and unenforceable.

Contracts Contrary to Statute

Statutes often set forth rules specifying which terms and clauses may be included in contracts and which are prohibited. We now examine several ways in which contracts may be contrary to statute and thus illegal.

Contracts to Commit a Crime   Any contract to commit a crime is in violation of a statute. Thus, a contract to sell illegal drugs in violation of criminal laws is unenforceable, as is a contract to cover up a corporation's violation of the Dodd-Frank Wall Street Reform and Consumer Protection Act.

Sometimes, the object or performance of a contract is rendered illegal by a statute *after* the parties entered into the contract. In that situation, the contract is considered to be discharged by law. (See the discussion of impossibility or impracticability of performance in Chapter 11.)

Usury   Almost every state has a statute that sets the maximum rate of interest that can be charged for different types of transactions, including ordinary loans. A lender who makes a loan at an interest rate above the lawful maximum commits **usury.**

Although usurious contracts are illegal, most states simply limit the interest that the lender may collect on the contract to the lawful maximum interest rate in that state. In a few states, the lender can recover the principal amount of the loan but no interest. In addition, states can make exceptions to facilitate business transactions. For instance, many states exempt corporate loans from the usury laws, and nearly all states allow higher interest rate loans for borrowers who could not otherwise obtain funds.

Usury Charging an illegal rate of interest.

Gambling   Gambling is the creation of risk for the purpose of assuming it. Traditionally, the states have deemed gambling contracts illegal and thus void. It is sometimes difficult, however, to distinguish a gambling contract from the risk sharing inherent in almost all contracts.

All states have statutes that regulate gambling, and many states allow certain forms of gambling, such as betting on horse races, poker machines, and charity-sponsored bingo. In addition, nearly all states allow state-operated lotteries as well as gambling on Native

American reservations. Even in states that permit certain types of gambling, though, courts often find that gambling contracts are illegal.

CASE EXAMPLE 10.30   Video poker machines are legal in Louisiana, but their use requires the approval of the state video gaming commission. Gaming Venture, Inc., did not obtain this approval before agreeing with Tastee Restaurant Corporation to install poker machines in some of its restaurants. For this reason, when Tastee allegedly reneged on the deal by refusing to install the machines, a state court held that their agreement was an illegal gambling contract and therefore void.[31] ●

Licensing Statutes   All states require members of certain professions—including physicians, lawyers, real estate brokers, accountants, architects, electricians, and stockbrokers—to have licenses. Some licenses are obtained only after extensive schooling and examinations, which indicate to the public that a special skill has been acquired. Others require only that the applicant be of good moral character and pay a fee.

Whether a contract with an unlicensed person is legal and enforceable depends on the purpose of the licensing statute. If the statute's purpose is to protect the public from unauthorized practitioners (such as unlicensed architects, attorneys, and electricians), then a contract involving an unlicensed practitioner is generally illegal and unenforceable. If the statute's purpose is merely to raise government revenues, however, a court may enforce the contract and fine the unlicensed person.

Contracts Contrary to Public Policy

Although contracts involve private parties, some are not enforceable because of the negative impact they would have on society. These contracts are said to be *contrary to public policy*. Examples include a contract to commit an immoral act, such as selling a child, and a contract that prohibits marriage. We look here at certain types of business contracts that are often found to be against public policy.

Learning Objective 5
Under what circumstances will a covenant not to compete be enforced? When will such covenants not be enforced?

Contracts in Restraint of Trade   Contracts in restraint of trade (anticompetitive agreements) usually adversely affect the public policy that favors competition in the economy. Typically, such contracts also violate one or more federal or state antitrust statutes (see Chapter 23).

An exception is recognized when the restraint is reasonable and is contained in an ancillary (secondary or subordinate) clause in a contract. Restraints called covenants not to compete are often included in contracts for the sale of an ongoing business and employment contracts, as we saw in Case 10.2 presented earlier.

Covenants Not to Compete and the Sale of an Ongoing Business   A covenant not to compete or a restrictive covenant (promise) may be created when a seller of a store agrees not to open a new store in a certain geographic area surrounding the old business. The agreement enables the purchaser to buy, and the seller to sell, the goodwill and reputation of an ongoing business without having to worry that the seller will open a competing business a block away. Provided the restrictive covenant is reasonable and is an ancillary part of the sale of an ongoing business, it is enforceable.

Covenants Not to Compete in Employment Contracts   As explained earlier, agreements not to compete (*noncompete agreements*) are sometimes included in employment contracts. People in middle- or upper-level management positions commonly agree not to work for

---

31. *Gaming Venture, Inc. v. Tastee Restaurant Corp.*, 996 So.2d 515 (La.App. 5 Cir. 2008).

competitors or not to start competing businesses for a specified period of time after termination of employment.

Such agreements are legal in most states so long as the specified period of time (of restraint) is not excessive in duration and the geographic restriction is reasonable. What constitutes a reasonable time period may be shorter in the online environment than in conventional employment contracts because the restrictions apply worldwide. To be reasonable, a restriction on competition must protect a legitimate business interest and must not be any greater than necessary to protect that interest.

Enforcement Problems   The laws governing the enforceability of covenants not to compete vary significantly from state to state. In some states, including Texas, such a covenant will not be enforced unless the employee has received some benefit in return for signing the noncompete agreement. This is true even if the covenant is reasonable as to time and area. If the employee receives no benefit, the covenant will be deemed void. California prohibits altogether the enforcement of covenants not to compete.

Occasionally, depending on the jurisdiction, courts will *reform* covenants not to compete. If a covenant is found to be unreasonable in time or geographic area, the court may convert the terms into reasonable ones and then enforce the reformed covenant. Such court actions present a problem, though, in that the judge implicitly becomes a party to the contract. Consequently, courts usually resort to contract **reformation** only when necessary to prevent undue burdens or hardships.

Reformation A court-ordered correction of a written contract so that it reflects the true intentions of the parties.

The court in the following case considered the enforceability of a covenant not to compete.

Case 10.3

Brown & Brown, Inc. v. Johnson
New York Supreme Court, Appellate Division, Fourth Department, 115 A.D.3d 162, 980 N.Y.S.2d 631 (2014).

Can a covenant not to service former clients apply to an actuarial analyst?

BACKGROUND AND FACTS   Brown & Brown, Inc., is a firm of insurance intermediaries—insurance agents, brokers, and consultants—in New York City. Brown hired Theresa Johnson to provide actuarial analysis. On Johnson's first day of work, she was asked to sign a nonsolicitation covenant, which prohibited her from soliciting or servicing any of Brown's clients for two years after the termination of her employment. The covenant specified that if any of its provisions were declared unenforceable, they should be modified and then enforced "to the maximum extent possible." Less than five years later, Johnson's employment with Brown was terminated, and she went to work for Lawley Benefits Group, LLC. Brown filed a suit in a New York state court against Johnson, seeking to enforce the nonsolicitation covenant. Johnson filed a motion to dismiss Brown's complaint. The court ruled in Brown's favor, and Johnson appealed.

IN THE WORDS OF THE COURT . . .
Opinion by WHALEN, J. [Judge]
    * * * *

A *non-solicitation covenant is overbroad and therefore unenforceable* if it seeks to bar the employee from soliciting

or providing services to clients with whom the employee never acquired a relationship through his or her employment. Here, the non-solicitation covenant purported to restrict Johnson from, *inter alia* [among other things], soliciting, diverting, servicing, or accepting, either directly or indirectly, "any insurance or bond business of any kind or character from any person, firm, corporation, or other entity that is a customer or account of the New York offices of the Company during the term of the Agreement" for two years following the termination of Johnson's employment, without regard to whether Johnson acquired a relationship with those clients. We conclude that the language of the non-solicitation covenant renders it overbroad and unenforceable. [Emphasis added.]

Plaintiffs contend * * * that * * * we nevertheless should partially enforce the covenant, inasmuch as plaintiffs seek to prevent Johnson from soliciting and servicing only those clients with whom Johnson actually developed a relationship during her employment with plaintiffs. We reject that contention. * * * Partial enforcement may be justified if the employer demonstrates

Case 10.3—Continues ➡

Case 10.3—Continued

an absence of overreaching, coercive use of dominant bargaining power, or other anti-competitive misconduct, but has in good faith sought to protect a legitimate business interest, consistent with reasonable standards of fair dealing. Factors weighing against partial enforcement are the imposition of the covenant in connection with hiring or continued employment[,] * * * the existence of coercion or a general plan of the employer to forestall competition, and the employer's knowledge that the covenant was overly broad. Here, it is undisputed that Johnson was not presented with the Agreement until her first day of work with plaintiffs, after Johnson already had left her previous employer. *Plaintiffs have made no showing that, in exchange for signing the Agreement, Johnson received any benefit from plaintiffs beyond her continued employment.* [Emphasis added.]

* * * The fact that the Agreement contemplated partial enforcement does not require partial enforcement. * * * Allowing a former employer the benefit of partial enforcement of overly broad restrictive covenants simply because the applicable agreement contemplated partial enforcement would * * * enhance the risk that employers will use their superior bargaining position to impose unreasonable anti-competitive restrictions, uninhibited by the risk that a court will void the entire agreement, leaving the employee free of any restraint. In our view, the fact that the Agreement here contemplated partial enforcement does not demonstrate the absence of overreaching on plaintiffs' part, but, rather, demonstrates that plaintiffs imposed the covenant in bad faith, knowing full well that it was overbroad. We therefore conclude that the non-solicitation covenant should not be partially enforced.

DECISION AND REMEDY   A state intermediate appellate court reversed the lower court's ruling and granted Johnson's motion to dismiss Brown's action with respect to the nonsolicitation covenant. The covenant was overbroad. Furthermore, it was not presented to Johnson until her first day of work, and she received no benefit for signing it beyond her continued employment.

THE LEGAL ENVIRONMENT DIMENSION   *How might Brown have phrased its covenant with Johnson in such a way that the covenant would have been enforced?*

WHAT IF THE FACTS WERE DIFFERENT?   *Suppose that instead of a nonsolicitation or noncompete agreement, Johnson had been asked to sign a covenant prohibiting her from disclosing Brown's confidential information or using it for her own purposes. Would the result have been different? Explain.*

Unconscionable Contracts or Clauses

A court ordinarily does not look at the fairness or equity of a contract. Persons are assumed to be reasonably intelligent, and the courts will not come to their aid just because they have made an unwise or foolish bargain.

Unconscionable A contract or clause that is void on the basis of public policy because one party was forced to accept terms that are unfairly burdensome and that unfairly benefit the stronger party.

In certain circumstances, however, bargains are so oppressive that the courts relieve innocent parties of part or all of their duties. Such bargains are deemed **unconscionable**[32] because they are so unscrupulous or grossly unfair as to be "void of conscience."

The Uniform Commercial Code incorporates the concept of unconscionability in its provisions with regard to the sale and lease of goods.[33] A contract can be unconscionable on either procedural or substantive grounds. *Procedural* unconscionability often involves inconspicuous print, unintelligible language ("legalese"), or the lack of an opportunity to read the contract or ask questions about its meaning. *Substantive* unconscionability occurs when contracts, or portions of contracts, are oppressive or overly harsh. For instance, a contract clause that gives the business entity free access to the courts but requires the other party to arbitrate any dispute with the firm may be unconscionable.

Exculpatory Clauses

Exculpatory Clause A clause that releases a contractual party from liability in the event of monetary or physical injury, no matter who is at fault.

Often closely related to the concept of unconscionability are **exculpatory clauses**, which release a party from liability in the event of monetary or physical injury *no matter who is at fault*. Indeed, courts sometimes refuse to enforce such clauses on the ground that they are unconscionable.

Most courts view exculpatory clauses with disfavor. Exculpatory clauses found in rental agreements for commercial property are frequently held to be contrary to public

---

32. Pronounced un-kon-shun-uh-bul.
33. See UCC 2–302 and 2A–719.

policy, and such clauses are almost always unenforceable in residential property leases. Courts also usually hold that exculpatory clauses are against public policy in the employment context.

Courts do enforce exculpatory clauses if they are reasonable, do not violate public policy, and do not protect parties from liability for intentional misconduct. The language used must not be ambiguous, and the parties must have been in relatively equal bargaining positions.

Businesses such as health clubs, racetracks, amusement parks, skiing facilities, horse-rental operations, golf-cart concessions, and skydiving organizations frequently use exculpatory clauses to limit their liability for patrons' injuries. **CASE EXAMPLE 10.31** Colleen Holmes participated in the Susan G. Komen Race for the Cure in St. Louis, Missouri. Her signed entry form included an exculpatory clause under which Holmes agreed to release the event sponsors from liability "for any injury or damages I might suffer in connection with my participation in this Event."

During the race, Holmes sustained injuries when she tripped and fell over an audiovisual box left on the ground by one of the sponsors. She filed a negligence suit against the sponsor whose employees had placed the box on the ground without barricades or warnings of its presence. The court held that the language used in the exculpatory clause clearly released all sponsors and their agents and employees from liability for future negligence. Holmes could not sue for the injuries she sustained during the race.[34] •

If a carnival swing is defective and causes an injury, can the swing's owner avoid liability if each participant signed an exculpatory clause?

Form

A contract that is otherwise valid may still be unenforceable if it is not in the proper form. Certain types of contracts are required to be in writing or evidenced by a memorandum or electronic record. The writing requirement does not mean that an agreement must be a formal written contract. An exchange of e-mails that evidences the parties' agreement usually is sufficient, provided that they are "signed," or agreed to, by the party against whom enforcement is sought.

Every state has a statute that stipulates what types of contracts must be in writing. We refer to such a statute as the **Statute of Frauds.** The actual name of the Statute of Frauds is misleading because the statute does not apply to fraud. Rather, it denies enforceability to certain contracts that do not comply with its writing requirements.

The following types of contracts are generally required to be in writing or evidenced by a written memorandum or electronic record:

1. Contracts involving interests in land.
2. Contracts that cannot *by their terms* be performed within *one year from the day after* the date of formation.
3. Collateral, or secondary, contracts, such as promises to answer for the debt or duty of another and promises by the administrator or executor of an estate to pay a debt of the estate personally—that is, out of her or his own pocket.
4. Promises made in consideration of marriage.
5. Under the Uniform Commercial Code, contracts for the sale of goods priced at $500 or more (see Chapter 12).

A contract that is oral when it is required to be evidenced by a writing or an electronic record is voidable by a party who does not wish to follow through with the agreement.

Statute of Frauds A state statute under which certain types of contracts must be in writing or in an electronic record to be enforceable.

"Wallace, have you forgotten our prenuptial contract? No whistling!"

---

34. *Holmes v. Multimedia KSDK, Inc.*, 395 S.W.3d 557, (Mo.App.E.D. 2013).

Reviewing . . . The Formation of Traditional and E-Contracts

Shane Durbin wanted to have a recording studio custom-built in his home. He sent invitations to a number of local contractors to submit bids on the project. Rory Amstel submitted the lowest bid, which was $20,000 less than any of the other bids Durbin received. Durbin called Amstel to ascertain the type and quality of the materials that were included in the bid and to find out if he could substitute a superior brand of acoustic tiles for the same bid price. Amstel said he would have to check into the price difference. The parties also discussed a possible start date for construction. Two weeks later, Durbin changed his mind and decided not to go forward with his plan to build a recording studio. Amstel filed a suit against Durbin for breach of contract. Using the information presented in the chapter, answer the following questions.

1. Did Amstel's bid meet the requirements of an offer? Explain.
2. Was there an acceptance of the offer? Why or why not?
3. How is an offer terminated? Assuming that Durbin did not inform Amstel that he was rejecting the offer, was the offer terminated at any time described here? Explain.

Debate This The terms and conditions in click-on agreements are so long and detailed that no one ever reads the agreements. Therefore, the act of clicking on "I agree" is not really an acceptance.

Key Terms

acceptance 262
agreement 257
bilateral contract 252
browse-wrap terms 268
click-on agreement 267
consideration 270
contract 250
contractual capacity 273
counteroffer 261
covenant not to compete 272
disaffirmance 274

e-contract 264
e-signature 268
exculpatory clause 278
executed contract 255
executory contract 255
express contract 255
forbearance 270
formal contract 254
forum-selection clause 265
implied contract 255
informal contract 254

mailbox rule 263
mirror image rule 261
objective theory of contracts 250
offer 257
option contract 260
past consideration 272
promise 249
record 269
reformation 277
rescission 272
revocation 260

shrink-wrap agreement 267
Statute of Frauds 279
unconscionable 278
unenforceable contract 256
unilateral contract 253
usury 275
valid contract 256
void contract 257
voidable contract 256

Chapter Summary: The Formation of Traditional and E-Contracts

An Overview of Contract Law	1. *Sources of contract law*—The common law governs all contracts except when it has been modified or replaced by statutory law, such as the Uniform Commercial Code (UCC), or by administrative agency regulations. 2. *The function of contracts*—Contract law establishes what kinds of promises will be legally binding and supplies procedures for enforcing legally binding promises, or agreements. 3. *Definition of a contract*—A contract is an agreement that can be enforced in court. It is formed by two or more competent parties who agree to perform or to refrain from performing some act now or in the future. 4. *Objective theory of contracts*—In contract law, intent is determined by objective facts, not by the personal or subjective intent, or belief, of a party. 5. *Requirements of a valid contract*—The four requirements of a valid contract are agreement, consideration, contractual capacity, and legality. 6. *Defenses to the enforceability of a contract*—Even if the four requirements of a valid contract are met, a contract may be unenforceable if it lacks voluntary consent or is not in the required form.

Chapter Summary: The Formation of Traditional and E-Contracts— Continued

Types of Contracts	1. *Bilateral*—A promise for a promise. 2. *Unilateral*—A promise for an act (acceptance is the completed—or substantial—performance of the contract by the offeree). 3. *Formal*—Requires a special form for contract formation. 4. *Informal*—Requires no special form for contract formation. 5. *Express*—Formed by words (oral, written, or a combination). 6. *Implied*—Formed at least in part by the conduct of the parties. 7. *Executed*—A fully performed contract. 8. *Executory*—A contract not yet fully performed. 9. *Valid*—A contract that has the four necessary contractual elements of agreement, consideration, capacity, and legality. 10. *Voidable*—A contract in which a party has the option of avoiding or enforcing the contractual obligation. 11. *Unenforceable*—A valid contract that cannot be enforced because of a legal defense. 12. *Void*—No contract exists, or there is a contract without legal obligations.

Agreement	1. *Requirements of the offer*—
	    a. Intent—There must be a serious, objective intention by the offeror to become bound by the offer. Nonoffer situations include (1) expressions of opinion, (2) statements of future intent, (3) preliminary negotiations, (4) generally, advertisements, catalogues, pricelists, and circulars, and (e) traditionally, agreements to agree in the future.
	    b. Definiteness—The terms of the offer must be sufficiently definite to be ascertainable by the parties or by a court.
	    c. Communication—The offer must be communicated to the offeree.
	 2. *Termination of the offer*—
	    a. By action of the parties—An offer can be revoked or withdrawn at any time before acceptance without liability. A counteroffer is a rejection of the original offer and the making of a new offer.
	    b. By operation of law—An offer can terminate by (a) lapse of time, (b) destruction of the subject matter, (c) death or incompetence of the parties, or (d) supervening illegality.
	 3. *Acceptance*—
	    a. Can be made only by the offeree or the offeree's agent.
	    b. Must be unequivocal. Under the common law (mirror image rule), if new terms or conditions are added to the acceptance, it will be considered a counteroffer.
	    c. Acceptance of a unilateral offer is effective on full performance of the requested act. Generally, no communication is necessary.
	    d. Acceptance of a bilateral offer can be communicated by the offeree by any authorized mode of communication and is effective on dispatch. If the offeror does not specify the mode of communication, acceptance can be made by any reasonable means. Usually, the same means used by the offeror or a faster means can be used.

E-Contracts	1. *Offer*—The terms of contract offers presented via the Internet should be as inclusive as the terms in an offer made in a written (paper) document. The offer should be displayed in an easily readable format and should include some mechanism, such as an "I agree" or "I accept" box, by which the customer may accept the offer. Because jurisdictional issues frequently arise with online transactions, the offer should include dispute-settlement provisions and a forum-selection clause. 2. *Click-on agreement*—An agreement created when a buyer, completing a transaction on a computer, is required to indicate her or his assent to be bound by the terms of an offer by clicking on a box that says, for example, "I agree." The courts have enforced click-on agreements, holding that by clicking on "I agree," the offeree has indicated acceptance by conduct. 3. *Shrink-wrap agreement*—An agreement whose terms are expressed inside a box in which the goods are packaged. The party who opens the box is informed that, by keeping the goods that are in the box, he or she agrees to the terms of the shrink-wrap agreement. The courts have often enforced shrink-wrap agreements, even if the purchaser-user of the goods did not read the terms of the agreement. A court may deem a shrink-wrap agreement unenforceable, however, if the buyer learns of the shrink-wrap terms after the parties entered into the agreement. 4. *Browse-wrap terms*—A term or condition of use that is presented when an online buyer downloads a product but does not require the buyer's explicit agreement. Such terms are usually unenforceable because the buyer has not agreed. 5. *E-Signature*—A federal law, the Electronic Signatures in Global and National Commerce Act (E-SIGN Act) gave validity to e-signatures by providing that no contract, record, or signature may be "denied legal effect" solely because it is in an electronic form. Almost all states have e-signature laws as well.

Continued

Chapter Summary: The Formation of Traditional and E-Contracts— Continued

E-Contracts—Continued	6. *The Uniform Transactions Act (UETA)*—This uniform act has been adopted, at least in part, by most states, to create rules to support the enforcement of e-contracts. The UETA provides for the validity of e-signatures and may ultimately create more uniformity among the states in this respect. Under the UETA, contracts entered into online, as well as other documents, are presumed to be valid. The UETA does not apply to certain transactions governed by the UCC or to wills or testamentary trusts.
Consideration	1. *Elements of consideration*—Consideration is the value given in exchange for a promise. A contract cannot be formed without sufficient consideration. Consideration is often broken down into two parts: a. Something of *legally sufficient value* must be given in exchange for the promise. This may consist of a promise, an act, or a forbearance. b. There must be a bargained-for exchange. 2. *Agreements that lack consideration*—Consideration is lacking in the following situations: a. *Preexisting duty*—Consideration is not legally sufficient if a party by law or by contract already has a preexisting duty to perform the action being offered as consideration for a new contract. b. *Past consideration*—Actions or events that have already taken place do not constitute legally sufficient consideration.
Contractual Capacity	1. *Minors*—A minor is a person who has not yet reached the age of majority. In virtually all states, the age of majority is eighteen for contract purposes. Contracts with minors are voidable at the option of the minor. 2. *Intoxication*—A contract with an intoxicated person is enforceable if, despite being intoxicated, the person understood the legal consequences of entering into the contract. A contract entered into by an intoxicated person is voidable at the option of the intoxicated person if the person was sufficiently intoxicated to lack mental capacity, even if the intoxication was voluntary. Courts rarely permit contracts to be avoided due to intoxication, however. 3. *Mental incompetence*—A contract made by a person whom a court has previously determined to be mentally incompetent is void. A contract made by a person with questionable mental competence can be either valid or voidable. If at the time the contract was formed, the person had the capacity to understand the contract, it is usually valid. If, at the time the contract was formed, the person lacked the capacity to understand the nature and consequences of it, then in the majority of states it is considered voidable.
Legality	1. *Contracts contrary to statute*—For a contract to be valid and enforceable, it must be formed for a legal purpose. A contract to do something that is prohibited by federal or state statutory law is illegal and, as such, void from the outset and thus unenforceable. Contracts contrary to statute include contracts to commit crimes as well as contracts that violate other laws, such as state laws setting the maximum interest rate that can be charged by a lender. They also include gambling contracts and some contracts with unlicensed professionals. 2. *Contracts contrary to public policy*—Contracts that are contrary to public policy are also not enforceable on the grounds of illegality. a. Contracts to reduce or restrain free competition are illegal and prohibited by statutes. An exception is a *covenant not to compete,* which is enforceable in many states if the terms are secondary to a contract (such as a contract for the sale of a business or an employment contract) and are reasonable as to time and area of restraint. b. When a contract or contract clause is so unfair that it is oppressive to one party, it may be deemed unconscionable. As such, it is illegal and cannot be enforced. c. An exculpatory clause is a clause that releases a party from liability in the event of monetary or physical injury, no matter who is at fault. In certain situations, exculpatory clauses may be contrary to public policy and thus unenforceable.
Form	A contract that is otherwise valid may not be enforceable if it is required to be evidenced by a writing or electronic record. Under the Statute of Frauds, the following types of contracts are required to be evidenced by a writing or record: 1. Contracts involving interests in land. 2. Contracts that cannot by their own terms be performed within one year from the day after the date of formation. 3. Collateral, or secondary, contracts, such as promises to answer for the debt or duty of another and promises by the administrator or executor of an estate to pay a debt of the estate personally (out of her or his own pocket). 4. Promises made in consideration of marriage. 5. Contracts for the sale of goods priced at $500 or more.

Issue Spotters

1. Fidelity Corporation offers to hire Ron to replace Monica, who has given Fidelity a month's notice of intent to quit. Fidelity gives Ron a week to decide whether to accept. Two days later, Monica decides not to quit and signs an employment contract with Fidelity for another year. The next day, Monica tells Ron of the new contract. Ron immediately faxes a formal letter of acceptance to Fidelity. Do Fidelity and Ron have a contract? Why or why not? (See *Agreement.*)

2. Dyna tells Ed that she will pay him $1,000 to set fire to her store so that she can collect under a fire insurance policy. Ed sets fire to the store, but Dyna refuses to pay. Can Ed recover? Why or why not? (See *Legality.*)

—Check your answers to the Issue Spotters against the answers provided in Appendix D at the end of this text.

For Review

1. What are the four basic elements necessary to the formation of a valid contract?
2. What is the difference between express and implied contracts?
3. What are the elements necessary for an effective acceptance?
4. How do shrink-wrap and click-on agreements differ from other contracts? How have traditional laws been applied to these agreements?
5. Under what circumstances will a covenant not to compete be enforced? When will such covenants not be enforced?

Business Scenarios and Case Problems

10–1. Unilateral Contract. Rocky Mountain Races, Inc., sponsors the "Pioneer Trail Ultramarathon" with an advertised first prize of $10,000. The rules require the competitors to run 100 miles from the floor of Blackwater Canyon to the top of Pinnacle Mountain. The rules also provide that Rocky reserves the right to change the terms of the race at any time. Monica enters the race and is declared the winner. Rocky offers her a prize of $1,000 instead of $10,000. Did Rocky and Monica have a contract? Explain. (See *Types of Contracts.*)

10–2. Online Acceptance. Anne is a reporter for *Daily Business Journal,* a print publication consulted by investors and other businesspersons. She often uses the Internet to perform research for the articles that she writes for the publication. While visiting the Web site of Cyberspace Investments Corp., Anne reads a pop-up window that states, "Our business newsletter, *E-Commerce Weekly,* is available at a one-year subscription rate of $5 per issue. To subscribe, enter your e-mail address below and click 'SUBSCRIBE.' By subscribing, you agree to the terms of the subscriber's agreement. To read this agreement, click 'AGREEMENT.' " Anne enters her e-mail address, but does not click on "AGREEMENT" to read the terms. Has Anne entered into an enforceable contract to pay for *E-Commerce Weekly?* Explain. (See *E-Contracts.*)

10–3. ⚖ **Spotlight on Taco Bell—Implied Contract.** Thomas Rinks and Joseph Shields developed Psycho Chihuahua, a caricature of a Chihuahua dog with a "do-not-back-down" attitude. They promoted and marketed the character through their company, Wrench, L.L.C. Ed Alfaro and Rudy Pollak, representatives of Taco Bell Corp., learned of Psycho Chihuahua and met with Rinks and Shields to talk about using the character as a Taco Bell "icon." Wrench sent artwork, merchandise, and marketing ideas to Alfaro, who promoted the character within Taco Bell. Alfaro asked Wrench to propose terms for Taco Bell's use of Psycho Chihuahua. Taco Bell did not accept Wrench's terms, but Alfaro continued to promote the character within the company. Meanwhile, Taco Bell hired a new advertising agency, which proposed an advertising campaign involving a Chihuahua. When Alfaro learned of this proposal, he sent the Psycho Chihuahua materials to the agency. Taco Bell made a Chihuahua the focus of its marketing but paid nothing to Wrench. Wrench filed a suit against Taco Bell in a federal court claiming that it had an implied contract with Taco Bell and that Taco Bell breached that contract. Do these facts satisfy the requirements for an implied contract? Why or why not? [*Wrench, L.L.C. v. Taco Bell Corp.,* 256 F.3d 446 (6th Cir. 2001), cert. denied, 534 U.S. 1114, 122 S.Ct. 921, 151 L.Ed.2d 805 (2002)] (See *Types of Contracts.*)

10–4. ⚖ **Business Case Problem with Sample Answer— Offer and Acceptance.** While gambling at Prairie Meadows Casino, Troy Blackford became angry and smashed a slot machine. He was banned from the premises. Despite the ban, he later gambled at the casino and won $9,387. When he tried to collect his winnings, the casino refused to pay. Blackford filed a suit for breach of contract, arguing that he and the casino had a contract because he had accepted its offer to gamble. Did the casino and Blackford have a contract? Discuss. [*Blackford v. Prairie Meadows Racetrack and Casino,* 778 N.W.2d 184 (Sup.Ct. Iowa 2010)] (See *Agreement.*)

—For a sample answer to Problem 10–4, go to Appendix E at the end of this text.

10–5. Consideration. On Brenda Sniezek's first day of work for the Kansas City Chiefs Football Club, she signed a document that purported to compel arbitration of any disputes that she might have with the Chiefs. In the document, Sniezek agreed to comply at all times with and be bound by the constitution and bylaws of the National Football League (NFL). She agreed to refer all disputes to the NFL Commissioner for a binding decision. On the Commissioner's decision, she agreed to release the Chiefs and others from any related claims. Nowhere in the document did the Chiefs agree to do anything. Was there consideration for the arbitration provision? Explain. [*Sniezek v. Kansas City Chiefs Football Club,* 402 S.W.3d 580, (Mo.App. W.D. 2013)] (See *Consideration.*)

10–6. Implied Contracts. Ralph Ramsey insured his car with Allstate Insurance Co. He also owned a house on which he maintained a homeowner's insurance policy with Allstate. Bank of America had a mortgage on the house and paid the insurance premiums on the homeowner's policy from Ralph's account. After Ralph died, Allstate canceled the car insurance. Ralph's son Douglas inherited the house. The bank continued to pay the premiums on the homeowner's policy, but from Douglas's account, and Allstate continued to renew the insurance. When a fire destroyed the house, Allstate denied coverage, however, claiming that the policy was still in Ralph's name. Douglas filed a suit in a federal district court against the insurer. Was Allstate liable under the homeowner's policy? Explain. [*Ramsey v. Allstate Insurance Co.,* 2013 WL 467327 (6th Cir. 2013)] (See *Types of Contracts.*)

10–7. Acceptance. Judy Olsen, Kristy Johnston, and their mother, Joyce Johnston, owned seventy-eight acres of real property on Eagle Creek in Meagher County, Montana. When Joyce died, she left her interest in the property to Kristy. Kristy wrote to Judy, offering to buy Judy's interest or to sell her own interest to Judy. The letter said to "please respond to Bruce Townsend." In a letter to Kristy—not to Bruce—Judy accepted Kristy's offer to sell her interest. By that time, however, Kristy had made the same offer to sell her interest to their brother Dave, and he had accepted. Did Judy and Kristy have an enforceable binding contract? Or did Kristy's offer specifying one exclusive mode of acceptance mean that Judy's reply was not effective? Discuss. [*Olsen v. Johnston,* 368 Mont. 347, 301 P.3d 791, (2013)] (See *Agreement.*)

10–8. Minors. D.V.G. (a minor) was injured in a one-car auto accident in Hoover, Alabama. The vehicle was covered by an insurance policy issued by Nationwide Mutual Insurance Co. Stan Brobston, D.V.G.'s attorney, accepted Nationwide's offer of $50,000 on D.V.G.'s behalf. Before the settlement could be submitted to an Alabama state court for approval, D.V.G. died from injuries received in a second, unrelated auto accident. Nationwide argued that it was not bound to the settlement because a minor lacks the capacity to contract and so cannot enter into a binding settlement without court approval. Should Nationwide be bound to the settlement? Why or why not? [*Nationwide Mutual Insurance Co. v. Wood,* 121 So.3d 982 (Ala. 2013)] (See *Contractual Capacity.*)

10–9. Agreement. Amy Kemper was seriously injured when her motorcycle was struck by a vehicle driven by Christopher Brown. Kemper's attorney wrote to Statewide Claims Services, the administrator for Brown's insurer, asking for "all the insurance money that Mr. Brown had under his insurance policy." In exchange, the letter indicated that Kemper would sign a "limited release" on Brown's liability, provided that it did not include any language requiring her to reimburse Brown or his insurance company for any of their incurred costs. Statewide then sent a check and release form to Kemper, but the release demanded that Kemper "place money in an escrow account in regards to any and all liens pending." Kemper refused the demand, claiming that Statewide's response was a counteroffer rather than an unequivocal acceptance of the settlement offer. Did Statewide and Kemper have an enforceable agreement? Discuss. [*Kemper v. Brown,* 754 S.E.2d 141 (Ga.App. 2014)] (See *Agreement.*)

10–10. ◆ A Question of Ethics—Covenants Not to Compete. Brendan Coleman created and marketed Clinex, a software billing program. Later, Retina Consultants, P.C., a medical practice, hired Coleman as a software engineer. Together, they modified the Clinex program to create Clinex-RE. Coleman signed an agreement to the effect that he owned Clinex, Retina owned Clinex-RE, and he would not market Clinex in competition with Clinex-RE. After Coleman quit Retina, he withdrew funds from a Retina bank account and marketed both forms of the software to other medical practices. At trial, the court entered a judgment enjoining (preventing) Coleman from marketing the software that was in competition with the software he had developed for Retina Consultants. The court also obligated Coleman to return the funds taken from the company's bank account. Coleman appealed. [*Coleman v. Retina Consultants, P.C.,* 286 Ga. 317, 687 S.E.2d 457 (2009)] (See *Legality.*)

1. Should the court uphold the noncompete clause? If so, why? If not, why not?

2. Should the court require Coleman to return the funds he withdrew from the company's accounts? Discuss fully.

CHAPTER 11

Contract Performance, Breach, and Remedies

(Gordon Saunders/Shutterstock.com)

CONTENTS

- Voluntary Consent
- Third Party Rights
- Performance and Discharge
- Damages
- Equitable Remedies
- Contract Provisions Limiting Remedies

LEARNING OBJECTIVES

The five learning objectives below are designed to help improve your understanding of the chapter. After reading this chapter, you should be able to answer the following questions:

1. What are the elements of fraudulent misrepresentation?
2. What is substantial performance?
3. When is a breach considered material, and what effect does that have on the other party's duty to perform a contract?
4. What is the standard measure of compensatory damages when a contract is breached?
5. What equitable remedies can a court grant, and in what circumstances will a court consider granting them?

"Men keep their engagements when it is to the advantage of both not to break them."
—Solon, Sixth century B.C.E., (Athenian legal reformer)

As pointed out in the chapter-opening quotation above, a contract will not be broken so long as "it is to the advantage of both" parties not to break it. In a perfect world, every party who signed a contract would perform his or her duties completely and in a timely fashion, thereby discharging (terminating) the contract. In the real world, however, things frequently become complicated.

Certainly, events often occur that may affect our performance or our ability to perform contractual duties. Just as rules are necessary to determine when a legally enforceable contract exists, so also are they required to determine when one of the parties can justifiably say, "I have fully performed, so I am now discharged from my obligations under this contract."

Additionally, the parties to a contract need to know what remedies are available to them if one party decides that he or she does not want to, or cannot, perform as promised. A *remedy* is the relief provided for an innocent party when the other party has breached the contract. It is the means employed to enforce a right or to redress an injury. The most common remedies available to a nonbreaching party include damages, rescission and restitution, specific performance, and reformation, all of which will be examined later in this chapter.

Voluntary Consent

An otherwise valid contract may still be unenforceable if the parties have not genuinely agreed to its terms. As mentioned in Chapter 10, a lack of *voluntary consent* (assent) can be used as a defense to the contract's enforceability.

Voluntary consent may be lacking because of a mistake, misrepresentation, undue influence, or duress—in other words, because there is no true "meeting of the minds." Generally, a party who demonstrates that he or she did not truly agree to the terms of a contract has a choice. The party can choose either to carry out the contract or to rescind (cancel) it and thus avoid the entire transaction.

Voluntary Consent The knowing and voluntary agreement to the terms of a contract. If voluntary consent is lacking, and the contract will be voidable.

Mistakes

We all make mistakes, so it is not surprising that mistakes are made when contracts are formed. In certain circumstances, contract law allows a contract to be avoided on the basis of mistake. It is important to distinguish between *mistakes of fact* and *mistakes of value or quality.*

Only a mistake of fact makes a contract voidable. Also, the mistake must involve some *material fact*—a fact that a reasonable person would consider important when determining his or her course of action.

EXAMPLE 11.1 Sung buys a violin from Bev for $250. Although the violin is very old, neither party believes that it is valuable. Later, however, an antiques dealer informs the parties that the violin is rare and worth thousands of dollars. Here, both parties were mistaken, but the mistake is a mistake of *value* rather than a mistake of *fact* that warrants contract rescission. Therefore, Bev cannot rescind the contract. ●

Mistakes of fact occur in two forms—*unilateral* and *bilateral,* as shown in Exhibit 11–1 that follows. A unilateral mistake is made by only *one* of the parties. A bilateral, or mutual, mistake is made by *both* of the contracting parties. We look next at these two types of mistakes.

Exhibit 11–1 Mistakes of Fact

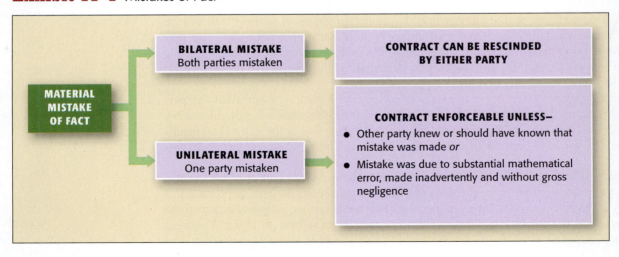

Unilateral Mistakes of Fact

A **unilateral mistake** is made by only one of the parties. In general, a unilateral mistake does not give the mistaken party any right to relief from the contract. Normally, the contract is enforceable.

EXAMPLE 11.2   Elena intends to sell her jet ski for $2,500. When she learns that Chin is interested in buying a used jet ski, she sends him an e-mail offering to sell the jet ski to him. When typing the e-mail, however, she mistakenly keys in the price of $1,500. Chin immediately sends Elena an e-mail reply accepting her offer. Even though Elena intended to sell her personal jet ski for $2,500, she has made a unilateral mistake and is bound by the contract to sell it to Chin for $1,500. ●

This general rule has at least two exceptions.[1] The contract may be enforceable if:

1. The *other* party to the contract knows or should have known that a mistake of fact was made.
2. The error was due to a substantial mathematical mistake in addition, subtraction, division, or multiplication and was made inadvertently and without gross (extreme) negligence. If, for instance, a contractor's bid was significantly low because he or she made a mistake in addition when totaling the estimated costs, any contract resulting from the bid normally may be rescinded.

Of course, in both situations, the mistake must still involve some material fact.

Bilateral (Mutual) Mistakes of Fact

A **bilateral mistake** is a "mutual misunderstanding concerning a basic assumption on which the contract was made."[2] When both parties are mistaken about the same material fact, the contract can be rescinded by either party.

A word or term in a contract may be subject to more than one reasonable interpretation. If the parties to the contract attach materially different meanings to the term, a court may allow the contract to be rescinded because there has been no true "meeting of the minds."

CASE EXAMPLE 11.3   L&H Construction Company contracted with Circle Redmont, Inc., to make a staircase and flooring system. Circle Redmont's original proposal was to "engineer, fabricate, and install" the system. Installation was later cut from the deal. In the final agreement, payment was due on Circle Redmont's "supervision" instead of "completion" of installation. But the final contract still included the wording, "engineer, fabricate, and install." Later, Circle Redmont claimed that this wording was a mistake. L&H insisted that installation was included and filed a suit against Circle Redmont.

The court held that the use of the word *install* in the contract was a mutual mistake. Circle Redmont's witnesses stated that the parties had agreed that Circle Redmont would only supervise the installation, not perform it. The court found the witnesses were credible, and ruled that installation was not included.[3] ●

Mistakes of Value

If a mistake concerns the future market value or quality of the object of the contract, the mistake is one of *value*, and the contract normally is enforceable. The reason for this is that value is variable. Depending on the time, place, and other circumstances, the same item may be worth considerably different amounts.

When parties form a contract, their agreement establishes the value of the object of their transaction—for the moment. Each party is considered to have assumed the risk that the value will change in the future or prove to be different from what he or she thought. Without this rule, almost any party who did not receive what she or he considered a fair bargain could argue mistake.

Unilateral Mistake A mistake that occurs when one party to a contract is mistaken as to a material fact.

> "Mistakes are the inevitable lot of mankind."
>
> Sir George Jessel, 1824–1883, (English jurist)

Bilateral Mistake A mistake that occurs when both parties to a contract are mistaken about the same material fact.

If an architect is mistaken about the future value of the project, is the contract still enforceable?

(shotbydave/iStockphoto.com)

---

1. *Restatement (Second) of Contracts*, Section 153.
2. *Restatement (Second) of Contracts*, Section 152.
3. *L&H Construction Co. v. Circle Redmont, Inc.*, 55 So.3d 630 (Fla.App. 2011).

Fraudulent Misrepresentation

Although fraud is a tort (see Chapter 5), it also affects the authenticity of the innocent party's consent to the contract. When an innocent party is fraudulently induced to enter into a contract, the contract normally can be avoided because that party has not *voluntarily* consented to its terms. Ordinarily, the innocent party can either rescind the contract and be restored to her or his original position or enforce the contract and seek damages for any harms resulting from the fraud.

Generally, fraudulent misrepresentation refers only to misrepresentation that is consciously false and is intended to mislead another. The person making the fraudulent misrepresentation knows or believes that the assertion is false or knows that she or he does not have a basis (stated or implied) for the assertion. Typically, fraudulent misrepresentation consists of the following elements:

1. A misrepresentation of a material fact must occur.
2. There must be an intent to deceive.
3. The innocent party must justifiably rely on the misrepresentation.
4. To collect damages, a party must have been harmed as a result of the misrepresentation.

Misrepresentation by Words or Actions

The misrepresentation can occur by words or actions. For instance, the statement "This sculpture was created by Michelangelo" is a misrepresentation of fact if another artist sculpted the statue. Similarly, if a customer asks to see only paintings by the decorative artist Paul Wright and the gallery owner immediately leads the customer over to paintings that were not done by Wright, the owner's actions can be a misrepresentation.

Misrepresentation also occurs when a party takes specific action to conceal a fact that is material to the contract. **CASE EXAMPLE 11.4**   Actor Tom Selleck contracted to purchase a horse named Zorro for his daughter from Dolores Cuenca. Cuenca acted as though Zorro was fit to ride in competitions, when in reality the horse suffered from a medical condition. Selleck filed a lawsuit against Cuenca for wrongfully concealing the horse's condition and won. A jury awarded Selleck more than $187,000 for Cuenca's misrepresentation by conduct.[4] ●

Injury to the Innocent Party

Most courts do not require a showing of injury when the action is to rescind the contract. These courts hold that because rescission returns the parties to the positions they held before the contract was made, a showing of injury to the innocent party is unnecessary.

In contrast, to recover damages caused by fraud, proof of harm is universally required. The measure of damages is ordinarily equal to the property's value had it been delivered as represented, less the actual price paid for the property. (What if someone pretends to be someone else online? Can the victim of the hoax prove injury sufficient to recover for fraudulent misrepresentation? See this chapter's *Online Developments* feature that follows for a discussion of this topic.)

PREVENTING LEGAL DISPUTES

If you are selling products or services, assume that all clients and customers are naïve and that they rely on your representations. Instruct employees to phrase their comments so that facts are clearly distinguished from opinions. If someone asks a question that is beyond an employee's knowledge, it is better for the employee to say "I don't know" than to guess and have the customer rely on a representation that turns out to be false. This can be particularly important when questions concern topics such as compatibility or speed of electronic and digital goods, software, or related services.

---

4. *Selleck v. Cuenca*, Case No. GIN056909, North County of San Diego, California, decided September 9, 2009.

ONLINE DEVELOPMENTS

"Catfishing": Is That Online "Friend" Who You Think It Is?

When you are communicating with a person you have met only online, how do you know that person is who she or he purports to be? After all, the person could turn out to be a "catfish." The term comes from *Catfish,* a 2010 film about a fake online persona.

According to a story told in the film, when live cod were shipped long distances, they were inactive and their flesh became mushy. When catfish were added to the tanks, the cod swam around and stayed in good condition. At the end of the film, a character says of the creator of the fake persona, "There are those people who are catfish in life. And they keep you on your toes. They keep you guessing, they keep you thinking, they keep you fresh."

Catfishing Makes National Headlines

Catfishing made headlines in 2012 when a popular Notre Dame football star supposedly fell victim to it. Linebacker Manti Te'o said that his girlfriend Lennay Kekua, a student at Stanford, had died of leukemia after a near-fatal car accident. Although Kekua had Facebook and Twitter accounts and Te'o had communicated with her online and by telephone for several years, reporters could find no evidence of her existence. Te'o later claimed that he had been a victim of a catfishing hoax. Others suggested that his friends created the persona and her tragic death to provide an inspirational story what would increase Te'o's chances of winning the Heisman trophy.

Is Online Fraudulent Misrepresentation Actionable?

Some victims of catfishing have turned to the courts, but they have had little success. A few have attempted to sue Internet service providers for allowing fake personas, but the courts have generally dismissed these suits.[a] Laws in some states make it a crime to impersonate someone online, but these laws generally do not apply to those who create totally fake personas.

Attempts to recover damages for fraudulent misrepresentation have generally failed to meet the requirement that there must be proof of actual injury. For instance, Paula Bonhomme developed an online romantic relationship with a man called Jesse. Jesse was actually a woman named Janna St. James, who also communicated with Bonhomme using her own name and pretending to be a friend of Jesse's.

St. James created a host of fictional characters, including an ex-wife and a son for Jesse. Bonhomme in turn sent gifts totaling more than $10,000 to Jesse and the other characters. After being told by St. James that Jesse had attempted suicide, Bonhomme suffered such emotional distress that she incurred more than $5,000 in bills for a therapist. Eventually, she was told that Jesse had died of liver cancer. When Bonhomme finally learned the truth, she suffered additional emotional distress, resulting in more expenses for a therapist and lost earnings due to her "affected mental state."

Although Bonhomme had incurred considerable expenses, the Illinois Supreme Court ruled that she could not bring a suit for fraudulent misrepresentation. The case involved only a "purely personal relationship" without any "commercial, transactional, or regulatory component." Bonhomme and St. James "were not engaged in any kind of business dealings or bargaining." Therefore, the truth of representations "made in the context of purely private personal relationships is simply not something the state regulates or in which the state possesses any kind of valid public policy interest."[b]

Critical Thinking

So far, victims of catfishing have had little success in the courts. Under what circumstances might a person be able to collect damages for fraudulent misrepresentation involving online impersonation?

a. See, for example, *Robinson v. Match.com, LLC,* 2012 WL 3263992 (N.D.Tex. 2012).

b. *Bonhomme v. St. James,* 970 N.E.2d 1 (Ill. 2012).

Undue Influence

Undue influence arises from relationships in which one party can greatly influence another party, thus overcoming that party's free will. A contract entered into under excessive or undue influence lacks voluntary consent and is therefore voidable.

In various types of relationships, one party may have the opportunity to dominate and unfairly influence another party. Minors and elderly people, for instance, are often under the influence of guardians (persons who are legally responsible for another). If a guardian induces a young or elderly ward (a person whom the guardian looks after) to enter into a contract that benefits the guardian, the guardian may have exerted undue influence.

Undue influence can arise from a number of fiduciary relationships, such as physician-patient, parent-child, husband-wife, or guardian-ward situations. When a contract enriches the dominant party in a fiduciary relationship (such as an attorney), the court will often *presume* that the contract was made under undue influence.

The essential feature of undue influence is that the party being taken advantage of does not, in reality, exercise free will in entering into a contract. It is not enough that a person is elderly or suffers from some physical or mental impairment. There must be clear and convincing evidence that the person did not act out of her or his free will. Similarly, the existence of a fiduciary relationship alone is insufficient to prove undue influence.

Duress

Agreement to the terms of a contract is not voluntary if one of the parties is *forced* into the agreement. The use of threats to force a party to enter into a contract is referred to as *duress*. In addition, blackmail or extortion to induce consent to a contract constitutes duress. Duress is both a defense to the enforcement of a contract and a ground for the rescission of a contract.

To establish duress, there must be proof of a threat to do something that the threatening party has no right to do. Generally, for duress to occur, the threatened act must be wrongful or illegal, and it must render the person incapable of exercising free will. A threat to exercise a legal right, such as the right to sue someone, ordinarily does not constitute duress.

Third Party Rights

Once it has been determined that a valid and legally enforceable contract exists, attention can turn to the rights and duties of the parties to the contract. A contract is a private agreement between the parties who have entered into it, and traditionally these parties alone have rights and liabilities under the contract. This principle is referred to as **privity of contract.** A *third party*—one who is not a direct party to a particular contract—normally does not have rights under that contract.

There are exceptions to the rule of privity of contract. One exception allows a party to a contract to transfer the rights or duties arising from the contract to another person through an *assignment* (of rights) or a *delegation* (of duties). Another exception involves a *third party beneficiary contract*—a contract in which the parties to the contract intend that the contract benefit a third party.

In a bilateral contract, the two parties have corresponding rights and duties. One party has a *right* to require the other to perform some task, and the other has a *duty* to perform it. The transfer of contractual *rights* to a third party is known as an **assignment.** The transfer of contractual *duties* to a third party is known as a **delegation.** An assignment or a delegation occurs *after* the original contract was made.

Assignments

In an assignment, the party assigning the rights to a third party is known as the *assignor,*[5] and the party receiving the rights is the *assignee.*[6] When rights under a contract are assigned unconditionally, the rights of the assignor are extinguished. The third party (the assignee)

Privity of Contract The relationship that exists between the promisor and the promisee of a contract.

Assignment The act of transferring to another all or part of one's rights arising under a contract.

Delegation The transfer of a contractual duty to a third party. The party delegating the duty (the delegator) to the third party (the delegatee) is still obliged to perform on the contract should the delegatee fail to perform.

---

5. Pronounced uh-sye-nore.
6. Pronounced uh-sye-nee.

has a right to demand performance from the other original party to the contract. The assignee takes only those rights that the assignor originally had, however.

Assignments are important because they are used in many types of business financing. Banks, for instance, frequently assign their rights to receive payments under their loan contracts to other firms, which pay for those rights.

CASE EXAMPLE 11.5 Edward Hosch entered into four loan agreements with Citicapital Commercial Corporation to finance the purchase of heavy construction equipment. A few months later, Citicapital merged into Citicorp Leasing, Inc., which was then renamed GE Capital Commercial, Inc. One year later, GE Capital assigned the loans to Colonial Pacific Leasing Corporation. When Hosch defaulted on the loans, Colonial provided a notice of default and demanded payment. Hosch failed to repay the loans, so Colonial sued to collect the amount due. The trial court granted summary judgment to Colonial, and the appellate court affirmed. There was sufficient evidence that the loans had been assigned to Colonial.[7] ●

As a general rule, all rights can be assigned. Exceptions are made, however, under certain circumstances, including the following:

1. The assignment is prohibited by statute.
2. The contract is personal.
3. The assignment significantly changes the risk or duties of the obligor.
4. The contract prohibits assignment.

Delegations

Just as a party can transfer rights through an assignment, a party can also transfer duties. Duties are not assigned, however, they are *delegated*. The party delegating the duties is the *delegator,* and the party to whom the duties are delegated is the *delegatee*. Normally, a delegation of duties does not relieve the delegator of the obligation to perform in the event that the delegatee fails to do so.

No special form is required to create a valid delegation of duties. As long as the delegator expresses an intention to make the delegation, it is effective. The delegator need not even use the word *delegate.*

As a general rule, any duty can be delegated. There are, however, some exceptions to this rule. Delegation is prohibited in the following circumstances:

1. When special trust has been placed in the *obligor* (the person contractually obligated to perform).
2. When performance depends on the personal skill or talents of the obligor.
3. When performance by a third party will vary materially from that expected by the *obligee* (the person to whom an obligation is owed) under the contract.
4. When the contract expressly prohibits delegation by including an *antidelegation clause.*

If a delegation of duties is enforceable, the obligee must accept performance from the delegatee. As noted, a valid delegation of duties does not relieve the delegator of obligations under the contract. Although there are many exceptions, the general rule today is that the obligee can sue both the delegatee and the delegator if the duties are not performed.

This piano teacher has signed a contract to give weekly piano lessons. Can the teacher delegate performance of this contract to another piano teacher?

(Aispix/Image Source/Shutterstock.com)

Third Party Beneficiaries

Another exception to the doctrine of privity of contract arises when the contract is intended to benefit a third party. When the original parties to the contract agree that the contract performance should be rendered to or directly benefit a third person, the third person becomes

---

7. *Hosch v. Colonial Pacific Leasing Corp.,* 313 Ga.App. 873, 722 S.E.2d 778 (2012).

Third Party Beneficiary   One for whose benefit a promise is made in a contract but who is not a party to the contract.

Intended Beneficiary   A third party for whose benefit a contract is formed. An intended beneficiary can sue the promisor if such a contract is breached.

an *intended* **third party beneficiary** of the contract. As the **intended beneficiary** of the contract, the third party has legal rights and can sue the promisor directly for breach of the contract.

    CASE EXAMPLE 11.6   The classic case that gave third party beneficiaries the right to bring a suit directly against a promisor was decided in 1859. The case involved three parties—Holly, Lawrence, and Fox. Holly had borrowed $300 from Lawrence. Shortly thereafter, Holly loaned $300 to Fox, who in return promised Holly that he would pay Holly's debt to Lawrence on the following day. When Lawrence failed to obtain the $300 from Fox, he sued Fox to recover the funds. The court had to decide whether Lawrence could sue Fox directly (rather than suing Holly). The court held that when "a promise [is] made for the benefit of another, he for whose benefit it is made may bring an action for its breach."[8] ●

    The law distinguishes between *intended* beneficiaries and *incidental* beneficiaries. An incidental beneficiary is a third person who receives a benefit from a contract even though that person's benefit is not the reason the contract was made. Because the benefit is unintentional, an incidental beneficiary cannot sue to enforce the contract. Only intended beneficiaries acquire legal rights in a contract.

    To determine whether a person was an intended beneficiary, courts consider whether it is reasonable for the beneficiary to believe that he or she had a right to enforce the contract. **CASE EXAMPLE 11.7**   Neumann Homes, Inc., contracted to make public improvements for the Village of Antioch, Illinois. Neumann subcontracted the grading work required under the contract to Lake County Grading Company. The subcontractor completed the work but was not paid in full. When Neumann declared bankruptcy, the subcontractor filed a suit against the Village to recover, claiming to be a third party beneficiary of the contract between the Village and Neumann. The court held in favor of the subcontractor. Under an Illinois statute, the Village was required to obtain a payment bond guaranteeing that a contractor would pay what was owed for the completion of any public works project. The court reasoned that this statute was intended to benefit subcontractors in public works contracts. Thus, it was reasonable for Lake County to believe that it was an intended third party beneficiary. Because the Village had failed to obtain a bond ensuring payment to subcontractors, Lake County could sue for breach of contract.[9] ●

> "There are occasions and causes and why and wherefore in all things."
>
> William Shakespeare,
> 1564–1616
> (English dramatist and poet)

Discharge   The termination of an obligation. In contract law, discharge occurs when the parties have fully performed their contractual obligations or when events, conduct of the parties, or operation of law releases the parties from performance.

Performance   In contract law, the fulfillment of one's duties arising under a contract with another; the normal way of discharging one's contractual obligations.

Performance and Discharge

The most common way to **discharge**, or terminate, one's contractual duties is by the **performance** of those duties. For example, a buyer and seller enter into an agreement via e-mail for the sale of a 2015 Lexus for $42,000. This contract will be discharged by performance when the buyer pays $42,000 to the seller and the seller transfers possession of the Lexus to the buyer.

    The duty to perform under any contract (including e-contracts) may be *conditioned* on the occurrence or nonoccurrence of a certain event, or the duty may be *absolute*. In this section, we look at conditions of performance and the degree of performance required. We then examine some other ways in which a contract can be discharged, including discharge by agreement of the parties and discharge by operation of law.

Conditions of Performance

In most contracts, promises of performance are not expressly conditioned or qualified. Instead, they are *absolute promises*. They must be performed, or the parties promising the acts will be in breach of contract.   **EXAMPLE 11.8**   Paloma Enterprises contracts

---

8. *Lawrence v. Fox*, 20 N.Y. 268 (1859).
9. *Lake County Grading Co. v. Village of Antioch*, 2013 IL App (2d) 120474, 985 N.E.2d 638 (2013).

to sell a truckload of organic produce to Tran for $10,000. The parties' promises are unconditional: Paloma will deliver the produce to Tran, and Tran will pay $10,000 to Paloma. The payment does not have to be made if the produce is not delivered. •

In some situations, however, performance is contingent on the occurrence or nonoccurrence of a certain event. A **condition** is a qualification in a contract based on a possible future event. The occurrence or nonoccurrence of the event will trigger the performance of a legal obligation or terminate an existing obligation under a contract.[10] If the condition is not satisfied, the obligations of the parties are discharged.

A condition that must be fulfilled before a party's performance can be required is called a **condition precedent**. The condition precedes the absolute duty to perform. Life insurance contracts frequently specify that certain conditions, such as passing a physical examination, must be met before the insurance company will be obligated to perform under the contract.

In addition, many contracts are conditioned on an independent appraisal of value. **EXAMPLE 11.9** Restoration Motors offers to buy Charlie's 1960 Cadillac limousine only if an expert appraiser estimates that it can be restored for less than a certain price. Thus, the parties' obligations are conditioned on the outcome of the appraisal. If the condition is not satisfied—that is, if the appraiser deems the cost to be above that price—their obligations are discharged. •

Discharge by Performance

The great majority of contracts are discharged by performance. The contract comes to an end when both parties fulfill their respective duties by performing the acts they have promised.

Performance can also be accomplished by *tender*. **Tender** is an unconditional offer to perform by a person who is ready, willing, and able to do so. Therefore, a seller who places goods at the disposal of a buyer has tendered delivery and can demand payment. A buyer who offers to pay for goods has tendered payment and can demand delivery of the goods.

Once performance has been tendered, the party making the tender has done everything possible to carry out the terms of the contract. If the other party then refuses to perform, the party making the tender can sue for breach of contract. There are two basic types of performance—*complete performance* and *substantial performance*.

Complete Performance
When a party performs exactly as agreed, there is no question as to whether the contract has been performed. When a party's performance is perfect, it is said to be complete. Normally, conditions expressly stated in a contract must fully occur in all respects for complete performance (strict performance) of the contract to take place. Any deviation breaches the contract and discharges the other party's obligations to perform.

Most construction contracts, for instance, require the builder to meet certain specifications. If the specifications are conditions, complete performance is required to avoid material breach (*material breach* will be discussed shortly). If the conditions are met, the other party to the contract must then fulfill her or his obligation to pay the builder.

If the parties to the contract did not expressly make the specifications a condition, however, and the builder fails to meet the specifications, performance is not complete. What effect does such a failure have on the other party's obligation to pay? The answer is part of the doctrine of *substantial performance*.

(1001nights/istockphoto.com)

When is a deal to sell a new car completed?

Condition A qualification, provision, or clause in a contractual agreement, the occurrence or nonoccurrence of which creates, suspends, or terminates the obligations of the contracting parties.

Condition Precedent In a contractual agreement, a condition that must be met before a party's promise becomes absolute.

Tender An unconditional offer to perform an obligation by a person who is ready, willing, and able to do so.

---

10. The *Restatement (Second) of Contracts*, Section 224, defines a condition as "an event, not certain to occur, which must occur, unless its nonoccurrence is excused, before performance under a contract becomes due."

Learning Objective 2
What is substantial performance?

Substantial Performance   A party who in good faith performs substantially all of the terms of a contract can enforce the contract against the other party under the doctrine of substantial performance. The basic requirements for performance to qualify as substantial performance are as follows:

1. The party must have performed in good faith. Intentional failure to comply with the contract terms is a breach of the contract.
2. The performance must not vary greatly from the performance promised in the contract. An omission, variance, or defect in performance is considered minor if it can easily be remedied by compensation (monetary damages).
3. The performance must create substantially the same benefits as those promised in the contract.

Courts decide whether the performance was substantial on a case-by-case basis, examining all of the facts of the particular situation. **CASE EXAMPLE 11.10**   Wisconsin Electric Power Company (WEPCO) contracted with Union Pacific Railroad to transport coal to WEPCO from mines in Colorado. The contract required WEPCO to notify Union Pacific monthly of how many tons of coal (below a specified maximum) it wanted to have shipped the next month. Union Pacific was to make "good faith reasonable efforts" to meet the schedule.

The contract also required WEPCO to supply the railcars. When WEPCO did not supply the railcars, Union Pacific used its own railcars and delivered 84 percent of the requested coal. In this situation, a federal court held that the delivery of 84 percent of the contracted amount constituted substantial performance.[11] •

Effect on Duty to Perform   If performance is substantial, the other party's duty to perform remains absolute (except that the party can sue for damages due to the minor deviations). In other words, the parties must continue performing under the contract (for instance, making payment to the party who substantially performed). If performance is not substantial, there is a *material breach* (to be discussed shortly), and the nonbreaching party is excused from further performance.

Measure of Damages   Because substantial performance is not perfect, the other party is entitled to damages to compensate for the failure to comply with the contract. The measure of the damages is the cost to bring the object of the contract into compliance with its terms, if that cost is reasonable under the circumstances.

If the cost is unreasonable, the measure of damages is the difference in value between the performance that was rendered and the performance that would have been rendered if the contract had been performed completely.

The following case is a classic illustration that there is no exact formula for deciding when a contract has been substantially performed.

---

11. *Wisconsin Electric Power Co. v. Union Pacific Railroad Co.*, 557 F.3d 504 (7th Cir. 2009).

Classic Case 11.1

Jacob & Youngs v. Kent
Court of Appeals of New York, 230 N.Y. 239, 129 N.E. 889 (1921).

BACKGROUND AND FACTS   The plaintiff, Jacob & Youngs, Inc., was a builder that had contracted with George Kent to construct a country residence for him. A specification in the building contract required that "all wrought-iron pipe must be well galvanized, lap welded pipe of the grade known as 'standard pipe' of Reading manufacture." Jacob & Youngs installed substantially similar pipe that was

(Lisa F. Young/Alamy)

Does a contractor have to use the exact brands specified in the contract?

Classic Case 11.1—Continued

not of Reading manufacture. When Kent became aware of the difference, he ordered the builder to remove all of the plumbing and replace it with the Reading type. To do so would have required removing finished walls that encased the plumbing—an expensive and difficult task. The builder explained that the plumbing was of the same quality, appearance, value, and cost as Reading pipe. When Kent refused to pay the $3,483.46 still owed for the work, Jacob & Youngs sued to compel payment. The trial court ruled in favor of Kent. The plaintiff appealed, and the appellate court reversed the trial court's decision. Kent then appealed to the Court of Appeals of New York, the state's highest court.

IN THE WORDS OF THE COURT . . .
CARDOZO, Justice.
    * * * *
    * * * The courts never say that one who makes a contract fills the measure of his duty by less than full performance. They do say, however, that *an omission, both trivial and innocent, will sometimes be atoned [compensated] for by allowance of the resulting damage, and will not always be the breach of a condition[.]* [Emphasis added.]
    * * * Where the line is to be drawn between the important and the trivial cannot be settled by a formula. * * * *We must weigh the purpose to be served, the desire to be gratified, the excuse for deviation from the letter, [and] the cruelty*

of enforced adherence. Then only can we tell whether *literal fulfillment is to be implied by law as a condition.* [Emphasis added.]
    * * * We think the measure of the allowance is not the cost of replacement, which would be great, but the difference in value, which would be either nominal or nothing. * * * The owner is entitled to the money which will permit him to complete, unless the cost of completion is grossly and unfairly out of proportion to the good to be attained.

DECISION AND REMEDY   New York's highest court affirmed the appellate court's decision, holding that Jacob & Youngs had substantially performed the contract.

THE LEGAL ENVIRONMENT DIMENSION   *The New York Court of Appeals found that Jacob & Youngs had substantially performed the contract. To what, if any, remedy was Kent entitled?*

IMPACT OF THIS CASE ON TODAY'S LEGAL ENVIRONMENT   *At the time of the Jacob & Youngs case, some courts did not apply the doctrine of substantial performance to disputes involving breaches of contract. This landmark decision contributed to a developing trend toward equity and fairness in those circumstances. Today, an unintentional and trivial deviation from the terms of a contract will not prevent its enforcement but will permit an adjustment in the value of its performance.*

Performance to the Satisfaction of Another

Contracts often state that completed work must personally satisfy one of the parties or a third person. When the subject matter of the contract is *personal*, the obligation is conditional, and performance must actually satisfy the party specified in the contract. For instance, contracts for portraits, works of art, and tailoring are considered personal because they involve matters of personal taste. Therefore, only the personal satisfaction of the party fulfills the condition—unless a court finds that the party is expressing dissatisfaction simply to avoid payment or otherwise is not acting in good faith.

Most other contracts need to be performed only to the satisfaction of a reasonable person unless they *expressly state otherwise*. When the subject matter of the contract is mechanical, courts are more likely to find that the performing party has performed satisfactorily if a reasonable person would be satisfied with what was done. **EXAMPLE 11.11**   Mason signs a contract with Jen to mount a new heat pump on a concrete platform to her satisfaction. Such a contract normally need only be performed to the satisfaction of a reasonable person. •

Material Breach of Contract

A **breach of contract** is the nonperformance of a contractual duty. The breach is *material* when performance is not at least substantial.[12] As mentioned earlier, when there is a material breach, the nonbreaching party is excused from

Learning Objective 3
When is a breach considered material, and what effect does that have on the other party's duty to perform a contract?

Breach of Contract The failure, without legal excuse, of a promisor to perform the obligations of a contract.

---
12. *Restatement (Second) of Contracts*, Section 241.

the performance of contractual duties. That party can also sue the breaching party for damages resulting from the breach.

EXAMPLE 11.12   When country singer Garth Brooks's mother died, he donated $500,000 to a hospital in his hometown to build a new women's health center named after his mother. After several years passed and the health center was not built, Brooks demanded a refund. The hospital refused, claiming that while it had promised to honor his mother in some way, it did not promise to build a women's health center. Brooks sued for breach of contract. A jury determined that the hospital's failure to build a women's health center and name it after Brooks's mother was a material breach of the contract. The jury awarded Brooks damages. ●

Material versus Minor Breach   If the breach is *minor* (not material), the nonbreaching party's duty to perform can sometimes be suspended until the breach has been remedied, but the duty to perform is not entirely excused. Once the minor breach has been cured, the nonbreaching party must resume performance of the contractual obligations.

CASE EXAMPLE 11.13   Marc and Bree Kohel agreed to buy a used Mazda from Bergen Auto Enterprises, LLC, doing business as Wayne Mazda, Inc. As part of the deal, the Kohels traded in their 2005 Nissan for a credit toward the purchase price. Wayne Mazda agreed to pay the balance of the loan the Kohels still owed on the Nissan. The Kohels took possession of the Mazda with temporary plates. Later, Wayne Mazda discovered that the Nissan was missing a vehicle identification number (VIN) tag. The dealer therefore refused to make the payment for the Nissan and also refused to give the Kohels permanent plates for the Mazda. The Kohels obtained a replacement VIN tag for the Nissan, but Wayne Mazda still refused to take their calls or supply permanent plates for the car.

The Kohels sued, claiming that Wayne Mazda's conduct was a material breach of the contract. The court agreed and ruled in favor of the plaintiffs. The Kohels had not been aware that their Nissan lacked a VIN tag (potentially a minor breach of the contract), and the dealership had examined the car twice before accepting it in trade. Although the Kohels had attempted to remedy the tag problem, the dealership had acted in an unreasonable manner, and that constituted a material breach of the contract.[13] ●

Discharges Nonbreaching Party from Further Performance   Any breach entitles the nonbreaching party to sue for damages, but only a material breach discharges the nonbreaching party from the contract. The policy underlying these rules allows a contract to go forward when only minor problems occur but allows it to be terminated if major difficulties arise.

CASE EXAMPLE 11.14   Su Yong Kim sold an apartment building with substandard plumbing that violated the city's housing code. The contract stated that Kim would have the plumbing fixed (brought up to code) within eight months. A year later, Kim still had not made the necessary repairs, so the buyers stopped making the payments due under the contract. A court found that Kim's failure to make the required repairs was a material breach because it defeated the purpose of the contract—to lease the building to tenants. Because Kim's breach was material, the buyers were no longer obligated to continue making payments under the contract.[14] ●

Anticipatory Repudiation
Before either party to a contract has a duty to perform, one of the parties may refuse to carry out his or her contractual obligations. This is called **anticipatory repudiation** of the contract.

(Shane Shaw/iStockphoto.com)

If a trade-in car is missing its vehicle identification number, can a dealership suspend performance of the sales contract for the other automobile?

Anticipatory Repudiation   An assertion or action by a party indicating that he or she will not perform an obligation that the party is contractually obligated to perform at a future time.

---

13. *Kohel v. Bergen Auto Enterprises, LLC*, 2013 WL 439970 (N.J.App. 2013).
14. *Kim v. Park*, 192 Or.App. 365, 86 P.3d 63 (2004).

When an anticipatory repudiation occurs, it is treated as a material breach of the contract, and the nonbreaching party is permitted to bring an action for damages immediately. The nonbreaching party can file suit even though the scheduled time for performance under the contract may still be in the future. Until the nonbreaching party treats an early repudiation as a breach, however, the repudiating party can retract her or his anticipatory repudiation by proper notice and restore the parties to their original obligations.[15]

An anticipatory repudiation is treated as a present, material breach for two reasons. First, the nonbreaching party should not be required to remain ready and willing to perform when the other party has already repudiated the contract. Second, the nonbreaching party should have the opportunity to seek a similar contract elsewhere and may have a duty to do so to minimize his or her loss.

Time for Performance   If no time for performance is stated in the contract, a *reasonable time* is implied.[16] If a specific time is stated, the parties must usually perform by that time. Unless time is expressly stated to be vital, though, a delay in performance will not destroy the performing party's right to payment.

When time is expressly stated to be "of the essence" or vital, the parties normally must perform within the stated time period because the time element becomes a condition. Even when the contract states that time is of the essence, a court may find that a party who fails to complain about the other party's delay has waived the breach of the time provision.

Discharge by Agreement

Any contract can be discharged by agreement of the parties. The agreement can be contained in the original contract, or the parties can form a new contract for the express purpose of discharging the original contract.

Discharge by Mutual Rescission
As you'll read later, *rescission* is the process by which a contract is canceled or terminated and the parties are returned to the positions they occupied prior to forming it. For **mutual rescission** to take place, the parties must make another agreement that also satisfies the legal requirements for a contract. There must be an *offer,* an *acceptance,* and *consideration*. Ordinarily, if the parties agree to rescind the original contract, their promises not to perform the acts stipulated in the original contract will be legal consideration for the second contract (the rescission).

Agreements to rescind most executory contracts (in which neither party has performed) are enforceable, even if the agreement is made orally and even if the original agreement was in writing. Under the Uniform Commercial Code (UCC), however, agreements to rescind a sales contract must be in writing (or contained in an electronic record) when the contract requires a written rescission.[17] Agreements to rescind contracts involving transfers of realty also must be evidenced by a writing or record.

When one party has fully performed, an agreement to cancel the original contract normally will *not* be enforceable unless there is additional consideration. Because the performing party has received no consideration for the promise to call off the original bargain, additional consideration is necessary to support a rescission contract.

Discharge by Novation
A contractual obligation may also be discharged through novation. A **novation** occurs when both of the parties to a contract agree to

Mutual Rescission An agreement between the parties to cancel their contract, releasing the parties from further obligations under the contract. The object of the agreement is to restore the parties to the positions they would have occupied had no contract ever been formed.

Novation The substitution, by agreement, of a new contract for an old one, with the rights under the old one being terminated. Typically, novation involves the substitution of a new party for one of the original parties to the contract.

---

15. See Uniform Commercial Code (UCC) 2–611.
16. See UCC 2–204.
17. UCC 2–209(2), (4).

substitute a third party for one of the original parties. The requirements of a novation are as follows:

1. A previous valid obligation.
2. An agreement by all parties to a new contract.
3. The extinguishing of the old obligation (discharge of the prior party).
4. A new contract that is valid.

EXAMPLE 11.15 Union Corporation enters into a contract to sell its pharmaceutical division to British Pharmaceuticals, Ltd. Before the transfer is completed, Union, British Pharmaceuticals, and a third company, Otis Chemicals, execute a new agreement to transfer all of British Pharmaceuticals' rights and duties in the transaction to Otis Chemicals. As long as the new contract is supported by consideration, the novation will discharge the original contract (between Union and British Pharmaceuticals) and replace it with the new contract (between Union and Otis Chemicals). •

A novation expressly or impliedly revokes and discharges a prior contract. The parties involved may expressly state in the new contract that the old contract is now discharged. If the parties do not expressly discharge the old contract, it will be impliedly discharged if the new contract's terms are inconsistent with the old contract's terms. It is this immediate discharge of the prior contract that distinguishes a novation from both an accord and satisfaction, which will be discussed shortly, and an assignment of all rights, discussed earlier in this chapter.

Discharge by Settlement Agreement

A compromise, or settlement agreement, that arises out of a genuine dispute over the obligations under an existing contract will be recognized at law. The agreement will be substituted as a new contract and will either expressly or impliedly revoke and discharge the obligations under the prior contract. In contrast to a novation, a substituted agreement does not involve a third party. Rather, the two original parties to the contract form a different agreement to substitute for the original one.

Discharge by Accord and Satisfaction

In an *accord and satisfaction,* the parties agree to accept performance that is different from the performance originally promised. An *accord* is a contract to perform some act to satisfy an existing contractual duty that is not yet discharged. A *satisfaction* is the performance of the accord agreement. An accord and its satisfaction discharge the original contractual obligation.

Once the accord has been made, the original obligation is merely suspended until the accord agreement is fully performed. If it is not performed, the obligee (the one to whom performance is owed) can file a lawsuit based on the original obligation or the accord.

EXAMPLE 11.16 Fahreed has a judgment against Ling for $8,000. Later, both parties agree that the judgment can be satisfied by Ling's transfer of his automobile to Fahreed. This agreement to accept the auto in lieu of $8,000 in cash is the accord. If Ling transfers the car to Fahreed, the accord is fully performed, and the debt is discharged. If Ling refuses to transfer the car, the accord is breached. Because the original obligation was merely suspended, Fahreed can sue Ling to enforce the original judgment for $8,000 in cash or bring an action for breach of the accord. •

Release An agreement in which one party gives up the right to pursue a legal claim against another party.

Release

A **release** is a contract in which one party forfeits the right to pursue a legal claim against the other party. It bars any further recovery beyond the terms stated in the release. Releases will generally be binding if they are (1) given in good faith, (2) stated in a signed writing (required by many states), and (3) accompanied by consideration.[18] Clearly,

---

18. Under the Uniform Commercial Code (UCC), a written, signed waiver or renunciation by an aggrieved party discharges any further liability for a breach, even without consideration [UCC 1–107].

parties are better off if they know the extent of their injuries or damages before signing releases.

Covenant Not to Sue Unlike a release, a **covenant not to sue** does not always prevent further recovery. The parties simply substitute a contractual obligation for some other type of legal action based on a valid claim. As the following *Spotlight Case* illustrates, a covenant not to sue can form the basis for a dismissal of the claims of either party to the covenant.

Covenant Not to Sue An agreement to substitute a contractual obligation for some other type of legal action based on a valid claim.

Spotlight on Nike

Case 11.2
Already, LLC v. Nike, Inc.
Supreme Court of the United States, ___ U.S. ___, 133 S.Ct. 721, 184 L.Ed.2d 553 (2013).

(CBsigns/Alamy)

COMPANY PROFILE *Bill Bowerman was a track coach at the University of Oregon, and Phil Knight was an accountant in Portland, Oregon, who had been a track athlete on Bowerman's team. In 1964, the two men shook hands, pledged $500 each, and formed Blue Ribbon Sports to distribute athletic footwear manufactured by a Japanese company. A decade later, Blue Ribbon became Nike, Inc., adopted the familiar "Swoosh" logo, and began marketing shoes of its own design. Today, with revenue approaching $30 billion, Nike's markets are global. Nike is the official sponsor of the National Football League in the United States, as well as other athletes and sports teams around the world.*

BACKGROUND AND FACTS Nike, Inc., designs, makes, and sells athletic footwear, including a line of shoes known as "Air Force 1s." Already, LLC, also designs and markets athletic footwear, including shoe lines known as "Sugars" and "Soulja Boys." Nike filed a suit in a federal district court against Already, alleging that Soulja Boys and Sugars infringed the Air Force 1 trademark. Already filed a counterclaim, contending that the Air Force 1 trademark was invalid. While the suit was pending, Nike issued a covenant not to sue, in which it promised not to raise any trademark claims against Already or any affiliated entity based on Already's existing footwear designs or any future Already designs similar to Already's current products. Nike then filed a motion to dismiss its own claims and to dismiss Already's counterclaim. Already opposed the dismissal of its counterclaim, but the court granted Nike's motion. The U.S. Court of Appeals for the Second Circuit affirmed. Already appealed to the United States Supreme Court. The question was whether Nike's covenant not to sue could result in the dismissal of Already's action to have Nike's trademark declared invalid. To answer this question, the Court used the voluntary cessation test.

IN THE WORDS OF THE COURT . . .
Chief Justice *ROBERTS* delivered the opinion of the Court.
* * * *
* * * A defendant cannot automatically moot a case simply by ending its unlawful conduct once sued. [A matter is moot if it involves no actual controversy. In the U.S. federal courts, moot cases are dismissed.] Otherwise, a defendant could engage in unlawful conduct, stop when sued to have the case declared moot, then pick up where he left off, repeating this cycle until he achieves all his unlawful ends. Given this concern, * * * *a defendant claiming that its voluntary compliance moots a case bears the formidable burden of showing that it is absolutely clear the allegedly wrongful behavior could not reasonably be expected to recur.* [This is the voluntary cessation test.] [Emphasis added.]
* * * *
We begin our analysis with the terms of the covenant:

[Nike] unconditionally and irrevocably covenants to refrain from making *any* claim(s) or demand(s) * * * against Already or *any* of its * * * related business entities * * * [including] distributors * * * and employees of such entities and *all* customers * * * on account of any *possible* cause of action based on or involving trademark infringement * * * relating to the NIKE Mark based on the appearance of *any* of Already's current and/or previous footwear product designs, and *any* colorable imitations thereof, regardless of whether that footwear is produced * * * or otherwise used in commerce.

The breadth of this covenant suffices to meet the burden imposed by the voluntary cessation test.

In addition, Nike originally argued that the Sugars and Soulja Boys infringed its trademark; in other words, Nike

Spotlight Case 11.2—Continues ➡

Spotlight Case 11.2—Continued

believed those shoes were "colorable imitations" of the Air Force 1s. Nike's covenant now allows Already to produce all of its existing footwear designs—including the Sugar and Soulja Boy—and any "colorable imitation" of those designs. * * * It is hard to imagine a scenario that would potentially infringe Nike's trademark and yet not fall under the covenant. Nike, having taken the position in court that there is no prospect of such a shoe, would be hard pressed to assert the contrary down the road. If such a shoe exists, the parties have not pointed to it, there is no evidence that Already has dreamt of it, and we cannot conceive of it. It sits, as far as we can tell, on a shelf between Dorothy's ruby slippers and Perseus's winged sandals.

* * * *

* * * Given the covenant's broad language, and given that Already has asserted no concrete plans to engage in conduct

not covered by the covenant, we can conclude the case is moot because the challenged conduct cannot reasonably be expected to recur.

DECISION AND REMEDY   The United States Supreme Court affirmed the judgment of the lower court. Under the covenant not to sue, Nike could not file a claim for trademark infringement against Already, and Already could not assert that Nike's trademark was invalid.

THE ECONOMIC DIMENSION   *Why would any party agree to a covenant not to sue?*

THE LEGAL ENVIRONMENT DIMENSION   *Which types of contracts are similar to a covenant not to sue? Explain.*

Discharge by Operation of Law

> "Law is a practical matter."
>
> Roscoe Pound, 1870–1964 (American jurist)

Under specified circumstances, contractual duties may be discharged by operation of law. These circumstances include material alteration of the contract, the running of the statute of limitations, bankruptcy, and the impossibility or impracticability of performance.

Material Alteration of the Contract
To discourage parties from altering written contracts, the law allows an innocent party to be discharged when the other party has materially altered a written contract without consent. For instance, a party alters a material term of a contract, such as the stated quantity or price, without the knowledge or consent of the other party. In this situation, the party who was unaware of the alteration can treat the contract as discharged or terminated.

Statutes of Limitations
As mentioned earlier in this text, statutes of limitations restrict the period during which a party can sue on a particular cause of action. After the applicable limitations period has passed, a suit can no longer be brought. The limitations period for bringing suits for breach of oral contracts usually is two to three years, and for written or otherwise recorded contracts, four to five years. Parties generally have ten to twenty years to file for recovery of amounts awarded in judgments, depending on state law.

Lawsuits for breach of a contract for the sale of goods generally must be brought within four years after the cause of action has accrued. By their original agreement, the parties can reduce this four-year period to not less than one year, but they cannot agree to extend it.

Bankruptcy
A proceeding in bankruptcy (see Chapter 13) attempts to allocate the debtor's assets to the creditors in a fair and equitable fashion. Once the assets have been allocated, the debtor receives a *discharge in bankruptcy*. A discharge in bankruptcy ordinarily prevents the creditors from enforcing most of the debtor's contracts. Partial payment of a debt *after* discharge in bankruptcy will not revive the debt.

Impossibility of Performance A doctrine under which a party to a contract is relieved of his or her duty to perform when performance becomes objectively impossible or totally impracticable (through no fault of either party).

Impossibility of Performance
After a contract has been made, supervening events (such as a fire) may make performance impossible in an objective sense. This is known as **impossibility of performance** and can discharge a contract. The doctrine of impossibility

of performance applies only when the parties could not have reasonably foreseen, at the time the contract was formed, the event that rendered performance impossible. Performance may also become so difficult or costly due to some unforeseen event that a court will consider it commercially unfeasible, or impracticable, as will be discussed later in the chapter.

Objective impossibility ("It can't be done") must be distinguished from *subjective impossibility* ("I'm sorry, I simply can't do it"). An example of subjective impossibility occurs when a party cannot deliver goods on time because of freight car shortages or cannot make payment on time because the bank is closed. In effect, in each of these situations the party is saying, "It is impossible for *me* to perform," not "It is impossible for *anyone* to perform." Accordingly, such excuses do not discharge a contract, and the nonperforming party is normally held in breach of contract.

When Performance Is Impossible   Three basic types of situations may qualify as grounds for the discharge of contractual obligations based on impossibility of performance:[19]

(Yuri Arcurs/Shutterstock.com)

1. *When one of the parties to a personal contract dies or becomes incapacitated prior to performance.*

   EXAMPLE 11.17   Frederic, a famous dancer, contracts with Ethereal Dancing Guild to play a leading role in its new ballet. Before the ballet can be performed, Frederic becomes ill and dies. His personal performance was essential to the completion of the contract. Thus, his death discharges the contract and his estate's liability for his nonperformance. ●

2. *When the specific subject matter of the contract is destroyed.*

   EXAMPLE 11.18   A-1 Farm Equipment agrees to sell Gunther the green tractor on its lot and promises to have the tractor ready for Gunther to pick up on Saturday. On Friday night, however, a truck veers off the nearby highway and smashes into the tractor, destroying it beyond repair. Because the contract was for this specific tractor, A-1's performance is rendered impossible owing to the accident. ●

3. *When a change in law renders performance illegal.*

   EXAMPLE 11.19   Hopper contracts with Playlist, Inc., to create a Web site through which users can post and share movies, music, and other forms of digital entertainment. Hopper goes to work. Before the site is operational, however, Congress passes the No Online Piracy in Entertainment (NOPE) Act. The NOPE Act makes it illegal to operate a Web site on which copyrighted works are posted without the copyright owners' consent. In this situation, the contract is discharged by operation of law. The purpose of the contract has been rendered illegal, and contract performance is objectively impossible. ●

Can an agreement that prohibits personal contact between two parties affect the performance of contracts between one of these parties and the other party's business? That was the question before the court in the case that follows.

The star dancer above has a contract to appear in five ballets during the winter season. If he breaks his leg before the season starts, is he still bound by the contract?

---

19. *Restatement (Second) of Contracts,* Sections 261–266; UCC 2–615.

Kolodin v. Valenti

New York Supreme Court, Appellate Division, First Department, 115 A.D.3d 197, 979 N.Y.S.2d 587 (2014).

BACKGROUND AND FACTS   Hilary Kolodin (also known as Hilary Kole), a jazz singer, was involved personally with John Valenti, the sole shareholder and president of Jayarvee, Inc. Jayarvee manages artists, produces recordings, and owns and operates the jazz club Birdland in New York City. Kolodin contracted professionally with Jayarvee for recording and management services. After Kolodin and Valenti's personal relationship deteriorated, Kolodin asked a New York state court

(auremar/Fotolia)

Can severe disagreement within a couple render a personal services contract impossible to perform?

Case 11.3—Continues ➡

Case 11.3—Continued

to issue a temporary protection order, alleging domestic abuse. The parties then agreed under a court-ordered stipulation to have no further contact with one another. The stipulation specified that "no contact shall include no third party contact, excepting counsel." Later, Kolodin filed a suit in a New York state court against Valenti, alleging breach of her Jayarvee contracts and seeking their rescission. The court declared the contracts between Kolodin and Jayarvee terminated. Valenti appealed.

IN THE WORDS OF THE COURT . . .
ACOSTA, J.P. [Judge Presiding]
* * * *

Impossibility excuses a party's performance only when the destruction of the subject matter of the contract or the means of performance makes performance objectively impossible. Moreover, the impossibility must be produced by an unanticipated event that could not have been foreseen or guarded against in the contract. [Emphasis added.]

In this case, performance of the contracts at issue has been rendered objectively impossible by law, since the stipulation destroyed the means of performance by precluding all contact between plaintiff and Valenti except by counsel.

Because of Valenti's central role in the operation of Jayarvee, performance of the contracts would necessarily require his input and, consequently, a violation of the stipulation. The recording and management contracts are for personal services, so they require substantial and ongoing communication between plaintiff and Jayarvee. * * * Jayarvee is a relatively small organization, with approximately 40 employees, and Valenti concedes that he "oversees the employees in their day-to-day activities for the corporation." Of course, employees of Valenti's company are third parties who fall within the ambit [realm] of the stipulation's "no contact" provision. For Jayarvee to perform the contracts—or, for that matter, for plaintiff to perform—the company's employees would need to serve as conduits for communications to plaintiff that originated with Valenti. That result would clearly violate the stipulation's prohibition of third-party contact.
* * * *

Nor * * * was it foreseeable at the time of contracting that plaintiff and Valenti would enter into an agreement to bar contact between each other. Valenti argues that the breakdown of his relationship with plaintiff constituted the grounds of impossibility on which plaintiff relies, and that the breakdown was foreseeable. Rather, the *stipulation* is what makes performance of the contracts impossible. Absent the stipulation (and the temporary order of protection that preceded it), Jayarvee and plaintiff could have lawfully performed the contracts despite plaintiff and Valenti's strained relationship * * * . Even if plaintiff could have foreseen that her relationship with Valenti would continue to deteriorate, it was not foreseeable that she and Valenti would enter into the stipulation.

DECISION AND REMEDY   A state intermediate appellate court affirmed the lower court's ruling. Performance of Kolodin's Jayarvee contracts was rendered objectively impossible by Kolodin and Valenti's stipulation. "In undertaking to perform recording and management contracts, the eventuality that the parties would subsequently stipulate to forbid contact with one another could not have been foreseen or guarded against."

THE LEGAL ENVIRONMENT DIMENSION   *Should Kolodin's role in bringing about the "no contact" stipulation through her request for a protection order have rendered the doctrine of impossibility inapplicable? Explain.*

WHAT IF THE FACTS WERE DIFFERENT?   *Suppose that the stipulation between Kolodin and Valenti had exempted Jayarvee's employees. Would the result have been different? Why or why not?*

Temporary Impossibility   An occurrence or event that makes performance temporarily impossible operates to suspend performance until the impossibility ceases. Once the temporary event ends, the parties ordinarily must perform the contract as originally planned.

   CASE EXAMPLE 11.20   Keefe Hurwitz contracted to sell his home in Louisiana to Wesley and Gwendolyn Payne for $241,500. Four days later, Hurricane Katrina made landfall and caused extensive damage to the house. Hurwitz refused to pay the cost ($60,000) for the necessary repairs before the deal closed. The Paynes filed a lawsuit to enforce the contract at the agreed-on price. Hurwitz argued that Hurricane Katrina had made it impossible for him to perform and had discharged his duties under the contract. The court, however, ruled that Hurricane Katrina had caused only a temporary impossibility. Hurwitz was required to pay for the necessary repairs and to perform the contract as written. He could not obtain a higher purchase price to offset the cost of the repairs.[20] •

Sometimes, the lapse of time and the change in circumstances surrounding the contract make it substantially more burdensome for the parties to perform the promised acts. In that situation, the contract is discharged. **CASE EXAMPLE 11.21** In 1942, actor Gene Autry was drafted into the U.S. Army. Being drafted rendered his contract with a Hollywood movie company temporarily impossible to perform, and it was suspended until the end of World War II in 1945. When Autry got out of the army, the purchasing power of the dollar had declined so much that performance of the contract would have been substantially burdensome to him. Therefore, the contract was discharged.[21] •

Commercial Impracticability   Courts may also excuse parties from their performance when it becomes much more difficult or expensive than the parties originally contemplated at the time the contract was formed. For someone to invoke the doctrine of **commercial impracticability** successfully, however, the anticipated performance must become *significantly* difficult or costly.[22] The added burden of performing not only must be extreme but also *must not have been known by the parties when the contract was made.* (See this chapter's *Beyond Our Borders* feature for a discussion of Germany's approach to impracticability and impossibility of performance.)

Frustration of Purpose   Closely allied with the doctrine of commercial impracticability is the doctrine of **frustration of purpose.** In principle, a contract will be discharged if supervening circumstances make it impossible to attain the purpose both parties had in mind when they made the contract. As with commercial impracticability and impossibility, the supervening event must not have been reasonably foreseeable at the time the contract was formed.

There are some differences between the doctrines, however. Commercial impracticability usually involves an event that increases the cost or difficulty of performance. In contrast, frustration of purpose typically involves an event that decreases the value of what a party receives under the contract.

See Exhibit 11–2 that follows for a summary of the ways in which a contract can be discharged.

> **Commercial Impracticability** A doctrine that may excuse the duty to perform a contract when performance becomes much more difficult or costly due to forces that neither party could control or contemplate at the time the contract was formed.

> **Frustration of Purpose** A court-created doctrine under which a party to a contract will be relieved of his or her duty to perform when the objective purpose for performance no longer exists due to reasons beyond that party's control.

---

20. *Payne v. Hurwitz,* 978 So.2d 1000 (La.App. 1st Cir. 2008).
21. *Autry v. Republic Productions,* 30 Cal.2d 144, 180 P.2d 888 (1947).
22. *Restatement (Second) of Contracts,* Section 264.

BEYOND OUR BORDERS

Impossibility or Impracticability of Performance in Germany

In the United States, when a party alleges that contract performance is impossible or impracticable because of circumstances unforeseen at the time the contract was formed, a court will either discharge the party's contractual obligations or hold the party to the contract. If the court agrees that the contract is impossible or impracticable to perform, the remedy is to rescind (cancel) the contract. Under German law, however, a court may reform a contract in light of economic developments. If an unforeseen event affects the foundation of the agreement, the court can alter the contract's terms to align with the parties' original expectations, thus making the contract fair to the parties.

Critical Thinking
When a contract becomes impossible or impracticable to perform, which remedy would a businessperson prefer—rescission or reformation? Explain your answer.

Exhibit 11–2 Contract Discharge

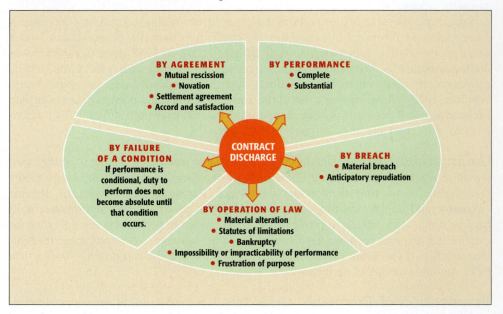

Damages

A breach of contract entitles the nonbreaching party to sue for monetary damages. Damages are designed to compensate a party for harm suffered as a result of another's wrongful act. In the context of contract law, damages compensate the nonbreaching party for the loss of the bargain. Often, courts say that innocent parties are to be placed in the position they would have occupied had the contract been fully performed.

Types of Damages

There are four broad categories of damages:

1. Compensatory (to cover direct losses and costs).
2. Consequential (to cover indirect and foreseeable losses).
3. Punitive (to punish and deter wrongdoing).
4. Nominal (to recognize wrongdoing when no monetary loss is shown).

Compensatory Damages   Damages that compensate the nonbreaching party for the *loss of the bargain* are known as *compensatory damages.* These damages compensate the injured party only for damages actually sustained and proved to have arisen directly from the loss of the bargain caused by the breach of contract. They simply replace what was lost because of the wrong or damage and, for this reason, are often said to "make the person whole." Courts will not award damages in an amount that leaves the nonbreaching party in a better position than he or she would have been in if the contract had not been breached.
CASE EXAMPLE 11.22   Janet Murley was the vice president of marketing at Hallmark Cards, Inc., until Hallmark eliminated her position as part of a corporate restructuring. Murley and Hallmark entered into a separation agreement under which she agreed not to work in the greeting card industry for eighteen months and not to disclose or use any of Hallmark's confidential information. In exchange, Hallmark gave Murley a $735,000 severance payment.

After eighteen months, Murley took a job with Recycled Paper Greetings (RPG) for $125,000 and disclosed confidential Hallmark information to RPG. Hallmark sued for breach of contract and won, and the jury awarded $860,000 in damages (the $735,000 severance payment and $125,000 that Murley received from RPG). Murley appealed. The appellate court held that Hallmark was only entitled to the return of the $735,000 severance payment. Hallmark was not entitled to the other $125,000 because that amount would leave Hallmark better off than it would have been if Murley had not breached the contract.[23] ●

Standard Measure   The standard measure of compensatory damages is the difference between the value of the breaching party's promised performance under the contract and the value of her or his actual performance. This amount is reduced by any loss that the injured party has avoided, however.

EXAMPLE 11.23   Randall contracts to perform certain services exclusively for Hernandez during the month of March for $4,000. Hernandez cancels the contract and is in breach. Randall is able to find another job during March but can earn only $3,000. He can sue Hernandez for breach and recover $1,000 as compensatory damages. Randall can also recover from Hernandez the amount that he spent to find the other job. ●

Learning Objective 4
What is the standard measure of compensatory damages when a contract is breached?

Expenses that are caused directly by a breach of contract—such as those incurred to obtain performance from another source—are known as *incidental damages*. Note that the measure of compensatory damages often varies by type of contract. (See the *Insight into Ethics* feature that follows for a discussion of the effect of breaching the terms of use in an online service contract.) Certain types of contracts deserve special mention.

---

23. *Hallmark Cards, Inc. v. Murley*, 703 F.3d 456 (8th Cir. 2013).

INSIGHT INTO ETHICS

THE EFFECT OF BREACHING AN ONLINE TESTING SERVICE'S TERMS OF USE

Increasingly, online testing services are available for almost any subject. Employers, for example, use online behavioral testing to evaluate the employability of applicants. Schools and counseling services can administer an online test to assess the probability that an adolescent is chemically dependent. California uses an online test to establish a driver impairment index for those who have been arrested for drunk driving.

Typical Terms and Conditions of Use

The majority of online testing services have a relatively short list of terms and conditions for using their tests. For example, most testing services require that fees be paid for each test and for its scoring.

Also, the school, employer, or other entity that is using the online test usually must agree that the persons who administer the test are qualified. In addition, the test user must agree that no decision or diagnosis can be made solely on the basis of the online test results.

Violation of the Online Terms

If the test user violates any of the terms and conditions, the implied contract with the testing service has been breached.

The following is a typical provision from an online testing service:

> When You Breach This Agreement: Each time you administer a test, the agreement granted herein will automatically terminate once the scoring has been provided to you. The Company has the right to terminate the authorization granted to you if you breach the terms and conditions of use for any test or if you violate the terms and conditions and obligations under this agreement. Once you breach your duties under this agreement, the Company will suffer immediate and irreparable damages. You therefore acknowledge that injunctive relief will be appropriate.

For Critical Analysis
Insight into the Social Environment
What possible "immediate and irreparable" damages might an online testing service experience if the test user breaches the contract?

Under what circumstances will a court award monetary damages for a breached sale-of-land contract?

(iStockphoto.com/Saturated)

Sale of Goods   In a contract for the sale of goods, the usual measure of compensatory damages is an amount equal to the difference between the contract price and the market price.[24]

EXAMPLE 11.24   Medik Laboratories contracts to buy ten model UTS network servers from Cal Industries for $4,000 each. Cal Industries, however, fails to deliver the ten servers to Medik. The market price of the servers at the time Medik learns of the breach is $4,500. Therefore, Medik's measure of damages is $5,000 (10 × $500), plus any incidental damages (expenses) caused by the breach. •

When the buyer breaches and the seller has not yet produced the goods, compensatory damages normally equal lost profits on the sale, not the difference between the contract price and the market price.

Sale of Land   Ordinarily, because each parcel of land is unique, the remedy for a seller's breach of a contract for a sale of real estate is specific performance. The buyer is awarded the parcel of property for which she or he bargained (*specific performance* will be discussed more fully later in this chapter). When the buyer is the party in breach, the measure of damages is typically the difference between the contract price and the market price of the land. The same measure is used when specific performance is not available (because the seller has sold the property to someone else, for example). The majority of states follow this rule.

A minority of states follow a different rule when the seller breaches the contract and the breach is not deliberate (intentional). These states limit the prospective buyer's damages to a refund of any down payment made plus any expenses incurred (such as fees for title searches, attorneys, and escrows). Thus, the minority rule effectively returns purchasers to the positions they occupied prior to the sale, rather than giving them the benefit of the bargain.

Construction Contracts   The measure of damages in a building or construction contract varies depending on which party breaches and when the breach occurs.

1. *Breach by owner.* The owner may breach at three different stages—before performance has begun, during performance, or after performance has been completed. If the owner breaches *before performance has begun,* the contractor can recover only the profits that would have been made on the contract (that is, the total contract price less the cost of materials and labor).

     If the owner breaches *during performance,* the contractor can recover the profits plus the costs incurred in partially constructing the building. If the owner breaches *after the construction has been completed,* the contractor can recover the entire contract price, plus interest.

2. *Breach by contractor.* When the construction contractor breaches the contract—either by failing to begin construction or by stopping work partway through the project—the measure of damages is the cost of completion. The cost of completion includes reasonable compensation for any delay in performance. If the contractor finishes late, the measure of damages is the loss of use.

3. *Breach by both owner and contractor.* When the performance of both parties—the construction contractor and the owner—falls short of what their contract required, the courts attempt to strike a fair balance in awarding damages.
     CASE EXAMPLE 11.25   Jamison Well Drilling, Inc., contracted to drill a well for Ed Pfeifer for $4,130. Jamison drilled the well and installed a storage tank. The well did

---

24. More specifically, the amount is the difference between the contract price and the market price at the time and place at which the goods were to be delivered or tendered. See Sections 2–708 and 2–713 of the Uniform Commercial Code (UCC).

not comply with state health department requirements, however, and failed repeated tests for bacteria. The health department ordered the well to be abandoned and sealed. Pfeifer used the storage tank but paid Jamison nothing. Jamison filed a suit to recover. The court held that Jamison was entitled to $970 for the storage tank but was not entitled to the full contract price because the well was not usable.[25] ●

The rules concerning the measurement of damages in breached construction contracts are summarized in Exhibit 11–3 that follows.

Consequential Damages   Foreseeable damages that result from a party's breach of contract are called **consequential damages,** or *special damages*. They differ from compensatory damages in that they are caused by special circumstances beyond the contract itself. They flow from the consequences, or results, of a breach. When a seller fails to deliver goods, knowing that the buyer is planning to use or resell those goods immediately, a court may award consequential damages for the loss of profits from the planned resale.

EXAMPLE 11.26   Marty contracts to buy a certain quantity of Quench, a specialty sports drink, from Nathan. Nathan knows that Marty has contracted with Ruthie to resell and ship the Quench within hours of its receipt. The beverage will then be sold to fans attending the Super Bowl. Nathan fails to timely deliver the Quench. Marty can recover the consequential damages—the loss of profits from the planned resale to Ruthie—caused by the nondelivery. (If Marty purchases Quench from another vender, he can also recover compensatory damages for the difference between the contract wholesale price and the market wholesale price.) ●

For the nonbreaching party to recover consequential damages, the breaching party must have known (or had reason to know) that special circumstances would cause the nonbreaching party to suffer an additional loss.

Punitive Damages   Punitive damages generally are not awarded in lawsuits for breach of contract. Because punitive damages are designed to punish a wrongdoer and set an example to deter similar conduct in the future, they have no legitimate place in contract law. A contract is simply a civil relationship between the parties. The law may compensate one party for the loss of the bargain—no more and no less. When a person's actions cause both a breach of contract and a tort (such as fraud), punitive damages may be available. Overall, though, punitive damages are almost never available in contract disputes.

Nominal Damages   When no actual damage or financial loss results from a breach of contract and only a technical injury is involved, the court may award *nominal damages* to the innocent party. Awards of nominal damages are often small, such as one

Consequential Damages   Special damages that compensate for a loss that does not directly or immediately result from the breach (for example, lost profits). For the plaintiff to collect consequential damages, they must have been reasonably foreseeable at the time the breach or injury occurred.

---

25. *Jamison Well Drilling, Inc. v. Pfeifer,* 2011 Ohio 521 (2011).

Exhibit 11–3 Measurement of Damages—Breach of Construction Contracts

PARTY IN BREACH	TIME OF BREACH	MEASUREMENT OF DAMAGES
Owner	Before construction has begun.	Profits (contract price less cost of materials and labor).
Owner	During construction.	Profits, plus costs incurred up to time of breach.
Owner	After construction is completed.	Full contract price, plus interest.
Contractor	Before construction has begun.	Cost in excess of contract price to complete work.
Contractor	Before construction is completed.	Generally, all costs incurred by owner to complete.

Mitigation of Damages A rule requiring
a plaintiff to do whatever is reasonable
to minimize the damages caused by the
defendant.

dollar, but they do establish that the defendant acted wrongfully. Most lawsuits for nominal damages are brought as a matter of principle under the theory that a breach has occurred and some damages must be imposed regardless of actual loss.

Mitigation of Damages

In most situations, when a breach of contract occurs, the innocent injured party is held to a duty to mitigate, or reduce, the damages that he or she suffers. Under this doctrine of **mitigation of damages,** the duty owed depends on the nature of the contract.

For instance, some states require a landlord to use reasonable means to find a new tenant if a tenant abandons the premises and fails to pay rent. If an acceptable tenant is found, the landlord is required to lease the premises to this tenant to mitigate the damages recoverable from the former tenant.

The former tenant is still liable for the difference between the amount of the rent under the original lease and the rent received from the new tenant. If the landlord has not taken reasonable steps to find a new tenant, a court will likely reduce any award made by the amount of rent the landlord could have received had he or she done so.

Liquidated Damages versus Penalties

Liquidated Damages An amount,
stipulated in a contract, that the parties to the
contract believe to be a reasonable estimate
of the damages that will occur in the event of
a breach.

Penalty A sum inserted into a contract, not
as a measure of compensation for its breach
but rather as a punishment for a default.
The agreement as to the amount will not be
enforced, and recovery will be limited to actual
damages.

A **liquidated damages** provision in a contract specifies that a certain dollar amount is to be paid in the event of a *future* default or breach of contract. (*Liquidated* means determined, settled, or fixed.)

Liquidated damages differ from penalties. Although a **penalty** also specifies a certain amount to be paid in the event of a default or breach of contract, it is designed to penalize the breaching party, not to make the innocent party whole. Liquidated damages provisions usually are enforceable. In contrast, if a court finds that a provision calls for a penalty, the agreement as to the amount will not be enforced, and recovery will be limited to actual damages.

Enforceability
To determine if a particular provision is for liquidated damages or for a penalty, a court must answer two questions:

1. When the contract was entered into, was it apparent that damages would be difficult to estimate in the event of a breach?
2. Was the amount set as damages a reasonable estimate and not excessive?

If the answers to both questions are yes, the provision normally will be enforced. If either answer is no, the provision usually will not be enforced.

CASE EXAMPLE 11.27   James Haber contracted with B-Sharp Musical Productions, Inc., to provide a particular band to perform at his son's bar mitzvah for $30,000. The contract contained a liquidated damages clause under which if Haber canceled within ninety days of the date of the bar mitzvah, he would still owe $30,000 to B-Sharp. If he canceled more than ninety days beforehand, Haber would owe B-Sharp half of that amount ($15,000).

Haber canceled less than ninety days before the bar mitzvah and refused to pay B-Sharp the $25,000 balance due under the contract. B-Sharp sued. The court held that the liquidated damages clause was enforceable. The court reasoned that the expense and possibility of rebooking a canceled performance could not be determined at the time of contracting and that the clause provided a reasonable amount of damages.[26] •

Liquidated Damages Common in Certain Contracts
Liquidated damages provisions are frequently used in construction contracts. For instance, a provision

---

26. *B-Sharp Musical Productions, Inc. v. Haber,* 27 Misc.3d 41, 899 N.Y.S.2d 792 (2010).

requiring a construction contractor to pay $300 for every day he or she is late in completing the project is a liquidated damages provision.

Such provisions are also common in contracts for the sale of goods. In addition, contracts with entertainers and professional athletes often include liquidated damages provisions. **EXAMPLE 11.28** A television network settled its contract dispute with *Tonight Show* host Conan O'Brien for $33 million. The amount of the settlement was somewhat less than the $40 million O'Brien could have received under a liquidated damages clause in his contract. •

Waiver of Breach

Under certain circumstances, a nonbreaching party may be willing to accept a defective performance of the contract. This knowing relinquishment of a legal right (that is, the right to require satisfactory and full performance) is called a **waiver.**

When a waiver of a breach of contract occurs, the party waiving the breach cannot take any later action on it. In effect, the waiver erases the past breach, and the contract continues as if the breach had never occurred. Of course, the waiver of breach of contract extends only to the matter waived and not to the whole contract. Businesspersons often waive breaches of contract to obtain whatever benefit is still possible out of the contract.

Ordinarily, a waiver by a contracting party will not operate to waive subsequent, additional, or future breaches of contract. This is always true when the subsequent breaches are unrelated to the first breach. A waiver can extend to subsequent defective performance if a reasonable person would conclude that similar defective performance in the future will be acceptable. The party who has rendered defective or less-than-full performance remains liable for the damages caused by the breach of contract. In effect, the waiver operates to keep the contract going.

Waiver An intentional, knowing relinquishment of a legal right.

Equitable Remedies

Sometimes, damages are an inadequate remedy for a breach of contract. In these situations, the nonbreaching party may ask the court for an equitable remedy. Equitable remedies include rescission and restitution, specific performance, and reformation.

Learning Objective 5
What equitable remedies can a court grant, and in what circumstances will a court consider granting them?

Rescission and Restitution

Rescission is essentially an action to undo, or terminate, a contract—to return the contracting parties to the positions they occupied prior to the transaction.[27] When fraud, a mistake, duress, undue influence, misrepresentation, or lack of capacity to contract is present, unilateral rescission is available. Rescission may also be available by statute. The failure of one party to perform entitles the other party to rescind the contract. The rescinding party must give prompt notice to the breaching party.

Generally, to rescind a contract, both parties must make **restitution** to each other by returning goods, property, or funds previously conveyed. If the property or goods can be returned, they must be. If the goods or property have been consumed, restitution must be made in an equivalent dollar amount.

Essentially, restitution involves the plaintiff's recapture of a benefit conferred on the defendant that has unjustly enriched her or him. **EXAMPLE 11.29** Katie contracts with Mikhail to design a house for her. Katie pays Mikhail $9,000 and agrees to make two more payments of

Restitution An equitable remedy under which a person is restored to his or her original position prior to loss or injury, or placed in the position he or she would have been in had the breach not occurred.

---

27. The rescission discussed here is *unilateral* rescission, in which only one party wants to undo the contract. In mutual rescission both parties agree to undo the contract. Mutual rescission discharges the contract. Unilateral rescission generally is available as a remedy for breach of contract.

$9,000 (for a total of $27,000) as the design progresses. The next day, Mikhail calls Katie and tells her that he has taken a position with a large architectural firm in another state and cannot design the house. Katie decides to hire another architect that afternoon. Katie can obtain restitution of the $9,000. ●

Restitution may be appropriate when a contract is rescinded, but the right to restitution is not limited to rescission cases. Because an award of restitution basically returns something to its rightful owner, a party can seek restitution in actions for breach of contract, tort actions, and other types of actions.

Specific Performance

Specific Performance An equitable remedy requiring exactly the performance that was specified in a contract; usually granted only when money damages would be an inadequate remedy and the subject matter of the contract is unique (for example, real property).

The equitable remedy of **specific performance** calls for the performance of the act promised in the contract. This remedy is attractive to a nonbreaching party because it provides the exact bargain promised in the contract. It also avoids some of the problems inherent in a suit for damages, such as collecting a judgment and arranging another contract. In addition, the actual performance may be more valuable than the monetary damages.

Normally, however, specific performance will not be granted unless the party's legal remedy (monetary damages) is inadequate.[28] For this reason, contracts for the sale of goods rarely qualify for specific performance. The legal remedy—monetary damages—is ordinarily adequate in such situations because substantially identical goods can be bought or sold in the market. Only if the goods are unique will a court grant specific performance. For instance, paintings, sculptures, or rare books or coins are so unique that monetary damages will not enable a buyer to obtain substantially identical substitutes in the market.

(dimdimich/iStockphoto.com)

Why would specific performance be preferred when antiques are the item in dispute?

Sale of Land   A court may grant specific performance to a buyer in an action for a breach of contract involving the sale of land. In this situation, the legal remedy of monetary damages may not compensate the buyer adequately because every parcel of land is unique: the same land in the same location obviously cannot be obtained elsewhere. Only when specific performance is unavailable (such as when the seller has sold the property to someone else) will monetary damages be awarded instead.

Contracts for Personal Services   Contracts for personal services require one party to work personally for another party. Courts generally refuse to grant specific performance of personal-service contracts because to order a party to perform personal services against his or her will amounts to a type of involuntary servitude.[29]

Moreover, the courts do not want to monitor contracts for personal services, which usually require the exercise of personal judgment or talent. **EXAMPLE 11.30** Nicole contracts with a surgeon to perform surgery to remove a tumor on her brain. If he refuses, the court would not compel (nor would Nicole want) the surgeon to perform under those circumstances. A court cannot ensure meaningful performance in such a situation. ●

If a contract is not deemed personal, the remedy at law of monetary damages may be adequate if substantially identical service (such as lawn mowing) is available from other persons.

---

28. *Restatement (Second) of Contracts*, Section 359.
29. Involuntary servitude, or slavery, is contrary to the public policy expressed in the Thirteenth Amendment to the U.S. Constitution.

Reformation

Reformation is an equitable remedy used when the parties have *imperfectly* expressed their agreement in writing. Reformation allows a court to rewrite the contract to reflect the parties' true intentions.

Exhibit 11–4 that follows graphically summarizes the remedies, including reformation, that are available to the nonbreaching party.

Reformation A court-ordered correction of a written contract so that it reflects the true intentions of the parties.

When Fraud or Mutual Mistake Is Present
Courts order reformation most often when fraud or mutual mistake (for example, a clerical error) is present. Typically, a party seeks reformation so that some other remedy may then be pursued.

EXAMPLE 11.31 If Carson contracts to buy a forklift from Yoshie but their contract mistakenly refers to a crane, a mutual mistake has occurred. Accordingly, a court can reform the contract so that it conforms to the parties' intentions and accurately refers to the forklift being sold. •

Written Contract Incorrectly States the Parties' Oral Agreement
A court will also reform a contract when two parties enter into a binding oral contract but later make an error when they attempt to put the terms into writing. Normally, a court will allow into evidence the correct terms of the oral contract, thereby reforming the written contract.

Covenants Not to Compete
Courts also may reform contracts when the parties have executed a written covenant not to compete (discussed in Chapter 10). If the covenant is for a valid and legitimate purpose (such as the sale of a business) but the area or time restraints of the covenant are unreasonable, reformation may occur. Some courts will reform the restraints by making them reasonable and then will enforce the entire contract as reformed. Other courts, however, will throw out the entire restrictive covenant as illegal.

Contract Provisions Limiting Remedies

A contract may include provisions stating that no damages can be recovered for certain types of breaches or that damages will be limited to a maximum amount. The contract may also provide that the only remedy for breach is replacement, repair, or refund of the purchase price. The contract may also provide that one party can seek injunctive relief if the other party breaches the contract. Provisions stating that no damages can be recovered are called *exculpatory clauses*

Exhibit 11–4 Remedies for Breach of Contract

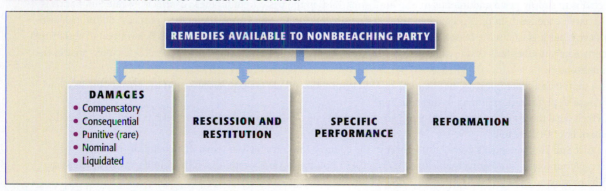

(see Chapter 10). Provisions that affect the availability of certain remedies are called *limitation-of-liability clauses.*

The UCC Allows Sales Contracts to Limit Remedies

The Uniform Commercial Code (UCC) provides that in a contract for the sale of goods, remedies can be limited. We will examine the UCC provisions on limited remedies in Chapter 12.

Enforceability of Limitation-of-Liability Clauses

Whether a limitation-of-liability clause in a contract will be enforced depends on the type of breach that is excused by the provision. Normally, a provision excluding liability for fraudulent or intentional injury will not be enforced. Likewise, a clause excluding liability for illegal acts, acts that are contrary to public policy, or violations of law will not be enforced. A clause that excludes liability for negligence may be enforced in some situations when the parties have roughly equal bargaining positions.

CASE EXAMPLE 11.32   Engineering Consulting Services, Ltd. (ECS), contracted with RSN Properties, Inc, a real estate developer. ECS was to perform soil studies for $2,200 and render an opinion on the use of septic systems in a particular subdivision being developed. A clause in the contract limited ECS's liability to RSN to the value of the engineering services or the sum of $50,000, whichever was greater.

ECS concluded that most of the lots were suitable for septic systems, so RSN proceeded with the development. RSN constructed the roads and water lines to the subdivision in reliance on ECS's conclusions, which turned out to be incorrect. RSN sued ECS for breach of contract and argued that the limitation of liability was against public policy and unenforceable. The court, however, enforced the limitation-of-liability clause as "a reasonable allocation of risks in an arm's-length business transaction."[30] ●

---

30. *RSN Properties, Inc. v. Engineering Consulting Services, Ltd.*, 301 Ga.App. 52, 686 S.E.2d 853 (2009).

Reviewing . . . Contract Performance, Breach, and Remedies

Val's Foods signs a contract to buy 1,500 pounds of basil from Sun Farms, a small organic herb grower, as long as an independent organization inspects the crop and certifies that it contains no pesticide or herbicide residue. Val's has a contract with several restaurant chains to supply pesto and intends to use Sun Farms' basil in the pesto to fulfill these contracts. While Sun Farms is preparing to harvest the basil, an unexpected hailstorm destroys half the crop. Sun Farms attempts to purchase additional basil from other farms, but it is late in the season and the price is twice the normal market price. Sun Farms is too small to absorb this cost and immediately notifies Val's that it will not fulfill the contract. Using the information presented in the chapter, answer the following questions.

1. Suppose that the basil does not pass the chemical-residue inspection. Which concept discussed in the chapter might allow Val's to refuse to perform the contract in this situation?

2. Under which legal theory or theories might Sun Farms claim that its obligation under the contract has been discharged by operation of law? Discuss fully.

3. Suppose that Sun Farms contacts every basil grower in the country and buys the last remaining chemical-free basil anywhere. Nevertheless, Sun Farms is able to ship only 1,475 pounds to Val's. Would this fulfill Sun Farms' obligations to Val's? Why or why not?

4. Now suppose that Sun Farms sells its operations to Happy Valley Farms. As a part of the sale, all three parties agree that Happy Valley will provide the basil as stated under the original contract. What is this type of agreement called?

_____

Debate This The doctrine of commercial impracticability should be abolished.

Key Terms

anticipatory repudiation 296
assignment 290
bilateral mistake 287
breach of contract 295
commercial impracticability 303
condition 293
condition precedent 293
consequential damages 307

covenant not to sue 299
delegation 290
discharge 292
frustration of purpose 303
impossibility of performance 300
intended beneficiary 292
liquidated damages 308
mitigation of damages 308

mutual rescission 297
novation 297
penalty 308
performance 292
privity of contract 290
release 298
reformation 311

restitution 309
specific performance 310
tender 293
third party beneficiary 292
unilateral mistake 287
voluntary consent 286
waiver 309

Chapter Summary: Contract Performance, Breach, and Remedies

Voluntary Consent	1. *Mistakes*—
	a. *Unilateral mistakes*—Generally, the party making the mistake is bound by the contract *unless* (a) the other party knows or should have known of the mistake or (b) the mistake is an inadvertent mathematical error—such as an error in addition or subtraction—committed without gross negligence.
	b. *Bilateral (mutual) mistakes*—When both parties are mistaken about the same material fact, such as identity, either party can avoid the contract. If the mistake concerns value or quality, either party can enforce the contract.
	2. *Fraudulent misrepresentation*—When fraud occurs, usually the innocent party can enforce or avoid the contract. To obtain damages, the innocent party must have suffered an injury.
	3. *Undue influence*—Undue influence arises from special relationships in which one party can greatly influence another party, thus overcoming that party's free will. Usually, the contract is voidable.
	4. *Duress*—Duress is the use of a threat, such as the threat of violence or serious economic loss, to force a party to enter a contract. The party forced to enter the contract can rescind the contract.
Third Party Rights	1. *Assignments*—An assignment is the transfer of rights under a contract to a third party. The third party to whom the rights are assigned has a right to demand performance from the other original party to the contract. Generally, all rights can be assigned, but there are a few exceptions, such as when a statute prohibits assignment or when the contract calls for personal services.
	2. *Delegations*—A delegation is the transfer of duties under a contract to a third party, who then assumes the obligation of performing the contractual duties previously held by the one making the delegation. As a general rule, any duty can be delegated, except in a few situations, such as when the contract expressly prohibits delegation or when performance depends on the personal skills of the original party.
	3. *Third party beneficiaries*—A third party beneficiary is one who benefits from a contract between two other parties. If the party was an intended beneficiary, then the third party has legal rights and can sue the promisor directly to enforce the contract. If the contract benefits the third party unintentionally, then the third party cannot sue to enforce the contract.
Performance and Discharge	1. *Conditions of performance*—Contract obligations are sometimes subject to conditions. A condition is a possible future event, the occurrence or nonoccurrence of which will trigger the performance of a contract obligation or terminate an existing obligation. A condition that must be fulfilled before a party's promise becomes absolute is called a *condition precedent*.
	2. *Discharge by performance*—A contract may be discharged by complete (strict) performance or by substantial performance. In some instances, performance must be to the satisfaction of another. Totally inadequate performance constitutes a material breach of contract. An anticipatory repudiation of a contract allows the other party to sue immediately for breach of contract.

Continued

Chapter Summary: Contract Performance, Breach, and Remedies—Continued

Performance and Discharge—Continued	3. *Discharge by agreement*—Parties may agree to discharge their contractual obligations in several ways: a. *By rescission*—The parties mutually agree to rescind (cancel) the contract. b. *By novation*—A new party is substituted for one of the primary parties to a contract. c. *By settlement agreement*—The parties agree to a new contract that replaces the old contract as a means of settling a dispute. d. *By accord and satisfaction*—The parties agree to render and accept performance different from that on which they originally agreed. e. *By release*—One party forfeits the right to pursue a legal claim against the other, barring further recovery. f. *By covenant not to sue*—The parties substitute a contractual obligation for some other type of legal action. 4. *Discharge by operation of law*—Parties' obligations under contracts may be discharged by operation of law owing to one of the following: a. Contract alteration. b. Statutes of limitations. c. Bankruptcy. d. Impossibility or impracticability of performance, including frustration of purpose.
Damages for Breach of Contract	Damages are the legal remedy designed to compensate the nonbreaching party for the loss of the bargain. By awarding monetary damages, the court tries to place the parties in the positions that they would have occupied had the contract been fully performed. 1. *Compensatory damages*—Damages that compensate the nonbreaching party for injuries actually sustained and proved to have arisen directly from the loss of the bargain resulting from the breach of contract. a. In breached contracts for the sale of goods, the usual measure of compensatory damages is the difference between the contract price and the market price. b. In breached contracts for the sale of land, the measure of damages is ordinarily the same as in contracts for the sale of goods. 2. *Consequential damages*—Damages resulting from special circumstances beyond the contract itself—the damages flow only from the consequences of a breach. For a party to recover consequential damages, the damages must be the foreseeable result of a breach of contract, and the breaching party must have known at the time the contract was formed that special circumstances existed that would cause the nonbreaching party to incur additional loss on breach of the contract. 3. *Mitigation of damages*—The nonbreaching party frequently has a duty to *mitigate* (lessen or reduce) the damages incurred as a result of the contract's breach. 4. *Liquidated damages*—Damages that may be specified in a contract as the amount to be paid to the nonbreaching party in the event the contract is breached in the future. Clauses providing for liquidated damages are enforced if the damages were difficult to estimate at the time the contract was formed and if the amount stipulated is reasonable. If the amount is construed to be a penalty, the clause will not be enforced. 5. *Waiver of breach*—If a party willingly accepts defective performance of a contract, this may operate as a waiver of the breach. The party waiving the breach cannot take later action on it. The party that rendered defective performance remains liable for any damages caused by the breach.
Equitable Remedies	1. *Rescission*—A remedy whereby a contract is canceled and the parties are restored to the positions that they occupied prior to the transaction. Available when fraud, a mistake, duress, or failure of consideration is present. The rescinding party must give prompt notice of the rescission to the breaching party. 2. *Restitution*—When a contract is rescinded, both parties must make restitution to each other by returning the goods, property, or funds previously conveyed. Restitution prevents the unjust enrichment of the parties. 3. *Specific performance*—An equitable remedy calling for the performance of the act promised in the contract. This remedy is available only in special situations—such as those involving contracts for the sale of unique goods or land—in which monetary damages would be an inadequate remedy. Specific performance is not available as a remedy in breached contracts for personal services. 4. *Reformation*—An equitable remedy allowing a contract to be "reformed," or rewritten, to reflect the parties' true intentions. Available when an agreement is imperfectly expressed in writing.
Contract Provisions Limiting Remedies	A contract may provide that no damages (or only a limited amount of damages) can be recovered in the event the contract is breached. Clauses excluding liability for fraudulent or intentional injury or for illegal acts cannot be enforced. Clauses excluding liability for negligence may be enforced if both parties hold roughly equal bargaining power.

Issue Spotters

1. Simmons finds a stone in his pasture that he believes to be quartz. Jenson, who also believes that the stone is quartz, contracts to purchase it for $10. Just before delivery, the stone is discovered to be a diamond worth $1,000. Is the contract enforceable? Why or why not? (See *Voluntary Consent.*)
2. Greg contracts to build a storage shed for Haney, who pays Greg in advance, but Greg completes only half the work. Haney pays Ipswich $500 to finish the shed. If Haney sues Greg, what would be the measure of recovery? (See *Damages.*)

—**Check your answers to the Issue Spotters against the answers provided in Appendix D at the end of this text.**

For Review

1. What are the elements of fraudulent misrepresentation?
2. What is substantial performance?
3. When is a breach considered material, and what effect does that have on the other party's duty to perform a contract?
4. What is the standard measure of compensatory damages when a contract is breached?
5. What equitable remedies can a court grant, and in what circumstances will a court consider granting them?

Business Scenarios and Case Problems

11–1. Conditions of Performance. The Caplans contract with Faithful Construction, Inc., to build a house for them for $360,000. The specifications state "all plumbing bowls and fixtures . . . to be Crane brand." The Caplans leave on vacation, and during their absence, Faithful is unable to buy and install Crane plumbing fixtures. Instead, Faithful installs Kohler brand fixtures, an equivalent in the industry. On completion of the building contract, the Caplans inspect the work, discover the substitution, and refuse to accept the house, claiming Faithful has breached the conditions set forth in the specifications. Discuss fully the Caplans' claim. (See *Performance and Discharge.*)

11–2. Impossibility of Performance. In the following situations, certain events take place after the contracts are formed. Discuss which of these contracts are discharged because the events render the contracts impossible to perform. (See *Performance and Discharge.*)

1. Jimenez, a famous singer, contracts to perform in your nightclub. He dies prior to performance.
2. Raglione contracts to sell you her land. Just before title is to be transferred, she dies.
3. Oppenheim contracts to sell you one thousand bushels of apples from her orchard in the state of Washington. Because of a severe frost, she is unable to deliver the apples.
4. Maxwell contracts to lease a service station for ten years. His principal income is from the sale of gasoline. Because of an oil embargo by foreign oil-producing nations, gasoline is rationed, cutting sharply into Maxwell's gasoline sales. He cannot make his lease payments.

11–3. Third Party Beneficiaries. Wilken owes Rivera $2,000. Howie promises Wilken that he will pay Rivera the $2,000 in return for Wilken's promise to give Howie's children guitar lessons. Is Rivera an intended beneficiary of the Howie-Wilken contract? Explain. (See *Third Party Rights.*)

11–4. Fraudulent Misrepresentation. Ricky and Sherry Wilcox hired Esprit Log and Timber Frame Homes to build a log house, which the Wilcoxes intended to sell. They paid Esprit $125,260 for materials and services. They eventually sold the home for $1,620,000 but sued Esprit due to construction delays. The logs were supposed to arrive at the construction site precut and predrilled, but that did not happen. So it took five extra months to build the house while the logs were cut and drilled one by one. The Wilcoxes claimed that the interest they paid on a loan for the extra construction time cost them about $200,000. The jury agreed and awarded them that much in damages, plus $250,000 in punitive damages and $20,000 in attorneys' fees. Esprit appealed, claiming that the evidence did not support the verdict because the Wilcoxes had sold the house for a good price. Is Esprit's argument credible? Why or why not? How should the court rule? [*Esprit Log and Timber Frame Homes, Inc. v. Wilcox,* 302 Ga. App. 550, 691 S.E.2d 344 (2010)] (See *Voluntary Consent.*)

11–5. ⚖ **Business Case Problem with Sample Answer—Consequential Damages.** After submitting the high bid at a foreclosure sale, David Simard entered into a contract to purchase real property in Maryland for $192,000. Simard defaulted (failed to pay) on the contract. A state court ordered the property to be resold at Simard's expense, as required by state law. The property was then resold for $163,000, but the second purchaser also defaulted on his contract. The court then ordered a second resale, resulting in a final price of $130,000. Assuming that Simard is liable for consequential damages, what is the extent of his liability? Is he liable for losses and expenses related to the first resale? If so, is he also liable for losses and expenses related to the second resale? Why or why not? [*Burson v. Simard,* 35 A.3d 1154 (Md. 2012)] (See *Damages.*)

—**For a sample answer to Problem 11–5, go to Appendix E at the end of this text.**

11–6. Liquidated Damages. Cuesport Properties, LLC, sold a condominium in Anne Arundel County, Maryland, to Critical Developments, LLC. As part of the sale, Cuesport agreed to build a wall between Critical Developments' unit and an adjacent unit within thirty days of closing. If Cuesport failed to do so, it was to pay $126 per day until completion. This was an estimate of the amount of rent that Critical Developments would lose until the wall was finished and the unit could be rented. Actual damages were otherwise difficult to estimate at the time of the contract. The wall was built on time, but without a county permit, and it did not comply with the county building code. Critical Developments did not modify the wall to comply with the code until 260 days after the date of the contract deadline for completion of the wall. Does Cuesport have to pay Critical Developments $126 for each of the 260 days? Explain. [*Cuesport Properties, LLC v. Critical Developments, LLC,* 209 Md.App. 607, 61 A.3d 91 (2013)] (See *Damages.*)

11–7. Material Breach. The Northeast Independent School District in Bexar County, Texas, hired STR Constructors, Ltd., to renovate a middle school. STR subcontracted the tile work in the school's kitchen to Newman Tile, Inc. (NTI). The project had already fallen behind schedule. As a result, STR allowed other workers to walk over and damage the newly installed tile before it had cured, forcing NTI to constantly redo its work. Despite NTI's requests for payment, STR remitted only half the amount due under their contract. When the school district refused to accept the kitchen, including the tile work, STR told NTI to quickly make the repairs. A week later, STR terminated their contract. Did STR breach the contract with NTI? Explain. [*STR Constructors, Ltd. v. Newman Tile, Inc.,* 395 S.W.3d 383 (Tex.App.—El Paso 2013)] (See *Performance and Discharge.*)

11–8. Conditions of Performance. Russ Wyant owned Humble Ranch in Perkins County, South Dakota. Edward Humble, whose parents had previously owned the ranch, was Wyant's uncle. Humble held a two-year option to buy the ranch. The option included specific conditions. Once it was exercised, the parties had thirty days to enter into a purchase agreement, and the seller could become the buyer's lender by matching the terms of the proposed financing. After the option was exercised, the parties engaged in lengthy negotiations, but Humble did not respond to Wyant's proposed purchase agreement nor advise him of available financing terms before the option expired. Six months later, Humble filed a suit against Wyant to enforce the option. Is Humble entitled to specific performance? Explain. [*Humble v. Wyant,* 843 N.W.2d 334 (S.Dak. 2014)] (See *Performance and Discharge.*)

11–9. ⬌ **A Question of Ethics—Remedies.** On a weekday, Tamara Cohen, a real estate broker, showed a townhouse owned by Ray and Harriet Mayer to Jessica Seinfeld, the wife of comedian Jerry Seinfeld. On the weekend, when Cohen was unavailable because her religious beliefs prevented her from working, the Seinfelds revisited the townhouse on their own and agreed to buy it. The contract stated that the "buyers will pay buyer's real estate broker's fees." [*Cohen v. Seinfeld,* 15 Misc.3d 1118(A), 839 N.Y.S.2d 432 (Sup. 2007)] (See *Equitable Remedies.*)

1. Is Cohen entitled to payment even though she was not available to show the townhouse to the Seinfelds on the weekend? Explain.

2. What obligation do parties involved in business deals owe to each other with respect to their religious beliefs? How might the situation in this case have been avoided?

11–10. 💡 **Critical-Thinking Managerial Question.** Ashu Malik owns a sixty-room motel on Highway 100 that you and your business partners are interested in purchasing. During the course of negotiations, Malik tells you that the motel netted $60,000 last year and that it will net at least $85,000 next year. The motel books, which Malik turns over to your firm right before the purchase, clearly show that Malik's motel netted only $30,000 last year. Also, Malik fails to tell you that a bypass to Highway 100 is being planned that will redirect most traffic away from the front of the motel. Your firm purchases the motel. During your first year of operating it, the motel nets $35,000. At this time, you learn of the previous low profitability of the motel and the planned bypass. Can your firm sue Malik for fraudulent misrepresentation? What are the elements that you need to prove? Discuss fully the probable success of your firm getting the money back. (See *Voluntary Consent.*)

CHAPTER 12

(Matthew Staver/Landov)

Sales, Leases, and Product Liability

CONTENTS

- The Scope of Articles 2 and 2A
- Formation of Sales and Lease Contracts
- Performance
- Remedies for Breach
- Warranties
- Product Liability

LEARNING OBJECTIVES

The five learning objectives below are designed to help improve your understanding of the chapter. After reading this chapter, you should be able to answer the following questions:

1. How do Article 2 and Article 2A of the UCC differ? What types of transactions does each article cover?

2. Under the UCC, if an offeree includes additional or different terms in an acceptance, will a contract result? If so, what happens to these terms?

3. What remedies are available to a seller or lessor when the buyer or lessee breaches the contract? What remedies are available to a buyer or lessee if the seller or lessor breaches the contract?

4. What implied warranties arise under the UCC?

5. What are the elements of a cause of action in strict product liability?

> "I am for free commerce with all nations."
> —George Washington, 1732–1799 (First president of the United States, 1789–1797)

When we turn to contracts for the sale and lease of goods, we move away from common law principles and into the area of statutory law. State statutory law governing sales and lease transactions is based on the Uniform Commercial Code (UCC), which, as mentioned in Chapter 1, has been adopted as law by all of the states.[1] You can gain an idea of the UCC's comprehensiveness by looking at Articles 2 amd 2A of the UCC in Appendix C.

The goal of the UCC is to simplify and to streamline commercial transactions. By facilitating commercial transactions, the UCC reflects the sentiment expressed in the chapter-opening quotation—free commerce will benefit our nation. The UCC allows parties to form sales and lease contracts without observing the same degree of formality used in forming other types of contracts. In addition, the UCC provides a framework of rules that are readily applicable to the numerous difficulties that can arise during sales and lease transactions, including those entered into online. We look at the important issue of whether online sales can be taxed in a feature later in this chapter.

---

1. Louisiana has not adopted Articles 2 and 2A, however.

At the conclusion of this chapter, we look at another area of tort law of particular importance to businesspersons—product liability. The manufacturers and sellers of products may incur *product liability* when product defects cause injury or property damage to consumers, users, or bystanders (people in the vicinity of the product when it fails). Although multimillion-dollar product liability claims often involve big automakers, pharmaceutical companies, or tobacco companies, many businesses face potential liability. For instance, in the last few years, there have been numerous reports of energy drinks, such as Monster, Red Bull, Rockstar, and 5-hour Energy, having serious adverse effects—especially on young people. Several lawsuits have been filed against Monster Beverage Corporation in California concerning the adverse effects of these products.

The Scope of Articles 2 and 2A

Article 2 of the UCC sets forth the requirements for *sales contracts,* as well as the duties and obligations of the parties involved in the sales contract. Article 2A covers similar issues for *lease contracts.* Bear in mind, however, that the parties to sales or lease contracts are free to agree to terms different from those stated in the UCC.

Article 2—The Sale of Goods

Sales Contract A contract for the sale of goods under which the ownership of goods is transferred from a seller to a buyer for a price.

Article 2 of the UCC (as adopted by state statutes) governs **sales contracts,** or contracts for the sale of goods. To facilitate commercial transactions, Article 2 modifies some of the common law contract requirements that were discussed in the previous chapters.

To the extent that it has not been modified by the UCC, however, the common law of contracts also applies to sales contracts. In other words, the common law requirements for a valid contract—agreement, consideration, capacity, and legality—that were discussed in Chapter 10 are also applicable to sales contracts.

In general, the rule is that whenever a conflict arises between a common law contract rule and the state statutory law based on the UCC, the UCC controls. Thus, when a UCC provision addresses a certain issue, the UCC rule governs. When the UCC is silent, the common law governs.

The relationship between general contract law and the law governing sales of goods is illustrated in Exhibit 12–1, which follows Case 12.1.

In regard to Article 2, keep two points in mind.

1. Article 2 deals with the sale of *goods.* It does not deal with real property (real estate), services, or intangible property such as stocks and bonds. Thus, if the subject matter of a dispute is goods, the UCC governs. If it is real estate or services, the common law applies.
2. In some situations, the rules can vary depending on whether the buyer or the seller is a *merchant.*

We look now at how the UCC defines a *sale, goods,* and *merchant status.*

Sale The passing of title to property from the seller to the buyer for a price.

What Is a Sale?   The UCC defines a **sale** as "the passing of title [evidence of ownership rights] from the seller to the buyer for a price" [UCC 2–106(1)]. The price may be payable in cash or in other goods or services. (See the *Online Developments* feature that appears later in this chapter for a discussion of whether states can impose taxes on online sales.)

In the following case, the court was asked to determine who owned the "personal property" damaged in a fire. How did the UCC's definition of a sale affect the answer to that question?

Case 12.1

Nautilus Insurance Co. v. Cheran Investments LLC

Court of Appeals of Nebraska, ___ N.W.2d ___, 2014 WL 292809 (2014).

(Shutterstock.com)

Who carries the risk of loss of personal property in a bar?

BACKGROUND AND FACTS   Under a contract with Cheran Investments LLC, Blasini Inc. agreed to buy the business assets of the Attic Bar & Grill in Omaha, Nebraska. The contract required Blasini to make a down payment and monthly payments until the price was fully paid. Blasini obtained insurance on the property from Nautilus Insurance Co. Less than three years later, a fire damaged the "personal property" in the Attic. Because the purchase price had not yet been fully paid, Nautilus filed an action in a Nebraska state court against several defendants, including Cheran, to determine who was entitled to the insurance proceeds for the damage. The court concluded that Blasini had "failed to consummate the purchase agreement" and declared Cheran the owner of the personal property. Blasini appealed, arguing that title to the Attic's assets had passed at the time of the sale.

IN THE WORDS OF THE COURT . . .

BISHOP, Judge.
    * * * *

    * * * The provisions of the U.C.C. apply to the instant purchase agreement. The purpose of the agreement was for Blasini to purchase the business assets of the bar * * * . The items specifically designated in the agreement were "the furniture, Security systems, Aloha accounting system, Television, Music system, refrigerators, kitchen equipment, and food and liquor inventory." The ledger attached to the agreement lists several of the bar's items and their values, including "kitchen equipment," "ice machine," "ATM," "snake," "speakers," "cutlery," and "furniture." The entire purchase price of $150,000 accounted for movable items of the bar, and no real estate, intellectual property, or goodwill was transferred under the purchase agreement.

    Under U.C.C. Section 2–401, unless otherwise explicitly agreed where delivery is to be made without moving the goods, *if the goods are at the time of contracting already identified and no documents are to be delivered, title passes at the time and place of contracting.* [Emphasis added.]
    * * * *

    In the present case, the evidence is that * * * Blasini contracted to [purchase] the business assets of the bar, evidenced by the signed purchase agreement. No physical delivery needed to be made because Blasini was to assume operation of the bar in which the goods were located. Under Section 2–401, therefore, "title" to the goods passed to Blasini at the time of contracting. The purchase agreement made no provision for when title passed to Blasini. Therefore, irrespective of whether Blasini paid the purchase price * * * , Blasini became the owner of the property in the purchase agreement.

DECISION AND REMEDY   A state intermediate appellate court reversed the lower court's ruling. The sale of the Attic's assets passed title to the goods to Blasini, who became the owner. The appellate court remanded the case to the lower court, however, to determine whether Blasini had breached the contract.

THE LEGAL ENVIRONMENT DIMENSION   *How does the UCC define a sale? Under that definition, did the court correctly determine the ownership of the "personal property" in the Attic at the time of the fire? Explain.*

WHAT IF THE FACTS WERE DIFFERENT?   *Suppose that Blasini had made no payments under the contract for the sale of the Attic's assets. How should that circumstance affect the disbursement of the insurance proceeds?*

What Are Goods?   To be characterized as a *good*, an item of property must be *tangible*, and it must be *movable*. **Tangible property** has physical existence—it can be touched or seen. **Intangible property**—such as corporate stocks and bonds, patents and copyrights, and ordinary contract rights—has only conceptual existence and thus does not come under Article 2. A *movable* item can be carried from place to place. Hence, real estate is excluded from Article 2.

Goods Associated with Real Estate   Goods *associated* with real estate often do fall within the scope of Article 2, however [UCC 2–107]. For instance, a contract for the sale

Tangible Property Property that has physical existence and can be distinguished by the senses of touch and sight.

Intangible Property Property that cannot be seen or touched but exists only conceptually, such as corporate stocks and bonds. Article 2 of the UCC does not govern intangible property.

Exhibit 12–1   The Law Governing Contracts

This exhibit graphically illustrates the relationship between general contract law and statutory law (UCC Articles 2 and 2A) governing contracts for the sale and lease of goods. Sales contracts are not governed exclusively by Article 2 of the UCC but are also governed by general contract law whenever it is relevant and has not been modified by the UCC.

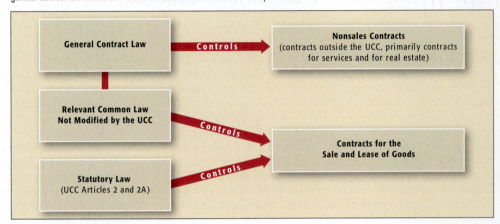

of minerals, oil, or gas is a contract for the sale of goods if *severance, or separation, is to be made by the seller.* Similarly, a contract for the sale of growing crops or timber to be cut is a contract for the sale of goods *regardless of who severs them from the land.*

Predominant-Factor Test A test courts use to determine whether a contract is primarily for the sale of goods or for the sale of services.

If a couple buys a concessions business that includes a truck, trailer, and tables and chairs, would this purchase be a sale of goods or of services?

(Marquis/Shutterstock.com)

Goods and Services Combined When contracts involve a combination of goods and services, courts generally use the **predominant-factor test** to determine whether a contract is primarily for the sale of goods or the sale of services.[2] If a court decides that a mixed contract is primarily a goods contract, *any* dispute, even a dispute over the services portion, will be decided under the UCC.

CASE EXAMPLE 12.1   Gene and Martha Jannusch agreed to sell Festival Foods, a concessions business, to Lindsey and Louann Naffziger for a price of $150,000. The deal included a truck, a trailer, freezers, roasters, chairs, tables, a fountain service, signs, and lighting. The Naffzigers paid $10,000 down with the balance to come from a bank loan. They took possession of the equipment and began to use it immediately in Festival Foods operations at various events.

After six events, the Naffzigers returned the truck and all the equipment, and wanted out of the deal because the business did not generate as much income as they expected. The Jannusches sued the Naffzigers for the balance due on the purchase price, claiming that the Naffzigers could no longer reject the goods under the UCC. The Naffzigers claimed that the UCC did not apply because the deal primarily involved the sale of a business rather than the sale of goods. The court found that the UCC governed under the predominant-factor test. The primary value of the contract was in the goods, not the value of the business. The parties had agreed on the essential terms of the contract (such as the price). Thus, a contract had been formed, and the Naffzigers had breached it. The Naffzigers took possession and control of all of the physical aspects of the business. Therefore, they had no right to return them.[3] ●

---

2. UCC 2–314(1) stipulate that serving food or drinks is a "sale of goods" for purposes of the implied warranty of merchantability, as will be discussed later in this chapter. The UCC also specifies that selling unborn animals or rare coins qualifies as a "sale of goods."
3. *Jannusch v. Naffziger,* 379 Ill.App.3d 381, 883 N.E.2d 711 (2008).

ONLINE DEVELOPMENTS

Taxing Web Purchases

In 1992, the United States Supreme Court ruled that an individual state cannot compel an out-of-state business that lacks a substantial physical presence within that state to collect and remit state taxes.[a] Although Congress has the power to pass legislation requiring out-of-state corporations to collect and remit state sales taxes, it has not yet done so. Thus, only online retailers that also have a physical presence within a state must collect state taxes on any Web sales made to residents of that state. (State residents are supposed to self-report their purchases and pay use taxes to the state, which they rarely do.)

Redefining Physical Presence

Several states have found a way to collect taxes on Internet sales made to state residents by out-of-state corporations—by redefining *physical presence*. In 2008, New York changed its tax laws in this manner. Now, an online retailer that pays any party within New York to solicit business for its products is considered a physical presence in the state and must collect state taxes. Since then, at least seventeen other states have made similar changes in their laws in an effort to increase their revenues by collecting sales tax from online retailers.

These new laws, often called the "Amazon tax" because they are largely aimed at Amazon.com, affect all online sellers, including Overstock.com and Drugstore.com. These tax laws especially affect those retailers that pay affiliates to direct traffic to their Web sites. These laws allow states to tax online commerce even though, to date, Congress has explicitly chosen not to tax Internet sales.

Local Governments Sue Online Travel Companies

Travelocity, Priceline.com, Hotels.com, and Orbitz.com are online travel companies (OTCs) that offer, among other things, hotel booking services. By 2014, more than twenty-five cities, including Atlanta, Charleston, Philadelphia, and San Antonio, had filed suits claiming that the OTCs owed taxes on hotel

reservations that they had booked. All of the cities involved in the suits impose a hotel occupancy tax, which is essentially a sales tax.

Initially, some cities won their cases, but more recently, they have been losing in court.[b] As of 2014, the OTCs had prevailed in eighteen of twenty-five cases nationwide. An exception is a 2014 case in Wyoming in which the state supreme court held that Travelocity, Priceline, Hotwire, Expedia, and Trip Network had to collect and remit sales tax.[c]

The Market Place Fairness Act

By the time you read this, online sales taxes may have become a reality for every online business that has annual revenues in excess of $1 million. For several years now, legislation called the Market Place Fairness Act has been introduced in the U.S. Senate. The act would allow states to collect sales taxes from online retailers for transactions within the state.

There are several problems with such legislation. The current tax system involves 9,600 taxing jurisdictions. Even one zip code may cover multiple taxing entities such as different cities and counties. Just consider that the Dallas–Fort Worth airport includes six separate taxing jurisdictions. Current software solutions for retailers that allow them to collect and remit sales taxes for different jurisdictions are extremely costly to install and operate. Overstock.com, for example, spent $1.3 million to add just one state to its sales tax collection system.

Critical Thinking

Some argue that if online retailers are required to collect and pay sales taxes in jurisdictions in which they have no physical presence, they have no democratic way to fight high taxes in those places. Is this an instance of taxation without representation? Discuss.

---

a. *Quill Corp. v. North Dakota,* 504 U.S. 298, 112 S.Ct. 1904, 119 L.Ed.2d 91 (1992).

b. *Travelscape, LLC v. South Carolina Department of Revenue,* 391 S.C. 89, 705 S.E.2d 28 (2011).

c. *Travelocity.com, LP v. Wyoming Dept of Revenue,* __ P.3d __, 2014 WL 1326388 (Wyo. 2014).

Who Is a Merchant?   Article 2 governs the sale of goods in general. It applies to sales transactions between all buyers and sellers. In a limited number of instances, though, the UCC presumes that special business standards ought to be imposed because

The buyer and the seller of aircraft parts are both merchants.

of merchants' relatively high degree of commercial expertise.[4] Such standards do not apply to the casual or inexperienced seller or buyer (consumer).

Section 2–104 sets forth three ways in which merchant status can arise:

1. A merchant is a person who *deals in goods of the kind* involved in the sales contract. Thus, a retailer, a whole-saler, or a manufacturer is a merchant of the goods sold in his or her business. A merchant for one type of goods is not necessarily a merchant for another type. For instance, a sporting goods retailer is a merchant when selling tennis rackets but not when selling a used computer.

2. A merchant is a person who, by occupation, *holds him-self or herself out as having knowledge and skill* unique to the practices or goods involved in the transaction. This broad definition may include banks or universities as merchants.

3. A person who *employs a merchant as a broker, agent, or other intermediary* has the status of merchant in that transaction. Hence, if an art collector hires a broker to purchase or sell art for her, the collector is considered a merchant in the transaction.

In summary, a person is a **merchant** when she or he, acting in a mercantile capacity, possesses or uses an expertise specifically related to the goods being sold. This basic dis-tinction is not always clear-cut. For instance, state courts appear to be split on whether farmers should be considered merchants.

Merchant A person who is engaged in the purchase and sale of goods. Under the UCC, a person who deals in goods of the kind involved in the sales contract or who holds herself or himself out as having skill or knowledge peculiar to the practices or goods being purchased or sold.

Article 2A—Leases

Leases of personal property (goods such as automobiles and industrial equipment) have become increasingly common. In this context, a lease is a transfer of the right to possess and use goods for a period of time in exchange for payment. Article 2A of the UCC was created to fill the need for uniform guidelines in this area.

Article 2A covers any transaction that creates a lease of goods or a sublease of goods [UCC 2A–102, 2A–103(1)(k)]. Article 2A is essentially a repetition of Article 2, except that it applies to leases of goods rather than sales of goods and thus varies to reflect dif-ferences between sales and lease transactions. (Note that Article 2A is not concerned with leases of real property, such as land or buildings.)

Article 2A defines a **lease agreement** as a lessor's and lessee's bargain with respect to the lease of goods, as found in their language and as implied by other circumstances [UCC 2A–103(1)(k)]. A **lessor** is one who transfers the right to the possession and use of goods under a lease. A **lessee** is one who acquires the right to the possession and use of goods under a lease. In other words, the lessee is the party who is leasing the goods from the lessor.

Article 2A applies to all types of leases of goods. Special rules apply to certain types of leases, however, including consumer leases (in which a business leases goods to a consumer "primarily for a personal, family, or household purpose") and finance leases (involving a lessor who buys goods from a supplier to lease to another).

Learning Objective 1
How do Article 2 and Article 2A of the UCC differ? What types of transactions does each article cover?

Lease Agreement In regard to the lease of goods, an agreement in which one person (the lessor) agrees to transfer the right to the possession and use of property to another person (the lessee) in exchange for rental payments.

Lessor One who transfers the right to the possession and use of goods to another in exchange for rental payments.

Lessee One who acquires the right to the possession and use of another's goods in exchange for rental payments.

---

4. The provisions that apply only to merchants deal principally with the Statute of Frauds, firm offers, confirmatory memoranda, warranties, and contract modification. They will be discussed later in this chapter.

Formation of Sales and Lease Contracts

As mentioned, Articles 2 and 2A of the UCC modify common law contract rules. Remember, though, that parties to sales and lease contracts are basically free to establish whatever terms they wish. A sales contract used by Starbucks Coffee Company follows this chapter as an exhibit to illustrate typical terms and clauses in contracts for the sale of goods.

The UCC comes into play when the parties either fail to provide certain terms in their contract or wish to change the effect of the UCC's terms in the contract's application. The UCC makes this very clear by its repeated use of such phrases as "unless the parties otherwise agree" and "absent a contrary agreement by the parties."

Offer

In general contract law, the moment a definite offer is met by an unqualified acceptance, a binding contract is formed. In commercial sales transactions, the verbal exchanges, correspondence, and actions of the parties may not reveal exactly when a binding contractual obligation arises. The UCC states that an agreement sufficient to constitute a contract can exist even if the moment of its making is undetermined [UCC 2–204(2), 2A–204(2)].

Open Terms   According to general contract law, an offer must be definite enough for the parties (and the courts) to ascertain its essential terms when it is accepted. In contrast, the UCC states that a sales or lease contract will not fail for indefiniteness even if one or more terms are left open as long as *both* of the following are true:

1. The parties intended to make a contract.
2. There is a reasonably certain basis for the court to grant an appropriate remedy [UCC 2–204(3), 2A–204(3)].

The UCC provides numerous provisions that can be used to fill the gaps in a contract. For instance, if the parties have not agreed on a price, the court will determine a "reasonable price at the time for delivery" [UCC 2–305(1)]. When the parties do not specify payment terms, payment is due at the time and place at which the buyer is to receive the goods [UCC 2–310(a)]. When no delivery terms are specified, the buyer normally takes delivery at the seller's place of business [UCC 2–308(a)].

Keep in mind, though, that if too many terms are left open, a court may find that the parties did not intend to form a contract. Also, the *quantity* of goods involved usually must be expressly stated in the contract. If the quantity term is left open, the courts will have no basis for determining a remedy.

PREVENTING LEGAL DISPUTES

If a business owner leaves certain terms of a sales or lease contract open, the UCC allows a court to supply the missing terms. Although this can sometimes be advantageous (to establish that a contract existed, for instance), it can also be a major disadvantage. If a party fails to state a price in the contract offer, for example, a court will impose a reasonable price by looking at the market price of similar goods *at the time of delivery*. Thus, instead of receiving the usual price for the goods, a business will receive what a court considers a reasonable price when the goods are delivered. Therefore, when goods are being sold or leased, the contract should clearly state any terms that are essential to the bargain, particularly the price. It is generally better to establish the terms of a contract than to leave it up to a court to determine what terms are reasonable after a dispute has arisen.

Merchant's Firm Offer   Under regular contract principles, an offer can be revoked at any time before acceptance. The major common law exception is an *option contract* (discussed in Chapter 10). The UCC creates a second exception for *firm offers* made by a merchant concerning the sale or lease of goods (regardless of whether or not the offeree is a merchant).

A **firm offer** arises when a merchant-offeror gives *assurances in a signed writing* that the offer will remain open. The merchant's firm offer is irrevocable without the necessity of consideration[5] for the stated period or, if no definite period is stated, a reasonable period (neither to exceed three months) [UCC 2–205, 2A–205].

> **EXAMPLE 12.2**   Osaka, a used-car dealer, e-mails a letter to Gomez on January 1, stating, "I have a used 2013 Toyota RAV4 on the lot that I'll sell you for $22,000 any time between now and January 31." This e-mail creates a firm offer, and Osaka will be liable for breach of contract if he sells the RAV4 to another person before January 31. ●

Acceptance

Acceptance of an offer to buy, sell, or lease goods generally may be made in any reasonable manner and by any reasonable means. The UCC permits acceptance of an offer to buy goods "either by a prompt *promise* to ship or by the prompt or current shipment of conforming or nonconforming goods" [UCC 2–206(1)(b)]. *Conforming goods* accord with the contract's terms, whereas *nonconforming goods* do not.

The prompt shipment of nonconforming goods constitutes both an acceptance, which creates a contract, and a breach of that contract. This rule does not apply if the seller *seasonably* (within a reasonable amount of time) notifies the buyer that the nonconforming shipment is offered only as an *accommodation,* or as a favor. The notice of accommodation must clearly indicate to the buyer that the shipment does not constitute an acceptance and that, therefore, no contract has been formed.

> **EXAMPLE 12.3**   McFarren Pharmacy orders five cases of Johnson & Johnson 3-by-5-inch gauze pads from H.T. Medical Supply, Inc. If H.T. ships five cases of Xeroform 3-by-5-inch gauze pads instead, the shipment acts as both an acceptance of McFarren's offer and a *breach* of the resulting contract. McFarren may sue H.T. for any appropriate damages. If, however, H.T. notifies McFarren that the Xeroform gauze pads are being shipped *as an accommodation*—because H.T. has only Xeroform pads in stock—the shipment will constitute a counteroffer, not an acceptance. A contract will be formed only if McFarren accepts the Xeroform gauze pads. ●

Communication of Acceptance   Under the common law, because a unilateral offer invites acceptance by performance, the offeree need not notify the offeror of performance unless the offeror would not otherwise know about it. In other words, a unilateral offer can be accepted by beginning performance.

The UCC is more stringent than the common law in this regard because it requires notification. Under the UCC, if the offeror is not notified within a reasonable time that the offeree has accepted the contract by beginning performance, then the offeror can treat the offer as having lapsed before acceptance [UCC 2–206(2), 2A–206(2)].

Additional Terms   Recall from Chapter 10 that under the common law, the mirror image rule requires that the terms of the acceptance exactly match those of the offer.
> **EXAMPLE 12.4**   Aldrich e-mails an offer to sell twenty Samsung Galaxy model 7.0 tablets to Beale. If Beale accepts the offer but changes it to require model 8.9 tablets, then there is no contract. ●

---

5. If the offeree pays consideration, then an option contract (not a merchant's firm offer) is formed.

Firm Offer An offer (by a merchant) that is irrevocable without consideration for a period of time (not longer than three months). A firm offer by a merchant must be in writing and must be signed by the offeror.

To avoid these problems, the UCC dispenses with the mirror image rule. Under the UCC, a contract is formed if the offeree's response indicates a *definite* acceptance of the offer, *even if the acceptance includes terms additional to or different from those contained in the offer* [UCC 2–207(1)]. Whether the additional terms become part of the contract depends, in part, on whether the parties are nonmerchants or merchants.

Rules When One Party or Both Parties Are Nonmerchants

If one (or both) of the parties is a *nonmerchant*, the contract is formed according to the terms of the original offer and does not include any of the additional terms in the acceptance [UCC 2–207(2)].

CASE EXAMPLE 12.5 OfficeSupplyStore.com sells office supplies on the Web. Employees of the Kansas City School District in Missouri ordered $17,642.54 worth of office supplies—without the authority or approval of their employer—from the Web site. The invoices accompanying the goods contained a *forum-selection clause* (see Chapter 10) that required all disputes to be resolved in California.

When the goods were not paid for, Office Supply filed suit in California. The Kansas City School District objected, arguing that the forum-selection clause was not binding. The court held that the forum-selection clause was not part of the parties' contract. The clause was an additional term included in the invoices delivered to a nonmerchant buyer (the school district) with the purchased goods. Therefore, the clause did not become part of the contract unless the buyer expressly agreed, which did not happen in this case.[6] ●

Rules When Both Parties Are Merchants

The drafters of the UCC created a special rule for merchants to avoid the "battle of the forms," which occurs when two merchants exchange separate standard forms containing different contract terms.

Under UCC 2–207(2), in contracts *between merchants,* the additional terms *automatically* become part of the contract *unless* one of the following conditions arises:

1. The original offer expressly limited acceptance to its terms.
2. The new or changed terms materially alter the contract.
3. The offeror objects to the new or changed terms within a reasonable period of time.

When determining whether an alteration is material, courts consider several factors. Generally, if the modification does not involve any unreasonable element of surprise or hardship for the offeror, a court will hold that the modification did not materially alter the contract.

Courts also consider the parties' prior dealings. **CASE EXAMPLE 12.6** WPS, Inc., submitted a proposal to manufacture equipment for Expro Americas, LLC, and Surface Production Systems, Inc. (SPS). Expro and SPS then submitted two purchase orders. WPS accepted the first purchase order in part, and the second order conditionally. Among other things, WPS's acceptance required that Expro and SPS give their "full release to proceed" and agree to "pay all valid costs associated with any order cancellation." The parties' negotiations continued, and Expro and SPS eventually submitted a third purchase order.

Although the third purchase order did not comply with all of WPS's requirements, it did give WPS full permission to proceed and agreed that Expro and SPS would pay all cancellation costs. With Expro's and SPS's knowledge, WPS then began working on that order. Expro and SPS later canceled the order and refused to pay the cancellation costs. When the dispute ended up in court, Expro and SPS claimed that the parties' contract was not enforceable because the additional terms in WPS's acceptance had materially altered the contract. The court found in favor of WPS. Expro and SPS had given a release to proceed that basically authorized WPS to go forward with manufacturing the equipment. Because "the parties

Learning Objective 2
Under the UCC, if an offeree includes additional or different terms in an acceptance, will a contract result? If so, what happens to these terms?

---

6. *OfficeSupplyStore.com v. Kansas City School Board,* 334 S.W.3d 574 (Kan. 2011).

operated as if they had additional time to resolve the outstanding differences," the court reasoned that Expro and SPS were contractually obligated to pay the cancellation costs.[7] •

Consideration

The common law rule that a contract requires consideration also applies to sales and lease contracts. Unlike the common law, however, the UCC does not require a contract *modification* to be supported by new consideration. The UCC states that an agreement modifying a contract for the sale or lease of goods "needs no consideration to be binding" [UCC 2–209(1), 2A–208(1)]. Of course, any contract modification must be made in good faith [UCC 1–304].

In some situations, an agreement to modify a sales or lease contract without consideration must be in writing to be enforceable. For instance, if the contract itself specifies that any changes to the contract must be in a signed writing, only those changes agreed to in a signed writing are enforceable.

Sometimes, when a consumer (nonmerchant) is buying goods from a merchant-seller, the merchant supplies a form that contains a prohibition against oral modification. In those situations, the consumer must sign a separate acknowledgment of the clause for it to be enforceable [UCC 2–209(2), 2A–208(2)]. Also, any modification that makes a sales contract come under Article 2's writing requirement (its Statute of Frauds, discussed next) usually requires a writing (or electronic record) to be enforceable.

The Statute of Frauds

The UCC contains Statute of Frauds provisions covering sales and lease contracts. Under these provisions, sales contracts for goods priced at $500 or more and lease contracts requiring total payments of $1,000 or more must be in a writing or record to be enforceable [UCC 2–201(1), 2A–201(1)]. (These low threshold amounts may eventually be raised.)

To satisfy the UCC's Statute of Frauds provisions, a writing, memorandum, or electronic record need only indicate that the parties intended to form a contract and be signed by the party against whom enforcement is sought. The contract normally will not be enforceable beyond the quantity of goods shown in the writing, however. All other terms can be proved in court by oral testimony. For leases, the writing must reasonably identify and describe the goods leased and the lease term.

The contract normally will not be enforceable beyond the quantity of goods shown in the writing, however. All other terms can be proved in court by oral testimony. For leases, the writing must reasonably identify and describe the goods leased and the lease term.

Special Rules for Contracts between Merchants   The UCC provides a special rule for merchants in sales transactions (there is no corresponding rule that applies to leases under Article 2A). Merchants can satisfy the Statute of Frauds if, after the parties have agreed orally, one of the merchants sends a signed written (or electronic) confirmation to the other merchant within a reasonable time.

The communication must indicate the terms of the agreement, and the merchant receiving the confirmation must have reason to know of its contents. Unless the merchant who receives the confirmation gives written notice of objection to its contents within ten days after receipt, the writing is sufficient against the receiving merchant, even though she or he has not signed it [UCC 2–201(2)].

EXAMPLE 12.7   Alfonso is a merchant-buyer in Cleveland. He contracts over the telephone to purchase $6,000 worth of spare aircraft parts from Goldstein, a merchant-seller in

---

7. *WPS, Inc. v. Expro Americas, LLC*, 369 S.W.3d 384 (Tex.App. 2012).

New York City. Two days later, Goldstein e-mails a signed confirmation detailing the terms of the oral contract, and Alfonso subsequently receives it. Alfonso does not notify Goldstein in writing (or e-mail) that he objects to the contents of the confirmation within ten days of receipt. Therefore, Alfonso cannot raise the Statute of Frauds as a defense against the enforcement of the oral contract. ●

Exceptions   The UCC defines three exceptions to the writing requirements of the Statute of Frauds [UCC 2–201(3), 2A–201(4)].

1. *Specially manufactured goods.* An oral contract will still be enforceable if it is for goods that are specially manufactured for a particular buyer and the seller has substantially started manufacturing the goods.
2. *Admissions.* When the party against whom enforcement is sought admits to making an oral contract, the contract is enforceable, but only as to the quantity of goods that the party admitted. **CASE EXAMPLE 12.8**   Gerald Lindgren, a farmer, agreed by phone to sell his crops to Glacial Plains Cooperative. The parties reached four oral agreements: two for the delivery of soybeans and two for the delivery of corn. Lindgren made the soybean deliveries and part of the first corn delivery, but he sold the rest of his corn to another dealer. Glacial Plains bought corn elsewhere, paying a higher price, and then sued Lindgren for breach of contract. In papers filed with the court, Lindgren acknowledged his oral agreements with Glacial Plains and admitted that he did not fully perform. The court applied the admissions exception and held that the four agreements were enforceable.[8] ●
3. *Partial performance.* An oral contract that has been partially performed (such as when some of the contracted goods have been paid for and accepted) will be enforceable to the extent that it has been performed. **CASE EXAMPLE 12.9**   Quality Pork International formed an oral contract with Rupari Food Services, Inc., which buys food products and sells them to retail operations. Quality was to ship three orders of pork to Star Food Processing, Inc., and Rupari was to pay for the products. Quality shipped the goods to Star and sent invoices to Rupari. Rupari billed Star for all three orders but paid Quality only for the first two. Quality filed a suit against Rupari to recover $44,051.98, the cost of the third order.

    The court held that even though Rupari had not signed a written contract or purchase order, it had accepted the goods and partially performed the contract by paying for the first two shipments. Rupari's conduct was sufficient to prove the existence of a contract, and the court required Rupari to pay for the last shipment.[9] ●

The exceptions just discussed and other ways in which sales law differs from general contract law are summarized in Exhibit 12–2 that follows.

Performance

The performance that is required of the parties under a sales or lease contract consists of the duties and obligations each party has under the terms of the contract. The basic obligation of the seller or lessor is to transfer and deliver the goods as stated in the contract, and the basic duty of the buyer or lessee is to accept and pay for the goods [UCC 2–301, 2A–516(1)].

---

8. *Glacial Plains Cooperative v. Lindgren,* 759 N.W.2d 661 (Min.App. 2009).
9. *Quality Pork International v. Rupari Food Services, Inc.,* 267 Neb. 474, 675 N.W.2d 642 (2004).

Exhibit 12–2 Major Differences between Contract Law and Sales Law

TOPIC	CONTRACT LAW	SALES LAW
Contract Terms	Contract must contain all material terms.	Open terms are acceptable, if parties intended to form a contract, but the contract is not enforceable beyond quantity term.
Acceptance	Mirror image rule applies. If additional terms are added in acceptance, counteroffer is created.	Additional terms will not negate acceptance unless acceptance is expressly conditioned on assent to the additional terms.
Contract Modification	Modification requires consideration.	Modification does not require consideration.
Irrevocable Offers	Option contracts (with consideration).	Merchants' firm offers (without consideration).
Statute of Frauds Requirements	All material terms must be included in the writing.	Writing is required only for the sale of goods priced at $500 or more, but the contract is not enforceable beyond the quantity specified. Merchants can satisfy the writing by a confirmation evidencing their agreement. Exceptions exist for (1) specially manufactured goods, (2) admissions, and (3) partial performance.

Keep in mind that "duties and obligations" under the terms of the contract include those specified by the agreement, by custom, and by the UCC. Thus, parties to a sales or lease contract may be bound not only by terms they expressly agreed on, but also by terms implied by custom, such as a customary method of weighing or measuring particular goods.

The obligations of good faith and commercial reasonableness underlie every sales and lease contract. The UCC's good faith provision, which can never be disclaimed, reads as follows: "Every contract or duty within this Act imposes an obligation of good faith in its performance or enforcement" [UCC 1–304]. *Good faith* means honesty in fact. For a merchant, it means honesty in fact and the observance of reasonable commercial standards of fair dealing in the trade [UCC 2–103(1)(b)]. In other words, merchants are held to a higher standard of performance or duty than are nonmerchants.

Obligations of the Seller or Lessor

As stated, the basic duty of the seller or lessor is to deliver the goods called for under the contract to the buyer or lessee. Goods that conform to the contract description in every way are called **conforming goods.** To fulfill the contract, the seller or lessor must either deliver or tender delivery of conforming goods to the buyer or lessee. **Tender of delivery** occurs when the seller or lessor makes conforming goods available and gives the buyer or lessee whatever notification is reasonably necessary to enable the buyer or lessee to take delivery [UCC 2–503(1), 2A–508(1)].

Tender must occur at a *reasonable hour* and in a *reasonable manner.* For example, a seller cannot call the buyer at 2:00 A.M. and say, "The goods are ready. I'll give you twenty minutes to get them." Unless the parties have agreed otherwise, the goods must be tendered for delivery at a reasonable hour and kept available for a reasonable time to enable the buyer to take possession [UCC 2–503(1)(a)].

Place of Delivery
The buyer and seller (or lessor and lessee) may agree that the goods will be delivered to a particular destination where the buyer or lessee will take possession. If the contract does not indicate where the goods will be delivered, then the place for delivery will be one of the following:

1. The *seller's place of business.*
2. The *seller's residence,* if the seller has no business location [UCC 2–308(a)].

Conforming Goods Goods that conform to the contract specifications.

Tender of Delivery Under the Uniform Commercial Code, a seller's or lessor's act of placing conforming goods at the disposal of the buyer or lessee and giving the buyer or lessee whatever notification is reasonably necessary to enable the buyer or lessee to take delivery.

3. The *location of the goods,* if both parties know at the time of contracting that the goods are located somewhere other than the seller's business [UCC 2–308(b)].

> **EXAMPLE 12.10**   Li Wan and Boyd both live in San Francisco. In San Francisco, Li Wan contracts to sell Boyd five used trucks, which both parties know are located in a Chicago warehouse. If nothing more is specified in the contract, the place of delivery for the trucks is Chicago. Li Wan may tender delivery by giving Boyd a document establishing that Boyd is legally entitled to possession. •

The Perfect Tender Rule   As previously noted, the seller or lessor has an obligation to ship or tender *conforming goods,* which the buyer or lessee is then obligated to accept and pay for according to the terms of the contract [UCC 2–507]. Under the common law, the seller was obligated to deliver goods that conformed with the terms of the contract in every detail. This is called the **perfect tender rule.**

The UCC preserves the perfect tender doctrine. It states that if goods or tender of delivery fails *in any respect* to conform to the contract, the buyer or lessee may accept the goods, reject the entire shipment, or accept part and reject part [UCC 2–601, 2A–509].

Because of the rigidity of the perfect tender rule, several exceptions to the rule have been created, some of which we discuss next.

Cure   The UCC does not specifically define the term **cure,** but it refers to the right of the seller or lessor to repair, adjust, or replace defective or nonconforming goods [UCC 2–508, 2A–513].

The seller or lessor has a right to attempt to "cure" a defect when the following are true:

1. A delivery is rejected because the goods were nonconforming.
2. The time for performance has not yet expired.
3. The seller or lessor provides timely notice to the buyer or lessee of the intention to cure.
4. The cure can be made *within the contract time for performance.*

Once the time for performance under the contract has expired, the seller or lessor no longer has a right to cure. Nevertheless, the seller or lessor can still cure if he or she has *reasonable grounds to believe that the nonconforming tender will be acceptable to the buyer or lessee* [UCC 2–508(2), 2A–513(2)].

Substitution of Carriers   Sometimes, an agreed-on manner of delivery (such as the use of a particular carrier to transport the goods) becomes impracticable or unavailable through no fault of either party. In that situation, if a commercially reasonable substitute is available, this substitute performance is sufficient tender to the buyer and must be used [UCC 2–614(1)]. The seller or lessor is required to arrange for a substitute carrier and normally is responsible for any additional shipping costs (unless the contract states otherwise).

Commercial Impracticability   As discussed in Chapter 11, occurrences unforeseen by either party when a contract was made may make performance commercially impracticable. When this occurs, the perfect tender rule no longer applies. The seller or lessor must, however, notify the buyer or lessee as soon as practicable that there will be a delay or nondelivery.

> **EXAMPLE 12.11**   Houston Oil Company, which receives its oil from the Middle East, has a contract to supply Northwest Fuels with one hundred thousand barrels of oil. Because of an oil embargo by the Organization of Petroleum Exporting Countries, Houston is unable to secure oil from the Middle East or any other source to meet the terms of the contract. This situation comes fully under the commercial impracticability exception to the perfect tender doctrine. •

Perfect Tender Rule A common law rule under which a seller was required to deliver to the buyer goods that conformed perfectly to the requirements stipulated in the sales contract. A tender of nonconforming goods would automatically constitute a breach of contract. Under the Uniform Commercial Code, the rule has been greatly modified.

Cure Under the Uniform Commercial Code, the right of a party who tenders nonconforming performance to correct his or her performance within the contract period.

If a buyer has accepted these blue pens in the past when she ordered black pens, is the seller justified in shipping blue pens again?

(Sadovnikova Olga/Shutterstock.com)

The doctrine of commercial impracticability does not extend to problems that could have been foreseen—such as an increase in cost resulting from inflation. The nonoccurrence of the contingency must have been a basic assumption on which the contract was made [UCC 2–615, 2A–405].

Destruction of Identified Goods   Sometimes, an unexpected event, such as a fire, totally destroys goods through no fault of either party before risk passes to the buyer or lessee. In such a situation, *if the goods were identified at the time the contract was formed,* the parties are excused from performance [UCC 2–613, 2A–221]. If the goods are only partially destroyed, however, the buyer or lessee can inspect them and either treat the contract as void or accept the damaged goods with a reduction in the contract price.

Obligations of the Buyer or Lessee

What happens to a contract for the sale of goods when those goods identified to the contract are completely destroyed by fire?

(AP Images/Joseph Kaczmarek)

The main obligation of the buyer or lessee under a sales or lease contract is to pay for the goods tendered in accordance with the contract. Once the seller or lessor has adequately tendered delivery, the buyer or lessee is obligated to accept the goods and pay for them according to the terms of the contract.

Payment   In the absence of any specific agreements, the buyer or lessee must make payment at the time and place the goods are *received* [UCC 2–310(a), 2A–516(1)]. When a sale is made on credit, the buyer is obligated to pay according to the specified credit terms (for example, 60, 90, or 120 days), not when the goods are received. The credit period usually begins on the *date of shipment* [UCC 2–310(d)]. Under a lease contract, a lessee must make the lease payment that was specified in the contract [UCC 2A–516(1)].

Payment can be made by any means agreed on between the parties—cash or any other method generally acceptable in the commercial world. If the seller demands cash, the seller must permit the buyer reasonable time to obtain it [UCC 2–511].

Right of Inspection   Unless the parties otherwise agree, or for C.O.D. (collect on delivery) transactions, the buyer or lessee has an absolute right to inspect the goods before making payment. This right allows the buyer or lessee to verify that the goods tendered or delivered conform to the contract. If the goods are not as ordered, the buyer or lessee has no duty to pay. *An opportunity for inspection is therefore a condition precedent to the right of the seller or lessor to enforce payment* [UCC 2–513(1), 2A–515(1)].

Inspection can take place at any reasonable place and time and in any reasonable manner. Generally, what is reasonable is determined by custom of the trade, past practices of the parties, and the like. The buyer bears the costs of inspecting the goods but can recover the costs from the seller if the goods do not conform and are rejected [UCC 2–513(2)].

Acceptance   After having had a reasonable opportunity to inspect the goods, the buyer or lessee can demonstrate acceptance in any of the following ways:

1. The buyer or lessee indicates (by words or conduct) to the seller or lessor that the goods are conforming or that he or she will retain them in spite of their nonconformity [UCC 2–606(1)(a), 2A–515(1)(a)].
2. The buyer or lessee *fails to reject* the goods within a reasonable period of time [UCC 2–602(1), 2–606(1)(b), 2A–515(1)(b)].
3. In sales contracts, the buyer will be deemed to have accepted the goods if he or she *performs any act inconsistent with the seller's ownership.* For instance, any use or resale of the goods—except for the limited purpose of testing or inspecting the goods—generally constitutes an acceptance [UCC 2–606(1)(c)].

If some of the goods delivered do not conform to the contract and the seller or lessor has failed to cure, the buyer or lessee can make a *partial* acceptance [UCC 2–601(c), 2A–509(1)]. The same is true if the nonconformity was not reasonably discoverable before acceptance. (In the latter situation, the buyer or lessee may be able to revoke the acceptance, as will be discussed later in this chapter.)

Anticipatory Repudiation

What if, before the time for contract performance, one party clearly communicates to the other the intention *not* to perform? As discussed in Chapter 11, such an action is a breach of the contract by *anticipatory repudiation*. When anticipatory repudiation occurs, the nonbreaching party has a choice of two responses:

1. Treat the repudiation as a final breach by pursuing a remedy.
2. Wait to see if the repudiating party will decide to honor the contract despite the avowed intention to renege [UCC 2–610, 2A–402].

In either situation, the nonbreaching party may suspend performance.

The UCC permits the breaching party to "retract" his or her repudiation (subject to some limitations). This can be done by any method that clearly indicates the party's intent to perform. Once retraction is made, the rights of the repudiating party under the contract are reinstated. There can be no retraction, however, if since the time of the repudiation the other party has canceled or materially changed position or otherwise indicated that the repudiation is final [UCC 2–611, 2A–403].

Remedies for Breach

When one party fails to carry out the performance promised in a contract, a breach occurs, and the aggrieved party looks for remedies. These remedies range from retaining the goods to requiring the breaching party's performance under the contract. The general purpose of these remedies is to put the aggrieved party "in as good a position as if the other party had fully performed." Remedies under the UCC are *cumulative* in nature. In other words, an innocent party to a breached sales or lease contract is not limited to one exclusive remedy. (Of course, a party still may not recover twice for the same harm.)

Remedies of the Seller or Lessor

When the buyer or lessee is in breach, the remedies available to the seller or lessor depend on the circumstances at the time of the breach, such as which party has possession of the goods. If the goods are in the buyer's or lessee's possession, the seller or lessor can sue to recover the purchase price of the goods or the lease payments due [UCC 2–709(1), 2A–529(1)]. If the breach occurs before the goods have been delivered to the buyer or lessee, the seller or lessor has the right to pursue the remedies discussed next.

The Right to Cancel the Contract
If the buyer or lessee breaches the contract, the seller or lessor can choose to simply cancel the contract [UCC 2–703(f), 2A–523(1)(a)]. The seller or lessor must notify the buyer or lessee of the cancellation, and at that point all remaining obligations of the seller or lessor are discharged. The buyer or lessee is not discharged from all remaining obligations, however. She or he is in breach, and the seller or lessor can pursue remedies available under the UCC for breach.

Learning Objective 3
What remedies are available to a seller or lessor when the buyer or lessee breaches the contract? What remedies are available to a buyer or lessee if the seller or lessor breaches the contract?

The Right to Withhold Delivery

In general, sellers and lessors can withhold delivery or discontinue performance of their obligations under sales or lease contracts when the buyers or lessees are in breach. [UCC 2–703(a), 2A–523(1)(c)]. The seller or lessor can also refuse to deliver the goods to a buyer or lessee who is insolvent (unable to pay debts as they become due) unless the buyer or lessee pays in cash [UCC 2–702(1), 2A–525(1)].

The Right to Resell or Dispose of the Goods

When a buyer or lessee breaches or repudiates the contract while the seller or lessor is in possession of the goods, the seller or lessor can resell or dispose of the goods. The seller can retain any profits made as a result of the sale and can hold the buyer or lessee liable for any loss [UCC 2–703(d), 2–706(1), 2A–523(1)(e), 2A–527(1)].

The seller must give the original buyer reasonable notice of the resale, unless the goods are perishable or will rapidly decline in value [UCC 2–706(2), (3)]. The resale can be private or public, and the goods can be sold as a unit or in parcels. Any resale of the goods must be made in good faith and in a commercially reasonable manner.

When the goods contracted for are unfinished at the time of the breach, the seller or lessor can do either of the following:

1. Cease manufacturing the goods and resell them for scrap or salvage value.
2. Complete the manufacture and resell or dispose of the goods, and hold the buyer or lessee liable for any deficiency.

In choosing between these two alternatives, the seller or lessor must exercise reasonable commercial judgment in order to mitigate the loss and obtain maximum value from the unfinished goods [UCC 2–704(2), 2A–524(2)].

The Right to Recover the Purchase Price or Lease Payments Due

An unpaid seller or lessor can bring an action to recover the purchase price or the payments due under the lease contract, plus incidental damages [UCC 2–709(1), 2A–529(1)]. If a seller or lessor is unable to resell or dispose of the goods and sues for the contract price or lease payments due, the goods must be held for the buyer or lessee. The seller or lessor can resell the goods at any time before collecting the judgment from the buyer or lessee. If the goods are resold, the net proceeds from the sale must be credited to the buyer or lessee because of the duty to mitigate damages.

A worker inspects returned goods that will be sold at Overstock.com. Is such a resale of these goods commercially acceptable?

(AP Images/Jim Urquhart)

The Right to Recover Damages

If a buyer or lessee repudiates a contract or wrongfully refuses to accept the goods, a seller or lessor can bring an action to recover the damages sustained. Ordinarily, the amount of damages equals the difference between the contract price or lease payments and the market price or lease payments at the time and place of tender of the goods, plus incidental damages [UCC 2–708(1), 2A–528(1)].

Remedies of the Buyer or Lessee

Like the remedies available to sellers and lessors, the remedies available to buyers and lessees depend on the circumstances existing at the time of the breach. If the seller or lessor refuses to deliver the goods or the buyer and lessee has rejected the goods, the basic remedies available to the buyer or lessee include those discussed next.

The Right to Cancel the Contract   When a seller or lessor fails to make proper delivery or repudiates the contract, the buyer or lessee can cancel, or rescind, the contract. The buyer or lessee is relieved of any further obligations under the contract but retains all rights to other remedies against the seller or lessor [UCC 2–711(1), 2A–508(1)(a)].

The Right to Obtain the Goods on Insolvency   If a buyer or lessee has partially or fully paid for goods that are in the possession of a seller or lessor who becomes insolvent, the buyer or lessee can obtain the goods. The seller or lessor must have become insolvent within ten days after receiving the first payment, and the goods must be identified to the contract. To exercise this right, the buyer or lessee must pay the seller or lessor any unpaid balance of the purchase price or lease payments [UCC 2–502, 2A–522].

The Right to Obtain Specific Performance   A buyer or lessee can obtain specific performance if the goods are unique or the remedy at law (monetary damages) is inadequate [UCC 2–716(1), 2A–521(1)]. Ordinarily, an award of damages is sufficient to place a buyer or lessee in the position she or he would have occupied if the seller or lessor had fully performed.

When the contract is for the purchase of a particular work of art or a similarly unique item, however, damages may not be sufficient. Under these circumstances, equity requires that the seller or lessor perform exactly by delivering the particular goods identified to the contract (the remedy of specific performance).

CASE EXAMPLE 12.12   Together, Doreen Houseman and Eric Dare bought a house and a pedigreed dog. When the couple separated, they agreed that Dare would keep the house (and pay Houseman for her interest in it) and that Houseman would keep the dog. Houseman allowed Dare to take the dog for visits, but after one visit, Dare kept the dog. Houseman filed a lawsuit seeking specific performance of their agreement. The court found that because pets have special subjective value to their owners, a dog can be considered a unique good. Thus, an award of specific performance was appropriate.[10] ●

The Right of Cover   In certain situations, buyers and lessees can protect themselves by obtaining **cover**—that is, by buying or leasing substitute goods for those that were due under the contract. This option is available when the seller or lessor repudiates the contract or fails to deliver the goods, or when a buyer or lessee has rightfully rejected goods or revoked acceptance.

In purchasing or leasing substitute goods, the buyer or lessee must act in good faith and without unreasonable delay [UCC 2–712, 2A–518]. The buyer or lessee can recover from the seller or lessor:

1. The difference between the cost of cover and the contract price (or lease payments).
2. Incidental damages that resulted from the breach.
3. *Consequential damages* to compensate for indirect losses (such as lost profits) resulting from the breach that were reasonably foreseeable at the time of contract formation. The amount of consequential damages is reduced by any amount the buyer or lessee saved as a result of the breach (such as when a buyer obtains cover without having to pay delivery charges that were part of the original sales contract).

Cover A buyer or lessee's purchase on the open market of goods to substitute for those promised but never delivered by the seller. Under the Uniform Commercial Code, if the cost of cover exceeds the cost of the contract goods, the buyer or lessee can recover the difference, plus incidental and consequential damages.

---

10. *Houseman v. Dare,* 405 N.J.Super. 538, 966 A.2d 24 (2009).

Buyers and lessees are not required to cover, and failure to do so will not bar them from using any other remedies available under the UCC. A buyer or lessee who fails to cover, however, risks collecting a lower amount of consequential damages. A court may reduce the consequential damages by the amount of the loss that could have been avoided had the buyer or lessee purchased or leased substitute goods.

The Right to Replevy Goods

Replevin An action to recover specific goods in the hands of a party who is wrongfully withholding them from the other party.

Buyers and lessees also have the right to replevy goods. **Replevin**[11] is an action to recover identified goods in the hands of a party who is unlawfully withholding them. Under the UCC, a buyer or lessee can replevy goods identified to the contract if the seller or lessor has repudiated or breached the contract. To maintain an action to replevy goods, buyers and lessees must usually show that they were unable to cover for the goods after making a reasonable effort [UCC 2–716(3), 2A–521(3)].

The Right to Recover Damages

If a seller or lessor repudiates the contract or fails to deliver the goods, the buyer or lessee can sue for damages. For the buyer, the measure of recovery is the difference between the contract price and the market price of the goods at the time the buyer *learned* of the breach. For the lessee, the measure is the difference between the lease payments and the lease payments that could be obtained for the goods at the time the lessee learned of the breach.

The market price or market lease payments are determined at the place where the seller or lessor was supposed to deliver the goods. The buyer or lessee can also recover incidental and consequential damages less the expenses that were saved as a result of the breach [UCC 2–713, 2A–519].

CASE EXAMPLE 12.13 Les Entreprises Jacques Defour & Fils, Inc., contracted to buy a thirty-thousand-gallon industrial tank from Dinsick Equipment Corporation for $70,000. Les Entreprises hired Xaak Transport, Inc., to pick up the tank, but when Xaak arrived at the pickup location, there was no tank. Les Entreprises paid Xaak $7,459 for its services and filed a suit against Dinsick. The court awarded compensatory damages of $70,000 for the tank and incidental damages of $7,459 for the transport. The parties had an enforceable contract, which Les Entreprises had substantially performed by paying for the tank. Dinsick failed to tender or deliver the tank, or to refund the price. The shipping costs were a necessary part of performance, so this was a reasonable expense.[12] ●

Fresh produce is loaded for delivery. Under what circumstances can the buyer reject this produce?

(AP Images/Mike Groll)

The Right to Reject the Goods

If either the goods or their tender fails to conform to the contract in any respect, the buyer or lessee can reject all of the goods or any commercial unit of the goods [UCC 2–601, 2A–509]. On rejecting the goods, the buyer or lessee may obtain cover or cancel the contract, and may seek damages just as if the seller or lessor had refused to deliver the goods.

The buyer or lessee must reject the goods within a reasonable amount of time after delivery or tender of delivery and must seasonably (timely) notify the seller or lessor [UCC 2–602(1), 2A–509(2)]. The buyer or lessee must also designate defects that are ascertainable by reasonable inspection. A merchant-buyer or lessee has a good faith obligation to follow any reasonable instructions received from the seller or lessor with respect to the goods [UCC 2–603, 2A–511].

---

11. Pronounced ruh-*pleh*-vun, derived from the Old French word *plevir*, meaning "to pledge."
12. *Les Entreprises Jacques Defour & Fils, Inc. v. Dinsick Equipment Corp.*, 2011 WL 307501 (N.D.Ill. 2011).

Revocation of Acceptance

Acceptance of the goods precludes the buyer or lessee from exercising the right of rejection, but it does not necessarily prevent the buyer or lessee from pursuing other remedies. In certain circumstances, a buyer or lessee is permitted to *revoke* his or her acceptance of the goods.

Acceptance of a lot or a commercial unit can be revoked if the nonconformity *substantially* impairs the value of the lot or unit *and* if one of the following factors is present:

1. Acceptance was based on the reasonable assumption that the nonconformity would be cured, and it has not been cured within a reasonable period of time [UCC 2–608(1)(a), 2A–517(1)(a)].
2. The failure of the buyer or lessee to discover the nonconformity was reasonably induced by either the difficulty of discovery before acceptance or by assurances made by the seller or lessor [UCC 2–608(1)(b), 2A–517(1)(b)].

Revocation of acceptance is not effective until notice is given to the seller or lessor. Notice must occur within a reasonable time after the buyer or lessee either discovers or *should have discovered* the grounds for revocation. Additionally, revocation must occur before the goods have undergone any substantial change (such as spoilage) not caused by their own defects [UCC 2–608(2), 2A–517(4)]. Once acceptance is revoked, the buyer or lessee can pursue remedies, just as if the goods had been rejected.

The Right to Recover Damages for Accepted Goods

A buyer or lessee who has accepted nonconforming goods may also keep the goods and recover damages [UCC 2–714(1), 2A–519(3)]. To do so, the buyer or lessee must notify the seller or lessor of the breach within a reasonable time after the defect was or should have been discovered. Failure to give notice of the defects (breach) to the seller or lessor bars the buyer or lessee from pursuing any remedy [UCC 2–607(3), 2A–516(3)].

Is two years after a sale of goods a reasonable time period in which to discover a defect in those goods and notify the seller of a breach? That was the question in the following case.

Spotlight on Baseball Cards

Case 12.2
Fitl v. Strek
Supreme Court of Nebraska, 269 Neb. 51, 690 N.W.2d 605 (2005).

A 1952 Mickey Mantle Topps baseball card.

(Justin Lane/EPA/Newscom)

BACKGROUND AND FACTS   In 1995, James Fitl attended a sports-card show in San Francisco, California, where he met Mark Strek, doing business as Star Cards of San Francisco, an exhibitor at the show. Later, on Strek's representation that a certain 1952 Mickey Mantle Topps baseball card was in near-mint condition, Fitl bought the card from Strek for $17,750. Strek delivered it to Fitl in Omaha, Nebraska, and Fitl placed it in a safe-deposit box.

In May 1997, Fitl sent the card to Professional Sports Authenticators (PSA), a sports-card grading service. PSA told Fitl that the card was ungradable because it had been discolored and doctored. Fitl complained to Strek, who replied that Fitl should have initiated a return of the card within "a typical grace period for the unconditional return of a card, . . . 7 days to 1 month" of its receipt. In August, Fitl sent the card to ASA Accugrade, Inc. (ASA), another grading service,

for a second opinion of the value. ASA also concluded that the card had been refinished and trimmed. Fitl filed a suit in a Nebraska state court against Strek, seeking damages. The court awarded Fitl $17,750, plus his court costs. Strek appealed to the Nebraska Supreme Court.

IN THE WORDS OF THE COURT . . .
WRIGHT, J. Judge.
    * * * *

Strek claims that the [trial] court erred in determining that notification of the defective condition of the baseball card 2 years after the date of purchase was timely pursuant to [UCC] 2–607(3)(a).

Spotlight Case 12.2—Continues ➡

Spotlight Case 12.2—Continued

* * * The [trial] court found that Fitl had notified Strek within a reasonable time after discovery of the breach. Therefore, our review is whether the [trial] court's finding as to the reasonableness of the notice was clearly erroneous.

Section 2–607(3)(a) states: "Where a tender has been accepted * * * the buyer must within a reasonable time after he discovers or should have discovered any breach notify the seller of breach or be barred from any remedy." [Under UCC 1–204(2)] *"what is a reasonable time for taking any action depends on the nature, purpose and circumstances of such action."* [Emphasis added.]

The notice requirement set forth in Section 2–607(3)(a) serves three purposes.

* * * The most important one is to enable the seller to make efforts to cure the breach by making adjustments or replacements in order to minimize the buyer's damages and the seller's liability. A second policy is to provide the seller a reasonable opportunity to learn the facts so that he may adequately prepare for negotiation and defend himself in a suit. A third policy * * * is the same as the policy behind statutes of limitation: to provide a seller with a terminal point in time for liability.

* * * *A party is justified in relying upon a representation made to the party as a positive statement of fact when an investigation would be required to ascertain its falsity.* In order for Fitl to have determined that the baseball card had been altered, he would have been required to conduct an investigation. We find that he was not required to do so. Once Fitl learned that the baseball card had been altered, he gave notice to Strek. [Emphasis added.]

* * * One of the most important policies behind the notice requirement * * * is to allow the seller to cure the breach by making adjustments or replacements to minimize the buyer's damages and the seller's liability. However, even if Fitl had learned immediately upon taking possession of the baseball card that it was not authentic and had notified Strek at that time, there is no evidence that Strek could have made any adjustment or taken any action that would have minimized his liability. In its altered condition, the baseball card was worthless.

* * * Earlier notification would not have helped Strek prepare for negotiation or defend himself in a suit because the damage to Fitl could not be repaired. Thus, the policies behind the notice requirement, to allow the seller to correct a defect, to prepare for negotiation and litigation, and to protect against stale claims at a time beyond which an investigation can be completed, were not unfairly prejudiced by the lack of an earlier notice to Strek. Any problem Strek may have had with the party from whom he obtained the baseball card was a separate matter from his transaction with Fitl, and an investigation into the source of the altered card would not have minimized Fitl's damages.

DECISION AND REMEDY   The state supreme court affirmed the decision of the lower court. Under the circumstances, notice of a defect in the card two years after its purchase was reasonable. The buyer had reasonably relied on the seller's representation that the card was "authentic" (which it was not), and when the defects were discovered, the buyer had given timely notice.

WHAT IF THE FACTS WERE DIFFERENT?   *Suppose that Fitl and Strek had included in their deal a written clause requiring Fitl to give notice of any defect in the card within "7 days to 1 month" of its receipt. Would the result have been different? Why or why not?*

THE LEGAL ENVIRONMENT DIMENSION   *What might a court award to a buyer who prevails in a dispute such as the one in this case?*

Additional Provisions Affecting Remedies

The parties to a sales or lease contract can vary their respective rights and obligations by contractual agreement. For instance, a seller and buyer can expressly provide for remedies in addition to those provided in the UCC. They can also specify remedies in lieu of those provided in the UCC (including liquidated damages clauses—see Chapter 11), or they can change the measure of damages.

A seller can provide that the buyer's only remedy on the seller's breach will be repair or replacement of the item. Alternatively, the seller can limit the buyer's remedy to return of the goods and refund of the purchase price.

In sales and lease contracts, an agreed-on remedy is in addition to those provided in the UCC unless the parties expressly agree that the remedy is exclusive of all others [UCC 2–719(1), 2A–503(1),(2)]. If the parties state that a remedy is *exclusive*, then it is the sole (only) remedy.

Warranties

The UCC has numerous rules governing product warranties as they occur in sales and lease contracts. Articles 2 (on sales) and 2A (on leases) designate several types of warranties that can arise in a sales or lease contract, including warranties of title, express warranties, and implied warranties.

Because a warranty imposes a duty on the seller or lessor, a breach of warranty is a breach of the seller's or lessor's promise. Assuming that the parties have not agreed to limit or modify the remedies available, if the seller or lessor breaches a warranty, the buyer or lessee can sue to recover damages from the seller or lessor. Under some circumstances, a breach of warranty can allow the buyer or lessee to rescind (cancel) the agreement.

Title Warranties

Under the UCC, three types of title warranties—*good title*, *no liens*, and *no infringements* —can automatically arise in sales and lease contracts [UCC 2–312, 2A–211]. Normally, a seller or lessor can disclaim or modify these title warranties only by including *specific language* in the contract. For example, sellers may assert that they are transferring only such rights, title, and interest as they have in the goods.

What title warranties did the seller of this pipe-cutting machine make to the buyer?

In most sales, sellers warrant that they have good and valid title to the goods sold and that the transfer of the title is rightful [UCC 2–312(1)(a)]. A second warranty of title protects buyers and lessees who are *unaware* of any encumbrances (claims, charges, or liabilities—usually called *liens*[13]) against goods at the time the contract is made [UCC 2–312(1) (b), 2A–211(1)]. This warranty protects buyers who, for instance, unknowingly purchase goods that are subject to a creditor's security interest (a *security interest* is an interest in the goods that secures payment or performance of an obligation). If a creditor legally repossesses the goods from a buyer *who had no actual knowledge of the security interest,* the buyer can recover from the seller for breach of warranty. (A buyer who has *actual knowledge of a security interest* has no recourse against a seller.) Article 2A affords similar protection for lessees [UCC 2A–211(1)].

Finally, when the seller or lessor is a merchant, he or she automatically warrants that the buyer or lessee takes the good *free of infringements*. In other words, a merchant promises that the goods delivered are free from any copyright, trademark, or patent claims of a third person [UCC 2–312(3), 2A–211(2)].

Express Warranties

A seller or lessor can create an **express warranty** by making representations concerning the quality, condition, description, or performance potential of the goods. Under UCC 2–313 and 2A–210, express warranties arise when a seller or lessor indicates any of the following:

1. That the goods conform to any *affirmation* (a declaration that something is true) *of fact* or *promise* that the seller or lessor makes to the buyer or lessee about the goods. Such affirmations or promises are usually made during the bargaining process. Statements such as "these drill bits will *easily* penetrate stainless steel—and without dulling" are express warranties.
2. That the goods conform to any *description* of them. For instance, a label that reads "Crate contains one 150-horsepower diesel engine" or a contract that calls for the delivery of a "wool coat" creates an express warranty that the content of the goods sold conforms to the description.
3. That the goods conform to any *sample or model* of the goods shown to the buyer or lessee.

Express Warranty A seller's or lessor's oral or written promise, ancillary to an underlying sales or lease agreement, as to the quality, description, or performance of the goods being sold or leased.

---

13. Pronounced *leens*. Liens will be discussed in Chapter 13.

Is this logo an express warranty?

(Arcady/Shutterstock.com)

Puffery A salesperson's exaggerated claims concerning the quality of goods offered for sale. Such claims involve opinions rather than facts and are not considered to be legally binding promises or warranties.

Implied Warranty A warranty that the law derives by implication or inference from the nature of the transaction or the relative situation or circumstances of the parties.

Implied Warranty of Merchantability A warranty that goods being sold or leased are reasonably fit for the ordinary purpose for which they are sold or leased, are properly packaged and labeled, and are of fair quality.

Learning Objective 4
What implied warranties arise under the UCC?

Express warranties can be found in a seller's or lessor's advertisement, brochure, or promotional materials, in addition to being made orally or in an express warranty provision in a sales or lease contract.

Basis of the Bargain   To create an express warranty, a seller or lessor does not have to use formal words such as *warrant* or *guarantee*. It is only necessary that a reasonable buyer or lessee would regard the representation as being part of the basis of the bargain [UCC 2–313(2), 2A–210(2)]. The UCC does not define "basis of the bargain," however, and it is a question of fact in each case whether a representation was made at such a time and in such a way that it induced the buyer or lessee to enter into the contract. Therefore, if an express warranty is not intended, the marketing agent or salesperson should not promise too much.

Statements of Opinion and Value   Only statements of fact create express warranties. A seller or lessor who makes a statement that merely relates to the value or worth of the goods, or states an opinion about or recommends the goods, does not create an express warranty [UCC 2–313(2), 2A–210(2)].

EXAMPLE 12.14   Suppose that a seller claims, "This is the best used car to come along in years. It has four new tires and a 250-horsepower engine rebuilt this year." The seller has made several *affirmations of fact* that can create a warranty: the automobile has an engine, it has a 250-horsepower engine, the engine was rebuilt this year, there are four tires on the automobile, and the tires are new.

The seller's *opinion* that the vehicle is "the best used car to come along in years," however, is known as *puffery* and creates no warranty. ● (**Puffery** is an expression of opinion by a seller or lessor that is not made as a representation of fact.) It is not always easy to determine whether a statement constitutes an express warranty or puffery. The reasonableness of the buyer's or lessee's reliance appears to be the controlling criterion in many cases.

Implied Warranties

An **implied warranty** is one that *the law derives* by inference from the nature of the transaction or the relative situations or circumstances of the parties. Under the UCC, merchants impliedly warrant that the goods they sell or lease are merchantable and, in certain circumstances, fit for a particular purpose. In addition, an implied warranty may arise from a course of dealing or usage of trade. We examine these three types of implied warranties in the following subsections.

Implied Warranty of Merchantability   Every sale or lease of goods made *by a merchant* who deals in goods of the kind sold or leased automatically gives rise to an **implied warranty of merchantability** [UCC 2–314, 2A–212]. For instance, a merchant who is in the business of selling ski equipment makes an implied warranty of merchantability every time he sells a pair of skis. A neighbor selling her skis at a garage sale does not (because she is not in the business of selling goods of this type).

To be *merchantable*, goods must be "reasonably fit for the ordinary purposes for which such goods are used." They must be of at least average, fair, or medium-grade quality. "Merchantable" food, for instance, is food that is fit to eat on the basis of consumer expectations [UCC 2–314(1)]. The goods must also be adequately packaged and labeled, and they must conform to the promises or affirmations of fact made on the container or label, if any.

CASE EXAMPLE 12.15   Darrell Shoop bought a Dodge Dakota truck that had been manufactured by DaimlerChrysler Corporation. Almost immediately, he had problems with the truck. During the first eighteen months, the engine, suspension, steering, transmission, and other components required repairs twelve times, including at least five times for the same defect, which remained uncorrected. Shoop eventually traded in the truck and filed a lawsuit against DaimlerChrysler for breach of the implied warranty of merchantability. The court held that Shoop could maintain an action against DaimlerChrysler and use the fact that the truck had required a significant number of repairs as evidence that it was unmerchantable.[14] •

Implied Warranty of Fitness for a Particular Purpose   The **implied warranty of fitness for a particular purpose** arises when any seller or lessor (merchant or nonmerchant) knows the particular purpose for which a buyer or lessee will use the goods *and* knows that the buyer or lessee is relying on the skill and judgment of the seller or lessor to select suitable goods [UCC 2–315, 2A–213].

A "particular purpose" of the buyer or lessee differs from the "ordinary purpose for which goods are used" (merchantability). Goods can be merchantable but unfit for a particular purpose. **EXAMPLE 12.16**   Shakira needs a gallon of paint to match the color of her living room walls—a light shade somewhere between coral and peach. She takes a sample to Lowe's and requests a gallon of paint of that color. Instead, she is given a gallon of bright blue paint. Here, the salesperson has not breached any warranty of implied merchantability—the bright blue paint is of high quality and suitable for interior walls—but he or she has breached an implied warranty of fitness for a particular purpose. •

A seller or lessor is not required to have actual knowledge of the buyer's or lessee's particular purpose, so long as the seller or lessor "has reason to know" the purpose. For an implied warranty to be created, however, the buyer or lessee must have relied on the skill or judgment of the seller or lessor in selecting or furnishing suitable goods.

Implied Warranty of Fitness for a Particular Purpose A warranty that goods sold or leased are fit for the particular purpose for which a buyer or lessee will use the goods.

Warranties Implied from Prior Dealings or Trade Custom

Implied warranties can also arise (or be excluded or modified) as a result of *course of dealing* (prior conduct between the parties) or *usage of trade* [UCC 2–314(3), 2A–212(3)]. In the absence of evidence to the contrary, when both parties to a sales or lease contract have knowledge of a well-recognized trade custom, the courts will infer that both parties intended for that trade custom to apply to their contract.

For instance, if it is an industry-wide custom to lubricate new cars before they are delivered to buyers and a dealer fails to do so, the dealer is liable for damages resulting from the breach of an implied warranty.

Warranty Disclaimers

The UCC generally permits warranties to be disclaimed or limited by specific and unambiguous language, provided that the buyer or lessee is protected from surprise. The manner in which a seller or lessor can disclaim warranties varies depending on the type of warranty. All oral express warranties can be disclaimed by including in the contract a written (or an electronically recorded) disclaimer in language that is clear and conspicuous, and called to a buyer's or lessee's attention [UCC 2–316(1), 2A–214(1)]. Note, however, that a buyer or lessee must be made aware of any warranty disclaimers or modifications *at the time the contract is formed.*

Generally, unless circumstances indicate otherwise, the implied warranties of merchantability and fitness are disclaimed by expressions such as "as is" or "with all faults."[15] To specifically disclaim an implied warranty of merchantability, a seller or lessor must

---

14. *Shoop v. DaimlerChrysler Corp.*, 371 Ill.App.3d 1058, 864 N.E.2d 785, 309 Ill.Dec. 544 (2007).
15. Note that some states have laws that forbid "as is" sales. Other states do not allow disclaimers of warranties of merchantability for consumer goods.

mention the word *merchantability*, but the disclaimer need not be written [UCC 2–316(2), 2A–214(2)]. To specifically disclaim an implied warranty of fitness for a particular purpose, the disclaimer *must* be in a writing (or record) and must be conspicuous. The word *fitness* does not have to be mentioned.

Product Liability

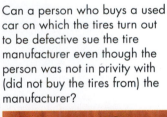

Product Liability The liability of manufacturers, sellers, and lessors of goods to consumers, users, and bystanders for injuries or damages that are caused by the goods.

Those who make, sell, or lease goods can be held liable for physical harm or property damage that those goods cause to a consumer, user, or bystander. This is called **product liability.** Product liability claims may be based on the theories of *negligence, misrepresentation,* and *strict liability.*

Negligence

If a manufacturer fails to exercise "due care" to make a product safe, a person who is injured by the product may sue the manufacturer for *negligence* (see Chapter 5).

Due Care Must Be Exercised   The manufacturer must exercise due care in designing the product, selecting the materials, using the appropriate production process, assembling the product, and placing adequate warnings on the label informing the user of dangers of which an ordinary person might not be aware. The duty of care also extends to the inspection and testing of any purchased products that are used in the final product sold by the manufacturer.

Privity of Contract Not Required   A product liability action based on negligence does not require *privity of contract* between the injured plaintiff and the defendant manufacturer. As was discussed in Chapter 11, *privity of contract* refers to the relationship that exists between the promisor and the promisee of a contract. Privity is the reason that only the parties to a contract normally can enforce that contract. In the context of product liability law, privity is not required. This means that a person who was injured by a defective product need not be the one who actually purchased the product to maintain a negligence suit against the manufacturer or seller of the product.

Can a person who buys a used car on which the tires turn out to be defective sue the tire manufacturer even though the person was not in privity with (did not buy the tires from) the manufacturer?

(Michael Temchine/AFP/Getty Images)

Misrepresentation

When a user or consumer is injured as a result of a manufacturer's or seller's fraudulent misrepresentation, the basis of liability may be the tort of fraud. The intentional mislabeling of packaged cosmetics, for instance, or the intentional concealment of a product's defects would constitute fraudulent misrepresentation. The misrepresentation must concern a material fact, and the seller must have intended to induce the buyer's reliance on the misrepresentation. Misrepresentation on a label or advertisement is enough to show an intent to induce the reliance of anyone who may use the product. In addition, the buyer must have relied on the misrepresentation.

Strict Product Liability

Under the doctrine of strict liability (see Chapter 5), people may be liable for the results of their acts regardless of their intentions or their exercise of reasonable care. In addition, liability does not depend on privity of contract. The law imposes strict product liability as a matter of public policy. This public policy rests on the following threefold assumption that:

1. Consumers should be protected against unsafe products.
2. Manufacturers and distributors should not escape liability for faulty products simply because they are not in privity of contract with the ultimate user of those products.
3. Manufacturers, sellers, and lessors of products generally are in a better position than consumers to bear the costs associated with injuries caused by their products—costs that they can ultimately pass on to all consumers in the form of higher prices.

California was the first state to impose strict product liability in tort on manufacturers. Today, the majority of states recognize strict product liability, although some state courts limit its application to situations involving personal injuries (rather than property damage).

Requirements for Strict Liability   After the *Restatement (Second) of Torts* was issued in 1964, Section 402A became a widely accepted statement of how the doctrine of strict liability should be applied to sellers of goods. The bases for an action in strict liability that are set forth in Section 402A of the *Restatement* can be summarized by the following six requirements. Depending on the jurisdiction, if these requirements are met, a manufacturer's liability to an injured party can be almost unlimited.

Learning Objective 5
What are the elements of a cause of action in strict product liability?

1. The product must be in a *defective condition* when the defendant sold it.
2. The defendant must normally be engaged in the *business of selling* (or otherwise distributing) that product.
3. The product must be *unreasonably dangerous* to the user or consumer because of its defective condition (in most states).
4. The plaintiff must incur *physical harm* to self or property by use or consumption of the product.
5. The defective condition must be the *proximate cause* of the injury or damage.
6. The *goods must not have been substantially changed* from the time the product was sold to the time the injury was sustained.

Proving a Defective Condition   Under these requirements, in any action against a manufacturer, seller, or lessor, the plaintiff does not have to show why or in what manner the product became defective. The plaintiff does, however, have to prove that the product was defective at the time it left the hands of the seller or lessor and that this defective condition made it "unreasonably dangerous" to the user or consumer. (See this chapter's *Beyond Our Borders* feature that follows for a discussion of how foreign suppliers were held liable for defective goods sold in the United States.) If the product was delivered in a safe condition and subsequent mishandling made it harmful to the user, the seller or lessor usually is not strictly liable.

Unreasonably Dangerous Products   The *Restatement* recognizes that many products cannot possibly be made entirely safe for all uses. Thus, sellers or lessors are held liable only for products that are *unreasonably* dangerous. A court may consider a product so defective as to be an **unreasonably dangerous product** in either of the following situations:

1. The product is dangerous beyond the expectation of the ordinary consumer.
2. A less dangerous alternative was economically feasible for the manufacturer, but the manufacturer failed to produce it.

As will be discussed next, a product may be unreasonably dangerous due to a flaw in the manufacturing process or in the design, or due to an inadequate warning.

Unreasonably Dangerous Product A product that is so defective that it is dangerous beyon the expection of an ordinary consumer or a product for which a less dangerous alternative was feasible but the manufacturer failed to produce it.

Product Defects—Restatement (Third) of Torts   The *Restatement (Third) of Torts: Products Liability* defines the three types of product defects that have

BEYOND OUR BORDERS

Imposing Product Liability as Far Away as China

Chinese drywall started being used in the construction of houses in the United States in 2003. By 2007, thousands of homes had been constructed with this product in Alabama, Florida, Louisiana, Mississippi, and a few other states. There was a problem, though—use of the Chinese drywall caused blackening and pitting of electrical wires. Homeowners began to notice an odor similar to rotten eggs. Air-conditioning

units started failing, as did ceiling fans, alarm systems, refrigerators, and other appliances.

Numerous lawsuits were filed against the Chinese drywall manufacturers, which initially fought the claims. When the number of lawsuits ran into the thousands, however, the Chinese companies decided to settle.

The estimated value of the settlement is between $800 million and $1 billion.

It includes an uncapped fund to pay for repairs for about 4,500 homes and a separate fund capped at $30 million that will be used to pay for health problems stemming from the defective Chinese drywall.

Critical Thinking
Could U.S. companies that sold Chinese drywall to consumers also be held liable for damages? Why or why not?

---

traditionally been recognized in product liability law—manufacturing defects, design defects, and inadequate warnings.

If this ladder collapses and the worker is injured, who could be held liable?

Manufacturing Defects   According to Section 2(a) of the *Restatement (Third) of Torts: Products Liability,* a product "contains a manufacturing defect when the product departs from its intended design even though all possible care was exercised in the preparation and marketing of the product." Basically, a manufacturing defect is a departure from a product's design specifications that results in products that are physically flawed, damaged, or incorrectly assembled. A glass bottle that is made too thin and explodes in a consumer's face has a manufacturing defect.

Usually, such defects occur when a manufacturer fails to assemble, test, or adequately check the quality of a product. Liability is imposed on the manufacturer regardless of whether the manufacturer's quality control efforts were "reasonable." The idea behind holding defendants strictly liable for manufacturing defects is to encourage greater investment in product safety and stringent quality control standards. (For more information on how effective quality control procedures can help businesses reduce their potential legal liability for breached warranties and defective products, see the *Linking Business Law to Corporate Management* feature at the end of this chapter.)

Design Defects   Unlike a product with a manufacturing defect, a product with a design defect is made in conformity with the manufacturer's design specifications, but nevertheless results in injury to the user because the design itself is flawed. The product's design creates an unreasonable risk to the user. A product "is defective in design when the foreseeable risks of harm posed by the product could have been reduced or avoided by the adoption of a reasonable alternative design by the seller or other distributor, or a predecessor in the commercial chain of distribution, and the omission of the alternative design renders the product not reasonably safe."[16]

To successfully assert a design defect, a plaintiff has to show that a reasonable alternative design was available and that the defendant's failure to adopt the alternative design rendered the product unreasonably dangerous. In other words, a manufacturer or other defendant is liable only when the harm was reasonably preventable.

A court can consider a broad range of factors in deciding claims of design defects. These factors include the magnitude and probability of the foreseeable risks, as well as the relative advantages and disadvantages of the product as designed and as it alternatively could have

---

16. *Restatement (Third) of Torts: Products Liability,* Section 2(b).

been designed. Basically, most courts engage in a risk-utility analysis, determining whether the risk of harm from the product as designed outweighs its utility to the user and to the public.

The court in the following case reviewed whether the plaintiff had satisfied the risk-utility test.

Case 12.3

Riley v. Ford Motor Co.
Court of Appeals of South Carolina, 408 S.C. 1, 757 S.E.2d 422 (2014).

(Mark Scheuern/Alamy)

BACKGROUND AND FACTS   Jasper County Sheriff Benjamin Riley was driving his Ford F-150 pickup truck near Ehrhardt, South Carolina, when it collided with another vehicle. The impact caused Riley's truck to leave the road and roll over. The driver's door of the truck opened in the collision, and Riley was ejected and killed. Riley's widow, Laura, as the representative of his estate, filed a product liability suit in a South Carolina state court against Ford Motor Company. The plaintiff alleged that the design of the truck's door-latch system allowed the door to open in the collision. The court awarded the estate $900,000 in damages "because of the stature of Riley and what he's done in life, what he's contributed to his family." Ford appealed, arguing that the plaintiff had not proved the existence of a reasonable alternative design.

IN THE WORDS OF THE COURT . . .
FEW, C.J. [Chief Justice]
    * * * *

* * * To satisfy the risk-utility test, a plaintiff must meet the requirement of showing a feasible alternative design. * * * *The very nature of feasible alternative design evidence entails the manufacturer's decision to employ one design over another. The weighing of costs and benefits attendant to that decision is the essence of the risk-utility test.* [Emphasis added.]

[Riley's 1998 F-150, a model that Ford called the PN96, contained a rod-linkage door-latch system.] The Estate * * * presented evidence of Ford's own alternative design for a [cable-linkage] door-latch system, which Ford used in F-150 trucks manufactured before Riley's 1998 model, and which Ford originally incorporated into the design of the 1998 model.
    * * * *

The Estate's primary evidence establishing the reasonableness and feasibility of the cable-linkage system was the fact that Ford designed, manufactured, and sold F-150 trucks with the cable-linkage door-latch system only three model years before Riley's PN96. In addition, the Estate presented extensive evidence concerning Ford's cable-linkage design. According to [a study conducted by Ford in 1994], the advantages of cables,

when compared to rods, included: (1) packaging—"cable systems require less package space"; (2) safety—"cable systems are more robust to crash"; (3) performance—"cable systems provide better performance to the customer"; and (4) manufacturing—"cable systems are easier for assembly plants to handle," "are tolerant to build variations between latch and handle," "reduce cost and reduce operator dependence," and "reduce complexity in service." The only disadvantage indicated by the report was that "cable systems are from two to three times as expensive as rods," costing $9.00 per door instead of $4.25 per door if Ford used a rod system. A second report Ford produced sometime after 1993, which compared rod and cable systems, concluded [that] cable systems "improved quality," were "easier to install," and were more "robust to door foreshortening." The only disadvantage listed was "higher cost"—"$0.85/door more than rods."

These reports demonstrate Ford conducted its own risk-utility analysis. Specifically, Ford considered the costs, safety and functionality associated with the alternative design and concluded the cable-linkage system was a feasible, if not superior, alternative design to the * * * rod system.

DECISION AND REMEDY   A state intermediate appellate court affirmed the lower court's ruling. Evidence showed that Ford knew of a reasonable alternative design for the rod-linkage door-latch system. Ford was aware of the system's safety problems and had conducted a risk-utility analysis of a cable-linkage system, concluding that it was a "feasible, if not superior, alternative."

THE LEGAL ENVIRONMENT DIMENSION   *By what means did the plaintiff most likely discover the defendant's studies of an alternative design?*

WHAT IF THE FACTS WERE DIFFERENT?   *Suppose that the plaintiff had not had the evidence cited in the court's opinion. How might the plaintiff have met the requirement to show a reasonable alternative design in that situation?*

Inadequate Warnings   A product may also be deemed defective because of inadequate instructions or warnings. A product will be considered defective "when the foreseeable risks of harm posed by the product could have been reduced or avoided by the provision of reasonable instructions or warnings by the seller or other distributor, or a predecessor in the commercial chain of distribution, and the omission of the instructions or warnings renders the product not reasonably safe."[17] Generally, a seller must also warn consumers of the harm that can result from the *foreseeable misuse* of its product.

Important factors for a court to consider include the risks of a product, the "content and comprehensibility" and "intensity of expression" of warnings and instructions, and the "characteristics of expected user groups." Courts apply a "reasonableness" test to determine if the warnings adequately alert consumers to the product's risks. For instance, children will likely respond more readily to bright, bold, simple warning labels, while educated adults might need more detailed information.

An action alleging that a product is defective due to an inadequate label can be based on state law. (For a discussion of a case involving a state law that required warning labels on violent video games, see this chapter's *Insight into Ethics* feature.)

Other Applications of Strict Liability

Almost all courts extend the strict liability of manufacturers and other sellers to injured bystanders. **EXAMPLE 12.17**   A forklift that Trent is operating will not go into reverse, and as a result, it runs into a bystander. In this situation, the bystander can sue the manufacturer of the defective forklift under strict liability (and possibly bring a negligence action against the forklift operator as well). •

Strict liability also applies to suppliers of component parts. **EXAMPLE 12.18**   Toyota buys brake pads from a subcontractor and puts them in Corollas without changing their composition. If those pads are defective, both the supplier of the brake pads and Toyota will be held strictly liable for the injuries caused by the defects. •

Defenses to Product Liability

Manufacturers, sellers, or lessors can raise several defenses to avoid liability for harms caused by their products. We look at some of these defenses in the following subsections.

Assumption of Risk

Assumption of risk can sometimes be used as a defense in a product liability action. To establish such a defense, the defendant must show that (1) the plaintiff knew and appreciated the risk created by the product defect and (2) the plaintiff voluntarily assumed the risk, even though it was unreasonable to do so.

Product Misuse

Similar to the defense of voluntary assumption of risk is that of product misuse, which occurs when a product is used for a purpose for which it was not intended. The courts have severely limited this defense, however, and it is now recognized as a defense *only when the particular use was not reasonably foreseeable.* If the misuse is foreseeable, the seller must take measures to guard against it.

Comparative Negligence

Developments in the area of comparative negligence, or fault (discussed in Chapter 5), have also affected the doctrine of strict liability. In the past, the plaintiff's conduct was not a defense to liability for a defective product. Today, courts in many jurisdictions consider the negligent or intentional actions of both the plaintiff and the defendant when apportioning liability and awarding damages.

---

17. *Restatement (Third) of Torts, Products Liability*, Section 2(c).

INSIGHT INTO ETHICS

WARNING LABELS FOR VIDEO GAMES

Almost every product that you purchase in the physical world has one or more warning labels. Indeed, some critics argue that these labels have become so long and ubiquitous that consumers ignore them. In other words, putting warnings on just about everything defeats their original purpose.

Until recently, video games have largely escaped mandated warning labels, although the video game industry has instituted a voluntary rating system to provide information about a video game's content. Each video game is assigned one of six age-specific ratings, ranging from "Early Childhood" to "Adults Only."

Should video games, whether downloaded or bought on a CD-ROM or DVD, have additional warnings to advise potential users (or their parents) that the games might be overly violent? When the California legislature enacted a law imposing restrictions and a labeling requirement on the sale or rental of "violent video games" to minors, this issue became paramount.[a]

Video Software Dealers Sue the State

The Video Software Dealers Association, along with the Entertainment Software Association, immediately brought a suit in federal district court seeking to invalidate the law. The court granted summary judgment in favor of the plaintiffs.

The act defined a violent video game as one in which "the range of options available to a player includes killing, maiming, dismembering, or sexually assaulting an image of a human being." While agreeing that some video games are unquestionably violent by everyday standards, the trial court pointed out that many video games are based on popular novels or motion pictures and have extensive plot lines.

Accordingly, the court found that the definition of a violent video game was unconstitutionally vague and thus violated the First Amendment's guarantee of freedom of speech. The court also noted the existence of the voluntary rating system. The U.S. Court of Appeals for the Ninth Circuit affirmed the district court's decision.[b]

The United States Supreme Court's Decision

The state of California appealed to the United States Supreme Court, but in 2011 the Court affirmed the decision in favor of the video game and software industries. The Court noted that video games are entitled to First Amendment protection. Because California had failed to show that the statute was justified by a compelling government interest and that the law was narrowly tailored to serve that interest, the Court ruled that the statute was unconstitutional.[c]

For Critical Analysis
Insight into the Social Environment

Should victims of a mass shooting be able to sue the manufacturer of a violent video game for a design defect if the shooter had been a devoted player of that game? Discuss.

---

a. California Civil Code Sections 1746–1746.5.

b. *Video Software Dealers Association v. Schwarzenegger,* 556 F.3d 950 (9th Cir. 2009).

c. *Brown v. Entertainment Merchants Association,* ___ U.S. ___, 131 S.Ct. 2729, 180 L.Ed.2d 708 (2011).

Thus, a defendant may be able to limit at least some of its liability for injuries caused by its defective product if it can show that the plaintiff's misuse of the product contributed to the injuries. When proved, comparative negligence differs from other defenses in that it does not completely absolve the defendant of liability, but it can reduce the amount of damages that will be awarded to the plaintiff.

Commonly Known Dangers   The dangers associated with certain products (such as sharp knives and guns) are so commonly known that manufacturers need not warn users of those dangers. If a defendant succeeds in convincing the court that a plaintiff's injury resulted from a commonly known danger, the defendant normally will not be liable.

Reviewing . . . Sales, Leases, and Product Liability

Guy Holcomb owns and operates Oasis Goodtime Emporium, an adult entertainment establishment. Holcomb wanted to create an adult Internet system for Oasis that would offer customers adult theme videos and "live" chat room programs using performers at the club. On May 10, Holcomb signed a work order authorizing Thomas Consulting Group (TCG) "to deliver a working prototype of a customer chat system, demonstrating the integration of live video and chatting in a Web browser." In exchange for creating the prototype, Holcomb agreed to pay TCG $64,697. On May 20, Holcomb signed an additional work order in the amount of $12,943 for TCG to install a customized firewall system. The work orders stated that Holcomb would make monthly installment payments to TCG, and both parties expected the work would be finished by September.

Due to unforeseen problems largely attributable to system configuration and software incompatibility, the project required more time than anticipated. By the end of the summer, the Web site was still not ready, and Holcomb had fallen behind in his payments to TCG. TCG threatened to cease work and file a suit for breach of contract unless the bill was paid. Rather than make further payments, Holcomb wanted to abandon the Web site project. Using the information presented in the chapter, answer the following questions.

1. Would a court be likely to decide that the transaction between Holcomb and TCG was covered by the Uniform Commercial Code (UCC)? Why or why not?
2. Would a court be likely to consider Holcomb a merchant under the UCC? Why or why not?
3. Did the parties have a valid contract under the UCC? Were any terms left open in the contract? If so, which terms? How would a court deal with open terms?
4. Suppose that Holcomb and TCG meet in October in an attempt to resolve their problems. At that time, the parties reach an oral agreement that TCG will continue to work without demanding full payment of the past due amounts and Holcomb will pay TCG $5,000 per week. Assuming the contract falls under the UCC, is the oral agreement enforceable? Why or why not?

Debate This The UCC should require the same degree of definiteness of terms, especially with respect to price and quantity, as contract law does.

LINKING BUSINESS LAW to Corporate Management
Quality Control

In this chapter, you learned that breaches of warranties and manufacturing and design defects can give rise to liability. Although it is possible to minimize liability through warranty disclaimers and various defenses to product liability claims, all businesspersons know that such disclaimers and defenses do not necessarily fend off expensive lawsuits.

The legal issues surrounding product liability and warranties relate directly to quality control. As all of your management courses will emphasize, quality control is a major issue facing

every manager in all organizations. Companies that have cost-effective quality control systems produce products with fewer manufacturing and design defects. As a result, these companies incur fewer potential and actual warranty and product liability lawsuits.

Three Types of Quality Control

Most management systems involve three types of quality control—preventive, concurrent, and feedback. They apply at different stages of the manufacturing process: preventive quality control occurs before the process begins, concurrent control takes place during the process, and feedback control occurs after it is finished.

In a typical manufacturing process, for example, preventive quality control might involve inspecting raw materials before they are put into the production process. Once the process begins, measuring and monitoring devices constantly assess quality standards as part of a concurrent quality control system. When the standards are not being met, employees correct the problem.

Once the manufacturing is completed, the products undergo a final quality inspection as part of the feedback quality control system. Of course, there are economic limits to how complete the final inspection will be. A refrigerator can be tested for an hour, a day, or a year. Management faces a trade-off. The less the refrigerator is tested, the sooner it gets to market and the faster the company receives its payment. The shorter the testing period, however, the higher the probability of a defect that will cost the manufacturer because of its expressed or implied warranties.

Total Quality Management (TQM)

Some managers attempt to reduce warranty and product liability costs by relying on a concurrent quality control system known as total quality management (TQM). This is an organization-wide effort to infuse quality into every activity in a company through continuous improvement.

Quality circles are a popular TQM technique. These are groups of six to twelve employees who volunteer to meet regularly to discuss problems and how to solve them. In a continuous stream manufacturing process, for example, a quality circle might consist of workers from different phases in the production process. Quality circles force changes in the production process that affect workers who are actually on the production line

Benchmarking is another technique used in TQM. In benchmarking, a company continuously measures its products against those of its toughest competitors or the industry leaders in order to identify areas for improvement. In the automobile industry, benchmarking enabled several Japanese firms to overtake U.S. automakers in terms of quality. Some argue that Toyota gained worldwide market share by effectively using this type of quality control management system.

Another TQM system is called *Six Sigma*. Motorola introduced the quality principles in this system in the late 1980s, but Six Sigma has now become a generic term for a quality control approach that takes nothing for granted. It is based on a five-step methodology: define, measure, analyze, improve, and control. Six Sigma controls emphasize discipline and a relentless attempt to achieve higher quality (and lower costs). A possible impediment to the institution of a Six Sigma program is that it requires a major commitment from top management because it may involve widespread changes throughout the entire organization.

Critical Thinking

Quality control leads to fewer defective products and fewer lawsuits. Consequently, managers know that quality control is important to their company's long-term financial health. At the same time, the more quality control managers impose on their organization, the higher the average cost per unit of whatever is produced and sold. How does a manager decide how much quality control to undertake?

Key Terms

conforming goods 328	implied warranty of fitness for a particular purpose 339	lessor 322	replevin 334
cover 333		merchant 322	sale 318
cure 329	implied warranty of merchantability 338	perfect tender rule 329	sales contract 318
express warranty 337	intangible property 319	predominant-factor test 320	tangible property 319
firm offer 324	lease agreement 322	product liability 340	tender of delivery 328
implied warranty 338	lessee 322	puffery 338	unreasonably dangerous product 341

Chapter Summary: Sales, Leases, and Product Liability

The Scope of Articles 2 and 2A	1. *Article 2 (sales)*—Article 2 of the UCC governs contracts for the sale of goods (tangible, movable personal property). The common law of contracts also applies to sales contracts to the extent that the common law has not been modified by the UCC. If there is a conflict between a common law rule and the UCC, the UCC controls. Special rules apply to merchants.
	2. *Article 2A (leases)*—Article 2A governs contracts for the lease of goods. Except that it applies to leases, instead of sales, of goods, Article 2A is essentially a repetition of Article 2 and varies only to reflect differences between sales and lease transactions.

Continued

Chapter Summary: Sales, Leases, and Product Liability—Continued

Formation of Sales and Lease Contracts	1. *Offer*—
	    a. Not all terms have to be included for a contract to be formed (only the quantity term must be specified).
	    b. The price does not have to be included for a contract to be formed.
	    c. Particulars of performance can be left open.
	    d. A written and signed offer by a *merchant*, covering a period of three months or less, is irrevocable without payment of consideration.
	2. *Acceptance*—
	    a. Acceptance may be made by any reasonable means of communication. It is effective when dispatched.
	    b. An offer can be accepted by a promise to ship or by prompt shipment of conforming goods, or by prompt shipment of nonconforming goods if not accompanied by a notice of accommodation.
	    c. Acceptance by performance requires notice within a reasonable time. Otherwise, the offer can be treated as lapsed.
	    d. A definite expression of acceptance creates a contract even if the terms of the acceptance differ from those of the offer, unless the different terms in the acceptance are expressly conditioned on the offeror's assent to those terms.
	3. *Consideration*—A modification of a contract for the sale of goods does not require consideration.
	4. *The Statute of Frauds*—All contracts for the sale of goods priced at $500 or more must be in a writing or electronic record that is signed by the party against whom enforcement is sought. A contract is not enforceable beyond the quantity shown in the writing.
	    a. When written confirmation of an oral contract *between merchants* is not objected to in writing by the receiver within ten days, the contract is enforceable.
	    b. Exceptions to the Statute of Frauds are made when the goods are specially manufactured, when the contract has been partially performed, and when there have been admissions.

Performance	1. The seller or lessor must tender *conforming goods* to the buyer or lessee. Tender must take place at a *reasonable hour* and in a *reasonable manner*. Under the perfect tender doctrine, the seller or lessor must tender goods that conform exactly to the terms of the contract [UCC 2–503(1), 2A–508(1)]. 2. If the seller or lessor tenders nonconforming goods prior to the performance date and the buyer or lessee rejects them, the seller or lessor may cure (repair or replace the goods) within the contract time for performance [UCC 2–508(1), 2A–513(1)]. 3. If the agreed-on means of delivery becomes impracticable or unavailable, the seller must substitute an alternative means (such as a different carrier) if one is available [UCC 2–614(1)]. 4. On tender of delivery by the seller or lessor, the buyer or lessee must pay for the goods at the time and place the goods are received, unless the sale is made on credit. 5. The buyer or lessee can show acceptance of delivered goods expressly in words or by conduct or by failing to reject the goods after a reasonable period of time following inspection or after having had a reasonable opportunity to inspect them [UCC 2–606(1), 2A–515(1)]. A buyer will be deemed to have accepted goods if he or she performs any act inconsistent with the seller's ownership [UCC 2–606(1)(c)]. 6. If, before the time for performance, either party clearly indicates to the other an intention not to perform, this is called anticipatory repudiation. Under UCC 2–610 and 2A–402, the nonbreaching party may either treat the breach as final by pursuing a remedy or wait and hope that the other party will perform. In either situation, the nonbreaching party may suspend performance.

Remedies for Breach	1. *Remedies of the seller or lessor*—When a buyer or lessee breaches the contract, a seller or lessor can withhold or discontinue performance. If the seller or lessor is still in possession of the goods, the seller or lessor can resell or dispose of the goods and hold the buyer or lessee liable for any loss [UCC 2–703(d), 2–706(1), 2A–523(1)(e), 2A–527(1)]. If the goods cannot be resold or disposed of, an unpaid seller or lessor can bring an action to recover the purchase price or payments due under the contract, plus incidental damages [UCC 2–709(1), 2A–529(1)]. If the buyer or lessee repudiates the contract or wrongfully refuses to accept goods, the seller or lessor can recover the damages that were sustained.
	2. *Remedies of the buyer or lessee*—When the seller or lessor breaches, the buyer or lessee can choose from a number of remedies, including the following:
	    a. Obtain specific performance (when the goods are unique and when the remedy at law is inadequate) [UCC 2–716(1), 2A–521(1)].
	    b. Obtain cover (in certain situations) [UCC 2–712, 2A–518].
	    c. Sue to recover damages [UCC 2–713, 2A–519].
	    d. Reject the goods [UCC 2–601, 2A–509].
	    e. Revoke acceptance (in certain circumstances) [UCC 2–608, 2A–517].
	    f. Accept the goods and recover damages [UCC 2–607, 2–714, 2–717, 2A–519].

Chapter Summary: Sales, Leases, and Product Liability—Continued

Remedies for Breach — Continued	3. The parties can agree to vary their respective rights and remedies in their agreement. If the contract states that a remedy is exclusive, then that is the sole remedy.

Warranties	1. *Title warranties*—The seller or lessor automatically warrants that he or she has good title, and that there are no liens or infringements on the property being sold or leased.
	2. *Express warranties*—An express warranty arises under the UCC when a seller or lessor indicates, as part of the basis of the bargain, that the goods conform to any of the following:
	  a. An affirmation or promise of fact.
	  b. A description of the goods.
	  c. A sample shown to the buyer or lessee [UCC 2–313, 2A–210].
	3. *Implied warranties*—
	  a. The implied warranty of merchantability automatically arises when the seller or lessor is a merchant who deals in the kind of goods sold or leased. The seller or lessor warrants that the goods sold or leased are of proper quality, are properly labeled, and are reasonably fit for the ordinary purposes for which such goods are used [UCC 2–314, 2A–212].
	  b. The implied warranty of fitness for a particular purpose arises when the buyer's or lessee's purpose or use is expressly or impliedly known by the seller or lessor and the buyer or lessee purchases or leases the goods in reliance on the seller's or lessor's selection [UCC 2–315, 2A–213].
	4. Warranties, both express and implied, can be disclaimed or qualified by a seller or lessor, but disclaimers generally must be specific and unambiguous, and often must be in writing.

Product Liability	1. *Liability based on negligence*—A manufacturer is liable for failure to exercise due care to any person who sustains an injury proximately caused by a negligently made (defective) product.
	2. *Strict liability requirements*—
	  a. The defendant must sell the product in a defective condition.
	  b. The defendant must normally be engaged in the business of selling that product.
	  c. The product must be unreasonably dangerous to the user or consumer because of its defective condition (in most states).
	  d. The plaintiff must incur physical harm to self or property by use or consumption of the product.
	  e. The defective condition must be the proximate cause of the injury or damage.
	  f. The goods must not have been substantially changed from the time the product was sold to the time the injury was sustained.
	3. *Product defects*—A product may be defective in its manufacture, its design, or the instructions or warnings that come with it.
	4. *Other applications of strict liability*—Manufacturers and other sellers are liable for harms suffered by bystanders as a result of defective products. Suppliers of component parts are strictly liable for defective parts that, when incorporated into a product, cause injuries to users.
	5. *Defenses to product liability*—
	  a. Assumption of risk—The user or consumer knew of the risk of harm and voluntarily assumed it.
	  b. Product misuse—The user or consumer misused the product in a way unforeseeable by the manufacturer.
	  c. Comparative negligence—Liability may be distributed between the plaintiff and the defendant under the doctrine of comparative negligence if the plaintiff's misuse of the product contributed to the risk of injury.
	  d. Commonly known dangers—If a defendant succeeds in convincing the court that a plaintiff's injury resulted from a commonly known danger, such as the danger associated with using a sharp knife, the defendant will not be liable.

Issue Spotters

1. E-Design, Inc., orders 150 computer desks. Fav-O-Rite Supplies, Inc., ships 150 printer stands. Is this an acceptance of the offer or a counteroffer? If it is an acceptance, is it a breach of the contract? What if Fav-O-Rite told E-Design it was sending the printer stands as "an accommodation"? (See *Formation of Sales and Lease Contracts*.)
2. Rim Corporation makes tire rims and sells them to Superior Vehicles, Inc., which installs them on cars. One set of rims is defective, which an inspection would reveal. Superior does not inspect the rims. The car with the defective rims is sold to Town Auto Sales, which sells the car to Uri. Soon, the car is in an accident caused by the defective rims, and Uri is injured. Is Superior Vehicles liable? Explain your answer. (See *Product Liability*.)

—Check your answers to the Issue Spotters against the answers provided in Appendix D at the end of this text.

For Review

1. How do Article 2 and Article 2A of the UCC differ? What types of transactions does each article cover?
2. Under the UCC, if an offeree includes additional or different terms in an acceptance, will a contract result? If so, what happens to these terms?
3. What remedies are available to a seller or lessor when the buyer or lessee breaches the contract? What remedies are available to a buyer or lessee if the seller or lessor breaches the contract?
4. What implied warranties arise under the UCC?
5. What are the elements of a cause of action in strict product liability?

Business Scenarios and Case Problems

12–1. Anticipatory Repudiation. Moore contracted in writing to sell her 2012 Hyundai Santa Fe to Hammer for $16,500. Moore agreed to deliver the car on Wednesday, and Hammer promised to pay the $16,500 on the following Friday. On Tuesday, Hammer informed Moore that he would not be buying the car after all. By Friday, Hammer had changed his mind again and tendered $16,500 to Moore. Moore, although she had not sold the car to another party, refused the tender and refused to deliver. Hammer claimed that Moore had breached their contract. Moore contended that Hammer's repudiation released her from her duty to perform under the contract. Who is correct, and why? (See *Performance.*)

12–2. Product Misuse. Five-year-old Cheyenne Stark was riding in the backseat of her parents' Ford Taurus. Cheyenne was not sitting in a booster seat. Instead, she was using a seatbelt designed by Ford, but was wearing the shoulder belt behind her back. The car was involved in a collision. As a result, Cheyenne suffered a spinal cord injury and was paralyzed from the waist down. The family filed a suit against Ford Motor Co., alleging that the seatbelt was defectively designed. Could Ford successfully claim that Cheyenne had misused the seatbelt? Why or why not? [*Stark v. Ford Motor Co.,* 693 S.E.2d 253 (N.C.App. 2010)] (See *Product Liability.*)

12–3. Additional Terms. B.S. International, Ltd. (BSI), makes costume jewelry. JMAM, LLC, is a wholesaler of costume jewelry. JMAM sent BSI a letter with the terms for orders, including the necessary procedure for obtaining credit for items that customers rejected. The letter stated, "By signing below, you agree to the terms." Steven Baracsi, BSI's owner, signed the letter and returned it. For six years, BSI made jewelry for JMAM, which resold it. Items rejected by customers were sent back to JMAM, but were never returned to BSI. BSI filed a suit against JMAM, claiming $41,294.21 for the unreturned items. BSI showed the court a copy of JMAM's terms. Across the bottom had been typed a "PS" requiring the return of rejected merchandise. Was this "PS" part of the contract? Discuss. [*B.S. International, Ltd. v. JMAM, LLC,* 13 A.3d 1057 (R.I. 2011)] (See *Formation of Sales and Lease Contracts.*)

12–4. Spotlight on Apple—Implied Warranties. Alan Vitt purchased an iBook G4 laptop computer from Apple, Inc. Shortly after the one-year warranty expired, the laptop failed to work due to a weakness in the product manufacture. Vitt sued Apple, arguing that the laptop should have lasted "at least a couple of years," which Vitt believed was a reasonable consumer expectation for a laptop. Vitt claimed that Apple's descriptions of the laptop as "durable," "rugged," "reliable," and "high performance" were affirmative statements concerning the quality and performance of the laptop, which Apple did not meet. How should the court rule? Why? [*Vitt v. Apple Computer, Inc.,* 2012 WL 627702 (9th Cir. 2012)] (See *Warranties.*)

12–5. Business Case Problem with Sample Answer— Nonconforming Goods. Padma Paper Mills, Ltd., converts waste paper into usable paper. In 2007, Padma entered into a contract with Universal Exports, Inc., under which Universal Exports certified that it would ship white envelope cuttings, and Padma paid $131,000 for the paper. When the shipment arrived, however, Padma discovered that Universal Exports had sent multicolored paper plates and other brightly colored paper products. Padma accepted the goods but notified Universal Exports that they did not conform to the contract. Can Padma recover even though it accepted the goods knowing that they were nonconforming? If so, how? [*Padma Paper Mills, Ltd. v. Universal Exports, Inc.,* 34 Misc.3d 1236(A) (N.Y.Sup. 2012)] (See *Remedies for Breach.*)

—For a sample answer to Problem 12–5, go to Appendix E at the end of this text.

12–6. The Statute of Frauds. Kendall Gardner agreed to buy from B&C Shavings, a specially built shaving mill to produce wood shavings for poultry processors. B&C faxed an invoice to Gardner reflecting a purchase price of $86,200, with a 30 percent down payment and the "balance due before shipment." Gardner paid the down payment. B&C finished the mill and wrote Gardner a letter telling him to "pay the balance due or you will lose the down payment." By then, Gardner had lost his customers for the wood shavings, could not pay the balance due, and asked for the return of his down payment. Did these parties have an enforceable contract under the Statute of Frauds? Explain. [*Bowen v. Gardner,* 2013 Ark.App. 52, 425 S.W.3d 875 (2013)] (See *Formation of Sales and Lease Contracts.*)

12–7. Implied Warranties. Bariven, S.A., agreed to buy 26,000 metric tons of powdered milk for $123.5 million from Absolute Trading Corp. to be delivered in shipments from China to Venezuela. After the first three shipments, China halted dairy exports due to the presence of melamine in some products. Absolute assured Bariven that its milk was safe, and when China resumed dairy exports, Absolute delivered sixteen more shipments. Tests of samples of the milk revealed that it contained dangerous levels of melamine. Did Absolute breach any implied warranties? Discuss. [*Absolute Trading Corp. v. Bariven S.A.,* 2013 WL 49735 (11th Cir. 2013)] (See *Warranties.*)

12–8. Product Liability. On Interstate 40 in North Carolina, Carroll Jett became distracted by a texting system in the cab of his tractor-trailer truck and smashed into several vehicles that were slowed or stopped in front of him. The crash injuried Barbara and Michael Durkee and others. The injured motorists filed a suit in a federal district court against Geologic Solutions, Inc., the maker of the texting system, alleging product liability. Was the accident caused by Jett's inattention or the texting device? Should a manufacturer be required to design a product that is incapable of distracting a driver? Discuss. [*Durkee v. Geologic Solutions, Inc.,* 2013 WL 14717 (4th Cir. 2013)] (See *Product Liability.*)

12–9. ⬌ **A Question of Ethics—Revocation of Acceptance.** Scotwood Industries, Inc., sells calcium chloride flake for use in ice melt products. Between July and September 2004, Scotwood delivered thirty-seven shipments of flake to Frank Miller & Sons, Inc. After each delivery, Scotwood billed Miller, which paid thirty-five of the invoices and processed 30 to 50 percent of the flake. In August, Miller began complaining about the product's quality. Scotwood assured Miller that it would remedy the situation. Finally, in October, Miller told Scotwood, "This is totally unacceptable. We are willing to discuss Scotwood picking up the material." Miller claimed that the flake was substantially defective because it was chunked. Calcium chloride maintains its purity for up to five years, but if it is exposed to and absorbs moisture, it chunks and becomes unusable. Scotwood sued to collect payment on the unpaid invoices. In response, Miller filed a counterclaim in a federal district court for breach of contract, seeking to recover based on revocation of acceptance, among other things. [*Scotwood Industries, Inc. v. Frank Miller & Sons, Inc.,* 435 F.Supp.2d 1160 (D.Kan. 2006)] (See *Remedies for Breach.*)

1. What is revocation of acceptance? How does a buyer effectively exercise this option? Do the facts in this case support this theory as a ground for Miller to recover damages? Why or why not?

2. Is there an ethical basis for allowing a buyer to revoke acceptance of goods and recover damages? If so, is there an ethical limit to this right? Discuss.

An Example of a Contract for the International Sale of Coffee

①② OVERLAND COFFEE IMPORT CONTRACT
OF THE
GREEN COFFEE ASSOCIATION
OF
NEW YORK CITY, INC.*

Contract Seller's No.: __504617__
Buyer's No.: __P9264__
Date: __10/11/16__

SOLD BY: __XYZ Co.__
TO: __Starbucks__

③ QUANTITY: __Five Hundred__ (__500__) (Bags) Tons of __Mexican__ coffee weighing about __152.117 lbs.__ per bag.

④ PACKAGING: Coffee must be packed in clean sound bags of uniform size made of sisal, henequen, jute, burlap, or similar woven material, without inner lining or outer covering of any material properly sewn by hand and/or machine. Bulk shipments are allowed if agreed by mutual consent of Buyer and Seller.

⑤ DESCRIPTION: __High grown Mexican Altura__

PRICE: At __Ten/$10.00 dollars__ U.S. Currency, per __lb.__ net, (U.S. Funds)
Upon delivery in Bonded Public Warehouse at __Laredo, TX__
(City and State)

⑥ PAYMENT: __Cash against warehouse receipts__

Bill and tender to DATE when all import requirements and governmental regulations have been satisfied, and coffee delivered or discharged (as per contract terms). Seller is obliged to give the Buyer two (2) calendar days free time in Bonded Public Warehouse following but not including date of tender.

⑦ ARRIVAL: During __December__ via __truck__
(Period)   (Method of Transportation)
from __Mexico__ for arrival at __Laredo, TX, USA__
(Country of Exportation)   (Country of Importation)
Partial shipments permitted.

⑧ ADVICE OF ARRIVAL: Advice of arrival with warehouse name and location, together with the quantity, description, marks and place of entry, must be transmitted directly, or through Seller's Agent/Broker, to the Buyer or his Agent/ Broker. Advice will be given as soon as known but not later than the fifth business day following arrival at the named warehouse. Such advice may be given verbally with written confirmation to be sent the same day.

⑨ WEIGHTS: (1) DELIVERED WEIGHTS: Coffee covered by this contract is to be weighed at location named in tender. Actual tare to be allowed.
(2) SHIPPING WEIGHTS: Coffee covered by this contract is sold on shipping weights. Any loss in weight exceeding __1/2__ percent at location named in tender is for account of Seller at contract price.
(3) Coffee is to be weighed within fifteen (15) calendar days after tender. Weighing expenses, if any, for account of __Seller__ (Seller or Buyer)

⑩ MARKINGS: Bags to be branded in English with the name of Country of Origin and otherwise to comply with laws and regulations of the Country of Importation, in effect at the time of entry, governing marking of import merchandise. Any expense incurred by failure to comply with these regulations to be borne by Exporter/Seller.

⑪ RULINGS: The "Rulings on Coffee Contracts" of the Green Coffee Association of New York City, Inc., in effect on the date this contract is made, is incorporated for all purposes as a part of this agreement, and together herewith, constitute the entire contract. No variation or addition hereto shall be valid unless signed by the parties to the contract.
Seller guarantees that the terms printed on the reverse hereof, which by reference are made a part hereof, are identical with the terms as printed in By-Laws and Rules of the Green Coffee Association of New York City, Inc., heretofore adopted.
Exceptions to this guarantee are:

⑫ ACCEPTED:
__XYZ Co.__
BY _____*DM*_____ Seller
_____ Agent
__Starbucks__
BY _____ Buyer
_____ Agent

COMMISSION TO BE PAID BY:
__Seller__

__ABC Brokerage__
Broker(s)

⑬ When this contract is executed by a person acting for another, such person hereby represents that he is fully authorized to commit his principal.

* Reprinted with permission of The Green Coffee Association of New York City, Inc.

(Shutterstock.com/Sergii Figurnyi)

An Example of a Contract for the International Sale of Coffee

1 This is a contract for a sale of coffee to be *imported* internationally. If the parties have their principal places of business located in different countries, the contract may be subject to the United Nations Convention on Contracts for the International Sale of Goods (CISG). If the parties' principal places of business are located in the United States, the contract may be subject to the Uniform Commercial Code (UCC).

2 Quantity is one of the most important terms to include in a contract. Without it, a court may not be able to enforce the contract.

3 Weight per unit (bag) can be exactly stated or approximately stated. If it is not so stated, usage of trade in international contracts determines standards of weight.

4 Packaging requirements can be conditions for acceptance and payment. Bulk shipments are not permitted without the consent of the buyer.

5 A description of the coffee and the "Markings" constitute express warranties (see Chapter 11). International contracts rely more heavily on descriptions and models or samples.

6 Under the UCC, parties may enter into a valid contract even though the price is not set. Under the CISG, a contract must provide for an exact determination of the price.

7 The terms of payment may take one of two forms: credit or cash. Credit terms can be complicated. A cash term can be simple, and payment can be made by any means acceptable in the ordinary course of business (for example, a personal check or a letter of credit). If the seller insists on actual cash, the buyer must be given a reasonable time to get it.

8 *Tender* means the seller has placed goods that conform to the contract at the buyer's disposition. This contract requires that the coffee meet all import regulations and that it be ready for pickup by the buyer at a "Bonded Public Warehouse." (A *bonded warehouse* is a place in which goods can be stored without payment of taxes until the goods are removed.)

9 The delivery date is significant because, if it is not met, the buyer may hold the seller in breach of the contract. Under this contract, the seller is given a "period" within which to deliver the goods, instead of a specific day. The seller is also given some time to rectify goods that do not pass inspection (see the "Guarantee" clause on the second page of the contract).

10 As part of a proper tender, the seller (or its agent) must inform the buyer (or its agent) when the goods have arrived at their destination.

11 In some contracts, delivered and shipping weights can be important. During shipping, some loss can be attributed to the type of goods (spoilage of fresh produce, for example) or to the transportation itself. A seller and buyer can agree on the extent to which either of them will bear such losses.

12 Documents are often incorporated in a contract by reference, because including them word for word can make a contract difficult to read. If the document is later revised, the entire contract might have to be reworked. Documents that are typically incorporated by reference include detailed payment and delivery terms, special provisions, and sets of rules, codes, and standards.

13 In international sales transactions, and for domestic deals involving certain products, brokers are used to form the contracts. When so used, the brokers are entitled to a commission.

(Continued)

An Example of a Contract for the International Sale of Coffee

TERMS AND CONDITIONS

14 · ARBITRATION: All controversies relating to, in connection with, or arising out of this contract, its modification, making or the authority or obligations of the signatories hereto, and whether involving the principals, agents, brokers, or others who actually subscribe hereto, shall be settled by arbitration in accordance with the "Rules of Arbitration" of the Green Coffee Association of New York City, Inc., as they exist at the time of the arbitration (including provisions as to payment of fees and expenses). Arbitration is the sole remedy hereunder, and it shall be held in accordance with the law of New York State, and judgment of any award may be entered in the courts of that State, or in any other court of competent jurisdiction. All notices or judicial service in reference to arbitration or enforcement shall be deemed given if transmitted as required by the aforesaid rules.

15 · GUARANTEE: (a) If all or any of the coffee is refused admission into the country of importation by reason of any violation of governmental laws or acts, which violation existed at the time the coffee arrived at Bonded Public Warehouse, seller is required, as to the amount not admitted and as soon as possible, to deliver replacement coffee in conformity to all terms and conditions of this contract, excepting only the Arrival terms, but not later than thirty (30) days after the date of the violation notice. Any payment made and expenses incurred for any coffee denied entry shall be refunded within ten (10) calendar days of denial of entry, and payment shall be made for the replacement delivery in accordance with the terms of this contract. Consequently, if Buyer removes the coffee from the Bonded Public Warehouse, Seller's responsibility as to such portion hereunder ceases.
(b) Contracts containing the overstamp "No Pass-No Sale" on the face of the contract shall be interpreted to mean: If any or all of the coffee is not admitted into the country of Importation in its original condition by reason of failure to meet requirements of the government's laws or Acts, the contract shall be deemed null and void as to that portion of the coffee which is not admitted in its original condition. Any payment made and expenses incurred for any coffee denied entry shall be refunded within ten (10) calendar days of denial of entry.

16 · CONTINGENCY: This contract is not contingent upon any other contract.

CLAIMS: Coffee shall be considered accepted as to quality unless within *fifteen* (15) calendar days after delivery at Bonded Public Warehouse or within *fifteen* (15) calendar days after all Government clearances have been received, whichever is later, either:
(a) Claims are settled by the parties hereto, or,
(b) Arbitration proceedings have been filed by one of the parties in accordance with the provisions hereof.
(c) If neither (a) nor (b) has been done in the stated period or if any portion of the coffee has been removed from the Bonded Public Warehouse before representative sealed samples have been drawn by the Green Coffee Association of New York City, Inc., in accordance with its rules, Seller's responsibility for quality claims ceases for that portion so removed.
(d) Any question of quality submitted to arbitration shall be a matter of allowance only, unless otherwise provided in the contract.

17 · DELIVERY: (a) No more than three (3) chops may be tendered for each lot of 250 bags.
(b) Each chop of coffee tendered is to be uniform in grade and appearance. All expense necessary to make coffee uniform shall be for account of seller.
(c) Notice of arrival and/or sampling order constitutes a tender, and must be given not later than the fifth business day following arrival at Bonded Public Warehouse stated on the contract.

18 · INSURANCE: Seller is responsible for any loss or damage, or both, until Delivery and Discharge of coffee at the Bonded Public Warehouse in the Country of Importation.

All Insurance Risks, costs and responsibility are for Seller's Account until Delivery and Discharge of coffee at the Bonded Public Warehouse in the Country of Importation.

Buyer's insurance responsibility begins from the day of importation or from the day of tender, whichever is later.

19 · FREIGHT: Seller to provide and pay for all transportation and related expenses to the Bonded Public Warehouse in the Country of Importation.

20 · EXPORT DUTIES/TAXES: Exporter is to pay all Export taxes, duties or other fees or charges, if any, levied because of exportation.

IMPORT DUTIES/TAXES: Any Duty or Tax whatsoever, imposed by the government or any authority of the Country of Importation, shall be borne by the Importer/Buyer.

21 · INSOLVENCY OR FINANCIAL FAILURE OF BUYER OR SELLER: If, at any time before the contract is fully executed, either party hereto shall meet with creditors because of inability generally to make payment of obligations when due, or shall suspend such payments, fail to meet his general trade obligations in the regular course of business, shall file a petition in bankruptcy or, for an arrangement, shall become insolvent, or commit an act of bankruptcy, then the other party may at his option, expressed in writing, declare the aforesaid to constitute a breach and default of this contract, and may, in addition to other remedies, decline to deliver further or make payment or may sell or purchase for the defaulter's account, and may collect damage for any injury or loss, or shall account for the profit, if any, occasioned by such sale or purchase.

This clause is subject to the provisions of (11 USC 365 (e) 1) if invoked.

22 · BREACH OR DEFAULT OF CONTRACT: In the event either party hereto fails to perform, or breaches or repudiates this agreement, the other party shall subject to the specific provisions of this contract be entitled to the remedies and relief provided for by the Uniform Commercial Code of the State of New York. The computation and ascertainment of damages, or the determination of any other dispute as to relief, shall be made by the arbitrators in accordance with the Arbitration Clause herein.

23 · Consequential damages shall not, however, be allowed.

An Example of a Contract for the International Sale of Coffee

14 Arbitration is the settling of a dispute by submitting it to a disinterested party (other than a court), which renders a decision. The procedures and costs can be provided for in an arbitration clause or incorporated through other documents. To enforce an award rendered in an arbitration, the winning party can "enter" (submit) the award in a court "of competent jurisdiction." For a general discussion of arbitration and other forms of dispute resolution (other than courts), see Chapter 3.

15 When goods are imported internationally, they must meet certain import requirements before being released to the buyer. See Chapter 7. Because of this, buyers frequently want a guaranty clause that covers the goods not admitted into the country and that either requires the seller to replace the goods within a stated time or allows the contract for those goods not admitted to be void.

16 In the "Claims" clause, the parties agree that the buyer has a certain time within which to reject the goods. The right to reject is a right by law and does not need to be stated in a contract. If the buyer does not exercise the right within the time specified in the contract, the goods will be considered accepted. See Chapter 12.

17 Many international contracts include definitions of terms so that the parties understand what they mean. Some terms are used in a particular industry in a specific way. Here, the word *chop* refers to a unit of like-grade coffee beans. The buyer has a right to inspect ("sample") the coffee. If the coffee does not conform to the contract, the seller must correct the nonconformity.

18 The "Delivery," "Insurance," and "Freight" clauses, with the "Arrival" clause on the first page of the contract, indicate that this is a destination contract. The seller has the obligation to deliver the goods to the destination, not simply deliver them into the hands of a carrier. Under this contract, the destination is a "Bonded Public Warehouse" in a specific location. The seller bears the risk of loss until the goods are delivered at their destination. Typically, the seller will have bought insurance to cover the risk.

19 Delivery terms are commonly placed in all sales contracts. Such terms determine who pays freight and other costs and, in the absence of an agreement specifying otherwise, who bears the risk of loss. International contracts may use these delivery terms, or they may use INCOTERMS, which are published by the International Chamber of Commerce. For example, the INCOTERM DDP (delivered duty paid) requires the seller to arrange shipment, obtain and pay for import or export permits, and get the goods through customs to a named destination.

20 Exported and imported goods are subject to duties, taxes, and other charges imposed by the governments of the countries involved. International contracts spell out who is responsible for these charges.

21 This clause protects a party if the other party should become financially unable to fulfill the obligations under the contract. Thus, if the seller cannot afford to deliver, or the buyer cannot afford to pay, for the stated reasons, the other party can consider the contract breached. This right is subject to "11 USC 365(e)(1)," which refers to a specific provision of the U.S. Bankruptcy Code dealing with executory contracts. Bankruptcy provisions are covered in Chapter 13.

22 In the "Breach or Default of Contract" clause, the parties agree that the remedies under this contract are the remedies (except for consequential damages) provided by the UCC, as in effect in the state of New York. The amount and "ascertainment" of damages, as well as other disputes about relief, are to be determined by arbitration. Breach of contract and contractual remedies in general are explained in Chapter 12. Arbitration is discussed in Chapter 3.

23 Three clauses frequently included in international contracts are omitted here. There is no choice-of-language clause designating the official language to be used in interpreting the contract terms. There is no choice-of-forum clause designating the place in which disputes will be litigated, except for arbitration (law of New York State). Finally, there is no *force majeure* clause relieving the sellers or buyers from nonperformance due to events beyond their control.

13 CHAPTER

Creditor-Debtor Relations and Bankruptcy

(Wavebreakmedia/Shutterstock.com)

CONTENTS

LEARNING OBJECTIVES

The five learning objectives below are designed to help improve your understanding of the chapter. After reading this chapter, you should be able to answer the following questions:

1. What is a prejudgment attachment? What is a writ of execution? How does a creditor use these remedies?

2. What is garnishment? When might a creditor undertake a garnishment proceeding?

3. In a bankruptcy proceeding, what constitutes the debtor's estate in property? What property is exempt from the estate under federal bankruptcy law?

4. What is the difference between an exception to discharge and an objection to discharge?

5. In a Chapter 11 reorganization, what is the role of the debtor in possession?

> "Capitalism without bankruptcy is like Christianity without hell."
> Frank Borman, 1928–present, (U.S. astronaut and businessman)

Many people in today's economy are struggling to pay their monthly debts. Although in the old days, debtors were punished and sometimes even sent to jail for failing to pay their debts, people today rarely go to jail. They have many other options. In this chapter, we discuss some basic laws that assist the debtor and creditor in resolving disputes.

We then turn to the topic of bankruptcy—a last resort in resolving debtor-creditor problems. As implied by the chapter-opening quotation, bankruptcy may be a necessary evil in our capitalistic society. Hence, every businessperson should have some understanding of the bankruptcy process that is outlined in this chapter. We also discuss in an *Online Developments* feature how some bankruptcy courts are using the Web and social media to communicate with the public.

Laws Assisting Creditors

Normally, creditors have no problem collecting the debts owed to them. When disputes arise over the amount owed, however, or when the debtor simply cannot or will not pay, what happens? Both the common law and statutory laws create various rights and remedies for creditors when a debtor **defaults** (fails to pay as promised). We discuss here some of these rights and remedies.

Default When a debtor fails to pay as promised.

Liens

A **lien** is an encumbrance on (claim against) property to satisfy a debt or protect a claim for the payment of a debt. Liens may arise under the common law (usually by possession of the property) or under statutory law. Statutory liens include *mechanic's liens,* whereas *artisan's liens* were recognized at common law. *Judicial liens* may be used by a creditor to collect on a debt before or after a judgment is entered by a court.

Lien A claim against specific property to satisfy a debt.

Liens can be an important tool for creditors because they generally take priority over other claims, except those of creditors who have a *perfected security interest* in the same property. (A *security interest* is an interest in a debtor's personal property—called *collateral*—that a seller, lender, or other creditor takes to secure payment of an obligation. *Perfection,* which is generally accomplished by filing a financing statement with a state official, is the legal process by which a creditor protects its security interest from the claims of others.) In fact, unless a statute provides otherwise, the holders of mechanic's and artisan's liens normally take priority even over creditors who have a perfected security interest in the property.

For liens other than mechanic's and artisan's liens, priority depends on whether the lien was obtained before the other creditor perfected its security interest. If the lien was obtained first, the lienholder has priority, but if the security interest was perfected first, the party with the perfected security interest has priority.

Mechanic's Liens

Sometimes, a person who has contracted for labor, services, or materials to be furnished for making improvements on real property does not immediately pay for the improvements. When that happens, the creditor can place a **mechanic's lien** on the property. A mechanic's lien creates a special type of debtor-creditor relationship in which the real estate itself becomes security for the debt.

Mechanic's Lien A statutory lien on the real property of another to ensure payment to a person who has performed work and furnished materials for the repair or improvement of that property.

EXAMPLE 13.1 Kirk contracts to paint Tanya's house for an agreed-on price to cover labor and materials. If Tanya refuses to pay or pays only a portion of the charges after the work is completed, a mechanic's lien against the property can be created. Kirk is then a lienholder, and the real property is encumbered (burdened) with the mechanic's lien for the amount owed.

If Tanya does not pay the lien, the property can be sold to satisfy the debt. Tanya must be given notice of the *foreclosure* (the process by which the creditor legally takes the debtor's property to satisfy a debt, discussed later in this chapter) and sale in advance, however. ●

State law governs the procedures that must be followed to create a mechanic's (or other statutory) lien. Generally, the lienholder must file a written notice of lien within a specific time period (usually within 60 to 120 days) from the last date that material or labor was provided. If the property owner fails to pay the debt, the lienholder is entitled to foreclose on the real estate and to sell it to satisfy the debt. The sale proceeds are used to pay the debt and the costs of the legal proceedings. The surplus, if any, is paid to the former owner.

Artisan's Liens

When a debtor fails to pay for labor and materials furnished for the repair or improvement of personal property, a creditor can recover payment through an **artisan's lien.**

Artisan's Lien A possessory lien on personal property of another person to ensure payment to a person who has made improvements on and added value to that property.

(Phil Augustavo/iStockphoto.com)

If the homeowner does not pay this painter, what can he do to recover payment?

Lienholder Must Retain Possession   In contrast to a mechanic's lien, an artisan's lien is *possessory.* The lienholder ordinarily must have retained possession of the property and have expressly or impliedly agreed to provide the services on a cash, not a credit, basis. The lien remains in existence as long as the lienholder maintains possession, and the lien is terminated once possession is *voluntarily* surrendered—unless the surrender is only temporary.

EXAMPLE 13.2   Kenzie takes a sapphire necklace that she inherited to a jewelry store to have it made into a ring and set of earrings. The store's owner agrees to reset the sapphires into custom jewelry for $4,000. Kenzie comes to pick up the jewelry but refuses to pay the $4,000 she owes. The jeweler can assert an artisan's lien on the jewelry in his possession until Kenzie pays. If the jeweler gives the jewelry to Kenzie (without requiring full payment), the lien disappears. ● As mentioned, artisan's liens usually take priority over other creditors' claims to the same property.

Foreclosure on Personal Property Possible   Modern statutes permit the holder of an artisan's lien to foreclose and sell the property subject to the lien to satisfy the debt. As with a mechanic's lien, the lienholder is required to give notice to the owner of the property before the foreclosure and sale. The sale proceeds are used to pay the debt and the costs of the legal proceedings, and the surplus, if any, is paid to the former owner.

Judicial Liens

When a debt is past due, a creditor can bring a legal action against the debtor to collect the debt. If the creditor is successful in the action, the court awards the creditor a judgment against the debtor (usually for the amount of the debt plus any interest and legal costs incurred in obtaining the judgment). Frequently, however, the creditor is unable to collect the awarded amount.

To ensure that a judgment in the creditor's favor will be collectible, the creditor may request that certain nonexempt property of the debtor be seized to satisfy the debt. (As will be discussed later in this chapter, under state or federal statutes, some kinds of property are exempt from attachment by creditors.) A court's order to seize the debtor's property is known as a *writ of attachment* if it is issued prior to a judgment in the creditor's favor. If the order is issued after a judgment, it is referred to as a *writ of execution.*

Attachment The legal process of seizing another's property under a court order to secure satisfaction of a judgment yet to be rendered.

Learning Objective 1

What is a prejudgment attachment? What is a writ of execution? How does a creditor use these remedies?

Writ of Attachment   In the context of judicial liens, **attachment** refers to a court-ordered seizure and taking into custody of property before a judgment is obtained on a past-due debt. Because attachment is a *prejudgment* remedy, it occurs either at the time a lawsuit is filed or immediately afterward.

A creditor must comply with the specific state's statutory restrictions and requirements. Under the due process clause of the Fourteenth Amendment to the U.S. Constitution, the debtor must be given notice and an opportunity to be heard (see Chapter 4). The creditor must have an enforceable right to payment of the debt under law and must follow certain procedures. Otherwise, the creditor can be liable for damages for wrongful attachment.

The typical procedure for attachment is as follows:

Writ of Attachment A writ used to enforce obedience to an order or judgment of the court.

1. The creditor files with the court an *affidavit* (a written statement, made under oath) stating that the debtor has failed to pay and indicating the statutory grounds under which attachment is sought.
2. The creditor must post a bond to cover at least the court costs, the value of the property attached, and the value of the loss of use of that property suffered by the debtor.
3. When the court is satisfied that all the requirements have been met, it issues a **writ of attachment,** which directs the sheriff or other officer to seize the debtor's nonexempt property. If the creditor prevails at trial, the seized property can be sold to satisfy the judgment.

Writ of Execution If a creditor wins a judgment against a debtor and the debtor will not or cannot pay the amount due, the creditor can request a **writ of execution** from the court. A writ of execution is an order that directs the sheriff to seize (levy) and sell any of the debtor's nonexempt real or personal property. The writ applies only to property that is within the court's geographic jurisdiction (usually the county in which the courthouse is located).

The proceeds of the sale are used to pay the judgment, accrued interest, and costs of the sale. Any excess is paid to the debtor. The debtor can pay the judgment and redeem the nonexempt property at any time before the sale takes place. (Because of exemption laws and bankruptcy laws, however, many judgments are practically uncollectible.)

Garnishment

An order for **garnishment** permits a creditor to collect a debt by seizing property of the debtor (such as wages or funds in a bank account) that is being held by a third party. As a result of a garnishment proceeding, the debtor's employer may be ordered by the court to turn over a portion of the debtor's wages to pay the debt.

CASE EXAMPLE 13.3 Helen Griffin failed to pay a debt she owed to Indiana Surgical Specialists. When Indiana Surgical filed a lawsuit to collect, the court issued a judgment in favor of Indiana Surgical and a garnishment order to withhold the appropriate amount from Griffin's earnings until her debt was paid. At the time, Griffin was working as an independent contractor (see Chapter 17 for a discussion of independent-contractor status) driving for a courier service. She claimed that her wages could not be garnished because she was not an employee. The court held that payments for the services of an independent contractor fall within the definition of earnings and can be garnished.[1] •

Many types of property can be garnished, including tax refunds, pensions, and trust funds—so long as the property is not exempt from garnishment and is in the possession of a third party.

Procedures

Garnishment can be a prejudgment remedy, requiring a hearing before a court, but it is most often a postjudgment remedy. State law governs garnishment actions, so the specific procedures vary from state to state. According to the laws in many states, the judgment creditor needs to obtain only one order of garnishment, which will then apply continuously to the judgment debtor's wages until the entire debt is paid. In other states, the judgment creditor must go back to court for a separate order of garnishment for each pay period.

Laws Limiting the Amount of Wages Subject to Garnishment

Both federal and state laws limit the amount that can be taken from a debtor's weekly take-home pay through garnishment proceedings.[2] Federal law provides a minimal framework to protect debtors from losing all their income to pay judgment debts.[3] State laws also provide dollar exemptions, and these amounts are often larger than those provided by federal law.

Under federal law, an employer cannot dismiss an employee because his or her wages are being garnished.

(Dan Prat/iStockphoto.com)

Under what conditions could a creditor obtain a writ of attachment on this speed boat?

Writ of Execution A writ that puts in force a court's decree or judgment.

Garnishment A legal process whereby a creditor appropriates a debtor's property or wages that are in the hands of a third party.

Learning Objective 2

What is garnishment? When might a creditor undertake a garnishment proceeding?

---

1. *Indiana Surgical Specialists v. Griffin*, 867 N.E.2d 260 (Ind.App. 2007).

2. A few states (for example, Texas) do not permit garnishment of wages by private parties except under a child-support order.

3. For example, the federal Consumer Credit Protection Act, 15 U.S.C. Sections 1601–1693r, provides that a debtor can retain either 75 percent of his or her disposable earnings per week or an amount equivalent to thirty hours of work paid at federal minimum wage rates, whichever is greater.

Creditors' Composition Agreements

Creditors' Composition Agreement An agreement formed between a debtor and his or her creditors in which the creditors agree to accept a lesser sum than that owed by the debtor in full satisfaction of the debt.

Creditors may contract with the debtor for discharge of the debtor's liquidated debts (debts that are definite, or fixed, in amount) on payment of a sum less than that owed. These agreements are referred to as **creditors' composition agreements** (or *composition agreements*) and usually are held to be enforceable unless they are formed under duress.

Suretyship and Guaranty

When a third person promises to pay a debt owed by another in the event that the debtor does not pay, either a *suretyship* or a *guaranty* relationship is created. Exhibit 13–1 illustrates these relationships. The third person's creditworthiness becomes the security for the debt owed.

Suretyship and guaranty provide creditors with the right to seek payment from the third party if the primary debtor, or *principal,* defaults on her or his obligations. At common law, there were significant differences in the liability of a surety and a guarantor, as discussed in the following subsections. Today, however, the distinctions outlined here have been abolished in some states.

(Callietat/iStockphoto.com)

How can a minor with little or no income convince a car dealer to sell him or her a car?

Suretyship An express contract in which a third party (the surety) promises to be primarily responsible for a debtor's obligation to a creditor.

Surety A third party who agrees to be primarily responsible for the debt of another.

Suretyship   A contract of strict **suretyship** is a promise made by a third person to be responsible for the debtor's obligation. It is an express contract between the **surety** (the third party) and the creditor.

In the strictest sense, the surety is primarily liable for the debt of the principal. The creditor can demand payment from the surety from the moment the debt is due. Moreover, the creditor need not exhaust all legal remedies against the principal debtor before holding the surety responsible for payment.

EXAMPLE 13.4   Roberto Delmar wants to obtain a loan from the bank to buy a used car. Because Roberto is still in college, the bank will not lend him the funds without a cosigner. Roberto's father, José Delmar, who has dealt with the bank before, agrees to cosign (add his signature to) the note, thereby becoming a surety and thus jointly liable for payment of the debt. When José Delmar cosigns the note, he becomes primarily liable to the bank. On the note's due date, the bank can seek payment from either Roberto or José Delmar, or both jointly. •

Guarantor A person who agrees to satisfy the debt of another (the debtor) only after the principal debtor defaults.

Guaranty   With a suretyship arrangement, the surety is *primarily* liable for the debtor's obligation. With a guaranty arrangement, the **guarantor**—the third person making the guaranty—is *secondarily* liable.

Liability Arises When Debtor Defaults   The guarantor can be required to pay the obligation *only after the principal debtor defaults,* and usually only after the creditor has made an attempt to collect from the debtor. The guaranty contract terms determine the extent and time of the guarantor's liability.

EXAMPLE 13.5   BX Enterprises, a small corporation, needs to borrow funds to meet its payroll. BX's president is Dawson, a wealthy businessperson who owns 70 percent of the company. The bank is skeptical about the creditworthiness of BX and requires Dawson to sign an agreement making herself personally liable for payment if BX does not pay off the loan. As a guarantor of the loan, Dawson cannot be held liable until BX is in default. •

The following case concerns a lender's attempt to recover on a loan guaranty.

Exhibit 13–1 Suretyship and Guaranty Parties

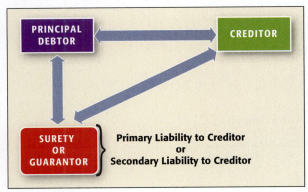

PRINCIPAL DEBTOR → CREDITOR

SURETY OR GUARANTOR

Primary Liability to Creditor
or
Secondary Liability to Creditor

Case 13.1

HSBC Realty Credit Corp. (USA) v. O'Neill

United States Court of Appeals, First Circuit, 745 F.3d 564 (2014).

(Richard Cummins/Encyclopedia/Corbis)

BACKGROUND AND FACTS   To finance a development project in Delaware, Brandywine Partners, LLC, borrowed $15.9 million from HSBC Realty Credit Corp. (USA). As part of the deal, Brian O'Neill, principal for Brandywine, signed a guaranty that designated him the "primary obligor" for $8.1 million of the loan. Brandywine defaulted, and HSBC filed a suit in a federal district court against O'Neill to recover on the guaranty. O'Neill filed a counterclaim, alleging fraud. The court granted HSBC's motion to dismiss O'Neill's counterclaim and issued a judgment in HSBC's favor. O'Neill appealed, still arguing that HSBC had fraudulently induced him to sign the guaranty.

IN THE WORDS OF THE COURT . . .
THOMPSON, Circuit Judge.
  * * * *
   O'Neill loudly protests that his fraudulent-inducement claim should have been enough to defeat HSBC's dismissal efforts. His theory rises or falls on his belief that two provisions in the project-loan agreement constitute false statements of material fact made to induce him to sign the guaranty and that he reasonably relied on those false statements to his detriment.
   The first provision he points to involves the * * * loan-to-value ratio, which he alleges put the collateral property's value at $26.5 million and is an HSBC representation that the chance of its having to call the $8.1 million guaranty was basically zero. HSBC made that representation, he adds, even though HSBC—and not he—knew that this was not the property's real value.
   The second project-loan-agreement provision he harps on provides that if Brandywine defaults, HSBC "can recover the obligations" by selling the property. He reads this contract language as an HSBC representation that it would move against the property before turning to his guaranty * * * . [But] we are unmoved. Merely to state the obvious, that proviso says that HSBC "can" proceed first against the property, not that it must do so.
   Ultimately—and unhappily for O'Neill—we must enforce the guaranty according to its terms, with the parties' rights ascertained [determined] from the written text. * * * Reliance

on supposed misrepresentations that contradict the terms of the parties' agreement is unreasonable as a matter of law and so cannot support a fraudulent-inducement claim. * * * The contract-inducing misrepresentations that O'Neill trumpets are irreconcilably at odds with the guaranty's express terms. * * * O'Neill specifically warranted in the guaranty that he was familiar with the collateral property's value, that the property did not operate as an inducement for him to make the guaranty, and that HSBC said nothing to induce him to execute the guaranty—all of which destroys his fraudulent-inducement thesis centered on the project-loan agreement's loan-to-value-ratio provision. He also agreed with the guaranty's tagging him as the primary obligor and with its allowing HSBC to go after him first to recoup the debt—provisions that put the kibosh on [put an end to] his other suggestion that HSBC must first seek recourse against the property. [Emphasis added.]
  * * * *
   The net result of all this is that O'Neill's inducement-based arguments fail.

DECISION AND REMEDY   The U.S. Court of Appeals for the First Circuit affirmed the lower court's judgment in favor of HSBC. The guaranty stated that O'Neill was familiar with the value of the property, that he was not relying on it as an inducement to sign the guaranty, and that HSBC made no representations to induce him to sign. The guaranty also provided that HSBC could enforce its rights against him without trying to recover on the property first.

THE E-COMMERCE DIMENSION   Do the principles applied to a written guaranty in this case also govern electronically recorded agreements and contracts entered into online? Why or why not?

WHAT IF THE FACTS WERE DIFFERENT?   Suppose that O'Neill had alleged a history of performance with HSBC that would have made his reliance on the complained-of representations reasonable. Could this have changed the result?

Writing or Record Required   Under the Statute of Frauds (see Chapter 10), a guaranty contract between the guarantor and the creditor must be in writing (or electronically recorded) to be enforceable unless the *main purpose* exception applies. The main purpose exception provides that if the main purpose of the guaranty agreement is to benefit the guarantor, then the contract need not be in writing to be enforceable.

Under the common law, a suretyship agreement did not need to be in writing to be enforceable, and oral surety agreements were sufficient. Today, however, some states require a writing (or electronic record) to enforce a suretyship.

Actions That Release the Surety and the Guarantor
Basically, the same actions will release a surety or a guarantor from an obligation. In general, the following rules apply to both sureties and guarantors, but for simplicity, we refer just to sureties:

1. *Material modification.* Making any material modification to the terms of the original contract—without the surety's consent—will discharge the surety's obligation. (The extent to which the surety is discharged depends on whether he or she was compensated and the amount of the loss suffered as a result of the modification. For example, a father who receives no consideration in return for acting as a surety on his daughter's loan will be completely discharged if the loan contract is modified without his consent.)
2. *Surrender of property.* If a creditor surrenders the collateral to the debtor or impairs the collateral without the surety's consent, these acts can reduce the obligation of the surety. If the creditor's actions reduce the value of the property used as collateral, the surety is released to the extent of any loss suffered.
3. *Payment or tender of payment.* Naturally, any payment of the principal obligation by the debtor or by another person on the debtor's behalf will discharge the surety from the obligation. Even if the creditor refused to accept payment of the principal debt when it was tendered, the obligation of the surety can be discharged (if the creditor knew about the suretyship).

Defenses of the Surety and the Guarantor
Generally, the surety or guarantor can also assert any of the defenses available to the principal debtor to avoid liability on the obligation to the creditor. A few exceptions do exist, however. They apply to both sureties and guarantors, although we refer just to sureties.

1. *Incapacity and bankruptcy.* Incapacity and bankruptcy are personal defenses, which can be asserted only by the person who is affected. Therefore, the surety cannot assert the principal debtor's incapacity or bankruptcy as a defense. A surety may assert his or her own incapacity or bankruptcy as a defense, however.
2. *Statute of limitations.* The surety cannot assert the statute of limitations as a defense. (In contrast, the principal debtor can claim the statute of limitations as a defense to payment.)
3. *Fraud.* If the creditor fraudulently induced the person to act as a surety on the debt, the surety can assert fraud as a defense. In most states, the creditor has a legal duty to inform the surety, before the formation of the suretyship contract, of material facts known by the creditor that would substantially increase the surety's risk. Failure to so inform may constitute fraud and renders the suretyship obligation voidable.

Rights of the Surety and the Guarantor
When the surety or guarantor pays the debt owed to the creditor, he or she acquires certain rights, as discussed next. Again, for simplicity, the discussion refers just to sureties.

Right of Subrogation The right of a surety or guarantor to stand in the place of (be substituted for) the creditors, giving the surety or guarantor the same legal rights against the debtor that the creditor had.

The Right of Subrogation   The surety has the legal **right of subrogation.** Simply stated, this means that any right that the creditor had against the debtor now becomes the right of the surety. Included are creditor rights in bankruptcy, rights to collateral possessed by the creditor, and rights to judgments obtained by the creditor. In short, the surety now stands in the shoes of the creditor and may pursue any remedies that were available to the creditor against the debtor.

CASE EXAMPLE 13.6 Guerrero Brothers, Inc. (GBI), contracted with the Public School System (PSS) to build a high school. Century Insurance Company (CIC) agreed to provide GBI with the required payment and performance bonds on the project. Thus, CIC acted as a surety of GBI's performance and promised to finish the project if GBI defaulted.

Four years after construction began, PSS canceled GBI's contract, and CIC fulfilled GBI's obligations by finishing construction of the school. Numerous disputes arose, and litigation ensued. Ultimately, PSS agreed to pay GBI $500,000 in contract funds. CIC then filed an action against GBI and PSS to recover the $867,000 it claimed PSS owed it for finishing the school. The court found that CIC, as a performing surety, was entitled to the remaining contract funds through the right of subrogation. It had performed GBI's obligations and therefore stepped into GBI's shoes and had the right to obtain payment from PSS.[4] •

The Right of Reimbursement The surety has a **right of reimbursement** from the debtor. Basically, the surety is entitled to receive from the debtor all outlays made on behalf of the suretyship arrangement. Such outlays can include expenses incurred as well as the actual amount of the debt paid to the creditor.

Right of Reimbursement The legal right of a person to be repaid or indemnified for costs, expenses, or losses incurred or expended on behalf of another.

The Right of Contribution Two or more sureties are called **co-sureties.** When a co-surety pays more than her or his proportionate share on a debtor's default, she or he is entitled to recover from the other co-sureties the amount paid above that surety's obligation. This is the **right of contribution.** Generally, a co-surety's liability either is determined by agreement or, in the absence of agreement, is set at the maximum liability under the suretyship contract.

Co-Surety A person who assumes liability jointly with another surety for the payment of an obligation.

Right of Contribution The right of a co-surety who pays more than her or his proportionate share on a debtor's default to recover the excess paid from other co-sureties.

EXAMPLE 13.7 Yasser and Itzhak, two co-sureties, are obligated under a suretyship contract to guarantee Jules's debt. Itzhak's maximum liability is $15,000, and Yasser's is $10,000. Jules owes $10,000 and is in default. Itzhak pays the creditor the entire $10,000.

In the absence of an agreement to the contrary, Itzhak can recover $4,000 from Yasser. The amount of the debt that Yasser agreed to cover ($10,000) is divided by the total amount that he and Itzhak together agreed to cover ($25,000). The result is multiplied by the amount of the default, yielding the amount that Yasser owes—$10,000 ÷ $25,000 × $10,000 = $4,000. •

PREVENTING LEGAL DISPUTES

Be careful when signing guaranty contracts. In particular, explicitly indicate if you are signing on behalf of a company rather than personally. If you are a corporate officer or director and you sign your name on a guaranty without indicating that you are signing as a representative of the corporation, you might be held personally liable. Although in some states a guaranty contract may be preferable to a suretyship contract, because it creates secondary rather than primary liability, a guaranty still involves substantial risk. Depending on the wording used in a guaranty contract, the extent of the guarantor's liability may be unlimited or may continue over a series of transactions. Be absolutely clear about the potential liability before agreeing to serve as a guarantor, and contact an attorney for guidance.

Mortgages

When individuals purchase real property, they typically borrow from a financial institution part or all of the funds needed to pay the purchase price. A **mortgage** is a written instrument that gives the creditor an interest in, or lien on, the debtor's real property as security for payment of a debt. The creditor is the *mortgagee,* and the debtor is the *mortgagor.*

Mortgage A written document that gives a creditor (the mortgagee) an interest in, or lien on, the debtor's (mortgagor's) real property as security for a debt.

---

4. *Century Insurance Co. v. Guerrero Brothers, Inc.,* 2010 WL 997112 (N.Mariana Islands 2010).

Down Payment The part of the purchase price of real property that is paid in cash up front, reducing the amount of the loan or mortgage.

Typically, as part of the mortgage loan, borrowers make a **down payment** (the part of the purchase price that is paid up front in cash). Lenders offer various types of mortgages to meet the needs of different borrowers, but a basic distinction is whether the interest rate is fixed or variable.

Why do many home buyers opt for thirty-year fixed-rate mortgages rather than adjustable-rate mortgages?

Fixed-Rate Mortgages

A *fixed-rate mortgage* has a fixed, or unchanging, rate of interest, so the payments remain the same for the duration of the loan. Lenders determine the interest rate for a standard fixed-rate mortgage loan based on a variety of factors, including the borrower's credit history, credit score, income, and debts. For a borrower to qualify, lenders typically require that the monthly mortgage payment (including principal, interest, taxes, and insurance) not exceed 28 percent of the person's monthly gross income.

Adjustable-Rate Mortgages

The rate of interest paid by the borrower changes periodically with an *adjustable-rate mortgage (ARM)*. Typically, the initial interest rate for an ARM is set at a relatively low fixed rate for a specified period, such as a year or three years. After that time, the interest rate adjusts annually or by some other period, such as biannually or monthly. The interest rate adjustment is calculated by adding a certain number of percentage points (called the margin) to an index rate (one of various government interest rates).

ARMs contractually shift the risk that the interest rate will change from the lender to the borrower. Borrowers will have lower initial payments if they are willing to assume the risk of interest rate changes.

Creditor Protection

When creditors extend mortgages, they are advancing a significant amount of funds for a number of years. Consequently, creditors take a number of steps to protect their interest, including the following:

1. *Requiring mortgage insurance.* One precaution is to require debtors to obtain private mortgage insurance if they do not make a down payment of at least 20 percent of the purchase price. For instance, if a borrower makes a down payment of only 5 percent of the purchase price, the creditor might require insurance covering 15 percent of the cost. Then, if the debtor defaults, the creditor repossesses the house and receives reimbursement from the insurer for the covered portion of the loan.

2. *Recording the mortgage.* The creditor will record the mortgage with the appropriate office in the county where the property is located. Recording ensures that the creditor is officially on record as holding an interest in the property. In essence, recording a mortgage perfects the lender's security interest in the property. A lender that fails to record a mortgage could find itself in the position of an unsecured creditor.

3. *Including contract provisions.* Creditors also include provisions in the mortgage contract that are aimed at protecting their investment. For instance, many lenders include a **prepayment penalty** clause, which requires the borrower to pay a penalty if the mortgage is repaid in full within a certain period. A prepayment penalty helps to protect the lender should the borrower refinance within a short time after obtaining a mortgage.

Prepayment penalty A provision in a mortgage loan contract that requires the borrower to pay a penalty if the mortgage is repaid in full within a certain period.

Mortgage Foreclosure

If the homeowner *defaults,* or fails to make the mortgage payments, the lender has the right to foreclose on the mortgaged property. **Foreclosure** is the legal process by which the lender repossesses and auctions off the property that has secured the loan.

Foreclosure is expensive and time consuming, though. It generally benefits neither the borrowers, who lose their homes, nor the lenders, which face the prospect of losses on their loans. Therefore, both lenders and borrowers are motivated to avoid foreclosure proceedings if possible.

Ways to Avoid Foreclosure

There are several possible methods of avoiding foreclosure. If the borrower might be able to make payments in the future, the lender may grant a **forbearance,** which is a postponement of part or all of the payments on a loan for a limited time. This option works well when the debtor can solve the problem by securing a new job, selling the property, or finding another acceptable solution.

The borrower and the lender may also enter into a **workout agreement**—a contract that describes their respective rights and responsibilities as they try to resolve the default without proceeding to foreclosure. Usually, the lender agrees to delay seeking foreclosure in exchange for the borrower providing additional financial information that might be used to modify the mortgage.

When a borrower is unable to make mortgage payments, a lender may agree to a **short sale**—that is, a sale of the property for less than the balance due on the mortgage loan. Typically, the borrower has to show some hardship, such as the loss of job, a decline in the value of the home, a divorce, or a death in the household. The lender often has approval rights in a short sale, so the sale process may take much longer than an ordinary real estate transaction.

Foreclosure Procedure

If all efforts to find another solution fail, the lender will proceed to foreclosure. The lender must strictly comply with the state statute governing foreclosures. Many problems arose in the last ten years because lenders, facing a record number of foreclosures during the recession, had difficulty complying with the required statutory formalities.

To bring a foreclosure action, a bank must have standing to sue (see Chapter 3). In the following case, the court had to decide whether a bank could foreclose a mortgage even though the bank could not prove when it became the owner of the borrower's promissory note.

When banks foreclose, they often end up owning the property.

Foreclosure A proceeding in which a mortgagee either takes title to or forces the sale of the mortgagor's property in satisfaction of a debt.

Forbearance The act of refraining from exercising a legal right. An agreement between the lender and the borrower in which the lender agrees to temporarily cease requiring mortgage payments, to delay foreclosure, or to accept smaller payments than previously scheduled.

Workout Agreement A formal contract between a debtor and his or her creditors in which the parties agree to negotiate a payment plan for the amount due on the loan instead of proceeding to foreclosure.

Short Sale A sale of real property for an amount that is less than the balance owed on the mortgage loan, usually due to financial hardship.

Spotlight on Chase Bank

Case 13.2
McLean v. JPMorgan Chase Bank, N.A.
District Court of Appeal of Florida, Fourth District, 79 So.3d 170 (2012).

How can Chase Bank foreclose on delinquent mortgages?

BACKGROUND AND FACTS On May 11, 2009, JPMorgan Chase Bank (Chase) filed a foreclosure action against Robert McLean. The complaint alleged that Chase was entitled to enforce the mortgage and promissory note on which McLean had defaulted. Nevertheless, the attached mortgage identified a different mortgagee and lender, and Chase claimed that the note had been "lost, stolen, or destroyed." When McLean filed a motion to dismiss, Chase produced a mortgage assignment dated May 14, 2009, which was three days after it had filed the lawsuit. Eventually, Chase also filed the original note. Although

Spotlight Case 13.2—Continues ➡

Spotlight Case 13.2—Continued

the indorsement to Chase was undated, Chase then filed a motion for summary judgment. The trial court granted Chase's motion even though the accompanying affidavit failed to show that Chase owned the mortgage or note when it had filed the complaint. McLean appealed.

IN THE WORDS OF THE COURT . . .
PER CURIAM. [By the Whole Court]
* * * *

A crucial element in any mortgage foreclosure proceeding is that the party seeking foreclosure must demonstrate that it has standing to foreclose.
* * * *

* * * A party's standing is determined at the time the lawsuit was filed. Stated another way, *"the plaintiff's lack of standing at the inception of the case is not a defect that may be cured by the acquisition of standing after the case is filed."* Thus, a party is not permitted to establish the right to maintain an action retroactively by acquiring standing to file a lawsuit after the fact. [Emphasis added.]
* * * *

In the present case, as is common in recent foreclosure cases, Chase did not attach a copy of the original note to its complaint, but instead [filed a claim] to re-establish a lost note. Later, however, Chase filed * * * the original promissory note, which bore a special endorsement in favor of Chase. [Thus,] * * * it obtained standing to foreclose, at least at some point.

Nonetheless, the record evidence is insufficient to demonstrate that Chase had standing to foreclose *at the time the lawsuit was filed.* [Emphasis in original.] The mortgage was assigned to Chase three days after Chase filed the instant foreclosure

complaint. While the original note contained an undated special endorsement in Chase's favor, the affidavit filed in support of summary judgment did not state when the endorsement was made to Chase. Furthermore, the affidavit, which was dated after the lawsuit was filed, did not specifically state when Chase became the owner of the note, nor did the affidavit indicate that Chase was the owner of the note before suit was filed.

We therefore reverse the summary judgment and corresponding final judgment of foreclosure. On remand, in order for Chase to be entitled to summary judgment, it must show * * * that it was the holder of the note on the date the complaint was filed ([meaning] that the note was endorsed to Chase on or before the date the lawsuit was filed). By contrast, if the evidence shows that the note was endorsed to Chase after the lawsuit was filed, then Chase had no standing at the time the complaint was filed, in which case the trial court should dismiss the instant lawsuit and Chase must file a new complaint.

DECISION AND REMEDY   The Florida appellate court held that Chase did not prove it had standing to foreclose against McLean. The court therefore reversed the trial court's grant of summary judgment.

THE LEGAL ENVIRONMENT DIMENSION   *If Chase cannot prove that it owned the note at the time of its complaint, what will happen next? Will Chase prevail? Why or why not?*

THE ETHICAL DIMENSION   *Why do states require strict compliance with the provisions of their foreclosure laws, such as the requirement in this case that the lender own the note at the time of the complaint?*

Right of Redemption The debtor's legal right to repurchase, or buy back, property before a foreclosure sale.

Redemption Rights
Every state allows a defaulting borrower to redeem the property before the foreclosure sale by paying the full amount of the debt, plus any interest and costs that have accrued. This is known as the **right of redemption**. The idea behind this right is that it is only fair for the borrower to have a chance to regain possession after default.

Some states even allow a borrower to repurchase property *after* a judicial foreclosure—called a *statutory right of redemption.* Generally, the borrower may exercise this right for up to one year from the time the house is sold at a foreclosure sale.[5] The borrower may retain possession of the property after the foreclosure sale until the statutory redemption period ends. If the borrower does not exercise the right of redemption, the new buyer receives title to and possession of the property.

---

5. Some states do not allow a borrower to waive the statutory right of redemption. This means that a buyer at auction must wait one year to obtain title to, and possession of, a foreclosed property.

Protection for Debtors

The law protects debtors as well as creditors. Certain property of the debtor, for example, is exempt under state law from creditors' actions. Consumer protection statutes (see Chapter 20) also protect debtors' rights. Of course, bankruptcy laws, which will be discussed shortly, are designed specifically to assist debtors in need of help.

In most states, certain types of real and personal property are exempt from execution or attachment. State exemption statutes usually include both real and personal property.

Exempted Real Property

Probably the most familiar exemption is the **homestead exemption.** Each state permits the debtor to retain the family home, either in its entirety or up to a specified dollar amount, free from the claims of unsecured creditors or trustees in bankruptcy.

The purpose of the homestead exemption is to ensure that the debtor will retain some form of shelter. (Note that federal bankruptcy law places a cap on the amount that debtors filing bankruptcy can claim is exempt under their states' homestead exemptions.)

In a few states, statutes allow the homestead exemption only if the judgment debtor has a family. If a judgment debtor does not have a family, a creditor may be entitled to collect the full amount realized from the sale of the debtor's home. In addition, the homestead exemption interacts with other areas of law and can sometimes operate to cancel out a portion of a lien on a debtor's real property.

CASE EXAMPLE 13.8   Antonio Stanley purchased a modular home from Yates Mobile Services Corporation. When Stanley failed to pay the purchase price of the modular home, Yates obtained a judicial lien against Stanley's property in the amount of $165,138. Stanley then filed for bankruptcy and asserted the homestead exemption. The court found that Stanley was entitled to avoid the lien to the extent that it impaired his exemption. Using a bankruptcy law formula, the court determined that the total impairment was $143,639 and that Stanley could avoid paying this amount to Yates. Thus, Yates was left with a judicial lien on Stanley's home in the amount of $21,499.[6] ●

Homestead Exemption A law permitting a debtor to retain the family home, either in its entirety or up to a specified dollar amount, free from the claims of unsecured creditors or trustees in bankruptcy.

Exempted Personal Property

Personal property that is most often exempt from satisfaction of judgment debts includes the following:

1. Household furniture up to a specified dollar amount.
2. Clothing and certain personal possessions, such as family pictures or a Bible.
3. A vehicle (or vehicles) for transportation (at least up to a specified dollar amount).
4. Certain classified animals, usually livestock but including pets.
5. Equipment that the debtor uses in a business or trade, such as tools or professional instruments, up to a specified dollar amount.

If a house is sold at auction to satisfy a debt, can the creditor always keep the full proceeds from that sale?

Bankruptcy Law

Bankruptcy law in the United States has two goals—to protect a debtor by giving him or her a fresh start, free from creditors' claims, and to ensure equitable treatment to creditors who are competing for the debtor's assets. Bankruptcy law is federal law, but state laws on

---

6. *In re Stanley,* 2010 WL 2103441 (M.D.N.C. 2010).

security interests, liens, judgments, and exemptions also play a role in federal bankruptcy proceedings.

Article I, Section 8, of the U.S. Constitution gave Congress the power to establish "uniform laws on the subject of bankruptcies throughout the United States." Federal bankruptcy legislation was first enacted in 1898 and since then has undergone several modifications, most recently in the 2005 Bankruptcy Reform Act.[7] Federal bankruptcy laws (as amended) are called the Bankruptcy Code or, more simply, the Code.

Bankruptcy Courts

Bankruptcy proceedings are held in federal bankruptcy courts, which are under the authority of U.S. district courts. Rulings from bankruptcy courts can be appealed to the district courts. The bankruptcy court holds the proceedings required to administer the estate of the debtor in bankruptcy (the *estate* consists of the debtor's assets, as will be discussed shortly). For a discussion of how bankruptcy courts are adapting to the use of social media, see this chapter's *Online Developments* feature.

Bankruptcy court judges are appointed for terms of fourteen years. A bankruptcy court can conduct a jury trial if the appropriate district court has authorized it and the parties to the bankruptcy consent.

Types of Bankruptcy Relief

The Bankruptcy Code is contained in Title 11 of the *United States Code* and has eight chapters. Chapters 1, 3, and 5 of the Code contain general definitional provisions, as well as provisions governing case administration, creditors, the debtor, and the estate. These three chapters normally apply to all kinds of bankruptcies.

Four chapters of the Code set forth the most important types of relief that debtors can seek:

Liquidation The sale of the nonexempt assets of a debtor and the distribution of the funds received to creditors.

1. Chapter 7 provides for **liquidation** proceedings (the selling of all nonexempt assets and the distribution of the proceeds to the debtor's creditors).
2. Chapter 11 governs reorganizations.
3. Chapter 12 (for family farmers and family fishermen) and 13 (for individuals) provide for the adjustment of debts by persons with regular incomes.[8]

Note that a debtor (except for a municipality) need not be insolvent[9] to file for bankruptcy relief under the Bankruptcy Code. Anyone obligated to a creditor can declare bankruptcy.

Special Requirements for Consumer-Debtors

Consumer-Debtor One whose debts result primarily from the purchases of goods for personal, family, or household use.

A **consumer-debtor** is a debtor whose debts result primarily from the purchase of goods for personal, family, or household use. The Bankruptcy Code requires that the clerk of the court give all consumer-debtors written notice of the general purpose, benefits, and costs of each chapter under which they might proceed. In addition, the clerk must provide

---

7. The full title of the act was the Bankruptcy Abuse Prevention and Consumer Protection Act of 2005, Pub. L. No. 109-8, 119 Stat. 23 (April 20, 2005).
8. There are no Chapters 2, 4, 6, 8, or 10 in Title 11. Such "gaps" are not uncommon in the *United States Code*. They occur because chapter numbers (or other subdivisional unit numbers) are sometimes reserved for future use when a statute is enacted. (A gap may also appear if a law has been repealed.)
9. The inability to pay debts as they become due is known as *equitable* insolvency. *Balance sheet* insolvency, which exists when a debtor's liabilities exceed assets, is not the test. Thus, debtors whose cash-flow problems become severe may petition for bankruptcy voluntarily or be forced into involuntary bankruptcy even though their assets far exceed their liabilities.

ONLINE DEVELOPMENTS

Live Chatting with Your State's Bankruptcy Court

Chatting on social media has become a way of life for most younger people in this country and elsewhere. Online chats preceded social media and are still used at retail Web sites. Today, some tech-savvy employees at bankruptcy courts are using the retail online chat model to answer questions about bankruptcy.

Arizona Was First to Use Live Chats

The U.S. Bankruptcy Court for the District of Arizona started live chatting several years ago. It added live chat to its Web site as part of a strategic initiative to educate the public about bankruptcy. Rather than leaving voice messages, people who access the court's Web site can send and receive text messages via an easy-to-use chat box. The court's goal is to respond to a live chat request within thirty seconds.

In 2011, New Mexico became the second state to add online chatting to its bankruptcy court's Web site. Nevada followed with its live chat in 2012.

The courts that have adopted online chatting average about ten chats a day. Most chats last less than ten minutes.

Who Uses Bankruptcy Court Chat Rooms?

At first, only individuals interested in filing for bankruptcy without an attorney used the live chat services. When paralegals learned that they could get quick answers to their questions online, they also began to use the services.

Then, during the real estate meltdown of the last few years, many real estate lawyers expanded into the area of bankruptcy law, often as a way to help their clients avoid foreclosure through bankruptcy filings. Many of these lawyers also have used live chat to expand their knowledge of bankruptcy law.

The Courts and Facebook

In this age of expanding social media, many courts have created their own Facebook pages. For example, the New Jersey Supreme Court, Superior Court, and Tax Court have a Facebook page that covers all three courts.

Increasingly, bankruptcy courts are posting announcements on their Facebook pages. Anyone who has signed up for Facebook can readily find announcements from the U.S. Bankruptcy Court for the Southern District of Mississippi. Information from the bankruptcy courts for Hawaii, New Mexico, Rhode Island, and Riverside, California, also is available on Facebook.

Critical Thinking

Are there any downsides to live chats with bankruptcy courts? If so, what are they?

---

consumer-debtors with information on the types of services available from credit counseling agencies.

Chapter 7—Liquidation

Liquidation under Chapter 7 of the Bankruptcy Code is probably the most familiar type of bankruptcy proceeding and is often referred to as an *ordinary,* or *straight, bankruptcy.* Put simply, a debtor in a liquidation bankruptcy turns all assets over to a **bankruptcy trustee,** a person appointed by the court to manage the debtor's funds. The trustee sells the nonexempt assets and distributes the proceeds to creditors. With certain exceptions, the remaining debts are then **discharged** (extinguished), and the debtor is relieved of the obligation to pay the debts.

Any "person"—defined as including individuals, partnerships, companies, corporations, and labor unions—may be a debtor in a liquidation proceeding. A husband and wife may file jointly for bankruptcy under a single petition. Railroads, insurance companies, banks, savings and loan associations, investment companies licensed by the Small Business

Bankruptcy Trustee A person who is appointed by the court or by creditors to manage the debtor's funds during bankruptcy.

Discharge In bankruptcy proceedings, the extinction of the debtor's dischargeable debts. The termination of an obligation.

Administration, and credit unions *cannot* be debtors in a liquidation bankruptcy, however. Other chapters of the Bankruptcy Code or other federal or state statutes apply to them.

A straight bankruptcy can be commenced by the filing of either a voluntary or an involuntary *petition in bankruptcy*—the document that is filed with a bankruptcy court to initiate bankruptcy proceedings. If a debtor files the petition, the bankruptcy is voluntary. If one or more creditors file a petition to force the debtor into bankruptcy, the bankruptcy is involuntary. We discuss both voluntary and involuntary bankruptcy proceedings under Chapter 7 in the following subsections.

Voluntary Bankruptcy

To bring a voluntary petition in bankruptcy, the debtor files official forms designated for that purpose in the bankruptcy court. The law now requires that *before* debtors can file a petition, they must receive credit counseling from an approved nonprofit agency within the 180-day period preceding the date of filing. Debtors filing a Chapter 7 petition must include a certificate proving that they have received individual or group counseling from an approved agency within the last 180 days (roughly six months).

A consumer-debtor who is filing for liquidation bankruptcy must confirm the accuracy of the petition's contents. The debtor must also state in the petition, at the time of filing, that he or she understands the relief available under other chapters of the Code and has chosen to proceed under Chapter 7.

Attorneys representing the consumer-debtors must file an affidavit stating that they have informed the debtors of the relief available under each chapter of the Bankruptcy Code. In addition, the attorneys must reasonably attempt to verify the accuracy of the consumer-debtors' petitions and schedules (described below). Failure to do so is considered perjury.

Chapter 7 Schedules   The voluntary petition must contain the following schedules:

1. A list of both secured and unsecured creditors, their addresses, and the amount of debt owed to each.
2. A statement of the financial affairs of the debtor.
3. A list of all property owned by the debtor, including property that the debtor claims is exempt.
4. A list of current income and expenses.
5. A certificate of credit counseling (as discussed previously).
6. Proof of payments received from employers within sixty days prior to the filing of the petition.
7. A statement of the amount of monthly income, itemized to show how the amount is calculated.
8. A copy of the debtor's federal income tax return for the most recent year ending immediately before the filing of the petition.

The official forms must be completed accurately, sworn to under oath, and signed by the debtor. To conceal assets or knowingly supply false information on these schedules is a crime under the bankruptcy laws.

With the exception of tax returns, failure to file the required schedules within forty-five days after the filing of the petition (unless an extension is granted) will result in an automatic dismissal of the petition. The debtor has up to seven days before the date of the first creditors' meeting to provide a copy of the most recent tax returns to the trustee.

Tax Returns during Bankruptcy

In addition, a debtor may be required to file a tax return at the end of each tax year while the case is pending and to provide a copy to the court. This may be done at the request of the court or of the **U.S. trustee**—a government official who performs administrative tasks that a bankruptcy judge would otherwise have to perform.

Any *party in interest* (a party, such as a creditor, who has a valid interest in the outcome of the proceedings) may make this request as well. Debtors may also be required to file tax returns during Chapter 11 and 13 bankruptcies.

U.S. Trustee A government official who performs certain administrative tasks that a bankruptcy judge would otherwise have to perform.

Substantial Abuse—Means Test

In the past, a bankruptcy court could dismiss a Chapter 7 petition for relief (discharge of debts) if the use of Chapter 7 would constitute a "substantial abuse" of bankruptcy law. Today, the law provides a *means test* to determine a debtor's eligibility for Chapter 7.

The purpose of the test is to keep upper-income people from abusing the bankruptcy process by filing for Chapter 7, as was thought to have happened in the past. The test forces more people to file for Chapter 13 bankruptcy rather than have their debts discharged under Chapter 7.

The Basic Formula

A debtor wishing to file for bankruptcy must complete the means test to determine whether she or he qualifies for Chapter 7. The debtor's average monthly income in recent months is compared with the median income in the geographic area in which the person lives. (The U.S. Trustee Program provides these data at its Web site.) If the debtor's income is below the median income, the debtor usually is allowed to file for Chapter 7 bankruptcy, as there is no presumption of bankruptcy abuse.

Applying the Means Test to Future Disposable Income

If the debtor's income is above the median income, then further calculations must be made to determine whether the person will have sufficient disposable income in the future to repay at least some of his or her unsecured debts. *Disposable income* is calculated by subtracting living expenses and secured debt payments, such as mortgage payments, from monthly income.

In making this calculation, the debtor's recent monthly income is presumed to continue for the next sixty months. Living expenses are the amounts allowed under formulas used by the Internal Revenue Service (IRS). The IRS allowances include modest allocations for food, clothing, housing, utilities, transportation (including a car payment), health care, and other necessities. (The U.S. Trustee Program's Web site also provides these amounts.) The allowances do not include expenditures for items such as cell phones and cable television service.

Can the Debtor Afford to Pay Unsecured Debts?

Once future disposable income has been estimated, that amount is used to determine whether the debtor will have income that could be applied to unsecured debts. The courts may also consider the debtor's bad faith or other circumstances indicating abuse.

CASE EXAMPLE 13.9 At thirty-three years old, Lisa Hebbring owned a home and a car, but had $11,124 in credit-card debt. Hebbring was earning $49,000 per year when she filed for Chapter 7 bankruptcy. Her petition listed monthly net income of $2,813 and expenditures of $2,897, for a deficit of $84.

In calculating her income, Hebbring excluded a $313 monthly deduction for contributions to retirement plans. The U.S. trustee filed a motion to dismiss Hebbring's petition due to substantial abuse, claiming that the retirement contributions should be disallowed. The court agreed and dismissed the Chapter 7 petition. Because Hebbring's retirement contributions were not reasonably necessary based on her age and financial circumstances, the court found that she was capable of paying her unsecured debts.[10] ●

Additional Grounds for Dismissal
As already noted, a court can dismiss a debtor's voluntary petition for Chapter 7 relief for substantial abuse or for failing to provide the necessary documents within the specified time.

In addition, a court might dismiss a Chapter 7 in two other situations. First, if the debtor has been convicted of a violent crime or a drug-trafficking offense, the victim can file a motion to dismiss the voluntary petition.[11] Second, if the debtor fails to pay postpetition domestic-support obligations (which include child and spousal support), the court may dismiss the debtor's petition.

Order for Relief
If the voluntary petition for bankruptcy is found to be proper, the filing of the petition will itself constitute an **order for relief.** (An order for relief is a court's grant of assistance to a petitioner.) Once a consumer-debtor's voluntary petition has been filed, the trustee and creditors must be given notice of the order for relief by mail not more than twenty days after entry of the order.

Involuntary Bankruptcy

An involuntary bankruptcy occurs when the debtor's creditors force the debtor into bankruptcy proceedings. An involuntary case cannot be filed against a charitable institution or a farmer (an individual or business that receives more than 50 percent of gross income from farming operations).

An involuntary petition should not be used as an everyday debt-collection device, and the Code provides penalties for the filing of frivolous petitions against debtors. If the court dismisses an involuntary petition, the petitioning creditors may be required to pay the costs and attorneys' fees incurred by the debtor in defending against the petition. If the petition was filed in bad faith, damages can be awarded for injury to the debtor's reputation. Punitive damages may also be awarded.

Requirements
For an involuntary action to be filed, the following requirements must be met:

1. If the debtor has twelve or more creditors, three or more of these creditors having unsecured claims totaling at least $15,325 must join in the petition.
2. If a debtor has fewer than twelve creditors, one or more creditors having a claim totaling $15,325 or more may file.[12]

Order for Relief
If the debtor challenges the involuntary petition, a hearing will be held, and the bankruptcy court will enter an order for relief if it finds either of the following:

1. The debtor is not paying debts as they come due.
2. A general receiver, assignee, or custodian took possession of, or was appointed to take charge of, substantially all of the debtor's property within 120 days before the filing of the petition.

Order for Relief A court's grant of assistance to a complainant. In bankruptcy proceedings, the order relieves the debtor of the immediate obligation to pay the debts listed in the bankruptcy petition.

"I hope that after I die, people will say of me: 'That guy sure owed me a lot of money.'"

Jack Handey, 1949–present (American humorist)

---

10. *Hebbring v. U.S. Trustee,* 463 F.3d 902 (9th Cir. 2006).
11. Note that the court may not dismiss a case on this ground if the debtor's bankruptcy is necessary to satisfy a claim for a domestic-support obligation.
12. 11 U.S.C. Section 303. The amounts stated in this chapter are in accordance with those computed on April 1, 2013.

If the court grants an order for relief, the debtor will be required to supply the same information in the bankruptcy schedules as in a voluntary bankruptcy.

Automatic Stay

The moment a petition, either voluntary or involuntary, is filed, an **automatic stay**, or suspension, of all actions by creditors against the debtor or the debtor's property normally goes into effect. In other words, once a petition has been filed, creditors cannot contact the debtor by phone or mail or start any legal proceedings to recover debts or to repossess property. (In some circumstances, a secured creditor or other party in interest may petition the bankruptcy court for relief from the automatic stay, as will be discussed shortly.)

If a creditor *knowingly* violates the automatic stay (a willful violation), any injured party, including the debtor, is entitled to recover actual damages, costs, and attorneys' fees, and may be awarded punitive damages as well. Until the bankruptcy proceeding is closed or dismissed, the automatic stay prohibits a creditor from taking any act to collect, assess, or recover a claim against the debtor that arose before the filing of the petition.

CASE EXAMPLE 13.10   Stefanie Kuehn filed for bankruptcy. When she requested a transcript from the university at which she obtained her master's degree, the university refused because she owed more than $6,000 in tuition. Kuehn complained to the court. The court ruled that the university violated the automatic stay by refusing to provide a transcript because it was attempting to collect an unpaid tuition debt.[13] ●

The Adequate Protection Doctrine   Underlying the Code's automatic-stay provision for a secured creditor is a concept known as *adequate protection*. The **adequate protection doctrine**, among other things, protects secured creditors from losing their security as a result of the automatic stay.

The bankruptcy court can provide adequate protection by requiring the debtor or trustee to make periodic cash payments or a one-time cash payment. The court can also require the debtor or trustee to provide additional collateral or replacement liens to the extent that the stay may actually cause the value of the property to decrease.

Exceptions to the Automatic Stay   The Code provides the following exceptions to the automatic stay:

1. Collection efforts can continue for domestic-support obligations, which include any debt owed to or recoverable by a spouse, a former spouse, a child of the debtor, that child's parent or guardian, or a governmental unit.
2. Proceedings against the debtor related to divorce, child custody or visitation, domestic violence, and support enforcement are not stayed.
3. Investigations by a securities regulatory agency (see Chapter 24) can continue.
4. Certain statutory liens for property taxes are not stayed.

Requests for Relief from the Automatic Stay   A secured creditor or other party in interest can petition the bankruptcy court for relief from the automatic stay. If a creditor or other party requests relief from the stay, the stay will automatically terminate sixty days after the request, unless the court grants an extension or the parties agree otherwise.

Secured Property   The automatic stay on secured property terminates forty-five days after the creditors' meeting (to be discussed shortly). The stay terminates unless the debtor redeems or reaffirms certain debts (*reaffirmation* will be discussed later in this chapter).

Automatic Stay In bankruptcy proceedings, the suspension of almost all litigation and other action by creditors against the debtor or the debtor's property.

Adequate Protection Doctrine A doctrine that protects secured creditors from losing their security as a result of an automatic stay on legal proceedings by creditors against the debtor once the debtor petitions for bankruptcy relief.

---

13. *In re Kuehn*, 563 F.3d 289 (7th Cir. 2009).

In other words, the debtor cannot keep the secured property (such as a financed automobile), even if she or he continues to make payments on it, without reinstating the rights of the secured party to collect on the debt.

Bad Faith   If the debtor had two or more bankruptcy petitions dismissed during the prior year, the Code presumes bad faith. In such a situation, the automatic stay does *not* go into effect until the court determines that the petition was filed in good faith.

Estate in Property

On the commencement of a liquidation proceeding under Chapter 7, an *estate in property* (sometimes called an *estate in bankruptcy*) is created. The estate consists of all the debtor's interests in property currently held, wherever located. The estate in bankruptcy includes all of the following:

1. *Community property* (property jointly owned by a husband and wife in certain states).
2. Property transferred in a transaction voidable by the trustee.
3. Proceeds and profits from the property of the estate.

Certain after-acquired property—such as gifts, inheritances, property settlements (from divorce), and life insurance death proceeds—to which the debtor becomes entitled *within 180 days after filing* may also become part of the estate.

Generally, though, the filing of a bankruptcy petition fixes a dividing line. Property acquired prior to the filing of the petition becomes property of the estate, and property acquired after the filing of the petition, except as just noted, remains the debtor's.

The Bankruptcy Trustee

Promptly after the order for relief in the liquidation proceeding has been entered, a trustee is appointed. The basic duty of the trustee is to collect the debtor's available estate and reduce it to cash for distribution, preserving the interests of both the debtor and the unsecured creditors. The trustee is held accountable for administering the debtor's estate.

To enable the trustee to accomplish this duty, the Code gives the trustee certain powers, stated in both general and specific terms. These powers must be exercised within two years of the order for relief.

Duties for Means Testing
The trustee is required to promptly review all materials filed by the debtor to determine if there is substantial abuse. Within ten days after the first meeting of the creditors (discussed shortly), the trustee must file a statement indicating whether the case is presumed to be an abuse under the means test. The trustee must provide a copy of this statement to all creditors within five days.

When there is a presumption of abuse, the trustee must either file a motion to dismiss the petition (or convert it to a Chapter 13 case) or file a statement explaining why a motion would not be appropriate. If the debtor owes a domestic-support obligation (such as child support), the trustee must provide written notice of the bankruptcy to the claim holder (a former spouse, for instance).

The Trustee's Powers
The trustee has the power to require persons holding the debtor's property at the time the petition is filed to deliver the property to the trustee.[14] To

---

14. Usually, though, the trustee takes constructive, rather than actual, possession of the debtor's property. For example, to obtain control of a debtor's business inventory, a trustee might change the locks on the doors to the business and hire a security guard.

enable the trustee to implement this power, the Code provides that the trustee has rights *equivalent* to those of certain other parties, such as a creditor who has a judicial lien. This power of a trustee, which is equivalent to that of a lien creditor, is known as *strong-arm power.*

In addition, the trustee has specific *powers of avoidance*. They enable the trustee to set aside (avoid) a sale or other transfer of the debtor's property and take the property back for the debtor's estate. These powers apply to voidable rights available to the debtor, preferences, and fraudulent transfers by the debtor. Each power is discussed in more detail below. In addition, a trustee can avoid certain statutory liens (creditors' claims against the debtor's property).

The debtor shares most of the trustee's avoidance powers. Thus, if the trustee does not take action to enforce one of the rights just mentioned, the debtor in a liquidation bankruptcy can enforce that right.

Voidable Rights

A trustee steps into the shoes of the debtor. Thus, any reason that a debtor can use to obtain the return of her or his property can be used by the trustee as well. These grounds include fraud, duress, incapacity, and mutual mistake.

EXAMPLE 13.11   Ben sells his boat to Tara. Tara gives Ben a check, knowing that she has insufficient funds in her bank account to cover the check. Tara has committed fraud. Ben has the right to avoid that transfer and recover the boat from Tara. If Ben files for bankruptcy relief under Chapter 7, the trustee can exercise the same right to recover the boat from Tara, and the boat becomes a part of the debtor's estate. ●

Preferences

A debtor is not permitted to transfer property or to make a payment that favors—or gives a **preference** to—one creditor over others. The trustee is allowed to recover payments made both voluntarily and involuntarily to one creditor in preference over another.

Preference   In bankruptcy proceedings, a property transfer or payment made by the debtor that favors one creditor over others.

To have made a recoverable preferential payment, an *insolvent* debtor must have transferred property, for a *preexisting* debt, within *ninety days* before the filing of the bankruptcy petition. The transfer must have given the creditor more than the creditor would have received as a result of the bankruptcy proceedings. The Code presumes that a debtor is insolvent during the ninety-day period before filing a petition.

If a **preferred creditor** (one who has received a preferential transfer from the debtor) has sold the property to an innocent third party, the trustee cannot recover the property from the innocent party. The preferred creditor, however, generally *can* be held accountable for the value of the property.

Preferred Creditor   In the context of bankruptcy, a creditor who has received a preferential transfer from a debtor.

Preferences to Insiders

Sometimes, the creditor receiving the preference is an insider. An *insider* is an individual, partner, partnership, corporation, or officer or director of a corporation (or a relative of one of these) who has a close relationship with the debtor. In this situation, the avoidance power of the trustee extends to transfers made within *one year* before filing. (If the transfer was fraudulent, as will be discussed shortly, the trustee can avoid transfers made within *two years* before filing.)

If the transfer occurred before the ninety-day period, however, the trustee must prove that the debtor was insolvent when the transfer occurred or that it was made to or for the benefit of an insider.

Transfers That Do Not Constitute Preferences

Not all transfers are preferences. To be a preference, the transfer must be made for something other than current consideration.

Most courts generally assume that payment for services rendered *within fifteen days* before the payment is not a preference. If a creditor receives payment in the ordinary course of business from an individual or business debtor, such as payment of last month's cell phone bill, the bankruptcy trustee cannot recover the payment.

To be recoverable, a preference must be a transfer for an antecedent (preexisting) debt, such as a year-old landscaping bill. In addition, the Code permits a consumer-debtor to transfer any property to a creditor up to a total value of $6,225 without the transfer's constituting a preference. Payment of domestic-support debts does not constitute a preference.

(Lissart/iStockphoto.com)

When is the sale of gold jewelry considered a fraudulent transfer?

Fraudulent Transfers   The trustee may avoid fraudulent transfers or obligations if they (1) were made within two years prior to the filing of the petition or (2) were made with actual intent to hinder, delay, or defraud a creditor. **EXAMPLE 13.12**   April is planning to petition for bankruptcy, so she sells her gold jewelry, worth $10,000, to a friend for $500. The friend agrees that in the future he will "sell" the jewelry back to April for the same amount. This is a fraudulent transfer that the trustee can undo. •

Transfers made for less than reasonably equivalent consideration are also vulnerable if the debtor thereby became insolvent or was left engaged in business with an unreasonably small amount of capital. When a fraudulent transfer is made outside the Code's two-year limit, creditors may seek alternative relief under state laws. Some state laws may allow creditors to recover transfers made up to three years before the filing of a petition.

Exemptions

As just described, the trustee takes control of the debtor's property in a Chapter 7 bankruptcy, but an individual debtor is entitled to exempt (exclude) certain property from the bankruptcy. The Bankruptcy Code exempts the following property:[15]

1. Up to $22,975 in equity in the debtor's residence and burial plot (the homestead exemption).
2. Interest in a motor vehicle up to $3,675.
3. Interest, up to $550 for a particular item, in household goods and furnishings, wearing apparel, appliances, books, animals, crops, and musical instruments (the aggregate total of all items is limited, however, to $12,250).
4. Interest in jewelry up to $1,550.
5. Interest in any other property up to $1,225, plus any unused part of the $22,975 homestead exemption up to $11,500.
6. Interest in any tools of the debtor's trade up to $2,300.
7. A life insurance contract owned by the debtor (other than a credit life insurance contract).
8. Certain interests in accrued dividends and interest under, or loan value of, life insurance contracts owned by the debtor, not to exceed $12,250.
9. Professionally prescribed health aids.
10. The right to receive Social Security and certain welfare benefits, alimony and support, certain retirement funds and pensions, and education savings accounts held for specific periods of time.
11. The right to receive certain personal-injury and other awards up to $22,975.

---

15. The dollar amounts stated in the Bankruptcy Code are adjusted automatically every three years on April 1 based on changes in the Consumer Price Index. The adjusted amounts are rounded to the nearest $25. The amounts stated in this chapter are in accordance with those computed on April 1, 2013.

Individual states have the power to pass legislation precluding debtors from using the federal exemptions within the state. A majority of the states have done this. In those states, debtors may use only state, not federal, exemptions. In the rest of the states, an individual debtor (or a husband and wife filing jointly) may choose either the exemptions provided under state law or the federal exemptions.

The Homestead Exemption

The Bankruptcy Code limits the amount of equity that can be claimed under the homestead exemption. In general, if the debtor acquired the homestead within three and a half years preceding the date of filing, the maximum equity exempted is $155,675, even if state law would permit a higher amount.

In addition, the state homestead exemption is available only if the debtor has lived in a state for two years before filing the bankruptcy petition. Furthermore, a debtor who has violated securities laws, been convicted of a felony, or engaged in certain other intentional misconduct may not be permitted to claim the homestead exemption.

Creditors' Meeting

Within a reasonable time after the order for relief has been granted (not more than forty days), the trustee must call a meeting of the creditors listed in the schedules filed by the debtor. The bankruptcy judge does not attend this meeting. The debtor is required to attend (unless excused by the court) and to submit to examination under oath by the creditors and the trustee. At the meeting, the trustee ensures that the debtor is aware of the potential consequences of bankruptcy and of his or her ability to file for bankruptcy under a different chapter of the Bankruptcy Code.

Creditors' Claims

To be entitled to receive a portion of the debtor's estate, each creditor normally files a *proof of claim* with the bankruptcy court clerk within ninety days of the creditors' meeting.[16] A proof of claim is necessary if there is any dispute concerning the claim. The proof of claim lists the creditor's name and address, as well as the amount that the creditor asserts is owed to the creditor by the debtor.

When the debtor has no assets—called a "no-asset case"—creditors are notified of the debtor's petition for bankruptcy but are instructed not to file a claim. In no-asset cases, the unsecured creditors will receive no payment, and most, if not all, of these debts will be discharged.

Distribution of Property

The Code provides specific rules for the distribution of the debtor's property to secured and unsecured creditors. If any amount remains after the priority classes of creditors have been satisfied, it is turned over to the debtor. Exhibit 13–2 that follows illustrates the collection and distribution of property in most voluntary bankruptcies.

Distribution to Secured Creditors
As noted earlier, secured creditors are creditors who received an interest in collateral to secure a debtor's payment or performance. The Code requires that consumer-debtors file a statement of intention with respect to the secured collateral. They can choose to pay off the debt and redeem the collateral,

---

16. This ninety-day rule applies in Chapter 12 and Chapter 13 bankruptcies as well.

Exhibit 13–2 Collection and Distribution of
Property in Most Voluntary Bankruptcies

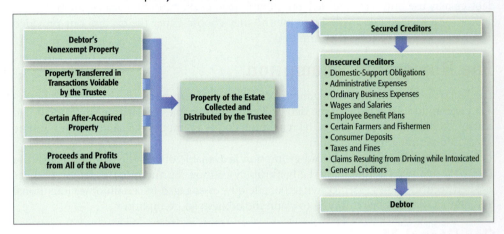

claim it is exempt, reaffirm the debt and continue making payments, or surrender the property to the secured party.

If the collateral is surrendered to the secured party, the secured creditor can enforce the security interest. The secured party can either (1) accept the property in full satisfaction of the debt or (2) sell the collateral and use the proceeds to pay off the debt. Thus, the secured party has priority over unsecured parties as to the proceeds from the disposition of the collateral. Should the collateral be insufficient to cover the secured debt owed, the secured creditor becomes an unsecured creditor for the difference.

Distribution to Unsecured Creditors   Bankruptcy law establishes an order of priority for classes of debts owed to *unsecured* creditors, and they are paid in the order of their priority. Each class must be fully paid before the next class is entitled to any of the remaining proceeds.

If there are insufficient proceeds to pay fully all the creditors in a class, the proceeds are distributed *proportionately* to the creditors in that class, and classes lower in priority receive nothing.

In almost all Chapter 7 bankruptcies, the funds will be insufficient to pay all creditors. The order of priority among classes of unsecured creditors is as follows (some of these classes involve cases against bankrupt businesses):

1. Claims for domestic-support obligations, such as child support and alimony.
2. Administrative expenses, including court costs, trustee fees, and attorneys' fees.
3. In an involuntary bankruptcy, expenses incurred by the debtor in the ordinary course of business.
4. Unpaid wages, salaries, and commissions earned within ninety days of the filing of the petition. The amount is capped for each claimant.
5. Unsecured claims for contributions to be made to employee benefit plans. The amount is capped for each claimant.
6. Consumer deposits given to the debtor before the petition was filed. The amount is capped for each claimant.
7. Certain taxes and penalties due to government units, such as income and property taxes.
8. Claims for death or personal injury resulting from the unlawful operation of a motor vehicle.
9. Claims of general creditors.

Which creditors have claims on the proceeds from liquidation sales?

(Wendell and Carolyn/iStockphoto.com)

If any amount remains after the priority classes of creditors have been satisfied, it is turned over to the debtor.

Discharge

From the debtor's point of view, the primary purpose of liquidation is to obtain a fresh start through a discharge of debts. Certain debts, however, are not dischargeable in bankruptcy. Also, certain debtors may not qualify to have all debts discharged in bankruptcy. These situations are discussed next.

Exceptions to Discharge   Claims that are not dischargeable in bankruptcy include the following:

1. Claims for back taxes accruing within two years prior to bankruptcy.
2. Claims for amounts borrowed by the debtor to pay federal taxes or any nondischargeable taxes.[17]
3. Claims against property or funds obtained by the debtor under false pretenses or by false representations.
4. Claims by creditors who were not notified of the bankruptcy. These claims did not appear on the schedules the debtor was required to file.
5. Claims based on fraud[18] or misuse of funds by the debtor while acting in a fiduciary capacity or claims involving the debtor's embezzlement or larceny.
6. Domestic-support obligations and property settlements as provided for in a separation agreement or divorce decree.
7. Claims for amounts due on a retirement account loan.
8. Claims based on willful or malicious conduct by the debtor toward another or the property of another.
9. Certain government fines and penalties.
10. Student loans, unless payment of the loans imposes an undue hardship on the debtor and the debtor's dependents. (For an example of what constitutes undue hardship, see *Case Example 13.13* that follows.)
11. Consumer debts of more than $650 for luxury goods or services owed to a single creditor incurred within ninety days of the order for relief.
12. Cash advances totaling more than $925 that are extensions of open-end consumer credit obtained by the debtor within seventy days of the order for relief.
13. Judgments against a debtor as a result of the debtor's operation of a motor vehicle while intoxicated.
14. Fees or assessments arising from property in a homeowners' association, as long as the debtor retained an interest in the property.
15. Taxes with respect to which the debtor failed to provide required or requested tax documents.

   CASE EXAMPLE 13.13   Keldric Mosley incurred student loans while attending Alcorn State University and then joined the U.S. Army Reserve Officers' Training Corps. He was injured during training and resigned from the Corps because of medical problems related to his injuries. Mosley worked briefly for several employers, but depressed and physically limited by his injuries, he was unable to keep any of the jobs. A federal bankruptcy court granted him a discharge under Chapter 7, but it did not include the student loans.

Learning Objective 4
What is the difference between an exception to discharge and an objection to discharge?

---

17. Taxes accruing within three years prior to bankruptcy are nondischargeable, including federal and state income taxes, employment taxes, taxes on gross receipts, property taxes, excise taxes, customs duties, and any other taxes for which the government claims the debtor is liable in some capacity. See 11 U.S.C. Sections 507(a)(8) and 523(a)(1).
18. Even if a debtor who is sued for fraud settles the lawsuit, the settlement agreement may not be discharged in bankruptcy because of the underlying fraud. See *Archer v. Warner*, 538 U.S. 314, 123 S.Ct. 1462, 155 L.Ed.2d 454 (2003).

Mosley became homeless and had a monthly income of only $210 in disability benefits, but he still owed $45,000 in student loans. He asked the bankruptcy court to reopen his case and discharge his student loans based on undue hardship. The court held that Mosley's medical problems, lack of skills, and "dire living conditions" made it unlikely that he would be able to hold a job and repay the loans. The court therefore discharged the debt, reasoning that Mosley could not maintain a minimal standard of living if forced to repay the loans.[19] ●

Objections to Discharge   In addition to the exceptions to discharge previously discussed, a bankruptcy court may also deny the discharge of debts based on the debtor's *conduct*. Grounds for denial of discharge to the debtor include the following:

1. The debtor's concealment or destruction of property with the intent to hinder, delay, or defraud a creditor.
2. The debtor's fraudulent concealment or destruction of financial records.
3. The grant of a discharge to the debtor within eight years before the petition was filed.
4. The debtor's failure to complete the required consumer education course.
5. Proceedings in which the debtor could be found guilty of a felony (basically, a court may not discharge any debt until the completion of felony proceedings against the debtor).

When a discharge is denied under any of these circumstances, the debtor's assets are still distributed to the creditors. After the bankruptcy proceeding, however, the debtor remains liable for the unpaid portion of all claims.

Effect of a Discharge   The primary effect of a discharge is to void, or set aside, any judgment on a discharged debt and prohibit any action to collect a discharged debt. A discharge does not affect the liability of a co-debtor.

Revocation of Discharge   A discharge may be revoked (taken back) within one year if it is discovered that the debtor acted fraudulently or dishonestly during the bankruptcy proceeding. If revocation occurs, a creditor whose claim was not satisfied in the distribution of the debtor's property can proceed with his or her claim against the debtor.

Reaffirmation of Debt

Reaffirmation Agreement An agreement between a debtor and a creditor in which the debtor voluntarily agrees to pay a debt dischargeable in bankruptcy.

An agreement to pay a debt dischargeable in bankruptcy is called a **reaffirmation agreement.** A debtor may wish to pay a debt—for instance, a debt owed to a family member, physician, bank, or some other creditor—even though the debt could be discharged in bankruptcy. Also, as noted previously, a debtor cannot retain secured property while continuing to pay without entering into a reaffirmation agreement.

Procedures   To be enforceable, reaffirmation agreements must be made before the debtor is granted a discharge. The agreement must be signed and filed with the court. Court approval is required unless the debtor is represented by an attorney during the negotiation of the reaffirmation and submits the proper documents and certifications. Even when the debtor is represented by an attorney, court approval may be required if it appears that the reaffirmation will result in undue hardship to the debtor.

When court approval is required, a separate hearing will take place. The court will approve the reaffirmation only if it finds that the agreement will not result in undue hardship to the debtor and that the reaffirmation is consistent with the debtor's best interests.

---

19. *In re Mosley*, 494 F.3d 1320 (11th Cir. 2007).

Required Disclosures To discourage creditors from engaging in abusive reaffirmation practices, the law provides specific language for disclosures that must be given to debtors entering into reaffirmation agreements. Among other things, these disclosures explain that the debtor is not required to reaffirm any debt. They also inform the debtor that liens on secured property, such as mortgages and cars, will remain in effect even if the debt is not reaffirmed.

The reaffirmation agreement must disclose the amount of the debt reaffirmed, the rate of interest, the date payments begin, and the right to rescind. The disclosures also caution the debtor: "Only agree to reaffirm a debt if it is in your best interest. Be sure you can afford the payments you agree to make."

The original disclosure documents must be signed by the debtor, certified by the debtor's attorney, and filed with the court at the same time as the reaffirmation agreement. A reaffirmation agreement that is not accompanied by the original signed disclosures will not be effective.

Chapter 11—Reorganization

The type of bankruptcy proceeding most commonly used by corporate debtors is the Chapter 11 *reorganization*. In a reorganization, the creditors and the debtor formulate a plan under which the debtor pays a portion of the debts and is discharged of the remainder. The debtor is allowed to continue in business. Although this type of bankruptcy is generally a corporate reorganization, any debtor (except a stockbroker or a commodities broker) who is eligible for Chapter 7 relief is eligible for relief under Chapter 11. Railroads are also eligible.

Congress has established a "fast-track" Chapter 11 procedure for small-business debtors whose liabilities do not exceed $2.49 million and who do not own or manage real estate. The fast track enables a debtor to avoid the appointment of a creditors' committee and also shortens the filing periods and relaxes certain other requirements. Because the process is shorter and simpler, it is less costly. (See the *Linking Business Law to Corporate Management* feature at the end of this chapter for suggestions on how small businesses can prepare for Chapter 11.)

The same principles that govern the filing of a liquidation (Chapter 7) petition apply to reorganization (Chapter 11) proceedings. The case may be brought either voluntarily or involuntarily. The automatic-stay provisions and its exceptions (such as substantial abuse), as well as the adequate protection doctrine, apply in reorganizations.

Workouts

In some instances, to avoid bankruptcy proceedings, creditors may prefer private, negotiated adjustments of creditor-debtor relations, also known as **workouts.** Often, these out-of-court workouts are much more flexible and thus more conducive to a speedy settlement. Speed is critical because delay is one of the most costly elements in any bankruptcy proceeding. Another advantage of workouts is that they avoid the various administrative costs of bankruptcy proceedings.

Workout An out-of-court agreement between a debtor and creditors that establishes a payment plan for discharging the debtor's debts.

Best Interests of the Creditors

Once a petition for Chapter 11 bankruptcy has been filed, a bankruptcy court, after notice and a hearing, can dismiss or suspend all proceedings at any time if dismissal or suspension would better serve the interests of the creditors. The Code also allows a court, after notice and a hearing, to dismiss a case under reorganization "for cause" when there is no

Learning Objective 5
In a Chapter 11 reorganization, what is the role of the debtor in possession?

Debtor in Possession (DIP) In Chapter 11 bankruptcy proceedings, a debtor who is allowed to continue in possession of the estate in property (the business) and to continue business operations.

reasonable likelihood of rehabilitation. Similarly, a court can dismiss when there is an inability to effect a plan or an unreasonable delay by the debtor that may harm the interests of creditors. A debtor whose petition is dismissed for these reasons can file a subsequent Chapter 11 petition in the future, however.

Debtor in Possession

On entry of the order for relief, the debtor generally continues to operate the business as a **debtor in possession (DIP)**. The court, however, may appoint a trustee (often referred to as a *receiver*) to operate the debtor's business if gross mismanagement of the business is shown or if appointing a trustee is in the best interests of the estate.

The DIP's role is similar to that of a trustee in a liquidation. The DIP is entitled to avoid preferential payments made to creditors and fraudulent transfers of assets. The DIP has the power to decide whether to cancel or assume obligations under prepetition executory contracts (those that are not yet performed) or unexpired leases. The DIP can also exercise a trustee's strong-arm powers.

Creditors' Committees

As soon as practicable after the entry of the order for relief, a creditors' committee of unsecured creditors is appointed.[20] This committee is often composed of the biggest suppliers to the business. The committee may consult with the trustee or the DIP concerning the administration of the case or the formulation of the plan. Additional creditors' committees may be appointed to represent special interest creditors.

Generally, no orders affecting the estate will be entered without the consent of the committee or after a hearing in which the judge is informed of the committee's position. As mentioned earlier, businesses with debts of less than $2.49 million that do not own or manage real estate can avoid creditors' committees. In these cases, orders can be entered without a committee's consent.

The Reorganization Plan

A reorganization plan to rehabilitate the debtor is a plan to conserve and administer the debtor's assets in the hope of an eventual return to successful operation and solvency. The plan must be fair and equitable and must do the following:

1. Designate classes of claims and interests.
2. Specify the treatment to be afforded to the classes of creditors. (The plan must provide the same treatment for all claims in a particular class.)
3. Provide an adequate means for the plan's execution. (Individual debtors are required to utilize postpetition assets as necessary to execute the plan.)
4. Provide for payment of tax claims over a five-year period.

Filing the Plan   Only the debtor may file a plan within the first 120 days after the date of the order for relief. This period may be extended, but not beyond eighteen months from the date of the order for relief. If the debtor does not meet the 120-day deadline or obtain an extension, and if the debtor fails to procure the required creditor consent (discussed next) within 180 days, any party may propose a plan. If a small-business debtor chooses to avoid a creditors' committee, the time for the debtor's filing is 180 days.

---

20. If the debtor has filed a reorganization plan accepted by the creditors, the trustee may decide not to call a meeting of the creditors.

Acceptance of the Plan   Once the plan has been developed, it is submitted to each class of creditors for acceptance. For the plan to be adopted, each class must accept it. A class has accepted the plan when a majority of the creditors, representing two-thirds of the amount of the total claim, vote to approve it.

The plan need not provide for full repayment to unsecured creditors. Instead, creditors receive a percentage of each dollar owed to them by the debtor.

Confirmation of the Plan   Confirmation is conditioned on the debtor's certifying that all postpetition domestic-support obligations have been paid in full. Even when all classes of creditors accept the plan, the court may refuse to confirm it if it is not "in the best interests of the creditors." For small-business debtors, if the plan meets the listed requirements, the court must confirm the plan within forty-five days (unless this period is extended).

The plan can be modified on the request of the debtor, the DIP, the trustee, the U.S. trustee, or a holder of an unsecured claim. If an unsecured creditor objects to the plan, specific rules apply to the value of property to be distributed under the plan. Tax claims must be paid over a five-year period.

Even if only one class of creditors has accepted the plan, the court may still confirm the plan under the Code's so-called **cram-down provision.** In other words, the court may confirm the plan over the objections of a class of creditors. Before the court can exercise this right of cram-down confirmation, it must be demonstrated that the plan does not discriminate unfairly against any creditors and is fair and equitable.

Cram-Down Provision A provision of the Bankruptcy Code that allows a court to confirm a debtor's Chapter 11 reorganization plan even though only one class of creditors has accepted it.

Discharge   The plan is binding on confirmation. Nevertheless, the law provides that confirmation of a plan does not discharge an individual debtor. *For individual debtors, the plan must be completed before discharge will be granted,* unless the court orders otherwise. For all other debtors, the court may order discharge at any time after the plan is confirmed.

The debtor is given a reorganization discharge from all claims not protected under the plan. This discharge does not apply to any claims that would be denied discharge under liquidation.

Bankruptcy Relief under Chapter 12 and Chapter 13

In addition to bankruptcy relief through liquidation and reorganization, the Code also provides for family-farmer and family-fisherman debt adjustments (Chapter 12), and individuals' repayment plans (Chapter 13).

Chapter 12—Family Farmers and Fishermen

To help relieve economic pressure on small farmers, Congress created Chapter 12 of the Bankruptcy Code. In 2005, Congress extended this protection to family fishermen, modified its provisions somewhat, and made it a permanent chapter in the Bankruptcy Code (previously, the statutes authorizing Chapter 12 had to be periodically renewed by Congress).

Definitions   For purposes of Chapter 12, a *family farmer* is one whose gross income is at least 50 percent farm dependent and whose debts are at least 50 percent farm related. The total debt for a family farmer must not exceed $4,031,575. A partnership or close corporation (see Chapter 15 in this textbook) at least 50 percent owned by the farm family can also qualify as a family farmer.[21]

---

21. Note that for a corporation or partnership to qualify under Chapter 12, at least 80 percent of the value of the firm's assets must consist of assets related to the farming operation.

A *family fisherman* is defined as one whose gross income is at least 50 percent dependent on commercial fishing operations[22] and whose debts are at least 80 percent related to commercial fishing. The total debt for a family fisherman must not exceed $1,868,200. As with family farmers, a partnership or closely held corporation can also qualify.

Filing the Petition

The procedure for filing a family-farmer or family-fisherman bankruptcy plan is very similar to the procedure for filing a repayment plan under Chapter 13. The debtor must file a plan not later than ninety days after the order for relief. The filing of the petition acts as an automatic stay against creditors' and co-obligors' actions against the estate.

A farmer or fisherman who has already filed a reorganization or repayment plan may convert it to a Chapter 12 plan. The debtor may also convert a Chapter 12 plan to a liquidation plan.

Content and Confirmation of the Plan

The content of a plan under Chapter 12 is basically the same as that of a Chapter 13 repayment plan. Generally, the plan must be confirmed or denied within forty-five days of filing.

Court confirmation of the plan is the same as for a repayment plan. The plan must provide for payment of secured debts at the value of the collateral. If the secured debt exceeds the value of the collateral, the remaining debt is unsecured.

For unsecured debtors, the plan must be confirmed if either (1) the value of the property to be distributed under the plan equals the amount of the claim or (2) the plan provides that all of the debtor's disposable income to be received in a three-year period (or longer, by court approval) will be applied to making payments. Disposable income is all income received less amounts needed to support the farmer or fisherman and his or her family and to continue the farming or commercial fishing operation. Completion of payments under the plan discharges all debts provided for by the plan.

Chapter 13—Individuals' Repayment Plans

Chapter 13 of the Bankruptcy Code provides for "Adjustment of Debts of an Individual with Regular Income." Individuals (not partnerships or corporations) with regular income who owe fixed (liquidated) unsecured debts of less than $383,175 or fixed secured debts of less than $1,149,525 may take advantage of bankruptcy repayment plans.

Among those eligible are salaried employees and sole proprietors, as well as individuals who live on welfare, Social Security, fixed pensions, or investment income. Many small-business debtors have a choice of filing under either Chapter 11 or Chapter 13. Repayment plans offer some advantages because they are less expensive and less complicated than reorganization or liquidation proceedings.

Filing the Petition

A Chapter 13 repayment plan case can be initiated only by the debtor's filing of a voluntary petition or by court conversion of a Chapter 7 petition (because of a finding of substantial abuse under the means test, for instance). Certain liquidation and reorganization cases may be converted to repayment plan cases with the consent of the debtor.[23]

A trustee, who will make payments under the plan, must be appointed. On the filing of a repayment plan petition, the automatic stay previously discussed takes effect. Although the stay applies to all or part of the debtor's consumer debt, it does not apply to any business debt incurred by the debtor or to any domestic-support obligations.

---

22. Commercial fishing operations include catching, harvesting, or raising fish, shrimp, lobsters, urchins, seaweed, shellfish, or other aquatic species or products.

23. A Chapter 13 repayment plan may be converted to a Chapter 7 liquidation at the request of the debtor or, under certain circumstances, by a creditor "for cause." A Chapter 13 case may be converted to a Chapter 11 case after a hearing.

Good Faith Requirement

The Bankruptcy Code imposes the requirement of good faith on a debtor at both the time of the filing of the petition and the time of the filing of the plan. The Code does not define good faith, but if the circumstances on the whole indicate bad faith, a court can dismiss a debtor's Chapter 13 petition.

Should a determination of good faith take into account whether a debtor includes Social Security income in the amount of disposable income to be dedicated to the payment of unsecured creditors under a Chapter 13 plan? That was the contention of the bankruptcy trustee in the following case.

Case 13.3

In re Welsh

United States Court of Appeals, Ninth Circuit, 711 F.3d 1120 (2013).

BACKGROUND AND FACTS David and Sharon Welsh filed a Chapter 13 petition. The bankruptcy trustee objected to the Welshes' proposed plan on the ground that it was not proposed in good faith. Specifically, the Welshes were making "minuscule" payments to unsecured claims while living in a $400,000 home, making payments on various luxury and unnecessary items, and failing to commit 100 percent of their disposable income to the plan (which would pay off only about $14,700 of $180,500 of the unsecured debt). Excluded from the plan was David's Social Security income because the Bankruptcy Code excludes Social Security income from the current monthly income calculation. The court ruled in the Welshes' favor. The Bankruptcy Appellate Panel for the Ninth Circuit affirmed the ruling. The trustee appealed to the U.S. Court of Appeals for the Ninth Circuit.

IN THE WORDS OF THE COURT . . .
RIPPLE, Senior Circuit Judge:
* * * *

In 2005, Congress * * * enacted the Bankruptcy Abuse Prevention and Consumer Protection Act ("BAPCPA"). The good faith requirement * * * remained the same, but there were significant changes with respect to the calculation of disposable income. Before the BAPCPA, bankruptcy judges had authority to determine a debtor's ability to pay based on the individual circumstances of each case and each debtor. Congress replaced this discretion with a detailed, mechanical means test, which requires debtors with above-median income to calculate their "disposable income" by subtracting specific expenses from "current monthly income," as defined by the Bankruptcy Code. For our purposes, several elements of this calculation are important. *The debtor begins with his "current monthly income," which, by definition, explicitly "excludes benefits received under the Social Security Act."* The debtor then subtracts living expenses based on the Internal Revenue Service's "Collection Financial Standards," a detailed series of averages for living expenses that the Service uses to calculate necessary expenditures for

delinquent taxpayers. The debtor also subtracts his averaged payments to secured creditors due during the following sixty months. [Emphasis added.]

As is the case here, the manner in which the means test calculates "disposable income" may underestimate the amount of actual funds that a taxpayer has available to pay unsecured creditors. A debtor who receives Social Security income * * * does not have to account for that income when calculating "disposable income" according to the means test. * * * The result may be that * * * little "disposable income," as that figure is calculated, remains to pay unsecured creditors.
* * * *

Here, the Trustee does not contend, of course, that the calculation of disposable income should have incorporated Social Security income; the statutory language is clearly to the contrary. Instead, he * * * maintains that the Welshes' failure to dedicate Mr. Welsh's Social Security income to the payment of unsecured creditors requires a conclusion that the plan was not proposed in good faith * * * . We cannot conclude, however, that a plan prepared completely in accordance with the very detailed calculations that Congress set forth is not proposed in good faith. To hold otherwise would be to allow the bankruptcy court to substitute its judgment of how much and what kind of income should be dedicated to the payment of unsecured creditors for the judgment of Congress. Such an approach would not only flout the express language of Congress, but also one of Congress's purposes in enacting the BAPCPA, namely to reduce the amount of discretion that bankruptcy courts previously had over the calculation of an above-median debtor's income and expenses.

DECISION AND REMEDY The U.S. Court of Appeals for the Ninth Circuit affirmed the Bankruptcy Appellate Panel's judgment in the Welshes' favor. The court of appeals concluded that "Congress's adoption of the BAPCPA forecloses a court's consideration of a debtor's Social Security income . . . as part of the inquiry into good faith."

Case 13.3—Continues ➡

Case 13.3—Continued

THE LEGAL ENVIRONMENT DIMENSION *In evaluating a debtor's petition, what factors should be part of a good faith analysis? Should consideration of disposable income play a role?*

THE ETHICAL DIMENSION *Why would Congress want to reduce the amount of discretion that bankruptcy courts have in calculating a debtor's income and expenses?*

The Repayment Plan

A plan of rehabilitation by repayment must provide for the following:

1. The turning over to the trustee of such future earnings or income of the debtor as is necessary for execution of the plan.
2. Full payment through deferred cash payments of all claims entitled to priority, such as taxes.[24]
3. Identical treatment of all claims within a particular class. (The Code permits the debtor to list co-debtors, such as guarantors or sureties, as a separate class.)

The repayment plan may provide either for payment of all obligations in full or for payment of a lesser amount. The debtor must begin making payments under the proposed plan within thirty days after the plan has been filed and must continue to make "timely" payments from her or his disposable income. If the debtor fails to make timely payments or to commence payments within the thirty-day period, the court can convert the case to a liquidation (Chapter 7) bankruptcy or dismiss the petition.

Length of the Plan The length of the payment plan can be three or five years, depending on the debtor's family income. If the debtor's family income is greater than the median family income in the relevant geographic area under the means test, the term of the proposed plan must be for three years.[25] The term may not exceed five years.

Confirmation of the Plan After the plan is filed, the court holds a confirmation hearing, at which interested parties (such as creditors) may object to the plan. The hearing must be held at least twenty days, but no more than forty-five days, after the meeting of the creditors. The debtor must have filed all prepetition tax returns and paid all postpetition domestic-support obligations before a court will confirm any plan.

The court will confirm a plan with respect to each claim of a secured creditor under any of the following circumstances:

1. If the secured creditors have accepted the plan.
2. If the plan provides that secured creditors retain their liens until there is payment in full or until the debtor receives a discharge.
3. If the debtor surrenders the property securing the claims to the creditors.

In addition, for a motor vehicle purchased within 910 days before the petition is filed, the plan must provide that a creditor who extended credit for part or all of the purchase price retains its lien until the entire debt is paid.

Discharge

After the debtor has completed all payments, the court grants a discharge of all debts provided for by the repayment plan. Generally, all debts are dischargeable except the following:

---

24. As with a Chapter 11 reorganization plan, full repayment of all claims is not always required.
25. See 11 U.S.C. Section 1322(d) for details on when the court will find that the Chapter 13 plan should extend to a five-year period.

1. Allowed claims not provided for by the plan.
2. Certain long-term debts provided for by the plan.
3. Certain tax claims and payments on retirement accounts.
4. Claims for domestic-support obligations.
5. Debts related to injury or property damage caused while driving under the influence of alcohol or drugs.

Reviewing . . . Creditor-Debtor Relations and Bankruptcy

Three months ago, Janet Hart's husband of twenty years died of cancer. Although he had medical insurance, he left Janet with outstanding medical bills of more than $50,000. Janet has worked at the local library for the past ten years, earning $1,500 per month. Since her husband's death, Janet also receives $1,500 in Social Security benefits and $1,100 in life insurance proceeds every month, for a total monthly income of $4,300. After she pays the mortgage payment of $1,500 and the amounts due on other debts, Janet has barely enough left to buy groceries for her family (she has two teenage daughters at home). She decides to file for Chapter 7 bankruptcy, hoping for a fresh start. Using the information presented in the chapter, answer the following questions.

1. What must Janet do *before* filing a petition for relief under Chapter 7?
2. How much time does Janet have after filing the bankruptcy petition to submit the required schedules? What happens if Janet does not meet the deadline?
3. Assume that Janet files a petition under Chapter 7. Further assume that the median family income in the geographic area in which Janet lives is $49,300. What steps would a court take to determine whether Janet's petition is presumed to be "substantial abuse" using the means test?
4. Suppose that the court determines that no *presumption* of substantial abuse applies in Janet's case. Nevertheless, the court finds that Janet does have the ability to pay at least a portion of the medical bills out of her disposable income. What would the court likely order in that situation?

Debate This   Rather than being allowed to file Chapter 7 bankruptcy petitions, individuals and couples should always be forced to make an effort to pay off their debts through Chapter 13.

LINKING BUSINESS LAW to Corporate Management

What Can You Do to Prepare for a Chapter 11 Reorganization?

Chapter 11 of the Bankruptcy Code expresses the broad public policy of encouraging commerce. To this end, Chapter 11 allows a financially troubled business firm to petition for reorganization in bankruptcy while it is still solvent so that the firm's business can continue. Small businesses, however, do not fare very well under Chapter 11. Although a few corporations that enter into Chapter 11 emerge as functioning entities, only a small number of companies survive the process.

Continued

Linking Business Law to Corporate Management—Continued

Plan Ahead

If you ever are a small-business owner contemplating Chapter 11 reorganization, you can improve your chances of being among the survivors by planning ahead. To ensure the greatest possibility of success, you should take action before, not after, entering bankruptcy proceedings. Discuss your financial troubles openly and cooperatively with creditors to see if you can agree on a workout or some other arrangement.

If you appear to have no choice but to file for Chapter 11 protection, try to persuade a lender to loan you funds to see you through the bankruptcy. If your business is a small corporation, you might try to negotiate a favorable deal with a major investor. For example, a small business could offer to transfer ownership of stock to the investor in return for a loan to pay the costs of the bankruptcy proceedings and an option to repurchase the stock when the firm becomes profitable again.

Consult with Creditors

Most important, you should form a Chapter 11 plan before entering bankruptcy proceedings. Consult with creditors in advance to see what kind of plan would be acceptable to them, and prepare your plan accordingly. Having an acceptable plan prepared before you file will expedite the proceedings and thus save substantially on costs.

Critical Thinking

More bankruptcy filings are under Chapter 11, which may increase the time needed to complete the proceedings. How might this affect the likelihood that a firm will be able to negotiate a workout agreement with its creditors?

Key Terms

adequate protection doctrine 373
artisan's lien 357
attachment 358
automatic stay 373
bankruptcy trustee 369
consumer-debtor 368
co-surety 363
cram-down provision 383
creditors' composition agreement 360
debtor in possession (DIP) 382

default 357
discharge 369
down payment 364
forbearance 365
foreclosure 365
garnishment 359
guarantor 360
homestead exemption 367
lien 357
liquidation 368

mechanic's lien 357
mortgage 363
order for relief 372
preference 375
preferred creditor 375
prepayment penalty 364
reaffirmation agreement 380
right of contribution 363
right of redemption 366
right of reimbursement 363

right of subrogation 362
short sale 365
surety 360
suretyship 360
U.S. trustee 371
workout 381
workout agreement 365
writ of attachment 358
writ of execution 359

Chapter Summary: Creditor-Debtor Relations and Bankruptcy

LAWS ASSISTING CREDITORS	

Liens	1. *Mechanic's lien*—A nonpossessory, filed lien on an owner's real estate for labor, services, or materials furnished to or used to make improvements on the realty.
	2. *Artisan's lien*—A possessory lien on an owner's personal property for labor performed or value added.
	3. *Judicial liens*—
	  a. *Writ of attachment*—A court-ordered seizure of property prior to a court's final determination of the creditor's rights to the property. Attachment is available only on the creditor's posting of a bond and strict compliance with the applicable state statutes.
	  b. *Writ of execution*—A court order directing the sheriff to seize (levy) and sell a debtor's nonexempt real or personal property to satisfy a court's judgment in the creditor's favor.

Garnishment	A collection remedy that allows the creditor to attach a debtor's funds (such as wages owed or bank accounts) and property that are held by a third person.
Creditors' Composition Agreements	A contract between a debtor and his or her creditors by which the debtor's debts are discharged by payment of a sum less than the amount that is actually owed.
Suretyship and Guaranty	Under contract, a third person agrees to be primarily or secondarily liable for the debt owed by the principal debtor. A creditor can turn to this third person for satisfaction of the debt.

Chapter Summary: Creditor-Debtor Relations and Bankruptcy—Continued

Mortgages	1. *Loans*—When individuals purchase real estate, they typically make a down payment and take out a mortgage loan for the balance of the purchase price. Different types of loans are available, including fixed-rate and adjustable-rate mortgages.
	2. *Lender protections*—To protect its interests, a creditor may (a) require private mortgage insurance if the down payment is less than 20 percent of the purchase price, (b) perfect its security interest by recording the mortgage in the appropriate office, and (c) include a prepayment penalty clause and a clause requiring the borrower to maintain homeowners' insurance in the mortgage contract.
	3. *Foreclosure*—If the borrower defaults, the entire mortgage debt is due and payable, and the lender can foreclose on the mortgaged property.
	   a. The foreclosure process allows a lender to repossess and auction the property but requires that the lender strictly comply with the relevant state statute.
	   b. Foreclosure can sometimes be avoided through a forbearance, a workout agreement, or a short sale.
	   c. The borrower has the right to purchase the property after default by paying the full amount of the debt, plus interest and costs, before the foreclosure sale.

PROTECTION FOR DEBTORS

Exemptions	Certain property of a debtor is exempt from creditors' actions under state laws. Each state permits a debtor to retain the family home, either in its entirety or up to a specified dollar amount, free from the claims of unsecured creditors or trustees in bankruptcy (homestead exemption).

BANKRUPTCY—A COMPARISON OF CHAPTERS 7, 11, 12, AND 13

Issue	Chapter 7	Chapter 11	Chapters 12 and 13
Purpose	Liquidation.	Reorganization.	Adjustment.
Who Can Petition	Debtor (voluntary) or creditors (involuntary).	Debtor (voluntary) or creditors (involuntary).	Debtor (voluntary) only.
Who Can Be a Debtor	Any "person" (including partnerships and corporations) except railroads, insurance companies, banks, savings and loan institutions, investment companies licensed by the U.S. Small Business Administration, and credit unions. Farmers and charitable institutions cannot be involuntarily petitioned.	Any debtor eligible for Chapter 7 relief; railroads are also eligible.	*Chapter 12*—Any family farmer (one whose gross income is at least 50 percent farm dependent and whose debts are at least 50 percent farm related) or family fisherman (one whose gross income is at least 50 percent dependent on and whose debts are at least 80 percent related to commercial fishing) or any partnership or close corporation at least 50 percent owned by a family farmer or fisherman, when total debt does not exceed $4,031,575 for a family farmer and $1,868,200 for a family fisherman. *Chapter 13*—Any individual (not partnerships or corporations) with regular income who owes fixed (liquidated) unsecured debts of less than $383,175 or fixed secured debts of less than $1,149,525.
Procedure Leading to Discharge	Nonexempt property is sold with proceeds to be distributed (in order) to priority groups. Dischargeable debts are terminated.	Plan is submitted. If it is approved and followed, debts are discharged.	Plan is submitted and must be approved if the value of the property to be distributed equals the amount of the claims or if the debtor turns over disposable income for a three-year or five-year period. If the plan is followed, debts are discharged.
Advantages	On liquidation and distribution, most debts are discharged, and the debtor has an opportunity for a fresh start.	Debtor continues in business. Creditors can either accept the plan, or it can be "crammed down" on them. The plan allows for the reorganization and liquidation of debts over the plan period.	Debtor continues in business or possession of assets. If the plan is approved, most debts are discharged after a three-year period.

Issue Spotters

1. Jorge contracts with Larry of Midwest Roofing to fix Jorge's roof. Jorge pays half of the contract price in advance. Larry and Midwest complete the job, but Jorge refuses to pay the rest of the price. What can Larry and Midwest do? (See *Laws Assisting Creditors*.)
2. After graduating from college, Tina works briefly as a salesperson before filing for bankruptcy. Tina's petition states that her only debts are student loans, taxes accruing within the last year, and a claim against her based on her misuse of customers' funds during her employment. Are these debts dischargeable in bankruptcy? Explain. (See *Chapter 7—Liquidation*.)

—**Check your answers to the Issue Spotters against the answers provided in Appendix D at the end of this text.**

For Review

1. What is a prejudgment attachment? What is a writ of execution? How does a creditor use these remedies?
2. What is garnishment? When might a creditor undertake a garnishment proceeding?
3. In a bankruptcy proceeding, what constitutes the debtor's estate in property? What property is exempt from the estate under federal bankruptcy law?
4. What is the difference between an exception to discharge and an objection to discharge?
5. In a Chapter 11 reorganization, what is the role of the debtor in possession?

Business Scenarios and Case Problems

13–1. Liens. Nabil is the owner of a relatively old home valued at $105,000. The home's electrical system is failing and the wiring needs to be replaced. He contracts with Kandhari Electrical to replace the electrical system. Kandhari performs the repairs, and on June 1 submits a bill of $10,000 to Nabil. Because of financial difficulties, Nabil does not pay the bill. Nabil's only asset is his home, but his state's homestead exemption is $60,000. Discuss fully Kandhari's remedies in this situation. (See *Laws Assisting Creditors*.)

13–2. Voluntary versus Involuntary Bankruptcy. Burke has been a rancher all her life, raising cattle and crops. Her ranch is valued at $500,000, almost all of which is exempt under state law. Burke has eight creditors and a total indebtedness of $70,000. Two of her largest creditors are Oman ($30,000 owed) and Sneed ($25,000 owed). The other six creditors have claims of less than $5,000 each. A drought has ruined all of Burke's crops and forced her to sell many of her cattle at a loss. She cannot pay off her creditors. (See *Chapter 7—Liquidation*.)

　　1. Under the Bankruptcy Code, can Burke, with a $500,000 ranch, voluntarily petition herself into bankruptcy? Explain.
　　2. Could either Oman or Sneed force Burke into involuntary bankruptcy? Explain.

13–3. Guaranty. Majestic Group Korea, Ltd., borrowed $1.5 million from Overseas Private Investment Corp. (OPIC) to finance a Ruby Tuesday's restaurant. Nam Koo Kim, the sole owner of Majestic, and his spouse, Hee Sun Kim, signed personal guaranties for full payment of the loan. Majestic defaulted. OPIC filed a suit against the Kims to recover. Hee claimed that she did not understand the extent of her liability when she signed the guaranty. Was Hee liable for the debt? Explain. [*Overseas Private Investment Corp. v. Kim*, 69 A.D.3d 1185, 895 N.Y.S.2d 217 (2010)] (See *Laws Assisting Creditors*.)

13–4. Foreclosure on Mortgages and Liens. LaSalle Bank loaned $8 million to Cypress Creek 1, LP, to build an apartment complex. The loan was secured by a mortgage. Cypress Creek hired contractors to provide concrete work, plumbing, carpentry, and other construction services. Cypress Creek went bankrupt, owing LaSalle $3 million. The contractors recorded mechanic's liens when they did not get paid for their work. The property was sold to LaSalle at a sheriff's sale for $1.3 million. The contractors claimed that they should be paid the amounts they were owed out of the $1.3 million and that the mechanic's liens should be satisfied before any funds were distributed to LaSalle for its mortgage. The trial court distributed the $1.3 million primarily to LaSalle, with only a small fraction going to the contractors. Do the liens come before the mortgage in priority of payment? Discuss. [*LaSalle Bank National Association v. Cypress Creek 1, LP*, 242 Ill.2d 231, 950 N.E.2d 1109 (2011)] (See *Mortgages*.)

13–5. Discharge in Bankruptcy. Monica Sexton filed a petition for Chapter 13 reorganization. One of her creditors was Friedman's Jewelers. Her petition misclassified Friedman's claim as $800 of unsecured debt. Within days, Friedman's filed proof of a secured claim for $300 and an unsecured claim for $462. Eventually, Friedman's was sent payments of about $300 by check. None of the checks were cashed. By then, Friedman's had filed its own petition under Chapter 11, Bankruptcy Receivables Management (BRM) had bought Friedman's unpaid accounts, and the checks had not been forwarded. Sexton received a discharge on the completion of her plan. BRM was not notified. BRM wrote to Sexton's attorney to ask about the status of her case, but received no response. BRM demanded that Sexton surrender the collateral on its claim. Sexton asked the court to impose sanctions on BRM for violating the discharge order. Was Sexton's debt to Friedman's dischargeable? Should BRM be sanctioned? Discuss. [*In re Sexton,* __ Bankr. __ (E.D.N.C. 2011)] (See *Chapter 7—Liquidation.*)

13–6. **Business Case Problem with Sample Answer— Automatic Stay.** Michelle Gholston leased a Chevy Impala from EZ Auto Van Rentals. In November 2011, Gholston filed for bankruptcy. Around November 21, the bankruptcy court notified EZ Auto of Gholston's bankruptcy and the imposition of an automatic stay. Nevertheless, because Gholston had fallen behind on her payments, EZ Auto repossessed the vehicle on November 28. Gholston's attorney then reminded EZ Auto about the automatic stay, but the company failed to return the car. As a result of the car's repossession, Gholston suffered damages that included emotional distress, lost wages, attorneys' fees, and car rental expenses. Can Gholston recover from EZ Auto? Why or why not? [*In re Gholston,* ___ Bankr. ___, 2012 WL 639288 (M.D.Fla. 2012)] (See *Chapter 7—Liquidation.*)

—For a sample answer to Problem 13–6, go to Appendix E at the end of this text.

13–7. **Guaranty.** Timothy Martinez, owner of Koenig & Vits, Inc. (K&V), guaranteed K&V's debt to Community Bank & Trust. The guaranty stated that the bank was not required to seek payment of the debt from any other source before enforcing the guaranty. K&V defaulted. Through a Wisconsin state court, the bank sought payment of $536,739.40, plus interest at the contract rate of 7.5 percent, from Martinez. Martinez argued that the bank could not enforce his guaranty while other funds were available to satisfy K&V's debt. For example, the debt might be paid out of the proceeds of a sale of corporate assets. Is this an effective defense to a guaranty? Why or why not? [*Community Bank & Trust v. Koenig & Vits, Inc.,* 346 Wis.2d 279 (Wis.App. 2013)] (See *Laws Assisting Creditors.*)

13–8. **Discharge in Bankruptcy.** Like many students, Barbara Hann financed her education partially through loans. These loans included three federally insured Stafford Loans of $7,500 each ($22,500 in total). Hann believed that she repaid the loans, but when she later filed a Chapter 13 petition, Educational Credit Management Corp. (ECMC) filed an

unsecured proof of claim based on the loans. Hann objected. At a hearing at which ECMC failed to appear, Hann submitted correspondence from the lender that indicated the loans had been paid. The court entered an order sustaining Hann's objection. Despite the order, can ECMC resume its effort to collect on Hann's loans? Explain. [*In re Hann,* 711 F.3d 235 (1st Cir. 2013)] (See *Chapter 7—Liquidation.*)

13–9. **Discharge.** Michael and Dianne Shankle divorced. An Arkansas state court ordered Michael to pay Dianne alimony and child support, as well as half of the $184,000 the couple had in investment accounts. Instead, he withdrew more than half of the investment funds and spent them. Over the next several years, the court repeatedly held Michael in contempt for failing to pay Dianne. Six years later, Michael filed for Chapter 7 bankruptcy, including in the petition's schedule the debt to Dianne of unpaid alimony, child support, and investment funds. Is Michael entitled to a discharge of this debt, or does it qualify as an exception? Why or why not? [*In re Shankle,* __ F.3d __, 2014 WL 486208 (5th Cir. 2014)] (See *Chapter 7—Liquidation.*)

13–10. **A Question of Ethics—Guaranty.** 73-75 Main Avenue, LLC, agreed to lease a portion of the commercial property at 73 Main Avenue, Norwalk, Connecticut, to PP Door Enterprise, Inc. Nan Zhang, as manager of PP Door, signed the lease agreement. The lessor required the principal officers of PP Door to execute personal guaranties. In addition, the principal officers agreed to provide the lessor with credit information. Apparently, both the lessor and the principals of PP Door signed the lease and guaranty agreements that were sent to PP Door's office. When PP Door failed to make monthly payments, 73-75 Main Avenue filed a suit against PP Door and its owner Li. At trial, Li testified that she was the sole owner of PP Door but denied that Zhang was its manager. She also denied signing the guaranty agreement. She claimed that she had signed the credit authorization form because Zhang had told her he was too young to have good credit. Li claimed to have no knowledge of the lease agreement. She did admit, however, that she had paid the rent. She claimed that Zhang had been in a car accident and had asked her to help pay his bills, including the rent at 73 Main Avenue. Li further testified that she did not see the name PP Door on the storefront of the leased location. [*73-75 Main Avenue, LLC v. PP Door Enterprise Inc.,* 120 Conn.App. 150, 991 A.2d 650 (2010)] (See *Laws Assisting Creditors.*)

1. Li argued that she was not liable on the lease agreement because Zhang was not authorized to bind her to the lease. Do the facts support Li? Why or why not?

2. Li claimed that the guaranty for rent was not enforceable against her. Why might the court agree?

UNIT 2 Cumulative Business Hypothetical

Samuel Polson has an idea for a new software application. Polson hires an assistant and invests a considerable amount of his own time and funds developing the application. To manufacture and market his application and develop other software, Polson needs financial capital.

1. Polson borrows $5,000 from his friend Michael Brant. Polson promises to repay Brant the $5,000 in three weeks. Brant, in urgent need of funds, borrows $5,000 from his friend Mary Viva and assigns his rights to the $5,000 Polson owes him to Viva in return for the loan. Viva notifies Polson of the assignment. Polson pays Brant the $5,000 on the date stipulated in their contract. Brant refuses to give the $5,000 to Viva, and Viva sues Polson. Is Polson obligated to pay Viva $5,000 also? Discuss.

2. Polson learns that a competitor, Trivan, Inc., has already filed for a patent on a nearly identical program and has manufactured and sold the software to some customers. Polson learns from a reliable source that Trivan paid Polson's assistant a substantial sum to obtain a copy of the program. What legal recourse does Polson have against Trivan? Discuss fully.

3. While Polson is developing his idea and founding his business, he has no income. To meet expenses, Polson and his wife begin a home-based baking business for which he orders and has installed a new model X23 McIntyre oven from a local company, Western Heating Appliances. One day, Polson is baking croissants. When he opens the oven, part of the door becomes detached. As he struggles with the door, his hands are badly burned, and he is unable to work for several months. Polson later learns that the hinge mechanism on the door was improperly installed. He wants to sue the oven's manufacturer to recover damages, including consequential damages for lost profits. In a product liability suit against the manufacturer, under what legal principles and doctrines might Polson recover damages? Discuss fully.

4. During the course of the events described in the preceding questions, the payments on Polson's mortgage, his various credit-card debts, and some loans that he took out to pay for his son's college tuition continue to come due. As his software business begins to generate revenue, Polson files for Chapter 7 liquidation. Polson hopes to be rid of his personal debts entirely, even though he believes he could probably pay his creditors off over a four-year period if he scrimped and used every cent available. Are all of Polson's personal debts dischargeable under Chapter 7, including the debts incurred for his son's education? Given that Polson could foreseeably pay off his debts over a four-year period, will the court allow Polson to obtain relief under Chapter 7? Why or why not?

Legal Reasoning Group Activity

Warranties. Milan purchased saffron extract, marketed as "America's Hottest New Way to a Flat Belly," online from Dr. Chen. The Web site stated that recently published studies showed a significant weight loss (more than 25 percent) for people who used pure saffron extract as a supplement *without diet and exercise*. Dr. Chen said that the saffron suppresses appetite by increasing levels of serotonin, which reduces emotional eating. Milan took the extract as directed without any resulting weight loss.

1. The first group will determine whether Dr. Chen's Web site made any express warranty on the saffron extract or its effectiveness in causing weight loss.

2. The second group will discuss whether the implied warranty of merchantability applies to the purchase of weight-loss supplements.

3. The third group will decide if Dr. Chen's sale of saffron extract breached the implied warranty of fitness for a particular purpose.

(track5/iStockphoto.com)

UNIT **3**

Business and Employment

UNIT CONTENTS

CHAPTER 14

Small Business Organizations

(Lisegagne/iStockphoto.com)

CONTENTS

- Sole Proprietorships
- Partnerships
- Limited Liability Partnerships
- Limited Partnerships
- Limited Liability Companies
- Franchises

LEARNING OBJECTIVES

The five learning objectives below are designed to help improve your understanding of the chapter. After reading this chapter, you should be able to answer the following questions:

1. What advantages and disadvantages are associated with the sole proprietorship?

2. What is meant by joint and several liability? Why is this often considered to be a disadvantage of doing business as a general partnership?

3. What advantages do limited liability partnerships offer to entrepreneurs that are not offered by general partnerships?

4. What are the key differences between the rights and liabilities of general partners and those of limited partners?

5. How are limited liability companies formed, and who decides how they will be managed and operated?

> "Why not go out on a limb? Isn't that where the fruit is?"
> —Frank Scully, 1892–1964, (American author)

Many Americans would agree with Frank Scully's comment in the chapter-opening quotation that to succeed in business one must "go out on a limb." Certainly, an entrepreneur's primary motive for undertaking a business enterprise is to make profits. An **entrepreneur** is by definition one who initiates and assumes the financial risks of a new enterprise and undertakes to provide or control its management. One of the first decisions an entrepreneur must make is which form of business organization will be most appropriate for the new endeavor.

In selecting an organizational form, the entrepreneur will consider a number of factors, including (1) ease of creation, (2) the liability of the owners, (3) tax considerations, and (4) the ability to raise capital. Keep these factors in mind as you read about the various forms of business organization. You may find it helpful to refer to Exhibit 15–3 in Chapter 15, which compares the major business forms in use today.

Traditionally, entrepreneurs have used three major forms to structure their business enterprises: the sole proprietorship, the partnership, and the corporation. In this chapter,

Entrepreneur One who initiates and assumes the financial risks of a new business enterprise and undertakes to provide or control its management.

we examine the forms of business most often used by small business enterprises, including two of these traditional forms—sole proprietorships and partnerships—as well as variations on partnerships, limited liability companies, and franchises. In Chapter 15, we will discuss the third major traditional form of business—the corporation.

Sole Proprietorships

Sole Proprietorship The simplest form of business, in which the owner is the business. The owner reports business income on his or her personal income tax return and is legally responsible for all debts and obligations incurred by the business.

The simplest form of business organization is a **sole proprietorship.** In this form, the owner is the business. Thus, anyone who does business without creating a separate business organization has a sole proprietorship. More than two-thirds of all U.S. businesses are sole proprietorships. They are usually small enterprises—about 99 percent of the sole proprietorships in the United States have revenues of less than $1 million per year. (For a discussion of how small business owners can protect themselves from cyber thieves, see the *Managerial Strategy* feature that follows.) Sole proprietors can own and manage any type of business, ranging from an informal, home-office or Web-based undertaking to a large restaurant or construction firm.

Learning Objective 1
What advantages and disadvantages are associated with the sole proprietorship?

Advantages of the Sole Proprietorship

A major advantage of the sole proprietorship is that the proprietor owns the entire business and has a right to receive all of the profits (because he or she assumes all of the risk). In addition, it is often easier and less costly to start a sole proprietorship than to start any other kind of business, as few legal formalities are involved.[1] One does not need to file any documents with the government to start a sole proprietorship (though a state business license may be required to operate certain businesses).

This sole proprietor enjoys full flexibility about how she runs her business. What are the downsides of this form of business organization?

This form of business organization also allows more flexibility than does a partnership or a corporation. The sole proprietor is free to make any decision she or he wishes concerning the business—including whom to hire, when to take a vacation, and what kind of business to pursue. In addition, the proprietor can sell or transfer all or part of the business to another party at any time and does not need approval from anyone else (as would be required from partners in a partnership or, normally, from shareholders in a corporation).

A sole proprietor pays only personal income taxes (including self-employment tax, which consists of Social Security and Medicare taxes) on the business's profits, which are reported as personal income on the proprietor's personal income tax return. Sole proprietors are also allowed to establish certain retirement accounts that are tax-exempt until the funds are withdrawn.

(YinYang/iStockphoto)

Disadvantages of the Sole Proprietorship

The major disadvantage of the sole proprietorship is that the proprietor alone bears the burden of any losses or liabilities incurred by the business enterprise. In other words, the sole proprietor has unlimited liability, or legal responsibility, for all obligations incurred in doing business. Any lawsuit against the business or its employees can lead to unlimited personal liability for the owner of a sole proprietorship. Creditors can go after the owner's personal assets to satisfy any business debts.

"Always tell yourself: The difference between running a business and ruining a business is I."

Anonymous

---

1. Although starting a sole proprietorship involves fewer legal formalities than other business organizational forms, even small sole proprietorships may need to comply with certain zoning requirements, obtain appropriate licenses, and the like.

MANAGERIAL STRATEGY

Small-Business Owners Now Have Recourse When Cyber Thieves Empty Their Bank Accounts

Between 150 and 200 cyber attacks on business organizations occur every day. Most of these attacks are initiated by cyber thieves in other countries, especially China and Russia. Thirty percent of the attacks are aimed at small businesses (those with fewer than 250 employees).

Who Is Responsible for the Loss due to a Fraudulent Fund Transfer? If cyber thieves cause you, an individual, to lose the funds in your bank account, usually your bank is responsible for the loss. The laws that protect individuals' bank accounts do not extend to small businesses, however. Nevertheless, some recent court decisions have allowed businesses to recover from their banks when their funds were fraudulently transferred.

In 2009, an employee at Experi-Metal, Inc., received an e-mail containing a link to a Web page with a Comerica Bank business connect form. Knowing that Comerica was the company's bank, the employee followed a further link and filled in the requested information. Experi-Metal had just been the victim of a phishing attack—the most common method used by cyber thieves to obtain the information needed for fraudulent fund transfers. Within minutes, cyber thieves transferred almost $2 million from Experi-Metal's account to bank accounts in China, Estonia, and Russia.

Experi-Metal sued Comerica, arguing, among other things, that the bank had not observed good faith when it accepted the online command for the wire transfers. Ultimately, the court found that the bank's employees had failed to meet reasonable commercial standards of fair dealing in not questioning the unusual size of the transfers and their destinations.[a]

A Small Business Wins an Appeal Pacto Construction Company did its banking with Ocean Bank (later acquired by People's United Bank). In 2009, cyber thieves installed malware in Pacto's computers. The malware recorded the keystrokes of Pacto's employees, thereby enabling the thieves to obtain the answers to the security questions posed by Ocean Bank for wire transfers. Over a five-day period, Ocean Bank approved wire transfers from Pacto's account for hundreds of thousands of dollars. The funds were sent to numerous individuals, none of whom had ever done business with Pacto. Although the bank's high-risk alert system indicated that the transfers might be fraudulent, the bank continued to allow them. Pacto sued the bank to recover its lost funds, but a U.S. district court ruled against Pacto.

On appeal, however, the reviewing court agreed with Pacto that Ocean Bank had not monitored the transactions effectively and should have notified Pacto before allowing them to be completed. These failures and others "rendered Ocean Bank's security procedures commercially unreasonable."[b]

MANAGERIAL IMPLICATIONS

Small-business owners now have some recourse if cyber thieves steal funds from their bank accounts. Nonetheless, small-business owners are well advised to be aware of potential cyber threats when they use banks' security procedures. Even though precedent makes recovery of funds stolen by cyber thieves now possible, few small companies have the resources to pursue a lawsuit against their banks.

BUSINESS QUESTIONS

1. Might there be any repercussions against small businesses because of recent decisions in their favor in cases involving cyber theft?
2. Why is it so difficult for banks to recover funds stolen online from their small-business customers?

---

a. *Experi-Metal, Inc. v. Comerica Bank*, 2011 WL 2433383 (E.D.Mich. 2011).

b. *Pacto Construction Co. v. People's United Bank, d/b/a Ocean Bank*, 684 F.3d 197 (1st Cir. 2012).

The sole proprietorship also has the disadvantage of lacking continuity on the death of the proprietor. When the owner dies, so does the business—it is automatically dissolved. Another disadvantage is that the proprietor's opportunity to raise capital is limited to personal funds and the funds of those who are willing to make loans.

The personal liability of the owner of a sole proprietorship was at issue in the following case.

Case 14.1

Quality Car & Truck Leasing, Inc. v. Sark

Court of Appeals of Ohio, Fourth District, 2013 -Ohio- 44, 2013 WL 139359 (2013).

(Shutterstock.com)

BACKGROUND AND FACTS   Michael Sark operated a logging business as a sole proprietorship. To acquire equipment for the business, Sark and his wife, Paula, borrowed funds from Quality Car & Truck Leasing, Inc. When his business encountered financial difficulties, Sark became unable to pay his creditors, including Quality. The Sarks sold their house (valued at $203,500) to their son, Michael, Jr., for one dollar but continued to live in it. Three months later, Quality obtained a judgment in an Ohio state court against the Sarks for $150,481.85 and then filed a claim to set aside the transfer of the house to Michael, Jr., as a fraudulent conveyance. From a decision in Quality's favor, the Sarks appealed, arguing that they did not intend to defraud Quality and that they were not actually Quality's debtors.

IN THE WORDS OF THE COURT . . .

KLINE, J. [Judge]

* * * *

The trial court found that summary judgment was proper under [Ohio Revised Code (R.C.) Section] 1336.04(A)(2)(a). That statute provides as follows:

> A transfer made or an obligation incurred by a debtor is fraudulent as to a creditor, whether the claim of the creditor arose before or after the transfer was made or the obligation was incurred, if the debtor made the transfer or incurred the obligation * * * without receiving a reasonably equivalent value in exchange for the transfer or obligation, and * * * the debtor was engaged or was about to engage in a business or a transaction for which the remaining assets of the debtor were unreasonably small in relation to the business or transaction.

The trial court found "that Michael Senior and Paula made a transfer without the exchange of reasonably equivalent value and that the debtor was engaged or was about to engage in a business * * * transaction for which the remaining assets of the debtor were unreasonably small in relation to the business or transaction."

* * * The Sarks argue that summary judgment was not proper because there is a genuine issue of material fact regarding whether they intended to defraud Quality Leasing. The Sarks'

argument fails because intent is not relevant to an analysis under R.C. Section 1336.04(A)(2)(a). *A creditor does not need to show that a transfer was made with intent to defraud in order to prevail under R.C. Section 1336.04(A)(2)(a). Thus, the Sarks cannot defeat summary judgment by showing that they did not act with fraudulent intent when Michael Senior and Paula transferred the Property to Michael Junior.* [Emphasis added.]

The Sarks also claim that summary judgment was improper because there is an issue of fact regarding whether Michael Senior and Paula are actually Quality Leasing's debtors. Michael Senior apparently returned the equipment that secured the debts owed to Quality Leasing. According to the Sarks, Quality Leasing's appraisals of the equipment showed that the value of the equipment would be enough to satisfy the debts.

The Sarks' argument, however, does not address the fact that they are clearly judgment debtors to Quality Leasing and that the judgment has not been satisfied. * * * The Sarks have not challenged the validity of the judgment against them nor have they shown that the judgment has been satisfied. Thus, there is no genuine issue of material fact regarding whether Paula and Michael Senior are debtors to Quality Leasing.

In conclusion, there is no genuine issue as to any material fact. Quality Leasing is entitled to judgment as a matter of law.

DECISION AND REMEDY   A state intermediate appellate court affirmed the lower court's judgment in Quality's favor. "Reasonable minds can come to only one conclusion, and that conclusion is adverse to the Sarks," said the court. The Sarks "are clearly judgment debtors to Quality Leasing and . . . the judgment has not been satisfied."

THE ECONOMIC DIMENSION   *What might the Sarks have done to avoid this dispute, as well as the loss of their home and their apparently declining business?*

THE ETHICAL DIMENSION   *Why did the Sarks take the unethical step of fraudulently conveying their home to their son? What should they have done instead?*

Partnerships

A *partnership* arises from an agreement, express or implied, between two or more persons to carry on a business for profit. Partners are co-owners of a business and have joint control over its operation and the right to share in its profits.

Partnerships are governed both by common law concepts—in particular, those relating to agency (discussed in Chapter 16)—and by statutory law. The National Conference of Commissioners on Uniform State Laws has drafted the Uniform Partnership Act (UPA), which governs the operation of partnerships *in the absence of express agreement* and has done much to reduce controversies in the law relating to partnerships. In other words, the partners are free to establish rules for their partnership that differ from those stated in the UPA.

The UPA has undergone several major revisions since it was first issued in 1914. Except for Louisiana, every state has adopted the UPA. The majority of states have adopted the most recent version of the UPA (as amended in 1997) to provide limited liability for partners in a limited liability partnership. We therefore base our discussion of the UPA in this chapter on the 1997 version of the act.

(Kzenon/iStockphoto)

What determines if a partnership exists between two individuals working together in the same business?

Agency Concepts and Partnership Law

When two or more persons agree to do business as partners, they enter into a special relationship with one another. To an extent, their relationship is similar to an agency relationship because each partner is deemed to be the agent of the other partners and of the partnership. The common law agency concepts you will read about in Chapter 16 thus apply—specifically, the imputation of knowledge of, and responsibility for, acts done within the scope of the partnership relationship. In their relations with one another, partners, like agents, are bound by fiduciary ties.

In one important way, however, partnership law is distinct from agency law. A partnership is based on a voluntary contract between two or more competent persons who agree to contribute financial capital, labor, and skill to a business with the understanding that profits and losses will be shared. In a nonpartnership agency relationship, the agent usually does not have an ownership interest in the business, nor is he or she obliged to bear a portion of the ordinary business losses.

When Does a Partnership Exist?

Conflicts sometimes arise over whether a business enterprise is legally a partnership, especially in the absence of a formal, written partnership agreement. The UPA defines a **partnership** as "an association of two or more persons to carry on as co-owners a business for profit" [UPA 101(6)]. Note that under the UPA a corporation is a "person" [UPA 101(10)]. The *intent* to associate is a key element of a partnership, and a person cannot join a partnership unless all of the other partners consent [UPA 401(i)].

Partnership An agreement by two or more persons to carry on, as co-owners, a business for profit.

In resolving disputes over whether partnership status exists, courts usually look for the following three essential elements, which are implicit in the UPA's definition of a partnership:

1. A sharing of profits and losses.
2. A joint ownership of the business.
3. An equal right to be involved in the management of the business.

Joint ownership of property, obviously, does not in and of itself create a partnership. In fact, the sharing of gross revenues and even profits from such ownership is usually not enough to create a partnership [UPA 202(c)(1), (2)]. **EXAMPLE 14.1** Chiang and Burke jointly own a piece of rural property. They lease the land to a farmer, with the understanding that—in lieu of set rental payments—they will receive a share of the profits from the farming operation conducted by the farmer. This arrangement normally would not make Chiang, Burke, and the farmer partners. •

Note, though, that although the sharing of profits from ownership of property does not prove the existence of a partnership, sharing *both profits and losses* usually does. **EXAMPLE 14.2** Syd and Drake start a business that sells fruit smoothies near a college campus. They open a joint bank account from which they pay for supplies and expenses, and they share the proceeds (and losses) that the smoothie stand generates. If a conflict arises as to their business relationship, a court will assume that a partnership exists unless the parties prove otherwise. ●

Entity versus Aggregate Theory of Partnerships

At common law, a partnership was treated only as an aggregate of individuals and never as a separate legal entity. Thus, at common law a suit could never be brought by or against the firm in its own name. Instead, each individual partner had to sue or be sued.

Today, in contrast, a majority of the states follow the UPA and treat a partnership as an entity for most purposes. For instance, a partnership usually can sue or be sued, collect judgments, and have all accounting procedures in the name of the partnership entity [UPA 201, 307(a)]. As an entity, a partnership may hold the title to real or personal property in its name rather than in the names of the individual partners. Additionally, federal procedural laws permit the partnership to be treated as an entity in suits in federal courts and bankruptcy proceedings.

For federal income tax purposes, however, the partnership is treated as an aggregate of the individual partners rather than a separate legal entity. The partnership is a pass-through entity and not a taxpaying entity. A **pass-through entity** is a business entity that has no tax liability because the entity's income is passed through to the owners, who pay taxes on it.

Thus, the income or losses the partnership incurs are "passed through" the entity framework and attributed to the partners on their individual tax returns. The partnership itself has no tax liability and is responsible only for filing an **information return** with the Internal Revenue Service. In other words, the firm itself pays no taxes. A partner's profit from the partnership (whether distributed or not) is taxed as individual income to the individual partner.

Partnership Formation

As a general rule, an agreement to form a partnership can be *oral, written,* or *implied by conduct.* Some partnership agreements, however, must be in writing to be legally enforceable under the Statute of Frauds (discussed in Chapter 10). A written partnership agreement, called **articles of partnership**, can include almost any terms that the parties wish, unless they are illegal or contrary to public policy or statute [UPA 103]. The agreement usually specifies the name and location of the business, the duration of the partnership, the purpose of the business, each partner's share of the profits, how the partnership will be managed, and how assets will be distributed on dissolution, among other things.

Duration of the Partnership
The partnership agreement can specify the duration of the partnership by stating that it will continue until a certain date or the completion of a particular project. A partnership that is specifically limited in duration is called a *partnership for a term.* Generally, withdrawing from a partnership for a term prematurely (prior to the expiration date) constitutes a breach of the agreement, and the responsible partner can be held liable for any resulting losses [UPA 602(b)(2)]. If no fixed duration is specified, the partnership is a *partnership at will.*

Partnership by Estoppel
Occasionally, persons who are not partners may nevertheless hold themselves out as partners and make representations that third parties rely on in dealing with them. In such a situation, a court may conclude that a *partnership by estoppel* exists. The law does not confer any partnership rights on these persons, but it may impose liability on them. This is also true when a partner represents, expressly or impliedly, that a nonpartner is a member of the firm [UPA 308].

Pass-Through Entity A business entity that has no tax liability. The entity's income is passed through to the owners, and the owners pay taxes on the income.

Information Return A tax return submitted by a partnership that only reports the income and losses earned by the business. The partnership as an entity does not pay taxes on the income received by the partnership.

Articles of Partnership A written agreement that sets forth each partner's rights and obligations with respect to the partnership.

When a partnership by estoppel is deemed to exist, the nonpartner is regarded as an agent whose acts are binding on the partnership [UPA 308]. **CASE EXAMPLE 14.3** Jackson Paper Manufacturing Company makes paper that is used by Stonewall Packaging, LLC. Jackson and Stonewall have officers and directors in common, and they share employees, property, and equipment. In reliance on Jackson's business reputation, Best Cartage, Inc., agreed to provide transportation services for Stonewall and bought thirty-seven tractor-trailers to use in fulfilling the contract. Best provided the services until Stonewall terminated the agreement.

Best filed a suit for breach of contract against Stonewall and Jackson, seeking $500,678 in unpaid invoices and consequential damages of $1,315,336 for the tractor-trailers it had purchased. Best argued that Stonewall and Jackson had a partnership by estoppel. The court agreed, finding that "defendants combined labor, skills, and property to advance their alleged business partnership." Jackson had negotiated the agreement on Stonewall's behalf, and a news release stated that Jackson had sought tax incentives for Stonewall. Jackson also had bought real estate, equipment, and general supplies for Stonewall with no expectation of payment from Stonewall to Jackson. This was sufficient to prove a partnership by estoppel.[2] ●

Rights of Partners

The rights of partners in a partnership relate to the following areas: management, interest in the partnership, compensation, inspection of books, accounting, and property. In the absence of provisions to the contrary in the partnership agreement, the law imposes the rights discussed here.

Management Rights
In a general partnership, all partners have equal rights in managing the partnership [UPA 401(f)]. Unless the partners agree otherwise, each partner has one vote in management matters *regardless of the proportional size of his or her interest in the firm.* Often, in a large partnership, partners agree to delegate daily management responsibilities to a management committee made up of one or more of the partners.

Decisions on ordinary matters connected with partnership business are made by majority rule, unless the agreement specifies otherwise. Decisions that significantly affect the nature of the partnership or that are outside the ordinary course of the partnership business, however, require the *unanimous* consent of the partners [UPA 301(2), 401(i), (j)]. Unanimous consent is typically required for such decisions as whether to admit new partners, amend the articles of partnership, engage in a new business, or undertake any act that would make further conduct of the partnership impossible.

Interest in the Partnership
Each partner is entitled to the proportion of business profits and losses that is designated in the partnership agreement. If the agreement does not apportion profits (indicate how the profits will be shared), the UPA provides that profits will be shared equally. If the agreement does not apportion losses, losses will be shared in the same ratio as profits [UPA 401(b)].

EXAMPLE 14.4 The partnership agreement for Rico and Brent provides for capital contributions of $60,000 from Rico and $40,000 from Brent, but it is silent as to how Rico and Brent will share profits or losses. In this situation, Rico and Brent will share both profits and losses equally. If their partnership agreement provided for profits to be shared in the same ratio as capital contributions, however, 60 percent of the profits would go to Rico, and 40 percent of the profits would go to Brent. If their partnership agreement was silent as to losses, losses would be shared in the same ratio as profits (60 percent and 40 percent, respectively). ●

"Forty for you, sixty for me—and equal partners we will be."

Anonymous

---

2. *Best Cartage, Inc. v. Stonewall Packaging, LLC,* 727 S.E.2d 291 (N.C.App. 2012).

Compensation   Devoting time, skill, and energy to partnership business is a partner's duty and generally is not a compensable service. Rather, as mentioned, a partner's income from the partnership takes the form of a distribution of profits according to the partner's share in the business. Partners can, of course, agree otherwise. For instance, the managing partner of a law firm often receives a salary—in addition to her or his share of profits—for performing special administrative duties, such as managing the office or personnel.

Who has the right to inspect a partnership's books and records?

Inspection of Books   Partnership books and records must be kept at the firm's principal business office and be accessible to all partners. Each partner has the right to receive (and the corresponding duty to produce) full and complete information concerning the conduct of all aspects of partnership business [UPA 403]. Every partner is entitled to inspect all books and records on demand and to make copies of the materials.

Accounting of Partnership Assets or Profits.   An accounting of partnership assets or profits is required to determine the value of each partner's share in the partnership. An accounting can be performed voluntarily, or it can be compelled by court order. Under UPA 405(b), a partner has the right to bring an action for an accounting during the term of the partnership, as well as on the partnership's dissolution and winding up.

Property Rights   Property acquired *by* a partnership is the property of the partnership and not of the partners individually [UPA 203]. Partnership property includes all property that was originally contributed to the partnership and anything later purchased by the partnership or in the partnership's name (except in rare circumstances) [UPA 204].

A partner may use or possess partnership property only on behalf of the partnership [UPA 401(g)]. A partner is *not* a co-owner of partnership property and has no right to sell, mortgage, or transfer partnership property to another. (A partner can assign her or his right to a share of the partnership profits to another to satisfy a debt, however.)

Duties and Liabilities of Partners

The duties and liabilities of partners are basically derived from agency law. Each partner is an agent of every other partner and acts as both a principal and an agent in any business transaction within the scope of the partnership agreement.

Each partner is also a general agent of the partnership in carrying out the usual business of the firm "or business of the kind carried on by the partnership" [UPA 301(1)]. Thus, every act of a partner concerning partnership business and "business of the kind," and every contract signed by that partner in the partnership's name, bind the firm.

One significant disadvantage associated with a traditional partnership is that partners are *personally* liable for the debts of the partnership. Moreover, the liability is essentially unlimited because the acts of one partner in the ordinary course of business subject the other partners to personal liability [UPA 305]. We examine here the fiduciary duties of partners, the authority of partners, and the liability of partners.

Fiduciary Duties   The fiduciary duties a partner owes to the partnership and to the other partners are the duty of loyalty and the duty of care [UPA 404(a)]. The duty of loyalty requires a partner to account to the partnership for "any property, profit, or benefit" derived by the partner from the partnership's business or the use of its property [UPA 404(b)]. A partner must also refrain from competing with the partnership in business or dealing with the firm as an adverse party. A partner's duty of care involves refraining from "grossly negligent or reckless conduct, intentional misconduct, or a knowing violation of law" [UPA 404(c)].

These duties may not be waived or eliminated in the partnership agreement, and in fulfilling them, each partner must act consistently with the obligation of good faith and fair dealing, which applies to all contracts, including partnership agreements [UPA 103(b), 404(d)]. The agreement can specify acts that the partners agree will violate a fiduciary duty.

Note that a partner may pursue his or her own interests without automatically violating these duties [UPA 404(e)]. The key is whether the partner has disclosed the interest to the other partners. **EXAMPLE 14.5** Jayne Trell, a partner at Jacoby & Meyers, owns a shopping mall. Trell may vote against a partnership proposal to open a competing mall, provided that she has fully disclosed her interest in the existing shopping mall to the other partners at the firm. ●

A partner can breach his or her duty of loyalty by self-dealing, misusing partnership property, disclosing trade secrets, or usurping a partnership business opportunity. The following case is a classic example.

> "Surround yourself with partners who are better than you are."
>
> David Ogilvy, 1911–1999,
> (Scottish advertising executive)

✳ Classic Case 14.2

Meinhard v. Salmon
Court of Appeals of New York, 249 N.Y. 458, 164 N.E. 545 (1928).

(Ugurhan Betin/iStockphoto.com)

What fiduciary duties does a partner have with respect to renewing a hotel lease?

BACKGROUND AND FACTS Walter Salmon negotiated a twenty-year lease for the Hotel Bristol in New York City. To pay for the conversion of the building into shops and offices, Salmon entered into an agreement with Morton Meinhard to assume half of the cost. They agreed to share the profits and losses from the joint venture (a *joint venture* is similar to a partnership but typically is created for a single project, whereas a partnership usually involves an ongoing business), but Salmon was to have the sole power to manage the building. Less than four months before the end of the lease term, the building's owner Elbridge Gerry approached Salmon about a project to raze the converted structure, clear five adjacent lots, and construct a single building across the whole property. Salmon agreed and signed a new lease in the name of his own business, Midpoint Realty Company, without telling Meinhard. When Meinhard learned of the deal, he filed a suit in a New York state court against Salmon. From a judgment in Meinhard's favor, Salmon appealed.

IN THE WORDS OF THE COURT . . .
CARDOZO, C.J. [Chief Justice]
 * * * *

Joint adventurers, like copartners, owe to one another, while the enterprise continues, the duty of the finest loyalty. Many forms of conduct permissible in a work-a-day world for those acting at arm's length are forbidden to those bound by fiduciary ties. * * * Not honesty alone, but the punctilio [strict observance of details] of an honor the most sensitive, is then the standard of behavior. As to this there has developed a tradition that is unbending and inveterate [entrenched]. Uncompromising rigidity has been the attitude of courts * * * when petitioned to undermine the rule of undivided loyalty.

 * * * The trouble about [Salmon's] conduct is that he excluded his coadventurer from any chance to compete, from any chance to enjoy the opportunity for benefit.

 * * * The very fact that Salmon was in control with exclusive powers of direction charged him the more obviously with the duty of disclosure, [because] only through disclosure could opportunity be equalized.

 * * * Authority is, of course, abundant that one partner may not appropriate to his own use a renewal of a lease, though its term is to begin at the expiration of the partnership. The lease at hand with its many changes is not strictly a renewal. Even so, the standard of loyalty for those in trust relations is without the fixed divisions of a graduated scale. * * * *A man obtaining [an] * * * opportunity * * * by the position he occupies as a partner is bound by his obligation to his copartners in such dealings not to separate his interest from theirs, but, if he acquires any benefit, to communicate it to them. Certain it is also that*

Case 14.2—Continues ➡

Case 14.2—Continued

there may be no abuse of special opportunities growing out of a special trust as manager or agent. [Emphasis added.]

* * * Very likely [Salmon] assumed in all good faith that with the approaching end of the venture he might ignore his coadventurer and take the extension for himself. He had given to the enterprise time and labor as well as money. He had made it a success. Meinhard, who had given money, but neither time nor labor, had already been richly paid. * * * [But] Salmon had put himself in a position in which thought of self was to be renounced, however hard the abnegation [self-denial]. He was much more than a coadventurer. He was a managing coadventurer. For him and for those like him the rule of undivided loyalty is relentless and supreme.

DECISION AND REMEDY   The Court of Appeals of New York held that Salmon breached his fiduciary duty by failing to inform Meinhard of the business opportunity and secretly taking advantage of it himself. The court granted Meinhard an interest "measured by the value of half of the entire lease."

WHAT IF THE FACTS WERE DIFFERENT?   *Suppose that Salmon had disclosed Gerry's proposal to Meinhard, who had said that he was not interested. Would the result in this case have been different? Explain.*

IMPACT OF THIS CASE ON TODAY'S LEGAL ENVIRONMENT   *This landmark case involved a joint venture, not a partnership. At the time, a member of a joint venture had only the duty to refrain from actively subverting the rights of the other members. The decision in this case imposed the highest standard of loyalty on joint-venture members. The duty is now the same in both joint ventures and partnerships. The eloquent language in this case that describes the standard of loyalty is frequently quoted approvingly by courts in cases involving partnerships.*

Authority of Partners

Under the UPA and agency law, a partner has the authority to bind a partnership in contract. A partner may also subject the partnership to tort liability under agency principles. When a partner is carrying on partnership business or business of the kind with third parties in the usual way, both the partner and the firm share liability.

If a partner acts within the scope of her or his authority, the partnership is legally bound to honor the partner's commitments to third parties. The partnership will not be liable, however, if the third parties know that the partner had no authority to commit the partnership. Agency concepts that we explore in Chapter 16 relating to actual (express and implied) authority, apparent authority, and ratification also apply to partnerships. The extent of implied authority is generally broader for partners than for ordinary agents, though.

Joint Liability of Partners

Joint Liability   In partnership law, partners share liability for partnership obligations and debts. Thus, if a third party sues a partner on a partnership debt, the partner has the right to insist that the other partners be sued with him or her.

At one time, each partner in a partnership generally was jointly liable for the partnership's obligations. **Joint liability** means that a third party must sue all of the partners as a group, but each partner can be held liable for the full amount.[3] If, for instance, a third party sues a partner on a partnership contract, the partner has the right to demand that the other partners be sued with her or him. In fact, if the third party does not sue all of the partners, the assets of the partnership cannot be used to satisfy the judgment. With joint liability, the partnership's assets must be exhausted before creditors can reach the partners' individual assets.[4]

Joint and Several Liability of Partners

In the majority of states, under UPA 306(a), partners are jointly and severally (separately or individually) liable for all

---

3. Under the prior version of the UPA, which is still in effect in a few states, partners were subject to joint liability on partnership debts and contracts, but not on partnership debts arising from torts.
4. For a case applying joint liability to partnerships, see *Shar's Cars, LLC v. Elder*, 97 P.3d 724 (Utah App. 2004).

partnership obligations, including contracts, torts, and breaches of trust. **Joint and several liability** means that a third party has the option of suing all of the partners together (jointly) or one or more of the partners separately (severally). All partners in a partnership can be held liable regardless of whether the partner participated in, knew about, or ratified the conduct that gave rise to the lawsuit. Normally, though, the partnership's assets must be exhausted before a creditor can enforce a judgment against a partner's separate assets [UPA 307(d)].

A judgment against one partner severally (separately) does not extinguish the others' liability. Those not sued in the first action normally may be sued subsequently, unless the court in the first action held that the partnership was in no way liable. If a plaintiff is successful in a suit against a partner or partners, he or she may collect on the judgment only against the assets of those partners named as defendants. A partner who commits a tort may be required to indemnify (reimburse) the partnership for any damages it pays—unless the tort was committed in the ordinary course of the partnership's business.

CASE EXAMPLE 14.6   Nicole Moren was a partner in Jax Restaurant. After work one day, Moren was called back to the restaurant to help in the kitchen. She brought her two-year-old-son, Remington, and placed him on the kitchen counter. While she was making pizzas, Remington reached into the dough press. His hand was crushed, causing permanent injuries. Through his father, Remington filed a suit against the partnership for negligence.

The partnership filed a complaint against Moren, arguing that it was entitled to indemnity (compensation or reimbursement) from Moren for her negligence. The court held in favor of Moren and ordered the partnership to pay damages to Remington. Moren was not required to indemnify the partnership because her negligence occurred in the ordinary course of the partnership's business.[5] ●

Partner's Dissociation

Dissociation occurs when a partner ceases to be associated with the carrying on of the partnership business. Although a partner always has the *power* to dissociate from the firm, he or she may not have the *right* to dissociate. Dissociation normally entitles the partner to have his or her interest purchased by the partnership and terminates his or her actual authority to act for the partnership and to participate with the partners in running the business. Otherwise, the partnership continues to do business without the dissociating partner.[6]

Events Causing Dissociation   Under UPA 601, a partner can be dissociated from a partnership in any of the following ways:

1. By the partner's voluntarily giving notice of an "express will to withdraw."
2. By the occurrence of an event agreed to in the partnership agreement.
3. By a unanimous vote of the other partners under certain circumstances, such as when a partner transfers substantially all of her or his interest in the partnership, or when it becomes unlawful to carry on partnership business with that partner.
4. By order of a court or arbitrator if the partner has engaged in wrongful conduct that affects the partnership business, breached the partnership agreement or violated a duty owed to the partnership or to the other partners, or engaged in conduct that makes it "not reasonably practicable to carry on the business in partnership with the partner" [UPA 601(5)].

---

5. *Moren v. Jax Restaurant,* 679 N.W.2d 165 (Minn.App. 2004).
6. Under the previous version of the UPA, when a partner dissociated from a partnership, the partnership was considered dissolved, its business had to be wound up, and the proceeds had to be distributed to creditors and among partners. The amendments to the UPA recognize that a partnership may not want to break up just because one partner has left the firm.

Joint and Several Liability In partnership law, a doctrine under which a plaintiff can file a lawsuit against all of the partners together (jointly) or one or more of the partners separately (severally, or individually). All partners in a partnership can be held liable regardless of whether the partner participated in, knew about, or ratified the conduct that gave rise to the lawsuit.

Learning Objective 2
What is meant by joint and several liability? Why is this often considered to be a disadvantage of doing business as a general partnership?

Dissociation The severance of the relationship between a partner and a partnership when the partner ceases to be associated with the carrying on of the partnership business.

Under what circumstances can partners be held personally liable for someone injured on partnership property?

(Sturti/iStockphoto.com)

5. By the partner's declaring bankruptcy, assigning his or her interest in the partnership for the benefit of creditors, or becoming physically or mentally incapacitated, or by the partner's death. Note that although the bankruptcy or death of a partner represents that partner's "dissociation" from the partnership, it is not an *automatic* ground for the partnership's dissolution (*dissolution* will be discussed shortly).

Wrongful Dissociation

As mentioned, a partner has the power to dissociate from a partnership at any time, but if she or he lacks the right to dissociate, then the dissociation is considered wrongful under the law [UPA 602]. When a partner's dissociation is in breach of the partnership agreement, for instance, it is wrongful.

EXAMPLE 14.7   Jenson & Burke's partnership agreement states that it is a breach of the agreement for any partner to assign partnership property to a creditor without the consent of the others. If a partner, Janis, makes such an assignment, she has not only breached the agreement but has also wrongfully dissociated from the partnership. •

Similarly, if a partner refuses to perform duties required by the partnership agreement—such as accounting for profits earned from the use of partnership property—this breach can be treated as wrongful dissociation. A partner who wrongfully dissociates is liable to the partnership and to the other partners for damages caused by the dissociation.

Effects of Dissociation

Dissociation (rightful or wrongful) terminates some of the rights of the dissociated partner, requires that the partnership purchase his or her interest, and alters the liability of both parties to third parties. On a partner's dissociation, his or her right to participate in the management and conduct of the partnership business terminates [UPA 603]. The partner's duty of loyalty also ends. A partner's duty of care continues only with respect to events that occurred before dissociation, unless the partner participates in winding up the partnership's business (to be discussed shortly).

EXAMPLE 14.8   Amy Pearson, a partner who leaves an accounting firm, Bubb & Pearson, can immediately compete with the firm for new clients. She must exercise care in completing ongoing client transactions, however, and must account to the firm for any fees received from the old clients based on those transactions. •

After a partner's dissociation, his or her interest in the partnership must be purchased according to the rules in UPA 701. The **buyout price** is based on the amount that would have been distributed to the partner if the partnership were wound up on the date of dissociation. Offset against the price are amounts owed by the partner to the partnership, including any damages for the partner's wrongful dissociation.

For two years after a partner dissociates from a continuing partnership, the partnership may be bound by the acts of the dissociated partner based on apparent authority [UPA 702]. In other words, the partnership may be liable to a third party with whom a dissociated partner enters into a transaction if the third party reasonably believed that the dissociated partner was still a partner. Similarly, a dissociated partner may be liable for partnership obligations entered into during a two-year period following dissociation [UPA 703].

Partnership Termination

The same events that cause dissociation can result in the end of the partnership if the remaining partners no longer wish to (or are unable to) continue the partnership business. The termination of a partnership is referred to as **dissolution**, which essentially means the commencement of the winding up process. **Winding up** is the process of collecting, liquidating, and distributing the partnership assets.

Buyout Price The amount payable to a partner on his or her dissociation from a partnership, based on the amount distributable to that partner if the firm were wound up on that date, and offset by any damages for wrongful dissociation.

Dissolution The formal disbanding of a partnership or a corporation.

Winding Up The second of two stages in the termination of a partnership or corporation, in which the firm's assets are collected, liquidated, and distributed, and liabilities are discharged.

Dissolution

Dissolution of a partnership generally can be brought about by the following:

1. Acts of the partners or, in a corporation, acts of the shareholders and board of directors.
2. The subsequent illegality of the firm's business.
3. The expiration of a time period stated in a partnership agreement or a certificate of incorporation.
4. Judicial decree.

Additionally, if the partnership agreement states that it will dissolve on a certain event, such as a partner's death or bankruptcy, then the occurrence of that event will dissolve the partnership. A partnership for a fixed term or a particular undertaking is dissolved by operation of law at the expiration of the term or on the completion of the undertaking.

Good Faith Each partner must exercise good faith when dissolving a partnership. Some state statutes allow partners injured by another partner's bad faith to file a tort claim for wrongful dissolution of a partnership.

CASE EXAMPLE 14.9 Attorneys Randall Jordan and Mary Helen Moses formed a two-member partnership in 2003. Although the partnership was for an indefinite term, Jordan ended the partnership in 2006 and asked the court for declarations concerning the partners' financial obligations. Moses, who had objected to ending the partnership, filed a claim against Jordan for wrongful dissolution and for appropriating $180,000 in fees that should have gone to the partnership. Ultimately, the court held in favor of Moses. A claim for wrongful dissolution of a partnership may be based on damages arising from the excluded partner's loss of "an existing, or continuing, business opportunity" or of income and material assets. Because Jordan had attempted to appropriate partnership assets through dissolution, Moses could sue for wrongful dissolution.[7] ●

Illegality or Impracticality Under the UPA, a court may order dissolution when it becomes obviously impractical for the firm to continue—for instance, if the business can only be operated at a loss [UPA 801(5)]. Even when one partner has brought a court action seeking to dissolve a partnership, the partnership continues to exist until it is legally dissolved by the court or by the parties' agreement.

CASE EXAMPLE 14.10 Clyde Webster, James Theis, and Larry Thomas formed T&T Agri-Partners Company to own and farm 180 acres in Illinois. Under the partnership agreement, the firm was to continue until January 31, 2010, unless it was dissolved. The death of any partner would dissolve the partnership. Webster died in 2002, but Theis and Thomas did not liquidate T&T and distribute its assets. Webster's estate filed a lawsuit against Theis, Thomas, and the partnership in state court, seeking to dissolve the partnership. The court ordered the defendants to dissolve the partnership and liquidate its assets. Because Theis and Thomas violated the clear provisions of the partnership agreement, it was unlawful for the partnership to continue after Webster's death.[8] ●

Does the death of any partner automatically dissolve the partnership?

(John Kwan/Shutterstock.com)

Winding Up

After dissolution, the partnership continues for the limited purpose of the winding up process. The partners cannot create new obligations on behalf of the partnership. They have authority only to complete transactions begun but not finished at the time of dissolution and to wind up the business of the partnership [UPA 803, 804(1)]. *Winding up* includes collecting and preserving partnership assets, discharging liabilities (paying debts), and accounting to each partner for the value of her or his interest in the

---

7. *Jordan v. Moses*, 291 Ga. 39, 727 S.E.2d 460 (2012).
8. *Estate of Webster v. Thomas*, 2013 WL 164041 (Ill.App. 2013).

partnership. Partners continue to have fiduciary duties to one another and to the firm during this process.

Both creditors of the partnership and creditors of the individual partners can make claims on the partnership's assets. In general, partnership creditors share proportionately with the partners' individual creditors in the assets of the partners' estates, which include their interests in the partnership. A partnership's assets are distributed according to the following priorities [UPA 807]:

1. Payment of debts, including those owed to partner and nonpartner creditors.
2. Return of capital contributions and distribution of profits to partners.

If the partnership's liabilities are greater than its assets, the partners bear the losses—in the absence of a contrary agreement—in the same proportion in which they shared the profits (rather than, for instance, in proportion to their contributions to the partnership's capital).

PREVENTING LEGAL DISPUTES

Before entering a partnership, agree on how the assets will be valued and divided in the event the partnership dissolves. Make express arrangements that will provide for a smooth dissolution. You and your partners can enter a buy-sell, or buyout, agreement, which provides that one or more partners will buy out the other or others, should the relationship deteriorate. Agreeing beforehand on who buys what, under what circumstances, and, if possible, at what price may eliminate costly negotiations or litigation later. Alternatively, your agreement can specify that one or more partners will determine the value of the interest being sold and that the other or others will decide whether to buy or sell.

Limited Liability Partnerships

Limited Liability Partnership (LLP)
A hybrid form of business organization that is used mainly by professionals who normally do business in a partnership. Like a partnership, an LLP is a pass-through entity for tax purposes, but the personal liability of the partners is limited.

The **limited liability partnership (LLP)** is a hybrid form of business designed mostly for professionals, such as attorneys and accountants, who normally do business as partners in a partnership. In fact, nearly all the big accounting firms are LLPs.

The major advantage of the LLP is that it allows a partnership to continue as a *pass-through entity* for tax purposes, but limits the personal liability of the partners. A special form of LLP is the *family limited liability partnership* (FLLP), in which the majority of the partners are persons related to each other, essentially as spouses, parents, grandparents, siblings, cousins, nephews, or nieces.

Formation

Learning Objective 3
What advantages do limited liability partnerships offer to entrepreneurs that are not offered by general partnerships?

LLPs must be formed and operated in compliance with state statutes, which often include provisions of the UPA. The appropriate form must be filed with a state agency, and the business's name must include either "Limited Liability Partnership" or "LLP" [UPA 1001, 1002]. In addition, an LLP must file an annual report with the state to remain qualified as an LLP in that state [UPA 1003].

In most states, it is relatively easy to convert a traditional partnership into an LLP because the firm's basic organizational structure remains the same. Additionally, all of the statutory and common law rules governing partnerships still apply (apart from those modified by the state's LLP statute).

Liability

The LLP allows professionals to avoid personal liability for the malpractice of other partners. A partner in an LLP is still liable for her or his own wrongful acts, such as negligence, however. Also liable is the partner who supervised the party who committed a wrongful act. This generally is true for all types of partners and partnerships, not just LLPs.

Although LLP statutes vary from state to state, generally each state statute limits the liability of partners in some way. For instance, Delaware law protects each innocent partner from the "debts and obligations of the partnership arising from negligence, wrongful acts, or misconduct." The UPA more broadly exempts partners from personal liability for any partnership obligation, "whether arising in contract, tort, or otherwise" [UPA 306(c)].

Limited Partnerships

We now look at a business organizational form that limits the liability of *some* of its owners—the **limited partnership (LP)**. LPs originated in medieval Europe and have been in existence in the United States since the early 1800s. In many ways, LPs are like the general partnerships discussed earlier in this chapter, but they differ from general partnerships in several ways. Hence, they are sometimes referred to as *special partnerships*.

An LP consists of at least one **general partner** and one or more **limited partners**. A general partner assumes responsibility for managing the partnership and so has full responsibility for the partnership and for all of its debts. A limited partner contributes funds or other property and owns an interest in the firm but is not involved in management responsibilities and is not personally liable for partnership debts beyond the amount of his or her investment. A limited partner can forfeit limited liability by taking part in the management of the business.

Most states and the District of Columbia have adopted the Revised Uniform Limited Partnership Act (RULPA), which we refer to in the following discussion.

Formation of the Limited Partnership

In contrast to the informal, private, and voluntary agreement that usually suffices for a general partnership, the formation of a limited partnership is a public and formal proceeding that must follow specific statutory requirements. Not only must a limited partnership have at least one general partner and one limited partner, but the partners must sign a **certificate of limited partnership.**

Like *articles of incorporation* (see Chapter 15), this certificate must include certain information such as the name, mailing address, and capital contribution of each general and limited partner. The certificate must be filed with the designated state official—under the RULPA, the secretary of state. The certificate is usually open to public inspection.

Liabilities of Partners in a Limited Partnership

General partners, unlike limited partners, are personally liable to the partnership's creditors. This policy can be circumvented in states that allow a corporation to be the general partner in a partnership. Because the corporation has limited liability by virtue of corporate laws, if a corporation is the general partner, no one in the limited partnership has personal liability.

In contrast to the personal liability of general partners, the liability of a limited partner is limited to the capital that she or he contributes or agrees to contribute to the partnership [RULPA 502]. Limited partners enjoy limited liability so long as they do not participate in management [RULPA 303].

A limited partner who participates in management will be just as liable as a general partner to any creditor who transacts business with the limited partnership and believes, based on the limited partner's conduct, that he or she is a general partner [RULPA 303]. How much actual review and advisement a limited partner can engage in before being exposed to liability is not always clear.

Limited Partnership (LP) A partnership consisting of one or more general partners (who manage the business and are liable to the full extent of their personal assets for debts of the partnership) and one or more limited partners (who contribute only assets and are liable only up to the extent of their contributions).

General Partner In a limited partnership, a partner who assumes responsibility for the management of the partnership and liability for all partnership debts.

Limited Partner In a limited partnership, a partner who contributes capital to the partnership but has no right to participate in the management and operation of the business. The limited partner assumes no liability for partnership debts beyond the capital contributed.

Certificate of Limited Partnership The basic document filed with a designated state official by which a limited partnership is formed.

Learning Objective 4
What are the key differences between the rights and liabilities of general partners and those of limited partners?

Dissociation and Dissolution of a Limited Partnership

A general partner has the power to voluntarily dissociate, or withdraw, from a limited partnership unless the partnership agreement specifies otherwise. A limited partner theoretically can withdraw from the partnership by giving six months' notice unless the partnership agreement specifies a term, which most do. Also, some states have passed laws prohibiting the withdrawal of limited partners.

In a limited partnership, a general partner's voluntary dissociation from the firm normally will lead to dissolution *unless* all partners agree to continue the business. Similarly, the bankruptcy, retirement, death, or mental incompetence of a general partner will cause the dissociation of that partner and the dissolution of the limited partnership unless the other members agree to continue the firm [RULPA 801].

Bankruptcy of a limited partner, however, does not dissolve the partnership unless it causes the bankruptcy of the firm. Death or an assignment of the interest of a limited partner does not dissolve a limited partnership [RULPA 702, 704, 705]. A limited partnership can be dissolved by court decree [RULPA 802].

On dissolution, creditors' claims, including those of partners who are creditors, take first priority. After that, partners and former partners receive unpaid distributions of partnership assets and, except as otherwise agreed, amounts representing returns on their contributions and amounts proportionate to their shares of the distributions [RULPA 804].

Limited Liability Companies

For many entrepreneurs and investors, the ideal business form would combine the tax advantages of the partnership form of business with the limited liability of the corporate enterprise. Although the limited partnership partially addresses these needs, the limited liability of limited partners is conditional: limited liability exists only so long as the limited partner does *not* participate in management.

This is one reason that every state has adopted legislation authorizing a form of business organization called the **limited liability company (LLC).** The LLC is a hybrid form of business enterprise that offers the limited liability of the corporation but the tax advantages of a partnership. Today, LLCs are a common form of business.

Like an LLP or LP, an LLC must be formed and operated in compliance with state law. About one-fourth of the states specifically require LLCs to have at least two owners, called **members.** In the rest of the states, although some LLC statutes are silent on this issue, one-member LLCs are usually permitted.

Formation of an LLC

To form an LLC, **articles of organization** must be filed with a central state agency—usually the secretary of state's office. Typically, the articles are required to set forth such information as the name of the business, its principal address, the name and address of a registered agent, the names of the owners, and information on how the LLC will be managed. The business's name must include the words "Limited Liability Company" or the initials "LLC." In addition to requiring that articles of organization be filed, a few states require that a notice of the intention to form an LLC be published in a local newspaper.

Sometimes, the future members of an LLC may enter into contracts on the entity's behalf before the LLC is formally formed. As you will read in Chapter 15, a similar process often occurs with corporations. Persons forming a corporation may enter into contracts during the process of incorporation but before the corporation becomes a legal entity. These contracts are referred to as preincorporation contracts. Once the corporation is formed

---

"A friendship founded on business is a good deal better than a business founded on friendship."

John D. Rockefeller, 1839–1937, (American industrialist)

Learning Objective 5
How are limited liability companies formed, and who decides how they will be managed and operated?

Limited Liability Company (LLC)
A hybrid form of business enterprise that offers the limited liability of the corporation but the tax advantages of a partnership.

Member A person who has an ownership interest in a limited liability company.

Articles of Organization The document filed with a designated state official by which a limited liability company is formed.

and adopts the preincorporation contract (by means of a *novation*, discussed in Chapter 11), it can then enforce the contract terms.

In dealing with the preorganization contracts of LLCs, courts may apply the well-established principles of corporate law relating to preincorporation contracts. **CASE EXAMPLE 14.11** 607 South Park, LLC, entered into a written agreement to sell a hotel to 607 Park View Associates, Ltd., whose general partner then assigned the rights to the hotel purchase to another company, 02 Development, LLC. At the time, 02 Development did not yet exist—it was legally created several months later. 607 South Park subsequently refused to sell the hotel to 02 Development, and 02 Development sued for breach of the purchase agreement. A California appellate court ruled that LLCs should be treated the same as corporations with respect to preorganization contracts. Although 02 Development did not exist when the agreement was executed, once it came into existence, it could enforce any preorganization contract made on its behalf.[9] ●

Some well-known companies, including Chrysler, Subway, and Dish Network, are limited liability companies.

Jurisdictional Requirements

One of the significant differences between LLCs and corporations has to do with federal jurisdictional requirements. Under the federal jurisdiction statute, a corporation is deemed to be a citizen of the state where it is incorporated and maintains its principal place of business. The statute does not mention the state citizenship of partnerships, LLCs, and other unincorporated associations, but the courts have tended to regard these entities as citizens of every state in which their members are citizens.

The state citizenship of an LLC may come into play when a party sues the LLC based on diversity of citizenship. Remember from Chapter 3 that when parties to a lawsuit are from different states and the amount in controversy exceeds $75,000, a federal court can exercise diversity jurisdiction. *Total* diversity of citizenship must exist, however. **EXAMPLE 14.12** Jen Fong, a citizen of New York, wishes to bring a suit against Skycel, an LLC formed under the laws of Connecticut. One of Skycel's members also lives in New York. Fong will not be able to bring a suit against Skycel in federal court on the basis of diversity jurisdiction because the defendant LLC is also a citizen of New York. The same would be true if Fong was bringing a suit against multiple defendants and one of the defendants lived in New York. ●

Advantages of the LLC

The LLC offers many advantages to businesspersons, which is why this form of business organization has become increasingly popular.

---

9. *02 Development, LLC v. 607 South Park, LLC,* 159 Cal.App.4th 609, 71 Cal.Rptr.3d 608 (2008). For a case in which a state court applied another corporate law principle (piercing the corporate veil) to LLCs, see *ORX Resources, Inc. v. MBW Exploration, LLC,* 32 So.3d 931 (La.App. 2010).

Limited Liability   A key advantage of the LLC is that the liability of members is limited to the amount of their investments. Although the LLC as an entity can be held liable for any loss or injury caused by the wrongful acts or omissions of its members, the members themselves generally are not personally liable.

Taxation   Another advantage is the flexibility of the LLC in regard to taxation. An LLC that has *two or more members* can choose to be taxed either as a partnership or as a corporation. As you will read in Chapter 15, a corporate entity must pay income taxes on its profits, and the shareholders pay personal income taxes on profits distributed as dividends. An LLC that wants to distribute profits to its members may prefer to be taxed as a partnership to avoid the "double taxation" that is characteristic of the corporate entity.

Unless an LLC indicates that it wishes to be taxed as a corporation, the IRS automatically taxes it as a partnership. This means that the LLC as an entity pays no taxes. Rather, as in a partnership, profits are "passed through" the LLC to the members who then personally pay taxes on the profits. If an LLC's members want to reinvest the profits in the business, however, rather than distribute the profits to members, they may prefer that the LLC be taxed as a corporation. Corporate income tax rates may be lower than personal tax rates. Part of the attractiveness of the LLC is this flexibility with respect to taxation.

For federal income tax purposes, one-member LLCs are automatically taxed as sole proprietorships unless they indicate that they wish to be taxed as corporations. With respect to state taxes, most states follow the IRS rules.

Management and Foreign Investors   Still another advantage of the LLC for businesspersons is the flexibility it offers in terms of business operations and management—as will be discussed shortly. Finally, because foreign investors can participate in an LLC, the LLC form of business is attractive as a way to encourage investment. For a discussion of business organizations in other nations that are similar to the LLC, see this chapter's *Beyond Our Borders* feature that follows.

BEYOND OUR BORDERS

Limited Liability Companies in Other Nations

Limited liability companies are not unique to the United States. Many nations have business forms that provide limited liability, although these organizations may differ significantly from our domestic limited liability companies (LLCs).

In Germany, the *GmbH*, or *Gesellschaft mit beschränkter Haftung* (which means "company with limited liability"), is a type of business entity that resembles the LLC. The GmbH is now the most widely used business form in Germany. A GmbH, however, is owned by shareholders and thus resembles a U.S. corporation in certain

respects. German laws also impose numerous restrictions on the operations and business transactions of GmbHs, whereas LLCs in the United States are not even required to have an operating agreement.

Business forms that limit the liability of owners can also be found in various other countries. Limited liability companies known as *limitadas* are common in many Latin American nations.

In France, a *société à responsabilité limitée* (meaning "society with limited liability") is an entity that provides business owners with limited liability. Although laws in the

United Kingdom and Ireland use the term *limited liability partnership*, the entities are similar to our domestic LLCs.

Japan has created a new type of business organization called the *godo kaisha (GK)*, which is also quite similar to an LLC in the United States.

Critical Thinking

Clearly, limited liability is an important aspect of doing business globally. Why might a nation limit the number of member-owners in a limited liability entity?

Disadvantages of the LLC

The main disadvantage of the LLC is that state LLC statutes are not uniform. Therefore, businesses that operate in more than one state may not receive consistent treatment in these states. Generally, most states apply to a foreign LLC (an LLC formed in another state) the law of the state where the LLC was formed. Difficulties can arise, though, when one state's court must interpret and apply another state's laws.

The LLC Operating Agreement

Under the Uniform Limited Liability Company Act (ULLCA), Section 103a, the members of an LLC can decide how to operate the various aspects of the business by forming an **operating agreement.** Operating agreements typically contain provisions relating to management, how profits will be divided, the transfer of membership interests, whether the LLC will be dissolved on the death or departure of a member, and other important issues.

Operating Agreement In a limited liability company, an agreement in which the members set forth the details of how the business will be managed and operated.

In many states, an operating agreement is not required for an LLC to exist, and if there is one, it need not be in writing. Generally, though, LLC members should protect their interests by forming a written operating agreement. As with any business arrangement, disputes may arise over any number of issues. If there is no agreement covering the topic under dispute, such as how profits will be divided, the state LLC statute will govern the outcome. For instance, most LLC statutes provide that if the members have not specified how profits will be divided, they will be divided equally among the members. When an issue is not covered by an operating agreement or by an LLC statute, the courts often apply the principles of partnership law.

Of course, the members of an LLC are bound to the operating agreement that they make. The agreement's provisions may become especially important in determining the relative rights of the parties when a dispute arises among the members, as the following case illustrates.

Case 14.3

(Getty Images)

Mekonen v. Zewdu
Court of Appeals of Washington, Division 1, 179 Wash.App. 1042 (2014).

BACKGROUND AND FACTS Green Cab Taxi and Disabled Service Association LLC ("Green Cab") is a taxi service company in King County, Washington. The operating agreement requires the members to pay weekly fees. Members who do not pay are in default and must return their taxi licenses to the company. In addition, a member in default cannot hold a seat on the board or withdraw from the company without the consent of all of the members. A disagreement arose among the members concerning the company's management, and several members, including Shumet Mekonen, withdrew from the company without the consent of the other members. Both sides continued to drive under the Green Cab name. Mekonen's group filed a suit in a Washington state court against a group of members who had not withdrawn, including Dessie Zewdu. In part, the Mekonen group sought the right to operate as Green Cab. The court held that the plaintiffs could not represent themselves as Green Cab and ordered them to return their taxi licenses to

the company. The plaintiffs appealed the order to return their licenses.

IN THE WORDS OF THE COURT . . .
LAU, J. [Judge]
    * * * *
    * * * The [lower] court found in defendants' favor regarding * * * the right of management and control over Green Cab. It found plaintiffs had no right to represent themselves as part of Green Cab's management or to operate under Green Cab's name.
    * * * *
    * * * Plaintiffs seek to retain the taxicab licenses affixed to the cars they own. According to Paragraph 6.4 of the LLC Operating

Case 14.3—Continues ➡

Case 14.3—Continued

Agreement, "the Company shall hold all rights to any taxi and other licenses and permits necessary to operate its vehicles." *The Plaintiffs have no right to use the taxicab licenses unless they are members of Green Cab LLC in good standing and are making any contributions toward the company's operating expenses that the board of directors deems necessary.* Plaintiffs admit that they withdrew their membership from Green Cab LLC and that they have paid no weekly fees since [their withdrawal]. As a result, the Plaintiffs have no legal right to retain the King County taxicab licenses currently in their possession. [Emphasis added.]

* * * The [lower] court deemed the members "defaulting members."

* * * *

* * * Plaintiffs admitted to default both in failing to make weekly payments and in withdrawing from the company in violation of article 5.6 of the operating agreement. That article states, "A Member may not withdraw as a Member prior to dissolution and commencement of winding up of the Company * * * without the written consent of all the other Members." The trial court imposed relief that was reasonably calculated to install defendants as the proper group to manage Green Cab

and to preserve their interests in operating the company * * * . Given the relative interests of the parties and the LLC, the trial court acted well within its discretion to order plaintiffs to return their taxi licenses.

DECISION AND REMEDY   A state intermediate appellate court upheld the lower court's order to the plaintiffs to return their taxi licenses to Green Cab. Under the provisions of the company's operating agreement, the plaintiffs, as "defaulting members," had no right to retain and use the licenses.

THE LEGAL ENVIRONMENT DIMENSION   *During discovery, the plaintiffs were asked to answer requests for admission, but they did not respond. Does it seem likely that their failure to answer affected the outcome? Why or why not?*

WHAT IF THE FACTS WERE DIFFERENT?   *Suppose that Green Cab had maintained a Web site on which it posted its operating agreement, conducted all intracompany business, and offered a forum where members could vent their complaints. How might the result have been different? Why?*

Management of an LLC

> "Business is the salt of life."
>
> Voltaire, 1694–1778, (French author)

Basically, there are two options for managing an LLC. The members may decide in their operating agreement to be either a "member-managed" LLC or a "manager-managed" LLC. Most LLC statutes and the ULLCA provide that unless the articles of organization specify otherwise, an LLC is assumed to be member managed [ULLCA 203(a)(6)].

In a *member-managed* LLC, all of the members participate in management, and decisions are made by majority vote [ULLCA 404(a)]. In a *manager-managed* LLC, the members designate a group of persons to manage the firm. The management group may consist of only members, both members and nonmembers, or only nonmembers.

Fiduciary Duties   Under the ULLCA, managers in a manager-managed LLC owe fiduciary duties to the LLC and its members, including the duty of loyalty and the duty of care [ULLCA 409(a), (h)]. (As you will read in Chapter 15, the same rule applies in corporate law. Corporate directors and officers owe fiduciary duties to the corporation and its shareholders.)

Because not all states have adopted the ULLCA, though, some state statutes provide that managers owe fiduciary duties only to the LLC and not to the LLC's members individually. Although to whom the duty is owed may seem insignificant at first glance, it can have a dramatic effect on the outcome of litigation.[10]

Decision-Making Procedures   The members of an LLC can also set forth in their operating agreement provisions governing decision-making procedures. For

---

10. See, for example, *Polk v. Polk,* 70 So.3d 363 (Ala. 2011).

instance, the agreement can include procedures for choosing or removing managers. Although most LLC statutes are silent on this issue, the ULLCA provides that members may choose and remove managers by majority vote [ULLCA 404(b)(3)].

Members may also specify in their agreement how voting rights will be apportioned. If they do not, LLC statutes in most states provide that voting rights are apportioned according to each member's capital contributions. Some states provide that, in the absence of an agreement to the contrary, each member has one vote.

(PhotoDisc/Getty Images)

Members of a manager-managed LLC hold a formal members' meeting. What is the difference between a member-managed LLC and a manager-managed LLC? How are managers typically chosen?

Dissociation and Dissolution of an LLC

Recall that in the context of partnerships, *dissociation* occurs when a partner ceases to be associated in the carrying on of the business. The same concept applies to limited liability companies. A member of an LLC has the *power* to dissociate from the LLC at any time, but he or she may not have the *right* to dissociate.

Under the ULLCA, the events that trigger a member's dissociation in an LLC are similar to the events causing a partner to be dissociated under the Uniform Partnership Act (UPA). These include voluntary withdrawal, expulsion by other members or by court order, bankruptcy, incompetence, and death. Generally, even if a member dies or otherwise dissociates from an LLC, the other members may continue to carry on LLC business, unless the operating agreement has contrary provisions.

Dissociation When a member dissociates from an LLC, he or she loses the right to participate in management and the right to act as an agent for the LLC. His or her duty of loyalty to the LLC also terminates, and the duty of care continues only with respect to events that occurred before dissociation.

Generally, the dissociated member also has a right to have his or her interest in the LLC bought by the other members of the LLC. The LLC's operating agreement may contain provisions establishing a buyout price, but if it does not, the member's interest is usually purchased at a fair value. In states that have adopted the ULLCA, the LLC must purchase the interest at "fair" value within 120 days after the dissociation.

If the member's dissociation violates the LLC's operating agreement, it is considered legally wrongful, and the dissociated member can be held liable for damages caused by the dissociation. **EXAMPLE 14.13** Chadwick and Barrel are members in an LLC. Chadwick manages the accounts, and Barrel, who has many connections in the community and is a skilled investor, brings in the business. If Barrel wrongfully dissociates from the LLC, the LLC's business will suffer, and Chadwick can hold Barrel liable for the loss of business resulting from her withdrawal. •

Dissolution Regardless of whether a member's dissociation was wrongful or rightful, normally the dissociated member has no right to force the LLC to dissolve. The remaining members can opt to either continue or dissolve the business. Members can also stipulate in their operating agreement that certain events will cause dissolution, or they can agree that they have the power to dissolve the LLC by vote. As with partnerships, a court can order an LLC to be dissolved in certain circumstances, such as when the members have engaged in illegal or oppressive conduct, or when it is no longer feasible to carry on the business.

CASE EXAMPLE 14.14   Three men—Walter Perkins, Gary Fordham, and David Thompson—formed Venture Sales, LLC, to develop a subdivision in Petal, Mississippi. Each of them contributed land and funds resulting in 466 acres of land and about $158,000 in cash. Perkins was an assistant coach for the Cleveland Browns, so he trusted Fordham and Thompson to develop the property.

More than ten years later, however, Fordham and Thompson still had not done anything with the property, although they had formed two other LLCs and developed two other subdivisions in the area. Fordham and Thompson claimed that they did not know when they could develop Venture's property and suggested selling it at a discounted price, but Perkins disagreed. Perkins then sought a judicial dissolution of Venture Sales. The court ordered a dissolution. Because Venture Sales was not meeting the economic purpose for which it was established (developing a subdivision), continuing the business was impracticable.[11] ●

Winding Up   When an LLC is dissolved, any members who did not wrongfully dissociate may participate in the winding up process. To wind up the business, members must collect, liquidate, and distribute the LLC's assets. Members may preserve the assets for a reasonable time to optimize their return, and they continue to have the authority to perform reasonable acts in conjunction with winding up. In other words, the LLC will be bound by the reasonable acts of its members during the winding up process.

Once all the LLC's assets have been sold, the proceeds are distributed to pay off debts to creditors first (including debts owed to members who are creditors of the LLC). The member's capital contributions are returned next, and any remaining amounts are then distributed to members in equal shares or according to their operating agreement.

Franchises

Instead of setting up a business to market their own products or services, many entrepreneurs opt to purchase a franchise. A **franchise** is defined as any arrangement in which the owner of a trademark, a trade name, or a copyright licenses others to use the trademark, trade name, or copyright in the selling of goods or services. A **franchisee** (the purchaser of a franchise) is generally legally independent of the **franchisor** (the seller of the franchise). At the same time, the franchisee is economically dependent on the franchisor's integrated business system. In other words, a franchisee can operate as an independent businessperson but still obtain the advantages of a regional or national organization.

Today, franchising companies and their franchisees account for a significant portion of all retail sales in this country. Well-known franchises include 7-Eleven, Holiday Inn, and McDonald's.

Types of Franchises

Because the franchising industry is so extensive and so many different types of businesses sell franchises, it is difficult to summarize the many types of franchises that now exist. Generally, though, the majority of franchises fall into one of three classifications: distributorships, chain-style business operations, or manufacturing or processing-plant arrangements. We briefly describe these types of franchises here.

Distributorship   A *distributorship* arises when a manufacturing concern (franchisor) licenses a dealer (franchisee) to sell its product. Often, a distributorship covers an exclusive territory. An example is an automobile dealership or beer distributorship.

Franchise Any arrangement in which the owner of a trademark, trade name, or copyright licenses another to use that trademark, trade name, or copyright in the selling of goods or services.

Franchisee One receiving a license to use another's (the franchisor's) trademark, trade name, or copyright in the sale of goods and services.

Franchisor One licensing another (the franchisee) to use the owner's trademark, trade name, or copyright in the selling of goods or services.

---

11. *Venture Sales, LLC v. Perkins*, 86 So.3d 910 (Miss.Sup. 2012).

EXAMPLE 14.15   Black Rain Beer Company distributes its brands of beer through a network of authorized wholesale distributors, each with an assigned territory. Marik signs a distributorship contract for the area from Gainesville to Ocala, Florida. If the contract states that Marik is the exclusive distributor in that area, then no other franchisee may distribute Black Rain beer in that region. •

Chain-Style Business Operation   In a *chain-style business operation,* a franchise operates under a franchisor's trade name and is identified as a member of a select group of dealers that engage in the franchisor's business. The franchisee is generally required to follow standardized or prescribed methods of operation. Often, the franchisor requires that the franchisee maintain certain standards of operation.

In addition, sometimes the franchisee is obligated to obtain materials and supplies exclusively from the franchisor. Examples of this type of franchise are McDonald's and most other fast-food chains. Chain-style franchises are also common in service-related businesses, including real estate brokerage firms, such as Century 21, and tax-preparing services, such as H&R Block, Inc.

(Sun Hai/Imagechina/AP Images)

Many franchises operate worldwide. McDonald's is what type of franchise?

Manufacturing or Processing-Plant Arrangement   In a *manufacturing or processing-plant arrangement,* the franchisor transmits to the franchisee the essential ingredients or formula to make a particular product. The franchisee then markets the product either at wholesale or at retail in accordance with the franchisor's standards. Examples of this type of franchise are Coca-Cola and other soft-drink bottling companies.

Laws Governing Franchising

Because a franchise relationship is primarily a contractual relationship, it is governed by contract law. If the franchise exists primarily for the sale of products manufactured by the franchisor, the law governing sales contracts as expressed in Article 2 of the Uniform Commercial Code applies (see Chapter 12).

Additionally, the federal government and most states have enacted laws governing certain aspects of franchising. Generally, these laws are designed to protect prospective franchisees from dishonest franchisors and to prohibit franchisors from terminating franchises without good cause.

Federal Regulation of Franchising   The federal government regulates franchising through laws that apply to specific industries and through the Franchise Rule, created by the Federal Trade Commission (FTC).

Industry-Specific Standards   Congress has enacted laws that protect franchisees in certain industries, such as automobile dealerships and service stations. These laws protect the franchisee from unreasonable demands and bad faith terminations of the franchise by the franchisor.

An automobile manufacturer–franchisor cannot make unreasonable demands of dealer-franchisees or set unrealistically high sales quotas. If an automobile manufacturer–franchisor terminates a franchise because of a dealer-franchisee's failure to comply with unreasonable demands, the manufacturer may be liable for damages.[12]

---

12. Automobile Dealers' Franchise Act of 1965, also known as the Automobile Dealers' Day in Court Act, 15 U.S.C. Sections 1221 *et seq.*

Similarly, federal law prescribes the conditions under which a franchisor of service stations can terminate the franchise.[13] Federal antitrust laws (discussed in Chapter 23) also apply in certain circumstances to prohibit certain types of anticompetitive agreements.

The Franchise Rule   The FTC's Franchise Rule requires franchisors to disclose certain material facts that a prospective franchisee needs to make an informed decision concerning the purchase of a franchise.[14] The rule was designed to enable potential franchisees to weigh the risks and benefits of an investment.

The rule requires the franchisor to make numerous written or electronic disclosures to prospective franchisees. For instance, if a franchisor provides projected earnings figures, the franchisor must indicate whether the figures are based on actual data or hypothetical examples. If a franchisor makes sales or earnings projections based on actual data for a specific franchise location, the franchisor must disclose the number and percentage of its existing franchises that have achieved this result.

All representations made to a prospective franchisee must have a reasonable basis. Franchisors are also required to explain termination, cancellation, and renewal provisions of the franchise contract to potential franchisees before the agreement is signed. (The Franchise Rule does *not* require franchisors to provide potential earnings figures, however, as discussed in this chapter's *Insight into Ethics* feature.) Those who violate the Franchise Rule are subject to substantial civil penalties, and the FTC can sue on behalf of injured parties to recover damages.

---

13. Petroleum Marketing Practices Act (PMPA) of 1979, 15 U.S.C. Sections 2801 *et seq.*
14. 16 C.F.R. Part 436.

INSIGHT INTO ETHICS

SHOULD FRANCHISORS HAVE TO GIVE PROSPECTIVE FRANCHISEES INFORMATION ABOUT POTENTIAL EARNINGS?

Entrepreneurs who are thinking about investing in a franchise almost invariably ask, "How much will I make?" Surprisingly, current law does not require franchisors to provide any information about the earnings potential of a franchise.

Voluntary Disclosure of Earnings Data

Franchisors can voluntarily choose to provide projected earnings in their disclosures but are not required to do so. If franchisors do include earnings data, they must indicate whether these figures are actual or hypothetical and have a reasonable basis for these claims. About 75 percent of franchisors choose *not* to provide information about earnings potential.

Franchisee Complaints

The failure of the FTC's Franchise Rule to require disclosure of earnings potential has led to many complaints from franchisees. After all, some franchisees invest their life savings in franchises that ultimately fail because of unrealistic earnings expectations. Moreover, the franchisee may be legally obliged to continue paying the franchisor even when the business is not turning a profit.

For instance, Thomas Anderson asked the franchisor, Rocky Mountain Chocolate Factory, Inc. (RMCF), and five of its franchisees for earnings information before he entered into a franchise agreement, but he did not receive any data. Although his chocolate franchise failed to become profitable, a court ordered Anderson and his partner to pay $33,109 in past due royalties and interest to RMCF (plus court costs and expenses).[a]

For Critical Analysis
Insight into the Business Environment
If the law required franchisors to provide estimates of potential earnings, would there be more or less growth in the number of franchises? Explain your answer.

---

a. *Rocky Mountain Chocolate Factory, Inc. v. SDMS, Inc.*, 2009 WL 579516 (D.Colo. 2009).

State Regulation of Franchising

State legislation varies but is often aimed at protecting franchisees from unfair practices and bad faith terminations by franchisors. Approximately fifteen states have laws similar to the federal rules requiring franchisors to provide presale disclosures to prospective franchisees.[15] Many state laws require that a disclosure document (known as the Franchise Disclosure Document, or FDD) be registered or filed with a state official. State laws may also require that the franchisor's advertising be submitted to the state for review or approval.

To protect franchisees, a state law might require the disclosure of information such as the actual costs of operation, recurring expenses, and profits earned, along with data substantiating these figures. State deceptive trade practices acts (see Chapter 20) may also apply and prohibit certain types of actions on the part of franchisors. To prevent arbitrary or bad faith terminations, state laws often prohibit termination without "good cause" or require that certain procedures be followed in terminating a franchising relationship.

(William Hamilton/The New Yorker Collection/www.cartoonbank.com.)

"You have written more than a book, Ms. McBean— you have written a franchise."

The Franchise Contract

The franchise relationship is defined by a contract between the franchisor and the franchisee. The franchise contract specifies the terms and conditions of the franchise and spells out the rights and duties of the franchisor and the franchisee. If either party fails to perform the contractual duties, that party may be subject to a lawsuit for breach of contract. Generally, statutes and case law governing franchising tend to emphasize the importance of good faith and fair dealing in franchise relationships.

Payment for the Franchise

The franchisee ordinarily pays an initial fee or lump-sum price for the franchise license (the privilege of being granted a franchise). This fee is separate from the various products that the franchisee purchases from or through the franchisor. The franchise agreement may also require the franchisee to pay a percentage of advertising costs and certain administrative expenses.

In some industries, the franchisor relies heavily on the initial sale of the franchise for realizing a profit. In other industries, the continued dealing between the parties brings profit to both. In most situations, the franchisor will receive a stated percentage of the annual (or monthly) sales or annual volume of business done by the franchisee.

Business Premises

The franchise agreement may specify whether the premises for the business must be leased or purchased outright. Sometimes, a building must be constructed or remodeled to meet the terms of the agreement. The agreement usually will specify whether the franchisor supplies equipment and furnishings for the premises or whether this is the responsibility of the franchisee.

Location of the Franchise

Typically, the franchisor will determine the territory to be served. Some franchise contracts give the franchisee exclusive rights, or "territorial rights," to a certain geographic area. Other franchise contracts, though they define the territory allotted to a particular franchise, either specifically state that the franchise is nonexclusive or are silent on the issue of territorial rights.

---

15. These states include California, Hawaii, Illinois, Indiana, Maryland, Michigan, Minnesota, New York, North Dakota, Oregon, Rhode Island, South Dakota, Virginia, Washington, and Wisconsin.

Many franchise cases involve disputes over territorial rights, and the implied covenant of good faith and fair dealing often comes into play in this area of franchising. If the franchise contract does not grant exclusive territorial rights to a franchisee and the franchisor allows a competing franchise to be established nearby, the franchisee may suffer a significant loss in profits. In this situation, a court may hold that the franchisor's actions breached an implied covenant of good faith and fair dealing.

Quality Control by the Franchisor

Although the day-to-day operation of the franchise business is normally left to the franchisee, the franchise agreement may provide for the amount of supervision and control agreed on by the parties. When the franchisee prepares a product, such as food, or provides a service, such as a motel, the contract often provides that the franchisor will establish certain standards for the facility. Typically, the contract will state that the franchisor is permitted to make periodic inspections to ensure that the standards are being maintained so as to protect the franchise's name and reputation.

As a general rule, the validity of a provision permitting the franchisor to establish and enforce certain quality standards is unquestioned. Because the franchisor has a legitimate interest in maintaining the quality of the product or service to protect its name and reputation, it can exercise greater control in this area than would otherwise be tolerated.

Termination of the Franchise

The duration of the franchise is a matter to be determined between the parties. Sometimes, a franchise will start out for a short period, such as a year, so that the franchisor can determine whether it wants to stay in business with the franchisee. Other times, the duration of the franchise contract correlates with the term of the lease for the business premises, and both are renewable at the end of that period.

Usually, the franchise agreement will specify that termination must be "for cause," such as death or disability of the franchisee, insolvency of the franchisee, breach of the franchise agreement, or failure to meet specified sales quotas. Most franchise contracts provide that notice of termination must be given. If no set time for termination is specified, then a reasonable time, with notice, will be implied. A franchisee must be given reasonable time to wind up the business—that is, to do the accounting and return the copyright or trademark or any other property of the franchisor.

When a franchisor rebrands its products, does that franchisor have remaining obligations to long-time franchisees who were selling the previous brand?

(Cai Zengle/Imaginechina/AP Images)

Wrongful Termination

Because a franchisor's termination of a franchise often has adverse consequences for the franchisee, much franchise litigation involves claims of wrongful termination. Generally, the termination provisions of contracts are more favorable to the franchisor. This means that the franchisee, who normally invests a substantial amount of time and funds to make the franchise operation successful, may receive little or nothing for the business on termination. The franchisor owns the trademark and hence the business.

It is in this area that statutory and case law become important. The federal and state laws discussed earlier attempt, among other things, to protect franchisees from the arbitrary or unfair termination of their franchises by the franchisors.

The Importance of Good Faith and Fair Dealing

Generally, both statutory law and case law emphasize the importance of good faith and fair dealing in terminating a franchise relationship. In determining whether a franchisor has acted in good faith when terminating a franchise agreement, the courts usually try to balance the rights of both parties.

If a court perceives that a franchisor has arbitrarily or unfairly terminated a franchise, the franchisee will be provided with a remedy for wrongful termination. If a franchisor's decision to terminate a franchise was made in the normal course of the franchisor's business operations, however, and reasonable notice of termination was given to the franchisee, in most instances a court will not consider the termination wrongful.

CASE EXAMPLE 14.16   Buddy House was in the construction business and had collaborated on projects with Holiday Inns Franchising, Inc., for decades. Many projects were undertaken without written contracts. Holiday Inn asked House to inspect a hotel in Texas to estimate the cost of renovating it to be a Holiday Inn. The parties agreed that House would buy and renovate the hotel and Holiday Inn would grant him a franchise for ten years. Holiday Inn assured House that his franchise license would be extended at the end of ten years provided that the hotel was run appropriately. House bought the hotel, renovated it, and operated it as Hotel Associates, Inc. (HAI), generating substantial profits.

Before the ten years had passed, Greg Aden, a Holiday Inn executive, developed a plan to license a different local hotel as a Holiday Inn instead of renewing House's franchise license. Aden stood to earn a commission from licensing the other hotel. House was not informed of Aden's plan. When HAI applied for an extension of its franchise, Holiday Inn asked for major renovations. HAI spent $3 million to comply with this request. Holiday Inn did not renew HAI's license, however, but instead granted a franchise to the other hotel. HAI sold its hotel for $5 million and filed a suit against Holiday Inn. The court found that Holiday Inn's conduct constituted bad faith and fraud. Holiday Inn had assured House that he would be relicensed at the end of ten years, and House was justified in believing that there were no obstacles to his relicensure. The court awarded HAI compensatory and punitive damages.[16] ●

_____

16. _Holiday Inn Franchising, Inc. v. Hotel Associates, Inc.,_ 2011 Ark.App. 147 (2011).

(Cengage Learning)

What actions by franchisors might constitute fraud?

Reviewing . . . Small Business Organizations

A bridge on a prominent public roadway in the city of Papagos, Arizona, was deteriorating and in need of repair. The city posted notices seeking proposals for an artistic bridge design and reconstruction. Davidson Masonry, LLC, which was owned and managed by Carl Davidson and his wife, Marilyn Rowe, submitted a bid for a decorative concrete project that incorporated artistic metalwork. They contacted Shana Lafayette, a local sculptor who specialized in large-scale metal forms, to help them design the bridge. The city selected their bridge design and awarded them the contract for a commission of $184,000. Davidson Masonry and Lafayette then entered into an agreement to work together on the bridge project. Davidson Masonry agreed to install and pay for concrete and structural work, and Lafayette agreed to install the metalwork at her expense. They agreed that overall profits would be split, with 25 percent going to Lafayette and 75 percent going to Davidson Masonry. Lafayette designed numerous metal sculptures of salmon that were incorporated into colorful decorative concrete forms designed by Rowe, while Davidson performed the structural engineering. Using the information presented in the chapter, answer the following questions.

1. Would Davidson Masonry automatically be taxed as a partnership or a corporation? Explain.
2. Is Davidson Masonry a member-managed or manager-managed LLC? Explain.

3. Suppose that during construction, Lafayette had entered into an agreement to rent space in a warehouse that was close to the bridge so that she could work on her sculptures near the site where they would be installed. She entered into the contract without the knowledge or consent of Davidson Masonry. In this situation, would a court be likely to hold that Davidson Masonry was bound by the contract that Lafayette entered? Why or why not?

4. Now suppose that Rowe has an argument with her husband and wants to withdraw from being a member of Davidson Masonry. What is the term for such a withdrawal, and what effect does it have on the LLC?

Debate This All franchisors should be required by law to provide a comprehensive estimate of the profitability of a prospective franchise based on the experiences of their existing franchisees.

Key Terms

articles of organization 410	entrepreneur 395	joint and several liability 405	member 410
articles of partnership 400	franchise 416	joint liability 404	operating agreement 413
buyout price 406	franchisee 416	limited liability company (LLC) 410	partnership 399
certificate of limited partnership 409	franchisor 416	limited liability partnership (LLP) 408	pass-through entity 400
dissociation 405	general partner 409	limited partner 409	sole proprietorship 396
dissolution 406	information return 400	limited partnership (LP) 409	winding up 406

Chapter Summary: Small Business Organizations

Sole Proprietorships	The simplest form of business organization that is used by anyone who does business without creating a separate organization. The owner is the business. The owner pays personal income taxes on all profits and is personally liable for all business debts.
Partnerships	1. A partnership is created by agreement of the parties. 2. A partnership is treated as an entity except for limited purposes. 3. Each partner pays a proportionate share of income taxes on the net profits of the partnership, whether or not they are distributed. The partnership files only an information return with the Internal Revenue Service. 4. Each partner has an equal voice in management unless the partnership agreement provides otherwise. 5. In the absence of an agreement, partners share profits equally and share losses in the same ratio as they share profits. 6. Partners have unlimited personal liability for partnership debts. 7. A partnership can be terminated by agreement or can be dissolved by action of the partners, operation of law (subsequent illegality), or court decree.
Limited Liability Partnerships (LLPs)	1. *Formation*—LLPs must be formed in compliance with state statutes. Typically, an LLP is formed by professionals who normally work together as partners in a partnership. Under most state LLP statutes, it is relatively easy to convert a traditional partnership into an LLP. 2. *Liability of partners*—LLP statutes vary, but under the UPA, professionals generally can avoid personal liability for acts committed by other partners. Partners in an LLP continue to be liable for their own wrongful acts and for the wrongful acts of those whom they supervise.
Limited Partnerships	1. *Formation*—A certificate of limited partnership must include information about the business and must be filed with the designated state official. The partnership consists of one or more general partners and one or more limited partners. 2. *Rights and liabilities of partners*—With some exceptions, the rights of partners are the same as the rights of partners in a general partnership. General partners have unlimited liability for partnership obligations. Limited partners are liable only to the extent of their contributions.

Chapter Summary: Small Business Organizations—Continued

Limited Partnerships—Continued	3. *Limited partners and management*—Only general partners can participate in management. Limited partners have no voice in management. If they do participate in management activities, they risk having liability as a general partner. 4. *Dissociation and dissolution*—Generally, a limited partnership can be dissolved in much the same way as an ordinary partnership. A general partner has the power to voluntarily dissociate unless the parties' agreement specifies otherwise. Some states limit the power of limited partners to voluntarily withdraw from the firm. The death or assignment of interest of a limited partner does not dissolve the partnership. Bankruptcy of a limited partner also will not dissolve the partnership unless it causes the bankruptcy of the firm.
Limited Liability Companies (LLCs)	1. *Formation*—Articles of organization must be filed with the appropriate state office—usually the office of the secretary of state—setting forth the name of the business, its principal address, the names of the owners (called members), and other relevant information. 2. *Advantages and disadvantages of the LLC*—Advantages of the LLC include limited liability, the option to be taxed as a partnership or as a corporation, and flexibility in deciding how the business will be managed and operated. The main disadvantage is the lack of uniformity in state LLC statutes. 3. *Operating agreement*—When an LLC is formed, the members decide, in an operating agreement, how the business will be managed and what rules will apply to the organization. 4. *Management*—An LLC may be managed by members only, by some members and some nonmembers, or by nonmembers only. 5. *Dissociation and dissolution*—Members of an LLC have the power to dissociate from the LLC at any time, but they may not have the right to dissociate. Dissociation does not always result in the dissolution of an LLC. The remaining members can choose to continue the business. Dissociated members have a right to have their interest purchased by the other members. If the LLC is dissolved, the business must be wound up and the assets sold. Creditors are paid first, and then members' capital investments are returned. Any remaining proceeds are distributed to members.

Franchises	1. *Types of franchises*—
	   a. Distributorship (for example, automobile dealerships).
	   b. Chain-style operation (for example, fast-food chains).
	   c. Manufacturing or processing-plant arrangement (for example, soft-drink bottling companies, such as Coca-Cola).
	2. *Laws governing franchising*—
	   a. Franchises are governed by contract law.
	   b. Franchises are also governed by federal and state statutory and regulatory laws.
	3. *The franchise contract*—The franchise relationship is defined by a contract between the franchisor and the franchisee. The contract normally spells out the following terms:
	   a. Payment for the franchise—Ordinarily, the contract requires the franchisee (purchaser) to pay an initial fee or lump-sum price for the franchise license.
	   b. Business premises and organization—Specifies whether the business premises will be leased or purchased by the franchisee. The franchisor may specify particular requirements for the form and capital structure of the business.
	   c. Location of the franchise—Specifies the territory to be served by the franchisee.
	   d. Quality control—The franchisor may require the franchisee to abide by certain standards of quality relating to the product or service offered.
	4. *Termination of the franchise*—Usually, the contract provides for the date and/or conditions of termination of the franchise arrangement. Both federal and state statutes attempt to protect franchisees from franchisors who unfairly or arbitrarily terminate franchises.

Issue Spotters

1. Gabriel, Harry, and Ida are members of Jeweled Watches, LLC. What are their options with respect to the management of their firm? (See *Limited Liability Companies.*)
2. Anchor Bottling Company and U.S. Beverages, Inc. (USB), enter into a franchise agreement that states that the franchise may be terminated at any time "for cause." Anchor fails to meet USB's specified sales quota. Does this constitute "cause" for termination? Why or why not? (See *Franchises.*)

—**Check your answers to the Issue Spotters against the answers provided in Appendix D at the end of this text.**

For Review

1. What advantages and disadvantages are associated with the sole proprietorship?
2. What is meant by joint and several liability? Why is this often considered to be a disadvantage of doing business as a general partnership?
3. What advantages do limited liability partnerships offer to entrepreneurs that are not offered by general partnerships?
4. What are the key differences between the rights and liabilities of general partners and those of limited partners?
5. How are limited liability companies formed, and who decides how they will be managed and operated?

Business Scenarios and Case Problems

14–1. Limited Liability Companies. John, Lesa, and Tabir form a limited liability company. John contributes 60 percent of the capital, and Lesa and Tabir each contribute 20 percent. Nothing is decided about how profits will be divided. John assumes that he will be entitled to 60 percent of the profits, in accordance with his contribution. Lesa and Tabir, however, assume that the profits will be divided equally. A dispute over the question arises, and ultimately a court has to decide the issue. What law will the court apply? In most states, what will result? How could this dispute have been avoided in the first place? Discuss fully. (See *Limited Liability Companies*.)

14–2. Dissolution of Limited Partnership. Dorinda, Luis, and Elizabeth form a limited partnership. Dorinda is a general partner, and Luis and Elizabeth are limited partners. Consider each of the separate events below, and discuss fully which would constitute a dissolution of the limited partnership. (See *Limited Partnerships*.)

1. Luis assigns his partnership interest to Ashley.
2. Elizabeth is petitioned into involuntary bankruptcy.
3. Dorinda dies.

14–3. Partnership Formation. Daniel is the owner of a chain of shoe stores. He hires Rubya to be the manager of a new store, which is to open in Grand Rapids, Michigan. Daniel, by written contract, agrees to pay Rubya a monthly salary and 20 percent of the profits. Without Daniel's knowledge, Rubya represents himself to Classen as Daniel's partner, showing Classen the agreement to share profits. Classen extends credit to Rubya. Rubya defaults. Discuss whether Classen can hold Daniel liable as a partner. (See *Partnerships*.)

14–4. **Business Case Problem with Sample Answer— LLC Operation.** After Hurricane Katrina, James Williford, Patricia Mosser, Marquetta Smith, and Michael Floyd formed Bluewater Logistics, LLC, to bid on construction contracts. Under Mississippi law, every member of a member-managed LLC is entitled to participate in managing the business. The operating agreement provided for a "super majority" 75 percent vote to remove a member "under any other circumstances that would jeopardize the company status" as a contractor. After Bluewater had completed more than $5 million in contracts, Smith told Williford that she, Mosser, and Floyd were exercising their "super majority"

vote to fire him. No reason was provided. Williford sued Bluewater and the other members. Did Smith, Mosser, and Floyd breach the state LLC statute, their fiduciary duties, or the Bluewater operating agreements? Discuss. [*Bluewater Logistics, LLC v. Williford*, 55 So.3d 148 (Miss. 2011)] (See *Limited Liability Companies*.)

—For a sample answer to Problem 14–4, go to Appendix E at the end of this text.

14–5. **Spotlight on Liberty Tax—Quality Control.** JTH Tax, Inc., doing business as Liberty Tax Service, provides tax preparation and related loan services through company-owned and franchised stores. Liberty's agreement with its franchisees reserved the right to control their ads. In operations manuals, Liberty provided step-by-step instructions, directions, and limitations regarding the franchisees' ads and retained the right to unilaterally modify the steps at any time. The California attorney general filed a suit in a California state court against Liberty, alleging that its franchisees had used misleading or deceptive ads regarding refund anticipation loans and e-refund checks. Can Liberty be held liable? Discuss. [*People v. JTH Tax, Inc.*, 212 Cal.App.4th 1219, 151 Cal.Rptr.3d 728 (1 Dist. 2013)] (See *Franchises*.)

14–6. Jurisdictional Requirements. Fadal Machining Centers, LLC, and MAG Industrial Automation Centers, LLC, sued a New Jersey–based corporation, Mid-Atlantic CNC, Inc., in federal district court. Ten percent of MAG was owned by SP MAG Holdings, a Delaware LLC. SP MAG had six members, including a Delaware limited partnership called Silver Point Capital Fund and a Delaware LLC called SPCP Group III. In turn, Silver Point and SPCP Group had a common member, Robert O'Shea, who was a New Jersey citizen. Assuming that the amount in controversy exceeds $75,000, does the district court have diversity jurisdiction? Why or why not? [*Fadal Machining Centers, LLC v. Mid-Atlantic CNC, Inc.*, 2012 WL 8669 (9th Cir. 2012)] (See *Limited Liability Companies*.)

14–7. Winding Up and Distribution of Assets. Dan and Lori Cole operated a Curves franchise exercise facility in Angola, Indiana, as a partnership. The firm leased commercial space from Flying Cat, LLC, for a renewable three-year term and renewed the lease for a second three-year term. But two years after the renewal, the Coles divorced. By the end of the second term, Flying Cat was owed more than $21,000 on the lease. Without telling the landlord about the divorce, Lori signed another extension. More rent went unpaid. Flying Cat obtained a judgment in an Indiana state court against the partnership for almost $50,000. Can Dan be held liable? Why or why not? [*Curves for Women Angola v. Flying Cat, LLC,* 983 N.E.2d 629 (Ind.App. 2013)] (See *Partnerships.*)

14–8. Partnerships. Karyl Paxton asked Christopher Sacco to work with her interior design business, Pierce Paxton Collections, in New Orleans. At the time, they were in a romantic relationship. Sacco was involved in every aspect of the business—bookkeeping, marketing, and design— but was not paid a salary. He was reimbursed, however, for expenses charged to his personal credit card, which Paxton also used. Sacco took no profits from the firm, saying that he wanted to "grow the business" and "build sweat equity." When Paxton and Sacco's personal relationship soured, she fired him. Sacco objected, claiming that they were partners. Is Sacco entitled to 50 percent of the profits of Pierce Paxton Collections? Explain. [*Sacco v. Paxton,* 133 So.3d 213 (La. App. 4th Cir. 2014)] (See *Partnerships.*)

14–9. ⬌ **A Question of Ethics—Wrongful Dissociation.** Elliot Willensky and Beverly Moran formed a partnership to buy, renovate, and sell a house. Moran agreed to finance the effort, which was to cost no more than $60,000. Willensky agreed to oversee the work, which was to be done in six months. Willensky lived in the house during the renovation. As the project progressed, Willensky incurred excessive and unnecessary expenses, misappropriated funds for his personal use,

did not pay bills on time, and did not keep Moran informed of the costs. More than a year later, the renovation was still not completed, and Willensky walked off the project. Moran completed the renovation, which ultimately cost $311,222, and sold the house. Moran then sued to dissolve the partnership and recover damages from Willensky for breach of contract and wrongful dissociation. [*Moran v. Willensky,* 395 S.W.3d 651 (Tenn.Ct.App. 2010)] (See *Partnerships.*)

1. Moran alleged that Willensky had wrongfully dissociated from the partnership. When did this dissociation occur? Why was his dissociation wrongful?

2. Which of Willensky's actions simply represent unethical behavior or bad management, and which constitute a breach of the agreement?

14–10. 💡 **Critical-Thinking Legal Environment Question.** Jordan Mendelson is interested in starting a kitchen franchise business. Customers will come to the business to assemble gourmet dinners and then take the prepared meals to their homes for cooking. The franchisor requires each store to use a specific layout and provides the recipes for various dinners, but the franchisee is not required to purchase the food products from the franchisor.

What general factors should Mendelson consider before entering a contract to start such a franchise? Is location important? Are there any laws that Mendelson should consider due to the fact that this franchise involves food preparation and sales? If the franchisor does not insist on a specific type of business entity, should Mendelson operate this business as a sole proprietorship? Why or why not? (See *Franchises.*)

Corporations

(Bershadsky Yuri/Shutterstock.com)

CONTENTS

- Nature and Classification
- Formation and Powers
- Piercing the Corporate Veil
- Directors and Officers
- Shareholders
- Major Business Forms Compared

LEARNING OBJECTIVES

The five learning objectives below are designed to help improve your understanding of the chapter. After reading this chapter, you should be able to answer the following questions:

1. What is a close corporation?

2. In what circumstances might a court disregard the corporate entity (pierce the corporate veil) and hold the shareholders personally liable?

3. What are the duties of corporate directors and officers?

4. Directors are expected to use their best judgment in managing the corporation. What must directors do to avoid liability for honest mistakes of judgment and poor business decisions?

5. What is a voting proxy? What is cumulative voting?

"A corporation is an artificial being, invisible, intangible, and existing only in contemplation of law."
—John Marshall, 1755–1835 (Chief justice of the United States Supreme Court, 1801–1835)

The corporation is a creature of statute. As John Marshall indicated in the chapter-opening quotation, a corporation is an artificial being, existing only in law and neither tangible nor visible. Its existence generally depends on state law, although some corporations, especially public organizations, are created under federal law. Each state has its own body of corporate law, and these laws are not entirely uniform.

The Model Business Corporation Act (MBCA) is a codification of modern corporation law that has been influential in the drafting and revision of state corporation statutes. Today, the majority of state statutes are guided by the revised version of the MBCA, which is often referred to as the Revised Model Business Corporation Act (RMBCA).

Keep in mind, however, that corporation laws vary considerably, even among the states that have used the MBCA or the RMBCA as a basis for their statutes, and several states do not follow either act. Consequently, individual state corporation laws should be relied on rather than the MBCA or the RMBCA.

Nature and Classification

A **corporation** is a legal entity created and recognized by state law. It can consist of one or more *natural persons* (as opposed to the artificial *legal person* of the corporation) identified under a common name. A corporation can be owned by a single person, or it can have hundreds, thousands, or even millions of owners (shareholders). Although the corporation substitutes itself for its shareholders in conducting corporate business and in incurring liability, its authority to act and the liability for its actions are separate and apart from the individuals who own it.

A corporation is recognized as a "person," and it enjoys many of the same rights and privileges under state and federal law that natural persons enjoy. For instance, corporations possess the same right of access to the courts as citizens and can sue or be sued. The constitutional guarantees of due process, free speech, and freedom from unreasonable searches and seizures also apply to corporations. Corporations also have a right under the First Amendment to fund political broadcasts (as was discussed in *Case Example 4.8* in Chapter 4).

> **Corporation** A legal entity formed in compliance with statutory requirements that is distinct from its shareholder-owners.

Corporate Personnel

In a corporation, the responsibility for the overall management of the firm is entrusted to a *board of directors*, whose members are elected by the shareholders. The board of directors hires *corporate officers* and other employees to run the daily business operations.

When an individual purchases a share of stock in a corporation, that person becomes a shareholder and thus an owner of the corporation. Unlike the members of a partnership, the body of shareholders can change constantly without affecting the continued existence of the corporation. A shareholder can sue the corporation, and the corporation can sue a shareholder. Also, under certain circumstances, a shareholder can sue on behalf of a corporation, as discussed later in this chapter.

The Limited Liability of Shareholders

One of the key advantages of the corporate form is the limited liability of its owners (shareholders). Corporate shareholders normally are not personally liable for the obligations of the corporation beyond the extent of their investments. In certain limited situations, however, a court can *pierce the corporate veil* and impose liability on shareholders for the corporation's obligations (see the discussion later in this chapter). Additionally, creditors often will not extend credit to small companies unless the shareholders assume personal liability, as guarantors, for corporate obligations.

Corporate Earnings and Taxation

When a corporation earns profits, it can either pass them on to shareholders in the form of **dividends** or retain them as profits. These **retained earnings**, if invested properly, will yield higher corporate profits in the future and thus cause the price of the company's stock to rise. Individual shareholders can then reap the benefits of these retained earnings in the capital gains that they receive when they sell their stock.

Whether a corporation retains its profits or passes them on to the shareholders as dividends, those profits are subject to income tax by various levels of government. Failure to pay taxes can lead to severe consequences. The state can suspend the entity's corporate status until the taxes are paid or even dissolve the corporation for failing to pay taxes.

Another important aspect of corporate taxation is that corporate profits can be subject to double taxation. The company pays tax on its profits. Then, if the profits are passed on

> **Dividend** A distribution to corporate shareholders of corporate profits or income, disbursed in proportion to the number of shares held.
>
> **Retained Earnings** The portion of a corporation's profits that has not been paid out as dividends to shareholders.

Many people believe that large corporations do not pay enough taxes.

to the shareholders as dividends, the shareholders must also pay income tax on them. The corporation normally does not receive a tax deduction for dividends it distributes to shareholders. This double-taxation feature is one of the major disadvantages of the corporate business form.

Criminal Acts and Tort Liability

Recall from Chapter 6 that under modern criminal law, a corporation may be held liable for the criminal acts of its agents and employees, provided the punishment is one that can be applied to the corporation. Although corporations cannot be imprisoned, they can be fined. (Of course, corporate directors and officers can be imprisoned, and many have been in recent years.) In addition, under sentencing guidelines for crimes committed by corporate employees (white-collar crimes), corporate lawbreakers can face fines amounting to hundreds of millions of dollars.[1]

CASE EXAMPLE 15.1   Brian Gauthier drove a dump truck for Angelo Todesca Corporation. The truck was missing its back-up alarm, but Angelo allowed Gauthier to continue driving it. At a worksite, Gauthier backed up to dump a load and struck and killed a police officer who was directing traffic. The state charged Angelo and Gauthier with the crime of vehicular homicide.

Angelo argued that a corporation could not be guilty of vehicular homicide because it cannot operate a vehicle. The court ruled that if an employee commits a crime "while engaged in corporate business that the employee has been authorized to conduct," the corporation can be held liable for the crime. Hence, the court held that Angelo Todesca Corporation was liable for Gauthier's negligent operation of its truck, which resulted in a person's death.[2] ●

A corporation is liable for the torts committed by its agents or officers within the course and scope of their employment. This principle applies to a corporation exactly as it applies to the ordinary agency relationships that we will discuss in Chapter 16. It follows the doctrine of *respondeat superior.*

The following case arose from a fraudulent scheme perpetrated by the officer of an investment firm through a separate investment fund that the officer controlled and managed. By the time investors filed a suit to recover the funds that they had lost, most of it was gone.

---

1. Note that the Sarbanes-Oxley Act of 2002, discussed in Chapter 2, stiffened the penalties for certain types of corporate crime and ordered the U.S. Sentencing Commission to revise the sentencing guidelines accordingly.
2. *Commonwealth v. Angelo Todesca Corp.,* 446 Mass. 128, 842 N.E.2d 930 (2006).

Case 15.1

Belmont v. MB Investment Partners, Inc.

United States Court of Appeals, Third Circuit, 708 F.3d 470 (2013).

BACKGROUND AND FACTS   In 1997, Mark Bloom formed North Hills, LP, as a stock investment fund. Bloom had sole authority over the fund's investments. Between 2001 and 2007, Bloom raised nearly $30 million from investors for the fund. At the time, Bloom was also an investment adviser and an officer and a director of MB Investment Partners, Inc. Investments in North Hills were administered by Bloom and other MB personnel, using MB's offices, computers, filing facilities, and office equipment. MB officers and directors were aware that Bloom was operating North Hills while he was also working at MB. In 2008, two investors in North Hills requested a full redemption of their investments. By that time, however, most of the money that had been invested in North Hills was

Case 15.1—Continued

gone. Bloom was arrested, and MB terminated him. Barry Belmont and other North Hills Investors filed a suit in a federal district court against MB, alleging fraud. From a summary judgment in MB's favor, the investors appealed.

IN THE WORDS OF THE COURT . . .
JORDAN, Circuit Judge.
* * * *
* * * North Hills was a Ponzi scheme that Bloom used to finance his lavish personal lifestyle, and, over time, he diverted at least $20 million from North Hills for his own personal use. Bloom used those funds to acquire multiple apartments and homes, furnishings, luxury cars and boats, and jewelry, and to fund parties and travel.
* * * *
* * * During the period of the North Hills fraud, MB did not have in place basic compliance procedures employed throughout the investment advising industry to identify and prevent fraud and self-dealing by MB employees and affiliates. Compliance weaknesses permitted Bloom to avoid required disclosures to MB about North Hills as a personal investment vehicle. *MB officers and directors failed to make basic inquiries about Bloom's operation of North Hills, and did not collect any information on North Hills or monitor sales of investments in North Hills to MB's own customers.* [Emphasis added.]
* * * *
* * * Bloom's violations * * * are beyond dispute, and the Investors argue that those violations may be imputed to MB as his employer.
* * * *The fraud of an officer of a corporation is imputed to the corporation when the officer's fraudulent contact was* *(1) in the course of his employment, and (2) for the benefit of the corporation.* This is true even if the officer's conduct was unauthorized, effected for his own benefit but clothed with apparent authority of the corporation, or contrary to instructions. The underlying reason is that a corporation can speak and act only through its agents and so must be accountable for any acts committed by one of its agents within his actual or apparent scope of authority and while transacting corporate business. [Emphasis added.]
* * * *
* * * We therefore conclude that imputation may be appropriate in this case, if the Investors can prove that the manner in which Bloom marketed North Hills to them while he was working for MB, and the apparent benefit to MB, made it appear that he marketed North Hills within the scope of his authority as a senior executive of MB.

DECISION AND REMEDY The U.S. Court of Appeals for the Third Circuit vacated the summary judgment in MB's favor and remanded the case for a trial with respect to the investors' claims against MB. Liability can be imputed (attributed) to a corporation for the acts of its agent committed within the scope of his or her authority.

THE LEGAL ENVIRONMENT DIMENSION *What circumstances in this case suggest that MB should be held liable for Bloom's fraud?*

THE ETHICAL DIMENSION *What public policy reasons support imputing (attributing) the fraud of a corporate officer to the corporation?*

Classification of Corporations

Corporations can be classified in several ways. The classification of a corporation normally depends on its location, purpose, and ownership characteristics, as described in the following subsections.

Domestic, Foreign, and Alien Corporations

A corporation is referred to as a **domestic corporation** by its home state (the state in which it incorporates). A corporation formed in one state but doing business in another is referred to in the second state as a **foreign corporation.** A corporation formed in another country (say, Mexico) but doing business in the United States is referred to in the United States as an **alien corporation.**

A corporation does not have an automatic right to do business in a state other than its state of incorporation. In some instances, it must obtain a *certificate of authority* in any state in which it plans to do business. Once the certificate has been issued, the corporation generally can exercise in that state all of the powers conferred on it by its home state. If a foreign corporation does business in a state without obtaining a certificate of authority,

Domestic Corporation In a given state, a corporation that does business in, and is organized under the law of, that state.

Foreign Corporation In a given state, a corporation that does business in the state without being incorporated therein.

Alien Corporation A designation in the United States for a corporation formed in another country but doing business in the United States.

(Ed Stock/iStockphoto.com)

Is AMTRAK a public or publicly held corporation?

the state can impose substantial fines and sanctions on the corporation, and sometimes even on its officers, directors, or agents.

Note that most state statutes specify certain activities, such as soliciting orders via the Internet, that are not considered doing business within the state. Thus, a foreign corporation normally does not need a certificate of authority to sell goods or services via the Internet or by mail.

Public and Private Corporations

A public corporation is one formed by the government to meet some political or governmental purpose. Cities and towns that incorporate are common examples. In addition, many federal government organizations, such as the U.S. Postal Service, the Tennessee Valley Authority, and AMTRAK, are public corporations.

Note that a public corporation is not the same as a *publicly held* corporation (often called a *public company*). A publicly held corporation is any corporation whose shares are publicly traded in securities markets, such as the New York Stock Exchange or the over-the-counter market.

In contrast to public corporations (*not* public companies), private corporations are created either wholly or in part for private benefit. Most corporations are private. Although they may serve a public purpose, as a public electric or gas utility does, they are owned by private persons rather than by the government.

Nonprofit Corporations

Corporations formed for purposes other than making a profit are called *nonprofit* or *not-for-profit* corporations. Private hospitals, educational institutions, charities, and religious organizations, for example, are frequently organized as nonprofit corporations. The nonprofit corporation is a convenient form of organization that allows various groups to own property and to form contracts without exposing the individual members to personal liability.

Close Corporations

Most corporate enterprises in the United States fall into the category of close corporations. A **close corporation** is one whose shares are held by members of a family or by relatively few persons. Close corporations are also referred to as *closely held, family,* or *privately held* corporations. Usually, the members of the small group constituting a close corporation are personally known to one another, and there is no trading market for the shares.

In practice, a close corporation is often operated like a partnership. Some states have enacted special statutory provisions that apply to close corporations. These provisions expressly permit close corporations to depart significantly from certain formalities required by traditional corporation law.[3]

Additionally, the RMBCA gives close corporations a substantial amount of flexibility in determining the rules by which they will operate [RMBCA 7.32]. If all of a corporation's shareholders agree in writing, the corporation can operate without directors, bylaws, annual or special shareholders' or directors' meetings, stock certificates, or formal records of shareholders' or directors' decisions.[4]

Close Corporation A corporation whose shareholders are limited to a small group of persons, often only family members. In a close corporation, the shareholders' rights to transfer shares to others are usually restricted.

Learning Objective 1
What is a close corporation?

---

3. For example, in some states (such as Maryland), a close corporation need not have a board of directors.

4. Shareholders cannot agree, however, to eliminate certain rights of shareholders, such as the right to inspect corporate books and records or the right to bring *derivative* actions (lawsuits on behalf of the corporation—discussed later in this chapter).

Management of Close Corporations A close corporation has a single shareholder or a closely knit group of shareholders, who usually hold the positions of directors and officers. Management of a close corporation resembles that of a sole proprietorship or a partnership. As a corporation, however, the firm must meet all specific legal requirements set forth in state statutes.

To prevent a majority shareholder from dominating a close corporation, the corporation may require that more than a simple majority of the directors approve any action taken by the board. Typically, this would apply only to extraordinary actions, such as changing the amount of dividends or dismissing an employee-shareholder, and not to ordinary business decisions.

Transfer of Shares in Close Corporations By definition, a close corporation has a small number of shareholders. Thus, the transfer of one shareholder's shares to someone else can cause serious management problems. The other shareholders may find themselves required to share control with someone they do not know or like.

EXAMPLE 15.2 Three brothers, Terry, Damon, and Henry Johnson, are the only shareholders of Johnson's Car Wash, Inc. Terry and Damon do not want Henry to sell his shares to an unknown third person. To avoid this situation, the corporation could restrict the transferability of shares to outside persons. Shareholders could be required to offer their shares to the corporation or the other shareholders before selling them to an outside purchaser. •

In fact, a few states have statutes that prohibit the transfer of close corporation shares unless certain persons—including shareholders, family members, and the corporation—are first given the opportunity to purchase the shares for the same price.

Control of a close corporation can also be stabilized through the use of a *shareholder agreement*. A shareholder agreement can provide for proportional control when one of the original shareholders dies. The deceased person's shares of stock in the corporation can be divided in such a way that the proportionate holdings of the survivors, and thus their proportionate control, can be maintained. Courts are generally reluctant to interfere with private agreements, including shareholder agreements.

Misappropriation of Close Corporation Funds Sometimes, a majority shareholder in a close corporation takes advantage of his or her position and misappropriates company funds. In such situations, the normal remedy for the injured minority shareholders is to have their shares appraised and to be paid the fair market value for them.

CASE EXAMPLE 15.3 John Murray, Stephen Hopkins, and Paul Ryan were officers, directors, employees, and majority shareholders of Olympic Adhesives, Inc. Merek Rubin was a minority shareholder. Murray, Hopkins, and Ryan were paid salaries. Twice a year, Murray, Hopkins, and Ryan paid themselves additional compensation—between 75 and 98 percent of Olympic's net profits. Rubin filed a suit against the majority shareholders, alleging that their compensation deprived him of his share of Olympic's profits. The court explained that a salary should reasonably relate to a corporate officer's ability and the quantity and quality of his or her services. Profits resulting from an officer's performance may also affect the amount of compensation. In this case, the court found that a reasonable amount of compensation would have been 10 percent of Olympic's average annual net sales. This was comparable to the average compensation for officers in similar firms.[5] •

S Corporations

A close corporation that meets the qualifying requirements specified in Subchapter S of the Internal Revenue Code can operate as an **S corporation**. If a corporation

S Corporation A close business corporation that has most corporate attributes, including limited liability, but qualifies under the Internal Revenue Code to be taxed as a partnership.

---

5. *Rubin v. Murray*, 79 Mass.App.Ct. 64, 943 N.E.2d 949 (2011).

has S corporation status, it can avoid the imposition of income taxes at the corporate level while retaining many of the advantages of a corporation, particularly limited liability. Among the numerous requirements for S corporation status, the following are the most important:

1. The corporation must be a domestic corporation.
2. The corporation must not be a member of an affiliated group of corporations.
3. The shareholders of the corporation must be individuals, estates, or certain trusts. Partnerships and nonqualifying trusts cannot be shareholders. Corporations can be shareholders under certain circumstances.
4. The corporation must have no more than one hundred shareholders.
5. The corporation must have only one class of stock, although all shareholders do not have to have the same voting rights.
6. No shareholder of the corporation may be a nonresident alien.

An S corporation is treated differently from a regular corporation for tax purposes. An S corporation is taxed like a partnership, so the corporate income passes through to the shareholders, who pay personal income tax on it. This treatment enables the S corporation to avoid the double taxation that is imposed on regular corporations. In addition, the shareholders' tax brackets may be lower than the tax bracket that the corporation would have been in if the tax had been imposed at the corporate level.

This tax saving is particularly attractive when the corporation wants to accumulate earnings for some future business purpose. If the corporation has losses, the S election allows the shareholders to use the losses to offset other taxable income. Nevertheless, because the limited liability company and the limited liability partnership (see Chapter 14) offer similar tax advantages and greater flexibility, the S corporation has lost much of its significance.

Professional Corporations

Professionals such as physicians, lawyers, dentists, and accountants can incorporate. Professional corporations typically are identified by the letters *S.C.* (service corporation), *P.C.* (professional corporation), or *P.A.* (professional association).

In general, the laws governing the formation and operation of professional corporations are similar to those governing ordinary business corporations. There are some differences in terms of liability, however, because the shareholder-owners are professionals who are held to a higher standard of conduct.

For liability purposes, some courts treat a professional corporation somewhat like a partnership and hold each professional liable for any malpractice committed within the scope of the business by the others in the firm. With the exception of malpractice or a breach of duty to clients or patients, a shareholder in a professional corporation generally cannot be held liable for the torts committed by other professionals at the firm.

Benefit Corporations

Benefit Corporation A for-profit corporation that seeks to have a material positive impact on society and the environment. This new business form is available by statute in a growing number of states.

A growing number of states have enacted legislation that creates a new corporate form called a *benefit corporation*. A **benefit corporation** is a for-profit corporation that seeks to have a material positive impact on society and the environment. Benefit corporations differ from traditional corporations in the following three ways:

1. *Purpose.* Although the corporation is designed to make a profit, its purpose is to benefit the public as a whole (rather than just to provide long-term shareholder value, as in ordinary corporations). The directors of a benefit corporation must, during the decision-making process, consider the impact of their decisions on society and the environment.
2. *Accountability.* Shareholders of a benefit corporation determine whether the company has achieved a material positive impact. Shareholders also have a right of private action, called a *benefit enforcement proceeding,* enabling them to sue the corporation if it fails to pursue or create public benefit.

3. *Transparency.* A benefit corporation must issue an annual benefit report on its overall social and environmental performance that uses a recognized third party standard to assess its performance. The report must be delivered to the shareholders and posted on a public Web site.

Formation and Powers

Up to this point, we have discussed some of the general characteristics of corporations. We now examine the process by which corporations come into existence. Incorporating a business is much simpler today than it was twenty years ago, and many states allow businesses to incorporate via the Internet. If the owners of a partnership or sole proprietorship wish to expand the business, they may decide to incorporate because a corporation can obtain more capital by issuing shares of stock.

Promotional Activities

In the past, preliminary steps were taken to organize and promote the business prior to incorporating. Contracts were made with investors and others on behalf of the future corporation. Today, due to the relative ease of forming a corporation in most states, persons incorporating their business rarely, if ever, engage in preliminary promotional activities.

Nevertheless, it is important for businesspersons to understand that they are personally liable for all preincorporation contracts made with investors, accountants, or others on behalf of the future corporation. This personal liability continues until the corporation assumes the preincorporation contracts by *novation* (discussed in Chapter 11).

Incorporation Procedures

Exact procedures for incorporation differ among states, but the basic steps are as follows:

1. Select a state of incorporation.
2. Secure the corporate name by confirming its availability.
3. Prepare the articles of incorporation.
4. File the articles of incorporation with the secretary of state and pay the specified fees.

Select the State of Incorporation The first step in the incorporation process is to select a state in which to incorporate. Because state corporation laws differ, individuals may look for the states that offer the most advantageous tax or other provisions. Another consideration is the fee that a particular state charges to incorporate, as well as the annual fees and the fees for specific transactions (such as stock transfers).

Delaware has historically had the least restrictive laws and provisions that favor corporate management. Consequently, many corporations, including a number of the largest, have incorporated there. Delaware's statutes permit firms to incorporate in that state and conduct business and locate their operating headquarters elsewhere. Most other states now permit this as well. Note, though, that close corporations, for reasons of convenience and cost, generally incorporate in the state where their principal shareholders live and work.

Secure the Corporate Name The choice of a corporate name is subject to state approval to ensure against duplication or deception. State statutes usually require that the secretary of state (or sometimes those incorporating the firm) run a check on the proposed name

> "A man to carry on a successful business must have imagination. He must see things as in a vision, a dream of the whole thing."
>
> Charles M. Schwab, 1862–1939 (American industrialist)

Forming a corporation requires several routine steps.

(spxChrome/iStockphoto.com)

in the state of incorporation. Once cleared, a name can be reserved for a short time, for a fee, pending the completion of the articles of incorporation. All corporate statutes require the corporation name to include the word *Corporation, Incorporated, Company,* or *Limited,* or abbreviations of these terms.

A new corporation's name cannot be the same as (or deceptively similar to) the name of an existing corporation doing business within the state. If those incorporating the firm contemplate doing business in other states or over the Internet, they also need to check on existing corporate names in those states as well. In addition, because the firm will want to use its name as its Internet domain name, the persons incorporating the firm will need to make sure that the domain name is available by checking the database of domain names at the Internet Corporation for Assigned Names and Numbers (ICANN).

EXAMPLE 15.4   If an existing corporation is named Digital Synergy, Inc., the state is unlikely to allow a new corporation to choose the name Digital Synergy Company. That name is deceptively similar to the first and could impliedly transfer part of the goodwill established by the first corporate user to the second corporation, thereby infringing on the first company's intellectual property rights. In addition, the new corporation could not use Digital Synergy Company as a domain name if the existing corporation used Digital Synergy, Inc., as its domain name. •

Prepare the Articles of Incorporation   The primary document needed to incorporate a business is the **articles of incorporation.** The articles include basic information about the corporation and serve as a primary source of authority for its future organization and business functions. The person or persons who execute (sign) the articles are called *incorporators.* Generally, the articles of incorporation *must* include the following information [RMBCA 2.02]:

> **Articles of Incorporation** The document containing basic information about the corporation that is filed with the appropriate governmental agency, usually the secretary of state, when a business is incorporated.

1. The name of the corporation.
2. The number of shares the corporation is authorized to issue. (For instance, a company might state that the aggregate number of shares that the corporation has the authority to issue is five thousand.)
3. The name and address of the corporation's initial *registered agent* (the person designated to receive legal documents on behalf of the corporation).
4. The name and address of each incorporator.

In addition, the articles *may* set forth other information, such as the names and addresses of the initial board of directors, the duration and purpose of the corporation, the par value of the corporation's shares, and other information pertinent to the rights and duties of the corporation's shareholders and directors.

Articles of incorporation vary widely depending on the size and type of corporation and the jurisdiction. Frequently, the articles do not provide much detail about the firm's operations, which are spelled out in the company's **bylaws** (internal rules of management adopted by the corporation at its first organizational meeting).

> **Bylaws** The internal rules of management adopted by a corporation or other association.

Duration and Purpose   A corporation has perpetual existence unless the articles state otherwise. The RMBCA does not require a specific statement of purpose to be included in the articles. A corporation can be formed for any lawful purpose. Some incorporators choose to specify the intended business activities ("to engage in the production and sale of agricultural products," for example). More often, though, the articles state that the corporation is organized for "any legal business," with no mention of specifics, to avoid the need for future amendments to the corporate articles.

Internal Organization   The articles can describe the internal management structure of the corporation, although this is usually included in the bylaws adopted after the corporation is formed. The articles of incorporation commence the corporation, whereas the bylaws are formed after commencement by the board of directors. Bylaws cannot conflict with the corporation statute or the articles of incorporation [RMBCA 2.06].

Under the RMBCA, shareholders may amend or repeal the bylaws. The board of directors may also amend or repeal the bylaws unless the articles of incorporation or provisions of the corporation statute reserve this power to the shareholders exclusively [RMBCA 10.20]. Typical bylaw provisions describe such matters as voting requirements for shareholders, the election of the board of directors, the methods of replacing directors, and the manner and time of holding shareholders' and board meetings. (These corporate activities will be discussed later in this chapter.)

File the Articles with the State   Once the articles of incorporation have been prepared, signed, and authenticated by the incorporators, they are sent to the appropriate state official, usually the secretary of state, along with the required filing fee. In most states, the secretary of state then stamps the articles as "Filed" and returns a copy of the articles to the incorporators. Once this occurs, the corporation officially exists.

First Organizational Meeting to Adopt Bylaws

After incorporation, the first organizational meeting must be held. Usually, the most important function of this meeting is the adoption of bylaws—the internal rules of management for the corporation. If the articles of incorporation named the initial board of directors, then the directors, by majority vote, call the meeting to adopt the bylaws and complete the company's organization. If the articles did not name the directors (as is typical), then the incorporators hold the meeting to elect the directors, adopt bylaws, and complete the routine business of incorporation (authorizing the issuance of shares and hiring employees, for example). The business transacted depends on the requirements of the state's corporation statute, the nature of the corporation, the provisions made in the articles, and the desires of the incorporators.

Improper Incorporation

The procedures for incorporation are very specific. If they are not followed precisely, others may be able to challenge the existence of the corporation. Errors in incorporation procedures can become important when, for example, a third party who is attempting to enforce a contract or bring a suit for a tort injury learns of them.

De Jure and De Facto Corporations   If a corporation has substantially complied with all conditions precedent to incorporation, the corporation is said to have *de jure* (rightful and lawful) existence. In most states and under RMBCA 2.03(b), the secretary of state's filing of the articles of incorporation is conclusive proof that all mandatory statutory provisions have been met [RMBCA 2.03(b)].

Sometimes, the incorporators fail to comply with all statutory mandates. If the defect is minor, such as an incorrect address listed on the articles of incorporation, most courts will overlook the defect and find that a corporation (*de jure*) exists. If the defect is substantial, however, such as a corporation's failure to hold an organizational meeting to adopt bylaws, the outcome will vary depending on the court. Some states, including Mississippi, New York, Ohio, and Oklahoma, still recognize the common law doctrine of *de facto* corporation, under which the corporation's status can be challenged by the state but not by third parties.[6]

---

6. See, for example, *In re Hausman*, 13 N.Y.3d 408, 921 N.E.2d 191, 893 N.Y.S.2d 499 (2009).

Many state courts, however, have interpreted their states' version of the RMBCA as abolishing the common law doctrine of *de facto* corporations. These states include Alaska, Arizona, the District of Columbia, New Mexico, Minnesota, Oregon, South Dakota, Tennessee, Utah, and Washington. In those states, if there is a substantial defect in complying with the incorporation statute, the corporation does not legally exist, and the incorporators are personally liable.

Corporation by Estoppel

If a business holds itself out to others as being a corporation but has made no attempt to incorporate, the firm may be estopped (prevented) from denying corporate status in a lawsuit by a third party. The doctrine of estoppel most commonly applies when a third party contracts with an entity that claims to be a corporation but has not filed articles of incorporation—or contracts with a person claiming to be an agent of a corporation that does not in fact exist.

When justice requires, courts in some states will treat an alleged corporation as if it were an actual corporation for the purpose of determining rights and liabilities in particular circumstances. Recognition of corporate status does not extend beyond the resolution of the problem at hand.

Corporate Financing

Securities Generally, stocks, bonds, and other items that represent an ownership interest in a corporation or a promise of repayment of debt by a corporation.

Stock An ownership (equity) interest in a corporation, measured in units of shares.

Bond A security that evidences a corporate (or government) debt.

Common Stock Shares of ownership in a corporation that give the owner of the stock a proportionate interest in the corporation with regard to control, earnings, and net assets.

Part of the process of corporate formation involves corporate financing. Corporations normally are financed by the issuance and sale of corporate **securities**, which include stocks and bonds. (See the *Online Developments* feature that follows for a discussion of how start-ups can seek financing online.)

Stocks, or *equity securities,* represent the purchase of ownership in the business firm. **Bonds** (debentures), or *debt securities,* represent the borrowing of funds by firms (and governments). Of course, not all debt is in the form of debt securities. For instance, some debt is in the form of accounts payable and notes payable, which typically are short-term debts. Bonds are simply a way for the corporation to split up its long-term debt so that it can be more easily marketed.

Bonds

Bonds are issued by business firms and by governments at all levels as evidence of the funds they are borrowing from investors. Bonds normally have a designated *maturity date*—the date when the principal, or face, amount of the bond is returned to the investor. They are sometimes referred to as *fixed-income securities* because their owners (that is, the creditors) receive fixed-dollar interest payments, usually semiannually, during the period of time before maturity. Because debt financing represents a legal obligation on the part of the corporation, various features and terms of a particular bond issue are specified in a lending agreement.

Today, physical paper shares are giving way to online proof of ownership.

(PhotoDisc)

Stocks

Issuing stocks is another way that corporations can obtain financing. Basically, as mentioned, stocks represent ownership in a business firm. The true ownership of a corporation is represented by **common stock.** Common stock provides a proportionate interest in the corporation with regard to (1) control (voting rights), (2) earnings, and (3) net assets. A shareholder's interest is generally in proportion to the number of shares he or she owns out of the total number of shares issued.

Firms are not obligated to return a principal amount per share to each holder of common stock, because no firm can

ONLINE DEVELOPMENTS

The New Era of Crowdfunding

Every new company needs funds to grow, but banks are generally unwilling to finance a company with prospects but no profits as of yet. Venture capitalists do finance young companies, but there are not enough of them to fund all the companies looking for help. Today, start-ups that are unable to attract venture capitalists have a new way to obtain funding—crowdfunding.

What Is Crowdfunding?

Crowdfunding is a cooperative activity in which people network and pool funds and other resources via the Internet to assist a cause or invest in a venture. Sometimes, crowdfunding is used to raise funds for charitable purposes, such as disaster relief, but increasingly it is being used to finance budding entrepreneurs. Several rock bands have financed tours in this way, and now ventures of all kinds are trying to raise funds through crowdfunding.

Crowdfunding Becomes More Specialized

Over a very short time, crowdfunding Web sites have proliferated. They offer partial ownership of start-ups in exchange for cash investments. At first, there were mostly generalized sites, such as Profounder.com and Startup Addict, but today the sites have become specialized.

If you are interested only in new mobile apps, for example, you can go to the Apps Funder (www.appsfunder.com). As you might imagine, many of the apps are games, but this site also has a more serious side. For instance, one new app that was funded involves sharing music scores. Another site, NewJelly (www.newjelly.com), raises funds for "dream" projects for artists and filmmakers.

Less Regulation Increases Crowdfunding's Appeal

Crowdfunding has taken off in many other countries, including France and Germany. Other countries' investor protection laws and regulations are often less stringent than U.S. laws, so we can expect to see more crowdfunding sites based abroad.

In 2012, President Barack Obama signed the JOBS Act (the acronym stands for "Jump-Start Our Business Start-Ups"), which relieved some of the regulatory burdens of securities laws (see in Chapter 24). Before enactment of this legislation, start-ups could look for financing only from investors who were "accredited," meaning that they had investment experience and a high net worth. If companies sought investment funds from the general public, they had to meet expensive and lengthy disclosure requirements. In 2013, the Securities and Exchange Commission removed the decades-old ban on public solicitation for private investments. In essence, this means that companies finally can advertise investment opportunities to the public, which will encourage growth of crowdfunding. Today, investing in start-ups will be more accessible to non-accredited investors.

Critical Thinking

What risks might be involved in crowdfunding investments?

---

ensure that the market price per share of its common stock will not decline over time. The issuing firm also does not have to guarantee a dividend. Indeed, some corporations never pay dividends. Holders of common stock are investors who assume a *residual* position in the overall financial structure of a business. In terms of receiving payment for their investments, they are last in line.

Preferred stock is stock with *preferences*. Usually, this means that holders of preferred stock have priority over holders of common stock as to dividends and payment on dissolution of the corporation. Holders of preferred stock may or may not have the right to vote. Holders of preferred stock have a stronger position than common shareholders with respect to dividends and claims on assets, but they will not share in the full prosperity of the firm if it grows successfully over time. Preferred stockholders do receive fixed dividends periodically, however, and they may benefit to some extent from changes in the market price of the shares.

Preferred Stock Stock that has priority over common stock as to payment of dividends and distribution of assets on the corporation's dissolution.

Venture Capital

Start-up businesses and high-risk enterprises often obtain venture capital financing. **Venture capital** is capital provided by professional, outside investors (*venture capitalists,* usually groups of wealthy investors and securities firms) to new business ventures. Venture capital investments are high risk—the investors must be willing to lose all of their invested funds—but offer the potential for well-above-average returns at some point in the future.

To obtain venture capital financing, the start-up business typically gives up a share of its ownership to the venture capitalists. In addition to funding, venture capitalists may provide managerial and technical expertise, and they nearly always are given some control over the new company's decisions. Many Internet-based companies, such as Google, were initially financed by venture capital.

Private Equity Capital

Private equity firms obtain their capital from wealthy investors in private markets. The firms use their **private equity capital** to invest in existing—often, publicly traded—corporations. Usually, they buy an entire corporation and then reorganize it. Sometimes, divisions of the purchased company are sold off to pay down debt. Ultimately, the private equity firm may sell shares in the reorganized (and perhaps more profitable) company to the public in an *initial public offering* (usually called an IPO—see Chapter 24). In this way, the private equity firm can make profits by selling its shares in the company to the public.

Corporate Powers

When a corporation is created, the express and implied powers necessary to achieve its purpose also come into existence.

Express Powers

The express powers of a corporation are found in its articles of incorporation, in the law of the state of incorporation, and in the state and federal constitutions. Corporate bylaws also establish the express powers of the corporation. Because state corporation statutes frequently provide default rules that apply if the company's bylaws are silent on an issue, it is important that the bylaws set forth the specific operating rules of the corporation. In addition, after the bylaws are adopted, the corporation's board of directors will pass resolutions that also grant or restrict corporate powers.

The following order of priority is used when conflicts arise among documents involving corporations:

1. The U.S. Constitution.
2. State constitutions.
3. State statutes.
4. The articles of incorporation.
5. Bylaws.
6. Resolutions of the board of directors.

Implied Powers

When a corporation is created, it acquires certain implied powers. Barring express constitutional, statutory, or other prohibitions, the corporation has the implied power to perform all acts reasonably appropriate and necessary to accomplish its corporate purposes. For this reason, a corporation has the implied power to borrow funds within certain limits, to lend funds, and to extend credit to those with whom it has a legal or contractual relationship.

To borrow funds, the corporation acts through its board of directors to authorize the loan. Most often, the president or chief executive officer of the corporation will execute the necessary documents on behalf of the corporation. In so doing, corporate officers have the implied power to bind the corporation in matters directly connected with the *ordinary* business affairs of the enterprise.

There is a limit to what a corporate officer can do, though. A corporate officer does not have the authority to bind the corporation to an action that will greatly affect the corporate purpose or undertaking, such as the sale of substantial corporate assets.

Ultra Vires Doctrine

The term **ultra vires** means "beyond the power." In corporate law, acts of a corporation that are beyond its express or implied powers are *ultra vires* acts.

In the past, most cases dealing with *ultra vires* acts involved contracts made for unauthorized purposes. Now, however, most private corporations are organized for "any legal business" and do not state a specific purpose, so the *ultra vires* doctrine has declined in importance in recent years. Today, cases that allege *ultra vires* acts usually involve nonprofit corporations or municipal (public) corporations.

CASE EXAMPLE 15.5   Four men formed a nonprofit corporation to create the Armenian Genocide Museum & Memorial (AGM&M). The bylaws appointed them as trustees (similar to corporate directors) for life. One of the trustees, Gerard L. Cafesjian, became the chair and president of AGM&M. Eventually, the relationship among the trustees deteriorated, and Cafesjian resigned.

The corporation then brought a suit claiming that Cafesjian had engaged in numerous *ultra vires* acts, self-dealing, and mismanagement. Although the bylaws required an 80 percent affirmative vote of the trustees to take action, Cafesjian had taken many actions without the board's approval. He had also entered into contracts for real estate transactions in which he had a personal interest. Because Cafesjian had taken actions that exceeded his authority and had failed to follow the rules set forth in the bylaws for board meetings, the court ruled that the corporation could go forward with its suit.[7] •

Piercing the Corporate Veil

Occasionally, the owners use a corporate entity to perpetrate a fraud, circumvent the law, or in some other way accomplish an illegitimate objective. In these situations, the court will ignore the corporate structure by **piercing the corporate veil** and exposing the shareholders to personal liability.

Generally, courts pierce the veil when the corporate privilege is abused for personal benefit or when the corporate business is treated so carelessly that it is indistinguishable from the controlling shareholder. In short, when the facts show that great injustice would result from the use of a corporation to avoid individual responsibility, a court will look behind the corporate structure to the individual shareholders.

Factors That Lead Courts to Pierce the Corporate Veil

The following are some of the factors that frequently cause the courts to pierce the corporate veil:

1. A party is tricked or misled into dealing with the corporation rather than the individual.
2. The corporation is set up never to make a profit or always to be insolvent, or it is too "thinly" capitalized—that is, it has insufficient capital at the time of formation to meet its prospective debts or other potential liabilities.

Ultra Vires A Latin term meaning "beyond the powers" that in corporate law, describes acts of management that are beyond the corporation's express and implied powers to undertake.

Piercing the Corporate Veil The action of a court to disregard the corporate entity and hold the shareholders personally liable for corporate debts and obligations.

Learning Objective 2
In what circumstances might a court disregard the corporate entity (pierce the corporate veil) and hold the shareholders personally liable?

---

7. *Armenian Assembly of America, Inc. v. Cafesjian*, 692 F.Supp.2d 20 (D.C. 2010).

Commingle To put funds or goods together into one mass so that they are mixed to such a degree that they no longer have separate identities.

3. The corporation is formed to evade an existing legal obligation.
4. Statutory corporate formalities, such as holding required corporation meetings, are not followed.
5. Personal and corporate interests are **commingled** (mixed together) to such an extent that the corporation has no separate identity.

The court looked for these factors in the circumstances of the following case.

Case 15.2

Dog House Investments, LLC v. Teal Properties, Inc.
Court of Appeals of Tennessee, ___ S.E.3d ___, 2014 WL 539530 (2014).

If leased property for dog kennels is flooded, what is the landlord's responsibility?

BACKGROUND AND FACTS Dog House Investments, LLC, operated a dog "camp" on property in Nashville, Tennessee, leased from Teal Properties, Inc., which was owned by Jerry Teal, its sole shareholder. Under the lease, the landlord promised to repair damage from fire or "other causes" that rendered the property "untenantable." Following a flood, Dog House notified Jerry that the property was "untenantable." Jerry assured Dog House that the flood damage was covered by insurance but took no steps to restore the property. The parties then agreed that Dog House would undertake the repairs and be reimbursed by Teal Properties.

Dog House spent $39,000 to repair the damage and submitted invoices for reimbursement. Teal Properties recovered $40,000 from its insurance company but did not pay Dog House. Close to bankruptcy, Dog House filed a suit in a Tennessee state court against Teal Properties and its owner. The court held Jerry personally liable for the repair costs. Jerry appealed.

IN THE WORDS OF THE COURT . . .
David R. FARMER, J. [Judge]
 * * * *

It is well-settled that courts may pierce the corporate veil and attribute the actions of a corporation to its shareholders when appropriate. *A party seeking to pierce the corporate veil bears the burden of demonstrating that the separate corporate entity is a sham or dummy or that disregarding the separate corporate entity is necessary to accomplish justice.* When determining whether piercing the corporate veil is appropriate, the court must consider whether the corporate entity has been used to work a fraud or injustice in contravention of public policy and also: [Emphasis added.]

(1) whether there was a failure to collect paid-in capital; (2) whether the corporation was grossly undercapitalized; (3) the nonissuance of stock certificates; (4) the sole ownership of stock by one individual; (5) the use of the same office or business location; (6) the employment of the same employees or attorneys; (7) the use of the corporation as an instrumentality or business conduit for an individual or another corporation; (8) the diversion of corporate assets by or to a stockholder or other entity to the detriment of creditors, or the manipulation of assets and liabilities in another; (9) the use of the corporation as a subterfuge in illegal transactions; (10) the formation and use of the corporation to transfer to it the existing liability of another person or entity; and (11) the failure to maintain arms length relationships among related entities.

No single factor is conclusive and not every factor must exist to pierce the corporate veil. The question depends on the specific facts and circumstances of the case. The equities, however, must substantially favor the party requesting the court to disregard the corporate status. The presumption of the corporation's separate identity should be set aside only with great caution and not precipitately [rashly].

In this case, Mr. Teal denied personal liability but admitted * * * that he owned the property leased by Dog House in Nashville. The trial court found that Teal Properties owns no property, has no assets, and has no cash except that which is deposited by Mr. Jerry Teal when he has the opportunity to do so; that Teal Properties receives rents and immediately pays it out to pay Mr. Teal's financial obligations; that Mr. Teal is the sole stockholder of Teal Properties and owns the corporation; and that Teal Properties has no purpose other than to collect the rent on properties owned by Mr. Teal. The trial court also found that Mr. Teal does not receive a salary from Teal Properties but utilizes its assets, including the flood insurance proceeds at issue in this case, to pay Mr. Teal's personal expenses and his personal obligations. The trial court found that Mr. Teal did not maintain an arms-length relationship with the corporation, and that it was, in fact, his alter ego. Mr. Teal does not dispute these findings * * * , but asserts that "there is no proof that Teal Properties is a sham or dummy corporation * * * ." We discern no error on the part of the trial court and affirm on this issue.

Case 15.2—Continued

DECISION AND REMEDY A state intermediate appellate court affirmed the lower court's decision. Teal Properties owned no property and had no assets. It received rent, but paid it immediately to Jerry Teal. "Mr. Teal did not maintain an arms-length relationship with the corporation, and that it was, in fact, his alter ego."

THE LEGAL ENVIRONMENT DIMENSION The trial court concluded, and the appellate court affirmed, that Teal Properties

had breached its contract with Dog House. What was the contract? How was it breached?

THE ETHICAL DIMENSION The failure of Teal Properties and Jerry Teal to reimburse Dog House for the repair costs placed the tenant in a dire financial situation. Does this consequence make the landlord's conduct unethical? Discuss.

A Potential Problem for Close Corporations

The potential for corporate assets to be used for personal benefit is especially great in a close corporation, in which the shares are held by a single person or by only a few individuals, usually family members. In such a situation, the separate status of the corporate entity and the sole shareholder (or family-member shareholders) must be carefully preserved. Certain practices invite trouble for the one-person or family-owned corporation, such as the commingling of corporate and personal funds or the shareholders' continuous personal use of corporate property (for example, vehicles).

Directors and Officers

Corporate directors, officers, and shareholders all play different roles within the corporate entity. Sometimes, actions that may benefit the corporation as a whole do not coincide with the separate interests of the individuals making up the corporation. In such situations, it is important to know the rights and duties of all participants in the corporate enterprise.

Directors

The board of directors is the ultimate authority in every corporation. Directors have responsibility for all policymaking decisions necessary to the management of all corporate affairs. The board selects and removes the corporate officers, determines the capital structure of the corporation, and declares dividends. Each director has one vote, and customarily the majority rules. The general areas of responsibility of the board of directors are shown in Exhibit 15–1 that follows.

Directors are sometimes inappropriately characterized as *agents,* (see Chapter 16) because they act on behalf of the corporation. No *individual* director, however, can act as an agent to bind the corporation. As a group, directors collectively control the corporation in a way that no agent is able to control a principal.

Few qualifications are legally required for directors. Only a handful of states impose minimum age and residency requirements. A director may be a shareholder, but this is not necessary (unless the articles of incorporation or bylaws require ownership).

Election of Directors Subject to statutory limitations, the number of directors is set forth in the corporation's articles or bylaws. Historically, the minimum number of directors has been three, but today many states permit fewer. Normally, the incorporators appoint the first board of directors at the time the corporation is created. The initial board

Are directors of a corporation agents of that corporation? Why or why not?

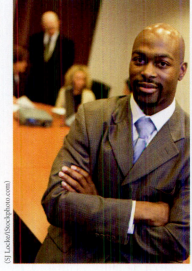

(SI Locke/iStockphoto.com)

Exhibit 15–1 Directors' Management Responsibilities

AUTHORIZE MAJOR CORPORATE POLICY DECISIONS	SELECT AND REMOVE CORPORATE OFFICERS AND OTHER MANAGERIAL EMPLOYEES, AND DETERMINE THEIR COMPENSATION	MAKE FINANCIAL DECISIONS
Examples: • Oversee major contract negotiations and management-labor negotiations. • Initiate negotiations on the sale or lease of corporate assets outside the regular course of business. • Decide whether to pursue new product lines or business opportunities.	*Examples:* • Search for and hire corporate executives and determine the elements of their compensation packages, including stock options. • Supervise managerial employees and make decisions regarding their termination.	*Examples:* • Make decisions regarding the issuance of authorized shares and bonds. • Decide when to declare dividends to be paid to shareholders.

serves until the first annual shareholders' meeting. Subsequent directors are elected by a majority vote of the shareholders.

A director usually serves for a term of one year—from annual meeting to annual meeting. Most state statutes permit longer and staggered terms. A common practice is to elect one-third of the board members each year for a three-year term. In this way, there is greater management continuity.

A director can be removed *for cause*—that is, for failing to perform a required duty—either as specified in the articles or bylaws or by shareholder action. If a director dies or resigns or if a new position is created through amendment of the articles or bylaws, either the shareholders or the board itself can fill the vacant position, depending on state law or the provisions of the bylaws.

Compensation of Directors

In the past, corporate directors rarely were compensated. Today, they are often paid at least nominal sums and may receive more substantial compensation in large corporations because of the time, work, effort, and especially risk involved. Most states permit the corporate articles or bylaws to authorize compensation for directors. In fact, the RMBCA states that unless the articles or bylaws provide otherwise, the directors may set their own compensation [RMBCA 8.11].

In many corporations, directors are also chief corporate officers (president or chief executive officer, for example) and receive compensation in their managerial positions. A director who is also an officer of the corporation is referred to as an **inside director,** whereas a director who does not hold a management position is an **outside director.** Typically, a corporation's board of directors includes both inside and outside directors.

Inside Director A member of the board of directors who is also an officer of the corporation.

Outside Director A member of the board of directors who does not hold a management position at the corporation.

Board of Directors' Meetings

The board of directors conducts business by holding formal meetings with recorded minutes. The dates of regular meetings are usually established in the articles or bylaws or by board resolution, and ordinarily no further notice is required.

Special meetings can be called, with notice sent to all directors. Most states allow directors to participate in board of directors' meetings from remote locations via telephone, Web conferencing, or Skype, provided that all the directors can simultaneously hear each other during the meeting [RMBCA 8.20].

Normally, a majority of the board of directors must be present to constitute a quorum [RMBCA 8.24]. (A **quorum** is the minimum number of members of a body of officials or other group that must be present in order for business to be validly transacted.) Some state

Quorum The number of members of a decision-making body that must be present before business may be transacted.

statutes specifically allow corporations to set a quorum as less than a majority but not less than one-third of the directors.[8]

Once a quorum is present, the directors transact business and vote on issues affecting the corporation. Each director present at the meeting has one vote.[9] Ordinary matters generally require a simple majority vote, but certain extraordinary issues may require a greater-than-majority vote.

Committees of the Board of Directors

When a board of directors has a large number of members and must deal with myriad complex business issues, meetings can become unwieldy. Therefore, the boards of large, publicly held corporations typically create committees, appoint directors to serve on individual committees, and delegate certain tasks to these committees. Committees focus on individual subjects and increase the efficiency of the board.

Two of the most common types of committees are the *executive committee* and the *audit committee*. An executive committee handles interim management decisions between board meetings. It is limited to making decisions about ordinary business matters, though, and does not have the power to declare dividends, amend the bylaws, or authorize the issuance of stock. The Sarbanes Oxley Act of 2002 requires all publicly held corporations to have an audit committee. The audit committee is responsible for the selection, compensation, and oversight of the independent public accountants that audit the firm's financial records.

Rights of Directors

A corporate director must have certain rights to function properly in that position and make informed policy decisions for the company. The *right to participation* means that directors are entitled to participate in all board of directors' meetings and have a right to be notified of these meetings. Because the dates of regular board meetings are usually specified in the bylaws, as noted earlier, no notice of these meetings is required. If special meetings are called, however, notice is required unless waived by the director.

A director also has the *right of inspection*, which means that each director can access the corporation's books and records, facilities, and premises. Inspection rights are essential for directors to make informed decisions and to exercise the necessary supervision over corporate officers and employees. This right of inspection is almost absolute and cannot be restricted (by the articles, bylaws, or any act of the board).

When a director becomes involved in litigation by virtue of her or his position or actions, the director may also have a *right to indemnification* (reimbursement) for legal costs, fees, and damages incurred. Most states allow corporations to indemnify and purchase liability insurance for corporate directors [RMBCA 8.51].

Whenever businesspersons serve as corporate directors or officers, they may at some point become involved in litigation as a result of their positions. To protect against personal liability, directors or officers should take several steps. First, they should make sure that the corporate bylaws explicitly give them a right to indemnification (reimbursement) for any costs incurred as a result of litigation, as well as any judgments or settlements stemming from a lawsuit. Second, they should have the corporation purchase directors' and officers' liability insurance (D&O insurance). Having D&O insurance policies enables the corporation to avoid paying the substantial costs involved in defending a particular director or officer.

PREVENTING LEGAL DISPUTES

> "I often feel like the director of a cemetery. I have a lot of people under me, but nobody listens!"
>
> General James Gavin, 1907–1990
> (U.S. Army lieutenant general)

---

8. See, for example, Delaware Code Annotated Title 8, Section 141(b), and New York Business Corporation Law Section 707, which both allow corporations to set a quorum at less than a majority.

9. Except in Louisiana, which allows a director to authorize another person to cast a vote in his or her place under certain circumstances.

Corporate Officers and Executives

Corporate officers and other executive employees are hired by the board of directors. At a minimum, most corporations have a president, one or more vice presidents, a secretary, and a treasurer. In most states, an individual can hold more than one office, such as president and secretary, and can be both an officer and a director of the corporation. In addition to carrying out the duties articulated in the bylaws, corporate and managerial officers act as agents of the corporation, and the ordinary rules of agency (discussed in Chapter 16) normally apply to their employment.

Corporate officers and other high-level managers are employees of the company, so their rights are defined by employment contracts. The board of directors normally can remove corporate officers at any time with or without cause and regardless of the terms of the employment contracts—although in so doing, the corporation may be liable for breach of contract.

The duties of corporate officers are similar to those of directors because both groups are involved in decision making and are in similar positions of control. We discuss those duties next.

Learning Objective 3
What are the duties of corporate directors and officers?

Duties and Liabilities of Directors and Officers

Directors and officers are deemed fiduciaries of the corporation because their relationship with the corporation and its shareholders is one of trust and confidence. As fiduciaries, directors and officers owe ethical—and legal—duties to the corporation and to the shareholders as a whole. These fiduciary duties include the duty of care and the duty of loyalty. (Directors and officers also have a duty not to destroy evidence in the event of a lawsuit involving the corporation.)

Duty of Care
Directors and officers must exercise due care in performing their duties. The standard of *due care* has been variously described in judicial decisions and codified in many state corporation codes. Generally, a director or officer is expected to act in good faith, to exercise the care that an ordinarily prudent person would exercise in similar circumstances, and to act in what he or she considers to be the best interests of the corporation [RMBCA 8.30].

Directors and officers whose failure to exercise due care results in harm to the corporation or its shareholders can be held liable for negligence (unless the *business judgment rule* applies, as will be discussed shortly). The prospect of liability may be one reason why corporate officers are using special software to help identify employees who might commit embezzlement. (See this chapter's *Insight into Ethics* feature that follows for a discussion of this topic.)

Duty to Make Informed and Reasonable Decisions   Directors and officers are expected to be informed on corporate matters and to conduct a reasonable investigation of the situation before making a decision. This means that they must do what is necessary to keep adequately informed: attend meetings and presentations, ask for information from those who have it, read reports, and review other written materials. In other words, directors and officers must investigate, study, and discuss matters and evaluate alternatives before making a decision. They cannot decide on the spur of the moment without adequate research.

Who hires corporate personnel?

(Bowden Images/iStockphoto.com)

INSIGHT INTO ETHICS

SOFTWARE TO HELP OFFICERS SPOT POTENTIAL EMBEZZLERS

Every year, dishonest employees embezzle millions of dollars from corporations around the world, and those funds are rarely recovered. Consequently, corporate officers are always looking for ways to prevent embezzlement. The typical way to "catch a thief" is to hire an accountant to look for anomalies in the firm's financial records. An alternative is to use linguistic software.

Linguistic Software Looks for Future Embezzlers

Accountants can detect embezzlers only after the crime, but linguistic software looks for employees who may become embezzlers in the future. The software scans e-mails for signs that employees are having financial troubles and thus might be prone to embezzlement. For example, if the software suddenly finds the phrase "under the gun" and similar phrases in a rash of e-mails sent by an employee, a red flag is raised.

The software also looks for signs that employees are unhappy in their jobs, such as e-mails with numerous references to the "evil" or "immoral" corporation. Another red flag is raised if an employee sends many messages asking the recipients to "call my cell phone," or to "come by my office." Such messages suggest that the employee wants to communicate without the call being recorded or without leaving a written record.

Insider Traders Can Be Detected, Too

Financial firms also have to be concerned that brokers might be obtaining inside information and using it for their own benefit. Financial Tracking Technologies developed a software program that combs through employees' calendars and travel expense claims. The goal is to find out which employees have come into contact with certain outside investors.

For Critical Analysis
Insight into the Legal Environment

Does a corporation's use of linguistic software to scan through its employees' electronic communications violate the employees' privacy? Why or why not? (Hint: Recall the discussion of the Electronic Communications Privacy Act in Chapter 9.)

Although directors and officers are expected to act in accordance with their own knowledge and training, they are also normally entitled to rely on information given to them by certain other persons. Most states and Section 8.30(b) of the RMBCA allow a director to make decisions in reliance on information furnished by competent officers or employees, professionals such as attorneys and accountants, and committees of the board of directors (on which the director does not serve). The reliance must be in good faith, of course, to insulate a director from liability if the information later proves to be inaccurate or unreliable.

Duty to Exercise Reasonable Supervision Directors are also expected to exercise a reasonable amount of supervision when they delegate work to corporate officers and employees. **EXAMPLE 15.6** Dale, a corporate bank director, fails to attend any board of directors' meetings for five years. In addition, Dale never inspects any of the corporate books or records and generally fails to supervise the efforts of the bank president and the loan committee. Meanwhile, Brennan, the bank president, who is a corporate officer, makes various improper loans and permits large overdrafts. In this situation, Dale (the corporate director) can be held liable to the corporation for losses resulting from the unsupervised actions of the bank president and the loan committee. ●

The Business Judgment Rule Directors and officers are expected to exercise due care and to use their best judgment in guiding corporate management, but they are not insurers of business success. Under the **business judgment rule**, a corporate

> "Executive ability is deciding quickly and getting somebody else to do the work."
>
> J. C. Pollard, 1946–present (British businessman)

Business Judgment Rule A rule that immunizes corporate management from liability for decisions that result in corporate losses or damages if the decision-makers took reasonable steps to become informed, had a rational basis for their decisions, and did not have a contract of interest with the corporation.

Learning Objective 4
Directors are expected to use their best judgment in managing the corporation. What must directors do to avoid liability for honest mistakes of judgment and poor business decisions?

director or officer will not be liable to the corporation or to its shareholders for honest mistakes of judgment and bad business decisions.

Courts give significant deference to the decisions of corporate directors and officers, and consider the reasonableness of a decision at the time it was made, without the benefit of hindsight. Thus, corporate decision makers are not subjected to second-guessing by shareholders or others in the corporation. The business judgment rule will apply as long as the director or officer:

1. Took reasonable steps to become informed about the matter.
2. Had a rational basis for his or her decision.
3. Did not have a conflict of interest between his or her personal interest and that of the corporation.

In fact, unless there is evidence of bad faith, fraud, or a clear breach of fiduciary duties, most courts will apply the rule and protect directors and officers who make bad business decisions from liability for those choices. Consequently, if there is a reasonable basis for a business decision, a court is unlikely to interfere with that decision, even if the corporation suffers as a result.

The business judgment rule does not apply when a director engages in fraud, dishonesty, or other intentional or reckless misconduct. **CASE EXAMPLE 15.7**   The board of directors of the Chugach Alaska Corporation (CAC) voted to remove Sheri Buretta as the chair and install Robert Henrichs. During his term, Henrichs acted without board approval, made decisions with only his supporters present, retaliated against directors who challenged his decisions, and ignored board rules for conducting meetings. Henrichs refused to comply with bylaws that required a special shareholders' meeting in response to a shareholder petition and personally mistreated directors, shareholders, and employees. After six months, the board voted to reinstall Buretta.

CAC filed a suit in an Alaska state court against Henrichs, alleging a breach of fiduciary duty. A jury found Henrichs liable, and the court barred him from serving on CAC's board for five years. The appellate court affirmed. Given the nature and seriousness of Henrichs's misconduct, the business judgment rule did not protect him.[10] ●

Duty of Loyalty   *Loyalty* can be defined as faithfulness to one's obligations and duties. In the corporate context, the duty of loyalty requires directors and officers to subordinate their personal interests to the welfare of the corporation. Directors cannot use corporate funds or confidential corporate information for personal advantage and must refrain from self-dealing.

For instance, a director should not oppose a transaction that is in the corporation's best interest simply because its acceptance may cost the director her or his position. Cases dealing with the duty of loyalty typically involve one or more of the following:

1. Competing with the corporation.
2. Usurping (taking advantage of) a corporate opportunity.
3. Having an interest that conflicts with the interest of the corporation.
4. Using information that is not available to the public to make a profit trading securities (*insider trading* will be discussed in Chapter 24).
5. Authorizing a corporate transaction that is detrimental to minority shareholders.
6. Selling control over the corporation.

The following classic case illustrates the conflict that can arise between a corporate official's personal interest and his or her duty of loyalty.

---

10. *Henrichs v. Chugach Alaska Corp.*, 250 P.3d 531 (Alaska Sup.Ct. 2011).

Classic Case 15.3

Guth v. Loft, Inc.
Supreme Court of Delaware, 23 Del.Ch. 255, 5 A.2d 503 (1939).

Pepsi-Cola got its start when the head of Loft Candy Company usurped a corporate opportunity.

(BrooklynScribe/Shutterstock.com)

BACKGROUND AND FACTS Loft, Inc., made and sold candies, syrups, beverages, and food from its offices and plant in Long Island City, New York. Loft operated 115 retail outlets in several states and also sold its products wholesale. Charles Guth was Loft's president. Guth and his family owned Grace Company, which made syrups for soft drinks in a plant in Baltimore, Maryland. Coca-Cola Company supplied Loft with cola syrup. Unhappy with what he felt was Coca-Cola's high price, Guth entered into an agreement with Roy Megargel to acquire the trademark and formula for Pepsi-Cola and form Pepsi-Cola Corporation. Neither Guth nor Megargel could finance the new venture, however, and Grace was insolvent. Without the knowledge of Loft's board, Guth used Loft's capital, credit, facilities, and employees to further the Pepsi enterprise. At Guth's direction, Loft made the concentrate for the syrup, which was sent to Grace to add sugar and water. Loft charged Grace for the concentrate but allowed forty months' credit. Grace charged Pepsi for the syrup but also granted substantial credit. Grace sold the syrup to Pepsi's customers, including Loft, which paid on delivery or within thirty days. Loft also paid for Pepsi's advertising. Finally, losing profits at its stores as a result of switching from Coca-Cola, Loft filed a suit in a Delaware state court against Guth, Grace, and Pepsi, seeking their Pepsi stock and an accounting. The court entered a judgment in the plaintiff's favor. The defendants appealed to the Delaware Supreme Court.

IN THE WORDS OF THE COURT . . .
LAYTON, Chief Justice, delivering the opinion of the court:
  * * * *

  Corporate officers and directors are not permitted to use their position of trust and confidence to further their private interests. * * * They stand in a fiduciary relation to the corporation and its stockholders. A public policy, existing through the years, and derived from a profound knowledge of human characteristics and motives, has established *a rule that demands of a corporate officer or director, peremptorily [not open for debate] and inexorably [unavoidably], the most scrupulous observance of his duty, not only affirmatively to protect the interests of the corporation committed to his charge, but also to refrain from doing anything that would work injury to the corporation* * * * . The rule that requires an undivided and unselfish loyalty to the corporation demands that there shall be no conflict between duty and self-interest. [Emphasis added.]
  * * * *

  * * * *If there is presented to a corporate officer or director a business opportunity which the corporation is financially able to undertake [that] is* * * * *in the line of the corporation's business and is of practical advantage to it* * * * *and, by embracing the opportunity, the self-interest of the officer or director will be brought into conflict with that of his corporation, the law will not permit him to seize the opportunity for himself.* * * * In such circumstances, * * * the corporation may elect to claim all of the benefits of the transaction for itself, and the law will impress a trust in favor of the corporation upon the property, interests and profits so acquired. [Emphasis added.]
  * * * *

  * * * The appellants contend that no conflict of interest between Guth and Loft resulted from his acquirement and exploitation of the Pepsi-Cola opportunity [and] that the acquisition did not place Guth in competition with Loft * * * . [In this case, however,] Guth was Loft, and Guth was Pepsi. He absolutely controlled Loft. His authority over Pepsi was supreme. As Pepsi, he created and controlled the supply of Pepsi-Cola syrup, and he determined the price and the terms. What he offered, as Pepsi, he had the power, as Loft, to accept. Upon any consideration of human characteristics and motives, he created a conflict between self-interest and duty. He made himself the judge in his own cause. * * * Moreover, a reasonable probability of injury to Loft resulted from the situation forced upon it. Guth was in the same position to impose his terms upon Loft as had been the Coca-Cola Company.

  * * * The facts and circumstances demonstrate that Guth's appropriation of the Pepsi-Cola opportunity to himself placed him in a competitive position with Loft with respect to a commodity essential to it, thereby rendering his personal interests incompatible with the superior interests of his corporation; and this situation was accomplished, not openly and with his own resources, but secretly and with the money and facilities of the corporation which was committed to his protection.

DECISION AND REMEDY The Delaware Supreme Court upheld the judgment of the lower court. The state supreme court was "convinced that the opportunity to acquire the Pepsi-Cola trademark and formula, goodwill and business belonged to [Loft], and that Guth, as its President, had no right to appropriate the opportunity to himself."

WHAT IF THE FACTS WERE DIFFERENT? Suppose that Loft's board of directors had approved Pepsi-Cola's use of the

Classic Case 15.3—Continues ➡

Classic Case 15.3—Continued

company's personnel and equipment. Would the court's decision have been different? Discuss.

IMPACT OF THIS CASE ON TODAY'S LEGAL ENVIRONMENT
This early Delaware decision was one of the first to set forth a test for determining when a corporate officer or director has breached the duty of loyalty. The test has two basic parts—whether the opportunity was reasonably related to the corporation's line of business, and whether the corporation was financially able to undertake the opportunity. The court also considered whether the corporation had an interest or expectancy in the opportunity and recognized that when the corporation had "no interest or expectancy, the officer or director is entitled to treat the opportunity as his own."

Conflicts of Interest   Corporate directors often have many business affiliations, and a director may sit on the board of more than one corporation. Of course, directors are precluded from entering into or supporting businesses that operate in direct competition with corporations on whose boards they serve. Their fiduciary duty requires them to make a full disclosure of any potential conflicts of interest that might arise in any corporate transaction [RMBCA 8.60].

Sometimes, a corporation enters into a contract or engages in a transaction in which an officer or director has a personal interest. The director or officer must make a *full disclosure* of that interest and must abstain from voting on the proposed transaction.

EXAMPLE 15.8   Southwood Corporation needs office space. Lambert Alden, one of its five directors, owns the building adjoining the corporation's main office building. He negotiates a lease with Southwood for the space, making a full disclosure to Southwood and the other four board directors. The lease arrangement is fair and reasonable, and it is unanimously approved by the other four directors. In this situation, Alden has not breached his duty of loyalty to the corporation, and thus the contract is valid. If it were otherwise, directors would be prevented from ever transacting business with the corporations they serve. •

"If it is not in the interest of the public, it is not in the interest of the business."

Joseph H. Defrees, 1812–1885
(U.S. congressman)

Shareholders

The acquisition of a share of stock makes a person an owner and shareholder in a corporation. Thus, shareholders own the corporation. Although they have no legal title to corporate property, such as buildings and equipment, they do have an equitable (ownership) interest in the firm.

As a general rule, shareholders have no responsibility for the daily management of the corporation, even if they are ultimately responsible for choosing the board of directors, which does have such control. Ordinarily, corporate officers and directors owe no duty to individual shareholders unless some contract or special relationship exists between them in addition to the corporate relationship. Their duty is to act in the best interests of the corporation and its shareholder-owners as a whole. In turn, as you will read later in this chapter, controlling shareholders owe a fiduciary duty to minority shareholders.

Shareholders' Powers

Shareholders must approve fundamental changes affecting the corporation before the changes can be implemented. Hence, shareholders are empowered to amend the articles of incorporation (charter) and bylaws, approve a merger or the dissolution of the corporation, and approve the sale of all or substantially all of the corporation's assets. Some of these powers are subject to prior board approval.

Members of the board of directors are elected and removed by a vote of the shareholders. The first board of directors is either named in the articles of incorporation or chosen by the incorporators to serve until the first shareholders' meeting. From that time on, the selection and retention of directors are exclusively shareholder functions.

Directors usually serve their full terms. If the shareholders judge them unsatisfactory, they are simply not reelected. Shareholders have the inherent power, however, to remove a director from office *for cause* (such as for breach of duty or misconduct) by a majority vote.[11] As mentioned earlier, some state statutes (and some corporate articles) permit removal of directors without cause by the vote of a majority of the holders of outstanding shares entitled to vote.

Shareholders' Meetings

Shareholders' meetings must occur at least annually. In addition, special meetings can be called to deal with urgent matters. A corporation must notify its shareholders of the date, time, and place of an annual or special shareholders' meeting at least ten days, but not more than sixty days, before the meeting date [RMBCA 7.05].[12] Notice of a special meeting must include a statement of the purpose of the meeting, and business transacted at the meeting is limited to that purpose.

(Rob Carr, File/AP Images)

Can nonshareholders speak at shareholder meetings?

Proxies   It is usually not practical for owners of only a few shares of stock of publicly traded corporations to attend shareholders' meetings. Therefore, the law allows stockholders to either vote in person or appoint another person as their agent to vote their shares at the meeting. The signed appointment form or electronic transmission authorizing an agent to vote the shares is called a **proxy** (from the Latin *procurare*, meaning "to manage, take care of").

Management often solicits proxies, but any person can solicit proxies to concentrate voting power. Proxies have been used by a group of shareholders as a device for taking over a corporation. Proxies normally are revocable (that is, they can be withdrawn), unless they are specifically designated as irrevocable. Under RMBCA 7.22(c), proxies last for eleven months, unless the proxy agreement provides for a longer period.

Proxy In corporate law, a written or electronically transmitted form in which a stockholder authorizes another party to vote the stockholder's shares in a certain manner.

Shareholder Proposals   When shareholders want to change a company policy, they can put their idea up for a shareholder vote. They can do this by submitting a shareholder proposal to the board of directors and asking the board to include the proposal in the proxy materials that are sent to all shareholders before meetings.

The Securities and Exchange Commission (SEC), which regulates the purchase and sale of securities (see Chapter 24), has special provisions relating to proxies and shareholder proposals. SEC Rule 14a-8 provides that all shareholders who own stock worth at least $1,000 are eligible to submit proposals for inclusion in corporate proxy materials. The corporation is required to include information on whatever proposals will be considered at the shareholders' meeting along with proxy materials.

Under the SEC's e-proxy rules,[13] all public companies must post their proxy materials on the Internet and notify shareholders how to find that information. Although the law

Learning Objective 5
What is a voting proxy? What is cumulative voting?

---

11. A director can often demand court review of removal for cause.
12. A shareholder can waive the requirement of written notice by signing a waiver form or, in some states, by attending the meeting without protesting the lack of written notice.
13. 17 C.F.R. Parts 240, 249, and 274.

requires proxy materials to be posted online, public companies may still choose among several options—including paper documents or a DVD sent by mail—for actually delivering the materials to shareholders.

Shareholder Voting
Shareholders exercise ownership control through the power of their votes. Corporate business matters are presented in the form of *resolutions,* which shareholders vote to approve or disapprove. Each shareholder is entitled to one vote per share of stock, although the articles of incorporation can exclude or limit voting rights, particularly for certain classes of shares. If a state statute requires specific voting procedures, the corporation's articles or bylaws must be consistent with the statute.

For shareholders to conduct business at a meeting, a quorum must be present. Generally, a quorum exists when shareholders holding more than 50 percent of the outstanding shares are present. In some states, obtaining the unanimous written consent of shareholders is a permissible alternative to holding a shareholders' meeting [RMBCA 7.25].

Once a quorum is present, voting can proceed. A majority vote of the shares represented at the meeting usually is required to pass resolutions. **EXAMPLE 15.9** Novo Pictures, Inc., has 10,000 outstanding shares of voting stock. Its articles of incorporation set the quorum at 50 percent of outstanding shares and provide that a majority vote of the shares present is necessary to pass resolutions concerning ordinary matters. Therefore, for this firm, a quorum of shareholders representing 5,000 outstanding shares must be present at a shareholders' meeting to conduct business. If exactly 5,000 shares are represented at the meeting, a vote of at least 2,501 of those shares is needed to pass a resolution. If 6,000 shares are represented, a vote of 3,001 is required. •

At times, more than a simple majority vote is required either by a state statute or by the corporate articles. Extraordinary corporate matters, such as a merger, consolidation, or dissolution of the corporation, require a higher percentage of all corporate shares entitled to vote [RMBCA 7.27].

Voting Lists
The corporation prepares the voting list prior to each meeting of the shareholders. Ordinarily, only persons whose names appear on the corporation's shareholder records as owners are entitled to vote. The voting list contains the name and address of each shareholder as shown on the corporate records on a given cutoff date, or *record date.* (Under RMBCA 7.07, the record date may be as much as seventy days before the meeting.) The voting list also includes the number of voting shares held by each owner. The list is usually kept at the corporate headquarters and is available for shareholder inspection [RMBCA 7.20].

Cumulative Voting
Most states permit, and many require, shareholders to elect directors by *cumulative voting,* which is a voting method designed to allow minority shareholders to be represented on the board of directors.

With cumulative voting, each shareholder is entitled to a total number of votes equal to the number of board members to be elected multiplied by the number of voting shares a shareholder owns. The shareholder can cast all of these votes for one candidate or split them among several nominees for director. All nominees stand for election at the same time. (When cumulative voting is not required either by statute or under the articles, the entire board can be elected by a simple majority of shares at a shareholders' meeting.)

Cumulative voting can best be understood through an example. **EXAMPLE 15.10** A corporation has 10,000 shares issued and outstanding. The minority shareholders hold 3,000 shares, and the majority shareholders hold the other 7,000 shares. Three members of the board are to be elected. The majority shareholders' nominees are Acevedo, Barkley, and Craycik. The minority shareholders' nominee is Drake. Can Drake be elected by the minority shareholders?

If cumulative voting is allowed, the answer is yes. Together, the minority shareholders have 9,000 votes (the number of directors to be elected times the number of shares held by the minority shareholders equals 3 times 3,000, which equals 9,000 votes). All of these votes can be cast to elect Drake. The majority shareholders have 21,000 votes (3 times 7,000 equals 21,000 votes), but these votes have to be distributed among their three nominees. The principle of cumulative voting is that no matter how the majority shareholders cast their 21,000 votes, they will not be able to elect all three directors if the minority shareholders cast all of their 9,000 votes for Drake, as illustrated in Exhibit 15–2 that follows. ●

Other Voting Techniques

Before a shareholders' meeting, a group of shareholders can agree in writing to vote their shares together in a specified manner. Such agreements, called *shareholder voting agreements,* usually are held to be valid and enforceable. A shareholder can also appoint a voting agent and vote by proxy.

Rights of Shareholders

Shareholders possess numerous rights. A significant right—the right to vote their shares—has already been discussed. We now look at some additional rights of shareholders.

Stock Certificates

In the past, corporations typically issued a **stock certificate** that evidenced ownership of a specified number of shares in the corporation. Only a few jurisdictions still require physical stock certificates, and shareholders there have the right to demand that the corporation issue certificates (or replace those that were lost or destroyed). Stock is intangible personal property, however, and the ownership right exists independently of the certificate itself.

In most states and under RMBCA 6.26, boards of directors may provide that shares of stock will be uncertificated, or "paperless"—that is, no actual, physical stock certificates will be issued. When shares are uncertificated, the corporation may be required to send each shareholder a letter or some other form of notice that contains the same information that traditionally appeared on the face of stock certificates. Notice of shareholders' meetings, dividends, and operational and financial reports are all distributed according to the recorded ownership listed in the corporation's books.

Stock Certificate A certificate issued by a corporation evidencing the ownership of a specified number of shares in the corporation.

Preemptive Rights

Sometimes, the articles of incorporation grant preemptive rights to shareholders [RMBCA 6.30]. With **preemptive rights,** a shareholder receives a preference over all other purchasers to subscribe to or purchase a prorated share of a new issue of stock. Generally, preemptive rights apply only to additional, newly issued stock sold for cash, and the preemptive rights must be exercised within a specified time period, which is usually thirty days.

A shareholder who is given preemptive rights can purchase the same percentage of the new shares being issued as she or he already holds in the company. This allows each shareholder to maintain her or his proportionate control, voting power, or financial interest in the corporation.

EXAMPLE 15.11 Tran Corporation authorizes and issues 1,000 shares of stock. Lebow purchases 100 shares, making her the owner of 10 percent of the company's stock.

Preemptive Rights Rights that entitle shareholders to purchase newly issued shares of a corporation's stock, equal in percentage to shares already held, before the stock is offered to outside buyers.

Exhibit 15–2 Results of Cumulative Voting

BALLOT	MAJORITY SHAREHOLDERS' VOTES			MINORITY SHAREHOLDERS' VOTES	DIRECTORS ELECTED
	Acevedo	Barkley	Craycik	Drake	
1	10,000	10,000	1,000	9,000	Acevedo/Barkley/Drake
2	9,001	9,000	2,999	9,000	Acevedo/Barkley/Drake
3	6,000	7,000	8,000	9,000	Barkley/Craycik/Drake

Subsequently, Tran, by vote of its shareholders, authorizes the issuance of another 1,000 shares (by amending the articles of incorporation). This increases its capital stock to a total of 2,000 shares. If preemptive rights have been provided, Lebow can purchase one additional share of the new stock being issued for each share she already owns—or 100 additional shares. Thus, she can own 200 of the 2,000 shares outstanding, and she will maintain her relative position as a shareholder. If preemptive rights are not allowed, her proportionate control and voting power may be diluted from that of a 10 percent shareholder to that of a 5 percent shareholder because of the issuance of the additional 1,000 shares. ●

Preemptive rights are most important in close corporations because each shareholder owns a relatively small number of shares but controls a substantial interest in the corporation. Without preemptive rights, it would be possible for a shareholder to lose his or her proportionate control over the firm.

Stock Warrant A certificate that grants the owner the option to buy a given number of shares of stock, usually within a set time period.

Stock Warrants   **Stock warrants** are rights to buy stock at a stated price by a specified date that are created by the company. Usually, when preemptive rights exist and a corporation is issuing additional shares, it issues its shareholders stock warrants. Warrants are often publicly traded on securities exchanges.

Dividends   As previously mentioned, a *dividend* is a distribution of corporate profits or income *ordered by the directors* and paid to the shareholders in proportion to their respective shares in the corporation. Dividends can be paid in cash, property, stock of the corporation that is paying the dividends, or stock of other corporations.[14]

State laws vary, but each state determines the general circumstances and legal requirements under which dividends are paid. State laws also control the sources of revenue to be used; only certain funds are legally available for paying dividends. Depending on state law, dividends may be paid from the following sources:

1. *Retained earnings.* All states allow dividends to be paid from retained earnings—the undistributed net profits earned by the corporation, including capital gains from the sale of fixed assets.
2. *Net profits.* A few states allow dividends to be issued from current net profits without regard to deficits in prior years.
3. *Surplus.* A number of states allow dividends to be paid out of any kind of surplus. For instance, earned surplus is the sum of a company's net profits over a period of time. It increases by the amount of each year's net income after dividend payments. Earned surplus is not extra cash, but shareholder equity. A company's board of directors may choose to pay dividends from the surplus or to use it for some other corporate purpose (such as for acquisitions).

Illegal Dividends   Sometimes, dividends are improperly paid from an unauthorized account, or their payment causes the corporation to become insolvent. Generally, shareholders must return illegal dividends only if they knew that the dividends were illegal when the payment was received (or if the dividends were paid when the corporation was insolvent). Whenever dividends are illegal or improper, the board of directors can be held personally liable for the amount of the payment.

Directors' Failure to Declare a Dividend   When directors fail to declare a dividend, shareholders can ask a court to compel the directors to meet and to declare a dividend. To succeed, the shareholders must show that the directors have acted so unreasonably in withholding the dividend that their conduct is an abuse of their discretion.

---

14. Technically, dividends paid in stock are not dividends. They maintain each shareholder's proportionate interest in the corporation.

A corporation might accumulate large cash reserves for a legitimate corporate purpose, such as expansion or research. The mere fact that the firm has sufficient earnings or surplus available to pay a dividend is not enough to compel directors to distribute funds that, in the board's opinion, should not be distributed. The courts are reluctant to interfere with corporate operations and will not compel directors to declare dividends unless abuse of discretion is clearly shown.

Inspection Rights

Shareholders in a corporation enjoy both common law and statutory inspection rights. The RMBCA provides that every shareholder is entitled to examine specified corporate records. The shareholder can inspect in person, or an attorney, accountant, or other authorized assistant can do so as the shareholder's agent.

The power of inspection is fraught with potential abuses, and the corporation is allowed to protect itself from them. For instance, a shareholder can properly be denied access to corporate records to prevent harassment or to protect trade secrets or other confidential corporate information. Some states require that a shareholder must have held his or her shares for a minimum period of time immediately preceding the demand to inspect or must hold a minimum number of outstanding shares.

Transfer of Shares

Corporate stock represents an ownership right in intangible personal property. The law generally recognizes the right to transfer stock to another person unless there are valid restrictions on its transferability. Although stock certificates are negotiable and freely transferable, transfer of stock in close corporations usually is restricted. These restrictions must be reasonable and may be set out in the bylaws or in a shareholder agreement. The existence of any restrictions on transferability must always be indicated on the face of the stock certificate.

When shares are transferred, a new entry is made in the corporate stock book to indicate the new owner. Until the corporation is notified and the entry is complete, all rights—including voting rights, the right to notice of shareholders' meetings, and the right to dividend distributions—remain with the current record owner.

Rights on Dissolution

When a corporation is dissolved and its outstanding debts and the claims of its creditors have been satisfied, the remaining assets are distributed to the shareholders in proportion to the percentage of shares owned by each shareholder. Certain classes of stock can be given priority. If no class of stock has been given preference in the distribution of assets on liquidation, then all of the stockholders share the remaining assets.

In some situations, shareholders can petition a court to have the corporation dissolved. The RMBCA permits any shareholder to initiate a dissolution proceeding when the directors are deadlocked, or have engaged in illegal, oppressive, or fraudulent conduct, or when corporate assets are being misapplied or wasted [RMBCA 14.30].

The Shareholder's Derivative Suit

When the corporation is harmed by the actions of a third party, the directors can bring a lawsuit in the name of the corporation against that party. If the corporate directors fail to bring a lawsuit, shareholders can do so "derivatively" in what is known as a **shareholder's derivative suit.** Before shareholders can bring a derivative suit, they must submit a written demand to the corporation, asking the board of directors to take appropriate action [RMBCA 7.40]. The directors then have ninety days in which to act. Only if they refuse to do so can the derivative suit go forward.

The right of shareholders to bring a derivative action is especially important when the wrong suffered by the corporation results from the actions of corporate directors or officers. This is because the directors and officers would probably be unwilling to take any action against themselves. Nevertheless, a court will dismiss a derivative suit if the majority of directors or an independent panel determines in good faith that the lawsuit is not in the

Shareholder's Derivative Suit A suit brought by a shareholder to enforce a corporate cause of action against a third party.

best interests of the corporation [RMBCA 7.44]. (Derivative actions are less common in other countries than in the United States, as this chapter's *Beyond Our Borders* feature that follows explains.)

When shareholders bring a derivative suit, they are not pursuing rights or benefits for themselves personally but are acting as guardians of the corporate entity. Therefore, if the suit is successful, any damages recovered normally go into the corporation's treasury, not to the shareholders personally.

Duties and Liabilities of Shareholders

One of the hallmarks of the corporate form of business organization is that shareholders are not personally liable for the debts of the corporation. If the corporation fails, shareholders can lose their investments, but generally that is the limit of their liability. As discussed earlier, in certain instances of fraud, undercapitalization, or careless observance of corporate formalities, a court will pierce the corporate veil and hold the shareholders individually liable. These situations are the exception, however, not the rule.

A shareholder can also be personally liable in certain other rare instances. One relates to illegal dividends, which were discussed previously. Another relates to *watered stock*.

Watered Stock Shares of stock issued by a corporation for which the corporation receives, as payment, less than the stated value of the shares.

Watered Stock
When a corporation issues shares for less than their fair market value, the shares are referred to as **watered stock**.[15] Usually, the shareholder who receives watered stock must pay the difference to the corporation (the shareholder is personally liable). In some states, the shareholder who receives watered stock may be liable to creditors of the corporation for unpaid corporate debts.

EXAMPLE 15.12 During the formation of a corporation, Gomez, one of the incorporators, transfers his property, Sunset Beach, to the corporation for 10,000 shares of stock. The stock has a specific face value (*par value*) of $100 per share, and thus the total price of the 10,000 shares is $1 million. After the property is transferred and the shares are issued, Sunset Beach is carried on the corporate books at a value of $1 million.

On appraisal, it is discovered that the market value of the property at the time of transfer was only $500,000. The shares issued to Gomez are therefore watered stock, and he is liable to the corporation for the difference between the value of the shares and the value of the property. ●

---

15. The phrase *watered stock* was originally used to describe cattle that were kept thirsty during a long drive and then were allowed to drink large quantities of water just before their sale. The increased weight of the "watered stock" allowed the seller to reap a higher profit.

BEYOND OUR BORDERS   Derivative Actions in Other Nations

Today, most of the claims brought against directors and officers in the United States are those alleged in shareholders' derivative suits. Other nations, however, put more restrictions on the use of such suits. German law, for example, does not provide for derivative litigation, and a corporation's duty to its employees is just as significant as its duty to its shareholder-owners. The United Kingdom has no statute authorizing derivative actions, which are permitted only to challenge directors' actions that the shareholders could not legally ratify. Japan authorizes derivative actions but also permits a company to sue the plaintiff-shareholder for damages if the action is unsuccessful.

Critical Thinking
Do corporations benefit from shareholders' derivative suits? If so, how?

Duties of Majority Shareholders

In certain instances, a majority shareholder who engages in oppressive conduct or attempts to exclude minority shareholders from receiving certain benefits can be held personally liable. In these situations, majority shareholders owe a fiduciary duty to the minority shareholders.

When a majority shareholder breaches her or his fiduciary duty to a minority shareholder, the minority shareholder can sue for damages. A common example of a breach of fiduciary duty occurs when the majority shareholders "freeze out" the minority shareholders and exclude them from certain benefits of participating in the firm.

CASE EXAMPLE 15.13 Brodie, Jordan, and Barbuto formed a close corporation to operate a machine shop. Each owned one-third of the shares in the company, and all three were directors. Brodie served as the corporate president for twelve years but thereafter met with the other shareholders only a few times a year. After disagreements arose, Brodie asked the company to purchase his shares, but his requests were refused.

A few years later, Brodie died, and his wife inherited his shares in the company. Jordan and Barbuto refused to perform a valuation of the company, denied her access to the corporate information she requested, did not declare any dividends, and refused to elect her as a director. In this situation, a court found that the majority shareholders had violated their fiduciary duty to Brodie's wife.[16] •

Major Business Forms Compared

As mentioned in Chapter 14, when deciding which form of business organization to choose, businesspersons normally consider several factors. These factors include the ease of creation, the liability of the owners, tax considerations, and the ability to raise capital. Each major form of business organization offers distinct advantages and disadvantages with respect to these and other factors.

Exhibit 15–3 that follows summarizes the essential advantages and disadvantages of each of the forms of business organization discussed in Chapter 14, as well as this chapter.

---

16. *Brodie v. Jordan,* 447 Mass. 866, 857 N.E.2d 1076 (2006).

Exhibit 15–3 Major Forms of Business Compared

CHARACTERISTIC	SOLE PROPRIETORSHIP	PARTNERSHIP	CORPORATION
Method of Creation	Created at will by owner.	Created by agreement of the parties.	Authorized by the state under the state's corporation law.
Legal Position	Not a separate entity. Owner is the business.	A traditional partnership is a separate legal entity in most states.	Always a legal entity separate and distinct from its owners—a legal fiction for the purposes of owning property and being a party to litigation.
Liability	Unlimited liability.	Unlimited liability.	Limited liability of shareholders—shareholders are not liable for the debts of the corporation.
Duration	Determined by owner; automatically dissolved on owner's death.	Terminated by agreement of the partners, but can continue to do business even when a partner dissociates from the partnership.	Can have perpetual existence.
Transferability of Interest	Interest can be transferred, but individual's proprietorship then ends.	Although partnership interest can be assigned, assignee does not have full rights of a partner.	Shares of stock can be transferred.

Continued

Exhibit 15–3 Major Forms of Business Compared—Continued

CHARACTERISTIC	SOLE PROPRIETORSHIP	PARTNERSHIP	CORPORATION
Management	Completely at owner's discretion.	Each partner has a direct and equal voice in management unless expressly agreed otherwise in the partnership agreement.	Shareholders elect directors, who set policy and appoint officers.
Taxation	Owner pays personal taxes on business income.	Each partner pays pro rata share of income taxes on net profits, whether or not they are distributed.	Double taxation—corporation pays income tax on net profits, with no deduction for dividends, and shareholders pay income tax on disbursed dividends they receive.
Organizational Fees, Annual License Fees, and Annual Reports	None or minimal.	None or minimal.	All required.
Transaction of Business in Other States	Generally no limitation.	Generally no limitation.[a]	Normally must qualify to do business and obtain certificate of authority.

CHARACTERISTIC	LIMITED PARTNERSHIP	LIMITED LIABILITY COMPANY	LIMITED LIABILITY PARTNERSHIP
Method of Creation	Created by agreement to carry on a business for profit. At least one party must be a general partner and the other(s) limited partner(s). Certificate of limited partnership is filed. Charter must be issued by the state.	Created by an agreement of the member-owners of the company. Articles of organization are filed. Charter must be issued by the state.	Created by agreement of the partners. A statement of qualification for the limited liability partnership is filed.
Legal Position	Treated as a legal entity.	Treated as a legal entity.	Generally, treated same as a traditional partnership.
Liability	Unlimited liability of all general partners. Limited partners are liable only to the extent of their capital contributions.	Member-owners' liability is limited to the amount of their capital contributions or investments.	Varies, but under the Uniform Partnership Act, liability of a partner for acts committed by other partners is limited.
Duration	By agreement in certificate, or by termination of the last general partner (retirement, death, and the like) or last limited partner.	Unless a single-member LLC, can have perpetual existence (same as a corporation).	Remains in existence until cancellation or revocation.
Transferability of Interest	Interest can be assigned (same as in a traditional partnership), but if assignee becomes a member with consent of other partners, certificate must be amended.	Member interests are freely transferable.	Interest can be assigned same as in a traditional partnership.
Management	General partners have equal voice or by agreement. Limited partners may not retain limited liability if they actively participate in management.	Member-owners can fully participate in management or can designate a group of persons to manage on behalf of the members.	Same as in a traditional partnership.
Taxation	Generally taxed as a partnership.	LLC is not taxed, and members are taxed personally on profits "passed through" the LLC.	Same as in a traditional partnership.
Organizational Fees, Annual License Fees, and Annual Reports	Organizational fee required, but others usually not required.	Organizational fee required. Others vary with states.	Fees are set by each state for filing statements of qualification, statements of foreign qualification, and annual reports.
Transaction of Business in Other States	Generally no limitation.	Generally no limitation, but may vary depending on state.	Must file a statement of foreign qualification before doing business in another state.

a. A few states have enacted statutes requiring that foreign partnerships qualify to do business within the state.

Reviewing . . . Corporations

David Brock is on the board of directors of Firm Body Fitness, Inc., which owns a string of fitness clubs in New Mexico. Brock owns 15 percent of the Firm Body stock, and he is also employed as a tanning technician at one of the fitness clubs. After the January financial report showed that Firm Body's tanning division was operating at a substantial net loss, the board of directors, led by Marty Levinson, discussed terminating the tanning operations. Brock successfully convinced a majority of the board that the tanning division was necessary to market the club's overall fitness package. By April, the tanning division's financial losses had risen. The board hired a business analyst who conducted surveys and determined that the tanning operations did not significantly increase membership. A shareholder, Diego Peñada, discovered that Brock owned stock in Sunglow, Inc., the company from which Firm Body purchased its tanning equipment. Peñada notified Levinson, who privately reprimanded Brock. Shortly afterward, Brock and Mandy Vail, who owned 37 percent of the Firm Body stock and also held shares of Sunglow, voted to replace Levinson on the board of directors. Using the information presented in the chapter, answer the following questions.

1. What duties did Brock, as a director, owe to Firm Body?
2. Does the fact that Brock owned shares in Sunglow establish a conflict of interest? Why or why not?
3. Suppose that Firm Body brought an action against Brock claiming that he had breached the duty of loyalty by not disclosing his interest in Sunglow to the other directors. What theory might Brock use in his defense?
4. Now suppose that Firm Body did not bring an action against Brock. What type of lawsuit might Peñada be able to bring based on these facts?

Debate This   The sole shareholder of an S corporation should not be able to avoid liability for the torts of his or her employees.

Key Terms

Chapter Summary: Corporations

Nature and Classification	A corporation is a legal entity distinct from its owners. Formal statutory requirements, which vary somewhat from state to state, must be followed in forming a corporation.
	1. *Corporate parties*—The shareholders own the corporation. They elect a board of directors to govern the corporation. The board of directors hires corporate officers and other employees to run the daily business of the firm.
	2. *Corporate taxation*—The corporation pays income tax on net profits, and shareholders pay income tax on the disbursed dividends that they receive from the corporation (double-taxation feature).
	3. *Torts and criminal acts*—The corporation is liable for the torts committed by its agents or officers within the course and scope of their employment. In some circumstances, a corporation can be held liable (and be fined) for the criminal acts of its agents and employees. In certain situations, corporate officers may be held personally liable for corporate crimes.

Continued

Chapter Summary: Corporations—Continued

Nature and Classification—Continued	4. *Domestic, foreign, and alien corporations*—A corporation is referred to as a domestic corporation within its home state (the state in which it incorporates). A corporation is referred to as a foreign corporation by any state that is not its home state. A corporation is referred to as an alien corporation if it originates in another country but does business in the United States.
	5. *Public and private corporations*—A public corporation is one formed by a government (for example, cities, towns, and public projects). A private corporation is one formed wholly or in part for private benefit. Most corporations are private corporations.
	6. *Nonprofit corporations*—Corporations formed without a profit-making purpose (for example, charitable, educational, and religious organizations and hospitals).
	7. *Close corporations*—Corporations owned by a family or a relatively small number of individuals. Transfer of shares is usually restricted, and the corporation cannot make a public offering of its securities.
	8. *S corporations*—Small domestic corporations (with no more than one hundred shareholders) that, under Subchapter S of the Internal Revenue Code, are given special tax treatment. These corporations allow shareholders to enjoy the limited legal liability of the corporate form but avoid its double-taxation feature.
	9. *Professional corporations*—Corporations formed by professionals (for example, physicians and lawyers) to obtain the benefits of incorporation (such as limited liability).
Formation and Powers	1. *Promotional activities*—Preliminary promotional activities are rarely if ever taken today. A person who enters contracts with investors and others on behalf of the future corporation is personally liable on all preincorporation contracts. Liability remains until the corporation is formed and assumes the contract by novation.
	2. *Incorporation procedures*—Exact procedures for incorporation differ among states, but the basic steps are as follows: (a) select a state of incorporation, (b) secure the corporate name by confirming its availability, (c) prepare the articles of incorporation, and (d) file the articles of incorporation with the secretary of state accompanied by payment of the specified fees.
	3. *Articles of incorporation*—The articles of incorporation must include the corporate name, the number of shares of stock the corporation is authorized to issue, the registered office and agent, and the names and addresses of the incorporators. The articles may (but are not required to) include additional information about the corporation's nature and purpose, duration, and internal organization. The state's filing of the articles of incorporation authorizes the corporation to conduct business.
	4. *The first organizational meeting*—A meeting is held after incorporation. The usual purpose of this meeting is to adopt the bylaws, or internal rules of the corporation, but other business, such as election of the board of directors may also take place.
	5. *Improper incorporation*—If a corporation has been improperly incorporated, the courts will sometimes impute corporate status to the firm by holding that it is a *de jure* corporation (cannot be challenged by the state or third parties) or a *de facto* corporation (can be challenged by the state but not by third parties). If a firm is neither a *de jure* nor a *de facto* corporation but represents itself to be a corporation and is sued as such by a third party, it may be held to be a corporation by estoppel.
	6. *Express powers*—The express powers of a corporation are found in the following laws and documents (listed according to their priority): federal constitution, state constitutions, state statutes, articles of incorporation, bylaws, and resolutions of the board of directors.
	7. *Implied powers*—Barring express constitutional, statutory, or other prohibitions, the corporation has the implied power to do all acts reasonably appropriate and necessary to accomplish its corporate purposes.
	8. *Ultra vires doctrine*—Any act of a corporation that is beyond its express or implied powers to undertake is an *ultra vires* act and may lead to a lawsuit by the shareholders, corporation, or state attorney general to enjoin or recover damages for the *ultra vires* acts.
Piercing the Corporate Veil	To avoid injustice, courts may pierce the corporate veil and hold a shareholder or shareholders personally liable for a judgment against the corporation. This usually occurs only when the corporation was established to circumvent the law, when the corporate form is used for an illegitimate or fraudulent purpose, or when the controlling shareholders commingle their personal interests with those of the corporation to such an extent that the corporation no longer has a separate identity.
Directors and Officers	1. *Director*—Directors are responsible for all policymaking decisions necessary to the management of all corporate affairs. Directors usually serve a one-year term, although their terms can be longer or staggered. Compensation is usually specified in the corporate articles or bylaws. The board of directors conducts business by holding formal meetings with recorded minutes.
	2. *Rights of directors*—Directors' rights include the rights of participation, inspection, compensation, and indemnification.
	3. *Corporate officers and executives*—Corporate officers and other executive employees are normally hired by the board of directors and have the rights defined by their employment contracts. The duties of corporate officers are the same as those of directors.
	4. *Duty of care*—Directors and officers are obligated to act in good faith, to use prudent business judgment in the conduct of corporate affairs, and to act in the corporation's best interests. If a director fails to exercise this duty of care, she or he can be answerable to the corporation and to the shareholders for breaching the duty.

Chapter Summary: Corporations—Continued

Directors and Officers—Continued	5. *The business judgment rule*—This rule immunizes directors and officers from liability when they acted in good faith, acted in the best interests of the corporation, and exercised due care. For the rule to apply, the directors and officers must have made an informed, reasonable, and loyal decision. 6. *Duty of loyalty*—Directors and officers have a fiduciary duty to subordinate their own interests to those of the corporation in matters relating to the corporation. 7. *Conflicts of interest*—To fulfill their duty of loyalty, directors and officers must make a full disclosure of any potential conflicts between their personal interests and those of the corporation.

Shareholders	1. *Shareholders' powers*—Shareholders' powers include the approval of all fundamental changes affecting the corporation and the election of the board of directors.
	2. *Shareholders' meetings*—Shareholders' meetings must occur at least annually. Special meetings can be called when necessary. Notice of the date, time, and place of the meeting (and its purpose, if it is specially called) must be sent to shareholders. Shareholders may vote by proxy (authorizing someone else to vote their shares) and may submit proposals to be included in the company's proxy materials sent to shareholders before meetings.
	3. *Shareholder voting*—Shareholder voting requirements and procedures are as follows:
	   a. A minimum number of shareholders (a quorum—generally, more than 50 percent of shares held) must be present at a meeting for business to be conducted. Resolutions are passed (usually) by simple majority vote.
	   b. The corporation must prepare voting lists of shareholders of record prior to each shareholders' meeting.
	   c. Cumulative voting may or may not be required or permitted. Cumulative voting gives minority shareholders a better chance to be represented on the board of directors.
	   d. A shareholder voting agreement (an agreement of shareholders to vote their shares together) is usually held to be valid and enforceable.
	4. *Rights of shareholders*—Shareholders have numerous rights, which may include the following:
	   a. The right to a stock certificate, preemptive rights, and the right to stock warrants (depending on the articles of incorporation).
	   b. The right to obtain a dividend (at the discretion of the directors).
	   c. The right to inspect the corporate records.
	   d. The right to transfer shares (this right may be restricted in close corporations).
	   e. The right to a share of corporate assets when the corporation is dissolved.
	   f. The right to sue on behalf of the corporation (bring a shareholder's derivative suit) when the directors fail to do so.
	5. *Duties and liabilities of shareholders*—Shareholders may be liable for the retention of illegal dividends and for the value of watered stock. In certain situations, majority shareholders may be regarded as having a fiduciary duty to minority shareholders and will be liable if that duty is breached.

Issue Spotters

1. Northwest Brands, Inc., is a small business incorporated in Minnesota. Its one class of stock is owned by twelve members of a single family. Ordinarily, corporate income is taxed at the corporate and shareholder levels. Is there a way for Northwest Brands to avoid this double taxation? Explain your answer. (See *Nature and Classification.*)
2. Wonder Corporation has an opportunity to buy stock in XL, Inc. The directors decide that instead of Wonder buying the stock, the directors will buy it. Yvon, a Wonder shareholder, learns of the purchase and wants to sue the directors on Wonder's behalf. Can she do it? Explain. (See *Shareholders.*)

—**Check your answers to the Issue Spotters against the answers provided in Appendix D at the end of this text.**

For Review

1. What is a close corporation?
2. In what circumstances might a court disregard the corporate entity (pierce the corporate veil) and hold the shareholders personally liable?
3. What are the duties of corporate directors and officers?

4. Directors are expected to use their best judgment in managing the corporation. What must directors do to avoid liability for honest mistakes of judgment and poor business decisions?

5. What is a voting proxy? What is cumulative voting?

Business Scenarios and Case Problems

15–1. Preincorporation. Cummings, Okawa, and Taft are recent college graduates who want to form a corporation to manufacture and sell personal computers. Peterson tells them he will set in motion the formation of their corporation. First, Peterson makes a contract with Owens for the purchase of a piece of land for $20,000. Owens does not know of the prospective corporate formation at the time the contract is signed. Second, Peterson makes a contract with Babcock to build a small plant on the property being purchased. Babcock's contract is conditional on the corporation's formation. Peterson secures all necessary subscription agreements and capitalization, and he files the articles of incorporation. Discuss whether the newly formed corporation, Peterson, or both are liable on the contracts with Owens and Babcock. Is the corporation automatically liable to Babcock on formation? Explain. (See *Formation and Powers.*)

15–2. Conflicts of Interest. Oxy Corp. is negotiating with the Wick Construction Co. for the renovation of the Oxy corporate headquarters. Wick, the owner of the Wick Construction Co., is also one of the five members of Oxy's board of directors. The contract terms are standard for this type of contract. Wick has previously informed two of the other directors of his interest in the construction company. Oxy's board approves the contract by a three-to-two vote, with Wick voting with the majority. Discuss whether this contract is binding on the corporation. (See *Directors and Officers.*)

15–3. Corporate Powers. Kora Nayenga and two business associates formed a corporation called Nayenga Corp. for the purpose of selling computer services. Kora, who owned 50 percent of the corporate shares, served as the corporation's president. Kora wished to obtain a personal loan from his bank for $250,000, but the bank required the note to be cosigned by a third party. Kora cosigned the note in the name of the corporation. Later, Kora defaulted on the note, and the bank sued the corporation for payment. The corporation asserted, as a defense, that Kora had exceeded his authority when he cosigned the note. Had he? Explain. (See *Formation and Powers.*)

15–4. ▲ **Spotlight on Smart Inventions—Piercing the Corporate Veil.** Thomas Persson and Jon Nokes founded Smart Inventions, Inc., to market household consumer products. The success of their first product, the Smart Mop, continued with later products, which were sold through infomercials. Persson and Nokes were the firm's officers and

equal shareholders, with Persson responsible for product development and Nokes in charge of day-to-day activities. By 1998, they had become dissatisfied with each other's efforts. Nokes represented the firm as financially "dying," "in a grim state, . . . worse than ever," and offered to buy all of Persson's shares for $1.6 million. Persson accepted.

On the day that they signed the agreement to transfer the shares, Smart Inventions began marketing a new product—the Tap Light. It was an instant success, generating millions of dollars in revenues. In negotiating with Persson, Nokes had intentionally kept the Tap Light a secret. Persson sued Smart Inventions, asserting fraud and other claims. Under what principle might Smart Inventions be liable for Nokes's fraud? Is Smart Inventions liable in this case? Explain. [*Persson v. Smart Inventions, Inc.,* 125 Cal.App.4th 1141, 23 Cal. Rptr.3d 335 (2 Dist. 2005)] (See *Piercing the Corporate Veil.*)

15–5. Close Corporations. Mark Burnett and Kamran Pourgol were the only shareholders in a corporation that built and sold a house. When the buyers discovered that the house exceeded the amount of square footage allowed by the building permit, Pourgol agreed to renovate the house to conform to the permit. No work was done, however, and Burnett filed a suit against Pourgol. Burnett claimed that, without his knowledge, Pourgol had submitted incorrect plans to obtain the building permit, misrepresented the extent of the renovation, and failed to fix the house. Was Pourgol guilty of misconduct? If so, how might it have been avoided? Discuss. [*Burnett v. Pourgol,* 83 A.D.3d 756, 921 N.Y.S.2d 280 (2 Dept. 2011)] (See *Nature and Classification.*)

15–6. ⚖ **Business Case Problem with Sample Answer— Rights of Shareholders.** Stanka Woods is the sole member of Hair Ventures, LLC. Hair Ventures owns 3 million shares of stock in Biolustré Inc. For several years, Woods and other Biolustré shareholders did not receive notice of shareholders' meetings or financial reports. On learning that Biolustré planned to issue more stock, Woods, through Hair Ventures, demanded to see Biolustré's books and records. Biolustré asserted that the request was not for a proper purpose. Does Woods have a right to inspect Biolustré's books and records? If so, what are the limits? Do any of those limits apply in this case? Explain. [*Biolustré Inc. v. Hair Ventures, LLC,* 2011 WL 540574 (Tex.App.—San Antonio 2011)] (See *Shareholders.*)

—**For a sample answer to Problem 15–6, go to Appendix E at the end of this text.**

15–7. Piercing the Corporate Veil. In 1997, Leon Greenblatt, Andrew Jahelka, and Richard Nichols incorporated Loop Corp. with only $1,000 of capital. Three years later, Banco Panamericano, Inc., which was run entirely by Greenblatt and owned by a Greenblatt family trust, extended a large line of credit to Loop. Loop's subsidiaries then participated in the credit, giving $3 million to Loop while acquiring a security interest in Loop itself. Loop then opened an account with Wachovia Securities, LLC, to buy stock shares using credit provided by Wachovia. When the stock values plummeted, Loop owed Wachovia $1.89 million. Loop also defaulted on its loan from Banco, but Banco agreed to lend Loop millions of dollars more.

Rather than repay Wachovia with the influx of funds, Loop gave the funds to closely related entities and "compensated" Nichols and Jahelka without issuing any W-2 forms (forms reporting compensation to the Internal Revenue Service). The evidence also showed that Loop made loans to other related entities and shared office space, equipment, and telephone and fax numbers with related entities. Loop also moved employees among related entities, failed to file its tax returns on time (or sometimes at all), and failed to follow its own bylaws. In a lawsuit brought by Wachovia, can the court hold Greenblatt, Jahelka, and Nichols personally liable by piercing the corporate veil? Why or why not? [*Wachovia Securities, LLC v. Banco Panamericano, Inc.,* 674 F.3d 743 (9th Cir. 2012)] (See *Piercing the Corporate Veil.*)

15–8. Duty of Loyalty. Kids International Corp. produced children's wear for Wal-mart and other retailers. Gila Dweck was a Kids director and its chief executive officer. Because she felt that she was not paid enough for the company's success, she started Success Apparel to compete with Kids. Success operated out of Kids' premises, used its employees, borrowed on its credit, took advantage of its business opportunities, and capitalized on its customer relationships. As an "administrative fee," Dweck paid Kids 1 percent of Success's total sales. Did Dweck breach any fiduciary duties? Explain. [*Dweck v. Nasser,* 2012 WL 3194069 (Del.Ch. 2012)] (See *Directors and Officers.*)

15–9. Piercing the Corporate Veil. Scott Snapp contracted with Castlebrook Builders, Inc., which was owned by Stephen Kappeler, to remodel a house. Kappeler estimated the cost at $500,000. Eventually, Snapp paid Kappeler more than $1.3 million. Snapp filed a suit in an Ohio state court against Castlebrook. During the trial, it was revealed that Castlebrook had issued no shares of stock. In addition, Kappeler had commingled personal and corporate funds. The minutes of the corporate meetings "all looked exactly the same." And Kappeler could not provide an accounting for the Snapp project—he could not explain double and triple charges or demonstrate that the amount Snapp paid had actually been spent on the project. Are these sufficient grounds to pierce the corporate veil? Explain. [*Snapp v. Castlebrook Builders, Inc.,* 2014 –Ohio- 163, __ Ohio App.3d __, 7 N.E.3d 574 (2014)] (See *Piercing the Corporate Veil.*)

15–10. ⬌ **A Question of Ethics—Directors and Officers Duties.** New Orleans Paddlewheels, Inc. (NOP), is a Louisiana corporation formed in 1982, when James Smith, Sr., and Warren Reuther were its only shareholders, with each holding 50 percent of the stock. NOP is part of a sprawling enterprise of tourism and hospitality companies in New Orleans. The positions on the board of each company were split equally between the Smith and Reuther families. At Smith's request, his son James Smith, Jr. (JES), became involved in the businesses. In 1999, NOP's board elected JES as president, to be in charge of day-to-day operations, and Reuther as chief executive officer (CEO), to be in charge of marketing and development. Over the next few years, animosity developed between Reuther and JES. In October 2001, JES terminated Reuther as CEO and denied him access to the offices and books of NOP and the other companies, literally changing the locks on the doors. At the next meetings of the boards of NOP and the overall enterprise, deadlock ensued, with the directors voting along family lines on every issue. Complaining that the meetings were a "waste of time," JES began to run the entire enterprise by taking advantage of an unequal balance of power on the companies' executive committees. In NOP's subsequent bankruptcy proceeding, Reuther filed a motion for the appointment of a trustee to formulate a plan for the firm's reorganization, alleging, among other things, misconduct by NOP's management. [*In re New Orleans Paddlewheels, Inc.,* 350 Bankr. 667 (E.D.La. 2006)] (See *Directors and Officers.*)

1. Was Reuther legally entitled to have access to the books and records of NOP and the other companies? JES maintained, among other things, that NOP's books were "a mess." Was JES's denial of that access unethical? Explain.

2. How would you describe JES's attempt to gain control of NOP and the other companies? Were his actions deceptive and self-serving in the pursuit of personal gain or legitimate and reasonable in the pursuit of a business goal? Discuss.

Agency Relationships

LEARNING OBJECTIVES

The five learning objectives below are designed to help improve your understanding of the chapter. After reading this chapter, you should be able to answer the following questions:

1. What is the difference between an employee and an independent contractor?
2. How do agency relationships arise?
3. What duties do agents and principals owe to each other?
4. When is a principal liable for the agent's actions with respect to third parties? When is the agent liable?
5. What are some of the ways in which an agency relationship can be terminated?

(Goodluz/iStockphoto.com)

> "[It] is a universal principle in the law of agency, that the powers of the agent are to be exercised for the benefit of the principal only, and not of the agent or of third parties."
>
> —Joseph Story, 1779–1845 (Associate justice of the United States Supreme Court, 1811–1844)

Agency A relationship between two parties in which one party (the agent) agrees to represent or act for the other (the principal).

One of the most common, important, and pervasive legal relationships is that of **agency.** In an agency relationship between two parties, one of the parties, called the *agent,* agrees to represent or act for the other, called the *principal.* The principal has the right to control the agent's conduct in matters entrusted to the agent, and the agent must exercise his or her powers "for the benefit of the principal only," as Justice Joseph Story indicated in the chapter-opening quotation.

By using agents, a principal can conduct multiple business operations, such as entering contracts, at the same time in different locations. Using agents provides clear benefits to principals, but agents also create liability for their principals. For this reason, small businesses sometimes attempt to retain workers as independent contractors or "permalancers," but this strategy may lead to problems with federal and state tax authorities, as you will read later in this chapter. Agency relationships are crucial to the business world. Indeed, the only way that some business entities can function is through their agents.

Agency Relationships

Section 1(1) of the *Restatement (Third) of Agency*[1] defines agency as "the fiduciary relation which results from the manifestation of consent by one person to another that the other shall act in his [or her] behalf and subject to his [or her] control, and consent by the other so to act." In other words, in a principal-agent relationship, the parties have agreed that the agent will act *on behalf and instead of* the principal in negotiating and transacting business with third parties.

The term **fiduciary** is at the heart of agency law. The term can be used both as a noun and as an adjective. When used as a noun, it refers to a person having a duty created by her or his undertaking to act primarily for another's benefit in matters connected with the undertaking. When used as an adjective, as in "fiduciary relationship," it means that the relationship involves trust and confidence.

Agency relationships commonly exist between employers and employees. Agency relationships may sometimes also exist between employers and independent contractors who are hired to perform special tasks or services.

Fiduciary As a noun, a person having a duty created by his or her undertaking to act primarily for another's benefit in matters connected with the undertaking. As an adjective, a relationship founded on trust and confidence.

Employer-Employee Relationships

Normally, all employees who deal with third parties are deemed to be agents. A salesperson in a department store, for instance, is an agent of the store's owner (the principal) and acts on the owner's behalf. Any sale of goods made by the salesperson to a customer is binding on the principal. Similarly, most representations of fact made by the salesperson with respect to the goods sold are binding on the principal.

Because employees who deal with third parties are generally deemed to be agents of their employers, agency law and employment law overlap considerably. Agency relationships, however, can exist outside an employer-employee relationship, so agency law has a broader reach than employment law. Additionally, agency law is based on the common law, whereas much employment law is statutory law.

Employment laws (state and federal) apply only to the employer-employee relationship. Statutes governing Social Security, withholding taxes, workers' compensation, unemployment compensation, workplace safety, employment discrimination, and the like (see Chapters 17 and 18) are applicable only if employer-employee status exists. *These laws do not apply to an independent contractor.*

Corporations could not operate without employing agents.

Learning Objective 1
What is the difference between an employee and an independent contractor?

Employer–Independent Contractor Relationships

Independent contractors are not employees because, by definition, those who hire them have no control over the details of their physical performance. Section 2 of the *Restatement (Third) of Agency* defines an **independent contractor** as follows:

> [An independent contractor is] a person who contracts with another to do something for him [or her] but who is not controlled by the other nor subject to the other's right to control with respect to his [or her] physical conduct in the performance of the undertaking. *He [or she] may or may not be an agent.* [Emphasis added.]

Building contractors and subcontractors are independent contractors. A property owner does not control the acts of either of these professionals. Truck drivers who own their equipment and hire themselves out on a per-job basis are independent contractors, but truck drivers who drive company trucks on a regular basis are usually employees.

Independent Contractor One who works for, and receives payment from, an employer but whose working conditions and methods are not controlled by the employer. An independent contractor is not an employee but may be an agent.

---

1. The *Restatement (Third) of Agency* is an authoritative summary of the law of agency and is often referred to by judges and other legal professionals.

The relationship between a person or firm and an independent contractor may or may not involve an agency relationship. To illustrate: An owner of real estate who hires a real estate broker to negotiate a sale of the property not only has contracted with an independent contractor (the broker) but also has established an agency relationship for the specific purpose of selling the property. Another example is an insurance agent, who is both an independent contractor and an agent of the insurance company for which she or he sells policies. (Note that an insurance *broker,* in contrast, normally is an agent of the person obtaining insurance and not of the insurance company.)

Determining Employee Status

The courts are frequently asked to determine whether a particular worker is an employee or an independent contractor. How a court decides this issue can have a significant effect on the rights and liabilities of the parties. Employers are required to pay certain taxes, such as Social Security and unemployment insurance taxes, for employees but not for independent contractors.

Criteria Used by the Courts
In determining whether a worker has the status of an employee or an independent contractor, the courts often consider the following questions:

1. How much control can the employer exercise over the details of the work? (If an employer can exercise considerable control over the details of the work, this would indicate employee status. This is perhaps the most important factor weighed by the courts in determining employee status.)
2. Is the worker engaged in an occupation or business distinct from that of the employer? (If so, this points to independent-contractor status, not employee status.)
3. Is the work usually done under the employer's direction or by a specialist without supervision? (If the work is usually done under the employer's direction, this would indicate employee status.)
4. Does the employer supply the tools at the place of work? (If so, this would indicate employee status.)
5. For how long is the person employed? (If the person is employed for a long period of time, this would indicate employee status.)
6. What is the method of payment—by time period or at the completion of the job? (Payment by time period, such as once every two weeks or once a month, would indicate employee status.)
7. What degree of skill is required of the worker? (If little skill is required, this may indicate employee status.)

Disputes Involving Employment Law   Sometimes, workers may benefit from having employee status—for tax purposes and to be protected under certain employment laws, for example. As mentioned earlier, federal statutes governing employment discrimination apply only when an employer-employee relationship exists. Protection under antidiscrimination statutes provides a significant incentive for workers to claim that they are employees rather than independent contractors.

   CASE EXAMPLE 16.1   A Puerto Rican television station, WIPR, contracted with a woman to co-host a television show. The woman signed a new contract for each episode and was committed to work for WIPR only during the filming of the episodes. WIPR paid her a lump sum for each contract and did not withhold any taxes. When the woman became pregnant, WIPR stopped contracting with her. She filed a lawsuit claiming that WIPR was discriminating against her in violation of federal antidiscrimination laws, but the court found in favor of WIPR. Because the parties had structured their relationship through repeated fixed-length contracts and had described the woman as an independent contractor on tax documents, she could not maintain an employment-discrimination suit.[2] •

Disputes Involving Tort Liability Whether a worker is an employee or an independent contractor can also affect the employer's liability for the worker's actions. In the following case, the court had to determine the status of an auto service company and its tow truck driver who assaulted the passenger of a vehicle the company had been hired to tow.

2. *Alberty-Vélez v. Corporación de Puerto Rico para la Difusión Pública*, 361 F.3d 1 (1st Cir. 2004).

Case 16.1

(Brian Stablyk/Getty Images)

Coker v. Pershad

Superior Court of New Jersey, Appellate Division, 2013 WL 1296271 (2013).

BACKGROUND AND FACTS AAA North Jersey, Inc., contracted with Five Star Auto Service to perform towing and auto repair services for AAA. Terence Pershad, the driver of a tow truck for Five Star, responded to a call to AAA for assistance by the driver of a car involved in an accident in Hoboken, New Jersey. Pershad got into a fight with Nicholas Coker, a passenger in the car, and assaulted Coker with a knife. Coker filed a suit in a New Jersey state court against Pershad, Five Star, and AAA. The court determined that Pershad was Five Star's employee and that Five Star was an independent contractor, not AAA's employee. Thus, AAA was "not responsible for the alleged negligence of its independent contractor, defendant Five Star, in hiring Mr. Pershad." Five Star entered into a settlement with Coker. Coker appealed the ruling in AAA's favor.

IN THE WORDS OF THE COURT . . .
PER CURIAM [By the Whole Court].
* * * *

The important difference between an employee and an independent contractor is that one who hires an independent contractor has no right of control over the manner in which the work is to be done. [Emphasis added.]
* * * *

* * * Plaintiff [Coker] argues AAA controlled the means and method of the work performed by Five Star. * * * Factors * * * [that] determine whether a principal maintains the right of control over an individual or a corporation claimed to be an independent contractor [include]:

(a) the extent of control which, by the agreement, the master may exercise over the details of the work;
(b) whether or not the one employed is engaged in a distinct occupation or business;
(c) the kind of occupation, with reference to whether, in the locality, the work is usually done under the direction of the employer or by a specialist without supervision;

(d) the skill required in the particular occupation;
(e) whether the employer or the workman supplies the * * * tools * * * ;
(f) the length of time for which the person is employed * * * .

Applying these factors to the facts of this case, it is clear AAA did not control the manner and means of Five Star's work. The Agreement specifically stated Five Star was an independent contractor. Five Star purchased its own trucks and any other necessary equipment. AAA assigned jobs to Five Star and Five Star completed the work without any further supervision by AAA. Five Star chose the employees to send on towing calls and the trucks and equipment the employees would use. [Emphasis added.]

Five Star was also in business for itself and performed auto repair services for principals and customers other than AAA. Five Star hired and fired its own employees * * * .
* * * *

Plaintiff also argues Five Star should be considered to be controlled by AAA because "providing towing and other roadside assistance is arguably the focus of the regular business of AAA." * * * [But] AAA is an automobile club that provides a wide variety of services to its members. It contracts with numerous service providers, such as gas stations, motels and other businesses, to provide these services. Thus, AAA is not solely in the towing business.

* * * AAA had used Five Star to provide towing services for approximately eight years and there is nothing in the record to demonstrate it lacked the skill needed to provide these services.

DECISION AND REMEDY A state intermediate appellate court affirmed the lower court's ruling. AAA could not be held liable for the actions of Five Star, its independent contractor, because "AAA did not control the manner and means of Five Star's work."

Case 16.1—Continues ➡

Case 16.1—Continued

THE LEGAL ENVIRONMENT DIMENSION   *Five Star's contract with AAA required Five Star to be available to provide service for AAA members. Does this support Coker's argument that Five Star was AAA's employee? Why or why not?*

MANAGERIAL IMPLICATIONS   *When an employment contract clearly designates one party as an independent contractor, the relationship between the parties is presumed to be that of employer and independent contractor. But this is only a presumption. Evidence can be introduced to show that the employer exercised sufficient control to establish the other party as an employee. The Internal Revenue Service is increasingly pursuing employers that it claims have wrongly classified employees as independent contractors. Thus, from a tax perspective, business managers need to ensure that all independent contractors fully control their own work.*

Criteria Used by the IRS

The Internal Revenue Service (IRS) has established its own criteria for determining whether a worker is an independent contractor or an employee. The most important factor in this determination is the degree of control the business exercises over the worker.

The IRS tends to closely scrutinize a firm's classification of its workers because, as mentioned, employers can avoid certain tax liabilities by hiring independent contractors instead of employees. Even when a firm classifies a worker as an independent contractor, the IRS may decide that the worker is actually an employee. In that situation, the employer will be responsible for paying any applicable Social Security, withholding, and unemployment taxes. Microsoft Corporation, for instance, was once ordered to pay back payroll taxes for hundreds of workers that the IRS determined had been misclassified as independent contractors.[3] (See this chapter's *Insight into Ethics* feature, which discusses the ethical ramifications of discouraging businesses from hiring independent contractors.)

Employee Status and "Works for Hire"

Under the Copyright Act of 1976, any copyrighted work created by an employee within the scope of her or his employment at the request of the employer is a "work for hire," and the *employer* owns the copyright to the work. When an employer hires an independent contractor—a freelance artist, writer, or computer programmer, for example—the independent contractor owns the copyright *unless* the parties agree in writing that the work is a "work for hire" and the work falls into one of nine specific categories, including audiovisual and other works.

CASE EXAMPLE 16.2   Artisan House, Inc., hired a professional photographer, Steven H. Lindner, owner of SHL Imaging, Inc., to take pictures of its products for the creation of color slides to be used by Artisan's sales force. Lindner controlled his own work and carefully chose the lighting and angles used in the photographs.

When Artisan published the photographs in a catalogue without Lindner's permission, SHL filed a lawsuit for copyright infringement. Artisan claimed that its publication of the photographs was authorized because they were works for hire. The court, however, held that SHL was an independent contractor and owned the copyrights to the photographs. Because SHL had not given Artisan permission (a license) to reproduce the photographs in other publications, Artisan was liable for copyright infringement.[4] •

---

3. See *Vizcaino v. U.S. District Court for the Western District of Washington,* 173 F.3d 713 (9th Cir. 1999).
4. *SHL Imaging, Inc. v. Artisan House, Inc.,* 117 F.Supp.2d 301 (S.D.N.Y. 2000).

INSIGHT INTO ETHICS

SHOULD SMALL BUSINESSES BE ALLOWED TO HIRE "PERMALANCERS"?

Freelancers, of course, are independent contractors. Now small businesses across the country are turning increasingly to *perma-lancers*—freelancers who stay on a business's payroll for years.

Business Advantages

From the business's perspective, the advantages are obvious—the cost savings from using freelancers rather than employees can be as much as 30 percent. The savings are because the business does not have to pay payroll and unemployment taxes or workers' compensation. Additionally, freelancers do not receive health-care and other benefits offered to employees. Finally, during an economic downturn, the business has more flexibility—it can let freelancers go quickly and usually without cost.

Taxation and Regulation Issues

The IRS and state tax authorities, however, view permalancers differently. In early 2010, the IRS launched an ongoing program that will examine six thousand companies to make sure that permanent workers have not been misclassified as independent contractors.

The Obama administration also revised some regulations to make it harder for businesses to classify workers as freelancers.

The IRS is targeting small businesses not only because they hire lots of freelancers but also because, unlike larger companies, they usually do not have on-staff attorneys to defend them and thus are likely to acquiesce when the IRS clamps down. But these efforts raise some ethical issues.

Certainly, the tax authorities will gain some revenues but at the cost of reducing the flexibility of small businesses. Another trade-off to consider is between the advantages that a business obtains from hiring permalancers and the disadvantages to those workers of having no employee benefits.

For Critical Analysis
Insight into the Social Environment

If businesses hire fewer workers as a result of the IRS's actions, are the taxes collected worth the possible increase in unemployment? Discuss.

Formation of Agencies

Agency relationships normally are consensual. They come about by voluntary consent and agreement between the parties. Generally, the agreement need not be in writing,[5] and consideration is not required.

A person must have contractual capacity to be a principal. Those who cannot legally enter into contracts directly should not be allowed to do so indirectly through an agent. Any person can be an agent, though, regardless of whether he or she has the capacity to enter a contract (including minors).

An agency relationship can be created for any legal purpose. An agency relationship that is created for an illegal purpose or that is contrary to public policy is unenforceable. **EXAMPLE 16.3** Sharp (the principal) contracts with McKenzie (the agent) to sell illegal narcotics. This agency relationship is unenforceable because selling illegal narcotics is a felony and is contrary to public policy. • It is also illegal for physicians and other licensed professionals to employ unlicensed agents to perform professional actions.

Generally, an agency relationship can arise in four ways: by agreement of the parties, by ratification, by estoppel, or by operation of law.

Learning Objective 2
How do agency relationships arise?

---

5. The following are two main exceptions to the statement that agency agreements need not be in writing: (1) Whenever agency authority empowers the agent to enter into a contract that the Statute of Frauds requires to be in writing, the agent's authority from the principal must likewise be in writing (this is called the *equal dignity rule,* which will be discussed in this chapter, and (2) a power of attorney, which confers authority to an agent, must be in writing.

If a homeowner contracted with a landscaper to hire a gardener, who is the agent of whom?

Agency by Agreement of the Parties

Most agency relationships are based on an express or implied agreement that the agent will act for the principal and that the principal agrees to have the agent so act. An agency agreement can take the form of an express written contract or be created by an oral agreement.
EXAMPLE 16.4   Reese asks Cary, a gardener, to contract with others for the care of his lawn on a regular basis. Cary agrees. An agency relationship is established between Reese (the principal) and Cary (the agent) for the lawn care. ●

An agency agreement can also be implied by conduct. **CASE EXAMPLE 16.5**   Gilbert Bishop was admitted to Laurel Creek Health Care Center suffering from various physical ailments. During an examination, Bishop told Laurel Creek staff that he could not use his hands well enough to write or hold a pencil, but he was otherwise found to be mentally competent. Bishop's sister, Rachel Combs, offered to sign the admissions forms, but it was Laurel Creek's policy to have the patient's spouse sign the admissions papers if the patient was unable to do so. Therefore, Gilbert asked Combs to get his wife, Anna, so that she could sign his admissions papers.

Combs then brought Anna to the hospital, and Anna signed the admissions paperwork, which contained a provision for mandatory arbitration. Later, the Bishops sued the hospital for negligence, and Laurel Creek sought to compel arbitration. The Bishops argued that Anna was not Bishop's agent and had no legal authority to make decisions for him, but the court concluded that an agency relationship between Bishop and his wife, Anna, had been formed by conduct.[6] ●

Agency by Ratification

Ratification A party's act of accepting or giving legal force to a contract or other obligation entered into by another that previously was not enforceable.

On occasion, a person who is in fact not an agent (or who is an agent acting outside the scope of her or his authority) may make a contract on behalf of another (a principal). If the principal affirms that contract by word or by action, an agency relationship is created by **ratification.** Ratification involves a question of intent, and intent can be expressed by either words or conduct. The basic requirements for ratification will be discussed later in this chapter.

Agency by Estoppel

When a principal causes a third person to believe that another person is his or her agent, and the third person deals with the supposed agent, the principal is "estopped to deny" the agency relationship. In such a situation, the principal's actions create the *appearance* of an agency that does not in fact exist. The third person must prove that she or he *reasonably* believed that an agency relationship existed, though. Facts and circumstances must show that an ordinary, prudent person familiar with business practice and custom would have been justified in concluding that the agent had authority.
CASE EXAMPLE 16.6   Francis Azur was president and chief executive officer of ATM Corporation of America. Michelle Vanek, Azur's personal assistant at ATM, reviewed his credit-card statements, among other duties. For seven years, Vanek took unauthorized cash advances from Azur's credit-card account with Chase Bank. The charges appeared on at least sixty-five monthly statements. When Azur discovered Vanek's fraud, he fired her and closed the account. He filed a suit against Chase, arguing that the bank should not have allowed Vanek to take cash advances. The court concluded that Azur (the principal) had given the bank reason to believe that Vanek (the agent) had authority. Therefore, Azur was estopped (prevented) from denying Vanek's authority.[7] ●

---

6. *Laurel Creek Health Care Center v. Bishop,* 2010 WL 985299 (Ky.App. 2010).
7. *Azur v. Chase Bank, USA, N.A.,* 601 F.3d 212 (3d Cir. 2010).

Note that the acts or declarations of a purported *agent* in and of themselves do not create an agency by estoppel. Rather, it is the deeds or statements of the *principal* that create an agency by estoppel.

Agency by Operation of Law

The courts may find an agency relationship in the absence of a formal agreement in other situations as well. This can occur in the family setting. When one spouse purchases certain necessaries and charges them to the other spouse's account, for example, the courts will often rule that the second spouse is liable to pay for the necessaries, either because of a social policy of promoting the general welfare of a spouse or because of a legal duty to supply necessaries to family members.

Agency by operation of law may also occur in emergency situations, when the agent's failure to act outside the scope of his or her authority would cause the principal substantial loss. If the agent is unable to contact the principal, the courts will often grant this emergency power. For instance, a railroad engineer may contract on behalf of her or his employer for medical care for an injured motorist hit by the train.

Duties of Agents and Principals

Learning Objective 3
What duties do agents and principals owe to each other?

Once the principal-agent relationship has been created, both parties have duties that govern their conduct. As mentioned previously, an agency relationship is *fiduciary*—one of trust. In a fiduciary relationship, each party owes the other the duty to act with the utmost good faith.

In general, for every duty of the principal, the agent has a corresponding right, and vice versa. When one party to the agency relationship violates his or her duty to the other party, the remedies available to the nonbreaching party arise out of contract and tort law. These remedies include monetary damages, termination of the agency relationship, an injunction, and required accountings.

(SJ Locke/iStockphoto.com)

Agent's Duties to the Principal

Generally, the agent owes the principal five duties: (1) performance, (2) notification, (3) loyalty, (4) obedience, and (5) accounting.

What five duties does a real estate agent owe to his clients?

Performance   An implied condition in every agency contract is the agent's agreement to use reasonable diligence and skill in performing the work. When an agent fails entirely to perform her or his duties, liability for breach of contract normally will result. The degree of skill or care required of an agent is usually that expected of a reasonable person under similar circumstances. Generally, this is interpreted to mean ordinary care. If an agent has claimed to possess special skill, however, failure to exercise that degree of skill constitutes a breach of the agent's duty.

Not all agency relationships are based on contract. In some situations, an agent acts gratuitously—that is, not for monetary compensation. A gratuitous agent cannot be liable for breach of contract, as there is no contract, but he or she can be subject to tort liability. Once a gratuitous agent has begun to act in an agency capacity, he or she has the duty to continue to perform in that capacity in an acceptable manner and is subject to the same standards of care and duty to perform as other agents.

Notification   An agent is required to notify the principal of all matters that come to her or his attention concerning the subject matter of the agency. This is the duty of notification, or the duty to inform. **EXAMPLE 16.7**   Lang, an artist, is about to negotiate a contract to sell a series of paintings to Barber's Art Gallery for $25,000. Lang's agent learns that Barber is insolvent and will be unable to pay for the paintings. The agent has a duty to inform Lang of this fact because it is relevant to the subject matter of the agency—the sale of Lang's paintings. •

Loyalty   Loyalty is one of the most fundamental duties in a fiduciary relationship. Basically, the agent has the duty to act *solely for the benefit of his or her principal* and not in the interest of the agent or a third party. For instance, an agent cannot represent two principals in the same transaction unless both know of the dual capacity and consent to it.

The duty of loyalty also means that any information or knowledge acquired through the agency relationship is considered confidential. It would be a breach of loyalty to disclose such information either during the agency relationship or after its termination.

In short, the agent's loyalty must be undivided. The agent's actions must be strictly for the benefit of the principal and must not result in any secret profit for the agent. **CASE EXAMPLE 16.8**   Don Cousins contracts with Leo Hodgins, a real estate agent, to negotiate the purchase of an office building. While working for Cousins, Hodgins discovers that the property owner will sell the building only as a package deal with another parcel, so he buys the two properties, intending to resell the building to Cousins. Hodgins has breached his fiduciary duties. As a real estate agent, Hodgins has a duty to communicate all offers to his principal and not to purchase the property secretly and then resell it to his principal. Hodgins is required to act in Cousins's best interests and can become the purchaser in this situation only with Cousins's knowledge and approval.[8] •

Obedience   When acting on behalf of a principal, an agent has a duty to follow all lawful and clearly stated instructions of the principal. Any deviation from such instructions is a violation of this duty.

During emergency situations, however, when the principal cannot be consulted, the agent may deviate from the instructions without violating this duty. Whenever instructions are not clearly stated, the agent can fulfill the duty of obedience by acting in good faith and in a manner reasonable under the circumstances.

Accounting   Unless an agent and a principal agree otherwise, the agent has the duty to keep and make available to the principal an account of all property and funds received and paid out on behalf of the principal. This includes gifts from third parties in connection with the agency. For instance, a gift from a customer to a salesperson for prompt deliveries made by the salesperson's firm, in the absence of a company policy to the contrary, belongs to the firm. The agent has a duty to maintain separate accounts for the principal's funds and for the agent's personal funds, and the agent must not intermingle these accounts.

Principal's Duties to the Agent

The principal also owes certain duties to the agent. These duties relate to compensation, reimbursement and indemnification, cooperation, and safe working conditions.

Compensation   In general, when a principal requests services from an agent, the agent reasonably expects payment. The principal therefore has a duty to pay the agent for services rendered. For instance, when an accountant or an attorney is asked to act as an

---

8. *Cousins v. Realty Ventures, Inc.*, 844 So.2d 860 (La.App. 5th Cir. 2003).

agent, an agreement to compensate the agent for service is implied. The principal also has a duty to pay that compensation in a timely manner. Unless the agency is gratuitous and the agent does not act in exchange for payment, the principal must pay the agreed-on value for the agent's services. If no amount has been expressly agreed on, the principal owes the agent the customary compensation for such services.

CASE EXAMPLE 16.9 Keith Miller worked as a sales representative for Paul M. Wolff Company, a subcontractor specializing in concrete finishing services. Sales representatives at Wolff are paid a 15 percent commission on projects that meet a 35 percent gross profit threshold, after the projects are completed and Wolff is paid. When Miller resigned, he asked for commissions on fourteen projects for which he had secured contracts. Wolff refused, so Miller sued. The court found that "an agent is entitled to receive commissions on sales that result from the agent's efforts," even after the employment or agency relationship ends. Miller had met the gross profit threshold on ten of the unfinished projects, and therefore he was entitled to more than $21,000 in commissions. (The court also awarded Miller nearly $75,000 in attorneys' fees and court costs.)[9] ●

> **PREVENTING LEGAL DISPUTES**
>
> Many disputes arise because the principal and agent did not specify how much the agent would be paid. To avoid such disputes, always state in advance, and in writing, the amount or rate of compensation that you will pay your agents. Even when dealing with salespersons, such as real estate agents, who customarily are paid a percentage of the value of the sale, it is best to explicitly state the rate of compensation.

Reimbursement and Indemnification Whenever an agent disburses funds at the request of the principal or to pay for necessary expenses in the reasonable performance of his or her agency duties, the principal has the duty to reimburse the agent for these payments. Agents cannot recover for expenses incurred through their own misconduct or negligence, though.

Subject to the terms of the agency agreement, the principal has the duty to compensate, or *indemnify*, an agent for liabilities incurred because of authorized and lawful acts and transactions. For instance, if the principal fails to perform a contract formed by the agent with a third party and the third party then sues the agent, the principal must compensate the agent for any costs incurred in defending against the lawsuit.

Additionally, the principal must indemnify (pay) the agent for the value of benefits that the agent confers on the principal. The amount of indemnification is usually specified in the agency contract. If it is not, the courts will look to the nature of the business and the type of loss to determine the amount. Note that this rule applies to acts by gratuitous agents as well. If the finder of a dog that becomes sick takes the dog to a veterinarian and pays the required fees for the veterinarian's services, the (gratuitous) agent is entitled to be reimbursed by the dog's owner for those fees.

Cooperation A principal has a duty to cooperate with the agent and to assist the agent in performing her or his duties. The principal must do nothing to prevent that performance.

When a principal grants an agent an exclusive territory, for instance, the principal creates an *exclusive agency* and cannot compete with the agent or appoint or allow another agent to so compete. If the principal does so, she or he may be liable for the agent's lost sales or profits.

EXAMPLE 16.10 River City Times Company (the principal) grants Emir (the agent) the right to sell its newspapers at a busy downtown intersection to the exclusion of all other

---

9. *Miller v. Paul M. Wolff Co.*, 178 Wash.App. 957, 316 P.3d 1113 (2014).

vendors. This creates an exclusive territory within which only Emir has the right to sell those newspapers. If River City Times allows another vendor to sell its papers on another corner of the same intersection, Emir can sue for lost profits. ●

Agent's Authority

An agent's authority to act can be either *actual* (express or implied) or *apparent*. If an agent contracts outside the scope of his or her authority, the principal may still become liable by ratifying the contract.

Express Authority

Express authority is authority declared in clear, direct, and definite terms. Express authority can be given orally or in writing.

Equal Dignity Rule
In most states, the **equal dignity rule** requires that if the contract being executed is or must be in writing, then the agent's authority must also be in writing. Failure to comply with the equal dignity rule can make a contract voidable *at the option of the principal.* The law regards the contract at that point as a mere offer. If the principal decides to accept the offer, the agent's authority must be ratified, or affirmed, in writing.

 EXAMPLE 16.11 Lee (the principal) orally asks Parkinson (the agent) to sell a ranch that Lee owns. Parkinson finds a buyer and signs a sales contract (a contract for an interest in realty must be in writing) on behalf of Lee to sell the ranch. The buyer cannot enforce the contract unless Lee subsequently ratifies Parkinson's agency status *in writing*. Once Parkinson's agency status is ratified, either party can enforce rights under the contract. ●

 Modern business practice allows exceptions to the equal dignity rule. An executive officer of a corporation normally is not required to obtain written authority from the corporation to conduct *ordinary* business transactions. The equal dignity rule also does not apply when an agent acts in the presence of a principal or when the agent's act of signing is merely perfunctory (automatic). Thus, if the principal negotiates a contract but is called out of town the day it is to be signed and orally authorizes his or her agent to sign the contract, the oral authorization is sufficient.

Power of Attorney
Giving an agent a **power of attorney** confers express authority.[10] The power of attorney normally is a written document and is usually notarized. (A document is notarized when a **notary public**—a person authorized by the state to attest to the authenticity of signatures—signs and dates the document and imprints it with his or her seal of authority.) Most states have statutory provisions for creating a power of attorney.

 A power of attorney can be special (permitting the agent to do specified acts only), or it can be general (permitting the agent to transact all business for the principal). Because a general power of attorney grants extensive authority to an agent to act on behalf of the principal in many ways, it should be used with great caution. Ordinarily, a power of attorney terminates on the incapacity or death of the person giving the power.[11]

---

10. An agent who holds the power of attorney is called an *attorney-in-fact* for the principal. The holder does not have to be an attorney-at-law (and often is not).
11. A durable power of attorney, however, continues to be effective despite the principal's incapacity. An elderly person, for example, might grant a durable power of attorney to provide for the handling of property and investments or specific health-care needs should she or he become incompetent.

Equal Dignity Rule A rule requiring that an agent's authority be in writing if the contract to be made on behalf of the principal must be in writing.

Power of Attorney Authorization for another to act as one's agent or attorney in either specified circumstances (special) or in all situations (general).

Notary Public A public official authorized to attest to the authenticity of signatures.

What functions does a notary public perform?

(Lucky Business/Shutterstock.com)

Implied Authority

An agent has the *implied authority* to do what is reasonably necessary to carry out his or her express authority and accomplish the objectives of the agency. Authority can also be implied by custom or inferred from the position the agent occupies.

EXAMPLE 16.12   Mueller is employed by Al's Supermarket to manage one of its stores. Al's has not expressly stated that Mueller has authority to contract with third persons. In this situation, though, authority to manage a business implies authority to do what is reasonably required (as is customary or can be inferred from a manager's position) to operate the business. A manager's implied authority typically includes forming contracts to hire employees, to buy merchandise and equipment, and to advertise the products sold in the store. •

If an employee-agent makes unauthorized use of his employer's computer data, has he committed a crime? See this chapter's *Online Developments* feature that follows for a discussion of this issue.

ONLINE DEVELOPMENTS

What Happens When an Agent Breaches Company Policy on the Use of Electronic Data?

Suppose that an employee-agent who is authorized to access company trade secrets contained in computer files takes those secrets to a competitor for whom the employee is about to begin working. Clearly, the agent has violated the ethical—and legal—duty of loyalty to the principal. Does this breach of loyalty mean that the employee's act of accessing the trade secrets was unauthorized?

The question has significant implications for both parties. If the action was unauthorized, the employee will be subject to state and federal laws prohibiting unauthorized access to computer information and data, including the Computer Fraud and Abuse Act (CFAA, discussed in Chapter 6). If the action was authorized, these laws will not apply.

Employees "Exceed Authorized Access" to Their Company's Database

David Nosal once worked for Korn/Ferry and had access to the company's confidential database. When he left, he encouraged several former colleagues who still worked there to join him in starting a competing firm. He asked them to access Korn/Ferry's database and download source lists, names, and client contact information before they quit. The employees had authority to access the database, but Korn/Ferry's policy forbade disclosure of confidential information.

The government filed charges against Nosal and his colleagues for violating the CFAA, among other things.

A Court Rules That Violating an Employer's Use Restrictions Is Not a Crime

The U.S. Court of Appeals for the Ninth Circuit refused to find that the defendants had violated the CFAA. The court ruled that the phrase "exceed authorized access" in the CFAA refers to restrictions on access, not restrictions on use. The court reasoned that Congress's intent in enacting the CFAA was to prohibit people from hacking into computers without authorization.

The court also stated that the CFAA should not be used to criminally prosecute persons who use data in an unauthorized or unethical way. The court pointed out that "adopting the government's interpretation would turn vast numbers of teens and pre-teens into juvenile delinquents—and their parents and teachers into delinquency contributors." Furthermore, "the effect this broad construction of the CFAA has on workplace conduct pales by comparison with its effect on everyone else who uses a computer, smart-phone, iPad, Kindle, Nook, X-box, Blu-Ray player or any other Internet-enabled device."[a]

Critical Thinking

If an employee accesses Facebook at work even though personal use of a workplace computer is against the employer's stated policies, can the employee be criminally prosecuted? Why or why not?

a. *United States. v. Nosal,* 676 F.3d 854 (9th Cir. 2012).

Apparent Authority

Apparent Authority Authority that is only apparent, not real. An agent's apparent authority arises when the principal causes a third party to believe that the agent has authority, even though she or he does not.

Actual authority (express or implied) arises from what the principal manifests *to the agent.* An agent has **apparent authority** when the principal, by either words or actions, causes a *third party* reasonably to believe that an agent has authority to act, even though the agent has no express or implied authority. If the third party changes his or her position in reliance on the principal's representations, the principal may be *estopped* (prevented) from denying that the agent had authority.

Apparent authority usually comes into existence through a principal's pattern of conduct over time. At issue in the following *Spotlight Case* was whether the manager of a horse breeding operation had the authority to bind the farm's owner in a contract guaranteeing breeding rights.

Spotlight on Apparent Authority of Managers

Case 16.2
Lundberg v. Church Farm, Inc.
Court of Appeals of Illinois, 502 N.E.2d 806, 151 Ill.App.3d 452 (1986).

Who can guarantee a minimum number of foals during a limited time period?

BACKGROUND AND FACTS Gilbert Church owned a horse breeding farm in Illinois managed by Herb Bagley. Advertisements for the breeding rights to one of Church Farm's stallions, Imperial Guard, directed all inquiries to "Herb Bagley, Manager." Vern and Gail Lundberg bred Thoroughbred horses. The Lundbergs contacted Bagley and executed a preprinted contract giving them breeding rights to Imperial Guard "at Imperial Guard's location," subject to approval of the mares by Church. Bagley handwrote a statement on the contract that guaranteed the Lundbergs "six live foals in the first two years." He then signed it "Gilbert G. Church by H. Bagley."

The Lundbergs bred four mares, which resulted in one live foal. Church then moved Imperial Guard from Illinois to Oklahoma. The Lundbergs sued Church for breaching the contract by moving the horse. Church claimed that Bagley was not authorized to sign contracts for Church or to change or add terms, but only to present preprinted contracts to potential buyers. Church testified that although Bagley was his farm manager and the contact person for breeding rights, Bagley had never before modified the preprinted forms or signed Church's name on these contracts. The jury found in favor of the Lundbergs and awarded $147,000 in damages. Church appealed.

IN THE WORDS OF THE COURT. . .
Justice *UNVERZAGT* delivered the opinion of the court:
* * * *

Defendant contends that plaintiffs have failed to establish that Bagley had apparent authority to negotiate and sign the Lundberg contract for Church Farm * * *.

The party asserting an agency has the burden of proving its existence * * * *but may do so by inference and circumstantial evidence.* * * * *Additionally, an agent may bind his principal by acts which the principal has not given him actual authority to perform, but which he appears authorized to perform.* * * * *An agent's apparent authority is that authority which* "the principal knowingly permits the agent to assume or which he holds his agent out as possessing. It is the authority that a reasonably prudent man, exercising diligence and discretion, in view of the principal's conduct, would naturally suppose the agent to possess." [Emphasis added.]

Plaintiffs produced evidence at trial that Gil Church approved the Imperial Guard advertisement listing Herb Bagley as Church Farm's manager, and directing all inquiries to him. Church also permitted Bagley to live on the farm and to handle its daily operations. Bagley was the only person available to visitors to the farm. Bagley answered Church Farm's phone calls, and there was a preprinted signature line for him on the breeding rights package.

The conclusion is inescapable that Gil Church affirmatively placed Bagley in a managerial position giving him complete control of Church Farm and its dealings with the public. We believe that this is just the sort of "holding out" of an agent by a principal that justifies a third person's reliance on the agent's authority.

We cannot accept defendant's contention that the Lundbergs were affirmatively obligated to seek out Church to ascertain

Spotlight Case 16.2—Continued

the actual extent of Bagley's authority. Where an agent has apparent authority to act, the principal will be liable in spite of any undisclosed limitations the principal has placed on that authority.

DECISION AND REMEDY The state appellate court affirmed the lower court's award of $147,000 to the Lundbergs. Because Church allowed circumstances to lead the Lundbergs to believe Bagley had authority, Church was bound by Bagley's actions.

THE LEGAL ENVIRONMENT DIMENSION *The court held that Church had allowed the Lundbergs to believe that Bagley was his agent. What steps could Church have taken to protect himself against a finding of apparent authority?*

THE ETHICAL DIMENSION *Does a principal have an ethical responsibility to inform an unaware third party that an apparent agent does not in fact have the authority to act on the principal's behalf? Explain.*

Ratification

As already mentioned, ratification occurs when the principal affirms an agent's *unauthorized* act. When ratification occurs, the principal is bound to the agent's act, and the act is treated as if it had been authorized by the principal *from the outset*. Ratification can be either express or implied.

If the principal does not ratify the contract, the principal is not bound, and the third party's agreement with the agent is viewed as merely an unaccepted offer. Because the third party's agreement is an unaccepted offer, the third party can revoke the offer at any time, without liability, before the principal ratifies the contract.

The requirements for ratification can be summarized as follows:

1. The agent must have acted on behalf of an identified principal who subsequently ratifies the action.
2. The principal must know of all material facts involved in the transaction. If a principal ratifies a contract without knowing all of the facts, the principal can rescind (cancel) the contract.
3. The principal must affirm the agent's act in its entirety.
4. The principal must have the legal capacity to authorize the transaction at the time the agent engages in the act and at the time the principal ratifies. The third party must also have the legal capacity to engage in the transaction.
5. The principal's affirmation must occur before the third party withdraws from the transaction.
6. The principal must observe the same formalities when approving the act done by the agent as would have been required to authorize it initially.

Liability in Agency Relationships

Frequently, a question arises as to which party, the principal or the agent, should be held liable for contracts formed by the agent or for torts or crimes committed by the agent. We look here at these aspects of agency law.

Liability for Contracts

Liability for contracts formed by an agent depends on how the principal is classified and on whether the actions of the agent were authorized or unauthorized. Principals are classified as disclosed, partially disclosed, or undisclosed.[12]

Learning Objective 4
When is a principal liable for the agent's actions with respect to third parties? When is the agent liable?

---

12. *Restatement (Third) of Agency,* Section 1.04(2).

Disclosed Principal A principal whose identity is known to a third party at the time the agent makes a contract with the third party.

Partially Disclosed Principal A principal whose identity is unknown by a third party, but the third party knows that the agent is or may be acting for a principal at the time the agent and the third party form a contract.

Undisclosed Principal A principal whose identity is unknown by a third party, and that person has no knowledge that the agent is acting for a principal at the time the agent and the third party form a contract.

A **disclosed principal** is a principal whose identity is known by the third party at the time the contract is made by the agent. A **partially disclosed principal** is a principal whose identity is not known by the third party, but the third party knows that the agent is or may be acting for a principal at the time the contract is made. **EXAMPLE 16.13** Sarah has contracted with a real estate agent to sell certain property. She wishes to keep her identity a secret, but the agent makes it clear to potential buyers of the property that the agent is acting in an agency capacity. In this situation, Sarah is a partially disclosed principal. •

An **undisclosed principal** is a principal whose identity is totally unknown by the third party, and the third party has no knowledge that the agent is acting in an agency capacity at the time the contract is made.

Authorized Acts   If an agent acts within the scope of her or his authority, normally the principal is obligated to perform the contract regardless of whether the principal was disclosed, partially disclosed, or undisclosed. Whether the agent may also be held liable under the contract, however, depends on the status of the principal.

Disclosed or Partially Disclosed Principal   A disclosed or partially disclosed principal is liable to a third party for a contract made by an agent who is acting within the scope of her or his authority. If the principal is disclosed, an agent has no contractual liability for the nonperformance of the principal or the third party.

If the principal is partially disclosed, in most states the agent is also treated as a party to the contract, and the third party can hold the agent liable for contractual nonperformance. In the following case, the court applied these principles to determine an agent's liability on a contract to install flooring in a commercial building.

Case 16.3

Stonhard, Inc. v. Blue Ridge Farms, LLC
New York Supreme Court, Appellate Division, Second Department, 114 A.D.3d 757, 980 N.Y.S.2d 507 (2014).

(IP Galantemik D.U./ iStockphoto.com)

Who is liable when the installer of food plant flooring is not paid?

BACKGROUND AND FACTS Stonhard, Inc., makes epoxy and urethane flooring and installs it in industrial and commercial buildings. Marvin Sussman entered into a contract with Stonhard to install flooring at Blue Ridge Farms, LLC, a food-manufacturing facility in Brooklyn, New York. Sussman did not disclose that he was acting as an agent for the facility's owner, Blue Ridge Foods, LLC. When Stonhard was not paid for the work, the flooring contractor filed a suit in a New York state court against the facility, its owner, and Sussman to recover damages for breach of contract. Stonhard filed a motion for summary judgment against the defendants, offering in support of the motion evidence of the contract entered into with Sussman. The court denied Stonhard's motion and dismissed the complaint against Sussman. Stonhard appealed.

IN THE WORDS OF THE COURT . . .
William F. *MASTRO*, J.P. [Judge Presiding], Reinaldo E. *RIVERA*, Sandra L. *SGROI*, and Jeffrey A. *COHEN*, JJ.
       * * * *

An agent who acts on behalf of a disclosed principal will generally not be liable for a breach of contract. A principal is considered to be disclosed if, at the time of a transaction conducted by an agent, the other party to the contract had notice that the agent was acting for the principal and of the principal's identity. *Knowledge of the real principal is the test, and this means actual knowledge, not suspicion.* The defense of agency in avoidance of contractual liability is an affirmative defense and the burden of establishing the disclosure of the agency relationship and the corporate existence and identity of the principal is upon he or she who asserts an agency relationship. [Emphasis added.]

The plaintiff established, *prima facie,* its entitlement to judgment as a matter of law on the complaint insofar as asserted against the defendant Marvin Sussman with evidence that it entered into a contract with Sussman of "Blue Ridge Farms," pursuant to which the plaintiff was to install flooring at the "Blue Ridge Farms" food manufacturing facility in Brooklyn,

Case 16.3—Continued

and Sussman failed to disclose that he was acting as an agent for the defendant Blue Ridge Foods, LLC, which owns the facility. * * * The documentary evidence submitted on the plaintiff's motion * * * indicates at best that Sussman was acting as an agent for a partially disclosed principal, in that the agency relationship was known, but the identity of the principal remained undisclosed. *As an agent for an undisclosed [or partially disclosed] principal, Sussman became personally liable under the contract.* [Emphasis added.]

Accordingly, the [lower] Court should have granted that branch of the plaintiff's motion which was for summary judgment on the complaint insofar as asserted against Sussman.

DECISION AND REMEDY A state intermediate appellate court reversed the lower court's dismissal of Stonhard's complaint and issued a summary judgment in the plaintiff's favor. The evidence of the parties' contract indicated that Sussman "at best" was acting as an agent for a partially disclosed principal (or he was acting as an agent for an undisclosed principal). In that capacity, Sussman was personally liable on the contract with Stonhard.

THE LEGAL ENVIRONMENT DIMENSION *The court ruled that Sussman was personally liable on the contract with Stonhard. Is the principal, Blue Ridge Foods, also liable? Explain.*

THE E-COMMERCE DIMENSION *The court cited "documentary evidence," which is evidence contained in documents, such as a contract offered to prove its terms. Could documentary evidence include a printout of e-mail exchanged between the parties?*

Undisclosed Principal When neither the fact of agency nor the identity of the principal is disclosed, the undisclosed principal is bound to perform just as if the principal had been fully disclosed at the time the contract was made. The agent is also liable as a party to the contract.

When a principal's identity is undisclosed and the agent is forced to pay the third party, the agent is entitled to be indemnified (compensated) by the principal. The principal had a duty to perform, even though his or her identity was undisclosed, and failure to do so will make the principal ultimately liable.

Once the undisclosed principal's identity is revealed, the third party generally can elect to hold either the principal or the agent liable on the contract. Conversely, the undisclosed principal can require the third party to fulfill the contract, *unless* (1) the undisclosed principal was expressly excluded as a party in the contract, (2) the contract is a negotiable instrument signed by the agent with no indication of signing in a representative capacity, or (3) the performance of the agent is personal to the contract, allowing the third party to refuse the principal's performance.

CASE EXAMPLE 16.14 Bobby Williams bought a car at Sherman Henderson's auto repair business in Monroe, Louisiana, for $3,000. Henderson negotiated and made the sale for the car's owner, Joe Pike, whose name was not disclosed. Williams drove the car to Memphis, Tennessee, where his daughter was a student. Three days after the sale, the car erupted in flames. Williams extinguished the blaze and contacted Henderson. The vehicle was soon stolen, which prevented Williams from returning it to Henderson. Williams later filed suits against both Pike and Henderson. The court noted that the state had issued Pike a permit to sell the car. The car was displayed for sale at Henderson's business, and Henderson actually sold it. This made Pike the principal and Henderson his agent. The fact that their agency relationship was not made clear to Williams made Pike an undisclosed principal. Williams could thus hold both Pike and Henderson liable for the condition of the car.[13] ●

Unauthorized Acts If an agent has no authority but nevertheless contracts with a third party, the principal cannot be held liable on the contract. It does not matter whether the principal was disclosed, partially disclosed, or undisclosed. The *agent* is liable,

---

13. *William v. Pike,* 58 So.3d 525 (2011).

however. **EXAMPLE 16.15**   Scranton signs a contract for the purchase of a truck, purportedly acting as an agent under authority granted by Johnson. In fact, Johnson has not given Scranton any such authority. Johnson refuses to pay for the truck, claiming that Scranton had no authority to purchase it. The seller of the truck is entitled to hold Scranton liable for payment. •

If the principal is disclosed or partially disclosed, the agent is liable to the third party as long as the third party relied on the agency status. The agent's liability here is based on the breach of an *implied warranty of authority,* not on breach of the contract itself.[14] An agent impliedly warrants that he or she has the authority to enter a contract on behalf of the principal. If the third party knows at the time the contract is made that the agent does not have authority—or if the agent expresses to the third party *uncertainty* as to the extent of her or his authority—then the agent is not personally liable.

Liability for Torts and Crimes

Obviously, any person, including an agent, is liable for her or his own torts and crimes. Whether a principal can also be held liable for an agent's torts and crimes depends on several factors. In some situations, a principal may be held liable not only for the torts of an agent but also for the torts committed by an independent contractor.

Principal's Tortious Conduct   A principal conducting an activity through an agent may be liable for harm resulting from the principal's own negligence or recklessness. Thus, a principal may be liable for giving improper instructions, authorizing the use of improper materials or tools, or establishing improper rules that resulted in the agent's committing a tort. **EXAMPLE 16.16**   Jack knows that Suki is not qualified to drive large trucks but nevertheless tells her to use the company truck to deliver some equipment to a customer. If someone is injured as a result, Jack (the principal) will be liable for his own negligence in giving improper instructions to Suki. •

Principal's Authorization of Agent's Tortious Conduct   A principal who authorizes an agent to commit a tort may be liable to persons or property injured thereby, because the act is considered to be the principal's. **EXAMPLE 16.17**   Selkow directs his agent, Warren, to cut the corn on specific acreage, which neither of them has the right to do. The harvest is therefore a trespass (a tort), and Selkow is liable to the owner of the corn. •

Note also that an agent acting at the principal's direction can be liable as a *tortfeasor* (one who commits a wrong, or tort), along with the principal, for committing the tortious act even if the agent was unaware of the wrongfulness of the act. Assume in *Example 16.17* that Warren, the agent, did not know that Selkow had no right to harvest the corn. Warren can be held liable to the owner of the field for damages, along with Selkow, the principal.

Liability for Agent's Misrepresentation   A principal is exposed to tort liability whenever a third person sustains a loss due to the agent's misrepresentation. The principal's liability depends on whether the agent was actually or apparently authorized to make representations and whether the representations were made within the scope of the agency. The principal is always directly responsible for an agent's misrepresentation made within the scope of the agent's authority.

EXAMPLE 16.18   Bassett is a demonstrator for Moore's products. Moore sends Bassett to a home show to demonstrate the products and to answer questions from consumers. Moore

When ski patrollers help an injured skier, is there an agency involved?

(Life Journeys/iStockphoto.com)

---

14. The agent is not liable on the contract because the agent was never intended personally to be a party to the contract.

has given Bassett authority to make statements about the products. If Bassett makes only true representations, all is fine, but if he makes false claims, Moore will be liable for any injuries or damages sustained by third parties in reliance on Bassett's false representations. ●

Liability for Agent's Negligence As mentioned, an agent is liable for his or her own torts. A principal may also be liable for harm an agent caused to a third party under the doctrine of *respondeat superior,*[15] a Latin term meaning "let the master respond." This doctrine is similar to the theory of strict liability discussed in Chapter 5. It imposes **vicarious liability**, or indirect liability, on the employer—that is, liability without regard to the personal fault of the employer—for torts committed by an employee in the course or scope of employment.

When an agent commits a negligent act, both the agent and the principal are liable. **CASE EXAMPLE 16.19** Aegis Communications hired Southwest Desert Images (SDI) to provide landscaping services for its property. An herbicide sprayed by SDI employee David Hoggatt entered the Aegis building through the air-conditioning system and caused Catherine Warner, an Aegis employee, to suffer a heart attack. Warner sued SDI and Hoggatt for negligence, but the lower court dismissed the suit against Hoggatt. On appeal, the court found that Hoggatt was also liable. An agent is not excused from responsibility for tortious conduct just because he is working for a principal.[16] ●

Determining the Scope of Employment The key to determining whether a principal may be liable for the torts of an agent under the doctrine of *respondeat superior* is whether the torts are committed within the scope of the agency or employment. The factors that courts consider in determining whether a particular act occurred within the course and scope of employment are as follows:

1. Whether the employee's act was authorized by the employer.
2. The time, place, and purpose of the act.
3. Whether the act was one commonly performed by employees on behalf of their employers.
4. The extent to which the employer's interest was advanced by the act.
5. The extent to which the private interests of the employee were involved.
6. Whether the employer furnished the means or instrumentality (such as a truck or a machine) by which the injury was inflicted.
7. Whether the employer had reason to know that the employee would do the act in question and whether the employee had ever done it before.
8. Whether the act involved the commission of a serious crime.

The Distinction between a "Detour" and a "Frolic" A useful insight into the "scope of employment" concept may be gained from the judge's classic distinction between a "detour" and a "frolic" in the case of *Joel v. Morison.*[17] In this case, the English court held that if a servant merely took a detour from his master's business, the master is responsible. If, however, the servant was on a "frolic of his own" and not in any way "on his master's business," the master is not liable. **EXAMPLE 16.20** While driving his employer's vehicle to call on a customer, Mandel decides to stop at the post office—which

Respondeat Superior A doctrine under which a principal or an employer is held liable for the wrongful acts committed by agents or employees while acting within the course and scope of their agency or employment.

Vicarious Liability Indirect liability imposed on a supervisory party (such as an employer) for the actions of a subordinate (such as an employee) because of the relationship between the two parties.

Under what circumstances could a school bus driver be charged individually with negligence?

(Scott Muthershaugh/Burlington Times-News/AP Images)

---

15. Pronounced ree-*spahn*-dee-uht soo-*peer*-ee-your.
16. *Warner v. Southwest Desert Images, LLC,* 218 Ariz. 121, 180 P.3d 986 (2008).
17. 6 Car. & P. 501, 172 Eng.Rep. 1338 (1834).

is one block off his route—to mail a personal letter. Mandel then negligently runs into a parked vehicle owned by Chan. In this situation, because Mandel's detour from the employer's business is not substantial, he is still acting within the scope of employment, and the employer is liable.

The result would be different if Mandel had decided to pick up a few friends for cocktails in another city and in the process had negligently run into Chan's vehicle. In that situation, the departure from the employer's business would be substantial, and the employer normally would not be liable to Chan for damages. Mandel would be considered to have been on a "frolic" of his own. ●

An employee going to and from work or to and from meals is usually considered outside the scope of employment. If travel is part of a person's position, however, such as a traveling salesperson or a regional representative of a company, then travel time is normally considered within the scope of employment.

Notice of Dangerous Conditions   The employer is charged with knowledge of any dangerous conditions discovered by an employee and pertinent to the employment situation. **EXAMPLE 16.21**   Brad, a maintenance employee in Martin's apartment building, notices a lead pipe protruding from the ground in the building's courtyard. Brad neglects either to fix the pipe or to inform Martin of the danger. John trips on the pipe and is injured. The employer is charged with knowledge of the dangerous condition regardless of whether or not Brad actually informed him. That knowledge is imputed to the employer by virtue of the employment relationship. ●

Liability for Agent's Intentional Torts   Most intentional torts that employees commit have no relation to their employment. Thus, their employers will not be held liable. Nevertheless, under the doctrine of *respondeat superior,* the employer can be liable for an employee's intentional torts that are committed within the course and scope of employment, just as the employer is liable for negligence. For instance, an employer is liable when an employee (such as a "bouncer" at a nightclub or a security guard at a department store) commits the tort of assault and battery or false imprisonment while acting within the scope of employment.

In addition, an employer who knows or should know that an employee has a propensity for committing tortious acts is liable for the employee's acts even if they ordinarily would not be considered within the scope of employment. For instance, if the employer hires a bouncer knowing that he has a history of arrests for assault and battery, the employer may be liable if the employee viciously attacks a patron in the parking lot after hours.

An employer may also be liable for permitting an employee to engage in reckless actions that can injure others. **EXAMPLE 16.22**   The owner of Bates Trucking observes an employee smoking while filling containerized trucks with highly flammable liquids. Failure to stop the employee will cause the employer to be liable for any injuries that result if a truck explodes. ●

Liability for Independent Contractor's Torts   Generally, an employer is not liable for physical harm caused to a third person by the negligent act of an independent contractor in the performance of the contract. This is because the employer does not have *the right to control* the details of an independent contractor's performance.

Exceptions to this rule are made in certain situations, though, such as when unusually hazardous activities are involved. Typical examples of such activities include blasting operations, the transportation of highly volatile chemicals, or the use of poisonous gases. In these situations, an employer cannot be shielded from liability merely by using an independent contractor. Strict liability is imposed on the employer-principal as a matter of law. Also, in some states, strict liability may be imposed by statute.

Liability for Agent's Crimes   An agent is liable for his or her own crimes. A principal or employer is not liable for an agent's crime even if the crime was committed within the scope of authority or employment—unless the principal participated by conspiracy or other action. In some jurisdictions, under specific statutes, a principal may be liable for an agent's violation—in the course and scope of employment—of regulations, such as those governing sanitation, prices, weights, and the sale of liquor.

Termination of Agency Relationships

Agency law is similar to contract law in that both an agency and a contract can be terminated *by an act of the parties* or *by operation of law.* Once the relationship between the principal and the agent has ended, the agent no longer has the right (*actual* authority) to bind the principal. For an agent's *apparent* authority to be terminated, though, third persons may also need to be notified that the agency has been terminated.

Termination by Act of the Parties

An agency may be terminated by act of the parties in any of the following ways:

1. *Lapse of time.* When an agency agreement specifies the time period during which the agency relationship will exist, the agency ends when that period expires. If no definite time is stated, the agency continues for a reasonable time and can be terminated at will by either party. What constitutes a "reasonable time" depends, of course, on the circumstances and the nature of the agency relationship.

2. *Purpose achieved.* If an agent is employed to accomplish a particular objective, such as the purchase of breeding stock for a cattle rancher, the agency automatically ends after the cattle have been purchased. If more than one agent is employed to accomplish the same purpose, such as the sale of real estate, the first agent to complete the sale automatically terminates the agency relationship for all the others.

3. *Occurrence of a specific event.* When an agency relationship is to terminate on the happening of a certain event, the agency automatically ends when the event occurs. If Posner appoints Rubik to handle her business affairs while she is away, the agency terminates when Posner returns.

4. *Mutual agreement.* The parties to an agency can cancel (rescind) their contract by mutually agreeing to terminate the agency relationship, even if it is for a specific duration.

5. *Termination by one party.* As a general rule, either party can terminate the agency relationship (the act of termination is called *revocation* if done by the principal and *renunciation* if done by the agent). Although both parties have the *power* to terminate the agency, they may not possess the *right.*

Learning Objective 5
What are some of the ways in which an agency relationship can be terminated?

Wrongful Termination   Wrongful termination can subject the canceling party to a suit for breach of contract (this topic will be discussed further in Chapter 17). **EXAMPLE 16.23**   Rawlins has a one-year employment contract with Munro to act as an agent in return for $65,000. Although Munro has the *power* to discharge Rawlins before the contract period expires, if he does so, he can be sued for breaching the contract because he had no *right* to terminate the agency. •

Notice of Termination   When the parties terminate an agency, it is the principal's duty to inform any third parties who know of the existence of the agency that it has been terminated. Although an agent's actual authority ends when the agency is terminated, an agent's *apparent authority* continues until the third party receives notice (from any source) that such authority has been terminated.

If the principal knows that a third party has dealt with the agent, the principal is expected to notify that person *directly*. For third parties who have heard about the agency but have not yet dealt with the agent, *constructive notice* is sufficient.[18]

No particular form is required for notice of agency termination to be effective. The principal can personally notify the agent, or the agent can learn of the termination through some other means.   **EXAMPLE 16.24**   Manning bids on a shipment of steel, and Stone is hired as an agent to arrange transportation of the shipment. When Stone learns that Manning has lost the bid, Stone's authority to make the transportation arrangement terminates. ● If the agent's authority is written, however, it normally must be revoked in writing.

Termination by Operation of Law

Termination of an agency by operation of law occurs in the circumstances discussed here. Note that when an agency terminates by operation of law, there is no duty to notify third persons.

Death or Insanity
The general rule is that the death or mental incompetence of either the principal or the agent automatically and immediately terminates an ordinary agency relationship. Knowledge of the death is not required.   **EXAMPLE 16.25**   Geer sends Tyron to China to purchase a rare painting. Before Tyron makes the purchase, Geer dies. Tyron's agent status is terminated at the moment of Geer's death, even though Tyron does not know that Geer has died. ● Some states, however, have enacted statutes changing this common law rule to make knowledge of the principal's death a requirement for agency termination.

Impossibility
When the specific subject matter of an agency is destroyed or lost, the agency terminates.   **EXAMPLE 16.26**   Bullard employs Gonzalez to sell Bullard's house, but before any sale, the house is destroyed by fire. In this situation, Gonzalez's agency and authority to sell Bullard's house terminate. ● Similarly, when it is impossible for the agent to perform the agency lawfully because of a change in the law, the agency terminates.

Changed Circumstances
When an event occurs that has such an unusual effect on the subject matter of the agency that the agent can reasonably infer that the principal will not want the agency to continue, the agency terminates.   **EXAMPLE 16.27**   Roberts hires Mullen to sell a tract of land for $20,000. Subsequently, Mullen learns that there is oil under the land and that the land is worth $1 million. The agency and Mullen's authority to sell the land for $20,000 are terminated. ●

Bankruptcy
If either the principal or the agent petitions for bankruptcy, the agency is *usually* terminated. In certain circumstances, as when the agent's financial status is irrelevant to the purpose of the agency, the agency relationship may continue. Insolvency (defined as the inability to pay debts when they become due or when liabilities exceed assets), as distinguished from bankruptcy, does not necessarily terminate the relationship.

War
When the principal's country and the agent's country are at war with each other, the agency is terminated. In this situation, the agency is automatically suspended or terminated because there is no way to enforce the legal rights and obligations of the parties.

---

18. *Constructive notice* is information or knowledge of a fact imputed by law to a person if he or she could have discovered the fact by proper diligence. Constructive notice is often accomplished by newspaper publication.

Reviewing . . . Agency Relationships

Lynne Meyer, on her way to a business meeting and in a hurry, stopped at a Buy-Mart store for a new car charger for her smartphone. There was a long line at one of the checkout counters, but a cashier, Valerie Watts, opened another counter and began loading the cash drawer. Meyer told Watts that she was in a hurry and asked Watts to work faster. Instead, Watts slowed her pace. At this point, Meyer hit Watts.

It is not clear whether Meyer hit Watts intentionally or, in an attempt to retrieve the car charger, hit her inadvertently. In response, Watts grabbed Meyer by the hair and hit her repeatedly in the back of the head, while Meyer screamed for help. Management personnel separated the two women and questioned them about the incident. Watts was immediately fired for violating the store's no-fighting policy. Meyer subsequently sued Buy-Mart, alleging that the store was liable for the tort (assault and battery) committed by its employee. Using the information presented in the chapter, answer the following questions.

1. Under what doctrine discussed in this chapter might Buy-Mart be held liable for the tort committed by Watts?
2. What is the key factor in determining whether Buy-Mart is liable under this doctrine?
3. How is Buy-Mart's potential liability affected by whether Watts's behavior constituted an intentional tort or a tort of negligence?
4. Suppose that when Watts applied for the job at Buy-Mart, she disclosed in her application that she had previously been convicted of felony assault and battery. Nevertheless, Buy-Mart hired Watts as a cashier. How might this fact affect Buy-Mart's liability for Watts's actions?

Debate This The doctrine of *respondeat superior* should be modified to make agents solely liable for their tortious (wrongful) acts committed within the scope of employment.

Key Terms

agency 462
apparent authority 474
disclosed principal 476
equal dignity rule 472

fiduciary 463
independent contractor 463
notary public 472

partially disclosed principal 476
power of attorney 472
ratification 468

respondeat superior 479
undisclosed principal 476
vicarious liability 479

Chapter Summary: Agency Relationships

Agency Relationships	In a *principal-agent* relationship, an agent acts on behalf of and instead of the principal in dealing with third parties. An employee who deals with third parties is normally an agent. An independent contractor is not an employee, and the employer has no control over the details of the person's physical performance. An independent contractor may or may not be an agent.
Formation of Agencies	Agency relationships may be formed by the following methods: 1. *Agreement*—The agency relationship is formed through express consent (oral or written) or implied by conduct. 2. *Ratification*—The principal either by act or by agreement ratifies the conduct of a person who is not in fact an agent. 3. *Estoppel*—The principal causes a third person to believe that another person is the principal's agent, and the third person acts to his or her detriment in reasonable reliance on that belief. 4. *Operation of law*—The agency relationship is based on a social duty or formed in emergency situations when the agent is unable to contact the principal and failure to act outside the scope of the agent's authority would cause the principal substantial loss.

Continued

Chapter Summary: Agency Relationships—Continued

Duties of Agents and Principals	1. *Duties of the agent*—
	    a. Performance—The agent must use reasonable diligence and skill in performing her or his duties.
	    b. Notification—The agent is required to notify the principal of all matters that come to his or her attention concerning the subject matter of the agency.
	    c. Loyalty—The agent has a duty to act solely for the benefit of the principal and not in the interest of the agent or a third party.
	    d. Obedience—The agent must follow all lawful and clearly stated instructions of the principal.
	    e. Accounting—The agent has a duty to make available to the principal records of all property and funds received and paid out on behalf of the principal.
	 2. *Duties of the principal*—
	    a. Compensation—The principal must pay the agreed-on value (or reasonable value) for the agent's services.
	    b. Reimbursement and indemnification—The principal must reimburse the agent for all funds disbursed at the request of the principal and for all funds that the agent disburses for necessary expenses in the reasonable performance of his or her agency duties.
	    c. Cooperation—A principal must cooperate with and assist an agent in performing her or his duties.

Agent's Authority	1. *Express authority*—Can be oral or in writing. Authorization must be in writing if the agent is to execute a contract that must be in writing. 2. *Implied authority*—Authority customarily associated with the position of the agent or authority that is deemed necessary for the agent to carry out expressly authorized tasks. 3. *Apparent authority*—Exists when the principal, by word or action, causes a third party reasonably to believe that an agent has authority to act, even though the agent has no express or implied authority. 4. *Ratification*—The affirmation by the principal of an agent's unauthorized action or promise. For the ratification to be effective, the principal must be aware of all material facts.

Liability in Agency Relationships	1. *Liability for contracts*—If the principal's identity is disclosed or partially disclosed at the time the agent forms a contract with a third party, the principal is liable to the third party under the contract if the agent acted within the scope of his or her authority.
	 2. *Liability for agent's negligence*—Under the doctrine of *respondeat superior,* the principal is liable for any harm caused to another through the agent's torts if the agent was acting within the scope of her or his employment at the time the harmful act occurred.
	 3. *Liability for agent's intentional torts*—Usually, employers are not liable for the intentional torts that their agents commit, unless:
	    a. The acts are committed within the scope of employment, and thus the doctrine of *respondeat superior* applies.
	    b. The employer knows or should know that the employee has a propensity for committing tortious acts.
	    c. The employer allowed the employee to engage in reckless acts that caused injury to another.
	    d. The agent's misrepresentation causes a third party to sustain damage, and the agent had either actual or apparent authority to act.
	 4. *Liability for independent contractor's torts*—A principal usually is not liable for harm caused by an independent contractor's negligence.
	 5. *Liability for agent's crimes*—An agent is responsible for his or her own crimes, even if the crimes were committed while the agent was acting within the scope of authority or employment. A principal will be liable for an agent's crime only if the principal participated by conspiracy or other action or (in some jurisdictions) if the agent violated certain government regulations in the course of employment.

Termination of Agency Relationships	1. *By act of the parties*— Notice to third parties is required when an agency is terminated by act of the parties. Direct notice is required for those who have previously dealt with the agency, but constructive notice will suffice for all other third parties. 2. *By operation of law*— Notice to third parties is not required when an agency is terminated by operation of law.

Issue Spotters

1. Dimka Corporation wants to build a new mall on a specific tract of land. Dimka contracts with Nadine to buy the property. When Nadine learns of the difference between the price that Dimka is willing to pay and the price at which the owner is willing to sell, she wants to buy the land and sell it to Dimka herself. Can she do this? Discuss. (See *Duties of Agent's and Principal's.*)
2. Davis contracts with Estee to buy a certain horse on her behalf. Estee asks Davis not to reveal her identity. Davis makes a deal with Farmland Stables, the owner of the horse, and makes a down payment. Estee does not pay the rest of the price.

Farmland Stables sues Davis for breach of contract. Can Davis hold Estee liable for whatever damages he has to pay? Why or why not? (See *Liability in Agency Relationships*.)

—**Check your answers to the Issue Spotters against the answers provided in Appendix D at the end of this text.**

For Review

1. What is the difference between an employee and an independent contractor?
2. How do agency relationships arise?
3. What duties do agents and principals owe to each other?
4. When is a principal liable for the agent's actions with respect to third parties? When is the agent liable?
5. What are some of the ways in which an agency relationship can be terminated?

Business Scenarios and Case Problems

16–1. Ratification by Principal. Springer, who was running for Congress, instructed his campaign staff not to purchase any campaign materials without his explicit authorization. In spite of these instructions, one of his campaign workers ordered Dubychek Printing Co. to print some promotional materials for Springer's campaign. When the printed materials arrived, Springer did not return them but instead used them during his campaign. When Springer failed to pay for the materials, Dubychek sued for recovery of the price.

Springer contended that he was not liable on the sales contract because he had not authorized his agent to purchase the printing services. Dubychek argued that the campaign worker was Springer's agent and that the worker had authority to make the printing contract. Additionally, Dubychek claimed that even if the purchase was unauthorized, Springer's use of the materials constituted ratification of his agent's unauthorized purchase. Is Dubychek correct? Explain. (See *Agent's Authority*.)

16–2. *Respondeat Superior.* ABC Tire Corp. hires Arnez as a traveling salesperson and assigns him a geographic area and time schedule in which to solicit orders and service customers. Arnez is given a company car to use in covering the territory. One day, Arnez decides to take his personal car to cover part of his territory. It is 11:00 A.M., and Arnez has just finished calling on all customers in the city of Tarrytown. His next appointment is at 2:00 P.M. in the city of Austex, twenty miles down the road. Arnez starts out for Austex, but halfway there he decides to visit a former college roommate who runs a farm ten miles off the main highway. Arnez is enjoying his visit with his former roommate when he realizes that it is 1:45 P.M. and that he will be late for the appointment in Austex. Driving at a high speed down the country road to reach the main highway, Arnez crashes his car into a tractor, severely injuring Thomas, the driver of the tractor. Thomas claims that he can hold ABC Tire Corp. liable for his injuries.

Discuss fully ABC's liability in this situation. (See *Liability in Agency Relationships*.)

16–3. 🔔 **Spotlight on Agency—Independent Contractors.** Frank Frausto delivered newspapers for Phoenix Newspapers, Inc., under a renewable six-month contract called a "Delivery Agent Agreement." The agreement identified Frausto as an independent contractor. Phoenix collected payments from customers and took complaints about delivery. Frausto was assigned the route for his deliveries and was required to deliver the papers within a certain time period each day. Frausto used his own vehicle to deliver the papers and had to provide proof of insurance to Phoenix. Phoenix provided him with health and disability insurance but did not withhold taxes from his weekly income. One morning while delivering papers, Frausto collided with a motorcycle ridden by William Santiago. Santiago filed a negligence action against Frausto and Phoenix. Phoenix argued that it should not be liable because Frausto was an independent contractor. What factors should the court consider in making its ruling? [*Santiago v. Phoenix Newspapers, Inc.,* 794 P.2d 138 (Ariz. 1990)] (See *Agency Relationships*.)

16–4. Employment Relationships. William Moore owned Moore Enterprises, a wholesale tire business. William's son, Jonathan, worked as a Moore Enterprises employee while he was in high school. Later, Jonathan started his own business, called Morecedes Tire. Morecedes regrooved tires and sold them to businesses, including Moore Enterprises. A decade after Jonathan started Morecedes, William offered him work with Moore Enterprises. On the first day, William told Jonathan to load certain tires on a trailer but did not tell him how to do it, and he was injured. Was Jonathan an independent contractor? Discuss. [*Moore v. Moore,* 152 Idaho 245, 269 P.3d 802 (2011)] (See *Agency Relationships*.)

16–5. Disclosed Principal. To display desserts in restaurants, Mario Sclafani ordered refrigeration units from Felix Storch,

Inc. Felix faxed a credit application to Sclafani. The application was faxed back with a signature that appeared to be Sclafani's. Felix delivered the units. When they were not paid for, Felix filed a suit against Sclafani to collect. Sclafani denied that he had seen the application or signed it. He testified that he referred all credit questions to "the girl in the office." Who was the principal? Who was the agent? Who is liable on the contract? Explain. [*Felix Storch, Inc. v. Martinucci Desserts USA, Inc.,* 30 Misc.2d 1217, 924 N.Y.S.2d 308 (Suffolk Co. 2011)] (See *Liability in Agency Relationships.*)

16–6. **Business Case Problem with Sample Answer— Liability for Contracts.** Thomas Huskin and his wife entered into a contract to have their home remodeled by House Medic Handyman Service. Todd Hall signed the contract as an authorized representative of House Medic. It turned out that House Medic was a fictitious name for Hall Hauling, Ltd. The contract did not indicate this, however, and Hall did not inform the Huskins about Hall Hauling. When a contract dispute later arose, the Huskins sued Todd Hall personally for breach of contract. Can Hall be held personally liable? Why or why not? [*Huskin v. Hall,* 2012 WL 553136 (Ohio Ct.App. 2012)] (See *Liability in Agency Relationships.*)

—For a sample answer to Problem 16–6, go to Appendix E at the end of this text.

16–7. **Agent's Duties to Principal.** William and Maxine Miller, shareholders of Claimsco International, Inc., filed a suit in an Illinois state court against the other shareholders, Michael Harris and Kenneth Hoxie, and John Verchota, the accountant who worked for all of them. The Millers alleged that Verchota owed them a duty, which he breached by following Harris's instructions to adjust Claimsco's books to maximize the Millers' financial liabilities, falsely reflect income to them without actually transferring that income, and unfairly disadvantage them compared to the other shareholders. Which duty are the Millers referring to? If the allegations can be proved, did Verchota breach this duty? Explain. [*Miller v.*

Harris, 985 N.E.2d 671, 368 Ill. Dec. 864 (Ill.App. 2 Dist. 2013)] (See *Duties of Agents and Principals.*)

16–8. **Determining Employee Status.** Nelson Ovalles worked as a cable installer for Cox Rhode Island Telecom, LLC, under an agreement with a third party, M&M Communications, Inc. The agreement stated that no employer-employee relationship existed between Cox and M&M's technicians, including Ovalles. Ovalles was required to designate his affiliation with Cox on his work van, clothing, and identification badge, but Cox had minimal contact with him and limited power to control the manner in which he performed his duties. Cox supplied cable wire and similar items, but the equipment was delivered to M&M, not to Ovalles. On a workday, while Ovalles was fulfilling a work order, his van rear-ended a car driven by Barbara Cayer. Is Cox liable to Cayer? Explain. [*Cayer v. Cox Rhode Island Telecom, LLC,* 85 A.3d 1140 (R.I. 2014)] (See *Agency Relationships.*)

16–9. **A Question of Ethics—Vicarious Liability.** Jamie Paliath worked as a real estate agent for Home Town Realty of Vandalia, LLC (the principal, a real estate broker). Torri Auer, a California resident, relied on Paliath's advice and assistance to buy three rental properties in Ohio. Before the sales, Paliath represented that each property was worth approximately twice as much as what Auer would pay, and there was a waiting list of prospective tenants. Paliath also stated that all of the property needed work and agreed to do it for certain prices. Nearly a year later, substantial work was still needed and only a few of the units had been rented. Auer sued Paliath and Home Town Realty for fraudulent misrepresentation. [*Auer v. Paliath,* 986 N.E.2d 1052 (Ohio App. 2013)] (See *Liability in Agency Relationships.*)

1. Were Paliath's representations to Auer within the scope of her employment? Explain. Will the court hold the principal (Home Town Realty) liable for the misrepresentations of the agent (Paliath)?

2. What is the ethical basis for imposing vicarious liability on a principal for an agent's tort?

CHAPTER 17

(Ed Stock/iStockphoto.com)

Employment, Immigration, and Labor Law

CONTENTS

- Employment at Will
- Wages, Hours, and Layoffs
- Family and Medical Leave
- Worker Health and Safety
- Income Security
- Employee Privacy Rights
- Immigration Law
- Labor Unions

LEARNING OBJECTIVES

The five learning objectives below are designed to help improve your understanding of the chapter. After reading this chapter, you should be able to answer the following questions:

1. What is the employment-at-will doctrine? When and why are exceptions to this doctrine made?
2. What federal statute governs working hours and wages?
3. Under the Family and Medical Leave Act, in what circumstances may an employee take family or medical leave?
4. What are the two most important federal statutes governing immigration and employment today?
5. What federal statute gave employees the right to organize unions and engage in collective bargaining?

"The employer generally gets the employees he deserves."
—Sir Walter Gilbey, 1831–1914 (English merchant)

Until the early 1900s, most employer-employee relationships were governed by the common law. Even today, as we will see, private employers have considerable freedom to hire and fire workers under the common law. (This is one reason that employers generally get the employees they deserve, as the chapter-opening quotation observed.)

Numerous statutes and administrative agency regulations, however, now govern the workplace. In this chapter and the next, we look at the most significant laws regulating employment relationships and at how these laws are changing to adapt to new technologies and new problems, such as the influx of illegal immigrants. We also consider some current controversies, such as the degree to which employers can regulate their employees' use of social media.

Employment at Will

Employment relationships have traditionally been governed by the common law doctrine of **employment at will,** which allows either the employer or the employee to end the relationship at any time and for any reason. Thus, employers can fire workers for any reason or for no reason, unless doing so violates an employee's statutory or contractual rights.

Employment at Will A common law doctrine under which either party may terminate an employment relationship at any time for any reason, unless a contract specifies otherwise.

Today, the majority of U.S. workers continue to have the legal status of "employees at will." Indeed, only one state (Montana) does not apply this doctrine. Nonetheless, federal and state statutes prevent the doctrine from being applied in a number of circumstances, and the courts have also created several exceptions.

Exceptions to the Employment-at-Will Doctrine

Learning Objective 1
What is the employment-at-will doctrine? When and why are exceptions to this doctrine made?

Because of the sometimes harsh effects of the employment-at-will doctrine for employees, the courts have carved out various exceptions to it. These exceptions are based on contract theory, tort theory, and public policy.

Exceptions Based on Contract Theory

Some courts have held that an *implied* employment contract exists between an employer and an employee. If an employee is fired outside the terms of the implied contract, he or she may succeed in an action for breach of contract even though no written employment contract exists.

What makes an employment contract "at will"?

EXAMPLE 17.1   BDI Enterprise's employment manual and personnel bulletin both state that, as a matter of policy, workers will be dismissed only for good cause. If an employee reasonably expects BDI to follow this policy, a court may find that there is an implied contract based on the terms stated in the manual and bulletin.[1] ● Generally, the employee's reasonable expectations are the key to whether an employment manual creates an implied contractual obligation.

An employer's oral promises to employees regarding discharge policy may also be considered part of an implied contract. If the employer fires a worker in a manner contrary to what was promised, a court may hold that the employer has violated the implied contract and is liable for damages. Most state courts will judge a claim of breach of an implied employment contract by traditional contract standards.

Courts in a few states have gone further and held that all employment contracts contain an implied covenant of good faith. This means that both sides promise to abide by the contract in good faith. If an employer fires an employee for an arbitrary or unjustified reason, the employee can claim that the covenant of good faith was breached and the contract violated.

Exceptions Based on Tort Theory

In a few situations, the discharge of an employee may give rise to an action for wrongful discharge under tort theories. Abusive discharge procedures may result in a suit for intentional infliction of emotional distress or defamation.

In addition, some courts have permitted workers to sue their employers under the tort theory of fraud. **EXAMPLE 17.2**   Goldfinch, Inc., induces a prospective employee to leave a lucrative job and move to another state by offering "a long-term job with a thriving business." In fact, Goldfinch is not only having significant financial problems but is also planning a merger that will result in the elimination of the position offered to the prospective employee. If the employee takes the job in reliance on Goldfinch's representations and is fired shortly thereafter, the employee may be able to bring an action against the employer for fraud. ●

Exceptions Based on Public Policy

The most common exception to the employment-at-will doctrine is made on the basis that the worker was fired for reasons that violate a fundamental public policy of the jurisdiction. Generally, the public policy involved must be expressed clearly in the jurisdiction's statutory law.

---

1. See, for example, *Janda v. U.S. Cellular Corp.,* 2011 IL App 103552, 961 N.E.2d 425 (1 Dist. 2011).

The public-policy exception may also apply to an employee who is discharged for **whistleblowing**—that is, telling government authorities, upper-level managers, or the media that her or his employer is engaged in some unsafe or illegal activity. Normally, however, whistleblowers seek protection from retaliatory discharge under federal and state statutory laws, such as the Whistleblower Protection Act of 1989.[2]

In the following case, an employer fired an employee after he complained about how his supervisor performed her job. The court had to decide whether the employee was protected by the employer's whistleblower policy even though it was implemented after he was hired.

Whistleblowing An employee's disclosure to government authorities, upper-level managers, or the media that the employer is engaged in unsafe or illegal activities.

---

2. 5 U.S.C. Section 1201.

Case 17.1

Waddell v. Boyce Thompson Institute for Plant Research, Inc.
Supreme Court of New York, Appellate Division, 92 A.D.3d 1172, 940 N.Y.S.2d 331 (2012).

(Galushko Sergey/Shutterstock.com)

BACKGROUND AND FACTS Donald Waddell worked as a business office supervisor for the Boyce Thompson Institute for Plant Research. Waddell did not have an employment contract for a fixed term. The Institute's employee manual said that his job was "terminable at the will of either the employee or [the Institute], at any time, with or without cause." Several months after hiring Waddell, the Institute implemented a whistleblower policy designed to encourage "the highest standards of financial reporting and lawful and ethical behavior." The whistleblower policy stated that the Institute would not retaliate against an employee for making a complaint "in good faith pursuant to this policy."

Waddell repeatedly told his supervisor, Sophia Darling, that she needed to file certain financial documents more promptly. Darling fired Waddell, telling him that his disrespectful and insubordinate conduct violated the Institute's Code of Conduct. Waddell then sued the Institute, and the trial court held that he failed to state a proper claim for breach of an implied contract. Waddell appealed.

IN THE WORDS OF THE COURT . . .
PETERS, J.P. [Justice Presiding]
* * * *

* * * It is well settled that, "absent an agreement establishing a fixed duration, an employment relationship is presumed to be a hiring at will, terminable at any time by either party." This presumption may be rebutted by proof establishing that "the employer made the employee aware of its express written policy limiting its right of discharge and that the employee detrimentally relied on that policy in accepting the employment."

Notably, "the requirements for such an implied contract of employment have been strictly construed, and the successful plaintiff must sustain an 'explicit and difficult pleading burden.'" [Emphasis added.]

* * * We find that plaintiff has failed to state a cause of action for breach of an implied contract. It is undisputed that the Whistleblower Policy had not been implemented until several months after plaintiff began employment with defendant. As such, [the trial court] correctly found that the essential element of detrimental reliance in accepting employment was lacking. Further, plaintiff did not allege that he forsook any other employment opportunities in reliance upon defendant's Whistleblower Policy or because of what he believed to be defendant's termination policy. Nor is the quality of plaintiff's service relevant in determining whether the presumption of at-will employment has been overcome. * * * Accordingly, plaintiff's claim for breach of an implied employment contract was properly dismissed.

DECISION AND REMEDY The New York appellate court found that Waddell did not state a proper claim for breach of contract. It therefore affirmed the judgment for the Institute.

THE LEGAL ENVIRONMENT DIMENSION *If Waddell had been allowed to bring a claim for breach of contract, how might his supervisor, Sophia Darling, have defended her conduct? Explain your answer.*

THE ETHICAL DIMENSION *Is the at-will employment doctrine fair to employees? Why or why not?*

Wrongful Discharge

Whenever an employer discharges an employee in violation of an employment contract or a statute protecting employees, the employee may bring an action for **wrongful discharge.** Even if an employer's actions do not violate any provisions in an employment contract or a statute, the employer may still be subject to liability under a common law doctrine, such as a tort theory or agency. For instance, if an employer discharges a female employee while publicly disclosing private facts about her sex life to her co-workers, the employee could bring a wrongful discharge suit (based on an invasion of privacy—see Chapter 5).

Note that in today's business world, an employment contract may be established or modified via e-mail exchanges. **CASE EXAMPLE 17.3** Robert Moroni negotiated a deal to provide consulting services for Medco Health Solutions, Inc., a third party administrator of prescription-drug plans. Medco's agent, Brian Griffin, sent Moroni an e-mail setting forth the details of the parties' agreement. Moroni e-mailed a counteroffer suggesting that he would work on Medco's projects two days a week for thirteen months, in exchange for $17,000 a month ($204,000 annually), plus travel expenses. Medco accepted via e-mail, and Moroni began performing the contract, but Medco refused to pay him. Moroni sued for breach of contract. Medco argued that no enforceable contract existed and that the e-mail showed only an agreement to agree. The court, however, ruled that the e-mail amounted to an agreement to the essential terms of an employment contract.[3] •

Wages, Hours, and Layoffs

In the 1930s, Congress enacted several laws to regulate the wages and working hours of employees, including the following:

1. The Davis-Bacon Act[4] requires contractors and subcontractors working on federal government construction projects to pay "prevailing wages" to their employees.
2. The Walsh-Healey Act[5] applies to U.S. government contracts. It requires that a minimum wage, as well as overtime pay at 1.5 times regular pay rates, be paid to employees of manufacturers or suppliers entering into contracts with agencies of the federal government.
3. The Fair Labor Standards Act (FLSA)[6] extended wage-hour requirements to cover all employers engaged in interstate commerce or in producing goods for interstate commerce, plus selected other types of businesses. The FLSA, as amended, provides the most comprehensive federal regulation of wages and hours today.

Child Labor

The FLSA prohibits oppressive child labor. Children under fourteen years of age are allowed to do certain types of work, such as deliver newspapers or work for their parents. They may also work in the entertainment industry and (with some exceptions) in agriculture. Children who are fourteen or fifteen years of age are allowed to work, but not in hazardous occupations. There are also numerous restrictions on how many hours per day (particularly on school days) and per week they can work.

Working times and hours are not restricted for persons between the ages of sixteen and eighteen, but they cannot be employed in hazardous jobs or in jobs detrimental to their health and well-being. None of these restrictions apply to individuals over the age of eighteen.

---

3. *Moroni v. Medco Health Solutions, Inc.,* 2008 WL 3539476 (E.D.Mich. 2008).
4. 40 U.S.C. Sections 276a–276a-5.
5. 41 U.S.C. Sections 35–45.
6. 29 U.S.C. Sections 201–260.

Wages and Hours

The FLSA provides that a **minimum wage** of $7.25 per hour must be paid to employees in covered industries (by the time you read this text, the minimum wage may be higher as President Barack Obama has proposed). Congress periodically revises this minimum wage. Additionally, many states have minimum wages. When the state minimum wage is greater than the federal minimum wage, the employee is entitled to the higher wage.

Minimum Wage The lowest wage, either by government regulation or union contract, that an employer may pay an hourly worker.

Overtime Exemptions

Under the FLSA, employees who work more than forty hours per week normally must be paid 1.5 times their regular pay for all hours over forty. Note that the FLSA overtime provisions apply only after an employee has worked more than forty hours per *week*. Thus, employees who work for ten hours a day, four days per week, are not entitled to overtime pay because they do not work more than forty hours per week.

Certain employees—usually executive, administrative, and professional employees, as well as outside salespersons and computer programmers—are exempt from the FLSA's overtime provisions. Employers are not required to pay overtime wages to exempt employees. Employers can voluntarily pay overtime to ineligible employees but cannot waive or reduce the overtime requirements of the FLSA. (Smartphones and other technology have raised new issues concerning overtime wages, as discussed in this chapter's *Beyond Our Borders* feature that follows.)

Administrative Employees   To qualify under the administrative employee exemption, the employee must be paid a salary, not hourly wages, and the employee's primary duty must be directly related to the management or general business operations of the employer. In addition, the employee's primary duty must include the exercise of discretion and independent judgment with respect to matters of significance.

CASE EXAMPLE 17.4   Patty Lee Smith was a pharmaceutical sales representative at Johnson and Johnson (J&J). She traveled to ten physicians' offices a day to promote the benefits of J&J's drug Concerta. Smith's work was unsupervised, she controlled her own schedule, and she received a salary of $66,000. When she filed a claim for overtime pay, the

> "By working faithfully eight hours a day, you may eventually get to be a boss and work twelve hours a day."
>
> Robert Frost, 1875–1963
> (American poet)

 BEYOND OUR BORDERS

Brazil Requires Employers to Pay Overtime for Use of Smartphones after Work Hours

U.S. workers are increasingly arguing that they should receive overtime pay for the time they spend staying connected to work through their iPads, smartphones, or other electronic devices. Indeed, many employers require their employees to carry a mobile device to keep in contact.

Checking e-mail, tweeting, and using LinkedIn or other employment-related apps can be considered work. If employees who are not exempt under the overtime regulations are required to use mobile devices after office hours,

the workers may have a valid claim to overtime wages. The FLSA is not clear about what constitutes work, however, so workers have difficulty showing they are entitled to overtime wages.

In Brazil, however, workers who answer work e-mails on their smartphones or other electronic devices after work are now entitled to receive overtime wages. E-mail from an employer is considered the equivalent of orders given directly to an employee, so it constitutes work. A few other nations also require payment to workers for staying

connected through smartphones and other devices after hours. France has even gone one step further and banned employers from sending e-mails and other electronic communications to their employees' smartphones and tablets after 6:00 P.M.

Critical Thinking

What are the pros and cons of paying overtime wages to workers who check e-mail and perform other work-related tasks electronically after hours?

court held that she was an administrative employee and therefore exempt from the FLSA's overtime provisions.[7] •

Executive Employees

An executive employee is one whose primary duty is management. An employee's primary duty is determined by what he or she does that is of principal value to the employer, not by how much time the employee spends doing particular tasks. An employer cannot deny overtime wages to an employee based only on the employee's job title, however, and must be able to show that the employee's primary duty qualifies her or him for an exemption.[8]

Layoffs

During the latest economic recession in the United States, hundreds of thousands of workers lost their jobs as many businesses disappeared. Other companies struggling to keep afloat reduced costs by restructuring their operations and downsizing their workforces, which meant layoffs. Here, we discuss the Worker Adjustment and Retraining Notification Act,[9] or WARN Act, which applies to employers with more than one hundred full-time employees.

Federal law requires large employers to provide sixty days' notice before implementing a mass layoff or closing an individual plant that employs more than fifty full-time workers. Employers must notify workers of mass layoffs, which means a layoff of at least one-third of the full-time employees at a particular job site.

The WARN Act is intended to give workers advance notice so that they can start looking for a new job while they are still employed and to alert state agencies so that they can provide training and other resources for displaced workers. Employers must provide advance notice of the layoff to the affected workers *or* their representative (if the workers are members of a labor union), as well as to state and local government authorities. Even companies that anticipate filing for bankruptcy normally must provide notice under the WARN Act before implementing a mass layoff.

Family and Medical Leave

In 1993, Congress passed the Family and Medical Leave Act (FMLA)[10] to allow employees to take time off from work for family or medical reasons. A majority of the states have similar legislation, and many employers maintain private family-leave plans for their workers. Recently, additional categories of FMLA leave have been created for military caregivers and for qualifying exigencies (emergencies) that arise due to military service.

Coverage and Applicability of the FMLA

The FMLA requires employers who have fifty or more employees to provide employees with up to twelve weeks of unpaid family or medical leave during any twelve-month period. The FMLA expressly covers private and public (government) employees who have worked for their employers for at least a year. An employee may take *family leave* to care for a newborn baby or a child recently placed for adoption or foster care. An employee can take *medical leave* when the employee or the employee's spouse, child, or parent has a "serious health condition" requiring care.

Learning Objective 3
Under the Family and Medical Leave Act, in what circumstances may an employee take family or medical leave?

A daughter helps her ailing father. Under what circumstances will she be protected by the Family and Medical Leave Act?

(Bowden Images/iStockphoto.com)

---

7. *Smith v. Johnson and Johnson*, 593 F.3d 280 (3d Cir. 2010).
8. See, for example, *Slusser v. Vantage Builders, Inc.*, 576 F.Supp.2d 1207 (D.N.M. 2008).
9. 29 U.S.C. Sections 2101 *et seq.*
10. 29 U.S.C. Sections 2601, 2611–2619, 2651–2654.

In addition, an employee caring for a family member with a serious injury or illness incurred as a result of military duty can take up to *twenty-six weeks of military caregiver leave* within a twelve-month period.[11] Also, an employee can take up to twelve weeks of *qualifying exigency* (emergency) *leave* to handle specified *nonmedical* emergencies when a spouse, parent, or child is in, or called to, active military duty.[12] For instance, when a spouse is deployed to Afghanistan, an employee may take exigency leave to arrange for child care or to deal with financial or legal matters.

When an employee takes FMLA leave, the employer must continue the worker's health-care coverage on the same terms as if the employee had continued to work. On returning from FMLA leave, most employees must be restored to their original position or to a comparable position (with nearly equivalent pay and benefits, for example). An important exception allows the employer to avoid reinstating a *key employee*—defined as an employee whose pay falls within the top 10 percent of the firm's workforce.

In the following case, an employee asked for medical leave to care for her mother on a trip to Las Vegas, Nevada.

---

11. 29 C.F.R. Section 825.200.
12. 29 C.F.R. Section 825.126.

Ballard v. Chicago Park District
United States Court of Appeals, Seventh Circuit, 741 F.3d 838 (2014).

BACKGROUND AND FACTS   Beverly Ballard worked for the Chicago Park District in Chicago, Illinois. She lived with her mother Sarah, who suffered from end-stage congestive heart failure. Beverly served as Sarah's primary caregiver with support from Horizon Hospice & Palliative Care. The hospice helped Sarah plan and secure funds for an end-of-life goal, a "family trip" to Las Vegas. To accompany Sarah as her caretaker, Beverly asked the Park District for unpaid time off under the Family Medical and Leave Act (FMLA). The employer refused. Beverly and Sarah took the trip as planned. Later, the Park District terminated Beverly for "unauthorized absences." She filed a suit in a federal district court against the employer. The court issued a decision in Beverly's favor. The Park District appealed, arguing that Beverly had been absent from work on a "recreational trip."

IN THE WORDS OF THE COURT . . .
FLAUM, Circuit Judge.
 * * * *

We begin with the text of the [FMLA]: an eligible employee is entitled to leave "in order to care for" a family member with a "serious health condition."
 * * * *

 * * * *The FMLA's text does not restrict care to a particular place or geographic location. For instance, it does not say that an employee is entitled to time off "to care *at home* for" a

family member. *The only limitation it places on care is that the family member must have a serious health condition.* We are reluctant, without good reason, to read in another limitation that Congress has not provided. [Emphasis added.]
 * * * *

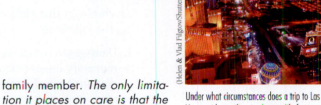

(Helen & Vlad Filgrow/Shutterstock)

Under what circumstances does a trip to Las Vegas with an ailing mother qualify for unpaid time off under the FMLA?

Sarah's basic medical, hygienic, and nutritional needs did not change while she was in Las Vegas, and Beverly continued to assist her with those needs during the trip. In fact, * * * Beverly's presence proved quite important indeed when a fire at the hotel made it impossible to reach their room, requiring Beverly to find another source of insulin and pain medicine. Thus, at the very least, [Beverly] requested leave in order to provide physical care.
 * * * *

 * * * The Park District describes [Beverly's] travel as a "recreational trip" or a "non-medically related pleasure trip." It also raises the specter that employees will help themselves to unpaid FMLA leave in order to take personal vacations, simply by bringing seriously ill family members along. So perhaps what the Park District means to argue is that the real reason Beverly requested leave was in order to take a free pleasure trip, and not in order to care for her mother. * * *

Case 17.2—Continues ➡

Case 17.2—Continued

However, * * * an employer concerned about the risk that employees will abuse the FMLA's leave provisions may of course require that requests be certified by the family member's health care provider. And any worries about opportunistic leave-taking in this case should be tempered by the fact that this dispute arises out of the hospice and palliative care context.

If Beverly had sought leave to care for her mother in Chicago, her request would have fallen within the scope of the FMLA. So too if Sarah had lived in Las Vegas instead of with her daughter, and Beverly had requested leave to care for her mother there. Ultimately, other than a concern that our straightforward reading will "open the door to increased FMLA requests," the Park District gives us no reason to treat the current scenario any differently.

DECISION AND REMEDY The U.S. Court of Appeals for the Seventh Circuit affirmed the lower court's judgment. Under the FMLA, an eligible employee is entitled to take leave from work to care for a family member with a serious health condition. The care is not restricted to a particular place (such as "at home").

THE LEGAL ENVIRONMENT DIMENSION *Under the FMLA, an employee is eligible for leave when he or she is needed to care for a family member. Should "needed to care for" be interpreted to cover only ongoing physical care? Discuss.*

WHAT IF THE FACTS WERE DIFFERENT? *Suppose that Beverly had requested leave to make arrangements for a change in Sarah's care, such as a transfer to a nursing home. Is it likely that the result would have been different? Explain.*

Violations of the FMLA

An employer that violates the FMLA can be required to provide various remedies, including the following:

1. Damages to compensate an employee for lost benefits, denied compensation, and actual monetary losses (such as the cost of providing for care of the family member) up to an amount equivalent to the employee's wages for twelve weeks (twenty-six weeks for military caregiver leave).
2. Job reinstatement.
3. Promotion, if a promotion has been denied.

Worker Health and Safety

Under the common law, employees who were injured on the job had to file lawsuits against their employers to obtain recovery. Today, numerous state and federal statutes protect employees and their families from the risk of accidental injury, death, or disease resulting from employment and provide a right to compensation for on-the-job injuries.

The Occupational Safety and Health Act

At the federal level, the primary legislation protecting employees' health and safety is the Occupational Safety and Health Act of 1970,[13] which is administered by the Occupational Safety and Health Administration (OSHA). The act imposes on employers a general duty to keep workplaces safe. In addition, the act prohibits employers from firing or discriminating against any employee who refuses to work when he or she believes a workplace is unsafe. OSHA has established specific safety standards for various industries that employers must follow.

The act also requires that employers post certain notices in the workplace, perform prescribed record keeping, and submit specific reports. For instance, employers with eleven

---

13. 29 U.S.C. Sections 553, 651–678.

or more employees are required to keep occupational injury and illness records for each employee. Each record must be made available for inspection when requested by an OSHA compliance officer.

Whenever a work-related injury or disease occurs, employers must make reports directly to OSHA. If an employee dies or three or more employees are hospitalized because of a work-related incident, the employer must notify OSHA within eight hours. A company that fails to do so will be fined and may also be prosecuted under state law. Following the incident, a complete inspection of the premises is mandatory.

State Workers' Compensation Laws

State **workers' compensation laws** establish an administrative procedure for compensating workers injured on the job. Instead of suing, an injured worker files a claim with the administrative agency or board that administers local workers' compensation claims.

Most workers' compensation statutes are similar. No state covers all employees. Typically, domestic workers, agricultural workers, temporary employees, and employees of common carriers (companies that provide transportation services to the public) are excluded, but minors are covered. Usually, the statutes allow employers to purchase insurance from a private insurer or a state fund to pay workers' compensation benefits in the event of a claim. Most states also allow employers to be self-insured—that is, employers that show an ability to pay claims do not need to buy insurance.

In general, there are only two requirements for an employee to receive benefits under a state workers' compensation law:

1. The existence of an employment relationship.
2. An *accidental* injury that *occurred on the job or in the course of employment,* regardless of fault. (An injury that occurs while an employee is commuting to or from work usually is not considered to have occurred on the job or in the course of employment and hence is not covered.)

An injured employee must notify her or his employer usually within thirty days of the accident. Generally, an employee must also file a workers' compensation claim with the appropriate state agency or board within sixty days to two years from the time the injury is first noticed, rather than from the time of the accident.

An employee's acceptance of workers' compensation benefits bars an employee from suing for injuries caused by the employer's negligence. A worker may sue an employer who *intentionally* injures him or her, however.

Workers' Compensation Laws State statutes that establish an administrative process for compensating workers for injuries that arise in the course of their employment, regardless of fault.

Income Security

Federal and state governments participate in insurance programs designed to protect employees and their families by covering the financial impact of retirement, disability, death, hospitalization, and unemployment. The key federal law on this subject is the Social Security Act.[14]

Social Security

The Social Security Act provides for old-age (retirement), survivors', and disability insurance. Hence, the act is often referred to as OASDI. Both employers and employees

---

14. 42 U.S.C. Sections 301–1397e.

(Social Security Administration)

Almost every aspect of Social Security programs is now online.

must "contribute" under the Federal Insurance Contributions Act (FICA)[15] to help pay for benefits that will partially make up for the employees' loss of income on retirement.

The basis for the employee's and the employer's contributions is the employee's annual wage base—the maximum amount of the employee's wages that are subject to the tax. The employer withholds the employee's FICA contribution from the employee's wages and ordinarily matches this contribution.

Retired workers are then eligible to receive monthly payments from the Social Security Administration, which administers the Social Security Act. Social Security benefits are fixed by statute but increase automatically with increases in the cost of living.

Medicare

Medicare is a federal government health-insurance program that is administered by the Social Security Administration for people sixty-five years of age and older and for some under the age of sixty-five who are disabled. It originally had two parts, one pertaining to hospital costs and the other to nonhospital medical costs, such as visits to physicians' offices.

Additional Coverage Options   Medicare now offers additional coverage options and a prescription-drug plan. People who have Medicare hospital insurance can also obtain additional federal medical insurance if they pay small monthly premiums, which increase as the cost of medical care increases.

Tax Contributions   Under FICA, both the employer and employee "contribute" to Social Security and Medicare. For Social Security, 12.4 percent of earned income up to an annual limit of $117,000 (for 2014) must be paid. Unlike Social Security, however, Medicare has no cap on the amount of wages subject to its tax. The Medicare tax rate is 2.9 percent. So even if an employee's salary is well above the cap for Social Security, he or she will still owe Medicare tax on the total earned income.

Thus, for Social Security and Medicare together, typically the employer and the employee each pay 7.65 percent (6.2 percent for Social Security + 1.45 percent for Medicare, which is half of the 12.4 and 2.9 percentages, respectively) up to the maximum wage base of $117,000. Any earned income above that threshold is taxed at 2.9 percent for Medicare. Self-employed persons pay both the employer and employee portions of the Social Security and Medicare taxes. Additionally, under the Affordable Care Act, high-income earners are subject to an additional Medicare tax of 0.9 percent (for a total rate of 3.8 percent).

Private Pension Plans

The major federal act regulating employee retirement plans is the Employee Retirement Income Security Act (ERISA).[16] Its provisions govern employers that have private pension funds for their employees.

ERISA created the Pension Benefit Guaranty Corporation (PBGC), an independent federal agency, to provide timely and uninterrupted payment of voluntary private pension benefits. The pension plans pay annual insurance premiums (at set rates adjusted for inflation) to the PBGC, which then pays benefits to participants in the event that a plan is unable to do so.

---

15. 26 U.S.C. Sections 3101–3125.
16. 29 U.S.C. Sections 1001 *et seq.*

ERISA does not require an employer to establish a pension plan. When a plan exists, however, ERISA specifies standards for its management, including investment of funds and record-keeping requirements. A key provision of ERISA concerns vesting. **Vesting** gives an employee a legal right to receive pension benefits at some future date when he or she stops working. ERISA establishes complex vesting rules. Generally, however, all employee contributions to pension plans vest immediately, and employee rights to employer contributions to a plan vest after five years of employment.

Vesting The creation of an absolute or unconditional right or power.

Unemployment Insurance

The Federal Unemployment Tax Act (FUTA)[17] created a state-administered system that provides unemployment compensation to eligible individuals who have lost their jobs. The FUTA and state laws require employers that fall under the provisions of the act to pay unemployment taxes at regular intervals. The proceeds from these taxes are then paid out to qualified unemployed workers.

To be eligible for unemployment compensation, a worker must be willing and able to work. Workers who have been fired for misconduct or who have voluntarily left their jobs are not eligible for benefits. Normally, workers must be actively seeking employment to continue receiving benefits. Temporary measures recently enacted in response to persistent high unemployment rates also allow some jobless persons to retain unemployment benefits while pursuing additional education and training.

COBRA

Federal law also enables workers to continue their health-care coverage after their jobs have been terminated—and the workers are thus no longer eligible for their employers' group health-insurance plans. The Consolidated Omnibus Budget Reconciliation Act (COBRA)[18] prohibits an employer from eliminating a worker's medical, optical, or dental insurance on the voluntary or involuntary termination of the worker's employment. The former employee—not the employer—pays the premiums under COBRA.

Employers, with some exceptions, must inform an employee of COBRA's provisions when the employee faces termination or a reduction of hours that would affect his or her eligibility for coverage under the plan. Only workers fired for gross misconduct are excluded from protection. An employer that does not comply with COBRA risks substantial penalties, such as a tax of up to 10 percent of the annual cost of the group plan or $500,000, whichever is less.

Employer-Sponsored Group Health Plans

The Health Insurance Portability and Accountability Act (HIPAA),[19] which was discussed in Chapter 4 in the context of privacy protections, contains provisions that affect employer-sponsored group health plans. HIPAA does not require employers to provide health insurance, but it does establish requirements for those that do provide such coverage. For instance, HIPAA strictly limits an employer's ability to exclude coverage for *preexisting conditions*, except pregnancy.

In addition, HIPAA restricts the manner in which covered employers collect, use, and disclose the health information of employees and their families. Employers must train employees, designate privacy officials, and distribute privacy notices to ensure that employees' health information is not disclosed to unauthorized parties.

17. 26 U.S.C. Sections 3301–3310.
18. 29 U.S.C. Sections 1161–1169.
19. 29 U.S.C.A. Sections 1181 *et seq.*

Failure to comply with HIPAA regulations can result in civil penalties of up to $100 per person per violation (with a cap of $25,000 per year). The employer is also subject to criminal prosecution for certain types of HIPAA violations and can face up to $250,000 in criminal fines and imprisonment for up to ten years if convicted.

Affordable Care Act

Under the Affordable Care Act[20] (ACA, commonly referred to as Obamacare), most employers with fifty or more full-time employees are required to offer health-insurance benefits. There is no requirement to provide health benefits if fewer than fifty people are employed. Any business offering health benefits to its employees (even if not legally required to do so) may be eligible for tax credits of up to 35 percent to offset the costs.

An employer who fails to provide health benefits as required under the statute can be fined up to $2,000 for each employee after the first thirty people. (This is known as the 50/30 rule: employers with fifty employees must provide insurance, and those failing to do so will be fined for each employee after the first thirty.) An employer who offers a plan that costs an employee more than 9.5 percent of the employee's income may receive a penalty of $3,000.

Employers will be fined for failing to provide benefits only if one of their employees receives a federal subsidy to buy health insurance through a health-insurance exchange. The act provided for these exchanges to establish marketplaces where business owners and individuals can compare premiums and purchase policies.

Employee Privacy Rights

In the last thirty years, concerns about the privacy rights of employees have arisen in response to the sometimes invasive tactics used by employers to monitor and screen workers. Perhaps the greatest privacy concern in today's employment arena has to do with electronic monitoring of employees' activities.

Employers often use video surveillance services to monitor employees. In addition, some employers engage in monitoring employee-generated e-mails.

(Joshua McKerrow/The Annapolis Capital/AP Images)

Electronic Monitoring

More than half of employers engage in some form of electronic monitoring of their employees. Many employers review employees' e-mail, blogs, instant messages, and tweets, as well as their social media, smartphone, and Internet use. Employers may also video their employees at work, record and listen to their telephone conversations and voice mail, and read their text messages and social media posts.

Employee Privacy Protection   Employees of private (nongovernment) employers have some privacy protection under tort law (see Chapter 5) and state constitutions. In addition, state and federal statutes may limit an employer's conduct in certain respects. For instance, as discussed in Chapter 9, the Electronic Communications Privacy Act prohibits employers from intercepting an employee's personal electronic communications unless they are made on devices and systems furnished by the employer. Nonetheless, employers do have considerable leeway to monitor employees in the workplace.

---

20. Pub. L. No. 111-148, 124 Stat. 119, March 23, 2010, codified in various sections of 42 U.S.C.

Private employers generally are free to use filtering software (discussed in Chapter 4) to block access to certain Web sites, such as sites containing sexually explicit images. The First Amendment's protection of free speech prevents only *government employers* from restraining speech by blocking Web sites.

Was There a Reasonable Expectation of Privacy?

When determining whether an employer should be held liable for violating an employee's privacy rights, the courts generally weigh the employer's interests against the employee's reasonable expectation of privacy. Normally, if employees have been informed that their communications are being monitored, they cannot reasonably expect those interactions to be private.

Also, if the employer provided the e-mail system, blog, or social media network that the employee used for communications, a court will typically hold that the employee did not have a reasonable expectation of privacy. For a discussion of how some employers are creating their own social media networks, see this chapter's *Online Developments* feature that follows.

If employees are *not* informed that certain communications are being monitored, however, the employer may be held liable for invading their privacy. Most employers that engage in electronic monitoring notify their employees about the monitoring. Nevertheless, a general policy may not sufficiently protect an employer who monitors forms of communications that the policy fails to mention. For instance, notifying employees that their e-mails and phone calls may be monitored does not necessarily protect an employer who monitors social media posts or text messages.

PREVENTING LEGAL DISPUTES

To avoid legal disputes, exercise caution when monitoring employees, and make sure that any monitoring is conducted in a reasonable place and manner. Establish written policies that include all types of electronic devices used by your employees—including employee-owned devices as well as those that the firm provides—and notify employees of how and when they may be monitored on these devices. Consider informing employees of the reasons for the monitoring. Explain what the concern is, what job repercussions could result, and what recourse employees have in the event that a negative action is taken against them. By providing more privacy protection to employees than is legally required, you can both avoid potential privacy complaints and give employees a sense that they retain some degree of privacy in their workplace, which can lead to greater job satisfaction.

Other Types of Monitoring

In addition to monitoring their employees' online activities, employers also engage in other types of employee screening and monitoring. The practices discussed next have often been challenged as violations of employee privacy rights.

Lie-Detector Tests

At one time, many employers required employees or job applicants to take polygraph examinations (lie-detector tests). Today, the Employee Polygraph Protection Act[21] generally prohibits employers from requiring employees or job applicants to take lie-detector tests or suggesting or requesting that they do so. The act also restricts employers' ability to use or ask about the results of any lie-detector test or to take any negative employment action based on the results.

Certain employers are exempt from these prohibitions. Federal, state, and local government employers, and certain security service firms, may conduct polygraph tests. In

> "We are rapidly entering the age of no privacy, where everyone is open to surveillance at all times; where there are no secrets."
>
> William O. Douglas, 1898–1980 (Associate justice of the United States Supreme Court, 1939–1975)

---

21. 29 U.S.C. Sections 2001 *et seq.*

ONLINE DEVELOPMENTS

Social Media in the Workplace Come of Age

What do corporate giant Dell, Inc., and relatively small Nikon Instruments have in common? They—and many other companies—have created internal social media networks using enterprise social networking software and systems, such as Salesforce.com, Chatter, Yammer, and Socialcast.

A glance at the posts on these internal networks reveals that they are quite different from typical posts on Facebook, LinkedIn, and Twitter. Rather than being personal, the tone is businesslike, and the posts deal with workplace concerns such as how a team is solving a problem or how to sell a new product.

Benefits and Pitfalls of Internal Social Media Networks

Internal social media networks offer businesses several advantages. Perhaps the most important is that employees can obtain real-time information about important issues such as production glitches. They can also exchange tips about how to deal with problems, such as difficult customers. News about the company's new products or those of a competitor is available immediately. Furthermore, employees spend much less time sorting through e-mail. Rather than wasting their fellow employees' time by sending mass e-mailings, workers can post messages or collaborate on presentations via the company's internal network.

Of course, the downside is that these networks may become polluted with annoying "white noise." If employees start posting comments about what they ate for lunch, for example, the system will lose much of its utility. Companies can prevent this from happening, though, by establishing explicit guidelines on what can be posted.

Keeping the Data Safe

Another concern is how to keep all that data and those corporate secrets safe. When a company sets up a social media network, it usually decides which employees can see which files and which employees will belong to each specific "social" group within the company. Often, the data created through a social media network are kept on the company's own servers in secure "clouds."

Critical Thinking

What problems might arise if data from an internal social media system are stored on third party servers?

---

addition, companies that manufacture and distribute controlled substances may perform lie-detector tests. Other employers may use polygraph tests when investigating losses attributable to theft, including embezzlement and the theft of trade secrets.

Drug Testing

In the interests of public safety and to reduce unnecessary costs, many employers, including the government, require their employees to submit to drug testing.

Public Employers   Government (public) employers are constrained in drug testing by the Fourth Amendment to the U.S. Constitution, which prohibits unreasonable searches and seizures (see Chapter 6). Drug testing of public employees is allowed by statute for transportation workers. Courts normally uphold drug testing of certain employees when drug use in a particular job may threaten public safety. Also, when there is a reasonable basis for suspecting public employees of drug use, courts often find that drug testing does not violate the Fourth Amendment.

Private Employers   The Fourth Amendment does not apply to drug testing conducted by private employers. Hence, the privacy rights and drug testing of private-sector employees are governed by state law, which varies from state to state. Many states have statutes that allow drug testing by private employers but put restrictions on when and how the testing may be performed. A collective bargaining agreement (to be discussed later in this chapter) may also provide protection against (or authorize) drug testing.

The permissibility of a private employee's drug test often hinges on whether the employer's testing was reasonable. Random drug tests and even "zero-tolerance" policies (which deny a "second chance" to employees who test positive for drugs) have been held to be reasonable.[22]

Federal government employees have long been required to submit to background checks as a condition of employment. Many workers who work at U.S. government facilities are employees of private contractors, not of the government. They generally have not been subject to background checks. Recent standards, however, now require background checks for all federal workers, including contract employees.

Genetic Testing
A serious privacy issue arose when some employers began conducting genetic testing of employees or prospective employees in an effort to identify individuals who might develop significant health problems in the future. To prevent the improper use of genetic information in employment and health insurance, in 2008 Congress passed the Genetic Information Nondiscrimination Act (GINA).[23]

Under GINA, employers cannot make decisions about hiring, firing, job placement, or promotion based on the results of genetic testing. GINA also prohibits group health plans and insurers from denying coverage or charging higher premiums based solely on a genetic predisposition to developing a specific disease in the future.

Immigration Law

The United States had no laws restricting immigration until the late nineteenth century. Today, the most important laws governing immigration and employment are the Immigration Reform and Control Act[24] (IRCA) and the Immigration Act.[25] Immigration law has become increasingly important in recent years. An estimated 12 million illegal immigrants now live in the United States, many of whom came to find jobs. Because U.S. employers face serious penalties if they hire illegal immigrants, it is necessary for businesspersons to have an understanding of immigration laws.

Immigration Reform and Control Act (IRCA)

When the IRCA was enacted in 1986, it provided amnesty to certain groups of illegal aliens living in the United States at the time. It also established a system that sanctions employers who hire illegal immigrants lacking work authorization.

The IRCA makes it illegal to hire, recruit, or refer for a fee someone not authorized to work in this country. Through Immigration and Customs Enforcement officers, the federal government conducts random compliance audits and engages in enforcement actions against employers who hire illegal immigrants.

I-9 Employment Verification
To comply with the IRCA, an employer must perform **I-9 verifications** for new hires, including those hired as "contractors" or "day

Learning Objective 4
What are the two most important federal statutes governing immigration and employment today?

I-9 Verification The process of verifying the employment eligibility and identity of a new worker. It must be completed within three days after the worker commences employment.

---

22. See, for example, *CITGO Asphalt Refining Co. v. Paper, Allied-Industrial, Chemical, and Energy Workers International Union Local No. 2-991*, 385 F.3d 809 (3d Cir. 2004).
23. 26 U.S.C. Section 9834; 42 U.S.C. Sections 300gg-53, 1320d-9, 2000ff-1 to 2000ff-11.
24. 29 U.S.C. Section 1802.
25. This act amended various provisions of the Immigration and Nationality Act of 1952, 8 U.S.C. Sections 1101 *et seq.*

(Konstantin L/Shutterstock.com)

Who is eligible for a permanent residence card?

workers" if they work under the employer's direct supervision. Form I-9, Employment Eligibility Verification, which is available from U.S. Citizenship and Immigration Services,[26] must be completed *within three days* of a worker's commencement of employment. The three-day period is to allow the employer to check the form's accuracy and to review and verify documents establishing the prospective worker's identity and eligibility for employment in the United States.

The employer must declare, under penalty of perjury, that an employee produced documents establishing his or her identity and legal employability. Acceptable documents include a U.S. passport establishing the person's citizenship or a document authorizing a foreign citizen to work in the United States, such as a Permanent Resident Card or an Alien Registration Receipt (discussed shortly).

Most legal actions for violations of I-9 rules are brought against employees who provide false information or documentation. If the employee enters false information on an I-9 form or presents false documentation, the employer can fire the worker, who then may be subject to deportation. Nevertheless, employers must be honest when verifying an employee's documentation: if an employer "should have known" that the worker was unauthorized, the employer has violated the rules.

Enforcement   U.S. Immigration and Customs Enforcement (ICE) is the largest investigative arm of the U.S. Department of Homeland Security. ICE has a general inspection program that conducts random compliance audits. Other audits may occur if the agency receives a written complaint alleging an employer's violations. Government inspections include a review of an employer's file of I-9 forms. The government does not need a subpoena or a warrant to conduct such an inspection.

If an investigation reveals a possible violation, ICE will bring an administrative action and issue a Notice of Intent to Fine, which sets out the charges against the employer. The employer has a right to a hearing on the enforcement action if a request is filed within thirty days. This hearing is conducted before an *administrative law judge* (see Chapter 19), and the employer has a right to counsel and to *discovery* (see Chapter 3). The typical defense in such actions is good faith or substantial compliance with the documentation provisions.

Penalties   An employer who violates the law by hiring an unauthorized alien is subject to substantial penalties. The employer may be fined up to $2,200 for each unauthorized employee for a first offense, $5,000 per employee for a second offense, and up to $11,000 for subsequent offenses. Criminal penalties, including additional fines and imprisonment for up to ten years, apply to employers who have engaged in a "pattern or practice of violations." A company may also be barred from future government contracts for violations.

The Immigration Act

Often, U.S. businesses find that they cannot hire sufficient domestic workers with specialized skills. For this reason, U.S. immigration laws have long made provisions for businesses to hire specially qualified foreign workers. The Immigration Act of 1990 placed caps on the number of visas (entry permits) that can be issued to immigrants each year.

Most temporary visas are set aside for workers who can be characterized as "persons of extraordinary ability," members of the professions holding advanced degrees, or other skilled workers and professionals. To hire such an individual, an employer must submit

---

26. U.S. Citizenship and Immigration Services is a federal agency that is part of the U.S. Department of Homeland Security.

a petition to ICE, which determines whether the job candidate meets the legal standards. Each visa is for a specific job, and there are legal limits on the employee's ability to change jobs once in the United States.

I-551 Alien Registration Receipts

A company seeking to hire a non-citizen worker may do so if the worker is self-authorized. This means that the worker either is a lawful permanent resident or has a valid temporary Employment Authorization Document. A lawful permanent resident can prove his or her status to an employer by presenting an **I-551 Alien Registration Receipt,** known as a "green card," or a properly stamped foreign passport.

Many immigrant workers are not already self-authorized, and employers may attempt to obtain labor certification, or green cards, for the immigrants they wish to hire. Approximately fifty thousand new green cards are issued each year. A green card can be obtained only for a person who is being hired for a permanent, full-time position. (A separate authorization system provides for the temporary entry and hiring of nonimmigrant visa workers.)

The employer must show that no U.S. worker is qualified, willing, and able to take the job. The government has detailed regulations governing the advertising of positions as well as the certification process.[27] Any U.S. applicants who meet the stated job qualifications must be interviewed for the position. The employer must also be able to show that the qualifications required for the job are a business necessity.

I-551 Alien Registration Receipt
A document, known as a "green card," that shows that a foreign-born individual can legally work in the United States.

The H-1B Visa Program

To obtain an H-1B visa, the potential employee must be qualified in a "specialty occupation," meaning that the individual has highly specialized knowledge and has attained a bachelor's or higher degree or its equivalent. Individuals with H-1B visas can stay in the United States for three to six years and can work only for the sponsoring employer.

The recipients of these visas include many high-tech workers, such as computer programmers and electronics specialists. A maximum of sixty-five thousand H-1B visas are set aside each year for new immigrants. That limit is typically reached within the first few weeks of the year. Consequently, many businesses, such as Microsoft, continue to lobby Congress to expand the number of H-1B visas available to immigrants.

"Immigration is the sincerest form of flattery."

Jack Paar, 1918–2004
(American entertainer)

Labor Unions

In the 1930s, in addition to wage-hour laws, the government also enacted the first of several labor laws. These laws protect employees' rights to join labor unions, to bargain with management over the terms and conditions of employment, and to conduct strikes.

Federal Labor Laws

Federal labor laws governing union-employer relations have developed considerably since the first law was enacted in 1932. Initially, the laws were concerned with protecting the rights and interests of workers. Subsequent legislation placed some restraints on unions and granted rights to employers. We look here at four major federal statutes regulating union-employer relations.

These construction workers argue for more jobs.

(Ed Stock/iStockphoto.com)

---

27. The most relevant regulations can be found at 20 C.F.R. Section 655 (for temporary employment) and 20 C.F.R. Section 656 (for permanent employment).

Learning Objective 5
What federal statute gave employees the right to organize unions and engage in collective bargaining?

Norris-LaGuardia Act   In 1932, Congress protected peaceful strikes, picketing, and boycotts in the Norris-LaGuardia Act.[28] The statute restricted the power of federal courts to issue injunctions against unions engaged in peaceful strikes. In effect, this act established a national policy permitting employees to organize.

National Labor Relations Act   One of the foremost statutes regulating labor is the National Labor Relations Act (NLRA).[29] This 1935 act established the rights of employees to engage in collective bargaining and to strike. The act also specifically defined a number of employer practices as unfair to labor:

1. Interference with the efforts of employees to form, join, or assist labor organizations or to engage in concerted activities for mutual aid or protection.
2. An employer's domination of a labor organization or contribution of financial or other support to it.
3. Discrimination in the hiring or awarding of tenure to employees based on union affiliation.
4. Discrimination against employees for filing charges under the act or giving testimony under the act.
5. Refusal to bargain collectively with the duly designated representative of the employees.

The National Labor Relations Board (NLRB)   The NLRA also created the National Labor Relations Board (NLRB) to oversee union elections and to prevent employers from engaging in unfair and illegal union activities and unfair labor practices. (To learn how NLRB rulings have affected social media policies, see this chapter's *Managerial Strategy* feature that follows.)

The NLRB has the authority to investigate employees' charges of unfair labor practices and to file complaints against employers in response to these charges. When violations are found, the NLRB may also issue a cease-and-desist order compelling the employer to stop engaging in the unfair practices. Cease-and-desist orders can be enforced by a federal appellate court if necessary. After the NLRB rules on claims of unfair labor practices, its decision may be appealed to a federal court.

CASE EXAMPLE 17.5   Roundy's, Inc., which operates a chain of stores in Wisconsin, became involved in a dispute with a local construction union. When union members started distributing "extremely unflattering" flyers outside the stores, Roundy's ejected them from the property. The NLRB filed a complaint against Roundy's for unfair labor practices. An administrative law judge ruled that Roundy's had violated the law by discriminating against the union, and a federal appellate court affirmed. It is an unfair labor practice for an employer to prohibit union members from distributing flyers outside a store when it allows nonunion members to do so.[30] ●

Good Faith Bargaining   Under the NLRA, employers and unions have a duty to bargain in good faith. Bargaining over certain subjects is mandatory, and a party's refusal to bargain over these subjects is an unfair labor practice that can be reported to the NLRB. In one case, for instance, an employer was required to bargain with the union over the use of hidden video surveillance cameras.[31]

Workers Protected by the NLRA   To be protected under the NLRA, an individual must be an *employee*, as that term is defined in the statute. Courts have long held that job applicants fall within the definition (otherwise, the NLRA's ban on discrimination in hiring would mean nothing). Additionally, the United States Supreme Court has held that individuals

---

28. 29 U.S.C. Sections 101–110, 113–115.
29. 20 U.S.C. Section 151.
30. *Roundy's, Inc. v. NLRB,* 647 F.3d 638 (7th Cir. 2012).
31. *National Steel Corp. v. NLRB,* 324 F.3d 928 (7th Cir. 2003).

MANAGERIAL STRATEGY

Many Companies Have to Revise Their Social Media Policies

Over the past few years, many companies have created social media policies for their employees. For example, Costco's policy used to read as follows:

> Any communication transmitted, stored or displayed electronically must comply with the policies outlined in the Costco Employee Agreement. Employees should be aware that statements posted electronically that damage the company, defame any individual or damage any person's reputation, or violate the policies outlined in the Costco Employee Agreement, may be subject to discipline up to and including termination of employment.

Since a ruling by the National Labor Relations Board (NLRB) in 2012, however, many companies have had to revise their policies.

The NLRB Rules on Protected "Concerted Activities" Section 7 of the National Labor Relations Act states: "Employees shall have the right to self-organization, to form, join, or assist labor organizations . . . and to engage in other *concerted activities* for the purpose of collective bargaining or *other mutual aid or protection.*" [Emphasis added.]

When employees challenged Costco's social media policy, the NLRB found that the policy violated the National Labor Relations Act because it was overly broad and did not specifically reference Section 7 activity. The ruling stated: "The broad prohibition against making statements that 'damage the company, defame any individual or damage any person's reputation' clearly encompasses concerted communications protesting the Respondent's [Costco's] treatment of its employees."[a]

The NLRB Continues to Strike Down Broad Prohibitions in Social Media Policies Since the ruling on Costco's social media policy, the NLRB has struck down similar policies at several companies, including EchoStar Technologies and Dish Network. The NLRB's general counsel has also issued three reports concluding that many companies' social media policies illegally restrict workers' exercise of their rights.

In one case, Karl Knauz BMW, a car dealership, had told its employees to always be "polite and friendly to our customers, vendors, and suppliers, as well as to your fellow employees." The NLRB found that this policy, like the one at Costco, was "unlawful because employees would reasonably construe its broad prohibition against disrespectful conduct and language which injures the image or reputation of the dealership" as encompassing Section 7 activity. In other words, the policy was overly broad because it could apply to discussions in which employees objected to their working conditions and sought the support of others in improving those conditions—which are protected activities.[b]

MANAGERIAL IMPLICATIONS

All companies that have social media policies should include a statement that any employee communications protected by Section 7 of the National Labor Relations Act are excluded from those policies. Companies can no longer have a policy that states that all social media posts must be "completely accurate and not misleading" because such a policy would be considered overbroad. Note also that companies cannot require their employees to report any unusual or inappropriate internal social media activity.

BUSINESS QUESTIONS

1. Employees meeting around the water cooler or coffee machine have always had the right to discuss work-related matters. Is a social media outlet simply a digital water cooler? Why or why not?

2. If your company instituted a policy stating that employees should "think carefully about 'friending' co-workers," would that policy be lawful? Why or why not?

---

a. *Costco Wholesale Corporation and United Food and Commercial Workers Union, Local 371*, Case 34-CA-01242, September 7, 2012, decision and order from NLRB (available at www.nlrb.gov/case/34–CA-012421).

b. www.nlrb.gov/category/case-number/13-CA-046452.

---

who are hired by a union to organize a company are to be considered employees of the company for NLRA purposes.[32]

Labor-Management Relations Act   The Labor-Management Relations Act (LMRA) (also called the Taft-Hartley Act)[33] was passed in 1947 to proscribe certain unfair

---

32. *NLRB v. Town & Country Electric, Inc.*, 516 U.S. 85, 116 S.Ct. 450, 133 L.Ed.2d 371 (1995).

33. 29 U.S.C. Sections 141 *et seq.*

Closed Shop A firm that requires union membership by its workers as a condition of employment, which is illegal.

Union Shop A firm that requires all workers, once employed, to become union members within a specified period of time as a condition of their continued employment.

Right-to-Work Law A state law providing that employees may not be required to join a union as a condition of retaining employment.

union practices, such as the *closed shop*. A **closed shop** requires union membership by its workers as a condition of employment.

Although the act made the closed shop illegal, it preserved the legality of the union shop. A **union shop** does not require membership as a prerequisite for employment but can, and usually does, require that workers join the union after a specified amount of time on the job.

The LMRA also prohibited unions from refusing to bargain with employers, engaging in certain types of picketing, and *featherbedding*—causing employers to hire more employees than necessary. The act also allowed individual states to pass their own **right-to-work laws,** which make it illegal for union membership to be required for *continued* employment in any establishment. Thus, union shops are technically illegal in the twenty-three states that have right-to-work laws.

Labor-Management Reporting and Disclosure Act In 1959, Congress enacted the Labor-Management Reporting and Disclosure Act (LMRDA).[34] The act established an employee bill of rights and reporting requirements for union activities. The act strictly regulates unions' internal business procedures, including union elections. For example, the LMRDA requires a union to hold regularly scheduled elections of officers using secret ballots. Ex-convicts are prohibited from holding union office. Moreover, union officials are accountable for union property and funds. Members have the right to attend and to participate in union meetings, to nominate officers, and to vote in most union proceedings.

Hot-Cargo Agreement An illegal agreement in which employers voluntarily agree with unions not to handle, use, or deal in the nonunion-produced goods of other employers.

The act also outlawed **hot-cargo agreements,** in which employers voluntarily agree with unions not to handle, use, or deal in goods produced by nonunion employees working for other employers.

The LMRDA holds union officers to a high standard of responsibility and ethical conduct in administering the affairs of their union. This standard was at the core of the dispute in the following case.

---

34. 29 U.S.C. Sections 401 *et seq.*

Case 17.3

Services Employees International Union v. National Union of Healthcare Workers
United States Court of Appeals, Ninth Circuit, 718 F.3d 1036 (2013).

BACKGROUND AND FACTS The Services Employees International Union (SEIU) consists of 2.2 million members who work in healthcare, public services, and property services. United Health Workers (UHW) is affiliated with SEIU and represents 150,000 healthcare workers in California. The SEIU, under its constitution, has the authority to realign local unions. The SEIU constitution also grants the SEIU the authority to place a local union into trusteeship "to protect the interests of the membership."

The SEIU proposed moving 150,000 long-term care workers from three separate unions, including 65,000 from the UHW, into a new union chartered by the SEIU. The UHW opposed the move. The SEIU placed the UHW into trusteeship. UHW officials blocked access to its buildings to prevent the trustees from entering, removed UHW property from the buildings, and instructed its members not to recognize the trustees'

authority. Meanwhile, the UHW officials, while still on the UHW payroll, created and promoted a new union—the National Union of Healthcare Workers (NUHW). The SEIU filed a suit in a federal district court against the NUHW and the UHW officials for breach of fiduciary duties. The jury returned a verdict against the NUHW and the UHW, on which the court entered a judgment. The defendants appealed.

IN THE WORDS OF THE COURT . . .
TALLMAN, Circuit Judge:
     * * * *

    Under Section 501 of the Labor Management Reporting and Disclosure Act ("LMRDA"), officers of labor unions are held to the highest standards of responsibility and ethical conduct in administering the affairs of the union. [Emphasis added.]

Case 17.3—Continued

The UHW defendants posit that they owed this duty to only the rank-and-file members of their local union. Because they subjectively believed their actions assisted those members by establishing a more democratic union with localized control, they maintain they have done no wrong under Section 501. Their argument ignores the fact that they diverted union resources to weaken their own union and form a rival union merely because they did not agree with the constitutionally permissible decision of the international union. *Because no construction of the LMRDA allows such conduct based merely on the defendants' subjective motives, we reject the defendants' argument.* [Emphasis added.]

The SEIU Executive Committee, under the authority given to it by both its constitution and the UHW constitution, carefully considered and adopted a measure it believed would better serve its members. The UHW officers disagreed, which they may do, and they voiced their opposition, which they also may do. What they may not do under the law is use their union's resources to actively obstruct implementation of the final decision.

* * * *

The judgment of liability was properly entered when a correctly instructed jury, on a sufficient factual record, found the defendants in breach of their fiduciary duties under Section 501 of the LMRDA.

DECISION AND REMEDY The U.S. Court of Appeals for the Ninth Circuit affirmed the lower court's judgment. Section 501 of the LMRDA creates a fiduciary duty owed by union officials to the union as an organization, not only the union's rank-and-file members. Officials who divert union resources to establish a new competing union breach this duty.

WHAT IF THE FACTS WERE DIFFERENT? *If the defendants in this case had only expressed their opinions against the SEIU's imposition of trusteeship and charter of a new union, could they have been held liable for a breach of fiduciary duty? Discuss.*

THE ETHICAL DIMENSION *What standard was at the core of the dispute in this case?*

Union Organization

Typically, the first step in organizing a union at a particular firm is to have the workers sign authorization cards. An **authorization card** usually states that the worker desires to have a certain union, such as the United Auto Workers, represent the workforce. If a majority of the workers sign authorization cards, the union organizers (unionizers) present the cards to the employer and ask for formal recognition of the union.

The employer is not required to recognize the union at this point in the process, but it may do so voluntarily on a showing of majority support. (Under pro-labor legislation that has been proposed repeatedly in recent years, the employer would be required to recognize the union as soon as a majority of the workers had signed authorization cards—without holding an election, as described next.)[35]

Authorization Card A card signed by an employee that gives a union permission to act on his or her behalf in negotiations with management.

Union Elections

If the employer refuses to voluntarily recognize the union after a majority of the workers sign authorization cards—or if less than 50 percent of the workers sign authorization cards—the union organizers present the cards to the NLRB with a petition for an election. For an election to be held, the unionizers must demonstrate that at least 30 percent of the workers to be represented support a union or an election on unionization.

The proposed union must also represent an *appropriate bargaining unit*. Not every group of workers can form a single union. One key requirement of an appropriate bargaining unit is a *mutuality of interest* among all the workers to be represented by the union. Factors considered in determining whether there is a mutuality of interest include the *similarity of the jobs* of all the workers to be unionized and their physical location.

If all of these requirements are met, an election is held. The NLRB supervises the election and ensures secret voting and voter eligibility. If the proposed union receives majority support in a fair election, the NLRB certifies the union as the bargaining representative for the employees.

---

35. If the proposed Employee Free Choice Act ever becomes law, some of the information stated here may change.

Union Election Campaigns

Many disputes between labor and management arise during union election campaigns. Generally, the employer has control over unionizing activities that take place on company property during working hours. Employers may thus limit the campaign activities of union supporters as long as the employer has a legitimate business reason for doing so. The employer may also reasonably limit the times and places that union solicitation occurs so long as the employer is not discriminating against the union.

EXAMPLE 17.6   A union is seeking to organize clerks at a department store owned by Amanti Enterprises. Amanti can prohibit all union solicitation in areas of the store open to the public because that activity could seriously interfere with the store's business. If Amanti allows solicitation for charitable causes in the workplace, however, it may not prohibit union solicitation. •

Collective Bargaining

If the NLRB certifies the union, the union becomes the *exclusive bargaining representative* of the workers. The central legal right of a union is to engage in collective bargaining on the members' behalf. **Collective bargaining** is the process by which labor and management negotiate the terms and conditions of employment, including wages, benefits, working conditions, and other matters.

Collective Bargaining The process by which labor and management negotiate the terms and conditions of employment, including working hours and workplace conditions.

The Union Negotiates with Management

Collective bargaining allows union representatives elected by union members to speak on behalf of the members at the bargaining table. When a union is officially recognized, it may demand to bargain with the employer and negotiate new terms or conditions of employment. In collective bargaining, as in most other business negotiations, each side uses its economic power to pressure or persuade the other side to grant concessions.

Both Sides Must Bargain in Good Faith

Bargaining does not mean that one side must give in to the other or that compromises must be made. It does mean that a demand to bargain with the employer must be taken seriously and that both sides must bargain in "good faith."

Good faith bargaining means that management, for instance, must be willing to meet with union representatives and consider the union's wishes when negotiating a contract. It would be bad faith for management to engage in a campaign to undermine the union among workers or to constantly shift position on disputed contract terms. Another example of bad faith would be for management to send bargainers who lack authority to commit the company to a contract. If an employer (or a union) refuses to bargain in good faith without justification, it has committed an unfair labor practice. The other party may then petition the NLRB for an order requiring good faith bargaining.

Strikes

Even when labor and management have bargained in good faith, they may be unable to reach a final agreement. When extensive collective bargaining has been conducted and an impasse results, the union may call a strike against the employer to pressure it into making concessions. In a **strike,** the unionized workers leave their jobs and refuse to work. The workers also typically picket the workplace, standing outside the facility with signs stating their complaints.

A strike is an extreme action. Striking workers lose their rights to be paid, and management loses production and may lose customers when orders cannot be filled. Labor law regulates the circumstances and conduct of strikes. Most strikes take the form of "economic strikes," which are initiated because the union wants a better contract. **EXAMPLE 17.7**   Teachers in Eagle Point, Oregon, engaged in an economic strike in 2012 after contract negotiations with

Strike An action undertaken by unionized workers when collective bargaining fails. The workers leave their jobs, refuse to work, and (typically) picket the employer's workplace.

the school district failed to bring an agreement on pay and working hours. The unionized teachers picketed outside the school building. Classes were canceled for a few weeks until the district found substitute teachers who filled in during the strike. •

The Right to Strike   The right to strike is guaranteed by the NLRA, within limits, and strike activities, such as picketing, are protected by the free speech guarantee of the First Amendment to the U.S. Constitution. Nonworkers have a right to participate in picketing an employer.

The NLRA also gives workers the right to refuse to cross a picket line of fellow workers who are engaged in a lawful strike. Employers are permitted to hire replacement workers to substitute for the workers who are on strike.

After a Strike Ends   In a typical economic strike over working conditions, the employer has a right to hire permanent replacements during the strike and need not terminate them when the economic strikers seek to return to work. In other words, striking workers are not guaranteed the right to return to their jobs after the strike if satisfactory replacement workers have been found. If the employer has not hired replacement workers to fill the strikers' positions, however, then the employer must rehire the economic strikers to fill any vacancies. Employers may not discriminate against former economic strikers, and those who are rehired retain their seniority rights.

Reviewing . . . Employment, Immigration, and Labor Law

Rick Saldona began working as a traveling salesperson for Aimer Winery in 1993. Sales constituted 90 percent of Saldona's work time. Saldona worked an average of fifty hours per week but received no overtime pay. In June 2016, Saldona's new supervisor, Caesar Braxton, claimed that Saldona had been inflating his reported sales calls and required Saldona to submit to a polygraph test. Saldona reported Braxton to the U.S. Department of Labor, which prohibited Aimer from requiring Saldona to take a polygraph test for this purpose. In August 2016, Saldona's wife, Venita, fell from a ladder and sustained a head injury while employed as a full-time agricultural harvester. Saldona delivered to Aimer's human resources department a letter from his wife's physician indicating that she would need daily care for several months, and Saldona took leave until December 2016. Aimer had sixty-three employees at that time. When Saldona returned to Aimer, he was informed that his position had been eliminated because his sales territory had been combined with an adjacent territory. Using the information presented in the chapter, answer the following questions.

1. Would Saldona have been legally entitled to receive overtime pay at a higher rate? Why or why not?
2. What is the maximum length of time Saldona would have been allowed to take leave to care for his injured spouse?
3. Under what circumstances would Aimer have been allowed to require an employee to take a lie-detector test?
4. Would Aimer likely be able to avoid reinstating Saldona under the *key employee* exception? Why or why not?

Debate This   The U.S. labor market is highly competitive, so state and federal laws that require overtime pay are unnecessary and should be abolished.

Key Terms

authorization card 507	hot-cargo agreement 506	right-to-work law 506	whistleblowing 489
closed shop 506	I-9 verification 501	strike 508	workers' compensation laws 495
collective bargaining 508	I-551 Alien Registration Receipt 503	union shop 506	wrongful discharge 490
employment at will 487	minimum wage 491	vesting 497	

Chapter Summary: Employment, Immigration, and Labor Law

Employment at Will	1. *Employment-at-will doctrine*—Under this common law doctrine, either party may terminate the employment relationship at any time and for any reason ("at will"). 2. *Exceptions to the employment-at-will doctrine*—Courts have made exceptions to the doctrine on the basis of contract theory, tort theory, and public policy. Whistleblowers have occasionally received protection under the common law for reasons of public policy. 3. *Wrongful discharge*—Whenever an employer discharges an employee in violation of an employment contract or statutory law protecting employees, the employee may bring a suit for wrongful discharge.
Wages, Hours, and Layoffs	1. *Davis-Bacon Act*—Requires contractors and subcontractors working on federal government construction projects to pay their employees "prevailing wages." 2. *Walsh-Healey Act*—Requires firms that contract with federal agencies to pay their employees a minimum wage and overtime pay. 3. *Fair Labor Standards Act*—Extended wage and hour requirements to cover all employers whose activities affect interstate commerce plus certain other businesses. The act has specific requirements in regard to child labor, maximum hours, and minimum wages. 4. *The Worker Adjustment and Retraining Notification (WARN) Act*—Applies to employers with at least one hundred full-time employees and requires that sixty days' advance notice of mass layoffs be given to affected employees or their representative (if workers are in a labor union).
Family and Medical Leave	The Family and Medical Leave Act (FMLA) requires employers with fifty or more employees to provide employees with up to twelve weeks of unpaid leave (twenty-six weeks for military caregiver leave) during any twelve-month period.
Worker Health and Safety	1. *Occupational Safety and Health Act*—Requires employers to meet specific safety and health standards that are established and enforced by the Occupational Safety and Health Administration (OSHA). 2. *State workers' compensation laws*—Establish an administrative procedure for compensating workers who are injured in accidents that occur on the job, regardless of fault.
Income Security	1. *Social Security and Medicare*—The Social Security Act provides for old-age (retirement), survivors', and disability insurance. Both employers and employees must make contributions under the Federal Insurance Contributions Act (FICA). The Social Security Administration also administers Medicare, a health-insurance program for older or disabled persons. 2. *Private pension plans*—The federal Employee Retirement Income Security Act (ERISA) establishes standards for the management of employer-provided pension plans. 3. *Unemployment insurance*—The Federal Unemployment Tax Act (FUTA) created a system that provides unemployment compensation to eligible individuals. Employers are taxed to cover the costs. 4. *COBRA*—The Consolidated Omnibus Budget Reconciliation Act (COBRA) requires employers to give employees, on termination of employment, the option of continuing their medical, optical, or dental insurance coverage for a certain period. 5. *HIPAA*—The Health Insurance Portability and Accountability Act (HIPAA) establishes requirements for employer-sponsored group health plans. The plans must also comply with various safeguards to ensure the privacy of employees' health information.
Employee Privacy Rights	In addition to the U.S. Constitution, tort law, state constitutions, and federal and state statutes may provide some protection for employees' privacy rights. Employer practices that are often challenged by employees as invasive of their privacy rights include electronic performance monitoring, lie-detector tests, drug testing, and genetic testing.
Immigration Law	1. *Immigration Reform and Control Act*—Prohibits employers from hiring illegal immigrants. The act is administered by U.S. Citizenship and Immigration Services. Compliance audits and enforcement actions are conducted by U.S. Immigration and Customs Enforcement. 2. *Immigration Act*—Limits the number of legal immigrants entering the United States by capping the number of visas (entry permits) that are issued each year.
Labor Unions	1. *Federal labor laws* include the Norris-LaGuardia Act, the National Labor Relations Act, the Labor-Management Relations Act, and the Labor-Management Reporting and Disclosure Act. 2. *Union organization*—Union campaign activities and elections must comply with federal labor laws and the NLRB. 3. *Collective bargaining*—The process by which labor and management negotiate the terms and conditions of employment (such as wages, benefits, and working conditions). The central legal right of a labor union is to engage in collective bargaining on the members' behalf. 4. *Strikes*—A strike occurs when unionized workers leave their jobs and refuse to work.

Issue Spotters

1. Erin, an employee of Fine Print Shop, is injured on the job. For Erin to obtain workers' compensation, does her injury have to have been caused by Fine Print's negligence? Does it matter whether the action causing the injury was intentional? Explain. (See *Worker Health and Safety*.)

2. Onyx applies for work with Precision Design Company, which tells her that it requires union membership as a condition of employment. She applies for work with Quality Engineering, Inc., which does not require union membership as a condition of employment but requires employees to join a union after six months on the job. Are these conditions legal? Why or why not? (See *Labor Unions*.)

—**Check your answers to the Issue Spotters against the answers provided in Appendix D at the end of this text.**

For Review

1. What is the employment-at-will doctrine? When and why are exceptions to this doctrine made?
2. What federal statute governs working hours and wages?
3. Under the Family and Medical Leave Act, in what circumstances may an employee take family or medical leave?
4. What are the two most important federal statutes governing immigration and employment today?
5. What federal statute gave employees the right to organize unions and engage in collective bargaining?

Business Scenarios and Case Problems

17–1. Wages and Hours. Calzoni Boating Co. is an interstate business engaged in manufacturing and selling boats. The company has five hundred nonunion employees. Representatives of these employees are requesting a four-day, ten-hours-per-day workweek, and Calzoni is concerned that this would require paying time and a half after eight hours per day. Which federal act is Calzoni thinking of that might require this? Will the act in fact require paying time and a half for all hours worked over eight hours per day if the employees' proposal is accepted? Explain. (See *Wages, Hours, and Layoffs*.)

17–2. Wrongful Discharge. Denton and Carlo were employed at an appliance plant. Their job required them to do occasional maintenance work while standing on a wire mesh twenty feet above the plant floor. Other employees had fallen through the mesh, and one was killed by the fall. When Denton and Carlo were asked by their supervisor to do work that would likely require them to walk on the mesh, they refused due to their fear of bodily harm or death. Because of their refusal to do the requested work, the two employees were fired from their jobs. Was their discharge wrongful? If so, under what federal employment law? To what federal agency or department should they turn for assistance? (See *Employment at Will*.)

17–3. ▮ **Spotlight on Coca Cola—Family and Medical Leave Act.** Jennifer Willis worked for Coca Cola Enterprises, Inc. (CCE), in Louisiana as a senior account manager. On a Monday in May 2003, Willis called her supervisor to tell him that she was sick and would not be able to work that day. She also said that she was pregnant, but she did not say she

was sick because of the pregnancy. On Tuesday, she called to ask where to report to work and was told that she could not return without a doctor's release. She said that she had a doctor's appointment on "Wednesday," which her supervisor understood to be the next day. Willis meant the following Wednesday.

For more than a week, Willis did not contact CCE. When she returned to work, she was told that she had violated CCE's "No Call/No Show" policy. Under this policy "an employee absent from work for three consecutive days without notifying the supervisor during that period will be considered to have voluntarily resigned." She was fired.

Willis filed a suit in a federal district court against CCE under the Family and Medical Leave Act (FMLA). To be eligible for FMLA leave, an employee must inform an employer of the reason for the leave. Did Willis meet this requirement? Did CCE's response to Willis's absence violate the FMLA? Explain. [*Willis v. Coca Cola Enterprises, Inc.,* 445 F.3d 413 (5th Cir. 2006)] (See *Family and Medical Leave*.)

17–4. Minimum Wage. Misty Cumbie worked as a waitress at the Vita Café in Portland, Oregon. The café was owned and operated by Woody Woo, Inc. Woody Woo paid its servers an hourly wage that was higher than the state's minimum wage, but the servers were required to contribute their tips to a "tip pool." Approximately one-third of the tip-pool funds went to the servers, and the rest was distributed to kitchen staff members, who otherwise rarely received tips for their services. Did this tip-pooling arrangement violate the minimum wage provisions of the Fair Labor Standards Act? Explain. [*Cumbie v. Woody Woo, Inc.,* 596 F.3d 577 (9th Cir. 2010)] (See *Wages, Hours, and Layoffs.*)

17–5. Business Case Problem with Sample Answer— Workers' Compensation. As a safety measure, Dynea USA, Inc., required an employee, Tony Fairbanks, to wear steel-toed boots. One of the boots caused a sore on Fairbanks's leg. The skin over the sore broke, and within a week, Fairbanks was hospitalized with a methicillin-resistant staphylococcus aureus (MRSA) infection. He filed a workers' compensation claim. Dynea argued that the MRSA bacteria that caused the infection had been on Fairbanks's skin before he came to work. What are the requirements to recover workers' compensation benefits? Does this claim qualify? Explain. [*Dynea USA, Inc. v. Fairbanks,* 241 Or.App. 311, 250 P.3d 389 (2011)] (See *Worker Health and Safety.*)

—**For a sample answer to Problem 17–5, go to Appendix E at the end of this text.**

17–6. Exceptions to the Employment-at-Will Doctrine. Li Li worked for Packard Bioscience, and Mark Schmeizl was her supervisor. In March 2000, Schmeizl told Li to call Packard's competitors, pretend to be a potential customer, and request "pricing information and literature." Li refused to perform the assignment. She told Schmeizl that she thought the work was illegal and recommended that he contact Packard's legal department. Although a lawyer recommended against the practice, Schmeizl insisted that Li perform the calls. Moreover, he later wrote negative performance reviews because she was unable to get the requested information when she called competitors and identified herself as a Packard employee. On June 1, 2000, Li was terminated on Schmeizl's recommendation. Can Li bring a claim for wrongful discharge? Why or why not? [*Li Li v. Canberra Industries,* 134 Conn.App. 448, 39 A.3d 789 (2012)] (See *Employment at Will.*)

17–7. Collective Bargaining. SDBC Holdings, Inc., acquired Stella D'oro Biscuit Co., a bakery in New York City. At the time, a collective bargaining agreement existed between Stella D'oro and Local 50, Bakery, Confectionary, Tobacco Workers and Grain Millers International Union. During negotiations to renew the agreement, Stella D'oro allowed Local 50 to examine and take notes on the company's financial statement and offered the union an opportunity to make its own copy. Stella D'oro, however, would not give Local 50 a copy. Did Stella D'oro engage in an unfair labor practice? Discuss. [*SDBC Holdings, Inc. v. National Labor Relations Board,* 711 F.3d 281 (2d Cir. 2013)] (See *Labor Unions.*)

17–8. Unemployment Compensation. Fior Ramirez worked as a housekeeper for Remington Lodging & Hospitality, a hotel in Atlantic Beach, Florida. After her father in the Dominican Republic suffered a stroke, she asked her employer for time off to be with him. Ramirez's manager, Katie Berkowski, refused the request. Two days later, Berkowski received a call from Ramirez to say that she was with her father. He died about a week later, and Ramirez returned to work, but Berkowski told her that she had abandoned her position. Ramirez applied for unemployment compensation. Under the applicable state statute, "an employee is disqualified from receiving benefits if he or she voluntarily left work without good cause." Does Ramirez qualify for benefits? Explain. [*Ramirez v. Reemployment Assistance Appeals Commission,* 135 So.3d 408 (Fla.App. 1 Dist. 2014)] (See *Income Security.*)

17–9. ⬌ A Question of Ethics—Immigration Work Status. Mohammad Hashmi, a citizen of Pakistan, entered the United States in 2002 on a student visa. Two years later, when he applied for a job at CompuCredit, he completed an I-9 form and checked the box to indicate that he was "a citizen or national of the United States." Soon after submitting that form, he married a U.S. citizen. Several months later, the federal immigration services claimed that Hashmi had misrepresented himself as a U.S. citizen. Hashmi contended that he had not misrepresented himself. At an administrative hearing, he testified that when he filled out the I-9 form he believed that he was a "national of the United States" because he was legally in the country under a student visa and was going to marry a U.S. citizen. He requested that his immigration status be adjusted to account for the fact that he was employed and married to an American. The immigration judge rejected that request and found that Hashmi had made a false claim on the I-9 form. He ruled that Hashmi was "inadmissible" to the United States and that his legal status in the country could not be amended because of his marriage or employment. Hashmi appealed. [*Hashmi v. Mukasey,* 533 F.3d 700 (8th Cir. 2008)] (See *Immigration Law.*)

1. Was it reasonable for Hashmi to think that he was a U.S. national? What if his misunderstanding was due to the fact that he was not proficient in the English language?

2. Should Hashmi's visa status be changed because of his marriage and employment? Why or why not? How should the appellate court rule in this case?

3. Should the court consider what happens to Hashmi's wife if he is denied legal status? In general, should the law consider the interests of family members when determining a person's immigration status? Explain.

CHAPTER 18

Employment Discrimination

(Andresr/Shutterstock.com)

CONTENTS

- Title VII of the Civil Rights Act
- Discrimination Based on Age
- Discrimination Based on Disability
- Defenses to Employment Discrimination
- Affirmative Action

LEARNING OBJECTIVES

The five learning objectives below are designed to help improve your understanding of the chapter. After reading this chapter, you should be able to answer the following questions:

1. Generally, what kind of conduct is prohibited by Title VII of the Civil Rights Act?
2. What is the difference between disparate-treatment discrimination and disparate-impact discrimination?
3. What remedies are available under Title VII of the Civil Rights Act?
4. What federal act prohibits discrimination based on age?
5. What are three defenses to claims of employment discrimination?

"Equal rights for all, special privileges for none."
—Thomas Jefferson, 1743–1826 (Third president of the United States, 1801–1809)

Out of the civil rights movement of the 1960s grew a body of law protecting employees against discrimination in the workplace. Legislation, judicial decisions, and administrative agency actions restrict employers from discriminating against workers on the basis of race, color, religion, national origin, gender, age, or disability. A class of persons defined by one or more of these criteria is known as a **protected class.** The laws designed to protect these individuals embody the sentiment expressed by Thomas Jefferson in the chapter-opening quotation.

The federal statutes discussed in this chapter prohibit **employment discrimination** against members of protected classes. Although this chapter focuses on federal statutes, many states have their own laws that protect employees against discrimination, and some provide more protection to employees than federal laws do.

Protected Class A group of persons protected by specific laws because of the group's defining characteristics, including race, color, religion, national origin, gender, age, and disability.

Employment Discrimination Treating employees or job applicants unequally on the basis of race, color, national origin, religion, gender, age, or disability.

(Lyndon Baines Johnson Presidential Library and Museum)

President Lyndon B. Johnson signs the Civil Rights Act in 1964. This legislation represented the most far-reaching set of antidiscrimination laws in modern times. Which groups in our country benefited most from this act?

Title VII of the Civil Rights Act

The most important statute covering employment discrimination is Title VII of the Civil Rights Act.[1] Title VII prohibits discrimination against employees, applicants, and union members on the basis of race, color, national origin, religion, or gender at any stage of employment.

Title VII applies to employers with fifteen or more employees and labor unions with fifteen or more members. Title VII also applies to labor unions that operate hiring halls (to which members go regularly to be rationed jobs as they become available), employment agencies, and state and local governing units or agencies. A special section of the act prohibits discrimination in most federal government employment.

The Equal Employment Opportunity Commission

Learning Objective 1
Generally, what kind of conduct is prohibited by Title VII of the Civil Rights Act?

The Equal Employment Opportunity Commission (EEOC) monitors compliance with Title VII. A victim of alleged discrimination must file a claim with the EEOC before bringing a suit against the employer. The EEOC may investigate the dispute and attempt to arrange an out-of-court settlement. If a voluntary agreement cannot be reached, the EEOC may file a suit against the employer on the employee's behalf. If the EEOC decides not to investigate the claim, the victim may bring her or his own lawsuit against the employer.

The EEOC does not investigate every claim of employment discrimination, regardless of the merits of the claim. Generally, it investigates only "priority cases," such as cases involving retaliatory discharge (firing an employee in retaliation for submitting a claim to the EEOC) and cases involving types of discrimination that are of particular concern to the EEOC.

In 2011, the United States Supreme Court limited the rights of employees to bring discrimination claims against their employer as a group, or class. **CASE EXAMPLE 18.1** A group of female employees sued Wal-Mart, the nation's largest private employer. The employees alleged that store managers who had discretion over pay and promotions were biased against women and disproportionately favored men. The United States Supreme Court ruled in favor of Wal-Mart, effectively blocking the class action (a lawsuit in which a small number of plaintiffs sue on behalf of a larger group). The Court held that the women could not maintain a class action because they had failed to prove a company-wide policy of discrimination that had a common effect on all women included in the class. Therefore, they could not maintain a class action.[2] ● This decision did not affect the rights of individual employees to sue under Title VII, however.

Intentional and Unintentional Discrimination

Disparate-Treatment Discrimination
A form of employment discrimination that results when an employer intentionally discriminates against employees who are members of protected classes.

Title VII prohibits both intentional and unintentional discrimination.

Intentional Discrimination   Intentional discrimination by an employer against an employee is known as **disparate-treatment discrimination**. Because intent

---

1. 42 U.S.C. Sections 2000e–2000e-17.
2. *Wal-Mart Stores, Inc. v. Dukes,* ___ U.S. ___, 131 S.Ct. 2541, 180 L.Ed.2d 374 (2011).

can be difficult to prove, courts have established certain procedures for resolving disparate-treatment cases. **EXAMPLE 18.2**   Samantha applies for employment with a construction firm and is rejected. If she sues on the basis of disparate-treatment discrimination in hiring, she must show that:

1. She is a member of a protected class.
2. She applied and was qualified for the job in question.
3. She was rejected by the employer.
4. The employer continued to seek applicants for the position or filled the position with a person not in a protected class.

If Samantha can meet these relatively easy requirements, she has made out a ***prima facie case*** of illegal discrimination. This means that she has met her initial burden of proof and will win unless the employer can present a legally acceptable defense. (Defenses to claims of employment discrimination will be discussed later in this chapter.)

The burden then shifts to the employer-defendant, who must articulate a legal reason for not hiring the plaintiff. For instance, the employer might say that Samantha was not hired because she lacked sufficient experience or training. To prevail, the plaintiff must then show that the employer's reason is a *pretext* (not the true reason) and that discriminatory intent actually motivated the employer's decision. ●

Prima Facie Case A case in which the plaintiff has produced sufficient evidence of his or her claim that the case will be decided for the plaintiff unless the defendant produces evidence to rebut it.

Unintentional Discrimination
Employers often use interviews and tests to choose from among a large number of applicants for job openings. Minimum educational requirements are also common. These practices and procedures may have an unintended discriminatory impact on a protected class.

Disparate-impact discrimination occurs when a protected group of people is adversely affected by an employer's practices, procedures, or tests, even though they do not appear to be discriminatory. In a disparate-impact discrimination case, the complaining party must first show statistically that the employer's practices, procedures, or tests are discriminatory in effect. Once the plaintiff has made out a *prima facie* case, the burden of proof shifts to the employer to show that the practices or procedures in question were justified. There are two ways of proving that disparate-impact discrimination exists, as discussed next.

Disparate-Impact Discrimination Discrimination that results from certain employer practices or procedures that, although not discriminatory on their face, have a discriminatory effect.

Learning Objective 2
What is the difference between disparate-treatment discrimination and disparate-impact discrimination?

Pool of Applicants   A plaintiff can prove a disparate impact by comparing the employer's workforce to the pool of qualified individuals available in the local labor market. The plaintiff must show that (1) as a result of educational or other job requirements or hiring procedures, (2) the percentage of nonwhites, women, or members of other protected classes in the employer's workforce (3) does not reflect the percentage of that group in the pool of qualified applicants. If the plaintiff can show a connection between the practice and the disparity, he or she has made out a *prima facie* case and need not provide evidence of discriminatory intent.

Rate of Hiring   A plaintiff can also prove disparate-impact discrimination by comparing the *selection rates* of whites and nonwhites (or members of another protected class). When a job requirement or hiring procedure excludes members of a protected class from an employer's workforce at a substantially higher rate than nonmembers, discrimination occurs, regardless of the racial balance in the employer's workforce.

The EEOC has devised a test, called the "four-fifths rule," to determine whether an employment selection procedure is discriminatory on its face. Under this rule, a selection rate for protected classes that is less than four-fifths, or 80 percent, of the rate for the group with the highest rate will generally be regarded as evidence of disparate impact. **EXAMPLE 18.3**   One hundred white applicants take an employment test, and fifty pass the test and are hired. One hundred minority applicants take the test, and twenty pass the test and are hired. Because twenty is less than four-fifths (80 percent) of fifty, the test would be considered discriminatory under the EEOC guidelines. •

Discrimination Based on Race, Color, and National Origin

Title VII prohibits employers from discriminating against employees or job applicants on the basis of race, color, or national origin. Race is interpreted broadly to apply to the ancestry or ethnic characteristics of a group of persons, such as Native Americans. National origin refers to discrimination based on a person's birth in another country or his or her ancestry or culture, such as Hispanic. (For a discussion of whether employers can legally discriminate against employees based on their appearance, see this chapter's *Insight into Ethics* feature that follows.)

If an employer's standards for selecting or promoting employees have a discriminatory effect on job applicants or employees in these protected classes, then a presumption of illegal discrimination arises. To avoid liability, the employer must then show that its standards have a substantial, demonstrable relationship to realistic qualifications for the job in question.

INSIGHT INTO ETHICS

APPEARANCE-BASED DISCRIMINATION

Research has shown that short men make statistically less income than tall men. It has also shown that compared with attractive individuals, less attractive people generally receive poorer performance reviews, lower salaries, and smaller damages awards if they win lawsuits. Should something be done about this?

Can "Lookism" Be Prohibited?

Although there is certainly evidence that appearance-based discrimination exists in the workplace and elsewhere, it is not so clear that it can be prohibited. In the 1970s, Michigan decided to do something about "lookism" and passed a law barring various kinds of appearance-based discrimination.[a] Whether because of the cost or the difficulty of proving this type of discrimination, however, only a few lawsuits based on the law have been filed each year. At least six cities have similar laws, but these laws also have not given rise to many lawsuits.

Federal and state laws prohibit discrimination against people who are clinically obese, but discrimination against those who are merely overweight is usually not illegal. Given that one study found that more than 40 percent of overweight women felt stigmatized by their employers, this remains a serious problem.

A Double Standard for Grooming

Women sometimes complain that they are held to different grooming standards in the workplace than their male counterparts. A female bartender at a casino in Nevada brought a lawsuit after she was fired for not complying with rules that required her to wear makeup and teased hair while male bartenders were just told to "look neat." The court ruled, however, that these allegations were not enough to outweigh an at-will employment contract.[b]

At the same time, women in senior management positions find that they can look "too sexy." A few years ago, a Citibank employee made headlines when she claimed that she was fired for her excessive sexiness, which supposedly distracted her male co-workers.

For Critical Analysis
Insight into Social Media

The majority of workers today post photographs of themselves, their families, and their friends on Facebook and other social media. How might this practice affect appearance-based discrimination in the workplace?

a. Michigan Compiled Laws Section 37.2202.

b. *Jespersen v. Harrah's Operating Co.*, 444 F.3d 1104 (9th Cir. 2006).

CASE EXAMPLE 18.4 Jiann Min Chang was an instructor at Alabama Agricultural and Mechanical University (AAMU). When AAMU terminated his employment, Chang filed a lawsuit claiming discrimination based on national origin. Chang established a *prima facie* case because he (1) was a member of a protected class, (2) was qualified for the job, (3) suffered an adverse employment action, and (4) was replaced by someone outside his protected class (a non-Asian instructor). AAMU, however, showed that Chang had argued with a university vice president and refused to comply with her instructions. The court ruled that the university had not renewed Chang's contract for a legitimate reason— insubordination—and therefore was not liable for unlawful discrimination.[3] •

Reverse Discrimination   Note that discrimination based on race can also take the form of *reverse discrimination,* or discrimination against "majority" individuals, such as white males. **CASE EXAMPLE 18.5** An African American woman fired four white men from their management positions at a school district. The men filed a lawsuit for racial discrimination, alleging that the woman was trying to eliminate white males from the department. The woman claimed that the terminations were part of a reorganization plan to cut costs. The jury sided with the men and awarded them nearly $3 million in damages. The verdict was upheld on appeal (though the damages award was reduced slightly).[4] •

A United States Supreme Court decision in 2009 has had a significant impact on disparate-impact and reverse discrimination litigation. **CASE EXAMPLE 18.6** The fire department in New Haven, Connecticut, administered a test to identify firefighters eligible for promotions. No African Americans and only two Hispanic firefighters passed the test. Fearing that it would be sued for discrimination if it based promotions on the test results, the city refused to use the results. The white firefighters (and one Hispanic) who had passed the test then sued the city, claiming reverse discrimination.

The United States Supreme Court held that an employer can engage in intentional discrimination to remedy an unintentional disparate impact only if the employer has "a strong basis in evidence" to believe that it will be successfully sued for disparate-impact discrimination "if it fails to take the race-conscious, discriminatory action." Mere fear of litigation was not sufficient reason for the city to discard its test results.[5] Subsequently, the city certified the test results and promoted the firefighters. •

Potential "Section 1981" Claims   Victims of racial or ethnic discrimination may also have a cause of action under 42 U.S.C. Section 1981. This section, which was enacted in 1866 to protect the rights of freed slaves, prohibits discrimination on the basis of race or ethnicity in the formation or enforcement of contracts. Because employment is often a contractual relationship, Section 1981 can provide an alternative basis for a plaintiff's action and is potentially advantageous because it does not place a cap on damages.

Discrimination Based on Religion

Title VII also prohibits government employers, private employers, and unions from discriminating against persons because of their religion. Employers cannot treat their employees more or less favorably based on their religious beliefs or practices and cannot require employees to participate in any religious activity (or forbid them from participating in one). **EXAMPLE 18.7** Jason Sewell claimed that his employer, a car dealership, fired him for not attending the weekly prayer meetings of dealership employees. If the dealership did require

---

3. *Jiann Min Chang v. Alabama Agricultural and Mechanical University,* 2009 WL 3403180 (11th Cir. 2009).
4. *Johnston v. School District of Philadelphia,* 2006 WL 999966 (E.D.Pa. 2006).
5. *Ricci v. DeStefano,* 557 U.S. 557, 129 S.Ct. 2658, 174 L.Ed.2d 490 (2009).

(JuanmoninofiStockphoto.com)

Under Title VII, can employers prohibit employees from participating in religious activities such as reciting prayers? Why or why not?

its employees to attend prayer gatherings and fired Sewell for not attending, he has a valid claim of religious discrimination. ●

Reasonable Accommodation   An employer must "reasonably accommodate" the religious practices of its employees, unless to do so would cause undue hardship to the employer's business. Employers must reasonably accommodate an employee's religious belief even if the belief is not based on the doctrines of a traditionally recognized religion, such as Christianity or Judaism, or a denomination, such as Baptist. The only requirement is that the belief be sincerely held by the employee.

Undue Hardship   If an employee's religion prohibits him or her from working on a certain day of the week or at a certain type of job, for instance, the employer must make a reasonable attempt to accommodate these religious requirements. A reasonable attempt to accommodate does not necessarily require the employer to permanently give an employee the requested day off, if to do so would cause the employer undue hardship.

   CASE EXAMPLE 18.8   Miguel Sánchez–Rodríguez sold cell phones in shopping malls for AT&T in Puerto Rico. After six years, Sánchez informed his supervisors that he had become a Seventh Day Adventist and could no longer work on Saturdays for religious reasons. AT&T responded that his inability to work on Saturdays would cause it hardship.

   As a reasonable accommodation, the company suggested that Sánchez swap schedules with others and offered him two other positions that did not require work on Saturdays. Sánchez could not find workers to swap shifts with him, however, and he declined the other jobs because they would result in less income. He began missing work on Saturdays.

   After a time, AT&T indicated that it would discipline him for any additional Saturdays that he missed. Eventually, he was placed on active disciplinary status. Sánchez resigned and filed a religious discrimination lawsuit against AT&T. The court found in favor of AT&T, and a federal appellate court affirmed. The company had made adequate efforts at accommodation by allowing Sánchez to swap shifts and offering him other positions that did not require work on Saturdays.[6] ●

Discrimination Based on Gender

Under Title VII, as well as other federal acts, employers are forbidden from discriminating against employees on the basis of gender. Employers are prohibited from classifying jobs as male or female and from advertising positions as male or female unless the employer can prove that the gender of the applicant is essential to the job.

Gender Must Be a Determining Factor   Generally, to succeed in a suit for gender discrimination, a plaintiff must demonstrate that gender was a determining factor in the employer's decision to fire or refuse to hire or promote her or him. Typically, this involves looking at all of the surrounding circumstances.

   CASE EXAMPLE 18.9   Wanda Collier worked for Turner Industries Group, LLC, in the maintenance department. She complained to her supervisor that Jack Daniell, the head of the department, treated her unfairly. Her supervisor told her that Daniell had a problem with her gender and was harder on women. The supervisor talked to Daniell but did not take any disciplinary action.

   A month later, Daniell confronted Collier, pushing her up against a wall and berating her. After this incident, Collier filed a formal complaint and kept a male co-worker with her at all times. A month later, she was fired. She subsequently filed a lawsuit alleging gender

"A sign that says 'men only' looks very different on a bathroom door than a courthouse door."

Thurgood Marshall, 1908–1993 (Associate justice of the United States Supreme Court, 1967–1991)

---

6. *Sánchez-Rodríquez v. AT&T Mobility Puerto Rico, Inc.,* 673 F.3d 1 (1st Cir. 2012).

discrimination. The court concluded that there was enough evidence that gender was a determining factor in Daniell's conduct to allow Collier's claims to go to a jury.[7] ●

Pregnancy Discrimination   The Pregnancy Discrimination Act,[8] amended Title VII and expanded the definition of gender discrimination to include discrimination based on pregnancy. Women affected by pregnancy, childbirth, or related medical conditions must be treated—for all employment-related purposes, including the receipt of benefits under employee benefit programs—the same as other persons not so affected but similar in ability to work.

Wage Discrimination   The Equal Pay Act[9] requires equal pay for male and female employees doing similar work at the same establishment. To determine whether the Equal Pay Act has been violated, a court will look to the primary duties of the two jobs— the job content rather than the job description controls. If the wage differential is due to "any factor other than gender," such as a seniority or merit system, then it does not violate the Equal Pay Act.

Congress also enacted the Lilly Ledbetter Fair Pay Act,[10] which made discriminatory wages actionable under federal law regardless of when the discrimination began. This act overturned a previous decision by the United States Supreme Court that had limited plaintiffs' time period to file a wage discrimination complaint to 180 days after the employer's decision.[11] Today, if a plaintiff continues to work for the employer while receiving discriminatory wages, the time period for filing a complaint is basically unlimited.

(Pablo Martinez Monsivais/AP Images)

President Obama signed the Lilly Ledbetter Fair Pay Act in 2009.

Constructive Discharge

The majority of Title VII complaints involve unlawful discrimination in decisions to hire or fire employees. In some situations, however, employees who leave their jobs voluntarily can claim that they were "constructively discharged" by the employer. **Constructive discharge** occurs when the employer causes the employee's working conditions to be so intolerable that a reasonable person in the employee's position would feel compelled to quit.

Constructive Discharge A termination of employment brought about by making the employee's working conditions so intolerable that the employee reasonably feels compelled to leave.

Proving Constructive Discharge   The plaintiff must present objective proof of intolerable working conditions, which the employer knew or had reason to know about yet failed to correct within a reasonable time period. Courts generally also require the employee to show causation—that the employer's unlawful discrimination caused the working conditions to be intolerable. Put a different way, the employee's resignation must be a foreseeable result of the employer's discriminatory action.

Although courts weigh the facts on a case-by-case basis, employee demotion is one of the most frequently cited reasons for a finding of constructive discharge, particularly when the employee was subjected to humiliation. **EXAMPLE 18.10**   Khalil's employer humiliates him in front of his co-workers by informing him that he is being demoted to an inferior position. Khalil's co-workers then continually insult and harass him about his national origin (he is from Iran). The employer is aware of this discriminatory treatment but does nothing to remedy the situation, despite repeated complaints from Khalil. After several months, Khalil quits his job and files a Title VII claim. In this situation, Khalil would likely have sufficient evidence to maintain an action for constructive discharge in violation of Title VII. ●

---

7. *Collier v. Turner Industries Group, LLC,* 797 F.Supp.2d 1029 (D. Idaho 2011).
8. 42 U.S.C. Section 2000e(k).
9. 29 U.S.C. Section 206(d).
10. Pub. L. No. 111-2, 123 Stat. 5 (January 5, 2009), amending 42 U.S.C. Section 2000e-5[e].
11. *Ledbetter v. Goodyear Tire Co.,* 550 U.S. 618, 127 S.Ct. 2162, 167 L.Ed.2d 982 (2007).

Applies to All Title VII Discrimination   Note that constructive discharge is a theory that plaintiffs can use to establish any type of discrimination claims under Title VII, including race, color, national origin, religion, gender, pregnancy, and sexual harassment. Constructive discharge has also been successfully used in situations involving discrimination based on age or disability (both of which will be discussed later in this chapter). Constructive discharge is most commonly asserted in cases involving sexual harassment, however.

When constructive discharge is claimed, the employee can pursue damages for loss of income, including back pay. These damages ordinarily are not available to an employee who left a job voluntarily.

Sexual Harassment

Sexual Harassment The demanding of sexual favors in return for job promotions or other benefits, or language or conduct that is so sexually offensive that it creates a hostile working environment.

Title VII also protects employees against **sexual harassment** in the workplace. Sexual harassment can take two forms: *quid pro quo* harassment and hostile-environment harassment. *Quid pro quo* is a Latin phrase that is often translated to mean "something in exchange for something else." *Quid pro quo* harassment occurs when sexual favors are demanded in return for job opportunities, promotions, salary increases, and the like.

According to the United States Supreme Court, hostile-environment harassment occurs when "the workplace is permeated with discriminatory intimidation, ridicule, and insult, that is sufficiently severe or pervasive to alter the conditions of the victim's employment and create an abusive working environment." [12]

The courts determine whether the sexually offensive conduct was sufficiently severe or pervasive to create a hostile environment on a case-by-case basis. Typically, a single incident of sexually offensive conduct is not enough to create a hostile environment (although there have been exceptions when the conduct was particularly objectionable). Note also that if the employee who is alleging sexual harassment has signed an employment contract with an arbitration clause, she or he will most likely be required to arbitrate the claim.

A court considers a number of factors in assessing the severity and pervasiveness of the alleged sexual harassment. As the following case shows, these factors include the nature and frequency of the conduct and whether it unreasonably interfered with the victim's work performance.

---

12. *Harris v. Forklift Systems*, 510 U.S. 17, 114 S.Ct. 367, 126 L.Ed.2d 295 (1993). See also *Billings v. Town of Grafton*, 515 F.3d 39 (1st Cir. 2008).

Case 18.1

Roberts v. Mike's Trucking, Ltd.
Court of Appeals of Ohio, Twelfth District, Madison County, 2014 -Ohio- 766, ___ Ohio App.3d ___, 9 N.E.3d 483 (2014).

(Gilles Lougassi/Shutterstock.com)

BACKGROUND AND FACTS   Teresa Roberts worked for Mike's Trucking, Ltd., in Columbus, Ohio. Her supervisor was the company's owner, Mike Culbertson. According to Roberts, Culbertson called her his "sexretary" and constantly talked about his sex life. He often invited her to sit on "Big Daddy's" lap, rubbed against her, trapped her at the door and asked for hugs or kisses, and asked if she needed help in the restroom. Roberts asked him to stop this conduct, to no avail. She became less productive and began to suffer anxiety attacks and high blood pressure. Roberts filed a suit in an Ohio state court

against Mike's, alleging a hostile work environment through sexual harassment in violation of Title VII. A jury decided in Roberts's favor, and Mike's appealed.

IN THE WORDS OF THE COURT . . .
HENDRICKSON, P.J. [Presiding Judge]
* * * *

* * * Conduct that is not severe or pervasive enough to create an objectively hostile or abusive work environment— an environment that a reasonable person would find hostile or

Case 18.1—Continued

abusive—is beyond Title VII's purview. Likewise, if the victim does not subjectively perceive the environment to be abusive, the conduct has not actually altered the conditions of the victim's employment, and there is no Title VII violation. Therefore, *the focus of this inquiry is: 1.) whether a reasonable person would find the environment objectively hostile; and 2.) whether the plaintiff subjectively found the conduct severe or pervasive.* [Emphasis added.]

* * * *

* * * Roberts' testimony was consistent with several witnesses affirming that Culbertson frequently engaged in a variety of conduct ranging from inappropriate discussions to groping women. The witnesses stated that Culbertson often discussed his sex life, asked Roberts and the women employees if they needed help in the bathroom * * * , referred to himself as "Big Daddy," asked Roberts and the women employees to sit in "Big Daddy's" lap, and asked them if they would give "Big Daddy" a hug.

The evidence established that the conduct occurred frequently. Roberts testified that throughout her employment, Culbertson's behavior became increasingly worse and that * * * he talked about sex hundreds of times, and attempted to corner her and hug and kiss her at least twice a week. [Former Mike's employees] testified that Culbertson talked about sex and asked the women if they needed help with the bathroom multiple times a week. The evidence also showed that the conduct became increasingly severe as Culbertson massaged Roberts [and] rubbed up against her * * * . Roberts testified that Culbertson's conduct was humiliating towards her as his

remarks were in front of others and she often became "furious" with him. Other employees reported Roberts becoming angry towards Culbertson. Roberts also established that Culbertson's conduct unreasonably interfered with her work performance as she stated she did not want to go to work anymore, she became less productive, and she suffered anxiety attacks. Her fiancé testified that Roberts has lost confidence and that she is now prescribed anti-anxiety medication.

Consequently, there was sufficient and substantial evidence to support the jury's finding that a reasonable person would find Culbertson's conduct created a hostile environment and Roberts found the conduct to be sufficiently severe or pervasive to affect her employment.

DECISION AND REMEDY A state intermediate appellate court affirmed the lower court's judgment in Roberts's favor. During the trial, other Mike's employees and Roberts's fiancé testified to corroborate Roberts's account. The evidence sufficiently established that Culbertson's conduct was severe or pervasive enough to create a hostile work environment for Roberts.

THE LEGAL ENVIRONMENT DIMENSION *Culbertson and some other witnesses testified that he did not engage in any sexually inappropriate behavior. Should an appellate court reverse a jury's decision simply due to contrary evidence? Why or why not?*

THE ETHICAL DIMENSION *Was Culbertson's conduct at any point unethical? Discuss.*

Harassment by Supervisors For an employer to be held liable for a supervisor's sexual harassment, the supervisor normally must have taken a *tangible employment action* against the employee. A **tangible employment action** is a significant change in employment status or benefits, such as when an employee is fired, refused a promotion, demoted, or reassigned to a position with significantly different responsibilities. Only a supervisor, or another person acting with the authority of the employer, can cause this sort of injury. A constructive discharge also qualifies as a tangible employment action.[13]

Tangible Employment Action A significant change in employment status or benefits, such as occurs when an employee is fired, refused a promotion, or reassigned to a lesser position.

The *Ellerth/Faragher* Affirmative Defense In 1998, the United States Supreme Court issued several important rulings that have had a lasting impact on cases alleging sexual harassment by supervisors.[14] The Court held that an employer (a city) was liable for a supervisor's harassment of employees even though the employer was unaware of the behavior. Although the city had a written policy against sexual

---

13. See, for example, *Pennsylvania State Police v. Suders*, 542 U.S. 129, 124 S.Ct. 2342, 159 L.Ed.2d 204 (2004).
14. *Burlington Industries, Inc. v. Ellerth*, 524 U.S. 742, 118 S.Ct. 2257, 141 L.Ed.2d 633 (1998); and *Faragher v. City of Boca Raton*, 524 U.S. 775, 118 S.Ct. 2275, 141 L.Ed.2d 662 (1998).

A presumed victim of sexual harassment attends a press conference with her attorney. What hurdles will she face in such litigation?

harassment, it had not distributed the policy to its employees and had not established any complaint procedures for employees who felt that they had been sexually harassed. In another case, the Court held that an employer can be liable for a supervisor's sexual harassment even though the employee does not suffer adverse job consequences.

The Court's decisions in these cases established what has become known as the *"Ellerth/Faragher* affirmative defense" to charges of sexual harassment. The defense has two elements:

1. That the employer has taken reasonable care to prevent and promptly correct any sexually harassing behavior (by establishing effective antiharassment policies and complaint procedures, for example).
2. That the plaintiff-employee unreasonably failed to take advantage of any preventive or corrective opportunities provided by the employer to avoid harm.

An employer that can prove both elements will not be liable for a supervisor's harassment.

Retaliation by Employers   Employers sometimes retaliate against employees who complain about sexual harassment or other Title VII violations. Retaliation can take many forms. An employer might demote or fire the person, or otherwise change the terms, conditions, and benefits of employment. Title VII prohibits retaliation, and employees can sue their employers.

In a *retaliation claim,* an individual asserts that she or he has suffered a harm as a result of making a charge, testifying, or participating in a Title VII investigation or proceeding. Plaintiffs do not have to prove that the challenged action adversely affected their workplace or employment. Instead, plaintiffs must show that the action was one that would likely have dissuaded a reasonable worker from making or supporting a charge of discrimination. Title VII's retaliation protection extends to an employee who speaks out about discrimination against another employee during an employer's internal investigation. The retaliation provision also protected an employee who was fired after his fiancée filed a gender discrimination claim against their employer.[15]

In the following case, a female law professor lost her job after she complained about comments made by her dean and colleagues. The court had to decide whether she had been retaliated against for engaging in protected conduct.

---

15. See *Thompson v. North American Stainless, LP,* ___ U.S. ___, 131 S.Ct. 863, 178 L.Ed.2d 694 (2011).

Case 18.2

Morales-Cruz v. University of Puerto Rico
United States Court of Appeals, First Circuit, 676 F.3d 220 (2012).

BACKGROUND AND FACTS   In 2003, Myrta Morales-Cruz began a tenure-track teaching position at the University of Puerto Rico School of Law. During Morales-Cruz's probationary period, one of her co-teachers in a law school clinic had an affair with one of their students, and it resulted in a pregnancy. In 2008,

Morales-Cruz wanted the university's administrative committee to approve a one-year extension for her tenure review. The law school's dean asked Morales-Cruz about her co-teacher's affair and criticized her for failing to report it. He later recommended granting the extension but called Morales-Cruz insecure,

Case 18.2—Continued

immature, and fragile. Similarly, a law school committee recommended granting the extension, but a dissenting professor commented that Morales-Cruz had shown poor judgment, in regard to the co-teacher's affair, had personality flaws, and had trouble with complex and sensitive situations.

Morales-Cruz learned about these comments and complained in writing to the university's chancellor. As a result, the dean then recommended denying the one-year extension, and the administrative committee ultimately did just that. When her employment was terminated, Morales-Cruz sued the university under Title VII. Among other things, she asserted that the dean had retaliated against her for complaining to the chancellor. The district court found that Morales-Cruz had not stated a proper retaliation claim under Title VII.

IN THE WORDS OF THE COURT . . .
SELYA, Circuit Judge.
* * * *

The amended complaint alleges that various officials described the plaintiff as "fragile," "immature," "unable to handle complex and sensitive issues," * * * and exhibiting "lack of judgment." These descriptors are admittedly unflattering—but they are without exception gender-neutral. All of them apply equally to persons of either gender * * * .
* * * *

* * * Title VII makes it unlawful for an employer to take materially adverse action against an employee "because he has opposed any practice made an unlawful employment practice by this subchapter." *To state a cause of action under this portion of the statute, the pleading must contain plausible*

allegations indicating that the plaintiff opposed a practice prohibited by Title VII and suffered an adverse employment action as a result of that opposition. [Emphasis added.]

The plaintiff alleges that she was retaliated against for writing to the Chancellor to complain about the "discriminatory" comments made in the course of her request for an extension. In support of this allegation, she points out that after she sent her letter the Dean reversed his position on her extension. This construct suffers from a fatal flaw: her factual allegations do not support a reasonable inference that she was engaging in protected conduct when she opposed the remarks made.

* * * The facts alleged * * * provide no reasonable basis for inferring that the comments cited reflected gender-based discrimination. Those comments were unarguably gender-neutral and do not afford an objectively reasonable foundation for a retaliation action.

DECISION AND REMEDY The U.S. Court of Appeals for the First Circuit held that Morales-Cruz could not bring a retaliation claim under Title VII. It therefore affirmed the district court's judgment for the University of Puerto Rico.

THE ETHICAL DIMENSION *Could Morales-Cruz's dean have had legitimate reasons for changing his mind about the one-year extension? If so, what might they have been?*

THE LEGAL ENVIRONMENT DIMENSION *What steps should employers take to reduce the likelihood that supervisors will retaliate against employees who make or support discrimination claims?*

Harassment by Co-Workers and Nonemployees When the harassment of co-workers, rather than supervisors, creates a hostile working environment, an employee may still have a cause of action against the employer. Normally, though, the employer will be held liable only if the employer knew, or should have known, about the harassment and failed to take immediate remedial action.

Occasionally, a court may also hold an employer liable for harassment by *nonemployees* if the employer knew about the harassment and failed to take corrective action. **EXAMPLE 18.11** Gordon, who owns and manages a Great Bites restaurant, knows that one of his regular customers, Dean, repeatedly harasses Sharon, a waitress. If Gordon does nothing and permits the harassment to continue, he may be liable under Title VII even though Dean is not an employee of the restaurant. •

Same-Gender Harassment In *Oncale v. Sundowner Offshore Services, Inc.,*[16] the United States Supreme Court held that Title VII protection extends to individuals who are sexually harassed by members of the same gender. Proving that the harassment in

---

16. 523 U.S. 75, 118 S.Ct. 998, 140 L.Ed.2d 207 (1998).

same-gender cases is "based on sex" can be difficult, though. It is usually easier to establish a case of same-gender harassment when the harasser is homosexual.

Sexual Orientation Harassment   Although federal law (Title VII) does not prohibit discrimination or harassment based on a person's sexual orientation, a growing number of states have enacted laws that prohibit sexual orientation discrimination in private employment. Some states, such as Oregon, explicitly prohibit discrimination based on a person's gender identity or expression. Also, many companies and organizations have voluntarily established nondiscrimination policies that include sexual orientation. For instance, the Boy Scouts of America and the National Football League (NFL) have changed their policies to allow members/players who are openly gay.

Online Harassment

Employees' online activities can create a hostile working environment in many ways. Racial jokes, ethnic slurs, or other comments contained in e-mail, text or instant messages, and social media or blog posts can become the basis for a claim of hostile-environment harassment or other forms of discrimination.

Nevertheless, employers may be able to avoid liability for online harassment if they take prompt remedial action. **EXAMPLE 18.12** While working at TriCom, Shonda Dean receives racially harassing e-mailed jokes from another employee. Shortly afterward, the company issues a warning to the offending employee about the proper use of the e-mail system and holds two meetings to discuss company policy on the use of the system. If Dean sues TriCom for racial discrimination, a court may find that because the employer took prompt remedial action, TriCom should not be held liable for its employee's racially harassing e-mails. ●

Remedies under Title VII

Employer liability under Title VII may be extensive. If the plaintiff successfully proves that unlawful discrimination occurred, he or she may be awarded reinstatement, back pay, retroactive promotions, and damages. Compensatory damages are available only in cases of intentional discrimination. Punitive damages may be recovered against a private employer only if the employer acted with malice or reckless indifference to an individual's rights.

The statute limits the total amount of compensatory and punitive damages that the plaintiff can recover from specific employers, depending on the size of the employer. The cap ranges from $50,000 for employers with one hundred or fewer employees to $300,000 for employers with more than five hundred employees.

Discrimination Based on Age

Age discrimination is potentially the most widespread form of discrimination, because anyone—regardless of race, color, national origin, or gender—could eventually be a victim. The Age Discrimination in Employment Act (ADEA)[17] prohibits employment discrimination on the basis of age against individuals forty years of age or older. The act also prohibits mandatory retirement for nonmanagerial workers.

For the act to apply, an employer must have twenty or more employees, and the employer's business activities must affect interstate commerce. The EEOC administers the ADEA, but the act also permits private causes of action against employers for age discrimination.

Learning Objective 3
What remedies are available under Title VII of the Civil Rights Act?

Learning Objective 4
What federal act prohibits discrimination based on age?

17. 29 U.S.C. Sections 621–634.

The ADEA includes a provision that extends protections against age discrimination to federal government employees.[18] This provision encompasses not only claims of age discrimination, but also claims of retaliation for complaining about age discrimination, which are not specifically mentioned in the statute.[19] Thus, the ADEA protects federal and private-sector employees from retaliation based on age-related complaints.

Procedures under the ADEA

The burden-shifting procedure under the ADEA differs from the procedure under Title VII as a result of a United States Supreme Court decision in 2009, which dramatically changed the burden of proof in age discrimination cases.[20] As explained earlier, if the plaintiff in a Title VII case can show that the employer was motivated, at least in part, by unlawful discrimination, the burden of proof shifts to the employer to articulate a legitimate nondiscriminatory reason. Thus, in cases in which the employer has a "mixed motive" for discharging an employee, the employer has the burden of proving its reason was legitimate.

Under the ADEA, in contrast, a plaintiff must show that the unlawful discrimination was not just *a* reason but *the* reason for the adverse employment action. In other words, the employee has the burden of establishing "but for" causation—that is, but for the plaintiff's age, the adverse action would not have happened.

Prima Facie **Case** To establish a *prima facie* case, the plaintiff must show that he or she was the following:

1. A member of the protected age group.
2. Qualified for the position from which he or she was discharged.
3. Discharged because of age discrimination.

Then the burden shifts to the employer.

Pretext If the employer offers a legitimate reason for its action, then the plaintiff must show that the stated reason is only a pretext and that the plaintiff's age was the real reason for the employer's decision.

When is firing an older worker considered age discrimination?

(StockLite/Shutterstock.com)

CASE EXAMPLE 18.13 Josephine Mora, a fund-raiser for Jackson Memorial Foundation, Inc., was sixty-two years old when the foundation's chief executive officer (CEO) fired her, citing errors and issues with professionalism. Mora filed a suit against the foundation, alleging age discrimination. She asserted that when she was fired, the CEO told her, "I need someone younger I can pay less." She had a witness who heard that statement and also heard the CEO say that Mora was "too old to be working here anyway." The CEO denied making these statements, and the foundation claimed that Mora was terminated for poor job performance.

A district court granted a summary judgment in the foundation's favor, and Mora appealed. A federal appellate court reversed, concluding that the lower court's analysis of causation was incorrect. The court held that a reasonable juror could have accepted that the CEO had made discriminatory remarks, and could have found these remarks were sufficient evidence of a discriminatory motive. If so, that would show that Mora was fired because of her age. The court therefore remanded the case back to the lower court for a trial.[21] •

---

18. See 29 U.S.C. Section 632(a) (2000 ed., Supp. V).
19. *Gomez-Perez v. Potter,* 553 U.S. 474, 128 S.Ct. 1931, 170 L.Ed.2d 887 (2008).
20. *Gross v. FBL Financial Services,* 557 U.S. 167, 129 S.Ct. 2343, 174 L.Ed.2d 119 (2009).
21. *Mora v. Jackson Memorial Foundation, Inc.,* 597 F.3d 1201 (2010).

State Employees Not Covered by the ADEA

Generally, the states are immune from lawsuits brought by private individuals in federal court—unless a state consents to the suit. This immunity stems from the United States Supreme Court's interpretation of the Eleventh Amendment (see Appendix B).

State immunity under the Eleventh Amendment is not absolute, however. In some situations, such as when fundamental rights are at stake, Congress has the power to abrogate (abolish) state immunity to private suits through legislation that unequivocally shows Congress's intent to subject states to private suits.[22]

As a general rule, though, the Court has found that state employers are immune from private suits brought by employees under the ADEA (for age discrimination, as noted above), the Americans with Disabilities Act[23] (for disability discrimination), and the Fair Labor Standards Act.[24] In contrast, state employers are not immune from the requirements of the Family and Medical Leave Act.[25]

Discrimination Based on Disability

The Americans with Disabilities Act (ADA)[26] prohibits disability-based discrimination in workplaces with fifteen or more workers (with the exception of state government employers, who are generally immune under the Eleventh Amendment, as just discussed). Basically, the ADA requires that employers reasonably accommodate the needs of persons with disabilities unless to do so would cause the employer to suffer an undue hardship. The ADA Amendments Act broadened the coverage of the ADA's protection.[27]

Procedures under the ADA

To prevail on a claim under the ADA, a plaintiff must show that he or she (1) has a disability, (2) is otherwise qualified for the employment in question, and (3) was excluded from the employment solely because of the disability. As in Title VII cases, a plaintiff must pursue her or his claim through the EEOC before filing an action in court for a violation of the ADA.

The EEOC may decide to investigate and perhaps even sue the employer on behalf of the employee. If the EEOC decides not to sue, then the employee is entitled to sue in court. The EEOC can bring a suit against an employer for disability-based discrimination even though the employee previously agreed to submit any job-related disputes to arbitration.

Plaintiffs in lawsuits brought under the ADA may obtain many of the same remedies available under Title VII. These include reinstatement, back pay, a limited amount of compensatory and punitive damages (for intentional discrimination), and certain other forms of relief. Repeat violators may be ordered to pay fines of up to $100,000.

What Is a Disability?

The ADA is broadly drafted to cover persons with a wide range of disabilities. Specifically, the ADA defines *disability* to include any of the following:

1. A physical or mental impairment that substantially limits one or more of an individual's major life activities.

---

22. *Tennessee v. Lane*, 541 U.S. 509, 124 S.Ct. 1978, 158 L.Ed.2d 820 (2004).
23. *Board of Trustees of the University of Alabama v. Garrett*, 531 U.S. 356, 121 S.Ct. 955, 148 L.Ed.2d 866 (2001).
24. *Alden v. Maine*, 527 U.S. 706, 119 S.Ct. 2240, 144 L.Ed.2d 636 (1999).
25. *Nevada Department of Human Resources v. Hibbs*, 538 U.S. 721, 123 S.Ct. 1972, 155 L.Ed.2d 953 (2003).
26. 42 U.S.C. Sections 12102–12118.
27. 42 U.S.C. Sections 12103 and 12205a.

2. A record of such impairment.

3. Being regarded as having such an impairment.

Health conditions that have been considered disabilities under the federal law include blindness, alcoholism, heart disease, cancer, muscular dystrophy, cerebral palsy, paraplegia, diabetes, acquired immune deficiency syndrome (AIDS), testing positive for the human immunodeficiency virus (HIV), and morbid obesity (defined as existing when an individual's weight is two times the normal weight for his or her height).

A separate provision in the ADA prevents employers from taking adverse employment actions based on stereotypes or assumptions about individuals who associate with people who have disabilities.[28] At one time, the courts focused on whether a person was disabled *after* the use of corrective devices or medication. With this approach, a person with severe myopia, or nearsightedness, which can be corrected with lenses, for instance, would not qualify as disabled because that individual's major life activities were not substantially impaired. In 2008, Congress amended the ADA to strengthen its protections and prohibit employers from considering mitigating measures or medications when determining if an individual has a disability. Disability is now determined on a case-by-case basis.

Reasonable Accommodation

The ADA does not require that employers accommodate the needs of job applicants or employees with disabilities who are not otherwise qualified for the work. If a job applicant or an employee with a disability can perform essential job functions with a reasonable accommodation, however, the employer must make the accommodation.

Required modifications may include installing ramps for a wheelchair, establishing more flexible working hours, creating or modifying job assignments, and creating or improving training materials and procedures. Generally, employers should give primary consideration to employees' preferences in deciding what accommodations should be made.

Undue Hardship

Employers who do not accommodate the needs of persons with disabilities must demonstrate that the accommodations will cause "undue hardship" in terms of being significantly difficult or expensive for the employer. Usually, the courts decide whether an accommodation constitutes an undue hardship on a case-by-case basis by looking at the employer's resources in relation to the specific accommodation.

EXAMPLE 18.14 Bryan Lockhart, who uses a wheelchair, works for a cell phone company that provides parking for its employees. Lockhart informs the company supervisors that the parking spaces are so narrow that he is unable to extend the ramp on his van that allows him to get in and out of the vehicle. Lockhart therefore requests that the company reasonably accommodate his needs by paying a monthly fee for him to use a larger parking space in an adjacent lot. In this situation, a court would likely find that it would not be an undue hardship for the employer to pay for additional parking for Lockhart. ●

Job Applications and Preemployment Physical Exams

Employers must modify their job-application process so that those with disabilities can compete for jobs with those who do not have disabilities. For instance, a job announcement might be modified to allow job applicants to respond by e-mail or letter, as well as by telephone, so that it does not discriminate against potential applicants with hearing impairments.

> "Jobs are physically easier, but the worker now takes home worries instead of an aching back."
>
> Homer Bigart, 1907–1991
> (American journalist)

---

28. 42 U.S.C. Section 12112(b)(4). Under this provision, an employer cannot, for instance, refuse to hire the parent of a child with a disability based on the assumption that the parent will miss work too often or be unreliable.

Employers are restricted in the kinds of questions they may ask on job-application forms and during preemployment interviews. Furthermore, they cannot require persons with disabilities to submit to preemployment physicals unless such exams are required of all other applicants. Employers can condition an offer of employment on the applicant's successfully passing a medical examination, but can disqualify the applicant only if the medical problems they discover would render the applicant unable to perform the job.

CASE EXAMPLE 18.15 When filling the position of delivery truck driver, a company cannot automatically screen out all applicants who are unable to meet the U.S. Department of Transportation's hearing standard. The company would first have to prove that drivers who are deaf are not qualified to perform the essential job function of driving safely and pose a higher risk of accidents than drivers who are not deaf.[29] ●

Substance Abusers Drug addiction is a disability under the ADA because drug addiction is a substantially limiting impairment. Those who are actually using illegal drugs are not protected by the act, however. The ADA protects only persons with *former* drug addictions—those who have completed or are now in a supervised drug-rehabilitation program. Individuals who have used drugs casually in the past are not protected under the act. They are not considered addicts and therefore do not have a disability (addiction).

People suffering from alcoholism are protected by the ADA. Employers cannot legally discriminate against employees simply because they are suffering from alcoholism. Of course, employers have the right to prohibit the use of alcohol in the workplace and can require that employees not be under the influence of alcohol while working.

Health-Insurance Plans Workers with disabilities must be given equal access to any health insurance provided to other employees. Employers cannot exclude preexisting health conditions from coverage. An employer can also put a limit, or cap, on health-care payments under its group health policy. Any such caps must be "applied equally to all insured employees" and not "discriminate on the basis of disability." Whenever a group health-care plan makes a disability-based distinction in its benefits, the plan violates the ADA (unless the employer can justify its actions under the business necessity defense, which will be discussed shortly).

Defenses to Employment Discrimination

Learning Objective 5
What are three defenses to claims of employment discrimination?

The first line of defense for an employer charged with employment discrimination is, of course, to assert that the plaintiff has failed to meet his or her initial burden of proving that discrimination occurred. Once a plaintiff succeeds in proving discrimination, the burden shifts to the employer to justify the discriminatory practice.

Possible justifications include that the discrimination was the result of a business necessity, a bona fide occupational qualification, a seniority system, a lack of motive, and after-acquired evidence of employee misconduct. In some situations, as noted earlier, an effective antiharassment policy and prompt remedial action when harassment occurs may shield employers from liability for sexual harassment under Title VII.

Business Necessity

Business Necessity A defense to alleged employment discrimination in which the employer demonstrates that an employment practice that discriminates against members of a protected class is related to job performance.

An employer may defend against a claim of disparate-impact (unintentional) discrimination by asserting that a practice that has a discriminatory effect is a **business necessity.** **EXAMPLE 18.16** If requiring a high school diploma is shown to have a discriminatory effect, an employer might argue that a high school education is necessary for workers to perform the job at a required level of competence. If the employer can demonstrate a

---

29. *Bates v. United Parcel Service, Inc.,* 465 F.3d 1069 (9th Cir. 2006).

definite connection between a high school education and job performance, the employer normally will succeed in this business necessity defense. ●

Bona Fide Occupational Qualification

Another defense applies when discrimination against a protected class is essential to a job—that is, when a particular trait is a **bona fide occupational qualification (BFOQ)**. Race, however, can never be a BFOQ.

Generally, courts have restricted the BFOQ defense to instances in which the employee's gender is essential to the job. **EXAMPLE 18.17**   A women's clothing store might legitimately hire only female sales attendants if part of an attendant's job involves assisting clients in the store's dressing rooms. Similarly, the Federal Aviation Administration can legitimately impose age limits for airline pilots—but an airline cannot impose weight limits only on female flight attendants. ●

Seniority Systems

An employer with a history of discrimination might have no members of protected classes in upper-level positions. Even if the employer now seeks to be unbiased, some employees may bring a lawsuit asking a court to order that minorities be promoted ahead of schedule to compensate for past discrimination. If no present intent to discriminate is shown, however, and if promotions or other job benefits are distributed according to a fair **seniority system** (in which workers with more years of service are promoted first or laid off last), the employer normally has a good defense against the suit.

A Lack of Motive

As indicated earlier, if the plaintiff in an employment discrimination case can successfully show that the employer was motivated, at least in part, by unlawful discrimination, the burden of proof then shifts. The employer then has to articulate a legitimate, nondiscriminatory reason for the challenged action.

Once the employer demonstrates a legitimate, nondiscriminatory reason for the action, the burden shifts back to the plaintiff to show that the reason is a pretext for discrimination. A plaintiff who cannot prove a discriminatory motive will be unable to establish his or her case, and the employer will have a defense against a charge of discrimination.

Sometimes, as in the following case, a court will assume that a plaintiff has established a *prima facie* case in order to consider both parties' evidence of the motive for the challenged action.

Bona Fide Occupational Qualification (BFOQ) Identifiable characteristics reasonably necessary to the normal operation of a particular business. These characteristics can include gender, national origin, and religion, but not race.

Seniority System A system in which those who have worked longest for an employer are first in line for promotions, salary increases, and other benefits, and are last to be laid off if the workforce must be reduced.

Case 18.3

Dees v. United Rentals North America, Inc.
United States Court of Appeals, Fifth Circuit, 2013 WL 28405 (2013).

(Spotmatik/Shutterstock.com)

BACKGROUND AND FACTS   In 2006, Ellis Dees, an African-American, applied to United Rentals for employment and was offered a position in St. Rose, Louisiana. Dees accepted. The first two years of his employment went smoothly, but his performance began to deteriorate in 2009. With increasing frequency, he marked equipment as fit, even though it was not working. His managers coached him, noted the incidents in his performance reviews, and gave him written warnings. After a final warning, Dees was fired. He was sixty-two years old. He filed a charge with the Equal Employment Opportunity Commission, alleging employment discrimination based on his race and age

Case 18.3—Continues ➡

Case 18.3—Continued

in violation of Title VII and the Age Discrimination in Employment Act (ADEA). After receiving a "right to sue" notice, he filed a suit in a federal district court against United Rentals. From a judgment in the employer's favor, Dees appealed.

IN THE WORDS OF THE COURT . . .

PER CURIAM [By the Whole Court]

* * * *

* * * [Under Title VII or the ADEA,] Dees first must make a *prima facie* case of discrimination based on age or race. To establish a *prima facie* case, Dees must show that he: (1) was a member of a protected group; (2) qualified for the position in question; (3) was subjected to an adverse employment action; and (4) received less favorable treatment due to his membership in the protected class than did other similarly situated employees who were not members of the protected class, under nearly identical circumstances.

If Dees makes a prima facie *case, the burden then shifts to United Rentals to articulate a legitimate, non-discriminatory reason for firing him.* If it does so, Dees must, as to his Title VII claim, offer sufficient evidence to create a genuine issue of material fact either (1) that United Rentals' reason is not true, but is instead a pretext for discrimination * * * ; or (2) that United Rentals' reason, while true, is only one of the reasons for its conduct, and another motivating factor is Dees' protected characteristic. [Emphasis added.]

* * * *

* * * The district court * * * determined that United Rentals had provided extensive evidence of a legitimate, non-discriminatory reason for Dees' termination—namely, unsatisfactory job performance. * * * The burden shifted back to Dees to produce evidence that United Rentals' reason was a pretext for discrimination.

The district court concluded that Dees had only made conclusory allegations that he was discriminated against.

* * * *

His termination notice states that he was terminated for failing to follow United Rentals' policy of ensuring that the batteries in rental equipment were in good working order prior to delivery of the equipment.

* * * Dees has presented nothing to tie United Rentals' final termination decision to a discriminatory motive. * * * Dees himself describes United Rentals as motivated by an "I ain't missing no rents" philosophy that encouraged renting out equipment regardless of its readiness. No evidence shows that United Rentals' philosophy also included discriminating against African–Americans or senior workers. Similarly, no evidence demonstrates that United Rentals' decision to discharge Dees was motivated by his race or age. * * * Dees' subjective belief that United Rentals discriminated against him is clearly insufficient to demonstrate pretext.

DECISION AND REMEDY   The federal appellate court affirmed the lower court's judgment in favor of United Rentals. The appellate court stated that "Dees failed to submit any evidence of discrimination and that this is fatal to his claims under Title VII and the ADEA."

WHAT IF THE FACTS WERE DIFFERENT?   *Suppose that rather than age discrimination, Dees had alleged employment discrimination on the basis of a disability. How would the steps to a decision on that allegation have been different?*

THE LEGAL ENVIRONMENT DIMENSION   *What did the plaintiff fail to do in submitting his side of the case? How did this failure affect his claims?*

After-Acquired Evidence of Employee Misconduct

Employers have also attempted to avoid liability for employment discrimination on the basis of *after-acquired evidence*—that is, evidence that the employer discovers after a lawsuit is filed—of an employee's misconduct. **EXAMPLE 18.18**   Pratt Legal Services fires Lucy, who sues Pratt for employer discrimination. During the pretrial investigation, Pratt discovers that Lucy made material misrepresentations on her job application. Had Pratt known of these misrepresentations, it would have had grounds to fire Lucy. ● The United States Supreme Court has held that after-acquired evidence cannot shield an employer entirely from liability for discrimination. It could, however, be used to limit the amount of damages of a lawsuit.

Affirmative Action

Affirmative Action   Job-hiring policies that give special consideration to members of protected classes in an effort to overcome present effects of past discrimination.

Federal statutes and regulations providing for equal opportunity in the workplace were designed to reduce or eliminate discriminatory practices with respect to hiring, retaining, and promoting employees. **Affirmative action** programs go further and attempt to "make up" for past patterns of discrimination by giving members of protected classes preferential treatment in hiring or promotion. During the 1960s, all federal and state government agencies, private companies that contracted to do business with the federal government, and institutions that received federal funding were required to implement affirmative action policies.

Title VII of the Civil Rights Act neither requires nor prohibits affirmative action. Thus, most private firms have not been required to implement affirmative action policies, though many have voluntarily done so. Affirmative action programs have been controversial, however, particularly when they have resulted in *reverse discrimination*.

Equal Protection Issues Because of their inherently discriminatory nature, affirmative action programs may violate the equal protection clause of the Fourteenth Amendment to the U.S. Constitution. Any federal, state, or local affirmative action program that uses racial or ethnic classifications as the basis for making decisions is subject to strict scrutiny (the highest standard to meet) by the courts.

Today, an affirmative action program normally is constitutional only if it attempts to remedy past discrimination and does not make use of quotas or preferences. Furthermore, once such a program has succeeded in the goal of remedying past discrimination, it must be changed or dropped.

States Can Prohibit Some states, including California, Maryland, Michigan, Virginia, and Washington, have enacted laws that prohibit affirmative action programs within their borders. The United States Supreme Court recognized that states have the power to enact such bans in 2014. **CASE EXAMPLE 18.19** Michigan voters passed an initiative to amend the state's constitution and prohibit publically funded colleges from granting preferential treatment to any group on the basis of race, sex, color, ethnicity, or national origin. The law also prohibited Michigan from considering race and gender in public hiring and contracting decisions.

A group that supports affirmative action programs in education sued the state's attorney general and others, claiming that the initiative deprived minorities of equal protection of the laws in violation of the U.S. Constitution. A federal appellate court found that the law violated the equal protection clause, but the United States Supreme Court reversed. The Supreme Court held that the courts do not have the power to set aside the amendment to the Michigan Constitution prohibiting affirmation action in public education, employment, and contracting. The Court explained that it was not deciding the constitutionality of a particular affirmative action program, but was only ruling that a state has the inherent power to ban affirmative action within that state.[30] •

---

30. *Schutte v. Coalition to Defend Affirmative Action, Integration and Immigrant Rights*, ___ U.S. ___, 134 S.Ct. 1623, 188 L.Ed.2d 613 (2014).

Reviewing . . . Employment Discrimination

Amaani Lyle, an African American woman, took a job as a scriptwriters' assistant at Warner Brothers Television Productions. She worked for the writers of *Friends*, a popular, adult-oriented television series. One of her essential job duties was to type detailed notes for the scriptwriters during brainstorming sessions in which they discussed jokes, dialogue, and story lines. The writers then combed through Lyle's notes after the meetings for script material. During these meetings, the three male scriptwriters told lewd and vulgar jokes and made sexually explicit comments and gestures. They often talked about their personal sexual experiences and fantasies, and some of these conversations were then used in episodes of *Friends*.

During the meetings, Lyle never complained that she found the writers' conduct offensive. After four months, she was fired because she could not type fast enough to keep up with the writers' conversations during the meetings. She filed a suit against

Warner Brothers alleging sexual harassment and claiming that her termination was based on racial discrimination. Using the information presented in the chapter, answer the following questions.

1. Would Lyle's claim of racial discrimination be for intentional (disparate-treatment) or unintentional (disparate-impact) discrimination? Explain.
2. Can Lyle establish a *prima facie* case of racial discrimination? Why or why not?
3. When she was hired, Lyle was told that typing speed was extremely important to her position. At the time, she maintained that she could type eighty words per minute, so she was not given a typing test. It later turned out that Lyle could type only fifty words per minute. What impact might typing speed have on Lyle's lawsuit?
4. Lyle's sexual-harassment claim is based on the hostile work environment created by the writers' sexually offensive conduct at meetings that she was required to attend. The writers, however, argue that their behavior was essential to the "creative process" of writing *Friends*, a show that routinely contained sexual innuendos and adult humor. Which defense discussed in the chapter might Warner Brothers assert using this argument?

Debate This Members of minority groups and women have made enough economic progress in the last several decades that they no longer need special legislation to protect them.

Key Terms

Chapter Summary: Employment Discrimination

Title VII of the Civil Rights Act	Title VII prohibits employment discrimination based on race, color, national origin, religion, or gender. 1. *Procedures*—Employees must file a claim with the Equal Employment Opportunity Commission (EEOC). The EEOC may sue the employer on the employee's behalf. If not, the employee may sue the employer directly. 2. *Types of discrimination*—Title VII prohibits both intentional (disparate-treatment) and unintentional (disparate-impact) discrimination. Disparate-impact discrimination occurs when an employer's practice, such as requiring a certain level of education, has the effect of discriminating against a protected class. Title VII also extends to discriminatory practices, such as various forms of harassment, in the online environment. 3. *Remedies for discrimination under Title VII*—Remedies include reinstatement, back pay, and retroactive promotions. Damages (both compensatory and punitive) may be awarded for intentional discrimination.
Discrimination Based on Age	The Age Discrimination in Employment Act (ADEA) prohibits employment discrimination on the basis of age against individuals forty years of age or older. Procedures for bringing a case under the ADEA are similar to those for bringing a case under Title VII.
Discrimination Based on Disability	The Americans with Disabilities Act (ADA) prohibits employment discrimination against persons with disabilities who are otherwise qualified to perform the essential functions of the jobs for which they apply. 1. *Procedures and remedies*—To prevail on a claim, the plaintiff must show that she or he has a disability, is otherwise qualified for the employment in question, and was excluded from it solely because of the disability. Procedures and remedies under the ADA are similar to those in Title VII cases. 2. *Definition of disability*—The ADA defines the term *disability* as a physical or mental impairment that substantially limits one or more major life activities, a record of such impairment, or being regarded as having such an impairment. 3. *Reasonable accommodation*—Employers are required to reasonably accommodate the needs of persons with disabilities through such measures as modifying the physical work environment and permitting more flexible work schedules.

Chapter Summary: Employment Discrimination—Continued

Defenses to Employment Discrimination	As defenses to claims of employment discrimination, employers may assert that the discrimination was required for reasons of business necessity, to meet a bona fide occupational qualification, or to maintain a legitimate seniority system, or a lack of motive.
Affirmative Action	Affirmative action programs attempt to "make up" for past patterns of discrimination by giving members of protected classes preferential treatment in hiring or promotion.

Issue Spotters

1. Ruth is a supervisor for a Subs & Suds restaurant. Tim is a Subs & Suds employee. The owner announces that some employees will be discharged. Ruth tells Tim that if he has sex with her, he can keep his job. Is this sexual harassment? Why or why not? (See *Title VII of the Civil Rights Act*.)
2. Koko, a person with a disability, applies for a job at Lively Sales Corporation for which she is well qualified, but she is rejected. Lively continues to seek applicants and eventually fills the position with a person who does not have a disability. Could Koko succeed in a suit against Lively for discrimination? Explain. (See *Discrimination Based on Disability*.)

—**Check your answers to the Issue Spotters against the answers provided in Appendix D at the end of this text.**

For Review

1. Generally, what kind of conduct is prohibited by Title VII of the Civil Rights Act?
2. What is the difference between disparate-treatment discrimination and disparate-impact discrimination?
3. What remedies are available under Title VII of the Civil Rights Act?
4. What federal act prohibits discrimination based on age?
5. What are three defenses to claims of employment discrimination?

Business Scenarios and Case Problems

18–1. Title VII Violations. Discuss fully whether either of the following actions would constitute a violation of Title VII of the 1964 Civil Rights Act, as amended. (See *Title VII of the Civil Rights Act*.)

1. Tennington, Inc., is a consulting firm and has ten employees. These employees travel on consulting jobs in seven states. Tennington has an employment record of hiring only white males.
2. Novo Films, Inc., is making a film about Africa and needs to employ approximately one hundred extras for this picture. To hire these extras, Novo advertises in all major newspapers in Southern California. The ad states that only African Americans need apply.

18–2. Religious Discrimination. Gina Gomez, a devout Roman Catholic, worked for Sam's Department Stores, Inc., in Phoenix, Arizona. Sam's considered Gomez a productive employee because her sales exceeded $200,000 per year. At the time, the store gave its managers the discretion to grant unpaid leave to employees but prohibited vacations or leave during the holiday season—October through December.

Gomez felt that she had a "calling" to go on a "pilgrimage" in October to Bosnia where some persons claimed to have had visions of the Virgin Mary. The Catholic Church had not designated the site an official pilgrimage site, the visions were not expected to be stronger in October, and tours were available at other times. The store managers denied Gomez's request for leave, but she had a nonrefundable ticket and left anyway. Sam's terminated her employment, and she could not find another job. Can Gomez establish a *prima facie* case of religious discrimination? Explain. (See *Title VII of the Civil Rights Act*.)

18–3. Spotlight on Dress Code Policies—Discrimination Based on Gender. Burlington Coat Factory Warehouse, Inc., had a dress code that required male salesclerks to wear business attire consisting of slacks, shirt, and a necktie. Female salesclerks, by contrast, were required to wear a smock so that customers could readily identify them. Karen O'Donnell and other female employees refused to wear the smock. Instead they reported to work in business attire and were suspended. After numerous suspensions, the female employees were fired for violating Burlington's dress code policy. All other conditions of employment, including salary, hours, and benefits, were the same for female and male employees. Was the dress code policy discriminatory? Why or why not? [*O'Donnell v. Burlington Coat Factory Warehouse, Inc.,* 656 F.Supp. 263 (S.D. Ohio 1987)] (See *Title VII of the Civil Rights Act.*)

18–4. Business Case Problem with Sample Answer— Retaliation by Employers. Entek International hired Shane Dawson, a male homosexual. Some of Dawson's co-workers, including his supervisor, made derogatory comments about his sexual orientation. Dawson's work deteriorated. He filed a complaint with Entek's human resources department. Two days later, he was fired. State law made it unlawful for an employer to discriminate against an individual based on sexual orientation. Could Dawson establish a claim for retaliation? Explain. [*Dawson v. Entek International,* 630 F.3d 928 (9th Cir. 2011)] (See *Title VII of the Civil Rights Act.*)

—For a sample answer to Problem 18–4, go to Appendix E at the end of this text.

18–5. Sexual Harassment by Co-Worker. Billie Bradford worked for the Kentucky Department of Community Based Services (DCBS). One of Bradford's co-workers, Lisa Stander, routinely engaged in extreme sexual behavior (such as touching herself and making crude comments) in Bradford's presence. Bradford and others regularly complained about Stander's conduct to their supervisor, Angie Taylor. Rather than resolve the problem, Taylor nonchalantly told Stander to stop, encouraged Bradford to talk to Stander, and suggested that Stander was just having fun. Assuming that Bradford was subjected to a hostile work environment, could DCBS be liable? Why or why not? [*Bradford v. Department of Community Based Services,* 2012 WL 360032 (E.D.Ky. 2012)] (See *Title VII of the Civil Rights Act.*)

18–6. Age Discrimination. Beginning in 1986, Paul Rangel was a sales professional for pharmaceutical company Sanofi-Aventis U.S., LLC (S-A). Rangel had satisfactory performance reviews until 2006, when S-A issued new expectations guidelines with sales call quotas and other standards that he failed to meet. After two years of negative performance reviews, Rangel—who was then more than forty years old—was terminated as part of a nationwide reduction of sales professionals who had not met the expectations guidelines. This sales force reduction also included younger workers. Did S-A engage in age discrimination? Discuss. [*Rangel v. Sanofi Aventis U.S. LLC,* 2013 WL 142040 (10th Cir. 2013)] (See *Discrimination Based on Age.*)

18–7. Discrimination Based on Disability. Cynthia Horn worked for Knight Facilities Management–GM, Inc., in Detroit, Michigan, as a janitor. When Horn developed a sensitivity to cleaning products, her physician gave her a "no exposure to cleaning solutions" restriction. Knight discussed possible accommodations with Horn. She suggested that restrooms be eliminated from her cleaning route or that she be provided with a respirator. Knight explained that she would be exposed to cleaning solutions in any situation and concluded that there was no work available within her physician's restriction. Has Knight violated the Americans with Disabilities Act by failing to provide Horn with the requested accommodations? Explain. [*Horn v. Knight Facilities Management–GM, Inc.,* __ F.3d __, 2014 WL 715711 (6th Cir. 2014)] (See *Discrimination Based on Disability.*)

18–8. Critical-Thinking Legal Environment Question. Why has the federal government limited the application of the statutes discussed in this chapter to firms with a specified number of employees, such as fifteen or twenty? Should these laws apply to all employers, regardless of size? Why or why not? (See *Title VII of the Civil Rights Act and Discrimination Based on Age and Disability.*)

18–9. A Question of Ethics—Discrimination Based on Disability. Titan Distribution, Inc., employed Quintak, Inc., to run its tire mounting and distribution operation in Des Moines, Iowa. Robert Chalfant worked for Quintak as a second-shift supervisor at Titan. He suffered a heart attack in 1992 and underwent heart bypass surgery in 1997. He also had arthritis. In July 2002, Titan decided to terminate Quintak. Chalfant applied to work at Titan. On his application, he described himself as having a disability. After a physical exam, Titan's doctor concluded that Chalfant could work in his current capacity, and he was notified that he would be hired. Despite the notice, Nadis Barucic, a Titan employee, wrote "not pass px" at the top of Chalfant's application, and he was not hired. He took a job with AMPCO Systems, a parking ramp management company. This work involved walking up to five miles a day and lifting more weight than he had at Titan. In September, Titan eliminated its second shift. Chalfant filed a suit in a federal district court against Titan, in part, under the Americans with Disabilities Act (ADA). Titan argued that the reason it had not hired Chalfant was not that he did not pass the physical, but no one—including Barucic—could explain why she had written "not pass px" on his application. Later, Titan claimed that Chalfant was not hired because the entire second shift was going to be eliminated. [*Chalfant v. Titan Distribution, Inc.,* 475 F.3d 982 (8th Cir. 2007)] (See *Discrimination Based on Disability.*)

1. What must Chalfant establish to make his case under the ADA? Can he meet these requirements? Explain.
2. In employment-discrimination cases, punitive damages can be appropriate when an employer acts with malice or reckless indifference to an employee's protected rights. Would an award of punitive damages to Chalfant be appropriate in this case? Discuss.

UNIT **3** Cumulative Business Hypothetical

....

Two brothers, Ray and Paul Ashford, start a business manufacturing a new type of battery system for hybrid automobiles. They hit the market at the perfect time, and the batteries are in great demand.

1. When Ray and Paul started their business, they contributed equal amounts of capital but did not sign a formal agreement. What type of business entity would they be presumed to have formed, and how would any profits be divided? If they want to limit their liability but still remain a small business enterprise, what are their options? Which type of limited liability organization would you recommend, and why?

2. As their business becomes more successful, Ray and Paul seek to raise significant capital to build a manufacturing plant. They decide to form a corporation called Ashford Motors, Inc. Outline the steps that Ray and Paul need to follow to incorporate their business.

3. Loren, one of Ashford's salespersons, anxious to make a sale, intentionally quotes a price to a customer that is $500 lower than Ashford has authorized for that particular product. The customer purchases the product at the quoted price. When Ashford learns of the deal, it claims that it is not legally bound to the sales contract because it did not authorize Loren to sell the product at that price. Is Ashford bound by the contract? Discuss fully.

4. One day Gina, an Ashford employee, suffered a serious burn when she accidentally spilled some acid on her hand. The accident occurred because another employee, who was suspected of using illegal drugs, carelessly bumped into her. Gina's hand required a series of skin grafts before it healed sufficiently to allow Gina to return to work. Gina wants to obtain compensation for her lost wages and medical expenses. Can she do so? If so, how?

5. Ashford provides health insurance for its two hundred employees, including Dan. For personal medical reasons, Dan takes twelve weeks of leave. During this period, can Dan continue his coverage under Ashford's health-insurance plan? After Dan returns to work, Ashford closes Dan's division and terminates the employees, including Dan. Can Dan continue his coverage under Ashford's health-insurance plan? If so, at whose expense?

6. Aretha, another employee at Ashford, is disgusted by the sexually offensive behavior of several male employees. She has complained to her supervisor on several occasions about the offensive behavior, but the supervisor merely laughs at her concerns. Aretha decides to bring a legal action against the company for sexual harassment. Does Aretha's complaint concern *quid pro quo* harassment or hostile-environment harassment? What federal statute protects employees from sexual harassment? What remedies are available under that statute? What procedures must Aretha follow in pursuing her legal action?

Legal Reasoning Group Activity

....

Racial Discrimination.   Two African American plaintiffs sued the producers of the reality television series *The Bachelor* and *The Bachelorette* for racial discrimination. The plaintiffs claimed that the shows have never featured persons of color in the lead roles. The plaintiffs also alleged that the producers failed to provide people of color who auditioned for the lead roles with the same opportunities to compete as white people who auditioned.

Legal Reasoning Group Activity—Continues ➡

Legal Reasoning Group Activity—Continued

1. The first group will assess whether the plaintiffs can establish a *prima facie* case of disparate-treatment (intentional) discrimination.
2. The second group will consider whether the plaintiffs can establish disparate-impact discrimination.
3. The third group will assume that the plaintiffs established a *prima facie* case and that the burden has shifted to the employer to articulate a legal reason for not hiring the plaintiffs. What legitimate reasons might the employer assert for not hiring the plaintiffs in this situation? Should the law require television producers to hire persons of color for lead roles in reality television shows? Discuss.

UNIT **4**

The Regulatory Environment

UNIT CONTENTS

CHAPTER 19

Powers and Functions of Administrative Agencies

(Skyhobo/iStockphoto.com)

LEARNING OBJECTIVES

The five learning objectives below are designed to help improve your understanding of the chapter. After reading this chapter, you should be able to answer the following questions:

1. How are federal administrative agencies created?
2. How do the three branches of government limit the power of administrative agencies?
3. What are the three basic functions of most administrative agencies?
4. What sequence of events must normally occur before an agency rule becomes law?
5. How do administrative agencies enforce their rules?

"Perhaps more values today are affected by [administrative] decisions than by those of all the courts."

—Robert H. Jackson, 1892–1954 (Associate justice of the United States Supreme Court, 1941–1954)

As the chapter-opening quotation suggests, government agencies established to administer the law have a significant impact on the day-to-day operation of the government and the economy. In its early years, the United States had a simple, nonindustrial economy with little regulation. As the economy has grown and become more complex, the size of government has also increased, and so has the number of administrative agencies.

In some instances, new agencies have been created in response to a crisis. In the wake of the financial crisis that led to the Great Recession, for example, Congress enacted the Dodd-Frank Wall Street Reform and Consumer Protection Act. Among other things, this statute created the Financial Stability Oversight Council to identify and respond to emerging risks in the financial system. It also created the Consumer Financial Protection Bureau to protect consumers from alleged abusive practices by financial institutions, including banks and nonbanks offering consumer financial products, mortgage lenders, and credit-card companies.

Administrative Law The body of law created by administrative agencies in order to carry out their duties and responsibilities.

As the number of agencies has multiplied, so have the rules, orders, and decisions that they issue. Today, there are rules covering almost every aspect of a business's operations (see the *Linking Business Law to Management* feature at the end of this chapter). The regulations that administrative agencies issue make up the body of **administrative law.** In this chapter, we explain the important principles of administrative law and their impact on businesses today.

Practical Significance

Unlike statutory law, administrative law is created by administrative agencies, not by legislatures, but it is nevertheless of overriding significance for businesses. When Congress—or a state legislature—enacts legislation, it typically adopts a rather general statute and leaves the statute's implementation to an **administrative agency,** which then creates the detailed rules and regulations necessary to carry out the statute. The administrative agency, with its specialized personnel, has the time, resources, and expertise to make the detailed decisions required for regulation.

Administrative Agency A federal or state government agency established to perform a specific function.

Administrative Agencies Exist at All Levels of Government

Administrative agencies are spread throughout the government. At the national level, numerous *executive agencies* exist within the cabinet departments of the executive branch. For instance, the Food and Drug Administration is within the U.S. Department of Health and Human Services. Executive agencies are subject to the authority of the president, who has the power to appoint and remove officers of federal agencies. Exhibit 19–1 that follows lists the cabinet departments and their most important subagencies.

There are also major *independent regulatory agencies* at the federal level, including the Federal Trade Commission, the Securities and Exchange Commission, and the Federal Communications Commission. The president's power is less pronounced in regard to independent agencies, whose officers serve for fixed terms and cannot be removed without just cause. See Exhibit 19–2 later in this chapter for a list of selected independent regulatory agencies and their principal functions.

There are administrative agencies at the state and local levels as well. Commonly, a state agency (such as a state pollution-control agency) is created as a parallel to a federal agency (such as the Environmental Protection Agency). Just as federal statutes take precedence over conflicting state statutes, so do federal agency regulations take precedence over conflicting state regulations. Because the rules of state and local agencies vary widely, we focus here on federal administrative law.

Agencies Provide a Comprehensive Regulatory Scheme

Often, administrative agencies at various levels of government work together and share the responsibility of creating and enforcing particular regulations.

EXAMPLE 19.1   When Congress enacted the Clean Air Act, it provided only general directions for the prevention of air pollution. The specific pollution-control requirements imposed on business are almost entirely the product of decisions made by the Environmental Protection Agency (EPA), which was created seven years later. Moreover, the EPA works with parallel environmental agencies at the state level to analyze existing data and determine the appropriate pollution-control standards. ●

Exhibit 19–1 Executive Departments and Important Subagencies

DEPARTMENT NAME	SELECTED SUBAGENCIES
State	Passport Office; Bureau of Diplomatic Security; Foreign Service; Bureau of Human Rights and Humanitarian Affairs; Bureau of Consular Affairs; Bureau of Intelligence and Research
Treasury	Internal Revenue Service; U.S. Mint
Interior	U.S. Fish and Wildlife Service; National Park Service; Bureau of Indian Affairs; Bureau of Land Management
Justice[a]	Federal Bureau of Investigation; Drug Enforcement Administration; Bureau of Prisons; U.S. Marshals Service
Agriculture	Soil Conservation Service; Agricultural Research Service; Food Safety and Inspection Service; Forest Service
Commerce[b]	Bureau of the Census; Bureau of Economic Analysis; Minority Business Development Agency; U.S. Patent and Trademark Office; National Oceanic and Atmospheric Administration
Labor[b]	Occupational Safety and Health Administration; Bureau of Labor Statistics; Employment Standards Administration; Office of Labor-Management Standards; Employment and Training Administration
Defense[c]	National Security Agency; Joint Chiefs of Staff; Departments of the Air Force, Navy, Army; service academies
Housing and Urban Development	Office of Community Planning and Development; Government National Mortgage Association; Office of Fair Housing and Equal Opportunity
Transportation	Federal Aviation Administration; Federal Highway Administration; National Highway Traffic Safety Administration; Federal Transit Administration
Energy	Office of Civilian Radioactive Waste Management; Office of Nuclear Energy; Energy Information Administration
Health and Human Services[d]	Food and Drug Administration; Centers for Medicare and Medicaid Services; Centers for Disease Control and Prevention; National Institutes of Health
Education[d]	Office of Special Education and Rehabilitation Services; Office of Elementary and Secondary Education; Office of Postsecondary Education; Office of Vocational and Adult Education
Veterans Affairs	Veterans Health Administration; Veterans Benefits Administration; National Cemetery System
Homeland Security	U.S. Citizenship and Immigration Services; Directorate of Border and Transportation Services; U.S. Coast Guard; Federal Emergency Management Agency

a. Formed from the Office of the Attorney General.
b. Formed from the Department of Commerce and Labor.
c. Formed from the Department of War and the Department of the Navy.
d. Formed from the Department of Health, Education, and Welfare.

Legislation and regulations have benefits—in *Example 19.1*, a cleaner environment than existed in decades past. At the same time, these benefits entail significant costs for business. The EPA has estimated the costs of compliance with the Clean Air Act at many tens of billions of dollars yearly. Although the agency has calculated that the overall benefits of its regulations often exceed their costs, the burden on business is substantial.

Agency Creation and Powers

Congress creates federal administrative agencies. By delegating some of its authority to make and implement laws, Congress can indirectly monitor a particular area in which it has passed legislation without becoming bogged down in the details relating to enforcement—details that are often best left to specialists.

Learning Objective 1
How are federal administrative agencies created?

Exhibit 19–2 Selected Independent Regulatory Agencies

NAME OF AGENCY	PRINCIPAL DUTIES
Federal Reserve System Board of Governors (the Fed)	Determines policy with respect to interest rates, credit availability, and the money supply.
Federal Trade Commission (FTC)	Prevents businesses from engaging in purported unfair trade practices; stops the formation of monopolies in the business sector; protects consumer rights.
Securities and Exchange Commission (SEC)	Regulates the nation's stock exchanges, in which shares of stock are bought and sold; enforces the securities laws, which require full disclosure of the financial profiles of companies that wish to sell stock and bonds to the public.
Federal Communications Commission (FCC)	Regulates all communications by telegraph, cable, telephone, radio, satellite, and television.
National Labor Relations Board (NLRB)	Protects employees' rights to join unions and bargain collectively with employers; attempts to prevent unfair labor practices by both employers and unions.
Equal Employment Opportunity Commission (EEOC)	Works to eliminate discrimination in employment based on religion, gender, race, color, disability, national origin, or age; investigates claims of discrimination.
Environmental Protection Agency (EPA)	Undertakes programs aimed at reducing air and water pollution; works with state and local agencies to help fight environmental hazards.
Nuclear Regulatory Commission (NRC)	Ensures that electricity-generating nuclear reactors in the United States are built and operated safely; regularly inspects operations of such reactors.

Enabling Legislation A statute enacted by Congress that authorizes the creation of an administrative agency and specifies the name, composition, and powers of the agency being created.

To create an administrative agency, Congress passes **enabling legislation**, which specifies the name, purposes, functions, and powers of the agency being created. Federal administrative agencies can exercise only those powers that Congress has delegated to them in enabling legislation. Through similar enabling acts, state legislatures create state administrative agencies.

Enabling Legislation—An Example

Congress created the Federal Trade Commission (FTC) in the Federal Trade Commission Act.[1] The act prohibits unfair and deceptive trade practices. It also describes the procedures that the agency must follow to charge persons or organizations with violations of the act, and it provides for judicial review of agency orders. The act grants the FTC the power to do the following:

1. Create "rules and regulations for the purpose of carrying out the Act."
2. Conduct investigations of business practices.
3. Obtain reports from interstate corporations concerning their business practices.
4. Investigate possible violations of federal antitrust statutes. (The FTC shares this task with the Antitrust Division of the U.S. Department of Justice.)
5. Publish findings of its investigations.
6. Recommend new legislation.
7. Hold trial-like hearings to resolve certain kinds of trade disputes that involve FTC regulations or federal antitrust laws.

The commission that heads the FTC is composed of five members, each of whom is appointed by the president, with the advice and consent of the Senate, for a term

---

1. 15 U.S.C. Sections 41–58.

of seven years. The president designates one of the commissioners to be the chair. Various offices and bureaus of the FTC undertake different administrative activities for the agency.

Agency Powers and the Constitution

Administrative agencies occupy an unusual niche in the U.S. governmental structure, because they exercise powers that are normally divided among the three branches of government. The constitutional principle of *checks and balances* allows each branch of government to act as a check on the actions of the other two branches. Furthermore, the U.S. Constitution authorizes only the legislative branch to create laws. Yet administrative agencies, to which the Constitution does not specifically refer, can make **legislative rules,** or *substantive rules,* that are as legally binding as laws that Congress passes.

Administrative agencies also issue **interpretive rules** that are not legally binding but simply indicate how an agency plans to interpret and enforce its statutory authority. **EXAMPLE 19.2** The Equal Employment Opportunity Commission periodically issues interpretive rules indicating how it plans to interpret the provisions of certain statutes, such as the Americans with Disabilities Act (see Chapter 18). These informal rules provide enforcement guidelines for agency officials. ●

Courts generally hold that Article I of the U.S. Constitution is the basis for all administrative law. Section 1 of that article grants all legislative powers to Congress and requires Congress to oversee the implementation of all laws. Article I, Section 8, gives Congress the power to make all laws necessary for executing its specified powers. Under what is known as the **delegation doctrine,** the courts interpret these passages as granting Congress the power to establish administrative agencies and delegate to them the power to create rules for implementing those laws.

The three branches of government exercise certain controls over agency powers and functions, as discussed next, but in many ways administrative agencies function independently. For this reason, administrative agencies, which constitute the **bureaucracy,** are sometimes referred to as the fourth branch of the U.S. government.

Executive Controls
The executive branch of government exercises control over agencies both through the president's power to appoint federal officers and through the president's veto power. The president may veto enabling legislation presented by Congress or congressional attempts to modify an existing agency's authority.

Legislative Controls
Congress exercises authority over agency powers through legislation. Congress gives power to an agency through enabling legislation and can take power away—or even abolish an agency altogether—through subsequent legislation. Legislative authority is required to fund an agency, and enabling legislation usually sets certain time and monetary limits on the funding of particular programs. Congress can always revise these limits.

In addition to its power to create and fund agencies, Congress has the authority to investigate the implementation of its laws and the agencies that it has created. Congress also has the power to "freeze" the enforcement of most federal regulations before the regulations take effect.

The question that a court faces when confronted with an agency's interpretation of a statute it administers is always whether the agency has acted within its statutory authority. At issue in the following case was an agency's authority under a statute enacted in the nineteenth century.

Legislative Rule An administrative agency rule that carries the same weight as a congressionally enacted statute.

Interpretive Rule An administrative agency rule that explains how the agency interprets and intends to apply the statutes it enforces.

Delegation Doctrine A doctrine based on the U.S. Constitution, which has been construed to allow Congress to delegate some of its power to administrative agencies to make and implement laws.

Bureaucracy The organizational structure, consisting of government bureaus and agencies, through which the government implements and enforces the laws.

Learning Objective 2
How do the three branches of government limit the power of administrative agencies?

Case 19.1

Loving v. Internal Revenue Service

United States Court of Appeals, District of Columbia Circuit, 742 F.3d 1013 (2014).

To what extent can the IRS regulate tax preparers?
(Aspen Photo/Shutterstock.com)

BACKGROUND AND FACTS The Internal Revenue Service (IRS) is a subagency of the U.S. Department of the Treasury. Responding to concerns about the performance of some paid tax-return preparers, the IRS issued a new rule. The rule required paid preparers to pass an initial certification exam, pay annual fees, and complete at least fifteen hours of continuing education courses each year. As authority for the rule, the IRS relied on a statute enacted in 1884 and recodified in 1982 that authorizes the agency to "regulate the practice of representatives of persons before the Department of the Treasury." Three independent preparers filed a suit in a federal district court against the IRS, contending that the rule exceeded the agency's authority. The court ruled in the plaintiffs' favor. The IRS appealed.

IN THE WORDS OF THE COURT . . .
KAVANAUGH, Circuit Judge.

* * * *

In our view, at least six considerations foreclose the IRS's interpretation of the statute.

First is the meaning of the key statutory term "representatives." * * * The term "representative" is traditionally and commonly defined as an agent with authority to bind others, a description that does not fit tax-return preparers.

Put simply, *tax-return preparers are not agents. They do not possess legal authority to act on the taxpayer's behalf. They cannot legally bind the taxpayer by acting on the taxpayer's behalf.* [Emphasis added.]

* * * *

Second is the meaning of the phrase "practice * * * before the Department of the Treasury."

* * * To "practice before" a court or agency ordinarily refers to practice during an investigation, adversarial hearing, or other adjudicative proceeding.

That is quite different from the process of filing a tax return. * * * *Tax-return preparers do not practice before the IRS when they simply assist in the preparation of someone else's tax return.* [Emphasis added.]

* * * *

Third is the history of [the statute]. The language [in the original statute included the phrase] "agents, attorneys, or other persons representing claimants."

That original language plainly would not encompass tax-return preparers. * * * When Congress re-codified the statute in 1982, Congress simplified the phrase * * * to the current "representatives of persons." But * * * Congress made clear in the statute itself that * * * the 1982 Act was designed "to revise, codify, and enact" the amended provisions "without substantive change."

* * * *

Fourth is the broader statutory framework.

* * * *

* * * [By enacting other statutes specific to tax-return preparers,] multiple Congresses have acted as if [the statute at the center of this case] did not extend so broadly as to cover tax-return preparers. * * * The meaning of one statute may be affected by other Acts, particularly where Congress has spoken * * * more specifically to the topic at hand. So it is here.

Fifth is the nature and scope of the authority being claimed by the IRS.

If we were to accept the IRS's interpretation of [the statute,] the IRS would be empowered for the first time to regulate hundreds of thousands of individuals in the multi-billion dollar tax-preparation industry. Yet nothing in the statute's text or the legislative record contemplates that vast expansion of the IRS's authority.

Sixth is the IRS's past approach to this statute. Until [now] the IRS never interpreted the statute to give it authority to regulate tax-return preparers.

* * * In light of the text, history, structure, and context of the statute, it becomes apparent that the IRS never before adopted its current interpretation for a reason: It is incorrect.

DECISION AND REMEDY The U.S. Court of Appeals for the District of Columbia Circuit affirmed the lower court's ruling. Under the IRS's interpretation of the statute, the agency "would be empowered for the first time to regulate hundreds of thousands of individuals in the multi-billion dollar tax-preparation industry." Nothing in the statute's text, history, structure, or context "contemplates that vast expansion of the IRS's authority."

THE LEGAL ENVIRONMENT DIMENSION *As a policy matter, some observers might argue that the IRS should be allowed to regulate tax-return preparers more strictly. Under the reasoning of the court, who has the authority to give effect to such a policy, and how would it be accomplished?*

WHAT IF THE FACTS WERE DIFFERENT? *Suppose that paid tax-return preparers actually represented their clients in proceedings before the IRS. Would the result in this case have been different? Why or why not?*

Judicial Controls   The judicial branch exercises control over agency powers through the courts' review of agency actions. The Administrative Procedure Act, discussed shortly, provides for judicial review of most agency decisions. Agency actions are not automatically subject to judicial review, however. The party seeking court review must first exhaust all administrative remedies under what is called the *exhaustion doctrine*. In other words, the complaining party normally must have gone through the administrative process (from complaint to hearing to final agency order, as described later in this chapter) before seeking court review.

The Administrative Procedure Act   In the absence of any directives from Congress concerning a particular agency procedure, the Administrative Procedure Act (APA)[2] applies. The APA sets forth rules and regulations that govern the procedures administrative agencies follow in performing their duties.

The Arbitrary and Capricious Test   One of Congress's goals in enacting the APA was to provide for more judicial control over administrative agencies. To that end, the APA provides that courts should "hold unlawful and set aside" agency actions found to be "arbitrary, capricious, an abuse of discretion, or otherwise not in accordance with law."[3] Under this standard, parties can challenge regulations as contrary to law or so irrational as to be arbitrary and capricious.

The arbitrary and capricious standard does not have a precise definition, but in applying it, courts typically consider whether the agency has done any of the following:

1. Failed to provide a rational explanation for its decision.
2. Changed its prior policy without justification.
3. Considered legally inappropriate factors.
4. Failed to consider a relevant factor.
5. Rendered a decision plainly contrary to the evidence.

Fair Notice   The APA also includes many requirements concerning the notice that regulatory agencies must give to those affected by its regulations. For example, an agency may change the way it applies a certain regulatory principle. Before the change can be carried out, the agency must give fair notice of what conduct will be expected in the future.

In the following *Spotlight Case,* a television network argued that an administrative agency failed to give fair notice of how it would apply certain regulations.

---

2. 5 U.S.C. Sections 551–706.
3. 5 U.S.C. Section 706(2)(A).

Spotlight on Fox Television

Case 19.2
Federal Communications Commission v. Fox Television Stations, Inc.
Supreme Court of the United States, __ U.S. __, 132 S.Ct. 2307, 183 L.Ed.2d 234 (2012).

(Daniel Stein/iStockphoto.com)

BACKGROUND AND FACTS   The 1934 Communications Act established a system of limited-term broadcast licenses subject to various conditions. One condition was the indecency ban, which prohibits the uttering of "any obscene, indecent, or profane language by means of radio communication." The Federal Communications Commission (FCC) first invoked this ban on indecent broadcasts in 1975. At that time, the FCC defined indecent speech as "language that describes, in terms patently

Spotlight Case 19.2—Continues ➡

Spotlight Case 19.2—Continued

offensive as measured by contemporary community standards for the broadcast medium, sexual or excretory activities or organs, at times of the day when there is a reasonable risk that children may be in the audience." Before 2004, one of the factors used by the FCC in determining whether a broadcaster had violated the ban was whether the offensive language had been repeated, or "dwelled on," in the broadcast.

If an offensive term was used just once in a broadcast, the FCC probably would not take any action. In 2004, however, the FCC changed this policy, declaring that an offensive term, such as the F-word, was actionably indecent even if it was used only once. In its 2004 ruling, the FCC specifically stated that previous FCC rulings allowing a "safe harbor" for a single utterance of an offensive term "were no longer good law." In 2006, the FCC applied this new rule to two Fox Television broadcasts, each of which contained a single use of the F-word, which had aired before the FCC's change in policy. After the FCC ruled that these broadcasts were actionably indecent, Fox appealed to the U.S. Court of Appeals for the Second Circuit for review. The appellate court reversed the agency's order. The FCC appealed to the United States Supreme Court.

IN THE WORDS OF THE COURT . . .
Justice *KENNEDY* delivered the opinion of the Court.

* * * *

A fundamental principle in our legal system is that laws which regulate persons or entities must give fair notice of conduct that is forbidden or required. This requirement of clarity in regulation is essential to the protections provided by the Due Process Clause of the Fifth Amendment. It requires the invalidation of laws that are impermissibly vague. A conviction or punishment fails to comply with due process if the statute or regulation under which it is obtained fails to provide a person of ordinary intelligence fair notice of what is prohibited, or is so standardless that it authorizes or encourages seriously discriminatory enforcement. As this Court has explained, a regulation is not vague because it may at times be difficult to prove an incriminating fact but rather because it is unclear as to what fact must be proved. [Emphasis added.]

The void for vagueness doctrine addresses at least two connected but discrete due process concerns: first, that regulated parties should know what is required of them so they may act accordingly; second, precision and guidance are necessary so that those enforcing the law do not act in an arbitrary or discriminatory way. * * *

These concerns are implicated here because, at the outset, the broadcasters claim they did not have * * * fair notice of

what was forbidden. Under the 2001 guidelines in force when the broadcasts occurred, a key consideration was whether the material dwelled on or repeated at length the offending description or depiction. In the 2004 order, issued after the broadcasts, the Commission changed course and held that fleeting expletives could be a statutory violation. In the challenged orders now under review the Commission applied the new principle * * * and determined fleeting expletives were actionably indecent. * * * The Commission policy in place at the time of the broadcasts gave no notice to Fox that a fleeting expletive could be indecent. * * *

* * * *

The Government raises two arguments in response, but neither is persuasive. * * * Though the Commission claims it will not consider the prior indecent broadcasts in any context, it has the statutory power to take into account any history of prior offenses when setting the level of a forfeiture penalty. * * * The Government's assurance it will elect not to do so is insufficient to remedy the constitutional violation.

In addition, * * * reputational injury provides further reason for granting relief to Fox. * * * The permanent Commission record describes in strongly disapproving terms the indecent material broadcast by Fox and Fox's efforts to protect children from being exposed to it. Commission sanctions on broadcasters for indecent material are widely publicized. The challenged orders could have an adverse impact on Fox's reputation that audiences and advertisers alike are entitled to take into account.

DECISION AND REMEDY The United States Supreme Court vacated the judgment of the U.S. Court of Appeals for the Second Circuit, which had ruled the FCC's order unconstitutional on different grounds. The Court noted that the regulations at the time the broadcasts took place did not cover "fleeting expletives." Therefore, Fox did not have fair notice of what was forbidden, and the standards applied to the broadcasts were impermissibly vague. The Court ordered the FCC's administrative order to be set aside.

THE LEGAL ENVIRONMENT DIMENSION *Technological advances have made it easier for broadcasters to "bleep out" offending words in the programs that they air. Does this development support a more or less stringent enforcement policy by the FCC? Explain.*

THE ETHICAL DIMENSION *Should an administrative agency be locked into its first interpretation of a statute? Why or why not?*

The Administrative Process

All federal agencies must follow specific procedural requirements as they go about fulfilling their three basic functions: rulemaking, enforcement, and adjudication. These three functions make up what is known as the **administrative process.** As mentioned earlier, the APA imposes requirements that all federal agencies must follow. This act is an integral part of the administrative process.

Rulemaking

The major function of an administrative agency is **rulemaking.** The APA defines a rule as "an agency statement of general or particular applicability and future effect designed to implement, interpret, or prescribe law and policy."[4] Regulations are sometimes said to be *legislative* because, like statutes, they have a binding effect. Thus, violators of agency rules may be punished. Because agency rules have such great legal force, the APA established procedures for agencies to follow in creating rules. Many rules must be adopted using the APA's *notice-and-comment rulemaking* procedure.

Notice-and-comment rulemaking involves three basic steps:

1. Notice of the proposed rulemaking.
2. A comment period.
3. The final rule.

The APA recognizes some limited exceptions to these procedural requirements, but they are seldom invoked. If the required procedures are violated, the resulting rule may be invalid.

The impetus for rulemaking may come from various sources, including Congress, the agency itself, or private parties, who may petition an agency to begin a rulemaking (or repeal a rule). For instance, environmental groups have petitioned for stricter air-pollution controls to combat global warming.

Notice of the Proposed Rulemaking When a federal agency decides to create a new rule, the agency publishes a notice of the proposed rulemaking proceedings in the *Federal Register,* a daily publication of the executive branch that prints government orders, rules, and regulations. The notice states where and when the proceedings will be held, the agency's legal authority for making the rule (usually its enabling legislation), and the terms or subject matter of the proposed rule.

Comment Period Following the publication of the notice of the proposed rulemaking proceedings, the agency must allow ample time for persons to comment on the proposed rule. The purpose of this comment period is to give interested parties the opportunity to express their views on the proposed rule in an effort to influence agency policy. The comments may be in writing or, if a hearing is held, may be given orally.

The agency need not respond to all comments, but it must respond to any significant comments that bear directly on the proposed rule. The agency responds by either modifying its final rule or explaining, in a statement accompanying the final rule, why it did not make any changes. In some circumstances, particularly when the procedure being used in a specific instance is less formal, an agency may accept comments after the comment period is closed.

The Final Rule After the agency reviews the comments, it drafts the final rule and publishes it in the *Federal Register.* A final rule must contain a "concise general statement

---

4. 5 U.S.C. Section 551(4).

Learning Objective 3
What are the three basic functions of most administrative agencies?

Administrative Process The procedure used by administrative agencies in the administration of law.

Rulemaking The actions of administrative agencies when formally adopting new regulations or amending old ones.

Notice-and-Comment Rulemaking A procedure in agency rulemaking that requires notice, opportunity for comment, and a published draft of the final rule.

Learning Objective 4
What sequence of events must normally occur before an agency rule becomes law?

of . . . basis and purpose" that describes the reasoning behind the rule.[5] The final rule may change the terms of the proposed rule, in light of the public comments, but cannot change the proposal too radically, or a new proposal and a new opportunity for comment are required. The final rule is later compiled along with the rules and regulations of other federal administrative agencies in the *Code of Federal Regulations*.

Final rules have binding legal effect unless the courts later overturn them. Because they are as binding as legislation, they are often referred to as legislative rules, as mentioned previously. If an agency failed to follow proper rulemaking procedures when it issued a final rule, however, the rule may not be binding. In reviewing a complaint against an agency, a court will examine whether the agency followed the APA's procedures.

CASE EXAMPLE 19.3   For many years, the Drug Enforcement Administration (DEA) allowed the production of hemp products, which contain only trace amounts of tetrahydrocannabinol (THC, a component of marijuana). Then the DEA published an interpretive rule that declared any product containing THC is considered a controlled substance (a drug whose availability is restricted). Subsequently, without following formal rulemaking procedures, the DEA declared that two legislative rules relating to hemp products were final. These rules effectively banned the possession and sale of the food products made by members of the Hemp Industries Association (HIA). The HIA petitioned the court for review, and the court held that the DEA's legislative rules were unenforceable because it had not followed its formal rulemaking procedures.[6] •

Investigation

Learning Objective 5
How do administrative agencies enforce their rules?

Although rulemaking is the most prominent agency activity, rule enforcement is also critical. Often, an agency itself enforces its rules. After final rules are issued, agencies conduct investigations to monitor compliance with those rules or the terms of the enabling statute. A typical agency investigation of this kind might begin when the agency receives a report of a possible violation.

Many agency rules also require compliance reporting from regulated entities, and such a report may trigger an enforcement investigation. For example, environmental regulators often require reporting of emissions.

Inspections and Tests
Many agencies gather information through on-site inspections. Sometimes, inspecting an office, a factory, or some other business facility is the only way to obtain the evidence needed to prove a regulatory violation. At other times, an inspection or test is used in place of a formal hearing to show the need to correct or prevent an undesirable condition.

Administrative inspections and tests cover a wide range of activities, including safety inspections of underground coal mines, safety tests of commercial equipment and automobiles, and environmental monitoring of factory emissions. An agency may also ask a firm or individual to submit certain documents or records to the agency for examination.

Normally, business firms comply with agency requests to inspect facilities or business records because it is in any firm's interest to maintain a good relationship with regulatory bodies. In some instances, however, such as when a firm thinks an agency's request is unreasonable and may be detrimental to the firm's interest, the firm may refuse to comply with the request. In such situations, an agency may resort to the use of a subpoena or a search warrant.

---

5. 5 U.S.C. Section 555(c).
6. *Hemp Industries Association v. Drug Enforcement Administration,* 357 F.3d 1012 (9th Cir. 2004).

Subpoenas   There are two basic types of subpoenas. The subpoena *ad testificandum*[7] (to testify) is an ordinary subpoena. It is a writ, or order, compelling a witness to appear at an agency hearing. The subpoena *duces tecum*[3] (bring it with you) compels an individual or organization to hand over books, papers, records, or documents to the agency. An administrative agency may use either type of subpoena to obtain testimony or documents.

There are limits on what an agency can demand. To determine whether an agency is abusing its discretion in pursuing information as part of an investigation, a court may consider such factors as the following:

1. *The purpose of the investigation.* An investigation must have a legitimate purpose. Harassment is an example of an improper purpose. An agency may not issue an administrative subpoena to inspect business records if the motive is to harass or pressure the business into settling an unrelated matter.
2. *The relevance of the information being sought.* Information is relevant if it reveals that the law is being violated or if it assures the agency that the law is not being violated.
3. *The specificity of the demand for testimony or documents.* A subpoena must, for example, adequately describe the material being sought.
4. *The burden of the demand on the party from whom the information is sought.* In responding to a request for information, a party must bear certain costs—for example, the cost of copying requested documents. A business generally is protected from revealing information such as trade secrets, however.

Search Warrants   The Fourth Amendment protects against unreasonable searches and seizures by requiring that in most instances a physical search for evidence must be conducted under the authority of a search warrant. An agency's search warrant is an order directing law enforcement officials to search a specific place for a specific item and seize it for the agency. Although it was once thought that administrative inspections were exempt from the warrant requirement, the United States Supreme Court held in *Marshall v. Barlow's, Inc.,*[9] that the requirement does apply to the administrative process.

Agencies can conduct warrantless searches in several situations. Warrants are not required to conduct searches in highly regulated industries. Firms that sell firearms or liquor, for example, are automatically subject to inspections without warrants. Sometimes, a statute permits warrantless searches of certain types of hazardous operations, such as coal mines. Also, a warrantless inspection in an emergency situation is normally considered reasonable.

Adjudication

After conducting an investigation of a suspected rule violation, an agency may initiate an administrative action against an individual or organization. Most administrative actions are resolved through negotiated settlements at their initial stages, without the need for formal **adjudication** (the resolution of the dispute through a hearing conducted by the agency).

Adjudication A proceeding in which an administrative law judge hears and decides issues that arise when an administrative agency charges a person or a firm with an agency violation.

Negotiated Settlements   Depending on the agency, negotiations may take the form of a simple conversation or a series of informal conferences. Whatever form the negotiations take, their purpose is to rectify the problem to the agency's satisfaction and eliminate the need for additional proceedings.

Settlement is an appealing option to firms for two reasons: to avoid appearing uncooperative and to avoid the expense involved in formal adjudication proceedings and in possible later appeals. Settlement is also an attractive option for agencies. To conserve their

7. Pronounced ad-tes-tee-fee-can-dum.
8. Pronounced doo-suhs tee-kum.
9. 436 U.S. 307, 98 S.Ct. 1816, 56 L.Ed.2d 305 (1978).

own resources and avoid formal actions, administrative agencies devote a great deal of effort to giving advice and negotiating solutions to problems.

Formal Complaints

If a settlement cannot be reached, the agency may issue a formal complaint against the suspected violator. **EXAMPLE 19.4** The Environmental Protection Agency (EPA) finds that Acme Manufacturing, Inc., is polluting groundwater in violation of federal pollution laws. The EPA issues a complaint against the violator in an effort to bring the plant into compliance with federal regulations. • This complaint is a public document, and a press release may accompany it. The party charged in the complaint responds by filing an answer to the allegations. If the charged party and the agency cannot agree on a settlement, the case will be adjudicated.

Agency adjudication involves a hearing before an **administrative law judge (ALJ)**. Under the APA, before the hearing takes place, the agency must issue a notice that includes the facts and law on which the complaint is based, the legal authority for the hearing, and its time and place.

Administrative Law Judge (ALJ) One who presides over an administrative agency hearing and has the power to administer oaths, take testimony, rule on questions of evidence, and make determinations of fact.

The Role of the Administrative Law Judge

The ALJ presides over the hearing and has the power to administer oaths, take testimony, rule on questions of evidence, and make determinations of fact. Technically, the ALJ is not an independent judge and works for the agency prosecuting the case. Nevertheless, the law requires an ALJ to be an unbiased adjudicator (judge).

Certain safeguards prevent bias on the part of the ALJ and promote fairness in the proceedings. For example, the APA requires that the ALJ be separate from an agency's investigative and prosecutorial staff. The APA also prohibits *ex parte* (private) communications between the ALJ and any party to an agency proceeding. Finally, provisions of the APA protect the ALJ from agency disciplinary actions unless the agency can show good cause for such an action.

Hearing Procedures

Hearing procedures vary widely from agency to agency. Administrative agencies generally exercise substantial discretion over the type of procedure that will be used. Frequently, disputes are resolved through informal adjudication proceedings that resemble arbitration. **EXAMPLE 19.5** The Federal Trade Commission (FTC) charges Good Foods, Inc., with deceptive advertising. Representatives of Good Foods and of the FTC, their counsel, and the ALJ meet in a conference room to resolve the dispute informally. •

A formal adjudicatory hearing, in contrast, resembles a trial in many respects. Prior to the hearing, the parties are permitted to undertake discovery—involving depositions, interrogatories, and requests for documents or other information, as described in Chapter 3—although the discovery process is not quite as extensive as it would be in a court proceeding. The hearing itself must comply with the procedural requirements of the APA and must also meet the constitutional standards of due process. The burden of proof in an enforcement proceeding is placed on the agency.

During the hearing, the parties may give testimony, present other evidence, and cross-examine adverse witnesses. A significant difference between a trial and an administrative agency hearing, though, is that normally much more information, including hearsay (secondhand information), can be introduced as evidence during an administrative hearing.

Initial Order An agency's disposition in a matter other than a rulemaking. An administrative law judge's initial order becomes final unless it is appealed.

Agency Orders

Following a hearing, the ALJ renders an **initial order,** or decision, on the case. Either party can appeal the ALJ's decision to the board or commission that governs the agency and can subsequently appeal the agency decision to a federal court of appeals. **EXAMPLE 19.6** The EPA issued a complaint against Acme Manufacturing, Inc., for polluting groundwater, as described in *Example 19.4*. The complaint resulted in a hearing before an ALJ, who ruled in the agency's favor. If Acme is dissatisfied with this decision, it can appeal to the EPA. If it is dissatisfied with the EPA's decision, it can appeal to a federal appeals court. ●

If no party appeals the case, the ALJ's decision becomes the **final order** of the agency. The ALJ's decision also becomes final if a party appeals and the commission and the court decline to review the case. If a party appeals and the case is reviewed, the final order comes from the commission's decision or (if that decision is appealed to a federal appellate court) that of the reviewing court. The administrative adjudication process is illustrated graphically in Exhibit 19–3 that follows.

In the following case, a federal appellate court reviewed the Drug Enforcement Administration's denial of a university professor's application to register to cultivate marijuana.

Final Order The final decision of an administrative agency on an issue.

Case 19.3

Craker v. Drug Enforcement Administration
United States Court of Appeals, First Circuit, 714 F.3d 17 (2013).

(Associated Press)

Can the DEA restrict marijuana supplies to be used in research?

BACKGROUND AND FACTS Dr. Lyle Craker, a professor in the University of Massachusetts's Department of Plant, Soil and Insect Sciences, applied to the Drug Enforcement Administration (DEA) for permission to register to manufacture marijuana for clinical research. He stated that "a second source of plant material is needed to facilitate privately funded Food and Drug Administration (FDA)-approved research into medical uses of marijuana, ensuring a choice of sources and an adequate supply of quality, research-grade marijuana for medicinal applications." An administrative law judge recommended that Craker's application be granted, but a DEA Deputy Administrator issued an order denying his application. Under the DEA's interpretation, the Controlled Substances Act (CSA) requires an applicant to prove both that effective controls against diversion of the marijuana for unapproved purposes are in place and that its supply and the competition to supply it are inadequate. The Administrator determined that the professor did not prove that effective controls against the marijuana's diversion were in place or that supply and competition were inadequate. Craker petitioned the U.S. Court of Appeals for the First Circuit to review the order.

IN THE WORDS OF THE COURT . . .
HOWARD, Circuit Judge.
  * * * *
Since 1968, the National Center for Natural Products Research ("NCNPR") at the University of Mississippi has held the necessary registration and a government contract to grow marijuana for research purposes. The contract is administered by the National Institute on Drug Abuse ("NIDA"), a component of the National Institutes of Health ("NIH"), which, in turn, is a component of the [U.S.] Department of Health and Human Services ("HHS"). The contract is opened for competitive

bidding every five years. The NCNPR is the only entity registered by the DEA to manufacture marijuana.
  * * * *
Dr. Craker's argument with respect to competition is essentially that there cannot be "adequately competitive conditions" when there is only one manufacturer of marijuana.

The Administrator * * * observed that NIDA had provided marijuana manufactured by the University of Mississippi either at cost or free to researchers, and that Dr. Craker had made no showing of how he could provide it for less * * * . Additionally, the Administrator noted that Dr. Craker is free to bid on the contract when it comes up for renewal.

*We see nothing improper in the Administrator's approach. The [CSA's] term "adequately competitive conditions" is not necessarily as narrow as the petitioner suggests. * * * That the current regime may not be the most competitive situation possible does not render it "inadequate."* [Emphasis added.]
  * * * *
In finding that Dr. Craker failed to demonstrate that the current supply of marijuana was not adequate and uninterrupted, the Administrator observed that there were over 1,000 kilograms of marijuana in NIDA possession, an amount which far exceeds present research demands and "any foreseeable" future demand. Dr. Craker does not dispute this finding, or that the current amount is more than ninety times the amount he proposes to supply. Instead, he argues that the adequacy of supply must not be measured against NIDA-approved research, but by whether the supply is adequate to supply projects approved by the FDA. But even if we were to accept his premise—which we don't—Dr. Craker fails to demonstrate that the supply is inadequate for those needs,

Case 19.3—Continues ➡

Case 19.3—Continued

either. He merely states that certain projects were rejected as "not bona-fide" by NIDA, a claim which does not address the adequacy of supply. The fact that Dr. Craker disagrees with the method by which marijuana research is approved does not undermine the substantial evidence that supports the Administrator's conclusion.

DECISION AND REMEDY The U.S. Court of Appeals for the First Circuit denied Craker's petition to review the agency's order "because the Administrator's interpretation of the CSA is

permissible and her findings are reasonable and supported by the evidence."

THE ECONOMIC DIMENSION *Why should a court wait to review an agency's order until the order has gone through the entire procedural process and can be considered final?*

THE LEGAL ENVIRONMENT DIMENSION *Did the court in this case appear to agree with the DEA's interpretation of the Controlled Substances Act? Why or why not?*

Exhibit 19–3 The Process of Formal Administrative Adjudication

Judicial Deference to Agency Decisions

When asked to review agency decisions, courts historically granted some deference (significant weight) to the agency's judgment, often citing the agency's expertise in the subject area of the regulation. This deference seems especially appropriate when applied to an agency's analysis of factual questions, but should it also extend to an agency's interpretation of its own legal authority? In *Chevron U.S.A., Inc. v. Natural Resources Defense Council, Inc.*,[10] the United States Supreme Court held that it should, thereby creating a standard of broadened deference to agencies on questions of legal interpretation.

The Holding of the *Chevron* Case

At issue in the *Chevron* case was whether the courts should defer to an agency's interpretation of a statute giving it authority to act. The Environmental Protection Agency (EPA) had interpreted the phrase "stationary source" in the Clean Air Act as referring to an entire manufacturing plant, and not to each facility within a plant. The agency's interpretation enabled it to adopt the so-called bubble policy, which allowed companies to offset increases in emissions in part of a plant with decreases elsewhere in the plant—an interpretation that reduced the pollution-control compliance costs faced by manufacturers. An environmental group challenged the legality of the EPA's interpretation.

The United States Supreme Court held that the courts should defer to an agency's interpretation of *law* as well as fact. The Court found that the agency's interpretation of the statute was reasonable and upheld the bubble policy. The Court's decision in the *Chevron* case created a new standard for courts to use when reviewing agency interpretations of law. The standard involves the following two questions:

1. Did Congress directly address the issue in dispute in the statute? If so, the statutory language prevails.
2. If the statute is silent or ambiguous, is the agency's interpretation "reasonable"? If it is, a court should uphold the agency's interpretation even if the court would have interpreted the law differently.

10. *467 U.S. 837, 104 S.Ct. 2778, 81 L.Ed.2d 694 (1984).*

When Courts Will Give *Chevron* Deference to Agency Interpretation

The notion that courts should defer to agencies on matters of law has been controversial. Under the holding of the *Chevron* case, when the meaning of a particular statute's language is unclear and an agency interprets it, the court must follow the agency's interpretation as long as it is reasonable. This has led to considerable discussion and litigation to test the boundaries of the *Chevron* holding.

For instance, are courts required to give deference to all agency interpretations or only to those that result from adjudication or formal rulemaking procedures? The United States Supreme Court has held that in order for agency interpretations to be assured *Chevron* deference, they must meet the formal legal standards for notice-and-comment rulemaking. Nevertheless, there are still gray areas, and many agency interpretations are challenged in court.

CASE EXAMPLE 19.7 The Federal Insurance Contributions Act (FICA) requires employees and employers to pay Social Security taxes on all wages. The FICA excludes wages paid for any service to a school "performed by a student who is enrolled and regularly attending classes." The Mayo Foundation for Medical Education and Research offers educational residency programs to doctors who seek instruction in a chosen specialty. In addition to receiving instruction, the doctors are paid to spend fifty to eighty hours a week caring for patients. The U.S. Treasury Department issued a rule providing that anyone who works forty or more hours per week is an employee, not a student. The Mayo Foundation asserted that the rule did not apply to its residents.

The United States Supreme Court upheld the rule, however. Congress gave the Treasury Department the authority to make rules to enforce the Internal Revenue Code. The employee rule was issued after notice-and-comment procedures, and it was based on a reasonable determination that imposing Social Security taxes on medical residents would further the purpose of the statute. The doctors were "the kind of workers that Congress intended to both contribute to and benefit from the Social Security system."[11] ●

Public Accountability

As a result of growing public concern over the powers exercised by administrative agencies, Congress passed several laws to make agencies more accountable through public scrutiny. We discuss here the most significant of these laws.

Freedom of Information Act

Enacted in 1966, the Freedom of Information Act (FOIA)[12] requires the federal government to disclose certain records to any person on request, even if no reason is given for the request. A request that complies with FOIA procedures need only contain a reasonable description of the information sought. An agency's failure to comply with such a request can be challenged in a federal district court. The media, industry trade associations, public-interest groups, and even companies seeking information about competitors rely on these FOIA provisions to obtain information from government agencies.

The FOIA exempts certain types of records, such as those involving national security, and those containing information that is personal or confidential.

---

11. *Mayo Foundation for Medical Education and Research v. United States,* ___ U.S. ___, 131 S.Ct. 704, 178 L.Ed.2d 588 (2011).
12. 5 U.S.C. Section 552.

Government in the Sunshine Act

Congress passed the Government in the Sunshine Act,[13] or open meeting law, in 1976. It requires that "every portion of every meeting of an agency" be open to "public observation." The act also requires procedures to ensure that the public is provided with adequate advance notice of the agency's scheduled meeting and agenda.

Like the FOIA, the Sunshine Act contains certain exceptions. Closed meetings are permitted when one of the following occurs:

1. The subject of the meeting concerns accusing any person of a crime.
2. Open meetings would frustrate implementation of future agency actions.
3. The subject of the meeting involves matters relating to future litigation or rulemaking.

Courts interpret these exceptions to allow open access whenever possible.

Regulatory Flexibility Act

Concern over the effects of regulation on the efficiency of businesses, particularly smaller ones, led Congress to pass the Regulatory Flexibility Act.[14] Under this act, whenever a new regulation will have a "significant impact upon a substantial number of small entities," the agency must conduct a regulatory flexibility analysis. The analysis must measure the cost that the rule would impose on small businesses and must consider less burdensome alternatives. The act also contains provisions to alert small businesses about forthcoming regulations. The act relieved small businesses of some record-keeping burdens, especially with regard to hazardous waste management.

Small Business Regulatory Enforcement Fairness Act

The Small Business Regulatory Enforcement Fairness Act (SBREFA)[15] allows Congress to review new federal regulations for at least sixty days before they take effect. This period gives opponents of the rules time to present their arguments to Congress.

The SBREFA also authorizes the courts to enforce the Regulatory Flexibility Act. This helps to ensure that federal agencies, such as the Internal Revenue Service, consider ways to reduce the economic impact of new regulations on small businesses. Federal agencies are required to prepare guides that explain in plain English how small businesses can comply with federal regulations.

> "Law . . . is a human institution, created by human agents to serve human ends."
>
> Harlan F. Stone, 1872–1946
> (Chief Justice of the United States Supreme Court, 1941–1946)

---

13. 5 U.S.C. Section 552b.
14. 5 U.S.C. Sections 601–612.
15. 5 U.S.C. Sections 801 *et seq.*

Reviewing . . . Powers and Functions of Administrative Agencies

Assume that the Securities and Exchange Commission (SEC) has a rule under which it enforces statutory provisions prohibiting insider trading only when the insiders make monetary profits for themselves. Then the SEC makes a new rule, declaring that it has the statutory authority to bring enforcement actions against individuals even if they did not personally profit from the insider trading. The SEC simply announces the new rule without conducting a rulemaking proceeding. A stockbrokerage firm objects and says that the new rule was unlawfully developed without opportunity for public comment. The brokerage firm challenges the rule in an action that ultimately is reviewed by a federal appellate court. Using the information presented in the chapter, answer the following questions.

1. Is the SEC an executive agency or an independent regulatory agency? Does it matter to the outcome of this dispute? Explain.

2. Suppose that the SEC asserts that it has always had the statutory authority to pursue persons for insider trading regardless of whether they personally profited from the transaction. This is the only argument the SEC makes to justify changing its enforcement rules. Would a court be likely to find that the SEC's action was arbitrary and capricious under the Administrative Procedure Act (APA)? Why or why not?

3. Would a court be likely to give *Chevron* deference to the SEC's interpretation of the law on insider trading? Why or why not?

4. Now assume that a court finds that the new rule is merely "interpretive." What effect would this determination have on whether the SEC had to follow the APA's rulemaking procedures?

Debate This Because an administrative law judge (ALJ) acts as both judge and jury, there should always be at least three ALJs in each administrative hearing.

LINKING BUSINESS LAW to Management

Dealing with Administrative Law

Whether you end up owning your own small business or working for a large corporation, you will be dealing with multiple aspects of administrative law. Recall that administrative law involves all of the rules, orders, and decisions of administrative agencies. At the federal level, these include the U.S. Food and Drug Administration, the Equal Employment Opportunity Commission, the National Labor Relations Board, and the U.S. Occupational Safety and Health Administration. All federal, state, and local government administrative agencies create rules that have the force of law. As a manager, you probably will have to pay more attention to administrative rules and regulations than to laws passed by local, state, and federal legislatures.

Federal versus State and Local Agency Regulations

The three levels of government create three levels of rules and regulations though their respective administrative agencies. You may face situations in which, for example, a state agency regulation and a federal agency regulation conflict. In general, federal agency regulations preempt, or take precedence over, conflicting state (or local) regulations.

As a manager, you will have to learn about agency regulations that pertain to your business activities. It will be up to you, as a manager or small-business owner, to ferret out those regulations

that are most important and could potentially create the most liability if you violate them.

When Should You Participate in the Rulemaking Process?

All federal agencies and many state agencies invite public comments on proposed rules. For example, suppose that you manage a large construction company and your state occupational safety agency proposes a new rule requiring every employee on a construction site to wear hearing protection. You believe that the rule will lead to a less safe environment because your employees will not be able to communicate easily with one another.

Should you spend time offering comments to the agency? As an efficient manager, you make a trade-off calculation: First, you determine the value of the time that you would spend in attempting to prevent or at least alter the proposed rule. Then you compare this implicit cost with your estimate of the potential benefits your company would receive if the rule were not put into place.

Be Prepared for Investigations

All administrative agencies have investigatory powers. Agencies' investigators usually have the power to search business premises, although normally they first have to obtain a search warrant. As

Continued

Linking Business Law to Management—Continued

a manager, you have the choice of cooperating with agency investigators or providing the minimum amount of assistance. If you receive investigators regularly, you will often opt for cooperation. In contrast, if your business is rarely investigated, you may decide that the on-site proposed inspection is overreaching. Then you must contact your company's attorney for advice on how to proceed.

If an administrative agency cites you for a regulatory violation, you will probably negotiate a settlement with the agency rather than take your case before an administrative law judge. You will have to weigh the cost of the negotiated settlement with the potential cost of fighting the enforcement action.

Management Involves Flexibility

Throughout your business career, you will face hundreds of administrative rules and regulations, investigations, and perhaps

enforcement proceedings for rule violations. You may sometimes be frustrated by seemingly meaningless regulations. You must accept that these are part of the legal environment in which you work. The rational manager looks at administrative law as just another parameter that he or she cannot easily alter.

Critical Thinking

Why are owner/operators of small businesses at a disadvantage relative to large corporations when they attempt to decipher complex regulations that apply to their businesses?

Key Terms

adjudication 549
administrative agency 540
administrative law 540
administrative law judge (ALJ) 550

administrative process 547
bureaucracy 543
delegation doctrine 543
enabling legislation 542

final order 551
initial order 550
interpretive rule 543

legislative rule 543
notice-and-comment rulemaking 547
rulemaking 547

Chapter Summary: Powers and Functions of Administrative Agencies

Agency Creation and Powers	1. Under the U.S. Constitution, Congress can delegate the implementation of its laws to government agencies. Congress can thus indirectly monitor an area in which it has passed laws without becoming bogged down in details relating to enforcement.
	 2. Administrative agencies are created by enabling legislation, which usually specifies the name, composition, and powers of the agency.
	 3. Agencies can create legislative rules, which are as binding as formal acts of Congress.
	 4. The three branches of government exercise controls over agency powers and functions.
	   a. Executive controls—The president can control agencies through appointments of federal officers and through vetoes of bills affecting agency powers.
	   b. Legislative controls—Congress can give power to an agency, take it away, increase or decrease the agency's funding, or abolish the agency.
	   c. Judicial controls—Administrative agencies are subject to the judicial review of the courts.
	   d. The Administrative Procedure Act of 1946 also limits agencies.

The Administrative Process	1. The administrative process consists of rulemaking, enforcement, and adjudication.
	 2. Agencies are authorized to create new regulations—their rulemaking function. This power is conferred on an agency in the enabling legislation.
	 3. Notice-and-comment rulemaking is the most common rulemaking procedure. It involves the publication of the proposed regulation in the *Federal Register,* followed by a comment period to allow private parties to comment on the proposed rule.
	 4. Administrative agencies investigate the entities that they regulate, both during the rulemaking process to obtain data and after rules are issued to monitor compliance.
	 5. The most important investigative tools available to an agency are the following:
	   a. Inspections and tests—Used to gather information and to correct or prevent undesirable conditions.
	   b. Subpoenas—Orders that direct individuals to appear at a hearing or to hand over specified documents.

Chapter Summary: Powers and Functions of Administrative Agencies —Continued

The Administrative Process— Continued	6. Limits on administrative investigations include the following:
	  a. The investigation must be for a legitimate purpose.
	  b. The information sought must be relevant, and the investigative demands must be specific and not unreasonably burdensome.
	  c. The Fourth Amendment protects companies and individuals from unreasonable searches and seizures by requiring search warrants in most instances.
	7. After a preliminary investigation, an agency may initiate an administrative action against an individual or organization by filing a complaint. Most such actions are resolved at this stage.
	8. If there is no settlement, the case is presented to an administrative law judge (ALJ) in a proceeding similar to a trial.
	9. After a case is concluded, the ALJ renders an initial order, which can be appealed by either party to the board or commission that governs the agency and ultimately to a federal appeals court. If no appeal is taken or the case is not reviewed, then the order becomes the final order of the agency. The charged party may be ordered to pay damages or to stop carrying on some specified activity.

Judicial Deference to Agency Decisions	1. When reviewing agency decisions, courts typically grant deference (significant weight or consideration) to an agency's findings of fact and interpretations of law. 2. If Congress directly addressed the issue in dispute when enacting the statute, courts must follow the statutory language. 3. If the statute is silent or ambiguous, a court will uphold an agency's decision if the agency's interpretation of the statute was reasonable, even if the court would have interpreted the law differently. (This is known as *Chevron* deference.) 4. An agency must follow notice-and-comment rulemaking procedures before it is entitled to judicial deference in its interpretation of the law.
Public Accountability	Congress has passed several laws to make agencies more accountable through public scrutiny. These laws include the Freedom of Information Act, the Government in the Sunshine Act, the Regulatory Flexibility Act, and the Small Business Regulatory Enforcement Fairness Act.

Issue Spotters

1. The U.S. Department of Transportation (DOT) sometimes hears an appeal from a party whose contract with the DOT has been canceled. An administrative law judge (ALJ) who works for the DOT hears this appeal. What safeguards promote the ALJ's fairness? (See *The Administrative Process.*)
2. Apples & Oranges Corporation learns that a federal administrative agency is considering a rule that will have a negative impact on the firm's ability to do business. Will the firm have any opportunity to express its opinion about the pending rule? Explain. (See *The Administrative Process.*)

—**Check your answers to the Issue Spotters against the answers provided in Appendix D at the end of this text.**

For Review

1. How are federal administrative agencies created?
2. How do the three branches of government limit the power of administrative agencies?
3. What are the three basic functions of most administrative agencies?
4. What sequence of events must normally occur before an agency rule becomes law?
5. How do administrative agencies enforce their rules?

Business Scenarios and Case Problems

19–1. Rulemaking. For decades, the Federal Trade Commission (FTC) resolved fair trade and advertising disputes through individual adjudications. In the 1960s, the FTC began setting forth rules that defined *unfair trade practices*. In cases involving violations of these rules, the due process rights of participants were more limited and did not include cross-examination. This was because, although anyone found violating a rule would receive a full adjudication, the legitimacy of the rule itself could not be challenged in the adjudication. Any party charged with violating a rule was almost certain to lose the adjudication. Affected parties complained to a court, arguing that their rights before the FTC were unduly limited by the new rules. What will the court examine to determine whether to uphold the new rules? (See *The Administrative Process*.)

19–2. Informal Rulemaking. Assume that the Food and Drug Administration (FDA), using proper procedures, adopts a rule describing its future investigations. This new rule covers all future circumstances in which the FDA wants to regulate food additives. Under the new rule, the FDA is not to regulate food additives without giving food companies an opportunity to cross-examine witnesses. Some time later, the FDA wants to regulate methylisocyanate, a food additive. The FDA conducts an informal rulemaking procedure, without cross-examination, and regulates methylisocyanate. Producers protest, saying that the FDA promised them the opportunity for cross-examination. The FDA responds that the Administrative Procedure Act does not require such cross-examination and that it is free to withdraw the promise made in its new rule. If the producers challenge the FDA in court, on what basis would the court rule in their favor? (See *The Administrative Process*.)

19–3. ▲ **Spotlight on Defense Contracts—Judicial Controls.** Under federal law, when accepting bids on a contract, an agency must hold "discussions" with all offerors. An agency may ask a single offeror for "clarification" of its proposal, however, without holding "discussions" with the others. Regulations define clarifications as "limited exchanges." In 2001, the U.S. Air Force asked for bids on a contract. The winning contractor would examine, assess, and develop means of integrating national intelligence assets with the U.S. Department of Defense space systems, to enhance the capabilities of the Air Force's Space Warfare Center. Among the bidders were Information Technology & Applications Corp. (ITAC) and RS Information Systems, Inc. (RSIS). The Air Force asked the parties for more information on their subcontractors but did not allow them to change their proposals. Determining that there were weaknesses in ITAC's bid, the Air Force awarded the contract to RSIS. ITAC filed a suit against the government, contending that the postproposal requests to RSIS, and its responses, were improper "discussions." Should the court rule in ITAC's favor? Why or why not? [*Information Technology & Applications Corp. v. United States,* 316 F.3d 1312 (Fed.Cir. 2003)]. (See *Agency Creation and Powers*.)

19–4. Rulemaking. The Investment Company Act prohibits a mutual fund from engaging in certain transactions in which there may be a conflict of interest between the manager of the fund and its shareholders. Under rules issued by the Securities and Exchange Commission (SEC), however, a fund that meets certain conditions may engage in an otherwise prohibited transaction. In 2004, the SEC added two

new conditions. A year later, the SEC reconsidered the new conditions in terms of the costs that they would impose on the funds. Within eight days, and without asking for public input, the SEC readopted the conditions. The U.S. Chamber of Commerce—which is both a mutual fund shareholder and an association with mutual fund managers among its members—asked a federal appellate court to review the new rules. The Chamber charged that in readopting the rules, the SEC relied on materials not in the "rulemaking record" without providing an opportunity for public comment. The SEC countered that the information was otherwise "publicly available." In adopting a rule, should an agency consider information that is not part of the rulemaking record? Why or why not? [*Chamber of Commerce of the United States v. Securities and Exchange Commission,* 443 F.3d 890 (D.C.Cir. 2006)] (See *The Administrative Process*.)

19–5. ⚖ **Business Case Problem with Sample Answer— Powers of the Agency.** A well-documented rise in global temperatures has coincided with a significant increase in the concentration of carbon dioxide in the atmosphere. Many scientists believe that the two trends are related, because when carbon dioxide is released into the atmosphere, it produces a greenhouse effect, trapping solar heat. Under the Clean Air Act (CAA), the Environmental Protection Agency (EPA) is authorized to regulate "any" air pollutants "emitted into . . . the ambient air" that in its "judgment cause, or contribute to, air pollution." A group of private organizations asked the EPA to regulate carbon dioxide and other "greenhouse gas" emissions from new motor vehicles. The EPA refused, stating that Congress last amended the CAA in 1990 without authorizing new, binding limits on auto emissions. Nineteen states, including Massachusetts, asked a district court to review the EPA's denial. Did the EPA have the authority to regulate greenhouse gas emissions from new motor vehicles? If so, was its stated reason for refusing to do so consistent with that authority? Discuss. [*Massachusetts v. Environmental Protection Agency,* 549 U.S. 497, 127 S.Ct. 1438, 167 L.Ed.2d 248 (2007)] (See *Agency Creation and Powers*.)

—**For a sample answer to Problem 19–5, go to Appendix E at the end of this text.**

19–6. Judicial Deference. After Dave Conley died of lung cancer, his widow filed for benefits under the Black Lung Benefits Act. To qualify for benefits under the act, exposure to coal dust must have been a substantial contributing factor to a person's death. Conley had been a coal miner, but he had also been a longtime smoker. At the benefits hearing, a physician testified that coal dust was a substantial factor in Conley's death. No evidence was presented to support this conclusion, however. The administrative law judge awarded benefits. On appeal, should a court defer to this decision? Discuss. [*Conley v. National Mines Corp.,* 595 F.3d 297 (6th Cir. 2010)] (See *Judicial Deference to Agency Decisions*.)

19–7. Arbitrary and Capricious Test. Michael Manin, an airline pilot, was twice convicted of disorderly conduct, a minor misdemeanor. To renew his flight certification with the National Transportation Safety Board (NTSB), Manin filed an application that asked him about his criminal history. He did not disclose his two convictions. When these came to light more than ten years later, Manin argued that he had not known that he was required to report convictions for minor misdemeanors. The NTSB's policy was to consider an applicant's understanding of what information a question sought before determining whether an answer was false. But without explanation, the agency departed from this policy, refused to consider Manin's argument, and revoked his certification. Was this action arbitrary or capricious? Explain. [*Manin v. National Transportation Safety Board*, 627 F.3d 1239 (D.C.Cir. 2011)] (See *Agency Creation and Powers*.)

19–8. Adjudication. Mechanics replaced a brake assembly on the landing gear of a CRJ–700 plane operated by GoJet Airlines, LLC. The mechanics installed gear pins to lock the assembly in place during the repair, but failed to remove one of the pins after they had finished. On the plane's next flight, a warning light alerted the pilots that the landing gear would not retract after takeoff. There was a potential for danger, but the pilots flew the CRJ–700 safely back to the departure airport. No one was injured, and no property was damaged. The Federal Aviation Administration (FAA) cited GoJet for violating FAA regulations by "carelessly or recklessly operating an unairworthy airplane." GoJet objected to the citation. To which court can GoJet appeal for review? On what ground might that court decline to review the case? [*GoJet Airlines, LLC v. F.A.A.*, 743 F.3d 1168 (8th Cir. 2014)] (See *The Administrative Process*.)

19–9. ⬌ A Question of Ethics—Rulemaking. To ensure highway safety and protect driver health, Congress charged federal agencies with regulating the hours of service of commercial motor vehicle operators. Between 1940 and 2003, the regulations that applied to long-haul truck drivers were mostly unchanged. In 2003, the Federal Motor Carrier Safety Administration (FMCSA) revised the regulations significantly, increasing the number of daily and weekly hours that drivers could work. The agency had not considered the impact of the changes on the health of the drivers, however, and the revisions were overturned. The FMCSA then issued a notice that it would reconsider the revisions and opened them up for public comment. The agency analyzed the costs to the industry and the crash risks due to driver fatigue under different options and concluded that the safety benefits of not increasing the hours were less than the economic costs. In 2005, the agency issued a rule that was nearly identical to the 2003 version. Public Citizen, Inc., and others, including the Owner-Operator Independent Drivers Association, asked a district court to review the 2005 rule as it applied to long-haul drivers. [*Owner-Operator Independent Drivers Association, Inc. v. Federal Motor Carrier Safety Administration*, 494 F.3d 188 (D.C.Cir. 2007)] (See *The Administrative Process*.)

1. The agency's cost-benefit analysis included new methods that were not disclosed to the public in time for comments. Was this unethical? Should the agency have disclosed the new methodology sooner? Why or why not?

2. The agency created a graph to show the risk of a crash as a function of the time a driver spent on the job. The graph plotted the first twelve hours of a day individually, but the rest of the time was depicted with an aggregate figure at the seventeenth hour. This made the risk at those hours appear to be lower. Is it unethical for an agency to manipulate data? Explain.

Consumer Protection

LEARNING OBJECTIVES

The five learning objectives below are designed to help improve your understanding of the chapter. After reading this chapter, you should be able to answer the following questions:

1. When will advertising be deemed deceptive?

2. What information must be listed on the labels of food products?

3. What law protects consumers against contaminated and misbranded foods and drugs?

4. What does Regulation Z require, and how does it relate to the Truth-in-Lending Act?

5. What federal statute is aimed at preventing inaccurate credit reporting?

(STILLFX/Shutterstock.com)

"The good of the people is the greatest law."
—Marcus Tullius Cicero, 106–43 B.C.E. (Roman politician and orator)

Congress has enacted a substantial amount of legislation to protect "the good of the people," to borrow a phrase from Marcus Tullius Cicero (see the chapter-opening quotation). All statutes, agency rules, and common law judicial decisions that attempt to protect the interests of consumers are classified as *consumer law.*

Today, countless federal and state laws attempt to protect consumers from unfair trade practices, unsafe products, discriminatory or unreasonable credit requirements, and other problems related to consumer transactions. Nearly every agency and department of the federal government has an office of consumer affairs, and most states have one or more such offices to help consumers. Also, typically the attorney general's office assists consumers at the state level.

In recent years, there has been a renewed interest in attempting to protect consumers in their dealings with credit-card companies, financial institutions, and insurance companies. Congress has enacted new credit-card regulations and financial reforms to regulate the nation's largest banks. Congress has also enacted health-care reforms and revised food safety laws.

In this chapter, we examine some of the major laws and regulations protecting consumers, focusing primarily on federal legislation. Realize, though, that state laws often provide more sweeping and significant protections for the consumer than do federal laws. Exhibit 20–1 that follows indicates many of the areas of consumer law that are regulated by federal statutes.

Deceptive Advertising

The Federal Trade Commission Act[1] (mentioned in Chapter 19) created the Federal Trade Commission (FTC) to carry out the broadly stated goal of preventing unfair and deceptive trade practices, including deceptive advertising.

A Reasonable Consumer Would Be Misled

Generally, **deceptive advertising** occurs if a reasonable consumer would be misled by the advertising claim. Vague generalities and obvious exaggerations are permissible. These claims are known as *puffery*. When a claim takes on the appearance of literal authenticity, however, it may create problems.

Deceptive Advertising Advertising that misleads consumers, either by making unjustified claims about a product's performance or by omitting a material fact concerning the product's composition or performance.

Claims That Appear to Be Based on Factual Evidence   Advertising that *appears* to be based on factual evidence but in fact is not reasonably supported by some evidence will be deemed deceptive. **CASE EXAMPLE 20.1**   MedLab, Inc., advertised that its weight-loss supplement ("The New Skinny Pill") would cause users to lose substantial amounts of weight rapidly. The ads claimed that "clinical studies prove" that people who take the pill lose "as much as 15 to 18 pounds per week and as much as 50 percent of all excess weight in just 14 days, without dieting or exercising." The FTC sued MedLab for deceptive advertising.

---

1. 15 U.S.C. Sections 41–58.

Exhibit 20–1   Selected Areas of Consumer Law
Regulated by Statutes

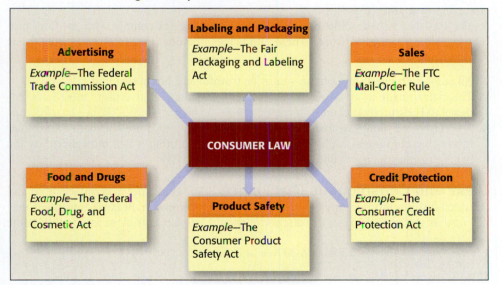

Were Campbell's claims that its soups helped fight heart disease truthful?

Bait-and-Switch Advertising Advertising a product at an attractive price and then telling the consumer that the advertised product is not available or is of poor quality and encouraging her or him to purchase a more expensive item.

An expert hired by the FTC to evaluate the claim testified that to lose this much weight, "a 200-pound individual would need to run between 57 and 68 miles every day"—the equivalent of more than two marathons per day. The court concluded that the advertisement was false and misleading, granted the FTC a summary judgment, and issued a permanent injunction to stop MedLab from running the ads.[2] ●

Claims Based on Half-Truths   Some advertisements contain "half-truths," meaning that the information is true but incomplete and, therefore, leads consumers to a false conclusion. **EXAMPLE 20.2**   The maker of Campbell's soups advertised that "most" Campbell's soups were low in fat and cholesterol and thus were helpful in fighting heart disease. What the ad did not say was that Campbell's soups were also high in sodium and that high-sodium diets may increase the risk of heart disease. Hence, the FTC ruled that the company's claims were deceptive. ● Advertising featuring an endorsement by a celebrity may be deemed deceptive if the celebrity does not actually use the product.

Bait-and-Switch Advertising

The FTC has issued rules that govern specific advertising techniques. One of the more important rules is contained in the FTC's "Guides Against Bait Advertising."[3] The rule is designed to prevent **bait-and-switch advertising**—that is, advertising a very low price for a particular item that will likely be unavailable to the consumer and then encouraging him or her to purchase a more expensive item.

The low price is the "bait" to lure the consumer into the store. The salesperson is instructed to "switch" the consumer to a different, more expensive item. According to the FTC guidelines, bait-and-switch advertising occurs if the seller refuses to show the advertised item, fails to have reasonable quantities of it available, fails to promise to deliver the advertised item within a reasonable time, or discourages employees from selling the item.

Online Deceptive Advertising

Deceptive advertising can occur in the online environment as well. The FTC actively monitors online advertising and has identified numerous Web sites that have made false or deceptive claims for products ranging from medical treatments for various diseases to exercise equipment and weight-loss aids.

The FTC has issued guidelines to help online businesses comply with the laws prohibiting deceptive advertising.[4] These guidelines include the following three basic requirements:

1. All ads—both online and offline—must be truthful and not misleading.
2. The claims made in an ad must be substantiated—that is, advertisers must have evidence to back up their claims.
3. Ads cannot be unfair, which the FTC defines as "likely to cause substantial consumer injury that consumers could not reasonably avoid and that is not outweighed by the benefit to consumers or competition."

Clear and Conspicuous Disclosure   The guidelines also call for "clear and conspicuous" disclosure of any qualifying or limiting information. Because consumers may not read an entire Web page, the disclosure should be placed as close as possible to the

---

2. *Federal Trade Commission v. MedLab, Inc,* 615 F.Supp.2d 1068 (N.D.Cal. 2009).
3. 16 C.F.R. Section 288.
4. *"Advertising and Marketing on the Internet: Rules of the Road,"* Federal Trade Commission, Sept. 2000, Web.

claim being qualified. The next-best location is on a section of the page to which a consumer can easily scroll. Generally, hyperlinks to a disclosure are recommended only for lengthy disclosures.

Spam Advertising

As discussed in Chapter 9, Congress passed the federal CAN-SPAM Act to combat the problems associated with unsolicited commercial e-mails, commonly referred to as spam. Many states have also passed consumer protection laws that regulate deceptive online advertising.

In the following case, an e-mail service provider claimed that an online marketing company had violated a California statute that prohibited deceptive content in e-mail advertising. The court had to decide whether the CAN-SPAM Act preempted the state statute (preemption was discussed in Chapter 4).

Case 20.1

(PressureUA/Shutterstock.com)

Hypertouch, Inc. v. ValueClick, Inc.

California Court of Appeal, Second District, 192 Cal.App.4th 805, 123 Cal.Rptr.3d 8 (2011).

BACKGROUND AND FACTS Hypertouch, Inc., provides e-mail service to customers located inside and outside California. ValueClick, Inc., and its subsidiaries provide online marketing services to third party advertisers that promote retail products. ValueClick contracts with these third party advertisers to place offers on its Web sites. ValueClick also contracts with affiliates that send out commercial e-mail advertisements. The advertisements include links redirecting consumers to promotions on ValueClick's Web sites.

If a consumer clicks through an e-mail advertisement and participates in a promotional offer, the affiliate that sent the initial e-mail is compensated for generating a customer "lead." The affiliate, rather than ValueClick, controls the content and headers of the e-mails. Hypertouch filed a complaint against ValueClick, its subsidiaries, and others for violating a California state statute that prohibits e-mail advertising that contains deceptive content and headings. The trial court held that the federal CAN-SPAM Act preempts the California statute and granted a summary judgment in favor of ValueClick. Hypertouch appealed.

IN THE WORDS OF THE COURT . . .
ZELON, J. [Judge]
* * * *

A determination whether Hypertouch's claims are preempted by federal law requires an analysis of both section 17529.5 [the California statute] and the CAN-SPAM Act. * * * *

In 2003, the California Legislature passed Senate Bill 186, which imposed broad restrictions on advertising in unsolicited commercial e-mail advertisements sent from or to a computer within California. * * * The Legislature concluded that, to effectively regulate the abuses associated with spam, it was

necessary to target not only the entities that send unsolicited commercial e-mail advertisements, but also the advertisers whose products and services are promoted in those e-mails[.]
* * * *

Like several other California consumer protection statutes targeting deceptive advertising practices, section 17529.5 dispenses with many of the elements associated with common law fraud, which normally requires the plaintiff to prove "(a) [a] misrepresentation . . .; (b) knowledge of falsity (or '*scienter*'); (c) intent to defraud, [that is,] to induce reliance; (d) justifiable reliance; and (e) resulting damage."
* * * *

The CAN-SPAM Act includes a provision that expressly preempts state statutes that regulate the use of commercial e-mail "except to the extent that any such statute . . . prohibits falsity or deception in any portion of a commercial [e-mail]." * * * [The legislative history indicates that the act] was intended "to implement 'one national standard' " regarding the content of commercial e-mail because "the patchwork of state laws had proven ineffective."

The legislative history also makes clear, however, that the Act's preemption provision was largely intended to target state statutes imposing content requirements on commercial e-mails, while leaving states free to regulate the use of deceptive practices in commercial e-mails in whatever manner they chose.
* * * *

The [preemption] clause does not reference either fraud or the common law, but rather permits any state law that prohibits " 'falsity and deception in any portion of a commercial electronic mail message.' " Congress "is certainly familiar with

Case 20.1—Continues ➡

Case 20.1—Continued

the word fraud and choose not to use it; the words 'falsity or deception' suggest broader application."

* * * [Furthermore,] at the time the CAN-SPAM Act was passed, Congress was aware that many states imposed liability for deceptive commercial e-mails without requiring reliance or other elements of common law fraud. Despite this knowledge, Congress chose not to use the word 'fraud' in the savings [preemption] provision, thereby suggesting that it intended the phrase "falsity or deception" to have a broader application.

* * * *

Rather than broadening the scope of prohibited content in commercial e-mail, California's decision to dispense with the elements of common law fraud was intended to create a more effective mechanism for eradicating the use of deceptive commercial e-mails. Section 17529.5 seeks to accomplish this goal in two ways. *First, the statute permits a recipient of a deceptive commercial e-mail to bring suit regardless of whether they were actually misled or harmed by the deceptive message.* This ensures that the use of deceptive e-mail will not go unpunished merely because it failed to mislead its targets. Second, imposing strict liability on the advertisers who benefit from (and are the ultimate cause of) deceptive e-mails, forces those entities to take a more active role in supervising the complex web of affiliates who are promoting their products. [Emphasis added.]

* * * *

*The numerous subject lines at issue in this suit contain a wide variety of different statements. Some simply state that the recipient of the e-mail can get a free gift ("Get a $300 gift card FREE" * * *), others suggest that the recipient can obtain something free for doing a particular task ("Let us know your opinion and win a free gift card" * * *).* [Emphasis added.]

[ValueClick has] made no effort to explain why a reasonable trier of fact could not conclude that many of the subject lines at issue here, such as those offering a free gift card with no qualifying language, would be likely to mislead a reasonable person. Instead, it targets isolated e-mails in the record, such as one e-mail with the subject line "GAP Promotion," and argues that those particular e-mails are, as a matter of law, not deceptive. Regardless of whether Respondent is correct that the isolated e-mails it cites are not likely to mislead the recipient, that alone does not entitle it to summary judgment on [Hypertouch's claims.]

DECISION AND REMEDY   The state appellate court held that California's anti-spam statute is not preempted by the federal CAN-SPAM Act, which exempts state laws that prohibit falsity or deception in commercial e-mail. The court therefore reversed the lower court's decision and remanded the case for trial.

THE E-COMMERCE DIMENSION   *Describe some ways in which the subject line of an e-mail advertisement might be deceptive.*

MANAGERIAL IMPLICATIONS   *Business owners and managers who engage in e-mail advertising or contract with online marketing companies for that purpose need to be aware of and comply with the applicable state laws. The online marketing company in this case claimed that it was not responsible for the deceptive content of the advertising because it did not send or initiate the e-mails—that was done by the affiliates—and it did not know that the e-mails were deceptive. The state court rejected this argument, however, finding that California's law applies more broadly to any entity that advertises in deceptive e-mails. This holding will aid plaintiffs who sue under California's antispam statute. It may also persuade courts in other states to apply the same reasoning and broadly interpret their state laws against deceptive online advertising.*

Federal Trade Commission Actions

The FTC receives complaints from many sources, including competitors of alleged violators, consumers, trade associations, Better Business Bureaus, and government organizations and officials. When the agency receives numerous and widespread complaints about a particular problem, it will investigate.

Formal Complaint

If the FTC concludes that a given advertisement is unfair or deceptive, it drafts a formal complaint, which is sent to the alleged offender. The company may agree to settle the complaint without further proceedings. If not, the FTC can conduct a hearing in which the company can present its defense.

Cease-and-Desist Order An administrative or judicial order prohibiting a person or business firm from conducting activities that an agency or court has deemed illegal.

FTC Orders

If the FTC succeeds in proving that an advertisement is unfair or deceptive, it usually issues a **cease-and-desist order** requiring the company to stop the challenged advertising. In some circumstances, it may also impose a sanction known as **counteradvertising**. This requires the company to advertise anew—in print, on the Internet, on radio, and on television—to inform the public about the earlier misinformation. The FTC sometimes institutes a **multiple product order**, which requires a firm to stop false advertising for all of its products, not just the product involved in the original action.

Restitution Possible When a company's deceptive ad leads to wrongful payments by consumers, the FTC may seek other remedies, including restitution. **CASE EXAMPLE 20.3** Verity International, Ltd., billed phone-line subscribers who accessed certain online pornography sites at the rate for international calls to Madagascar. When consumers complained about the charges, Verity told them that the charges were valid and had to be paid, or the consumers would face further collection actions. A federal appellate court held that this representation of "uncontestability" was deceptive and a violation of the FTC Act. The court ordered Verity to pay nearly $18 million in restitution to consumers.[5] ●

Counteradvertising New advertising that is undertaken to correct earlier false claims that were made about a product.

Multiple Product Order An order requiring a firm that has engaged in deceptive advertising to cease and desist from false advertising in regard to all the firm's products.

False Advertising Claims under the Lanham Act

The Lanham Act, which protects trademarks as discussed in Chapter 8, also covers false advertising claims. To state a successful claim for false advertising under this act, a business must establish (1) an injury to a commercial interest in reputation or sales, (2) direct causation of the injury by false or deceptive advertising, and (3) a loss of business from buyers who were deceived by the advertising.

The dispute between the parties in the following case focused initially on a mimicked microchip. When the case reached the United States Supreme Court, the question was whether Static Control Components, Inc., could sue Lexmark International, Inc., for false advertising under the Lanham Act.

---

5. *Federal Trade Commission v. Verity International, Ltd.*, 443 F.3d 48 (2d Cir. 2006).

Case 20.2

(Jo K. Media/iStockphoto.com)

Lexmark International, Inc. v. Static Control Components, Inc.
United States Supreme Court, ___ U.S. ___, 134 S.Ct. 1377, 188 L.Ed.2d 392 (2014).

BACKGROUND AND FACTS Lexmark International, Inc., sells the only style of toner cartridges that work with the company's laser printers. Other businesses—known as remanufacturers—acquire and refurbish used Lexmark cartridges to sell in competition with the cartridges sold by Lexmark. Static Control Components, Inc., makes and sells components for the remanufactured cartridges, including microchips that mimic the chips in Lexmark's cartridges. Lexmark released ads claiming that Static Control's microchips illegally infringed Lexmark's patents. Lexmark then filed a suit in a federal district court against Static Control, alleging violations of intellectual property law.

Static Control counterclaimed, alleging that Lexmark had engaged in false advertising in violation of the Lanham Act. The court dismissed the counterclaim. On Static Control's appeal, the U.S. Court of Appeals for the Sixth Circuit reversed the dismissal. Lexmark appealed to the United States Supreme Court.

IN THE WORDS OF THE COURT . . .
Justice *SCALIA* delivered the opinion of the Court.
 * * * *

First, * * * a statutory cause of action extends only to plaintiffs whose interests fall within the zone of interests protected by the law invoked.
 * * * *

* * * To come within the zone of interests in a suit for false advertising under [the Lanham Act,] a plaintiff must allege an injury to a commercial interest in reputation or sales.
 * * * *

Second, * * * a statutory cause of action is limited to plaintiffs whose injuries are proximately caused by violations of the statute.

Case 20.2—Continues ➡

Case 20.2—Continued

* * * *

* * * A plaintiff suing under [the Lanham Act] ordinarily must show economic or reputational injury flowing directly from the deception wrought by the defendant's advertising; and that occurs when deception of consumers causes them to withhold trade from the plaintiff.

* * * *

Applying those principles to Static Control's false-advertising claim, we conclude that Static Control comes within the class of plaintiffs whom Congress authorized to sue under [the Lanham Act].

To begin, Static Control's alleged injuries—lost sales and damage to its business reputation—are injuries to precisely the sorts of commercial interests the Act protects. *Static Control is suing not as a deceived consumer, but [in the words of the statute] as a "person engaged in * * * commerce within the control of Congress" whose position in the marketplace has been damaged by Lexmark's false advertising.* There is no doubt that it is within the zone of interests protected by the statute. [Emphasis added.]

Static Control also sufficiently alleged that its injuries were proximately caused by Lexmark's misrepresentations.

First, Static Control alleged that Lexmark disparaged its business and products by asserting that Static Control's business was illegal. *When a defendant harms a plaintiff's reputation by casting aspersions on its business, the plaintiff's injury flows directly from the audience's belief in the disparaging statements.* [Emphasis added.]

* * * *

The District Court emphasized that Lexmark and Static Control are not direct competitors [since Static Control is not itself a remanufacturer]. But when a party claims reputational injury from disparagement, competition is not required for proximate cause; and that is true even if the defendant's aim was to harm its immediate competitors, and the plaintiff merely suffered collateral damage.

In addition, Static Control adequately alleged proximate causation by alleging that it designed, manufactured, and sold microchips that both (1) were necessary for, and (2) had no other use than, refurbishing Lexmark toner cartridges. It follows from that allegation that any false advertising that reduced the remanufacturers' business necessarily injured Static Control as well.

DECISION AND REMEDY   The United States Supreme Court affirmed the lower court's ruling. Static Control had adequately pleaded the elements of a cause of action under the Lanham Act for false advertising. The Supreme Court's decision clarified that businesses do not need to be direct competitors to bring an action for false advertising under the act.

THE LEGAL ENVIRONMENT DIMENSION   *Under the Court's ruling in this case, is Static Control now entitled to relief? Explain your answer.*

WHAT IF THE FACTS WERE DIFFERENT?   *Suppose that Lexmark had issued a retraction of its ad claims before this case reached the Supreme Court. Would the outcome have been different? Discuss.*

Telemarketing and Fax Advertising

The Telephone Consumer Protection Act (TCPA)[6] prohibits telephone solicitation using an automatic telephone dialing system or a prerecorded voice. In addition, most states have statutes regulating telephone solicitation. The TCPA also makes it illegal to transmit ads via fax without first obtaining the recipient's permission. (Similar issues have arisen with respect to spam e-mail—see Chapter 9.)

Statutory Remedies   The Federal Communications Commission (FCC) enforces the TCPA. The FCC imposes substantial fines ($11,000 each day) on companies that violate the junk fax provisions of the act and even fined one company as much as $5.4 million.[7]

The TCPA also gives consumers a right to sue for either $500 for each violation of the act or for the actual monetary losses resulting from a violation, whichever is greater. If a court

---

6. 47 U.S.C. Sections 227 *et seq.*
7. See *Missouri ex rel. Nixon v. American Blast Fax, Inc.,* 323 F.3d 649 (8th Cir. 2003); *cert. denied,* 540 U.S. 1104, 124 S.Ct. 1043, 157 L.Ed.2d 888 (2004).

finds that a defendant willfully or knowingly violated the act, the court has the discretion to treble (triple) the amount of damages awarded.

Fraudulent Telemarketing
The Telemarketing and Consumer Fraud and Abuse Prevention Act[8] directed the FTC to establish rules governing telemarketing and to bring actions against fraudulent telemarketers.

The FTC's Telemarketing Sales Rule (TSR)[9] requires a telemarketer to identify the seller's name, describe the product being sold, and disclose all material facts related to the sale (such as the total cost of the goods being sold). The TSR makes it illegal for telemarketers to misrepresent information or facts about their goods or services. A telemarketer must also remove a consumer's name from its list of potential contacts if the customer so requests.

An amendment to the TSR established the national Do Not Call Registry. Telemarketers must refrain from calling those consumers who have placed their names on the list. Significantly, the TSR applies to any offer made to consumers in the United States—even if the offer comes from a foreign firm. Thus, the TSR helps to protect consumers from illegal cross-border telemarketing operations.

Advertising is essential to business. Before you advertise via faxes, however, you should know the applicable rules and be aware that the FCC aggressively enforces these rules. Make sure that all fax advertisements comply with the Telephone Consumer Protection Act and any state laws on faxes. Educate and train your employees about these laws. Do not send faxes without first obtaining the recipient's permission, and develop effective opt-out procedures so that anyone who no longer wants to receive faxes can notify you. Keep reliable records of the faxes you send, and maintain these records for at least four years. Do not purchase lists of fax numbers from outsiders. Avoiding consumer complaints about unwanted faxes and phone calls is the best way to avoid potentially significant liability.

PREVENTING LEGAL DISPUTES

Labeling and Packaging

A number of federal and state laws deal specifically with the information given on labels and packages. In general, labels must be accurate, and they must use words that are easily understood by the ordinary consumer. In some instances, labels must specify the raw materials used in the product, such as the percentage of cotton, nylon, or other fiber used in a garment. In other instances, the products must carry a warning, such as those required on cigarette packages and advertising.[10]

Fuel Economy Labels on Automobiles

The Energy Policy and Conservation Act[11] requires automakers to attach an information label to every new car. The label must include the Environmental Protection Agency's fuel economy estimate for the vehicle. In the following case, the buyer of a new car complained that the vehicle had failed to achieve the fuel economy estimate advertised in the automaker's brochure and listed on the label.

Does federal law preempt state deceptive advertising laws with respect to published fuel economy estimates?

(Reed Saxon/AP Images)

8. 15 U.S.C. Sections 6101–6108.
9. 16 C.F.R. Sections 310.1–310.8.
10. 15 U.S.C. Sections 1331–1341.
11. 49 U.S.C. Section 32908(b)(1).

Spotlight on Honda

Case 20.3
Paduano v. American Honda Motor Co.
California Court of Appeal, Fourth District, 169 Cal.App.4th 1453, 88 Cal.Rptr.3d 90 (2009).

(Evox Productions/Alamy Limited)

Can a buyer sue Honda if the stated gas mileage is greater than actual mileage?

BACKGROUND AND FACTS In 2004, Gaetano Paduano bought a new Honda Civic Hybrid in California. The information label on the car stated that the fuel economy estimates from the Environmental Protection Agency (EPA) were forty-seven miles per gallon (mpg) for city driving and forty-eight mpg for highway driving. Honda's sales brochure added, "Just drive the Hybrid like you would a conventional car and save on fuel bills." Paduano soon became frustrated with the car's fuel economy, which was less than half of the EPA's estimate. When American Honda Motor Company refused to repurchase the vehicle, Paduano filed a suit in a California state court against the automaker, alleging deceptive advertising in violation of the state's Consumer Legal Remedies Act and Unfair Competition Law. Honda argued that the federal Energy Policy and Conservation Act (EPCA), which prescribed the EPA's fuel economy estimate, preempted Paduano's claims (see Chapter 4). The court issued a summary judgment in Honda's favor. Paduano appealed to a state intermediate appellate court.

IN THE WORDS OF THE COURT
AARON, J. [Judge]
    * * * *

The basic rules of preemption are not in dispute: *Under the supremacy clause of the United States Constitution, Congress has the power to preempt state law concerning matters that lie within the authority of Congress. In determining whether federal law preempts state law, a court's task is to discern congressional intent. Congress's express intent in this regard will be found when Congress explicitly states that it is preempting state authority.* [Emphasis added.]
    * * * *

Honda * * * argues that [the EPCA] prevents Paduano from pursuing his * * * claims. That provision states in pertinent part,

> When a requirement under [the EPCA] is in effect, a State or a political subdivision of a State may adopt or enforce a law or regulation on disclosure of fuel economy or fuel operating costs for an automobile covered by [the EPCA] only if the law or regulation is identical to that requirement.

* * * Honda goes on to assert that "Paduano's deceptive advertising and misrepresentation claims would impose *non identical* disclosure requirements."

Contrary to Honda's characterization * * * , Paduano's claims are based on statements Honda made in its advertising brochure to the effect that one may drive a Civic Hybrid in the same manner as one would a conventional car, and need not do anything "special," in order to achieve the beneficial fuel economy of the EPA estimates. * * * Paduano is challenging * * * Honda's * * * commentary in which it alludes to those estimates in a manner that may give consumers the misimpression that they will be able to achieve mileage close to the EPA estimates while driving a Honda hybrid in the same manner as they would a conventional vehicle. Paduano does not seek to require Honda to provide "additional alleged facts" regarding the Civic Hybrid's fuel economy, as Honda suggests, but rather, seeks to prevent Honda from making misleading claims about how easy it is to achieve better fuel economy. Contrary to Honda's assertions, if Paduano were to prevail on his claims, Honda would not have to do anything differently with regard to its disclosure of the EPA mileage estimates.
    * * * *

* * * Allowing states to regulate false advertising and unfair business practices may further the goals of the EPCA, and we reject Honda's claim.

DECISION AND REMEDY The state intermediate appellate court concluded that federal law did not preempt Paduano's claims concerning Honda's advertising. The court reversed the lower court's judgment and remanded the case.

THE ETHICAL DIMENSION *Suppose that the defendant automaker had opposed this action solely to avoid paying damages to the purchaser of a car that had proved to be a "lemon." Would this have been unethical? Explain.*

THE LEGAL ENVIRONMENT DIMENSION *What does the interpretation of the law in this case suggest to businesspersons who sell products labeled with statements mandated by federal or state law?*

Food Labeling

Because the quality and safety of food are so important to consumers, several statutes deal specifically with food labeling. The Fair Packaging and Labeling Act requires that food product labels identify (1) the product, (2) the net quantity of the contents (and, if the number of servings is stated, the size of a serving), (3) the manufacturer, and (4) the packager or distributor. The act includes additional requirements concerning descriptions on packages, savings claims, components of nonfood products, and standards for the partial filling of packages.

Learning Objective 2
What information must be listed on the labels of food products?

Nutritional Content of Food Products

Food products must bear labels detailing the nutritional content, including the number of calories and the amounts of various nutrients that the food contains. The Nutrition Labeling and Education Act[12] requires standard nutrition facts (including the amount and type of fat that the food contains) to be listed on food labels and regulates the use of such terms as *fresh* and *low fat*.

The U.S. Food and Drug Administration (FDA) and the U.S. Department of Agriculture (USDA) are the primary agencies that issue regulations on food labeling. These rules are published in the *Federal Register* and updated annually. For instance, labels on fresh meats, vegetables, and fruits must indicate where the food originated so that consumers can know whether their food was imported.

Caloric Content of Restaurant Foods

The health-care reforms enacted by Congress in 2010 included provisions aimed at combating obesity in the United States. All restaurant chains with twenty or more locations are required to post the caloric content of the foods on their menus so that customers will know how many calories they are eating.[13] Foods offered through vending machines must also be labeled so that their caloric content is visible to would-be purchasers.

In addition, restaurants must post guidelines on the number of calories that an average person requires daily so that customers can determine what portion of a day's calories a particular food will provide. The hope is that consumers, armed with this information, will consider the number of calories when they make their food choices. The federal law on menu labeling supersedes all state and local laws already in existence.

Sales

A number of statutes protect consumers by requiring the disclosure of certain terms in sales transactions and providing rules governing unsolicited merchandise and home or door-to-door sales, mail-order sales, and referral sales. The FTC has regulatory authority in this area, as do other federal agencies.

The Federal Reserve Board of Governors, for instance, has issued a regulation that governs credit provisions associated with sales contracts (Regulation Z[14]—discussed later in this chapter). Many states and the FTC have **"cooling-off" laws** that permit the buyers of goods sold door to door to cancel their contracts within three business days. The FTC rule further requires that consumers be notified in Spanish of this right if the oral negotiations for the sale were in that language.

"Cooling-Off" Laws Laws that allow buyers to cancel door-to-door sales contracts within three business days.

---

12. 21 U.S.C. Section 343.1.
13. See Section 4205 of the Patient Protection and Affordable Care Act, Pub. L. No. 111-148, 124 Stat. 119 (March 23, 2010).
14. 12 C.F.R. Sections 226.1–226.30.

Telephone and Mail-Order Sales

The FTC Mail or Telephone Order Merchandise Rule amended the FTC Mail-Order Rule.[15] The rule provides specific protections for consumers who purchase goods over the phone, through the mail, by fax, or via the Internet. Merchants must ship orders within the time promised in their advertisements and notify consumers when orders cannot be shipped on time. The rule also requires merchants to issue a refund within a specified period of time when a consumer cancels an order.

In addition, under the Postal Reorganization Act,[16] a consumer who receives *unsolicited* merchandise sent by U.S. mail can keep it, throw it away, or dispose of it in any manner that she or he sees fit. The recipient will not be obligated to the sender.

Online Sales

The FTC and other federal agencies have brought numerous enforcement actions against those who perpetrate online fraud (see the discussion of wire fraud in Chapter 6). Nonetheless, protecting consumers from fraudulent and deceptive sales practices conducted via the Internet has proved to be a challenging task.

Faced with economic recession, job losses, mounting debt, and dwindling savings, many consumers are looking for any source of income. The number of consumers who have fallen prey to Internet fraud has grown in recent years. Complaints to the FTC about sales of fraudulent business opportunities, such as work-at-home offers and real estate systems, nearly tripled from 2008 to 2014. About 10 percent of U.S. adults claim to have been victims of online fraud.

Protection of Health and Safety

Labeling and packaging laws (discussed earlier) promote consumer health and safety. Nevertheless, there is a significant distinction between regulating the information dispensed about a product and regulating the actual content of the product. The classic example is tobacco products. Tobacco companies must label their products to warn consumers about the health hazards associated with their use, but the sale of tobacco products has not been subjected to significant restrictions. Here, we examine various laws that regulate the actual products made available to consumers.

The Federal Food, Drug, and Cosmetic Act

The most important federal legislation regulating food and drugs is the Federal Food, Drug, and Cosmetic Act (FDCA).[17] The act protects consumers against adulterated (contaminated) and misbranded foods and drugs.

Food Safety   The FDCA establishes food standards, specifies safe levels of potentially hazardous food additives, and provides classifications of foods and food advertising. Most of these statutory requirements are monitored and enforced by the Food and Drug Administration (FDA).

Tainted Foods   In recent years, many people in the United States have contracted food poisoning from eating foods that were contaminated—often with salmonella or E. coli

---

15. 16 C.F.R. Sections 435.1–435.2.
16. 39 U.S.C. Section 3009.
17. 21 U.S.C. Sections 301–393.

bacteria. There have been high-profile recalls of peanut products, eggs, and beef. Tainted cantaloupes killed thirty-three people.

Modernization Legislation   In 2011, Congress enacted the Food Safety Modernization Act (FSMA)[18] to provide greater government control over the U.S. food safety system. The FSMA gives the FDA authority to directly recall any food products that it suspects are tainted (rather than relying on the producers to recall items).

The act requires any person who manufactures, processes, packs, distributes, receives, holds, or imports food products to pay a fee and register with the U.S. Department of Health and Human Services. (There are some exceptions for small farmers.) The act also requires owners and operators of facilities to analyze and identify food safety hazards, implement preventive controls, monitor effectiveness, and take corrective actions.

The FSMA also places more restrictions on importers of food and requires them to verify that imported foods meet U.S. safety standards. In 2013, the FDA proposed new rules to implement the FSMA, but most of these rules have not been finalized. Given that some members of the food industry have expressed concerns about aspects of the proposed rules, it may be several years before final rules implementing the FSMA are in place.

Drugs   The FDA also has the responsibility of ensuring that drugs are safe and effective before they are marketed to the public. Because the FDA must ensure the safety of new medications, there is always a delay before drugs are available to the public, and this sometimes leads to controversy.

CASE EXAMPLE 20.4   A group of citizens petitioned the FDA to allow everyone access to Plan B—the morning-after birth control pill—without a prescription. The FDA denied the petition and continued to require women under the age of seventeen to obtain a prescription. The group appealed to a federal district court, claiming that the prescription requirement can delay access to the pill. The pill should be taken as soon as possible after sexual intercourse, preferably within twenty-four hours.

The court ruled in favor of the plaintiffs and ordered the FDA to make the morning-after pill available to people of any age without a prescription. Shortly after the decision in 2013, the FDA changed its policy to allow anyone to obtain the morning-after pill without a prescription.[19] ●

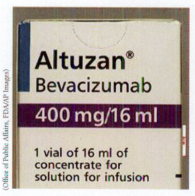

(Office of Public Affairs, FDA/AP Images)

Can the FDA prevent fake drugs from being sold to consumers?

The Consumer Product Safety Act

In 1972, the Consumer Product Safety Act[20] created the first comprehensive scheme of regulation over matters of consumer safety. The act also established the Consumer Product Safety Commission (CPSC), which has far-reaching authority over consumer safety.

The CPSC's Authority   The CPSC conducts research on the safety of individual consumer products and maintains a clearinghouse on the risks associated with various products. The Consumer Product Safety Act authorizes the CPSC to do the following:

1. Set safety standards for consumer products.
2. Ban the manufacture and sale of any product that the commission believes poses an "unreasonable risk" to consumers. (Products banned by the CPSC have included various types of fireworks, cribs, and toys, as well as many products containing asbestos or vinyl chloride.)

---

18. Pub. L. No. 111-353, 124 Stat. 3885 (January 4, 2011). This statute affected numerous parts of Title 21 of the U.S.C.
19. *Tummino v. Hamburg*, 936 F.Supp.2d 162 (E.D.N.Y. 2013).
20. 15 U.S.C. Sections 2051–2083.

3. Remove from the market any products it believes to be imminently hazardous. The CPSC frequently works in conjunction with manufacturers to voluntarily recall defective products from stores. **EXAMPLE 20.5** In cooperation with the CPSC, Kolcraft Enterprises, Inc., recalled one million infant play yards because of a defective latch that could cause a rail to fall, posing a risk to children. ●

4. Require manufacturers to report on any products already sold or intended for sale if the products have proved to be hazardous.

5. Administer other product-safety legislation, including the Child Protection and Toy Safety Act of 1969[21] and the Federal Hazardous Substances Act of 1960.[22]

Notification Requirements

The Consumer Product Safety Act requires the distributors of consumer products to notify the CPSC immediately if they receive information that a product "contains a defect which . . . creates a substantial risk to the public" or "an unreasonable risk of serious injury or death."

CASE EXAMPLE 20.6 A company that sold juicers received twenty-three letters from customers complaining that during operation the juicer had suddenly exploded, sending pieces of glass and razor-sharp metal across the room. The government sued the company because it had waited more than six months before notifying the CPSC. The court held that the company had violated that law and ordered it to pay damages.[23] ●

Health-Care Reforms

In 2010, the health-care reforms enacted by Congress went into effect and gave Americans new rights and benefits with regard to health care.[24] By 2014, these laws prohibited certain insurance company practices, such as denying coverage for preexisting conditions.

Expanded Coverage for Children and Seniors

The reforms expanded access to health care by enabling more children to obtain health-insurance coverage. In addition, the reforms allowed young adults (under age twenty-six) to remain on their parents' health insurance. The act also ended lifetime and most annual limits on care, and gave patients access to recommended preventive services (such as cancer screening, vaccinations, and well-baby checks) without cost. Medicare recipients now receive a 50 percent discount on name-brand drugs, and the gap in Medicare's prescription drug coverage will be eliminated by 2020.

Controlling Costs of Health Insurance

In an attempt to control the rising costs of health insurance, the law places restrictions on insurance companies. Insurance companies must spend at least 85 percent of all premium dollars collected from large employers (80 percent of the premiums collected from individuals and small employers) on benefits and quality improvement. If insurance companies do not meet these goals, they must provide rebates to consumers. Additionally, states can require insurance companies to justify their premium increases to be eligible to participate in the new health-insurance exchanges.

---

21. 15 U.S.C. Section 1262(e).
22. 15 U.S.C. Sections 1261–1273.
23. *United States v. Mirama Enterprises, Inc.*, 185 F.Supp.2d 1148 (S.D.Cal. 2002).
24. Patient Protection and Affordable Health Care Act of 2010, Pub. L. No. 111-148, 124 Stat. 119 (March 23, 2010); and the Health Care and Education Reconciliation Act of 2010, Pub. L. No. 111-152, 124 Stat. 1029 (March 30, 2010).

Credit Protection

Credit protection is one of the most important aspects of consumer protection legislation. Nearly 80 percent of U.S. consumers have credit cards, and most carry a balance on these cards, which amounts to about $2.5 trillion of debt nationwide. In 2010, Congress established a new agency, the Consumer Financial Protection Bureau, to oversee the practices of banks, mortgage lenders, and credit-card companies.[25]

The Truth-in-Lending Act

A key statute regulating the credit and credit-card industries is the Truth-in-Lending Act (TILA), the name commonly given to Title 1 of the Consumer Credit Protection Act (CCPA), as amended.[26] The TILA is basically a *disclosure law*. It is administered by the Federal Reserve Board and requires sellers and lenders to disclose credit terms or loan terms (such as the annual percentage rate, or APR, and any finance charges) so that individuals can shop around for the best financing arrangements.

Learning Objective 4
What does Regulation Z require, and how does it relate to the Truth-in-Lending Act?

Application TILA requirements apply only to persons who, in the ordinary course of business, lend funds, sell on credit, or arrange for the extension of credit. Thus, sales or loans made between two consumers do not come under the act. Additionally, this law protects only debtors who are *natural* persons (as opposed to the artificial "person" of a corporation) and does not extend to other legal entities.

Disclosure Requirements The disclosure requirements are found in **Regulation Z**, issued by the Federal Reserve Board of Governors. If the contracting parties are subject to the TILA, the requirements of Regulation Z apply to any transaction involving an installment sales contract that calls for payment to be made in more than four installments. Transactions subject to Regulation Z typically include installment loans, retail and installment sales, car loans, home-improvement loans, and certain real estate loans if the amount of financing is less than $25,000.

Regulation Z A set of rules issued by the Federal Reserve Board of Governors to implement the provisions of the Truth-in-Lending Act.

Under the provisions of the TILA, all of the terms of a credit instrument must be clearly and conspicuously disclosed. A lender must disclose the annual percentage rate (APR), finance charge, amount financed, and total payments (the sum of the amount loaned, plus any fees, finance charges, and interest at the end of the loan). The TILA provides for contract rescission (cancellation) if a creditor fails to follow the *exact* procedures required by the act.

Equal Credit Opportunity The Equal Credit Opportunity Act (ECOA) amended the TILA in 1974. The ECOA prohibits the denial of credit solely on the basis of race, religion, national origin, color, gender, marital status, or age. The act also prohibits credit discrimination on the basis of whether an individual receives certain forms of income, such as public-assistance benefits.

Under the ECOA, a creditor may not require the signature of an applicant's spouse, or a cosigner, on a credit instrument if the applicant qualifies under the creditor's standards of creditworthiness for the amount requested. **CASE EXAMPLE 20.7** T.R. Hughes, Inc., and

Which federal law prohibits discrimination for credit-card applications?

(Teekid/iStockphoto.com)

---

25. Title 10 of the Restoring American Financial Stability Act of 2010, S.B. 3217, April 15, 2010.
26. 15 U.S.C. Sections 1601–1693r.

Summit Pointe, LLC, obtained financing from Frontenac Bank to construct two real estate developments near St. Louis, Missouri. The bank also required the builder, Thomas R. Hughes, and his wife, Carolyn Hughes, to sign personal guaranty agreements for the loans.

When the borrowers failed to make the loan payments, the bank sued the two companies and Thomas and Carolyn Hughes personally, and foreclosed on the properties. Carolyn claimed that personal guaranty contracts that she signed were obtained in violation of the ECOA. The court held that because the applicant, Thomas R. Hughes, was creditworthy, the personal guarantees of Carolyn Hughes were obtained in violation of the ECOA and therefore unenforceable.[27]

Credit-Card Rules   The TILA also contains provisions regarding credit cards. One provision limits the liability of a cardholder to $50 per card for unauthorized charges made before the creditor is notified that the card has been lost. If a consumer received an *unsolicited* credit card in the mail that is later stolen, the company that issued the card cannot charge the consumer for any unauthorized charges.

Another provision requires credit-card companies to disclose the balance computation method that is used to determine the outstanding balance, and to state when finance charges begin to accrue. Other provisions set forth procedures for resolving billing disputes with the credit-card company. These procedures may be used if, for instance, a cardholder wishes to withhold payment for a faulty product purchased with a credit card.

Amendments to Credit-Card Rules   Amendments to TILA's credit-card rules that became effective in 2010 added the following protections:

1. A company may not retroactively increase the interest rates on existing card balances unless the account is sixty days delinquent.
2. A company must provide forty-five days' advance notice to consumers before changing its credit-card terms.
3. Monthly bills must be sent to cardholders twenty-one days before the due date.
4. The interest rate charged on a customer's credit-card balance may not be increased except in specific situations, such as when a promotional rate ends.
5. A company may not charge fees to a customer for being over his or her credit-card limit except in specified situations.
6. When the customer has balances at different interest rates, payments in excess of the minimum amount due must be applied first to the balance with the highest rate (for instance, a higher interest rate is commonly charged for cash advances).
7. A company may not compute finance charges based on the previous billing cycle (a practice known as double-cycle billing, which hurts consumers because they are charged interest for the previous cycle even though they have paid the bill in full).

The Fair Credit Reporting Act

Learning Objective 5
What federal statute is aimed at preventing inaccurate credit reporting?

The Fair Credit Reporting Act (FCRA)[28] protects consumers against inaccurate credit reporting and requires that lenders and other creditors report correct, relevant, and up-to-date information. The act provides that consumer credit reporting agencies may issue credit reports to users only for specified purposes. Legitimate purposes include the extension of credit, the issuance of insurance policies, and in response to a consumer's request.

27. *Frontenac Bank v. T.R. Hughes, Inc.*, 404 S.W.3d 272 (Mo.App. 2012).
28. 15 U.S.C. Sections 1681 *et seq.*

Consumer Notification and Inaccurate Information

Any time a consumer is denied credit or insurance on the basis of his or her credit report, the consumer must be notified of that fact and of the name and address of the credit reporting agency that issued the report. The same notice must be sent to consumers who are charged more than others ordinarily would be for credit or insurance because of their credit reports.

Under the FCRA, consumers can request the source of any information used by the credit agency, as well as the identity of anyone who has received an agency's report. Consumers are also permitted to have access to the information contained about them in a credit reporting agency's files. If a consumer discovers that the agency's files contain inaccurate information, the agency, on the consumer's written request, must investigate the disputed information. Any unverifiable or erroneous information must be deleted within a reasonable period of time.

On the consumer's written (or electronic) request, the agency must conduct a systematic examination of its records. Any unverifiable or erroneous information must be deleted within a reasonable period of time.

How does the Fair Credit Reporting Act protect consumers?

Remedies for Violations

An agency that fails to comply with the act is liable for actual damages, plus additional damages not to exceed $1,000 and attorneys' fees. Creditors and other companies that use information from credit reporting agencies may also be liable for violations of the FCRA. The United States Supreme Court has held that an insurance company's failure to notify new customers that they were paying higher insurance rates as a result of their credit scores was a *willful* violation of the FCRA.[29]

CASE EXAMPLE 20.8 Branch Banking & Trust Company of Virginia (BB&T) gave Rex Saunders an auto loan but failed to give him a payment coupon book and rebuffed his attempts to make payments on the loan. Eventually, BB&T discovered its mistake and demanded full payment, plus interest and penalties. When payment was not immediately forthcoming, BB&T declared that Saunders was in default. It then repossessed the car and forwarded adverse credit information about Saunders to credit reporting agencies without noting that Saunders disputed the information. Saunders filed a lawsuit alleging violations of the FCRA and was awarded $80,000 in punitive damages. An appellate court found that the damages award was reasonable, given BB&T's willful violation.[30] ●

The Fair and Accurate Credit Transactions Act

Congress passed the Fair and Accurate Credit Transactions (FACT) Act to combat identity theft.[31] The act established a national fraud alert system so that consumers who suspect that they have been or may be victimized by identity theft can place an alert in their credit files. The act also requires the major credit reporting agencies to provide consumers with a free copy of their credit reports every twelve months.

Another provision requires account numbers on credit-card receipts to be truncated (shortened) so that merchants, employees, and others who have access to the receipts cannot obtain a consumer's name and full credit-card number. The act also mandates that financial institutions work with the FTC to identify "red flag" indicators of identity theft and to develop rules for disposing of sensitive credit information.

> "Credit is a system whereby a person who can't pay gets another person who can't pay to guarantee that he can pay."
>
> Charles Dickens, 1812–1870 (English novelist)

---

29. *Safeco Insurance Co. of America v. Burr,* 551 U.S. 47, 127 S.Ct. 2201, 167 L.Ed.2d 1045 (2007).
30. *Saunders v. Branch Banking & Trust Co. of Virginia,* 526 F.3d 142 (4th Cir. 2008).
31. Pub. L. No. 108-159, 117 Stat. 1952 (December 4, 2003).

The Fair Debt Collection Practices Act

The Fair Debt Collection Practices Act (FDCPA)[32] attempts to curb abuses by collection agencies. The act applies only to specialized debt-collection agencies and attorneys who regularly attempt to collect debts on behalf of someone else, usually for a percentage of the amount owed. Creditors attempting to collect debts are not covered by the act unless, by misrepresenting themselves, they cause the debtors to believe that they are collection agencies. A debt collector who fails to comply with the act is liable for actual damages, plus additional damages not to exceed $1,000 and attorneys' fees.

Requirements of the Act   Under the FDCPA, a collection agency may *not* do any of the following:

1. Contact the debtor at the debtor's place of employment if the debtor's employer objects.
2. Contact the debtor at inconvenient or unusual times (such as three o'clock in the morning), or at any time if the debtor is being represented by an attorney.
3. Contact third parties other than the debtor's parents, spouse, or financial adviser about payment of a debt unless a court authorizes such action.
4. Harass or intimidate the debtor (by using abusive language or threatening violence, for instance) or make false or misleading statements (such as posing as a police officer).
5. Communicate with the debtor at any time after receiving notice that the debtor is refusing to pay the debt, except to advise the debtor of further action to be taken by the collection agency.

Validation Notice An initial notice to a debtor from a collection agency informing the debtor that he or she has thirty days to challenge the debt and request verification.

The FDCPA also requires a collection agency to include a **validation notice** whenever it initially contacts a debtor for payment of a debt or within five days of that initial contact. The notice must state that the debtor has thirty days in which to dispute the debt and to request a written verification of the debt from the collection agency. The debtor's request for debt validation must be in writing.

Enforcement of the Act   The enforcement of the FDCPA is primarily the responsibility of the Federal Trade Commission. The act provides that a debt collector who fails to comply with the act is liable for actual damages, plus additional damages not to exceed $1,000 and attorneys' fees.

Debt collectors who violate the act are exempt from liability if they can show that the violation was not intentional and resulted from a bona fide error—regardless of existing procedures that were adapted to avoid such an error. The "bona fide error" defense typically has been applied to mistakes of fact or clerical errors.

---

32. 15 U.S.C. Section 1692.

Reviewing . . . Consumer Protection

Leota Sage saw a local motorcycle dealer's newspaper advertisement offering a MetroRider EZ electric scooter for $1,699. When she went to the dealership, however, she learned that the EZ model had been sold out. The salesperson told Sage that he still had the higher-end MetroRider FX model in stock for $2,199 and would sell her one for $1,999. Sage was disappointed but decided to purchase the FX model. When Sage said that she wished to purchase the scooter on credit, she was directed to the dealer's credit department. As she filled out the credit forms, the clerk told Sage, who is an Asian American, that she would need a cosigner to obtain a loan. Sage could not understand why she would need a cosigner and asked to speak to the store manager.

The manager apologized, told her that the clerk was mistaken, and said that he would "speak to" the clerk about that. The manager completed Sage's credit application, and Sage then rode the scooter home. Seven months later, Sage received a letter from the manufacturer informing her that a flaw had been discovered in the scooter's braking system and that the model had been recalled. Using the information presented in the chapter, answer the following questions.

1. Did the dealer engage in deceptive advertising? Why or why not?
2. Suppose that Sage had ordered the scooter through the dealer's Web site but the dealer was unable to deliver it by the date promised. What would the FTC have required the merchant to do in that situation?
3. Assuming that the clerk required a cosigner based on Sage's race or gender, what act prohibits such credit discrimination?
4. What organization has the authority to ban the sale of scooters based on safety concerns?

Debate This Laws against bait-and-switch advertising should be abolished because no consumer is ever forced to buy anything.

Key Terms

bait-and-switch advertising 562
cease-and-desist order 564
"cooling-off" laws 569
counteradvertising 565
deceptive advertising 561
multiple product order 565
Regulation Z 573
validation notice 576

Chapter Summary: Consumer Protection

Deceptive Advertising	1. *Definition of deceptive advertising*—Generally, an advertising claim will be deemed deceptive if it would mislead a reasonable consumer.
	2. *Bait-and-switch advertising*—Advertising a lower-priced product (the bait) to lure consumers into the store and then telling them the product is unavailable and urging them to buy a higher-priced product (the switch) is prohibited by the FTC.
	3. *Online deceptive advertising*—The FTC has issued guidelines to help online businesses comply with the laws prohibiting deceptive advertising.
	4. *FTC actions against deceptive advertising*—
	  a. Cease-and-desist orders—Requiring the advertiser to stop the challenged advertising.
	  b. Counteradvertising—Requiring the advertiser to advertise to correct the earlier misinformation.

Labeling and Packaging	Manufacturers must comply with the labeling or packaging requirements for their specific products. In general, all labels must be accurate and not misleading.
Sales	Federal and state statutes and regulations govern certain practices of sellers who solicit over the telephone or through the mails and protect consumers to some extent against fraudulent and deceptive online sales practices.
Protection of Health and Safety	1. *Food and drugs*—The Federal Food, Drug, and Cosmetic Act protects consumers against adulterated and misbranded foods and drugs. The act establishes food standards, specifies safe levels of potentially hazardous food additives, and sets classifications of food and food advertising. 2. *Consumer product safety*—The Consumer Product Safety Act seeks to protect consumers from injury from hazardous products. The Consumer Product Safety Commission has the power to remove products that are deemed imminently hazardous from the market and to ban the manufacture and sale of hazardous products.

Continued

Chapter Summary: Consumer Protection—Continued

Credit Protection	1. *Consumer Credit Protection Act, Title I (Truth-in-Lending Act, or TILA)*—A disclosure law that requires sellers and lenders to disclose credit terms or loan terms in certain transactions, including retail and installment sales and loans, car loans, home-improvement loans, and certain real estate loans. Additionally, the TILA provides for the following:
	   a. Equal credit opportunity—Creditors are prohibited from discriminating on the basis of race, religion, marital status, gender, national origin, color, or age.
	   b. Credit-card protection—Liability of cardholders for unauthorized charges is limited to $50, providing notice requirements are met. Consumers are not liable for unauthorized charges made on unsolicited credit cards. The act also sets out procedures to be used in settling disputes between credit-card companies and their cardholders.
	2. *Fair Credit Reporting Act*—Entitles consumers to request verification of the accuracy of a credit report and to have unverified or false information removed from their files.
	3. *Fair and Accurate Credit Transaction Act*—Combats identity theft by establishing a national fraud alert system. Requires account numbers to be truncated and credit reporting agencies to provide one free credit report per year to consumers.
	4. *Fair Debt Collection Practices Act*—Prohibits debt collectors from using unfair debt-collection practices, such as contacting the debtor at his or her place of employment if the employer objects or at unreasonable times, contacting third parties about the debt, and harassing the debtor.

Issue Spotters

1. United Pharmaceuticals, Inc., believes that it has developed a new drug that will be effective in the treatment of patients with AIDS. The drug has had only limited testing, but United wants to make the drug widely available as soon as possible. To market the drug, what must United prove to the U.S. Food and Drug Administration? (See *Protection of Health and Safety.*)
2. Gert buys a notebook computer from EZ Electronics. She pays for it with her credit card. When the computer proves defective, she asks EZ to repair or replace it, but EZ refuses. What can Gert do? (See *Credit Protection.*)

—Check your answers to the Issue Spotters against the answers provided in Appendix D at the end of this text.

For Review

1. When will advertising be deemed deceptive?
2. What information must be listed on the labels of food products?
3. What law protects consumers against contaminated and misbranded foods and drugs?
4. What does Regulation Z require, and how does it relate to the Truth-in-Lending Act?
5. What federal statute is aimed at preventing inaccurate credit reporting?

Business Scenarios and Case Problems

20–1. Unsolicited Merchandise. Andrew, a resident of California, received an advertising circular in the U.S. mail announcing a new line of regional cookbooks distributed by the Every-Kind Cookbook Co. Andrew didn't want any books and threw the circular away. Two days later, Andrew received in the mail an introductory cookbook entitled *Lower Mongolian Regional Cookbook*, as announced in the circular, on a "trial basis" from Every-Kind. Andrew was not interested but did not go to the trouble to return the cookbook. Every-Kind demanded payment of $20.95 for the *Lower Mongolian Regional Cookbook*. Discuss whether Andrew can be required to pay for the book. (See *Sales.*)

20–2. Credit-Card Rules. Maria Ochoa receives two new credit cards on May 1. She has solicited one of them from Midtown Department Store, and the other arrives unsolicited from High-Flying Airlines. During the month of May, Ochoa makes numerous credit-card purchases from Midtown Department Store, but she does not use the High-Flying Airlines card. On May 31, a burglar breaks into Ochoa's home and steals both credit cards, along with other items.

Ochoa notifies the Midtown Department Store of the theft on June 2, but she fails to notify High-Flying Airlines. Using the Midtown credit card, the burglar makes a $500 purchase on June 1 and a $200 purchase on June 3. The burglar then charges a vacation flight on the High-Flying Airlines card for $1,000 on June 5. Ochoa receives the bills for these charges and refuses to pay them. Discuss Ochoa's liability for the charges. (See *Credit Protection*.)

20–3. **Spotlight on McDonald's—Food Labeling.** McDonald's Corp.'s Happy Meal® meal selection consists of an entrée, a small order of french fries, a small drink, and a toy. In the early 1990s, McDonald's began to aim its Happy Meal marketing at children aged one to three. In 1995, McDonald's began making nutritional information for its food products available in documents known as "McDonald's Nutrition Facts." Each document lists the food items that the restaurant serves and provides a nutritional breakdown, but the Happy Meal is not included.

Marc Cohen filed a suit in an Illinois state court, alleging, among other things, that McDonald's had violated a state law prohibiting consumer fraud and deceptive business practices by failing to adhere to the Nutrition Labeling and Education Act (NLEA). The NLEA sets out different requirements for products specifically intended for children under the age of four—generally, the products' labels cannot declare the percent of daily value of nutritional components. Would this requirement be readily understood by a consumer who is not familiar with nutritional standards? Why or why not? Should a state court impose such regulations? Explain. [*Cohen v. McDonald's Corp.,* 347 Ill.App.3d 627, 808 N.E.2d 1, 283 Ill.Dec. 451 (1 Dist. 2004)] (See *Labeling and Packaging*.)

20–4. **Debt Collection.** 55th Management Corp. in New York City owns residential property that it leases to various tenants. In June 2000, claiming that one of the tenants, Leslie Goldman, owed more than $13,000 in back rent, 55th retained Jeffrey Cohen, an attorney, to initiate nonpayment proceedings. Cohen filed a petition in a New York state court against Goldman, seeking recovery of the unpaid rent and at least $3,000 in attorneys' fees. After receiving notice of the petition, Goldman filed a suit in a federal district court against Cohen. Goldman contended that the notice of the petition constituted an initial contact that, under the Fair Debt Collection Practices Act (FDCPA), required a validation notice. Because Cohen did not give Goldman a validation notice at the time or within five days of the notice of the petition, Goldman argued that Cohen was in violation of the FDCPA. Should the filing of a suit in a state court be considered "communication," requiring a debt collector to provide a validation notice under the FDCPA? Why or why not? [*Goldman v. Cohen,* 445 F.3d 152 (2d Cir. 2006)] (See *Credit Protection*.)

20–5. **Food Labeling.** The Nutrition Labeling and Education Act (NLEA) requires packaged food to have a "Nutrition Facts" panel that sets out "nutrition information," including "the total number of calories" per serving. Before the 2010 health-care reforms enacted provisions on menu labeling (discussed in this chapter), restaurants were exempt from this requirement. The NLEA also regulated nutritional content claims, such as "low sodium," that a purveyor might choose to add to a label. The NLEA permitted a state or city to require restaurants to disclose nutrition information about the food they serve, but expressly preempted state or local attempts to regulate nutritional content claims.

New York City Health Code Section 81.50 requires 10 percent of the restaurants in the city, including McDonald's, Burger King, and KFC, to post calorie content information on their menus. The New York State Restaurant Association (NYSRA) filed a suit in a federal district court, contending that the NLEA preempts Section 81.50. (Under the U.S. Constitution, state or local laws that conflict with federal laws are preempted.) Was the NYSRA correct? Explain. [*New York State Restaurant Association v. New York City Board of Health,* 556 F.3d 114 (2d Cir. 2009)] (See *Labeling and Packaging*.)

20–6. **Deceptive Advertising.** Brian Cleary and Rita Burke filed a suit against cigarette maker Philip Morris USA, Inc., seeking class-action status for a claim of deceptive advertising. Cleary and Burke claimed that "light" cigarettes, such as Marlboro Lights, were advertised as safer than regular cigarettes, even though the health effects are the same. They contended that the tobacco companies concealed the true nature of light cigarettes. Philip Morris correctly claimed that it was authorized by the government to advertise cigarettes, including light cigarettes. Assuming that is true, should the plaintiffs still be able to bring a deceptive advertising claim against the tobacco company? Why or why not? [*Cleary v. Philip Morris USA, Inc.,* 683 F.Supp.2d 730 (N.D.Ill. 2010)] (See *Deceptive Advertising*.)

20–7. **Business Case Problem with Sample Answer— Fair Debt-Collection Practices.** Bank of America hired Atlantic Resource Management, LLC, to collect a debt from Michael E. Engler. Atlantic called Engler's employer and asked his supervisor about the company's policy concerning the execution of warrants. It then told the supervisor that, to stop the process, Engler needed to call Atlantic about "Case Number 37291 NY0969" during the first three hours of his next shift. When Engler's supervisor told him about the call, Engler feared that he might be arrested, and he experienced discomfort, embarrassment, and emotional distress at work. Can Engler recover under the Fair Debt Collection Practices Act? Why or why not? [*Engler v. Atlantic Resource Management, LLC,* 2012 WL 464728 (W.D.N.Y. 2012)] (See *Credit Protection*.)

—For a sample answer to Problem 20–7, go to Appendix E at the end of this text.

20–8. **Deceptive Advertising.** Innovative Marketing, Inc. (IMI), sold "scareware"—computer security software. IMI's Internet ads redirected consumers to sites where they were told that a scan of their computers had detected dangerous files— viruses, spyware, and "illegal" pornography. In fact, no scans were conducted. Kristy Ross, an IMI cofounder and vice president, reviewed and edited the ads, and was aware of the many complaints that consumers had made about them. An individual can be held liable under the Federal Trade Commission Act's prohibition of deceptive acts or practices if the person (1) participated directly in the deceptive practices or had the authority to control them, and (2) had or should have had knowledge of them. Were IMI's ads deceptive? If so, can Ross be held liable? Explain. [*Federal Trade Commission v. Ross, Inc.,* 743 F.3d 886 (4th Cir. 2014)] (See *Deceptive Advertising.*)

20–9. 💡 **Critical-Thinking Legal Environment Question.** Many states have enacted laws that go even further than federal law to protect consumers. These laws vary tremendously from state to state. Generally, is having different laws fair to sellers who may be prohibited from engaging in a practice in one state that is legal in another? How might these different laws affect a business? Is it fair that residents of one state have more protection than residents of another?

20–10. ↔ **A Question of Ethics—Fair Debt-Collection Practices.** Barry Sussman graduated from law school, but also served time in prison for attempting to collect debts by posing as an FBI agent. He theorized that if a debt-collection business collected only debts that it owned as a result of buying checks written on accounts with insufficient funds (NSF checks), it would not be subject to the Federal Debt Collection Practices Act (FDCPA). Sussman formed Check Investors, Inc., to act on his theory. Check Investors bought more than 2.2 million NSF checks, with an estimated face value of about $348 million, for pennies on the dollar. Check Investors added a fee of $125 or $130 (more than the legal limit in most states) to the face amount of each check and aggressively pursued its drawer to collect. The firm's employees were told to accuse drawers of being criminals and to threaten them with arrest and prosecution. The threats were false. Check Investors never took steps to initiate a prosecution. The employees contacted the drawers' family members and used "saturation phoning"—phoning a drawer numerous times in a short period. They used abusive language, referring to drawers as "deadbeats," "retards," "thieves," and "idiots." Between January 2000 and January 2003, Check Investors netted more than $10.2 million from its efforts. [*Federal Trade Commission v. Check Investors, Inc.,* 502 F.3d 159 (3d Cir. 2007)] (See *Credit Protection.*)

1. The Federal Trade Commission filed a suit in a federal district court against Check Investors and others, alleging, in part, violations of the FDCPA. Was Check Investors a "debt collector," collecting "debts," within the meaning of the FDCPA? If so, did its methods violate the FDCPA? Were its practices unethical? What might Check Investors argue in its defense? Discuss.

2. Are "deadbeats" the primary beneficiaries of laws such as the FDCPA? If not, how would you characterize debtors who default on their obligations?

CHAPTER 21

Environmental Law

(AVT/iStockphoto.com)

CONTENTS

- Common Law Actions
- Government Regulation
- Air Pollution
- Water Pollution
- Toxic Chemicals
- Hazardous Wastes

LEARNING OBJECTIVES

The five learning objectives below are designed to help improve your understanding of the chapter. After reading this chapter, you should be able to answer the following questions:

1. Under what common law theories can polluters be held liable?
2. What is contained in an environmental impact statement, and who must file one?
3. What federal statute regulates air pollution?
4. What are three main goals of the Clean Water Act?
5. What is Superfund? What categories of persons are liable under Superfund?

"Man, however, much he may like to pretend the contrary, is part of nature."

—Rachel Carson, 1907–1964 (American writer and conservationist)

As the chapter-opening quotation observes, we are all "part of nature." Concern over the degradation of the environment has increased over time in response to the environmental effects of population growth, urbanization, and industrialization. Environmental protection is not without a price, however. For many businesses, the costs of complying with environmental regulations are high, and for some they may seem too high. A constant tension exists between the desirability of increasing profits and productivity and the need to protect the environment.

To a great extent, environmental law consists of statutes passed by federal, state, or local governments and regulations issued by administrative agencies. Before examining statutory and regulatory environmental laws, however, we look at the remedies against environmental pollution that are available under the common law.

Learning Objective 1
Under what common law theories
can polluters be held liable?

Common Law Actions

Common law remedies against environmental pollution originated centuries ago in England. Those responsible for operations that created dirt, smoke, noxious odors, noise, or toxic substances were sometimes held liable under common law theories of nuisance or negligence. Today, injured individuals continue to rely on the common law to obtain damages and injunctions against business polluters.

Nuisance

Nuisance A common law doctrine under which persons may be held liable for using their property in a manner that unreasonably interferes with others' rights to use or enjoy their own property.

Under the common law doctrine of **nuisance,** persons may be held liable if they use their property in a manner that unreasonably interferes with others' rights to use or enjoy their own property. In these situations, the courts commonly balance the harm caused by the pollution against the costs of stopping it.

Courts have often denied injunctive relief on the ground that the hardships that would be imposed on the polluter and on the community are relatively greater than the hardships suffered by the plaintiff. **EXAMPLE 21.1**   Hewitt's Factory causes neighboring landowners to suffer from smoke, soot, and vibrations. The factory, however, may be left in operation if it is the core of the local economy. The injured parties may be awarded only monetary damages, which may include compensation for the decrease in the value of their property caused by Hewitt's operation. ●

To obtain relief from pollution under the nuisance doctrine, a property owner may have to identify a distinct harm separate from that affecting the general public. This harm is referred to as a "private" nuisance. Under the common law, individuals were denied *standing* (access to the courts—see Chapter 3) unless they suffered a harm distinct from the harm suffered by the public at large. Some states still require this. A public authority (such as a state's attorney general), though, can sue to abate a "public" nuisance.

Negligence and Strict Liability

An injured party may sue a business polluter in tort under the negligence and strict liability theories discussed in Chapter 5. The basis for a negligence action is the business's failure to use reasonable care toward the party whose injury was foreseeable and caused by the lack of reasonable care. For instance, employees might sue an employer whose failure to use proper pollution controls contaminated the air and caused the employees to suffer respiratory illnesses. Lawsuits for personal injuries caused by exposure to a toxic substance, such as asbestos, radiation, or hazardous waste, have given rise to a growing body of tort law known as **toxic torts.**

Toxic Tort A civil wrong arising from exposure to a toxic substance, such as asbestos, radiation, or hazardous waste.

Businesses that engage in ultrahazardous activities—such as the transportation of radioactive materials—are strictly liable for any injuries the activities cause. In a strict liability action, the injured party does not need to prove that the business failed to exercise reasonable care.

Government Regulation

All levels of government in the United States regulate some aspect of the environment. In this section, we look at some of the ways in which the federal, state, and local governments control business activities and land use in the interests of environmental preservation and protection.

State and Local Regulations

In addition to the federal regulations to be discussed shortly, many states have enacted laws to protect the environment. State laws may restrict a business's discharge of chemicals into the air or water, or regulate its disposal of toxic wastes. States may also regulate the disposal or recycling of other wastes, including glass, metal, plastic containers, and paper. Additionally, states may restrict emissions from motor vehicles.

City, county, and other local governments also regulate some aspects of the environment. For instance, local zoning laws may be designed to inhibit or regulate the growth of cities and suburbs or to protect the natural environment. In the interest of safeguarding the environment, such laws may prohibit certain land uses.

Even when zoning laws permit a business's proposed development, the plans may have to be altered to lessen the development's impact on the environment. In addition, cities and counties may impose rules regulating methods of waste removal, the appearance of buildings, the maximum noise level, and other aspects of the local environment.

State and local regulatory agencies also play a significant role in implementing federal environmental legislation. Typically, the federal government relies on state and local governments to enforce federal environmental statutes and regulations such as those regulating air quality.

Federal Regulations

Congress has passed a number of statutes to control the impact of human activities on the environment. Exhibit 21–1 that follows lists and summarizes the major federal environmental statutes discussed in this chapter. Most of these statutes are designed to address pollution in the air, water, or land. Some specifically regulate toxic chemicals, including pesticides, herbicides, and hazardous wastes.

Environmental Regulatory Agencies
The primary federal agency regulating environmental law is the Environmental Protection Agency (EPA), which was created in 1970 to coordinate federal environmental responsibilities. Other federal agencies with authority for regulating specific environmental matters include the Department of the Interior, the Department of Defense, the Department of Labor, the Food and Drug Administration, and the Nuclear Regulatory Commission. All federal agencies must take environmental factors into consideration when making significant decisions. In addition, as mentioned, state and local agencies play an important role in enforcing federal environmental legislation.

Most federal environmental laws provide that citizens can sue to enforce environmental regulations if government agencies fail to do so—or to limit enforcement actions if agencies go too far in their actions. Typically, a threshold hurdle in such suits is meeting the requirements for standing to sue.

Environmental Impact Statements
The National Environmental Policy Act[1] requires that an **environmental impact statement (EIS)** be prepared for every major federal action that significantly affects the quality of the environment. An EIS must analyze the following:

1. The impact on the environment that the action will have.
2. Any adverse effects on the environment and alternative actions that might be taken.
3. Any irreversible effects the action might generate.

An action qualifies as "major" if it involves a substantial commitment of resources (monetary or otherwise). An action is "federal" if a federal agency has the power to control it. **EXAMPLE 21.2** Development of a ski resort by a private developer on federal land may require an EIS. Construction or operation of a nuclear plant, which requires a federal permit, or creation of a dam as part of a federal project requires an EIS. ●

Environmental Impact Statement (EIS)
A formal analysis required for any major federal action that will significantly affect the quality of the environment to determine the action's impact and explore alternatives.

Learning Objective 2
What is contained in an environmental impact statement, and who must file one?

---

1. 42 U.S.C. Sections 4321–4370d.

Exhibit 21–1 Major Federal Environmental Statutes

POPULAR NAME	PURPOSE	STATUTE REFERENCE
Rivers and Harbors Appropriations Act	To prohibit ships and manufacturers from discharging and depositing refuse in navigable waterways.	33 U.S.C. Sections 401–418.
Federal Insecticide, Fungicide, and Rodenticide Act	To control the use of pesticides and herbicides.	7 U.S.C. Sections 136–136y.
Federal Water Pollution Control Act	To eliminate the discharge of pollutants from major sources into navigable waters.	33 U.S.C. Sections 1251–1387.
Clean Air Act	To control air pollution from mobile and stationary sources.	42 U.S.C. Sections 7401–7671q.
National Environmental Policy Act	To limit environmental harm from federal government activities.	42 U.S.C. Sections 4321–4370d.
Ocean Dumping Act	To prohibit the dumping of radiological, chemical, and biological warfare agents and high-level radioactive waste into the ocean.	16 U.S.C. Sections 1401–1445.
Endangered Species Act	To protect species that are threatened with extinction.	16 U.S.C. Sections 1531–1544.
Safe Drinking Water Act	To regulate pollutants in public drinking water systems.	42 U.S.C. Sections 300f–300j-25.
Resource Conservation and Recovery Act	To establish standards for hazardous waste disposal.	42 U.S.C. Sections 6901–6986.
Toxic Substances Control Act	To regulate toxic chemicals and chemical compounds.	15 U.S.C. Sections 2601–2692.
Superfund	To regulate the clean-up of hazardous waste—disposal sites.	42 U.S.C. Sections 9601–9675.
Oil Pollution Act	To establish liability for the clean-up of navigable waters after oil spills.	33 U.S.C. Sections 2701–2761.
Small Business Liability Relief and Brownfields Revitalization Act	To allow developers who comply with state voluntary clean-up programs to avoid federal liability for the properties that they decontaminate and develop.	42 U.S.C. Section 9628.

If an agency decides that an EIS is unnecessary, it must issue a statement supporting this conclusion. Private individuals, consumer interest groups, businesses, and others who believe that a federal agency's activities threaten the environment often use EISs as a means to challenge those activities.

What law governs discharge of pollutants into water?

(Wonderisland/Shutterstock.com)

Air Pollution

Federal involvement with air pollution goes back to the 1950s and 1960s, when Congress authorized funds for air-pollution research and enacted the Clean Air Act.[2] The Clean Air Act, as amended, provides the basis for issuing regulations to control multistate air pollution. It covers both mobile sources (such as automobiles and other vehicles) and stationary sources (such as electric utilities and industrial plants) of pollution.

Mobile Sources

Regulations governing air pollution from automobiles and other mobile sources specify pollution standards and establish time schedules for meeting the standards. The EPA periodically updates the pollution standards in light of new developments and data, usually reducing the amount of emissions allowed.

---

2. 42 U.S.C. Sections 7401–7671q.

Reducing Emissions over the Long Term   The Obama administration announced a long-term goal of reducing emissions of nitrogen oxide and other pollutants, including those from automobiles, by 80 percent by 2050. In 2010, the administration ordered the EPA to develop national standards regulating fuel economy and emissions for medium- and heavy-duty trucks, starting with 2014 models.

Greenhouse Gases   A growing concern is that greenhouse gases, such as carbon dioxide (CO_2), may contribute to global warming. The Clean Air Act, as amended, however, does not specifically mention CO_2 emissions. Therefore, until 2009, the EPA did not regulate CO_2 emissions from motor vehicles.   **CASE EXAMPLE 21.3**   Environmental groups and several states sued the EPA in an effort to force the agency to regulate CO_2 emissions. When the case reached the United States Supreme Court, the EPA argued that the plaintiffs lacked *standing*. The agency claimed that because global warming has widespread effects, an individual plaintiff could not show the particularized harm required for standing. The agency also maintained that it did not have authority under the Clean Air Act to address global climate change and regulate CO_2.

The Court, however, ruled that Massachusetts had standing because its coastline, including state-owned lands, faced a threat from rising sea levels potentially caused by global warming. The Court also held that the Clean Air Act's broad definition of air pollutant gives the EPA authority to regulate CO_2 and requires the EPA to regulate any air pollutants that might "endanger public health or welfare." Accordingly, the Court ordered the EPA to determine whether CO_2 was a pollutant that endangered the public health.[3] • The EPA later concluded that greenhouse gases, including CO_2 emissions, do constitute a public danger.

Learning Objective 3
What federal statute regulates air pollution?

> "There's so much pollution in the air now that if it weren't for our lungs, there'd be no place to put it all."
>
> Robert Orben, 1927–present
> (American comedian)

Stationary Sources

The Clean Air Act authorizes the EPA to establish air-quality standards for stationary sources (such as manufacturing plants) but recognizes that the primary responsibility for preventing and controlling air pollution rests with state and local governments.

The EPA sets primary and secondary levels of ambient standards— that is, the maximum permissible levels of certain pollutants—and the states formulate plans to achieve those standards. Different standards apply depending on whether the sources of pollution are located in clean areas or polluted areas and whether they are existing sources or major new sources.

Hazardous Air Pollutants   The EPA standards are aimed at controlling hazardous air pollutants—those likely to cause death or serious irreversible or incapacitating illness, such as cancer, or neurological and reproductive damage. The Clean Air Act requires the EPA to list all regulated hazardous air pollutants on a prioritized schedule. In all, nearly two hundred substances, including asbestos, benzene, beryllium, cadmium, and vinyl chloride, have been classified as hazardous. They are emitted from stationary sources by a variety of business activities, including smelting (melting ore to produce metal), dry cleaning, house painting, and commercial baking.

Maximum Achievable Control Technology   Instead of establishing specific emissions standards for each hazardous air pollutant, the Clean Air Act requires major sources of pollutants to use pollution-control equipment that represents the *maximum achievable control technology,* or MACT, to reduce emissions. The EPA issues guidelines as to what equipment meets this standard.[4]

Why are stationary sources of air pollution regulated differently than mobile sources?

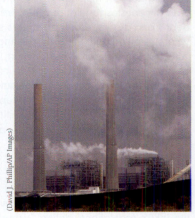

(David J. Phillip/AP Images)

---

3. *Massachusetts v. EPA,* 549 U.S. 497, 127 S.Ct. 1438, 167 L.Ed.2d 248 (2007).
4. The EPA has also issued rules to regulate hazardous air pollutants emitted by landfills. See 40 C.F.R. Sections 60.750–60.759.

Violations of the Clean Air Act

For violations of emission limits under the Clean Air Act, the EPA can assess civil penalties of up to $25,000 per day. Additional fines of up to $5,000 per day can be assessed for other violations, such as failing to maintain the required records. To penalize those who find it more cost-effective to violate the act than to comply with it, the EPA is authorized to obtain a penalty equal to the violator's economic benefits from noncompliance. Persons who provide information about violators may be paid up to $10,000. Private individuals can also sue violators.

Those who knowingly violate the act may be subject to criminal penalties, including fines of up to $1 million and imprisonment for up to two years (for false statements or failures to report violations). Corporate officers are among those who may be subject to these penalties. The phrase "knowingly violate" was at the center of the dispute in an individual's appeal of his conviction for violations of the Clean Air Act.

Case 21.1

United States v. O'Malley
United States Court of Appeals, Seventh Circuit, 739 F.3d 1001 (2014).

(Heather Faye Bath/Getty Images)

Is a license required for asbestos removal?

BACKGROUND AND FACTS Duane O'Malley owned and operated Origin Fire Protection. Michael Pinski hired Origin to remove and dispose of 2,200 feet of insulation from a building Pinski owned in Kankakee, Illinois. The insulation contained asbestos, which Pinski, O'Malley, and O'Malley's employees recognized. O'Malley did not have a license to remove asbestos, and none of his employees were trained in complying with federal asbestos regulations. Nevertheless, Origin removed the debris and disposed of it at various sites, including a vacant lot where it spilled onto the soil, resulting in cleanup costs of nearly $50,000. In a federal district court, a jury convicted O'Malley of removing, transporting, and dumping asbestos in violation of the Clean Air Act. The court sentenced him to 120 months of imprisonment, three years of supervised release, a fine of $15,000, and $47,085.70 in restitution to the Environmental Protection Agency (EPA). O'Malley appealed.

IN THE WORDS OF THE COURT . . .
TINDER, Circuit Judge.
* * * *

On appeal to this court, O'Malley * * * claims that because the [EPA's regulations] define "asbestos-containing material" as only six types of regulated asbestos, the government was required to prove that O'Malley knew that the asbestos in the building was one of the six forms of regulated asbestos. He asserts that the government did not present evidence to demonstrate O'Malley's knowledge of the type of asbestos in the building.
* * * *

O'Malley is correct that not all forms of asbestos are subject to regulation. The Clean Air Act [under Section 7412] authorizes

the regulation of hazardous air pollutants, one of which is asbestos. "Because asbestos is not typically emitted through a conveyance designed and constructed to emit or capture it, such as a pipe or smokestack, but rather escapes from more diffuse sources such as open construction or demolition sites, EPA adopted a work-practice standard for the handling of asbestos in building demolition and renovation." * * * The work practice standard promulgated for the handling of asbestos applies only to the six types of "regulated asbestos-containing material (RACM)," [which includes "friable asbestos material"]. "Friable asbestos material" is defined as "any material containing more than 1 percent asbestos * * * that, when dry, can be crumbled, pulverized, or reduced to powder by hand pressure." Thus, there is no question that the material in [this case]—which was both friable and contained asbestos at concentrations ranging from four percent to forty-eight percent—was indeed "regulated asbestos-containing material."
* * * *

The Clean Air Act makes it a crime for any person to "knowingly violate any * * * requirement or prohibition of * * * Section 7412, * * * including a requirement of any rule" promulgated under Section 7412. * * * The district court instructed the jury on the knowledge elements as follows: "The government must prove * * * the defendant knew that asbestos-containing material was in the building." [Emphasis added.]

O'Malley argues that the knowledge element instruction should have required the government to prove that the defendant knew that regulated asbestos-containing material, not simply asbestos-containing material, was in the building. But this cannot be correct. * * * The phrase "knowingly violates" does

Case 21.1—Continued

not "carv[e] out an exception to the general rule that ignorance of the law is no excuse." The *mens rea* [criminal intent] required by the phrase is one that is higher than strict liability * * * . But it is certainly much lower than specific intent, especially when, as here, "dangerous * * * materials are involved," because "the probability of regulation is so great that anyone who is aware that he is in possession of them or dealing with them must be presumed to be aware of the regulation." The very fact that O'Malley was knowingly working with asbestos-containing material met the *mens rea* requirement.

DECISION AND REMEDY   The U.S. Court of Appeals for the Seventh Circuit affirmed the lower court's judgment. The appellate court disagreed with O'Malley's claim that the government was required to prove he knew the asbestos was one of the six types of regulated asbestos. "The very fact that O'Malley was knowingly working with asbestos-containing material met the *mens rea* requirement."

WHAT IF THE FACTS WERE DIFFERENT?   *Suppose that O'Malley had been licensed to remove the asbestos. Would the result have been different? Why or why not?*

THE ETHICAL DIMENSION   *How did O'Malley's violation of environmental laws also violate the standards of ethics discussed in Chapter 2?*

Water Pollution

Water pollution stems mostly from industrial, municipal, and agricultural sources. Pollutants entering streams, lakes, and oceans include organic wastes, heated water, sediments from soil runoff, nutrients (including fertilizers and human and animal wastes), and toxic chemicals and other hazardous substances. We look here at laws and regulations governing water pollution.

Federal regulations governing the pollution of water can be traced back to the 1899 Rivers and Harbors Appropriations Act.[5] These regulations prohibited ships and manufacturers from discharging or depositing refuse in navigable waterways without a permit. In 1948, Congress passed the Federal Water Pollution Control Act (FWPCA),[6] but its regulatory system and enforcement powers proved to be inadequate.

The Clean Water Act

In 1972, amendments to the FWPCA—known as the Clean Water Act (CWA)—established the following goals: (1) make waters safe for swimming, (2) protect fish and wildlife, and (3) eliminate the discharge of pollutants into the water. The amendments set specific time schedules, which were extended by amendment and by the Water Quality Act.[7] Under these schedules, the EPA limits the discharge of various types of pollutants based on the technology available for controlling them.

Learning Objective 4
What are three main goals of the Clean Water Act?

Permit System for Point Source Emissions   The CWA established a permit system, called the *National Pollutant Discharge Elimination System (NPDES),* for regulating discharges from "point sources" of pollution. Point sources include industrial, municipal (such as sewer pipes and sewage treatment plants), and agricultural facilities.[8] Under this system, industrial, municipal, and agricultural polluters must apply for permits before discharging wastes into surface waters.

---

5. 33 U.S.C. Sections 401–418.
6. 33 U.S.C. Sections 1251–1387.
7. This act amended 33 U.S.C. Section 1251.
8. 33 U.S.C. Section 1342.

(BW Folson/Shutterstock.com)

Can urban storm-water runoff be discharged into navigable waters?

NPDES permits can be issued by the EPA and authorized state agencies and Indian tribes, but only if the discharge will not violate water-quality standards (both federal and state standards). Special requirements must be met to discharge toxic chemicals and residue from oil spills. NPDES permits must be renewed every five years. Although initially the NPDES system focused mainly on industrial wastewater, it was later expanded to cover storm water discharges.

CASE EXAMPLE 21.4   Two environmental organizations sued the county of Los Angeles and the Los Angeles County Flood Control District for violations of the Clean Water Act. The plaintiffs alleged that the county and the district were discharging urban storm water runoff into navigable waters in violation of the law. The levels of pollutants detected in four rivers—the Santa Clara River, the Los Angeles River, the San Gabriel River, and Malibu Creek—exceeded the limits allowed by the county's NPDES permit. All parties agreed that the rivers did not meet water-quality standards, but the county and district argued that they were not responsible for discharging storm water carrying pollutants into the rivers. Ultimately, a federal appellate court held that the defendants were responsible for the pollution discharged in two of the rivers. Because the district operated a monitoring station on those two rivers, it was aware that the excessive pollution violated CWA standards, and that was sufficient to impose liability.[9] ●

Standards for Equipment   Regulations generally specify that the *best available control technology,* or BACT, be installed. The EPA issues guidelines as to what equipment meets this standard. Essentially, the guidelines require the most effective pollution-control equipment available.

New sources must install BACT equipment before beginning operations. Existing sources are subject to timetables for the installation of BACT equipment and must immediately install equipment that utilizes the *best practical control technology,* or BPCT. The EPA also issues guidelines as to what equipment meets this standard.

The EPA must take into account many factors when issuing and updating its rules. Some provisions of the CWA instruct the EPA to weigh the cost of the technology required relative to the benefits achieved. The provision that covers power plants, however, neither requires nor prohibits a cost-benefit analysis. The question in the following case was whether the EPA could base its decision on such an analysis anyway.

---

9. *Natural Resources Defense Council, Inc. v. County of Los Angeles,* 673 F.3d 880 (9th Cir. 2011).

Entergy Corp. v. Riverkeeper, Inc.

Supreme Court of the United States, 556 U.S. 208, 129 S.Ct. 1498, 173 L.Ed.2d 369 (2009).

(Jelle vd Wolf/Shutterstock.com)

BACKGROUND AND FACTS   As part of its implementation of the Clean Water Act, the Environmental Protection Agency (EPA) has developed two sets of rules that apply to the cooling systems of power plants. Phase I rules require new power plants to restrict their inflow of water "to a level commensurate with that which can be attained by a closed-cycle recirculating cooling water system." Phase II rules apply "national performance standards" to more than five hundred existing plants but do not require closed-cycle cooling systems. The EPA found that converting these facilities to closed-cycle operations would cost $3.5 billion per year. The facilities would then produce less power while burning the same amount of coal. Moreover, other

Case 21.2—Continued

technologies can attain nearly the same results as closed-cycle systems. Phase II rules also allow a variance from the national performance standards if a facility's cost of compliance "would be significantly greater than the benefits." Environmental organizations, including Riverkeeper, Inc., challenged the Phase II regulations, arguing that existing plants should be required to convert to closed-cycle systems. The U.S. Court of Appeals for the Second Circuit issued a ruling in the plaintiffs' favor. Power-generating companies, including Entergy Corporation, appealed to the United States Supreme Court.

IN THE WORDS OF THE COURT . . .
Justice *SCALIA* delivered the opinion of the Court.
 * * * *

In setting the Phase II national performance standards and providing for site-specific cost-benefit variances, the EPA relied on its view that [the] "best technology available" standard permits consideration of the technology's costs and of the relationship between those costs and the environmental benefits produced.

* * * The "best" technology—that which is "most advantageous"—may well be the one that produces the most of some good, here a reduction in adverse environmental impact. But "best technology" may also describe the technology that most efficiently produces some good. *In common parlance one could certainly use the phrase "best technology" to refer to that which produces a good at the lowest per-unit cost, even if it produces a lesser quantity of that good than other available technologies.* [Emphasis added.]

* * * This latter reading is [not] precluded by the statute's use of the phrase "for minimizing adverse environmental impact." *Minimizing * * * is a term that admits of degree and is not necessarily used to refer exclusively to the "greatest possible reduction."* [Emphasis added.]

Other provisions in the Clean Water Act also suggest the agency's interpretation. When Congress wished to mandate the greatest feasible reduction in water pollution, it did so in plain language: The provision governing the discharge of toxic pollutants into the Nation's waters requires the EPA to set "effluent limitations which shall require the elimination of discharges of all pollutants * * * ." The less ambitious goal of "minimizing adverse environmental impact" suggests, we think, that the agency retains some discretion to determine the extent of reduction that is warranted under the circumstances. That determination could plausibly involve a consideration of the benefits derived from reductions and the costs of achieving them.

* * * [Under other Clean Water Act provisions that impose standards on sources of pollution,] the EPA is instructed to consider, among other factors, "the total cost of application of technology in relation to the * * * benefits to be achieved."
 * * * *

This * * * comparison of * * * statutory factors * * * leads us to the conclusion that it was well within the bounds of reasonable interpretation for the EPA to conclude that cost-benefit analysis is not categorically forbidden.
 * * * *

While not conclusive, it surely tends to show that the EPA's current practice is a reasonable and hence legitimate exercise of its discretion to weigh benefits against costs that the agency has been proceeding in essentially this fashion for over 30 years.

DECISION AND REMEDY The United States Supreme Court concluded that the EPA permissibly relied on a cost-benefit analysis to set national performance standards and to allow for variances from those standards as part of the Phase II regulations. The Court reversed the lower court's judgment and remanded the case.

THE ETHICAL DIMENSION *In this case, aquatic organisms were most directly at risk. Is it acceptable to apply cost-benefit analyses to situations in which the lives of people are directly affected? Explain.*

THE GLOBAL DIMENSION *In analyzing the costs and benefits of an action that affects the environment, should a line be drawn at a nation's borders? Why or why not?*

Wetlands

The CWA prohibits the filling or dredging of **wetlands** unless a permit is obtained from the Army Corps of Engineers. The EPA defines *wetlands* as "those areas that are inundated or saturated by surface or ground water at a frequency and duration sufficient to support . . . vegetation typically adapted for life in saturated soil conditions."

Wetlands are thought to be vital to the ecosystem because they filter streams and rivers and provide habitat for wildlife. In the past, the EPA's broad interpretation of what constitutes a wetland generated substantial controversy, but the courts have considerably scaled back the CWA's protection of wetlands in recent years.

Wetlands Water-saturated, protected areas of land that support wildlife and cannot be filled in or dredged without a permit.

"Among the treasures of our land is water—fast becoming our most valuable, most prized, most critical resource."

Dwight D. Eisenhower,
1890–1969
(Thirty-fourth president of the United States, 1953–1961)

Violations of the Clean Water Act

Under the CWA, violators are subject to a variety of civil and criminal penalties. Depending on the violation, civil penalties range from $10,000 per day to $25,000 per day, but not more than $25,000 per violation. Criminal penalties, which apply only if a violation was intentional, range from a fine of $2,500 per day and imprisonment for up to one year to a fine of $1 million and fifteen years' imprisonment. Injunctive relief and damages can also be imposed. The polluting party can be required to clean up the pollution or pay for the cost of doing so.

In the following case, landowners filed a lawsuit challenging an EPA order finding that they had violated the CWA. The United States Supreme Court had to decide whether the federal courts could review the EPA's decision.

Case 21.3

Sackett v. Environmental Protection Agency
Supreme Court of the United States, ____ U.S. ____, 132 S.Ct. 1367, 182 L.Ed.2d 367 (2012).

(W. Britten/iStockphoto.com)

BACKGROUND AND FACTS To build a home in Idaho, Michael and Chantell Sackett filled part of their residential lot with dirt and rock. A few months later, they received a compliance order from the Environmental Protection Agency (EPA). The order asserted that, because their property was near a major lake, the Sacketts had polluted wetlands in violation of the Clean Water Act. The order required the Sacketts to restore their property immediately, and they faced heavy fines of $75,000 a day. The Sacketts requested a hearing with the EPA. When a hearing was denied, they sued the EPA in federal district court, asserting, among other things, that the compliance order was "arbitrary and capricious" under the Administrative Procedure Act (APA). The district court found that it could not review the EPA's compliance order. On appeal, a federal appellate court affirmed, concluding that the Sacketts had to wait for the EPA to bring an enforcement action against them. The United States Supreme Court granted *certiorari* to resolve the matter.

IN THE WORDS OF THE COURT . . .
Justice *SCALIA* delivered the opinion of the Court.
    * * * *
    * * * The APA * * * provides for judicial review of "final agency action for which there is no other adequate remedy in a court." We consider first whether the compliance order is final agency action. There is no doubt it is agency action, which the APA defines as including even a "failure to act." But is it *final*? It has all of the hallmarks of APA finality that our opinions establish. Through the order, the EPA " 'determined' " " 'rights or obligations.' " By reason of the order, the Sacketts have the legal obligation to "restore" their property according to an agency-approved Restoration Work Plan, and must give the EPA access

to their property and to "records and documentation related to the conditions at the Site." Also, " 'legal consequences . . . flow' " from issuance of the order. * * * The order exposes the Sacketts to double penalties in a future enforcement proceeding.

    The issuance of the compliance order also marks the " 'consummation' " of the agency's decision-making process. As the Sacketts learned when they unsuccessfully sought a hearing, * * * [the] compliance order * * * [was] not subject to further agency review. * * *

    The APA's judicial review provision also requires that the person seeking APA review of final agency action have "no other adequate remedy in a court[.]" In Clean Water Act enforcement cases, judicial review ordinarily comes by way of a civil action brought by the EPA * * * . But the Sacketts cannot initiate that process, and each day they wait for the agency to drop the hammer, they accrue * * * an additional $75,000 in potential liability.
        * * * *

    * * * Compliance orders * * * can obtain quick remediation through voluntary compliance. The Government warns that the EPA is less likely to use the orders if they are subject to judicial review. That may be true—but it will be true for all agency actions subjected to judicial review. * * * *There is no reason to think that the Clean Water Act was uniquely designed to enable the strong-arming of regulated parties into "voluntary compliance" without the opportunity for judicial review* * * * . Compliance orders will remain an effective means of securing prompt voluntary compliance in those many cases where there is no substantial basis to question their validity. [Emphasis added.]

Case 21.3—Continued

DECISION AND REMEDY The United States Supreme Court held that the Sacketts could challenge the EPA's compliance order in federal court. The Court reversed the judgment of the federal appellate court.

THE LEGAL ENVIRONMENT DIMENSION *What does the Court's decision in this case mean for people and businesses that face compliance orders? Are they more or less likely to acquiesce to orders they find objectionable? Why?*

THE ENVIRONMENTAL DIMENSION *Is it appropriate to impose significant fines on citizens when they violate environmental laws? Discuss.*

Drinking Water

The Safe Drinking Water Act[10] requires the EPA to set maximum levels for pollutants in public water systems. Public water system operators must come as close as possible to meeting the EPA's standards by using the best available technology that is economically and technologically feasible.

Under the act, each supplier of drinking water is required to send every household that it supplies with water an annual statement describing the source of its water. Suppliers must also disclose the level of any contaminants contained in the water and any possible health concerns associated with the contaminants.

The EPA is particularly concerned about contamination from underground sources, such as pesticides and wastes leaked from landfills or disposed of in underground injection wells. Many of these substances are associated with cancer and may cause damage to the central nervous system, liver, and kidneys. Although some evidence suggests that trace amounts of pharmaceuticals may be entering the nation's drinking water, the law does not yet require suppliers to test for or report these substances. The drugs come from prescription medications taken by humans and antibiotics and other medications given to livestock.

Oil Pollution

When more than 10 million gallons of oil leaked into Alaska's Prince William Sound from the *Exxon Valdez* supertanker in 1989, Congress responded by passing the Oil Pollution Act.[11] (At that time, the *Exxon Valdez* disaster was the worst oil spill in U.S. history, but the British Petroleum oil spill in the Gulf of Mexico in 2010 surpassed it.) Under this act, any onshore or offshore oil facility, oil shipper, vessel owner, or vessel operator that discharges oil into navigable waters or onto an adjoining shore can be liable for clean-up costs and damages.

Toxic Chemicals

Today, the control of toxic chemicals used in agriculture and in industry has become increasingly important.

---

10. 42 U.S.C. Sections 300f to 300j-25.
11. 33 U.S.C. Sections 2701–2761.

Pesticides and Herbicides

Under the Federal Insecticide, Fungicide, and Rodenticide Act (FIFRA),[12] pesticides and herbicides must be (1) registered before they can be sold, (2) certified and used only for approved applications, and (3) used in limited quantities when applied to food crops.

The EPA can cancel or suspend registration of substances that are identified as harmful and may also inspect factories where the chemicals are made. There must be no more than a one-in-a-million risk to people of developing cancer from any kind of exposure to the substance, including eating food that contains pesticide residues.[13]

It is a violation of FIFRA to sell a pesticide or herbicide that is unregistered or has had its registration canceled or suspended. It is also a violation to sell a pesticide or herbicide with a false or misleading label or to destroy or deface any labeling required under the act. Penalties for commercial dealers include imprisonment for up to one year and a fine of up to $25,000. Farmers and other private users of pesticides or herbicides who violate the act are subject to a $1,000 fine and incarceration for up to thirty days.

Note that a state can also regulate the sale and use of federally registered pesticides. **CASE EXAMPLE 21.5**   The EPA conditionally registered Strongarm, a weed-killing pesticide, in 2000. Dow Agrosciences, LLC, immediately sold Strongarm to Texas peanut farmers. When the farmers applied it, however, Strongarm damaged their crops while failing to control the growth of weeds. The farmers sued Dow, but the lower courts ruled that FIFRA preempted their claims. The farmers appealed to the United States Supreme Court. The Supreme Court held that under a specific provision of FIFRA, a state can regulate the sale and use of federally registered pesticides so long as the regulation does not permit anything that FIFRA prohibits.[14] •

Toxic Substances

The Toxic Substances Control Act[15] was passed to regulate chemicals and chemical compounds that are known to be toxic and to institute investigation of any possible harmful effects from new chemical compounds. The act applies to compounds such as asbestos and polychlorinated biphenyls, popularly known as PCBs.

The regulations authorize the EPA to require that manufacturers, processors, and other organizations planning to use chemicals first determine their effects on human health and the environment. The EPA can regulate substances that potentially pose an imminent hazard or an unreasonable risk of injury to health or the environment. The EPA may require special labeling, limit the use of a substance, set production quotas, or prohibit the use of a substance altogether.

Hazardous Wastes

Some industrial, agricultural, and household wastes pose more serious threats than others. If not properly disposed of, these toxic chemicals may present a substantial danger to human health and the environment. If released into the environment, they may contaminate public drinking water resources.

---

12. *7 U.S.C. Sections 135–136y.*
13. 21 U.S.C. Section 346a.
14. *Bates v. Dow Agrosciences, LLC,* 544 U.S. 431, 125 S.Ct. 1788, 161 L.Ed.2d 687 (2005).
15. 15 U.S.C. Sections 2601–2692.

Resource Conservation and Recovery Act

Congress passed the Resource Conservation and Recovery Act (RCRA)[16] in reaction to concern over the effects of hazardous waste materials on the environment. The RCRA required the EPA to determine which forms of solid waste should be considered hazardous and to establish regulations to monitor and control hazardous waste disposal.

The act also requires all producers of hazardous waste materials to label and package properly any hazardous waste to be transported. Amendments to the RCRA decrease the use of land containment in the disposal of hazardous waste and require smaller generators of hazardous waste to comply with the act.

Under the RCRA, a company may be assessed a civil penalty of up to $25,000 for each violation. Penalties are based on the seriousness of the violation, the probability of harm, and the extent to which the violation deviates from RCRA requirements. Criminal penalties include fines of up to $50,000 for each day of violation, imprisonment for up to two years (in most instances), or both.[17] Criminal fines and the period of imprisonment can be doubled for certain repeat offenders.

Who must pay for the cleanup of leaking hazardous waste?

Superfund

Congress passed the Comprehensive Environmental Response, Compensation, and Liability Act (CERCLA),[18] commonly known as Superfund, to regulate the clean-up of leaking hazardous waste–disposal sites. A special federal fund was created for that purpose.

CERCLA, as amended, has four primary elements:

1. It established an information-gathering and analysis system that enables the government to identify chemical dump sites and determine the appropriate action.
2. It authorized the EPA to respond to hazardous substance emergencies and to arrange for the clean-up of a leaking site directly if the persons responsible for the problem fail to clean up the site.
3. It created a Hazardous Substance Response Trust Fund (also called Superfund) to pay for the clean-up of hazardous sites using funds obtained through taxes on certain businesses.
4. It allowed the government to recover the cost of clean-up from the persons who were (even remotely) responsible for hazardous substance releases.

Potentially Responsible Parties Superfund provides that when a release or a threatened release of hazardous chemicals from a site occurs, the EPA can clean up the site and recover the cost of the clean-up from the following persons:

1. The person who generated the wastes disposed of at the site.
2. The person who transported the wastes to the site.
3. The person who owned or operated the site at the time of the disposal.
4. The current owner or operator.

A person falling within one of these categories is referred to as a **potentially responsible party (PRP)**. If the PRPs do not clean up the site, the EPA can clean up the site and recover the clean-up costs from the PRPs.

Learning Objective 5
What is Superfund? What categories of persons are liable under Superfund?

Potentially Responsible Party (PRP)
A party liable for the costs of cleaning up a hazardous waste–disposal site under the Comprehensive Environmental Response, Compensation, and Liability Act.

---

16. 42 U.S.C. Sections 6901 *et seq.*
17. 42 U.S.C. Section 6928(a),(d).
18. 42 U.S.C. Sections 9601–9675.

Superfund imposes strict liability on PRPs, and that liability cannot be avoided through transfer of ownership. Thus, selling a site where hazardous wastes were disposed of does not relieve the seller of liability, and the buyer also becomes liable for the clean-up. Liability also extends to businesses that merge with or buy corporations that have violated CERCLA.

Joint and Several Liability   Liability under Superfund is usually joint and several—that is, a person who generated *only a fraction of the hazardous waste* disposed of at the site may nevertheless be liable for *all* of the clean-up costs. CERCLA authorizes a party who has incurred clean-up costs to bring a "contribution action" against any other person who is liable or potentially liable for a percentage of the costs.

Reviewing . . . Environmental Law

Residents of Lake Caliopa, Minnesota, began noticing an unusually high number of lung ailments among their population. Several concerned local citizens pooled their resources and commissioned a study of the frequency of these health conditions per capita in Lake Caliopa as compared with national averages. The study concluded that residents of Lake Caliopa experienced four to seven times the rate of frequency of asthma, bronchitis, and emphysema as the population nationwide. During the study period, citizens began expressing concerns about the large volumes of smog emitted by the Cotton Design apparel manufacturing plant on the outskirts of town. The plant had opened its production facility two miles east of town beside the Tawakoni River and employed seventy workers.

Just downstream on the Tawakoni River, the city of Lake Caliopa operated a public waterworks facility, which supplied all city residents with water. The Minnesota Pollution Control Agency required Cotton Design to install new equipment to control air and water pollution. Later, citizens brought a lawsuit in a Minnesota state court against Cotton Design for various respiratory ailments allegedly caused or compounded by smog from Cotton Design's factory. Using the information presented in the chapter, answer the following questions.

1. Under the common law, what would each plaintiff be required to identify in order to be given relief by the court?
2. What standard for limiting emissions into the air does Cotton Design's pollution-control equipment have to meet?
3. If Cotton Design's emissions violated the Clean Air Act, how much can the EPA assess in fines per day?
4. What information must the city send to every household that it supplies with water?

Debate This   The courts should reject all cases in which the wetlands in question do not consist of actual bodies of water that exist during the entire year.

Key Terms

environmental impact statement (EIS) 583   potentially responsible party (PRP) 593   toxic tort 582   wetlands 589
nuisance 582

Chapter Summary: Environmental Law

Common Law Actions	1. *Nuisance*—A common law doctrine under which actions against pollution-causing activities may be brought. In some states, an action is permissible only if an individual suffers a harm separate and distinct from that of the general public. 2. *Negligence and strict liability*—Parties may recover damages for injuries sustained as a result of a firm's pollution-causing activities if they can demonstrate that the harm was a foreseeable result of the firm's failure to exercise reasonable care (negligence). Businesses engaging in ultrahazardous activities are liable for whatever injuries the activities cause, regardless of whether the firms exercise reasonable care.

Government Regulations	1. *State and local regulations*—Activities affecting the environment are controlled at the local and state levels through regulations relating to land use, the disposal and recycling of garbage and waste, and pollution-causing activities in general.
	2. *Federal regulations*—
	   a. Environmental protection agencies—The primary agency regulating environmental law is the federal Environmental Protection Agency (EPA), which administers most federal environmental policies and statutes.
	   b. Assessing environmental impact—The National Environmental Policy Act imposes environmental responsibilities on all federal agencies and requires the preparation of an environmental impact statement (EIS) for every major federal action. An EIS must analyze the action's impact on the environment, its adverse effects and possible alternatives, and its irreversible effects on environmental quality.

Air Pollution	1. *Mobile sources*—Automobiles and other vehicles are mobile sources of air pollution, and the EPA establishes pollution-control standards and time schedules for meeting these standards. 2. *Stationary sources*—The Clean Air Act requires the EPA to list all regulated hazardous air pollutants that are emitted from stationary sources on a prioritized schedule. These include substances such as asbestos, mercury, and vinyl chloride that are known to cause harm to humans. Major sources of air pollution are required to use the *maximum achievable control technology* to reduce emissions.
Water Pollution	1. *Clean Water Act*—This act amended an earlier federal law by setting specific time schedules to improve water quality. The act also requires cities and businesses to obtain a permit before discharging waste into navigable waters. The EPA limits discharges of various pollutants based on the technology available for controlling them. 2. *Wetlands*—Certain water-saturated areas are designated wetlands and protected from dredging or filling without a permit. This is intended to provide natural habitat to support wildlife, such as migratory birds. 3. *Drinking water*—Federal law requires the EPA to set maximum levels for pollutants in public water systems and requires public systems to use the best available technology to prevent contamination from underground sources. Each supplier of public water must send to every household it supplies with water an annual statement describing the water's source, the level of any contaminants, and any possible health concerns associated with these contaminants. 4. *Oil pollution*—Federal law provides that any offshore or onshore oil facility, oil shipper, vessel owner, or vessel operator that discharges oil into navigable waters or onto a shoreline is liable for clean-up costs and damages.
Toxic Chemicals	The federal government regulates the pesticides and herbicides that can be used in agriculture, as well as the use and transportation of chemical compounds known to be toxic.
Hazardous Wastes	Federal laws regulate the disposal of certain types of industrial, agricultural, and household wastes that present serious dangers to human health and the environment. These hazardous wastes must be properly labeled and packaged before they can be transported. Moreover, under Superfund, when a hazardous substance is released into the environment, the EPA can clean up the site and recover the costs from a broad array of potentially responsible parties.

Issue Spotters

1. Resource Refining Company's plant emits smoke and fumes. Resource's operation includes a short railway system, and trucks enter and exit the grounds continuously. Constant vibrations from the trains and trucks rattle nearby residential neighborhoods. The residents sue Resource. Are there any reasons why the court might refuse to issue an injunction against Resource's operation? Explain. (See *Common Law Actions*.)
2. ChemCorp generates hazardous wastes from its operations. Disposal Trucking Company transports those wastes to Eliminators, Inc., which owns a hazardous waste–disposal site. Eliminators sells the property on which the disposal site

is located to Fluid Properties, Inc. If the Environmental Protection Agency cleans up the site, from whom can it recover the cost? (See *Hazardous Wastes*.)

—**Check your answers to the Issue Spotters against the answers provided in Appendix D at the end of this text.**

For Review

1. Under what common law theories can polluters be held liable?
2. What is contained in an environmental impact statement, and who must file one?
3. What federal statute regulates air pollution?
4. What are three main goals of the Clean Water Act?
5. What is Superfund? What categories of persons are liable under Superfund?

Business Scenarios and Case Problems

21–1. Clean Air Act. Current scientific knowledge indicates that there is no safe level of exposure to a cancer-causing agent. In theory, even one molecule of such a substance has the potential for causing cancer. Section 112 of the Clean Air Act requires that all cancer-causing substances be regulated to ensure a margin of safety. Some environmental groups have argued that all emissions of such substances must be eliminated if a margin of safety is to be reached. Such a total elimination would likely shut down many major U.S. industries. Should the Environmental Protection Agency totally eliminate all emissions of cancer-causing chemicals? Discuss. (See *Air Pollution*.)

21–2. Environmental Laws. Fruitade, Inc., is a processor of a soft drink called Freshen Up. Fruitade uses returnable bottles, which it cleans with a special acid to allow for further beverage processing. The acid is diluted with water and then allowed to pass into a navigable stream. Fruitade crushes its broken bottles and throws the crushed glass into the stream. Discuss fully any environmental laws that Fruitade has violated. (See *Water Pollution*.)

21–3. Environmental Laws. Moonbay is a home-building corporation that primarily develops retirement communities. Farmtex owns a number of feedlots in Sunny Valley. Moonbay purchased 20,000 acres of farmland in the same area and began building and selling homes on this acreage. In the meantime, Farmtex continued to expand its feedlot business, and eventually only 500 feet separated the two operations. Because of the odor and flies from the feedlots, Moonbay found it difficult to sell the homes in its development. Moonbay wants to enjoin (prevent) Farmtex from operating its feedlot in the vicinity of the retirement home development. Under what common law theory would Moonbay file this action? Has Farmtex violated any federal environmental laws? Discuss. (See *Common Law Actions*.)

21–4. ⚖ **Business Case Problem with Sample Answer— Environmental Impact Statement.** The U.S. National Park Service (NPS) manages the Grand Canyon

National Park in Arizona under a management plan that is subject to periodic review. In 2006, after nine years of background work and the completion of a comprehensive environmental impact statement, the NPS issued a new management plan for the park. The plan allowed for the continued use of rafts on the Colorado River, which runs through the Grand Canyon. The number of rafts was limited, however. Several environmental groups criticized the plan because they felt that it still allowed too many rafts on the river. The groups asked a federal appellate court to overturn the plan, claiming that it violated the wilderness status of the national park. When can a federal court overturn a determination by an agency such as the NPS? Explain. *[River Runners for Wilderness v. Martin,* 593 F.3d 1064 (9th Cir. 2010)] (See *Government Regulation*.)

—**For a sample answer to Problem 21–4, go to Appendix E at the end of this text.**

21–5. Superfund. A by-product of phosphate fertilizer production is pyrite waste, which contains arsenic and lead. From 1884 to 1906, seven phosphate fertilizer plants operated on a forty-three-acre site in Charleston, South Carolina. Planters Fertilizer & Phosphate Co. bought the site in 1906 and continued to make fertilizer. In 1966, Planters sold the site to Columbia Nitrogen Corp. (CNC), which also operated the fertilizer plants. In 1985, CNC sold the site to James Holcombe and J. Henry Fair. Holcombe and Fair subdivided and sold the site to Allwaste Tank Cleaning Inc., Robin Hood Container Express, the city of Charleston, and Ashley II of Charleston, Inc. Ashley spent almost $200,000 cleaning up the contaminated soil. Who can be held liable for the cost? Why? *[PCS Nitrogen Inc. v. Ashley II of Charleston LLC,* 714 F.3d 161 (4th Cir. 2013)] (See *Hazardous Wastes*.)

21–6. Environmental Impact Statements. The U.S. Forest Service (USFS) proposed a travel management plan (TMP) for the Beartooth Ranger District in the Pryor and Absaroka Mountains in the Custer National Forest of southern

Montana. The TMP would convert unauthorized user-created routes within the wilderness to routes authorized for motor vehicle use and would permit off-road "dispersed vehicle camping" within 300 feet of the routes, with some seasonal restrictions. The TMP would ban cross-country motorized travel outside the designated routes. Is an environmental impact statement required before the USFS implements the TMP? If so, what aspects of the environment should the USFS consider in preparing it? Discuss. [*Pryors Coalition v. Weldon,* __ F.3d __, 2014 WL 46468 (9th Cir. 2014)] (See *Government Regulation.*)

21–7. 💡 **Critical-Thinking Legal Environment Question.** It has been estimated that for every dollar spent cleaning up hazardous waste sites, administrative agencies spend seven dollars in overhead. Can you think of any way to trim these administrative costs? Explain. (See *Hazardous Wastes.*)

21–8. ↔ **A Question of Ethics—Clean Air Act.** In the Clean Air Act, Congress allowed California, which has particular problems with clean air, to adopt its own standard for emissions from cars and trucks. California's standard is subject to the approval of the Environmental Protection Agency (EPA) based on certain criteria. Congress also allowed other states to adopt California's standard after the EPA's approval. In 2004, in an effort to address global warming, the California Air Resources Board amended the state's standard to attain "the maximum feasible and cost-effective reduction of GHG [greenhouse gas] emissions from motor vehicles." The

regulation, which applies to new passenger vehicles and light-duty trucks for 2009 and later, imposes decreasing limits on emissions of carbon dioxide through 2016. While EPA approval was pending, Vermont and other states adopted similar standards. Green Mountain Chrysler Plymouth Dodge Jeep and other auto dealers, automakers, and associations of automakers filed a suit in a federal district court against George Crombie (then the secretary of the Vermont Agency of Natural Resources) and others, seeking relief from the state regulations. [*Green Mountain Chrysler Plymouth Dodge Jeep v. Crombie,* 508 F.Supp.2d 295 (D.Vt. 2007)] (See *Air Pollution.*)

1. Under the Environmental Policy and Conservation Act (EPCA) of 1975, the National Highway Traffic Safety Administration sets fuel economy standards for new cars. The plaintiffs argued, among other things, that the EPCA, which prohibits states from adopting separate fuel economy standards, preempts Vermont's GHG regulation. Do the GHG rules equate to the fuel economy standards? Discuss.

2. Do Vermont's rules tread on the efforts of the federal government to address global warming internationally? Who should regulate GHG emissions? The federal government? The state governments? Both? Neither? Why?

3. The plaintiffs claimed that they would go bankrupt if they were forced to adhere to the state's GHG standards. Should they be granted relief on this basis? Does history support their claim? Explain.

22 **CHAPTER**

Real Property and Land-Use Control

LEARNING OBJECTIVES

The five learning objectives below are designed to help improve your understanding of the chapter. After reading this chapter, you should be able to answer the following questions:

1. What is a fixture, and how does it relate to real property rights?
2. What is an easement? Describe three ways that easements are created.
3. What are the requirements for acquiring property by adverse possession?
4. What limitations may be imposed on the rights of property owners?
5. What is the purpose of zoning laws?

(Marje/iStockphoto.com)

"The right of property is the most sacred of all the rights of citizenship."
—Jean-Jacques Rousseau, 1712–1778 (French writer and philosopher)

From earliest times, property has provided a means for survival. Primitive peoples lived off the fruits of the land, eating the vegetation and wildlife. Later, as the vegetation was cultivated and the wildlife domesticated, property provided farmland and pasture.

Throughout history, property has continued to be an indicator of family wealth and social position. Indeed, an individual's right to his or her property has become, in the words of Jean-Jacques Rousseau, one of the "most sacred of all the rights of citizenship."

In this chapter, we examine the nature of real property and the ways in which it can be owned and transferred. We even consider the sale of a haunted house in this chapter's *Spotlight Case*. We also discuss leased property and landlord-tenant relationships.

The Nature of Real Property

Real property consists of land and the buildings, plants, and trees that are on it. Real property also includes subsurface and airspace rights, as well as personal property that has become permanently attached to real property. Whereas personal property is movable, real property—also called *real estate* or *realty*—is immovable.

Land

Land includes the soil on the surface of the earth and the natural or artificial structures that are attached to it. It further includes all the waters contained on or under the surface and much, but not necessarily all, of the airspace above it. The exterior boundaries of land extend down to the center of the earth and up to the farthest reaches of the atmosphere (subject to certain qualifications).

Airspace and Subsurface Rights

The owner of real property has rights to the airspace above the land, as well as to the soil and minerals underneath it. Limitations on either airspace rights or subsurface rights normally must be indicated on the document that transfers title at the time of purchase. When no such limitations, or *encumbrances,* are noted, a purchaser generally can expect to have an unlimited right to possession of the property.

Who owns the airspace above residential land?

Airspace Rights Disputes concerning airspace rights may involve the right of commercial and private planes to fly over property and the right of individuals and governments to seed clouds and produce rain artificially. Flights over private land normally do not violate property rights unless the flights are so low and so frequent that they directly interfere with the owner's enjoyment and use of the land. Leaning walls or buildings and projecting eave spouts or roofs may also violate the airspace rights of an adjoining property owner.

Subsurface Rights In many states, land ownership may be separated, in that the surface of a piece of land and the subsurface may have different owners. Subsurface rights can be extremely valuable, as these rights include the ownership of minerals, oil, and natural gas. Subsurface rights would be of little value, however, if the owner could not use the surface to exercise those rights. Hence, a subsurface owner has a right (called a *profit,* to be discussed later in this chapter) to go onto the surface of the land to, for example, discover and mine minerals.

When ownership is separated into surface and subsurface rights, each owner can pass title to what she or he owns without the consent of the other owner. Of course, conflicts can arise between the surface owner's use of the property and the subsurface owner's need to extract minerals, oil, or natural gas. In that situation, one party's interest may become subservient (secondary) to the other party's interest either by statute or by case law.

If the owners of the subsurface rights excavate (dig), they are absolutely liable if their excavation causes the surface to collapse. Many states have statutes that also make the excavators liable for any damage to structures on the land. Typically, these statutes provide precise requirements for excavations of various depths.

Plant Life and Vegetation

Plant life, both natural and cultivated, is also considered to be real property. In many instances, the natural vegetation, such as trees, adds greatly to the value of the realty. When a parcel of land is sold and the land has growing crops on it, the sale includes the crops, unless otherwise specified in the sales contract. When crops are sold by themselves, however, they are considered to be personal property or goods. Consequently, the sale of crops

"The meek shall inherit the earth, but not the mineral rights."

J. Paul Getty, 1892–1976
(American entrepreneur and industrialist)

is a sale of goods and thus is governed by the Uniform Commercial Code (UCC, discussed in Chapter 12) rather than by real property law.

Fixtures

Learning Objective 1
What is a fixture, and how does it relate to real property rights?

Fixture An item of personal property that has become so closely associated with real property that it is legally regarded as part of that real property.

Certain personal property can become so closely associated with the real property to which it is attached that the law views it as real property. Such property is known as a **fixture**—an item *affixed* to realty, meaning that it is attached to the real property in a permanent way. The item may be attached, embedded into, or permanently situated on the property by means of cement, plaster, bolts, nails, roots, or screws. The fixture can be physically attached to the real property, be attached to another fixture, or even be without any actual physical attachment to the land (such as a statue). As long as the owner intends the property to be a fixture, normally it will be a fixture.

Fixtures are included in the sale of land if the sales contract does not provide otherwise. The sale of a house includes the land and the house and the garage on the land, as well as the cabinets, plumbing, and windows. Because these are permanently affixed to the property, they are considered to be a part of it. Certain items, such as drapes and window-unit air conditioners, are difficult to classify. Thus, a contract for the sale of a house or commercial realty should indicate which items of this sort are included in the sale.

(Songbird839/iStockphoto.com)

Under what circumstances is an industrial-quality irrigation system considered a fixture?

CASE EXAMPLE 22.1   Sand & Sage Farm had an eight-tower center-pivot irrigation system bolted to a cement slab and connected to an underground well. The bank held a mortgage note on the farm secured by "all buildings, improvements, and fixtures." The farm's owners had also used the property as security for other loans, but the contracts for those loans did not specifically mention fixtures or the irrigation system. Later, when Sand & Sage filed for bankruptcy, a dispute arose between the bank and another creditor over the irrigation system. The court held that the irrigation system was a fixture because it was firmly attached to the land and integral to the operation of the farm. Therefore, the bank's security interest had priority over the other creditor's interest.[1] ●

PREVENTING LEGAL DISPUTES

When real property is being sold, transferred, or subjected to a security interest, make sure that any contract specifically lists which fixtures are to be included. Without such a list, the parties may have very different ideas as to what is being transferred with the real property (or included as collateral for a loan). It is much simpler and less expensive to itemize fixtures in a contract than to engage in litigation.

Ownership Interests and Leases

Ownership of property is an abstract concept that cannot exist independently of the legal system. No one can actually possess or *hold* a piece of land, the airspace above it, the earth below it, and all the water contained on it. The legal system therefore recognizes certain rights and duties that constitute ownership interests in real property.

Property ownership is often viewed as a bundle of rights. One who possesses the entire bundle of rights is said to hold the property in *fee simple*, which is the most complete form of ownership. When only some of the rights in the bundle are transferred to another

---

1. *In re Sand & Sage Farm & Ranch, Inc.*, 266 Bankr. 507 (D.Kans. 2001).

person, the effect is to limit the ownership rights of both the transferor of the rights and the recipient.

Traditionally, ownership interests in real property were referred to as *estates in land,* which include fee simple estates, life estates, and leasehold estates. We examine these estates in land, forms of concurrent ownership, and certain other interests in real property that is owned by others in the following subsections.

Ownership in Fee Simple

In a **fee simple absolute,** the owner has the greatest aggregation of rights, privileges, and power possible. The owner can give the property away or dispose of the property by *deed* (the instrument used to transfer property, as will be discussed later in this chapter) or by will. When there is no will, the fee simple ownership interest passes to the owner's legal heirs on her or his death. A fee simple is potentially infinite in duration and is assigned forever to a person and her or his heirs without limitation or condition. The owner has the rights of *exclusive* possession and use of the property.

The rights that accompany a fee simple include the right to use the land for whatever purpose the owner sees fit. Of course, other laws, including applicable zoning, noise, and environmental laws, may limit the owner's ability to use the property in certain ways. A person who uses his or her property in a manner that unreasonably interferes with others' right to use or enjoy their own property can be liable for the tort of *nuisance* (discussed in Chapter 21).

CASE EXAMPLE 22.2 Nancy and James Biglane owned and lived in a building in Natchez, Mississippi. Next door to the Biglanes' property was a popular bar called the Under the Hill Saloon that featured live music. During the summer, the Saloon, which had no air-conditioning, opened its windows and doors, and live music echoed up and down the street. The Biglanes installed extra insulation, thicker windows, and air-conditioning units in their building.

Nevertheless, the noise from the Saloon kept them awake at night. Eventually, they sued the owners of the Saloon for nuisance. The court held that the noise from the bar unreasonably interfered with the Biglanes' right to enjoy their property and enjoined (prevented) the Saloon from opening its windows and doors while playing music.[2] ●

Fee Simple Absolute An ownership interest in land in which the owner has the greatest possible aggregation of rights, privileges, and power.

Life Estates

A **life estate** is an estate that lasts for the life of some specified individual. A **conveyance,** or transfer of real property, "to A for his life" creates a life estate. In a life estate, the life tenant's ownership rights cease to exist on the life tenant's death. The life tenant has the right to use the land, provided that he or she commits no **waste** (injury to the land). In other words, the life tenant cannot use the land in a manner that would adversely affect its value.

The life tenant is entitled to any rents generated by the land and can harvest crops from the land. If mines and oil wells are already on the land, the life tenant can extract minerals and oil and is entitled to the royalties, but he or she cannot exploit the land by creating new wells or mines.

The life tenant can create liens, *easements* (discussed shortly), and leases, but none can extend beyond the life of the tenant. In addition, with few exceptions, the owner of a life estate has an exclusive right to possession during her or his life.

Along with these rights, the life tenant also has some duties—to keep the property in repair and to pay property taxes. In short, the owner of the life estate has the same rights as a fee simple owner except that the life tenant must maintain the value of the property during her or his tenancy.

Life Estate An interest in land that exists only for the duration of the life of a specified individual, usually the holder of the estate.

Conveyance The transfer of title to real property from one person to another by deed or other document.

Waste The abuse or destructive use of real property by one who is in rightful possession of the property but who does not have title to it.

---

2. *Biglane v. Under the Hill Corp.,* 949 So.2d 9 (Miss.Sup. 2007).

Concurrent Ownership

Concurrent ownership Joint ownership.

Persons who share ownership rights simultaneously in particular property (including real property and personal property) are said to have **concurrent ownership.** There are two principal types of concurrent ownership: *tenancy in common* and *joint tenancy.* Concurrent ownership rights can also be held in a *tenancy by the entirety* or as *community property,* although these types of concurrent ownership are less common.

Tenancy in Common Co-ownership of property in which each party owns an undivided interest that passes to his or her heirs at death.

Tenancy in Common
The term **tenancy in common** refers to a form of co-ownership in which each of two or more persons owns an undivided interest in the property. The interest is undivided because each tenant shares rights in the whole property. On the death of a tenant in common, that tenant's interest in the property passes to her or his heirs.

EXAMPLE 22.3 Four friends purchase a condominium unit in Hawaii together as tenants in common. This means that each of them has an ownership interest (one-fourth) in the whole. If one of the four owners dies a year after the purchase, his ownership interest passes to his heirs (his wife and children, for example) rather than to the other tenants in common. ●

Unless the co-tenants have agreed otherwise, a tenant in common can transfer her or his interest in the property to another without the consent of the remaining co-owners. In most states, it is presumed that a co-tenancy is a tenancy in common unless there is specific language indicating the intent to establish a joint tenancy (discussed next).

Joint Tenancy The joint ownership of property by two or more co-owners in which each co-owner owns an undivided portion of the property. On the death of one of the joint tenants, his or her interest automatically passes to the surviving joint tenants.

Joint Tenancy
In a **joint tenancy,** each of two or more persons owns an undivided interest in the property, but a deceased joint tenant's interest passes to the surviving joint tenant or tenants.

Right of Survivorship   The right of a surviving joint tenant to inherit a deceased joint tenant's ownership interest—referred to as a *right of survivorship*—distinguishes a joint tenancy from a tenancy in common. **EXAMPLE 22.4** Jerrold and Eva are married and purchase a house as joint tenants. The title to the house clearly expresses the intent to create a joint tenancy because it says "to Jerrold and Eva as joint tenants with right of survivorship." Jerrold has three children from a prior marriage. If Jerrold dies, his interest in the house automatically passes to Eva rather than to his children from the prior marriage. ●

Termination of a Joint Tenancy   Although a joint tenant can transfer her or his rights by sale or gift to another without the consent of the other joint tenants, doing so terminates the joint tenancy. The person who purchases the property or receives it as a gift becomes a tenant in common, not a joint tenant. **EXAMPLE 22.5** Three brothers, Brody, Saul, and Jacob, own a parcel as joint tenants. Brody is experiencing financial difficulties and sells his interest in the property to Beth. The sale terminates the joint tenancy, and now Beth, Saul, and Jacob hold the property as tenants in common. ●

A joint tenant's interest can also be levied against—that is seized by court order—to satisfy the tenant's judgment creditors. If this occurs, the joint tenancy terminates, and the remaining owners hold the property as tenants in common. (Judgment creditors can also seize the interests of tenants in a tenancy in common.)

Tenancy by the Entirety The joint ownership of property by a husband and wife. Neither party can transfer his or her interest in the property without the consent of the other.

Tenancy by the Entirety
A less common form of shared ownership of real property by husband and wife is a **tenancy by the entirety.** It differs from a joint tenancy in that neither spouse may separately transfer his or her interest during his or her lifetime unless the other spouse consents. In some states in which statutes give the wife the right to convey her property, this form of concurrent ownership has effectively been abolished. A divorce, either spouse's death, or mutual agreement will terminate a tenancy by the entirety.

Community Property   A limited number of states[3] allow property to be owned by a married couple as **community property.** If property is held as community property, each spouse technically owns an undivided one-half interest in the property. This type of ownership applies to most property acquired by the husband or the wife during the course of the marriage. It generally does *not* apply to property acquired prior to the marriage or to property acquired by gift or inheritance as separate property during the marriage. After a divorce, community property is divided equally in some states and according to the discretion of the court in other states.

Leasehold Estates

A **leasehold estate** is created when a real property owner or lessor (landlord) agrees to convey the right to possess and use the property to a lessee (tenant) for a certain period of time. In every leasehold estate, the tenant has a *qualified* right to exclusive, though *temporary,* possession. (The tenant's rights are qualified by the landlord's right to enter onto the premises to ensure that the tenant is not causing damage to the property.) The tenant can use the land—for instance, by harvesting crops—but cannot injure it by such activities as cutting down timber to sell or by extracting oil.

Here, we look at the types of leasehold estates, or tenancies, that can be created when real property is leased.

Fixed-Term Tenancy

Fixed-Term Tenancy   A **fixed-term tenancy,** also called a *tenancy for years,* is created by an express contract stating that the property is leased for a specified period of time, such as a month, a year, or a period of years. Signing a one-year lease to occupy an apartment, for instance, creates a tenancy for years.

Note that the term need not be specified by date and can be conditioned on the occurrence of an event, such as leasing a cabin for the summer or an apartment during Mardi Gras. At the end of the period specified in the lease, the lease ends (without notice), and possession of the property returns to the lessor. If the tenant dies during the period of the lease, the lease interest passes to the tenant's heirs as personal property. Often, leases include renewal or extension provisions.

Periodic Tenancy

Periodic Tenancy   With a **periodic tenancy,** the lease does not specify how long it is to last but does specify that rent is to be paid at certain intervals. This type of tenancy is automatically renewed for another rental period unless properly terminated. **EXAMPLE 22.6**   Jewel, LLC, enters into a lease with Capital Properties. The lease states, "Rent is due on the tenth day of every month." This provision creates a periodic tenancy from month to month. • This type of tenancy can also extend from week to week or from year to year. A periodic tenancy sometimes arises after the lease term ends when the landlord allows the tenant to retain possession and continue paying monthly or weekly rent.

Under the common law, the landlord or tenant must give at least one period's notice to the other party before terminating a periodic tenancy. If the tenancy is month to month, for instance, one month's notice must be given. Today, however, state statutes often require a different period of notice before the termination of a tenancy.

Will this couple necessarily share equally in all income earned during their marriage?

Community Property   A form of concurrent ownership of property in which each spouse owns an undivided one-half interest in property acquired during the marriage.

Leasehold Estate   An interest in real property that gives a tenant a qualified right to possess and/or use the property for a limited time under a lease.

Fixed-term Tenancy   A type of tenancy under which property is leased for a specified period of time, such as a month, a year, or a period of years; also called a *tenancy for years.*

Periodic Tenancy   A lease interest in land for an indefinite period involving payment of rent at fixed intervals, such as week to week, month to month, or year to year.

---

3. These states include Alaska, Arizona, California, Idaho, Louisiana, Nevada, New Mexico, Texas, Washington, and Wisconsin. Puerto Rico allows property to be owned as community property as well.

Tenancy at Will A type of tenancy under which either party can terminate the tenancy without notice; usually arises when a tenant who has been under a tenancy for years retains possession, with the landlord's consent, after the tenancy for years has terminated.

Tenancy at Sufferance A type of tenancy under which one who, after rightfully being in possession of leased premises, continues (wrongfully) to occupy the property after the lease has been terminated. The tenant has no rights to possess the property and occupies it only because the person entitled to evict the tenant has not done so.

Nonpossessory Interest In the context of real property, an interest that involves the right to use land but not the right to possess it.

Easement A nonpossessory right, established by express or implied agreement, to make limited use of another's property without removing anything from the property.

Profit In real property law, the right to enter onto another's property and remove something of value from that property.

Tenancy at Will

With a **tenancy at will,** either party can terminate the tenancy without notice. This type of tenancy can arise if a landlord rents property to a tenant "for as long as both agree" or allows a person to live on the premises without paying rent. Tenancy at will is rare today because, as mentioned, most state statutes require a landlord to provide some period of notice to terminate a tenancy. States may also require a landowner to have sufficient cause (reason) to end a residential tenancy.

Tenancy at Sufferance

The mere possession of land without right is called a **tenancy at sufferance.** A tenancy at sufferance is not a true tenancy because it is created when a tenant *wrongfully* retains possession of property. Whenever a tenancy for years or a periodic tenancy ends and the tenant continues to retain possession of the premises without the owner's permission, a tenancy at sufferance is created.

Nonpossessory Interests

In contrast to the types of property interests just described, some interests in land do not include any rights to possess the property. These interests are therefore known as **nonpossessory interests.** They include easements, profits, and licenses.

An **easement** is the right of a person to make limited use of another person's real property without taking anything from the property. An easement, for instance, can be the right to walk or drive across another's property. In contrast, a **profit** is the right to go onto land owned by another and take away some part of the land itself or some product of the land. **EXAMPLE 22.7** Akmed owns The Dunes. Akmed gives Carmen the right to go there to remove all the sand and gravel that she needs for her cement business. Carmen has a profit. ●

Easements and profits can be classified as either *appurtenant* or *in gross*. Because easements and profits are similar and the same rules apply to both, we discuss them together.

Easement or Profit Appurtenant

An easement or profit *appurtenant* arises when the owner of one piece of land has a right to go onto (or remove something from) an adjacent piece of land owned by another. The land that is benefited by the easement is called the *dominant estate,* and the land that is burdened is called the *servient estate.*

Because easements appurtenant are intended to *benefit the land,* they run (are conveyed) with the land when it is transferred. **EXAMPLE 22.8** Acosta has a right to drive his car across Green's land, which is adjacent to Acosta's land. This right-of-way over Green's property is an easement appurtenant to Acosta's property and can be used only by Acosta. If Acosta sells his land, the easement runs with the land to benefit the new owner. ●

Easement or Profit in Gross

In an easement or profit *in gross,* the right to use or take things from another's land is given to one who does not own an adjacent tract of land. These easements are intended to *benefit a particular person or business,* not a particular piece of land, and cannot be transferred.

EXAMPLE 22.9 Avery owns a parcel of land with a marble quarry. Avery conveys (transfers) to Classic Stone Corporation the right to come onto her land and remove up to five hundred pounds of marble per day. Classic Stone owns a profit in gross and cannot transfer this right to another. ● Similarly, when a utility company is granted an easement to run its power lines across another's property, it obtains an easement in gross.

Creation of an Easement or Profit

Most easements and profits are created by an express grant in a contract, deed (discussed shortly), or *will*. This allows the parties to include terms defining the extent and length of time of use. In some situations, an easement or profit can also be created without an express agreement.

An easement or profit may arise by *implication* when the circumstances surrounding the division of a parcel of property imply its existence. **EXAMPLE 22.10** Barrow divides a

Learning Objective 2
What is an easement? Describe three ways that easements are created.

parcel of land that has only one well for drinking water. If Barrow conveys the half without a well to Jarad, a profit by implication arises because Jarad needs drinking water. ●

An easement may also be created by *necessity*. An easement by necessity does not require a division of property for its existence. A person who rents an apartment, for example, has an easement by necessity in the private road leading up to the apartment building.

An easement arises by *prescription* when one person exercises an easement, such as a right-of-way, on another person's land without the landowner's consent, and the use is apparent and continues for the length of time required by the applicable statute of limitations. (In much the same way, title to property may be obtained by *adverse possession*, as will be discussed shortly in this chapter.)

In the following case, an easement had been created by an express grant in a deed. The grant did not specify the easement's precise location, however.

Case 22.1

Baker v. Walnut Bowls, Inc.

Missouri Court of Appeals, Southern District, Division Two, 423 S.W.3d 293 (2014).

(Woodygraphs/Shutterstock.com)

If an easement's location is not precisely fixed, is it still valid?

BACKGROUND AND FACTS Junior and Wilma Thompson sold twenty-one acres of their fifty acres of land in Lebanon, Missouri, to Walnut Bowls, Inc. The deed expressly reserved an easement to the Thompsons' remaining twenty-nine acres, but did not fix a precise location. James and Linda Baker subsequently bought the rest of the Thompsons' land. Decades later, on learning of the easement, a potential buyer of Walnut Bowls' property refused to go through with the sale. Walnut Bowls then put steel cables across its driveway entrances, installed a lock and chain on an access gate, and bolted a "No Trespassing" sign facing the Bakers' property. At about the same time, the Bakers filed a suit in a Missouri state court to determine the location of the easement. Citing the lack of an express location, the court held that there was no easement. The Bakers appealed.

IN THE WORDS OF THE COURT . . .
Jeffrey W. BATES, J. [Judge]
    * * * *

An easement may be created even though its precise location is not described in the grant. If the location is not precisely fixed when the easement is first created, the grantee is entitled to a convenient, reasonable and accessible use. When the location of the easement is unknown initially, the location can subsequently be fixed by express agreement or inferred from proof of the use of a particular way. *If the easement is not fixed by subsequent express agreement or selection, however, the trial court must fix the location of the easement. In doing so, the easement holder is entitled to a convenient, reasonable and accessible use.* [Emphasis added.]
    * * * *

The grant creating the Bakers' easement did not fix its precise location. As the trial court found, there was no evidence of

any express agreement concerning the easement's location or any way to infer its location from past use. By stopping there and concluding that there was no easement at all, however, the trial court misapplied the law. On remand, the court should undertake to outline a route of access consistent with the interests of convenience, and reasonable, accessible use. Once a definite route is determined, the judgment must contain a legal description of the easement. The trial court has the inherent authority to order a survey to establish a proper legal description.

DECISION AND REMEDY A state intermediate appellate court reversed the decision of the lower court and remanded the case for further proceedings. If a grant or other agreement does not precisely fix an easement's location, and it cannot be inferred from past use, "it is the trial court's obligation to fix the location of the easement so as to provide the easement holder with convenient, reasonable and accessible use."

THE LEGAL ENVIRONMENT DIMENSION *In Missouri, ten years is the period for the acquisition of an interest in land by adverse possession. Could Walnut Bowls have successfully argued that it had acquired the Bakers' easement by adverse possession? Explain.*

WHAT IF THE FACTS WERE DIFFERENT? *Suppose that the Bakers' only route to their property was Walnut Bowls' driveway, but that the deed had not granted an easement. Could the Bakers have acquired an easement by other means? Discuss.*

Termination of an Easement or Profit
An easement or profit can be terminated or extinguished in several ways. The simplest way is to deed it back to the owner of the land that is burdened by it. Another way is to abandon it and create evidence of intent to relinquish the right to use it. Mere nonuse will not extinguish an easement or profit *unless the nonuse is accompanied by an overt act showing the intent to abandon*. Also, if the owner of an easement or profit becomes the owner of the property burdened by it, then it is merged into the property.

License In the context of real property, a revocable right or privilege to enter onto another person's land.

License
In the context of real property, a **license** is the revocable right to enter onto another person's land. It is a personal privilege that arises from the consent of the owner of the land and can be revoked by the owner. A ticket to attend a movie at a theater or a concert is an example of a license.

In essence, a license grants a person the authority to enter the land of another and perform a specified act or series of acts without obtaining any permanent interest in the land. When a person with a license exceeds the authority granted and undertakes an action that is not permitted, the property owner can sue that person for the tort of trespass.

CASE EXAMPLE 22.11 A Catholic church granted Prince Realty Management, LLC, a three-month license to use a three-foot strip of its property adjacent to Prince's property. The license authorized Prince to "put up plywood panels," creating a temporary fence to protect Prince's property during the construction of a new building. During the license's term, Prince installed steel piles and beams on the licensed property. When Prince ignored the church's demands that these structures be removed, the church sued Prince for trespass. The court held that because the license allowed only temporary structures and Prince had exceeded its authority by installing steel piles and beams, the church was entitled to damages.[4] •

Transfer of Ownership

Ownership interests in real property are frequently transferred (conveyed) by sale, and the terms of the transfer are specified in a real estate sales contract. Often, real estate brokers or agents who are licensed by the state assist the buyers and sellers during the sales transaction.

Real property ownership can also be transferred by gift, by will or inheritance, by possession, or by *eminent domain*. When ownership rights in real property are transferred, the type of interest being transferred and the conditions of the transfer normally are set forth in a *deed* executed by the person who is conveying the property.

Real Estate Sales Contracts

In some ways, a sale of real estate is similar to a sale of goods because it involves a transfer of ownership, often with specific warranties. A sale of real estate, however, is generally a more complicated transaction that involves certain formalities that are not required in a sale of goods. Usually, after lengthy negotiations (involving offers, counteroffers, and responses), the parties enter into a detailed contract setting forth their agreement. A contract for a sale of land includes such terms as the purchase price, the type of deed the buyer will receive, the condition of the premises, and any items that will be included.

Unless the buyer pays cash for the property, he or she must obtain financing through a mortgage loan. Real estate sales contracts are often contingent on the buyer's ability to obtain financing at or below a specified rate of interest. The contract may also be contingent

---

4. *Roman Catholic Church of Our Lady of Sorrows v. Prince Realty Management, LLC,* 47 A.D.3d 909, 850 N.Y.S.2d 569 (2008).

on the buyer's sale of other real property, the seller's acquisition of title insurance, or the completion of a survey of the property and its passing one or more inspections. Normally, the buyer is responsible for having the premises inspected for physical or mechanical defects and for insect infestation.

Implied Warranties in the Sale of New Homes
Most states recognize a warranty—the **implied warranty of habitability**—in the sale of new homes. The seller of a new house warrants that it will be fit for human habitation even if the deed or contract of sale does not include such a warranty.

Essentially, the seller is warranting that the house is in reasonable working order and is of reasonably sound construction. Thus, under this warranty, the seller of a new home is in effect a guarantor of its fitness. In some states, the warranty protects not only the first purchaser but any subsequent purchaser as well.

Implied Warranty of Habitability
An implied promise by a seller of a new house that the house is fit for human habitation. Also, the implied promise by a landlord that rented residential premises are habitable.

Seller's Duty to Disclose Hidden Defects
In most jurisdictions, courts impose on sellers a duty to disclose any known defect that materially affects the value of the property and that the buyer could not reasonably discover. Failure to disclose such a material defect gives the buyer the right to rescind the contract and to sue for damages based on fraud or misrepresentation. There is usually a limit to the time within which the buyer can bring a suit against the seller based on the defect, however.

CASE EXAMPLE 22.12   Matthew Humphrey partially renovated a house in Louisiana and sold it to Terry and Tabitha Whitehead for $67,000. A few months after the Whiteheads moved in, they discovered rotten wood behind the tile in the bathroom and experienced problems with the fireplace and the plumbing. Two years later, the Whiteheads filed a suit against Humphrey seeking to rescind the sale. They argued that the plumbing problems were a latent defect that the seller had failed to disclose. Evidence revealed that prior to the sale, the parties were made aware of issues regarding the sewer system and that corrective actions were taken. At the time of the sale, the toilets flushed, and neither side realized that the latent defects had not been resolved. The court ruled that rescission was not warranted because the Whiteheads had waited too long after their discovery to file a claim against Humphrey.[5] ●

In the following *Spotlight Case,* the court had to decide whether a buyer—who was not told that the house he had purchased was allegedly haunted—had the right to rescind the sales contract.

---

5. *Whitehead v. Humphrey,* 954 So.2d 859 (La.App. 2007).

Spotlight on Sales of Haunted Houses

Case 22.2
Stambovsky v. Ackley
Supreme Court, Appellate Division, New York, 572 N.Y.S.2d 672, 169 A.D.2d 254 (1991).

(C. Cahill/iStockphoto.com)

BACKGROUND AND FACTS Jeffrey Stambovsky signed a contract to buy Helen Ackley's house in Nyack, New York. After the contract was signed, Stambovsky discovered that the house was widely reputed to be haunted. The Ackley family claimed to have seen poltergeists on numerous occasions over the previous nine years. The Ackleys had been interviewed about the house in both a national publication *(Reader's Digest)* and the local newspaper.

The house was included on a walking tour of Nyack, New York, as "a riverfront Victorian (with ghost)." When Stambovsky learned of the house's reputation, he sued to rescind the contract, alleging that Ackley and her real estate agent had made material misrepresentations when they failed to disclose Ackley's belief that the home was haunted.

Spotlight Case 22.2—Continues ➡

Spotlight Case 22.2—Continued

IN THE WORDS OF THE COURT . . .

Justice *RUBIN* delivered the opinion of the Court.

* * * *

While I agree with [the trial court] that the real estate broker, as agent for the seller, is under no duty to disclose to a potential buyer the phantasmal reputation of the premises and that, in his pursuit of a legal remedy for fraudulent misrepresentation against the seller, plaintiff hasn't a ghost of a chance, I am nevertheless moved by the spirit of equity to allow the buyer to seek rescission of the contract of sale and recovery of his down payment. New York law fails to recognize any remedy for damages incurred as a result of the seller's mere silence, applying instead the strict rule of caveat emptor. Therefore, the theoretical basis for granting relief, even under the extraordinary facts of this case, is elusive if not ephemeral.

* * * *

The doctrine of caveat emptor *requires that a buyer act prudently to assess the fitness and value of his purchase and operates to bar the purchaser who fails to exercise due care from seeking the equitable remedy of rescission.* * * * Applying the strict rule of caveat emptor to a contract involving a house possessed by poltergeists conjures up visions of a psychic or medium routinely accompanying the structural engineer and Terminix man on an inspection of every home subject to a contract of sale. It portends that the prudent attorney will establish an escrow account lest the subject of the transaction come back to haunt him and his client—or pray that his malpractice insurance coverage extends to supernatural disasters. In the interest of avoiding such untenable consequences, the notion that a haunting is a condition which can and should be ascertained upon reasonable inspection of the premises is a hobgoblin which should be exorcised from the body of legal precedent and laid quietly to rest. [Emphasis added.]

* * * *

In the case at bar, defendant seller deliberately fostered the public belief that her home was possessed. Having undertaken to inform the public at large, to whom she has no legal relationship, about the supernatural occurrences on her property, she may be said to owe no less a duty to her contract vendee. It has been remarked that the occasional modern cases which permit a seller to take unfair advantage of a buyer's ignorance so long as he is not actively misled are "singularly unappetizing" (Prosser, Law of Torts [Section] 106, at 696 [4th ed. 1971]). Where, as here, the seller not only takes unfair advantage of the buyer's ignorance but has created and perpetuated a condition about which he is unlikely to even inquire, enforcement of the contract (in whole or in part) is offensive to the court's sense of equity. Application of the remedy of rescission, within the bounds of the narrow exception to the doctrine of caveat emptor set forth herein, is entirely appropriate to relieve the unwitting purchaser from the consequences of a most unnatural bargain.

DECISION AND REMEDY   The New York appellate court found that the doctrine of *caveat emptor* did not apply in this case. The court reinstated Stambovsky's claim for rescission of the purchase contract and the down payment.

THE ETHICAL DIMENSION   *In not disclosing the house's reputation to Stambovsky, was Ackley's behavior unethical? If so, was it unethical because she knew something he did not, or was it unethical because of the nature of the information she omitted? What if Ackley had failed to mention that the roof leaked or that the well was dry—conditions that a buyer would normally investigate? Explain your answer.*

THE LEGAL ENVIRONMENT DIMENSION   *Why did the court decide that applying the strict rule of caveat emptor was inappropriate in this case? How would applying this doctrine increase costs for the purchaser?*

Deeds

Deed A document by which title to real property is passed.

Possession and title to land are passed from person to person by means of a **deed**—the instrument of conveyance of real property. Unlike a contract, a deed does not have to be supported by legally sufficient consideration. To be valid, a deed must include the following:

1. The names of the buyer (*grantee*) and the seller (*grantor*).
2. Words indicating an intent to convey the property (for example, "I hereby bargain, sell, grant, or give").
3. A legally sufficient description of the land.
4. The grantor's (and usually her or his spouse's) signature.
5. Delivery of the deed.

Warranty Deeds   Different types of deeds provide different degrees of protection against defects of title. A **warranty deed** makes the greatest number of *covenants*, or promises, from the grantor to the grantee and thus provides the greatest protection against defects of title. In most states, special language is required to create a general warranty deed.

Warranty deeds commonly include the following:

1. A covenant that the grantor has the title to, and the power to convey, the property.
2. A covenant of quiet enjoyment (a warranty that the buyer will not be disturbed in her or his possession of the land).
3. A covenant that transfer of the property is made without knowledge of adverse claims of third parties.

Generally, the warranty deed makes the grantor liable for all defects of title during the time that the property was held by the grantor and previous titleholders. **EXAMPLE 22.13**   Julio sells a two-acre lot and office building by warranty deed to Daniel. Subsequently, a third person shows up who has better title than Julio had and forces Daniel off the property. Here, the covenant of quiet enjoyment has been breached. Daniel can sue Julio to recover the purchase price of the land, plus any other damages incurred as a result. ●

Special Warranty Deeds   In contrast to a warranty deed, a **special warranty deed**, which is also referred to as a *limited warranty deed*, warrants only that the grantor or seller held good title during his or her ownership of the property. In other words, the grantor is not warranting that there were no defects of title when the property was held by previous owners.

If the special warranty deed discloses all liens or other encumbrances, the seller will not be liable to the buyer if a third person subsequently interferes with the buyer's ownership. If the third person's claim arises out of, or is related to, some act of the seller, however, the seller will be liable to the buyer for damages.

Quitclaim Deeds   A **quitclaim deed** offers the least amount of protection against defects of title. Basically, a quitclaim deed conveys to the grantee whatever interest the grantor had. Therefore, if the grantor had no interest, then the grantee receives no interest.

Quitclaim deeds are often used when the seller, or grantor, is uncertain as to the extent of his or her rights in the property. They may also be used to release a party's interest in a particular parcel of property, such as in divorce settlements or business dissolutions when the grantors are dividing up their interests in real property.

Recording Statutes   Every jurisdiction has **recording statutes**, which allow deeds to be recorded for a fee. Deeds are recorded in the county where the property is located. Recording a deed gives notice to the public that a certain person is now the owner of a particular parcel of real estate. Thus, prospective buyers can check the public records to see whether there have been earlier transactions creating interests or rights in specific parcels of real property.

Will or Inheritance

Property that is transferred on an owner's death is passed either by will or by state inheritance laws. If the owner of land dies with a will, the land passes in accordance with the terms of the will. If the owner dies without a will, state inheritance statutes prescribe how and to whom the property will pass.

Warranty Deed A deed that provides the greatest amount of protection for the grantee, in that the grantor promises that she or he has title to the property conveyed in the deed, that there are no undisclosed encumbrances on the property, and that the grantee will enjoy quiet possession of the property.

Special Warranty Deed A deed that warrants only that the grantor held good title during his or her ownership of the property and does not warrant that there were no defects of title when the property was held by previous owners.

Quitclaim Deed A deed that conveys only whatever interest the grantor had in the property and therefore offers the least amount of protection against defects of title.

Recording Statutes Statutes that allow deeds, mortgages, and other real property transactions to be recorded so as to provide notice to future purchasers or creditors of an existing claim on the property.

Adverse Possession

Adverse Possession The acquisition of title to real property by occupying it openly, without the consent of the owner, for a period of time specified by a state statute. The occupation must be actual, exclusive, open, continuous, and in opposition to all others, including the owner.

Adverse possession is a means of obtaining title to land without delivery of a deed. Essentially, when one person possesses the property of another for a certain statutory period of time (three to thirty years, with ten years being most common), that person, called the *adverse possessor*, acquires title to the land and cannot be removed from it by the original owner. The adverse possessor may ultimately obtain a perfect title just as if there had been a conveyance by deed.

Requirements for Adverse Possession   For property to be held adversely, four elements must be satisfied:

1. Possession must be *actual and exclusive*—that is, the possessor must take sole physical occupancy of the property.
2. The possession must be *open, visible, and notorious,* not secret or clandestine. The possessor must occupy the land for all the world to see.
3. Possession must be *continuous and peaceable for the required period of time.* This requirement means that the possessor must not be interrupted in the occupancy by the true owner or by the courts.
4. Possession must be *hostile and adverse.* In other words, the possessor must claim the property as against the whole world. He or she cannot be living on the property with the permission of the owner.

Purpose of the Doctrine   There are a number of public-policy reasons for the adverse possession doctrine. These include society's interest in resolving boundary disputes, determining title when title to property is in question, and ensuring that real property remains in the stream of commerce. More fundamentally, policies behind the doctrine include rewarding possessors for putting land to productive use and punishing owners who sit on their rights too long and do not take action when they see adverse possession.

CASE EXAMPLE 22.14 Charles Scarborough and Mildred Rollins were adjoining landowners, sharing one common boundary. Based on Rollins's survey of the property, Rollins believed that she owned a portion of a gravel road located to the south of the apartment buildings she owned. In contrast, Scarborough believed that the gravel road was located totally on his property and that he owned some property north of the gravel road toward Rollins's apartment buildings. Scarborough filed a complaint seeking to receive quiet title to the property and prove he was the sole owner. The court ruled that Rollins owned a portion of the gravel road by adverse possession. She had used it openly for more than thirty-five years, it was generally thought to be part of her apartment complex, and she had paid taxes on it.[6] ●

How might this gravel road change ownership through adverse possession?

(Gali Estrange/Shutterstock.com)

Limitations on Property Rights

No ownership rights in real property can ever really be absolute—that is, an owner of real property cannot always do whatever she or he wishes on or with the property. Nuisance and environmental laws, for example, restrict certain types of activities.

Holding the property is also conditional on the payment of property taxes. Zoning laws and building permits frequently restrict one's use of realty. In addition, if a property owner fails to pay debts, the property may be seized to satisfy judgment creditors.

---

6. *Scarborough v. Rollins,* 44 So.3d 381 (2010).

In short, the rights of every property owner are subject to certain conditions and limitations. We look here at some of the important ways in which owners' rights in real property can be limited.

Eminent Domain

Even ownership in fee simple absolute is limited by a superior ownership. The U.S. government has an ultimate ownership right in all land. This right, known as **eminent domain,** is sometimes referred to as the *condemnation power* of government to take land for public use. It gives the government the right to acquire possession of real property in the manner directed by the U.S. Constitution and the laws of the state whenever the public interest requires it.

Eminent Domain The power of a government to take land from private citizens for public use on the payment of just compensation.

Public Use Requirement   Property may be taken only for public use, not for
private benefit. **EXAMPLE 22.15** When a new public highway is to be built, the government must decide where to build it and how much land to condemn. After the government determines that a particular parcel of land is necessary for public use, it will first offer to buy the property. If the owner refuses the offer, the government brings a judicial (**condemnation**) proceeding to obtain title to the land. Then, in another proceeding, the court determines the *fair value* of the land, which usually is approximately equal to its market value. ●

Condemnation The process of taking private property for public use through the government's power of eminent domain.

When the government uses its power of eminent domain to acquire land owned by a private party, a **taking** occurs. Under the *takings clause* of the Fifth Amendment to the U.S. Constitution, the government must pay "just compensation" to the property owner. State constitutions contain similar provisions.

Taking The taking of private property by the government for public use through the power of eminent domain.

Economic Development   In 2005, the United States Supreme Court ruled that
the power of eminent domain may be used to further economic development.[7] Since that decision, a majority of state legislatures have passed laws limiting the power of state governments to use eminent domain, particularly for urban redevelopment projects that benefit private developers.

The following case involved condemnation actions brought by a town to acquire rights-of-way for a natural gas pipeline to be constructed through the town. The issue was whether the pipeline was for public use, even though it was not built to furnish natural gas to the residents of that town.

7. *Kelo v. City of New London, Connecticut,* 545 U.S. 469, 125 S.Ct. 2655, 162 L.Ed.2d 439 (2005).

Case 22.3

(Lingbeek/iStockphoto.com)

Town of Midland v. Morris
Court of Appeals of North Carolina, 704 S.E.2d 329 (2011).

BACKGROUND AND FACTS The Transcontinental Pipeline transports and distributes natural gas from the Gulf of Mexico to the northeastern United States. The city of Monroe, North Carolina, decided to supply its citizens and the surrounding area with natural gas by constructing a direct connection between its natural gas distribution system and the Transcontinental Pipeline. To construct the connecting pipeline, Monroe needed to acquire the rights to property along a forty-two-mile route.

To do this, Monroe entered into an agreement with the town of Midland under which Midland would acquire the property (either by voluntary transfer or by eminent domain) and grant an easement to Monroe. In exchange, Midland would have the right to install a tap on the pipeline and receive discounted natural gas services.

Case 22.3—Continues ➡

Case 22.3—Continued

In 2008, Midland began the process of acquiring the property necessary for construction of the pipeline. When negotiations for voluntary acquisitions of the rights-of-way failed, Midland exercised its eminent domain authority to condemn the needed property. Midland filed fifteen condemnation actions, which the property owners (including Harry Morris) challenged. The trial court ruled in favor of Midland, and the property owners appealed. The property owners claimed, among other things, that Midland's condemnation of the property was not for public use or benefit because Midland had no concrete plans to furnish natural gas services from the pipeline to the city and its citizens.

IN THE WORDS OF THE COURT . . .
STEPHENS, Judge.
* * * *

Property Owners first argue that because Midland neither currently provides natural gas services to its citizens, nor currently has any plans to provide natural gas to its citizens in the future, the condemnations were undertaken in violation of the statutes governing eminent domain. We disagree.
* * * *

* * * *We find it manifest [obvious] that Midland may acquire property by condemnation to establish a gas transmission and distribution system, even in the absence of a concrete, immediate plan to furnish gas services to its citizens.* [Emphasis added.]

While we acknowledge the existence of the requirement that the public enterprise be established and conducted for the city and its citizens, we conclude that this requirement is satisfied by Midland's placement of a tap on the Pipeline and by Midland's acquisition of the right to low-cost natural gas. Further, * * * *there is nothing in the record to indicate that Midland will never offer natural gas services to its citizens. In fact, Midland's contracted-for right to install a tap on the Pipeline "from which to operate and supply its own natural gas distribution utility for the benefit of Midland's utility customers" indicates just the opposite: that Midland will, eventually, furnish natural gas services to its citizens.* [Emphasis added.]
* * * *

Property Owners further argue that Midland's condemnations violate [the state's statute] because the condemnations are not "for the public use or benefit."
* * * *

Despite the disjunctive language of this statutory requirement, our courts have determined the propriety of a condemnation under [the statute] based on the condemnation's satisfaction of both a "public use test" and a "public benefit test."

The first approach—the public use test—asks whether the public has a right to a definite use of the condemned property. The second approach—the public benefit test—asks whether some benefit accrues to the public as a result of the desired condemnation.

Under the public use test, "the principal and dispositive determination is whether the general public has a right to a definite use of the property sought to be condemned." * * * Applying this test to the present case in the appropriate context, there is nothing to indicate that gas services—were they to be provided by Midland—would be available to anything less than the entire population. Accordingly, there can be no doubt that the Midland condemnations would pass the public use test * * * .
* * * *

Under the public benefit test, *"a given condemnor's desired use of the condemned property in question is for 'the public use or benefit' if that use would contribute to the general welfare and prosperity of the public at large."* In this case, we must take care in defining Midland's "desired use" of the property. Midland is condemning the property to run the Pipeline and to control a tap on the Pipeline, not to immediately provide gas to the citizens of Midland. Accordingly, it is the *availability* of natural gas that must contribute to the general welfare and prosperity of the public at large. [Emphasis added.]

As noted by our Courts, the construction and extension of public utilities, and especially the concomitant commercial and residential growth, provide a clear public benefit to local citizens. * * * Midland's tap on the Pipeline, and its potential to provide natural gas service, likely will spur growth, as well as provide Midland with an advantage in industrial recruitment. These opportunities must be seen as public benefits accruing to the citizens of Midland, such that Midland's condemnations are for the public benefit.

DECISION AND REMEDY   The appellate court affirmed the lower court's decision that Midland had lawfully exercised its eminent domain power. Even though Midland might never tap into the pipeline, the condemnation satisfied the public use test because it gave the citizens of Midland a right to a definite use of the condemned property. Furthermore, the availability of natural gas benefited the public at large because it would likely contribute to growth and enhance the general prosperity of Midland.

THE ETHICAL DIMENSION   *Is it fair that a city can exercise its eminent domain power to take property even though the property will not be used immediately to benefit the city's residents? Why or why not?*

THE ECONOMIC DIMENSION   *The town of Midland—and its taxpaying citizens—had to pay fair value to fifteen property owners for the property it acquired through eminent domain. Is it right to make the citizens of one town pay for a pipeline constructed primarily to benefit another town? Discuss.*

Inverse Condemnation

Typically, a government agency exercises the power of eminent domain through litigation or negotiation and pays compensation to the landowner whose property is seized. **Inverse condemnation,** in contrast, occurs when a government simply takes private property from a landowner without paying any compensation, thereby forcing the landowner to sue the government for compensation.

The taking can be physical, as when a government agency uses or occupies the land, or it may be constructive, as when an agency regulation results in loss of property value. The United States Supreme Court has held that even temporary flooding of land by the government may result in liability under the takings clause.[8]

CASE EXAMPLE 22.16   In Walton County, Florida, water flows through a ditch from Oyster Lake to the Gulf of Mexico. When Hurricane Opal caused the water to rise in Oyster Lake, Walton County reconfigured the drainage to divert the overflow onto the nearby property of William and Patricia Hemby. The flow was eventually restored to pre-Opal conditions, but during a later emergency, water was diverted onto the Hembys' property again. This diversion was not restored.

The Hembys filed a suit against the county. After their deaths, their daughter Cozette Drake pursued the claim. The court found that by allowing the water diversion, created during emergency conditions, to remain on Drake's property long after the emergency had passed, the county had engaged in a permanent or continuous physical invasion. This invasion rendered Drake's property useless and deprived her of its beneficial enjoyment. Drake was therefore entitled to receive compensation from the county.[9] ●

Restrictive Covenants

A private restriction on the use of land is known as a **restrictive covenant**. If the restriction is binding on the party who purchases the property originally and on subsequent purchasers as well, it is said to "run with the land." A covenant running with the land must be in writing (usually it is in the deed), and subsequent purchasers must have reason to know about it.

EXAMPLE 22.17   In the course of developing a fifty-lot suburban subdivision, Levitt records a declaration of restrictions that effectively limits construction on each lot to one single-family house. Each lot's deed includes a reference to the declaration with a provision that the purchaser and her or his successors are bound to those restrictions. Thus, each purchaser assumes ownership with notice of the restrictions. If an owner attempts to build a duplex (or any structure that does not comply with the restrictions) on a lot, the other owners may obtain a court order enjoining the construction.

Alternatively, Levitt might simply have included the restrictions on the subdivision's map, filed the map in the appropriate public office, and included a reference to the map in each deed. In this way, each owner would also have been held to have constructive notice of the restrictions. ●

Land-Use Control and Zoning

The rules and regulations that collectively manage the development and use of land are known as **zoning laws.** Zoning laws were first used in the United States to segregate slaughterhouses, distilleries, kilns, and other businesses that might pose a nuisance to nearby residences. The growth of modern urban areas has led to an increased need to organize uses of land. Today, zoning laws enable the government of a municipality—a town, city, or

---

Inverse Condemnation The taking of private property by the government without payment of just compensation as required by the U.S. Constitution. The owner must sue the government to recover just compensation.

Restrictive Covenant A private restriction on the use of land that is binding on the party that purchases the property originally as well as on subsequent purchasers. If its benefit or obligation passes with the land's ownership, it is said to "run with the land."

Learning Objective 5
What is the purpose of zoning laws?

Zoning Laws Laws that divide a municipality into districts and prescribe the use to which property within each district may be put.

---

8. *Arkansas Game and Fish Commission v. United States,* ___ U.S. ___, 133 S.Ct. 511, 184 L.Ed.2d 417 (2012).
9. *Drake v. Walton County,* 6 So.3d 717 (Fla.App. 2009).

county—to control the speed and type of development within its borders by creating different zones and regulating the use of property allowed in each zone.

The United States Supreme Court has held that zoning is a constitutional exercise of a government's police powers.[10] Therefore, as long as its zoning ordinances are rationally related to the health, safety, or welfare of the community, a municipal government has broad discretion to carry out zoning as it sees fit.

Purpose and Scope of Zoning Laws

The purpose of zoning laws is to manage the land within a community in a way that encourages sustainable and organized development while controlling growth in a manner that serves the interests of the community. One of the basic elements of zoning is the classification of land by permissible use as part of a comprehensive municipal plan, but zoning extends to other aspects of land use as well.

Permissible Uses of Land

Residential Use   Use of land for construction of buildings for human habitation only.

Commercial Use   Use of land for business activities only. Also called *business use.*

Industrial Use   Use of land for light or heavy manufacturing, shipping, or heavy transportation.

Permissible Uses of Land   Municipalities generally divide their available land into districts according to the land's present and potential future uses. Typically, land is classified into the following types of permissible uses:

1. *Residential.* In areas dedicated for **residential use,** landowners can construct buildings for human habitation.
2. *Commercial.* Land assigned for business activities is designated as being for **commercial use,** sometimes called business use. An area with a number of retail stores, offices, supermarkets, and hotels might be designated as a commercial or business district. Land used for entertainment purposes, such as movie theaters and sports stadiums, also falls into this category, as does land used for government activities.
3. *Industrial.* Areas designated for **industrial use** typically encompass light and heavy manufacturing, shipping, and heavy transportation. For instance, undeveloped land with easy access to highways and railroads might be classified as suitable for future use by industry. Although industrial uses can be profitable for a city seeking to raise tax revenue, such uses can also result in noise, smoke, or vibrations that interfere with others' enjoyment of their property. Consequently, areas zoned for industrial use generally are kept as far as possible from residential districts and some commercial districts.
4. *Conservation districts.* Some municipalities also establish certain areas that are dedicated to carrying out local soil and water conservation efforts—for instance, wetlands (see Chapter 21) might be designated as a conservation district.

A city's residential, commercial, and industrial districts may be divided, in turn, into subdistricts. For instance, zoning ordinances regulate the type, density, size, and approved uses of structures within a given district. Thus, a residential district may be divided into low-density (single-family homes with large lots), high-density (single- and multiple-family homes with small lots), and planned-unit (condominiums or apartments) subdistricts.

Other Zoning Restrictions   Zoning rules extend to much more than the permissible use of land. In residential districts, for instance, an ordinance may require a house or garage to be set back a specific number of feet from a neighbor's property line.

In commercial districts, zoning rules may attempt to maintain a certain visual aesthetic. Therefore, businesses may be required to construct buildings of a certain height and width so that they conform to the style of other commercial buildings in the area.

Businesses may also be required to provide parking for patrons or take other measures to manage traffic. Sometimes, municipalities limit construction of new businesses

---

10. *Village of Euclid v. Ambler Realty Co.,* 272 U.S. 365, 47 S.Ct. 114, 71 L.Ed. 303 (1926).

to prevent traffic congestion. Zoning laws may even attempt to regulate the public morals of the community. For instance, cities commonly impose severe restrictions on the location and operation of adult businesses.

Exceptions to Zoning Laws

Zoning restrictions are not absolute. It is impossible for zoning laws to account for every contingency. The purpose of zoning is to enable the municipality to control development but not to prevent it altogether or limit the government's ability to adapt to changing circumstances or unforeseen needs. Hence, legal processes have been developed to allow for exceptions to zoning laws. Here, we look at these exceptions, known as *variances* and *special-use permits,* as well as at the *special incentives* that governments may offer to encourage certain kinds of development.

(MCT/Getty Images)

What entities determine zoning classifications?

Variances   When a property owner wants to use his or her land in a manner not permitted by zoning rules, she or he can request a **variance,** which allows an exception to the rules. The property owner requesting the variance must demonstrate that the requested variance:

1. Is necessary for reasonable development.
2. Is the least intrusive solution to the problem.
3. Will not alter the essential character of the neighborhood.

Hardship Situations   Property owners normally request variances in *hardship situations* (when complying with the zoning rules would be too difficult or costly due to existing property conditions). **EXAMPLE 22.18**   Lin Wang, a homeowner, wants to replace her single-car garage with a two-car garage, but if she does so, the garage will be closer to her neighbor's property than is permitted by the zoning rules. In this situation, she may ask for a variance. She can claim that the configuration of her property (where the current garage is located) makes it difficult and costly to comply with the zoning code, so compliance would create a hardship for her. ●

Similarly, a church might request a variance from height restrictions in order to erect a new steeple. Or a furniture store might ask for a variance from *footprint* limitations so that it can expand its showroom (a building's footprint is the area of ground that it covers).

Note that the hardship may not be self-created. In other words, a person usually cannot buy property with zoning regulations in effect and then argue that a variance is needed for the property to be used for the owner's intended purpose.

Public Hearing   In almost all instances, before a variance is granted, there must be a public hearing with adequate notice to neighbors who may object to the exception. After the public hearing, a hearing examiner appointed by the municipality (or the local zoning board or commission) determines whether to grant the exception. When a variance is granted, it applies only to the specific parcel of land for which it was requested and does not create a regulation-free zone.

Special-Use Permits   Sometimes, zoning laws permit a use, but only if the property owner complies with specific requirements to ensure that the proposed use does not harm the immediate neighborhood. In such instances, the zoning board will issue **special-use permits,** also called conditional-use permits.

Variance A form of relief from zoning laws that is granted to a property owner to allow the property to be used in a manner not permitted by zoning regulations.

Special-Use Permit A permit that allows an exemption to zoning regulations for a particular piece of property as long as the property owner complies with specific requirements to ensure that the proposed use does not affect the characteristics of the area.

EXAMPLE 22.19 An area is designated as a residential district, but small businesses are permitted to operate there so long as they do not affect the characteristics of the neighborhood. A bank asks the zoning board for a special-use permit to open a branch in the area.

At the public hearing, the bank's managers demonstrate that the branch will be housed in a building that conforms to the style of other structures in the area. The bank also shows that adequate parking will be available and that landscaping will shield the parking lot from public view. Unless there are strong objections from the branch's prospective neighbors, the board will likely grant the permit. ●

Special Incentives In addition to granting exceptions to zoning regulations, municipalities may also wish to encourage certain kinds of development. To do so, they offer incentives, often in the form of lower tax rates or tax credits.

For instance, to attract new businesses that will provide jobs for local citizens and increase the tax base, a city may offer incentives in the form of lower property tax rates for a period of years. Similarly, homeowners may receive tax credits for historical preservation if they renovate and maintain older homes.

Tax credits provided by cities and towns may encourage construction firms to utilize "green" construction techniques that are more sustainable. **EXAMPLE 22.20** Ryan Orley, of Orley Construction, LLC, knows that a building's thermal load (the amount of heat that must be removed over a given time period) depends, in part, on its orientation to the sun. A change in the building's orientation may entail a higher cost initially but save on air-conditioning expenses later. Ryan convinces his client that it is worth the extra cost to have the building redesigned to minimize the long-term cost of air-conditioning. Ryan also conducts research and discovers that the tax credit available from the city will help cover the additional construction costs. ●

Reviewing . . . Real Property and Land-Use Control

Vern Shoepke purchased a two-story home from Walter and Eliza Bruster in the town of Roche, Maine. The warranty deed did not specify what covenants would be included in the conveyance. The property was adjacent to a public park that included a popular Frisbee golf course. (Frisbee golf is a sport similar to golf but using Frisbees.) Wayakichi Creek ran along the north end of the park and along Shoepke's property. The deed allowed Roche citizens the right to walk across a five-foot-wide section of the lot beside Wayakichi Creek as part of a two-mile public trail system. Teenagers regularly threw Frisbee golf discs from the walking path behind Shoepke's property over his yard to the adjacent park. Shoepke habitually shouted and cursed at the teenagers, demanding that they not throw objects over his yard. Using the information presented in the chapter, answer the following questions.

1. What is the term for the right of Roche citizens to walk across Shoepke's land on the trail?
2. What covenants would most courts infer were included in the warranty deed that was used in the property transfer from the Brusters to Shoepke?
3. Suppose that Shoepke wants to file a trespass lawsuit against some teenagers who continually throw Frisbees over his land. Shoepke discovers, however, that when the city put in the Frisbee golf course, the neighborhood homeowners signed an agreement that limited their right to complain about errant Frisbees. What is this type of promise or agreement called in real property law?

Debate This Under no circumstances should a local government be able to condemn property in order to sell it later to real estate developers for private use.

Key Terms

Chapter Summary: Real Property and Land-Use Control

The Nature of Real Property	Real property (also called real estate or realty) is immovable. It includes land, subsurface and airspace rights, plant life and vegetation, and fixtures.

Ownership Interests and Leases	1. *Fee simple absolute* — The most complete form of ownership.
	2. *Life estate* — An estate that lasts for the life of a specified individual, during which time the individual is entitled to possess, use, and benefit from the estate. The life tenant's ownership rights cease to exist on her or his death.
	3. *Nonpossessory interest* — An interest that involves the right to use real property but not to possess it. Easements, profits, and licenses are nonpossessory interests.
	4. *Leasehold estate* — An interest in real property that is held for only a limited period of time, as specified in the lease agreement. Types of tenancies include the following:
	   a. Fixed-term tenancy — Tenancy for a period of time stated by express contract.
	   b. Periodic tenancy — Tenancy for a period determined by the frequency of rent payments and automatically renewed unless proper notice is given.
	   c. Tenancy at will — Tenancy for as long as both parties agree. No notice of termination is required.
	   d. Tenancy at sufferance — Possession of land without legal right.

Transfer of Ownership	1. *By deed* — When real property is sold or transferred as a gift, title to the property is conveyed by means of a deed. A deed must meet specific legal requirements. A *warranty deed* provides the most extensive protection against defects of title. A *quitclaim deed* conveys to the grantee only whatever interest the grantor had in the property. A deed may be recorded in the manner prescribed by *recording statutes* in the appropriate jurisdiction to give third parties notice of the owner's interest. 2. *By will or inheritance* — If the owner dies after having made a valid will, the land passes as specified in the will. If the owner dies without having made a will, the heirs inherit according to state inheritance statutes. 3. *By adverse possession* — When a person possesses the property of another for a statutory period of time (ten years is the most common), that person acquires title to the property, provided the possession is actual and exclusive, open and visible, continuous and peaceable, and hostile and adverse (without the permission of the owner).
Limitations on Property Rights	1. *Eminent domain* — The government's power to take land for public use, with just compensation, when the public interest requires the taking. 2. *Restrictive covenant* — A private restriction on the use of land (often included in a deed). 3. *Inverse condemnation* — A government's taking of private property without paying compensation to the property owner, as when an agency restricts the use of private property, thereby lowering its value.
Land-Use Control and Zoning	Each state regulates land use within its boundaries, typically through municipal planning boards and zoning authorities. Zoning laws divide an area into districts to which specific land-use regulations apply. Certain areas are designated for residential use, commercial use, or industrial use. A property owner who wants an exception from zoning regulations can seek a variance or a special-use permit.

Issue Spotters

1. Bernie sells his house to Consuela under a warranty deed. Later, Delmira appears, holding a better title to the house than Consuela has. Delmira wants Consuela off the property. What can Consuela do? (See *Transfer of Ownership*.)

2. Grey owns a commercial building in fee simple. Grey transfers temporary possession of the building to Haven Corporation. Can Grey enter the building without Haven Corporation's permission? Explain. (See *Ownership Interests and Leases*.)

—**Check your answers to the Issue Spotters against the answers provided in Appendix D at the end of this text.**

For Review

1. What is a fixture, and how does it relate to real property rights?
2. What is an easement? Describe three ways that easements are created.
3. What are the requirements for acquiring property by adverse possession?
4. What limitations may be imposed on the rights of property owners?
5. What is the purpose of zoning laws?

Business Scenarios and Case Problems

22–1. Property Ownership. Twenty-two years ago, Lorenz was a wanderer. At that time, he decided to settle down on an unoccupied, three-acre parcel of land that he did not own. People in the area told him that they had no idea who owned the property. Lorenz built a house on the land, got married, and raised three children while living there. He fenced in the land, installed a gate with a sign above it that read "Lorenz's Homestead," and removed trespassers. Lorenz is now confronted by Joe Reese, who has a deed in his name as owner of the property. Reese, claiming ownership of the land, orders Lorenz and his family off the property. Discuss who has the better "title" to the property. (See *Transfer of Ownership*.)

22–2. Zoning. The county intends to rezone an area from industrial use to residential use. Land within the affected area is largely undeveloped, but nonetheless it is expected that the proposed action will reduce the market value of the affected land by as much as 50 percent. Will the landowners be successful in suing to have the action declared a taking of their property, entitling them to just compensation? Why or why not? (See *Land-Use Control and Zoning*.)

22–3. Eminent Domain. Some Catholic organizations proposed to build a private independent middle school in a run-down neighborhood in Philadelphia, Pennsylvania. They asked the Redevelopment Authority of the City of Philadelphia to acquire specific land for the project and sell it to them for a nominal price. The land included a house on North Eighth Street owned by Mary Smith, whose daughter Veronica lived there with her family. The Authority offered Smith $12,000 for the house and initiated a taking of the property. Smith filed a suit in state court against the Authority, admitting that the house was a "substandard structure in a blighted area," but arguing that the taking was unconstitutional because its beneficiary was private. The Authority asserted that only the public purpose of the taking should be considered, not the status of the property's developer. On what basis can a

government entity use the power of eminent domain to take property? What are the limits to this power? How should the court rule? Why? (See *Limitations on Property Rights*.)

22–4. Ownership in Fee Simple. Thomas and Teresa Cline built a house on 76 acres next to Roy Berg's home in Virginia. The homes were about 1,800 feet apart but in view of each other. After several disagreements between the parties, Berg equipped an 11-foot tripod with motion sensors and floodlights that intermittently illuminated the Clines' home. Berg also installed surveillance cameras that tracked some of the movement on the Clines' property. The cameras transmitted on an open frequency, which could be received by any television within range. The Clines asked Berg to turn off, or at least redirect, the lights. When he refused, they erected a fence for 200 feet along the parties' common property line. The 32-foot-high fence consisted of 20 utility poles spaced 10 feet apart with plastic wrap stretched between the poles. This effectively blocked the lights and cameras. Berg filed a suit against the Clines in a Virginia state court, complaining that the fence interfered unreasonably with his use and enjoyment of his property. He asked the court to order the Clines to take the fence down. What are the limits on an owner's use of property? How should the court rule in this case? Why? [*Cline v. Berg*, 273 Va. 142, 639 S.E.2d 231 (2007)] (See *Ownership Interests and Leases*.)

22–5. Zoning and Variances. Joseph and Lois Ryan hired a contractor to build a home in Weston, Connecticut. The contractor submitted plans to the town that included a roof height of thirty-eight feet for the proposed dwelling. This exceeded the town's roof-height restriction of thirty-five feet. The contractor and the architect revised the plans to meet the restriction, and the town approved the plans and issued a zoning permit and a building permit. After the roof was constructed, a code enforcement officer discovered that it measured thirty-seven feet, seven inches high.

The officer issued a cease-and-desist order requiring the Ryans to "remove the height violation and bring the structure into compliance." The Ryans appealed to the zoning board, claiming that the error was not theirs but that of their general contractor and architect. The zoning board upheld the cease-and-desist order but later granted the Ryans a variance because "the roof height was out of compliance by approximately two feet, . . . the home [was] perched high on the land and [was] not a detriment to the neighborhood, and . . . the hardship was created by the contractor's error." Neighbors (including Curtis Morikawa) appealed to a court.

They argued that the hardship claimed was solely economic. In addition, they argued that even though it was unintended, the hardship was self-created. The trial court ruled in favor of the neighbors, and the Ryans appealed. How should the court rule? Were there legitimate grounds for granting a variance? Discuss. [*Morikawa v. Zoning Board of Appeals of Town of Weston*, 126 Conn.App. 400, 11 A.3d 735 (2011)] (See *Land-Use Control and Zoning*.)

22–6. **Business Case Problem with Sample Answer— Adverse Possession.** The McKeag family operated a marina on their lakefront property in Bolton, New York. For more than forty years, the McKeags used a section of property belonging to their neighbors, the Finleys, as a beach for the marina's customers. The McKeags also stored a large float on the beach during the winter months, built their own retaining wall, and planted bushes and flowers there. The McKeags prevented others from using the property, including the Finleys. Nevertheless, the families always had a friendly relationship, and one of the Finleys gave the McKeags permission to continue using the beach in 1992. He also reminded them of his ownership several times, to which they said nothing. The McKeags also asked for permission to mow grass on the property and once apologized for leaving a jet ski there. Can the McKeags establish adverse possession over the statutory period of ten years? Why or why not? [*McKeag v. Finley*, 939 N.Y.S.2d 644 (N.Y.App.Div. 2012)] (See *Transfer of Ownership*.)

—For a sample answer to Problem 22–6, go to Appendix E at the end of this text.

22–7. Real Estate Sales Contracts. A California state statute requires sellers to provide a real estate "Transfer Disclosure Statement" (TDS) to buyers of residential property consisting of one to four dwelling units. Required disclosures include information about significant defects, including hazardous materials, encroachments, easements, fill, settling, flooding, drainage problems, neighborhood noise, damage from natural disasters, and lawsuits. Mark Hartley contracted with Randall Richman to buy Richman's property in Ventura, California. The property included a commercial building and a residential duplex with two dwelling units. Richman did not provide a TDS, claiming that it was not required because the property was "mixed use"—that is, it included both a commercial building and a residential building. Hartley refused to go through with the deal. Did Hartley breach their contract, or did Richman's failure to provide a TDS excuse Hartley's nonperformance? Discuss. [*Richman v. Hartley*, 224 Cal.App.4th 1182, 169 Cal.Rptr.3d 475 (2 Dist. 2014)] (See *Transfer of Ownership*.)

22–8. **Critical-Thinking Legal Environment Question.** Garza Construction Co. erects a silo (a grain storage facility) on Reeve's ranch. Garza also lends Reeve funds to pay for the silo under an agreement providing that the silo is not to become part of the land until Reeve completes the loan payments. Before the silo is paid for, Metropolitan State Bank, the mortgage holder on Reeve's land, forecloses on the property. Metropolitan contends that the silo is a fixture to the realty and that the bank is therefore entitled to the proceeds from its sale. Garza argues that the silo is personal property and that the proceeds should therefore go to Garza. Is the silo a fixture? Why or why not? (See *The Nature of Real Property*.)

22–9. **A Question of Ethics—Adverse Possession.** Alana Mansell built a garage on her property that encroached on the property of her neighbor, Betty Hunter, by fourteen feet. Hunter knew of the encroachment and informally agreed to it, but she did not transfer ownership of the property to Mansell. A survey twenty-eight years later confirmed the encroachment, and Hunter sought the removal of the garage. Mansell asked a court to declare that she was the owner of the property by adverse possession. [*Hunter v. Mansell*, 240 P.3d 469 (Colo.App. 2010)] (See *Transfer of Ownership*.)

1. Did Mansell obtain title by adverse possession? Would the open occupation of the property for nearly thirty years be in Mansell's favor? Why or why not?

2. Was her conduct in any way unethical? Discuss.

23 CHAPTER

Antitrust Law and Promoting Competition

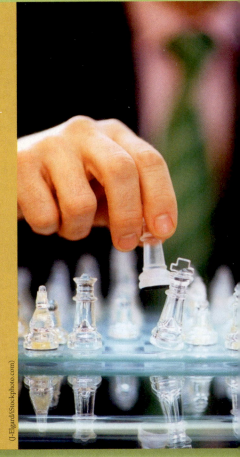

(J. Elgard/iStockphoto.com)

CONTENTS

- The Sherman Antitrust Act
- Section 1 of the Sherman Act
- Section 2 of the Sherman Act
- The Clayton Act
- Enforcement and Exemptions
- U.S. Antitrust Laws in the Global Context

LEARNING OBJECTIVES

The five learning objectives below are designed to help improve your understanding of the chapter. After reading this chapter, you should be able to answer the following questions:

1. What is a monopoly? What is market power? How do these concepts relate to each other?
2. What anticompetitive activities are prohibited by Section 1 of the Sherman Act?
3. What type of activity is prohibited by Section 2 of the Sherman Act?
4. What are the four major provisions of the Clayton Act, and what types of activities do these provisions prohibit?
5. What agencies of the federal government enforce the federal antitrust laws?

> "Competition is not only the basis of protection to the consumer but is the incentive to progress."
> —Herbert Hoover, 1874–1964 (Thirty-first president of the United States, 1929–1933)

Antitrust Law Laws protecting commerce from unlawful restraints and anticompetitive practices.

The laws regulating economic competition in the United States are referred to as **antitrust laws.** They include the Sherman Antitrust Act,[1] the Clayton Act,[2] and the Federal Trade Commission Act,[3] passed by Congress to further curb anticompetitive or unfair business practices. Congress later amended these acts to broaden and strengthen their coverage. We examine these major federal antitrust statutes in this chapter.

The basis of antitrust legislation is the desire to foster competition. Antitrust legislation was initially created—and continues to be enforced—because of our society's belief that competition leads to lower prices and generates more product information. As President Herbert Hoover indicated in the chapter-opening quotation, competition not only protects the consumer, but also provides "the incentive to progress."

---

1. 15 U.S.C. Sections 1–7.
2. 15 U.S.C. Sections 12–27.
3. 15 U.S.C. Sections 41–58.

Consumers and society as a whole benefit when producers strive to develop better products that they can sell at lower prices to beat the competition. This is still true today, which is why the government is concerned about the pricing of e-books, as you will read later in this chapter.

The Sherman Antitrust Act

Today's antitrust laws are the direct descendants of common law actions intended to limit *restraints of trade* (agreements between or among firms that have the effect of reducing competition in the marketplace). Such actions date to the fifteenth century in England.

After the Civil War (1861–1865), the American public became increasingly concerned about declining competition in the marketplace. Large corporate enterprises were attempting to reduce or eliminate competition by legally tying themselves together in contracts to create *business trusts* (unincorporated organizations with limited liability). The most powerful of these trusts, the Standard Oil trust, is examined in this chapter's *Landmark in the Legal Environment* feature that follows.

In 1890, Congress passed "An Act to Protect Trade and Commerce against Unlawful Restraints and Monopolies"—commonly known as the Sherman Antitrust Act or, more simply, as the Sherman Act. The Sherman Act became (and still is) one of the government's most powerful weapons in the effort to maintain a competitive economy.

Major Provisions of the Sherman Act

Sections 1 and 2 contain the main provisions of the Sherman Act:

1. "Every contract, combination in the form of trust or otherwise, or conspiracy, in restraint of trade or commerce among the several States, or with foreign nations, is hereby declared to be illegal [and is a felony punishable by a fine and/or imprisonment]."
2. "Every person who shall monopolize, or attempt to monopolize, or combine or conspire with any other person or persons, to monopolize any part of the trade or commerce among the several States, or with foreign nations, shall be deemed guilty of a felony [and is similarly punishable]."

Differences between Section 1 and Section 2

These two sections of the Sherman Act are quite different. Violation of Section 1 requires two or more persons, as a person cannot contract or combine or conspire alone. Thus, the essence of the illegal activity is *the act of joining together*. Section 2, though, can apply either to one person or to two or more persons because it refers to "every person." Thus, unilateral conduct can result in a violation of Section 2.

The cases brought under Section 1 of the Sherman Act differ from those brought under Section 2. Section 1 cases are often concerned with finding an agreement (written or oral)

One of Standard Oil's refineries in Richmond, California, around 1900.

LANDMARK IN THE LEGAL ENVIRONMENT

The Sherman Antitrust Act of 1890

The author of the Sherman Antitrust Act, Senator John Sherman, was the brother of the famous Civil War general William Tecumseh Sherman and a recognized financial authority. Sherman had been concerned for years about diminishing competition in U.S. industry and the emergence of monopolies, such as the Standard Oil trust.

The Standard Oil Trust By 1890, the Standard Oil trust had become the foremost petroleum refining and marketing combination in the United States. Streamlined, integrated, and centrally controlled, Standard Oil maintained an indisputable monopoly over the industry. The trust controlled 90 percent of the U.S. market for refined petroleum products, making it impossible for small producers to compete with such a leviathan.

The increasing consolidation in U.S. industry, and particularly the Standard Oil trust, came to the attention of the public in March 1881. Henry Demarest Lloyd, a young journalist from Chicago, published an article in the *Atlantic Monthly* entitled "The Story of a Great Monopoly." The article argued that the U.S. petroleum industry was dominated by one firm—Standard Oil. Lloyd's article was so popular that the issue was reprinted six times. It marked the beginning of the U.S. public's growing concern over monopolies.

The Passage of the Sherman Antitrust Act The common law regarding trade regulation was not always consistent.

Certainly, it was not very familiar to the members of Congress. The public concern over large business integrations and trusts was familiar, however. In 1888, 1889, and again in 1890, Senator Sherman introduced in Congress bills designed to destroy the large combinations of capital that, he felt, were creating a lack of balance within the nation's economy.

Sherman told Congress that the Sherman Act "does not announce a new principle of law, but applies old and well-recognized principles of the common law."[a] In 1890, the Fifty-First Congress enacted the bill into law. Generally, the act prohibits business combinations and conspiracies that restrain trade and commerce, as well as certain monopolistic practices.

Application to Today's Legal Environment *The Sherman Antitrust Act remains very relevant to today's world. Since the widely publicized monopolization case against Microsoft Corporation in 2001,[b] the U.S. Department of Justice and state attorneys general have brought numerous Sherman Act cases against other corporations, including eBay, Intel, and Philip Morris.[c]*

---

a. 21 *Congressional Record* 2456 (1890).
b. *United States v. Microsoft Corp.*, 253 F.3d 34 (D.C.Cir. 2001).
c. See, for example, *United States v. Philip Morris USA, Inc.*, 566 F.3d 1095 (D.C.Cir. 2009); *In re eBay Seller Antitrust Litigation*, 545 F.Supp.2d 1027 (N.D.Cal. 2008); and *In re Intel Corp. Microprocessor Antitrust Litigation*, 2007 WL 137152 (D.Del. 2007).

Learning Objective 1

What is a monopoly? What is market power? How do these concepts relate to each other?

Monopoly A market in which there is a single seller or a very limited number of sellers.

Monopoly Power The ability of a monopoly to dictate what takes place in a given market.

Market Power The power of a firm to control the market price of its product. A monopoly has the greatest degree of market power.

that leads to a restraint of trade. Section 2 cases deal with the structure of a monopoly that already exists in the marketplace. The term **monopoly** generally is used to describe a market in which there is a single seller or a very limited number of sellers. Whereas Section 1 focuses on agreements that are restrictive—that is, agreements that have a wrongful purpose—Section 2 addresses the misuse of **monopoly power** in the marketplace.

Monopoly power exists when a firm has an extreme amount of **market power**—the power to affect the market price of its product. Both Section 1 and Section 2 seek to curtail market practices that result in undesired monopoly pricing and output behavior. For a case to be brought under Section 2, however, the "threshold" or "necessary" amount of monopoly power must already exist. We illustrate the different requirements for violating these two sections of the Sherman Act in Exhibit 23–1 that follows.

Jurisdictional Requirements

The Sherman Act applies only to restraints that have a substantial impact on interstate commerce. Generally, any activity that substantially affects interstate commerce falls within the scope of the Sherman Act. As will be discussed later in this chapter, the Sherman Act

Exhibit 23–1 Required Elements of a Sherman Act Violation

SECTION 1 VIOLATION REQUIREMENTS	SECTION 2 VIOLATION REQUIREMENTS
1. An agreement between two or more parties that 2. Unreasonably restrains competition and 3. Affects interstate commerce.	1. The possession of monopoly power in the relevant market, and 2. Willful acquisition or maintenance of that power as distinguished from its growth or development as a consequence of a superior product, business acumen, or historic accident.

also extends to U.S. nationals abroad who are engaged in activities that have an effect on U.S. foreign commerce. Federal courts have exclusive jurisdiction over antitrust cases brought under the Sherman Act. State laws regulate local restraints on competition, and state courts decide claims brought under those laws.

Section 1 of the Sherman Act

The underlying assumption of Section 1 of the Sherman Act is that society's welfare is harmed if rival firms are permitted to join in an agreement that consolidates their market power or otherwise restrains competition. The types of trade restraints that Section 1 of the Sherman Act prohibits generally fall into two broad categories: *horizontal restraints* and *vertical restraints,* both of which will be discussed shortly. First, though, we look at the rules that the courts may apply when assessing the anticompetitive impact of alleged restraints on trade.

Learning Objective 2
What anticompetitive activities are prohibited by Section 1 of the Sherman Act?

Per Se Violations versus the Rule of Reason

Some restraints are so blatantly and substantially anticompetitive that they are deemed ***per se* violations**—illegal *per se* (on their face, or inherently)—under Section 1. Other agreements, however, even though they result in enhanced market power, do not *unreasonably* restrain trade. Using what is called the **rule of reason**, the courts analyze anticompetitive agreements that allegedly violate Section 1 of the Sherman Act to determine whether they actually constitute reasonable restraints on trade.

Per Se Violation A restraint of trade that is so anticompetitive that it is deemed inherently (*per se*) illegal.

Rule of Reason A test used to determine whether an anticompetitive agreement constitutes a reasonable restraint on trade. Courts consider such factors as the purpose of the agreement, its effect on competition, and whether less restrictive means could have been used.

Why the Rule of Reason Was Developed
The need for a rule-of-reason analysis of some agreements in restraint of trade is obvious—if the rule of reason had not been developed, almost any business agreement could conceivably be held to violate the Sherman Act. Justice Louis Brandeis effectively phrased this sentiment in *Chicago Board of Trade v. United States*, a case decided in 1918:

> Every agreement concerning trade, every regulation of trade, restrains. To bind, to restrain, is of their very essence. The true test of legality is whether the restraint imposed is such as merely regulates and perhaps thereby promotes competition or whether it is such as may suppress or even destroy competition.[4]

Factors Courts Consider under the Rule of Reason
When analyzing an alleged Section 1 violation under the rule of reason, a court will consider several factors. These factors include the purpose of the agreement, the parties' market ability to implement the agreement to achieve that purpose, and the effect or potential effect of the agreement on competition. Another factor that a court might consider is whether the parties could have relied on less restrictive means to achieve their purpose.

---

4. 246 U.S. 231, 38 S.Ct. 242, 62 L.Ed. 683 (1918).

CASE EXAMPLE 23.1 The National Football League (NFL) includes thirty-two separately owned professional football teams. Each team has its own name, colors, and logo, and owns related intellectual property that it markets through National Football League Properties (NFLP). Until 2000, the NFLP granted nonexclusive licenses to a number of vendors, permitting them to manufacture and sell apparel bearing NFL team insignias. American Needle, Inc., was one of those licensees.

In late 2000, the teams authorized the NFLP to grant exclusive licenses, and the NFLP granted Reebok International, Ltd., an exclusive ten-year license to manufacture and sell trademarked headwear for all thirty-two teams. It then declined to renew American Needle's nonexclusive license. American Needle sued, claiming that the NFL teams, the NFLP, and Reebok had violated Section 1 of the Sherman Act. The United States Supreme Court agreed. The Court concluded that the agreement among the NFL teams to license their intellectual property exclusively through the NFLP to Reebok constituted concerted activity.[5] ●

Recently, a question was raised regarding whether the bundling together high-demand and low-demand television channels in cable and satellite programming packages violates the Sherman Act. Bundling forces consumers to pay for channels they do not watch to have access to channels they watch regularly. **CASE EXAMPLE 23.2** A group of consumers sued NBC Universal, the Walt Disney Company, and other programmers, as well as cable and satellite distributors. The consumers claimed that the defendants, through their control of high-demand programming, exercised market power that made it impossible for any distributor to offer unbundled programs. A federal appellate court ruled in favor of the defendants and dismissed the case. The court reasoned that Sherman Act applies to actions that diminish competition and that the bundling of channels does not injure competition.[6] ●

Horizontal Restraints

Horizontal Restraint Any agreement that restrains competition between rival firms competing in the same market.

The term **horizontal restraint** is encountered frequently in antitrust law. A horizontal restraint is any agreement that in some way restrains competition between rival firms competing in the same market. Horizontal restraints may include price-fixing, group boycotts, market divisions, and trade associations.

Price-Fixing Agreement An agreement between competitors to fix the prices of products or services at a certain level.

Price Fixing
Any **price-fixing agreement**—an agreement among competitors to fix prices—constitutes a *per se* violation of Section 1. The agreement on price need not be explicit: as long as it restricts output or artificially fixes price, it violates the law.

CASE EXAMPLE 23.3 Independent oil producers in Texas and Louisiana were caught between falling demand due to the Great Depression of the 1930s and increasing supply from newly discovered oil fields in the region. In response to these conditions, a group of the major refining companies agreed to buy "distress" gasoline (excess supplies) from the independents so as to dispose of it in an "orderly manner." Although there was no explicit agreement as to price, it was clear that the purpose of the agreement was to limit the supply of gasoline on the market and thereby raise prices.

There may have been good reasons for the agreement. Nonetheless, the United States Supreme Court recognized the potentially adverse effects that such an agreement could have on open and free competition. The Court held that the reasonableness of a price-fixing agreement is never a defense. Any agreement that restricts output or artificially fixes price is a *per se* violation of Section 1.[7] ●

Price-fixing cartels (groups) are commonplace in today's business world, particularly among global companies. For instance, in 2011, Samsung Electronics, Sharp Corporation,

---

5. *American Needle, Inc. v. National Football League*, 560 U.S. 183, 130 S.Ct. 2201, 176 L.Ed.2d 947 (2010).
6. *Brantley v. NBC Universal, Inc.*, 675 F.3d 1192 (9th Cir. 2012).
7. *United States v. Socony-Vacuum Oil Co.*, 310 U.S. 150, 60 S.Ct. 811, 84 L.Ed. 1129 (1940).

and five other makers of liquid crystal displays (LCDs) for notebooks and other devices agreed to pay more than $553 million to settle price-fixing claims against them. See this chapter's *Online Developments* feature that follows for a discussion of price-fixing allegations in the e-book industry.

Price-fixing accusations are also frequently made against drug manufacturers. **CASE EXAMPLE 23.4** The manufacturer of the prescription drug Cardizem CD, which can help prevent heart attacks, was about to lose its patent on the drug. Another company developed a generic version in anticipation of the patent expiring. After the two firms became involved in litigation over the patent, the first company agreed to pay the second company $40 million per year not to market the generic version until their dispute

(Peter J. Kovacs/Shutterstock.com)

What major companies tried to fix LCD prices?

ONLINE DEVELOPMENTS

The Justice Department Goes after E-Book Pricing

In 2012, the U.S. Justice Department filed a lawsuit against five major book publishers and Apple, Inc., charging that they had conspired to fix the prices of e-books. According to the thirty-six-page complaint, publishing executives met "in private rooms for dinner in upscale Manhattan restaurants" to discuss ways to limit e-book price competition. As a result, claims the Justice Department, consumers paid "tens of millions of dollars more for e-books than they otherwise would have paid."

The E-Book Market Explodes

E-books were only a niche product until a few years ago when Amazon.com released its first Kindle e-book reader. To sell more Kindles, Amazon offered thousands of popular books for downloading at $9.99 per e-book. Amazon kept 50 percent and gave 50 percent to the publishers, who had to agree to Amazon's pricing. Although Amazon lost on its e-book sales, it made up the losses by selling more Kindles.

Enter Apple's iPad

When the iPad entered the scene, Apple and the book publishers agreed to use Apple's "agency" model, which allowed the publishers to set their own prices while Apple kept 30 percent as a commission. Apple was already using this model for games and apps for its iPhones and iPads.

The Justice Department, however, decided that because the publishers chose prices that were relatively similar, price fixing was evident. Nowhere in the Justice Department's complaint did it acknowledge that the agency model is the standard approach for many types of sales. Indeed, the Justice Department claimed that the agency model is *per se* illegal and "would not have occurred without the conspiracy among

the defendants." Yet the model is used in many industries and has been upheld by federal courts for years.

Amazon Still Leads but Not by Much

When the Kindle was king, Amazon had 90 percent of the e-book market. Since the advent of the the iPad, Barnes & Noble's Nook, and other e-book readers, Kindle's market share has fallen to 60 percent because of increased competition. E-books now cost anywhere from zero to $14.99.

(Photo by Bill Stryker)

It's *Gone with the Wind* All Over Again

During the Great Depression, the federal government brought a similar antitrust lawsuit. At the time, Macy's, the department store chain, sold books at a steep discount. It was selling *Gone with the Wind* for the equivalent of $15 in today's dollars, whereas smaller stores charged double or triple that price. Publishers and booksellers lobbied for protection from what they called predatory pricing. Ultimately, the federal government did not prevail, but for a while, retail book prices remained high.

Critical Thinking

The publishing business is in dire straits today with retail bookstores going bankrupt and publishers laying off hundreds of employees. Why do you think the declining book business was worthy of so much attention from the Justice Department?

was resolved. This agreement was held to be a *per se* violation of the Sherman Act because it restrained competition between rival firms and delayed the entry of generic versions of Cardizem into the market.[8] ●

Group Boycotts

Group Boycott An agreement by two or more sellers to refuse to deal with a particular person or firm.

A **group boycott** is an agreement by two or more sellers to refuse to deal with (boycott) a particular person or firm. Such group boycotts have been held to constitute *per se* violations of Section 1 of the Sherman Act. Section 1 has been violated if it can be demonstrated that the boycott or joint refusal to deal was undertaken with the intention of eliminating competition or preventing entry into a given market. Some boycotts, such as group boycotts against a supplier for political reasons, may be protected under the First Amendment right to freedom of expression, however.

Horizontal Market Division

It is a *per se* violation of Section 1 of the Sherman Act for competitors to divide up territories or customers. **EXAMPLE 23.5** Alred Office Supply, Belmont Business, and Carlson's, Inc., compete against each other in the states of Kansas, Nebraska, and Oklahoma. The three firms agree that Alred will sell products only in Kansas, Belmont will sell only in Nebraska, and Carlson's will sell only in Oklahoma. This concerted action reduces marketing costs and allows all three (assuming there is no other competition) to raise the price of the goods sold in their respective states.

The same violation would take place if the three firms agreed to divide up their customers by having Alred sell only to institutional purchasers (such as governments and schools) in all three states, Belmont only to wholesalers, and Carlson only to retailers. ●

Trade Associations

Businesses in the same general industry or profession frequently organize trade associations to pursue common interests. A trade association may engage in various joint activities such as exchanging information, representing the members' business interests before governmental bodies, conducting advertising campaigns, and setting regulatory standards to govern the industry or profession.

Generally, the rule of reason is applied to many of these horizontal actions. If a court finds that a trade association practice or agreement that restrains trade is sufficiently beneficial both to the association and to the public, it may deem the restraint reasonable.

Concentrated Industry An industry in which a single firm or a small number of firms control a large percentage of market sales.

In concentrated industries, however, trade associations can be, and have been, used as a means to facilitate anticompetitive actions, such as fixing prices or allocating markets. A **concentrated industry** is one in which either a single firm or a small number of firms control a large percentage of market sales. When trade association agreements have substantially anticompetitive effects, a court will consider them to be in violation of Section 1 of the Sherman Act.

Vertical Restraints

Vertical Restraint A restraint of trade created by an agreement between firms at different levels in the manufacturing and distribution process.

A **vertical restraint** of trade results from an agreement between firms at different levels in the manufacturing and distribution process. In contrast to horizontal relationships, which occur at the same level of operation, vertical relationships encompass the entire chain of production. The chain of production normally includes the purchase of inventory, basic manufacturing, distribution to wholesalers, and eventual sale of a product at the retail level. When a single firm carries out two or more of the separate functional phases, it is considered to be a **vertically integrated firm.**

Vertically Integrated Firm A firm that carries out two or more functional phases (manufacturing, distribution, and retailing, for example) of the chain of production.

Even though firms operating at different functional levels are not in direct competition with one another, they are in competition with other firms. Thus, agreements between

---

8. *In re Cardizem CD Antitrust Litigation,* 332 F.3d 896 (6th Cir. 2003).

firms standing in a vertical relationship may affect competition. Some vertical restraints are *per se* violations of Section 1. Others are judged under the rule of reason.

Territorial or Customer Restrictions

In arranging for the distribution of its products, a manufacturing firm often wishes to insulate dealers from direct competition with other dealers selling the product. To do so, it may institute territorial restrictions or attempt to prohibit wholesalers or retailers from reselling the product to certain classes of buyers, such as competing retailers.

Territorial and customer restrictions were once considered *per se* violations of Section 1, but in 1977, the United States Supreme Court held that they should be judged under the rule of reason. **CASE EXAMPLE 23.6** GTE Sylvania, Inc., limited the number of retail franchises that it granted in any given geographic area and required them to sell only Sylvania products. Sylvania retained sole discretion to increase the number of retailers in an area. When Sylvania decided to open a new franchise, it terminated the franchise of Continental T.V., Inc. Continental sued, claiming that Sylvania's vertically restrictive franchise system violated Section 1. The Supreme Court found that "vertical restrictions promote interbrand competition by allowing the manufacturer to achieve certain efficiencies in the distribution of his products." Therefore, Sylvania's vertical system, which was not price restrictive, did not constitute a *per se* violation of Section 1 of the Sherman Act.[9] ●

The decision in the *Continental* case marked a definite shift from rigid characterization of these kinds of vertical restraints to a more flexible, economic analysis of the restraints under the rule of reason. A firm may have legitimate reasons for imposing territorial or customer restrictions, and not all such restrictions harm competition.

Resale Price Maintenance Agreements

An agreement between a manufacturer and a distributor or retailer in which the manufacturer specifies what the retail prices of its products must be is referred to as a **resale price maintenance agreement.** Such agreements were also once considered to be *per se* violations of Section 1. In 1997, however, the United States Supreme Court ruled that *maximum* resale price maintenance agreements should be judged under the rule of reason.[10] The setting of a maximum price that retailers and distributors can charge for a manufacturer's products may sometimes increase competition and benefit consumers. In 2007, the Supreme Court held that *minimum* resale price maintenance agreements should also be judged under the rule of reason.[11]

Resale Price Maintenance Agreement
An agreement between a manufacturer and a retailer in which the manufacturer specifies what the retail prices of its products must be.

Section 2 of the Sherman Act

Section 1 of the Sherman Act prohibits certain concerted, or joint, activities that restrain trade. In contrast, Section 2 condemns "every person who shall monopolize, or attempt to monopolize." Thus, two distinct types of behavior are subject to sanction under Section 2: *monopolization* and *attempts to monopolize.*

One tactic that may be involved in either offense is **predatory pricing.** Predatory pricing involves an attempt by one firm to drive its competitors from the market by selling its product at prices substantially *below* the normal costs of production. Once the competitors are eliminated, the firm will presumably attempt to recapture its losses and go on to earn higher profits by driving prices up far above their competitive levels.

Learning Objective 3
What type of activity is prohibited by Section 2 of the Sherman Act?

Predatory Pricing The pricing of a product below cost with the intent to drive competitors out of the market.

---

9. *Continental T.V., Inc. v. GTE Sylvania, Inc.,* 433 U.S. 36, 97 S.Ct. 2549, 53 L.Ed.2d 568 (1977).
10. *State Oil Co. v. Khan,* 522 U.S. 3, 118 S.Ct. 275, 139 L.Ed.2d 199 (1997).
11. *Leegin Creative Leather Products, Inc. v. PSKS, Inc.,* 551 U.S. 877, 127 S.Ct. 2705, 168 L.Ed.2d 623 (2007).

Monopolization

Monopolization The possession of monopoly power in the relevant market and the willful acquisition or maintenance of that power, as distinguished from growth or development as a consequence of a superior product, business acumen, or historic accident.

The United States Supreme Court has defined the offense of **monopolization** as involving two elements: "(1) the possession of monopoly power in the relevant market and (2) the willful acquisition or maintenance of [that] power as distinguished from growth or development as a consequence of a superior product, business acumen, or historic accident."[12] A violation of Section 2 requires that both these elements—monopoly power and an intent to monopolize—be established.

Monopoly Power
The Sherman Act does not define *monopoly*. In economic theory, monopoly refers to control of a single market by a single entity. It is well established in antitrust law, however, that a firm may be deemed a monopolist even though it is not the sole seller in a market.

Additionally, size alone does not determine whether a firm is a monopoly. **EXAMPLE 23.7** A "mom and pop" grocery located in the isolated town of Happy Camp, Idaho, is a monopolist if it is the only grocery serving that particular market. Size in relation to the market is what matters because monopoly involves the power to affect prices. ●

Monopoly power may be proved by direct evidence that the firm used its power to control prices and restrict output.[13] Usually, however, there is not enough evidence to show that the firm was intentionally controlling prices, so the plaintiff has to offer indirect, or circumstantial, evidence of monopoly power.

(Seth Perlman/AP Images)

To prove monopoly power indirectly, the plaintiff must show that the firm has a dominant share of the relevant market and that there are significant barriers to new competitors entering that market. **CASE EXAMPLE 23.8** DuPont manufactures and sells para-aramid fiber, a synthetic fiber used to make body armor, fiber-optic cables, and tires, among other things. Although several companies around the world manufacture this fiber, only three sell in the U.S. market—DuPont (based in the United States), Teijin (based in the Netherlands), and Kolon Industries, Inc. (based in Korea). DuPont is the industry leader and, at times, has produced 60 percent of all para-aramid fibers purchased in the United States.

After DuPont brought suit against Kolon for theft and misappropriation of trade secrets, Kolon counterclaimed that DuPont had illegally monopolized and attempted to monopolize the U.S. para-aramid market in violation of Section 2. Kolon claimed that DuPont had illegally used multiyear supply agreements for all of its high-volume para-aramid customers to deter competition. A federal appellate court, however, found that there was insufficient proof that DuPont possessed monopoly power in the U.S. market during the relevant time period (between 2006 and 2009). Additionally, the court concluded that Kolon had not showed that the supply agreements foreclosed competition. Therefore, the court held in favor of DuPont on the antitrust claims.[14] ●

Relevant Market
Before a court can determine whether a firm has a dominant market share, it must define the relevant market. The relevant market consists of two elements: a relevant product market and a relevant geographic market.

Relevant Product Market   The relevant product market includes all products that, although produced by different firms, have identical attributes, such as sugar. It also includes products that are reasonably interchangeable for the purpose for which they are produced. Products will be considered reasonably interchangeable if consumers treat them as acceptable substitutes.

---

12. *United States v. Grinnell Corp.*, 384 U.S. 563, 86 S.Ct. 1698, 16 L.Ed.2d 778 (1966).
13. See, for example, *Broadcom Corp. v. Qualcomm, Inc.*, 501 F.3d 297 (3d Cir. 2007).
14. *Kolon Industries, Inc. v. E.I. DuPont de Nemours & Co.*, 748 F.3d 160 (4th Cir. 2014).

Establishing the relevant product market is often a key issue in monopolization cases because the way the market is defined may determine whether a firm has monopoly power. By defining the product market narrowly, the degree of a firm's market power is enhanced.

CASE EXAMPLE 23.9   Whole Foods Market, Inc., wished to acquire Wild Oats Markets, Inc., its main competitor in nationwide high-end organic food supermarkets. The Federal Trade Commission (FTC) filed a Section 2 claim against Whole Foods to prevent the merger. The FTC argued that the relevant product market consisted of only "premium natural and organic supermarkets" rather than all supermarkets, as Whole Foods maintained. An appellate court accepted the FTC's narrow definition of the relevant market and remanded the case to the lower court to decide what remedies were appropriate, as the merger had already taken place. Whole Foods and the FTC later entered into a settlement that required Whole Foods to divest (sell or give up control over) thirteen stores, most of which were formerly Wild Oats outlets.[15] ●

Relevant Geographic Market   The second component of the relevant market is the geographic extent of the market. For products that are sold nationwide, the geographic market encompasses the entire United States. If transportation costs are significant or a producer and its competitors sell in only a limited area (one in which customers have no access to other sources of the product), the geographic market is limited to that area. A national firm may thus compete in several distinct areas and have monopoly power in one area but not in another.

Generally, the geographic market is that section of the country within which a firm can increase its price a bit without attracting new sellers or without losing many customers to alternative suppliers outside that area. Of course, the Internet and e-commerce are changing the notion of the size and limits of a geographic market. It may become difficult to perceive any geographic market as local, except for products that are not easily transported, such as concrete. The reality is that we live in a global world, including one for commerce.

The Intent Requirement
Monopoly power, in and of itself, does not constitute the offense of monopolization under Section 2 of the Sherman Act. The offense also requires an *intent* to monopolize.

Why Intent Is Required   A dominant market share may be the result of business acumen or the development of a superior product. It may simply be the result of a historic accident. In these situations, the acquisition of monopoly power is not an antitrust violation. Indeed, it would be contrary to society's interest to condemn every firm that acquired a position of power because it was well managed and efficient and marketed a product desired by consumers.

Inferred from Anticompetitive Conduct   If a firm possesses market power as a result of carrying out some purposeful act to acquire or maintain that power through anticompetitive means, then it is in violation of Section 2. In most monopolization cases, intent may be inferred from evidence that the firm had monopoly power and engaged in anticompetitive behavior.

CASE EXAMPLE 23.10   When Navigator, the first popular graphical Internet browser by Netscape Communications Corporation, was introduced, Microsoft, Inc., perceived a threat to its dominance of the operating-system market. Microsoft developed a competing browser, Internet Explorer, and then began to require computer makers that wanted to install the Windows operating

Why did Netscape sue Microsoft?

(AP Photo)

---

15. *FTC v. Whole Foods Market, Inc.,* 548 F.3d 1028 (D.C.Cir. 2008); and 592 F.Supp.2d 107 (D.D.C. 2009).

system to also install Explorer and exclude Navigator. Microsoft included codes in Windows that would cripple the operating system if Explorer was deleted, and paid Internet service providers to distribute Explorer and exclude Navigator. Because of this pattern of exclusionary conduct, a court found Microsoft guilty of monopolization. Microsoft's pattern of conduct could be rational only if the firm knew that it possessed monopoly power.[16] ●

PREVENTING LEGAL DISPUTES

Because exclusionary conduct can have legitimate efficiency-enhancing effects, it can be difficult to determine when conduct will be viewed as anticompetitive and a violation of Section 2 of the Sherman Act. Thus, a business that possesses monopoly power must be careful that its actions cannot be inferred to be evidence of intent to monopolize. Even if your business does not have a dominant market share, you would be wise to take precautions.

Make sure that you can articulate clear, legitimate reasons for the particular conduct or contract and that you do not provide any direct evidence (damaging e-mails, for example) of an intent to exclude competitors. A court will be less likely to infer the intent to monopolize if the specific conduct was aimed at increasing output and lowering per-unit costs, improving product quality, or protecting a patented technology or innovation.

Unilateral Refusals to Deal

Group boycotts, discussed earlier, are also joint refusals to deal—sellers acting as a group jointly refuse to deal with another business or individual. These group refusals are subject to close scrutiny under Section 1 of the Sherman Act. A single manufacturer acting unilaterally, though, normally is free to deal, or not to deal, with whomever it wishes.[17]

Why did the smallest Aspen ski resort sue Aspen Skiing Company?

(M. Kaminski/iStockphoto.com)

Nevertheless, in limited circumstances, a unilateral refusal to deal will violate antitrust laws. These instances involve offenses proscribed under Section 2 of the Sherman Act and occur only if (1) the firm refusing to deal has—or is likely to acquire—monopoly power and (2) the refusal is likely to have an anticompetitive effect on a particular market.

CASE EXAMPLE 23.11 Aspen Skiing Company, the owner of three of the four major downhill ski areas in Aspen, Colorado, refused to continue participating in a jointly offered six-day "all Aspen" lift ticket. The Supreme Court ruled that Aspen Skiing's refusal to cooperate with its smaller competitor was a violation of Section 2 of the Sherman Act. Because the company owned three-fourths of the local ski areas, it had monopoly power, and thus its unilateral refusal had an anticompetitive effect on the market.[18] ●

Attempts to Monopolize

Attempted Monopolization An action by a firm that involves anticompetitive conduct, the intent to gain monopoly power, and a "dangerous probability" of success in achieving monopoly power.

Section 2 also prohibits **attempted monopolization** of a market, which requires proof of the following three elements:

1. Anticompetitive conduct.
2. The specific intent to exclude competitors and garner monopoly power.
3. A "dangerous" probability of success in achieving monopoly power. The probability cannot be dangerous unless the alleged offender possesses some degree of market power. Only *serious* threats of monopolization are condemned as violations.

---

16. *United States v. Microsoft Corp.,* 253 F.3d 34 (D.C.Cir. 2001). Microsoft has faced numerous antitrust claims and has settled a number of lawsuits in which it was accused of antitrust violations and anticompetitive tactics.

17. See, for example, *Pacific Bell Telephone Co. v. Linkline Communications, Inc.,* 555 U.S. 438, 129 S.Ct. 1109, 172 L.Ed.2d 836 (2009).

18. *Aspen Skiing Co. v. Aspen Highlands Skiing Corp.,* 472 U.S. 585, 105 S.Ct. 2847, 86 L.Ed.2d 467 (1985).

As mentioned earlier, predatory pricing is a form of anticompetitive conduct that, in theory, could be used by firms that are attempting to monopolize. (Predatory pricing may also lead to claims of price discrimination, discussed next.) Predatory bidding involves the acquisition and use of *monopsony power,* which is market power on the *buy* side of a market. This may occur when a buyer bids up the price of an input too high for its competitors to pay, causing them to leave the market. The predatory bidder may then attempt to drive down input prices to reap above-competitive profits and recoup any losses it suffered in bidding up the prices.

The question in the following *Spotlight Case* was whether a claim of predatory bidding was sufficiently similar to a claim of predatory pricing so that the same antitrust test should apply to both.

Spotlight on Weyerhaeuser Co.

Case 23.1
Weyerhaeuser Co. v.
Ross-Simmons Hardwood Lumber Co.
Supreme Court of the United States, 549 U.S. 312, 127 S.Ct. 1069, 166 L.Ed.2d 911 (2007).

Was predatory bidding on the price of alder logs tantamount to predatory pricing and therefore illegal?

BACKGROUND AND FACTS   Weyerhaeuser Company entered the Pacific Northwest's hardwood lumber market in 1980. By 2000, Weyerhaeuser owned six mills processing 65 percent of the red alder logs in the region. Meanwhile, Ross-Simmons Hardwood Lumber Company operated a single competing mill. When the prices of logs rose and those for lumber fell, Ross-Simmons suffered heavy losses. Several million dollars in debt, the mill closed in 2001. Ross-Simmons filed a suit in a federal district court against Weyerhaeuser, alleging attempted monopolization under Section 2 of the Sherman Act. Ross-Simmons claimed that Weyerhaeuser used its dominant position in the market to bid up the prices of logs and prevent its competitors from being profitable. Weyerhaeuser argued that the antitrust test for predatory pricing applies to a claim of predatory bidding and that Ross-Simmons had not met this standard. The district court ruled in favor of the plaintiff, a federal appellate court affirmed, and Weyerhaeuser appealed.

IN THE WORDS OF THE COURT . . .
Justice *THOMAS* delivered the opinion of the Court.
* * * *

Predatory-pricing and predatory-bidding claims are analytically similar. This similarity results from the close theoretical connection between monopoly and monopsony. The kinship between monopoly and monopsony suggests that similar legal standards should apply to claims of monopolization and to claims of monopsonization.

* * * Both claims involve the deliberate use of unilateral pricing measures for anticompetitive purposes. And both claims logically require firms to incur short-term losses on the chance that they might reap supracompetitive [above-competitive] profits in the future.
* * * *

* * *   "Predatory pricing schemes are rarely tried, and even more rarely successful."
Predatory pricing requires a firm to suffer certain losses in the short term on the chance of reaping supracompetitive profits in the future. A rational business will rarely make this sacrifice. The same reasoning applies to predatory bidding. [Emphasis added.]
* * * *

* * * A failed predatory-pricing scheme may benefit consumers. * * * Failed predatory-bidding schemes can also * * * benefit consumers.

In addition, predatory bidding presents less of a direct threat of consumer harm than predatory pricing. A predatory-pricing scheme ultimately achieves success by charging higher prices to consumers. By contrast, a predatory-bidding scheme could succeed with little or no effect on consumer prices because a predatory bidder does not necessarily rely on raising prices in the output market to recoup its losses.
* * * *

* * * [Thus] our two-pronged [predatory pricing] test should apply to predatory-bidding claims.

* * * A plaintiff must prove that the alleged predatory bidding led to below-cost pricing of the predator's outputs. That is, the predator's bidding on the buy side must have caused the cost of the relevant output to rise above the revenues generated in the sale of those outputs. * * * Given the multitude of procompetitive ends served by higher bidding for inputs, the risk of chilling procompetitive behavior with too lax a liability standard is * * * serious * * *. Consequently, only higher bidding that leads to below-cost pricing in the relevant output market will suffice as a basis for liability for predatory bidding.

Spotlight Case 23.1—Continues ➡

Spotlight Case 23.1—Continued

A predatory-bidding plaintiff also must prove that the defendant has a dangerous probability of recouping the losses incurred in bidding up input prices through the exercise of monopsony power. Absent proof of likely recoupment, a strategy of predatory bidding makes no economic sense because it would involve short-term losses with no likelihood of offsetting long-term gains.

Ross-Simmons has conceded that it has not satisfied [this] standard. Therefore, its predatory-bidding theory of liability cannot support the jury's verdict.

DECISION AND REMEDY The United States Supreme Court held that the antitrust test that applies to claims of predatory pricing also applies to claims of predatory bidding. Because Ross-Simmons conceded that it had not met this standard, the Court vacated the lower court's judgment and remanded the case.

WHAT IF THE FACTS WERE DIFFERENT? *Logs represent up to 75 percent of a mill's total costs. Efficient equipment can increase both the speed at which lumber can be recovered from a log and the amount of lumber recovered. The Court noted that "Ross-Simmons appears to have engaged in little efficiency-enhancing investment." If Ross-Simmons had invested in state-of-the-art technology, how might the circumstances in this case have been different?*

THE ECONOMIC DIMENSION *Why does a plaintiff alleging predatory bidding have to prove that the defendant's "bidding on the buy side caused the cost of the relevant output to rise above the revenues generated in the sale of those outputs"?*

The Clayton Act

Learning Objective 4
What are the four major provisions of the Clayton Act, and what types of activities do these provisions prohibit?

In 1914, Congress enacted the Clayton Act. The act was aimed at specific anticompetitive or monopolistic practices that the Sherman Act did not cover. The substantive provisions of the act—set out in Sections 2, 3, 7, and 8—deal with four distinct forms of business behavior, which are declared illegal but not criminal. For each provision, the act states that the behavior is *illegal only if it tends to substantially lessen competition or to create monopoly power.*

Section 2—Price Discrimination

Price Discrimination A seller's act of charging competing buyers different prices for identical products or services.

Section 2 of the Clayton Act prohibits **price discrimination**, which occurs when a seller charges different prices to competing buyers for identical goods or services. Congress strengthened this section by amending it with the passage of the Robinson-Patman Act in 1936.

As amended, Section 2 prohibits price discrimination that cannot be justified by differences in production costs, transportation costs, or cost differences due to other reasons. In short, a seller is prohibited from charging a lower price to one buyer than is charged to that buyer's competitor.

"Becoming number one is easier than remaining number one."

Bill Bradley, 1943–present
(American politician and athlete)

Requirements To violate Section 2, the seller must be engaged in interstate commerce, the goods must be of like grade and quality, and goods must have been sold to two or more purchasers. In addition, the effect of the price discrimination must be to substantially lessen competition, tend to create a monopoly, or otherwise injure competition. Without proof of an actual injury resulting from the price discrimination, the plaintiff cannot recover damages.

Note that price discrimination claims can arise from discounts, offsets, rebates, or allowances given to one buyer over another. Giving favorable credit terms, delivery, or freight charges to only some buyers can also lead to allegations of price discrimination. For instance, offering goods to different customers at the same price but including free delivery for certain buyers may violate Section 2 in some circumstances.

Defenses   There are several statutory defenses to liability for price discrimination.

1. *Cost justification.* If the seller can justify the price reduction by demonstrating that a particular buyer's purchases saved the seller costs in producing and selling the goods, the seller will not be liable for price discrimination.

2. *Meeting competitor's prices.* If the seller charged the lower price in a good faith attempt to meet an equally low price of a competitor, the seller will not be liable for price discrimination. **CASE EXAMPLE 23.12** Water Craft was a retail dealership of Mercury Marine outboard motors in Baton Rouge, Louisiana. Mercury Marine also sold its motors to other dealers in the Baton Rouge area. When Water Craft discovered that Mercury was selling its outboard motors at a substantial discount to Water Craft's largest competitor, it filed a price discrimination lawsuit against Mercury. The court ruled in favor of Mercury Marine, however, because it was able to show that the discounts given to Water Craft's competitor were made in good faith to meet the low price charged by another manufacturer of marine motors.[19] ●

3. *Changing market conditions.* A seller may lower its price on an item in response to changing conditions affecting the market for or the marketability of the goods concerned. Thus, if an advance in technology makes a particular product less marketable than it was previously, a seller can lower the product's price.

Section 3—Exclusionary Practices

Under Section 3 of the Clayton Act, sellers or lessors cannot condition the sale or lease of goods on the buyer's or lessee's promise not to use or deal in the goods of the seller's competitor. In effect, this section prohibits two types of vertical agreements involving exclusionary practices—*exclusive-dealing contracts* and *tying arrangements*.

Exclusive-Dealing Contracts
A contract under which a seller forbids a buyer to purchase products from the seller's competitors is called an **exclusive-dealing contract.** A seller is prohibited from making an exclusive-dealing contract under Section 3 if the effect of the contract is "to substantially lessen competition or tend to create a monopoly."

CASE EXAMPLE 23.13 In a classic case decided by the United States Supreme Court in 1949, Standard Oil Company, the largest gasoline seller in the nation at that time, made exclusive-dealing contracts with independent stations in seven western states. The contracts involved 16 percent of all retail outlets, with sales amounting to approximately 7 percent of all retail sales in that market. The market was substantially concentrated because the seven largest gasoline suppliers all used exclusive-dealing contracts with their independent retailers. Together, these suppliers controlled 65 percent of the market.

The Court looked at market conditions after the arrangements were instituted and found that market shares were extremely stable and entry into the market was apparently restricted. Because competition was "foreclosed in a substantial share" of the relevant market, the Court held that Section 3 of the Clayton Act had been violated.[20] ● Note that since the Supreme Court's 1949 decision, a number of subsequent decisions have called the holding in this case into doubt.[21]

Today, it is clear that to violate antitrust law, an exclusive-dealing agreement (or *tying arrangement*, discussed next) must qualitatively and substantially harm competition. To prevail, a plaintiff must present affirmative evidence that the performance of the agreement will foreclose competition and harm consumers.

Exclusive-Dealing Contract An agreement under which a seller forbids a buyer to purchase products from the seller's competitors.

---

19. *Water Craft Management, LLC v. Mercury Marine*, 457 F.3d 484 (5th Cir. 2006).
20. *Standard Oil Co. of California v. United States*, 337 U.S. 293, 69 S.Ct. 1051, 93 L.Ed. 1371 (1949).
21. See, for example, *Illinois Tool Works, Inc. v. Independent Ink, Inc.*, 547 U.S. 28, 126 S.Ct. 1281, 164 L.Ed.2d 26 (2006); and *Stop & Shop Supermarket Co. v. Blue Cross & Blue Shield of Rhode Island*, 373 F.3d 57 (1st Cir. 2004).

Tying Arrangements

When a seller conditions the sale of a product (the tying product) on the buyer's agreement to purchase another product (the tied product) produced or distributed by the same seller, a **tying arrangement** results. The legality of a tying arrangement (or *tie-in sales agreement*) depends on many factors, particularly the purpose of the agreement and its likely effect on competition in the relevant markets (the market for the tying product and the market for the tied product).

EXAMPLE 23.14 Morshigi Precision, Inc., manufactures laptop hardware and provides repair service for the hardware. Morshigi also makes and markets software, but the company will provide support for buyers of the software only if they also buy its hardware service. This is a tying arrangement. Depending on the purpose of the agreement and the effect of the agreement on competition in the market for the two products, the agreement may be illegal. ●

Section 3 of the Clayton Act has been held to apply only to commodities, not to services. Some tying arrangements, however, can also be considered agreements that restrain trade in violation of Section 1 of the Sherman Act. Thus, cases involving tying arrangements of services have been brought under Section 1 of the Sherman Act. Although earlier cases condemned tying arrangements as illegal *per se*, courts now evaluate tying agreements under the rule of reason.

In the following case, a concertgoer claimed that a promoter's inclusion of a parking fee in the price of a ticket was an unlawful tying arrangement.

Case 23.2

Batson v. Live Nation Entertainment, Inc.
United States Court of Appeals, Seventh Circuit, 746 F.3d 827 (2014).

BACKGROUND AND FACTS James Batson bought a nonrefundable ticket to see the American rock band O.A.R. from Live Nation Entertainment, Inc., at the Charter One Pavilion in Chicago, Illinois. The face of the ticket noted that the price included a $9 parking fee. Batson did not have a car to park. In fact, he had walked to the concert venue and bought the ticket at the box office just before the performance. Feeling stung to be charged for parking that he did not want, Batson filed a suit in a federal district court against Live Nation. He argued that the bundled fee was unfair because consumers were forced to pay it or forego the concert. He asserted that this was a tying arrangement in violation of Section 1 of the Sherman Act. The court dismissed the suit. Batson appealed.

IN THE WORDS OF THE COURT . . .
WOOD, Chief Judge.
    * * * *
    * * * A tying arrangement exists when a seller exploits power over one product (the tying product) to force the buyer to accept a second product (the tied product). Such an arrangement violates Section 1 of the Sherman Act if the seller has appreciable economic power in the tying product market and if the arrangement affects a substantial volume of commerce in the tied market.

Can Live Nation include a parking fee for all of its tickets?

Applying those principles here, we would need to find that Live Nation had enough power in some market (O.A.R. concerts? Live music concerts? Entertainment in Chicago?) to permit it to force people to spend money for useless parking rights (the tied product). But is it possible to regard O.A.R. concerts or the Charter One Pavilion as a meaningful product market? * * * *A single popular venue is not a stand-alone relevant market.* We are dubious here * * * that the Charter One Pavilion in Chicago has that much clout. Even if it does, however, Batson has failed to allege anything that would plausibly show that Live Nation's parking tie-in has affected a substantial volume of commerce in parking (we presume parking in Chicago, but that is unclear). Indeed, Batson all but concedes this point and instead invites us to break new ground by finding that a tying arrangement violates federal antitrust law if its anticompetitive effect is felt in the tying product market. We decline the invitation. We are not the arbiters of fair prices for Illinois, and *if the requisite market power is missing, the antitrust laws do not prohibit a seller from asking consumers to pay a higher price for a package.* [Emphasis added.]
    * * * *

Case 23.2—Continued

While we understand why a consumer who does not want parking would prefer to purchase a concert ticket unbundled from that benefit, there is no rule that requires everything to be sold on a fully unbundled basis.

* * * *

There are times when consumers are required to accept a package deal in order to get the part of the package they want. An airline passenger with no luggage may prefer the cost of baggage to be decoupled from the cost of a seat, and a * * * student may prefer to pay lower tuition and avoid "free" pizza days. But while some people may find these bundles annoying, or even unfair, the tie is not illegal unless the standards [for a violation of antitrust law] * * * have been met.

DECISION AND REMEDY The U.S. Court of Appeals for the Seventh Circuit affirmed the dismissal of Batson's claim. "While

we understand why a consumer who does not want parking would prefer to purchase a concert ticket unbundled from that benefit, there is no rule that requires everything to be sold on a fully unbundled basis."

THE LEGAL ENVIRONMENT DIMENSION *Why aren't tying arrangements illegal per se? Under the rule of reason, in what circumstance would a tying arrangement violate Section 1 of the Sherman Act?*

WHAT IF THE FACTS WERE DIFFERENT? *Suppose that instead of noting on the ticket that the price included a parking fee, Live Nation had simply charged $9 more for the ticket and announced that there was "free" parking for all who needed it. Would the result have been different? Why or why not?*

Section 7—Mergers

Under Section 7 of the Clayton Act, a person or business organization cannot hold stock and/or assets in another entity "where the effect . . . may be to substantially lessen competition." Section 7 is the statutory authority for preventing mergers or acquisitions among firms that could result in monopoly power or a substantial lessening of competition in the marketplace.

A crucial consideration in most merger cases is the **market concentration** of a product or business. Determining market concentration involves allocating percentage market shares among the various companies in the relevant market. When a small number of companies control a large share of the market, the market is concentrated. **EXAMPLE 23.15** If the four largest grocery stores in Chicago accounted for 80 percent of all retail food sales, the market clearly would be concentrated in those four firms. If one of these stores absorbed the assets and liabilities of another, so the other ceased to exist, the result would be a merger that would further concentrate the market and thereby possibly diminish competition. ●

Market Concentration The degree to which a small number of firms control a large percentage of a relevant market.

Competition, however, is not necessarily diminished solely as a result of market concentration, and courts will consider other factors in determining whether a merger will violate Section 7. One factor of particular importance in evaluating the effects of a merger is whether the merger will make it more difficult for *potential* competitors to enter the relevant market.

Horizontal Mergers Mergers between firms that compete with each other in the same market are called **horizontal mergers.** If a horizontal merger creates an entity with a significant market share, the merger initially will be presumed illegal because it increases market concentration.

Horizontal Merger A merger between two firms that are competing in the same market.

When analyzing the legality of a horizontal merger, however, the courts also consider three other factors: the overall concentration of the relevant product market, the relevant market's history of tending toward concentration, and whether the apparent design of the merger is to establish market power or to restrict competition.

Vertical Mergers A **vertical merger** occurs when a company at one stage of production acquires a company at a higher or lower stage of production. An example of a vertical merger is a company merging with one of its suppliers or retailers. Whether a vertical merger is illegal generally depends on several factors, such as whether the merger would produce a firm controlling an undue percentage share of the relevant market.

The courts also analyze whether the merger would result in a significant increase in the concentration of firms in that market, the barriers to entry into the market, and the apparent intent of the merging parties. Mergers that do not prevent competitors of either merging firm from competing in a segment of the market are legal.

Section 8—Interlocking Directorates

Section 8 of the Clayton Act deals with *interlocking directorates*—that is, the practice of having individuals serve as directors on the boards of two or more competing companies simultaneously. Specifically, no person may be a director in two or more competing corporations at the same time if either of the corporations has capital, surplus, or undivided profits aggregating more than $29,945,000 or competitive sales of $2,994,500 or more. The FTC adjusts the threshold amounts each year. (The amounts given here are those announced by the FTC in 2014.)

The reasoning behind the FTC's prohibition of interlocking directorates is that if two competing businesses share the same officers and directors, the firms are unlikely to compete with one another, or to compete aggressively. If directors or officers do not comply with this prohibition, they may be liable under the Clayton Act.

Enforcement and Exemptions

The federal agencies that enforce the federal antitrust laws are the U.S. Department of Justice (DOJ) and the Federal Trade Commission (FTC). The FTC was established in 1914 by the Federal Trade Commission Act. Section 5 of that act condemns all forms of anticompetitive behavior that are not covered under other federal antitrust laws.

Enforcement by Federal Agencies

Only the DOJ can prosecute violations of the Sherman Act, which can be either criminal or civil offenses. Violations of the Clayton Act are not crimes, but the act can be enforced by either the DOJ or the FTC through civil proceedings.

The DOJ or the FTC may ask the courts to impose various remedies, including **divestiture** (making a company give up one or more of its operating functions) and dissolution. A meatpacking firm, for instance, might be forced to divest itself of control or ownership of butcher shops.

The FTC has the sole authority to enforce violations of Section 5 of the Federal Trade Commission Act. FTC actions are effected through administrative orders, but if a firm violates an FTC order, the FTC can seek court sanctions for the violation.

Enforcement by Private Parties

A private party who has been injured as a result of a violation of the Sherman Act or the Clayton Act can sue for **treble damages** (three times the actual damages suffered) and attorneys' fees. In some instances, private parties may also seek injunctive relief to prevent antitrust violations. A party wishing to sue under the Sherman Act must prove that:

1. The antitrust violation either caused or was a substantial factor in causing the injury that was suffered.

2. The unlawful actions of the accused party affected business activities of the plaintiff that were protected by the antitrust laws.

Exemptions from Antitrust Laws

There are many legislative and constitutional limitations on antitrust enforcement. Most of the statutory or judicially created exemptions to antitrust laws apply in such areas as labor, insurance, and foreign trade, and are listed in Exhibit 23–2 that follows.

One of the most significant of these exemptions covers joint efforts by businesspersons to obtain legislative, judicial, or executive action. Under this exemption, Blu-ray producers can jointly lobby Congress to change the copyright laws without being held liable for attempting to restrain trade. Another exemption covers professional baseball teams.

(Courtesy of the Federal Trade Commission)

What antitrust enforcement powers does the Federal Trade Commission have?

U.S. Antitrust Laws in the Global Context

U.S. antitrust laws have a broad application. Not only may persons in foreign nations be subject to their provisions, but the laws may also be applied to protect foreign consumers and competitors from violations committed by U.S. business firms. Consequently, *foreign persons*, a term that by definition includes foreign governments, may sue under U.S. antitrust laws in U.S. courts.

Exhibit 23–2 Exemptions to Antitrust Enforcement

EXEMPTION	SOURCE AND SCOPE
Labor	Clayton Act—Permits unions to organize and bargain without violating antitrust laws and specifies that strikes and other labor activities normally do not violate any federal law.
Agricultural associations	Clayton Act and Capper-Volstead Act—Allow agricultural cooperatives to set prices.
Fisheries	Fisheries Cooperative Marketing Act—Allows the fishing industry to set prices.
Insurance companies	McCarran-Ferguson Act—Exempts the insurance business in states in which the industry is regulated.
Exporters	Webb-Pomerene Act—Allows U.S. exporters to engage in cooperative activity to compete with similar foreign associations. Export Trading Company Act—Permits the U.S. Department of Justice to exempt certain exporters.
Professional baseball	The United States Supreme Court has held that professional baseball is exempt because it is not "interstate commerce."[a]
Oil marketing	Interstate Oil Compact—Allows states to set quotas on oil to be marketed in interstate commerce.
Defense activities	Defense Production Act—Allows the president to approve, and thereby exempt, certain activities to further the military defense of the United States.
Small businesses' cooperative research	Small Business Administration Act—Allows small firms to undertake cooperative research.
State actions	The United States Supreme Court has held that actions by a state are exempt if the state clearly articulates and actively supervises the policy behind its action.[b]
Regulated industries	Industries (such as airlines) are exempt when a federal administrative agency (such as the Federal Aviation Administration) has primary regulatory authority.
Businesspersons' joint efforts to seek government action	Cooperative efforts by businesspersons to obtain legislative, judicial, or executive action are exempt unless it is clear that an effort is "objectively baseless" and is an attempt to make anticompetitive use of government processes.[c]

a. *Federal Baseball Club of Baltimore, Inc. v. National League of Professional Baseball Clubs*, 259 U.S. 200, 42 S.Ct. 465, 66 L.Ed. 898 (1922). A federal district court has held that this exemption applies only to the game's reserve system. (Under the reserve system, teams hold players' contracts for the players' entire careers. The reserve system generally is being replaced by the free agency system.) See *Piazza v. Major League Baseball*, 831 F.Supp. 420 (E.D.Pa. 1993).
b. See *Parker v. Brown*, 317 U.S. 341, 63 S.Ct. 307, 87 L.Ed. 315 (1943).
c. *Eastern Railroad Presidents Conference v. Noerr Motor Freight, Inc.*, 365 U.S. 127, 81 S.Ct. 523, 5 L.Ed.2d 464 (1961); and *United Mine Workers of America v. Pennington*, 381 U.S. 657, 89 S.Ct. 1585, 14 L.Ed.2d 626 (1965). These two cases established the exception often referred to as the *Noerr-Pennington* doctrine.

The Extraterritorial Application of U.S. Antitrust Laws

Section 1 of the Sherman Act provides for the extraterritorial effect of the U.S. antitrust laws. The United States is a major proponent of free competition in the global economy, and thus any conspiracy that has a *substantial effect* on U.S. commerce is within the reach of the Sherman Act. The violation may even occur outside the United States, and foreign persons including governments can be sued for violation of U.S. antitrust laws. Before U.S. courts will exercise jurisdiction and apply antitrust laws, it must be shown that the alleged violation had a substantial effect on U.S. commerce. U.S. jurisdiction is automatically invoked, however, when a *per se* violation occurs.

If a domestic firm, for example, joins a foreign cartel to control the production, price, or distribution of goods, and this cartel has a *substantial effect* on U.S. commerce, a *per se* violation may exist. Hence, both the domestic firm and the foreign cartel could be sued for violation of the U.S. antitrust laws. Likewise, if a foreign firm doing business in the United States enters into a price-fixing or other anticompetitive agreement to control a portion of U.S. markets, a *per se* violation may exist.

In the following case, the court had to decide whether an alleged anticompetitive conspiracy had a substantial effect on U.S. commerce.

Case 23.3

Carrier Corp. v. Outokumpu Oyj

United States Court of Appeals, Sixth Circuit, 673 F.3d 430 (2012).

Why did Carrier sue Outokumpu Oyj?

BACKGROUND AND FACTS Carrier Corporation is a U.S. firm that manufactures air-conditioning and refrigeration (ACR) equipment. To make these products, Carrier uses ACR copper tubing bought from Outokumpu Oyj, a Finnish company. Carrier is one of the world's largest purchasers of ACR copper tubing. The Commission of the European Communities (EC) found that Outokumpu had conspired with other companies to fix ACR tubing prices in Europe. Carrier then filed a lawsuit in a U.S. court, alleging that the cartel had also conspired to fix prices in the United States by agreeing that only Outokumpu would sell ACR tubing in the U.S. market. The district court dismissed Carrier's claim for lack of jurisdiction. Carrier appealed.

IN THE WORDS OF THE COURT . . .
Karen Nelson *MOORE*, Circuit Judge.
     * * * *

Carrier's complaint describes, in some detail, an elaborate worldwide conspiracy in which the U.S. market for ACR copper tubing was assigned to Outokumpu. Furthermore, *Carrier alleges that this conspiracy caused the price of goods purchased within the United States to increase, which in turn caused a direct antitrust injury.* In support of these allegations, the complaint references numerous specific dates during which the * * * cartel met and the various agreements its members entered into. *Assuming that these allegations are true, as we must, we conclude that Carrier has met any applicable*

requirement that it allege a [substantial] effect on U.S. commerce. [Emphasis added.]

Outokumpu, which attached the full EC decision to its motion to dismiss, counters that many of the details contained in the complaint are drawn from [an] EC * * * decision that found no evidence that the cartel's focus extended beyond Europe. * * * As a consequence, Outokumpu argues that any details regarding specific meetings and agreements occurring during the [cartel] meetings are of no assistance to Carrier because they relate only to a European conspiracy.

We are [not] persuaded by this argument. * * * The EC * * * decision clearly states that "insofar as the activities of the cartel relate to sales in countries that are not members of the Community * * * they lie outside the scope of this Decision." Thus, any silence on the part of the EC decision as to U.S. markets may simply reflect the limited scope of the decision.
     * * * *

Furthermore, Carrier offers additional circumstantial allegations that corroborate its claim that the market-allocation scheme extended to the United States. Although Carrier's complaint provides numerous circumstantial allegations, of particular interest is its claim that [Outokumpu's competitors] initially refrained from aggressively competing for Carrier's U.S. business until 2003, and then suddenly began doing so at that time. It is true that the mere fact that competitors do not intrude upon one another's markets does not necessarily mean that an illegal market-allocation

Case 23.3—Continued

scheme is taking place. When two companies refrain from entering a market and then suddenly do so after a cartel dissolves, however, there are good grounds for suspicion.

DECISION AND REMEDY The federal appellate court found that the district court had jurisdiction over Carrier's Sherman Act claims. It therefore reversed the district court's judgment for the defendants.

THE LEGAL ENVIRONMENT DIMENSION *When this case proceeds, should the district court apply the rule of reason? Why or why not?*

WHAT IF THE FACTS WERE DIFFERENT? *Suppose that Carrier had engaged in anticompetitive conduct that affected Outokumpu. Discuss fully whether the foreign firm would be protected from illegal competition by the U.S. firm.*

The Application of Foreign Antitrust Laws

Large U.S. companies increasingly need to worry about the application of foreign antitrust laws as well. The European Union, in particular, has stepped up its enforcement actions against antitrust violators, as discussed in this chapter's *Beyond Our Borders* feature.

Many other nations also have laws that promote competition and prohibit trade restraints. For instance, Japanese antitrust laws forbid unfair trade practices, monopolization, and restrictions that unreasonably restrain trade. China's antitrust rules restrict monopolization and price fixing (although China has claimed that the government may set prices on exported goods without violating these rules). Indonesia, Malaysia, South Korea, and Vietnam all have statutes protecting competition. Argentina, Brazil, Chile, Peru, and several other Latin American countries have adopted modern antitrust laws as well.

Most of these antitrust laws apply extraterritorially, as U.S. antitrust laws do. This means that a U.S. company may be subject to another nation's antitrust laws if the company's conduct has a substantial effect on that nation's commerce. For instance, South Korea once fined Intel, Inc., the world's largest semiconductor chip maker, $25 million for antitrust violations.

 BEYOND OUR BORDERS   **The European Union's Expanding Role in Antitrust Litigation**

The European Union (EU) has laws promoting competition that are stricter in many respects than those of the United States. Although the EU's laws provide only for civil, rather than criminal, penalties, the rules define more conduct as anticompetitive than U.S. laws do.

The EU actively pursues antitrust violators, especially individual companies and cartels that engage in alleged monopolistic conduct. For example, the EU fined chip-making giant Intel, Inc., $1.44 billion in an antitrust case. According to European regulators, Intel offered computer manufacturers and retailers price discounts and marketing subsidies if they agreed to buy Intel's chips rather than the chips produced by Intel's main competitor in Europe. The EU has also fined Microsoft Corporation more than $2 billion in the last twelve years for anticompetitive conduct.

The EU is investigating Google, Inc., for potentially violating European antitrust laws by thwarting competition in Internet search engines. Ironically, in 2011, Microsoft—which has paid substantial fines to the EU for anticompetitive conduct—filed its own complaint with the EU against Google. Among other things, Microsoft claims that Google has unlawfully restricted competing search engines from accessing YouTube, content from book publishers, advertiser data, and more. (A similar case brought against Google in the United States, for monopolizing or attempting to monopolize Internet search engines, was dismissed in 2011.[a])

Critical Thinking
Some commentators argue that EU regulators are too focused on reining in powerful U.S. technology companies, such as Microsoft and Intel. How might the large fines imposed by the EU on successful U.S. technology firms affect competition in the United States?

---

a. See *TradeComet.com, LLC v. Google, Inc.*, 647 F.3d 472 (2d Cir. 2011).

Reviewing . . . Antitrust Law and Promoting Competition

The Internet Corporation for Assigned Names and Numbers (ICANN) is a nonprofit entity that organizes Internet domain names. It is governed by a board of directors elected by various groups with commercial interests in the Internet. One of ICANN's functions is to authorize an entity to serve as a registrar for certain "top level domains" (TLDs). ICANN entered into an agreement with VeriSign to provide registry services for the ".com" TLD in accordance with ICANN's specifications. VeriSign complained that ICANN was restricting the services that it could make available as a registrar and was blocking new services, imposing unnecessary conditions on those services, and setting prices at which the services were offered. VeriSign claimed that ICANN's control of the registry services for domain names violated Section 1 of the Sherman Act. Using the information presented in the chapter, answer the following questions.

1. Should ICANN's actions be judged under the rule of reason or be deemed a *per se* violation of Section 1 of the Sherman Act? Explain.
2. Should ICANN's actions be viewed as a horizontal or a vertical restraint of trade? Explain.
3. Does it matter that ICANN's directors are chosen by groups with a commercial interest in the Internet? Why or why not?
4. If the dispute is judged under the rule of reason, what might be ICANN's defense for having a standardized set of registry services that must be used?

Debate This   The Internet and the rise of e-commerce have rendered our antitrust concepts and laws obsolete.

Key Terms

antitrust law 620	horizontal merger 635	monopoly power 622	rule of reason 623
attempted monopolization 630	horizontal restraint 624	*per se* violation 623	treble damages 636
concentrated industry 626	market concentration 635	predatory pricing 627	tying arrangement 634
divestiture 636	market power 622	price discrimination 632	vertically integrated firm 626
exclusive-dealing contract 633	monopolization 628	price-fixing agreement 624	vertical merger 636
group boycott 626	monopoly 622	resale price maintenance agreement 627	vertical restraint 626

Chapter Summary: Antitrust Law and Promoting Competition

The Sherman Antitrust Act	1. *Major provisions*—
	     a. Section 1—Prohibits contracts, combinations, and conspiracies in restraint of trade.
	       (1) Horizontal restraints subject to Section 1 include price-fixing agreements, group boycotts (joint refusals to deal), horizontal market divisions, and trade association agreements.
	       (2) Vertical restraints subject to Section 1 include territorial or customer restrictions, resale price maintenance agreements, and refusals to deal.
	     b. Section 2—Prohibits monopolies and attempts to monopolize.
	 2. *Jurisdictional requirements*—The Sherman Act applies only to activities that have a significant impact on interstate commerce.
	 3. *Interpretive rules*—
	     a. *Per se* rule—Applied to restraints on trade that are so inherently anticompetitive that they cannot be justified and are deemed illegal as a matter of law.
	     b. Rule of reason—Applied when an anticompetitive agreement may be justified by legitimate benefits. Under the rule of reason, the lawfulness of a trade restraint will be determined by the purpose and effects of the restraint.

Chapter Summary: Antitrust Law and Promoting Competition— Continued

The Clayton Act	The major provisions are as follows:
	1. *Section 2*—As amended by the Robinson-Patman Act, prohibits a seller engaged in interstate commerce from price discrimination that substantially lessens competition.
	2. *Section 3*—Prohibits exclusionary practices, such as exclusive-dealing contracts and tying arrangements, when the effect may be to substantially lessen competition.
	3. *Section 7*—Prohibits mergers when the effect may be to substantially lessen competition or to tend to create a monopoly.
	a. A horizontal merger initially will be presumed unlawful if the entity created by the merger will have a significant market share.
	b. A vertical merger will be unlawful if the merger prevents competitors of either merging firm from competing in a segment of the market that otherwise would be open to them, resulting in a substantial lessening of competition.
	4. *Section 8*—Prohibits interlocking directorates.
Enforcement and Exemptions	1. *Enforcement*—The U.S. Department of Justice and the Federal Trade Commission enforce the federal antitrust laws. Private parties who have been injured as a result of violations of the Sherman Act or Clayton Act may bring civil suits, and, if successful, they may be awarded treble damages and attorneys' fees.
	2. *Exemptions*—Numerous exemptions from the antitrust laws have been created. See Exhibit 23–2 for a list of significant exemptions.
U.S. Antitrust Laws in the Global Context	1. *Application of U.S. laws*—U.S. antitrust laws can be applied in foreign nations to protect foreign consumers and competitors. Foreign governments and persons can also bring actions under U.S. antitrust laws. Section 1 of the Sherman Act applies to any conspiracy that has a substantial effect on U.S. commerce.
	2. *Application of foreign laws*—Many other nations also have laws that promote competition and prohibit trade restraints, and some are more restrictive than U.S. laws. These foreign antitrust laws are increasingly being applied to U.S. firms.

Issue Spotters

1. Under what circumstances would Pop's Market, a small store in a small, isolated town, be considered a monopolist? If Pop's is a monopolist, is it in violation of Section 2 of the Sherman Act? Why or why not? (See *Section 2 of the Sherman Act*.)
2. Maple Corporation conditions the sale of its syrup on the buyer's agreement to buy Maple's pancake mix. What factors would a court consider to decide whether this arrangement violates the Clayton Act? (See *The Clayton Act*.)

—**Check your answers to the Issue Spotters against the answers provided in Appendix D at the end of this text.**

For Review

1. What is a monopoly? What is market power? How do these concepts relate to each other?
2. What anticompetitive activities are prohibited by Section 1 of the Sherman Act?
3. What type of activity is prohibited by Section 2 of the Sherman Act?
4. What are the four major provisions of the Clayton Act, and what types of activities do these provisions prohibit?
5. What agencies of the federal government enforce the federal antitrust laws?

Business Scenarios and Case Problems

23–1. Antitrust Laws. Allitron, Inc., and Donovan, Ltd., are interstate competitors selling similar appliances, principally in the states of Illinois, Indiana, Kentucky, and Ohio. Allitron and Donovan agree that Allitron will no longer sell in Indiana and Ohio and that Donovan will no longer sell in Illinois and Kentucky. Have Allitron and Donovan violated any antitrust laws? If so, which law? Explain. (See *The Clayton Act*.)

23–2. Tying Arrangement. John Sheridan owned a Marathon gas station franchise. He sued Marathon Petroleum Co. under Section 1 of the Sherman Act and Section 3 of the Clayton Act, charging it with illegally tying the processing of credit-card sales to the gas station. As a condition of obtaining a Marathon dealership, dealers had to agree to let the franchisor process credit cards. They could not shop around to see if credit-card processing could be obtained at a lower price from another source. The district court dismissed the case for failure to state a claim. Sheridan appealed. Is there a tying arrangement? If so, does it violate the law? Explain. [*Sheridan v. Marathon Petroleum Co.,* 530 F.3d 590 (7th Cir. 2008)] (See *The Clayton Act.*)

23–3. Monopolization. When Deer Valley Resort Co. (DVRC) was developing its ski resort in the Wasatch Mountains near Park City, Utah, it sold parcels of land in the resort village to third parties. Each sales contract reserved the right of approval over the conduct of certain businesses on the property, including ski rentals. For fifteen years, DVRC permitted Christy Sports, LLC, to rent skis in competition with DVRC's ski rental outlet. When DVRC opened a new midmountain ski rental outlet, it revoked Christy's permission to rent skis. This meant that most skiers who flew into Salt Lake City and shuttled to Deer Valley had few choices: they could carry their ski equipment with them on their flights, take a shuttle into Park City and look for cheaper ski rentals there, or rent from DVRC. Christy filed a suit in a federal district court against DVRC. Was DVRC's action an attempt to monopolize in violation of Section 2 of the Sherman Act? Why or why not? [*Christy Sports, LLC v. Deer Valley Resort Co.,* 555 F.3d 1188 (10th Cir. 2009)] (See *Section 2 of the Sherman Act.*)

23–4. Price Fixing. Together, EMI, Sony BMG Music Entertainment, Universal Music Group Recordings, Inc., and Warner Music Group Corp. produced, licensed, and distributed 80 percent of the digital music sold in the United States. The companies formed MusicNet to sell music to online services that sold the songs to consumers. MusicNet required all of the services to sell the songs at the same price and subject to the same restrictions. Digitization of music became cheaper, but MusicNet did not change its prices. Did MusicNet violate the antitrust laws? Explain. [*Starr v. Sony BMG Music Entertainment,* 592 F.3d 314 (2d Cir. 2010)] (See *Section 2 of the Sherman Act.*)

23–5.   Business Case Problem with Sample Answer— Price Discrimination. Dayton Superior Corp. sells its products in interstate commerce to several companies, including Spa Steel Products, Inc. The purchasers often compete directly with each other for customers. From 2005 to 2007, one of Spa Steel's customers purchased Dayton Superior's products from two of Spa Steel's competitors. According to the customer, Spa Steel's prices were always 10 to 15 percent higher for the same products. As a result, Spa Steel lost sales to at least that customer and perhaps others. Spa Steel wants to sue Dayton Superior for price discrimination. Which requirements for such a claim under Section 2 of the Clayton Act does Spa Steel satisfy? What additional facts will it need to prove? [*Dayton Superior Corp. v. Spa Steel Products, Inc.,* 2012 WL 113663 (N.D.N.Y. 2012)] (See *The Clayton Act.*)

—**For a sample answer to Problem 23–5, go to Appendix E at the end of this text.**

23–6. Section 1 of the Sherman Act. The National Collegiate Athletic Association (NCAA) and the National Federation of State High School Associations (NFHS), in an effort to enhance player safety and reduce technology-driven home runs and other big hits, set a standard for non-wood baseball bats to ensure that aluminum and composite bats performed like wood bats. Marucci Sports, LLC, makes non-wood bats. Under the new standard, four of Marucci's eleven products were decertified for use in high school and collegiate games. Marucci filed suit against the NCAA and the NFHS under Section 1 of the Sherman Act. At trial, Marucci's evidence focused on injury to its own business. Did the NCAA and NFHS's standard restrain trade in violation of the Sherman Act? Explain. [*Marucci Sports, L.L.C. v. National Collegiate Athletic Association,* 751 F.3d 368 (2014)] (See *Section 1 of the Sherman Act.*)

23–7.   Critical-Thinking Legal Environment Question. Critics of antitrust law claim that in the long run, competitive market forces will eliminate private monopolies unless they are fostered by government regulation. Can you think of any examples of monopolies that continue to be fostered by government in the United States? (See *Section 2 of the Sherman Act.*)

23–8.   A Question of Ethics—Section 1 of the Sherman Act. In the 1990s, DuCoa, L.P., made choline chloride, a B-complex vitamin essential for the growth and development of animals. DuCoa, Bioproducts, Inc., and Chinook Group, Ltd., each had one-third of the U.S. market for choline chloride. To stabilize the market and keep the price of the vitamin higher than it would otherwise have been, the companies agreed to fix the price and allocate market share by deciding which of them would offer the lowest price to each customer. At times, however, the companies disregarded the agreement. During an increase in competitive activity in August 1997, Daniel Rose became president of DuCoa. The next month, a subordinate advised him of the conspiracy. By February 1998, Rose had begun to implement a strategy to persuade DuCoa's competitors to rejoin the conspiracy. By April, the three companies had reallocated their market shares and increased their prices. In June, the U.S. Department of Justice began to investigate allegations of price fixing in the vitamin market. Ultimately, a federal district court convicted Rose of conspiracy to violate Section 1 of the Sherman Act. [*United States v. Rose,* 449 F.3d 627 (5th Cir. 2006)] (See *Section 1 of the Sherman Act.*)

1. The court "enhanced" Rose's sentence to thirty months' imprisonment, one year of supervised release, and a $20,000 fine based, among other things, on his role as "a manager or supervisor" in the conspiracy. Rose appealed this enhancement to the U.S. Court of Appeals for the Fifth Circuit. Was it fair to increase Rose's sentence on this ground? Why or why not?

2. Was Rose's participation in the conspiracy unethical? If so, how might Rose have behaved ethically instead? If not, could any of the participants' conduct be considered unethical? Explain.

CHAPTER 24

Investor Protection and Corporate Governance

(Just ASC/Shutterstock.com)

LEARNING OBJECTIVES

The five learning objectives below are designed to help improve your understanding of the chapter. After reading this chapter, you should be able to answer the following questions:

1. What is meant by the term *securities*?
2. What are the two major statutes regulating the securities industry?
3. What is insider trading? Why is it prohibited?
4. What are some of the features of state securities laws?
5. What certification requirements does the Sarbanes-Oxley Act impose on corporate executives?

> "You are remembered for the rules you break."
> —General Douglas MacArthur, 1880–1964 (U.S. Army general)

After the stock market crash of 1929, Congress enacted legislation to regulate securities markets. **Securities** generally are defined as any instruments representing corporate ownership (stock) or debts (bonds). The goal of regulation was to provide investors with more information to help them make buying and selling decisions about securities and to prohibit deceptive, unfair, and manipulative practices.

Today, the sale and transfer of securities are heavily regulated by federal and state statutes and by government agencies. Moreover, the Securities and Exchange Commission (SEC) has implemented new regulations since Congress passed the Dodd-Frank Wall Street Reform and Consumer Protection Act,[1] in reaction to the economic recession. We discuss the role of the SEC in the regulation of securities laws in this chapter's *Landmark in the Legal Environment* feature that follows.

Despite all efforts to regulate the securities markets, people continue to break the rules and are often remembered for it, as observed in the chapter-opening quotation. Violations are not always clear, though. Consider what happened when Facebook went public and issued stock in 2012. Facebook and its underwriters at Morgan Stanley determined that

Security Generally, a stock, bond, note, debenture, warrant, or other instrument representing an ownership interest in a corporation or a promise of repayment of debt by a corporation.

---

1. Pub. L. No. 111-203, July 21, 2010, 124 Stat. 1376; 12 U.S.C. Sections 5301 *et seq.*

LANDMARK IN THE LEGAL ENVIRONMENT

The Securities and Exchange Commission

In 1931, in the wake of the stock market crash of 1929, the U.S. Senate passed a resolution calling for an extensive investigation of securities trading. The investigation led, ultimately, to the enactment of the Securities Act of 1933, which is also known as the *truth-in-securities* bill. In the following year, Congress passed the Securities Exchange Act. This 1934 act created the Securities and Exchange Commission (SEC).

Major Responsibilities of the SEC   The SEC was created as an independent regulatory agency with the function of administering the 1933 and 1934 acts. Its major responsibilities in this respect are as follows:

1. Interprets federal securities laws and investigates securities law violations.
2. Issues new rules and amends existing rules.
3. Oversees the inspection of securities firms, brokers, investment advisers, and ratings agencies.
4. Oversees private regulatory organizations in the securities, accounting, and auditing fields.
5. Coordinates U.S. securities regulation with federal, state, and foreign authorities.

The SEC's Expanding Regulatory Powers   Since its creation, the SEC's regulatory functions have gradually been increased by legislation granting it authority in different areas. For example, to curb further securities fraud, the Securities Enforcement Remedies and Penny Stock Reform Act of 1990[a] was enacted to expand the SEC's enforcement options and allow SEC administrative law

judges to hear cases involving more types of alleged securities law violations. In addition, the act provides that courts can prevent persons who have engaged in securities fraud from serving as officers and directors of publicly held corporations. The Securities Acts Amendments of 1990 authorized the SEC to seek sanctions against those who violate foreign securities laws.[b]

The National Securities Markets Improvement Act of 1996 expanded the power of the SEC to exempt persons, securities, and transactions from the requirements of the securities laws.[c] (This part of the act is also known as the Capital Markets Efficiency Act.) The act also limited the authority of the states to regulate certain securities transactions and particular investment advisory firms.[d] The Sarbanes-Oxley Act of 2002,[e] which you will read about later in this chapter, further expanded the authority of the SEC by directing the agency to issue new rules relating to corporate disclosure requirements and by creating an oversight board to regulate public accounting firms.

Application to Today's Legal Environment   *The SEC is working to make the regulatory process more efficient and more relevant to today's securities trading practices. To this end, the SEC has embraced modern technology and communications methods, especially the Internet, more completely than many other federal agencies have. For example, the agency now requires—not just allows—companies to file certain information electronically so that it can be posted on the SEC's EDGAR (Electronic Data Gathering, Analysis, and Retrieval) database.*

b. 15 U.S.C. Section 78a.
c. 15 U.S.C. Sections 77z-3, 78mm.
d. 15 U.S.C. Section 80b-3a.
e. 15 U.S.C. Sections 7201 *et seq.*

a. 15 U.S.C. Section 77g.

---

there was enough interest by investors to justify an opening price of $38 per share. Within a few weeks, however, the value of a share was $25.75—30 percent below the original price. A rash of lawsuits were filed, and government regulators began an investigation. Many suspected that Facebook had provided information only to underwriters and certain (institutional) investors rather than making it available to all investors. Such an action is a violation of the securities laws, as you will read in this chapter.

Securities Act of 1933

The Securities Act[2] governs initial sales of stock by businesses. The act was designed to prohibit various forms of fraud and to stabilize the securities industry by requiring that all essential information concerning the issuance of securities be made available to the investing

2. 15 U.S.C. Sections 77–77aa.

public. Basically, the purpose of this act is to require disclosure. The 1933 act provides that all securities transactions must be registered with the SEC or be exempt from registration requirements.

What Is a Security?

Section 2(1) of the Securities Act contains a broad definition of securities, which generally include the following:[3]

1. Instruments and interests commonly known as securities, such as preferred and common stocks, treasury stocks, bonds, debentures, and stock warrants.
2. Any interests, such as stock options, puts, calls, or other types of privilege on a security or on the right to purchase a security or a group of securities in a national security exchange.
3. Notes, instruments, or other evidence of indebtedness, including certificates of interest in a profit-sharing agreement and certificates of deposit.
4. Any fractional undivided interest in oil, gas, or other mineral rights.
5. Investment contracts, which include interests in limited partnerships and other investment schemes.

(National Archives)

During the stock market crash of 1929, hordes of investors crowded Wall Street to find out the latest news. How did the "crash" affect stock trading in the years thereafter?

The *Howey* Test In interpreting the act, the United States Supreme Court has held that an **investment contract** is any transaction in which a person (1) invests (2) in a common enterprise (3) reasonably expecting profits (4) derived *primarily* or *substantially* from others' managerial or entrepreneurial efforts. Known as the *Howey* test, this definition continues to guide the determination of what types of contracts can be considered securities.[4]

CASE EXAMPLE 24.1 Alpha Telcom sold, installed, and maintained pay-phone systems. As part of its pay-phone program, Alpha guaranteed buyers a 14 percent return on their investment. Alpha was operating at a net loss, however, and continually borrowed funds to pay investors the fixed rate of return it had promised. Eventually, the company filed for bankruptcy, and the SEC brought an action alleging that Alpha had violated the Securities Act of 1933. A federal court concluded that Alpha's pay-phone program was a security because it involved an investment contract.[5] ●

Investment Contract In securities law, a transaction in which a person invests in a common enterprise reasonably expecting profits that are derived primarily from the efforts of others.

Learning Objective 1
What is meant by the term *securities*?

Many Types of Securities For our purposes, it is probably convenient to think of securities in their most common forms—stocks and bonds issued by corporations. Bear in mind, though, that securities can take many forms, including interests in whiskey, cosmetics, worms, beavers, boats, vacuum cleaners, muskrats, and cemetery lots. Almost any stake in the ownership or debt of a company can be considered a security. Investment contracts in condominiums, franchises, limited partnerships in real estate, and oil or gas or other mineral rights have qualified as securities.

Securities are not limited to stocks and bonds but can encompass a wide variety of legal claims. The analysis hinges on the nature of the transaction rather than on the particular instrument or rights involved. Because Congress enacted securities laws to regulate investments, in whatever form and by whatever name they are called, almost any type of security that might be sold as an investment can be subject to securities laws. When in doubt about whether an investment transaction involves securities, seek the advice of a specialized attorney.

PREVENTING LEGAL DISPUTES

---

3. 15 U.S.C. Section 77b(1). Amendments in 1982 added stock options.
4. *SEC v. W. J. Howey Co.*, 328 U.S. 293, 66 S.Ct. 1100, 90 L.Ed. 1244 (1946).
5. *SEC v. Alpha Telcom, Inc.*, 187 F.Supp.2d 1250 (2002). See also *SEC v. Edwards*, 540 U.S. 389, 124 S.Ct. 892, 157 L.Ed.2d 813 (2004), in which the United States Supreme Court held that an investment scheme offering contractual entitlement to a fixed rate of return can be an investment contract and therefore can be considered a security under federal law.

Registration Statement

Section 5 of the Securities Act broadly provides that a security must be *registered* before being offered to the public unless it qualifies for an exemption. The issuing corporation must file a *registration statement* with the SEC and must provide all investors with a *prospectus*.

A **prospectus** is a written disclosure document that describes the security being sold, the financial operations of the issuing corporation, and the investment or risk attaching to the security. The prospectus also serves as a selling tool for the issuing corporation.

The SEC now allows an issuer to deliver its prospectus to investors electronically via the Internet.[6] In principle, the registration statement and the prospectus supply sufficient information to enable unsophisticated investors to evaluate the financial risk involved.

Prospectus A written document required by securities laws when a security is being sold. The prospectus describes the security, the financial operations of the issuing corporation, and the risk attaching to the security so that investors will have sufficient information to evaluate the risk involved in purchasing the security.

Contents of the Registration Statement

The registration statement must be written in plain English and fully describe the following:

1. The securities being offered for sale, including their relationship to the issuer's other capital securities.
2. The corporation's properties and business (including a financial statement certified by an independent public accounting firm).
3. The management of the corporation, including managerial compensation, stock options, pensions, and other benefits. Any interests of directors or officers in any material transactions with the corporation must be disclosed.
4. How the corporation intends to use the proceeds of the sale.
5. Any pending lawsuits or special risk factors.

All companies, both domestic and foreign, must file their registration statements electronically so that they can be posted on the SEC's EDGAR (Electronic Data Gathering, Analysis, and Retrieval) database. The EDGAR database includes material on *initial public offerings* (IPOs), proxy statements, corporations' annual reports, registration statements, and other documents that have been filed with the SEC. Investors can access the database via the Internet (www.sec.gov/edgar.shtml) to obtain information that can be used to make investment decisions.

Registration Process

The registration statement does not become effective until after it has been reviewed and approved by the SEC (unless it is filed by a *well-known seasoned issuer,* as will be discussed shortly). The 1933 act restricted the types of activities that an issuer can engage in at each stage in the registration process.

Prefiling Period   During the *prefiling period* (before filing the registration statement), the issuer normally cannot sell or offer to sell the securities. Once the registration statement has been filed, a waiting period begins while the SEC reviews the registration statement for completeness.[7]

Waiting Period   During the *waiting period,* the securities can be offered for sale but cannot be sold by the issuing corporation. Only certain types of offers are allowed. All issuers can distribute a *preliminary prospectus,* which contains most of the information that will be included in the final prospectus but often does not include a price.

---

6. Basically, an electronic prospectus must meet the same requirements as a printed prospectus. The SEC has special rules that address situations in which the graphics, images, or audio files in a printed prospectus cannot be reproduced in an electronic form. 17 C.F.R. Section 232.304.
7. The waiting period must last at least twenty days but always extends much longer because the SEC invariably requires numerous changes and additions to the registration statement.

Most issuers can also use a *free-writing prospectus* during this period (although some inexperienced issuers will need to file a preliminary prospectus first).[8] A **free-writing prospectus** is any type of written, electronic, or graphic offer that describes the issuer or its securities and includes a legend indicating that the investor may obtain the prospectus at the SEC's Web site.

Posteffective Period   Once the SEC has reviewed and approved the registration statement and the waiting period is over, the registration is effective, and the *posteffective period* begins. The issuer can now offer and sell the securities without restrictions. If the company issued a preliminary or free-writing prospectus to investors, it must provide those investors with a final prospectus either before or at the time they purchase the securities. The issuer can require investors to download the final prospectus from a Web site if it notifies them of the appropriate Internet address.

Well-Known Seasoned Issuers

In 2005, the SEC revised the registration process and loosened some of the restrictions on large, experienced issuers.[9] The rules created new categories of issuers depending on their size and presence in the market and provided a simplified registration process for these issuers. The large, well-known securities firms that issue most securities have the greatest flexibility.

A firm that has issued at least $1 billion in securities in the previous three years or has at least $700 million of value of outstanding stock in the hands of the public is considered a *well-known seasoned issuer* (WKSI). WKSIs can file registration statements the day they announce a new offering and are not required to wait for SEC review and approval. They can also use a free-writing prospectus at any time, even during the prefiling period.

Exempt Securities and Transactions

Certain types of securities are exempt from the registration requirements of the 1933 Securities Act. These securities—which generally can also be resold without being registered—are summarized in Exhibit 24–1 that follows under the "Exempt Securities" heading.[10] The exhibit also lists and describes certain transactions that are exempt from registration requirements under various SEC regulations.

The transaction exemptions are the most important because they are very broad and can enable an issuer to avoid the high cost and complicated procedures associated with registration. Because the coverage of the exemptions overlaps somewhat, an offering may qualify for more than one. Therefore, many sales of securities occur without registration. Even when a transaction is exempt from the registration requirements, the offering is still subject to the antifraud provisions of the 1933 act (as well as those of the 1934 act, to be discussed later in this chapter).

Regulation A Offerings

Securities issued by an issuer that has offered less than $5 million in securities during any twelve-month period are exempt from registration.[11] Under Regulation A,[12] the issuer must file with the SEC a notice of the issue and an offering circular, which must also be provided to investors before the sale. This is a much simpler and less expensive process than the procedures associated with full registration.

Free-Writing Prospectus A written, electronic, or graphic offer that is used during the waiting period and describes securities that are being offered for sale, or describes the issuing corporation and includes a legend indicating that the investor may obtain the prospectus at the Securities and Exchange Commission's Web site.

---

8. See SEC Rules 164 and 433.
9. Securities Offering Reform, codified at 17 C.F.R. Sections 200, 228, 229, 230, 239, 240, 243, 249, and 274. 15 U.S.C. Section 77c.
10. 15 U.S.C. Section 77c.
11. 15 U.S.C. Section 77c(b).
12. 17 C.F.R. Sections 230.251–230.263.

Exhibit 24–1 Exemptions for Securities Offerings under the 1933 Securities Act

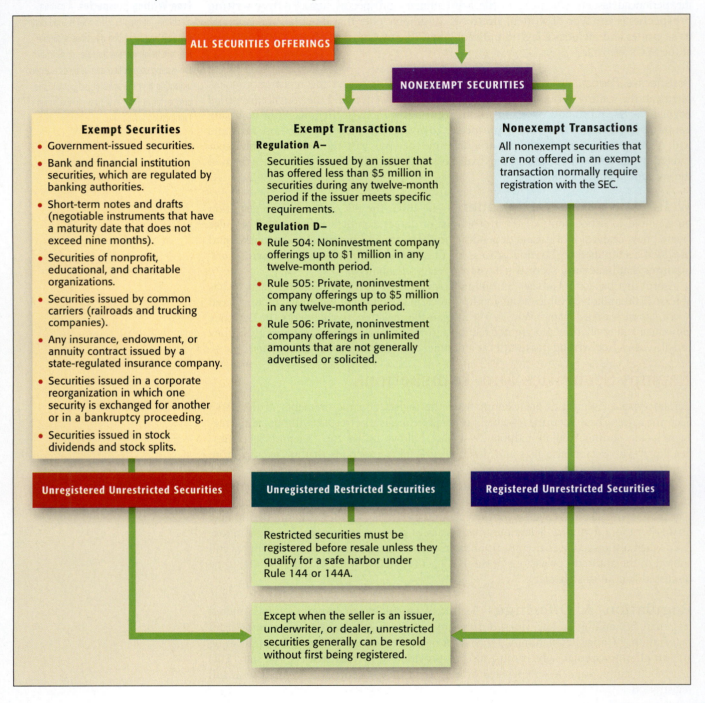

Testing the Waters   Companies are allowed to "test the waters" for potential interest before preparing the offering circular. To *test the waters* means to determine potential interest without actually selling any securities or requiring any commitment on the part of those who express interest. Small-business issuers (companies with annual revenues of less than $25 million) can use an integrated registration and reporting system that uses simpler forms than the full registration system.

Using the Internet Some companies have sold their securities via the Internet using Regulation A. **EXAMPLE 24.2** The Spring Street Brewing Company became the first company to sell securities via an online initial public offering (IPO). Spring Street raised about $1.6 million—without having to pay any commissions to brokers or underwriters. ● Such online IPOs are particularly attractive to small companies and start-up ventures that may find it difficult to raise capital from institutional investors or through underwriters.

Small Offerings—Regulation D

The SEC's Regulation D contains several exemptions from registration requirements (Rules 504, 505, and 506) for offers that either involve a small dollar amount or are made in a limited manner.

Rule 504 Rule 504 is the exemption used by most small businesses. It provides that non-investment company offerings up to $1 million in any twelve-month period are exempt. Noninvestment companies are firms that are not engaged primarily in the business of investing or trading in securities. (In contrast, an **investment company** is a firm that buys a large portfolio of securities and professionally manages it on behalf of many smaller shareholders/owners. A **mutual fund** is a type of investment company.)
EXAMPLE 24.3 Zeta Enterprises is a limited partnership that develops commercial property. Zeta intends to offer $600,000 of its limited partnership interests for sale between June 1 and May 31. Because an interest in a limited partnership meets the definition of a security (discussed earlier in this chapter), this offering would be subject to the registration and prospectus requirements of the Securities Act of 1933. Under Rule 504, however, the sales of Zeta's interests are exempt from these requirements because Zeta is a noninvestment company making an offering of less than $1 million in a twelve-month period. Therefore, Zeta can sell its limited partnership interests without filing a registration statement with the SEC or issuing a prospectus to any investor. ●

Rule 505 Another exemption is available under Rule 505 for private, noninvestment company offerings up to $5 million in any twelve-month period. The offer may be made to an unlimited number of *accredited investors* and up to thirty-five unaccredited investors. **Accredited investors** include banks, insurance companies, investment companies, employee benefit plans, the issuer's executive officers and directors, and persons whose income or net worth exceeds a certain threshold.

The SEC must be notified of the sales, and precautions must be taken because these restricted securities may be resold only by registration or in an exempt transaction. No general solicitation or advertising is allowed. The issuer must provide any unaccredited investors with disclosure documents that generally are the same as those used in registered offerings.

Rule 506—Private Placement Exemption Rule 506 exempts private, noninvestment company offerings in unlimited amounts that are not generally solicited or advertised. This exemption is often referred to as the *private placement* exemption because it exempts "transactions not involving any public offering."[13] To qualify for the exemption, the issuer must believe that each unaccredited investor has sufficient knowledge or experience in financial matters to be capable of evaluating the investment's merits and risks.[14]

The private placement exemption is perhaps most important to firms that want to raise funds through the sale of securities without registering them. **EXAMPLE 24.4** Citco Corporation needs to raise capital to expand its operations. Citco decides to make a private $10 million offering of its common stock directly to two hundred accredited investors and thirty highly sophisticated, but unaccredited, investors. Citco provides all of these investors with a prospectus and material information about the firm, including its most recent financial statements.

Investment Company A company that acts on the behalf of many smaller shareholders-owners by buying a large portfolio of securities and professionally managing that portfolio.

Mutual Fund A specific type of investment company that continually buys or sells to investors shares of ownership in a portfolio.

Accredited Investor In the context of securities offerings, "sophisticated" investors, such as banks, insurance companies, investment companies, the issuer's executive officers and directors, and persons whose income or net worth exceeds certain limits.

---

13. 15 U.S.C. Section 77d(2).
14. 17 C.F.R. Section 230.506.

As long as Citco notifies the SEC of the sale, this offering will likely qualify for the private placement exemption. The offering is nonpublic and not generally advertised. There are fewer than thirty-five unaccredited investors, and each of them possesses sufficient knowledge and experience to evaluate the risks involved. The issuer has provided all purchasers with the material information. Thus, Citco will *not* be required to comply with the registration requirements of the Securities Act. ●

Resales and Safe Harbor Rules

Most securities can be resold without registration. The Securities Act provides exemptions for resales by most persons other than issuers or underwriters. The average investor who sells shares of stock does not have to file a registration statement with the SEC.

Resales of restricted securities, however, trigger the registration requirements unless the party selling them complies with Rule 144 or Rule 144A. These rules are sometimes referred to as "safe harbors."

Rule 144   Rule 144 exempts restricted securities from registration on resale if all of the following conditions are met:

1. There is adequate current public information about the issuer. ("Adequate current public information" refers to the reports that certain companies are required to file under the Securities Exchange Act of 1934.)
2. The person selling the securities has owned them for at least six months if the issuer is subject to the reporting requirements of the 1934 act.[15] If the issuer is not subject to the 1934 act's reporting requirements, the seller must have owned the securities for at least one year.
3. The securities are sold in certain limited amounts in unsolicited brokers' transactions.
4. The SEC is notified of the resale.[16]

Rule 144A   Securities that at the time of issue are not of the same class as securities listed on a national securities exchange or quoted in a U.S. automated interdealer quotation system may be resold under Rule 144A.[17] They may be sold only to a qualified institutional buyer (an institution, such as an insurance company or a bank that owns and invests at least $100 million in securities). The seller must take reasonable steps to ensure that the buyer knows that the seller is relying on the exemption under Rule 144A.

Violations of the 1933 Act

It is a violation of the Securities Act of 1933 to intentionally defraud investors by misrepresenting or omitting facts in a registration statement or prospectus. Liability is also imposed on those who are negligent for not discovering the fraud. Selling securities before the effective date of the registration statement or under an exemption for which the securities do not qualify also results in liability.

Remedies

Criminal violations are prosecuted by the U.S. Department of Justice. Violators may be fined up to $10,000, imprisoned for up to five years, or both.

---

15. Before 2008, when amendments to Rule 144 became effective, the holding period was one year if the issuer was subject to the reporting requirements of the 1934 act. See the revised SEC Rules and Regulations at 72 Federal Rules 71546-01, 2007 WL 4368599, Release No. 33-8869. This reduced holding period allows nonpublic issuers to raise capital electronically from private and overseas sources more quickly.
16. 17 C.F.R. Section 230.144.
17. 17 C.F.R. Section 230.144A.

The SEC is authorized to seek civil sanctions against those who willfully violate the 1933 act. It can request an injunction to prevent further sales of the securities involved or ask the court to grant other relief, such as an order to a violator to refund profits. Parties who purchase securities and suffer harm as a result of false or omitted statements may also bring suits in a federal court to recover their losses and other damages.

Defenses   There are three basic defenses to charges of violations under the 1933 act. A defendant can avoid liability by proving any of the following:

1. The statement or omission was not material.
2. The plaintiff knew about the misrepresentation at the time of purchasing the stock.
3. The defendant exercised *due diligence* in preparing the registration and reasonably believed at the time that the statements were true.

The due diligence defense is the most important because it can be asserted by any defendant, except the issuer of the stock. The defendant must prove that she or he reasonably believed, at the time the registration statement became effective, that the statements in it were true and there were no omissions of material facts.

CASE EXAMPLE 24.5   Blackstone Group, LP, manages investments, nearly 40 percent of which are corporate private equity investments. In preparation for an initial public offering (IPO), Blackstone filed a registration statement with the SEC. At the time, Blackstone's corporate private equity investments included FGIC Corporation (which insured investments in subprime mortgages) and Freescale Semiconductor, Inc. Before the IPO, FGIC's customers began to suffer large losses, and Freescale had recently lost an exclusive contract to make wireless 3G chipsets for Motorola, Inc. (its largest customer). The losses suffered by these two companies would affect Blackstone. Nevertheless, Blackstone's registration statement did not mention the impact on its revenue of the investments in FGIC and Freescale.

Martin Litwin and others who invested in Blackstone's IPO filed a suit in a federal district court against Blackstone and its officers, alleging material omissions from the statement. Blackstone argued as a defense that the omissions were not material, and the lower court dismissed the case. The plaintiffs appealed. A federal appellate court ruled in favor of the plaintiffs. The plaintiffs' allegations were sufficient that Blackstone had omitted material information that it was required to disclose under the securities laws for the case to go to trial.[18] ●

When Blackstone Group filed for an initial public offering with the SEC, did it have to disclose the declining profitability of some of its private equity investments?

Securities Exchange Act of 1934

The 1934 Securities Exchange Act provides for the regulation and registration of securities exchanges, brokers, dealers, and national securities associations, such as the National Association of Securities Dealers (NASD). Unlike the 1933 act, which is a one-time disclosure law, the 1934 act provides for continuous periodic disclosures by publicly held corporations to enable the SEC to regulate subsequent trading.

The Securities Exchange Act applies to companies that have assets in excess of $10 million and five hundred or more shareholders. These corporations are referred to as *Section 12 companies* because they are required to register their securities under Section 12 of the 1934 act. Section 12 companies must file reports with the SEC annually and quarterly, and sometimes even monthly if specified events occur (such as a merger). Other provisions in the 1934 act require all securities brokers and dealers to be registered, to keep detailed records of their activities, and to file annual reports with the SEC.

The act also authorizes the SEC to engage in market surveillance to deter undesirable market practices such as fraud, market manipulation (attempts at illegally influencing

Learning Objective 2
What are the two major statutes regulating the securities industry?

---

18. *Litwin v. Blackstone Group, LP,* 634 F.3d 706 (2d Cir. 2011).

stock prices), and misrepresentation. In addition, the act provides for the SEC's regulation of proxy solicitations for voting (discussed in Chapter 15).

Section 10(b), SEC Rule 10b-5, and Insider Trading

Section 10(b) is one of the more important sections of the Securities Exchange Act. This section proscribes the use of any manipulative or deceptive mechanism in violation of SEC rules and regulations. Among the rules that the SEC has promulgated pursuant to the 1934 act is **SEC Rule 10b-5,** which prohibits the commission of fraud in connection with the purchase or sale of any security.

SEC Rule 10b-5 A rule of the Securities and Exchange Commission that prohibits the commission of fraud in connection with the purchase or sale of any security. It is unlawful to make any untrue statement of a material fact or to omit a material fact if doing so causes the statement to be misleading.

SEC Rule 10b-5 applies to almost all cases concerning the trading of securities, whether on organized exchanges, in over-the-counter markets, or in private transactions. Generally, the rule covers just about any form of security, and the securities need not be registered under the 1933 act for the 1934 act to apply.

Private parties can sue for securities fraud under the 1934 act and SEC rules. The basic elements of a securities fraud action are as follows:

1. A *material misrepresentation* (or omission) in connection with the purchase and sale of securities.
2. *Scienter* (a wrongful state of mind).
3. *Reliance* by the plaintiff on the material misrepresentation.
4. An *economic loss.*
5. *Causation,* meaning that there is a causal connection between the misrepresentation and the loss.

Insider Trading The purchase or sale of securities on the basis of information that has not been made available to the public.

Learning Objective 3
What is insider trading?
Why is it prohibited?

Insider Trading   One of the major goals of Section 10(b) and SEC Rule 10b-5 is to prevent so-called **insider trading,** which occurs when persons buy or sell securities on the basis of information that is not available to the public. Corporate directors, officers, and others such as majority shareholders, for instance, often have advance inside information that can affect the future market value of the corporate stock. Obviously, if they act on this information, their positions give them a trading advantage over the general public and other shareholders.

The 1934 Securities Exchange Act defines inside information and extends liability to those who take advantage of such information in their personal transactions when they know that the information is unavailable to those with whom they are dealing. Section 10(b) of the 1934 act and SEC Rule 10b-5 apply to anyone who has access to or receives information of a nonpublic nature on which trading is based—not just to corporate "insiders."

A government official outlines what he believes was an insider trading scandal that involved computer company Dell, Inc.

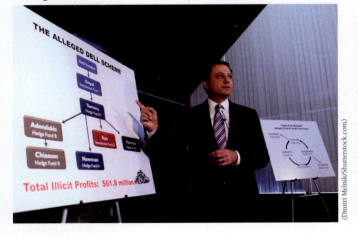

(Dmitri Melnik/Shutterstock.com)

Disclosure under SEC Rule 10b-5   Any material omission or misrepresentation of material facts in connection with the purchase or sale of a security may violate not only the Securities Act but also the antifraud provisions of Section 10(b) of the 1934 act and SEC Rule 10b-5. The key to liability (which can be civil or criminal) under Section 10(b) and SEC Rule 10b-5 is whether the insider's information is *material.*

The following are some examples of material facts calling for disclosure under SEC Rule 10b-5:

1. Fraudulent trading in the company's stock by a broker-dealer.
2. A dividend change (whether up or down).

3. A contract for the sale of corporate assets.
4. A new discovery, a new process, or a new product.
5. A significant change in the firm's financial condition.
6. Potential litigation against the company.

Note that any one of these facts, by itself, is not *automatically* considered a material fact. Rather, it will be regarded as a material fact if it is significant enough that it would likely affect an investor's decision as to whether to purchase or sell the company's securities.

EXAMPLE 24.6 Sheen, Inc., is the defendant in a class-action product liability suit that its attorney, Paula Frasier, believes that the company will lose. Frasier has advised Sheen's directors, officers, and accountants that the company will likely have to pay a substantial damages award. Sheen plans to make a $5 million offering of newly issued stock before the date when the trial is expected to end. Sheen's potential liability and the financial consequences to the firm are material facts that must be disclosed because they are significant enough to affect an investor's decision as to whether to purchase the stock. ●

The following is a classic decision interpreting materiality under SEC Rule 10b-5.

Classic Case 24.1

Securities and Exchange Commission v. Texas Gulf Sulphur Co.
United States Court of Appeals, Second Circuit, 401 F.2d 833 (1968).

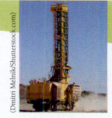

(Dmitri Melnik/Shutterstock.com)

After sample drilling revealed potential mineral deposits, company executives made substantial stock purchases. Did they violate insider-trading laws?

HISTORICAL AND ENVIRONMENTAL SETTING *In 1957, the Texas Gulf Sulphur Company began exploring for minerals in eastern Canada. In March 1959, aerial geophysical surveys were conducted over more than fifteen thousand square miles of the area. The operations revealed numerous variations in the conductivity of the rock, which indicated a remarkable concentration of commercially exploitable minerals. One site of such variations was near Timmins, Ontario. On October 29 and 30, 1963, a ground survey of the site near Timmins indicated a need to drill for further evaluation.*

BACKGROUND AND FACTS On November 12, 1963, the Texas Gulf Sulphur Company (TGS) drilled a hole that appeared to yield a core with an exceedingly high mineral content, although further drilling would be necessary to establish whether there was enough ore to be mined commercially. TGS kept secret the results of the core sample. After learning of the ore discovery, officers and employees of the company made substantial purchases of TGS's stock or accepted stock options (rights to purchase stock). On April 11, 1964, an unauthorized report of the mineral find appeared in the newspapers. On the following day, April 12, TGS issued a press release that played down the discovery and stated that it was too early to tell whether the ore find would be significant.

Later on, TGS announced a strike of at least 25 million tons of ore. The news led to a substantial increase in the price of TGS stock. The Securities and Exchange Commission (SEC) brought a suit in a federal district court against the officers and employees of TGS for violating the insider-trading prohibition of SEC

Rule 10b-5. The officers and employees argued that the prohibition did not apply. They reasoned that the information on which they had traded was not material, as the find had not been commercially proved. The trial court held that most of the defendants had not violated SEC Rule 10b-5, and the SEC appealed.

IN THE WORDS OF THE COURT . . .
WATERMAN, Circuit Judge.
 * * * *

 * * * Whether facts are material within Rule 10b-5 when the facts relate to a particular event and are undisclosed by those persons who are knowledgeable thereof *will depend at any given time upon a balancing of both the indicated probability that the event will occur and the anticipated magnitude of the event in light of the totality of the company activity.* Here, * * * knowledge of the possibility, which surely was more than marginal, of the existence of a mine of the vast magnitude indicated by the remarkably rich drill core located rather close to the surface (suggesting mineability by the less expensive open-pit method) within the confines of a large anomaly (suggesting an extensive region of mineralization) might well have affected the price of TGS stock and would certainly have been an important fact to a reasonable, if speculative, investor in deciding whether he should buy, sell, or hold. [Emphasis added.]

Classic Case 24.1—Continues ➡

Classic Case 24.1—Continued

* * * *

    * * * A major factor in determining whether the * * * discovery was a material fact is the importance attached to the drilling results by those who knew about it. * * * The timing by those who knew of it of their stock purchases * * * —purchases in some cases by individuals who had never before purchased * * * TGS stock—virtually compels the inference that the insiders were influenced by the drilling results.

DECISION AND REMEDY The appellate court ruled in favor of the SEC. All of the trading by insiders who knew of the mineral find before its true extent had been publicly announced had violated SEC Rule 10b-5.

WHAT IF THE FACTS WERE DIFFERENT? *Suppose that further drilling revealed that there was not enough ore at this site for it to be mined commercially. Would the defendants still have been liable for violating SEC Rule 10b-5? Why or why not?*

IMPACT OF THIS CASE ON TODAY'S LEGAL ENVIRONMENT *This landmark case affirmed the principle that the test of whether information is "material," for SEC Rule 10b-5 purposes, is whether it would affect the judgment of reasonable investors. The corporate insiders' purchases of stock and stock options indicated that they were influenced by the results and that the information about the drilling results was material. The courts continue to cite this case when applying SEC Rule 10b-5 to other cases of alleged insider trading.*

Outsiders and SEC Rule 10b-5 The traditional insider-trading case involves true insiders—corporate officers, directors, and majority shareholders who have access to (and trade on) inside information. Increasingly, liability under Section 10(b) of the 1934 act and SEC Rule 10b-5 is being extended to certain "outsiders"—those persons who trade on inside information acquired indirectly. Two theories have been developed under which outsiders may be held liable for insider trading: the *tipper/tippee theory* and the *misappropriation theory.*

Tipper/Tippee Theory Anyone who acquires inside information as a result of a corporate insider's breach of his or her fiduciary duty can be liable under SEC Rule 10b-5. This liability extends to **tippees** (those who receive "tips" from insiders) and even remote tippees (tippees of tippees).

    The key to liability under this theory is that the inside information must be obtained as a result of someone's breach of a fiduciary duty to the corporation whose shares are involved in the trading. The tippee is liable under this theory only if the following requirements are met:

Tippee A person who receives inside information.

1. There is a breach of a duty not to disclose inside information.
2. The disclosure is made in exchange for personal benefit.
3. The tippee knows (or should know) of this breach and benefits from it.

"The way to stop financial 'joy-riding' is to arrest the chauffeur, not the automobile."

Woodrow Wilson, 1856–1924
(Twenty-eighth president of the United States, 1913–1921)

Misappropriation Theory Liability for insider trading may also be established under the misappropriation theory. This theory holds that an individual who wrongfully obtains (misappropriates) inside information and trades on it for her or his personal gain should be held liable because, in essence, she or he stole information rightfully belonging to another.

    The misappropriation theory has been controversial because it significantly extends the reach of SEC Rule 10b-5 to outsiders who ordinarily would *not* be deemed fiduciaries of the corporations in whose stock they trade. It is not always wrong to disclose material, nonpublic information about a company to another person. Nevertheless, a person who obtains the information and trades securities on it can be liable.

    CASE EXAMPLE 24.7 Patricia Rocklage was the wife of Scott Rocklage, the CEO of Cubist Pharmaceuticals, Inc. Scott had sometimes disclosed material, nonpublic information about Cubist to Patricia. She had always kept the information confidential. When Scott told Patricia that one of Cubist's key drugs had failed its clinical trial, however, Patricia informed her brother, William Beaver, who owned Cubist stock. Beaver sold his Cubist shares and tipped his friend David Jones, who sold his shares. When Cubist publicly announced the trial results, the price of its stock dropped. Beaver and Jones avoided significant losses by selling when they did. The SEC filed a lawsuit against Patricia, Beaver, and Jones. The court found all three defendants guilty of insider trading under the misappropriation theory.[19] ●

Insider Reporting and Trading—Section 16(b)

Section 16(b) of the 1934 act provides for the recapture by the corporation of all profits realized by an insider on any purchase and sale or sale and purchase of the corporation's stock within any six-month period.[20] It is irrelevant whether the insider actually uses inside information—*all such **short-swing profits** must be returned to the corporation.*

In this context, *insiders* means officers, directors, and large stockholders of Section 12 corporations (those owning at least 10 percent of the class of equity securities registered under Section 12 of the 1934 act). To discourage such insiders from using nonpublic information about their companies for their personal benefit in the stock market, they must file reports with the SEC concerning their ownership and trading of the corporation's securities.

Section 16(b) applies not only to stock but also to warrants, *options* (discussed later in this chapter), and securities convertible into stock. In addition, the courts have fashioned complex rules for determining profits. Note that the SEC exempts a number of transactions under Rule 16b-3.[21] For all of these reasons, corporate insiders are wise to seek specialized counsel before trading in the corporation's stock. Exhibit 24–2 that follows compares the effects of SEC Rule 10b-5 and Section 16(b).

Short-Swing Profits Profits earned by a purchase and sale, or sale and purchase, of the same security within a six-month period. Under Section 16(b) of the 1934 Securities Exchange Act, the profits must be returned to the corporation if earned by company insiders from transactions in the company's stock.

The Private Securities Litigation Reform Act of 1995

The disclosure requirements of SEC Rule 10b-5 had the unintended effect of deterring the disclosure of forward-looking information. To understand why, consider an example.

---

19. *SEC v. Rocklage,* 470 F.3d 1 (1st Cir. 2006).
20. A person who expects the price of a particular stock to decline can realize profits by "selling short"—selling at a high price and repurchasing later at a lower price to cover the "short sale."
21. 17 C.F.R. Section 240.16b-3.

Exhibit 24–2 Comparison of Coverage, Application, and Liability under SEC Rule 10b-5 and Section 16(b)

AREA OF COMPARISON	SEC RULE 10b-5	SECTION 16(b)
What is the subject matter of the transaction?	Any security (does not have to be registered).	Any security (does not have to be registered).
What transactions are covered?	Purchase or sale.	Short-swing purchase and sale or short-swing sale and purchase.
Who is subject to liability?	Almost anyone with inside information under a duty to disclose—including officers, directors, controlling shareholders, and tippees.	Officers, directors, and certain shareholders who earn 10 percent or more.
Is omission or misrepresentation necessary for liability?	Yes.	No.
Are there any exempt transactions?	No.	Yes, there are a number of exemptions.
Who may bring an action?	A person transacting with an insider, the SEC, or a purchaser or seller damaged by a wrongful act.	A corporation or a shareholder by derivative action.

EXAMPLE 24.8   QT Company announces that its projected earnings in a future time period will be a certain amount, but the forecast turns out to be wrong. The earnings are in fact much lower, and the price of QT's stock is affected—negatively. The shareholders then file suit against the company, alleging that the directors violated SEC Rule 10b-5 by disclosing misleading financial information. ●

In an attempt to rectify this problem and promote disclosure, in 1995 Congress passed the Private Securities Litigation Reform Act (PSLRA). Among other things, the PSLRA provides a "safe harbor" for publicly held companies that make forward-looking statements, such as financial forecasts. Those who make such statements are protected against liability for securities fraud if they include "meaningful cautionary statements identifying important factors that could cause actual results to differ materially from those in the forward-looking statement."[22]

The PSLRA also affected the level of detail required in securities fraud complaints. Plaintiffs must specify each misleading statement and say how it led them to a mistaken belief.

Limitations on Class Actions

After the Private Securities Litigation Reform Act was passed, a number of securities class-action suits were filed in state courts to skirt its requirements. In response to this problem, Congress passed the Securities Litigation Uniform Standards Act (SLUSA).[23] The act placed stringent limits on the ability of plaintiffs to bring class-action suits in state courts against firms whose securities are traded on national stock exchanges. SLUSA not only prevents the purchasers and sellers of securities from bringing class-action fraud claims under state securities laws, but also applies to investors who are fraudulently induced to hold on to their securities.[24]

Regulation of Proxy Statements

Section 14(a) of the Securities Exchange Act regulates the solicitation of proxies (see Chapter 15) from shareholders of Section 12 companies. The SEC regulates the content of proxy statements. Whoever solicits a proxy must fully and accurately disclose in the proxy statement all of the facts that are pertinent to the matter on which the shareholders are to vote. SEC Rule 14a-9 is similar to the antifraud provisions of SEC Rule 10b-5. Remedies for violations are extensive, ranging from injunctions to prevent a vote from being taken to monetary damages.

Violations of the 1934 Act

As mentioned earlier, violations of Section 10(b) of the Securities Exchange Act and SEC Rule 10b-5, including insider trading, may be subject to criminal or civil liability.

Scienter Requirement

For either criminal or civil sanctions to be imposed, *scienter* must exist—that is, the violator must have had an intent to defraud or knowledge of her or his misconduct. *Scienter* can be proved by showing that the defendant made false statements or wrongfully failed to disclose material facts. In some situations, *scienter* can even be proved by showing that the defendant was consciously reckless as to the truth or falsity of his or her statements.

CASE EXAMPLE 24.9   Alvin Gebhart and Jack Archer started a business venture purchasing mobile home parks (MHPs) from owners and converting them to resident

---

22. 15 U.S.C. Sections 77z-2, 78u-5.
23. Pub. L. No. 105-353. This act amended many sections of Title 15 of the *United States Code*.
24. See *Merrill Lynch, Pierce, Fenner & Smith, Inc. v. Dabit,* 547 U.S. 71, 126 S.Ct. 1503, 164 L.Ed.2d 179 (2006).

ownership. They formed MHP Conversions, LP, to facilitate the conversion process and issue promissory notes that were sold to investors to raise funds for the purchases. Archer ran the MHP program, and Gebhart sold the promissory notes. Gebhart sold nearly $2.4 million in MHP promissory notes to clients, who bought notes based on the Gebhart's positive statements about the investment.

During the time Gebhart was selling the notes, however, he never actually looked into the finances of the MHP program. He relied entirely on information that Archer gave him, some of which was not true. When Gebhart was later sued for securities fraud, a federal appellate court concluded that there was sufficient evidence of *scienter*. Gebhart knew that he had no knowledge of the financial affairs of MHP, and he had been consciously reckless as to the truth or falsity of his statements about investing in MHP.[25] ●

In a complaint alleging violations of Section 10(b) and Rule 10b-5, the plaintiff must state facts giving rise to an inference of *scienter* (knowledge that an action was illegal or that statements were false) at least as likely as any plausible opposing inference. Opposing inferences and their proof were at issue in the following case.

---

25. *Gebhart v. SEC*, 595 F.3d 1034 (9th Cir. 2010).

Case 24.2

City of Livonia Employees' Retirement System and Local 295/Local 851 v. Boeing Co.
United States Court of Appeals, Seventh Circuit, 711 F.3d 754 (2013).

What was one of the consequences of the delay in Boeing's 787 Dreamliner's first flight?

BACKGROUND AND FACTS Between May 4 and June 22, 2009, Boeing Co. made announcements implying that its Dreamliner, a new plane that had not yet flown, was on track for its "First Flight" (a significant milestone in the development of new aircraft), scheduled for June 30. Meanwhile, however, the plane failed important stress tests, and on June 23, Boeing canceled the scheduled flight. This foretold a delay in the delivery of the Dreamliner to the airlines. Boeing's stock price dropped more than 10 percent. On behalf of all persons who had bought Boeing stock between May 4 and June 22, investors filed a suit in a federal district court alleging that the company, its chief executive officer (W. James McNerney), and the head of its commercial aircraft division (Scott Carson) were guilty of securities fraud. The investors claimed that when these executives announced that the Dreamliner was on track, they knew that the flight would likely be postponed. The court dismissed the suit, and the plaintiffs appealed.

IN THE WORDS OF THE COURT . . .
POSNER, Circuit Judge.
* * * *

There is no securities fraud by hindsight. The law does not require public disclosure of mere risks of failure. No prediction—even a prediction that the sun will rise tomorrow—has a 100 percent probability of being correct. The future is shrouded in uncertainty. *If a mistaken prediction is deemed a fraud, there*

will be few predictions, including ones that are well grounded, as no one wants to be held hostage to an unknown future. [Emphasis added.]

Any sophisticated purchaser of a product that is still on the drawing boards knows, moreover, that its market debut may be delayed, or indeed that the project may be abandoned before it yields salable product. The purchasers of the Dreamliner protected themselves against the possibility of delay in delivery by reserving the right to cancel their orders; there are no allegations regarding cancellation penalties, or for that matter penalties imposed on Boeing for delivery delays. And therefore * * * the defendants * * * had, so far as appears, little incentive to delay the announcement of the postponement.

Without a motive to commit securities fraud, [businesspersons] are unlikely to commit it. A more plausible inference than that of fraud is that the defendants, unsure whether they could fix the problem by the end of June, were reluctant to tell the world "we have a problem and maybe it will cause us to delay the First Flight and maybe not, but we're working on the problem and we hope we can fix it in time to prevent any significant delay, but we can't be sure, so stay tuned." There is a difference * * * between a duty of truthfulness and a duty of candor, or between a lie and reticence. *There is no duty of total corporate transparency—no rule that every hitch or glitch, every pratfall, in*

Case 24.2—Continues ➡

Case 24.2—Continued

a company's operations must be disclosed in real time, forming a running commentary, a baring of the corporate innards, day and night. [Emphasis added.]

* * * *

* * * The * * * complaint alleged [that] what McNerney and Carson knew about the likely postponement of the First Flight * * * was confirmed by "internal e-mails" of Boeing. The reference to internal e-mails implied that someone inside Boeing was aiding the plaintiffs. But as no such person was identified, the judge could not determine whether such e-mails * * * existed.

Allegations * * * merely implying unnamed confidential sources of damaging information require a heavy discount. The sources may be ill-informed, may be acting from spite rather than knowledge, may be misrepresented, may even be nonexistent * * * . The district judge therefore rightly refused to give any weight to the "internal e-mails" to which the complaint referred.

DECISION AND REMEDY The U.S. Court of Appeals for the Seventh Circuit affirmed the lower court's dismissal of the plaintiffs' complaint. The investors' allegation that company executives knew about the First Flight's likely postponement was insufficient to establish *scienter,* because it was based on internal company e-mails provided by an unidentified source.

THE LEGAL ENVIRONMENT DIMENSION *The document at the center of the dispute in this case was the plaintiffs' complaint. What must a complaint state to properly allege violations of Section 10(b) and Rule 10b-5?*

THE ETHICAL DIMENSION *Should the court impose sanctions on the lawyers who filed the complaint in this case based on allegations from unnamed confidential sources? Discuss.*

Scienter Not Required for Section 16(b) Violations

Violations of Section 16(b) include the sale by insiders of stock acquired less than six months before the sale (or less than six months after the sale if selling short). These violations are subject to civil sanctions. Liability under Section 16(b) is strict liability. Neither *scienter* nor negligence is required.

Criminal Penalties

For violations of Section 10(b) and Rule 10b-5, an individual may be fined up to $5 million, imprisoned for up to twenty years, or both. A partnership or a corporation may be fined up to $25 million. Section 807 of the Sarbanes-Oxley Act provides that for a *willful* violation of the 1934 act, the violator may be imprisoned for up to twenty-five years in addition to being fined.

For a defendant to be convicted in a criminal prosecution under the securities laws, there can be no reasonable doubt that the defendant knew he or she was acting wrongfully. A jury is not allowed merely to speculate that the defendant may have acted willfully. **CASE EXAMPLE 24.10** Martha Stewart, founder of a well-known media and homemaking empire, was charged with intentionally deceiving investors based on public statements she made. Stewart's stockbroker allegedly had informed Stewart that the head of ImClone Systems, Inc., was selling his shares in that company. Stewart then sold her ImClone shares. The next day, ImClone announced that the U.S. Food and Drug Administration had not approved Erbitux, the company's greatly anticipated medication.

After the government began investigating Stewart's ImClone trades, she publicly stated that she had previously instructed her stockbroker to sell her ImClone stock if the price fell to $60 per share. The government prosecutor claimed that Stewart's statement showed she had the intent to deceive investors. The court, however, acquitted Stewart on this charge because "to find the essential element of criminal intent beyond a reasonable doubt, a rational juror would have to speculate."[26] ●

---

26. *United States v. Stewart,* 305 F.Supp.2d 368 (S.D.N.Y. 2004). Stewart was later convicted on other charges relating to her ImClone trading that did not require proof of intent.

In the following case, the defendant argued that he should not have been convicted for securities fraud because the government had failed to prove the offense.

Case 24.3

United States v. Newton

United States Court of Appeals, Eleventh Circuit, 2014 WL 1045685 (2014).

Real American Brands once owned and operated a Billy Martin's western wear retail boutique in Trump Plaza.

BACKGROUND AND FACTS   Douglas Newton was the president and sole director of Real American Brands, Inc. (RLAB), which owned the Billy Martin's USA brand and operated a Billy Martin's retail boutique at Trump Plaza in New York City. (Billy Martin, one-time manager of the New York Yankees, co-founded Billy Martin's, a western wear store.) Newton agreed to pay kickbacks to Chris Russo, whom he believed to be the manager of a pension fund, to induce the fund to buy restricted shares of RLAB stock. Newton later arranged for his friend Yan Skwara to pay similar kickbacks for the fund's purchase of stock in U.S. Farms, Inc. Skwara was the chief executive officer and president of U.S. Farms. In fact, the pension fund was fictitious—Newton and Skwara had been dealing with agents of the Federal Bureau of Investigation (FBI). Newton and Skwara were charged with securities fraud. Skwara pleaded guilty. A federal district court jury convicted Newton. Sentenced to thirty months' imprisonment, Newton appealed.

IN THE WORDS OF THE COURT . . .
SCHLESINGER, * * * Judge.
      * * * *

The government, according to Defendant, never established the central allegation in this case—that the stock was sold at an artificially inflated price. * * * Evidence supports Defendant's conviction beyond a reasonable doubt, and Defendant fails to demonstrate that his conviction [is] shocking or a manifest miscarriage of justice.

Moreover, the record refutes Defendant's assertions. The evidence at trial established that the 30 percent kickbacks made the price of the stock irrelevant. The parties involved cared only about the kickback payments, not the stock price. In addition, because of the kickbacks, the pension fund purchased restricted shares at the higher price set for freely-traded shares. Thus, the kickback itself artificially increased the stock price. The pension fund paid $20,000 for stock that should have cost only $14,000—absent the $6,000 bribe. *Ample evidence existed for the jury to conclude that the fraudulent scheme caused the pension fund to pay inflated prices for the restricted shares of stock.* [Emphasis added.]

Likewise, Defendant's contention that there was no evidence that he made any misrepresentation material to the fraud lacks merit. A "scheme to defraud" has been broadly defined, and it may include more than fraudulent misrepresentations. * * * The Government merely needs to show that the accused intended to defraud his victim and that his or her communications were reasonably calculated to deceive persons of ordinary prudence and comprehension.

The evidence here demonstrated that Defendant engaged in a scheme to defraud the pension fund beneficiaries by making undisclosed kickbacks to induce the purchase of stock at inflated prices. While the undercover FBI agents initiated the deal and proposed the terms, Defendant voluntarily joined the scheme, and then urged Skwara to participate for Defendant's own gain. Furthermore, Defendant attempted to conceal the kickback agreement with a fictitious consulting agreement, and numerous e-mails referring to advice he never received. Finally, Defendant's words and conduct, as captured on the recorded tapes played at the trial, demonstrated his intent to defraud the pension fund investors. Accordingly, there was no miscarriage of justice.

DECISION AND REMEDY   The U.S. Court of Appeals for the Eleventh Circuit affirmed Newton's conviction and sentence for securities fraud. The evidence supported the conviction beyond a reasonable doubt. "Accordingly, there was no miscarriage of justice."

THE LEGAL ENVIRONMENT DIMENSION   *The crimes of mail and wire fraud were discussed in Chapter 6. Could these defendants have been convicted of those crimes? Explain.*

THE ETHICAL DIMENSION   *What is the difference between a sales commission or a transaction fee and a kickback? Why is a kickback unethical? Discuss.*

Civil Sanctions   The SEC can also bring suit in a federal district court against anyone violating or aiding in a violation of the 1934 act or SEC rules by purchasing or selling a security while in the possession of material nonpublic information.[27] The violation must occur on or through the facilities of a national securities exchange or from or through a broker or dealer.

A court may assess a penalty for as much as triple the profits gained or the loss avoided by the guilty party.[28] The Insider Trading and Securities Fraud Enforcement Act increased the number of persons who may be subject to civil liability for insider trading and gave the SEC authority to pay monetary rewards to informants.[29]

Private parties may also sue violators of Section 10(b) and Rule 10b-5. A private party may obtain rescission (cancellation) of a contract to buy securities or damages to the extent of the violator's illegal profits. Those found liable have a right to seek contribution from those who share responsibility for the violations, including accountants, attorneys, and corporations. For violations of Section 16(b), a corporation can bring an action to recover the short-swing profits.

State Securities Laws

Learning Objective 4
What are some of the features of state securities laws?

Today, every state has its own corporate securities laws, or "blue sky laws," that regulate the offer and sale of securities within its borders. (The phrase *blue sky laws* dates to a 1917 decision by the United States Supreme Court in which the Court declared that the purpose of such laws was to prevent "speculative schemes which have no more basis than so many feet of 'blue sky.'"[30]) Article 8 of the Uniform Commercial Code, which has been adopted by all of the states, also imposes various requirements relating to the purchase and sale of securities.

Requirements under State Securities Laws

Typically, state laws have disclosure requirements and antifraud provisions, many of which are patterned after Section 10(b) of the Securities Exchange Act and SEC Rule 10b-5. State laws also provide for the registration of securities offered or issued for sale within the state and impose disclosure requirements.

Methods of registration, required disclosures, and exemptions from registration vary among states. Unless an exemption from registration is applicable, issuers must register or qualify their stock with the appropriate state official, often called a *corporations commissioner.* Additionally, most state securities laws regulate securities brokers and dealers.

Concurrent Regulation

State securities laws apply mainly to intrastate transactions. Since the adoption of the 1933 and 1934 federal securities acts, the state and federal governments have regulated securities concurrently. Issuers must comply with both federal and state securities laws, and exemptions from federal law are not exemptions from state laws.

The dual federal and state system has not always worked well, particularly during the early 1990s, when the securities markets underwent considerable expansion. Today, most

---

27. 15 U.S.C. Section 78u(d)(2)(A).

28. Profit or loss is defined as "the difference between the purchase or sale price of the security and the value of that security as measured by the trading price of the security at a reasonable period of time after public dissemination of the nonpublic information." 15 U.S.C. Section 78u(d)(2)(C).

29. 15 U.S.C. Section 78u-1.

30. *Hall v. Geiger-Jones Co.,* 242 U.S. 539, 37 S.Ct. 217, 61 L.Ed. 480 (1917).

of the duplicate regulations have been eliminated, and the SEC has exclusive power to regulate most national securities activities. The National Conference of Commissioners on Uniform State Laws also substantially revised the Uniform Securities Act in 2002 to coordinate state and federal securities regulation and enforcement efforts. Seventeen states have adopted the most recent version of the Uniform Securities Act.[31]

Corporate Governance

Corporate governance can be narrowly defined as the relationship between a corporation and its shareholders. Some argue for a broader definition—that corporate governance specifies the rights and responsibilities among different participants in the corporation, such as the board of directors, managers, shareholders, and other stakeholders, and spells out the rules and procedures for making decisions on corporate affairs. Regardless of the way it is defined, effective corporate governance requires more than just compliance with laws and regulations.

Effective corporate governance is essential in large corporations because corporate ownership (by shareholders) is separated from corporate control (by officers and managers). Under these circumstances, officers and managers may attempt to advance their own interests at the expense of the shareholders. The well-publicized corporate scandals in the first decade of the 2000s clearly illustrate the reasons for concern about managerial opportunism. See this chapter's *Insight into Ethics* that follows for a discussion of shareholder control over compensation of corporate executives.

Corporate Governance A set of policies specifying the rights and responsibilities of the various participants in a corporation and spelling out the rules and procedures for making corporate decisions.

---

31. At the time this book went to press, the Uniform Securities Act had been adopted in Georgia, Hawaii, Idaho, Indiana, Iowa, Kansas, Maine, Michigan, Minnesota, Mississippi, Missouri, New Mexico, Oklahoma, South Carolina, South Dakota, Vermont, and Wisconsin, as well as in the U.S. Virgin Islands.

INSIGHT INTO ETHICS

SHAREHOLDER "SAY-ON-PAY"

Over the last several years, executive compensation has become a hotly debated issue. Many critics argue that the chief executive officers (CEOs) of public companies are paid too much, especially in comparison with the wages earned by the average worker.

The Dodd-Frank Wall Street Reform and Consumer Protection Act includes a "say-on-pay" provision that gives shareholders the right to vote on executive compensation for senior executives at every public U.S. company. These votes on executive pay are nonbinding, however—the board of directors does not have to abide by them. Furthermore, more than 90 percent of shareholder votes on executive pay have been in favor of the proposed compensation plans. For example, in 2013 only 58 (about 3 percent) of the companies got less than 50 percent of shareholder support for their executive compensation packages.

Despite the "say-on-pay" provision, the average compensation for a CEO in 2014 was more than $10.5 million, up 13 percent from the previous year. A typical U.S. employee would have to work about a month to earn what a CEO earns in an hour.

For Critical Analysis
Insight into the Social Environment
Why do you think that shareholders continue to vote to approve large executive compensation packages?

Attempts at Aligning the Interests of Officers with Those of Shareholders

Stock Option A right to buy a given number of shares of stock at a set price, usually within a specified time period.

Some corporations have sought to align the financial interests of their officers with those of the company's shareholders by providing the officers with **stock options,** which enable them to purchase shares of the corporation's stock at a set price. When the market price rises above that level, the officers can sell their shares for a profit. Because a stock's market price generally increases as the corporation prospers, the options give the officers a financial stake in the corporation's well-being and supposedly encourage them to work hard for the benefit of the shareholders.

Options have turned out to be an imperfect device for providing effective governance, however. Executives in some companies have been tempted to "cook" the company's books in order to keep share prices higher so that they could sell their stock for a profit. Executives in other corporations have experienced no losses when share prices dropped because their options were "repriced" so that they did not suffer from the share price decline. Thus, although stock options theoretically can motivate officers to protect shareholder interests, stock option plans have sometimes become a way for officers to take advantage of shareholders.

Stock options are valuable when the market price of a company's share rises greatly. Why?

(Richard Drew, File/AP Images)

With stock options generally failing to work as planned, there has been an outcry for more "outside" directors (those with no formal employment affiliation with the company). The theory is that independent directors will more closely monitor the actions of corporate officers. Hence, today we see more boards with outside directors. Note, though, that outside directors may not be truly independent of corporate officers. They may be friends or business associates of the leading officers.

The Goal Is to Promote Accountability

Effective corporate governance standards are designed to address problems (such as those just briefly discussed) and to motivate officers to make decisions that promote the financial interests of the company's shareholders. Generally, corporate governance entails corporate decision-making structures that monitor employees (particularly officers) to ensure that they are acting for the benefit of the shareholders. Thus, corporate governance involves, at a minimum:

1. The audited reporting of financial progress at the corporation, so managers can be evaluated.
2. Legal protections for shareholders, so that violators of the law, who attempt to take advantage of shareholders, can be punished for misbehavior and victims may recover damages for any associated losses.

The Company Benefits   Effective corporate governance may have considerable practical significance. Firms that are more accountable to shareholders typically report higher profits, higher sales growth, higher firm value, and other economic advantages. Thus, a corporation that provides better corporate governance in the form of greater accountability to investors may also have a higher valuation than a corporation that is less concerned about governance.

"Honesty is the single most important factor having a direct bearing on the final success of an individual, corporation, or product."

Ed McMahon, 1923–2009
(American entertainer)

Governance and Corporation Law   State corporation statutes set up the legal framework for corporate governance. Under the corporate law of Delaware, where most major companies incorporate, all corporations must have certain structures of corporate governance in place. The most important structure, of course, is the board of directors because the board makes the major decisions about the future of the corporation.

The Board of Directors   Under corporate law, a corporation must have a board of directors elected by the shareholders. Almost anyone can become a director, though some organizations, such as the New York Stock Exchange, require certain standards of service for directors of their listed corporations.

Directors are responsible for ensuring that the corporation's officers are operating wisely and in the exclusive interest of shareholders. The directors receive reports from the officers and give them managerial directions. In reality, though, corporate directors devote a relatively small amount of time to monitoring officers.

Ideally, shareholders would monitor the directors' supervision of the officers. In practice, however, it can be difficult for shareholders to monitor directors and hold them responsible for corporate failings. Although the directors can be sued for failing to do their jobs effectively, directors are rarely held personally liable.

The Audit Committee   A crucial committee of the board of directors is the *audit committee,* which oversees the corporation's accounting and financial reporting processes, including both internal and outside auditors. Unless the committee members have sufficient expertise and are willing to spend the time to carefully examine the corporation's bookkeeping methods, however, the audit committee may be ineffective.

The audit committee also oversees the corporation's "internal controls," which are the measures taken to ensure that reported results are accurate. As an example, these controls—carried out largely by the company's internal auditing staff—help to determine whether a corporation's debts are collectible. If the debts are not collectible, it is up to the audit committee to make sure that the corporation's financial officers do not simply pretend that payment will eventually be made.

The Compensation Committee   Another important committee of the board of directors is the *compensation committee.* This committee monitors and determines the compensation the company's officers are paid. As part of this process, it is responsible for assessing the officers' performance and for designing a compensation system that will better align the officers' interests with those of the shareholders.

The Sarbanes-Oxley Act

As discussed in Chapter 2, Congress passed the Sarbanes-Oxley Act in 2002. The act separately addresses certain issues relating to corporate governance. Generally, the act attempts to increase corporate accountability by imposing strict disclosure requirements and harsh penalties for violations of securities laws. Among other things, the act requires chief corporate executives to take responsibility for the accuracy of financial statements and reports that are filed with the SEC.

Additionally, the act requires that certain financial and stock-transaction reports be filed with the SEC earlier than was required under the previous rules. The act also created a new entity, called the Public Company Accounting Oversight Board, which regulates and oversees public accounting firms. Other provisions of the act established private civil actions and expanded the SEC's remedies in administrative and civil actions.

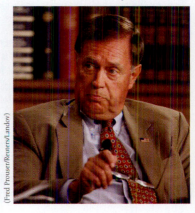

Michael Oxley is a former member of the U.S. House of Representatives and the cosponsor of the Sarbanes-Oxley Act.

(Fred Prouser/Reuters/Landov)

Because of the importance of this act for corporate leaders and for those dealing with securities transactions, we highlight some of its key provisions relating to corporate accountability in Exhibit 24–3 that follows.

More Internal Controls and Accountability

The Sarbanes-Oxley Act also introduced direct *federal* corporate governance requirements for public companies (companies whose shares are traded in the public securities markets). The law addressed many of the corporate governance procedures just discussed and created new requirements in an attempt to make the system work more effectively. The requirements deal with independent monitoring of company officers by both the board of directors and auditors.

Sections 302 and 404 of Sarbanes-Oxley require high-level managers (the most senior officers) to establish and maintain an effective system of internal controls, including "disclosure controls and procedures" to ensure that company financial reports are accurate and timely and to document financial results prior to reporting. Moreover, senior management must reassess the system's effectiveness annually. Some companies had to take expensive steps to bring their internal controls up to the new federal standard. After the act was passed, hundreds of companies reported that they had identified and corrected shortcomings in their internal control systems.

Exhibit 24–3 Some Key Provisions of the Sarbanes-Oxley Act Relating to Corporate Accountability

Certification Requirements—Under Section 906 of the Sarbanes-Oxley Act, the chief executive officers (CEOs) and chief financial officers (CFOs) of most major companies listed on public stock exchanges must certify financial statements that are filed with the SEC. CEOs and CFOs have to certify that filed financial reports "fully comply" with SEC requirements and that all of the information reported "fairly represents in all material respects, the financial conditions and results of operations of the issuer."

Under Section 302 of the act, CEOs and CFOs of reporting companies are required to certify that a signing officer reviewed each quarterly and annual filing with the SEC and that none contained untrue statements of material fact. Also, the signing officer or officers must certify that they have established an internal control system to identify all material information and that any deficiencies in the system were disclosed to the auditors.

Effectiveness of Internal Controls on Financial Reporting—Under Section 404(a), all public companies are required to assess the effectiveness of their internal control over financial reporting. Section 404(b) requires independent auditors to report on management's assessment of internal controls, but companies with a public float of less than $75 million are exempted from this requirement.

Loans to Directors and Officers—Section 402 prohibits any reporting company, as well as any private company that is filing an initial public offering, from making personal loans to directors and executive officers (with a few limited exceptions, such as for certain consumer and housing loans).

Protection for Whistleblowers—Section 806 protects "whistleblowers"—employees who report ("blow the whistle" on) securities violations by their employers—from being fired or in any way discriminated against by their employers.

Blackout Periods—Section 306 prohibits certain types of securities transactions during "blackout periods"—periods during which the issuer's ability to purchase, sell, or otherwise transfer funds in individual account plans (such as pension funds) is suspended.

Enhanced Penalties for—

- *Violations of Section 906 Certification Requirements*—A CEO or CFO who certifies a financial report or statement filed with the SEC knowing that the report or statement does not fulfill all of the requirements of Section 906 will be subject to criminal penalties of up to $1 million in fines, ten years in prison, or both. *Willful* violators of the certification requirements may be subject to $5 million in fines, twenty years in prison, or both.

- *Violations of the Securities Exchange Act*—Penalties for securities fraud under the 1934 act were also increased (as discussed earlier in this chapter). Individual violators may be fined up to $5 million, imprisoned for up to twenty years, or both. *Willful* violators may be imprisoned for up to twenty-five years in addition to being fined.

- *Destruction or Alteration of Documents*—Anyone who alters, destroys, or conceals documents or otherwise obstructs any official proceeding will be subject to fines, imprisonment for up to twenty years, or both.

- *Other Forms of White-Collar Crime*—The act stiffened the penalties for certain criminal violations, such as federal mail and wire fraud, and ordered the U.S. Sentencing Commission to revise the sentencing guidelines for white-collar crimes (see Chapter 6).

Statute of Limitations for Securities Fraud—Section 804 provides that a private right of action for securities fraud may be brought no later than two years after the discovery of the violation or five years after the violation, whichever is earlier.

Exemptions for Smaller Companies

The Sarbanes-Oxley Act initially required all public companies to have an independent auditor file a report with the SEC on management's assessment of internal controls. In 2010, however, Congress enacted an exemption for smaller companies in an effort to reduce compliance costs. Public companies with a market capitalization, or public float (price times total shares publicly owned), of less than $75 million no longer need to have an auditor report on management's assessment of internal controls.

Certification and Monitoring Requirements

Section 906 requires that chief executive officers (CEOs) and chief financial officers (CFOs) certify that the information in the corporate financial statements "fairly represents in all material respects, the financial conditions and results of operations of the issuer." This requirement makes officers directly accountable for the accuracy of their financial reporting and avoids any "ignorance defense" if shortcomings are later discovered.

Sarbanes-Oxley also includes requirements to improve directors' monitoring of officers' activities. All members of the corporate audit committee for public companies must be outside directors. The audit committee must have a written charter that sets out its duties and provides for performance appraisal.

Online Securities Fraud

A major problem facing the SEC today is how to enforce the antifraud provisions of the securities laws in the online environment. The SEC filed the first cases involving illegal online securities offerings back in 1999. Since then, the SEC has brought a variety of Internet-related fraud cases and regularly issues interpretive releases to explain how securities laws apply in the online environment.

Online Investment Scams and Newsletters

An ongoing problem is how to curb online investment scams. As discussed in Chapters 6 and 9, the Internet has created a new vehicle for criminals to use to commit fraud and has provided them with new ways of targeting innocent investors. The criminally inclined can use spam, online newsletters and bulletin boards, chat rooms, blogs, social media, and tweets to spread false information and perpetrate fraud. For a relatively small cost, criminals can even build sophisticated Web pages to facilitate their investment scams.

Hundreds of online investment newsletters provide free information on stocks. Legitimate online newsletters can help investors gather valuable information, but some of these newsletters are used for fraud. The law allows companies to pay people who write these newsletters to tout their securities, but the newsletters are required to disclose who paid for the advertising. Many fraudsters either fail to disclose or lie about who paid them. Thus, an investor reading an online newsletter may believe that the information is unbiased, when in fact the fraudsters will directly profit by convincing investors to buy or sell particular stocks.

Fraudulent E-Mails

There are countless variations of investment scams, most of which promise spectacular returns for small investments. A person might receive spam e-mail that falsely claims the earnings potential of a home business can "turn $5 into $60,000 in just three to six weeks." A few years ago, an investment scam claimed "your stimulus package has arrived" and promised recipients that they could make $100,000 a year using their home computers.

Learning Objective 5
What certification requirements does the Sarbanes-Oxley Act impose on corporate executives?

"Make money your God and it will plague you like the devil."

Henry Fielding, 1707–1754
(English author)

Although most people are dubious of the bogus claims made in spam messages, such offers can be more attractive during times of economic recession. Often, investment scams are simply the electronic version of pyramid schemes in which the participants attempt to profit solely by recruiting new participants.

Ponzi Schemes

Although securities fraud is increasingly occurring online, schemes conducted primarily offline have not disappeared. Recently, the SEC has filed an increasing number of enforcement actions against perpetrators of *Ponzi schemes*. Since 2010, the SEC has brought more than a hundred enforcement actions against nearly two hundred individuals and two hundred and fifty entities for carrying out Ponzi schemes. It has also barred more than sixty-five persons from working in the securities industry.

Ponzi schemes sometimes target U.S. residents and convince them to invest in offshore companies or banks.   **CASE EXAMPLE 24.11**   In 2012, Texas billionaire R. Allen Stanford, of the Stanford Financial Group, was convicted for orchestrating a $7 billion scheme to defraud more than five thousand investors. Stanford had advised clients to buy certificates of deposit with improbably high interest rates from his Antigua-based Stanford International Bank. Although some early investors were paid returns from the funds provided by later investors, Stanford used $1.6 billion of the funds for personal purchases. He also falsified financial statements that were filed with the SEC and reportedly paid more than $100,000 in bribes to an Antigua official to ensure that the bank would not be audited.[32] ●

---

32. *United States v. Stanford*, 2012 WL 1699459 (S.D. Tex. 2012).

Reviewing . . . Investor Protection and Corporate Governance

Dale Emerson served as the chief financial officer for Reliant Electric Company, a distributor of electricity serving portions of Montana and North Dakota. Reliant was in the final stages of planning a takeover of Dakota Gasworks, Inc., a natural gas distributor that operated solely within North Dakota. Emerson went on a weekend fishing trip with his uncle, Ernest Wallace. Emerson mentioned to Wallace that he had been putting in a lot of extra hours at the office planning a takeover of Dakota Gasworks. When he returned from the fishing trip, Wallace purchased $20,000 worth of Reliant stock. Three weeks later, Reliant made a tender offer to Dakota Gasworks stockholders and purchased 57 percent of Dakota Gasworks stock. Over the next two weeks, the price of Reliant stock rose 72 percent before leveling out. Wallace then sold his Reliant stock for a gross profit of $14,400. Using the information presented in the chapter, answer the following questions.

1. Would registration with the SEC be required for Dakota Gasworks securities? Why or why not?
2. Did Emerson violate Section 10(b) of the Securities Exchange Act of 1934 and SEC Rule 10b-5? Why or why not?
3. What theory or theories might a court use to hold Wallace liable for insider trading?
4. Under the Sarbanes-Oxley Act, who would be required to certify the accuracy of financial statements filed with the SEC?

Debate This Insider trading should be legalized.

Key Terms

accredited investor 649
corporate governance 661
free-writing prospectus 647
insider trading 652

investment company 649
investment contract 645
mutual fund 649

prospectus 646
SEC Rule 10b-5 652
security 643

short-swing profits 655
stock option 662
tippee 654

Chapter Summary: Investor Protection and Corporate Governance

Securities Act of 1933	Prohibits fraud and stabilizes the securities industry by requiring disclosure of all essential information relating to the issuance of securities to the investing public. 1. *Registration requirements*—Securities, unless exempt, must be registered with the SEC before being offered to the public. The *registration statement* must include detailed financial information about the issuing corporation; the intended use of the proceeds of the securities being issued; and certain disclosures, such as interests of directors or officers and pending lawsuits. 2. *Prospectus*—The issuer must provide investors with a *prospectus* that describes the security being sold, the issuing corporation, and the risk attaching to the security. 3. *Exemptions*—The SEC has exempted certain offerings from the requirements of the 1933 Securities Act. Exemptions may be determined on the basis of the size of the issue, whether the offering is private or public, and whether advertising is involved. Exemptions are summarized in Exhibit 24–1.

Securities Exchange Act of 1934	Provides for the regulation and registration of securities exchanges, brokers, dealers, and national securities associations (such as the NASD). Maintains a continuous disclosure system for all corporations with securities on the securities exchanges and for those companies that have assets in excess of $10 million and five hundred or more shareholders (Section 12 companies).
	 1. *SEC Rule 10b-5 [under Section 10(b) of the 1934 act]*—
	   a. Applies to almost all trading of securities—a firm's securities do not have to be registered under the 1933 act for the 1934 act to apply.
	   b. Applies to insider trading by corporate officers, directors, majority shareholders, and any persons receiving inside information (information not available to the public) who base their trading on this information.
	   c. Liability for insider trading may be based on the tipper/tippee or the misappropriation theory.
	   d. May be violated by failing to disclose "material facts" that must be disclosed under this rule.
	   e. Liability for violations can be civil or criminal.
	 2. *Insider trading [under Section 16(b) of the 1934 act]*—To prevent corporate insiders from taking advantage of inside information, the 1934 act requires officers, directors, and shareholders owning 10 percent or more of the issued stock of a corporation to turn over to the corporation all short-term profits (called *short-swing profits*) realized from the purchase and sale or sale and purchase of corporate stock within any six-month period.
	 3. *Regulation of proxies*—The SEC regulates the content of proxy statements sent to shareholders of Section 12 companies. Section 14(a) is essentially a disclosure law, with provisions similar to the antifraud provisions of SEC Rule 10b-5.

State Securities Laws	All states have corporate securities laws (*blue sky laws*) that regulate the offer and sale of securities within state borders. These laws are designed to prevent "speculative schemes which have no more basis than so many feet of 'blue sky.'" States regulate securities concurrently with the federal government. The Uniform Securities Act, which has been adopted by seventeen states and is being considered by several others, is designed to promote coordination and reduce duplication between state and federal securities regulation.
Corporate Governance	1. *Definition*—Corporate governance involves a set of policies specifying the rights and responsibilities of the various participants in a corporation and spelling out the rules and procedures for making decisions on corporate affairs. 2. *The need for corporate governance*—Corporate governance is necessary in large corporations because corporate ownership (by the shareholders) is separated from corporate control (by officers and managers). This separation of corporate ownership and control can often result in conflicting interests. Corporate governance standards address such issues. 3. *Sarbanes-Oxley Act*—This act attempts to increase corporate accountability by imposing strict disclosure requirements and harsh penalties for violations of securities laws.
Online Securities Fraud	The SEC today faces how to enforce the antifraud provisions of the securities laws in the online environment. Internet-related forms of securities fraud include numerous types of investment scams, fraudulent e-mails, and Ponzi schemes.

Issue Spotters

1. When a corporation wishes to issue certain securities, it must provide sufficient information for an unsophisticated investor to evaluate the financial risk involved. Specifically, the law imposes liability for making a false statement or omission that is "material." What sort of information would an investor consider material? (See *Securities Exchange Act of 1934.*)
2. Lee is an officer of Magma Oil, Inc. Lee knows that a Magma geologist has just discovered a new deposit of oil. Can Lee take advantage of this information to buy and sell Magma stock? Why or why not? (See *Securities Exchange Act of 1934.*)

—**Check your answers to the Issue Spotters against the answers provided in Appendix D at the end of this text.**

For Review

1. What is meant by the term *securities*?
2. What are the two major statutes regulating the securities industry?
3. What is insider trading? Why is it prohibited?
4. What are some of the features of state securities laws?
5. What certification requirements does the Sarbanes-Oxley Act impose on corporate executives?

Business Scenarios and Case Problems

24–1. Registration Requirements. Langley Brothers, Inc., a corporation incorporated and doing business in Kansas, decides to sell common stock worth $1 million to the public. The stock will be sold only within the state of Kansas. Joseph Langley, the chair of the board, says the offering need not be registered with the Securities and Exchange Commission. His brother, Harry, disagrees. Who is right? Explain. (See *Securities Act of 1933.*)

24–2. Registration. Huron Corp. has 300,000 common shares outstanding. The owners of these outstanding shares live in several different states. Huron has decided to split the 300,000 shares two for one. Will Huron Corp. have to file a registration statement and prospectus on the 300,000 new shares to be issued as a result of the split? Explain. (See *Securities Act of 1933.*)

24–3. Violations of the 1934 Act. To comply with accounting principles, a company that engages in software development must either "expense" the cost (record it immediately on the company's financial statement) or "capitalize" it (record it as a cost incurred in increments over time). If the project is in the pre- or post-development stage, the cost must be expensed. Otherwise it may be capitalized. Capitalizing a cost makes a company look more profitable in the short term. Digimarc Corp. announced that it had improperly capitalized software development costs over at least the previous eighteen months. The errors resulted in $2.7 million in overstated earnings, requiring a restatement of prior financial statements. Zucco Partners, LLC, which had bought Digimarc stock within the relevant period, filed a suit in a federal district court against the firm. Zucco claimed that it could show that there had been disagreements within Digimarc over its accounting. Is this sufficient to establish a violation of SEC Rule 10b-5? Why or why not? [*Zucco Partners, LLC v. Digimarc Corp.*, 552 F.3d 981 (9th Cir. 2009)] (See *Securities Exchange Act of 1934.*)

24–4. Insider Trading. Jabil Circuit, Inc., is a publicly traded electronics and technology company. A group of shareholders who owned Jabil stock from 2001 to 2007 sued the company and its auditors, directors, and officers for insider trading. Stock options were a part of Jabil's compensation for executives. Sometimes, stock options were backdated to a point in time when the stock price was lower, so the options would be worth more to certain company executives. Backdating is not illegal so long as it is reported, but Jabil did not report the fact that backdating had occurred. Thus, expenses were underreported, and net income was overstated by millions of dollars. The shareholders claimed that by rigging the stock price through backdating, the executives had engaged in insider trading and could pick favorable purchase prices and that there was a general practice of selling stock before unfavorable news about the company was reported to the public. The shareholders, however, had no specific information about these stock trades or when (or even if) a particular executive was aware of any accounting errors during the time of any backdating purchases. Were the shareholders' allegations sufficient to assert that insider trading had occurred under Rule 10b-5? Why or why not? [*Edward J. Goodman Life Income Trust v. Jabil Circuit, Inc.*, 594 F.3d 783 (11th Cir. 2010)] (See *Securities Exchange Act of 1934.*)

24–5. ⚖ **Business Case Problem with Sample Answer—Violations of the 1934 Act.** Matrixx Initiatives, Inc., makes and sells over-the-counter pharmaceutical products. Its core brand is Zicam, which accounts for 70 percent of its sales. Matrixx received reports that some consumers had lost their sense of smell (a condition called *anosmia*) after using Zicam Cold Remedy. Four product liability suits were filed against Matrixx, seeking damages for anosmia. In public statements relating to revenues and product safety, however, Matrixx did not reveal this information. James Siracusano and other Matrixx investors filed a suit in a federal district court against the company and its executives under Section 10(b) of the Securities Exchange Act of 1934 and SEC Rule 10b-5, claiming that the statements were misleading because they did not disclose the information about the product liability suits. Matrixx argued that to be material, information must consist of a statistically significant number of adverse events that require disclosure. Because Siracusano's claim did not allege that Matrixx knew of a statistically significant number of adverse events, the company contended that the claim should be dismissed. What is the standard for materiality in this context? Should Siracusano's claim be dismissed? Explain. [*Matrixx Initiatives, Inc. v. Siracusano,* __ U.S. __, 131 S.Ct. 1309, 179 L.Ed.2d 398 (2011)] (See *Securities Exchange Act of 1934.*)

—For a sample answer to Problem 24–5, go to Appendix E at the end of this text.

24–6. Disclosure under SEC Rule 10b-5. Dodona I, LLC, invested $4 million in two securities offerings from Goldman, Sachs & Co. The investments were in collateralized debt obligations (CDOs). Their value depended on residential mortgage-backed securities (RMBS), whose value in turn depended on the performance of subprime residential mortgages. Before marketing the CDOs, Goldman had noticed several "red flags" relating to investments in the subprime market, in which it had invested heavily. To limit its risk, Goldman began betting against subprime mortgages, RMBS, and CDOs, including the CDOs it had sold to Dodona. In an internal e-mail, one Goldman official commented that the company had managed to "make some lemonade from some big old lemons." Nevertheless, Goldman's marketing materials provided only boilerplate statements about the risks of investing in the securities. The CDOs were later downgraded to junk status, and Dodona suffered a major loss while Goldman profited. Assuming that Goldman did not affirmatively misrepresent any facts about the CDOs, can Dodona still recover under SEC Rule 10b-5? If so, how? [*Dodona I, LLC v. Goldman, Sachs & Co.,* 847 F.Supp.2d 624 (S.D.N.Y. 2012)] (See *Securities Exchange Act of 1934.*)

24–7. Violations of the 1933 Act. Three shareholders of iStorage sought to sell their stock through World Trade Financial Corp. The shares were restricted securities—securities acquired in an unregistered, private sale. Restricted securities typically bear a "restrictive" legend clearly stating that they cannot be resold in the public marketplace. This legend had been wrongly removed from the iStorage shares, however. Information about the company that was publicly available included the fact that, despite a ten-year life, it had no operating history or earnings. In addition, it had net losses of about $200,000, and its stock was thinly traded. Without investigating the company or the status of its stock, World Trade sold more than 2.3 million shares to the public on behalf of the three customers. Did World Trade violate the Securities Act of 1933? Discuss. [*World Trade Financial Corp. v. Securities and Exchange Commission,* 739 F.3d 1243 (9th Cir. 2014)] (See *Securities Act of 1933.*)

24–8. ⬌ A Question of Ethics—Violations of the 1934 Act. Melvin Lyttle told John Montana and Paul Knight about a "Trading Program" that purportedly would buy and sell securities in deals that were fully insured, as well as monitored and controlled by the Federal Reserve Board. Without checking the details or even verifying whether the program existed, Montana and Knight, with Lyttle's help, began to sell interests in the program to investors. For a minimum investment of $1 million, the investors were promised extraordinary rates of return—from 10 percent to as much as 100 percent per week—without risk. They were also told that the program would "utilize banks that can ensure full bank integrity of The Transaction whose undertaking[s] are in complete harmony with international banking rules and protocol and who [sic] guarantee maximum security of a Funder's Capital Placement Amount." Nothing was required but the investors' funds and their silence—the program was to be kept secret. Over a four-month period, Montana raised nearly $23 million from twenty-two investors. The promised gains did not accrue, however. Instead, Montana, Lyttle, and Knight depleted the investors' funds in high-risk trades or spent the funds on themselves. [*SEC v. Montana,* 464 F.Supp.2d 772 (S.D.Ind. 2006)] (See *Securities Exchange Act of 1934.*)

1. The Securities and Exchange Commission (SEC) filed a suit against Montana alleging violations of Section 10(b) and SEC Rule 10b-5. What is required to establish a violation of these laws? Explain how and why the facts in this case meet, or fail to meet, these requirements.

2. Ultimately, about half of the investors recouped the amount they had invested. Should the others be considered at least partly responsible for their own losses? Discuss.

UNIT 4 Cumulative Business Hypothetical

Falwell Motors, Inc., is a large corporation that manufactures automobile batteries.

1. The Federal Trade Commission (FTC) learns that one of the retail stores that sells Falwell's batteries engages in deceptive advertising practices. What actions can the FTC take against the retailer?

2. For years, Falwell has shipped the toxic waste created by its manufacturing process to a waste-disposal site in the next county. The waste site has become contaminated by leakage from toxic waste containers delivered to the site by other manufacturers. Can Falwell be held liable for clean-up costs, even though its containers were not the ones that leaked? If so, what is the extent of its liability?

3. Falwell faces stiff competition from Alchem, Inc., another battery manufacturer. To acquire control over Alchem, Falwell makes a tender offer to Alchem's shareholders. If Falwell succeeds in its attempt and Alchem is merged into Falwell, will the merger violate any antitrust laws? Suppose that the merger falls through. The vice president of Falwell's battery division and the president of Alchem agree to divide up the market between them, so they will not have to compete for customers. Is this agreement legal? Explain.

4. One of Falwell's employees learns that Falwell is contemplating a takeover of a rival. The employee tells her husband about the possibility. The husband calls their broker, who purchases shares in the target corporation for the employee and her husband, as well as for himself. Has the employee violated any securities law? Has her husband? Has the broker? Explain.

Legal Reasoning Group Activity

Violations of Securities Laws. Karel Svoboda, a credit officer for Rogue Bank, evaluated and approved his employer's extensions of credit to clients. These responsibilities gave Svoboda access to nonpublic information about the clients' earnings, performance, acquisitions, and business plans from confidential memos, e-mail, and other sources. Svoboda devised a scheme with Alena Robles, an independent accountant, to use this information to trade securities. Pursuant to their scheme, Robles traded in the securities of more than twenty different companies and profited by more than $2 million. Svoboda also executed trades for his own profit of more than $800,000, despite their agreement that Robles would do all of the trading. Aware that their scheme violated Rogue Bank's policy, they attempted to conduct their trades to avoid suspicion. When the bank questioned Svoboda about his actions, he lied, refused to cooperate, and was fired.

1. The first group will determine whether Svoboda or Robles committed any crimes.

2. The second group will decide whether Svoboda or Robles are subject to civil liability. If so, who could file a suit and on what ground? What are the possible sanctions?

3. A third group will identify any defenses that Svoboda or Robles could raise, and determine their likelihood of success.

How to Brief Cases and Analyze Case Problems

How to Brief Cases

To fully understand the law with respect to business, you need to be able to read and understand court decisions. To make this task easier, you can use a method of case analysis that is called *briefing*. There is a fairly standard procedure that you can follow when you "brief" any court case. You must first read the case opinion carefully. When you feel you understand the case, you can prepare a brief of it.

Although the format of the brief may vary, typically it will present the essentials of the case under headings such as those listed below.

1. **Citation.** Give the full citation for the case, including the name of the case, the date it was decided, and the court that decided it.
2. **Facts.** Briefly indicate (a) the reasons for the lawsuit; (b) the identity and arguments of the plaintiff(s) and defendant(s), respectively; and (c) the lower court's decision—if appropriate.
3. **Issue.** Concisely phrase, in the form of a question, the essential issue before the court. (If more than one issue is involved, you may have two—or even more—questions here.)
4. **Decision.** Indicate here—with a "yes" or "no," if possible—the court's answer to the question (or questions) in the *Issue* section above.
5. **Reason.** Summarize as briefly as possible the reasons given by the court for its decision (or decisions) and the case or statutory law relied on by the court in arriving at its decision.

An Example of a Briefed Sample Court Case

As an example of the format used in briefing cases, we present here a briefed version of the sample court case that was presented in the appendix to Chapter 1 as Exhibit 1A–3.

EXPERIENCE HENDRIX L.L.C.
v. HENDRIXLICENSING.COM LTD.
United States Court of Appeals, Ninth Circuit, 742 F.3d 377 (2014).

FACTS Experience Hendrix, LLC, a company formed by the sole heir of Jimi Hendrix, owns trademarks—including "Hendrix"—that it uses to market and license Hendrix-related merchandise online and in brick-and-mortar stores throughout the United States. Andrew Pitsicalis owns, or has licenses to use, photos and other art depicting Hendrix. Pitsicalis does business in brick-and-mortar stores and online through his Web sites, hendrixlicensing.com and

hendrixartwork.com. Alleging trademark infringement, Experience Hendrix filed a suit in a federal district court against Pitsicalis. The court issued a summary judgment in Experience Hendrix's favor and enjoined Pitsicalis's infringing activity. The court also awarded damages of $60,000, which were reduced from the jury's award of $366,650. Both parties appealed to the U.S. Court of Appeals for the Ninth Circuit. Pitsicalis argued that he had not infringed Experience Hendrix's trademark, and Experience Hendrix sought to reinstate the jury's award.

ISSUE Did Pitsicalis's domain names, hendrixlicensing.com and hendrixartwork.com, infringe Experience Hendrix's trademark "Hendrix?" If so, was there sufficient evidence to support the jury's award?

DECISION Yes, to both questions. The U.S. Court of Appeals for the Ninth Circuit affirmed the lower court's decision that Pitsicalis's domain names infringed the "Hendrix" mark. But the appellate court reversed the lower court's decision to reduce the amount of the award and remanded the case for a new trial on the issue of damages.

REASON Pitsicalis defended his use of the trademark "Hendrix" in his domain names as nominative fair use. This defense applies when the defendant uses the plaintiff's mark to describe the plaintiff's product. The lower court rejected this defense, concluding that Pitsicalis used "Hendrix" in his domain names to refer, not to Experience Hendrix's products, but to Pitsicalis's own products and services (licensing and marketing Hendrix-related goods). This use of another's trademark is not protected under the nominative fair use defense. As for the amount of damages, the evidence that supported the jury's award included a "significant" decline in Experience Hendrix's licensing revenue during the period in which Pitsicalis was earning revenue from similar, infringing merchandise. The jury had before it financial documents that showed the decline.

Review of Sample Court Case

Next, we provide a review of the briefed version to indicate the kind of information included in each section.

CITATION The name of the case is *Experience Hendrix L.L.C. v. Hendrixlicensing.com Ltd.* Experience Hendrix is the plaintiff. Hendrixlicensing.com is the defendant. The U.S. Court of Appeals for the Ninth Circuit decided this case in 2014. The citation states that this case can be found in volume 742 of the *Federal Reporter, Third Series,* on page 377.

FACTS The *Facts* section identifies the plaintiff and the defendant, and describes the events leading up to the suit and the allegations made by the plaintiff. Because this case was decided by a U.S. courts of appeals, the lower court's ruling, the party appealing, and the appellant's contention on appeal are included as well.

ISSUE The *Issue* section presents the central issue (or issues) decided by the court. In this case, the court considers whether the domain names hendrixlicensing.com and hendrixartwork.com infringed Experience Hendrix's trademark "Hendrix," and if so, whether there was sufficient evidence to support the jury's award.

DECISION The *Decision* section includes the court's decision on the issues before it. The decision reflects the opinion of the judge or justice hearing the case. Here, the court determined that Pitsicalis's domain names infringed the "Hendrix" mark and that there was sufficient evidence to support the jury's award. Decisions by appellate courts are frequently phrased in reference to the lower court's decision. That is, the appellate court may "affirm" the lower court's ruling or "reverse" it. In addition, a case may be remanded, or sent back to the lower court, for further proceedings.

REASON The *Reason* section identifies the laws and legal principles that the court applied in coming to its conclusion in the case. The relevant law here included the defendant's assertion of the nominative fair use defense. This section also explains the court's application of the law to the facts of the case.

Analyzing Case Problems

In addition to learning how to brief cases, students of business law and the legal environment also find it helpful to know how to analyze case problems. Part of the study of business law and the legal environment usually involves analyzing case problems, such as those included in this text at the end of each chapter.

For each case problem in this book, we provide the relevant background and facts of the lawsuit and the issue before the court. When you are assigned one of these problems, your job will be to determine how the court should decide the issue, and why. In other words, you will need to engage in legal analysis and reasoning. Here, we offer some suggestions on how to make this task less daunting. We begin by presenting a sample problem:

> While Janet Lawson, a famous pianist, was shopping in Quality Market, she slipped and fell on a wet floor in one of the aisles. The floor had recently been mopped by one of the store's employees, but there were no signs warning customers that the floor in that area was wet. As a result of the fall, Lawson injured her right arm and was unable to perform piano concerts for the next six months. Had she been able to perform the scheduled concerts, she would have

earned approximately $60,000 over that period of time. Lawson sued Quality Market for this amount, plus another $10,000 in medical expenses. She claimed that the store's failure to warn customers of the wet floor constituted negligence and therefore the market was liable for her injuries. Will the court agree with Lawson? Discuss.

Understand the Facts

This may sound obvious, but before you can analyze or apply the relevant law to a specific set of facts, you must clearly understand those facts. In other words, you should read through the case problem carefully—more than once, if necessary—to make sure you understand the identity of the plaintiff(s) and defendant(s) in the case and the progression of events that led to the lawsuit.

In the sample case problem just given, the identity of the parties is fairly obvious. Janet Lawson is the one bringing the suit—therefore, she is the plaintiff. Quality Market, against whom she is bringing the suit, is the defendant. Some of the case problems you may work on have multiple plaintiffs or defendants. Often, it is helpful to use abbreviations for the parties. To indicate a reference to a plaintiff, for example, the *pi* symbol—π—is often used, and a defendant is denoted by a *delta*—Δ—a triangle.

The events leading to the lawsuit are also fairly straightforward. Lawson slipped and fell on a wet floor, and she contends that Quality Market should be liable for her injuries because it was negligent in not posting a sign warning customers of the wet floor.

When you are working on case problems, realize that the facts should be accepted as they are given. For example, in our sample problem, it should be accepted that the floor was wet and that there was no sign. In other words, avoid making conjectures, such as "Maybe the floor wasn't too wet," or "Maybe an employee was getting a sign to put up," or "Maybe someone stole the sign." Questioning the facts as they are presented only adds confusion to your analysis.

Legal Analysis and Reasoning

Once you understand the facts given in the case problem, you can begin to analyze the case. Recall from Chapter 1 that the IRAC method is a helpful tool to use in the legal analysis and reasoning process. IRAC is an acronym for Issue, Rule, Application, Conclusion. Applying this method to our sample problem would involve the following steps:

1. First, you need to decide what legal **issue** is involved in the case. In our sample case, the basic issue is whether Quality Market's failure to warn customers of the wet floor constituted negligence. As discussed in Chapter 5, negligence is a *tort*—a civil wrong. In a tort lawsuit, the plaintiff seeks to be compensated for another's wrongful act. A defendant will be deemed negligent if he or she breached a duty of care owed to the plaintiff and the breach of that duty caused the plaintiff to suffer harm.

2. Once you have identified the issue, the next step is to determine what **rule of law** applies to the issue. To make this determination, you will want to review carefully the text of the chapter in which the relevant rule of law for the problem appears. Our sample case problem involves the tort of negligence, which is covered in Chapter 5. The applicable rule of law is the tort law principle that business owners owe a duty to exercise reasonable care to protect their customers ("business invitees"). Reasonable care, in this context, includes either removing—or warning customers of—*foreseeable* risks about which the owner *knew* or *should have known.* Business owners need not warn customers of "open and obvious" risks, however. If a business owner breaches this duty of care (fails to exercise the appropriate degree of care toward customers), and the breach of duty causes a customer to be injured, the business owner will be liable to the customer for the customer's injuries.

3. The next—and usually the most difficult—step in analyzing case problems is the **application** of the relevant rule of law to the specific facts of the case you are studying. In our sample problem, applying the tort law principle just discussed presents few difficulties. An employee of the store had mopped the floor in the aisle where Lawson slipped and fell, but no sign was present indicating that the floor was wet. That a customer might fall on a wet floor is clearly a foreseeable risk. Therefore, the failure to warn customers about the wet floor was a breach of the duty of care owed by the business owner to the store's customers.

4. Once you have completed Step 3 in the IRAC method, you should be ready to draw your **conclusion.** In our sample problem, Quality Market is liable to Lawson for her injuries, because the market's breach of its duty of care caused Lawson's injuries.

The fact patterns in the case problems presented in this text are not always as simple as those presented in our sample problem. Often, for example, a case has more than one plaintiff or defendant. A case may also involve more than one issue and have more than one applicable rule of law. Furthermore, in some case problems the facts may indicate that the general rule of law should not apply. For example, suppose that a store employee advised Lawson not to walk on the floor in the aisle because it was wet, but Lawson decided to walk on it anyway. This fact could alter the outcome of the case because the store could then raise the defense of assumption of risk (see Chapter 12). Nonetheless, a careful review of the chapter should always provide you with the knowledge you need to analyze the problem thoroughly and arrive at accurate conclusions.

The Constitution of the United States

Preamble

We the People of the United States, in Order to form a more perfect Union, establish Justice, insure domestic Tranquility, provide for the common defence, promote the general Welfare, and secure the Blessings of Liberty to ourselves and our Posterity, do ordain and establish this Constitution for the United States of America.

Article I

Section 1. All legislative Powers herein granted shall be vested in a Congress of the United States, which shall consist of a Senate and House of Representatives.

Section 2. The House of Representatives shall be composed of Members chosen every second Year by the People of the several States, and the Electors in each State shall have the Qualifications requisite for Electors of the most numerous Branch of the State Legislature.

No Person shall be a Representative who shall not have attained to the Age of twenty five Years, and been seven Years a Citizen of the United States, and who shall not, when elected, be an Inhabitant of that State in which he shall be chosen.

Representatives and direct Taxes shall be apportioned among the several States which may be included within this Union, according to their respective Numbers, which shall be determined by adding to the whole Number of free Persons, including those bound to Service for a Term of Years, and excluding Indians not taxed, three fifths of all other Persons. The actual Enumeration shall be made within three Years after the first Meeting of the Congress of the United States, and within every subsequent Term of ten Years, in such Manner as they shall by Law direct. The Number of Representatives shall not exceed one for every thirty Thousand, but each State shall have at Least one Representative; and until such enumeration shall be made, the State of New Hampshire shall be entitled to chuse three, Massachusetts eight, Rhode Island and Providence Plantations one, Connecticut five, New York six, New Jersey four, Pennsylvania eight, Delaware one, Maryland six, Virginia ten, North Carolina five, South Carolina five, and Georgia three.

When vacancies happen in the Representation from any State, the Executive Authority thereof shall issue Writs of Election to fill such Vacancies.

The House of Representatives shall chuse their Speaker and other Officers; and shall have the sole Power of Impeachment.

Section 3. The Senate of the United States shall be composed of two Senators from each State, chosen by the Legislature thereof, for six Years; and each Senator shall have one Vote.

Immediately after they shall be assembled in Consequence of the first Election, they shall be divided as equally as may be into three Classes. The Seats of the Senators of the first Class shall be vacated at the Expiration of the second Year, of the second Class at the Expiration of the fourth Year, and of the third Class at the Expiration of the sixth Year, so that one third may be chosen every second Year; and if Vacancies happen by Resignation, or otherwise, during the Recess of the Legislature of any State, the Executive thereof may make temporary Appointments until the next Meeting of the Legislature, which shall then fill such Vacancies.

No Person shall be a Senator who shall not have attained to the Age of thirty Years, and been nine Years a Citizen of the United States, and who shall not, when elected, be an Inhabitant of that State for which he shall be chosen.

The Vice President of the United States shall be President of the Senate, but shall have no Vote, unless they be equally divided.

The Senate shall chuse their other Officers, and also a President pro tempore, in the Absence of the Vice President, or when he shall exercise the Office of President of the United States.

The Senate shall have the sole Power to try all Impeachments. When sitting for that Purpose, they shall be on Oath or Affirmation. When the President of the United States is tried, the Chief Justice shall preside: And no Person shall be convicted without the Concurrence of two thirds of the Members present.

Judgment in Cases of Impeachment shall not extend further than to removal from Office, and disqualification to hold and enjoy any Office of honor, Trust, or Profit under the United States: but the Party convicted shall nevertheless be liable and subject to Indictment, Trial, Judgment, and Punishment, according to Law.

Section 4. The Times, Places and Manner of holding Elections for Senators and Representatives, shall be prescribed in each State by the Legislature thereof; but the Congress may at any time by Law make or alter such Regulations, except as to the Places of chusing Senators.

The Congress shall assemble at least once in every Year, and such Meeting shall be on the first Monday in December, unless they shall by Law appoint a different Day.

Section 5. Each House shall be the Judge of the Elections, Returns, and Qualifications of its own Members, and a Majority of each shall constitute a Quorum to do Business; but a smaller Number may adjourn from day to day, and may be authorized to compel the Attendance of absent Members, in such Manner, and under such Penalties as each House may provide.

Each House may determine the Rules of its Proceedings, punish its Members for disorderly Behavior, and, with the Concurrence of two thirds, expel a Member.

Each House shall keep a Journal of its Proceedings, and from time to time publish the same, excepting such Parts as may in their Judgment require Secrecy; and the Yeas and Nays of the Members of either House on any question shall, at the Desire of one fifth of those Present, be entered on the Journal.

Neither House, during the Session of Congress, shall, without the Consent of the other, adjourn for more than three days, nor to any other Place than that in which the two Houses shall be sitting.

Section 6. The Senators and Representatives shall receive a Compensation for their Services, to be ascertained by Law, and paid out of the Treasury of the United States. They shall in all Cases, except Treason, Felony and Breach of the Peace, be privileged from Arrest during their Attendance at the Session of their respective Houses, and in going to and returning from the same; and for any Speech or Debate in either House, they shall not be questioned in any other Place.

No Senator or Representative shall, during the Time for which he was elected, be appointed to any civil Office under the Authority of the United States, which shall have been created, or the Emoluments whereof shall have been increased during such time; and no Person holding any Office under the United States, shall be a Member of either House during his Continuance in Office.

Section 7. All Bills for raising Revenue shall originate in the House of Representatives; but the Senate may propose or concur with Amendments as on other Bills.

Every Bill which shall have passed the House of Representatives and the Senate, shall, before it become a Law, be presented to the President of the United States; If he approve he shall sign it, but if not he shall return it, with his Objections to the House in which it shall have originated, who shall enter the Objections at large on their Journal, and proceed to reconsider it. If after such Reconsideration two thirds of that House shall agree to pass the Bill, it shall be sent together with the Objections, to the other House, by which it shall likewise be reconsidered, and if approved by two thirds of that House, it shall become a Law. But in all such Cases the Votes of both Houses shall be determined by Yeas and Nays, and the Names of the Persons voting for and against the Bill shall be entered on the Journal of each House respectively. If any Bill shall not be returned by the President within ten Days (Sundays excepted) after it shall have been presented to him, the Same shall be a Law, in like Manner as if he had signed it, unless the Congress by their Adjournment prevent its Return in which Case it shall not be a Law.

Every Order, Resolution, or Vote, to which the Concurrence of the Senate and House of Representatives may be necessary (except on a question of Adjournment) shall be presented to the President of the United States; and before the Same shall take Effect, shall be approved by him, or being disapproved by him, shall be repassed by two thirds of the Senate and House of Representatives, according to the Rules and Limitations prescribed in the Case of a Bill.

Section 8. The Congress shall have Power To lay and collect Taxes, Duties, Imposts and Excises, to pay the Debts and provide for the common Defence and general Welfare of the United States; but all Duties, Imposts and Excises shall be uniform throughout the United States;

To borrow Money on the credit of the United States;

To regulate Commerce with foreign Nations, and among the several States, and with the Indian Tribes;

To establish an uniform Rule of Naturalization, and uniform Laws on the subject of Bankruptcies throughout the United States;

To coin Money, regulate the Value thereof, and of foreign Coin, and fix the Standard of Weights and Measures;

To provide for the Punishment of counterfeiting the Securities and current Coin of the United States;

To establish Post Offices and post Roads;

To promote the Progress of Science and useful Arts, by securing for limited Times to Authors and Inventors the exclusive Right to their respective Writings and Discoveries;

To constitute Tribunals inferior to the supreme Court;

To define and punish Piracies and Felonies committed on the high Seas, and Offenses against the Law of Nations;

To declare War, grant Letters of Marque and Reprisal, and make Rules concerning Captures on Land and Water;

To raise and support Armies, but no Appropriation of Money to that Use shall be for a longer Term than two Years;

To provide and maintain a Navy;

To make Rules for the Government and Regulation of the land and naval Forces;

To provide for calling forth the Militia to execute the Laws of the Union, suppress Insurrections and repel Invasions;

To provide for organizing, arming, and disciplining, the Militia, and for governing such Part of them as may be employed in the Service of the United States, reserving to the States respectively, the Appointment of the Officers, and the Authority of training the Militia according to the discipline prescribed by Congress;

To exercise exclusive Legislation in all Cases whatsoever, over such District (not exceeding ten Miles square) as may, by Cession of particular States, and the Acceptance of Congress, become the Seat of the Government of the United States, and to exercise like Authority over all Places purchased by the Consent of the Legislature of the State in which the Same shall be, for the Erection of Forts, Magazines, Arsenals, dock-Yards, and other needful Buildings;—And

To make all Laws which shall be necessary and proper for carrying into Execution the foregoing Powers, and all other Powers vested by this Constitution in the Government of the United States, or in any Department or Officer thereof.

Section 9. The Migration or Importation of such Persons as any of the States now existing shall think proper to admit, shall not be prohibited by the Congress prior to the Year one thousand eight hundred and eight, but a Tax or duty may be imposed on such Importation, not exceeding ten dollars for each Person.

The privilege of the Writ of Habeas Corpus shall not be suspended, unless when in Cases of Rebellion or Invasion the public Safety may require it.

No Bill of Attainder or ex post facto Law shall be passed.

No Capitation, or other direct, Tax shall be laid, unless in Proportion to the Census or Enumeration herein before directed to be taken.

No Tax or Duty shall be laid on Articles exported from any State.

No Preference shall be given by any Regulation of Commerce or Revenue to the Ports of one State over those of another: nor shall Vessels bound to, or from, one State be obliged to enter, clear, or pay Duties in another.

No Money shall be drawn from the Treasury, but in Consequence of Appropriations made by Law; and a regular Statement and Account of the Receipts and Expenditures of all public Money shall be published from time to time.

No Title of Nobility shall be granted by the United States: And no Person holding any Office of Profit or Trust under them, shall, without the Consent of the Congress, accept of any present, Emolument, Office, or Title, of any kind whatever, from any King, Prince, or foreign State.

Section 10. No State shall enter into any Treaty, Alliance, or Confederation; grant Letters of Marque and Reprisal; coin Money; emit Bills of Credit; make any Thing but gold and silver Coin a Tender in Payment of Debts; pass any Bill of Attainder, ex post facto Law, or Law impairing the Obligation of Contracts, or grant any Title of Nobility.

No State shall, without the Consent of the Congress, lay any Imposts or Duties on Imports or Exports, except what may be absolutely necessary for executing its inspection Laws: and the net Produce of all Duties and Imposts, laid by any State on Imports or Exports, shall be for the Use of the Treasury of the United States; and all such Laws shall be subject to the Revision and Controul of the Congress.

No State shall, without the Consent of Congress, lay any Duty of Tonnage, keep Troops, or Ships of War in time of Peace, enter into any Agreement or Compact with another State, or with a foreign Power, or engage in War, unless actually invaded, or in such imminent Danger as will not admit of delay.

Article II

Section 1. The executive Power shall be vested in a President of the United States of America. He shall hold his Office during the Term of four Years, and, together with the Vice President, chosen for the same Term, be elected, as follows:

Each State shall appoint, in such Manner as the Legislature thereof may direct, a Number of Electors, equal to the whole Number of Senators and Representatives to which the State may be entitled in the Congress; but no Senator or Representative, or Person holding an Office of Trust or Profit under the United States, shall be appointed an Elector.

The Electors shall meet in their respective States, and vote by Ballot for two Persons, of whom one at least shall not be an Inhabitant of the same State with themselves. And they shall make a List of all the Persons voted for, and of the Number of Votes for each; which List they shall sign and certify, and transmit sealed to the Seat of the Government of the United States, directed to the President of the Senate. The President of the Senate shall, in the Presence of the Senate and House of Representatives, open all the Certificates, and the Votes shall then be counted. The Person having the greatest Number of Votes shall be the President, if such Number be a Majority of the whole Number of Electors appointed; and if there be more than one who have such Majority, and have an equal Number of Votes, then the House of Representatives shall immediately chuse by Ballot one of them for President; and if no Person have a Majority, then from the five highest on the List the said House shall in like Manner chuse the President. But in chusing the President, the Votes shall be taken by States, the Representation from each State having one Vote; A quorum for this Purpose shall consist of a Member or Members from two thirds of the States, and a Majority of all the States shall be necessary to a Choice. In every Case, after the Choice of the President, the Person having the greater Number of Votes of the Electors shall be the Vice President. But if there should remain two or more who have equal Votes, the Senate shall chuse from them by Ballot the Vice President.

The Congress may determine the Time of chusing the Electors, and the Day on which they shall give their Votes; which Day shall be the same throughout the United States.

No person except a natural born Citizen, or a Citizen of the United States, at the time of the Adoption of this Constitution, shall be eligible to the Office of President; neither shall any Person be eligible to that Office who shall not have attained to the Age of thirty five Years, and been fourteen Years a Resident within the United States.

In Case of the Removal of the President from Office, or of his Death, Resignation or Inability to discharge the Powers and Duties of the said Office, the same shall devolve on the Vice President, and the Congress may by Law provide for the Case of Removal, Death, Resignation or Inability, both of the President and Vice President, declaring what Officer shall then act as President, and such Officer shall act accordingly, until the Disability be removed, or a President shall be elected.

The President shall, at stated Times, receive for his Services, a Compensation, which shall neither be increased nor diminished during the Period for which he shall have been elected, and he shall not receive within that Period any other Emolument from the United States, or any of them.

Before he enter on the Execution of his Office, he shall take the following Oath or Affirmation: "I do solemnly swear (or affirm) that I will faithfully execute the Office of President of the United States, and will to the best of my Ability, preserve, protect and defend the Constitution of the United States."

Section 2. The President shall be Commander in Chief of the Army and Navy of the United States, and of the Militia of the several States, when called into the actual Service of the United States; he may require the Opinion, in writing, of the principal Officer in each of the executive Departments, upon any Subject relating to the Duties of their respective Offices, and he shall have Power to grant Reprieves and Pardons for Offenses against the United States, except in Cases of Impeachment.

He shall have Power, by and with the Advice and Consent of the Senate to make Treaties, provided two thirds of the Senators present concur; and he shall nominate, and by and with the Advice and Consent of the Senate, shall appoint Ambassadors, other public Ministers and Consuls, Judges of the supreme Court, and all other Officers of the United States, whose Appointments are not herein otherwise provided for, and which shall be established by Law; but the Congress may by Law vest the Appointment of such inferior Officers, as they think proper, in the President alone, in the Courts of Law, or in the Heads of Departments.

The President shall have Power to fill up all Vacancies that may happen during the Recess of the Senate, by granting Commissions which shall expire at the End of their next Session.

Section 3. He shall from time to time give to the Congress Information of the State of the Union, and recommend to their Consideration such Measures as he shall judge necessary and expedient; he may, on extraordinary Occasions, convene both Houses, or either of them, and in Case of Disagreement between them, with Respect to the Time of Adjournment, he may adjourn them to such Time as he shall think proper; he shall receive Ambassadors and other public Ministers; he shall take Care that the Laws be faithfully executed, and shall Commission all the Officers of the United States.

Section 4. The President, Vice President and all civil Officers of the United States, shall be removed from Office on Impeachment for, and Conviction of, Treason, Bribery, or other high Crimes and Misdemeanors.

Article III

Section 1. The judicial Power of the United States, shall be vested in one supreme Court, and in such inferior Courts as the Congress may from time to time ordain and establish. The Judges, both of the supreme and inferior Courts, shall hold their Offices during good Behaviour, and shall, at stated Times, receive for their Services a Compensation, which shall not be diminished during their Continuance in Office.

Section 2. The judicial Power shall extend to all Cases, in Law and Equity, arising under this Constitution, the Laws of the United States, and Treaties made, or which shall be made, under their Authority;—to all Cases affecting Ambassadors, other public Ministers and Consuls;—to all Cases of admiralty and maritime Jurisdiction;—to Controversies to which the United States shall be a Party;—to Controversies between two or more States;—between a State and Citizens of another State;—between Citizens of different States;—between Citizens of the same State claiming Lands under Grants of different States, and between a State, or the Citizens thereof, and foreign States, Citizens or Subjects.

In all Cases affecting Ambassadors, other public Ministers and Consuls, and those in which a State shall be a Party, the supreme Court shall have original Jurisdiction. In all the other Cases before mentioned, the supreme Court shall have appellate Jurisdiction, both as to Law and Fact, with such Exceptions, and under such Regulations as the Congress shall make.

The Trial of all Crimes, except in Cases of Impeachment, shall be by Jury; and such Trial shall be held in the State where the said Crimes shall have been committed; but when not committed within any State, the Trial shall be at such Place or Places as the Congress may by Law have directed.

Section 3. Treason against the United States, shall consist only in levying War against them, or, in adhering to their Enemies, giving them Aid and Comfort. No Person shall be convicted of Treason unless on the Testimony of two Witnesses to the same overt Act, or on Confession in open Court.

The Congress shall have Power to declare the Punishment of Treason, but no Attainder of Treason shall work Corruption of Blood, or Forfeiture except during the Life of the Person attainted.

Article IV

Section 1. Full Faith and Credit shall be given in each State to the public Acts, Records, and judicial Proceedings of every other State. And the Congress may by general Laws prescribe the Manner in which such Acts, Records and Proceedings shall be proved, and the Effect thereof.

Section 2. The Citizens of each State shall be entitled to all Privileges and Immunities of Citizens in the several States.

A Person charged in any State with Treason, Felony, or other Crime, who shall flee from Justice, and be found in another State, shall on Demand of the executive Authority of the State from which he fled, be delivered up, to be removed to the State having Jurisdiction of the Crime.

No Person held to Service or Labour in one State, under the Laws thereof, escaping into another, shall, in Consequence of any Law or Regulation therein, be discharged from such Service or Labour, but shall be delivered up on Claim of the Party to whom such Service or Labour may be due.

Section 3. New States may be admitted by the Congress into this Union; but no new State shall be formed or erected within the Jurisdiction of any other State; nor any State be formed by the Junction of two or more States, or Parts of States, without the

Consent of the Legislatures of the States concerned as well as of the Congress.

The Congress shall have Power to dispose of and make all needful Rules and Regulations respecting the Territory or other Property belonging to the United States; and nothing in this Constitution shall be so construed as to Prejudice any Claims of the United States, or of any particular State.

Section 4. The United States shall guarantee to every State in this Union a Republican Form of Government, and shall protect each of them against Invasion; and on Application of the Legislature, or of the Executive (when the Legislature cannot be convened) against domestic Violence.

Article V

The Congress, whenever two thirds of both Houses shall deem it necessary, shall propose Amendments to this Constitution, or, on the Application of the Legislatures of two thirds of the several States, shall call a Convention for proposing Amendments, which, in either Case, shall be valid to all Intents and Purposes, as part of this Constitution, when ratified by the Legislatures of three fourths of the several States, or by Conventions in three fourths thereof, as the one or the other Mode of Ratification may be proposed by the Congress; Provided that no Amendment which may be made prior to the Year One thousand eight hundred and eight shall in any Manner affect the first and fourth Clauses in the Ninth Section of the first Article; and that no State, without its Consent, shall be deprived of its equal Suffrage in the Senate.

Article VI

All Debts contracted and Engagements entered into, before the Adoption of this Constitution shall be as valid against the United States under this Constitution, as under the Confederation.

This Constitution, and the Laws of the United States which shall be made in Pursuance thereof; and all Treaties made, or which shall be made, under the Authority of the United States, shall be the supreme Law of the Land; and the Judges in every State shall be bound thereby, any Thing in the Constitution or Laws of any State to the Contrary notwithstanding.

The Senators and Representatives before mentioned, and the Members of the several State Legislatures, and all executive and judicial Officers, both of the United States and of the several States, shall be bound by Oath or Affirmation, to support this Constitution; but no religious Test shall ever be required as a Qualification to any Office or public Trust under the United States.

Article VII

The Ratification of the Conventions of nine States shall be sufficient for the Establishment of this Constitution between the States so ratifying the Same.

Amendment I [1791]

Congress shall make no law respecting an establishment of religion, or prohibiting the free exercise thereof; or abridging the freedom of speech, or of the press; or the right of the people peaceably to assembly, and to petition the Government for a redress of grievances.

Amendment II [1791]

A well regulated Militia, being necessary to the security of a free State, the right of the people to keep and bear Arms, shall not be infringed.

Amendment III [1791]

No Soldier shall, in time of peace be quartered in any house, without the consent of the Owner, nor in time of war, but in a manner to be prescribed by law.

Amendment IV [1791]

The right of the people to be secure in their persons, houses, papers, and effects, against unreasonable searches and seizures, shall not be violated, and no Warrants shall issue, but upon probable cause, supported by Oath or affirmation, and particularly describing the place to be searched, and the persons or things to be seized.

Amendment V [1791]

No person shall be held to answer for a capital, or otherwise infamous crime, unless on a presentment or indictment of a Grand Jury, except in cases arising in the land or naval forces, or in the Militia, when in actual service in time of War or public danger; nor shall any person be subject for the same offence to be twice put in jeopardy of life or limb; nor shall be compelled in any criminal case to be a witness against himself, nor be deprived of life, liberty, or property, without due process of law; nor shall private property be taken for public use, without just compensation.

Amendment VI [1791]

In all criminal prosecutions, the accused shall enjoy the right to a speedy and public trial, by an impartial jury of the State and district wherein the crime shall have been committed, which district shall have been previously ascertained by law, and to be informed of the nature and cause of the accusation; to be confronted with the witnesses against him; to have compulsory process for obtaining witnesses in his favor, and to have the Assistance of Counsel for his defence.

Amendment VII [1791]

In Suits at common law, where the value in controversy shall exceed twenty dollars, the right of trial by jury shall be preserved, and no fact tried by jury, shall be otherwise re-examined in any Court of the United States, than according to the rules of the common law.

Amendment VIII [1791]

Excessive bail shall not be required, nor excessive fines imposed, nor cruel and unusual punishments inflicted.

Amendment IX [1791]

The enumeration in the Constitution, of certain rights, shall not be construed to deny or disparage others retained by the people.

Amendment X [1791]

The powers not delegated to the United States by the Constitution, nor prohibited by it to the States, are reserved to the States respectively, or to the people.

Amendment XI [1798]

The Judicial power of the United States shall not be construed to extend to any suit in law or equity, commenced or prosecuted against one of the United States by Citizens of another State, or by Citizens or Subjects of any Foreign State.

Amendment XII [1804]

The Electors shall meet in their respective states, and vote by ballot for President and Vice-President, one of whom, at least, shall not be an inhabitant of the same state with themselves; they shall name in their ballots the person voted for as President, and in distinct ballots the person voted for as Vice-President, and they shall make distinct lists of all persons voted for as President, and of all persons voted for as Vice-President, and of the number of votes for each, which lists they shall sign and certify, and transmit sealed to the seat of the government of the United States, directed to the President of the Senate;—The President of the Senate shall, in the presence of the Senate and House of Representatives, open all the certificates and the votes shall then be counted;—The person having the greatest number of votes for President, shall be the President, if such number be a majority of the whole number of Electors appointed; and if no person have such majority, then from the persons having the highest numbers not exceeding three on the list of those voted for as President, the House of Representatives shall choose immediately, by ballot, the President. But in choosing the President, the votes shall be taken by states, the representation from each state having one vote; a quorum for this purpose shall consist of a member or members from two-thirds of the states, and a majority of all states shall be necessary to a choice. And if the House of Representatives shall not choose a President whenever the right of choice shall devolve upon them, before the fourth day of March next following, then the Vice-President shall act as President, as in the case of the death or other constitutional disability of the President.—The person having the greatest number of votes as Vice-President, shall be the Vice-President, if such number be a majority of the whole number of Electors appointed, and if no person have a majority, then from the two highest numbers on the list, the Senate shall choose the Vice-President; a quorum for the purpose shall consist of two-thirds of the whole number of Senators, and a majority of the whole number shall be necessary to a choice. But no person constitutionally ineligible to the office of President shall be eligible to that of Vice-President of the United States.

Amendment XIII [1865]

Section 1. Neither slavery nor involuntary servitude, except as a punishment for crime whereof the party shall have been duly convicted, shall exist within the United States, or any place subject to their jurisdiction.

Section 2. Congress shall have power to enforce this article by appropriate legislation.

Amendment XIV [1868]

Section 1. All persons born or naturalized in the United States, and subject to the jurisdiction thereof, are citizens of the United States and of the State wherein they reside. No State shall make or enforce any law which shall abridge the privileges or immunities of citizens of the United States; nor shall any State deprive any person of life, liberty, or property, without due process of law; nor deny to any person within its jurisdiction the equal protection of the laws.

Section 2. Representatives shall be apportioned among the several States according to their respective numbers, counting the whole number of persons in each State, excluding Indians not taxed. But when the right to vote at any election for the choice of electors for President and Vice President of the United States, Representatives in Congress, the Executive and Judicial officers of a State, or the members of the Legislature thereof, is denied to any of the male inhabitants of such State, being twenty-one years of age, and citizens of the United States, or in any way abridged, except for participation in rebellion, or other crime, the basis of representation therein shall be reduced in the proportion which the number of such male citizens shall bear to the whole number of male citizens twenty-one years of age in such State.

Section 3. No person shall be a Senator or Representative in Congress, or elector of President and Vice President, or hold any office, civil or military, under the United States, or under any State, who having previously taken an oath, as a member of Congress, or as an officer of the United States, or as a member of any State legislature, or as an executive or judicial officer of any State, to support the Constitution of the United States, shall have engaged in insurrection or rebellion against the same, or given aid or comfort to the enemies thereof. But Congress may by a vote of two-thirds of each House, remove such disability.

Section 4. The validity of the public debt of the United States, authorized by law, including debts incurred for payment of pensions and bounties for services in suppressing insurrection or rebellion, shall not be questioned. But neither the United States nor any State shall assume or pay any debt or obligation incurred in aid of insurrection or rebellion against the United States, or any claim for the loss or emancipation of any slave; but all such debts, obligations and claims shall be held illegal and void.

Section 5. The Congress shall have power to enforce, by appropriate legislation, the provisions of this article.

Amendment XV [1870]

Section 1. The right of citizens of the United States to vote shall not be denied or abridged by the United States or by any State on account of race, color, or previous condition of servitude.

Section 2. The Congress shall have power to enforce this article by appropriate legislation.

Amendment XVI [1913]

The Congress shall have power to lay and collect taxes on incomes, from whatever source derived, without apportionment among the several States, and without regard to any census or enumeration.

Amendment XVII [1913]

Section 1. The Senate of the United States shall be composed of two Senators from each State, elected by the people thereof, for six years; and each Senator shall have one vote. The electors in each State shall have the qualifications requisite for electors of the most numerous branch of the State legislatures.

Section 2. When vacancies happen in the representation of any State in the Senate, the executive authority of such State shall issue writs of election to fill such vacancies: *Provided*, That the legislature of any State may empower the executive thereof to make temporary appointments until the people fill the vacancies by election as the legislature may direct.

Section 3. This amendment shall not be so construed as to affect the election or term of any Senator chosen before it becomes valid as part of the Constitution.

Amendment XVIII [1919]

Section 1. After one year from the ratification of this article the manufacture, sale, or transportation of intoxicating liquors within, the importation thereof into, or the exportation thereof from the United States and all territory subject to the jurisdiction thereof for beverage purposes is hereby prohibited.

Section 2. The Congress and the several States shall have concurrent power to enforce this article by appropriate legislation.

Section 3. This article shall be inoperative unless it shall have been ratified as an amendment to the Constitution by the legislatures of the several States, as provided in the Constitution, within seven years from the date of the submission hereof to the States by the Congress.

Amendment XIX [1920]

Section 1. The right of citizens of the United States to vote shall not be denied or abridged by the United States or by any State on account of sex.

Section 2. Congress shall have power to enforce this article by appropriate legislation.

Amendment XX [1933]

Section 1. The terms of the President and Vice President shall end at noon on the 20th day of January, and the terms of Senators and Representatives at noon on the 3d day of January, of the years in which such terms would have ended if this article had not been ratified; and the terms of their successors shall then begin.

Section 2. The Congress shall assemble at least once in every year, and such meeting shall begin at noon on the 3d day of January, unless they shall by law appoint a different day.

Section 3. If, at the time fixed for the beginning of the term of the President, the President elect shall have died, the Vice President elect shall become President. If the President shall not have been chosen before the time fixed for the beginning of his term, or if the President elect shall have failed to qualify, then the Vice President elect shall act as President until a President shall have qualified; and the Congress may by law provide for the case wherein neither a President elect nor a Vice President elect shall have qualified, declaring who shall then act as President, or the manner in which one who is to act shall be selected, and such person shall act accordingly until a President or Vice President shall have qualified.

Section 4. The Congress may by law provide for the case of the death of any of the persons from whom the House of Representatives may choose a President whenever the right of choice shall have devolved upon them, and for the case of the death of any of the persons from whom the Senate may choose a Vice President whenever the right of choice shall have devolved upon them.

Section 5. Sections 1 and 2 shall take effect on the 15th day of October following the ratification of this article.

Section 6. This article shall be inoperative unless it shall have been ratified as an amendment to the Constitution by the legislatures of three-fourths of the several States within seven years from the date of its submission.

Amendment XXI [1933]

Section 1. The eighteenth article of amendment to the Constitution of the United States is hereby repealed.

Section 2. The transportation or importation into any State, Territory, or possession of the United States for delivery or use therein of intoxicating liquors, in violation of the laws thereof, is hereby prohibited.

Section 3. This article shall be inoperative unless it shall have been ratified as an amendment to the Constitution by conventions in the several States, as provided in the Constitution, within seven years from the date of the submission hereof to the States by the Congress.

Amendment XXII [1951]

Section 1. No person shall be elected to the office of the President more than twice, and no person who has held the office of President, or acted as President, for more than two years of a term to which some other person was elected President shall be elected to the office of President more than once. But this Article shall not apply to any person holding the office of President when this Article was proposed by the Congress, and shall not prevent any person who may be holding the office of President, or acting as President, during the term within which this Article becomes operative from holding the office of President or acting as President during the remainder of such term.

Section 2. This article shall be inoperative unless it shall have been ratified as an amendment to the Constitution by the legislatures of three-fourths of the several States within seven years from the date of its submission to the States by the Congress.

Amendment XXIII [1961]

Section 1. The District constituting the seat of Government of the United States shall appoint in such manner as the Congress may direct:

A number of electors of President and Vice President equal to the whole number of Senators and Representatives in Congress to which the District would be entitled if it were a State, but in no event more than the least populous state; they shall be in addition to those appointed by the states, but they shall be considered, for the purposes of the election of President and Vice President, to be electors appointed by a state; and they shall meet in the District and perform such duties as provided by the twelfth article of amendment.

Section 2. The Congress shall have power to enforce this article by appropriate legislation.

Amendment XXIV [1964]

Section 1. The right of citizens of the United States to vote in any primary or other election for President or Vice President, for electors for President or Vice President, or for Senator or Representative in Congress, shall not be denied or abridged by the United States, or any State by reason of failure to pay any poll tax or other tax.

Section 2. The Congress shall have power to enforce this article by appropriate legislation.

Amendment XXV [1967]

Section 1. In case of the removal of the President from office or of his death or resignation, the Vice President shall become President.

Section 2. Whenever there is a vacancy in the office of the Vice President, the President shall nominate a Vice President who shall take office upon confirmation by a majority vote of both Houses of Congress.

Section 3. Whenever the President transmits to the President pro tempore of the Senate and the Speaker of the House of Representatives his written declaration that he is unable to discharge the powers and duties of his office, and until he transmits to them a written declaration to the contrary, such powers and duties shall be discharged by the Vice President as Acting President.

Section 4. Whenever the Vice President and a majority of either the principal officers of the executive departments or of such other body as Congress may by law provide, transmit to the President pro tempore of the Senate and the Speaker of the House of Representatives their written declaration that the President is unable to discharge the powers and duties of his office, the Vice President shall immediately assume the powers and duties of the office as Acting President.

Thereafter, when the President transmits to the President pro tempore of the Senate and the Speaker of the House of Representatives his written declaration that no inability exists, he shall resume the powers and duties of his office unless the Vice President and a majority of either the principal officers of the executive department or of such other body as Congress may by law provide, transmit within four days to the President pro tempore of the Senate and the Speaker of the House of Representatives their written declaration that the President is unable to discharge the powers and duties of his office. Thereupon Congress shall decide the issue, assembling within forty-eight hours for that purpose if not in session. If the Congress, within twenty-one days after receipt of the latter written declaration, or, if Congress is not in session, within twenty-one days after Congress is required to assemble, determines by two-thirds vote of both Houses that the President is unable to discharge the powers and duties of his office, the Vice President shall continue to discharge the same as Acting President; otherwise, the President shall resume the powers and duties of his office.

Amendment XXVI [1971]

Section 1. The right of citizens of the United States, who are eighteen years of age or older, to vote shall not be denied or abridged by the United States or by any State on account of age.

Section 2. The Congress shall have power to enforce this article by appropriate legislation.

Amendment XXVII [1992]

No law, varying the compensation for the services of the Senators and Representatives, shall take effect, until an election of Representatives shall have intervened.

The Uniform Commercial Code (Articles 2 and 2A)

(Adopted in fifty-two jurisdictions; all fifty States, although Louisiana has adopted only Articles 1, 3, 4, 7, 8, and 9; the District of Columbia; and the Virgin Islands.)

The code consists of the following articles:

Article

1. General Provisions
2. Sales
2A. Leases
3. Negotiable Instruments
4. Bank Deposits and Collections
4A. Fund Transfers
5. Letters of Credit
6. Repealer of Article 6—Bulk Transfers and [Revised] Article 6—Bulk Sales
7. Warehouse Receipts, Bills of Lading and Other Documents of Title
8. Investment Securities
9. Secured Transactions
10. Effective Date and Repealer
11. Effective Date and Transition Provisions

Article 1
GENERAL PROVISIONS

Part 1   General Provisions

§ 1–101.   Short Titles.

(a) This [Act] may be cited as Uniform Commercial Code.

(b) This article may be cited as Uniform Commercial Code–Uniform Provisions.

§ 1–102.   Scope of Article.

This article applies to a transaction to the extent that it is governed by another article of [the Uniform Commercial Code].

§ 1–103.   Construction of [Uniform Commercial Code] to Promote Its Purpose and Policies; Applicability of Supplemental Principles of Law.

(a) [The Uniform Commercial Code] must be liberally construed and applied to promote its underlying purposes and policies, which are:

(1) to simplify, clarify, and modernize the law governing commercial transactions;

(2) to permit the continued expansion of commercial practices through custom, usage, and agreement of the parties; and

(3) to make uniform the law among the various jurisdictions.

(b) Unless displaced by the particular provisions of [the Uniform Commercial Code], the principles of law and equity, including the law merchant and the law relative to capacity to contract, principal and agent, estoppel, fraud, misrepresentation, duress, coercion, mistake, bankruptcy, and other validating or invalidating cause, supplement its provisions.

§ 1–104.   Construction Against Implicit Repeal.

This Act being a general act intended as a unified coverage of its subject matter, no part of it shall be deemed to be impliedly repealed by subsequent legislation if such construction can reasonably be avoided.

§ 1–105.   Severability.

If any provision or clause of [the Uniform Commercial Code] or its application to any person or circumstance is held invalid, the invalidity does not affect other provisions or applications of [the Uniform Commercial Code] which can be given effect without the invalid provision or application, and to this end the provisions of [the Uniform Commercial Code] are severable.

§ 1–106.   Use of Singular and Plural; Gender.

In [the Uniform Commercial Code], unless the statutory context otherwise requires:

(1) words in the singular number include the plural, and those in the plural include the singular; and

(2) words of any gender also refer to any other gender.

§ 1–107.   Section Captions.

Section captions are part of [the Uniform Commercial Code].

§ 1–108.   Relation to Electronic Signatures in Global and National Commerce Act.

This article modifies, limits, and supersedes the Federal Electronic Signatures in Global and National Commerce Act, 15 U.S.C. Sections 7001 et seq., except that nothing in this article modifies, limits, or supersedes section 7001(c) of that act or authorizes electronic delivery of any of the notices described in section 7003(b) of that Act.

Part 2   General Definitions and Principles of Interpretation

§ 1–201.   General Definitions.

Subject to additional definitions contained in the subsequent Articles of this Act which are applicable to specific Articles or Parts thereof, and unless the context otherwise requires, in this Act:

(1) "Action", in the sense of a judicial proceeding, includes recoupment, counterclaim, set-off, suit in equity, and any other proceedings in which rights are determined.

(2) "Aggrieved party" means a party entitled to resort to a remedy.

(3) "Agreement", as distinguished from "contract", means the bargain of the parties in fact, as found in their language or by implication from other circumstances, including course of performance, course of dealing, or usage of trade as provided in Section 1–303.

(4) "Bank" means a person engaged in the business of banking and includes a savings bank, savings and loan association, credit union, and trust company.

(5) "Bearer" means a person in control of a negotiable electronic document of title or a person in possession of a negotiable instrument, negotiable tangible document of title, or certificated security that is payable to bearer or indorsed in blank.

(6) "Bill of lading" means a document of title evidencing the receipt of goods for shipment issued by a person engaged in the business of directly or indirectly transporting or forwarding goods. The term does not include a warehouse receipt.

(7) "Branch" includes a separately incorporated foreign branch of a bank.

(8) "Burden of establishing" a fact means the burden of persuading the trier of fact that the existence of the fact is more probable than its nonexistence.

(9) "Buyer in ordinary course of business" means a person that buys goods in good faith, without knowledge that the sale violates the rights of another person in the goods, and in the ordinary course from a person, other than a pawnbroker, in the business of selling goods of that kind. A person buys goods in the ordinary course if the sale to the person comports with the usual or customary practices in the kind of business in which the seller is engaged or with the seller's own usual or customary practices. A person that sells oil, gas, or other minerals at the wellhead or minehead is a person in the business of selling goods of that kind. A buyer in ordinary course of business may buy for cash, by exchange of other property, or on secured or unsecured credit, and may acquire goods or documents of title under a pre-existing contract for sale. Only a buyer that takes possession of the goods or has a right to recover the goods from the seller under Article 2 may be a buyer in ordinary course of business. A person that acquires goods in a transfer in bulk or as security for or in total or partial satisfaction of a money debt is not a buyer in ordinary course of business.

(10) "Conspicuous", with reference to a term, means so written, displayed, or presented that a reasonable person against which it is to operate ought to have noticed it. Whether a term is "conspicuous" or not is a decision for the court. Conspicuous terms include the following:

(A) a heading in capitals equal to or greater in size than the surrounding text, or in contrasting type, font, or color to the surrounding text of the same or lesser size; and

(B) language in the body of a record or display in larger type than the surrounding text, or in contrasting type, font, or color to the surrounding text of the same size, or set off from surrounding text of the same size by symbols or other marks that call attention to the language.

(11) "Consumer" means an individual who enters into a transaction primarily for personal, family, or household purposes.

(12) "Contract", as distinguished from "agreement", means the total legal obligation that results from the parties' agreement as determined by [the Uniform Commercial Code] as supplemented by any other laws.

(13) "Creditor" includes a general creditor, a secured creditor, a lien creditor and any representative of creditors, including an assignee for the benefit of creditors, a trustee in bankruptcy, a receiver in equity and an executor or administrator of an insolvent debtor's or assignor's estate.

(14) "Defendant" includes a person in the position of defendant in a counterclaim, cross-action, or third-party claim.

(15) "Delivery" with respect to an electronic document of title means voluntary transfer of control and with respect to an instrument, a tangible document of title, or chattel paper means voluntary transfer of possession.

(16) "Document of title" means a record (i) that in regular course of business or financing is treated as adequately evidencing that the person in possession or control of the record is entitled to receive, control, hold, and dispose of the record and the goods the record covers and (ii) that purports to be issued by or addressed to a bailee and to cover goods in the bailee's possession which are either identified or are fungible portions of an identified mass. The term includes a bill of lading, transport document, dock warrant, dock receipt, warehouse receipt, and order for delivery of goods. An electronic document of title means a document of title evidenced by a record consisting of information stored in an electronic medium. A tangible document of title means a document of title evidenced by a record consisting of information that is inscribed on a tangible medium.

(17) "Fault" means a default, breach, or wrongful act or omission.

(18) "Fungible goods" means:

(A) goods of which any unit, by nature or usage of trade, is the equivalent of any other like unit; or

(B) goods that by agreement are treated as equivalent.

(19) "Genuine" means free of forgery or counterfeiting.

(20) "Good faith," except as otherwise provided in Article 5, means honesty in fact and the observance of reasonable commercial standards of fair dealing.

(21) "Holder" means:

(A) the person in possession of a negotiable instrument that is payable either to bearer or to an identified person that is the person in possession;

(B) the person in possession of a negotiable tangible document of title if the goods are deliverable either to bearer or to the order of the person in possession; or

(C) the person in control of a negotiable electronic document of title.

(22) "Insolvency proceeding" includes an assignment for the benefit of creditors or other proceeding intended to liquidate or rehabilitate the estate of the person involved.

(23) "Insolvent" means:

    (A) having generally ceased to pay debts in the ordinary course of business other than as a result of bona fide dispute;

    (B) being unable to pay debts as they become due; or

    (C) being insolvent within the meaning of federal bankruptcy law.

(24) "Money" means a medium of exchange currently authorized or adopted by a domestic or foreign government. The term includes a monetary unit of account established by an intergovernmental organization or by agreement between two or more countries.

(25) "Organization" means a person other than an individual.

(26) "Party", as distinguished from "third party", means a person that has engaged in a transaction or made an agreement subject to [the Uniform Commercial Code].

(27) "Person" means an individual, corporation, business trust, estate, trust, partnership, limited liability company, association, joint venture, government, governmental subdivision, agency, or instrumentality, public corporation, or any other legal or commercial entity.

(28) "Present value" means the amount as of a date certain of one or more sums payable in the future, discounted to the date certain by use of either an interest rate specified by the parties if that rate is not manifestly unreasonable at the time the transaction is entered into or, if an interest rate is not so specified, a commercially reasonable rate that takes into account the facts and circumstances at the time the transaction is entered into.

(29) "Purchase" means taking by sale, lease, discount, negotiation, mortgage, pledge, lien, security interest, issue or reissue, gift, or any other voluntary transaction creating an interest in property.

(30) "Purchaser" means a person that takes by purchase.

(31) "Record" means information that is inscribed on a tangible medium or that is stored in an electronic or other medium and is retrievable in perceivable form.

(32) "Remedy" means any remedial right to which an aggrieved party is entitled with or without resort to a tribunal.

(33) "Representative" means a person empowered to act for another, including an agent, an officer of a corporation or association, and a trustee, executor, or administrator of an estate.

(34) "Right" includes remedy.

(35) "Security interest" means an interest in personal property or fixtures which secures payment or performance of an obligation. "Security interest" includes any interest of a consignor and a buyer of accounts, chattel paper, a payment intangible, or a promissory note in a transaction that is subject to Article 9. "Security interest" does not include the special property interest of a buyer of goods on identification of those goods to a contract for sale under Section 2–401, but a buyer may also acquire a "security interest" by complying with Article 9. Except as otherwise provided in Section 2–505, the right of a seller or lessor of goods under Article 2 or 2A to retain or acquire possession of the goods is not a "security interest", but a seller or lessor may also acquire a "security interest" by complying with Article 9. The retention or reservation of title by a seller of goods notwithstanding shipment or delivery to the buyer under Section 2–401 is limited in effect to a reservation of a "security interest." Whether a transaction in the form of a lease creates a "security interest" is determined pursuant to Section 1–203.

(36) "Send" in connection with a writing, record, or notice means:

    (A) to deposit in the mail or deliver for transmission by any other usual means of communication with postage or cost of transmission provided for and properly addressed and, in the case of an instrument, to an address specified thereon or otherwise agreed, or if there be none to any address reasonable under the circumstances; or

    (B) in any other way to cause to be received any record or notice within the time it would have arrived if properly sent.

(37) "Signed" includes using any symbol executed or adopted with present intention to adopt or accept a writing.

(38) "State" means a State of the United States, the District of Columbia, Puerto Rico, the United States Virgin Islands, or any territory or insular possession subject to the jurisdiction of the United States.

(39) "Surety" includes a guarantor or other secondary obligor.

(40) "Term" means a portion of an agreement that relates to a particular matter.

(41) "Unauthorized signature" means a signature made without actual, implied, or apparent authority. The term includes a forgery.

(42) "Warehouse receipt" means a document of title issued by a person engaged in the business of storing goods for hire.

(43) "Writing" includes printing, typewriting, or any other intentional reduction to tangible form. "Written" has a corresponding meaning.

As amended in 2003.

§ 1–202.   Notice; Knowledge.

(a) Subject to subsection (f), a person has "notice" of a fact if the person:

    (1) has actual knowledge of it;

    (2) has received a notice or notification of it; or

    (3) from all the facts and circumstances known to the person at the time in question, has reason to know that it exists.

(b) "Knowledge" means actual knowledge. "Knows" has a corresponding meaning.

(c) "Discover", "learn", or words of similar import refer to knowledge rather than to reason to know.

(d) A person "notifies" or "gives" a notice or notification to another person by taking such steps as may be reasonably required to inform the other person in ordinary course, whether or not the other person actually comes to know of it.

(e) Subject to subsection (f), a person "receives" a notice or notification when:

    (1) it comes to that person's attention; or

    (2) it is duly delivered in a form reasonable under the circumstances at the place of business through which the contract was made or at another location held out by that person as the place for receipt of such communications.

(f) Notice, knowledge, or a notice or notification received by an organization is effective for a particular transaction from the time it is brought to the attention of the individual conducting that transaction and, in any event, from the time it would have been brought to the individual's attention if the organization had exercised due diligence. An organization exercises due diligence if it maintains reasonable routines for communicating significant information to the person conducting the transaction and there is reasonable compliance with the routines. Due diligence does not require an individual acting for the organization to communicate information unless the communication is part of the individual's regular duties or the individual has reason to know of the transaction and that the transaction would be materially affected by the information.

§ 1–203.   Lease Distinguished from Security Interest.

(a) Whether a transaction in the form of a lease creates a lease or security interest is determined by the facts of each case.

(b) A transaction in the form of a lease creates a security interest if the consideration that the lessee is to pay the lessor for the right to possession and use of the goods is an obligation for the term of the lease and is not subject to termination by the lessee, and:

    (1) the original term of the lease is equal to or greater than the remaining economic life of the goods;

    (2) the lessee is bound to renew the lease for the remaining economic life of the goods or is bound to become the owner of the goods;

    (3) the lessee has an option to renew the lease for the remaining economic life of the goods for no additional consideration or for nominal additional consideration upon compliance with the lease agreement; or

    (4) the lessee has an option to become the owner of the goods for no additional consideration or for nominal additional consideration upon compliance with the lease agreement.

(c) A transaction in the form of a lease does not create a security interest merely because:

    (1) the present value of the consideration the lessee is obligated to pay the lessor for the right to possession and use of the goods is substantially equal to or is greater than the fair market value of the goods at the time the lease is entered into;

    (2) the lessee assumes risk of loss of the goods;

    (3) the lessee agrees to pay, with respect to the goods, taxes, insurance, filing, recording, or registration fees, or service or maintenance costs;

    (4) the lessee has an option to renew the lease or to become the owner of the goods;

    (5) the lessee has an option to renew the lease for a fixed rent that is equal to or greater than the reasonably predictable fair market rent for the use of the goods for the term of the renewal at the time the option is to be performed; or

    (6) the lessee has an option to become the owner of the goods for a fixed price that is equal to or greater than the reasonably predictable fair market value of the goods at the time the option is to be performed.

(d) Additional consideration is nominal if it is less than the lessee's reasonably predictable cost of performing under the lease agreement if the option is not exercised. Additional consideration is not nominal if:

    (1) when the option to renew the lease is granted to the lessee, the rent is stated to be the fair market rent for the use of the goods for the term of the renewal determined at the time the option is to be performed; or

    (2) when the option to become the owner of the goods is granted to the lessee, the price is stated to be the fair market value of the goods determined at the time the option is to be performed.

(e) The "remaining economic life of the goods" and "reasonably predictable" fair market rent, fair market value, or cost of performing under the lease agreement must be determined with reference to the facts and circumstances at the time the transaction is entered into.

§ 1–204.   Value.

Except as otherwise provided in Articles 3, 4, [and] 5, [and 6], a person gives value for rights if the person acquires them:

    (1) in return for a binding commitment to extend credit or for the extension of immediately available credit, whether or not drawn upon and whether or not a charge-back is provided for in the event of difficulties in collection;

    (2) as security for, or in total or partial satisfaction of, a preexisting claim;

    (3) by accepting delivery under a preexisting contract for purchase; or

    (4) in return for any consideration sufficient to support a simple contract.

§ 1–205.   Reasonable Time; Seasonableness.

(a) Whether a time for taking an action required by [the Uniform Commercial Code] is reasonable depends on the nature, purpose, and circumstances of the action.

(b) An action is taken seasonably if it is taken at or within the time agreed or, if no time is agreed, at or within a reasonable time.

§ 1–206.   Presumptions.

Whenever [the Uniform Commercial Code] creates a "presumption" with respect to a fact, or provides that a fact is "presumed," the trier of fact must find the existence of the fact unless and until evidence is introduced that supports a finding of its nonexistence.

Part 3   Territorial Applicability and General Rules

§ 1–301.   Territorial Applicability; Parties' Power to Choose Applicable Law.

(a) In this section:

    (1) "Domestic transaction" means a transaction other than an international transaction.

    (2) "International transaction" means a transaction that bears a reasonable relation to a country other than the United States.

(b) This section applies to a transaction to the extent that it is governed by another article of the [Uniform Commercial Code].

(c) Except as otherwise provided in this section:

(1) an agreement by parties to a domestic transaction that any or all of their rights and obligations are to be determined by the law of this State or of another State is effective, whether or not the transaction bears a relation to the State designated; and

(2) an agreement by parties to an international transaction that any or all of their rights and obligations are to be determined by the law of this State or of another State or country is effective, whether or not the transaction bears a relation to the State or country designated.

(d) In the absence of an agreement effective under subsection (c), and except as provided in subsections (e) and (g), the rights and obligations of the parties are determined by the law that would be selected by application of this State's conflict of laws principles.

(e) If one of the parties to a transaction is a consumer, the following rules apply:

(1) An agreement referred to in subsection (c) is not effective unless the transaction bears a reasonable relation to the State or country designated.

(2) Application of the law of the State or country determined pursuant to subsection (c) or (d) may not deprive the consumer of the protection of any rule of law governing a matter within the scope of this section, which both is protective of consumers and may not be varied by agreement: (A) of the State or country in which the consumer principally resides, unless subparagraph (B) applies; or (B) if the transaction is a sale of goods, of the State or country in which the consumer both makes the contract and take delivery of those goods, if such State or country is not the State or country in which the consumer principally resides.

(f) An agreement otherwise effective under subsection (c) is not effective to the extent that application of the law of the State or country designated would be contrary to a fundamental policy of the State or country whose law would govern in the absence of agreement under subsection (d).

(g) To the extent that [the Uniform Commercial Code] governs a transaction, if one of the following provisions of [the Uniform Commercial Code] specifies the applicable law, that provision governs and a contrary agreement is effective only to the extent permitted by the law so specified: (1) Section 2–402; (2) Sections 2A–105 and 2A–106; (3) Section 4–102; (4) Section 4A–507; (5) Section 5–116; [(6) Section 6–103;] (7) Section 8–110; (8) Sections 9–301 through 9–307.

§ 1–302.   Variation by Agreement.

(a) Except as otherwise provided in subsection (b) or elsewhere in [the Uniform Commercial Code], the effect of provisions of [the Uniform Commercial Code] may be varied by agreement.

(b) The obligations of good faith, diligence, reasonableness, and care prescribed by [the Uniform Commercial Code] may not be disclaimed by agreement. The parties, by agreement, may determine the standards by which the performance of those obligations is to be measured if those standards are not manifestly unreasonable. Whenever [the Uniform Commercial Code] requires an action to be taken within a reasonable time, a time that is not manifestly unreasonable may be fixed by agreement.

(c) The presence in certain provisions of [the Uniform Commercial Code] of the phrase "unless otherwise agreed", or words of similar import, does not imply that the effect of other provisions may not be varied by agreement under this section.

§ 1–303.   Course of Performance, Course of Dealing, and Usage of Trade.

(a) A "course of performance" is a sequence of conduct between the parties to a particular transaction that exists if:

(1) the agreement of the parties with respect to the transaction involves repeated occasions for performance by a party; and

(2) the other party, with knowledge of the nature of the performance and opportunity for objection to it, accepts the performance or acquiesces in it without objection.

(b) A "course of dealing" is a sequence of conduct concerning previous transactions between the parties to a particular transaction that is fairly to be regarded as establishing a common basis of understanding for interpreting their expressions and other conduct.

(c) A "usage of trade" is any practice or method of dealing having such regularity of observance in a place, vocation, or trade as to justify an expectation that it will be observed with respect to the transaction in question. The existence and scope of such a usage must be proved as facts. If it is established that such a usage is embodied in a trade code or similar record, the interpretation of the record is a question of law.

(d) A course of performance or course of dealing between the parties or usage of trade in the vocation or trade in which they are engaged or of which they are or should be aware is relevant in ascertaining the meaning of the parties' agreement, may give particular meaning to specific terms of the agreement, and may supplement or qualify the terms of the agreement. A usage of trade applicable in the place in which part of the performance under the agreement is to occur may be so utilized as to that part of the performance.

(e) Except as otherwise provided in subsection (f), the express terms of an agreement and any applicable course of performance, course of dealing, or usage of trade must be construed whenever reasonable as consistent with each other. If such a construction is unreasonable:

(1) express terms prevail over course of performance, course of dealing, and usage of trade;

(2) course of performance prevails over course of dealing and usage of trade; and

(3) course of dealing prevails over usage of trade.

(f) Subject to Section 2–209 and Section 2A–208, a course of performance is relevant to show a waiver or modification of any term inconsistent with the course of performance.

(g) Evidence of a relevant usage of trade offered by one party is not admissible unless that party has given the other party notice that the court finds sufficient to prevent unfair surprise to the other party.

§ 1–304.   Obligation of Good Faith.

Every contract or duty within [the Uniform Commercial Code] imposes an obligation of good faith in its performance and enforcement.

§ 1–305.   Remedies to be Liberally Administered.

(a) The remedies provided by [the Uniform Commercial Code] must be liberally administered to the end that the aggrieved party may be put in as good a position as if the other party had fully performed but neither consequential or special damages nor penal damages may be had except as specifically provided in [the Uniform Commercial Code] or by other rule of law.

(b) Any right or obligation declared by [the Uniform Commercial Code] is enforceable by action unless the provision declaring it specifies a different and limited effect.

§ 1–306.   Waiver or Renunciation of Claim or Right After Breach.

A claim or right arising out of an alleged breach may be discharged in whole or in part without consideration by agreement of the aggrieved party in an authenticated record.

§ 1–307.   *Prima Facie* Evidence by Third-Party Documents.

A document in due form purporting to be a bill of lading, policy or certificate of insurance, official weigher's or inspector's certificate, consular invoice, or any other document authorized or required by the contract to be issued by a third party is *prima facie* evidence of its own authenticity and genuineness and of the facts stated in the document by the third party.

§ 1–308.   Performance or Acceptance Under Reservation of Rights.

(a) A party that with explicit reservation of rights performs or promises performance or assents to performance in a manner demanded or offered by the other party does not thereby prejudice the rights reserved. Such words as "without prejudice," "under protest," or the like are sufficient.

(b) Subsection (a) does not apply to an accord and satisfaction.

§ 1–309.   Option to Accelerate at Will.

A term providing that one party or that party's successor in interest may accelerate payment or performance or require collateral or additional collateral "at will" or when the party "deems itself insecure," or words of similar import, means that the party has power to do so only if that party in good faith believes that the prospect of payment or performance is impaired. The burden of establishing lack of good faith is on the party against which the power has been exercised.

§ 1–310.   Subordinated Obligations.

An obligation may be issued as subordinated to performance of another obligation of the person obligated, or a creditor may subordinate its right to performance of an obligation by agreement with either the person obligated or another creditor of the person obligated. Subordination does not create a security interest as against either the common debtor or a subordinated creditor.

Article 2
SALES

Part 1   Short Title, General Construction and Subject Matter

§ 2–101.   Short Title.

This Article shall be known and may be cited as Uniform Commercial Code—Sales.

§ 2–102.   Scope; Certain Security and Other Transactions Excluded From This Article.

Unless the context otherwise requires, this Article applies to transactions in goods; it does not apply to any transaction which although in the form of an unconditional contract to sell or present sale is intended to operate only as a security transaction nor does this Article impair or repeal any statute regulating sales to consumers, farmers or other specified classes of buyers.

§ 2–103.   Definitions and Index of Definitions.

(1) In this Article unless the context otherwise requires

    (a) "Buyer" means a person who buys or contracts to buy goods.

    (b) "Good faith" in the case of a merchant means honesty in fact and the observance of reasonable commercial standards of fair dealing in the trade.

    (c) "Receipt" of goods means taking physical possession of them.

    (d) "Seller" means a person who sells or contracts to sell goods.

(2) Other definitions applying to this Article or to specified Parts thereof, and the sections in which they appear are:

"Acceptance". Section 2–606.

"Banker's credit". Section 2–325.

"Between merchants". Section 2–104.

"Cancellation". Section 2–106(4).

"Commercial unit". Section 2–105.

"Confirmed credit". Section 2–325.

"Conforming to contract". Section 2–106.

"Contract for sale". Section 2–106.

"Cover". Section 2–712.

"Entrusting". Section 2–403.

"Financing agency". Section 2–104.

"Future goods". Section 2–105.

"Goods". Section 2–105.

"Identification". Section 2–501.

"Installment contract". Section 2–612.

"Letter of Credit". Section 2–325.

"Lot". Section 2–105.

"Merchant". Section 2–104.

"Overseas". Section 2–323.

"Person in position of seller". Section 2–707.

"Present sale". Section 2–106.

"Sale". Section 2–106.

"Sale on approval". Section 2–326.

"Sale or return". Section 2–326.

"Termination". Section 2–106.

(3) The following definitions in other Articles apply to this Article:

"Check". Section 3–104.

"Consignee". Section 7–102.

"Consignor". Section 7–102.

"Consumer goods". Section 9–109.

"Dishonor". Section 3–507.

"Draft". Section 3–104.

(4) In addition Article 1 contains general definitions and principles of construction and interpretation applicable throughout this Article.

As amended in 1994 and 1999.

§ 2–104.   Definitions: "Merchant"; "Between Merchants"; "Financing Agency".

(1) "Merchant" means a person who deals in goods of the kind or otherwise by his occupation holds himself out as having knowledge or skill peculiar to the practices or goods involved in the transaction or to whom such knowledge or skill may be attributed by his employment of an agent or broker or other intermediary who by his occupation holds himself out as having such knowledge or skill.

(2) "Financing agency" means a bank, finance company or other person who in the ordinary course of business makes advances against goods or documents of title or who by arrangement with either the seller or the buyer intervenes in ordinary course to make or collect payment due or claimed under the contract for sale, as by purchasing or paying the seller's draft or making advances against it or by merely taking it for collection whether or not documents of title accompany the draft. "Financing agency" includes also a bank or other person who similarly intervenes between persons who are in the position of seller and buyer in respect to the goods (Section 2–707).

(3) "Between merchants" means in any transaction with respect to which both parties are chargeable with the knowledge or skill of merchants.

§ 2–105.   Definitions: Transferability; "Goods"; "Future" Goods; "Lot"; "Commercial Unit".

(1) "Goods" means all things (including specially manufactured goods) which are movable at the time of identification to the contract for sale other than the money in which the price is to be paid, investment securities (Article 8) and things in action. "Goods" also includes the unborn young of animals and growing crops and other identified things attached to realty as described in the section on goods to be severed from realty (Section 2–107).

(2) Goods must be both existing and identified before any interest in them can pass. Goods which are not both existing and identi-

fied are "future" goods. A purported present sale of future goods or of any interest therein operates as a contract to sell.

(3) There may be a sale of a part interest in existing identified goods.

(4) An undivided share in an identified bulk of fungible goods is sufficiently identified to be sold although the quantity of the bulk is not determined. Any agreed proportion of such a bulk or any quantity thereof agreed upon by number, weight or other measure may to the extent of the seller's interest in the bulk be sold to the buyer who then becomes an owner in common.

(5) "Lot" means a parcel or a single article which is the subject matter of a separate sale or delivery, whether or not it is sufficient to perform the contract.

(6) "Commercial unit" means such a unit of goods as by commercial usage is a single whole for purposes of sale and division of which materially impairs its character or value on the market or in use. A commercial unit may be a single article (as a machine) or a set of articles (as a suite of furniture or an assortment of sizes) or a quantity (as a bale, gross, or carload) or any other unit treated in use or in the relevant market as a single whole.

§ 2–106.   Definitions: "Contract"; "Agreement"; "Contract for Sale"; "Sale"; "Present Sale"; "Conforming" to Contract; "Termination"; "Cancellation".

(1) In this Article unless the context otherwise requires "contract" and "agreement" are limited to those relating to the present or future sale of goods. "Contract for sale" includes both a present sale of goods and a contract to sell goods at a future time. A "sale" consists in the passing of title from the seller to the buyer for a price (Section 2–401). A "present sale" means a sale which is accomplished by the making of the contract.

(2) Goods or conduct including any part of a performance are "conforming" or conform to the contract when they are in accordance with the obligations under the contract.

(3) "Termination" occurs when either party pursuant to a power created by agreement or law puts an end to the contract otherwise than for its breach. On "termination" all obligations which are still executory on both sides are discharged but any right based on prior breach or performance survives.

(4) "Cancellation" occurs when either party puts an end to the contract for breach by the other and its effect is the same as that of "termination" except that the cancelling party also retains any remedy for breach of the whole contract or any unperformed balance.

§ 2–107.   Goods to Be Severed From Realty: Recording.

(1) A contract for the sale of minerals or the like (including oil and gas) or a structure or its materials to be removed from realty is a contract for the sale of goods within this Article if they are to be severed by the seller but until severance a purported present sale thereof which is not effective as a transfer of an interest in land is effective only as a contract to sell.

(2) A contract for the sale apart from the land of growing crops or other things attached to realty and capable of severance without material harm thereto but not described in subsection (1) or of timber to be cut is a contract for the sale of goods within this Article whether

the subject matter is to be severed by the buyer or by the seller even though it forms part of the realty at the time of contracting, and the parties can by identification effect a present sale before severance.

(3) The provisions of this section are subject to any third party rights provided by the law relating to realty records, and the contract for sale may be executed and recorded as a document transferring an interest in land and shall then constitute notice to third parties of the buyer's rights under the contract for sale.

As amended in 1972.

Part 2   Form, Formation and Readjustment of Contract

§ 2–201.   Formal Requirements; Statute of Frauds.

(1) Except as otherwise provided in this section a contract for the sale of goods for the price of $500 or more is not enforceable by way of action or defense unless there is some writing sufficient to indicate that a contract for sale has been made between the parties and signed by the party against whom enforcement is sought or by his authorized agent or broker. A writing is not insufficient because it omits or incorrectly states a term agreed upon but the contract is not enforceable under this paragraph beyond the quantity of goods shown in such writing.

(2) Between merchants if within a reasonable time a writing in confirmation of the contract and sufficient against the sender is received and the party receiving it has reason to know its contents, its satisfies the requirements of subsection (1) against such party unless written notice of objection to its contents is given within ten days after it is received.

(3) A contract which does not satisfy the requirements of subsection (1) but which is valid in other respects is enforceable

   (a) if the goods are to be specially manufactured for the buyer and are not suitable for sale to others in the ordinary course of the seller's business and the seller, before notice of repudiation is received and under circumstances which reasonably indicate that the goods are for the buyer, has made either a substantial beginning of their manufacture or commitments for their procurement; or

   (b) if the party against whom enforcement is sought admits in his pleading, testimony or otherwise in court that a contract for sale was made, but the contract is not enforceable under this provision beyond the quantity of goods admitted; or

   (c) with respect to goods for which payment has been made and accepted or which have been received and accepted (Sec. 2–606).

§ 2–202.   Final Written Expression:
Parol or Extrinsic Evidence.

Terms with respect to which the confirmatory memoranda of the parties agree or which are otherwise set forth in a writing intended by the parties as a final expression of their agreement with respect to such terms as are included therein may not be contradicted by evidence of any prior agreement or of a contemporaneous oral agreement but may be explained or supplemented

   (a) by course of dealing or usage of trade (Section 1–205) or by course of performance (Section 2–208); and

   (b) by evidence of consistent additional terms unless the court finds the writing to have been intended also as a complete and exclusive statement of the terms of the agreement.

§ 2–203.   Seals Inoperative.

The affixing of a seal to a writing evidencing a contract for sale or an offer to buy or sell goods does not constitute the writing a sealed instrument and the law with respect to sealed instruments does not apply to such a contract or offer.

§ 2–204.   Formation in General.

(1) A contract for sale of goods may be made in any manner sufficient to show agreement, including conduct by both parties which recognizes the existence of such a contract.

(2) An agreement sufficient to constitute a contract for sale may be found even though the moment of its making is undetermined.

(3) Even though one or more terms are left open a contract for sale does not fail for indefiniteness if the parties have intended to make a contract and there is a reasonably certain basis for giving an appropriate remedy.

§ 2–205.   Firm Offers.

An offer by a merchant to buy or sell goods in a signed writing which by its terms gives assurance that it will be held open is not revocable, for lack of consideration, during the time stated or if no time is stated for a reasonable time, but in no event may such period of irrevocability exceed three months; but any such term of assurance on a form supplied by the offeree must be separately signed by the offeror.

§ 2–206.   Offer and Acceptance in Formation of Contract.

(1) Unless other unambiguously indicated by the language or circumstances

   (a) an offer to make a contract shall be construed as inviting acceptance in any manner and by any medium reasonable in the circumstances;

   (b) an order or other offer to buy goods for prompt or current shipment shall be construed as inviting acceptance either by a prompt promise to ship or by the prompt or current shipment of conforming or nonconforming goods, but such a shipment of non-conforming goods does not constitute an acceptance if the seller seasonably notifies the buyer that the shipment is offered only as an accommodation to the buyer.

(2) Where the beginning of a requested performance is a reasonable mode of acceptance an offeror who is not notified of acceptance within a reasonable time may treat the offer as having lapsed before acceptance.

§ 2–207.   Additional Terms in Acceptance or Confirmation.

(1) A definite and seasonable expression of acceptance or a written confirmation which is sent within a reasonable time operates as an acceptance even though it states terms additional to or different from those offered or agreed upon, unless acceptance is expressly made conditional on assent to the additional or different terms.

(2) The additional terms are to be construed as proposals for addition to the contract. Between merchants such terms become part of the contract unless:

(a) the offer expressly limits acceptance to the terms of the offer;

(b) they materially alter it; or

(c) notification of objection to them has already been given or is given within a reasonable time after notice of them is received.

(3) Conduct by both parties which recognizes the existence of a contract is sufficient to establish a contract for sale although the writings of the parties do not otherwise establish a contract. In such case the terms of the particular contract consist of those terms on which the writings of the parties agree, together with any supplementary terms incorporated under any other provisions of this Act.

§ 2–208.   Course of Performance or Practical Construction.

(1) Where the contract for sale involves repeated occasions for performance by either party with knowledge of the nature of the performance and opportunity for objection to it by the other, any course of performance accepted or acquiesced in without objection shall be relevant to determine the meaning of the agreement.

(2) The express terms of the agreement and any such course of performance, as well as any course of dealing and usage of trade, shall be construed whenever reasonable as consistent with each other; but when such construction is unreasonable, express terms shall control course of performance and course of performance shall control both course of dealing and usage of trade (Section 1–205).

(3) Subject to the provisions of the next section on modification and waiver, such course of performance shall be relevant to show a waiver or modification of any term inconsistent with such course of performance.

§ 2–209.   Modification, Rescission and Waiver.

(1) An agreement modifying a contract within this Article needs no consideration to be binding.

(2) A signed agreement which excludes modification or rescission except by a signed writing cannot be otherwise modified or rescinded, but except as between merchants such a requirement on a form supplied by the merchant must be separately signed by the other party.

(3) The requirements of the statute of frauds section of this Article (Section 2–201) must be satisfied if the contract as modified is within its provisions.

(4) Although an attempt at modification or rescission does not satisfy the requirements of subsection (2) or (3) it can operate as a waiver.

(5) A party who has made a waiver affecting an executory portion of the contract may retract the waiver by reasonable notification received by the other party that strict performance will be required of any term waived, unless the retraction would be unjust in view of a material change of position in reliance on the waiver.

§ 2–210.   Delegation of Performance; Assignment of Rights.

(1) A party may perform his duty through a delegate unless otherwise agreed or unless the other party has a substantial interest in having his original promisor perform or control the acts required by the contract. No delegation of performance relieves the party delegating of any duty to perform or any liability for breach.

(2) Except as otherwise provided in Section 9–406, unless otherwise agreed, all rights of either seller or buyer can be assigned except where the assignment would materially change the duty of the other party, or increase materially the burden or risk imposed on him by his contract, or impair materially his chance of obtaining return performance. A right to damages for breach of the whole contract or a right arising out of the assignor's due performance of his entire obligation can be assigned despite agreement otherwise.

(3) The creation, attachment, perfection, or enforcement of a security interest in the seller's interest under a contract is not a transfer that materially changes the duty of or increases materially the burden or risk imposed on the buyer or impairs materially the buyer's chance of obtaining return performance within the purview of subsection (2) unless, and then only to the extent that, enforcement actually results in a delegation of material performance of the seller. Even in that event, the creation, attachment, perfection, and enforcement of the security interest remain effective, but (i) the seller is liable to the buyer for damages caused by the delegation to the extent that the damages could not reasonably by prevented by the buyer, and (ii) a court having jurisdiction may grant other appropriate relief, including cancellation of the contract for sale or an injunction against enforcement of the security interest or consummation of the enforcement.

(4) Unless the circumstances indicate the contrary a prohibition of assignment of "the contract" is to be construed as barring only the delegation to the assignee of the assignor's performance.

(5) An assignment of "the contract" or of "all my rights under the contract" or an assignment in similar general terms is an assignment of rights and unless the language or the circumstances (as in an assignment for security) indicate the contrary, it is a delegation of performance of the duties of the assignor and its acceptance by the assignee constitutes a promise by him to perform those duties. This promise is enforceable by either the assignor or the other party to the original contract.

(6) The other party may treat any assignment which delegates performance as creating reasonable grounds for insecurity and may without prejudice to his rights against the assignor demand assurances from the assignee (Section 2–609).

As amended in 1999.

Part 3   General Obligation and Construction of Contract
§ 2–301.   General Obligations of Parties.

The obligation of the seller is to transfer and deliver and that of the buyer is to accept and pay in accordance with the contract.

§ 2–302.   Unconscionable Contract or Clause.

(1) If the court as a matter of law finds the contract or any clause of the contract to have been unconscionable at the time it was made

the court may refuse to enforce the contract, or it may enforce the remainder of the contract without the unconscionable clause, or it may so limit the application of any unconscionable clause as to avoid any unconscionable result.

(2) When it is claimed or appears to the court that the contract or any clause thereof may be unconscionable the parties shall be afforded a reasonable opportunity to present evidence as to its commercial setting, purpose and effect to aid the court in making the determination.

§ 2–303.   Allocations or Division of Risks.

Where this Article allocates a risk or a burden as between the parties "unless otherwise agreed", the agreement may not only shift the allocation but may also divide the risk or burden.

§ 2–304.   Price Payable in Money, Goods, Realty, or Otherwise.

(1) The price can be made payable in money or otherwise. If it is payable in whole or in part in goods each party is a seller of the goods which he is to transfer.

(2) Even though all or part of the price is payable in an interest in realty the transfer of the goods and the seller's obligations with reference to them are subject to this Article, but not the transfer of the interest in realty or the transferor's obligations in connection therewith.

§ 2–305.   Open Price Term.

(1) The parties if they so intend can conclude a contract for sale even though the price is not settled. In such a case the price is a reasonable price at the time for delivery if

(a) nothing is said as to price; or

(b) the price is left to be agreed by the parties and they fail to agree; or

(c) the price is to be fixed in terms of some agreed market or other standard as set or recorded by a third person or agency and it is not so set or recorded.

(2) A price to be fixed by the seller or by the buyer means a price for him to fix in good faith.

(3) When a price left to be fixed otherwise than by agreement of the parties fails to be fixed through fault of one party the other may at his option treat the contract as cancelled or himself fix a reasonable price.

(4) Where, however, the parties intend not to be bound unless the price be fixed or agreed and it is not fixed or agreed there is no contract. In such a case the buyer must return any goods already received or if unable so to do must pay their reasonable value at the time of delivery and the seller must return any portion of the price paid on account.

§ 2–306.   Output, Requirements and Exclusive Dealings.

(1) A term which measures the quantity by the output of the seller or the requirements of the buyer means such actual output or requirements as may occur in good faith, except that no quantity unreasonably disproportionate to any stated estimate or in the absence of a stated estimate to any normal or otherwise comparable prior output or requirements may be tendered or demanded.

(2) A lawful agreement by either the seller or the buyer for exclusive dealing in the kind of goods concerned imposes unless otherwise agreed an obligation by the seller to use best efforts to supply the goods and by the buyer to use best efforts to promote their sale.

§ 2–307.   Delivery in Single Lot or Several Lots.

Unless otherwise agreed all goods called for by a contract for sale must be tendered in a single delivery and payment is due only on such tender but where the circumstances give either party the right to make or demand delivery in lots the price if it can be apportioned may be demanded for each lot.

§ 2–308.   Absence of Specified Place for Delivery.

Unless otherwise agreed

(a) the place for delivery of goods is the seller's place of business or if he has none his residence; but

(b) in a contract for sale of identified goods which to the knowledge of the parties at the time of contracting are in some other place, that place is the place for their delivery; and

(c) documents of title may be delivered through customary banking channels.

§ 2–309.   Absence of Specific Time Provisions; Notice of Termination.

(1) The time for shipment or delivery or any other action under a contract if not provided in this Article or agreed upon shall be a reasonable time.

(2) Where the contract provides for successive performances but is indefinite in duration it is valid for a reasonable time but unless otherwise agreed may be terminated at any time by either party.

(3) Termination of a contract by one party except on the happening of an agreed event requires that reasonable notification be received by the other party and an agreement dispensing with notification is invalid if its operation would be unconscionable.

§ 2–310.   Open Time for Payment or Running of Credit; Authority to Ship Under Reservation.

Unless otherwise agreed

(a) payment is due at the time and place at which the buyer is to receive the goods even though the place of shipment is the place of delivery; and

(b) if the seller is authorized to send the goods he may ship them under reservation, and may tender the documents of title, but the buyer may inspect the goods after their arrival before payment is due unless such inspection is inconsistent with the terms of the contract (Section 2–513); and

(c) if delivery is authorized and made by way of documents of title otherwise than by subsection (b) then payment is due at the time and place at which the buyer is to receive the documents regardless of where the goods are to be received; and

(d) where the seller is required or authorized to ship the goods on credit the credit period runs from the time of shipment but post-dating the invoice or delaying its dispatch will correspondingly delay the starting of the credit period.

§ 2–311.   Options and Cooperation Respecting Performance.

(1) An agreement for sale which is otherwise sufficiently definite (subsection (3) of Section 2–204) to be a contract is not made invalid by the fact that it leaves particulars of performance to be specified by one of the parties. Any such specification must be made in good faith and within limits set by commercial reasonableness.

(2) Unless otherwise agreed specifications relating to assortment of the goods are at the buyer's option and except as otherwise provided in subsections (1)(c) and (3) of Section 2–319 specifications or arrangements relating to shipment are at the seller's option.

(3) Where such specification would materially affect the other party's performance but is not seasonably made or where one party's cooperation is necessary to the agreed performance of the other but is not seasonably forthcoming, the other party in addition to all other remedies

(a) is excused for any resulting delay in his own performance; and

(b) may also either proceed to perform in any reasonable manner or after the time for a material part of his own performance treat the failure to specify or to cooperate as a breach by failure to deliver or accept the goods.

§ 2–312.   Warranty of Title and Against Infringement; Buyer's Obligation Against Infringement.

(1) Subject to subsection (2) there is in a contract for sale a warranty by the seller that

(a) the title conveyed shall be good, and its transfer rightful; and

(b) the goods shall be delivered free from any security interest or other lien or encumbrance of which the buyer at the time of contracting has no knowledge.

(2) A warranty under subsection (1) will be excluded or modified only by specific language or by circumstances which give the buyer reason to know that the person selling does not claim title in himself or that he is purporting to sell only such right or title as he or a third person may have.

(3) Unless otherwise agreed a seller who is a merchant regularly dealing in goods of the kind warrants that the goods shall be delivered free of the rightful claim of any third person by way of infringement or the like but a buyer who furnishes specifications to the seller must hold the seller harmless against any such claim which arises out of compliance with the specifications.

§ 2–313.   Express Warranties by Affirmation, Promise, Description, Sample.

(1) Express warranties by the seller are created as follows:

(a) Any affirmation of fact or promise made by the seller to the buyer which relates to the goods and becomes part of the basis of the bargain creates an express warranty that the goods shall conform to the affirmation or promise.

(b) Any description of the goods which is made part of the basis of the bargain creates an express warranty that the goods shall conform to the description.

(c) Any sample or model which is made part of the basis of the bargain creates an express warranty that the whole of the goods shall conform to the sample or model.

(2) It is not necessary to the creation of an express warranty that the seller use formal words such as "warrant" or "guarantee" or that he have a specific intention to make a warranty, but an affirmation merely of the value of the goods or a statement purporting to be merely the seller's opinion or commendation of the goods does not create a warranty.

§ 2–314.   Implied Warranty: Merchantability; Usage of Trade.

(1) Unless excluded or modified (Section 2–316), a warranty that the goods shall be merchantable is implied in a contract for their sale if the seller is a merchant with respect to goods of that kind. Under this section the serving for value of food or drink to be consumed either on the premises or elsewhere is a sale.

(2) Goods to be merchantable must be at least such as

(a) pass without objection in the trade under the contract description; and

(b) in the case of fungible goods, are of fair average quality within the description; and

(c) are fit for the ordinary purposes for which such goods are used; and

(d) run, within the variations permitted by the agreement, of even kind, quality and quantity within each unit and among all units involved; and

(e) are adequately contained, packaged, and labeled as the agreement may require; and

(f) conform to the promises or affirmations of fact made on the container or label if any.

(3) Unless excluded or modified (Section 2–316) other implied warranties may arise from course of dealing or usage of trade.

§ 2–315.   Implied Warranty: Fitness for Particular Purpose.

Where the seller at the time of contracting has reason to know any particular purpose for which the goods are required and that the buyer is relying on the seller's skill or judgment to select or furnish suitable goods, there is unless excluded or modified under the next section an implied warranty that the goods shall be fit for such purpose.

§ 2–316.   Exclusion or Modification of Warranties.

(1) Words or conduct relevant to the creation of an express warranty and words or conduct tending to negate or limit warranty shall be construed wherever reasonable as consistent with each other; but subject to the provisions of this Article on parol or extrinsic evidence (Section 2–202) negation or limitation is inoperative to the extent that such construction is unreasonable.

(2) Subject to subsection (3), to exclude or modify the implied warranty of merchantability or any part of it the language must mention merchantability and in case of a writing must be conspicuous, and to exclude or modify any implied warranty of fitness the exclusion must be by a writing and conspicuous. Language to

exclude all implied warranties of fitness is sufficient if it states, for example, that "There are no warranties which extend beyond the description on the face hereof."

(3) Notwithstanding subsection (2)

(a) unless the circumstances indicate otherwise, all implied warranties are excluded by expressions like "as is", "with all faults" or other language which in common understanding calls the buyer's attention to the exclusion of warranties and makes plain that there is no implied warranty; and

(b) when the buyer before entering into the contract has examined the goods or the sample or model as fully as he desired or has refused to examine the goods there is no implied warranty with regard to defects which an examination ought in the circumstances to have revealed to him; and

(c) an implied warranty can also be excluded or modified by course of dealing or course of performance or usage of trade.

(4) Remedies for breach of warranty can be limited in accordance with the provisions of this Article on liquidation or limitation of damages and on contractual modification of remedy (Sections 2–718 and 2–719).

§ 2–317.   Cumulation and Conflict of Warranties Express or Implied.

Warranties whether express or implied shall be construed as consistent with each other and as cumulative, but if such construction is unreasonable the intention of the parties shall determine which warranty is dominant. In ascertaining that intention the following rules apply:

(a) Exact or technical specifications displace an inconsistent sample or model or general language of description.

(b) A sample from an existing bulk displaces inconsistent general language of description.

(c) Express warranties displace inconsistent implied warranties other than an implied warranty of fitness for a particular purpose.

§ 2–318.   Third Party Beneficiaries of Warranties Express or Implied.

Note: If this Act is introduced in the Congress of the United States this section should be omitted. (States to select one alternative.)

Alternative A

A seller's warranty whether express or implied extends to any natural person who is in the family or household of his buyer or who is a guest in his home if it is reasonable to expect that such person may use, consume or be affected by the goods and who is injured in person by breach of the warranty. A seller may not exclude or limit the operation of this section.

Alternative B

A seller's warranty whether express or implied extends to any natural person who may reasonably be expected to use, consume or be affected by the goods and who is injured in person by breach of the warranty. A seller may not exclude or limit the operation of this section.

Alternative C

A seller's warranty whether express or implied extends to any person who may reasonably be expected to use, consume or be affected by the goods and who is injured by breach of the warranty. A seller may not exclude or limit the operation of this section with respect to injury to the person of an individual to whom the warranty extends.

As amended 1966.

§ 2–319.   F.O.B. and F.A.S. Terms.

(1) Unless otherwise agreed the term F.O.B. (which means "free on board") at a named place, even though used only in connection with the stated price, is a delivery term under which

(a) when the term is F.O.B. the place of shipment, the seller must at that place ship the goods in the manner provided in this Article (Section 2–504) and bear the expense and risk of putting them into the possession of the carrier; or

(b) when the term is F.O.B. the place of destination, the seller must at his own expense and risk transport the goods to that place and there tender delivery of them in the manner provided in this Article (Section 2–503);

(c) when under either (a) or (b) the term is also F.O.B. vessel, car or other vehicle, the seller must in addition at his own expense and risk load the goods on board. If the term is F.O.B. vessel the buyer must name the vessel and in an appropriate case the seller must comply with the provisions of this Article on the form of bill of lading (Section 2–323).

(2) Unless otherwise agreed the term F.A.S. vessel (which means "free alongside") at a named port, even though used only in connection with the stated price, is a delivery term under which the seller must

(a) at his own expense and risk deliver the goods alongside the vessel in the manner usual in that port or on a dock designated and provided by the buyer; and

(b) obtain and tender a receipt for the goods in exchange for which the carrier is under a duty to issue a bill of lading.

(3) Unless otherwise agreed in any case falling within subsection (1)(a) or (c) or subsection (2) the buyer must seasonably give any needed instructions for making delivery, including when the term is F.A.S. or F.O.B. the loading berth of the vessel and in an appropriate case its name and sailing date. The seller may treat the failure of needed instructions as a failure of cooperation under this Article (Section 2–311). He may also at his option move the goods in any reasonable manner preparatory to delivery or shipment.

(4) Under the term F.O.B. vessel or F.A.S. unless otherwise agreed the buyer must make payment against tender of the required documents and the seller may not tender nor the buyer demand delivery of the goods in substitution for the documents.

§ 2–320.   C.I.F. and C. & F. Terms.

(1) The term C.I.F. means that the price includes in a lump sum the cost of the goods and the insurance and freight to the named destination. The term C. & F. or C.F. means that the price so includes cost and freight to the named destination.

(2) Unless otherwise agreed and even though used only in connection with the stated price and destination, the term C.I.F. destination or its equivalent requires the seller at his own expense and risk to

(a) put the goods into the possession of a carrier at the port for shipment and obtain a negotiable bill or bills of lading covering the entire transportation to the named destination; and

(b) load the goods and obtain a receipt from the carrier (which may be contained in the bill of lading) showing that the freight has been paid or provided for; and

(c) obtain a policy or certificate of insurance, including any war risk insurance, of a kind and on terms then current at the port of shipment in the usual amount, in the currency of the contract, shown to cover the same goods covered by the bill of lading and providing for payment of loss to the order of the buyer or for the account of whom it may concern; but the seller may add to the price the amount of the premium for any such war risk insurance; and

(d) prepare an invoice of the goods and procure any other documents required to effect shipment or to comply with the contract; and

(e) forward and tender with commercial promptness all the documents in due form and with any indorsement necessary to perfect the buyer's rights.

(3) Unless otherwise agreed the term C. & F. or its equivalent has the same effect and imposes upon the seller the same obligations and risks as a C.I.F. term except the obligation as to insurance.

(4) Under the term C.I.F. or C. & F. unless otherwise agreed the buyer must make payment against tender of the required documents and the seller may not tender nor the buyer demand delivery of the goods in substitution for the documents.

§ 2–321.   C.I.F. or C. & F.: "Net Landed Weights"; "Payment on Arrival"; Warranty of Condition on Arrival.

Under a contract containing a term C.I.F. or C. & F.

(1) Where the price is based on or is to be adjusted according to "net landed weights", "delivered weights", "out turn" quantity or quality or the like, unless otherwise agreed the seller must reasonably estimate the price. The payment due on tender of the documents called for by the contract is the amount so estimated, but after final adjustment of the price a settlement must be made with commercial promptness.

(2) An agreement described in subsection (1) or any warranty of quality or condition of the goods on arrival places upon the seller the risk of ordinary deterioration, shrinkage and the like in transportation but has no effect on the place or time of identification to the contract for sale or delivery or on the passing of the risk of loss.

(3) Unless otherwise agreed where the contract provides for payment on or after arrival of the goods the seller must before payment allow such preliminary inspection as is feasible; but if the goods are lost delivery of the documents and payment are due when the goods should have arrived.

§ 2–322.   Delivery "Ex-Ship".

(1) Unless otherwise agreed a term for delivery of goods "ex-ship" (which means from the carrying vessel) or in equivalent language is not restricted to a particular ship and requires delivery from a ship which has reached a place at the named port of destination where goods of the kind are usually discharged.

(2) Under such a term unless otherwise agreed

(a) the seller must discharge all liens arising out of the carriage and furnish the buyer with a direction which puts the carrier under a duty to deliver the goods; and

(b) the risk of loss does not pass to the buyer until the goods leave the ship's tackle or are otherwise properly unloaded.

§ 2–323.   Form of Bill of Lading Required in Overseas Shipment; "Overseas".

(1) Where the contract contemplates overseas shipment and contains a term C.I.F. or C. & F. or F.O.B. vessel, the seller unless otherwise agreed must obtain a negotiable bill of lading stating that the goods have been loaded on board or, in the case of a term C.I.F. or C. & F., received for shipment.

(2) Where in a case within subsection (1) a bill of lading has been issued in a set of parts, unless otherwise agreed if the documents are not to be sent from abroad the buyer may demand tender of the full set; otherwise only one part of the bill of lading need be tendered. Even if the agreement expressly requires a full set

(a) due tender of a single part is acceptable within the provisions of this Article on cure of improper delivery (subsection (1) of Section 2–508); and

(b) even though the full set is demanded, if the documents are sent from abroad the person tendering an incomplete set may nevertheless require payment upon furnishing an indemnity which the buyer in good faith deems adequate.

(3) A shipment by water or by air or a contract contemplating such shipment is "overseas" insofar as by usage of trade or agreement it is subject to the commercial, financing or shipping practices characteristic of international deep water commerce.

§ 2–324.   "No Arrival, No Sale" Term.

Under a term "no arrival, no sale" or terms of like meaning, unless otherwise agreed,

(a) the seller must properly ship conforming goods and if they arrive by any means he must tender them on arrival but he assumes no obligation that the goods will arrive unless he has caused the non-arrival; and

(b) where without fault of the seller the goods are in part lost or have so deteriorated as no longer to conform to the contract or arrive after the contract time, the buyer may proceed as if there had been casualty to identified goods (Section 2–613).

§ 2–325.   "Letter of Credit" Term; "Confirmed Credit".

(1) Failure of the buyer seasonably to furnish an agreed letter of credit is a breach of the contract for sale.

(2) The delivery to seller of a proper letter of credit suspends the buyer's obligation to pay. If the letter of credit is dishonored, the seller may on seasonable notification to the buyer require payment directly from him.

(3) Unless otherwise agreed the term "letter of credit" or "banker's credit" in a contract for sale means an irrevocable credit issued by a financing agency of good repute and, where the shipment is overseas, of good international repute. The term "confirmed credit" means that the credit must also carry the direct obligation of such an agency which does business in the seller's financial market.

§ 2–326.   Sale on Approval and Sale or Return; Rights of Creditors.

(1) Unless otherwise agreed, if delivered goods may be returned by the buyer even though they conform to the contract, the transaction is

   (a) a "sale on approval" if the goods are delivered primarily for use, and

   (b) a "sale or return" if the goods are delivered primarily for resale.

(2) Goods held on approval are not subject to the claims of the buyer's creditors until acceptance; goods held on sale or return are subject to such claims while in the buyer's possession.

(3) Any "or return" term of a contract for sale is to be treated as a separate contract for sale within the statute of frauds section of this Article (Section 2–201) and as contradicting the sale aspect of the contract within the provisions of this Article or on parol or extrinsic evidence (Section 2–202).

As amended in 1999.

§ 2–327.   Special Incidents of Sale on Approval and Sale or Return.

(1) Under a sale on approval unless otherwise agreed

   (a) although the goods are identified to the contract the risk of loss and the title do not pass to the buyer until acceptance; and

   (b) use of the goods consistent with the purpose of trial is not acceptance but failure seasonably to notify the seller of election to return the goods is acceptance, and if the goods conform to the contract acceptance of any part is acceptance of the whole; and

   (c) after due notification of election to return, the return is at the seller's risk and expense but a merchant buyer must follow any reasonable instructions.

(2) Under a sale or return unless otherwise agreed

   (a) the option to return extends to the whole or any commercial unit of the goods while in substantially their original condition, but must be exercised seasonably; and

   (b) the return is at the buyer's risk and expense.

§ 2–328.   Sale by Auction.

(1) In a sale by auction if goods are put up in lots each lot is the subject of a separate sale.

(2) A sale by auction is complete when the auctioneer so announces by the fall of the hammer or in other customary manner. Where a bid is made while the hammer is falling in acceptance of a prior bid the auctioneer may in his discretion reopen the bidding or declare the goods sold under the bid on which the hammer was falling.

(3) Such a sale is with reserve unless the goods are in explicit terms put up without reserve. In an auction with reserve the auctioneer may withdraw the goods at any time until he announces completion of the sale. In an auction without reserve, after the auctioneer calls for bids on an article or lot, that article or lot cannot be withdrawn unless no bid is made within a reasonable time. In either case a bidder may retract his bid until the auctioneer's announcement of completion of the sale, but a bidder's retraction does not revive any previous bid.

(4) If the auctioneer knowingly receives a bid on the seller's behalf or the seller makes or procures such as bid, and notice has not been given that liberty for such bidding is reserved, the buyer may at his option avoid the sale or take the goods at the price of the last good faith bid prior to the completion of the sale. This subsection shall not apply to any bid at a forced sale.

Part 4   Title, Creditors and Good Faith Purchasers
§ 2–401.   Passing of Title; Reservation for Security; Limited Application of This Section.

Each provision of this Article with regard to the rights, obligations and remedies of the seller, the buyer, purchasers or other third parties applies irrespective of title to the goods except where the provision refers to such title. Insofar as situations are not covered by the other provisions of this Article and matters concerning title became material the following rules apply:

(1) Title to goods cannot pass under a contract for sale prior to their identification to the contract (Section 2–501), and unless otherwise explicitly agreed the buyer acquires by their identification a special property as limited by this Act. Any retention or reservation by the seller of the title (property) in goods shipped or delivered to the buyer is limited in effect to a reservation of a security interest. Subject to these provisions and to the provisions of the Article on Secured Transactions (Article 9), title to goods passes from the seller to the buyer in any manner and on any conditions explicitly agreed on by the parties.

(2) Unless otherwise explicitly agreed title passes to the buyer at the time and place at which the seller completes his performance with reference to the physical delivery of the goods, despite any reservation of a security interest and even though a document of title is to be delivered at a different time or place; and in particular and despite any reservation of a security interest by the bill of lading

   (a) if the contract requires or authorizes the seller to send the goods to the buyer but does not require him to deliver them at destination, title passes to the buyer at the time and place of shipment; but

   (b) if the contract requires delivery at destination, title passes on tender there.

(3) Unless otherwise explicitly agreed where delivery is to be made without moving the goods,

(a) if the seller is to deliver a document of title, title passes at the time when and the place where he delivers such documents; or

(b) if the goods are at the time of contracting already identified and no documents are to be delivered, title passes at the time and place of contracting.

(4) A rejection or other refusal by the buyer to receive or retain the goods, whether or not justified, or a justified revocation of acceptance revests title to the goods in the seller. Such revesting occurs by operation of law and is not a "sale".

§ 2–402.   Rights of Seller's Creditors Against Sold Goods.

(1) Except as provided in subsections (2) and (3), rights of unsecured creditors of the seller with respect to goods which have been identified to a contract for sale are subject to the buyer's rights to recover the goods under this Article (Sections 2–502 and 2–716).

(2) A creditor of the seller may treat a sale or an identification of goods to a contract for sale as void if as against him a retention of possession by the seller is fraudulent under any rule of law of the state where the goods are situated, except that retention of possession in good faith and current course of trade by a merchant-seller for a commercially reasonable time after a sale or identification is not fraudulent.

(3) Nothing in this Article shall be deemed to impair the rights of creditors of the seller

(a) under the provisions of the Article on Secured Transactions (Article 9); or

(b) where identification to the contract or delivery is made not in current course of trade but in satisfaction of or as security for a pre-existing claim for money, security or the like and is made under circumstances which under any rule of law of the state where the goods are situated would apart from this Article constitute the transaction a fraudulent transfer or voidable preference.

§ 2–403.   Power to Transfer; Good Faith Purchase of Goods; "Entrusting".

(1) A purchaser of goods acquires all title which his transferor had or had power to transfer except that a purchaser of a limited interest acquires rights only to the extent of the interest purchased. A person with voidable title has power to transfer a good title to a good faith purchaser for value. When goods have been delivered under a transaction of purchase the purchaser has such power even though

(a) the transferor was deceived as to the identity of the purchaser, or

(b) the delivery was in exchange for a check which is later dishonored, or

(c) it was agreed that the transaction was to be a "cash sale", or

(d) the delivery was procured through fraud punishable as larcenous under the criminal law.

(2) Any entrusting of possession of goods to a merchant who deals in goods of that kind gives him power to transfer all rights of the entruster to a buyer in ordinary course of business.

(3) "Entrusting" includes any delivery and any acquiescence in retention of possession regardless of any condition expressed between the parties to the delivery or acquiescence and regardless of whether the procurement of the entrusting or the possessor's disposition of the goods have been such as to be larcenous under the criminal law.

(4) The rights of other purchasers of goods and of lien creditors are governed by the Articles on Secured Transactions (Article 9), Bulk Transfers (Article 6) and Documents of Title (Article 7).

As amended in 1988.

Part 5   Performance

§ 2–501.   Insurable Interest in Goods; Manner of Identification of Goods.

(1) The buyer obtains a special property and an insurable interest in goods by identification of existing goods as goods to which the contract refers even though the goods so identified are nonconforming and he has an option to return or reject them. Such identification can be made at any time and in any manner explicitly agreed to by the parties. In the absence of explicit agreement identification occurs

(a) when the contract is made if it is for the sale of goods already existing and identified;

(b) if the contract is for the sale of future goods other than those described in paragraph (c), when goods are shipped, marked or otherwise designated by the seller as goods to which the contract refers;

(c) when the crops are planted or otherwise become growing crops or the young are conceived if the contract is for the sale of unborn young to be born within twelve months after contracting or for the sale of crops to be harvested within twelve months or the next normal harvest season after contracting whichever is longer.

(2) The seller retains an insurable interest in goods so long as title to or any security interest in the goods remains in him and where the identification is by the seller alone he may until default or insolvency or notification to the buyer that the identification is final substitute other goods for those identified.

(3) Nothing in this section impairs any insurable interest recognized under any other statute or rule of law.

§ 2–502.   Buyer's Right to Goods on Seller's Insolvency.

(1) Subject to subsections (2) and (3) and even though the goods have not been shipped a buyer who has paid a part or all of the price of goods in which he has a special property under the provisions of the immediately preceding section may on making and keeping good a tender of any unpaid portion of their price recover them from the seller if:

(a) in the case of goods bought for personal, family, or household purposes, the seller repudiates or fails to deliver as required by the contract; or

(b) in all cases, the seller becomes insolvent within ten days after receipt of the first installment on their price.

(2) The buyer's right to recover the goods under subsection (1)(a) vests upon acquisition of a special property, even if the seller had not then repudiated or failed to deliver.

(3) If the identification creating his special property has been made by the buyer he acquires the right to recover the goods only if they conform to the contract for sale.

As amended in 1999.

§ 2–503.   Manner of Seller's Tender of Delivery.

(1) Tender of delivery requires that the seller put and hold conforming goods at the buyer's disposition and give the buyer any notification reasonably necessary to enable him to take delivery. The manner, time and place for tender are determined by the agreement and this Article, and in particular

(a) tender must be at a reasonable hour, and if it is of goods they must be kept available for the period reasonably necessary to enable the buyer to take possession; but

(b) unless otherwise agreed the buyer must furnish facilities reasonably suited to the receipt of the goods.

(2) Where the case is within the next section respecting shipment tender requires that the seller comply with its provisions.

(3) Where the seller is required to deliver at a particular destination tender requires that he comply with subsection (1) and also in any appropriate case tender documents as described in subsections (4) and (5) of this section.

(4) Where goods are in the possession of a bailee and are to be delivered without being moved

(a) tender requires that the seller either tender a negotiable document of title covering such goods or procure acknowledgment by the bailee of the buyer's right to possession of the goods; but

(b) tender to the buyer of a non-negotiable document of title or of a written direction to the bailee to deliver is sufficient tender unless the buyer seasonably objects, and receipt by the bailee of notification of the buyer's rights fixes those rights as against the bailee and all third persons; but risk of loss of the goods and of any failure by the bailee to honor the non-negotiable document of title or to obey the direction remains on the seller until the buyer has had a reasonable time to present the document or direction, and a refusal by the bailee to honor the document or to obey the direction defeats the tender.

(5) Where the contract requires the seller to deliver documents

(a) he must tender all such documents in correct form, except as provided in this Article with respect to bills of lading in a set (subsection (2) of Section 2–323); and

(b) tender through customary banking channels is sufficient and dishonor of a draft accompanying the documents constitutes non-acceptance or rejection.

§ 2–504.   Shipment by Seller.

Where the seller is required or authorized to send the goods to the buyer and the contract does not require him to deliver them at a particular destination, then unless otherwise agreed he must

(a) put the goods in the possession of such a carrier and make such a contract for their transportation as may be reasonable having regard to the nature of the goods and other circumstances of the case; and

(b) obtain and promptly deliver or tender in due form any document necessary to enable the buyer to obtain possession of the goods or otherwise required by the agreement or by usage of trade; and

(c) promptly notify the buyer of the shipment.

Failure to notify the buyer under paragraph (c) or to make a proper contract under paragraph (a) is a ground for rejection only if material delay or loss ensues.

§ 2–505.   Seller's Shipment under Reservation.

(1) Where the seller has identified goods to the contract by or before shipment:

(a) his procurement of a negotiable bill of lading to his own order or otherwise reserves in him a security interest in the goods. His procurement of the bill to the order of a financing agency or of the buyer indicates in addition only the seller's expectation of transferring that interest to the person named.

(b) a non-negotiable bill of lading to himself or his nominee reserves possession of the goods as security but except in a case of conditional delivery (subsection (2) of Section 2–507) a non-negotiable bill of lading naming the buyer as consignee reserves no security interest even though the seller retains possession of the bill of lading.

(2) When shipment by the seller with reservation of a security interest is in violation of the contract for sale it constitutes an improper contract for transportation within the preceding section but impairs neither the rights given to the buyer by shipment and identification of the goods to the contract nor the seller's powers as a holder of a negotiable document.

§ 2–506.   Rights of Financing Agency.

(1) A financing agency by paying or purchasing for value a draft which relates to a shipment of goods acquires to the extent of the payment or purchase and in addition to its own rights under the draft and any document of title securing it any rights of the shipper in the goods including the right to stop delivery and the shipper's right to have the draft honored by the buyer.

(2) The right to reimbursement of a financing agency which has in good faith honored or purchased the draft under commitment to or authority from the buyer is not impaired by subsequent discovery of defects with reference to any relevant document which was apparently regular on its face.

§ 2–507.   Effect of Seller's Tender; Delivery on Condition.

(1) Tender of delivery is a condition to the buyer's duty to accept the goods and, unless otherwise agreed, to his duty to pay for them. Tender entitles the seller to acceptance of the goods and to payment according to the contract.

(2) Where payment is due and demanded on the delivery to the buyer of goods or documents of title, his right as against the seller to retain or dispose of them is conditional upon his making the payment due.

§ 2–508.   Cure by Seller of Improper Tender or Delivery; Replacement.

(1) Where any tender or delivery by the seller is rejected because non-conforming and the time for performance has not yet expired, the seller may seasonably notify the buyer of his intention to cure and may then within the contract time make a conforming delivery.

(2) Where the buyer rejects a non-conforming tender which the seller had reasonable grounds to believe would be acceptable with or without money allowance the seller may if he seasonably notifies the buyer have a further reasonable time to substitute a conforming tender.

§ 2–509.   Risk of Loss in the Absence of Breach.

(1) Where the contract requires or authorizes the seller to ship the goods by carrier

   (a) if it does not require him to deliver them at a particular destination, the risk of loss passes to the buyer when the goods are duly delivered to the carrier even though the shipment is under reservation (Section 2–505); but

   (b) if it does require him to deliver them at a particular destination and the goods are there duly tendered while in the possession of the carrier, the risk of loss passes to the buyer when the goods are there duly so tendered as to enable the buyer to take delivery.

(2) Where the goods are held by a bailee to be delivered without being moved, the risk of loss passes to the buyer

   (a) on his receipt of a negotiable document of title covering the goods; or

   (b) on acknowledgment by the bailee of the buyer's right to possession of the goods; or

   (c) after his receipt of a non-negotiable document of title or other written direction to deliver, as provided in subsection (4)(b) of Section 2–503.

(3) In any case not within subsection (1) or (2), the risk of loss passes to the buyer on his receipt of the goods if the seller is a merchant; otherwise the risk passes to the buyer on tender of delivery.

(4) The provisions of this section are subject to contrary agreement of the parties and to the provisions of this Article on sale on approval (Section 2–327) and on effect of breach on risk of loss (Section 2–510).

§ 2–510.   Effect of Breach on Risk of Loss.

(1) Where a tender or delivery of goods so fails to conform to the contract as to give a right of rejection the risk of their loss remains on the seller until cure or acceptance.

(2) Where the buyer rightfully revokes acceptance he may to the extent of any deficiency in his effective insurance coverage treat the risk of loss as having rested on the seller from the beginning.

(3) Where the buyer as to conforming goods already identified to the contract for sale repudiates or is otherwise in breach before risk of their loss has passed to him, the seller may to the extent of any deficiency in his effective insurance coverage treat the risk of loss as resting on the buyer for a commercially reasonable time.

§ 2–511.   Tender of Payment by Buyer; Payment by Check.

(1) Unless otherwise agreed tender of payment is a condition to the seller's duty to tender and complete any delivery.

(2) Tender of payment is sufficient when made by any means or in any manner current in the ordinary course of business unless the seller demands payment in legal tender and gives any extension of time reasonably necessary to procure it.

(3) Subject to the provisions of this Act on the effect of an instrument on an obligation (Section 3–310), payment by check is conditional and is defeated as between the parties by dishonor of the check on due presentment.

As amended in 1994.

§ 2–512.   Payment by Buyer Before Inspection.

(1) Where the contract requires payment before inspection non-conformity of the goods does not excuse the buyer from so making payment unless

   (a) the non-conformity appears without inspection; or

   (b) despite tender of the required documents the circumstances would justify injunction against honor under this Act (Section 5–109(b)).

(2) Payment pursuant to subsection (1) does not constitute an acceptance of goods or impair the buyer's right to inspect or any of his remedies.

As amended in 1995.

§ 2–513.   Buyer's Right to Inspection of Goods.

(1) Unless otherwise agreed and subject to subsection (3), where goods are tendered or delivered or identified to the contract for sale, the buyer has a right before payment or acceptance to inspect them at any reasonable place and time and in any reasonable manner. When the seller is required or authorized to send the goods to the buyer, the inspection may be after their arrival.

(2) Expenses of inspection must be borne by the buyer but may be recovered from the seller if the goods do not conform and are rejected.

(3) Unless otherwise agreed and subject to the provisions of this Article on C.I.F. contracts (subsection (3) of Section 2–321), the buyer is not entitled to inspect the goods before payment of the price when the contract provides

   (a) for delivery "C.O.D." or on other like terms; or

   (b) for payment against documents of title, except where such payment is due only after the goods are to become available for inspection.

(4) A place or method of inspection fixed by the parties is presumed to be exclusive but unless otherwise expressly agreed it does not postpone identification or shift the place for delivery or for passing the risk of loss. If compliance becomes impossible, inspection shall be as provided in this section unless the place or method fixed was clearly intended as an indispensable condition failure of which avoids the contract.

§ 2-514.   When Documents Deliverable on Acceptance; When on Payment.

Unless otherwise agreed documents against which a draft is drawn are to be delivered to the drawee on acceptance of the draft if it is payable more than three days after presentment; otherwise, only on payment.

§ 2-515.   Preserving Evidence of Goods in Dispute.

In furtherance of the adjustment of any claim or dispute

(a) either party on reasonable notification to the other and for the purpose of ascertaining the facts and preserving evidence has the right to inspect, test and sample the goods including such of them as may be in the possession or control of the other; and

(b) the parties may agree to a third party inspection or survey to determine the conformity or condition of the goods and may agree that the findings shall be binding upon them in any subsequent litigation or adjustment.

Part 6   Breach, Repudiation and Excuse
§ 2-601.   Buyer's Rights on Improper Delivery.

Subject to the provisions of this Article on breach in installment contracts (Section 2-612) and unless otherwise agreed under the sections on contractual limitations of remedy (Sections 2-718 and 2-719), if the goods or the tender of delivery fail in any respect to conform to the contract, the buyer may

(a) reject the whole; or

(b) accept the whole; or

(c) accept any commercial unit or units and reject the rest.

§ 2-602.   Manner and Effect of Rightful Rejection.

(1) Rejection of goods must be within a reasonable time after their delivery or tender. It is ineffective unless the buyer seasonably notifies the seller.

(2) Subject to the provisions of the two following sections on rejected goods (Sections 2-603 and 2-604),

(a) after rejection any exercise of ownership by the buyer with respect to any commercial unit is wrongful as against the seller; and

(b) if the buyer has before rejection taken physical possession of goods in which he does not have a security interest under the provisions of this Article (subsection (3) of Section 2-711), he is under a duty after rejection to hold them with reasonable care at the seller's disposition for a time sufficient to permit the seller to remove them; but

(c) the buyer has no further obligations with regard to goods rightfully rejected.

(3) The seller's rights with respect to goods wrongfully rejected are governed by the provisions of this Article on Seller's remedies in general (Section 2-703).

§ 2-603.   Merchant Buyer's Duties as to Rightfully Rejected Goods.

(1) Subject to any security interest in the buyer (subsection (3) of Section 2-711), when the seller has no agent or place of business at the market of rejection a merchant buyer is under a duty after rejection of goods in his possession or control to follow any reasonable instructions received from the seller with respect to the goods and in the absence of such instructions to make reasonable efforts to sell them for the seller's account if they are perishable or threaten to decline in value speedily. Instructions are not reasonable if on demand indemnity for expenses is not forthcoming.

(2) When the buyer sells goods under subsection (1), he is entitled to reimbursement from the seller or out of the proceeds for reasonable expenses of caring for and selling them, and if the expenses include no selling commission then to such commission as is usual in the trade or if there is none to a reasonable sum not exceeding ten per cent on the gross proceeds.

(3) In complying with this section the buyer is held only to good faith and good faith conduct hereunder is neither acceptance nor conversion nor the basis of an action for damages.

§ 2-604.   Buyer's Options as to Salvage of Rightfully Rejected Goods.

Subject to the provisions of the immediately preceding section on perishables if the seller gives no instructions within a reasonable time after notification of rejection the buyer may store the rejected goods for the seller's account or reship them to him or resell them for the seller's account with reimbursement as provided in the preceding section. Such action is not acceptance or conversion.

§ 2-605.   Waiver of Buyer's Objections by Failure to Particularize.

(1) The buyer's failure to state in connection with rejection a particular defect which is ascertainable by reasonable inspection precludes him from relying on the unstated defect to justify rejection or to establish breach

(a) where the seller could have cured it if stated seasonably; or

(b) between merchants when the seller has after rejection made a request in writing for a full and final written statement of all defects on which the buyer proposes to rely.

(2) Payment against documents made without reservation of rights precludes recovery of the payment for defects apparent on the face of the documents.

§ 2-606.   What Constitutes Acceptance of Goods.

(1) Acceptance of goods occurs when the buyer

(a) after a reasonable opportunity to inspect the goods signifies to the seller that the goods are conforming or that he will take or retain them in spite of their nonconformity; or

(b) fails to make an effective rejection (subsection (1) of Section 2–602), but such acceptance does not occur until the buyer has had a reasonable opportunity to inspect them; or

(c) does any act inconsistent with the seller's ownership; but if such act is wrongful as against the seller it is an acceptance only if ratified by him.

(2) Acceptance of a part of any commercial unit is acceptance of that entire unit.

§ 2–607.   Effect of Acceptance; Notice of Breach; Burden of Establishing Breach After Acceptance; Notice of Claim or Litigation to Person Answerable Over.

(1) The buyer must pay at the contract rate for any goods accepted.

(2) Acceptance of goods by the buyer precludes rejection of the goods accepted and if made with knowledge of a non-conformity cannot be revoked because of it unless the acceptance was on the reasonable assumption that the non-conformity would be seasonably cured but acceptance does not of itself impair any other remedy provided by this Article for non-conformity.

(3) Where a tender has been accepted

(a) the buyer must within a reasonable time after he discovers or should have discovered any breach notify the seller of breach or be barred from any remedy; and

(b) if the claim is one for infringement or the like (subsection (3) of Section 2–312) and the buyer is sued as a result of such a breach he must so notify the seller within a reasonable time after he receives notice of the litigation or be barred from any remedy over for liability established by the litigation.

(4) The burden is on the buyer to establish any breach with respect to the goods accepted.

(5) Where the buyer is sued for breach of a warranty or other obligation for which his seller is answerable over

(a) he may give his seller written notice of the litigation. If the notice states that the seller may come in and defend and that if the seller does not do so he will be bound in any action against him by his buyer by any determination of fact common to the two litigations, then unless the seller after seasonable receipt of the notice does come in and defend he is so bound.

(b) if the claim is one for infringement or the like (subsection (3) of Section 2–312) the original seller may demand in writing that his buyer turn over to him control of the litigation including settlement or else be barred from any remedy over and if he also agrees to bear all expense and to satisfy any adverse judgment, then unless the buyer after seasonable receipt of the demand does turn over control the buyer is so barred.

(6) The provisions of subsections (3), (4) and (5) apply to any obligation of a buyer to hold the seller harmless against infringement or the like (subsection (3) of Section 2–312).

§ 2–608.   Revocation of Acceptance in Whole or in Part.

(1) The buyer may revoke his acceptance of a lot or commercial unit whose non-conformity substantially impairs its value to him if he has accepted it

(a) on the reasonable assumption that its nonconformity would be cured and it has not been seasonably cured; or

(b) without discovery of such non-conformity if his acceptance was reasonably induced either by the difficulty of discovery before acceptance or by the seller's assurances.

(2) Revocation of acceptance must occur within a reasonable time after the buyer discovers or should have discovered the ground for it and before any substantial change in condition of the goods which is not caused by their own defects. It is not effective until the buyer notifies the seller of it.

(3) A buyer who so revokes has the same rights and duties with regard to the goods involved as if he had rejected them.

§ 2–609.   Right to Adequate Assurance of Performance.

(1) A contract for sale imposes an obligation on each party that the other's expectation of receiving due performance will not be impaired. When reasonable grounds for insecurity arise with respect to the performance of either party the other may in writing demand adequate assurance of due performance and until he receives such assurance may if commercially reasonable suspend any performance for which he has not already received the agreed return.

(2) Between merchants the reasonableness of grounds for insecurity and the adequacy of any assurance offered shall be determined according to commercial standards.

(3) Acceptance of any improper delivery or payment does not prejudice the party's right to demand adequate assurance of future performance.

(4) After receipt of a justified demand failure to provide within a reasonable time not exceeding thirty days such assurance of due performance as is adequate under the circumstances of the particular case is a repudiation of the contract.

§ 2–610.   Anticipatory Repudiation.

When either party repudiates the contract with respect to a performance not yet due the loss of which will substantially impair the value of the contract to the other, the aggrieved party may

(a) for a commercially reasonable time await performance by the repudiating party; or

(b) resort to any remedy for breach (Section 2–703 or Section 2–711), even though he has notified the repudiating party that he would await the latter's performance and has urged retraction; and

(c) in either case suspend his own performance or proceed in accordance with the provisions of this Article on the seller's right to identify goods to the contract notwithstanding breach or to salvage unfinished goods (Section 2–704).

§ 2–611.   Retraction of Anticipatory Repudiation.

(1) Until the repudiating party's next performance is due he can retract his repudiation unless the aggrieved party has since the repudiation cancelled or materially changed his position or otherwise indicated that he considers the repudiation final.

(2) Retraction may be by any method which clearly indicates to the aggrieved party that the repudiating party intends to perform,

but must include any assurance justifiably demanded under the provisions of this Article (Section 2–609).

(3) Retraction reinstates the repudiating party's rights under the contract with due excuse and allowance to the aggrieved party for any delay occasioned by the repudiation.

§ 2–612. "Installment Contract"; Breach.

(1) An "installment contract" is one which requires or authorizes the delivery of goods in separate lots to be separately accepted, even though the contract contains a clause "each delivery is a separate contract" or its equivalent.

(2) The buyer may reject any installment which is non-conforming if the non-conformity substantially impairs the value of that installment and cannot be cured or if the non-conformity is a defect in the required documents; but if the non-conformity does not fall within subsection (3) and the seller gives adequate assurance of its cure the buyer must accept that installment.

(3) Whenever non-conformity or default with respect to one or more installments substantially impairs the value of the whole contract there is a breach of the whole. But the aggrieved party reinstates the contract if he accepts a non-conforming installment without seasonably notifying of cancellation or if he brings an action with respect only to past installments or demands performance as to future installments.

§ 2–613. Casualty to Identified Goods.

Where the contract requires for its performance goods identified when the contract is made, and the goods suffer casualty without fault of either party before the risk of loss passes to the buyer, or in a proper case under a "no arrival, no sale" term (Section 2–324) then

(a) if the loss is total the contract is avoided; and

(b) if the loss is partial or the goods have so deteriorated as no longer to conform to the contract the buyer may nevertheless demand inspection and at his option either treat the contract as voided or accept the goods with due allowance from the contract price for the deterioration or the deficiency in quantity but without further right against the seller.

§ 2–614. Substituted Performance.

(1) Where without fault of either party the agreed berthing, loading, or unloading facilities fail or an agreed type of carrier becomes unavailable or the agreed manner of delivery otherwise becomes commercially impracticable but a commercially reasonable substitute is available, such substitute performance must be tendered and accepted.

(2) If the agreed means or manner of payment fails because of domestic or foreign governmental regulation, the seller may withhold or stop delivery unless the buyer provides a means or manner of payment which is commercially a substantial equivalent. If delivery has already been taken, payment by the means or in the manner provided by the regulation discharges the buyer's obligation unless the regulation is discriminatory, oppressive or predatory.

§ 2–615. Excuse by Failure of Presupposed Conditions.

Except so far as a seller may have assumed a greater obligation and subject to the preceding section on substituted performance:

(a) Delay in delivery or non-delivery in whole or in part by a seller who complies with paragraphs (b) and (c) is not a breach of his duty under a contract for sale if performance as agreed has been made impracticable by the occurrence of a contingency the nonoccurrence of which was a basic assumption on which the contract was made or by compliance in good faith with any applicable foreign or domestic governmental regulation or order whether or not it later proves to be invalid.

(b) Where the causes mentioned in paragraph (a) affect only a part of the seller's capacity to perform, he must allocate production and deliveries among his customers but may at his option include regular customers not then under contract as well as his own requirements for further manufacture. He may so allocate in any manner which is fair and reasonable.

(c) The seller must notify the buyer seasonably that there will be delay or non-delivery and, when allocation is required under paragraph (b), of the estimated quota thus made available for the buyer.

§ 2–616. Procedure on Notice Claiming Excuse.

(1) Where the buyer receives notification of a material or indefinite delay or an allocation justified under the preceding section he may by written notification to the seller as to any delivery concerned, and where the prospective deficiency substantially impairs the value of the whole contract under the provisions of this Article relating to breach of installment contracts (Section 2–612), then also as to the whole,

(a) terminate and thereby discharge any unexecuted portion of the contract; or

(b) modify the contract by agreeing to take his available quota in substitution.

(2) If after receipt of such notification from the seller the buyer fails so to modify the contract within a reasonable time not exceeding thirty days the contract lapses with respect to any deliveries affected.

(3) The provisions of this section may not be negated by agreement except in so far as the seller has assumed a greater obligation under the preceding section.

Part 7 Remedies
§ 2–701. Remedies for Breach of Collateral Contracts Not Impaired.

Remedies for breach of any obligation or promise collateral or ancillary to a contract for sale are not impaired by the provisions of this Article.

§ 2–702. Seller's Remedies on Discovery of Buyer's Insolvency.

(1) Where the seller discovers the buyer to be insolvent he may refuse delivery except for cash including payment for all goods theretofore delivered under the contract, and stop delivery under this Article (Section 2–705).

(2) Where the seller discovers that the buyer has received goods on credit while insolvent he may reclaim the goods upon demand

made within ten days after the receipt, but if misrepresentation of solvency has been made to the particular seller in writing within three months before delivery the ten day limitation does not apply. Except as provided in this subsection the seller may not base a right to reclaim goods on the buyer's fraudulent or innocent misrepresentation of solvency or of intent to pay.

(3) The seller's right to reclaim under subsection (2) is subject to the rights of a buyer in ordinary course or other good faith purchaser under this Article (Section 2–403). Successful reclamation of goods excludes all other remedies with respect to them.

§ 2–703.   Seller's Remedies in General.

Where the buyer wrongfully rejects or revokes acceptance of goods or fails to make a payment due on or before delivery or repudiates with respect to a part or the whole, then with respect to any goods directly affected and, if the breach is of the whole contract (Section 2–612), then also with respect to the whole undelivered balance, the aggrieved seller may

(a) withhold delivery of such goods;

(b) stop delivery by any bailee as hereafter provided (Section 2–705);

(c) proceed under the next section respecting goods still unidentified to the contract;

(d) resell and recover damages as hereafter provided (Section 2–706);

(e) recover damages for non-acceptance (Section 2–708) or in a proper case the price (Section 2–709);

(f) cancel.

§ 2–704.   Seller's Right to Identify Goods to the Contract Notwithstanding Breach or to Salvage Unfinished Goods.

(1) An aggrieved seller under the preceding section may

(a) identify to the contract conforming goods not already identified if at the time he learned of the breach they are in his possession or control;

(b) treat as the subject of resale goods which have demonstrably been intended for the particular contract even though those goods are unfinished.

(2) Where the goods are unfinished an aggrieved seller may in the exercise of reasonable commercial judgment for the purposes of avoiding loss and of effective realization either complete the manufacture and wholly identify the goods to the contract or cease manufacture and resell for scrap or salvage value or proceed in any other reasonable manner.

§ 2–705.   Seller's Stoppage of Delivery in Transit or Otherwise.

(1) The seller may stop delivery of goods in the possession of a carrier or other bailee when he discovers the buyer to be insolvent (Section 2–702) and may stop delivery of carload, truckload, planeload or larger shipments of express or freight when the buyer repudiates or fails to make a payment due before delivery or if for any other reason the seller has a right to withhold or reclaim the goods.

(2) As against such buyer the seller may stop delivery until

(a) receipt of the goods by the buyer; or

(b) acknowledgment to the buyer by any bailee of the goods except a carrier that the bailee holds the goods for the buyer; or

(c) such acknowledgment to the buyer by a carrier by reshipment or as warehouseman; or

(d) negotiation to the buyer of any negotiable document of title covering the goods.

(3) (a) To stop delivery the seller must so notify as to enable the bailee by reasonable diligence to prevent delivery of the goods.

(b) After such notification the bailee must hold and deliver the goods according to the directions of the seller but the seller is liable to the bailee for any ensuing charges or damages.

(c) If a negotiable document of title has been issued for goods the bailee is not obliged to obey a notification to stop until surrender of the document.

(d) A carrier who has issued a non-negotiable bill of lading is not obliged to obey a notification to stop received from a person other than the consignor.

§ 2–706.   Seller's Resale Including Contract for Resale.

(1) Under the conditions stated in Section 2–703 on seller's remedies, the seller may resell the goods concerned or the undelivered balance thereof. Where the resale is made in good faith and in a commercially reasonable manner the seller may recover the difference between the resale price and the contract price together with any incidental damages allowed under the provisions of this Article (Section 2–710), but less expenses saved in consequence of the buyer's breach.

(2) Except as otherwise provided in subsection (3) or unless otherwise agreed resale may be at public or private sale including sale by way of one or more contracts to sell or of identification to an existing contract of the seller. Sale may be as a unit or in parcels and at any time and place and on any terms but every aspect of the sale including the method, manner, time, place and terms must be commercially reasonable. The resale must be reasonably identified as referring to the broken contract, but it is not necessary that the goods be in existence or that any or all of them have been identified to the contract before the breach.

(3) Where the resale is at private sale the seller must give the buyer reasonable notification of his intention to resell.

(4) Where the resale is at public sale

(a) only identified goods can be sold except where there is a recognized market for a public sale of futures in goods of the kind; and

(b) it must be made at a usual place or market for public sale if one is reasonably available and except in the case of goods which are perishable or threaten to decline in value speedily the seller must give the buyer reasonable notice of the time and place of the resale; and

(c) if the goods are not to be within the view of those attending the sale the notification of sale must state the place where the goods are located and provide for their reasonable inspection by prospective bidders; and

(d) the seller may buy.

(5) A purchaser who buys in good faith at a resale takes the goods free of any rights of the original buyer even though the seller fails to comply with one or more of the requirements of this section.

(6) The seller is not accountable to the buyer for any profit made on any resale. A person in the position of a seller (Section 2–707) or a buyer who has rightfully rejected or justifiably revoked acceptance must account for any excess over the amount of his security interest, as hereinafter defined (subsection (3) of Section 2–711).

§ 2–707.   "Person in the Position of a Seller".

(1) A "person in the position of a seller" includes as against a principal an agent who has paid or become responsible for the price of goods on behalf of his principal or anyone who otherwise holds a security interest or other right in goods similar to that of a seller.

(2) A person in the position of a seller may as provided in this Article withhold or stop delivery (Section 2–705) and resell (Section 2–706) and recover incidental damages (Section 2–710).

§ 2–708.   Seller's Damages for Non-Acceptance or Repudiation.

(1) Subject to subsection (2) and to the provisions of this Article with respect to proof of market price (Section 2–723), the measure of damages for non-acceptance or repudiation by the buyer is the difference between the market price at the time and place for tender and the unpaid contract price together with any incidental damages provided in this Article (Section 2–710), but less expenses saved in consequence of the buyer's breach.

(2) If the measure of damages provided in subsection (1) is inadequate to put the seller in as good a position as performance would have done then the measure of damages is the profit (including reasonable overhead) which the seller would have made from full performance by the buyer, together with any incidental damages provided in this Article (Section 2–710), due allowance for costs reasonably incurred and due credit for payments or proceeds of resale.

§ 2–709.   Action for the Price.

(1) When the buyer fails to pay the price as it becomes due the seller may recover, together with any incidental damages under the next section, the price

(a) of goods accepted or of conforming goods lost or damaged within a commercially reasonable time after risk of their loss has passed to the buyer; and

(b) of goods identified to the contract if the seller is unable after reasonable effort to resell them at a reasonable price or the circumstances reasonably indicate that such effort will be unavailing.

(2) Where the seller sues for the price he must hold for the buyer any goods which have been identified to the contract and are still in his control except that if resale becomes possible he may resell them at any time prior to the collection of the judgment. The net

proceeds of any such resale must be credited to the buyer and payment of the judgment entitles him to any goods not resold.

(3) After the buyer has wrongfully rejected or revoked acceptance of the goods or has failed to make a payment due or has repudiated (Section 2–610), a seller who is held not entitled to the price under this section shall nevertheless be awarded damages for non-acceptance under the preceding section.

§ 2–710.   Seller's Incidental Damages.

Incidental damages to an aggrieved seller include any commercially reasonable charges, expenses or commissions incurred in stopping delivery, in the transportation, care and custody of goods after the buyer's breach, in connection with return or resale of the goods or otherwise resulting from the breach.

§ 2–711.   Buyer's Remedies in General; Buyer's Security Interest in Rejected Goods.

(1) Where the seller fails to make delivery or repudiates or the buyer rightfully rejects or justifiably revokes acceptance then with respect to any goods involved, and with respect to the whole if the breach goes to the whole contract (Section 2–612), the buyer may cancel and whether or not he has done so may in addition to recovering so much of the price as has been paid

(a) "cover" and have damages under the next section as to all the goods affected whether or not they have been identified to the contract; or

(b) recover damages for non-delivery as provided in this Article (Section 2–713).

(2) Where the seller fails to deliver or repudiates the buyer may also

(a) if the goods have been identified recover them as provided in this Article (Section 2–502); or

(b) in a proper case obtain specific performance or replevy the goods as provided in this Article (Section 2–716).

(3) On rightful rejection or justifiable revocation of acceptance a buyer has a security interest in goods in his possession or control for any payments made on their price and any expenses reasonably incurred in their inspection, receipt, transportation, care and custody and may hold such goods and resell them in like manner as an aggrieved seller (Section 2–706).

§ 2–712.   "Cover"; Buyer's Procurement of Substitute Goods.

(1) After a breach within the preceding section the buyer may "cover" by making in good faith and without unreasonable delay any reasonable purchase of or contract to purchase goods in substitution for those due from the seller.

(2) The buyer may recover from the seller as damages the difference between the cost of cover and the contract price together with any incidental or consequential damages as hereinafter defined (Section 2–715), but less expenses saved in consequence of the seller's breach.

(3) Failure of the buyer to effect cover within this section does not bar him from any other remedy.

§ 2–713.   Buyer's Damages for Non-Delivery or Repudiation.

(1) Subject to the provisions of this Article with respect to proof of market price (Section 2–723), the measure of damages for non-delivery or repudiation by the seller is the difference between the market price at the time when the buyer learned of the breach and the contract price together with any incidental and consequential damages provided in this Article (Section 2–715), but less expenses saved in consequence of the seller's breach.

(2) Market price is to be determined as of the place for tender or, in cases of rejection after arrival or revocation of acceptance, as of the place of arrival.

§ 2–714.   Buyer's Damages for Breach in Regard to Accepted Goods.

(1) Where the buyer has accepted goods and given notification (subsection (3) of Section 2–607) he may recover as damages for any non-conformity of tender the loss resulting in the ordinary course of events from the seller's breach as determined in any manner which is reasonable.

(2) The measure of damages for breach of warranty is the difference at the time and place of acceptance between the value of the goods accepted and the value they would have had if they had been as warranted, unless special circumstances show proximate damages of a different amount.

(3) In a proper case any incidental and consequential damages under the next section may also be recovered.

§ 2–715.   Buyer's Incidental and Consequential Damages.

(1) Incidental damages resulting from the seller's breach include expenses reasonably incurred in inspection, receipt, transportation and care and custody of goods rightfully rejected, any commercially reasonable charges, expenses or commissions in connection with effecting cover and any other reasonable expense incident to the delay or other breach.

(2) Consequential damages resulting from the seller's breach include

(a) any loss resulting from general or particular requirements and needs of which the seller at the time of contracting had reason to know and which could not reasonably be prevented by cover or otherwise; and

(b) injury to person or property proximately resulting from any breach of warranty.

§ 2–716.   Buyer's Right to Specific Performance or Replevin.

(1) Specific performance may be decreed where the goods are unique or in other proper circumstances.

(2) The decree for specific performance may include such terms and conditions as to payment of the price, damages, or other relief as the court may deem just.

(3) The buyer has a right of replevin for goods identified to the contract if after reasonable effort he is unable to effect cover for such goods or the circumstances reasonably indicate that such effort will be unavailing or if the goods have been shipped under reservation and satisfaction of the security interest in them has been made or tendered. In the case of goods bought for personal, family, or household purposes, the buyer's right of replevin vests upon acquisition of a special property, even if the seller had not then repudiated or failed to deliver.

As amended in 1999.

§ 2–717.   Deduction of Damages From the Price.

The buyer on notifying the seller of his intention to do so may deduct all or any part of the damages resulting from any breach of the contract from any part of the price still due under the same contract.

§ 2–718.   Liquidation or Limitation of Damages; Deposits.

(1) Damages for breach by either party may be liquidated in the agreement but only at an amount which is reasonable in the light of the anticipated or actual harm caused by the breach, the difficulties of proof of loss, and the inconvenience or nonfeasibility of otherwise obtaining an adequate remedy. A term fixing unreasonably large liquidated damages is void as a penalty.

(2) Where the seller justifiably withholds delivery of goods because of the buyer's breach, the buyer is entitled to restitution of any amount by which the sum of his payments exceeds

(a) the amount to which the seller is entitled by virtue of terms liquidating the seller's damages in accordance with subsection (1), or

(b) in the absence of such terms, twenty per cent of the value of the total performance for which the buyer is obligated under the contract or $500, whichever is smaller.

(3) The buyer's right to restitution under subsection (2) is subject to offset to the extent that the seller establishes

(a) a right to recover damages under the provisions of this Article other than subsection (1), and

(b) the amount or value of any benefits received by the buyer directly or indirectly by reason of the contract.

(4) Where a seller has received payment in goods their reasonable value or the proceeds of their resale shall be treated as payments for the purposes of subsection (2); but if the seller has notice of the buyer's breach before reselling goods received in part performance, his resale is subject to the conditions laid down in this Article on resale by an aggrieved seller (Section 2–706).

§ 2–719.   Contractual Modification or Limitation of Remedy.

(1) Subject to the provisions of subsections (2) and (3) of this section and of the preceding section on liquidation and limitation of damages,

(a) the agreement may provide for remedies in addition to or in substitution for those provided in this Article and may limit or alter the measure of damages recoverable under this Article, as by limiting the buyer's remedies to return of the goods and repayment of the price or to repair and replacement of nonconforming goods or parts; and

(b) resort to a remedy as provided is optional unless the remedy is expressly agreed to be exclusive, in which case it is the sole remedy.

(2) Where circumstances cause an exclusive or limited remedy to fail of its essential purpose, remedy may be had as provided in this Act.

(3) Consequential damages may be limited or excluded unless the limitation or exclusion is unconscionable. Limitation of consequential damages for injury to the person in the case of consumer goods is *prima facie* unconscionable but limitation of damages where the loss is commercial is not.

§ 2–720. Effect of "Cancellation" or "Rescission" on Claims for Antecedent Breach.

Unless the contrary intention clearly appears, expressions of "cancellation" or "rescission" of the contract or the like shall not be construed as a renunciation or discharge of any claim in damages for an antecedent breach.

§ 2–721. Remedies for Fraud.

Remedies for material misrepresentation or fraud include all remedies available under this Article for non-fraudulent breach. Neither rescission or a claim for rescission of the contract for sale nor rejection or return of the goods shall bar or be deemed inconsistent with a claim for damages or other remedy.

§ 2–722. Who Can Sue Third Parties for Injury to Goods.

Where a third party so deals with goods which have been identified to a contract for sale as to cause actionable injury to a party to that contract

(a) a right of action against the third party is in either party to the contract for sale who has title to or a security interest or a special property or an insurable interest in the goods; and if the goods have been destroyed or converted a right of action is also in the party who either bore the risk of loss under the contract for sale or has since the injury assumed that risk as against the other;

(b) if at the time of the injury the party plaintiff did not bear the risk of loss as against the other party to the contract for sale and there is no arrangement between them for disposition of the recovery, his suit or settlement is, subject to his own interest, as a fiduciary for the other party to the contract;

(c) either party may with the consent of the other sue for the benefit of whom it may concern.

§ 2–723. Proof of Market Price: Time and Place.

(1) If an action based on anticipatory repudiation comes to trial before the time for performance with respect to some or all of the goods, any damages based on market price (Section 2–708 or Section 2–713) shall be determined according to the price of such goods prevailing at the time when the aggrieved party learned of the repudiation.

(2) If evidence of a price prevailing at the times or places described in this Article is not readily available the price prevailing within any reasonable time before or after the time described or at any other place which in commercial judgment or under usage of trade would serve as a reasonable substitute for the one described may be used, making any proper allowance for the cost of transporting the goods to or from such other place.

(3) Evidence of a relevant price prevailing at a time or place other than the one described in this Article offered by one party is not admissible unless and until he has given the other party such notice as the court finds sufficient to prevent unfair surprise.

§ 2–724. Admissibility of Market Quotations.

Whenever the prevailing price or value of any goods regularly bought and sold in any established commodity market is in issue, reports in official publications or trade journals or in newspapers or periodicals of general circulation published as the reports of such market shall be admissible in evidence. The circumstances of the preparation of such a report may be shown to affect its weight but not its admissibility.

§ 2–725. Statute of Limitations in Contracts for Sale.

(1) An action for breach of any contract for sale must be commenced within four years after the cause of action has accrued. By the original agreement the parties may reduce the period of limitation to not less than one year but may not extend it.

(2) A cause of action accrues when the breach occurs, regardless of the aggrieved party's lack of knowledge of the breach. A breach of warranty occurs when tender of delivery is made, except that where a warranty explicitly extends to future performance of the goods and discovery of the breach must await the time of such performance the cause of action accrues when the breach is or should have been discovered.

(3) Where an action commenced within the time limited by subsection (1) is so terminated as to leave available a remedy by another action for the same breach such other action may be commenced after the expiration of the time limited and within six months after the termination of the first action unless the termination resulted from voluntary discontinuance or from dismissal for failure or neglect to prosecute.

(4) This section does not alter the law on tolling of the statute of limitations nor does it apply to causes of action which have accrued before this Act becomes effective.

Article 2A
LEASES

Part 1 General Provisions

§ 2A–101. Short Title.

This Article shall be known and may be cited as the Uniform Commercial Code—Leases.

§ 2A–102. Scope.

This Article applies to any transaction, regardless of form, that creates a lease.

§ 2A–103.   Definitions and Index of Definitions.

(1) In this Article unless the context otherwise requires:

(a) "Buyer in ordinary course of business" means a person who in good faith and without knowledge that the sale to him [or her] is in violation of the ownership rights or security interest or leasehold interest of a third party in the goods buys in ordinary course from a person in the business of selling goods of that kind but does not include a pawnbroker. "Buying" may be for cash or by exchange of other property or on secured or unsecured credit and includes receiving goods or documents of title under a pre-existing contract for sale but does not include a transfer in bulk or as security for or in total or partial satisfaction of a money debt.

(b) "Cancellation" occurs when either party puts an end to the lease contract for default by the other party.

(c) "Commercial unit" means such a unit of goods as by commercial usage is a single whole for purposes of lease and division of which materially impairs its character or value on the market or in use. A commercial unit may be a single article, as a machine, or a set of articles, as a suite of furniture or a line of machinery, or a quantity, as a gross or carload, or any other unit treated in use or in the relevant market as a single whole.

(d) "Conforming" goods or performance under a lease contract means goods or performance that are in accordance with the obligations under the lease contract.

(e) "Consumer lease" means a lease that a lessor regularly engaged in the business of leasing or selling makes to a lessee who is an individual and who takes under the lease primarily for a personal, family, or household purpose [, if the total payments to be made under the lease contract, excluding payments for options to renew or buy, do not exceed $_____].

(f) "Fault" means wrongful act, omission, breach, or default.

(g) "Finance lease" means a lease with respect to which:

(i) the lessor does not select, manufacture or supply the goods;

(ii) the lessor acquires the goods or the right to possession and use of the goods in connection with the lease; and

(iii) one of the following occurs:

(A) the lessee receives a copy of the contract by which the lessor acquired the goods or the right to possession and use of the goods before signing the lease contract;

(B) the lessee's approval of the contract by which the lessor acquired the goods or the right to possession and use of the goods is a condition to effectiveness of the lease contract;

(C) the lessee, before signing the lease contract, receives an accurate and complete statement designating the promises and warranties, and any disclaimers of warranties, limitations or modifications of remedies, or liquidated damages, including those of a third party, such as the manufacturer of the goods, provided to the lessor by the person supplying the goods in connection with or as part of the contract by which the lessor acquired the goods or the right to possession and use of the goods; or

(D) if the lease is not a consumer lease, the lessor, before the lessee signs the lease contract, informs the lessee in writing (a) of the identity of the person supplying the goods to the lessor, unless the lessee has selected that person and directed the lessor to acquire the goods or the right to possession and use of the goods from that person, (b) that the lessee is entitled under this Article to any promises and warranties, including those of any third party, provided to the lessor by the person supplying the goods in connection with or as part of the contract by which the lessor acquired the goods or the right to possession and use of the goods, and (c) that the lessee may communicate with the person supplying the goods to the lessor and receive an accurate and complete statement of those promises and warranties, including any disclaimers and limitations of them or of remedies.

(h) "Goods" means all things that are movable at the time of identification to the lease contract, or are fixtures (Section 2A–309), but the term does not include money, documents, instruments, accounts, chattel paper, general intangibles, or minerals or the like, including oil and gas, before extraction. The term also includes the unborn young of animals.

(i) "Installment lease contract" means a lease contract that authorizes or requires the delivery of goods in separate lots to be separately accepted, even though the lease contract contains a clause "each delivery is a separate lease" or its equivalent.

(j) "Lease" means a transfer of the right to possession and use of goods for a term in return for consideration, but a sale, including a sale on approval or a sale or return, or retention or creation of a security interest is not a lease. Unless the context clearly indicates otherwise, the term includes a sublease.

(k) "Lease agreement" means the bargain, with respect to the lease, of the lessor and the lessee in fact as found in their language or by implication from other circumstances including course of dealing or usage of trade or course of performance as provided in this Article. Unless the context clearly indicates otherwise, the term includes a sublease agreement.

(l) "Lease contract" means the total legal obligation that results from the lease agreement as affected by this Article and any other applicable rules of law. Unless the context clearly indicates otherwise, the term includes a sublease contract.

(m) "Leasehold interest" means the interest of the lessor or the lessee under a lease contract.

(n) "Lessee" means a person who acquires the right to possession and use of goods under a lease. Unless the context clearly indicates otherwise, the term includes a sublessee.

(o) "Lessee in ordinary course of business" means a person who in good faith and without knowledge that the lease to him [or her] is in violation of the ownership rights or security interest or leasehold interest of a third party in the goods, leases in ordinary course from a person in the business of selling or leasing goods of that kind but does not include a pawnbroker. "Leasing" may be for cash or by exchange of other property or on secured or unsecured credit and includes receiving goods or documents of title under a pre-existing lease contract but does not include a transfer in bulk or as security for or in total or partial satisfaction of a money debt.

(p) "Lessor" means a person who transfers the right to possession and use of goods under a lease. Unless the context clearly indicates otherwise, the term includes a sublessor.

(q) "Lessor's residual interest" means the lessor's interest in the goods after expiration, termination, or cancellation of the lease contract.

(r) "Lien" means a charge against or interest in goods to secure payment of a debt or performance of an obligation, but the term does not include a security interest.

(s) "Lot" means a parcel or a single article that is the subject matter of a separate lease or delivery, whether or not it is sufficient to perform the lease contract.

(t) "Merchant lessee" means a lessee that is a merchant with respect to goods of the kind subject to the lease.

(u) "Present value" means the amount as of a date certain of one or more sums payable in the future, discounted to the date certain. The discount is determined by the interest rate specified by the parties if the rate was not manifestly unreasonable at the time the transaction was entered into; otherwise, the discount is determined by a commercially reasonable rate that takes into account the facts and circumstances of each case at the time the transaction was entered into.

(v) "Purchase" includes taking by sale, lease, mortgage, security interest, pledge, gift, or any other voluntary transaction creating an interest in goods.

(w) "Sublease" means a lease of goods the right to possession and use of which was acquired by the lessor as a lessee under an existing lease.

(x) "Supplier" means a person from whom a lessor buys or leases goods to be leased under a finance lease.

(y) "Supply contract" means a contract under which a lessor buys or leases goods to be leased.

(z) "Termination" occurs when either party pursuant to a power created by agreement or law puts an end to the lease contract otherwise than for default.

(2) Other definitions applying to this Article and the sections in which they appear are:

"Accessions". Section 2A–310(1).
"Construction mortgage". Section 2A–309(1)(d).
"Encumbrance". Section 2A–309(1)(e).
"Fixtures". Section 2A–309(1)(a).
"Fixture filing". Section 2A–309(1)(b).
"Purchase money lease". Section 2A–309(1)(c).

(3) The following definitions in other Articles apply to this Article:

"Accounts". Section 9–106.
"Between merchants". Section 2–104(3).
"Buyer". Section 2–103(1)(a).
"Chattel paper". Section 9–105(1)(b).
"Consumer goods". Section 9–109(1).
"Document". Section 9–105(1)(f).
"Entrusting". Section 2–403(3).
"General intangibles". Section 9–106.
"Good faith". Section 2–103(1)(b).
"Instrument". Section 9–105(1)(i).
"Merchant". Section 2–104(1).
"Mortgage". Section 9–105(1)(j).
"Pursuant to commitment". Section 9–105(1)(k).
"Receipt". Section 2–103(1)(c).
"Sale". Section 2–106(1).
"Sale on approval". Section 2–326.
"Sale or return". Section 2–326.
"Seller". Section 2–103(1)(d).

(4) In addition Article 1 contains general definitions and principles of construction and interpretation applicable throughout this Article.

As amended in 1990 and 1999.

§ 2A–104.   Leases Subject to Other Law.

(1) A lease, although subject to this Article, is also subject to any applicable:

(a) certificate of title statute of this State: (list any certificate of title statutes covering automobiles, trailers, mobile homes, boats, farm tractors, and the like);

(b) certificate of title statute of another jurisdiction (Section 2A–105); or

(c) consumer protection statute of this State, or final consumer protection decision of a court of this State existing on the effective date of this Article.

(2) In case of conflict between this Article, other than Sections 2A–105, 2A–304(3), and 2A–305(3), and a statute or decision referred to in subsection (1), the statute or decision controls.

(3) Failure to comply with an applicable law has only the effect specified therein.

As amended in 1990.

§ 2A–105.   Territorial Application of Article to Goods Covered by Certificate of Title.

Subject to the provisions of Sections 2A–304(3) and 2A–305(3), with respect to goods covered by a certificate of title issued under a statute of this State or of another jurisdiction, compliance and the effect of compliance or noncompliance with a certificate of title statute are governed by the law (including the conflict of laws rules) of the jurisdiction issuing the certificate until the earlier of (a) surrender of the certificate, or (b) four months after the goods are removed from that jurisdiction and thereafter until a new certificate of title is issued by another jurisdiction.

§ 2A–106.   Limitation on Power of Parties to Consumer Lease to Choose Applicable Law and Judicial Forum.

(1) If the law chosen by the parties to a consumer lease is that of a jurisdiction other than a jurisdiction in which the lessee resides at the time the lease agreement becomes enforceable or within 30 days thereafter or in which the goods are to be used, the choice is not enforceable.

(2) If the judicial forum chosen by the parties to a consumer lease is a forum that would not otherwise have jurisdiction over the lessee, the choice is not enforceable.

§ 2A–107.   Waiver or Renunciation of Claim or Right After Default.

Any claim or right arising out of an alleged default or breach of warranty may be discharged in whole or in part without consideration by a written waiver or renunciation signed and delivered by the aggrieved party.

§ 2A–108.   Unconscionability.

(1) If the court as a matter of law finds a lease contract or any clause of a lease contract to have been unconscionable at the time it was made the court may refuse to enforce the lease contract, or it may enforce the remainder of the lease contract without the unconscionable clause, or it may so limit the application of any unconscionable clause as to avoid any unconscionable result.

(2) With respect to a consumer lease, if the court as a matter of law finds that a lease contract or any clause of a lease contract has been induced by unconscionable conduct or that unconscionable conduct has occurred in the collection of a claim arising from a lease contract, the court may grant appropriate relief.

(3) Before making a finding of unconscionability under subsection (1) or (2), the court, on its own motion or that of a party, shall afford the parties a reasonable opportunity to present evidence as to the setting, purpose, and effect of the lease contract or clause thereof, or of the conduct.

(4) In an action in which the lessee claims unconscionability with respect to a consumer lease:

(a) If the court finds unconscionability under subsection (1) or (2), the court shall award reasonable attorney's fees to the lessee.

(b) If the court does not find unconscionability and the lessee claiming unconscionability has brought or maintained an action he [or she] knew to be groundless, the court shall award reasonable attorney's fees to the party against whom the claim is made.

(c) In determining attorney's fees, the amount of the recovery on behalf of the claimant under subsections (1) and (2) is not controlling.

§ 2A–109.   Option to Accelerate at Will.

(1) A term providing that one party or his [or her] successor in interest may accelerate payment or performance or require collateral or additional collateral "at will" or "when he [or she] deems himself [or herself] insecure" or in words of similar import must be construed to mean that he [or she] has power to do so only if he [or she] in good faith believes that the prospect of payment or performance is impaired.

(2) With respect to a consumer lease, the burden of establishing good faith under subsection (1) is on the party who exercised the power; otherwise the burden of establishing lack of good faith is on the party against whom the power has been exercised.

Part 2   Formation and Construction of Lease Contract
§ 2A–201.   Statute of Frauds.

(1) A lease contract is not enforceable by way of action or defense unless:

(a) the total payments to be made under the lease contract, excluding payments for options to renew or buy, are less than $1,000; or

(b) there is a writing, signed by the party against whom enforcement is sought or by that party's authorized agent, sufficient to indicate that a lease contract has been made between the parties and to describe the goods leased and the lease term.

(2) Any description of leased goods or of the lease term is sufficient and satisfies subsection (1)(b), whether or not it is specific, if it reasonably identifies what is described.

(3) A writing is not insufficient because it omits or incorrectly states a term agreed upon, but the lease contract is not enforceable under subsection (1)(b) beyond the lease term and the quantity of goods shown in the writing.

(4) A lease contract that does not satisfy the requirements of subsection (1), but which is valid in other respects, is enforceable:

(a) if the goods are to be specially manufactured or obtained for the lessee and are not suitable for lease or sale to others in the ordinary course of the lessor's business, and the lessor, before notice of repudiation is received and under circumstances that reasonably indicate that the goods are for the lessee, has made either a substantial beginning of their manufacture or commitments for their procurement;

(b) if the party against whom enforcement is sought admits in that party's pleading, testimony or otherwise in court that a lease contract was made, but the lease contract is not enforceable under this provision beyond the quantity of goods admitted; or

(c) with respect to goods that have been received and accepted by the lessee.

(5) The lease term under a lease contract referred to in subsection (4) is:

(a) if there is a writing signed by the party against whom enforcement is sought or by that party's authorized agent specifying the lease term, the term so specified;

(b) if the party against whom enforcement is sought admits in that party's pleading, testimony, or otherwise in court a lease term, the term so admitted; or

(c) a reasonable lease term.

§ 2A–202. Final Written Expression: Parol or Extrinsic Evidence.

Terms with respect to which the confirmatory memoranda of the parties agree or which are otherwise set forth in a writing intended by the parties as a final expression of their agreement with respect to such terms as are included therein may not be contradicted by evidence of any prior agreement or of a contemporaneous oral agreement but may be explained or supplemented:

(a) by course of dealing or usage of trade or by course of performance; and

(b) by evidence of consistent additional terms unless the court finds the writing to have been intended also as a complete and exclusive statement of the terms of the agreement.

§ 2A–203. Seals Inoperative.

The affixing of a seal to a writing evidencing a lease contract or an offer to enter into a lease contract does not render the writing a sealed instrument and the law with respect to sealed instruments does not apply to the lease contract or offer.

§ 2A–204. Formation in General.

(1) A lease contract may be made in any manner sufficient to show agreement, including conduct by both parties which recognizes the existence of a lease contract.

(2) An agreement sufficient to constitute a lease contract may be found although the moment of its making is undetermined.

(3) Although one or more terms are left open, a lease contract does not fail for indefiniteness if the parties have intended to make a lease contract and there is a reasonably certain basis for giving an appropriate remedy.

§ 2A–205. Firm Offers.

An offer by a merchant to lease goods to or from another person in a signed writing that by its terms gives assurance it will be held open is not revocable, for lack of consideration, during the time stated or, if no time is stated, for a reasonable time, but in no event may the period of irrevocability exceed 3 months. Any such term of assurance on a form supplied by the offeree must be separately signed by the offeror.

§ 2A–206. Offer and Acceptance in Formation of Lease Contract.

(1) Unless otherwise unambiguously indicated by the language or circumstances, an offer to make a lease contract must be construed as inviting acceptance in any manner and by any medium reasonable in the circumstances.

(2) If the beginning of a requested performance is a reasonable mode of acceptance, an offeror who is not notified of acceptance within a reasonable time may treat the offer as having lapsed before acceptance.

§ 2A–207. Course of Performance or Practical Construction.

(1) If a lease contract involves repeated occasions for performance by either party with knowledge of the nature of the performance and opportunity for objection to it by the other, any course of performance accepted or acquiesced in without objection is relevant to determine the meaning of the lease agreement.

(2) The express terms of a lease agreement and any course of performance, as well as any course of dealing and usage of trade, must be construed whenever reasonable as consistent with each other; but if that construction is unreasonable, express terms control course of performance, course of performance controls both course of dealing and usage of trade, and course of dealing controls usage of trade.

(3) Subject to the provisions of Section 2A–208 on modification and waiver, course of performance is relevant to show a waiver or modification of any term inconsistent with the course of performance.

§ 2A–208. Modification, Rescission and Waiver.

(1) An agreement modifying a lease contract needs no consideration to be binding.

(2) A signed lease agreement that excludes modification or rescission except by a signed writing may not be otherwise modified or rescinded, but, except as between merchants, such a requirement on a form supplied by a merchant must be separately signed by the other party.

(3) Although an attempt at modification or rescission does not satisfy the requirements of subsection (2), it may operate as a waiver.

(4) A party who has made a waiver affecting an executory portion of a lease contract may retract the waiver by reasonable notification received by the other party that strict performance will be required of any term waived, unless the retraction would be unjust in view of a material change of position in reliance on the waiver.

§ 2A–209. Lessee under Finance Lease as Beneficiary of Supply Contract.

(1) The benefit of the supplier's promises to the lessor under the supply contract and of all warranties, whether express or implied, including those of any third party provided in connection with or as part of the supply contract, extends to the lessee to the extent of the lessee's leasehold interest under a finance lease related to the supply contract, but is subject to the terms warranty and of the supply contract and all defenses or claims arising therefrom.

(2) The extension of the benefit of supplier's promises and of warranties to the lessee (Section 2A–209(1)) does not: (i) modify the rights and obligations of the parties to the supply contract, whether arising therefrom or otherwise, or (ii) impose any duty or liability under the supply contract on the lessee.

(3) Any modification or rescission of the supply contract by the supplier and the lessor is effective between the supplier and the lessee unless, before the modification or rescission, the supplier has received notice that the lessee has entered into a finance lease

related to the supply contract. If the modification or rescission is effective between the supplier and the lessee, the lessor is deemed to have assumed, in addition to the obligations of the lessor to the lessee under the lease contract, promises of the supplier to the lessor and warranties that were so modified or rescinded as they existed and were available to the lessee before modification or rescission.

(4) In addition to the extension of the benefit of the supplier's promises and of warranties to the lessee under subsection (1), the lessee retains all rights that the lessee may have against the supplier which arise from an agreement between the lessee and the supplier or under other law.

As amended in 1990.

§ 2A–210. Express Warranties.

(1) Express warranties by the lessor are created as follows:

(a) Any affirmation of fact or promise made by the lessor to the lessee which relates to the goods and becomes part of the basis of the bargain creates an express warranty that the goods will conform to the affirmation or promise.

(b) Any description of the goods which is made part of the basis of the bargain creates an express warranty that the goods will conform to the description.

(c) Any sample or model that is made part of the basis of the bargain creates an express warranty that the whole of the goods will conform to the sample or model.

(2) It is not necessary to the creation of an express warranty that the lessor use formal words, such as "warrant" or "guarantee," or that the lessor have a specific intention to make a warranty, but an affirmation merely of the value of the goods or a statement purporting to be merely the lessor's opinion or commendation of the goods does not create a warranty.

§ 2A–211. Warranties Against Interference and Against Infringement; Lessee's Obligation Against Infringement.

(1) There is in a lease contract a warranty that for the lease term no person holds a claim to or interest in the goods that arose from an act or omission of the lessor, other than a claim by way of infringement or the like, which will interfere with the lessee's enjoyment of its leasehold interest.

(2) Except in a finance lease there is in a lease contract by a lessor who is a merchant regularly dealing in goods of the kind a warranty that the goods are delivered free of the rightful claim of any person by way of infringement or the like.

(3) A lessee who furnishes specifications to a lessor or a supplier shall hold the lessor and the supplier harmless against any claim by way of infringement or the like that arises out of compliance with the specifications.

§ 2A–212. Implied Warranty of Merchantability.

(1) Except in a finance lease, a warranty that the goods will be merchantable is implied in a lease contract if the lessor is a merchant with respect to goods of that kind.

(2) Goods to be merchantable must be at least such as

(a) pass without objection in the trade under the description in the lease agreement;

(b) in the case of fungible goods, are of fair average quality within the description;

(c) are fit for the ordinary purposes for which goods of that type are used;

(d) run, within the variation permitted by the lease agreement, of even kind, quality, and quantity within each unit and among all units involved;

(e) are adequately contained, packaged, and labeled as the lease agreement may require; and

(f) conform to any promises or affirmations of fact made on the container or label.

(3) Other implied warranties may arise from course of dealing or usage of trade.

§ 2A–213. Implied Warranty of Fitness for Particular Purpose.

Except in a finance of lease, if the lessor at the time the lease contract is made has reason to know of any particular purpose for which the goods are required and that the lessee is relying on the lessor's skill or judgment to select or furnish suitable goods, there is in the lease contract an implied warranty that the goods will be fit for that purpose.

§ 2A–214. Exclusion or Modification of Warranties.

(1) Words or conduct relevant to the creation of an express warranty and words or conduct tending to negate or limit a warranty must be construed wherever reasonable as consistent with each other; but, subject to the provisions of Section 2A–202 on parol or extrinsic evidence, negation or limitation is inoperative to the extent that the construction is unreasonable.

(2) Subject to subsection (3), to exclude or modify the implied warranty of merchantability or any part of it the language must mention "merchantability", be by a writing, and be conspicuous. Subject to subsection (3), to exclude or modify any implied warranty of fitness the exclusion must be by a writing and be conspicuous. Language to exclude all implied warranties of fitness is sufficient if it is in writing, is conspicuous and states, for example, "There is no warranty that the goods will be fit for a particular purpose".

(3) Notwithstanding subsection (2), but subject to subsection (4),

(a) unless the circumstances indicate otherwise, all implied warranties are excluded by expressions like "as is" or "with all faults" or by other language that in common understanding calls the lessee's attention to the exclusion of warranties and makes plain that there is no implied warranty, if in writing and conspicuous;

(b) if the lessee before entering into the lease contract has examined the goods or the sample or model as fully as desired or has refused to examine the goods, there is no implied warranty with regard to defects that an examination ought in the circumstances to have revealed; and

(c) an implied warranty may also be excluded or modified by course of dealing, course of performance, or usage of trade.

(4) To exclude or modify a warranty against interference or against infringement (Section 2A–211) or any part of it, the language must be specific, be by a writing, and be conspicuous, unless the circumstances, including course of performance, course of dealing, or usage of trade, give the lessee reason to know that the goods are being leased subject to a claim or interest of any person.

§ 2A–215.   Cumulation and Conflict of Warranties Express or Implied.

Warranties, whether express or implied, must be construed as consistent with each other and as cumulative, but if that construction is unreasonable, the intention of the parties determines which warranty is dominant. In ascertaining that intention the following rules apply:

(a) Exact or technical specifications displace an inconsistent sample or model or general language of description.

(b) A sample from an existing bulk displaces inconsistent general language of description.

(c) Express warranties displace inconsistent implied warranties other than an implied warranty of fitness for a particular purpose.

§ 2A–216.   Third-Party Beneficiaries of Express and Implied Warranties.

Alternative A

A warranty to or for the benefit of a lessee under this Article, whether express or implied, extends to any natural person who is in the family or household of the lessee or who is a guest in the lessee's home if it is reasonable to expect that such person may use, consume, or be affected by the goods and who is injured in person by breach of the warranty. This section does not displace principles of law and equity that extend a warranty to or for the benefit of a lessee to other persons. The operation of this section may not be excluded, modified, or limited, but an exclusion, modification, or limitation of the warranty, including any with respect to rights and remedies, effective against the lessee is also effective against any beneficiary designated under this section.

Alternative B

A warranty to or for the benefit of a lessee under this Article, whether express or implied, extends to any natural person who may reasonably be expected to use, consume, or be affected by the goods and who is injured in person by breach of the warranty. This section does not displace principles of law and equity that extend a warranty to or for the benefit of a lessee to other persons. The operation of this section may not be excluded, modified, or limited, but an exclusion, modification, or limitation of the warranty, including any with respect to rights and remedies, effective against the lessee is also effective against the beneficiary designated under this section.

Alternative C

A warranty to or for the benefit of a lessee under this Article, whether express or implied, extends to any person who may reasonably be expected to use, consume, or be affected by the goods and who is injured by breach of the warranty. The operation of this section may not be excluded, modified, or limited with respect to injury to the person of an individual to whom the warranty extends, but an exclusion, modification, or limitation of the warranty, including any with respect to rights and remedies, effective against the lessee is also effective against the beneficiary designated under this section.

§ 2A–217.   Identification.

Identification of goods as goods to which a lease contract refers may be made at any time and in any manner explicitly agreed to by the parties. In the absence of explicit agreement, identification occurs:

(a) when the lease contract is made if the lease contract is for a lease of goods that are existing and identified;

(b) when the goods are shipped, marked, or otherwise designated by the lessor as goods to which the lease contract refers, if the lease contract is for a lease of goods that are not existing and identified; or

(c) when the young are conceived, if the lease contract is for a lease of unborn young of animals.

§ 2A–218.   Insurance and Proceeds.

(1) A lessee obtains an insurable interest when existing goods are identified to the lease contract even though the goods identified are nonconforming and the lessee has an option to reject them.

(2) If a lessee has an insurable interest only by reason of the lessor's identification of the goods, the lessor, until default or insolvency or notification to the lessee that identification is final, may substitute other goods for those identified.

(3) Notwithstanding a lessee's insurable interest under subsections (1) and (2), the lessor retains an insurable interest until an option to buy has been exercised by the lessee and risk of loss has passed to the lessee.

(4) Nothing in this section impairs any insurable interest recognized under any other statute or rule of law.

(5) The parties by agreement may determine that one or more parties have an obligation to obtain and pay for insurance covering the goods and by agreement may determine the beneficiary of the proceeds of the insurance.

§ 2A–219.   Risk of Loss.

(1) Except in the case of a finance lease, risk of loss is retained by the lessor and does not pass to the lessee. In the case of a finance lease, risk of loss passes to the lessee.

(2) Subject to the provisions of this Article on the effect of default on risk of loss (Section 2A–220), if risk of loss is to pass to the lessee and the time of passage is not stated, the following rules apply:

(a) If the lease contract requires or authorizes the goods to be shipped by carrier

(i) and it does not require delivery at a particular destination, the risk of loss passes to the lessee when the goods are duly delivered to the carrier; but

(ii) if it does require delivery at a particular destination and the goods are there duly tendered while in the possession of the carrier, the risk of loss passes to the lessee when the goods are there duly so tendered as to enable the lessee to take delivery.

(b) If the goods are held by a bailee to be delivered without being moved, the risk of loss passes to the lessee on acknowledgment by the bailee of the lessee's right to possession of the goods.

(c) In any case not within subsection (a) or (b), the risk of loss passes to the lessee on the lessee's receipt of the goods if the lessor, or, in the case of a finance lease, the supplier, is a merchant; otherwise the risk passes to the lessee on tender of delivery.

§ 2A–220. Effect of Default on Risk of Loss.

(1) Where risk of loss is to pass to the lessee and the time of passage is not stated:

(a) If a tender or delivery of goods so fails to conform to the lease contract as to give a right of rejection, the risk of their loss remains with the lessor, or, in the case of a finance lease, the supplier, until cure or acceptance.

(b) If the lessee rightfully revokes acceptance, he [or she], to the extent of any deficiency in his [or her] effective insurance coverage, may treat the risk of loss as having remained with the lessor from the beginning.

(2) Whether or not risk of loss is to pass to the lessee, if the lessee as to conforming goods already identified to a lease contract repudiates or is otherwise in default under the lease contract, the lessor, or, in the case of a finance lease, the supplier, to the extent of any deficiency in his [or her] effective insurance coverage may treat the risk of loss as resting on the lessee for a commercially reasonable time.

§ 2A–221. Casualty to Identified Goods.

If a lease contract requires goods identified when the lease contract is made, and the goods suffer casualty without fault of the lessee, the lessor or the supplier before delivery, or the goods suffer casualty before risk of loss passes to the lessee pursuant to the lease agreement or Section 2A–219, then:

(a) if the loss is total, the lease contract is avoided; and

(b) if the loss is partial or the goods have so deteriorated as to no longer conform to the lease contract, the lessee may nevertheless demand inspection and at his [or her] option either treat the lease contract as avoided or, except in a finance lease that is not a consumer lease, accept the goods with due allowance from the rent payable for the balance of the lease term for the deterioration or the deficiency in quantity but without further right against the lessor.

Part 3 Effect of Lease Contract
§ 2A–301. Enforceability of Lease Contract.

Except as otherwise provided in this Article, a lease contract is effective and enforceable according to its terms between the parties, against purchasers of the goods and against creditors of the parties.

§ 2A–302. Title to and Possession of Goods.

Except as otherwise provided in this Article, each provision of this Article applies whether the lessor or a third party has title to the goods, and whether the lessor, the lessee, or a third party has possession of the goods, notwithstanding any statute or rule of law that possession or the absence of possession is fraudulent.

§ 2A–303. Alienability of Party's Interest Under Lease Contract or of Lessor's Residual Interest in Goods; Delegation of Performance; Transfer of Rights.

(1) As used in this section, "creation of a security interest" includes the sale of a lease contract that is subject to Article 9, Secured Transactions, by reason of Section 9–109(a)(3).

(2) Except as provided in subsections (3) and Section 9–407, a provision in a lease agreement which (i) prohibits the voluntary or involuntary transfer, including a transfer by sale, sublease, creation or enforcement of a security interest, or attachment, levy, or other judicial process, of an interest of a party under the lease contract or of the lessor's residual interest in the goods, or (ii) makes such a transfer an event of default, gives rise to the rights and remedies provided in subsection (4), but a transfer that is prohibited or is an event of default under the lease agreement is otherwise effective.

(3) A provision in a lease agreement which (i) prohibits a transfer of a right to damages for default with respect to the whole lease contract or of a right to payment arising out of the transferor's due performance of the transferor's entire obligation, or (ii) makes such a transfer an event of default, is not enforceable, and such a transfer is not a transfer that materially impairs the propsect of obtaining return performance by, materially changes the duty of, or materially increases the burden or risk imposed on, the other party to the lease contract within the purview of subsection (4).

(4) Subject to subsection (3) and Section 9–407:

(a) if a transfer is made which is made an event of default under a lease agreement, the party to the lease contract not making the transfer, unless that party waives the default or otherwise agrees, has the rights and remedies described in Section 2A–501(2);

(b) if paragraph (a) is not applicable and if a transfer is made that (i) is prohibited under a lease agreement or (ii) materially impairs the prospect of obtaining return performance by, materially changes the duty of, or materially increases the burden or risk imposed on, the other party to the lease contract, unless the party not making the transfer agrees at any time to the transfer in the lease contract or otherwise, then, except as limited by contract, (i) the transferor is liable to the party not making the transfer for damages caused by the transfer to the extent that the damages could not reasonably be prevented by the party not making the transfer and (ii) a court having jurisdiction may grant other appropriate relief, including cancellation of the lease contract or an injunction against the transfer.

(5) A transfer of "the lease" or of "all my rights under the lease", or a transfer in similar general terms, is a transfer of rights and, unless the language or the circumstances, as in a transfer for security, indicate the contrary, the transfer is a delegation of duties by the transferor to the transferee. Acceptance by the transferee constitutes a promise by the transferee to perform those duties. The promise is enforceable by either the transferor or the other party to the lease contract.

(6) Unless otherwise agreed by the lessor and the lessee, a delegation of performance does not relieve the transferor as against the other party of any duty to perform or of any liability for default.

(7) In a consumer lease, to prohibit the transfer of an interest of a party under the lease contract or to make a transfer an event of default, the language must be specific, by a writing, and conspicuous.

As amended in 1990 and 1999.

§ 2A–304.   Subsequent Lease of Goods by Lessor.

(1) Subject to Section 2A–303, a subsequent lessee from a lessor of goods under an existing lease contract obtains, to the extent of the leasehold interest transferred, the leasehold interest in the goods that the lessor had or had power to transfer, and except as provided in subsection (2) and Section 2A–527(4), takes subject to the existing lease contract. A lessor with voidable title has power to transfer a good leasehold interest to a good faith subsequent lessee for value, but only to the extent set forth in the preceding sentence. If goods have been delivered under a transaction of purchase the lessor has that power even though:

(a) the lessor's transferor was deceived as to the identity of the lessor;

(b) the delivery was in exchange for a check which is later dishonored;

(c) it was agreed that the transaction was to be a "cash sale"; or

(d) the delivery was procured through fraud punishable as larcenous under the criminal law.

(2) A subsequent lessee in the ordinary course of business from a lessor who is a merchant dealing in goods of that kind to whom the goods were entrusted by the existing lessee of that lessor before the interest of the subsequent lessee became enforceable against that lessor obtains, to the extent of the leasehold interest transferred, all of that lessor's and the existing lessee's rights to the goods, and takes free of the existing lease contract.

(3) A subsequent lessee from the lessor of goods that are subject to an existing lease contract and are covered by a certificate of title issued under a statute of this State or of another jurisdiction takes no greater rights than those provided both by this section and by the certificate of title statute.

As amended in 1990.

§ 2A–305.   Sale or Sublease of Goods by Lessee.

(1) Subject to the provisions of Section 2A–303, a buyer or sublessee from the lessee of goods under an existing lease contract obtains, to the extent of the interest transferred, the leasehold interest in the goods that the lessee had or had power to transfer, and

except as provided in subsection (2) and Section 2A–511(4), takes subject to the existing lease contract. A lessee with a voidable leasehold interest has power to transfer a good leasehold interest to a good faith buyer for value or a good faith sublessee for value, but only to the extent set forth in the preceding sentence. When goods have been delivered under a transaction of lease the lessee has that power even though:

(a) the lessor was deceived as to the identity of the lessee;

(b) the delivery was in exchange for a check which is later dishonored; or

(c) the delivery was procured through fraud punishable as larcenous under the criminal law.

(2) A buyer in the ordinary course of business or a sublessee in the ordinary course of business from a lessee who is a merchant dealing in goods of that kind to whom the goods were entrusted by the lessor obtains, to the extent of the interest transferred, all of the lessor's and lessee's rights to the goods, and takes free of the existing lease contract.

(3) A buyer or sublessee from the lessee of goods that are subject to an existing lease contract and are covered by a certificate of title issued under a statute of this State or of another jurisdiction takes no greater rights than those provided both by this section and by the certificate of title statute.

§ 2A–306.   Priority of Certain Liens Arising by Operation of Law.

If a person in the ordinary course of his [or her] business furnishes services or materials with respect to goods subject to a lease contract, a lien upon those goods in the possession of that person given by statute or rule of law for those materials or services takes priority over any interest of the lessor or lessee under the lease contract or this Article unless the lien is created by statute and the statute provides otherwise or unless the lien is created by rule of law and the rule of law provides otherwise.

§ 2A–307.   Priority of Liens Arising by Attachment or Levy on, Security Interests in, and Other Claims to Goods.

(1) Except as otherwise provided in Section 2A–306, a creditor of a lessee takes subject to the lease contract.

(2) Except as otherwise provided in subsection (3) and in Sections 2A–306 and 2A–308, a creditor of a lessor takes subject to the lease contract unless the creditor holds a lien that attached to the goods before the lease contract became enforceable.

(3) Except as otherwise provided in Sections 9–317, 9–321, and 9–323, a lessee takes a leasehold interest subject to a security interest held by a creditor of the lessor.

As amended in 1990 and 1999.

§ 2A–308.   Special Rights of Creditors.

(1) A creditor of a lessor in possession of goods subject to a lease contract may treat the lease contract as void if as against the creditor retention of possession by the lessor is fraudulent under any statute or rule of law, but retention of possession in good

faith and current course of trade by the lessor for a commercially reasonable time after the lease contract becomes enforceable is not fraudulent.

(2) Nothing in this Article impairs the rights of creditors of a lessor if the lease contract (a) becomes enforceable, not in current course of trade but in satisfaction of or as security for a pre-existing claim for money, security, or the like, and (b) is made under circumstances which under any statute or rule of law apart from this Article would constitute the transaction a fraudulent transfer or voidable preference.

(3) A creditor of a seller may treat a sale or an identification of goods to a contract for sale as void if as against the creditor retention of possession by the seller is fraudulent under any statute or rule of law, but retention of possession of the goods pursuant to a lease contract entered into by the seller as lessee and the buyer as lessor in connection with the sale or identification of the goods is not fraudulent if the buyer bought for value and in good faith.

§ 2A–309.   Lessor's and Lessee's Rights When Goods Become Fixtures.

(1) In this section:

(a) goods are "fixtures" when they become so related to particular real estate that an interest in them arises under real estate law;

(b) a "fixture filing" is the filing, in the office where a mortgage on the real estate would be filed or recorded, of a financing statement covering goods that are or are to become fixtures and conforming to the requirements of Section 9–502(a) and (b);

(c) a lease is a "purchase money lease" unless the lessee has possession or use of the goods or the right to possession or use of the goods before the lease agreement is enforceable;

(d) a mortgage is a "construction mortgage" to the extent it secures an obligation incurred for the construction of an improvement on land including the acquisition cost of the land, if the recorded writing so indicates; and

(e) "encumbrance" includes real estate mortgages and other liens on real estate and all other rights in real estate that are not ownership interests.

(2) Under this Article a lease may be of goods that are fixtures or may continue in goods that become fixtures, but no lease exists under this Article of ordinary building materials incorporated into an improvement on land.

(3) This Article does not prevent creation of a lease of fixtures pursuant to real estate law.

(4) The perfected interest of a lessor of fixtures has priority over a conflicting interest of an encumbrancer or owner of the real estate if:

(a) the lease is a purchase money lease, the conflicting interest of the encumbrancer or owner arises before the goods become fixtures, the interest of the lessor is perfected by a fixture filing before the goods become fixtures or within ten

days thereafter, and the lessee has an interest of record in the real estate or is in possession of the real estate; or

(b) the interest of the lessor is perfected by a fixture filing before the interest of the encumbrancer or owner is of record, the lessor's interest has priority over any conflicting interest of a predecessor in title of the encumbrancer or owner, and the lessee has an interest of record in the real estate or is in possession of the real estate.

(5) The interest of a lessor of fixtures, whether or not perfected, has priority over the conflicting interest of an encumbrancer or owner of the real estate if:

(a) the fixtures are readily removable factory or office machines, readily removable equipment that is not primarily used or leased for use in the operation of the real estate, or readily removable replacements of domestic appliances that are goods subject to a consumer lease, and before the goods become fixtures the lease contract is enforceable; or

(b) the conflicting interest is a lien on the real estate obtained by legal or equitable proceedings after the lease contract is enforceable; or

(c) the encumbrancer or owner has consented in writing to the lease or has disclaimed an interest in the goods as fixtures; or

(d) the lessee has a right to remove the goods as against the encumbrancer or owner. If the lessee's right to remove terminates, the priority of the interest of the lessor continues for a reasonable time.

(6) Notwithstanding paragraph (4)(a) but otherwise subject to subsections (4) and (5), the interest of a lessor of fixtures, including the lessor's residual interest, is subordinate to the conflicting interest of an encumbrancer of the real estate under a construction mortgage recorded before the goods become fixtures if the goods become fixtures before the completion of the construction. To the extent given to refinance a construction mortgage, the conflicting interest of an encumbrancer of the real estate under a mortgage has this priority to the same extent as the encumbrancer of the real estate under the construction mortgage.

(7) In cases not within the preceding subsections, priority between the interest of a lessor of fixtures, including the lessor's residual interest, and the conflicting interest of an encumbrancer or owner of the real estate who is not the lessee is determined by the priority rules governing conflicting interests in real estate.

(8) If the interest of a lessor of fixtures, including the lessor's residual interest, has priority over all conflicting interests of all owners and encumbrancers of the real estate, the lessor or the lessee may (i) on default, expiration, termination, or cancellation of the lease agreement but subject to the agreement and this Article, or (ii) if necessary to enforce other rights and remedies of the lessor or lessee under this Article, remove the goods from the real estate, free and clear of all conflicting interests of all owners and encumbrancers of the real estate, but the lessor or lessee must reimburse any encumbrancer or owner of the real estate who is not the lessee and who has not otherwise agreed for the cost of repair of any physical injury, but not for any diminution in value of the real estate caused by the absence of the goods removed

or by any necessity of replacing them. A person entitled to reimbursement may refuse permission to remove until the party seeking removal gives adequate security for the performance of this obligation.

(9) Even though the lease agreement does not create a security interest, the interest of a lessor of fixtures, including the lessor's residual interest, is perfected by filing a financing statement as a fixture filing for leased goods that are or are to become fixtures in accordance with the relevant provisions of the Article on Secured Transactions (Article 9).

As amended in 1990 and 1999.

§ 2A–310. Lessor's and Lessee's Rights When Goods Become Accessions.

(1) Goods are "accessions" when they are installed in or affixed to other goods.

(2) The interest of a lessor or a lessee under a lease contract entered into before the goods became accessions is superior to all interests in the whole except as stated in subsection (4).

(3) The interest of a lessor or a lessee under a lease contract entered into at the time or after the goods became accessions is superior to all subsequently acquired interests in the whole except as stated in subsection (4) but is subordinate to interests in the whole existing at the time the lease contract was made unless the holders of such interests in the whole have in writing consented to the lease or disclaimed an interest in the goods as part of the whole.

(4) The interest of a lessor or a lessee under a lease contract described in subsection (2) or (3) is subordinate to the interest of

  (a) a buyer in the ordinary course of business or a lessee in the ordinary course of business of any interest in the whole acquired after the goods became accessions; or

  (b) a creditor with a security interest in the whole perfected before the lease contract was made to the extent that the creditor makes subsequent advances without knowledge of the lease contract.

(5) When under subsections (2) or (3) and (4) a lessor or a lessee of accessions holds an interest that is superior to all interests in the whole, the lessor or the lessee may (a) on default, expiration, termination, or cancellation of the lease contract by the other party but subject to the provisions of the lease contract and this Article, or (b) if necessary to enforce his [or her] other rights and remedies under this Article, remove the goods from the whole, free and clear of all interests in the whole, but he [or she] must reimburse any holder of an interest in the whole who is not the lessee and who has not otherwise agreed for the cost of repair of any physical injury but not for any diminution in value of the whole caused by the absence of the goods removed or by any necessity for replacing them. A person entitled to reimbursement may refuse permission to remove until the party seeking removal gives adequate security for the performance of this obligation.

§ 2A–311. Priority Subject to Subordination.

Nothing in this Article prevents subordination by agreement by any person entitled to priority.

As added in 1990.

Part 4 Performance of Lease Contract: Repudiated, Substituted and Excused

§ 2A–401. Insecurity: Adequate Assurance of Performance.

(1) A lease contract imposes an obligation on each party that the other's expectation of receiving due performance will not be impaired.

(2) If reasonable grounds for insecurity arise with respect to the performance of either party, the insecure party may demand in writing adequate assurance of due performance. Until the insecure party receives that assurance, if commercially reasonable the insecure party may suspend any performance for which he [or she] has not already received the agreed return.

(3) A repudiation of the lease contract occurs if assurance of due performance adequate under the circumstances of the particular case is not provided to the insecure party within a reasonable time, not to exceed 30 days after receipt of a demand by the other party.

(4) Between merchants, the reasonableness of grounds for insecurity and the adequacy of any assurance offered must be determined according to commercial standards.

(5) Acceptance of any nonconforming delivery or payment does not prejudice the aggrieved party's right to demand adequate assurance of future performance.

§ 2A–402. Anticipatory Repudiation.

If either party repudiates a lease contract with respect to a performance not yet due under the lease contract, the loss of which performance will substantially impair the value of the lease contract to the other, the aggrieved party may:

(a) for a commercially reasonable time, await retraction of repudiation and performance by the repudiating party;

(b) make demand pursuant to Section 2A–401 and await assurance of future performance adequate under the circumstances of the particular case; or

(c) resort to any right or remedy upon default under the lease contract or this Article, even though the aggrieved party has notified the repudiating party that the aggrieved party would await the repudiating party's performance and assurance and has urged retraction. In addition, whether or not the aggrieved party is pursuing one of the foregoing remedies, the aggrieved party may suspend performance or, if the aggrieved party is the lessor, proceed in accordance with the provisions of this Article on the lessor's right to identify goods to the lease contract notwithstanding default or to salvage unfinished goods (Section 2A–524).

§ 2A–403. Retraction of Anticipatory Repudiation.

(1) Until the repudiating party's next performance is due, the repudiating party can retract the repudiation unless, since the repudiation, the aggrieved party has cancelled the lease contract or materially changed the aggrieved party's position or otherwise indicated that the aggrieved party considers the repudiation final.

(2) Retraction may be by any method that clearly indicates to the aggrieved party that the repudiating party intends to perform under the lease contract and includes any assurance demanded under Section 2A–401.

(3) Retraction reinstates a repudiating party's rights under a lease contract with due excuse and allowance to the aggrieved party for any delay occasioned by the repudiation.

§ 2A–404.   Substituted Performance.

(1) If without fault of the lessee, the lessor and the supplier, the agreed berthing, loading, or unloading facilities fail or the agreed type of carrier becomes unavailable or the agreed manner of delivery otherwise becomes commercially impracticable, but a commercially reasonable substitute is available, the substitute performance must be tendered and accepted.

(2) If the agreed means or manner of payment fails because of domestic or foreign governmental regulation:

(a) the lessor may withhold or stop delivery or cause the supplier to withhold or stop delivery unless the lessee provides a means or manner of payment that is commercially a substantial equivalent; and

(b) if delivery has already been taken, payment by the means or in the manner provided by the regulation discharges the lessee's obligation unless the regulation is discriminatory, oppressive, or predatory.

§ 2A–405.   Excused Performance.

Subject to Section 2A–404 on substituted performance, the following rules apply:

(a) Delay in delivery or nondelivery in whole or in part by a lessor or a supplier who complies with paragraphs (b) and (c) is not a default under the lease contract if performance as agreed has been made impracticable by the occurrence of a contingency the nonoccurrence of which was a basic assumption on which the lease contract was made or by compliance in good faith with any applicable foreign or domestic governmental regulation or order, whether or not the regulation or order later proves to be invalid.

(b) If the causes mentioned in paragraph (a) affect only part of the lessor's or the supplier's capacity to perform, he [or she] shall allocate production and deliveries among his [or her] customers but at his [or her] option may include regular customers not then under contract for sale or lease as well as his [or her] own requirements for further manufacture. He [or she] may so allocate in any manner that is fair and reasonable.

(c) The lessor seasonally shall notify the lessee and in the case of a finance lease the supplier seasonally shall notify the lessor and the lessee, if known, that there will be delay or nondelivery and, if allocation is required under paragraph (b), of the estimated quota thus made available for the lessee.

§ 2A–406.   Procedure on Excused Performance.

(1) If the lessee receives notification of a material or indefinite delay or an allocation justified under Section 2A–405, the lessee may by written notification to the lessor as to any goods involved, and with respect to all of the goods if under an installment lease contract the value of the whole lease contract is substantially impaired (Section 2A–510):

(a) terminate the lease contract (Section 2A–505(2)); or

(b) except in a finance lease that is not a consumer lease, modify the lease contract by accepting the available quota in substitution, with due allowance from the rent payable for the balance of the lease term for the deficiency but without further right against the lessor.

(2) If, after receipt of a notification from the lessor under Section 2A–405, the lessee fails so to modify the lease agreement within a reasonable time not exceeding 30 days, the lease contract lapses with respect to any deliveries affected.

§ 2A–407.   Irrevocable Promises: Finance Leases.

(1) In the case of a finance lease that is not a consumer lease the lessee's promises under the lease contract become irrevocable and independent upon the lessee's acceptance of the goods.

(2) A promise that has become irrevocable and independent under subsection (1):

(a) is effective and enforceable between the parties, and by or against third parties including assignees of the parties, and

(b) is not subject to cancellation, termination, modification, repudiation, excuse, or substitution without the consent of the party to whom the promise runs.

(3) This section does not affect the validity under any other law of a covenant in any lease contract making the lessee's promises irrevocable and independent upon the lessee's acceptance of the goods.

As amended in 1990.

Part 5   Default

A. In General

§ 2A–501.   Default: Procedure.

(1) Whether the lessor or the lessee is in default under a lease contract is determined by the lease agreement and this Article.

(2) If the lessor or the lessee is in default under the lease contract, the party seeking enforcement has rights and remedies as provided in this Article and, except as limited by this Article, as provided in the lease agreement.

(3) If the lessor or the lessee is in default under the lease contract, the party seeking enforcement may reduce the party's claim to judgment, or otherwise enforce the lease contract by self-help or any available judicial procedure or nonjudicial procedure, including administrative proceeding, arbitration, or the like, in accordance with this Article.

(4) Except as otherwise provided in Section 1–106(1) or this Article or the lease agreement, the rights and remedies referred to in subsections (2) and (3) are cumulative.

(5) If the lease agreement covers both real property and goods, the party seeking enforcement may proceed under this Part as to the goods, or under other applicable law as to both the real property and the goods in accordance with that party's rights and remedies in

respect of the real property, in which case this Part does not apply. As amended in 1990.

§ 2A–502.   Notice After Default.

Except as otherwise provided in this Article or the lease agreement, the lessor or lessee in default under the lease contract is not entitled to notice of default or notice of enforcement from the other party to the lease agreement.

§ 2A–503.   Modification or Impairment of Rights and Remedies.

(1) Except as otherwise provided in this Article, the lease agreement may include rights and remedies for default in addition to or in substitution for those provided in this Article and may limit or alter the measure of damages recoverable under this Article.

(2) Resort to a remedy provided under this Article or in the lease agreement is optional unless the remedy is expressly agreed to be exclusive. If circumstances cause an exclusive or limited remedy to fail of its essential purpose, or provision for an exclusive remedy is unconscionable, remedy may be had as provided in this Article.

(3) Consequential damages may be liquidated under Section 2A–504, or may otherwise be limited, altered, or excluded unless the limitation, alteration, or exclusion is unconscionable. Limitation, alteration, or exclusion of consequential damages for injury to the person in the case of consumer goods is *prima facie* unconscionable but limitation, alteration, or exclusion of damages where the loss is commercial is not *prima facie* unconscionable.

(4) Rights and remedies on default by the lessor or the lessee with respect to any obligation or promise collateral or ancillary to the lease contract are not impaired by this Article.

As amended in 1990.

§ 2A–504.   Liquidation of Damages.

(1) Damages payable by either party for default, or any other act or omission, including indemnity for loss or diminution of anticipated tax benefits or loss or damage to lessor's residual interest, may be liquidated in the lease agreement but only at an amount or by a formula that is reasonable in light of the then anticipated harm caused by the default or other act or omission.

(2) If the lease agreement provides for liquidation of damages, and such provision does not comply with subsection (1), or such provision is an exclusive or limited remedy that circumstances cause to fail of its essential purpose, remedy may be had as provided in this Article.

(3) If the lessor justifiably withholds or stops delivery of goods because of the lessee's default or insolvency (Section 2A–525 or 2A–526), the lessee is entitled to restitution of any amount by which the sum of his [or her] payments exceeds:

(a) the amount to which the lessor is entitled by virtue of terms liquidating the lessor's damages in accordance with subsection (1); or

(b) in the absence of those terms, 20 percent of the then present value of the total rent the lessee was obligated to pay for

the balance of the lease term, or, in the case of a consumer lease, the lesser of such amount or $500.

(4) A lessee's right to restitution under subsection (3) is subject to offset to the extent the lessor establishes:

(a) a right to recover damages under the provisions of this Article other than subsection (1); and

(b) the amount or value of any benefits received by the lessee directly or indirectly by reason of the lease contract.

§ 2A–505.   Cancellation and Termination and Effect of Cancellation, Termination, Rescission, or Fraud on Rights and Remedies.

(1) On cancellation of the lease contract, all obligations that are still executory on both sides are discharged, but any right based on prior default or performance survives, and the cancelling party also retains any remedy for default of the whole lease contract or any unperformed balance.

(2) On termination of the lease contract, all obligations that are still executory on both sides are discharged but any right based on prior default or performance survives.

(3) Unless the contrary intention clearly appears, expressions of "cancellation," "rescission," or the like of the lease contract may not be construed as a renunciation or discharge of any claim in damages for an antecedent default.

(4) Rights and remedies for material misrepresentation or fraud include all rights and remedies available under this Article for default.

(5) Neither rescission nor a claim for rescission of the lease contract nor rejection or return of the goods may bar or be deemed inconsistent with a claim for damages or other right or remedy.

§ 2A–506.   Statute of Limitations.

(1) An action for default under a lease contract, including breach of warranty or indemnity, must be commenced within 4 years after the cause of action accrued. By the original lease contract the parties may reduce the period of limitation to not less than one year.

(2) A cause of action for default accrues when the act or omission on which the default or breach of warranty is based is or should have been discovered by the aggrieved party, or when the default occurs, whichever is later. A cause of action for indemnity accrues when the act or omission on which the claim for indemnity is based is or should have been discovered by the indemnified party, whichever is later.

(3) If an action commenced within the time limited by subsection (1) is so terminated as to leave available a remedy by another action for the same default or breach of warranty or indemnity, the other action may be commenced after the expiration of the time limited and within 6 months after the termination of the first action unless the termination resulted from voluntary discontinuance or from dismissal for failure or neglect to prosecute.

(4) This section does not alter the law on tolling of the statute of limitations nor does it apply to causes of action that have accrued before this Article becomes effective.

§ 2A-507. Proof of Market Rent: Time and Place.

(1) Damages based on market rent (Section 2A-519 or 2A-528) are determined according to the rent for the use of the goods concerned for a lease term identical to the remaining lease term of the original lease agreement and prevailing at the times specified in Sections 2A-519 and 2A-528.

(2) If evidence of rent for the use of the goods concerned for a lease term identical to the remaining lease term of the original lease agreement and prevailing at the times or places described in this Article is not readily available, the rent prevailing within any reasonable time before or after the time described or at any other place or for a different lease term which in commercial judgment or under usage of trade would serve as a reasonable substitute for the one described may be used, making any proper allowance for the difference, including the cost of transporting the goods to or from the other place.

(3) Evidence of a relevant rent prevailing at a time or place or for a lease term other than the one described in this Article offered by one party is not admissible unless and until he [or she] has given the other party notice the court finds sufficient to prevent unfair surprise.

(4) If the prevailing rent or value of any goods regularly leased in any established market is in issue, reports in official publications or trade journals or in newspapers or periodicals of general circulation published as the reports of that market are admissible in evidence. The circumstances of the preparation of the report may be shown to affect its weight but not its admissibility.

As amended in 1990.

B. Default by Lessor

§ 2A-508. Lessee's Remedies.

(1) If a lessor fails to deliver the goods in conformity to the lease contract (Section 2A-509) or repudiates the lease contract (Section 2A-402), or a lessee rightfully rejects the goods (Section 2A-509) or justifiably revokes acceptance of the goods (Section 2A-517), then with respect to any goods involved, and with respect to all of the goods if under an installment lease contract the value of the whole lease contract is substantially impaired (Section 2A-510), the lessor is in default under the lease contract and the lessee may:

(a) cancel the lease contract (Section 2A-505(1));

(b) recover so much of the rent and security as has been paid and is just under the circumstances;

(c) cover and recover damages as to all goods affected whether or not they have been identified to the lease contract (Sections 2A-518 and 2A-520), or recover damages for nondelivery (Sections 2A-519 and 2A-520);

(d) exercise any other rights or pursue any other remedies provided in the lease contract.

(2) If a lessor fails to deliver the goods in conformity to the lease contract or repudiates the lease contract, the lessee may also:

(a) if the goods have been identified, recover them (Section 2A-522); or

(b) in a proper case, obtain specific performance or replevy the goods (Section 2A-521).

(3) If a lessor is otherwise in default under a lease contract, the lessee may exercise the rights and pursue the remedies provided in the lease contract, which may include a right to cancel the lease, and in Section 2A-519(3).

(4) If a lessor has breached a warranty, whether express or implied, the lessee may recover damages (Section 2A-519(4)).

(5) On rightful rejection or justifiable revocation of acceptance, a lessee has a security interest in goods in the lessee's possession or control for any rent and security that has been paid and any expenses reasonably incurred in their inspection, receipt, transportation, and care and custody and may hold those goods and dispose of them in good faith and in a commercially reasonable manner, subject to Section 2A-527(5).

(6) Subject to the provisions of Section 2A-407, a lessee, on notifying the lessor of the lessee's intention to do so, may deduct all or any part of the damages resulting from any default under the lease contract from any part of the rent still due under the same lease contract.

As amended in 1990.

§ 2A-509. Lessee's Rights on Improper Delivery; Rightful Rejection.

(1) Subject to the provisions of Section 2A-510 on default in installment lease contracts, if the goods or the tender or delivery fail in any respect to conform to the lease contract, the lessee may reject or accept the goods or accept any commercial unit or units and reject the rest of the goods.

(2) Rejection of goods is ineffective unless it is within a reasonable time after tender or delivery of the goods and the lessee seasonably notifies the lessor.

§ 2A-510. Installment Lease Contracts: Rejection and Default.

(1) Under an installment lease contract a lessee may reject any delivery that is nonconforming if the nonconformity substantially impairs the value of that delivery and cannot be cured or the nonconformity is a defect in the required documents; but if the nonconformity does not fall within subsection (2) and the lessor or the supplier gives adequate assurance of its cure, the lessee must accept that delivery.

(2) Whenever nonconformity or default with respect to one or more deliveries substantially impairs the value of the installment lease contract as a whole there is a default with respect to the whole. But, the aggrieved party reinstates the installment lease contract as a whole if the aggrieved party accepts a nonconforming delivery without seasonably notifying of cancellation or brings an action with respect only to past deliveries or demands performance as to future deliveries.

§ 2A-511. Merchant Lessee's Duties as to Rightfully Rejected Goods.

(1) Subject to any security interest of a lessee (Section 2A-508(5)), if a lessor or a supplier has no agent or place of business at the

market of rejection, a merchant lessee, after rejection of goods in his [or her] possession or control, shall follow any reasonable instructions received from the lessor or the supplier with respect to the goods. In the absence of those instructions, a merchant lessee shall make reasonable efforts to sell, lease, or otherwise dispose of the goods for the lessor's account if they threaten to decline in value speedily. Instructions are not reasonable if on demand indemnity for expenses is not forthcoming.

(2) If a merchant lessee (subsection (1)) or any other lessee (Section 2A–512) disposes of goods, he [or she] is entitled to reimbursement either from the lessor or the supplier or out of the proceeds for reasonable expenses of caring for and disposing of the goods and, if the expenses include no disposition commission, to such commission as is usual in the trade, or if there is none, to a reasonable sum not exceeding 10 percent of the gross proceeds.

(3) In complying with this section or Section 2A–512, the lessee is held only to good faith. Good faith conduct hereunder is neither acceptance or conversion nor the basis of an action for damages.

(4) A purchaser who purchases in good faith from a lessee pursuant to this section or Section 2A–512 takes the goods free of any rights of the lessor and the supplier even though the lessee fails to comply with one or more of the requirements of this Article.

§ 2A–512. Lessee's Duties as to Rightfully Rejected Goods.

(1) Except as otherwise provided with respect to goods that threaten to decline in value speedily (Section 2A–511) and subject to any security interest of a lessee (Section 2A–508(5)):

(a) the lessee, after rejection of goods in the lessee's possession, shall hold them with reasonable care at the lessor's or the supplier's disposition for a reasonable time after the lessee's seasonable notification of rejection;

(b) if the lessor or the supplier gives no instructions within a reasonable time after notification of rejection, the lessee may store the rejected goods for the lessor's or the supplier's account or ship them to the lessor or the supplier or dispose of them for the lessor's or the supplier's account with reimbursement in the manner provided in Section 2A–511; but

(c) the lessee has no further obligations with regard to goods rightfully rejected.

(2) Action by the lessee pursuant to subsection (1) is not acceptance or conversion.

§ 2A–513. Cure by Lessor of Improper Tender or Delivery; Replacement.

(1) If any tender or delivery by the lessor or the supplier is rejected because nonconforming and the time for performance has not yet expired, the lessor or the supplier may seasonably notify the lessee of the lessor's or the supplier's intention to cure and may then make a conforming delivery within the time provided in the lease contract.

(2) If the lessee rejects a nonconforming tender that the lessor or the supplier had reasonable grounds to believe would be acceptable with or without money allowance, the lessor or the supplier may have a further reasonable time to substitute a conforming tender if he [or she] seasonably notifies the lessee.

§ 2A–514. Waiver of Lessee's Objections.

(1) In rejecting goods, a lessee's failure to state a particular defect that is ascertainable by reasonable inspection precludes the lessee from relying on the defect to justify rejection or to establish default:

(a) if, stated seasonably, the lessor or the supplier could have cured it (Section 2A–513); or

(b) between merchants if the lessor or the supplier after rejection has made a request in writing for a full and final written statement of all defects on which the lessee proposes to rely.

(2) A lessee's failure to reserve rights when paying rent or other consideration against documents precludes recovery of the payment for defects apparent on the face of the documents.

§ 2A–515. Acceptance of Goods.

(1) Acceptance of goods occurs after the lessee has had a reasonable opportunity to inspect the goods and

(a) the lessee signifies or acts with respect to the goods in a manner that signifies to the lessor or the supplier that the goods are conforming or that the lessee will take or retain them in spite of their nonconformity; or

(b) the lessee fails to make an effective rejection of the goods (Section 2A–509(2)).

(2) Acceptance of a part of any commercial unit is acceptance of that entire unit.

§ 2A–516. Effect of Acceptance of Goods; Notice of Default; Burden of Establishing Default after Acceptance; Notice of Claim or Litigation to Person Answerable Over.

(1) A lessee must pay rent for any goods accepted in accordance with the lease contract, with due allowance for goods rightfully rejected or not delivered.

(2) A lessee's acceptance of goods precludes rejection of the goods accepted. In the case of a finance lease, if made with knowledge of a nonconformity, acceptance cannot be revoked because of it. In any other case, if made with knowledge of a nonconformity, acceptance cannot be revoked because of it unless the acceptance was on the reasonable assumption that the nonconformity would be seasonably cured. Acceptance does not of itself impair any other remedy provided by this Article or the lease agreement for nonconformity.

(3) If a tender has been accepted:

(a) within a reasonable time after the lessee discovers or should have discovered any default, the lessee shall notify the lessor and the supplier, if any, or be barred from any remedy against the party notified;

(b) except in the case of a consumer lease, within a reasonable time after the lessee receives notice of litigation for infringement or the like (Section 2A–211) the lessee shall notify the lessor or be barred from any remedy over for liability established by the litigation; and

(c) the burden is on the lessee to establish any default.

(4) If a lessee is sued for breach of a warranty or other obligation for which a lessor or a supplier is answerable over the following apply:

(a) The lessee may give the lessor or the supplier, or both, written notice of the litigation. If the notice states that the person notified may come in and defend and that if the person notified does not do so that person will be bound in any action against that person by the lessee by any determination of fact common to the two litigations, then unless the person notified after seasonable receipt of the notice does come in and defend that person is so bound.

(b) The lessor or the supplier may demand in writing that the lessee turn over control of the litigation including settlement if the claim is one for infringement or the like (Section 2A–211) or else be barred from any remedy over. If the demand states that the lessor or the supplier agrees to bear all expense and to satisfy any adverse judgment, then unless the lessee after seasonable receipt of the demand does turn over control the lessee is so barred.

(5) Subsections (3) and (4) apply to any obligation of a lessee to hold the lessor or the supplier harmless against infringement or the like (Section 2A–211).

As amended in 1990.

§ 2A–517.   Revocation of Acceptance of Goods.

(1) A lessee may revoke acceptance of a lot or commercial unit whose nonconformity substantially impairs its value to the lessee if the lessee has accepted it:

(a) except in the case of a finance lease, on the reasonable assumption that its nonconformity would be cured and it has not been seasonably cured; or

(b) without discovery of the nonconformity if the lessee's acceptance was reasonably induced either by the lessor's assurances or, except in the case of a finance lease, by the difficulty of discovery before acceptance.

(2) Except in the case of a finance lease that is not a consumer lease, a lessee may revoke acceptance of a lot or commercial unit if the lessor defaults under the lease contract and the default substantially impairs the value of that lot or commercial unit to the lessee.

(3) If the lease agreement so provides, the lessee may revoke acceptance of a lot or commercial unit because of other defaults by the lessor.

(4) Revocation of acceptance must occur within a reasonable time after the lessee discovers or should have discovered the ground for it and before any substantial change in condition of the goods which is not caused by the nonconformity. Revocation is not effective until the lessee notifies the lessor.

(5) A lessee who so revokes has the same rights and duties with regard to the goods involved as if the lessee had rejected them.

As amended in 1990.

§ 2A–518.   Cover; Substitute Goods.

(1) After a default by a lessor under the lease contract of the type described in Section 2A–508(1), or, if agreed, after other default by the lessor, the lessee may cover by making any purchase or lease of or contract to purchase or lease goods in substitution for those due from the lessor.

(2) Except as otherwise provided with respect to damages liquidated in the lease agreement (Section 2A–504) or otherwise determined pursuant to agreement of the parties (Sections 1–102(3) and 2A–503), if a lessee's cover is by lease agreement substantially similar to the original lease agreement and the new lease agreement is made in good faith and in a commercially reasonable manner, the lessee may recover from the lessor as damages (i) the present value, as of the date of the commencement of the term of the new lease agreement, of the rent under the new lease agreement applicable to that period of the new lease term which is comparable to the then remaining term of the original lease agreement minus the present value as of the same date of the total rent for the then remaining lease term of the original lease agreement, and (ii) any incidental or consequential damages, less expenses saved in consequence of the lessor's default.

(3) If a lessee's cover is by lease agreement that for any reason does not qualify for treatment under subsection (2), or is by purchase or otherwise, the lessee may recover from the lessor as if the lessee had elected not to cover and Section 2A–519 governs.

As amended in 1990.

§ 2A–519.   Lessee's Damages for Non-Delivery, Repudiation, Default, and Breach of Warranty in Regard to Accepted Goods.

(1) Except as otherwise provided with respect to damages liquidated in the lease agreement (Section 2A–504) or otherwise determined pursuant to agreement of the parties (Sections 1–102(3) and 2A–503), if a lessee elects not to cover or a lessee elects to cover and the cover is by lease agreement that for any reason does not qualify for treatment under Section 2A–518(2), or is by purchase or otherwise, the measure of damages for non-delivery or repudiation by the lessor or for rejection or revocation of acceptance by the lessee is the present value, as of the date of the default, of the then market rent minus the present value as of the same date of the original rent, computed for the remaining lease term of the original lease agreement, together with incidental and consequential damages, less expenses saved in consequence of the lessor's default.

(2) Market rent is to be determined as of the place for tender or, in cases of rejection after arrival or revocation of acceptance, as of the place of arrival.

(3) Except as otherwise agreed, if the lessee has accepted goods and given notification (Section 2A–516(3)), the measure of damages for non-conforming tender or delivery or other default by a lessor is the loss resulting in the ordinary course of events from the lessor's default as determined in any manner that is reasonable together with incidental and consequential damages, less expenses saved in consequence of the lessor's default.

(4) Except as otherwise agreed, the measure of damages for breach of warranty is the present value at the time and place of acceptance of the difference between the value of the use of the goods accepted and the value if they had been as warranted for the lease term, unless special circumstances show proximate damages of a different amount, together with incidental and consequential damages, less expenses saved in consequence of the lessor's default or breach of warranty.

As amended in 1990.

§ 2A–520.   Lessee's Incidental and Consequential Damages.

(1) Incidental damages resulting from a lessor's default include expenses reasonably incurred in inspection, receipt, transportation, and care and custody of goods rightfully rejected or goods the acceptance of which is justifiably revoked, any commercially reasonable charges, expenses or commissions in connection with effecting cover, and any other reasonable expense incident to the default.

(2) Consequential damages resulting from a lessor's default include:

(a) any loss resulting from general or particular requirements and needs of which the lessor at the time of contracting had reason to know and which could not reasonably be prevented by cover or otherwise; and

(b) injury to person or property proximately resulting from any breach of warranty.

§ 2A–521.   Lessee's Right to Specific Performance or Replevin.

(1) Specific performance may be decreed if the goods are unique or in other proper circumstances.

(2) A decree for specific performance may include any terms and conditions as to payment of the rent, damages, or other relief that the court deems just.

(3) A lessee has a right of replevin, detinue, sequestration, claim and delivery, or the like for goods identified to the lease contract if after reasonable effort the lessee is unable to effect cover for those goods or the circumstances reasonably indicate that the effort will be unavailing.

§ 2A–522.   Lessee's Right to Goods on Lessor's Insolvency.

(1) Subject to subsection (2) and even though the goods have not been shipped, a lessee who has paid a part or all of the rent and security for goods identified to a lease contract (Section 2A–217) on making and keeping good a tender of any unpaid portion of the rent and security due under the lease contract may recover the goods identified from the lessor if the lessor becomes insolvent within 10 days after receipt of the first installment of rent and security.

(2) A lessee acquires the right to recover goods identified to a lease contract only if they conform to the lease contract.

C. Default by Lessee

§ 2A–523.   Lessor's Remedies.

(1) If a lessee wrongfully rejects or revokes acceptance of goods or fails to make a payment when due or repudiates with respect to a part or the whole, then, with respect to any goods involved, and with respect to all of the goods if under an installment lease contract the value of the whole lease contract is substantially impaired (Section 2A–510), the lessee is in default under the lease contract and the lessor may:

(a) cancel the lease contract (Section 2A–505(1));

(b) proceed respecting goods not identified to the lease contract (Section 2A–524);

(c) withhold delivery of the goods and take possession of goods previously delivered (Section 2A–525);

(d) stop delivery of the goods by any bailee (Section 2A–526);

(e) dispose of the goods and recover damages (Section 2A–527), or retain the goods and recover damages (Section 2A–528), or in a proper case recover rent (Section 2A–529)

(f) exercise any other rights or pursue any other remedies provided in the lease contract.

(2) If a lessor does not fully exercise a right or obtain a remedy to which the lessor is entitled under subsection (1), the lessor may recover the loss resulting in the ordinary course of events from the lessee's default as determined in any reasonable manner, together with incidental damages, less expenses saved in consequence of the lessee's default.

(3) If a lessee is otherwise in default under a lease contract, the lessor may exercise the rights and pursue the remedies provided in the lease contract, which may include a right to cancel the lease. In addition, unless otherwise provided in the lease contract:

(a) if the default substantially impairs the value of the lease contract to the lessor, the lessor may exercise the rights and pursue the remedies provided in subsections (1) or (2); or

(b) if the default does not substantially impair the value of the lease contract to the lessor, the lessor may recover as provided in subsection (2).

As amended in 1990.

§ 2A–524.   Lessor's Right to Identify Goods to Lease Contract.

(1) After default by the lessee under the lease contract of the type described in Section 2A–523(1) or 2A–523(3)(a) or, if agreed, after other default by the lessee, the lessor may:

(a) identify to the lease contract conforming goods not already identified if at the time the lessor learned of the default they were in the lessor's or the supplier's possession or control; and

(b) dispose of goods (Section 2A–527(1)) that demonstrably have been intended for the particular lease contract even though those goods are unfinished.

(2) If the goods are unfinished, in the exercise of reasonable commercial judgment for the purposes of avoiding loss and of effective realization, an aggrieved lessor or the supplier may either complete manufacture and wholly identify the goods to the lease contract or cease manufacture and lease, sell, or otherwise dispose of the goods for scrap or salvage value or proceed in any other reasonable manner.

As amended in 1990.

§ 2A–525.   Lessor's Right to Possession of Goods.

(1) If a lessor discovers the lessee to be insolvent, the lessor may refuse to deliver the goods.

(2) After a default by the lessee under the lease contract of the type described in Section 2A–523(1) or 2A–523(3)(a) or, if agreed, after other default by the lessee, the lessor has the right to take possession of the goods. If the lease contract so provides, the lessor may require the lessee to assemble the goods and make them available to the lessor at a place to be designated by the lessor which is reasonably convenient to both parties. Without removal, the lessor may render unusable any goods employed in trade or business, and may dispose of goods on the lessee's premises (Section 2A–527).

(3) The lessor may proceed under subsection (2) without judicial process if that can be done without breach of the peace or the lessor may proceed by action.

As amended in 1990.

§ 2A–526.   Lessor's Stoppage of Delivery in Transit or Otherwise.

(1) A lessor may stop delivery of goods in the possession of a carrier or other bailee if the lessor discovers the lessee to be insolvent and may stop delivery of carload, truckload, planeload, or larger shipments of express or freight if the lessee repudiates or fails to make a payment due before delivery, whether for rent, security or otherwise under the lease contract, or for any other reason the lessor has a right to withhold or take possession of the goods.

(2) In pursuing its remedies under subsection (1), the lessor may stop delivery until

   (a) receipt of the goods by the lessee;

   (b) acknowledgment to the lessee by any bailee of the goods, except a carrier, that the bailee holds the goods for the lessee; or

   (c) such an acknowledgment to the lessee by a carrier via reshipment or as warehouseman.

(3) (a) To stop delivery, a lessor shall so notify as to enable the bailee by reasonable diligence to prevent delivery of the goods.

   (b) After notification, the bailee shall hold and deliver the goods according to the directions of the lessor, but the lessor is liable to the bailee for any ensuing charges or damages.

   (c) A carrier who has issued a nonnegotiable bill of lading is not obliged to obey a notification to stop received from a person other than the consignor.

§ 2A–527.   Lessor's Rights to Dispose of Goods.

(1) After a default by a lessee under the lease contract of the type described in Section 2A–523(1) or 2A–523(3)(a) or after the lessor refuses to deliver or takes possession of goods (Section 2A–525 or 2A–526), or, if agreed, after other default by a lessee, the lessor may dispose of the goods concerned or the undelivered balance thereof by lease, sale, or otherwise.

(2) Except as otherwise provided with respect to damages liquidated in the lease agreement (Section 2A–504) or otherwise determined pursuant to agreement of the parties (Sections 1–102(3) and 2A–503), if the disposition is by lease agreement substantially similar to the original lease agreement and the new lease agreement is made in good faith and in a commercially reasonable manner, the lessor may recover from the lessee as damages (i) accrued and unpaid rent as of the date of the commencement of the term of the new lease agreement, (ii) the present value, as of the same date, of the total rent for the then remaining lease term of the original lease agreement minus the present value, as of the same date, of the rent under the new lease agreement applicable to that period of the new lease term which is comparable to the then remaining term of the original lease agreement, and (iii) any incidental damages allowed under Section 2A–530, less expenses saved in consequence of the lessee's default.

(3) If the lessor's disposition is by lease agreement that for any reason does not qualify for treatment under subsection (2), or is by sale or otherwise, the lessor may recover from the lessee as if the lessor had elected not to dispose of the goods and Section 2A–528 governs.

(4) A subsequent buyer or lessee who buys or leases from the lessor in good faith for value as a result of a disposition under this section takes the goods free of the original lease contract and any rights of the original lessee even though the lessor fails to comply with one or more of the requirements of this Article.

(5) The lessor is not accountable to the lessee for any profit made on any disposition. A lessee who has rightfully rejected or justifiably revoked acceptance shall account to the lessor for any excess over the amount of the lessee's security interest (Section 2A–508(5)).

As amended in 1990.

§ 2A–528.   Lessor's Damages for Non-acceptance, Failure to Pay, Repudiation, or Other Default.

(1) Except as otherwise provided with respect to damages liquidated in the lease agreement (Section 2A–504) or otherwise determined pursuant to agreement of the parties (Section 1–102(3) and 2A–503), if a lessor elects to retain the goods or a lessor elects to dispose of the goods and the disposition is by lease agreement that for any reason does not qualify for treatment under Section 2A–527(2), or is by sale or otherwise, the lessor may recover from the lessee as damages for a default of the type described in Section 2A–523(1) or 2A–523(3)(a), or if agreed, for other default of the lessee, (i) accrued and unpaid rent as of the date of the default if the lessee has never taken possession of the goods, or, if the lessee has taken possession of the goods, as of the date the lessor repossesses the goods or an earlier date on which the lessee makes a tender of the goods to the lessor, (ii) the present value as of the date determined under clause (i) of the total rent for the then remaining lease term of the original lease agreement minus the present value as of the same date of the market rent as the place where the goods are

located computed for the same lease term, and (iii) any incidental damages allowed under Section 2A–530, less expenses saved in consequence of the lessee's default.

(2) If the measure of damages provided in subsection (1) is inadequate to put a lessor in as good a position as performance would have, the measure of damages is the present value of the profit, including reasonable overhead, the lessor would have made from full performance by the lessee, together with any incidental damages allowed under Section 2A–530, due allowance for costs reasonably incurred and due credit for payments or proceeds of disposition.

As amended in 1990.

§ 2A–529.   Lessor's Action for the Rent.

(1) After default by the lessee under the lease contract of the type described in Section 2A–523(1) or 2A–523(3)(a) or, if agreed, after other default by the lessee, if the lessor complies with subsection (2), the lessor may recover from the lessee as damages:

> (a) for goods accepted by the lessee and not repossessed by or tendered to the lessor, and for conforming goods lost or damaged within a commercially reasonable time after risk of loss passes to the lessee (Section 2A–219), (i) accrued and unpaid rent as of the date of entry of judgment in favor of the lessor (ii) the present value as of the same date of the rent for the then remaining lease term of the lease agreement, and (iii) any incidental damages allowed under Section 2A–530, less expenses saved in consequence of the lessee's default; and

> (b) for goods identified to the lease contract if the lessor is unable after reasonable effort to dispose of them at a reasonable price or the circumstances reasonably indicate that effort will be unavailing, (i) accrued and unpaid rent as of the date of entry of judgment in favor of the lessor, (ii) the present value as of the same date of the rent for the then remaining lease term of the lease agreement, and (iii) any incidental damages allowed under Section 2A–530, less expenses saved in consequence of the lessee's default.

(2) Except as provided in subsection (3), the lessor shall hold for the lessee for the remaining lease term of the lease agreement any goods that have been identified to the lease contract and are in the lessor's control.

(3) The lessor may dispose of the goods at any time before collection of the judgment for damages obtained pursuant to subsection (1). If the disposition is before the end of the remaining lease term of the lease agreement, the lessor's recovery against the lessee for damages is governed by Section 2A–527 or Section 2A–528, and the lessor will cause an appropriate credit to be provided against a judgment for damages to the extent that the amount of the judgment exceeds the recovery available pursuant to Section 2A–527 or 2A–528.

(4) Payment of the judgment for damages obtained pursuant to subsection (1) entitles the lessee to the use and possession of the goods not then disposed of for the remaining lease term of and in accordance with the lease agreement.

(5) After default by the lessee under the lease contract of the type described in Section 2A–523(1) or Section 2A–523(3)(a) or, if agreed, after other default by the lessee, a lessor who is held not entitled to rent under this section must nevertheless be awarded damages for non-acceptance under Sections 2A–527 and 2A–528.

As amended in 1990.

§ 2A–530.   Lessor's Incidental Damages.

Incidental damages to an aggrieved lessor include any commercially reasonable charges, expenses, or commissions incurred in stopping delivery, in the transportation, care and custody of goods after the lessee's default, in connection with return or disposition of the goods, or otherwise resulting from the default.

§ 2A–531.   Standing to Sue Third Parties for Injury to Goods.

(1) If a third party so deals with goods that have been identified to a lease contract as to cause actionable injury to a party to the lease contract (a) the lessor has a right of action against the third party, and (b) the lessee also has a right of action against the third party if the lessee:

> (i) has a security interest in the goods;

> (ii) has an insurable interest in the goods; or

> (iii) bears the risk of loss under the lease contract or has since the injury assumed that risk as against the lessor and the goods have been converted or destroyed.

(2) If at the time of the injury the party plaintiff did not bear the risk of loss as against the other party to the lease contract and there is no arrangement between them for disposition of the recovery, his [or her] suit or settlement, subject to his [or her] own interest, is as a fiduciary for the other party to the lease contract.

(3) Either party with the consent of the other may sue for the benefit of whom it may concern.

§ 2A–532.   Lessor's Rights to Residual Interest.

In addition to any other recovery permitted by this Article or other law, the lessor may recover from the lessee an amount that will fully compensate the lessor for any loss of or damage to the lessor's residual interest in the goods caused by the default of the lessee.

As added in 1990.

APPENDIX D

Answers to *Issue Spotters*

Chapter 1

1. No. The U.S. Constitution is the supreme law of the land and applies to all jurisdictions. A law in violation of the Constitution (in this question, the First Amendment to the Constitution) will be declared unconstitutional.

2. Case law includes courts' interpretations of statutes, as well as constitutional provisions and administrative rules. Statutes often codify common law rules. For these reasons, a judge might rely on the common law as a guide to the intent and purpose of a statute.

Chapter 2

1. When a corporation decides to respond to what it sees as a moral obligation to correct for past discrimination by adjusting pay differences among its employees, an ethical conflict is raised between the firm and its employees and between the firm and its shareholders. This dilemma arises directly out of the effect such a decision has on the firm's profits. If satisfying this obligation increases profitability, then the dilemma is easily resolved in favor of "doing the right thing."

2. Maybe. On the one hand, it is not the company's "fault" when a product is misused. Also, keeping the product on the market is not a violation of the law, and stopping sales would hurt profits. On the other hand, suspending sales could reduce suffering and could prevent negative publicity that might occur if sales continued.

Chapter 3

1. Tom could file a motion for a directed verdict. This motion asks the judge to direct a verdict for Tom on the ground that Sue presented no evidence that would justify granting her relief. The judge grants the motion if there is insufficient evidence to raise an issue of fact.

2. Yes. Submission of the dispute to mediation or nonbinding arbitration is mandatory, but compliance with the decision of the mediator or arbitrator is voluntary.

Chapter 4

1. No. Even if commercial speech is not related to illegal activities or misleading, it may be restricted if a state has a substantial government interest that cannot be achieved by less restrictive means. In this case, the interest in energy conservation is substantial, but it could be achieved by less restrictive means. That would be the utilities' defense against the enforcement of this state law.

2. Yes. The tax would limit the liberty of some persons, such as out-of-state businesses, so it is subject to a review under the equal protection clause. Protecting local businesses from out-of-state competition is not a legitimate government objective. Thus, such a tax would violate the equal protection clause.

Chapter 5

1. Probably. To recover on the basis of negligence, the injured party as a plaintiff must show that the truck's owner owed the plaintiff a duty of care, that the owner breached that duty, that the plaintiff was injured, and that the breach caused the injury. In this problem, the owner's actions breached the duty of reasonable care. The billboard falling on the plaintiff was the direct cause of the injury, not the plaintiff's own negligence. Thus, liability turns on whether the plaintiff can connect the breach of duty to the injury. This involves the test of proximate cause—the question of foreseeability. The consequences to the injured party must have been a foreseeable result of the owner's carelessness.

2. The company might defend against this electrician's claim by asserting that the electrician should have known of the risk and, therefore, the company had no duty to warn. According to the problem, the danger is common knowledge in the electrician's field and should have been apparent to this electrician, given his years of training and experience. In other words, the company most likely had no need to warn the electrician of the risk.

    The firm could also raise comparative negligence. Both parties' negligence, if any, could be weighed and the liability distributed proportionately. The defendant could furthermore assert assumption of risk, claiming that the electrician voluntarily entered into a dangerous situation, knowing the risk involved.

Chapter 6

1. Yes. With respect to the gas station, Dana has obtained goods by false pretenses. She might also be charged with the crimes of larceny and forgery, and most states have special statutes covering illegal use of credit cards.

2. Yes. The Counterfeit Access Device and Computer Fraud and Abuse Act of 1984 provides that a person who accesses a computer online, without permission, to obtain classified data—such as consumer credit files in a credit agency's database—is subject to criminal prosecution. The crime has two elements: accessing the computer without permission and taking data. It is a felony if done for private financial gain. Penalties include fines and imprisonment for up to twenty years. The victim of the theft can also bring a civil suit against the criminal to obtain damages and other relief.

Chapter 7

1. Under the principle of comity, a U.S court would defer and give effect to foreign laws and judicial decrees that are consistent with U.S. law and public policy.

2. The practice described in this Issue Spotter is known as dumping, which is regarded as an unfair international trade practice. Dumping is the sale of imported goods at "less than fair value." Based on the price of those goods in the exporting country, an extra tariff—known as an antidumping duty—can be imposed on the imports.

Chapter 8

1. Yes, Roslyn has committed theft of trade secrets. Lists of suppliers and customers cannot be patented, copyrighted, or trademarked, but the information they contain is protected against appropriation by others as trade secrets. And most likely, Roslyn signed a contract, agreeing not to use this information outside her employment by Organic. But even without this contract, Organic could have made a convincing case against its ex-employee for a theft of trade secrets.

2. This is patent infringement. A software maker in this situation might best protect its product, save litigation costs, and profit from its patent by the use of a license. In the context of this problem, a license would grant permission to sell a patented item. (A license can be limited to certain purposes and to the licensee only.)

Chapter 9

1. Karl may have committed trademark infringement. Search engines compile their results by looking through Web sites' keyword fields. Key words, or meta tags, increase the likelihood that a site will be included in search engine results, even if the words have no connection to the site.

A site that appropriates the key words of other sites with more frequent hits will appear in the same search engine results as the more popular sites. But using another's trademark as a key word without the owner's permission normally constitutes trademark infringement. Of course, some uses of another's trademark as a meta tag may be permissible if the use is reasonably necessary and does not suggest that the owner authorized or sponsored the use.

2. Yes. This may be an instance of trademark dilution. Dilution occurs when a trademark is used, without permission, in a way that diminishes the distinctive quality of the mark. Dilution does not require proof that consumers are likely to be confused by the use of the unauthorized mark. The products involved do not have to be similar. Dilution does require, however, that a mark be famous when the dilution occurs.

Chapter 10

1. No. Revocation of an offer may be implied by conduct inconsistent with the offer. When Fidelity Corporation rehired Monica, and Ron learned of the hiring, the offer was revoked. His acceptance was too late.

2. No. This contract, although not fully executed, is for an illegal purpose and therefore is void. A void contract gives rise to no legal obligation on the part of any party. A contract that is void is no contract. There is nothing to enforce.

Chapter 11

1. No, the contract can be avoided because Simmons and Jenson have made a bilateral mistake. The issue is whether the mistake involves the identity of the stone (quartz versus diamond) or the value of the stone ($10 versus $1,000). Because both parties were mistaken as to the true character of the subject matter, the contract can be rescinded by either. Had either party known that the stone was some type of gem, then even though its exact nature was unknown (diamond), the mistake would be one of value, not fact, and the contract would not be rescindable.

2. A nonbreaching party is entitled to his or her benefit of the bargain under the contract. Here, the innocent party is entitled to be put in the position she would have been in if the contract had been fully performed. The measure of the benefit is the cost to complete the work ($500). These are compensatory damages.

Chapter 12

1. A shipment of nonconforming goods constitutes an acceptance and a breach, unless the seller seasonably notifies the buyer that the nonconforming shipment does not constitute an acceptance and is offered only as an accommodation. Without the notification, the shipment is an acceptance and a breach. Thus, here the shipment was both an acceptance and a breach.

2. Yes. The manufacturer is liable for the injuries to the user of the product. A manufacturer is liable for its failure to exercise due care to any person who sustains an injury proximately caused by a negligently made (defective) product. In this problem, the failure to inspect is a failure to use due care.

Chapter 13

1. Each of the parties can place a mechanic's lien on the debtor's property. If the debtor does not pay what is owed, the property can be sold to satisfy the debt. The only requirements are that the lien be filed within a specific time from the time of the work, depending on the state statute, and notice of the foreclosure and sale must be given to the debtor in advance.

2. No. Besides the claims listed in this problem, the debts that cannot be discharged in bankruptcy include amounts borrowed to pay back taxes and goods obtained by fraud. Also not dischargeable in bankruptcy are debts that were not listed in the petition, domestic support obligations, certain cash advances, and others.

Chapter 14

1. The members of a limited liability company (LLC) may designate a group to run their firm—then, the firm is considered a manager-managed LLC. The group may include only members, only nonmembers, or members and nonmembers. If, instead, all members participate in management, the firm is a member-managed LLC. In fact, unless the members agree otherwise, all members are considered to participate in the management of the firm.

2. Yes. Failing to meet a specified sales quota can constitute a breach of a franchise agreement. If the franchisor is acting in good faith, "cause" may also include the death or disability of the franchisee, the insolvency of the franchisee, and a breach of another term of the franchise agreement.

Chapter 15

1. Yes. Small businesses that meet certain requirements can qualify as S corporations, created specifically to permit small businesses to avoid double taxation. The six requirements of an S corporation are (1) the firm must be a domestic corporation, (2) the firm must not be a member of an affiliated group of corporations, (3) the firm must have less than a certain number of shareholders, (4) the shareholders must be individuals, estates, or qualified trusts (or corporations in some cases), (5) there can be only one class of stock, and (6) no shareholder can be a nonresident alien.

2. Yes. A shareholder can bring a derivative suit on behalf of a corporation, if some wrong is done to the corporation. Normally, any damages recovered go into the corporate treasury.

Chapter 16

1. No. Nadine, as an agent, is prohibited from taking advantage of the agency relationship to obtain property that the principal (Dimka Corporation) wants to purchase. This is the duty of loyalty that arises with every agency relationship.

2. Yes. A principal has a duty to indemnify (reimburse) an agent for liabilities incurred because of authorized and lawful acts and transactions and for losses suffered because of the principal's failure to perform his or her duties.

Chapter 17

1. Workers' compensation laws establish a procedure for compensating workers who are injured on the job. Instead of suing to collect benefits, an injured worker notifies the employer of the injury and files a claim with the appropriate state agency. The right to recover is normally determined without regard to negligence or fault, but intentionally inflicted injuries are not covered. Unlike the potential for recovery in a lawsuit based on negligence or fault,

recovery under a workers' compensation statute is limited to the specific amount designated in the statute for the employee's injury.

2. No. A closed shop (a company that requires union membership as a condition of employment) is illegal. A union shop (a company that does not require union membership as a condition of employment but requires workers to join the union after a certain time on the job) is illegal in a state with a right-to-work law, which makes it illegal to require union membership for continued employment.

Chapter 18

1. Yes. One type of sexual harassment occurs when a request for sexual favors is a condition of employment, and the person making the request is a supervisor or acts with the authority of the employer. A tangible employment action, such as continued employment, may also lead to the employer's liability for the supervisor's conduct. That the injured employee is a male and the supervisor a female, instead of the other way around, would not affect the outcome. Same-gender harassment is also actionable.

2. Yes, Koko could succeed in a discrimination suit if she can show that she was not hired solely because of her disability. The other elements for a discrimination suit based on a disability are that the plaintiff (1) has a disability and (2) is otherwise qualified for the job. Both of these elements appear to be satisfied in this scenario.

Chapter 19

1. Under the Administrative Procedure Act (APA), the ALJ must be separate from the agency's investigative and prosecutorial staff. *Ex parte* communications between the ALJ and a party to a proceeding are prohibited. Under the APA, an ALJ is exempt from agency discipline except on a showing of good cause.

2. Yes. Administrative rulemaking starts with the publication of a notice of the rulemaking in the *Federal Register*. Among other details, this notice states where and when the proceedings, such as a public hearing, will be held. Proponents and opponents can offer their comments and concerns regarding the pending rule. After the agency reviews all the comments from the proceedings, it considers what was presented and drafts the final rule.

Chapter 20

1. Under an extensive set of procedures established by the U.S. Food and Drug Administration, which administers the federal Food, Drug, and Cosmetic Act, drugs must be shown to be effective as well as safe before they may be marketed to the public. In general, manufacturers are responsible for ensuring that the drugs they offer for sale are free of any substances that could injure consumers.

2. Under the Truth-in-Lending Act, a buyer who wishes to withhold payment for a faulty product purchased with a credit card must follow specific procedures to settle the dispute. The credit card issuer then must intervene and attempt to settle the dispute.

Chapter 21

1. Yes. On the ground that the hardships that would be imposed on the polluter and on the community are greater than the hardships suffered by the residents, the court might deny an injunction. If the plant is the core of the local economy, for instance, the residents may be awarded only damages.

2. The Comprehensive Environmental Response, Compensation, and Liability Act of 1980 regulates the clean-up of hazardous waste disposal sites. Any potentially responsible party can be charged with the entire cost of cleaning up a site. Potentially responsible parties include the person that generated the waste (ChemCorp), the person that transported the waste to the site (Disposal), the person that owned or operated the site at the time of the disposal (Eliminators), and the current owner or operator of the site (Fluid). A party held responsible for the entire cost may be able to recoup some of it in a lawsuit against other potentially responsible parties.

Chapter 22

1. This is a breach of the warranty deed's covenant of quiet enjoyment. Consuela can sue Bernie and recover the purchase price of the house, plus any damages.

2. Yes. An owner of a fee simple has the most rights possible—he or she can give the property away, sell it, transfer it by will, use it for almost any purpose, possess it to the exclusion of all the world, or, as in this case, transfer possession for any period of time. The party to whom possession is transferred can also transfer her or his interest (usually only with the owner's permission) for any lesser period of time.

Chapter 23

1. Size alone does not determine whether a firm is a monopoly—size in relation to the market is what matters. A small store in a small, isolated town is a monopolist if it is the only store serving that market. Monopoly involves the power to affect prices and output. If a firm has sufficient market power to control prices and exclude competition, that firm has monopoly power. Monopoly power in itself is not a violation of Section 2 of the Sherman Act. The offense also requires an intent to acquire or maintain that power through anticompetitive means.

2. This agreement is a tying arrangement. The legality of a tying arrangement depends on the purpose of the agreement, the agreement's likely effect on competition in the relevant markets (the market for the tying product and the market for the tied product), and other factors. Tying arrangements for commodities are subject to Section 3 of the Clayton Act. Tying arrangements for services can be agreements in restraint of trade in violation of Section 1 of the Sherman Act.

Chapter 24

1. The average investor is not concerned with minor inaccuracies but with facts that if disclosed would tend to deter him or her from buying the securities. These would include material facts that have an important bearing on the condition of the issuer and its business—such as liabilities, loans to officers and directors, customer delinquencies, and pending lawsuits.

2. No. The Securities Exchange Act of 1934 extends liability to officers and directors in their personal transactions for taking advantage of inside information when they know it is unavailable to the persons with whom they are dealing.

Sample Answers for *Business Case Problems with Sample Answer*

Problem 1–6. *Law around the World.* The key differences between common law and civil law systems relate to how judges decide cases. In the common law system, courts decide new cases with reference to former decisions, or precedents. Judges attempt to be consistent and to decide similar cases in a similar way, basing their decisions on the principles suggested by earlier cases. Each interpretation becomes part of the law on the subject and serves as a legal precedent, forming the doctrine called *stare decisis.* Common law systems exist in Australia, Canada, India, Ireland, and New Zealand, as well as the United States.

Most of the other European nations base their legal systems on Roman civil law. Civil law is codified law—an ordered grouping of legal principles enacted into law by a legislature or governing body. In a civil law system, the primary source of law is a statutory code, and case precedents are not judicially binding as they are in a common law system. Nonetheless, judges in such systems commonly refer to previous decisions as sources of legal guidance. The difference is that in a civil law system, judges are not bound by precedent, and the doctrine of *stare decisis* does not apply.

Problem 2–6. *Online Privacy.* Facebook created a program that makes decisions for users. Many believe that privacy is an extremely important right that should be fiercely protected. Thus, using duty-based ethics, any program that has a default setting of giving out information is unethical. Facebook should create the program as an opt-in program.

In addition, under the Kantian categorical imperative, if every company used opt-out programs that allowed the disclosure of potentially personal information, privacy might become merely theoretical. If privacy were reduced or eliminated, the world might not be a better place. From a utilitarian or outcome-based approach, an opt-out program might offer the benefits of being easy to created and start, as well as making it easy to recruit partner programs. On the negative side, the program would eliminate users' ability to chose whether to disclose information about themselves. An opt-in program would maintain that user control but might entail higher start-up costs because it would require more marketing to users up front to persuade them to opt in.

Problem 3–8. *Discovery.* Yes, the items that were deleted from a Facebook page can be recovered. Normally, a party must hire an expert to recover material in an electronic format, and this can be time consuming and expensive.

Electronic evidence, or e-evidence, consists of all computer-generated or electronically recorded information, such as posts on Facebook and other social media sites. The effect that e-evidence can have in a case depends on its relevance and what it reveals. In the facts presented in this problem, Isaiah should be sanctioned—he should be required to cover Allied's cost to hire the recovery expert and attorney's fees to confront the misconduct. In a jury trial, the court might also instruct the jury to presume that any missing items are harmful to Isaiah's case. If all of the material is retrieved and presented at the trial, any prejudice (disadvantage) to Allied's case might thereby be mitigated (lessened). If not, of course, the court might go so far as to order a new trial.

In the actual case on which this problem is based, Allied hired an expert, who determined that Isaiah had in fact removed some photos and other items from his Facebook page. After the expert testified about the missing material, Isaiah provided Allied with all of it, including the photos that he had deleted. Allied sought a retrial, but the court instead reduced the amount of Isaiah's damages by the amount that it cost Allied to address his "misconduct."

Problem 4–6. *Establishment Clause.* The establishment clause prohibits the government from passing laws or taking actions that promote religion or show a preference for one religion over another. In assessing a government action, the courts look at the predominant purpose of the action and ask whether the action has the effect of endorsing religion.

Although here DeWeese claimed to have a nonreligious purpose for displaying the poster of the Ten Commandments in a courtroom, his own statements showed a religious purpose. These statements reflected his views about "warring" legal philosophies and his belief that "our legal system is based on moral absolutes from divine law handed down by God through the Ten Commandments." This plainly constitutes a religious purpose that violates the establishment clause because it has the effect of endorsing Judaism or Christianity over other religions. In the case on which this problem is based, the court ruled in favor of the American Civil Liberties Union.

Problem 5–8. *Negligence.* Negligence requires proof that (a) the defendant owed a duty of care to the plaintiff, (b) the defendant breached that duty, (c) the defendant's breach caused the plaintiff's injury, and (d) the plaintiff suffered a legally recognizable injury. With respect to the duty of care, a business owner has a duty to use reasonable care to protect business invitees. This duty includes an obligation to discover and correct or warn of unreasonably dangerous conditions that the owner of the premises should reasonably foresee might endanger an invitee. Some risks are so obvious that an owner need not warn of them. But even if a risk is obvious, a business owner may not be excused from the duty to protect the business's customers from foreseeable harm.

Because Lucario was the Weatherford's business invitee, the hotel owed her a duty of reasonable care to make its premises safe for her use. The balcony ran nearly the entire width of the window in Lucario's room. She could have reasonably believed that the window was a means of access to the balcony. The window/balcony configuration was dangerous, however, because the window opened wide enough for an adult to climb out, but the twelve-inch gap between one side of the window and the balcony was unprotected. This unprotected gap opened to a drop of more than three stories to a concrete surface below.

Should the hotel have anticipated the potential harm to a guest opening the window in Room 59 and attempting to access the balcony? The hotel encouraged guests to "step out onto the balcony" to smoke. The dangerous window/balcony configuration could have been remedied at a minimal cost. These circumstances could be perceived as creating an "unreasonably dangerous" condition. And it could be concluded that the hotel created or knew of the condition and failed to take reasonable steps to warn of it or correct it. Of course, the Weatherford might argue that the window/balcony configuration was so obvious that the hotel was not liable for Lucario's fall.

In the actual case on which this problem is based, the court concluded that the Weatherford did not breach its duty of care to Lucario. On McMurtry's appeal, a state intermediate appellate court held that this conclusion was in error, vacated the lower court's judgment in favor of the hotel on this issue, and remanded the case.

Problem 6–8. *Criminal Liability.* Yes, Green exhibited the required mental state to establish criminal liability. A wrongful mental state *(mens rea)* is one of the elements typically required to establish criminal liability. The required mental state, or intent, is indicated in an applicable statute or law. For example, for murder, the required mental state is the intent to take another's life. A court can also find that the required mental state is present when a defendant's acts are reckless or criminally negligent. A defendant is criminally reckless if he or she consciously disregards a substantial and unjustifiable risk.

In this problem, Green was clearly aware of the danger to which he was exposing people on the street below, but he did not indicate that he specifically intended to harm anyone. The risk of death created by his conduct, however, was obvious. He must have known what was likely to happen if a bottle or plate thrown from the height of twenty-six stories hit a pedestrian or the windshield of an occupied motor vehicle on the street below. Despite his claim that he was intoxicated, he was sufficiently aware to stop throwing things from the balcony when he saw police in the area, and he later recalled what he had done and what had happened.

In the actual case on which this problem is based, after a jury trial, Green was convicted of reckless endangerment. On appeal,

a state intermediate appellate court affirmed the conviction, based in part on the reasoning just stated.

Problem 7–6. *Sovereign Immunity.* The doctrine of sovereign immunity exempts foreign nations from the jurisdiction of U.S. courts, subject to certain conditions. The Foreign Sovereign Immunities Act (FSIA) of 1976 codifies this doctrine and exclusively governs the circumstances in which an action may be brought in a U.S. court against a foreign nation.

A foreign state is not immune from the jurisdiction of U.S. courts when the state (a) waives immunity, (b) engages in commercial activity, or (c) commits a tort in the United States or violates certain international laws. Under the FSIA, a foreign state includes its political subdivisions and "instrumentalities"—departments and agencies. A commercial activity is a regular course of commercial conduct, transaction, or act that is carried out by the foreign state within the United States or has a direct effect in the United States.

The details of what constitutes a commercial activity are left to the courts. But it seems clear that a foreign government can be considered to engage in commercial activity when, instead of regulating a market, the government participates in it. In other words, when a foreign state, or its political subdivisions or instrumentalities, performs the type of actions in which a private party engages in commerce, the state's actions are likewise commercial.

In the facts of this problem, Iran engaged in commercial activity outside the United States by making and marketing its counterfeit versions of Bell's Model 206 Series helicopters. This activity caused a direct effect in the United States by the consumer confusion that will likely result from Iran's unauthorized use of Bell's trade dress. Thus, the court can exercise jurisdiction in these circumstances, and Iran may be as liable as a private party would be for the same acts.

In the actual case on which this problem is based, Iran did not respond to Bell's complaint. The court held that it had jurisdiction under the FSIA's commercial activity exception, as just explained. The court entered a default judgment against Iran and awarded damages and an injunction to Bell.

Problem 8–4. *Trade Secrets.* Some business information that cannot be protected by trademark, patent, or copyright law is protected against appropriation by competitors as trade secrets. Trade secrets consist of anything that makes a company unique and that would have value to a competitor—customer lists, plans, research and development, pricing information, marketing techniques, and production techniques, for example. Theft of trade secrets is a federal crime.

In this problem, the documents in the boxes in the car could constitute trade secrets. But a number of factors suggest that a finding of theft and imposition of liability would not be appropriate. The boxes were not marked in any way that would indicate they contained confidential information. The boxes were stored in an employee's car. The alleged thief was the employee's spouse, not a CPR competitor, and she apparently had no idea what was in the boxes. Leaving trade secrets so accessible does not show an effort to protect the information.

In the case on which this problem is based, the court dismissed Jones's claim, in part on the reasoning just stated.

Problem 9–6. *Privacy.* No, Rolfe did not have a privacy interest in the information obtained by the subpoenas issued to Midcontinent Communications. The courts have held that the right to privacy is guaranteed by the U.S. Constitution's Bill of Rights, and some state constitutions contain an explicit guarantee of the right. A person must have a reasonable expectation of privacy, though, to maintain a suit or to assert a successful defense for an invasion of privacy.

People clearly have a reasonable expectation of privacy when they enter their personal banking or credit-card information online. They also have a reasonable expectation that online companies will follow their own privacy policies. But people do not have a reasonable expectation of privacy in statements made on Twitter and other data that they publicly disseminate. In other words, there is no violation of a subscriber's right to privacy when a third party Internet service provider receives a subpoena and discloses the subscriber's information.

Here, Rolfe supplied his e-mail address and other personal information, including his Internet protocol address, to Midcontinent. In other words, Rolfe publicly disseminated this information. Law enforcement officers obtained this information from Midcontinent through the subpoenas issued by the South Dakota state court. Rolfe provided his information to Midcontinent—he has no legitimate expectation of privacy in that information.

In the actual case on which this problem is based, Rolfe was charged with, and convicted of, possessing, manufacturing, and distributing child pornography, as well as other crimes. As part of the proceedings, the court found that Rolfe had no expectation of privacy in the information that he made available to Midcontinent. On appeal, the South Dakota Supreme Court upheld the conviction.

Problem 10–4. *Offer and Acceptance.* No, a contract was not formed in this case. As the Iowa Supreme Court pointed out, the parties must voluntarily agree to enter into a contract. Courts determine whether an offer has been made objectively—not subjectively.

Under the *Restatement of Contracts (Second)*, "the test for an offer is whether it induces a reasonable belief in the recipient that [the recipient] can, by accepting, bind the sender." The offeror may decide to whom to extend the offer. According to the *Restatement*, an offer may create a power of acceptance in a specified person or in one or more of a specified group or class of persons, acting separately or together.

The court hearing this case explained: "In this situation, Prairie Meadows is the offeror. It makes an offer to its patrons that, if accepted by wagering an amount and the patron wins, it will pay off the wager. Simply stated, the issue is whether Prairie Meadows made an offer to Blackford. Because Prairie Meadows has the ability to determine the class of individuals to whom the offer is made, it may also exclude certain individuals. Blackford had been banned for life from the casino. . . . Under an objective test, unless the

ban had been lifted, Blackford could not have reasonably believed he was among the class of individuals invited to accept Prairie Meadows's offer."

In the actual case on which this problem is based, the jury found that the ban against Blackford had not been lifted and, therefore, Prairie Meadows had not extended him an offer to wager. Because there was no offer to him, no contract could result. The state supreme court therefore reversed the decision of the state appellate court and affirmed the trial court's judgment.

Problem 11–5. *Consequential Damages.* Simard is liable only for the losses and expenses related to the first resale. Simard could reasonably anticipate that his breach would require another sale and that the sales price might be less than what he agreed to pay. Therefore, he should be liable for the difference between his sales price and the first resale price ($29,000), plus any expenses arising from the first resale. Simard is not liable, however, for any expenses and losses related to the second resale. After all, Simard did not cause the second purchaser's default, and he could not reasonably foresee that default as a probable result of his breach.

Problem 12–5. *Nonconforming Goods.* Padma Paper Mills notified Universal Exports about its breach, so Padma has two ways to recover even though it accepted the goods.

Padma's first option is to argue that it revoked its acceptance, giving it the right to reject the goods. To revoke acceptance, Padma would have to show that (a) the nonconformity substantially impaired the value of the shipment, (b) it predicated its acceptance on a reasonable assumption that Universal Exports would cure the nonconformity, and (c) Universal Exports did not cure the nonconformity within a reasonable time.

Padma's second option is to keep the goods and recover for the damages caused by Universal Exports' breach. Under this option, Padma could recover at least the difference between the value of the goods as promised and their value as accepted.

Problem 13–6. *Automatic Stay.* Gholston can recover damages because EZ Auto willfully violated the automatic stay. EZ Auto repossessed the car even though it received notice of the automatic stay from the bankruptcy court. Moreover, EZ Auto retained the car even after it was reminded of the stay by Gholston's attorney. Thus, EZ Auto knew about the automatic stay and violated it intentionally. Because Gholston suffered direct damages as a result, she can recover from EZ Auto.

Problem 14–4. *LLC Operation.* No. One Bluewater member could not unilaterally "fire" another member without providing a reason. Part of the attractiveness of the limited liability company (LLC) as a form of business enterprise is its flexibility. The members can decide how to operate the business through an operating agreement. For example, the agreement can set forth procedures for choosing or removing members or managers.

Here, the Bluewater operating agreement provided for a "super majority" vote to remove a member under circumstances that would jeopardize the firm's contractor status. Thus, one Bluewater member could not unilaterally "fire" another member without providing a reason. In fact, a majority of the members could not terminate the other's interest in the firm without providing a reason. Moreover, the only acceptable reason would be a circumstance that undercut the firm's status as a contractor.

The flexibility of the LLC business form relates to its framework, not to its members' capacity to violate its operating agreement. In the actual case on which this problem is based, Smith attempted to "fire" Williford without providing a reason. In Williford's suit, the court issued a judgment in his favor.

Problem 15–6. *Rights of Shareholders.* Yes. Woods has a right to inspect Biolustré's books and records. Every shareholder is entitled to examine corporate records. A shareholder can inspect the books in person or through an agent such as an attorney, accountant, or other authorized assistant.

The right of inspection is limited to the inspection and copying of corporate books and records for a proper purpose. This is because the power of inspection is fraught with potential for abuse—for example, it can involve the disclosure of trade secrets and other confidential information. Thus, a corporation is allowed to protect itself.

Here, Woods, through Hair Ventures, has the right to inspect Biolustré's books and records. She has a proper purpose for the inspection—to obtain information about Biolustré's financial situation. She, and other shareholders, had not received notice of shareholders' meetings or corporate financial reports for years, or notice of Biolustré's plan to issue additional stock. Hair Ventures had a substantial investment in the company. In the actual case on which this problem is based, the court ordered Biolustré to produce its books and records for Hair Ventures' inspection.

Problem 16–6. *Liability for Contracts.* Hall may be held personally liable. Hall could not be an agent for House Medic because it was a fictitious name and not a real entity. Moreover, when the contract was formed, Hall did not disclose his true principal, which was Hall Hauling, Ltd. Thus, Hall may be held personally liable as a party to the contract.

Problem 17–5. *Workers' Compensation.* Fairbanks's claim qualifies for workers' compensation benefits. To recover benefits under state workers' compensation laws, the requirements are that the injury (a) was accidental and (b) occurred on the job or in the course of employment. Fault is not an issue. The employee must file a claim with the appropriate state agency or board that administers local workers' compensation claims.

In this problem, Fairbanks's claim for workers' compensation benefits appears to have been timely filed with the appropriate state agency. The focus of the dispute is on the second requirement listed—an accidental injury that occurred on the job or in the course of employment. Dynea required its employees to wear certain boots as a safety measure. One of the boots caused a sore on Fairbanks's leg. The sore developed into a pustule and broke into a lesion. Within a week, Fairbanks was hospitalized with an MRSA infection.

Dynea argued that the bacteria were on Fairbanks's skin before he came to work. Even if this were true, however, it was the rubbing of the boot that caused the sore through which the bacteria entered his body. This fact fulfills the second requirement for the recovery of workers' compensation benefits.

In the actual case on which this problem is based, the court issued a decision in favor of Fairbanks's claim for benefits.

Problem 18–4. *Retaliation by Employers.* Yes. Dawson could establish a claim for retaliation. Title VII prohibits retaliation. In a retaliation claim, an individual asserts that she or he suffered harm as a result of making a charge, testifying, or participating in a Title VII investigation or proceeding. To prove retaliation, a plaintiff must show that the challenged action was one that would likely have dissuaded a reasonable worker from making or supporting a charge of discrimination.

In this problem, under applicable state law, it was unlawful for an employer to discriminate against an individual based on sexual orientation. Dawson was subjected to derision on the part of co-workers, including his supervisor, based on his sexual orientation. He filed a complaint with his employer's human resources department. Two days later, he was fired. The proximity in time and the other circumstances, especially the supervisor's conduct, would support a retaliation claim. Also, the discharge would likely have dissuaded Dawson, or any reasonable worker, from making a claim of discrimination. In the actual case on which this problem is based, the court held that Dawson offered enough evidence that "a reasonable trier of fact could find in favor of Dawson on his retaliation claim."

Problem 19–5. *Powers of the Agency.* The United States Supreme Court held that greenhouse gases fit within the Clean Air Act's (CAA's) definition of "air pollutant." Thus, the Environmental Protection Agency (EPA) has the authority under that statute to regulate the emission of such gases from new motor vehicles. According to the Court, the definition, which includes "any" air pollutant, embraces all airborne compounds "of whatever stripe."

The EPA's focus on Congress's 1990 amendments (or their lack) does not indicate the original intent behind the statute (and its amendments before 1990). Nothing in the statute suggests that Congress meant to curtail the agency's power to treat greenhouse gases as air pollutants. In other words, the agency has a preexisting mandate to regulate "any air pollutant" that may endanger the public welfare.

The EPA also argued that, even if it had the authority to regulate greenhouse gases, the agency would not exercise that authority because any regulation would conflict with other administration priorities. The Court acknowledged that the CAA conditions EPA action on the agency's formation of a "judgment," but explained that judgment must relate to whether a pollutant "cause[s], or contribute[s] to, air pollution which may reasonably be anticipated to endanger public health or welfare."

Thus, the EPA can avoid issuing regulations only if the agency determines that greenhouse gases do not contribute to climate change (or if the agency reasonably explains why it cannot or will not determine whether they do). The EPA's refusal to regulate was thus "arbitrary, capricious, or otherwise not in accordance with law." The Court remanded the case for the EPA to "ground its reasons for action or inaction in the statute."

Problem 20–7. *Fair Debt-Collection Practices.* Engler may recover under the Fair Debt Collection Practices Act (FDCPA). Atlantic is subject to the FDCPA because it is a debt-collection agency, and it was attempting to collect a debt on behalf of Bank of America. Atlantic also used offensive tactics to collect from Engler. After all, Atlantic gave Engler's employer the false impression that Engler was a criminal, had a pending case, and was about to be arrested. Finally, Engler suffered harm because he experienced discomfort, embarrassment, and distress as a result of Atlantic's abusive conduct. Engler may recover actual damages, statutory damages, and attorneys' fees from Atlantic.

Problem 21–4. *Environmental Impact Statement.* When an agency acts in an arbitrary and capricious manner, then the court has grounds for intervention. Otherwise, the court defers to the expertise of the agency, as revealed in the record.

Here, the environmental impact statement (EIS) was comprehensive, and the National Park Service (NPS) had credible reason to believe that the use of rafts on the river did not damage the wilderness status of portions of the park. Since the NPS acted within its statutory guidelines and followed proper procedure in its decision making, the court would not intervene in the agency's decision. The appellate court found that the plaintiffs had failed to establish that the NPS acted in an arbitrary and capricious manner when it adopted the plan.

Problem 22–6. *Adverse Possession.* The McKeags satisfied the first three requirements for adverse possession:

1. Their possession was actual and exclusive because they used the beach and prevented others from doing so, including the Finleys,
2. Their possession was open, visible, and notorious because they made improvements to the beach and regularly kept their belongings there.
3. Their possession was continuous and peaceable for the required ten years. They possessed the property for more than four decades, and they even kept a large float there during the winter months.

Nevertheless, the McKeags' possession was *not* hostile and adverse, which is the fourth requirement. The Finleys had substantial evidence that they gave the McKeags permission to use the beach. Rather than reject the Finleys' permission as unnecessary, the McKeags sometimes said nothing and other times seemingly affirmed that the property belonged to the Finleys. Thus, because the McKeags did not satisfy all four requirements, they cannot establish adverse possession.

Problem 23–5. *Price Discrimination.* Spa Steel satisfies most of the requirements for a price discrimination claim under Section 2 of the Clayton Act. Dayton Superior is engaged in interstate commerce, and it sells goods of like grade and quality to at least three purchasers. Moreover, Spa Steel can show that, because it sells Dayton Superior's products at a higher price, it lost business and thus suffered an injury.

To recover, however, Spa Steel will also need to prove that Dayton Superior charged Spa Steel's competitors a lower price for the same product. Spa Steel cannot recover if its prices were higher for reasons related to its own business, such as having a higher overhead or seeking a larger profit.

Problem 24–5. *Violations of the 1934 Act.* An omission or misrepresentation of a material fact in connection with the purchase or sale of a security may violate Section 10(b) of the Securities Exchange Act of 1934 and SEC Rule 10b-5. The key question is whether the omitted or misrepresented information is material. A fact, by itself, is not automatically material.

A fact will be regarded as material only if it is significant enough that it would likely affect an investor's decision as to whether to buy or sell the company's securities. For example, a company's potential liability in a product liability suit and the financial consequences to the firm are material facts that must be disclosed because they affect an investor's decision to buy stock in the company.

In this case, the plaintiffs' claim should not be dismissed. To prevail on their claim that the defendants made material omissions in violation of Section 10(b) and SEC Rule 10-5, the plaintiffs must prove that the omission was material. Their complaint alleged the omission of information linking Zicam and anosmia (loss of the sense of smell) and plausibly suggested that reasonable investors would have viewed this information as material. Zicam products account for 70 percent of Matrixx's sales. Matrixx received reports of consumers who suffered anosmia after using Zicam Cold Remedy.

In public statements discussing revenues and product safety, Matrixx did not disclose this information. But the information was significant enough to likely affect a consumer's decision to use the product, and this would affect the company's revenue and ultimately the commercial viability of the product. The information was therefore significant enough to likely affect an investor's decision whether to buy or sell Matrixx's stock, and this would affect the stock price. Thus, the plaintiffs' allegations were sufficient. Contrary to the defendants' assertion, statistical sampling is not required to show materiality—reasonable investors could view reports of adverse events as material even if the reports did not provide statistically significant evidence.

Glossary

A

Acceptance The act of voluntarily agreeing, through words or conduct, to the terms of an offer, thereby creating a contract.

Accredited Investor In the context of securities offerings, "sophisticated" investors, such as banks, insurance companies, investment companies, the issuer's executive officers and directors, and persons whose income or net worth exceeds certain limits.

Actionable Capable of serving as the basis of a lawsuit. An actionable claim can be pursued in a lawsuit or other court action.

Act of State Doctrine A doctrine providing that the judicial branch of one country will not examine the validity of public acts committed by a recognized foreign government within its own territory.

Actual Malice The deliberate intent to cause harm that exists when a person makes a statement with either knowledge of its falsity or reckless disregard of the truth. Actual malice is required to establish defamation against public figures.

Actus reus A guilty (prohibited) act. The commission of a prohibited act is one of the two essential elements required for criminal liability, the other element being the intent to commit a crime.

Adequate Protection Doctrine A doctrine that protects secured creditors from losing their security as a result of an automatic stay on legal proceedings by creditors against the debtor once the debtor petitions for bankruptcy relief.

Adjudication A proceeding in which an administrative law judge hears and decides issues that arise when an administrative agency charges a person or a firm with an agency violation.

Administrative Agency A federal or state government agency established to perform a specific function.

Administrative Law The body of law created by administrative agencies in order to carry out their duties and responsibilities.

Administrative Law Judge (ALJ) One who presides over an administrative agency hearing and has the power to administer oaths, take testimony, rule on questions of evidence, and make determinations of fact.

Administrative Process The procedure used by administrative agencies in the administration of law.

Adverse Possession The acquisition of title to real property by occupying it openly, without the consent of the owner, for a period of time specified by a state statute. The occupation must be actual, exclusive, open, continuous, and in opposition to all others, including the owner.

Affirmative Action Job-hiring policies that give special consideration to members of protected classes in an effort to overcome present effects of past discrimination.

Agency A relationship between two parties in which one party (the agent) agrees to represent or act for the other (the principal).

Agreement A mutual understanding or meeting of the minds between two or more individuals regarding the terms of a contract.

Alien Corporation A designation in the United States for a corporation formed in another country but doing business in the United States.

Alternative Dispute Resolution (ADR) The resolution of disputes in ways other than those involved in the traditional judicial process, such as negotiation, mediation, and arbitration.

Answer Procedurally, a defendant's response to the plaintiff's complaint.

Anticipatory Repudiation An assertion or action by a party indicating that he or she will not perform an obligation that the party is contractually obligated to perform at a future time.

Antitrust Law Laws protecting commerce from unlawful restraints and anticompetitive practices.

Apparent Authority Authority that is only apparent, not real. An agent's apparent authority arises when the principal causes a third party to believe that the agent has authority, even though she or he does not.

Appropriation In tort law, the use by one person of another person's name, likeness, or other identifying characteristic without permission and for the benefit of the user.

Arbitration The settling of a dispute by submitting it to a disinterested third party (other than a court), who renders a decision.

Arbitration Clause A clause in a contract that provides that, in the event of a dispute, the parties will submit the dispute to arbitration rather than litigate the dispute in court.

Arson The intentional burning of a building.

Articles of Incorporation The document containing basic information about the corporation that is filed with the appropriate governmental agency, usually the secretary of state, when a business is incorporated.

Articles of Organization The document filed with a designated state official by which a limited liability company is formed.

Articles of Partnership A written agreement that sets forth each partner's rights and obligations with respect to the partnership.

Artisan's Lien A possessory lien on personal property of another person to ensure payment to a person who has made improvements on and added value to that property.

Assault Any word or action intended to make another person fearful of immediate physical harm—a reasonably believable threat.

Assignment The act of transferring to another all or part of one's rights arising under a contract.

Assumption of Risk A defense to negligence. A plaintiff may not recover for injuries or damage suffered from risks he or she knows of and has voluntarily assumed.

Attachment The legal process of seizing another's property under a court order to secure satisfaction of a judgment yet to be rendered.

Attempted Monopolization An action by a firm that involves anticompetitive conduct, the intent to gain monopoly power, and a "dangerous probability" of success in achieving monopoly power.

Authorization Card A card signed by an employee that gives a union permission to act on his or her behalf in negotiations with management.

Automatic Stay In bankruptcy proceedings, the suspension of almost all litigation and other action by creditors against the debtor or the debtor's property.

Award The monetary compensation given to a party at the end of a trial or other proceeding.

B

Bait-and-Switch Advertising Advertising a product at an attractive price and then telling the consumer that the advertised product is not available or is of poor quality and encouraging her or him to purchase a more expensive item.

Bankruptcy Court A federal court of limited jurisdiction that handles only bankruptcy proceedings, which are governed by federal bankruptcy law.

Bankruptcy Trustee A person who is appointed by the court or by creditors to manage the debtor's funds during bankruptcy.

Battery Unexcused, harmful or offensive, physical contact with another that is intentionally performed.

Benefit Corporation A for-profit corporation that seeks to have a material positive impact on society and the environment. This new business form is available by statute in a growing number of states.

Beyond a Reasonable Doubt The standard of proof used in criminal cases.

Bilateral Contract A type of contract that arises when a promise is given in exchange for a return promise.

Bilateral Mistake A mistake that occurs when both parties to a contract are mistaken about the same material fact.

Bill of Rights The first ten amendments to the U.S. Constitution.

Binding Authority Any source of law that a court *must* follow when deciding a case.

Bona Fide Occupational Qualification (BFOQ) Identifiable characteristics reasonably necessary to the normal operation of a particular business. These characteristics can include gender, national origin, and religion, but not race.

Bond A security that evidences a corporate (or government) debt.

Botnet Short for robot network—a group of computers that run an application that is controlled and manipulated only by the software source. Usually this term is reserved for networks that have been infected by malicious software.

Breach The failure to perform a legal obligation.

Breach of Contract The failure, without legal excuse, of a promisor to perform the obligations of a contract.

Brief A written summary or statement prepared by one side in a lawsuit to explain its case to the judge.

Browse-Wrap Term A term or condition of use that is presented when an online buyer downloads a product but that does not require the buyer's explicit agreement.

Bureaucracy The organizational structure, consisting of government bureaus and agencies, through which the government implements and enforces the laws.

Burglary The unlawful entry or breaking into a building with the intent to commit a felony.

Business Ethics What constitutes right or wrong behavior and the application of moral principles in a business context.

Business Invitee A person, such as a customer or a client, who is invited onto business premises by the owner of those premises for business purposes.

Business Judgment Rule A rule that immunizes corporate management from liability for decisions that result in corporate losses or damages if the decision-makers took reasonable steps to become informed, had a rational basis for their decisions, and did not have a contract of interest with the corporation.

Business Necessity A defense to alleged employment discrimination in which the employer demonstrates that an employment practice that discriminates against members of a protected class is related to job performance.

Business Tort Wrongful interference with another's business rights and relationships.

Buyout Price The amount payable to a partner on his or her dissociation from a partnership, based on the amount distributable to that partner if the firm were wound up on that date, and offset by any damages for wrongful dissociation.

Bylaws The internal rules of management adopted by a corporation or other association.

C

Case Law The rules of law announced in court decisions. Case law interprets statutes, regulations, constitutional provisions, and other case law.

Categorical Imperative An ethical guideline developed by Immanuel Kant under which an action is evaluated in terms of what would

happen if everybody else in the same situation, or category, acted the same way.

Causation in Fact An act or omission without which an event would not have occurred.

Cease-and-Desist Order An administrative or judicial order prohibiting a person or business firm from conducting activities that an agency or court has deemed illegal.

Certificate of Limited Partnership The basic document filed with a designated state official by which a limited partnership is formed.

Certification Mark A mark used by one or more persons, other than the owner, to certify the region, materials, mode of manufacture, quality, or other characteristic of specific goods or services.

Checks and Balances The principle under which the powers of the national government are divided among three separate branches—the executive, legislative, and judicial branches—each of which exercises a check on the actions of the others.

Choice-of-Language Clause A clause in a contract designating the official language by which the contract will be interpreted in the event of a disagreement over the contract's terms.

Choice-of-Law Clause A clause in a contract designating the law (such as the law of a particular state or nation) that will govern the contract.

Citation A reference to a publication in which a legal authority—such as a statute or a court decision—or other source can be found.

Civil Law The branch of law dealing with the definition and enforcement of all private or public rights, as opposed to criminal matters.

Civil Law System A system of law derived from Roman law that is based on codified laws (rather than on case precedents).

Click-On Agreement An agreement that arises when an online buyer clicks on "I agree," or otherwise indicates her or his assent to be bound by the terms of an offer.

Close Corporation A corporation whose shareholders are limited to a small group of persons, often only family members. In a close corporation, the shareholders' rights to transfer shares to others are usually restricted.

Closed Shop A firm that requires union membership by its workers as a condition of employment, which is illegal.

Cloud Computing The delivery to users of on-demand services from third-party servers over a network.

Collective Bargaining The process by which labor and management negotiate the terms and conditions of employment, including working hours and workplace conditions.

Collective Mark A mark used by members of a cooperative, association, union, or other organization to certify the region, materials, mode of manufacture, quality, or other characteristic of specific goods or services.

Comity The principle by which one nation defers to and gives effect to the laws and judicial decrees of another nation. This recognition is based primarily on respect.

Commerce Clause The provision in Article I, Section 8, of the U.S. Constitution that gives Congress the power to regulate interstate commerce.

Commercial Impracticability A doctrine that may excuse the duty to perform a contract when performance becomes much more difficult or costly due to forces that neither party could control or contemplate at the time the contract was formed.

Commercial Use Use of land for business activities only. Also called *business use.*

Commingle To put funds or goods together into one mass so that they are mixed to such a degree that they no longer have separate identities.

Common Law The body of law developed from custom or judicial decisions in English and U.S. courts, not attributable to a legislature.

Common Stock Shares of ownership in a corporation that give the owner of the stock a proportionate interest in the corporation with regard to control, earnings, and net assets.

Community Property A form of concurrent ownership of property in which each spouse owns an undivided one-half interest in property acquired during the marriage.

Comparative Negligence A rule in tort law, used in the majority of states, that reduces the plaintiff's recovery in proportion to the plaintiff's degree of fault, rather than barring recovery completely.

Compelling Government Interest A test of constitutionality that requires the government to have convincing reasons for passing any law that restricts fundamental rights, such as free speech, or distinguishes among people based on a suspect trait.

Compensatory Damages A monetary award equivalent to the actual value of injuries or damage sustained by the aggrieved party.

Complaint The pleading made by a plaintiff alleging wrongdoing on the part of the defendant. When filed with a court, the complaint initiates a lawsuit.

Computer Crime The unlawful use of a computer or network to take or alter data, or to gain the use of computers or services without authorization.

Concentrated Industry An industry in which a single firm or a small number of firms control a large percentage of market sales.

Concurrent Jurisdiction Jurisdiction that exists when two different courts have the power to hear a case.

Concurrent Ownership Joint ownership.

Concurring Opinion A court opinion by one or more judges or justices who agree with the majority but want to make or emphasize a point that was not made or emphasized in the majority's opinion.

Condemnation The process of taking private property for public use through the government's power of eminent domain.

Condition A qualification, provision, or clause in a contractual agreement, the occurrence or nonoccurrence of which creates, suspends, or terminates the obligations of the contracting parties.

Condition Precedent In a contractual agreement, a condition that must be met before a party's promise becomes absolute.

Confiscation A government's taking of a privately owned business or personal property without a proper public purpose or an award of just compensation.

Conforming Goods Goods that conform to the contract specifications.

Consequential Damages Special damages that compensate for a loss that does not directly or immediately result from the breach (for example, lost profits). For the plaintiff to collect consequential damages, they must have been reasonably foreseeable at the time the breach or injury occurred.

Consideration The value given in return for a promise or performance in a contractual agreement.

Constitutional Law The body of law derived from the U.S. Constitution and the constitutions of the various states.

Constructive Discharge A termination of employment brought about by making the employee's working conditions so intolerable that the employee reasonably feels compelled to leave.

Consumer-Debtor One whose debts result primarily from the purchases of goods for personal, family, or household use.

Contract A set of promises constituting an agreement between parties, giving each a legal duty to the other and also the right to seek a remedy for the breach of the promises or duties.

Contractual Capacity The legal ability to enter into contracts. The threshold mental capacity required by law for a party who enters into a contract to be bound by that contract.

Contributory Negligence A rule in tort law, used in only a few states, that completely bars the plaintiff from recovering any damages if the damage suffered is partly the plaintiff's own fault.

Conversion Wrongfully taking or retaining possession of an individual's personal property and placing it in the service of another.

Conveyance The transfer of title to real property from one person to another by deed or other document.

Cookie A small file sent from a Web site and stored in a user's Web browser to track the user's Web-browsing activities.

"Cooling-Off" Laws Laws that allow buyers to cancel door-to-door sales contracts within a certain period of time, such as three business days.

Copyright The exclusive right of an author or originator of a literary or artistic production to publish, print, sell, or otherwise use that production for a statutory period of time.

Corporate Governance A set of policies specifying the rights and responsibilities of the various participants in a corporation and spelling out the rules and procedures for making corporate decisions.

Corporate Social Responsibility (CSR) The idea that corporations can and should act ethically and be accountable to society for their actions.

Corporation A legal entity formed in compliance with statutory requirements that is distinct from its shareholder-owners.

Correspondent Bank A bank in which another bank has an account (and vice versa) for the purpose of facilitating fund transfers.

Cost-Benefit Analysis A decision-making technique that involves weighing the costs of a given action against the benefits of that action.

Co-Surety A person who assumes liability jointly with another surety for the payment of an obligation.

Counteradvertising New advertising that is undertaken to correct earlier false claims that were made about a product.

Counterclaim A claim made by a defendant in a civil lawsuit against the plaintiff. In effect, the defendant is suing the plaintiff.

Counteroffer An offeree's response to an offer in which the offeree rejects the original offer and at the same time makes a new offer.

Covenant Not to Compete A contractual promise of one party to refrain from competing with another party for certain period of time and within a certain geographic area.

Covenant Not to Sue An agreement to substitute a contractual obligation for some other type of legal action based on a valid claim.

Cover A buyer or lessee's purchase on the open market of goods to substitute for those promised but never delivered by the seller. Under the Uniform Commercial Code, if the cost of cover exceeds the cost of the contract goods, the buyer or lessee can recover the difference, plus incidental and consequential damages.

Cram-Down Provision A provision of the Bankruptcy Code that allows a court to confirm a debtor's Chapter 11 reorganization plan even though only one class of creditors has accepted it.

Creditors' Composition Agreement An agreement formed between a debtor and his or her creditors in which the creditors agree to accept a lesser sum than that owed by the debtor in full satisfaction of the debt.

Crime A wrong against society proclaimed in a statute and, if committed, punishable by society through fines, imprisonment, or death.

Criminal Law The branch of law that defines and punishes wrongful actions committed against the public.

Cure Under the Uniform Commercial Code, the right of a party who tenders nonconforming performance to correct his or her performance within the contract period.

Cyber Crime A crime that occurs in the online environment rather than in the physical world.

Cyber Fraud Any misrepresentation knowingly made over the Internet with the intention of deceiving another for the purpose of obtaining property or funds.

Cyberlaw An informal term used to refer to all laws governing transactions conducted via the Internet.

Cybersquatting The act of registering a domain name that is the same as, or confusingly similar to, the trademark of another and then offering to sell that domain name back to the trademark owner.

Cyber Tort A tort committed via the Internet.

D

Damages A monetary award sought as a remedy for a breach of contract or a tortious action.

Debtor in Possession (DIP) In Chapter 11 bankruptcy proceedings, a debtor who is allowed to continue in possession of the estate in property (the business) and to continue business operations.

Deceptive Advertising Advertising that misleads consumers, either by making unjustified claims about a product's performance or by omitting a material fact concerning the product's composition or performance.

Deed A document by which title to real property is passed.

Defamation Anything published or publicly spoken that causes injury to another's good name, reputation, or character.

Default When a debtor fails to pay as promised.

Default Judgment A judgment entered by a court against a defendant who has failed to appear in court to answer or defend against the plaintiff's claim.

Defendant One against whom a lawsuit is brought, or the accused person in a criminal proceeding.

Defense A reason offered and alleged by a defendant in an action or lawsuit as to why the plaintiff should not recover or establish what she or he seeks.

Delegation The transfer of a contractual duty to a third party. The party delegating the duty (the delegator) to the third party (the delegatee) is still obliged to perform on the contract should the delegatee fail to perform.

Delegation Doctrine A doctrine based on the U.S. Constitution, which has been construed to allow Congress to delegate some of its power to administrative agencies to make and implement laws.

Deposition The testimony of a party to a lawsuit or a witness taken under oath before a trial.

Disaffirmance The legal avoidance, or setting aside, of a contractual obligation.

Discharge The termination of an obligation. In contract law, discharge occurs when the parties have fully performed their contractual obligations or when events, conduct of the parties, or operation of law releases the parties from performance. In bankruptcy proceedings, the extinction of the debtor's dischargeable debts.

Disclosed Principal A principal whose identity is known to a third party at the time the agent makes a contract with the third party.

Discovery A method by which the opposing parties obtain information from each other to prepare for trial.

Disparagement of Property An economically injurious falsehood about another's product or property.

Disparate-Impact Discrimination Discrimination that results from certain employer practices or procedures that, although not discriminatory on their face, have a discriminatory effect.

Disparate-Treatment Discrimination A form of employment discrimination that results when an employer intentionally discriminates against employees who are members of protected classes.

Dissenting Opinion A court opinion that presents the views of one or more judges or justices who disagree with the majority's decision.

Dissociation The severance of the relationship between a partner and a partnership when the partner ceases to be associated with the carrying on of the partnership business.

Dissolution The formal disbanding of a partnership or a corporation.

Distributed Network A network that can be used by persons located (distributed) around the country or the globe to share computer files.

Distribution Agreement A contract between a seller and a distributor of the seller's products setting out the terms and conditions of the distributorship.

Diversity of Citizenship A basis for federal court jurisdiction over a lawsuit between citizens of different states and countries.

Divestiture A company's sale of one or more of its divisions' operating functions under court order as part of the enforcement of the antitrust laws.

Dividend A distribution to corporate shareholders of corporate profits or income, disbursed in proportion to the number of shares held.

Docket The list of cases entered on a court's calendar and thus scheduled to be heard by the court.

Domain Name The series of letters and symbols used to identify site operators on the Internet; Internet "addresses."

Domestic Corporation In a given state, a corporation that does business in, and is organized under the law of, that state.

Double Jeopardy The Fifth Amendment requirement that prohibits a person from being tried twice for the same criminal offense.

Down Payment The part of the purchase price of real property that is paid in cash up front, reducing the amount of the loan or mortgage.

Dram Shop Act A state statute that imposes liability on the owners of bars and taverns, as well as those who serve alcoholic drinks to the public, for injuries resulting from accidents caused by intoxicated persons when the sellers or servers of alcoholic drinks contributed to the intoxication.

Due Process Clause The provisions in the Fifth and Fourteenth Amendments that guarantee that no person shall be deprived of life, liberty, or property without due process of law. State constitutions often include similar clauses.

Dumping The sale of goods in a foreign country at a price below the price charged for the same goods in the domestic market.

Duress Unlawful pressure brought to bear on a person, causing the person to perform an act that she or he would not otherwise perform.

Duty-based Ethics An ethical philosophy rooted in the idea that every person has certain duties to others, including both humans and the planet. Those duties may be derived from religious principles or from other philosophical reasoning.

Duty of Care The duty of all persons, as established by tort law, to exercise a reasonable amount of care in their dealings with others. Failure to exercise due care, which is normally determined by the reasonable person standard, constitutes the tort of negligence.

E

Easement A nonpossessory right, established by express or implied agreement, to make limited use of another's property without removing anything from the property.

E-Contract A contract that is formed electronically.

E-Evidence A type of evidence that consists of all computer-generated or electronically recorded information.

Embezzlement The fraudulent appropriation of funds or other property by a person who was entrusted with the funds or property.

Eminent Domain The power of a government to take land from private citizens for public use on the payment of just compensation.

Employment at Will A common law doctrine under which either party may terminate an employment relationship at any time for any reason, unless a contract specifies otherwise.

Employment Discrimination Treating employees or job applicants unequally on the basis of race, color, national origin, religion, gender, age, or disability.

Enabling Legislation A statute enacted by Congress that authorizes the creation of an administrative agency and specifies the name, composition, and powers of the agency being created.

Entrapment A defense in which a defendant claims that he or she was induced by a public official to commit a crime that he or she would otherwise not have committed.

Entrepreneur One who initiates and assumes the financial risks of a new business enterprise and undertakes to provide or control its management.

Environmental Impact Statement (EIS) A formal analysis required for any major federal action that will significantly affect the quality of the environment to determine the action's impact and explore alternatives.

Equal Dignity Rule A rule requiring that an agent's authority be in writing if the contract to be made on behalf of the principal must be in writing.

Equal Protection Clause The provision in the Fourteenth Amendment that requires state governments to treat similarly situated individuals in a similar manner.

Equitable Principles and Maxims General propositions or principles of law that have to do with fairness (equity).

E-Signature An electronic sound, symbol, or process attached to or logically associated with a record and adopted by a person with the intent to sign the record.

Establishment Clause The provision in the First Amendment that prohibits the government from establishing any state-sponsored religion or enacting any law that promotes religion or favors one religion over another.

Ethical Reasoning A reasoning process in which an individual links his or her moral convictions or ethical standards to the particular situation at hand.

Ethics Moral principles and values applied to social behavior.

Exclusionary Rule A rule that prevents evidence that is obtained illegally or without a proper search warrant—and any evidence derived from illegally obtained evidence—from being admissible in court.

Exclusive-Dealing Contract An agreement under which a seller forbids a buyer to purchase products from the seller's competitors.

Exclusive Jurisdiction Jurisdiction that exists when a case can be heard only in a particular court or type of court.

Exculpatory Clause A clause that releases a contractual party from liability in the event of monetary or physical injury, no matter who is at fault.

Executed Contract A contract that has been fully performed by both parties.

Executory Contract A contract that has not yet been fully performed.

Export The sale of goods and services by domestic firms to buyers located in other countries.

Express Contract A contract in which the terms of the agreement are stated in words, oral or written.

Express Warranty A seller's or lessor's oral or written promise, ancillary to an underlying sales or lease agreement, as to the quality, description, or performance of the goods being sold or leased.

Expropriation A government's seizure of a privately owned business or personal property for a proper public purpose and with just compensation.

F

Federal Form of Government A system of government in which the states form a union and the sovereign power is divided between the central government and the member states.

Federal Question A question that pertains to the U.S. Constitution, an act of Congress, or a treaty and provides a basis for federal jurisdiction in a case.

Fee Simple Absolute An ownership interest in land in which the owner has the greatest possible aggregation of rights, privileges, and power.

Felony A crime—such as arson, murder, rape, or robbery—that carries the most severe sanctions, ranging from more than one year in a state or federal prison to the death penalty.

Fiduciary As a noun, a person having a duty created by his or her undertaking to act primarily for another's benefit in matters connected with the undertaking. As an adjective, a relationship founded on trust and confidence.

Filtering Software A computer program that is designed to block access to certain Web sites, based on their content.

Final Order The final decision of an administrative agency on an issue.

Firm Offer An offer (by a merchant) that is irrevocable without consideration for a period of time (not longer than three months). A firm offer by a merchant must be in writing and must be signed by the offeror.

Fixed-term Tenancy A type of tenancy under which property is leased for a specified period of time, such as a month, a year, or a period of years; also called a *tenancy for years.*

Fixture An item of personal property that has become so closely associated with real property that it is legally regarded as part of that real property.

Forbearance The act of refraining from an action that one has a legal right to undertake. An agreement between the lender and the borrower in which the lender agrees to temporarily cease requiring mortgage payments, to delay foreclosure, or to accept smaller payments than previously scheduled.

Force Majeure Clause A provision in a contract stipulating that certain unforeseen events—such as war, political upheavals, or acts of God—will excuse a party from liability for nonperformance of contractual obligations.

Foreclosure A proceeding in which a mortgagee either takes title to or forces the sale of the mortgagor's property in satisfaction of a debt.

Foreign Corporation In a given state, a corporation that does business in the state without being incorporated therein.

Foreign Exchange Market A worldwide system in which foreign currencies are bought and sold.

Forgery The fraudulent making or altering of any writing in a way that changes the legal rights and liabilities of another.

Formal Contract An agreement that by law requires a specific form for its validity.

Forum-Selection Clause A provision in a contract designating the court, jurisdiction, or tribunal that will decide any disputes arising under the contract.

Franchise Any arrangement in which the owner of a trademark, trade name, or copyright licenses another to use that trademark, trade name, or copyright in the selling of goods or services.

Franchisee One receiving a license to use another's (the franchisor's) trademark, trade name, or copyright in the sale of goods and services.

Franchisor One licensing another (the franchisee) to use the owner's trademark, trade name, or copyright in the selling of goods or services.

Fraudulent Misrepresentation Any misrepresentation, either by misstatement or by omission of a material fact, knowingly made with the intention of deceiving another and on which a reasonable person would and does rely to his or her detriment.

Free Exercise Clause The provision in the First Amendment that prohibits the government from interfering with people's religious practices or forms of worship.

Free-Writing Prospectus A written, electronic, or graphic offer that is used during the waiting period and describes securities that are being offered for sale, or describes the issuing corporation and includes a legend indicating that the investor may obtain the prospectus at the Securities and Exchange Commission's Web site.

Frustration of Purpose A court-created doctrine under which a party to a contract will be relieved of his or her duty to perform when the objective purpose for performance no longer exists due to reasons beyond that party's control.

G

Garnishment A legal process whereby a creditor appropriates a debtor's property or wages that are in the hands of a third party.

General Partner In a limited partnership, a partner who assumes responsibility for the management of the partnership and liability for all partnership debts.

Good Samaritan Statute A state statute stipulating that persons who provide emergency services to, or rescue, someone in peril cannot be sued for negligence unless they act recklessly, thereby causing further harm.

Goodwill In the business context, the valuable reputation of a business viewed as an intangible asset.

Grand Jury A group of citizens who decide, after hearing the state's evidence, whether probable cause exists for believing that a crime has been committed and that a trial ought to be held.

Group Boycott An agreement by two or more sellers to refuse to deal with a particular person or firm.

Guarantor A person who agrees to satisfy the debt of another (the debtor) only after the principal debtor defaults.

H

Hacker A person who uses computers to gain unauthorized access to data.

Historical School A school of legal thought that looks to the past to determine what the principles of contemporary law should be.

Homestead Exemption A law permitting a debtor to retain the family home, either in its entirety or up to a specified dollar amount, free from the claims of unsecured creditors or trustees in bankruptcy.

Horizontal Merger A merger between two firms that are competing in the same market.

Horizontal Restraint Any agreement that restrains competition between rival firms competing in the same market.

Hot-Cargo Agreement An illegal agreement in which employers voluntarily agree with unions not to handle, use, or deal in the nonunion-produced goods of other employers.

I

I-9 Verification The process of verifying the employment eligibility and identity of a new worker. It must be completed within three days after the worker commences employment.

I-551 Alien Registration Receipt A document, known as a "green card," that shows that a foreign-born individual can legally work in the United States.

Identity Theft The illegal use of someone else's personal information to access the victim's financial resources.

Implied Contract A contract formed in whole or in part from the conduct of the parties.

Implied Warranty A warranty that the law derives by implication or inference from the nature of the transaction or the relative situation or circumstances of the parties.

Implied Warranty of Fitness for a Particular Purpose A warranty that goods sold or leased are fit for the particular purpose for which a buyer or lessee will use the goods.

Implied Warranty of Habitability An implied promise by a seller of a new house that the house is fit for human habitation. Also, the implied promise by a landlord that rented residential premises are habitable.

Implied Warranty of Merchantability A warranty that goods being sold or leased are reasonably fit for the ordinary purpose for which they are sold or leased, are properly packaged and labeled, and are of fair quality.

Impossibility of Performance A doctrine under which a party to a contract is relieved of his or her duty to perform when performance becomes objectively impossible or totally impracticable (through no fault of either party).

Independent Contractor One who works for, and receives payment from, an employer but whose working conditions and methods are not controlled by the employer. An independent contractor is not an employee but may be an agent.

Indictment A formal charge by a grand jury that there is probable cause to believe that a named person has committed a crime.

Industrial Use Use of land for light or heavy manufacturing, shipping, or heavy transportation.

Informal Contract A contract that does not require a specific form or method of creation to be valid.

Information A formal accusation or complaint (without an indictment) issued in certain types of actions by a government prosecutor.

Information Return A tax return submitted by a partnership that only reports the income and losses earned by the business. The partnership as an entity does not pay taxes on the income received by the partnership.

Initial Order An agency's disposition in a matter other than a rulemaking. An administrative law judge's initial order becomes final unless it is appealed.

Inside Director A member of the board of directors who is also an officer of the corporation.

Insider Trading The purchase or sale of securities on the basis of information that has not been made available to the public.

Intangible Property Property that cannot be seen or touched but exists only conceptually, such as corporate stocks and bonds. Article 2 of the UCC does not govern intangible property.

Intellectual Property Property resulting from intellectual and creative processes.

Intended Beneficiary A third party for whose benefit a contract is formed. An intended beneficiary can sue the promisor if such a contract is breached.

Intentional Tort A wrongful act knowingly committed.

International Law The law that governs relations among nations.

International Organization An organization that is composed mainly of member nations and usually established by treaty—for example, the United Nations.

Internet Service Provider (ISP) A business or organization that offers users access to the Internet and related services.

Interpretive Rule An administrative agency rule that explains how the agency interprets and intends to apply the statutes it enforces.

Interrogatories A series of written questions for which written answers are prepared by a party to a lawsuit, usually with the assistance of the party's attorney, and then signed under oath.

Inverse Condemnation The taking of private property by the government without payment of just compensation as required by the U.S. Constitution. The owner must sue the government to recover just compensation.

Investment Company A company that acts on the behalf of many smaller shareholders-owners by buying a large portfolio of securities and professionally managing that portfolio.

Investment Contract In securities law, a transaction in which a person invests in a common enterprise reasonably expecting profits that are derived primarily from the efforts of others.

J

Joint and Several Liability In partnership law, a doctrine under which a plaintiff can file a lawsuit against all of the partners together (jointly) or one or more of the partners separately (severally, or individually). All partners in a partnership can be held liable regardless of whether the partner participated in, knew about, or ratified the conduct that gave rise to the lawsuit.

Joint Liability In partnership law, partners share liability for partnership obligations and debts. Thus, if a third party sues a partner on a partnership debt, the partner has the right to insist that the other partners be sued with him or her.

Joint Tenancy The joint ownership of property by two or more co-owners in which each co-owner owns an undivided portion of the property. On the death of one of the joint tenants, his or her interest automatically passes to the surviving joint tenants.

Judicial Review The process by which a court decides on the constitutionality of legislative enactments and actions of the executive branch.

Jurisdiction The authority of a court to hear and decide a specific case.

Jurisprudence The science or philosophy of law.

Justiciable Controversy A controversy that is not hypothetical or academic but real and substantial; a requirement that must be satisfied before a court will hear a case.

L

Larceny The wrongful taking and carrying away of another person's personal property with the intent to permanently deprive the owner of the property.

Law A body of enforceable rules governing relationships among individuals and between individuals and their society.

Lease Agreement In regard to the lease of goods, an agreement in which one person (the lessor) agrees to transfer the right to the possession and use of property to another person (the lessee) in exchange for rental payments.

Leasehold Estate An interest in real property that gives a tenant a qualified right to possess and/or use the property for a limited time under a lease.

Legal Positivism A school of legal thought centered on the assumption that there is no law higher than the laws created by a national govern-ment. Laws must be obeyed, even if they are unjust, to prevent anarchy.

Legal Realism A school of legal thought that holds that the law is only one factor to be considered when deciding cases and that social and economic circumstances should also be taken into account.

Legislative Rule An administrative agency rule that carries the same weight as a congressionally enacted statute.

Lessee One who acquires the right to the possession and use of another's goods in exchange for rental payments.

Lessor One who transfers the right to the possession and use of goods to another in exchange for rental payments.

Letter of Credit A written document in which the issuer (usually a bank) promises to honor drafts or other demands for payment by third persons in accordance with the terms of the instrument.

Liability The state of being legally responsible (liable) for something, such as a debt or obligation.

Libel Defamation in writing or another form having the quality of permanence (such as a digital recording).

License An agreement by the owner of intellectual property to permit another to use a trademark, copyright, patent, or trade secret for certain limited purposes. A revocable right or privilege of a person to come on another person's land.

Lien A claim against specific property to satisfy a debt.

Life Estate An interest in land that exists only for the duration of the life of a specified individual, usually the holder of the estate.

Limited Liability Company (LLC) A hybrid form of business enterprise that offers the limited liability of the corporation but the tax advantages of a partnership.

Limited Liability Partnership (LLP) A hybrid form of business organization that is used mainly by professionals who normally do business in a partnership. Like a partnership, an LLP is a pass-through entity for tax purposes, but the personal liability of the partners is limited.

Limited Partner In a limited partnership, a partner who contributes capital to the partnership but has no right to participate in the management and operation of the business. The limited partner assumes no liability for partnership debts beyond the capital contributed.

Limited Partnership (LP) A partnership consisting of one or more general partners (who manage the business and are liable to the full extent of their personal assets for debts of the partnership) and one or more limited partners (who contribute only assets and are liable only up to the extent of their contributions).

Liquidated Damages An amount, stipulated in a contract, that the parties to the contract believe to be a reasonable estimate of the damages that will occur in the event of a breach.

Liquidation The sale of the nonexempt assets of a debtor and the distribution of the funds received to creditors.

Litigation The process of resolving a dispute through the court system.

Long Arm Statute A state statute that permits a state to exercise jurisdiction over nonresident defendants.

M

Mailbox Rule A common law rule that acceptance takes effect, and thus a contract is formed, at the time the offeree sends or delivers the acceptance using the communication mode expressly or impliedly authorized by the offeror.

Majority Opinion A court opinion that represents the views of the majority (more than half) of the judges or justices deciding the case.

Malpractice Professional misconduct or the lack of the requisite degree of skill as a professional. Negligence—the failure to exercise due care—on the part of a professional, such as a physician, is commonly referred to as malpractice.

Market Concentration The degree to which a small number of firms control a large percentage of a relevant market.

Market Power The power of a firm to control the market price of its product. A monopoly has the greatest degree of market power.

Mechanic's Lien A statutory lien on the real property of another to ensure payment to a person who has performed work and furnished materials for the repair or improvement of that property.

Mediation A method of settling disputes outside the courts by using the services of a neutral third party, who acts as a communicating agent between the parties and assists them in negotiating a settlement.

Member A person who has an ownership interest in a limited liability company.

Mens rea The wrongful mental state ("guilty mind"), or intent, that is one of the key requirements to establish criminal liability for an act.

Merchant A person who is engaged in the purchase and sale of goods. Under the UCC, a person who deals in goods of the kind involved in the sales contract or who holds herself or himself out as having skill or knowledge peculiar to the practices or goods being purchased or sold.

Metadata Data that are automatically recorded by electronic devices and provide information about who created a file and when, and who accessed, modified, or transmit-

ted it on their hard drives. Can be described as data about data.

Meta Tag A key word in a document that can serve as an index reference to the document. Online search engines return results based, in part, on the tags in Web documents.

Minimum Wage The lowest wage, either by government regulation or union contract, that an employer may pay an hourly worker.

Mirror Image Rule A common law rule that requires the terms of the offeree's acceptance to exactly match the terms of the offeror's offer for a valid contract to be formed.

Misdemeanor A lesser crime than a felony, punishable by a fine or incarceration in jail for up to one year.

Mitigation of Damages A rule requiring a plaintiff to do whatever is reasonable to minimize the damages caused by the defendant.

Money Laundering Engaging in financial transactions to conceal the identity, source, or destination of illegally gained funds.

Monopolization The possession of monopoly power in the relevant market and the willful acquisition or maintenance of that power, as distinguished from growth or development as a consequence of a superior product, business acumen, or historic accident.

Monopoly A market in which there is a single seller or a very limited number of sellers.

Monopoly Power The ability of a monopoly to dictate what takes place in a given market.

Moral Minimum The minimum degree of ethical behavior expected of a business firm, which is usually defined as compliance with the law.

Mortgage A written document that gives a creditor (the mortgagee) an interest in, or lien on, the debtor's (mortgagor's) real property as security for a debt.

Motion for a Directed Verdict A motion for the judge to take the decision out of the hands of the jury and to direct a verdict for the party making the motion on the ground that the other party has not produced sufficient evidence to support her or his claim.

Motion for a New Trial A motion asserting that the trial was so fundamentally flawed (because of error, newly discovered evidence, prejudice, or another reason) that a new trial is necessary to prevent a miscarriage of justice.

Motion for Judgment N.O.V. A motion requesting the court to grant judgment in favor of the party making the motion on the ground that the jury's verdict against him or her was unreasonable and erroneous.

Motion for Judgment on the Pleadings A motion by either party to a lawsuit at the close of the pleadings requesting the court to decide the issue solely on the pleadings without proceeding to trial. The motion will be granted only if no facts are in dispute.

Motion for Summary Judgment A motion requesting the court to enter a judgment without proceeding to trial. The motion can be based on evidence outside the pleadings and will be granted only if no facts are in dispute.

Motion to Dismiss A pleading in which a defendant admits the facts as alleged by the plaintiff but asserts that the plaintiff's claim to state a cause of action has no basis in law.

Multiple Product Order An order requiring a firm that has engaged in deceptive advertising to cease and desist from false advertising in regard to all the firm's products.

Mutual Fund A specific type of investment company that continually buys or sells to investors shares of ownership in a portfolio.

Mutual Rescission An agreement between the parties to cancel their contract, releasing the parties from further obligations under the contract. The object of the agreement is to restore the parties to the positions they would have occupied had no contract ever been formed.

N

National Law Law that pertains to a particular nation (as opposed to international law).

Natural Law The oldest school of legal thought, based on the belief that the legal system should reflect universal ("higher") moral and ethical principles that are inherent in human nature.

Negligence The failure to exercise the standard of care that a reasonable person would exercise in similar circumstances.

Negligence *Per Se* An action or failure to act in violation of a statutory requirement.

Negotiation A process in which parties attempt to settle their dispute informally, with or without attorneys to represent them.

Nonpossessory Interest In the context of real property, an interest that involves the right to use land but not the right to possess it.

Normal Trade Relations (NTR) Status A legal trade status granted to member countries of the World Trade Organization.

Notary Public A public official authorized to attest to the authenticity of signatures.

Notice-and-Comment Rulemaking A procedure in agency rulemaking that requires notice, opportunity for comment, and a published draft of the final rule.

Novation The substitution, by agreement, of a new contract for an old one, with the rights under the old one being terminated. Typically, novation involves the substitution of a new party for one of the original parties to the contract.

Nuisance A common law doctrine under which persons may be held liable for using their property in a manner that unreasonably interferes with others' rights to use or enjoy their own property.

O

Objective Theory of Contracts The view that contracting parties shall only be bound by terms that can objectively be inferred from promises made.

Offer A promise or commitment to perform or refrain from performing some specified act in the future.

Online Dispute Resolution (ODR) The resolution of disputes with the assistance of organizations that offer dispute-resolution services via the Internet.

Operating Agreement In a limited liability company, an agreement in which the members set forth the details of how the business will be managed and operated.

Option Contract A contract under which the offeror cannot revoke the offer for a stipulated time period (because the offeree has given consideration for the offer to remain open).

Order for Relief A court's grant of assistance to a complainant. In bankruptcy proceedings, the order relieves the debtor of the immediate obligation to pay the debts listed in the bankruptcy petition.

Ordinance A regulation enacted by a city or county legislative body that becomes part of that state's statutory law.

Outcome-based Ethics An ethical philosophy that focuses on the impacts of a decision on society or on key stakeholders.

Outside Director A member of the board of directors who does not hold a management position at the corporation.

P

Partially Disclosed Principal A principal whose identity is unknown by a third party, but the third party knows that the agent is or may be acting for a principal at the time the agent and the third party form a contract.

Partnership An agreement by two or more persons to carry on, as co-owners, a business for profit.

Pass-Through Entity A business entity that has no tax liability. The entity's income is passed through to the owners, and the owners pay taxes on the income.

Past Consideration An act that has already taken place at the time a contract is made and that ordinarily, by itself, cannot be consideration for a later promise to pay for the act.

Patent A property right granted by the federal government that gives an inventor an exclusive right to make, use, sell, or offer to sell an invention in the United States for a limited time.

Peer-to-Peer (P2P) Networking The sharing of resources (such as files, hard drives, and processing styles) among multiple computers without the requirement of a central network server.

Penalty A sum inserted into a contract, not as a measure of compensation for its breach but rather as a punishment for a default. The agreement as to the amount will not be enforced, and recovery will be limited to actual damages.

Per Curiam Opinion A court opinion that does not indicate which judge or justice authored the opinion.

Perfect Tender Rule A common law rule under which a seller was required to deliver to the buyer goods that conformed perfectly to the requirements stipulated in the sales contract. A tender of nonconforming goods would automatically constitute a breach of contract. Under the Uniform Commercial Code, the rule has been greatly modified.

Performance In contract law, the fulfillment of one's duties arising under a contract with another; the normal way of discharging one's contractual obligations.

Periodic Tenancy A lease interest in land for an indefinite period involving payment of rent at fixed intervals, such as week to week, month to month, or year to year.

Per Se Violation A restraint of trade that is so anticompetitive that it is deemed inherently (*per se*) illegal.

Persuasive Authority Any legal authority or source of law that a court may look to for guidance but need not follow when making its decision.

Petty Offense The least serious kind of criminal offense, such as a traffic or building-code violation.

Phishing An e-mail fraud scam in which the messages purport to be from legitimate businesses to induce individuals into revealing their personal financial data, passwords, or other information.

Piercing the Corporate Veil The action of a court to disregard the corporate entity and hold the shareholders personally liable for corporate debts and obligations.

Plaintiff One who initiates a lawsuit.

Plea Bargaining The process by which a criminal defendant and the prosecutor work out an agreement to dispose of the criminal case, subject to court approval.

Pleadings Statements by the plaintiff and the defendant that detail the facts, charges, and defenses of a case.

Plurality Opinion A court opinion that is joined by the largest number of the judges or justices hearing the case, but less than half of the total number.

Police Powers Powers possessed by the states as part of their inherent sovereignty. These powers may be exercised to protect or promote the public order, health, safety, morals, and general welfare.

Potentially Responsible Party (PRP) A party liable for the costs of cleaning up a hazardous waste–disposal site under the Comprehensive Environmental Response, Compensation, and Liability Act.

Power of Attorney Authorization for another to act as one's agent or attorney in either specified circumstances (special) or in all situations (general).

Precedent A court decision that furnishes an example or authority for deciding subsequent cases involving identical or similar legal principles or facts.

Predatory Pricing The pricing of a product below cost with the intent to drive competitors out of the market.

Predominant-Factor Test A test courts use to determine whether a contract is primarily for the sale of goods or for the sale of services.

Preemption A doctrine under which certain federal laws preempt, or take precedence over, conflicting state or local laws.

Preemptive Rights Rights that entitle shareholders to purchase newly issued shares of a corporation's stock, equal in percentage to shares already held, before the stock is offered to outside buyers.

Preference In bankruptcy proceedings, a property transfer or payment made by the debtor that favors one creditor over others.

Preferred Creditor In the context of bankruptcy, a creditor who has received a preferential transfer from a debtor.

Preferred Stock Stock that has priority over common stock as to payment of dividends and distribution of assets on the corporation's dissolution.

Prepayment penalty A provision in a mortgage loan contract that requires the borrower to pay a penalty if the mortgage is repaid in full within a certain period.

Price Discrimination A seller's act of charging competing buyers different prices for identical products or services.

Price-Fixing Agreement An agreement between competitors to fix the prices of products or services at a certain level.

Prima Facie Case A case in which the plaintiff has produced sufficient evidence of his or her claim that the case will be decided for the plaintiff unless the defendant produces evidence to rebut it.

Primary Source of Law A document that establishes the law on a particular issue, such as a constitution, a statute, an administrative rule, or a court decision.

Principle of Rights The belief that human beings have certain fundamental rights. Whether an action or decision is ethical depends on how it affects the rights of various groups, such as owners, employees, consumers, suppliers, the community, and society.

Private Equity Capital Funds invested by a private equity firm in an existing corporation, usually to purchase and reorganize it.

Privilege A special right, advantage, or immunity granted to a person or a class of persons, such as a judge's absolute privilege to avoid liability for defamation over statements made in the courtroom during a trial.

Privity of Contract The relationship that exists between the promisor and the promisee of a contract.

Probable Cause Reasonable grounds for believing that a search should be conducted or that a person should be arrested.

Probate Court A state court of limited jurisdiction that conducts proceedings relating to the settlement of a deceased person's estate.

Procedural Law Law that establishes the methods of enforcing the rights established by substantive law.

Product Liability The liability of manufacturers, sellers, and lessors of goods to consumers, users, and bystanders for injuries or damages that are caused by the goods.

Profit In real property law, the right to enter onto another's property and remove something of value from that property.

Promise A declaration by a person (the promisor) to do or not to do a certain act.

Prospectus A written document required by securities laws when a security is being sold. The prospectus describes the security, the financial operations of the issuing corporation, and the risk attaching to the security so that investors will have sufficient information to evaluate the risk involved in purchasing the security.

Protected Class A group of persons protected by specific laws because of the group's defining characteristics, including race, color, religion, national origin, gender, age, and disability.

Proximate Cause Legal cause. It exists when the connection between an act and an injury is strong enough to justify imposing liability.

Proxy In corporate law, a written or electronically transmitted form in which a stockholder authorizes another party to vote the stockholder's shares in a certain manner.

Puffery A salesperson's exaggerated claims concerning the quality of goods offered for sale. Such claims involve opinions rather than facts and are not considered to be legally binding promises or warranties.

Punitive Damages Monetary damages that may be awarded to a plaintiff to punish the defendant and deter similar conduct in the future.

Q

Question of Fact In a lawsuit, an issue that involves only disputed facts, and not what the law is on a given point.

Question of Law In a lawsuit, an issue involving the application or interpretation of a law.

Quitclaim Deed A deed that conveys only whatever interest the grantor had in the property and therefore offers the least amount of protection against defects of title.

Quorum The number of members of a decision-making body that must be pre-sent before business may be transacted.

Quota A set limit on the amount of goods that can be imported.

R

Ratification A party's act of accepting or giving legal force to a contract or other obligation entered into by another that previously was not enforceable.

Reaffirmation Agreement An agreement between a debtor and a creditor in which the debtor voluntarily agrees to pay a debt dischargeable in bankruptcy.

Reasonable Person Standard The standard of behavior expected of a hypothetical "reasonable person." It is the standard against which negligence is measured and that must be observed to avoid liability for negligence.

Record Information that is either inscribed on a tangible medium or stored in an electronic or other medium and is retrievable.

Recording Statutes Statutes that allow deeds, mortgages, and other real property transactions to be recorded so as to provide notice to future purchasers or creditors of an existing claim on the property.

Reformation A court-ordered correction of a written contract so that it reflects the true intentions of the parties.

Regulation Z A set of rules issued by the Federal Reserve Board of Governors to implement the provisions of the Truth-in-Lending Act.

Release An agreement in which one party gives up the right to pursue a legal claim against another party.

Remedy The relief given to an innocent party to enforce a right or compensate for the violation of a right.

Replevin An action to recover specific goods in the hands of a party who is wrongfully withholding them from the other party.

Reply Procedurally, a plaintiff's response to a defendant's answer.

Resale Price Maintenance Agreement An agreement between a manufacturer and a retailer in which the manufacturer specifies what the retail prices of its products must be.

Rescission A remedy whereby a contract is canceled and the parties are returned to the positions they occupied before the contract was made.

Residential Use Use of land for construction of buildings for human habitation only.

Res Ipsa Loquitur A doctrine under which negligence may be inferred simply because an event occurred, if it is the type of event that would not occur in the absence of negligence. Literally, the term means "the facts speak for themselves."

Respondeat Superior A doctrine under which a principal or an employer is held liable for the wrongful acts committed by agents or employees while acting within the course and scope of their agency or employment.

Restitution An equitable remedy under which a person is restored to his or her original position prior to loss or injury, or placed in the position he or she would have been in had the breach not occurred.

Restrictive Covenant A private restriction on the use of land that is binding on the party that purchases the property originally as well as on subsequent purchasers. If its benefit or obligation passes with the land's ownership, it is said to "run with the land."

Retained Earnings The portion of a corporation's profits that has not been paid out as dividends to shareholders.

Revocation The withdrawal of a contract offer by the offeror. Unless an offer is irrevocable, it can be revoked at any time prior to acceptance without liability.

Right of Contribution The right of a co-surety who pays more than her or his proportionate share on a debtor's default to recover the excess paid from other co-sureties.

Right of Redemption The debtor's legal right to repurchase, or buy back, property before a foreclosure sale.

Right of Reimbursement The legal right of a person to be repaid or indemnified for costs, expenses, or losses incurred or expended on behalf of another.

Right of Subrogation The right of a surety or guarantor to stand in the place of (be substituted for) the creditors, giving the surety or guarantor the same legal rights against the debtor that the creditor had.

Right-to-Work Law A state law providing that employees may not be required to join a union as a condition of retaining employment.

Robbery The act of forcefully and unlawfully taking personal property of any value from another.

Rulemaking The actions of administrative agencies when formally adopting new regulations or amending old ones.

Rule of Four A rule of the United States Supreme Court under which the Court will not issue a writ of *certiorari* unless at least four justices approve of the decision to issue the writ.

Rule of Reason A test used to determine whether an anticompetitive agreement constitutes a reasonable restraint on trade. Courts consider such factors as the purpose of the agreement, its effect on competition, and whether less restrictive means could have been used.

S

Sale The passing of title to property from the seller to the buyer for a price.

Sales Contract A contract for the sale of goods under which the ownership of goods is transferred from a seller to a buyer for a price.

S Corporation A close business corporation that has most corporate attributes, including limited liability, but qualifies under the Internal Revenue Code to be taxed as a partnership.

Search Warrant An order granted by a public authority, such as a judge, that authorizes law enforcement personnel to search particular premises or property.

Secondary Source of Law A publication that summarizes or interprets the law, such as a legal encyclopedia, a legal treatise, or an article in a law review.

SEC Rule 10b-5 A rule of the Securities and Exchange Commission that prohibits the commission of fraud in connection with the purchase or sale of any security. It is unlawful to make any untrue statement of a material fact or to omit a material fact if doing so causes the statement to be misleading.

Securities Generally, stocks, bonds, and other items that represent an ownership interest in a corporation or a promise of repayment of debt by a corporation.

Security Generally, a stock, bond, note, debenture, warrant, or other instrument representing an ownership interest in a corporation or a promise of repayment of debt by a corporation.

Self-Defense The legally recognized privilege to do what is reasonably necessary to protect oneself, one's property, or someone else against injury by another.

Self-Incrimination Giving testimony in a trial or other legal proceeding that could expose the person testifying to criminal prosecution.

Seniority System A system in which those who have worked longest for an employer are first in line for promotions, salary increases, and other benefits, and are last to be laid off if the workforce must be reduced.

Service Mark A trademark that is used to distinguish the services (rather than the products) of one person or company from those of another.

Service of Process The delivery of the complaint and summons to the defendant.

Sexual Harassment The demanding of sexual favors in return for job promotions or other benefits, or language or conduct that is so sexually offensive that it creates a hostile working environment.

Shareholder's Derivative Suit A suit brought by a shareholder to enforce a corporate cause of action against a third party.

Short Sale A sale of real property for an amount that is less than the balance owed on the mortgage loan, usually due to financial hardship.

Short-Swing Profits Profits earned by a purchase and sale, or sale and purchase, of the same security within a six-month period. Under Section 16(b) of the 1934 Securities Exchange Act, the profits must be returned to the corporation if earned by company insiders from transactions in the company's stock.

Shrink-Wrap Agreement An agreement whose terms are expressed in a document located inside a box in which goods (usually software) are packaged.

Slander Defamation in oral form.

Slander of Quality (Trade Libel) The publication of false information about another's product, alleging that it is not what its seller claims.

Slander of Title The publication of a statement that denies or casts doubt on another's legal ownership of any property, causing financial loss to that property's owner.

Small Claims Court A special court in which parties can litigate small claims without an attorney.

Social Media Forms of communication through which users create and share information, ideas, messages, and other content via the Internet.

Sole Proprietorship The simplest form of business, in which the owner is the business. The owner reports business income on his or her personal income tax return and is legally responsible for all debts and obligations incurred by the business.

Sovereign Immunity A doctrine that immunizes foreign nations from the jurisdiction of U.S. courts when certain conditions are satisfied.

Spam Bulk, unsolicited (junk) e-mail.

Special-Use Permit A permit that allows an exemption to zoning regulations for a particular piece of property as long as the property owner complies with specific requirements to ensure that the proposed use does not affect the characteristics of the area.

Special Warranty Deed A deed that warrants only that the grantor held good title during his or her ownership of the property and does not warrant that there were no defects of title when the property was held by previous owners.

Specific Performance An equitable remedy requiring exactly the performance that was specified in a contract; usually granted only when money damages would be an inadequate remedy and the subject matter of the contract is unique (for example, real property).

Stakeholders Groups, other than the company's shareholders, that are affected by corporate decisions. Stakeholders include employees, customers, creditors, suppliers, and the community in which the corporation operates.

Standing to Sue The legal requirement that an individual must have a sufficient stake in a controversy before he or she can bring a lawsuit.

Stare Decisis A common law doctrine under which judges are obligated to follow the precedents established in prior decisions.

Statute of Frauds A state statute under which certain types of contracts must be in writing or in an electronic record to be enforceable.

Statutory Law The body of law enacted by legislative bodies (as opposed to constitutional law, administrative law, or case law).

Stock An ownership (equity) interest in a corporation, measured in units of shares.

Stock Certificate A certificate issued by a corporation evidencing the ownership of a specified number of shares in the corporation.

Stock Option A right to buy a given number of shares of stock at a set price, usually within a specified time period.

Stock Warrant A certificate that grants the owner the option to buy a given number of shares of stock, usually within a set time period.

Strict Liability Liability regardless of fault, which is imposed on those engaged in abnormally dangerous activities, on persons who keep dangerous animals, and on manufacturers or sellers that introduce into commerce defective and unreasonably dangerous goods.

Strike An action undertaken by unionized workers when collective bargaining fails. The workers leave their jobs, refuse to work, and (typically) picket the employer's workplace.

Substantive Law Law that defines, describes, regulates, and creates legal rights and obligations.

Summons A document informing a defendant that a legal action has been commenced against her or him and that the defendant must appear in court on a certain date to answer the plaintiff's complaint.

Supremacy Clause The requirement in Article VI of the U.S. Constitution that provides that the Constitution, laws, and treaties of the United States are "the supreme Law of the Land."

Surety A third party who agrees to be primarily responsible for the debt of another.

Suretyship An express contract in which a third party (the surety) promises to be primarily responsible for a debtor's obligation to a creditor.

Symbolic Speech Nonverbal expressions of beliefs. Symbolic speech, which includes gestures, movements, and articles of clothing, is given substantial protection by the courts.

T

Taking The taking of private property by the government for public use through the power of eminent domain.

Tangible Employment Action A significant change in employment status or benefits, such as occurs when an employee is fired, refused a promotion, or reassigned to a lesser position.

Tangible Property Property that has physical existence and can be distinguished by the senses of touch and sight.

Tariff A tax on imported goods.

Tenancy at Sufferance A type of tenancy under which one who, after rightfully being in possession of leased premises, continues (wrongfully) to occupy the property after the lease has been terminated. The tenant has no rights to possess the property and occupies it only because the person entitled to evict the tenant has not done so.

Tenancy at Will A type of tenancy under which either party can terminate the tenancy without notice; usually arises when a tenant who has been under a tenancy for years retains possession, with the landlord's consent, after the tenancy for years has terminated.

Tenancy by the Entirety The joint ownership of property by a husband and wife. Neither party can transfer his or her interest in the property without the consent of the other.

Tenancy in Common Co-ownership of property in which each party owns an undivided interest that passes to his or her heirs at death.

Tender An unconditional offer to perform an obligation by a person who is ready, willing, and able to do so.

Tender of Delivery Under the Uniform Commercial Code, a seller's or lessor's act of placing conforming goods at the disposal of the buyer or lessee and giving the buyer or lessee whatever notification is reasonably necessary to enable the buyer or lessee to take delivery.

Third Party Beneficiary One for whose benefit a promise is made in a contract but who is not a party to the contract.

Tippee A person who receives inside information.

Tort A wrongful act (other than a breach of contract) that results in harm or injury to another and leads to civil liability.

Tortfeasor One who commits a tort.

Toxic Tort A civil wrong arising from exposure to a toxic substance, such as asbestos, radiation, or hazardous waste.

Trade Dress The image and overall appearance ("look and feel") of a product that is protected by trademark law.

Trademark A distinctive word, symbol, or design that identifies the manufacturer as the source of particular goods and distinguishes its products from those made or sold by others.

Trade Name A name that a business uses to identify itself and its brand. A trade name that is the same as the company's trademarked product is protected as a trademark, and unique trade names are protected under the common law.

Trade Secret A formula, device, idea, process, or other information used in a business that gives the owner a competitve advantage in the marketplace.

Transferred Intent A legal principle under which a person who intends to harm one individual, but unintentionally harms a second person, can be liable to the second victim for an intentional tort.

Treaty A formal international agreement negotiated between two nations or among several nations. In the United States, all treaties must be approved by the Senate.

Treble Damages Damages that, by statute, are three times the amount of actual damages suffered.

Trespass to Land Entry onto, above, or below the surface of land owned by another without the owner's permission or legal authorization.

Trespass to Personal Property Wrongfully taking or harming the personal property of another or otherwise interfering with the lawful owner's possession of personal property.

Triple Bottom Line Focuses on a corporation's profits, its impact on people, and its impact on the planet.

Tying Arrangement A seller's act of conditioning the sale of a product or service on the buyer's agreement to purchase another product or service from the seller.

Typosquatting A form of cybersquatting that relies on mistakes, such as typographical errors, made by Internet users when inputting information into a Web browser.

U

Ultra Vires A Latin term meaning "beyond the powers" that in corporate law, describes acts of management that are beyond the corporation's express and implied powers to undertake.

Unconscionable A contract or clause that is void on the basis of public policy because one party was forced to accept terms that are unfairly burdensome and that unfairly benefit the stronger party.

Undisclosed Principal A principal whose identity is unknown by a third party, and that person has no knowledge that the agent is acting for a principal at the time the agent and the third party form a contract.

Unenforceable Contract A valid contract rendered unenforceable by some statute or law.

Uniform Law A model law developed by the National Conference of Commissioners on Uniform State Laws for the states to consider enacting into statute.

Unilateral Contract A contract that results when an offer can be accepted only by the offeree's performance.

Unilateral Mistake A mistake that occurs when one party to a contract is mistaken as to a material fact.

Union Shop A firm that requires all workers, once employed, to become union members within a specified period of time as a condition of their continued employment.

Unreasonably Dangerous Product A product that is so defective that it is dangerous beyon the expection of an ordinary consumer or a product for which a less dangerous alternative was feasible but the manufacturer failed to produce it.

U.S. Trustee A government official who performs certain administra-tive tasks that a bankruptcy judge would otherwise have to perform.

Usury Charging an illegal rate of interest.

Utilitarianism An approach to ethical reasoning in which an action is evaluated in terms of its consequences for those whom it will affect. A "good" action is one that results in the greatest good for the greatest number of people.

V

Validation Notice An initial notice to a debtor from a collection agency informing the debtor that he or she has thirty days to challenge the debt and request verification.

Valid Contract A contract that results when the elements necessary for contract formation are present.

Variance A form of relief from zoning laws that is granted to a property owner to allow the property to be used in a manner not permitted by zoning regulations.

Venture Capital Financing provided by professional, outside investors (venture capitalists) to new business ventures.

Venue The geographic district in which a legal action is tried and from which the jury is selected.

Vertically Integrated Firm A firm that carries out two or more functional phases (manufacturing, distribution, and retailing, for example) of the chain of production.

Vertical Merger The acquisition by a company at one stage of production of a company at a higher or lower stage of production (such as a company merging with one of its suppliers or retailers).

Vertical Restraint A restraint of trade created by an agreement between firms at different levels in the manufacturing and distribution process.

Vesting The creation of an absolute or unconditional right or power.

Vicarious Liability Indirect liability imposed on a supervisory party (such as an employer) for the actions of a subordinate (such as an employee) because of the relationship between the two parties.

Virus A type of malware that is transmitted between computers and attempts to do deliberate damage to systems and data.

Void Contract A contract having no legal force or binding effect.

Voidable Contract A contract that may be legally avoided at the option of one or both of the parties.

Voir Dire An important part of the jury selection process in which the attorneys question prospective jurors about their backgrounds, attitudes, and biases to ascertain whether they can be impartial jurors.

Voluntary Consent The knowing and voluntary agreement to the terms of a contract. If voluntary consent is lacking, and the contract will be voidable.

W

Waiver An intentional, knowing relinquishment of a legal right.

Warranty Deed A deed that provides the greatest amount of protection for the grantee, in that the grantor promises that she or he has title

to the property conveyed in the deed, that there are no undisclosed encumbrances on the property, and that the grantee will enjoy quiet possession of the property.

Waste The abuse or destructive use of real property by one who is in rightful possession of the property but who does not have title to it.

Watered Stock Shares of stock issued by a corporation for which the corporation receives, as payment, less than the stated value of the shares.

Wetlands Water-saturated, protected areas of land that support wildlife and cannot be filled in or dredged without a permit.

Whistleblowing An employee's disclosure to government authorities, upper-level managers, or the media that the employer is engaged in unsafe or illegal activities.

White-Collar Crime Nonviolent crime committed by individuals or corporations to obtain a personal or business advantage.

Winding Up The second of two stages in the termination of a partnership or corporation, in which the firm's assets are collected, liquidated, and distributed, and liabilities are discharged.

Workers' Compensation Laws State statutes that establish an administrative process for compensating workers for injuries that arise in the course of their employment, regardless of fault.

Workout An out-of-court agreement between a debtor and creditors

that establishes a payment plan for discharging the debtor's debts.

Workout Agreement A formal contract between a debtor and his or her creditors in which the parties agree to negotiate a payment plan for the amount due on the loan instead of proceeding to foreclosure.

Worm A type of malware that is designed to copy itself from one computer to another without human interaction. A worm can copy itself automatically and can replicate in great volume and with great speed. Worms, for example, can send out copies of themselves to every contact in your e-mail address book.

Writ of Attachment A writ used to enforce obedience to an order or judgment of the court.

Writ of Certiorari A writ from a higher court asking a lower court for the record of a case.

Writ of Execution A writ that puts in force a court's decree or judgment.

Wrongful Discharge An employer's termination of an employee's employment in violation of the law or an employment contract.

Z

Zoning Laws Laws that divide a municipality into districts and prescribe the use to which property within each district may be put.

Table of Cases

For your convenience and reference, here is a list of all the cases mentioned in this text, including those within the footnotes, features, and case problems. Any case that was an excerpted case for a chapter is given special emphasis by having its title **boldfaced**.

Index

C

Q

LANDMARK IN THE LEGAL ENVIRONMENT

BEYOND OUR BORDERS